Ethnic Information Sources of the United States

SECOND EDITION

A Guide to Organizations, Agencies, Foundations, Institutions, Media, Commercial and Trade Bodies, Government Programs, Research Institutes, Libraries and Museums, Religious Organizations, Banking Firms, Festivals and Fairs, Travel and Tourist Offices, Airlines and Ship Lines, Bookdealers and Publishers' Representatives, and Books, Pamphlets, and Audiovisuals on Specific Ethnic Groups

Paul Wasserman
Managing Editor

Alice E. Kennington
Associate Editor

Volume 1

Ethnic Peoples: Afghans—Italians

Gale Research Company • Book Tower • Detroit, Michigan 48226

Editorial Staff Manager: Effie T. Knight

Editorial Assistants: Gayle Batty, Sharon Luy, Jacqueline O'Brien, Todd Stockslager

Library of Congress Catalog Card Number 76-4642
ISBN 0-8103-0367-1
ISSN 0738-1719

CONTENTS

In addition to the listing in the Contents, a supplemental alphabetical GUIDE TO ETHNIC ARRANGEMENT is presented on page xvii of this volume

Volume 1

Section 1

Ethnic Peoples

Volume 2

Section 1 (Continued)

Ethnic Peoples

Section 2

INTRODUCTION

A continuing characteristic of our times is the widespread interest in ethnic affairs and in the origins of the varied groups that have been drawn to these shores. The cultural diversity of the United States is currently perceived as the basis for a thriving social system. No longer is there pressure to deny the distinctions among assorted national, religious, and cultural groups.

Purpose and Scope

Ethnic Information Sources of the United States, second edition, brings together in one source information about the various ethnic groups that comprise the U.S. populace. It is intended for use by individuals who have come to the United States from foreign countries as visitors or permanent residents; by individuals whose ancestors or relatives by marriage belong to particular ethnic groups; by people who plan to live or travel in a foreign region; by those who engage in commerce or trade with specific ethnic groups; and by students, educators, librarians, and others interested in learning about distinctive ethnic lines and the countries from which they are drawn or who require information about the rich details of history, culture, customs, values, politics, and problems of ethnic groups in the United States.

Topics and resources (embassies, fraternal organizations, museums, etc.) covered in this book are discussed in detail in the section titled "Scope and Arrangement of This Book," beginning on page xiii.

A complete index to all organizations will be found in Volume 2.

Exclusions

While *Ethnic Information Sources of the United States* is committed to the identification and description of as many sources of information on ethnic groups as possible, it does not cover Blacks, American Indians, or Eskimos, since these racial groups are extensively treated in many other sources.

New Features in This Edition

The present volume updates and extends the coverage of the first edition, issued in 1976, and incorporates several additional features. A general chapter has been added for groups, especially study centers, which focus on ethnicity as a phenomenon in itself rather than on any particular ethnic group. For each of these organizations, details are provided about the specific ethnic areas that they treat, the focus of their work, and the range of activities and information sources that they make available. This new section, found in Volume 2, also provides information on the many festivals devoted to the celebration of ethnic heritage and lists some of the periodicals and reference works covering the ethnic picture as a whole.

Additional Ethnic Classifications

A new category has been added for Asians, a group that warrants specific attention because of the growing number of study groups that either treat the Asian region as a whole or focus on a component of it, such as South, Southeast, or East Asia. Information about Buddhists is now included in this Asian section, although ethnically-based Buddhist groups are still listed in the pertinent ethnic section. Similarly, information about Moslems is now found primarily under the general Arab classification, although a few non-Arab Moslem groups are treated in the ethnic groupings to which they belong.

The Indochinese are an added ethnic category in this work because of the increasing importance of their recent migratory movements. Although it may be considered an artificial designation, "Indochinese" is widely used to refer to the several distinct ethnic groups originating in Southeast Asia, including Vietnamese, Laotians, Cambodians, Hmong, etc. The grouping is a particularly interesting one because it is currently in the process of formation, following much the same course as have other ethnic groups arriving in America: first, a proliferation of local organizations, followed by consolidation at regional and national levels. With the Indochinese there are, at present, hundreds of local, ethnically-oriented, mutual assistance associations; but regional and national structure is so far provided largely by *American* organizations, especially voluntary agencies assisting in refugee resettlement, organization, orientation, etc.

Finally, in response to the suggestions of a number of those who commented on the content and arrangement of the first edition, the Byelorussians receive specific and separate treatment in this new edition.

Methods of Compilation

Information for this publication has been collected through a wide range of methods, including comprehensive correspondence with key agencies, questionnaire distribution, library research, interviews with experts and embassy officials, discussions with representatives of travel and tourist offices, and the exploration of many unique and unusual sources in the literature and organizational systems of the ethnic groups themselves. Of great significance has been the contribution of many ethnically oriented organizations. These serve as valuable sources of information on the customs, language, history, country of origin, and way of life of the particular ethnic group with which they are affiliated. It is these organizations that typically assume responsibility for keeping alive the ethnic heritage and languages by distributing newspapers, magazines, and other publications reflective of the original cultures.

Acknowledgments

An especially important source of information has been the Washington embassies of numerous foreign countries. To all of those embassy officials who provided advice, assistance, and informational materials, we owe special gratitude. In particular, the editors would like to express their appreciation for the detailed interviews and helpful information provided by the following:

Dr. Rudolf Lennkh, Third Secretary, Embassy of Austria

Mr. Eygheni Z. Kirilov, Third Secretary, Embassy of Bulgaria

Ms. Merle Fabian, Librarian, Embassy of Canada

Ms. Maria B. de Pincus, Cultural Department, Embassy of Chile

Ms. Cecilia Isaacs, Cultural Attache, Embassy of Colombia

Ms. Ligia G. Haas, Counselor, Embassy of Costa Rica

Mr. Josef Stary, Third Secretary, Embassy of Czechoslovakia

Mr. Piedad de Suro, Counselor for Cultural and Press Affairs, Embassy of Ecuador

Ms. Bacon and Mr. Alain Gouhier, Press and Information Service, Embassy of France

Mr. Michael Poetschke, Embassy of the German Democratic Republic

Ms. Eudoxia Cutler, Administrative Attache, and Mr. Alexis Phylactopoulos, Press Counselor, Embassy of Greece

Ms. Maria Z. Landis, Counselor, Embassy of Guatemala

Mr. Eddy V. Etienne, First Secretary, Embassy of Haiti

Ms. Patricia Casteneda, Cultural Attache, Embassy of Honduras

Dr. Tibor Keszthelyi, Counselor, Embassy of Hungary

Mr. Sverrir Haukur Gunnlaugsson, Minister-Counselor, Embassy of Iceland

Mr. Prahasto, Assistant to the Educational and Cultural Attache, Embassy of Indonesia

Ms. Jeanne Trabulsi, Jordan Information Bureau

Ms. Susan Loeffter, Office of Cultural and Information Attache, Embassy of Korea

Mr. Valdemars Kreicbergs, Counselor, Legation of Latvia

Mr. Alfred Mady, Executive Director, Lebanese Information and Reseach Center; and Ms. Micheline Abi-Samra, First Secretary, Embassy of Lebanon

Dr. Stasys A. Backis, Charge d'Affaires, Legation of Lithuania

G.N. Nair, First Secretary, Embassy of Malaysia

Mr. Alberto Campillo, Cultural Counselor, Embassy of Mexico

Mr. Syed Iqbal Hussain, Assistant Attache, Press Affairs, Embassy of Pakistan

Dr. Antonio Correa, Charge d'Affairs, Embassy of Panama

Ms. M. Cristina Samudio-Hamuy Price, Cultural Attache, Embassy of Paraguay

Ms. Natalia Macedo, Attache, Embassy of Peru

Ms. Tessie Paynor, Cultural Section, Embassy of the Philippines

Ms. Margaret Romaniuk, Information Officer, Embassy of Poland

Mr. Mario Godinho De Matos, Embassy of Portugal

Major P.B.C. Dharmapala, First Secretary, Embassy of Sri Lanka

Mr. Pierre-Yves Simonin, Cultural Counselor, Embassy of Switzerland

Mr. Ridha Hamada, Attache for Cultural and Consular Affairs, Embassy of Tunisia

Ms. Nurinisa Bayramoglu, Assistant Press Attache, Embassy of Turkey

Ms. Vera Beliak, Office of the Information Counselor, Embassy of the Union of Soviet Socialist Republics

Mr. Slavko Kruljevic, Attache for Consular Affairs, Embassy of Yugoslavia

The editors also owe a strong debt of gratitude to the following individuals who helped with particular groups, as well as with general problems:

Ms. Carmen Rodriquez, of the former Ethnic Heritage Center, Department of Education

Mr. Thaddeus C. Radzialowski, formerly of the National Endowment for the Humanities, and now at Southwest State University, Marshall, Minnesota

For Afghans: Dr. Louis Dupree, Universities Field Staff International; Ms. Mary Ann Siegfried, Afghanistan Council, Asia Society

For Arabs: Mr. John Richardson, formerly of the National Association of Arab Americans, now President of the Center for Middle East Policy; Mr. Neal Lendenmann, National Association of Arab Americans; Joseph Haiek, Editor, New Circle Magazine; Nassar Asi, Islamic Center, Washington, D.C.

For Armenians: Mr. Ross Varian, Mr. Laurens Ayvazian, and Ms. Susan Carlin, Armenian Assembly of America

For Basques: Ms. Janet Inda, North American Basque Organizations, Inc.

For Byelorussians: Mr. Vitaut Kipel, New York Public Library

For Chinese: Mr. Henry Hu, Coordination Council for North American Affairs

For Cubans: Ms. Deni Blackburn, Office of Refugee Resettlement

For Hungarians: Mr. Istvan B. Gereben, Executive Secretary, Coordinating Council of Hungarian Organizations in North America

For Indochinese: Ms. Thora Frank, American Red Cross; Mr. Ed Sponga, Office of Refugee Resettlement; Mr. Robert Frankel, formerly of the Indochinese Refugee Action Center, now of Refugee Policy Group; Ms. Diana Bui and Mr. Le Xuan Khoa, Indochinese Refugee Action Center; Mr. Nguyen Ngoc Bich, Georgetown University

For Iranians: Mr. Z.N. Araghi and Mr. F. Darui, Iranian Freedom Foundation

For Italians: Mr. Maurice T. Perilli, of the former Il Popolo Italiano newspaper

For Jews: Mr. Hank Siegel, B'nai B'rith

For Poles: Dr. Edward C. Rozanski, Archivist, Polish American Congress

For Scots: Mr. Fergus McLarty, Saint Andrew's Society of the State of New York

For Spanish-Speaking: Mr. Angel Hurtado, Museum of Modern Art of Latin America

For Turks: Ms. Colleen Darko, Executive Secretary, Assembly of Turkish American Associations

For Ukrainians: Dr. George N. Krywolap, Archivist, Ukrainian Youth Association

For Welsh: Arturo L. Roberts, Editor, Ninnau newspaper

In the last months of manuscript preparation, Ms. Gayle Batty assumed responsibility for assembling and verifying a number of the sections; special thanks is given for her perceptive and patient participation. Acknowledgment must also be made of the important contribution of Patti Hilley and Linda Stemmy, typists of the present work, who prepared a very difficult manuscript with patience and intelligence; and to Sharon Luy, Jacqueline O'Brien, and Todd Stockslager for proofreading and indexing this work.

SCOPE AND ARRANGEMENT OF THIS BOOK

Section 1, Ethnic Peoples, is arranged alphabetically. In general, each ethnic group is identified with an individual foreign country of origin. There are, however, separate sections for some ethnic peoples who no longer constitute independent nations, such as the Armenian, Basque, Byelorussian, Estonian, Latvian, Lithuanian, Scottish, Ukrainian, and Welsh peoples. Since most of the information sources for the English are also about the British, English and British are combined in one section. Ethnic peoples constituting a cultural minority within a nation are in some cases combined with the culturally related group, rather than with the political division. For instance, French Canadians are grouped under French-Speaking Peoples and Moravian religious sects under Germans.

In addition to the listing in the Contents, a supplemental alphabetical GUIDE TO ETHNIC ARRANGEMENT is presented on page xvii of this volume

Within each Ethnic Peoples division, information sources are arranged under 27 major headings, although some headings may be omitted for lack of material. The headings used follow a related arrangement rather than alphabetical order:

EMBASSY AND CONSULATES. Supplies addresses and telephone numbers of foreign government embassies and subordinate offices. In two cases a legation is listed in place of an embassy. Addresses and telephone numbers are given for consulates general serving areas of the country and for consulates serving major cities. Arrangement is alphabetical according to the name of the city.

MISSION TO THE UNITED NATIONS. Where applicable, supplies address and telephone number of the United Nations mission or observer in New York City.

INFORMATION OFFICES. Includes addresses and telephone numbers for designated information offices. Often the information office is located at the New York City consulate or consulate general, but with a different telephone number. Government-sponsored tourist offices also serve as information offices.

TOURIST AND TRAVEL OFFICES. Includes addresses and telephone numbers for foreign government tourist and travel offices in the United States, arranged in alphabetical order of the cities where offices are located. In some cases the primary or headquarters office is listed first.

FRATERNAL ORGANIZATIONS. Social and fraternal benefit organizations composed of ethnic peoples in the United States or people interested in the ethnic group. Each entry ordinarily includes the address, telephone number, date founded, title and name of a designated officer, a description of the organization's activities, and a list of publications. Emphasis is on national, regional, or large city organizations. Arrangement is alphabetical according to the name of the organization.

PROFESSIONAL ORGANIZATIONS. Follows an arrangement similar to that for fraternal organizations.

PUBLIC AFFAIRS ORGANIZATIONS. Ethnic political action groups, labor organizations, and other organizations involved with public affairs issues.

CULTURAL AND EDUCATIONAL ORGANIZATIONS. Educational organizations and those concerned with the history, literature, art, music, dancing, customs, and other cultural aspects of ethnic peoples.

FOUNDATIONS. Provides information similar to that for fraternal and other organizations. In addition to a directing officer, the donor of the foundation funds is usually listed.

CHARITABLE ORGANIZATIONS. Organizations whose primary function is to supply aid to ethnic peoples. Some fraternal, professional, and other designated organizations also undertake charitable programs.

RELIGIOUS ORGANIZATIONS. Central or national religious organizations composed of ethnic peoples in this country and missionary organizations concerned with foreign countries.

RESEARCH CENTERS AND SPECIAL INSTITUTES. Research centers connected with universities and independent special institutes engaged in research studies of ethnic peoples in the United States or in foreign countries. Information is given about the areas of research and the types of studies pursued.

U.S. GOVERNMENT PROGRAMS. Specific government programs, such as the one for Indochinese refugees in the United States. Other important government programs for ethnic peoples that benefit minority groups in general are not included. Ethnic activities of the U.S. Library of Congress are discussed under the heading Special Libraries and Subject Collections.

MUSEUMS. Limited to museums in the United States devoted entirely or primarily to a particular ethnic group. Although their ethnic collections may be much more extensive, large city museums covering many different ethnic peoples and subject areas are omitted.

SPECIAL LIBRARIES AND SUBJECT COLLECTIONS. Limited to special libraries in the United States devoted entirely or primarily to a particular ethnic group. Separate ethnic collections are identified, but collections of ethnic materials integrated within a library's other holdings are not ordinarily included, even though they may be far more extensive than the collections that have been included here.

NEWSPAPERS AND NEWSLETTERS. Ethnic newspapers and newsletters published in the United States in a foreign language or in English, or in both English and a foreign language. Also includes newspapers and newsletters in English produced in foreign countries or by foreign governments for use in the United States, such as embassy newsletters. The title and translation of the title, date established, editor, publisher, address, and language of the newspaper or newsletter are usually given, as well as a brief description of the content. Entries are arranged alphabetically by title.

MAGAZINES. Ethnic magazines published in the United States and English editions of foreign magazines. The same type of information is given as for newspapers and newsletters. Again, arrangement is alphabetical by title.

RADIO PROGRAMS. Names, addresses, and telephone numbers of radio stations in the United States broadcasting programs in foreign languages. Arrangement is geographical by state and city. The number of hours of programming is normally provided. Foreign radio stations broadcasting shortwave radio programs to the United States in English or a foreign language are also included.

TELEVISION PROGRAMS. Follows the same arrangement as that for radio programs.

BANK BRANCHES IN THE U.S. Addresses and telephone numbers for branches of foreign banks located in United States cities. Names of the foreign banks are in alphabetical order.

COMMERCIAL AND TRADE ORGANIZATIONS. Names, addresses, telephone numbers, dates founded, titles and names of designated officers, descriptions of the organizations' activities, and lists of publications for organizations in the United States concerned with foreign trade and commerce. In some cases, such as chambers of commerce, only the name, address, and telephone number are given. Commercial companies, such as oil companies, are included only if they are controlled by a foreign government. Individual private export and import companies are excluded, although associations of such companies are listed. Names of the organizations are in alphabetical order.

FESTIVALS, FAIRS, AND CELEBRATIONS. Descriptions of ethnic festivities held in various parts of the United States, with approximate dates and addresses of organizations or people to contact. If no address is given, information about exact dates or other information may be obtained by writing to the chamber of commerce in the town or city listed. Arranged geographically by state and city.

AIRLINE OFFICES. Names, addresses, and telephone numbers for foreign airlines maintaining offices in the United States, as well as information about available flights. Arrangement is alphabetical by the name of the airline.

SHIP LINES. Names, addresses, and telephone numbers in the United States and information about foreign ship line routes. Arranged alphabetically by name of the ship line.

BOOKDEALERS AND PUBLISHERS' REPRESENTATIVES. Dealers in foreign books and publishers' representatives listed alphabetically by name, along with addresses and telephone numbers. Alphabetization is by last name of the owner of the company, rather than by first names or initials.

BOOKS AND PAMPHLETS. The first part is restricted to bibliographies of materials about foreign countries and to publications produced in English in foreign countries or in the United States by foreign government organizations for distribution here. Many of the pamphlets and paperback books described are updated and issued under new titles as more recent material and statistics become available, and new editions with the same title may be issued.

The second part deals with books about ethnic peoples in America. With a few exceptions, they have been published in the United States. In addition to bibliographic information, annotations have been included for most of the entries.

Arrangement in both parts of this section is alphabetical by title. Most of the materials are in the English language.

AUDIOVISUAL MATERIAL. Descriptions of maps, pictures, and films. In a few cases, cassettes, sets of slides, and filmstrips are included. Films are listed alphabetically by title.

GUIDE TO ETHNIC ARRANGEMENT

AFGHANS—See also: ASIANS

ALBANIANS

ALGERIANS—See also: ARABS; FRENCH-SPEAKING PEOPLES

ARABS (Includes MOSLEMS)—See also: Individual Arab Peoples

ARCADIANS—See: FRENCH-SPEAKING PEOPLES

ARGENTINES—See also: SPANISH-SPEAKING PEOPLES

ARMENIANS

ASIANS (Includes BUDDHISTS)—See also: Individual Asian Peoples

ASSYRIANS—See: IRAQIS

AUSTRALIANS

AUSTRIANS—See also: GERMANS

BAHRAINIANS—See: ARABS

BASQUES

BELGIANS (Includes FLEMISH)—See also: FRENCH-SPEAKING PEOPLES

BOLIVIANS—See also: SPANISH-SPEAKING PEOPLES

BRAZILIANS—See also: PORTUGUESE

BRITISH (Includes CORNISH; ENGLISH; MANX)—See also: IRISH; SCOTS; WELSH

BULGARIANS—See also: SLAVIC PEOPLES

BURMESE—See also: ASIANS

BYELORUSSIANS—See also: RUSSIANS; SLAVIC PEOPLES

CAJUNS—See: FRENCH-SPEAKING PEOPLES

CANADIANS—See also: FRENCH-SPEAKING PEOPLES

CARPATHO-RUSSIANS—See: RUSSIANS

CEYLONESE—See: SRI LANKIANS

CHICANOS—See: MEXICANS

CHILEANS—See also: SPANISH-SPEAKING PEOPLES

CHINESE—See also: ASIANS

COLOMBIANS—See also: SPANISH-SPEAKING PEOPLES

CORNISH—See: BRITISH

COSTA RICANS—See also: SPANISH-SPEAKING PEOPLES

CRETANS—See: GREEKS

CROATIANS—See: YUGOSLAVS

CUBANS—See also: SPANISH-SPEAKING PEOPLES

CZECHOSLOVAKIANS (Includes SLOVAKS)—See also: SLAVIC PEOPLES

DANES—See also: SCANDINAVIANS

DOMINICANS—See also: SPANISH-SPEAKING PEOPLES

DUTCH

EAST INDIANS—See: INDIANS

ECUADORIANS—See also: SPANISH-SPEAKING PEOPLES

EGYPTIANS—See also: ARABS

ENGLISH—See: BRITISH

ESTONIANS

FILIPINOS—See also: ASIANS

FINNS—See also: SCANDINAVIANS

FLEMISH—See: BELGIANS

FRENCH-CANADIANS—See: FRENCH-SPEAKING PEOPLES

FRENCH-SPEAKING PEOPLES (Includes ARCADIANS; CAJUNS; FRENCH CANADIANS; HUGUENOTS)—See also: ALGERIANS; BELGIANS; HAITIANS; MOROCCANS; TUNISIANS

GERMANS (Includes MENNONITES; MORAVIANS; PENNSYLVANIA DUTCH)

GREEKS (Includes CRETANS)

GUATEMALANS—See also: SPANISH-SPEAKING PEOPLES

HAITIANS—See also: FRENCH-SPEAKING PEOPLES

HAWAIIANS

HEBREWS—See: JEWS

HINDUS—See: INDIANS

HONDURANS—See also: SPANISH-SPEAKING PEOPLES

HUGUENOTS—See: FRENCH-SPEAKING PEOPLES

HUNGARIANS (Includes MAGYARS)

ICELANDERS—See also: SCANDINAVIANS

INDIANS (East Indians) (Includes HINDUS)—See also: ASIANS

INDOCHINESE (Includes CAMBODIANS; HMONG; LAOTIANS; VIETNAMESE)—See also: ASIANS

INDONESIANS

IRANIANS (Persians)—See also: ARABS

IRAQIS (Includes ASSYRIANS)—See also: ARABS

IRISH—See also: BRITISH

ISRAELIS—See: JEWS

ITALIANS

JAMAICANS

JAPANESE—See also: ASIANS

JEWS (Includes HEBREWS AND ISRAELIS)

JORDANIANS—See also: ARABS

KOREANS—See also: ASIANS

KUWAITIS—See also: ARABS

LATIN AMERICANS—See: SPANISH-SPEAKING PEOPLES

LATVIANS

LEBANESE—See also: ARABS

LIBYANS—See: ARABS

LITHUANIANS

MACEDONIANS—See: BULGARIANS; GREEKS; YUGOSLAVS

MAGYARS—See: HUNGARIANS

MALAYSIANS—See also: ASIANS

MALTESE

MANX—See: BRITISH

MENNONITES—See: GERMANS

MEXICANS (Includes CHICANOS)—See also: SPANISH-SPEAKING PEOPLES

MORAVIANS—See: GERMANS

MOROCCANS—See also: ARABS; FRENCH-SPEAKING PEOPLES

NETHERLANDERS—See: DUTCH

NEW ZEALANDERS

NICARAGUANS—See also: SPANISH-SPEAKING PEOPLES

NORWEGIANS—See also: SCANDINAVIANS

PAKISTANIS—See also: ASIANS

PALESTINIANS—See: ARABS

PANAMANIANS—See also: SPANISH-SPEAKING PEOPLES

PARAGUAYANS—See also: SPANISH-SPEAKING PEOPLES

PENNSYLVANIA DUTCH—See: GERMANS

PERSIANS—See: IRANIANS

PERUVIANS—See also: SPANISH-SPEAKING PEOPLES

POLES—See also: SLAVIC PEOPLES

PORTUGUESE

PUERTO RICANS—See also: SPANISH-SPEAKING PEOPLES

QATARIS—See: ARABS

ROMANIANS

RUSSIANS (Includes CARPATHO-RUSSIANS)—See also: ARMENIANS; BYELORUSSIANS; ESTONIANS; LATVIANS; LITHUANIANS; SLAVIC PEOPLES: UKRAINIANS

SALVADORIANS—See also: SPANISH-SPEAKING PEOPLES

SAUDI ARABIANS—See also: ARABS

SCANDINAVIANS—See also: DANES; FINNS; ICELANDERS; NORWEGIANS; SWEDES

SCOTS—See also: BRITISH

SERBS—See: YUGOSLAVS

SIAMESE—See: THAIS

SILESIANS—See: GERMANS; POLES

SLAVIC PEOPLES (Slavonic Peoples)—See also: BULGARIANS; BYELORUSSIANS; CZECHOSLOVAKIANS; POLES; RUSSIANS; UKRAINIANS; YUGOSLAVS

SLAVONIC PEOPLES—See: SLAVIC PEOPLES

SLOVAKS—See: CZECHOSLOVAKIANS

SLOVENES—See: YUGOSLAVS

SPANISH-SPEAKING PEOPLES (Includes CARRIBEANS; LATIN AMERICANS)—See also: Individual Peoples of Latin America

SRI LANKANS (Ceylonese)

SWEDES—See also: SCANDINAVIANS

SWISS

SYRIANS—See also: ARABS

THAIS (Siamese)—See also: ASIANS

TUNISIANS—See also: ARABS; FRENCH-SPEAKING PEOPLES

TURKS

UKRAINIANS—See also: RUSSIANS; SLAVIC PEOPLES

UNITED ARAB EMIRATES—See: ARABS

UNITED KINGDOM—See: BRITISH; IRISH; SCOTS; WELSH

URUGUAYANS—See also: SPANISH-SPEAKING PEOPLES

VENEZUELANS—See also: SPANISH-SPEAKING PEOPLES

WELSH—See also: BRITISH

YEMENI—See: ARABS

YUGOSLAVS (Includes CROATIANS; SERBS; SLOVENES)—See also: SLAVIC PEOPLES

Section 1

Ethnic Peoples: Afghans—Italians

AFGHANS
See also: ASIANS

Embassy and Consulates

EMBASSY OF THE DEMOCRATIC REPUBLIC OF AFGHANISTAN
2341 Wyoming Avenue, Northwest
Washington, D.C. 20008 (202) AD4-3770

CONSULATE GENERAL
122-126 West 30th Street
New York, New York 10001 (212) 736-8150

Mission to the United Nations

PERMANENT MISSION OF THE DEMOCRATIC REPUBLIC OF AFGHANISTAN TO THE UNITED NATIONS
866 United Nations Plaza, 4th Floor
New York, New York 10017 (212) 754-1191

Information Offices

AFGHAN TOURIST INFORMATION
845 North Michigan Avenue
Chicago, Illinois 60602 (312) 944-4223

Public Affairs Organizations

AFGHAN ASSOCIATION OF FREEDOM FIGHTERS
F.D.R. Post Office, Box 5301
New York, New York 10022

AFGHAN INFORMATION CENTER OF FREEDOM HOUSE
20 West 40th Street
New York, New York 10018

Makes public information coming from Afghanistan from those working against the Russian domination of the country.

COMMITTEE OF CONCERNED SCHOLARS FOR AFGHANISTAN
Post Office Box 40053
Washington, D.C. 20016

Gathers and circulates information about Afghanistan of importance in American policy making.

FREE AFGHANISTAN
6 Divinity Avenue
Cambridge, Massachusetts 02138

Works against the Soviet seizure of power in Afghanistan.

SOLIDARITY COUNCIL OF AFGHANISTAN FREEDOM ORGANIZATIONS IN AMERICA
Post Office Box 1216
Pacific Palisades, California 90272
President: Dr. Erfan Fetrat

Cultural and Educational Organizations

AFGHAN COUNCIL OF THE ASIA SOCIETY
725 Park Avenue
New York, New York 10021 Founded 1960

A major function of the Afghan Council is to introduce the American public to Afghan culture, including the performing and visual arts, archeology, handicrafts, politics and history. Contributes to the production and distribution of educational materials; prepares art exhibitions.
Publications: Afghanistan Council Newsletter, three times a year; Occasional Papers and Special Papers.

AFGHANISTAN STUDIES ASSOCIATION
c/o Center for Afghanistan Studies
University of Nebraska, Adm. 238
60th and Dodge
Omaha, Nebraska 68182
Secretary of Executive Committee: (402) 554-2376
Thomas E. Gouttierre Founded 1971

Scholars, development practitioners, students and others interested in promoting or being participants in the study of Afghanistan. Purposes are to expand and develop Afghanistan studies; to collect and disseminate pertinent information; to facilitate contact, cooperation and exchange of information among scholars of Afghanistan; to identify research opportunities and stimulate sources of support for research, teaching and cultural programs; to assist planning of research projects to be conducted in Afghanistan; to maintain liaison with government, education, scholarly

and cultural institutions concerned with Afghanistan studies; to assist Afghan (national) scholars in carrying on their professional goals in the United States. Maintains library of 2,000 volumes and list of scholars active in the Afghanistan field. Affiliated with the Association of Asian Studies and Middle East Studies Association.
Publication: Newsletter, three times a year.

Charitable Organizations

AFGHAN COMMUNITY IN AMERICA
139-15 95th Avenue
Jamaica, New York 11346 (212) 658-3737
Chairman: Habib Mayer Founded 1980

A non-profit organization for the purpose of providing non-military assistance to those persons made needy by the present war in Afghanistan, wherever they be located, and to solicit contributions and gifts of any kind toward that end.

AFGHAN COMMUNITY IN WASHINGTON, D.C.
Post Office Box 28156
Washington, D.C. 20005

AFGHAN RELIEF COMMITTEE
3839 Rodman Street, Northwest
Washington, D.C. 20016
Director: Ogden Williams (202) 362-8797

AFGHANISTAN RELIEF COMMITTEE, INCORPORATED
40 Exchange Place, Suite 1301
New York, New York 10005 (212) 344-6617
President: Gordon A. Thomas
Director: Janik Raden (212) 483-1000

Provides charitable, educational, humanitarian and benevolent assistance to the people of Afghanistan wherever they are located, either directly or through organizations with similar purposes. Solicits funds and in-kind donations for this purpose.

AID FOR AFGHAN REFUGEES
1052 Oak Street
San Francisco, California 94117 (415) 863-1450
President: Michael Griffin Founded 1980

Active in aid to Afghan refugees in Pakistan as well as in assisting with the resettlement of refugees in Northern California.

AMERICAN AID FOR AFGHANS
6443 Southwest Beaverton Highway
Portland, Oregon 97221

Solicits funds for the purchase and delivery of supplies to the freedom fighters in Afghanistan. Also functions as an educational organization.

Research Centers and Special Institutes

AFGHANISTAN RESEARCH MATERIALS SURVEY
Department of Economics
University of Southern California
University Park
Los Angeles, California 90007
Director: Professor Nake M. Kamrany (213) 454-1708

With assistance from the National Endowment for the Humanities and the University of Southern California, this research group is endeavoring to assemble a comprehensive bibliography of all published materials on Afghanistan as well as the major unpublished writings, in all the major European languages as well as Dari (Persian), Pashto and Urdu. It is also intended to provide guides to the most significant archival collections in the United States and Europe.

CENTER FOR AFGHAN STUDIES
University of Nebraska at Omaha
Post Office Box 688 (402) 554-2376
Director: Thomas E. Gouttierre Founded 1972

Offers courses in Afghan history, Afghan geography, Islamic law, and related fields, as well as language training in Dari (Kabuli Persian). Maintains a library collection of Afghan primary and secondary materials, including holdings in Dari, Pashto, and English dealing with Afghanistan. Sponsors a week-long series of seminars, informative talks, panel discussions, and movies by well-known Afghans each year during the spring semester. Publishes occasional papers consisting of bibliographic and research studies.
Publication: Afghanistan Studies Association Newsletter, annual.

Special Libraries and Subject Collections

AFGHANISTAN STUDIES ASSOCIATION
See: Cultural and Educational Organizations

Newspapers and Newsletters

AFGHANISTAN COUNCIL NEWSLETTER. Quarterly. Publisher: Afghanistan Council of the Asia Society, 725 Park Avenue, New York, New York 10021.

Publishes news of Afghan organizations in this country, excerpts from the world press concerning Afghanistan, feature articles, book reviews and an update on what is happening in Afghanistan.

Commercial and Trade Organizations

AFGHAN AMERICAN TRADING COMPANY, INCORPORATED
122-126 West 30th Street
New York, New York 10001 (212) 736-8150

Organized to promote trade between the United States and Afghanistan. Partially controlled by the government of Afghanistan.

Airline Offices

ARIANA, AFGHAN AIRLINES COMPANY, LIMITED
535 Fifth Avenue
New York, New York 10017 (212) 697-3660

Books and Pamphlets

AFGHAN STUDIES. By Louis Dupree. Hanover, New Hampshire, American Universities Field Staff, 1976.

A summary of Afghan studies in various countries as well as the United States. Includes a selected bibliography.

AFGHANISTAN. By Louis Dupree. Princeton University Press, 1980.

A paperback edition of the original 1973 text brought up to date by epilogues covering the period after the coup 1973 and the Soviet invasion in 1980.

AFGHANISTAN-LAND IN TRANSITION. By Mary Bradley Watkins. Van Nostrand, 1963.

AFGHANISTAN 1980. By Louis Dupree. Hanover, New Hampshire, American Universities Field Staff, 1980.

An update on Afghanistan since the occupation of the country by Russia.

ANNOTATED BIBLIOGRAPHY OF AFGHANISTAN. 3rd edition. By Donald N. Wilber. New Haven, Connecticut, Human Relations Area Files, 1968.

Contains more than 1,200 book and periodical items in a classified list on physical, social, and humanistic aspects of the country. Materials in many languages are included, published in and outside of Afghanistan.

BIBLIOGRAPHIC CLASSIFICATION OF MATERIALS ON AFGHANISTAN SINCE 1968. Afghan Council of the Asia Society, 1973.

BIBLIOGRAPHY OF AMERICAN PERIODICAL LITERATURE OF AFGHANISTAN; 1890-1946. By Leila Poullada. Afghan Council of the Asia Society, 1979.

A JOURNEY THROUGH AFGHANISTAN: A MEMORIAL. By David Chaffetz. Chicago, Illinois, Regnery Gateway Incorporated, 1981.

UNDECLARED WAR. Kabul, Information Department of the Democratic Republic of Afghanistan, 1980.

A pro-Soviet discussion of the political situation in Afghanistan.

Audiovisual Material

FILMS

AFGHAN EXODUS. Color. Videocassette. 52 minutes. By Andre Signer. Granada Television International, London and New York, 1980.

AFGHANISTAN. 16mm. Color and sound. 15 minutes. ACI Films, 1972.

Takes a look at the people, customs, and landscape of Afghanistan.

AFGHANISTAN: ASIAN LAND IN TRANSITION. 35mm. Black and white. 41 frames. Includes narration guide. Visual Education Consultants, 1974.

Explores the history and geography of the country of Afghanistan. Shows how the people of Afghanistan are adapting to the gradual pace of change and modernization in their country.

AFGHANS. Slide-tape production. 15 minutes. Available from Aid for Afghan Refugees (AFAR), 1052 Oak Street, San Francisco, California 94117.

Introduces Afghanistan to Americans.

LIVING IN ASIA TODAY: AMONG THE MARKETS OF AFGHANISTAN. 35mm with phono disc. Color. 52 frames. Also issued with phono tape in cassette. Coronet Instructional Media, 1972.

Describes items that people bring to sell at the markets in Afghanistan, and tells what they buy there in order to show ways of life in that country. For elementary grades.

THE PAINTED TRUCK. 16mm. Color and sound. 28 minutes. By Judith Hallet, Stanley Hallet, and Sebastian C. Schroeder. Released by Film Images/Radim Films, 1973.

Follows the adventures of a multi-colored, muraled panel truck loaded with rice, soap, wheat, wood, melons, and seasoned truck travelers, as it journeys across the Hajigak Pass from Kabul to Bamian.

ALBANIANS

Mission to the United Nations

ALBANIAN MISSION
250 East 87th Street, 21st Floor
New York, New York 10028 (212) 722-1831

Fraternal Organizations

FREE ALBANIA ORGANIZATION
397 B West Broadway
South Boston, Massachusetts 02127 (617) 269-5192
President: William Johns Founded 1940

Persons of Albanian birth or descent. Organized to keep alive the traditions and customs of Albania.
Publication: Liria (Liberty), weekly.

PAN-ALBANIAN FEDERATION OF AMERICA, VATRA
517 East Broadway
South Boston, Massachusetts 02127 (617) 269-6787
President: Andrea Elia Founded 1912

Albanians, over 18 years of age, living in the United States. Sponsors cultural and charitable activities; publishes books on Albanian subjects. Educational foundation gives scholarships to college students of Albanian extraction. Also known as: Vatra (Albanian word for "hearth").
Publication: Dielli (The Sun), weekly.

Religious Organizations

ALBANIAN AMERICAN CATHOLIC LEAGUE, INCORPORATED
4221 Park Avenue and East Tremont Avenue
Bronx, New York 10457 (212) 792-4044
President: Joseph J. Oroshi Founded 1962

Combines educational, health and welfare and religious objectives.
Publication: Jeta Katholike Shqiptare (Catholic Albanian Life), quarterly.

ALBANIAN ORTHODOX ARCHDIOCESE IN AMERICA
529 East Broadway
South Boston, Massachusetts 02127 (617) 268-1275
Primate: Rt. Reverend Bishop Mark Fosburg
Chancellor: Arthur Liolin

A member of the autocephalous Orthodox Church in America, established in 1908, which ministers to Albanians in the United States.
Publication: The Vineyard (Vreshta), quarterly.

ALBANIAN ORTHODOX DIOCESE OF AMERICA
54 Burroughs Street
Jamaica Plain, Massachusetts 02130
President of the Diocese Council:
His Grace Bishop Mark (Lipa) (617) 524-0477

This diocese is under the ecclesiastical jurisdiction of the Ecumenical Patriarchate of Constantinople (Istanbul). It was organized in 1950 as a canonical body ministering to the Albanian faithful.
Publication: Drita e Vertete (The True Light), monthly.

FIRST ALBANIAN TEKE BEKTASHIANE IN AMERICA
21749 Northline Road
Taylor, Michigan 48180 (313) 287-3646
President: Sadik Shemsuden Founded 1954

A religious order. Maintains a small library and reading room.
Publication: Zeri I Bektashizmes (The Voice of Bektashism), irregular.

Special Libraries and Subject Collections

FAN S. NOLI LIBRARY
St. George Albanian Orthodox Cathedral
South Boston, Massachusetts 02127

Subjects: Albanians in America. Special Collection: Papers of Fan S. Noli. Holdings: Archival materials, newspapers and periodicals.

Newspapers and Newsletters

DIELLI (The Sun). 1909-. Monthly. Editor: Xhevat Kallanxheia. Publisher: Pan Albanian Federation of America, 517 East Broadway, South Boston, Massachusetts 02127. In Albanian and English.

Publishes articles on social, cultural, ethnic, and political issues of special interest to Albanians.

LIRIA (Liberty). 1942-. Bimonthly. Editor: Dhimitri R. Nikolla. Publisher: Free Albania Organization, 397 B West Broadway, South Boston, Massachusetts 02127. In Albanian and English.

Prints information on cultural and social events in the Albanian ethnic community.

STRUGGLE OF THE KOSSOVARS BULLETIN. 1978. Quarterly. Publisher: Albanians of Yugoslavia, Union of the Kossovars, 189-10 33rd Avenue, Flushing, New York 11358.

ZERI I BEKTASHIZMES (The Voice of Bektashism). 1954-. Irregular. Publisher: First Albanian Bektashi Tekke in America, 21749 Northline, Taylor, Michigan 48180. In Albanian.

Official publication of the Bektashi religious order.

Magazines

DRITA E VERTETE (The True Light). 1958-. Monthly. Editor: Reverend Fr. Ilia Katre. Publisher: Albanian Orthodox Diocese of America, Post Office Box 18162, Station A, Boston, Massachusetts 02118. In Albanian and English.

Prints religious articles concerning the Orthodox faith and covers activities of the Bishop of the Albanian Orthodox Church, as well as news of developments within various church communities. Also includes articles dealing with Albanian culture, history, ethnic traditions, and current problems within Albanian communities in the United States.

JETA KATHOLIKE SHQIPTARE (Catholic Albanian Life). 1966-. Quarterly. Editor: Reverend Joseph J. Oroshi. Publisher: Albanian American Catholic League, Incorporated, 4221 Park Avenue and East Tremont Avenue, Bronx, New York 10457. In Albanian.

Carries articles dealing with religious, social, cultural, and political issues of interest to Albanians in the United States. Includes Bible translations and a special section concerning activities of the Albanian Catholic Church.

SHQIPTARI I LIRE (The Free Albanian). 1957-. Annual. Publisher: Free Albania Committee, 150 Fifth Avenue, Room 1103, New York, New York 10011. In Albanian.

Features articles concerned with various developments in Communist Albania for the purpose of exposing the denial of human, political, and other rights of the Albanian people by the Communist regime. Also covers resettlement problems of Albanian political refugees in the United States. Reports on political, cultural, religious, and social activities in the United States and abroad.

VRESHTA (The Vine). Quarterly. Editor: Metropolitan Fan S. Noli, Memorial Library, 529 East Broadway, South Boston, Massachusetts 02127. In Albanian and English.

ZERI I BALLIT (The Voice). 1950-. Quarterly. Editor: Dr. Begeja Halim. Publisher: Balli Kombetar Organization, 158-23 84th Drive, Jamaica, New York 11432. In Albanian.

Radio Programs

Massachusetts - Worcester

WORC - 8 Portland Street, Worcester, Massachusetts 01608, (617) 799-0581. Albanian programs, 1 hour weekly.

Bookdealers and Publishers' Representatives

CO-OP BOOKS
Post Office Box 2436
Tallahassee, Florida 32304 (904) 222-6677

FAM BOOK SERVICE
69 Fifth Avenue
New York, New York 10003 (212) 243-3737

Books and Pamphlets

THE ALBANIAN STRUGGLE IN THE OLD WORLD AND NEW. Boston, prepared by Federal Writers' Project of Massachusetts, 1939.

The most basic treatment to date on Albanian immigration.

THE ALBANIANS IN AMERICA: THE FIRST ARRIVALS. By Constantine A. Demo. Boston, Society "Fatbardhesia" of Katundi, 1960.

Discusses assimilation and acculturation of the first Albanian immigrants from a personal point of view. In English and Albanian.

FIFTIETH ANNIVERSARY BOOK OF THE ALBANIAN ORTHODOX CHURCH IN AMERICA, 1908-1958. By Fan S. Noli. Boston, Pan-Albanian Federation of America, 1960.

Describes the history of Albanian Orthodoxy in America.

ALGERIANS
See also: ARABS; FRENCH-SPEAKING PEOPLES

Embassy and Consulates

EMBASSY OF THE DEMOCRATIC AND POPULAR REPUBLIC OF ALGERIA
2118 Kalorama Road, Northwest
Washington, D.C. 20008 (202) 328-5300

CULTURAL ATTACHE
Watergate Office Building
2600 Virginia Avenue
Washington, D.C. 20037 (202) 328-5334

Mission to the United Nations

ALGERIAN MISSION
15 East 47th Street
New York, New York 10017 (212) 750-1960

Books and Pamphlets

ALGERIA. By the Arab Information Center with the cooperation of the Permanent Mission of Algeria to the United Nations. New York, Arab Information Center, 1973.

An illustrated pamphlet summarizing information about the country, its history, government, people, economic development, foreign trade, and tourism.

ALGERIA. By Richard I. Lawless. Oxford, England and Santa Barbara, California. Clio Press, 1980. (World Bibliographical Series).

An annotated bibliography of works dealing with Algeria's history, geography, economy, politics, and people. Includes a map of Algeria.

ALGERIAN PANORAMA; A Select Bibliographical Survey, 1965-1966. African Bibliographic Center. New York, Negro Universities Press, 1969.

ALGERIAN VINE AND WINE. By the Algerian Office for Marketing Wine and Other Viticultural Products, Algiers.

A brochure about wine production in ancient and modern times in Algeria and the various kinds of wine manufactured. Illustrated with color photographs and a fold-out map of winegrowing districts in Algeria.

THE ECONOMIC, SOCIAL AND POLITICAL DEVELOPMENT OF ALGERIA AND LIBYA. By John Vidergar. Monticello, Illinois, Vance Bibliographies, 1978.

This bibliography lists materials that show the current economic, social and political conditions in Algeria and Libya as well as how these conditions emerged. Materials are those that have been published in the 1970's with the majority of the entries by French authors.

THE FACES OF ALGERIA: AGRICULTURAL DEVELOPMENT. Algiers, Algerian Ministry of Information and Culture, 1971.

Discusses the physical characteristics of Algeria; evolution and methods of agricultural production; principal products; enlargement of productive capacities through land reform and improvement; protection and reclamation from erosion; use of scientific advances; and careful planning. One in a collection of 24 booklets on various aspects of Algeria.

THE FACES OF ALGERIA: THE FOUR-YEAR PLAN, 1971-1974. Algiers, Algerian Ministry of Information and Culture.

Covers overall predictions of the plan and projections for separate sectors in agriculture, industry, education, communication, transportation, housing, health, and tourism. Illustrated with tables and graphs.

THE FACES OF ALGERIA: TRANSPORT. Algiers, Algerian Ministry of Information, 1970.

Contains sections dealing with problems, plans, and developments in land transport, maritime transport, air transport, and professional training for various types of transport.

Audiovisual Material

MAPS

OASIS. Algiers, Algerian Ministry of Information and Culture.

One in a series of maps showing seven regions of Algeria. Gives the location of the oases and connecting roads, along with a text describing places of interest and special features of the region. Color photographs cover the reverse side of the map. Approximately 16 by 17 inches.

FILMS

ALGERIAN SAHARA. 16 mm. Color and sound. 29 minutes. By Ontario Educational Communications Authority. Released by Films, Incorporated, Wilmette, Illinois, 1976, made 1975.

Examines the Algerian Sahara from a geographical, historical, and demographic viewpoint. Explores subtle changes that are being brought about by technology. Also discusses nationalization of the oil industry, farming cooperatives, and agrarian reform programs.

The Office of the Cultural Attache of the Embassy of the Democratic and Popular Republic of Algeria, 2600 Virginia Avenue, Washington, D.C. 20037, will provide a list of documentary and feature films in French.

ARABS
(Includes MOSLEMS)
See also: Individual Arab Peoples

Information Offices

ARAB INFORMATION CENTERS

168 North Michigan Avenue
Chicago, Illinois 60601 (312) 368-0523

6060 North Central Expressway
Dallas, Texas 75206 (214) 369-3023

747 Third Avenue, 25th Floor
New York, New York 10017 (212) 838-8700

210 Post Street
San Francisco, California
94108 (415) 986-5911

1100 17th Street, Northwest
Washington, D.C. 20009 (202) 265-3210

PALESTINE INFORMATION OFFICE
1337 22nd Street, Northwest
Washington, D.C. 20037
Director: Hasan Rahman (202) 466-3348

Fraternal Organizations

AMERICAN ARABIC ASSOCIATION
Post Office Box 18217
Boston, Massachusetts 02118 (617) 396-8040
President: Fred Howard Founded 1960

Engages in humanitarian activities related to the Middle East such as Boys Town in Jericho and Project Loving Care for needy Arab Christian and Muslim children in Jerusalem and other parts of the Middle East. Sponsors exhibits of Arab art crafts, and literature, lectures, television and radio programs, study programs and other cultural and educational activities to interpret the Arab world to Americans. Monitors media and other communication outlets in order to counter anti-Arab stereotyping and discrimination. Presents AMARA awards in recognition of patriotic and humanitarian service towards peace in the Middle East.
Publications: AMARA Newsletter; also publishes pamphlets and greeting cards (Project Loving Care).

AMERICAN FEDERATION OF RAMALLAH
Post Office Box 2422 (313) 478-7687
Livonia, Michigan 48152 Founded 1959

The Ramallahites are Christians who trace their origins to the city of Ramallah on the West Bank territory. The various Ramallah local clubs maintain links with Ramallah by raising money to support needy families, hospitals and study abroad. Engages in social activities as well as cultural and educational pursuits such as workshops, films and lectures to contribute to the understanding of the Palestinian problem.

ARAB AMERICAN ASSOCIATION
Post Office Box 20041 (513) 961-0456
Cincinnati, Ohio 45220 (513) 793-6195
Director: Hasan A. Hammami Founded 1967

Activities of the Association relate primarily to Arab Americans, Americans of Arab descent and Arab residents in the greater Cincinnati area as well as to the image of Arabs in general the United States. Social, educational, cultural and informational activities are sponsored with the aim of improving attitudes and behavior towards Arab Americans, Arabs and the Arab world on the basis of enlightened mutual interests and interdependence. Supports strong ties between the United States and the Arab world and a just and lasting peace in the Middle East.
Publications: Arab American Association Newsletter, bimonthly.

ARAB WOMEN'S COUNCIL
Post Office Box 11048
Washington, D.C. 20008 (202) 363-4890
President: Nuha Alhegelan Founded 1982

Arab and Arab-American women. To inform the public on Arab women and the Arab culture. Initiated a hunger strike to protest Israel's blockage of food and water to west Beirut, Lebanon in July, 1982. Conducts seminars for Arab-American women. Maintains speakers bureau and charitable program.
Publications: Facts About the War in Lebanon, semiweekly.

Professional Organizations

ARAB AMERICAN MEDICAL ASSOCIATION
Post Office Box 1500 (213) 872-0428
Encino, California 91426 Founded 1973

Members of the medical professions who are of Arab descent. Holds scientific lectures and symposia in relation to medicine in the Middle East. Sponsors a crippled child from the Middle East for medical and surgical treatment. Engages in social activities.

MIDDLE EAST LIBRARIANS' ASSOCIATION
Main Library, Room 310
1858 Neil Avenue Mall
Ohio State University
Columbus, Ohio 43210
Secretary - Treasurer: Marsha McClintock (614) 422-8389
Founded 1972

Librarians and others interested in those aspects of librarianship which support the study or dissemination of information about the Middle East since the rise of Islam. Purposes are: to facilitate communication among members through meetings and publications; to improve the quality of area librarianship through the development of standards for the profession and education of Middle East library specialists; to compile and disseminate information concerning Middle East libraries and collections and represent the judgment of the members in matters affecting them; to encourage cooperation among members and Middle East libraries, especially in the acquisition of materials and the development of bibliographic controls; to cooperate with other library and area organizations in projects of mutual concern and benefit; to promote research in and development of indexing and automated techniques as applied to Middle East materials.
Publications: MELA Notes, 3 times a year; Membership Directory, annual.

NATIONAL ARAB AMERICAN MEDICAL ASSOCIATION
c/o Los Angeles Chapter
Post Office Box 1500
Encino, California 91426 (213) 872-0428
Secretary: Floyd A. Nassif M.D. Founded 1980

Established to contribute to progress within the medical profession; to provide professional relations among members of the medical professions in the United States and Arab countries, to create friendly relations among health field professionals who share a common cultural heritage; to provide assistance to medical students, interns and residents of Arabic background; to encourage and coordinate efforts to supply medicines and medical aid to the poor and needy of Arab countries and to those of Arabic background in the United States. Sponsors medical scholarships.

Public Affairs Organizations

AMERICAN-ARAB ANTI-DISCRIMINATION COMMITTEE
1611 Connecticut Avenue, Northwest
Washington, D.C. 20009
Executive Director: James J. Zogby (202) 797-7662
Founded 1980

Grassroots organization representing Arab Americans. To protect the rights of people of Arab descent; to promote and defend the Arab-American heritage, and to serve the needs of the Arab-American community. Works through its Action Network and Media Monitoring Groups to end, by legal means, the stereotyping of Arabs in the media and discrimination against Americans in employment, education, and politics. Organizes protests against racist advertisements and other media.
Publications: Issues, monthly; Report (in English and Arabic), monthly.

AMERICAN-ARAB RELATIONS COMMITTEE
Box 416
New York, New York 10017 (212) 682-1154
President: Dr. M. T. Mehdi Founded 1964

Composed of "persons concerned about the goal of improving American-Arab relations and the establishment of peace and democracy in Palestine." Non-sectarian group which does not take stands on problems of the Arab world and inter-Arab relations or on domestic issues within the United States. Some 60 percent of members are Americans of Arab origin. "An organization of the moderates; Committee is opposed to fascism, anti-Semitism and Zionism." Activities have included picketing and demonstrations, filing lawsuits and registering complaints with the Federal Communications Commission about slanted portrayal of Arabs by communications media. Offers special services to American Arabs in their process of becoming full citizens; has met with Jewish groups to formulate a peace plan for the Middle East. Maintains speakers bureau. Formerly (1978) Action Committee on American-Arab Relations.
Publications: Action (English-Arabic newspaper), weekly; Yearbook.

AMERICAN COMMUNITY FOR MIDDLE EAST JUSTICE
Post Office Box 521
Cedar Rapids, Iowa 52406
Contact: Bill Aossey

Muslim and Christian Arabs engaged in improving understanding of the Arab tradition in the American media.

CENTER FOR MIDDLE EAST POLICY
1763 N Street, Northwest
Washington, D.C. 20036 (202) 296-7152
President: John P. Richardson Founded 1981

Furthers understanding of Middle East issues among the industrialized nations (United States, Europe and Japan) by organizing visits among government officials of the various countries, sponsoring a series of congressional luncheons at which knowledgeable speakers examine trade, energy, security, cultural and political matters, and arranging lecture tours and seminars. Disseminates European and Japanese editorial opinion about the Middle East to major newspapers in the United States.
Publication: Newsletter, monthly.

COALITION FOR STRATEGIC STABILITY IN THE MIDDLE EAST
c/o Mr. Chris Gersten
1125 17th Street, Northwest
Washington, D.C. 20006
Chairman: Clifford P. Chase

According to an advertisement in the New York Times, October 18, 1981, the coalition questions the United States Middle East policy aimed at forming "a broad anti-Soviet alliance of moderate Muslim states." Believes it is unwise to base the West's opposition to Soviet expansionism in the Middle East on "unreliable and authoritarian monarchical regimes such as Saudi Arabia," especially after the revolution in Iran. Opposes the sale of sophisticated military technology (such as the AWACS plane) to these regimes, and calls for increased United States military presence in the region to meet the Soviet threat. Calls for America's Middle Eastern allies to increase their cooperation in their own defense by leasing military bases to the United States and through support for the Camp David peace process and other international initiatives aimed at the Soviet Union.

COMMUNITY FOR SOCIAL JUSTICE IN THE MIDDLE EAST AND NORTH AFRICA
Fox Hall, Room 224
American University
Washington, D.C. 20016
Executive Director: Katherine Knight (202) 686-7925

An independent research group established by the Center for Mediterranean Studies. Seeks to unite people from differing orientations interested in the problems of social and economic justice in the Middle East and North Africa. Goal is the establishment of an efficient, humanistic and creative society through the promotion of political participation, advancement of responsive institutions, and the attempt to balance traditional culture with self-development. Community activities include the collection and distribution of information on social change, sponsorship of research, publications, symposiums and curriculum development, and the expansion of communication between organizations and institutions in the Middle East and similar groups worldwide.

MIDDLE EAST RESEARCH AND INFORMATION PROJECT
Post Office Box 3122
Columbia Heights Station
Washington, D.C. 20010 (202) 667-1188
Executive Officer: Judith Tucker Founded 1970

Collective of part- or full-time researchers on the Middle East area. To provide information, research and analysis of United States involvement in the Middle East revolutionary movements and political and economic developments. Provides speakers; conducts seminars and slide and media shows.
Publication: Reports, 9 times a year.

MIDDLE EAST RESOURCE CENTER
1322 18th Street, Northwest
Washington, D.C. 20036 (202) 659-6846
Coordinator: Janice Murphy Founded 1975

Resource and information distribution center aimed at informing Washington based non-governmental offices, congressional offices and national media about issues pertinent to the Middle East conflict, with particular emphasis on the Palestinian people. Advocates recognition of the Palestine Liberation Organization as a representative of the Palestinian people and establishment of a Palestinian state. Coordinates requests for speakers on the Middle East with local and visiting experts and representatives. Conducts research; holds press conferences.
Publication: Palestine/Israel Bulletin, monthly.

NATIONAL ASSOCIATION OF ARAB AMERICANS
1825 Connecticut Avenue, Northwest, No. 211
Washington, D.C. 20009 (202) 797-7757
Executive Director: David Sadd Founded 1972

United States citizens of Arab ancestry and interested individuals. Objectives are: to encourage and promote friendship between the people of the United States and of Arab countries; to engage in political, social, cultural and educational activities for the purpose of maintaining political action and involvement in the United States; to give support and assistance to citizens of Arab ancestry throughout the United States; to assist them in any endeavor to attain positions of local, state and national office; to support and assist members of Congress and others in the United States government who support these objectives; to maintain communication with the appropriate officials in Washington, D.C., the United Nations and elsewhere in the continental limits of the United States; to exchange opinions, formulate plans and conduct dialogue for the avowed purpose of encouraging better relations between the United States and Arab countries. Conducts seminars and conferences. Compiles statistics. Maintains speakers bureau; conducts research programs.
Publications: Counterpoint, monthly; Focus, bimonthly; Voice, quarterly; Middle East Business Survey, annual; also publishes monographs, reprints and handbooks.

NOVEMBER 29 COALITION
Post Office Box 115
New York, New York 10113 (212) 695-2686

Named for day declared by the United Nations as International Day of Solidarity with the Palestinian people. Conducts teach-ins.

PALESTINE ARAB DELEGATION
Post Office Box 1855
New York, New York 10063 (212) 838-6320
Director: Issa Nakhleh Founded 1956

Organized "to present the views of the Palestine Arabs in the special political committee of the United Nations during the United Nations General Assembly and rally support for the liberation of their homeland from the illegal Zionist occupation." Provides speakers for meetings. Publishes pamphlets and press releases. Formerly known as the Palestine Arab Refugee Office.

PALESTINE CONGRESS OF NORTH AMERICA
Post Office Box 9621
Washington, D.C. 20016 (202) 244-5573
Executive Officer: Jawad George Founded 1979

Goals are to build a better image for all Arab peoples and to develop a stronger political lobby on behalf of a Middle East solution that will provide Palestinians with their own homeland. Supports official Palestine Liberation Organization policy that aims to "establish an independent Palestinian state and see the end of the Zionist Israeli government."

PALESTINE HUMAN RIGHTS CAMPAIGN

20 East Jackson, Room 1111
Chicago, Illinois 60604
Executive Officer: Don Wagner (312) 987-1830

Post Office Box 3033
Washington, D.C. 20010 (202) 296-5089
Chairman: James J. Zogby Founded 1977

Defends the rights of Palestinians living in occupied territories. Using the United Nations Universal Declaration of Human Rights as its guide, the Campaign endeavors to see basic human rights and freedoms enforced for the Palestinian people. Supports victims and their attorneys, and investigates and publishes information on human rights violations.
Publications: Palestine Human Rights Bulletin, monthly; Shahak Papers (translations of Israeli press materials), monthly; also publishes position papers and translations.

SEARCH FOR JUSTICE AND EQUALITY IN PALESTINE
Post Office Box 53
Waverly Station
Boston, Massachusetts 02179
Acting Executive Director: Cheri Hanks (617) 899-9665
Founded 1971

To educate American leaders and the public on the Arab-Israeli conflict and to seek an American Middle East policy that supports a just Palestinian-Israeli settlement on the basis of the inalienable rights of both peoples. Urges Americans to recognize that justice for the Palestinians and security for Israeli Jews are "interdependent and not mutually exclusive"; encourages Americans to oppose both anti-Jewish and anti-Arab forms of prejudice, and to realize that "an exemplary opposition to anti-Semitism entails no obligation to support the policies of the State of Israel." Maintains dialogues between Palestinians and American Jews; supports

Israeli human rights groups. Operates speakers bureau. Affiliated with Middle East Resource Center. Publication: Palestine/Israel Bulletin, 10 times a year.

Cultural and Educational Organizations

AMERICA-MIDEAST EDUCATIONAL AND TRAINING SERVICES
1717 Massachusetts Avenue, Northwest
Washington, D.C. 20036 (202) 797-7900
President: Orin D. Parker Founded 1951

Americans interested in the Middle East. Purpose is to "improve the quality of educational and cultural exchanges to the mutual benefit of the peoples of the Middle East and of the United States." Provides information, counseling, admissions and orientation services for students and sponsors from the Middle East and North Africa, including translation and certification of credentials where not provided by government ministries and educational institutions; orientation for students prior to departure for the United States; administration and supervision of scholarship programs sponsored by governments, institutions and companies under contracts; and interviews as requested by American universities for students applying directly for admission or scholarship aid. Maintains overseas offices. Formerly (1977) American Friends of the Middle East.
Publications: Human Resource Developments, quarterly; also publishes Cultures of the Islamic Middle East and other materials on education in Middle East and North Africa.

AMERICAN-ARAB AFFAIRS COUNCIL
1730 M Street, Northwest, Suite 411
Washington, D.C. 20036
President and Executive Director: George A. Naifeh (202) 296-6767
Founded 1979

A non-profit organization established to explore current developments affecting United States - Arab relations. Offers a program of publications, lectures and seminars that provide interested Americans with scholarly discussion of issues of concern to both Americans and Arabs. Activities are guided by advisory committees in the field of diplomacy, economics, education, and the media, composed of Americans distinguished for their knowledge of United States - Arab affairs.
Publications: American Arab Affairs (journal), quarterly; Special Reports, irregular; also publishes books.

AMERICAN ASSOCIATION OF TEACHERS OF ARABIC
Oriental Institute
University of Chicago
1155 East 58th Street
Chicago, Illinois 60637
Executive Secretary: Carolyn G. Killean (312) 753-2473
Founded 1963

College and university teachers and scholars in the fields of Arabic studies, language, linguistics, and literature. Promotes annual Arabic Translation Contest and awards two prizes.
Publications: Al-Arabiyya, annual; Newsletter, annual.

AMERICAN COUNCIL ON THE MIDDLE EAST
c/o Frank C. Sakran
Mechanicsville, Maryland 20659
Executive Secretary: Frank C. Sakran (301) 884-3531
Founded 1967

Scholars working for a "just and lasting peace in the Middle East." Conducts educational seminars.

AMERICAN PROFESSORS FOR PEACE IN THE MIDDLE EAST
9 East 40th Street (212) 532-5005
New York, New York 10016 Founded 1967

Campus based organization concerned with working for a lasting peace in the Middle East, through study and analysis. Organizes academic conferences, briefing sessions and lecture tours by Middle East specialists. The organization is not committed to a specific policy but only for a just and lasting peace between Israel and her Arab neighbors. Maintains political arm called the American Academic Association for Peace in the Middle East.

AMERICANS FOR MIDDLE EAST UNDERSTANDING
475 Riverside Drive, Room 771
New York, New York 10115
Executive Director: Dr. John F. Mahoney (212) 870-2053
Founded 1967

Fosters better understanding in America about the history, goals and values of Middle East people as well as an understanding of the forces that are shaping American policy there. Distributes educational material to churches, schools and libraries. Maintains speakers bureau.
Publications: The Link (newsletter), five times a year; Public Affairs Series of Pamphlets, irregular; also publishes books on the Middle East.

ARAB-AMERICAN COUNCIL FOR CULTURAL AND ECONOMIC EXCHANGE
c/o Mohsen A. Bagnied
3445 Mildred Drive
Falls Church, Virginia 22042 (703) 536-1969
Chairman: Mohsen A. Bagnied Founded 1976

To promote cultural, economic and educational exchanges between the United States and the Arab world. Organizes delegations from business, government and academic institutions to travel to the Middle East.

ARABIC MATERIALS DEVELOPMENT CENTER
611 Church Street
Ann Arbor, Michigan 48104
Director: Frederick W. Bertolaet (313) 763-9946

Prepares teaching materials for Arabic-speaking children.

ASSOCIATION OF ARAB-AMERICAN UNIVERSITY GRADUATES
556 Trapelo Road
Belmont, Massachusetts 02178 (617) 484-5483
Administrative Director: Najla Deuny Founded 1967

Promotes knowledge and understanding of cultural, scientific, and educational matters between the Arab and American peoples. Establishes links among Arab-American professionals and promotes their professional activities and projects. Assists in the development of the Arab World by providing the professional services of its membership. Sponsors symposia and a speakers bureau. Presents awards annually.
Publications: Newsletter, bimonthly; Arab Studies, quarterly; also publishes information papers, books and monographs on contemporary Arab society, culture and politics.

ASSOCIATION OF MUSLIM SOCIAL SCIENTISTS
Post Office Box 38
Plainfield, Indiana 46168 (317) 839-8157
President: Dr. Talat Sultan Founded 1972

Professors and graduate students in the social sciences and humanities. Objectives are: to encourage members to conduct studies and research in their areas of specialization; to assist in developing Islamic positions on contemporary issues and to apply them to studies and researches; to generate Islamic thought through critical and scientific inquiry and disseminate it through various means; to aid in the professional development and introduction of placement opportunities. Sponsors research projects. Cooperates with other Islamic organizations of similar nature.
Publications: Bulletin, quarterly; Newsletters, four times a year; Proceedings of Conferences, annual; Proceedings of Seminars, annual.

ISLAM CENTENNIAL FOURTEEN
4900 Massachusetts Avenue, Northwest
Washington, D.C. 20016
Executive Director: Honorable William R. Crawford (202) 966-5633
Founded 1979

To promote a better understanding in the United States of the Muslim culture through a series of cultural and educational activities. Commemorated the fourteenth centennial of the founding of Islam on November 9, 1980. Publicizes nationwide events and programs recognizing the anniversary of Islam; acts as a resource and information clearinghouse; provides speakers. Bestows grants to universities and institutions for research, curricula, development and publications. Major projects are a documentary film production for television, museum and educational showing and a traveling museum exhibition, the Heritage of Islam, featuring Islamic arts, sciences, history and cultural contributions.
Publications: Newsletter, bimonthly; also publishes Islam: An Introduction (information kit).

MIDDLE EAST INSTITUTE
1761 N Street, Northwest
Washington, D.C. 20036 (202) 785-1141
President: L. Dean Brown Founded 1946

Government officials, scholars, business executives, students and others interested in the Middle East. To stimulate an interest in the history, culture, politics, economy and languages of the Middle East, through lectures, conferences and programs of all kinds; to provide, through a 15,000 volume research library, up-to-date, complete and objective information about the Middle East. Maintains film library; provides classes in modern Middle Eastern languages.
Publications: Middle East Journal, quarterly; Annual Conference Record; also publishes books on the Middle East and a Twenty-Year Index of the Middle East Journal.

MIDDLE EAST PEACE PROJECT
339 Lafayette Street
New York, New York 10012 (212) 475-4300
Director: Allan Solomonow Founded 1969

Individuals and national peace and religious groups committed to: nonviolent resolution of the conflict in the Middle East; peace and justice for all peoples in the Middle East; the right of Israel to exist in peace and security; the right of Palestinians to a state of their own; a Middle East that does not become a battleground for East and West, oil, an arms race, or nuclear weapons. Strives for a mutually satisfactory settlement to bring together the

Palestinian and Israeli peoples. Serves as resource center and clearinghouse for Middle East peace work; organizes Middle East tours; sponsors programs to encourage discussion between Palestinians, Jews, and Americans. Seeks to increase public awareness of the Middle East situation. Distributes articles, translations, books, and a monthly resources and information kit. Affiliated with Fellowship of Reconciliation. Formerly (1976) Committee on New Alternatives in the Middle East.

MIDDLE EAST STUDIES ASSOCIATION OF NORTH AMERICA
Department of Oriental Studies
University of Arizona
Tucson, Arizona 85721
Executive Secretary: Michael E. Bonnie — (602) 626-5850
Founded 1966

Scholars, students and individuals with interests in the Middle East "to promote high standards of scholarship and instruction in the area, to facilitate communication among scholars and to foster cooperation among persons and organizations concerned with the scholarly study of the Middle East, including the area from Morocco to Pakistan and from Turkey to the Sudan." MESA is concerned with this area primarily since the rise of Islam and from the viewpoint of the social science and humanities disciplines. Sponsors Visiting Scholars Program enabling Middle Eastern scholars to lecture at North American universities.
Publications: International Journal of Middle East Studies, quarterly; Newsletter, 3 times a year; Bulletin, semiannual; Abstracts of Papers Delivered at Annual Meeting, annual; Roster of MESA Fellows, annual; Directory of Graduate and Undergraduate Programs and Courses in Middle East Studies in the United States, Canada and Abroad, biennial.

MUSLIM STUDENTS' ASSOCIATION
Post Office Box 38
Plainfield, Indiana 46168
Secretary General: Rabie Hassan Ahmed — (317) 839-8157
Founded 1963

Students, immigrants and United States citizens who are of the Muslim faith or who are interested in Islam. To make Islam better understood by Muslims and non-Muslims. Programs and activities include: Islamic centers and mosques; Sunday schools; correspondence courses; scholarships; library; hostel; educational programs for women, youth, children and adults; special programs for professional groups (doctors, engineers, businessmen); co-operative fund. Conducts seminars and leadership training program. Maintains library and speakers bureau.
Publications: Islamic Horizons, monthly; Al-Itthad, quarterly; Annual Report; also publishes books, manuals, films and slides, tapes.

NEAR EAST COLLEGE ASSOCIATION
380 Madison Avenue
New York, New York 10017
Administrative Director: Walter Prosser — (212) 490-8770
Founded 1919

American sponsored educational institutions in the Near and Middle East including: American University of Beirut, Anatolia College, Athens College in Greece, International College, Robert College of Istanbul, and Sofia American Schools. Association exists only as a conduit for gifts and grants to the member institutions.

ORGANIZATION OF ARAB STUDENTS IN THE U.S.A. AND CANADA
Post Office Box 25302
Chicago, Illinois 60625
Founded 1952

Arab college students organized to present the interests and aspirations of the Arab students in the United States, disseminate true and adequate information about the Arab people, promote better understanding and closer relations with the various student organizations inside and outside the United States, and establish stronger ties with the American people through mutual understanding. Conducts research on all aspects of life in the Middle East and North Africa.
Publications: News, bimonthly; Arab Student Bulletin, quarterly; Year Book; also publishes information and statements on the Arab world, and convention reports.

Foundations

AMERICAN ARAB ETHNIC STUDIES FOUNDATION
4367 Beverly Boulevard
Los Angeles, California 90004
Director: Joseph Haiek — (213) 666-1212

Aids research in sociological, demographic, historical and cultural aspects of Arab American ethnic groups. Maintains library and archives.

AMERICAN PALESTINE EDUCATION FOUNDATION
Post Office Box 3729
Washington, D.C. 20007 (202) 244-2642
Executive Director: Shukri Abed Founded 1977

Administers scholarships for Palestine students to study in the United States. Sponsors educational projects in the Arab community in Israel.

ARAB AMERICAN CULTURAL FOUNDATION
2435 Virginia Avenue, Northwest
Post Office Box 3761
Washington, D.C. 20007
Executive Director: Claudette Shwiry (202) 338-1200
Chairman: Dr. Hisham Sharabi Founded 1980

Founded to extend and deepen the knowledge of Arab culture, particularly modern Arab culture, among the people of the United States. Seeks to emcompass a broad range of Arab culture, by presenting performing artists and musicians, painters, scholars and creative writers to the American public. Also sponsors programs by gifted Arab Americans and Western experts on the Arab world. Activities include lectures, symposia, workshops in music, poetry readings, exhibitions of painting, sculpture and photography, and performance of traditional music and modern compositions.

ATTIYEH FOUNDATION
1806 T Street, Northwest, Suite 201
Washington, D.C. 20009 (202) 745-3936
Executive Director: Paula Stinson Founded 1980

Founded to build understanding between the American people and Arab peoples. Sponsors speaking tours, art exhibits, and educational projects, such as the distribution of Sesame Street books in Arabic to Arabic-speaking children in the United States and an essay contest on the Israeli-Palestinian war. Activities are concentrated in the West and Midwest. Awards grants to institutions.

FOUNDATION FOR MIDDLE EAST PEACE
1522 K Street, Northwest, Suite 202
Washington, D.C. 20005 (202) 347-8241
President: Merle Thorpe Founded 1979

Awards grants to projects which are directed toward understanding the Israeli-Palestinian conflict and contributes to a just peace for both peoples.

NEAR EAST FOUNDATION
29 Broadway, Suite 1125
New York, New York 10006 (212) 269-0600
President: John M. Sutton Founded 1915

Not a membership organization; supported by voluntary contributions from individuals and corporations. "To assist governments of newly developing nations to launch programs of rural and community improvement that, as rapidly as possible, become the full responsibility of that government in matters of operation, financing and personnel." Conducts programs in areas of rural development, education, food production and agriculture, public health, social welfare and construction, housing and planning. Countries of operation include Egypt, Jordan, Lesotho, Liberia, Mali, Swaziland, Tanzania and Togo. Formerly (1930) Near East Relief.
Publications: News, semiannual; Annual Report.

Charitable Organizations

AMER MEDICAL DIVISION, AMERICAN NEAR EAST REFUGEE AID
1522 K Street, Northwest, No. 202
Washington, D.C. 20005 (202) 347-2558
Director: Ann Barhoum Founded 1948

Since 1971 has operated as a division of American Near East Refugee Aid. Solicits and ships medical supplies and pharmaceuticals for use by Palestine refugees in the Middle East. Formerly (1963) American Middle East Relief; (1978) American Middle East Rehabilitation.

AMERICAN NEAR EAST REFUGEE AID
1522 K Street, Northwest, No. 202
Washington, D.C. 20005 (202) 347-2558
President: Peter Gubser Founded 1968

Organizations associated with refugee relief; interested individuals. Formed "to provide assistance to Palestinian refugees and other needy individuals in the Arab world and to further American understanding of the Arab refugee problem." Sponsors projects to bring electricity into rural areas; helps support agricultural cooperatives; provides assistance to a four-year nursing school for young Palestinians; helps to provide education and skills training for Palestinian children; sponsors literacy classes and job-training programs for adults. Conducts fundraising appeals for Palestinian relief and socio-economic development; prepares and distributes information materials on the Middle East crisis.
Publication: Newsletter, quarterly.

CATHOLIC NEAR EAST WELFARE ASSOCIATION
1011 First Avenue
New York, New York 10022
National Secretary: John G. Nolan — (212) 826-1480
Founded 1926

Catholic organization of individuals and unrelated groups. Raises funds to assist humanitarian projects in 18 countries, primarily in the Near and Middle East; pays costs of education for native priests and sisters and provides money for chapels and rectories, orphanages, convents and schools. Promotes interest in the Eastern Rites and the problems of church unity. Affiliated with Pontifical Mission for Palestine.
Publication: Catholic Near East Magazine, quarterly.

NAJDA (Women Concerned about the Middle East)
Post Office Box 7152
Berkeley, California 94707 — (415) 655-6879
President: Tina Niccach — Founded 1960

Formed to give aid to refugees in the Middle East. Awards scholarships to Palestinian women. Sponsors educational and civic activities.
Publications: Najda Newsletter, monthly; also publishes books.

PALESTINE AID SOCIETY
904 Woodward Tower
Detroit, Michigan 48226 — (313) 961-7252
President: Anan Jabara — Founded 1977

Voluntary organization with chapters in Canada, Europe and the Middle East. Supports projects of Najdeh in Lebanon such as construction of bomb shelters, expenses of kindergartens and refugee camps, establishment of embroidery workshops for Palestine and Lebanon widows. Raises funds for charitable and self-help projects by selling embroideries from the workshops and sponsoring social and educational events.

PALESTINE CONGRESS EMERGENCY RELIEF FUND
Post Office Box 9621
Washington, D.C. 20016 — (202) 244-5573

Coordinates procurement of medical supplies and health professionals.

PONTIFICAL MISSION FOR PALESTINE
1011 First Avenue
New York, New York 10022 — (212) 826-1480
President: John G. Nolan — Founded 1949

Catholic organization of individuals and unrelated groups. Cooperates with the United Nations Relief and Works Agency and other voluntary agencies in providing Palestinian refugees in Lebanon, Syria, Jordan and the Gaza Strip with food, clothing, shelter, medical aid, vocational training and religious care. Affiliated with Catholic Near East Welfare Association.

UNITED PALESTINIAN APPEAL
2025 Eye Street, Northwest, Suite 916
Washington, D.C. 20006
Chairman: Mohammad Tarbush — (202) 659-5007
Contact Person: Nora Zein — Founded 1980

Founded by a group of philanthropic Palestinians to raise funds to alleviate suffering on the West Bank, Gaza and other parts of the Middle East. Gives aid to clinics, hospitals, schools and orphanages. Sponsors scholarships and grants, aid to farmers and peasants. Attempts to improve social, economic and human conditions of the Palestinians.

U.S. OMEN
Post Office Box 85249
Los Angeles, California 90072

A California-based relief organization working in the Middle East.

Religious Organizations

AMERICAN DRUZE SOCIETY
8213 Corteland Drive
Knoxville, Tennessee 37919
Executive Secretary: Kathy Jaber Stephenson — (615) 691-9080

CEDAR RAPIDS ISLAMIC CENTER AND MOSQUE
2999 First Avenue, Southwest
Cedar Rapids, Iowa 52404 — (515) 362-0857

COUNCIL OF ISLAMIC ORGANIZATIONS OF AMERICA
676 St. Marks Avenue
Brooklyn, New York 11216
President: Hajj Amir Hassam

FEDERATION OF ISLAMIC ASSOCIATIONS IN THE U.S. AND CANADA
25351 Five Mile Road
Redford Township, Michigan 48259 (313) 535-0014
Secretary General: Nihad Hamed Founded 1951

Religious, political, social, and educational organization which acts as an umbrella for Muslim groups in the United States and Canada. Objectives are to: defend the human rights of Muslims and all oppressed people through democratic, political means; promote the spirit, ethics, philosophy, and culture of Muslim heritage; answer questions and correct misconceptions about Islam; promote friendly relations between Muslims and non-Muslims of North America. Sponsors seminars on religious affairs; conducts charitable program and specialized education; sponsors youth programs and bestows scholarships for the study of Islam; holds receptions for Arab ambassadors; sponsors talks by representatives from the League of Arab States; distributes literature to schools, universities, and libraries. Maintains library of religious and political books on Middle East affairs.
Publications: Muslim Star, monthly; also publishes books and issues press releases.

ISLAMIC ASSOCIATION OF NORTHERN TEXAS
609 North Bagdad
Grand Praire, Texas 75050

THE ISLAMIC CENTER
15571 Joy Road at Greenfield
Detroit, Michigan 48238

THE ISLAMIC CENTER
2551 Massachusetts Avenue, Northwest
Washington, D.C. 20008 (202) 265-8504
Director: Mohammad Asi Founded 1949

The national center for the Moslem community in the United States. Conducts religious services, lectures, and discussions. Holds religious and language classes during the week and an Islamic Weekend School. Welcomes and assists converts to the faith of Islam. Performs marriage ceremonies in accordance with Islamic law and procedure. Maintains a Moslem cemetery. Also maintains a small library. Disseminates information about Islam, its history and civilization.
Publications: Bulletin; Islamic Calendar; also books and pamphlets on Islamic topics.

ISLAMIC CENTER OF CLEVELAND
9400 Detroit Avenue
Cleveland, Ohio 44120

ISLAMIC CENTER OF GREATER ST. LOUIS
3843 West Pine Boulevard
St. Louis, Missouri 63108 (314) 534-9672

ISLAMIC CENTER OF JERSEY CITY
17 Park Street
Jersey City, New Jersey 07304

ISLAMIC CENTER OF NEW YORK
1 Riverside Drive
New York, New York 10023 (212) 362-6800
Director: Hosny M. Garber Founded 1966

Founded to serve the religious and cultural needs of the 100,000-member Muslim community in the metropolitan New York area and to contribute to the well-being of the Muslims in America at large. Serves as a source of information about Islam, its history, civilization, and people. Conducts a weekend religious school. Maintains a library of about 8,000 volumes.

ISLAMIC CENTER OF SOUTHERN CALIFORNIA
4345 Vermont Avenue South
Los Angeles, California 90037 (213) 384-5783

ISLAMIC COMMUNITY, INCORPORATED
5110 Nineteenth Avenue
Brooklyn, New York 11204

ISLAMIC FOUNDATION OF SOUTHERN CALIFORNIA
9752 West Thirteenth Street
Garden Grove, California 92643 (714) 531-1722

ISLAMIC MISSION OF AMERICA
143 State Street
Brooklyn, New York 11201 (212) 875-6607
Director: Hajja Khadijah Faisal Founded 1938

Dedicated to the propagation of the Islamic faith. Prepares students for missionary work. Maintains a mosque in Brooklyn, New York, and an institute for teaching religion and Arabic.

ISLAMIC SOCIETY OF ORANGE COUNTY
Post Office Box 1330 B
Garden Grove, California 92642
Director: Dr. Muzammil Siddiqi (714) 963-7053

MOSLEM MOSQUE
104 Powers Street
Brooklyn, New York 11211 (212) 387-0835
President: Jack Gambitsky Founded 1907

Founded to perpetuate the religion and faith of Islam, and to provide a mosque for religious services. Formerly called the American Mohammedan Society.

MOSQUE FOUNDATION OF NEW JERSEY
80 Grandview Avenue
North Caldwell, New Jersey 07547

MUSLIM COMMUNITY CENTER
1651 North Kedzie Avenue
Chicago, Illinois 60647

NORTH AMERICAN ISLAMIC TRUST
10900 West Washington Street
Indianapolis, Indiana 46231 (317) 839-9248
General Manager: Muhammad Badr Founded 1973

Publishes, prints and distributes Islamic books and religious supplies. Maintains small library of Arabic and English works on Islam. Affiliated with Muslim Students' Association of the United States and Canada.

Research Centers and Special Institutes

AMERICAN INSTITUTE OF ISLAMIC STUDIES
c/o The Director
Post Office Box 10191
Denver, Colorado 80210 (303) 936-0108
Director: Charles Geddes Founded 1965

Academic research and educational services institution. Aim is to further the knowledge and understanding about the faith, history and culture of Islam and the contemporary Muslim world and to create a climate of mutual respect and friendship between peoples of all races, religious beliefs, nationalities, and cultures; provide accurate, unbiased information and educational materials on the history, culture and faith of Islam and the Muslim world, and a means of communication among students, scholars and research and teaching institutions. Encourages and supports the preparation and publication of scholarly materials. Conducts seminars, colloquia and meetings; sponsors exhibitions, films and lectures. Maintains a reference collection; the Muslim Bibliographic Center and a library of 7,500 volumes including a special collection of bibliographic materials. Plans to construct a research center and library and to establish a fellowship program.
Publications: Newsletter, 3 times a year; also publishes Bibliographic Series. Is currently preparing A Retrospective Catalogue and International Union List of Arabic Periodicals; A Guide to Reference Materials for Islamic Studies; An Annotated Bibliography of Bibliographies on the Muslim Peoples; A Guide to Periodicals in Western Languages Dealing with Islamic, Near Eastern, and North African Studies, and An International Directory of Institutes and Societies Interested in Islam and the Muslim World.

CENTER FOR ARAB-ISLAMIC STUDIES
Post Office Box 543
Brattleboro, Vermont 05301 (802) 257-0872
President: Samir Abed-Rabbo Founded 1980

Not a membership organization; board of directors is composed of educators. Objectives are to: promote deeper understanding between the American and Moslem peoples; study aspects of Arab/Islamic affairs. Sponsors symposia and lectures.
Publication: Search (journal), quarterly.

CENTER FOR CONTEMPORARY ARAB STUDIES
Georgetown University
Room 501, Intercultural Center
Washington, D.C. 20057 (202) 623-3128
Director: Dr. Michael Hudson Founded 1975

Offers courses leading to a Master's degree in Arab Studies, the only such program in the United States. Sponsors lectures, films and special cultural programs for the interested public. Provides a media service for current Arab questions. Conducts a research and publication program primarily in Arab-related international affairs, economics and history.
Publication: CCAS News, monthly newsletter.

CENTER FOR ISLAMIC AND ARABIAN DEVELOPMENT STUDIES
Duke University
2114 Campus Drive
Durham, North Carolina 27706
Director: Dr. Ralph Braibanti

Recently established research activity at Duke University, for conduct of research and instruction on Islamic civilization and political development of the Arabian peninsula.

CENTER FOR MIDDLE EAST STUDIES
Johns Hopkins University
1740 Massachusetts Avenue
Washington, D.C. 20036 (202) 785-6256
Director: Professor Fouad Ajami Founded 1960

Integral unit of Johns Hopkins University School of Advanced International Studies, located in Washington, D.C. Supported by parent institution and private foundations. Principal fields of research are in Middle East, specifically Israel, Turkey and Arabic-speaking states, including studies on political modernization and development, conflict and revolutionary change, parties and elites, the military, Islamic culture, law and institutions, contemporary political thought, ideological development with an emphasis on nationalism, economic trends and international politics. Also provides graduate instruction in these subjects and courses in Turkish and modern literary Arabic. Holds frequent lectures and discussions on aspects of the Middle East. Research results published in professional journals and monographs.

CENTER FOR MIDDLE EASTERN STUDIES
Harvard University
1737 Cambridge Street
Cambridge, Massachusetts 02138
Director: Professor Dennis Skiotis (617) 495-4055
Founded 1954

Integral unit of Faculty of Arts and Sciences at Harvard University, operating under an interdepartmental faculty committee. Supported by parent institution, United States Government, industry and research grants. Research is concentrated in the social sciences and the humanities, including interdisciplinary studies on culture, economics, history, languages and literatures of Middle East, with particular emphasis on modern period. Also provides instruction and research training for graduate students of the University. Research results published in two series of special study monographs by Harvard University Press, professional journals and doctoral theses.

CENTER FOR MIDDLE EASTERN STUDIES
University of California at Berkeley
215 Moses Hall
Berkeley, California 94720 (415) 642-8208
Director: Ira M. Lapidus Founded 1979

An integral part of the Institute of International Studies at the University of California at Berkeley. Interdisciplinary and interdepartmental area studies center offering courses in Middle East related fields of anthropology, art and art history, classics, comparative literature, economics, environmental design, geography, history, linguistics, Near Eastern Studies, Oriental languages, political science, psychology and sociology. Supports a lecture series, film acquisitions, reading room, faculty-student colloquium, extension courses, speakers bureau, travel awards, course development and symposia.
Publication: Newsletter, quarterly.

CENTER FOR MIDDLE EASTERN STUDIES
University of Chicago
1130 East 59th Street (312) 643-0800
Chicago, Illinois 60637 ext. 4548
Director: Dr. Richard Chambers Founded 1961

Non-degree granting academic unit of University of Chicago; formerly called Near East and African Committee. Supported by parent institution and research grants. Studies: Middle Eastern cultures in medieval and modern times from both humanistic and social science perspectives. Also promotes and integrates scholarly study of these cultures at the University, administers a program of graduate fellowships and brings to the University visiting scholars for seminars and lectures. Holds periodic seminars attended by staff members, fellows and guests; also sponsors international conferences. Maintains a large Middle East area library. Research results published in books, monographs and professional journals.

CENTER FOR MIDDLE EASTERN STUDIES
University of Texas
Austin, Texas 78712
Director: Dr. Paul Ward English (512) 471-3881
Founded 1960

Integral unit of University of Texas. Supported by parent institution and federal funding. Conducts research in anthropology, art history, economics, geography, government, history, languages, linguistic analyses of Middle Eastern languages and preparation of teaching materials. Also coordinates instruction in Middle Eastern languages and area studies at the University and administers interdisciplinary undergraduate program in Middle Eastern studies. Maintains a reading library of English language publications and a vernacular Middle East collection.
Publications: Modern Middle East Series and Middle East Monographs; research results published in professionsl journals, books and monographs.

CENTER FOR NEAR EASTERN AND NORTH AFRICAN STUDIES
University of Michigan
144 Lane Hall
Ann Arbor, Michigan 48109
Director: Dr. Ernest T. Abdel-Massih — (313) 764-0350
Founded 1961

Integral unit of College of Literature, Science and the Arts at University of Michigan, operating under an executive committee. Supported by parent institution, United States Government and Foundations. Studies in ancient, medieval and modern peoples and cultures of the Near East and North Africa, including multidisciplinary research in cultural continuity and change, anthropology, art history, economics, geography, history, linguistics and politics, also literary studies. Also provides instruction in these fields and in Near Eastern languages and literatures at the University and coordinates and facilitates interdepartmental training and research on the area. Holds special lectures and research colloquia. Maintains a reference library in addition to research collections in the University system. Research results published in occasional papers, books and periodical literature.

GUSTAVE E. VON GRUNEBAUM CENTER FOR NEAR EASTERN STUDIES
University of California at Los Angeles
405 Hilgard Avenue
Los Angeles, California 90024 — (213) 825-4668
Director: Malcolm H. Kerr — Founded 1957

Integral unit of University of California at Los Angeles; previously known as Near Eastern Center. Supported by parent institution, Unites States Government and foundations. Performs research in phases of development of the Near East since the rise of Islam, particularly concerned with social science and language research in the area and with cultural relations of the area with the West, the Byzantine and Slavic world and Islamic Africa. Participates in program of inter-university American research centers in Cairo, Egypt, Ankara, Turkey, and Tehran, Iran, Middle and Near Eastern language area studies at the University and activities such as archaeological excavations in the Near East and provides research and training facilities aimed at integration of language instruction with social sciences essential to understanding of Middle Eastern background in anthropology, art, economics, geography, history, political science and sociology. Also sponsors international meetings organized to deal with specific problems. Utilizes Near Eastern section of 100,000 volumes plus 4,000 Arabic, Persian and Turkish manuscripts in University Research Library; Research results published in monographs and books.

INSTITUTE FOR MEDITERRANEAN AFFAIRS
1078 Madison Avenue
New York, New York 10028
President: Seymour Maxwell Finger — (212) 988-1725
Founded 1957

"Independent group investigating the basic problems of the Mediterranean area with a view to finding and proposing peaceful and permanent solutions to these problems. An immediate objective is analyzing the underlying tensions in the Eastern Mediterranean." Holds conferences, seminars, symposia and study panels; maintains library of 2,000 volumes on the Middle East and North Africa.
Publications: Mediterranean Survey, irregular; has also published several reports and studies on the Middle East in book form.

INSTITUTE FOR PALESTINE STUDIES
United States Office
Post Office Box 19449
Washington, D.C. 20036 — (202) 745-0868
Director: Carolyn Gates — Founded 1963

Public officials, professors and businessmen. Private Arab non-profit research organization designed to promote better understanding of the Palestine. Conducts research programs. Washington office distributes publications of Institute in Beirut, Lebanon such as Arabs Under Israeli Occupation, annual; International Documents on Palestine, annual; U.N. Documents on Palestine, annual; anthologies, reprints and monographs (in Arabic, English, French, Spanish).
Publication: Journal of Palestine Studies, quarterly.

INSTITUTE OF ARAB STUDIES
556 Trapelo Road
Belmont, Massachusetts 02178 — (617) 484-3262
Director: Muhammad Hallaj — Founded 1979

Founded by a group of Arab American scholars to further research on the Arab world, its history, economics, art and architecture, language, literature, music, philolosophies, cosmologies and religions. Offers fellowships and scholarships to writers, artists, poets, scholars and professionals. Maintains a research library for scholars and interested public. Holds lectures, conferences and seminars.
Publications: Newsletter, irregular; Arab Studies Quarterly (co-publisher with Association of Arab-American University Graduates); also publishes books and monographs.

MIDDLE EAST CENTER
University of Utah
Salt Lake City, Utah 84112 (801) 322-6181
Director: Dr. Khosrow Mostofi Founded 1960

Integral unit of University of Utah, administratively within its College of Humanities. Supported by parent institution. Specializes in Middle East languages and area studies and compilations of readers, monographs, books and articles dealing with Islamic and Middle East studies including development of Persian achievement tests, translation of a Turkish novel and archaeological excavations in Petra. Also provides undergraduate training in Arabic or Persian and graduate training in Middle East studies in Arabic, Hebrew, Persian and Turkish through Department of Languages and in cooperation with 11 other academic departments at the University. Holds intensive seminars, annual conferences and public lectures. Maintains a library of 100,000 volumes. Research results published in professional journals, books, monographs and readers.

MIDDLE EAST INSTITUTE
Columbia University
420 West 118th Street
New York, New York 10027
Director: Professor J.C. Hurewitz (212) 280-2584
Founded 1954

Integral unit of School of International Affairs at Columbia University; formerly called Near and Middle East Institute. Supported by parent institution and a variety of funds. Researches current problems in history, economics, government, international relations and languages of the Middle East from rise of Islam to the present, with primary focus on Nineteenth and Twentieth Centuries. Also serves as coordinator of Middle East studies at the University by sponsoring and overseeing interdisciplinary pre- and postdoctoral programs on the Middle East. Maintains a library of 60,000 pamphlets and newspapers on the Middle East from Turkey to Pakistan.
Publications: Modern Middle East Studies (serially); research results published in professional journals, books and in series.

MIDDLE EAST STUDIES
Columbia University
Department of Middle East Languages and Cultures
609 Kent Hall (212) 280-2556
New York, New York 10027 (212) 280-2560
Director: Pierre Cachia Founded 1954

Offers courses in philology, history, literatures and religions of the area extending from North Africa to the Himalayas at undergraduate through Ph.D level. Graduate degrees are avialable in the following linguistic groups: Altaic and Turkic, Ancient Semitic, Arabic, Armenian, Central Asian, Hebrew, Indic and Iranian.

MIDDLE EAST STUDIES CENTER
Portland State University
Portland, Oregon 97207 (503) 229-3609
Director: Dr. Frederick J. Cox Founded 1959

Integral unit of Portland State University. Supported by parent institution. Concentrates on cultural, political and economic problems in the Middle East, including studies on Arabic literature, reading and writing systems, Turkish history, English as a foreign language and Persian history and literature. Maintains a special Middle East collection in the University library. Research results published in professional journals and books.

MIDDLE EAST STUDIES COMMITTEE
Pennsylvania State University
603 Liberal Arts Tower
University Park, Pennsylvania 16802 (814) 863-0061
Director: Arthur Goldschmidt, Jr. Founded 1972

Offers courses on Middle Eastern history from Muhammed to the present, the politics of the Middle East and Biblical studies.

MIDDLE EAST STUDIES PROGRAM
University of Connecticut
Storrs, Connecticut 06268 (203) 486-3028
Director: Ramon Knauerhase Founded 1980

Concentrates on problems in the Middle East from Morocco to Afghanistan.

MIDDLE EAST STUDIES PROGRAM
University of Wisconsin
1146 Van Hise
Madison, Wisconsin 53706 (608) 263-1825
Director: Kemel H. Karpat Founded 1974

Program treats problems in the Middle East and North Africa as well as Soviet Muslims in Central Asia.

NEAR EAST CENTER
University of Washington
219 Denny Hall (DH-20)
Seattle, Washington 98195 (206) 543-6033
Director: Farhat J. Ziadeh Founded 1975

Areas of research range from ethnomusicology to urban planning, anthropology, languages (Turkish, Persian, Arabic, Hebrew, Ugarite, Akkadian), Islamic history, art, architecture, linguistics, Asian languages and literature, geography, political science, archeology, comparative literature, comparative religion, international law and Islamic law.

NEAR EASTERN AND JUDAIC STUDIES PROGRAM
Brandeis University
Waltham, Massachusetts 02154 (617) 647-2647
Chairman: Professor Marvin Fox Founded 1948

Research activity of Near Eastern and Judaic Studies Department at Brandeis University. Supported by parent institution. Principal fields of research: Ancient Near Eastern, modern Near Eastern and Jewish history, Biblical and Islamic Studies, medieval and modern Jewish philosophy, studies on the American Jewish community and modern Hebrew literature. Maintains a library of 90,000 volumes on ancient and modern Near East, Biblical and Islamic studies, medieval and modern Jewish philosophy, studies on American Jewish community and modern Hebrew literature. Holds periodic public lectures and seminars. Research results published in professional journals and monographs.

ORIENTAL INSTITUTE
University of Chicago
1155 East 58th Street
Chicago, Illinois 60637
Director: Dr. John A. Brinkman (312) 753-2471
Founded 1919

Integral unit of University of Chicago. Supported by parent institution, endowment income and gifts. Principal field of research is in the ancient Near East, including archaeological field studies on ancient man, excavation and recovery of artifacts and interpretation of origin and development of civilization. Holds monthly lectures for its lay members. Maintains a museum exhibiting the Institute's finds and containing "largest and most representative collection of objects of ancient Near Eastern culture and art west of the Alleghenies". Research results published in books, illustrated reports, monographs and maps.

PROGRAM IN NEAR EASTERN STUDIES
Princeton University
110 Jones Hall
Princeton, New Jersey 08540 (609) 452-4272
Director: Dr. John H. Marks Founded 1947

Research activity at Princeton University. Supported by parent institution, United States Government, industry and foundation grants. Studies: all aspects of the modern Near East, including geographical studies of area from North Africa to Afghanistan and Islamic cultures of Asia and Africa, also interdisciplinary studies in history, social science and the humanities. Also trains graduate and undergraduate students of the University for specialized work and careers relating to the Near East. Holds biannual Near East conference for scholars, officials of governments and international agencies and corporation executives, special research conferences, seminars and bimonthly informal talks by guests. Maintains a library of 150,000 volumes on all aspects of Islamic and Near Eastern societies. Research results published in books and monographs.
Publications: Proceedings of Biannual Near East Conference, biannually; Princeton Near East Papers, irregularly; and Princeton Studies in the Modern Near East, irregularly.

SEMITIC MUSEUM
Harvard University
6 Divinity Avenue
Cambridge, Massachusetts 02138
Director: Professor Frank Moore Cross, Jr. (617) 495-4631
Founded 1889

Integral unit of Harvard University. Supported by parent institution and research grants. Principal fields of research are in the civilizations and history of Near East in ancient times. Also conducts explorations in western Asia and maintains collections of antiquities recovered in expeditions in northern Iraq, central Palestine and Sinai.

Museums

ANDERSON COLLEGE MUSEUM OF BIBLE AND NEAR EASTERN STUDIES
School of Theology Building
1123 East Third Street
Anderson College
Anderson, Indiana 46011 (317) 649-9071
Director: Gustav Jeeninga Founded 1963

Collections include archaeological objects related to Biblical and Near Eastern Studies.

THE BADE INSTITUTE OF BIBLICAL ARCHEOLOGY
1798 Scenic Avenue
Berkeley, California 94709 (415) 848-0529
Director: John H. Otwell Founded 1930

Collections center on biblical archaelogy and artifacts from Egypt, Syria, Cyprus, Greece and Rome. Offers guided tours, lectures, formally organized education programs for children, adults, and undergraduate and graduate students, and permanent and traveling exhibitions. Affiliated with the Pacific School of Religion.

ORIENTAL INSTITUTE MUSEUM, UNIVERSITY OF CHICAGO
1155 East 58th Street
Chicago, Illinois 60637
Director: John A. Brinkman (312) 753-2475
Curator: John Carswell Founded 1919

Collections cover art and archaeology of the Ancient Near East, Egypt, Assyria, Babylonia, Syria, Palestine, Anatolia, Nubia, Iran, Early Christian and Islamic material. Research is conducted in Near Eastern archaeology, sculpture, decorative arts; Ancient Near Eastern languages and Islamic langauges. Offers guided tours; lectures; films; formally organized education programs for adults, undergraduate and graduate students affiliated with University of Chicago; docent program; intermuseum loan, permanent and temporary exhibitions; manuscript collections and museum shop.
Publications: Guide to N.E. Collections of the Oriental Institute Museum; exhibition catalogs.

SEMITIC MUSEUM
Harvard University
6 Divinity Avenue
Cambridge, Massachusetts 02138
Director: Frank Moore Cross, Jr.
Curator: Father Carney E. S. Gavin (617) 495-4631
Founded 1887

Features religious and archaeological exhibits from Babylonia, Assyria, Hittite lands, Egypt, Arabia, Phoenicia, and Syria. Research is conducted in Semitic languages, history and Near East archeology. Offers guided tours, lectures, television programs, educational programs, intermuseum loans, school loans, permanent, temporary and traveling exhibition. Affiliated with Harvard University.
Publication : Harvard Semitic Series; Newsletter.

THE UNIVERSITY MUSEUM, UNIVERSITY OF PENNSYLVANIA
33rd and Spruce Streets
Philadelphia, Pennsylvania 19104 (215) 243-4000
Director: Martin Biddle Founded 1889

Collections include the Near Eastern, Syro-Palestinan, Egyptian and Mediterranean archeology, anthropology and ethnology as well as in other fields. Maintains library on archeological collections. Has museum shop. Offers guided tours, lectures, films, concerts, travel program, docent program, classes, intermuseum and school loans, permanent, temporary and traveling exhibitions.
Publications: Expedition, quarterly; MASCA Journal; Museum monographs.

Special Libraries and Subject Collections

ANTIOCHIAN ORTHODOX CHRISTIAN ARCHDIOCESE OF NORTH AMERICA - LIBRARY
358 Mountain Road (201) 871-1355
Englewood, New Jersey 07631 Founded 1895

Subjects: History of Arab Orthodox Christians in North America. Holdings: Books, periodicals, archives. Services: Reading room, copying.
Publication: The Word Magazine (Al-Kalimat), 10 times a year.

ARAB-AMERCIAN ASSOCIATION LIBRARY
Post Office Box 20041 (513) 751-3603
Cincinnati, Ohio 45220 Founded 1967

Holdings: Books, audiovisual materials.

ARAB INFORMATION CENTER - LEAGUE OF ARAB STATES
747 Third Avenue
New York, New York 10017
Information Officer: Marwan Kanafani (212) 838-8700
Founded 1955

Subjects: Arab history, statistics, description and travel; Islamic history; Arab art and literature; Arab current events; Middle East economics. Special Collections: Arab League documents; United Nations documents. Holdings: Books; photographs, films, and filmstrips; journals and other serials; newspapers. Services: Center not open to public. Information papers and documents of the Arab League are available for free distribution to libraries and schools.
Publications: Palestine Digest, monthly; Arab Report; also publishes booklets and other publications on the twenty Arab countries.

CENTER FOR MIDDLE EASTERN STUDIES - LIBRARY
HARVARD UNIVERSITY
Coolidge Hall
1737 Cambridge Street
Cambridge, Massachusetts 02138 (617) 495-2173
Librarian: Julie M. Blattner Founded 1959

Subjects: History of Islam; ancient and modern Middle East - Turkey, Iran, Egypt, Syria, Jordan, Israel, Libya, North Africa, Caucasus, Central Asia. Special Collections: Army maps of Middle Eastern area. Holdings: Books, bound periodical volumes and pamphlets, journals and other serials. Services: Library may be consulted by special arrangement only.

GEORGE CAMP KEISER LIBRARY - MIDDLE EAST INSTITUTE
1761 N Street, Northwest
Washington, D.C. 20036 (202) 785-1141
Librarian: Lois M. Khairallah Founded 1946

Subjects: North Africa and Middle East - history, culture, religion, economics, philosophy, literature. Special Collections: George Camp Keiser Collection of the art of the Middle East; Richard D. Robinson Collection of books and documents relating to the development of modern Turkey. Holdings: Books; bound periodical volumes; vertical files and binders, chronological clipping file on Middle East, 1956-1972; journals and other serials; newspapers. Services: Interlibrary loans; library open to public; only Institute members may borrow materials.

INDIANA UNIVERSITY - NEAR EASTERN COLLECTION
Bloomington, Indiana 47405
Librarian: James W. Pollock (812) 337-3403

Subjects: Arabic, Hebrew, Persian and Turkish languages and literatures. Special Collections: Near East languages and literatures. Holdings: Books; bound periodical volumes; journals and other serials; newspapers. Services: Interlibrary loans; copying; collection open to public with identification.

ISLAMIC CENTER OF NEW YORK LIBRARY
1 Riverside Drive (212) 362-6800
New York, New York 10023 Founded 1966

Subjects: Islamic history and culture.

LIBRARY OF CONGRESS - AFRICAN & MIDDLE EASTERN DIVISION
John Adams Building, Room 1040C
Washington, D.C. 20540
Chief: Dr. Julian W. Witherell (202) 287-7937

Remarks: The Library of Contress has extensive holdings of books, newspapers, manuscripts, periodicals, and other material relating to nations of Africa and the Middle East. Detailed reference services on the 750,000 western-language volumes relating to this area in the Library's general collections is provided by the division's African, Hebraic, and Near East sections. In addition, the Hebraic Section has custody of over 109,000 volumes in Hebrew, Yiddish, and cognate languages covering such topics as the Bible, ancient Middle East, and Jews and Judaism throughout the world. The Near East Section has holdings of more than 104,000 volumes in Arabic, Turkish, Persian, and other languages of an area of responsibility that extends from Afghanistan to Morocco, excluding Israel. Both the Hebraic and Near East sections maintain union catalogs relating to their respective areas of responsibility, while the African Section has a card index of citations to Africana periodical literature.

LIBRARY OF CONGRESS - LAW LIBRARY - NEAR EASTERN AND AFRICAN LAW DIVISION
James Madison Memorial Building
Room 240
Washington, D.C. 20540
Chief: Zuhair E. Jwaideh (202) 287-5073

Subjects: Legal materials on all subjects covering the Middle Eastern countries; law of the North African countries; British-African law; French-African law; Roman-Dutch-African law; religious law (Jewish, Christian and Islamic); tribal and customary African law; international law.

MIDDLE EAST LIBRARY - UNIVERSITY OF MINNESOTA
S50 Wilson Library
309 19th Avenue, South
Minneapolis, Minnesota 55455 (612) 373-7804
Head: Nassif Youssif Founded 1967

Subjects: Arabic, Hebrew, Persian and Turkish languages, literature and history. Special Collections: Middle Eastern vernaculars. Holdings: Books; bound periodical volumes; journals and other serials; newspapers. Services: Interlibrary loans; library open to public with permission from the administration.

MIDDLE EAST LIBRARY - UNIVERSITY OF UTAH
Marriott Library
Salt Lake City, Utah 84112
Assistant Professor: Dr. P. Rashid Wu (801) 581-6208

Subjects: Humanities and social sciences in the Middle East. Special Collections: Papyrus and paper documents; manuscript Korans; early Arabic imprints and paleography manuscripts; Abushady Literature Collection; Abushady personal papers; Martin Levey Collection on the History of Science; Martin Levey papers and offprints; Mount Sinai manuscripts on microfilm. Holdings: Books; bound periodical volumes; microfilm of Middle East newspapers; Arabic manuscripts on microfilm; microfilms of Syriac and Arabic manuscripts; Arabic manuscripts on history of science; journals and other serials; newspapers. Services: Interlibrary loans; copying; library (except vault material) open to students and faculty.
Publications: Aziz S. Atiya Library for Middle East Studies; Arabic Collection, 1968; Supplement, including indexes, 1971.

MIDDLE EAST STUDIES CENTER - LIBRARY - PORTLAND STATE UNIVERSITY
Box 751
Portland, Oregon 97207
Director: C. Thomas Pfingsten (503) 229-3609

Subjects: Arabic, Hebrew, Persian, Turkish. Holdings: Books in vernacular languages; additional volumes in Western languages to supplement area studies. Services: Interlibrary loans; copying; library open to public through the University's Main Library.

MUSLIM BIBLIOGRAPHIC CENTER - AMERICAN INSTITUTE OF ISLAMIC STUDIES
Box 10398
Denver, Colorado 80210 (303) 936-0108
Director: C. L. Geddes Founded 1965

Subjects: Islamic, Muslim culture; North African, Southeast Asian and Near Eastern bibliography. Holdings: Books and bound periodical volumes; microfilms in bibliographic collection; microfilms in Islamic collection; journals and other serials. Services: Interlibrary loans; copying; center open to public by appointment.
Publications: Bibliographic series, irregular - sold through bookstores; Islamic Studies Newsletter - free upon request.

MUSLIM LIBRARY - AHMADIYYA MOVEMENT IN ISLAM
2141 Leroy Place, Northwest
Washington, D.C. 20008
Information Director: Ata Ullah Kaleem (202) 232-3737

Subjects: Islamic theology; history of different countries and religions. Special Collections: Work of Hazrat Ahmad the Promised Messiah on Islam and other religions. Holdings: Books; bound periodical volumes; other cataloged items; newspapers and periodicals; journals and other serials; newspapers. Services: Library open to public for reference use only.
Publication: Muslim Sunrise, quarterly.

NORTH AMERICAN ISLAMIC TRUST INCORPORATED - LIBRARY
10900 West Washington Street
Indianapolis, Indiana 46227
General Manager: Muhammad Badr (317) 839-4248
Founded 1973

Subjects: Islam.
Publications: List of publications - available on request.

OHIO STATE UNIVERSITY - MIDDLE EAST/ ISLAMICA READING ROOM
Thompson Library, Room 320
1858 Neil Avenue Mall
Columbus, Ohio 43210
Middle East Librarian: Marsha McClintock (614) 422-3362
Founded 1977

Subjects: Arabic, Persian and Turkish history, languages and general reference. Holdings: Books and bound periodical volumes; journals and other serials; newspapers. Services: Interlibrary loans; copying; library open to public.

PRINCETON UNIVERSITY - NEAR EAST COLLECTIONS
Firestone Library
Princeton, New Jersey 08544
Curator: Eric Ormsby (609) 452-3279

Subjects: Arabic, Persian, Turkish and Hebrew languages and literatures. Special Collections: Garrett Collection of Near Eastern Manuscripts. Services: Interlibrary loans; copying; library open to public.

SAINT EPHREM EDUCATIONAL CENTER LIBRARY
1555 South Meridian Road
Youngstown, Ohio 44511 (216) 792-1532
Librarian: Helen Catherman Founded 1978

Subjects: Arabic and Aramaic languages; history of Maronite Catholics in America. Holdings: Books; archives; manuscripts.

SEMITIC REFERENCE LIBRARY - YALE UNIVERSITY
314 Sterling Memorial Library
Yale University Library
New Haven, Connecticut 06520
Near East Bibliographer: Edward A. Jajko — Founded 1930

Subjects: Comparative Semitics; Hebrew, Arabic and other Semitic languages (except Akkadian).

SEMITICS LIBRARY - INSTITUTE OF CHRISTIAN ORIENTAL RESEARCH - CATHOLIC UNIVERSITY OF AMERICA
Mullen Library, Room 18
Washington, D.C. 20064
Curator: Carolyn T. Lee — (202) 635-5091

Subjects: Coptic, Syriac, Arabic, Biblical Hebrew, Cuneiform languages, Christian Orient. Special Collections: Collection of the Institute of Christian Oriental Research, begun from the personal library of the founder, Monsignor H. Hyvernat. Holdings: Books; bound periodical volumes; photographs of Coptic manuscripts in Paris and Naples; photographs of Coptic manuscripts in Pierpont Morgan Library; offprints and department members papers; correspondence of Monsignor Hyvernat; bound miscellanea (Christian Orient studies); journals and other serials.

UNIVERSITY OF TEXAS, AUSTIN - MIDDLE EAST COLLECTION
General Libraries, MAI 316
Austin, Texas 78712
Librarian: Abazar Sepehri — (512) 471-4675

Subjects: Arabic and Persian language and literature; general Middle East studies in the vernacular. Holdings: Books; bound periodical volumes; microfilm; journals and other serials. Services: Interlibrary loans; copying; library open to public. Publication: Library Guide.

Newspapers and Newsletters

AAUG NEWSLETTER. 1968-. Quarterly. Editor: Carole Bohn. Publisher: Association of Arab-American University Graduates, Post Office Box 7391, North End Station, Detroit, Michigan 48202.

Provides information about the association and its members, who are American professionals of Arab descent. Includes book reviews.

ACTION. 1969-. Weekly. Editor: Dr. M. T. Mehdi. Publisher: American-Arab Relations Committee, Post Office Box 416, New York, New York 10017. In English.

Covers news of the Middle East and the United States. Focuses mainly on the liberation of Palestine. A section of the newspaper is devoted to editorials and letters to the editor.

AMERICAN-ARAB MESSAGE. 1950-. Weekly. Editor and publisher: Reverend M. A. Karoub, 17514 Woodward, Highland Park, Detroit, Michigan 48203. In English and Arabic.

Publishes general, local, and religious news of interest to Arab-Islamic communities.

AMIDEAST REPORT. 1971-. Quarterly. Editor: Joan L. Berum. Publisher: America-Mideast Educational & Training Services, Incorporated, 1717 Massachusetts Avenue, Northwest, Washington, D.C. 20036.

Provides feature articles and news briefs on educational developments in the Middle East and North Africa, along with information on activities of the organization. Includes listings of teaching opportunities in the area, book reviews, and announcements of newly published resources.

ANERA NEWSLETTER. 1969-. Quarterly. Editor: Sara C. Gentry. Publisher: American Near East Refugee Aid, 1522 K Street, Northwest, Suite 202, Washington, D.C. 20005.

Focuses on matters relating to the human rights of the Palestinian people in the Middle East crisis and the agency's work in community development, education, medical aid, and other forms of refugee assistance. Centers on a single topic in each issue, dealing with such subjects as Jerusalem, the Occupied Territories, religion (an outline of the major religious beliefs in the Middle East), or Arab women.

ARAB ECONOMIC REVIEW. 1973-. Quarterly. Publisher: United States-Arab Chamber of Commerce (Pacific), Incorporated, 433 California Street, Suite 920, San Francisco, California 94104. In English.

Transmits business news of interest to persons and firms engaged in trade with the Arab countries of the Middle East. Concentrates on the Western part of the United States.

ARRAYH. 1974-. Weekly. Editor: Mustaja El Dabbas. Publisher: El Dabbas Brothers, 3304 Germantown Avenue, Philadelphia, Pennsylvania 19140. In English and Arabic.

Presents current news from and about the Middle East, national news of interest to the Arab community in the United States, some local coverage of Arab American events, editorial comment and cultural features.

BULLETIN OF THE AMERICAN ARAB ASSOCIATION. 1951-. 10 times a year. Editor: I. F. Yusif. Publisher: American Arab Association for Commerce & Industry Incorporated, Suite 1060, 342 Madison Avenue, New York, New York 10017.

Prints business news and analyses of interest to firms engaged in commerce with Arab countries.

HABIBI. 1974-. Monthly. Editor and Publisher: Robert C. Zalot, Post Office Box 4081, Mountain View, California 94040.

Publishes on Middle Eastern dance, music and culture.

THE HERITAGE. 1963-. Biweekly. Editor: Louis Sahadi. Publisher: Dr. N. K. Basile, 30 East 40th Street, New York, New York 10016. In English.

Reports on world news, especially as concerning Middle East issues, United States and Middle East relations and the global Arab community.

AL-ISLAAH (The Reform). 1931-. Semimonthly. Editor and publisher: Alphonse Chaurize, 480 Canal Street, New York, New York 10013. In Arabic and English.

Publishes general news of special interest to Arabs. The content is devoted mainly to editorials, rather than to news articles.

ISLAMIC HORIZONS. Bimonthly. Editor: T. Tariq Quraishi. Publisher: Muslim Students Association, Post Office Box 38, Plainfield, Indiana 46168. In English.

Newsletter of the organization.

THE LINK. 1967-. Bimonthly. Publisher: Americans for Middle East Understanding, Incorporated, Room 771, 475 Riverside Drive, New York, New York 10115. In English.

Newsletter of the organization.

AL-MASHRIQ (The Orient). 1924-. Weekly. Editor and publisher: Hannah Yatooma, 25639 Southwood, Southfield, Michigan 48075. In Arabic.

Reports and comments on current news events of interest to Arab people throughout the world. Carries editorials pertaining to major issues in the countries of the Middle East. Covers cultural and social activities of Iraqis and other Arabic communities in the United States.

MELA NOTES. 1973-. 3 times a year. Editor: James W. Pollock. Publisher: Middle East Librarians Association, University of Chicago Library, Room 560, Chicago, Illinois 60637.

Presents news of the activities of the association and its members. Includes book reviews, bibliographies, and other information of value to Middle East librarians.

MIDDLE EAST AND NORTH AFRICAN NOTES. 1970-. Biweekly. Editor: David W. Carr. Publisher: National Foreign Trade Council, 10 Rockefeller Plaza, New York, New York 10020. In English.

Publicizes new construction projects and economic developments in the Middle East and North Africa. Includes news of significant government actions affecting foreign trade, investment climates, and major industrial and mineral projects.

MIDEAST BUSINESS EXCHANGE. 1976-. Monthly. Editor and publisher: Joseph R. Haiek, Mideast Business Exchange, 1650 Flower Street, Glendale, California 91201. In English.

Articles on current economic conditions and trade opportunities in the markets of the Middle East and North Africa, primarily the Arab world, Iran and Pakistan.

MIDEAST OBSERVER IN WASHINGTON. 1977-. Biweekly. Editor and publisher: Allan C. Kellum, Post Office Box 2397, Washington, D.C. 20013.

Reports on congressional votes pertaining to Arab and Middle East political and commercial interests.

NAJDA NEWSLETTER. Bimonthly. Publisher: Najda: Women Concerned about the Middle East, Post Office Box 7152, Berkeley, California 94707. In English.

Reports on activities of the organization in the fields of aid and education.

NEAR EAST FOUNDATION NEWS. 1963-. Semi-annual. Editor: Arthur H. Whitman. Publisher: Near East Foundation, 54 East 64th Street, New York, New York 10021. In English.

Publishes articles related to the Near East Foundation program in the Middle East and Africa and the personnel associated with the program. (The foundation operates primarily in countries with a low per capita income, under $300 per year.) Carries summaries of articles relating to public health, agricultural issues, education, and all phases of rural development in these areas; editorials about food production and health problems. Includes book reviews.

NEW AL - HODA (The New Guidance). 1896-. Weekly. Editor: Fred Koury. Publisher: New Al - Hoda Incorporated, 34 West 28th Street, New York, New York 10001. In Arabic.

ORANGE CRESCENT. 1974-. Monthly. Editor: Dr. Muzammil Siddiqi. Publisher: The Islamic Society of Orange County, Post Office Box 1330 B, Garden Grove, California 92642. In English.

Newsletter of the Society.

PALESTINE/ISRAEL BULLETIN. 1977-. 10 times a year. Publisher: Search for Justice and Equality in Palestine, Post Office Box 53, Waverly Station, Boston, Massachusetts 02179 and Middle East Resource Center, 1322 18th Street, Northwest, Washington, D.C. 20036. In English.

Reports on current events in the Israeli/Palestinian conflict.

PCNA NEWSLETTER. 1982-. Monthly. Publisher: Palestine Congress of North America, Post Office Box 9621, Washington, D.C. 20016. In English.

Prints news of organizational activities in all regions of the United States and Canada as well as political commentary supporting the Palestinian cause and cultural features. Includes regular supplements called Mideast Commentary and Palestine Report, the latter reporting on life among Palestinians in Israeli and other countries.

POLITICAL FOCUS. 1978-. Biweekly. Editor: Neal Lendenmann. Publisher: National Association of Arab Americans, 1825 Connecticut Avenue, Northwest, Washington, D.C. 20009.

Newsletter covering political events and policies pertaining to Arab interests. Includes editorial comment and news analysis.

SOUT AL MOUGTAREB. 1976-. Monthly. Editor and publisher: Michael M. Hattar, Box 27212, Los Angeles, California 90027. In Arabic.

VOICE. 1973-. Quarterly. Publisher: National Association of Arab Americans, 1825 Connecticut Avenue, Northwest, Washington, D.C. 20009. In English.

Carries news of the association's many activities centered in the Washington main office as well as those conducted by the various chapters throughout the United States.

WASHINGTON REPORT ON MIDDLE EAST AFFAIRS. 1982-. 22 times a year. Editor: John Law. Publisher: American Educational Trust, 918 16th Street, Northwest, Washington, D.C. 20006. In English.

Gives a survey of United States relations with Middle East countries. Includes editorial comment, book reviews and personality profile.

Magazines

AL-ALAM AL-JADID (The New World). 1962-. Weekly. Editor and publisher: Yusuf Antone, 2413 Woodward, Berkley, Michigan 48072. In Arabic.

Publishes news and articles on political, social, cultural, and religious life of Arabs in Arab countries and in the United States. Illustrated.

ALAM ATTIJARAT. 1966-. Monthly. Editor: Samir Atallah. Publisher: Hugh M. Hyde, 386 Park Avenue South, New York, New York 10016. In Arabic.

A magazine reporting on business developments.

AMERICAN ARAB AFFAIRS. 1982-. Quarterly. Editor: Erik R. Peterson. Publisher: American Arab Affairs Council, 1730 M Street, Northwest, Suite 411, Washington, D.C. 20036. In English.

Publishes analyses of current diplomatic, political, economic and social developments that affect United States - Arab relations. Also includes book reviews.

ARAB PERSPECTIVES. 1980-. Monthly. Editor and publisher: Marwan Kanafani. Publisher: Arab Information Center, 747 Third Avenue, New York, New York 10017. In English.

Prints articles about the political, social and economic aspects of the Arab world. Profiles an Arab country in each issue. Also includes poetry and stories, cultural articles, interviews, book reviews and reprints of documents.

ARAB STUDENT BULLETIN. 1982-. Quarterly. Publisher: Organization of Arab Students in the United States and Canada, Post Office Box 25302, Chicago, Illinois 60625. In English.

Prints articles dealing with political and social issues related to the Middle East conflict. Includes organizational news and book reviews.

ARAB STUDIES QUARTERLY. 1979-. Quarterly. Editors: Ibrahim Abu-Lughod and Edward Said. Publisher: Association of Arab-American University Graduates, Post Office Box 7391, North End Station, Detroit, Michigan 48202. In English.

A multidisciplinary journal presenting a critical Arab-centric approach to the study of Arab people. Essays are concerned primarily with the humanities and social sciences. Attempts to treat the Arabs comprehensively as a coherent historical and social entity.

ARAMCO WORLD MAGAZINE. 1949-. Bimonthly. Editor: Paul F. Hoye. Publisher: Aramco, 1345 Avenue of the Americas, New York, New York 10019. In English.

Features Arab-related articles of general interest on exploration, culture, wildlife and society. Beautifully illustrated.

AL-BAYAN (The Statement). 1910-. Weekly. Editor and publisher: Raji Daher, 126 La Belle, Detroit, Michigan 48214. In Arabic.

Contains news of general and local interest. Merged with Nahdat-al-Arab (Arab Progress) in 1970.

INTERNATIONAL INSIGHT. 1981-. Bimonthly. Editor and publisher: George A. Nader, Post Office Box 723, Cleveland, Ohio 44107. In English.

Publishes articles analyzing social, political, economic and historical issues underlying the conflict areas of the world with special focus on the Middle East.

INTERNATIONAL JOURNAL OF MIDDLE EAST STUDIES. 1970-. Quarterly. Editor: AFAF Lutfi Al-Sayyed Marsot. Publisher: Cambridge University Press, 32 East 57th Street, New York, New York 10022. In English.

Presents research essays in social and cultural history of the Middle East.

AL-ITTIHAD (Unity). 1963-. Quarterly. Editor: M. Tariq Quraishi. Publisher: Muslim Students' Association of the United States and Canada, Post Office Box 38, Plainfield, Indiana 46168. In English.

Prints articles relating social, political and cultural issues to the Islamic faith.

JOURNAL FOR PALESTINE STUDIES. 1971-. Quarterly. Editor: Hisham Sharabi. Publisher: Institute for Palestine Studies, Washington Office, Post Office Box 19449, Washington, D.C. 20036.

A scholarly journal treating various aspects of Palestinian history, politics and culture.

JOURNAL OF NEAR EASTERN STUDIES. 1884-. Quarterly. Editor: Robert D. Biggs. Publisher: University of Chicago Press, Attention: J. Dotzauer, 5801 Ellis Avenue, Chicago, Illinois 60637

Scholarly articles are published on the archeology and anthropology of the Near East.

MIDDLE EAST EXECUTIVE REPORTS. 1978-. Monthly. Editor: Joseph P. Saba. Publisher: Gary A. Brown, 1115 Massachusetts Avenue, Northwest, Washington, D.C. 20005.

Publishes articles on business and law in the context of the Middle East.

THE MIDDLE EAST JOURNAL. 1947-. Quarterly. Editor: Richard B. Parker. Publisher: Middle East Institute, 1761 N Street, Northwest, Washington, D.C. 20036. In English.

Articles deal with social, political and economic problems of the Middle East.

MIDDLE EAST PERSPECTIVE. 1968-. Monthly. Editor: Dr. Alfred Lienthal. Publisher: Middle East Perspective, 850 Seventh Avenue, New York, New York 10019. In English.

A journal of international relations with emphasis on Middle East problems.

MUSLIM WORLD. 1911-. Quarterly. Editor: Dr. Willem A. Bijlefeld. Publisher: Hartford Seminary Foundation, 77 Sherman Street, Hartford, Connecticut 06105. In English.

Devoted to studies of Islam and Christian-Muslim relations.

NEAR EAST BUSINESS. 1976-. 9 times a year. Editor: Martha Downing. Publisher: Johnston International Publishing Corporation, 386 Park Avenue, South, New York, New York 10016. In English.

Keeps readers informed of business policies and events in the Near East.

NEWS CIRCLE. 1972-. Monthly. Editor and publisher: Joseph Haiek, 1650 Flower Street, Glendale, California 91201. In English and Arabic.

Prints articles on American Arab community affairs and general news from the national and international scene of interest to the community. Includes editorial comment, a profile of an Arab American, and interviews.

OUR HERITAGE: VOICE OF THE AMERICAN DRUZE SOCIETY. 1980-. Quarterly. Editor: Kathy Jaber Stephenson. Publisher: Our Heritage, American Druze Society, 8213 Corteland Drive, Knoxville, Tennessee 37919. In English.

Prints articles on the Druze community in the United States and in the Middle East.

PALESTINE PERSPECTIVES. 1978-. Monthly. Publisher: Palestine Information Office, Post Office Box 57042, Washington, D.C. 20037. In English.

Brings interviews, news briefs, excerpts and editorial comment in support of the Palestine Liberation cause.

U.S.-ARAB COMMERCE. Bimonthly. Editor: Jack Dobson. Publisher: Mohamed A. Baghal, U.S.-Arab Chamber of Commerce, One World Trade Center, Suite 4657, New York, New York 10048. In English.

Publishes economic and political reports, concerning the Middle East.

THE VOICE. 1980-. Monthly. Editor: Ihsan Al-Kuraishi, 7452 North Milwaukee Avenue, Niles, Illinois 60648. In English and Arabic.

A magazine specializing in political articles about Arab issues.

Radio Programs

Colorado - Denver

KPOF - 3455 West 83rd Avenue, Denver, Colorado 80030, (303) 428-0910. Arabic programs, 1 hour weekly.

Illinois - Chicago

WSBC - 4949 West Belmont Avenue, Chicago, Illinois 60641, (312) 777-1700. Arabic programs, 1 hour weekly.

New Jersey - South Orange

WSOU (FM) - 400 South Orange Avenue, South Orange, New Jersey 07079, (201) 762-8950. Arabic programs, 1 hour weekly.

Television Programs

California - Los Angeles

KSCI - 1950 Cortner Avenue, West Los Angeles, California 90808, (213) 479-8081. Arabic programs, 1 hour weekly.

KWHY-TV - 5545 Sunset Boulevard, Los Angeles, California 90028, (213) 466-5441. Arabic programs.

Michigan - Detroit

WGPR-TV - 3140 East Jefferson Avenue, Detroit, Michigan 48207, (313) 259-8862. Arabic programs.

Bank Branches in the U.S.

BANQUE ARABE ET INTERNATIONALE D'INVESTISSEMENT
1290 Avenue of the Americas
New York, New York 10019 (212) 541-8340

UBAF ARAB AMERICAN BANK
345 Park Avenue
New York, New York 10154 (212) 223-1500

Jointly owned by four American banks, eleven Arab banks (two of them central banks) and five Arab consortium banks.

Commercial and Trade Organizations

AMERICAN-ARAB ASSOCIATION FOR COMMERCE AND INDUSTRY
342 Madison Avenue
New York, New York 10173
Executive Director: Jamal A. Sa'd (212) 986-7229

United States firms (oil, transportation, automotive, finance, machinery, etc.) interested in promoting and expanding trade between the United States, the Middle East, and North Africa. Co-sponsored four trade missions covering the Near East, Arabian Gulf area, and North Africa. Holds frequent industry workshops. Formerly known as the American Egyptian Society.
Publication: Bulletin, ten times a year.

AMERICAN-ARAB CHAMBER OF COMMERCE
319 World Trade Building
Houston, Texas 77002 (713) 222-6152

ARAB INTERNATIONAL CENTER FOR COMMERCE AND INDUSTRY
437 Madison Avenue
New York, New York 10022 (212) 355-3305

ARABIA PACIFIC ASIA BUSINESS COUNCIL
125 Merchant Street
Honolulu, Hawaii 96813 (808) 531-8141

MIDAMERICA-ARAB CHAMBER OF COMMERCE, INCORPORATED
Suite 2050
135 South LaSalle Street
Chicago, Illinois 60603 (312) 782-4654

U.S.-ARAB CHAMBER OF COMMERCE
One World Trade Center, Suite 4657
New York, New York 10048
Executive Director: Mohamed A. Baghal (212) 432-0655
Founded 1967

Corporations and businesses interested in working and trading with the Arab world. Promotes commerce, trade and mutual understanding between the United States and countries of the Arab world. Sponsors conferences and trade missions; disseminates information. Maintains commercial library.
Publications: U.S.-Arab Commerce, bimonthly; Annual Report; Directory, annual.

U.S.-ARAB CHAMBER OF COMMERCE (PACIFIC), INCORPORATED
Suite 920
433 California Street
San Francisco, California 94104 (415) 397-5663

U.S.-ARAB CHAMBER OF COMMERCE
(WASHINGTON CHAPTER)
Suite 627
1625 Eye Street, Northwest
Washington, D.C. 20006 (202) 293-6975

Festivals, Fairs, and Celebrations

Rhode Island - Pawtucket

MID-EAST FESTIVAL
Pawtucket, Rhode Island

An Arabic theme is carried out in the festival through the music, dancing and food. Held in early August for two days.
Contact: Rhode Island Department of Economic Development, Tourist Promotion Division, One Weybosset Hill, Providence, Rhode Island 02903.

Bookdealers and Publishers' Representatives

ALADDIN INTERNATIONAL LANGUAGE SYSTEMS
Post Office Box 2348
1327 Rockville Pike
Rockville, Maryland 20852 (301) 340-8988

GEORGE A. BERNSTEIN
(antiquarian Islamica)
GPO Box 1439
Brooklyn, New York 11202 (212) 875-7582

BIBLIOTHECA ISLAMICA, INCORPORATED
Box 14174 University Station
Minneapolis, Minnesota 55414

CRESCENT IMPORTS & PUBLICATION
(Books from the Middle East)
Post Office Box 7827
Ann Arbor, Michigan 48107 (313) 665-3492

CULTURAL INTEGRATION FELLOWSHIP BOOKSTORE
(Arabic, Bengali, Chinese, Hindi, and Sanskrit publications)
3494 21st Street
San Francisco, California 94110 (415) 648-6777

DAR AL KUTUB WAL NASHRAT AL ISLAMIYYA
(Arabic, French, German, Urdu)
Post Office Box 207
New Brunswick, New Jersey
08901 (201) 249-6961

THE EAST AND WEST SHOP
(books about the Middle East)
4 Appleblossom Lane
Newtown, Connecticut 06470 (203) 426-0661

FITZHUGH BOOKS INCORPORATED
(books about the Arab world)
Box 113
Farmingdale, New York 11735 (212) 425-2122

GRANMA BOOKSTORE
(Arabic, Persian, and Spanish materials)
2509 Telegraph Avenue
Berkeley, California 94704 (415) 841-9744

HAKIM'S BOOKSTORE
(publications in Arabic)
210 South 52nd Street
Philadelphia, Pennsylvania
19139 (215) 474-9495

INTERNATIONAL BOOK CENTRE
(Arabic books)
Post Office Box 295
Troy, Michigan 48099 (313) 879-8436

ISLAMIC BOOK SERVICES

10900 West Washington Street
Indianapolis, Indiana 45231 (317) 839-8150

Route 1, Box 664
Plainfield, Indiana 46188 (317) 839-8159

ISLAMIC PRODUCTIONS INTERNATIONAL, INCORPORATED
(books, records, cassettes, and other materials about Islam)
739 West Sixth Street
Tucson, Arizona 85701

JERUSALEM CORNER
(Arabic and Spanish)
554 Broadway
El Cajon, California 92021 (714) 447-4573

KAZI PUBLICATIONS
(Arabic books)
1529 North Wells
Chicago, Illinois 60610 (312) 642-1291

MAY DAY BOOKS & PUBLICATIONS
(Arabic, Chinese, Persian, Spanish books)
3134 East Davison
Detroit, Michigan 48212 (313) 893-0523

MCBLAIN BOOKS
(books on the Middle East)
Post Office Box 971
Des Moines, Iowa 50304 (515) 274-3033

MIDDLE EAST PRESS CENTER
626 North Manhattan Place No. 6
Los Angeles, California 90004 (213) 463-3382

PARAGON BOOK GALLERY, LIMITED
(imported and antiquarian books on the Middle East)
14 East 38th Street
New York, New York 10016 (212) 532-4920

SUFIAN & TAHER COMPANY
6519 Hollywood Boulevard
Hollywood, California 90028 (213) 467-4624

TEC BOOKS LIMITED (Librarie de Documentation Technique SA)
(Arabic)
41 William
Pittsburgh, Pennsylvania 12901 (518) 561-0005

Books and Pamphlets

AMERICAN DOCTORAL DISSERTATIONS ON THE ARAB WORLD, 1883-1974. By George Dimitri Selim. Washington, D.C., United States Library of Congress, 1976.

Covers dissertations in science and technology, humanities, and social sciences pertaining to Arabic-speaking countries of the Middle East and North Africa and communities where the Arabic language is spoken. Also includes titles related to Islam as a religion. Contains an author-subject index. A new edition is in press.

AN ANNOTATED BIBLIOGRAPHY OF BOOKS AND PERIODICALS IN ENGLISH DEALING WITH HUMAN RELATIONS IN THE ARAB STATES OF THE MIDDLE EAST. By Jean T. Burke. Beirut, American University of Beirut, 1956.

This bibliography deals with materials concerning Arabs and some non-Arab minorities and is limited to works covering the modern period (particularly post-war literature). Divided into 13 sections according to subject classification.

ARAB CULTURE AND SOCIETY IN CHANGE; A Partially Annotated Bibliography of Books and Articles in English, French, German and Italian. By Center for Study of the Modern Arab World. New York, Near East Books Company, 1973.

This bibliography is concerned with the Arab countries of the Middle East and North Africa and covers the period from the beginning of World Wat I to 1973. It also treats the interplay of the modern and traditional values and concepts in Arab society.

ARAB-ISLAMIC BIBLIOGRAPHY: THE MIDDLE EAST LIBRARY COMMITTEE GUIDE. Edited by Diana Grimwood - Jones. Hassocks, England, Harvester Press, Atlantic Highland, New Jersey, Humanities Press, 1977.

A general bibliography on the study of Islamic disciplines. Each section is arranged in chronological order.

THE ARAB WORLD. New York, Arab Information Center.

Gives a brief description of each of the twenty Arab states, including the major tourist attractions, the population, currency and where to obtain further information.

ARABESQUE. New York, Arab Information Center.

A portfolio of informational brochures and fact sheets on various topics such as medicine and mathematics, calligraphy, Islamic art motifs, the Arabic alphabet, music and musical instruments, early explorers and settlers in the New World, the Arabic language and script and festive recipes.

ARABIC HISTORICAL WRITING, 1975 AND 1976: AN ANNOTATED BIBLIOGRAPHY OF BOOKS IN HISTORY FROM ALL PARTS OF THE ARAB WORLD. By Fawzi Abdulrazak. London, Mansell, 1979.

A listing of Arabic books which covers the general history and the history of Arab and Muslim governments. Majority of the works are from 1975 and 1976 though some are from 1973 and 1974.

BIBLIOGRAPHIC LISTS OF THE ARAB WORLD. By Dar al-Katub al-Misriyah. Cairo, National Library Press, 1960-63. Nos. 1-10.

Easch issue lists nineteenth and twentieth century works in various languages. Contents: 1. Algeria; 2. Palestine; 3. North Region (Syria); 4. Lebanon; 5. Iraq; 6. Sudan; 7. Al Maghrib; 8. Tunisia; 9. Libya; 10. Arabian Peninsula. In English and Arabic.

THE CONTEMPORARY MIDDLE EAST, 1948-1973; A Selective and Annotated Bibliography. By George Nicholas Atiyeh. Boston, G. K. Hall, 1975.

A list of the basic literature on selected topics in the social sciences. Most entries are for works in English, French, German, Italian, Spanish and some works in Arabic, Turkish and Persian.

A CUMULATION OF SELECTED AND ANNOTATED BIBLIOGRAPHY OF ECONOMIC LITERATURE ON THE ARABIC-SPEAKING COUNTRIES OF THE MIDDLE EAST, 1938-1960. By London. University School of Oriental and African Studies. Boston, Hall, 1967.

A selected, classified and annotated list of books, reports, monographs, official documents and ephemera on the economics of the Arabic-speaking countries of the Middle East. Works are in English, French and Arabic.

GOVERNMENT AND POLITICS IN THE ARABIAN PENINSULA. By Norman L. Cigar. Monticello, Illinois, Vance Bibliographies, 1979.

Lists the main contributions on government and politics, with emphasis on domestic issues, ideologies and personalities in the 1960's and 1970's.

GOVERNMENT AND POLITICS OF THE MIDDLE EAST. By Norman L. Cigar. Monticello, Illinois, Vance Bibliographies, 1979.

Lists works on politics and government in the Middle East since 1945, with emphasis on the internal development of the region.

AL-HADITH: INTRODUCTION AND SAMPLE TEXTS. Washington, D.C., Islamic Center.

THE HOLY QUR'AN. English translation and commentary by Yusuf Ali. Washington, D.C., Islamic Center.

The Arabic text of the Koran with English translation and commentary in one bound edition.

INSIDE THE ARAB MIND; A Bibliographic Survey of Literature in Arabic on Arab Nationalism and Unity, with an Annotated List of English-Language Books and Articles. By Fahim I. Qubain. Arlington, Virginia, Middle East Associates, 1960.

Arabic titles are translated into English. In both sections the annotations are in English.

INTERNATIONAL AND REGIONAL POLITICS IN THE MIDDLE EAST AND NORTH AFRICA: A GUIDE TO INFORMATION SOURCES. By Ann Schulz. Detroit, Gale Research Company, 1977.

INTRODUCTION TO THE HISTORY OF THE MUSLIM EAST, A BIBLIOGRAPHICAL GUIDE. By Jean Sauvaget. Berkeley, University of California Press, 1965.

ISLAMIC RELIGIOUS KNOWLEDGE. By Dr. Muhammad Abdul-Rauf. Washington, D.C., Islamic Center.

A three-volume set of books on Islam.

LOVE, BROTHERHOOD AND EQUALITY IN ISLAM. Islamabad, Pakistan Publications.

Describes Islamic precepts of love and equality before Law, citing incidents from the past and passages from the Quran. Extends concept of equality to economics and social philosophy.

THE MIDDLE EAST: A SELECTED BIBLIOGRAPHY OF RECENT WORKS, 1960-1969. Washington, D.C., Middle East Institute, 1969.

An annotated bibliography on the Middle East divided according to the various countries making up the Middle East, with other sections on Islam, geography and social and cultural change.

MIDDLE EAST AND ISLAM; A Bibliographical Introduction. Edited by Derek Hopwood and Diana Grimwood-Jones. Switzerland, Inter Documentation Company, 1972.

MIDDLE EAST AND NORTH AFRICA: A BIBLIOGRAPHY FOR UNDERGRADUATE LIBRARIES. By Harry Howard. Williamsport, Pennsylvania, Bro-Dart Publishing Company, 1971.

Designed for use by librarians in undergraduate colleges and universities, the bibliography is arranged both by subject and country. The first part is the general section followed by division into countries. Grading of entries (based on importance for collections) is provided.

MIDDLE EAST SOCIAL SCIENCE BIBLIOGRAPHY; Books and Articles on the Social Sciences Published in Arab Countries of the Middle East in 1955-1960. By the United Nations Educational, Scientific and Cultural Organization, Middle East Science Cooperation Office. Cairo, 1961.

A classified list of about 1,200 items, in Western languages as well as in Arabic. Includes an author index.

MIDDLE EAST, THE STRATEGIC HUB: A BIBLIOGRAPHIC SURVEY OF LITERATURE. By the United States Department of the Army, Army Library. Washington, D.C., Headquarters, Department of the Army, 1978.

Divided into six chapters, this bibliographic survey covers issues like war and peace in the Middle East, unsettled issues between Arabs and Israelis, and national perspectives of the states of the Middle East. The appendices include background notes on the Middle East countries and maps (inserted in a back pocket).

THE MODERN MIDDLE EAST: A GUIDE TO RESEARCH TOOLS IN THE SOCIAL SCIENCES. By Reeva S. Simon. Boulder, Colorado, Westview Press, 1978.

This guide is designed as a handbook for those doing research on the Modern Middle East. The work concentrates on research tools in modern history, political science, sociology, and anthropology. It is based on materials in Arabic, Hebrew, Persian, Turkish and the Western languages in the collections of the Columbia University Libraries and the New York Public Library.

THE NEAR AND MIDDLE EAST: AN INTRODUCTION TO HISTORY AND BIBLIOGRAPHY. By Roderic H. Davison. Washington, D.C., Service Center for Teachers of History, 1959.

A bibliographic essay on the history of the Near and Middle East. All works cited are in English only and arranged in an alphabetical list at the end of the book.

THE NEAR EAST (SOUTH-WEST ASIA AND NORTH AFRICA); A Bibliographic Study. By Jalal Zuwiyyah. Metuchen, New Jersey, Scarecrow Press, 1973.

Based on the holdings of the Library of the State University of New York at Binghamton, this bibliography is divided into four parts: Near East (Swana) region, individual countries of Swana, an index of authors and an index of titles.

PALESTINE AND THE ARAB-ISRAELI CONFLICT: AN ANNOTATED BIBLIOGRAPHY. Edited by Walid Khalidi and Jull Khadduri. Oxford, Pennsylvania, Institute for Palestine Studies, 1974.

Provides an annotated listing of more than 4,500 books, periodical articles, documents, and dissertations. Covers the period from 1880 to 1971. Most of the works are in English, but Hebrew, Arabic, Russian, German, and French materials are included. The editors are affiliated with the Beirut Institute for Palestine Studies.

PEOPLE'S DEMOCRATIC REPUBLIC OF YEMEN. By the Arab Information Center with the cooperation of the Permanent Mission of the People's Democratic Republic of Yemen to the United Nations. New York, League of Arab States, 1974.

An illustrated pamphlet presenting brief information concerning the country and its history, government, economy, trade, education, health, and tourism. Includes a map.

POLITICAL ECONOMY OF THE MIDDLE EAST; A Computerized Guide to the Literature. By Ali Mohammad Fatemi. Akron, Ohio, Department of Economics, University of Akron, 1970.

A guide to abstracts and annotated lists of books, dissertations, special studies and articles related to economic development and international trade of the Middle East. There are three sections to the book: subject index (ascending numerical order), author index and KWICIR (Key Word in Context Information Retrieval).

THE POLITICS OF AFRICAN AND MIDDLE EASTERN STATES: AN ANNOTATED BIBLIOGRAPHY. By Anne Gordon Drabek. Oxford, Pergamon Press, 1976.

This annotated bibliography concentrates on the states or countries after independence. The majority of the materials treat all aspects of internal political development.

THE PROPHET AND ISLAM. By Stanley L. Poole. Washington, D.C., Islamic Center.

QATAR. By the Arab Information Center. New York, League of Arab States, 1974.

Describes briefly the country, its history, government, people, economic development, trade, transportation, social services, and sites of interest.

QATAR. New York, Aramtek Corporation.

A booklet stressing Qatar's developmental potential and telling about the country and its people, government, schools, health services, trade, transportation, banks and finance, communications, energy, industry, farming and fishing. Includes colored photographs, maps and general information.

SCIENCE AND ISLAM. By Mohammad Zia-ul-haq. Islamabad, Ministry of Information and Broadcasting, 1980.

A speech given by the President of Pakistan in 1979 outlining the general course of scientific progress for Muslim countries.

SOCIAL JUSTICE AND ROLE OF LAW IN ISLAM. Islamabad, Pakistan Publications, 1979.

Points out the close connection between Islamic precepts and social justice, brotherhood and equality. Islamic law is understood as a means to do justice and restore imbalance in the quest for an ideal society.

THE SOUTHERN ARABIAN PENINSULA: SOCIAL AND ECONOMIC DEVELOPMENT. By John J. Vidergar. Monticello, Illinois, Council of Planning Librarians, 1978.

Provides a listing of books that contain information on the social and economic history of the Arabian peninsula as well as studies on the impact of oil development on the states of the Arabian peninsula.

THE STATUS OF WOMEN IN THE ARAB WORLD. By Shwikar Elwan. New York, League of Arab States, 1974.

A lecture delivered at a seminar on the Middle East held at the Church Center for the United Nations on March 22, 1974. Considers the liberating effect Islam first had on the status of women and how it declined under Byzantine and Persian influence. Describes the more recent emancipation attempts in the nineteenth and twentieth centuries, the progress of female education and the impact of social change on Arab families and the status of women through increasing industrialization and urbanization. Looks at Muslim legal restrictions and the differences among various Arab countries with regard to women.

THIS IS BAHRAIN. Bahrain, Gulf Public Relations.

An informational booklet about the country published periodically. Each issue includes color maps, a list of diplomatic missions, places to eat, hotels, a short history of the country and description of its government, as well as feature articles on such topics as wildlife, gardens or economic progress. Additionally detailed information is provided for the tourist on many aspects of daily life.

UNITED ARAB EMIRATES. UAE, Ministry of Information and Culture.

A brochure telling about the region's scenic attractions, historical sites, customs and folklore and commercial importance. Illustrated in color.

UNITED ARAB EMIRATES. UAE, Ministry of Information and Culture.

A large poster with several smaller pictures on the verso and text telling about the member emirates, governmental structure, the drive for economic development and agricultural progress.

URBANIZATION IN THE ARAB WORLD: A SELECTED BIBLIOGRAPHY. By Aghil Barbar. Monticello, Illinois, Council of Planning Librarians, 1977.

This bibliography covers works on urban growth in the Arab world, largely Islamic urbanization. Includes a number of studies done in western languages especially English and French.

YEMEN ARAB REPUBLIC. By the Arab Information Center with the cooperation of the Permanent Mission of Yemen Arab Republic to the United Nations. New York, Arab Information Center, 1973.

An illustrated pamphlet providing information on present and past conditions in Yemen, including economic and political development, trade, education, health, and tourism.

YEMEN ARAB REPUBLIC. Washington, D.C., Embassy of the Yemen Arab Republic.

Informational booklet about North Yemen, telling about its history, form of government, development and economic planning, geographic characteristics and places to visit. Includes pictures and maps.

ARAB AMERICANS

ARAB AMERICANS ALMANAC. Edited by Joseph R. Haiek. Los Angeles, News Circle Publishing Company, 1983.

Covers: Arab American communities, organizations, churches and mosques, leaders, and newspapers and radio programs. Entries include: Name (of community, organization, church, newspaper, etc.), address. Who's who section includes biographical material. Arrangement: Five directory sections: Arab American communities in United States; cultural, political and other local and national organizations; biographical sketches of prominent Arab American personalities; churches and mosques; newspapers and radio programs. Published biennially.

ARAB-AMERICANS AND THEIR ORGANIZATIONS. Edited by Sheba Mittelman. New York, American Jewish Committee, 1978.

Covers: Arab American political, social, religious, and other groups in the United States. Entries include: Organization name, address.

THE ARAB AMERICANS: STUDIES IN ASSIMILATION. Edited by Elaine Hagopian and Ann Paden. Wilmette, Illinois, Medina University Press International, 1969.

A collection of essays dealing with diverse aspects such as Arab nationalism and ways of assimilation in urban areas.

THE ARAB COMMUNITY IN THE CHICAGO AREA. By Abdul Jalil al Tahir. Chicago, University of Chicago Press, 1952.

A comparative study of the Christian Syrians and the Muslim Palestinians in Chicago and its suburbs.

THE ARAB MOSLEMS IN THE UNITED STATES: Religion and Assimilation. By Abdo A. Elkholy. New Haven, College and University Press, 1966.

Compares the degree of adjustment and resistance to change of Arab Moslem communities in Toledo, Ohio, and Detroit, Michigan. Deals with their historical background and present situations, their ethnic-religious patterns, and generational differences.

ARABIC SPEAKING COMMUNITIES IN AMERICAN CITIES. Edited by Barbara C. Aswad. New York, Center for Migration Studies of New York, Incorporated and Association of Arab-American University Graduates, Incorporated, 1974.

Presents previously unpublished social science studies about people from the Arabic-speaking Middle East living in American cities. Discusses their activities, associations, churches, mosques, family life, occupations, assimulation, and ethnic divergence from community life.

THE ARABS IN AMERICA, 1492-1977: A CHRONOLOGY AND FACT BOOK. Edited by Beverlee Turner Mehdi. Dobbs Ferry, New York, Oceana Publications, 1978. (Ethnic Chronology Series, No. 31)

A history of Arabs in the United States with illustrative documents, appendices and bibliography.

THE ARABS IN THE UNITED STATES: A STUDY OF AN ARAB-AMERICAN COMMUNITY. By Ibrahim Othman. Ammau, Shashaa, 1974.

Focus is on the Christian Arab community of Springfield, Massachusetts.

THE CIVIL RIGHTS OF ARAB-AMERICANS: "THE SPECIAL MEASURES." Edited by M. C. Bassiouni. North Dartmouth, Massachusetts, Arab-American University Graduates, 1974.

The thesis of this collection, that Arab-Americans were harrassed during the Nixon administration, is addressed by several legal scholars.

THE IMMIGRANT ARAB COMMUNITY IN NEW YORK CITY. By Ishaq Y. Qutub. East Lansing, Michigan, 1962.

Audiovisual Material

CALENDAR

THE ISLAMIC CALENDAR. Washington, D.C., Islamic Center.

Gives times of prayer in English, Islamic dates, holidays, and festivals. Also includes addresses of Islamic centers and mosques in North America.

CASSETTES

ESSENTIALS OF ISLAM. Tucson, Arizona, Islamic Productions International.

LIFE HISTORY OF THE PROPHET MUHAMMAD. Tucson, Arizona, Islamic Productions International.

PRINCIPLES OF MUSLIM PRAYER. Tucson, Arizona, Islamic Productions International.

FILMS

ALKHALIJ - THE GULF. 16 mm. Color and sound. 29 minutes. By Caltex Petroleum Corporation. Made by Rayant Pictures Limited, London. Released by Association-Sterling Films, 1974.

A survey of the history, the development, and the current life-styles of people living in a number of states in the Persian Gulf area, including Bahrain, Qatar, and the United Arab Emirates.

THE ARAB IDENTITY: WHO ARE THE ARABS? 16 mm. Color and sound. 26 minutes. (The Arab Experience) By Yorkshire Television. New York, Learning Corporation of America, 1976.

Points out the diversity of culture of some 125 million Arabs, while noting the unifying power of their centuries-old heritage. Comments on the strength of the Islamic faith and the impact of modernizing and Westernizing influences.

THE ARAB-ISRAELI CONFLICT. 16 mm. Color and sound. 20 minutes. By Atlantis Productions, 1974.

An analysis of the basic political and territorial problems between the Arabs and the Israelis. Discusses the relative positions of the opposing views by tracing the historical origins of the Arab-Israeli conflict, with emphasis on the events that have occurred since the first Arab-Israeli War in 1948.

BEYOND THE MIRAGE. 16 mm. Color and sound. 29 minutes. New York, Jewish Chautauqua Society, 1970.

Describes opportunities for mutual understanding and peaceful coexistence between Arabs and Jews in Israel.

COMPARATIVE GEOGRAPHY: A CHANGING CULTURE. 16 mm. Color and sound. 17 minutes. By Yehuda Tarmu. Santa Monica, California, BFA Educational Media, 1970.

Discusses the Bedouins and their history as nomadic desert tribes for centuries. Shows how the Israeli Government has constructed permanent housing developments in the desert and explains the impact this cultural change will have on the Bedouin way of life.

DISCOVERY GOES TO ISRAEL. 16 mm. Color and sound. 21 minutes. By Daniel Wilson for American Broadcasting Company. Released by International Film Bureau, Chicago, 1970.

Portrays a traditional Arab family living in Israel in the village of Ramah. Also shows a view of life in the port of Haifa, where the Arab-Jewish center is working to bridge the gap between the Arab and Jewish cultures.

FAMILIES OF THE WORLD - YEMEN. 16 mm. Color and sound. 19 minutes. By United Nations Children's Fund. Journal Films, Evanston, Illinois, 1976.

Explores family life in Yemen. Highlights changing roles for young people against a background of Arabian traditional patterns. Shows a teenage boy from a poor family who is taking advantage of the educational opportunities open to him and a young girl from a wealthy family who has cast aside the traditional role of Arab women as she pursues a teaching career.

THE HOLY QUR'AN: A HISTORICAL SURVEY OF CALLIGRAPHY IN THE QUR'AN. 16 mm. Color and sound. 18 minutes. By Inca Films. Phoenix Films, New York, 1978.

Traces the evolution of calligraphic styles in the Koran from the introduction of the Kufic script in the eighth century to contemporary Koranic recordings.

IN ARAB LANDS - AN AGE OF CHANGE. 16 mm. Color and sound. 28 minutes. By Sunset Films, Incorporated. Bechtel Corporation, Bechtel Incorporated, and Bechtel Power Corporation, San Francisco, 1979.

Filmed in Saudi Arabia, Kuwait, the United Arab Emirates, and Spain. Discusses the history of the Arab peoples, the beginning and spread of the Islamic faith, and the Arabs' contributions to Western culture and scientific knowledge in earlier centuries. Also shows changes taking place in the Arabian Peninsula as the people proceed with industrialization and new social programs to improve their standard of living.

ISLAM. 16 mm. Color and sound. 17 minutes. (Altars of the World) By Lew Ayres. Doubleday Multimedia, Irvine, California, 1976, made 1975.

Explains the rituals, symbols, and teachings of Islam, including its history and growth, Muhammad's role, the Koran, and the Pillars of Fire.

ISLAM, THE PROPHET AND THE PEOPLE. 16 mm. Color and sound. 34 minutes. Also issued in super 8 mm and as videocassette. By RAI, Rome, and Texture Films. Released in the United States by Texture Films, 1975.

Traces the history and growth of the Islamic faith in the Middle East and describes the basic beliefs of Muslims today.

ISLAM: THERE IS NO GOD BUT GOD. 16 mm. Color and sound. 52 minutes. Also issued as videocassette. By BBC-TV. Time-Life Multimedia, New York, 1978.

Visits Egypt to explore the experience of Islamic worship. Includes interviews with a number of Moslems who discuss their personal attitudes and approaches to their religion.

MIDDLE EAST, JOURNEY INTO THE FUTURE. 16 mm. Color and sound. 15 minutes. By Vladimir Bibic Film Productions. Barr Films, Pasadena, California, 1978.

Shows, through the story of a Middle Eastern village farmer, the hardships encountered by a culture whose people are forced to move from the past to the future.

MIDEAST - ARTS, CRAFTS, AND ARCHITECTURE. 16 mm. Color and sound. 18 minutes. By Vocational & Industrial Films Limited. BFA Educational Media, Santa Monica, California, 1977.

Focuses on the arts and crafts of the Middle East, including rug making, miniature painting, mosiacs, leather bookbinding, and calligraphy. Points out various Middle Eastern architectural styles and examines the role of the Islamic religion in shaping artistic activity and expression.

MIDEAST - ECONOMIC DEVELOPMENT. 16 mm. Color and sound. 18 minutes. By Vocational & Industrial Films Limited. BFA Educational Media, Santa Monica, California, 1977.

Discusses the economic development of the Middle East. Explores the impact of oil on the region and examines the plans of Mideast nations to build a lasting economic future.

MIDEAST - ISLAM, THE UNIFYING FORCE. 16 mm. Color and sound. 17 minutes. By Vocational & Industrial Films Limited. BFA Educational Media, Santa Monica, California, 1977.

Investigates the history, beliefs, and practices of the Islamic faith and examines its role in the lives of Muslims. Discusses Islam's significance as a unifying force among the majority of people and governments in the Middle East.

MIDEAST - LAND AND PEOPLE. 16 mm. Color and sound. 20 minutes. By Vocational & Industrial Films Limited. BFA Educational Media, Santa Monica, California, 1977.

Describes the varied geographical regions and diverse cultural groups found in the Middle East.

MIDEAST - PIONEERS OF SCIENCE. 16 mm. Color and sound. 20 minutes. By Vocational & Industrial Films Limited. BFA Educational Media, Santa Monica, California, 1977.

Enumerates various contributions to modern civilization originating in the Middle East, including the wheel and axle, writing, the use of the decimal point, anesthetics, our number system, and others.

PROMISED LAND, TROUBLED LAND. 16 mm. Black and white. Sound. 14 minutes. By Hearst Metrotone News, 1973.

Tells of major events during the centuries of smouldering conflict that have shaped history in the Middle East from ancient days to modern times.

FILMS ABOUT ARAB AMERICANS

JOURNEY TO THE WEST. 16 mm. Color and sound. Washington, D.C., Middle East Educational Trust, Incorporated.

A documentary showing the adaptation, accomplishments and common heritage of immigrants to the United States from Arab lands.

ARGENTINES
See also: SPANISH-SPEAKING PEOPLES

Embassy and Consulates

EMBASSY OF THE ARGENTINE REPUBLIC
1600 New Hampshire Avenue, Northwest
Washington, D.C. 20009 (202) 387-0705/13

Office of the Economic and Commercial Counselor
555 Madison Avenue, 31st Floor
New York, New York 10022 (212) 759-6477

Permanent Mission to the OAS
2232 Massachusetts Avenue, Northwest
Washington, D.C. 20008 (202) 387-4170/4142/4146

CONSULATES GENERAL

819 Edificio Mercantil
Av. Ponce de Leon, Parada 27
Hato Rey, Puerto Rico 00918 (809) 754-6501

International Trade Mart, Suite 915
2 Canal Street
New Orleans, Louisiana 70130 (504) 523-2823

12 West 56th Street
New York, New York 10019 (212) 397-1400

870 Market Street
San Francisco, California 94102 (415) 982-3050

CONSULATES

204/5 Keyser Building
Calvert and Redwood Street
Baltimore, Maryland 21202 (301) 837-0444

20 North Clark, Suite 602
Chicago, Illinois 60602 (312) 263-7435

2000 South Post Oak Road
Suite 1810
Houston, Texas 77056 (713) 871-8935

World Trade Center Building
350 South Figueroa
Los Angeles, California 90071 (213) 687-8884

25 Southeast Second Avenue
Miami, Florida 33131 (305) 373-7794

Mission to the United Nations

ARGENTINE MISSION
One United Nations Plaza, 25th Floor
New York, New York 10017 (212) 688-6300

Public Affairs Organizations

ARGENTINE INFORMATION SERVICE CENTER
Post Office Box 4233
2700 Bancroft Way
Berkeley, California 94704
Executive Officer: Anya Thompson (415) 548-7615
Founded 1976

Seeks freedom for political prisoners in Argentina and restoration of their democratic rights. Presents slide shows; sponsors speakers. Compiles statistics on kidnapped persons in Argentina.
Publications: Argentina Outreach, quarterly; also issues Rebellion in Patagonia (film).

COMMISSION FOR HUMAN RIGHTS IN ARGENTINA
Post Office Box 2635
Washington, D.C. 20013
Representative: Gino Lofredo (202) 296-8340
Founded 1976

Main objective is to contribute to the defense of human rights and to the restoration of democratic liberties in Argentina. Conducts research into repression and violations of human rights in Argentina and publishes results; maintains case files, press clippings and files of testimonies of victims.
Publications: Bulletin, monthly; Information Packets, monthly; also publishes books.

Cultural and Educational Organizations

SAN MARTIN SOCIETY OF WASHINGTON, D.C.
Post Office Box 33
McLean, Virginia 22101
President: Christian Garcia-Godoy
Founded 1977

Organization of individuals interested in the study of Argentine General Jose de San Martin and the

South American liberation movements which he led. Purposes are to pool efforts in order to make available in the English language the ideals held by San Martin; to promote understanding and solidarity between the peoples of the Americas; and to stimulate study and historic research on San Martin's life and work. Sponsors periodic commemorative ceremonies, including San Martin's birthday (February 25, 1778), Argentine Independence Day (July 9, 1816) and the anniversary of San Martin's death (August 17, 1850). Maintains collection of books, broadsides, document photocopies, medals, iconography and biographical archives.
Publications: San Martin News, quarterly; has also published selected bibliography of San Martin (English).

Bank Branches in the U.S.

BANCO DE LA NACION ARGENTINA
299 Park Avenue
New York, New York 10017 (212) 754-0200

135 South LaSalle Street,
22nd Floor
Chicago, Illinois 60603 (312) 580-1700

BANCO DE LA PROVINCIA DE BUENOS AIRES
650 Fifth Avenue
New York, New York 10022 (212) 397-7650

BANCO INTERNATIONAL OF BUENOS AIRES
277 Park Avenue
New York, New York 10017 (212) 683-5524.

Commercial and Trade Organizations

ARGENTINE-AMERICAN CHAMBER OF COMMERCE
50 West 34th
New York, New York 10001 (212) 564-3855

Publishes Argentine-American Business Review and Directory, annually.

Airline Offices

ARGENTINE AIRLINES (Aerolineas Argentinas)
North American Headquarters:
9 Rockefeller Plaza
New York, New York 10020 (212) 974-3370

Provides international services from South America to North America and Europe. Other offices in the United States: Boston, Chicago, Houston, Los Angeles, Miami, San Francisco, and Washington.

Ship Lines

ARGENTINE LINES
1115 American Bank Building (504) 522-3492
New Orleans, Louisiana 70130 527-6710

Argentine flag freighters carry freight and some passengers between New Orleans and Buenos Aires, Argentina.

E.L.M.A. (Empresas Lineas Maritimas Argentinas)
1 World Trade Center, Suite 2611
New York, New York 10048 (212) 432-0877

Books and Pamphlets

ARGENTINA. Buenos Aires, Ministry of Foreign Relations and Culture.

A booklet describing Argentina, its sociology, history, geography, economy, science and technology, sports, art, culture and tourism. Many illustrations, some in color.

ARGENTINA. Buenos Aires, Secretary of Public Information, 1981.

Lavish color illustrations accompany articles on newspapers in Argentina, flowers, the thinker Alberdi, mate, humor, the stock exchange, export of grains, the Tierra de Fuego region, ceramics in Argentina and the medium-sized tank.

ARGENTINA'S INCREDIBLE WILDLIFE. By William G. Conway and Roger Payne. Washington, D.C., National Geographic Society, 1976. Separately bound and distributed by the Argentine Embassy, Washington, D.C.

Includes three photographic essays by Des and Jan Bartlett: Argentina protects its Wildlife Treasures, Where Two Worlds Meet, and At Home with Right Whales, all about the Patagonia region of Argentina.

HISTORICAL DICTIONARY OF ARGENTINA. By Ione S. Wright and Lisa M. Nekhom. Metuchen, New Jersey, Scarecrow Press, 1977.

A sourcebook of historical and contemporary facts and

statistics about people, places, events, geography and political organizations. Includes a bibliography.

A SELECTED ANNOTATED BIBLIOGRAPHY OF ENVIRONMENTAL STUDIES OF ARGENTINA, CHILE, AND URUGUAY. Compiled by Vincent J. Creasi. Washington, U.S. Air Force Environmental Technical Applications Center, 1970.

An annotated bibliography available from the National Technical Information Service in Springfield, Virginia.

Audiovisual Material

FILMS

ALLIANCE FOR PROGRESS. 16mm. Black and white with sound. 108 minutes. By Julio Luduena, Argentina, 1972. Released in the United States by Tricontinental Film Center, 1973.

An allegory on the present-day political situation in Argentina which describes a revolution which would lead to a new social order as one possible resolution of the situation.

ARGENTINA: CULTURE. 16mm. Color and sound. 15 minutes. Embassy of Argentina, Cultural Department, Washington, D.C., 1981.

ARGENTINA-LAND OF PEACE AND FUTURE. 16mm. Color and sound. 30 minutes. Embassy of Argentina, Cultural Department, Washington, D.C., 1980.

ARGENTINA TODAY. 16mm. Color and sound. 20 minutes. Embassy of Argentina, Cultural Department, Washington, D.C., 1977.

ARGENTINA: TOURISM AND ECONOMY. 16mm. Color and sound. 26 minutes. Embassy of Argentina, Cultural Department, Washington, D.C., 1981.

ARGENTINA WITH OPEN ARMS. 16mm. Color and sound. 11 minutes. Embassy of Argentina, Cultural Department, Washington, D.C., 1980.

ARGENTINE SOUTHERN RIVERS. 16mm. Color and sound. 15 minutes. Embassy of Argentina, Cultural Department, Washington, D.C.

CHILE AND ARGENTINA. 16mm. Color and sound. 19 minutes. By William Claiborne, Incorporated. Latin American series: A Focus on People. New York, Sterling Educational Films, 1973.

Examines the social and political structure of Chile and Argentina. Discusses the non-Spanish background of half the population, European aspects of life, and problems arising from high expectations and low productivity.

COSQUIN: CITY OF FOLKLORE. 16mm. Color and sound. 14 minutes. Also available on videocassette. Museum of Modern Art of Latin America, Organization of American States, Washington, D. C., 1970.

Visits the folk festival celebrated annually in Cosquin, Argentina, and its market place.

THE GAUCHO. 16mm. Color and sound. 15 minutes. Embassy of Argentina, Cultural Department, Washington, D.C.

Shows the life of Argentina's "cowboy".

GEOGRAPHY OF SOUTH AMERICA: ARGENTINA, PARAGUAY, URUGUAY. 16mm. Color and sound. 11 minutes. Coronet Instructional Media, Chicago, 1977.

Presents a view of life in the cities and on the farms and ranches of Argentina, Paraguay, and Uruguay, the three nations sharing the Plata-Parana River system. Shows similarities and contrasts among the people, lands, and cultures of these countries.

VOYAGE TO THE BOTTOM OF THE WORLD. 16mm. Color and sound. 24 minutes. Hayden Productions, Dublin, California, 1977.

A promotional film for Prudential Lines' sea cruise from Buenos Aires through the Strait of Magellan to Valparaiso. Also issued in Portuguese and Spanish.

ARMENIANS

Information Offices

ARMENIAN ASSEMBLY OF AMERICA
INCORPORATED
1420 N Street, Northwest,
Suite 101
Washington, D.C. 20005 (202) 332-3434

4250 Wilshire Boulevard, Suite 212
Los Angeles, California 90010 (213) 933-5238

Fraternal Organizations

ARMENIAN PROGRESSIVE LEAGUE OF AMERICA
1605 Cahuenga Boulevard, Suite 200
Hollywood, California 90028

Established to inform Armenians about life in the homeland; to work for democracy and peace.

ARMENIAN YOUTH FEDERATION OF AMERICA
212 Stuart Street
Boston, Massachusetts 02116 (617) 926-3860
Director: Stephen Dulgarian Founded 1933

1501 Venice Boulevard
Los Angeles, California 90006
Director: Sarkis Ghazarian (213) 380-2936

North American young people (13-30 years old) of Armenian parentage. Committed to efforts to liberate the Armenian national homeland and to provide Armenian youth with an understanding and appreciation of their ethnic heritage. Sponsors AYF junior organization (10-16 years of age). Supports summer camps at Franklin, Massachusetts and Kern County, California. Sponsors general scholarship program for study in liberal arts; conducts special scholarship competition for study of government, international law, history and political science. Youth branch of the Armenian Revolutionary Federation of America. Formerly called ARF Tzeghagrons. Publication: Armenian Weekly.

HOMENETMEN ASSOCIATION
109 Langdon Avenue
Watertown, Massachusetts 02172
President: Bedros Garabedian (617) 926-0715

KNIGHTS OF VARTAN
844 Ormond Avenue
Drexel Hill, Pennsylvania 19029
Commander: Harry Chilingerian

Dedicated to the moral and cultural uplift of its members and the community. A non-sectarian, non-political, and non-denominational, fraternal organization which emphasizes patriotism, discipline, and contribution to cultural, educational, religious, and charitable institutions on a national and international level.

UNION OF MARASH ARMENIANS
Central Committee
Post Office Box 95
New Town Branch
Boston, Massachusetts 02258

Professional Organizations

ARMENIAN LAWYERS ASSOCIATION
12744 Milbank
Studio City, California 91604
President: Michael Hachigian (213) 985-0543

ARMENIAN MEDICAL ASSOCIATION
Boston University School of Medicine
80 East Concord Street
Boston, Massachusetts
President: Dr. Aram Cholanian (617) 643-1700
Founded 1972

Physicians of Armenian origin who wish to support the following goals: to assist young Armenians to obtain medical education and a good start in their profession; to foster contact with physicians in Armenia by personal contact and assistance with medical facilities; to give medical help to the Armenian community.

ARMENIAN PROFESSIONAL SOCIETY
215 West Mariners View Lane
La Canada, California 91011
President: Ms. Seda Marootian (213) 790-7271

ARMENIAN SCIENTIFIC ASSOCIATION OF AMERICA
c/o Mr. Nerses Almoian
30 Half Moon Lane
Irvington, New York 10533

ARMENIAN TEACHERS ASSOCIATION
4220 Dixie Canyon Avenue
Sherman Oaks, California 91403
President: Ms. Sara Chitjian

Public Affairs Organizations

ARMENIAN CONGRESS OF CALIFORNIA
1252 LaGranada Drive
Thousand Oaks, California 91360
President: Dr. J. Michael Hagopian (805) 495-4031

ARMENIAN DEMOCRATIC LEAGUE
755 Mount Auburn Street
Watertown, Massachusetts 02172
President: Ara Kalayjian (617) 924-4420

ARMENIAN NATIONAL COMMITTEE-EASTERN REGION
212 Stuart Street
Boston, Massachusetts 02116
Chairman: Harry Derderian (617) 426-9842

ARMENIAN NATIONAL COMMITTEE-WESTERN REGION
1501 Venice Boulevard
Los Angeles, California 90006
Chairman: Ms. Salpi Ghazarian (213) 380-6129

Functions as an information center.

ARMENIAN REVOLUTIONARY FEDERATION OF AMERICA
212 Stuart Street
Boston, Massachusetts 02116
Secretary and Editor: Dr. Kevork Donabadian (617) 426-8479

Publications: Asbarez, daily; Hairenik (Fatherland), daily except Sunday and Monday; Armenian Weekly (in English); Armenian Review, quarterly.

ARMENIAN RIGHTS COUNCIL OF AMERICA
c/o Nor Or
7466 Beverly Boulevard, Suite 101
Los Angeles, California 90036
Western Chairman: Dr. Arto Poladian (213) 933-3298

1073 Palisades Avenue
Fort Lee, New Jersey 07024
Eastern Chairman: Nubar Dorian (201) 224-5343

SOCIAL DEMOCRAT HUNCHAKIAN PARTY OF AMERICA
353 Forest Avenue, or
Post Office Box 742
Paramus, New Jersey 07652

Cultural and Educational Organizations

ARMENIAN ALLIED ARTS ASSOCIATION
5410 West Adams
Los Angeles, California 90016 (213) 937-2870
Chairman: Leon Partamanian

ARMENIAN ARTISTS ASSOCIATION OF AMERICA
Box 140
Watertown, Massachusetts 02172
President: Richard Tashjian Founded 1973

Sponsors special exhibitions and other educational programs to inform the public about Armenian art and artists. Active primarily in the Boston area.

ARMENIAN ASSEMBLY OF AMERICA, INCORPORATED
1420 N Street, Northwest, Suite 101
Washington, D.C. 20005 (202) 332-3434
Director: Ross Vartian Founded 1972

4250 Wilshire Boulevard, Suite 212
Los Angeles, California 90010 (213) 933-5238

A national, nonprofit coalition office for the Armenian-American community. Serves as an information clearinghouse on issues of importance and concern to the Armenian people. Fosters greater participation in the federal structures via a grants service and intership program.
Publications: Armenian Assembly of America Newsletter, quarterly; Federal Grants Handbook Annual; Federation of Armenian Student Clubs of America Newsletter, bimonthly.

ARMENIAN CULTURAL ASSOCIATION
212 Stuart Street
Boston, Massachusetts 02116
President: Dr. Kevork Donoyan

ARMENIAN LITERARY SOCIETY
114 First Street
Yonkers, New York 10704 (914) 237-5751
Secretary: K.N. Magarian Founded 1956

Individuals of Armenian descent interested in Armenian literature. Purposes are: to help Armenian authors morally and financially by promoting and distributing their publications; to organize lectures about literature and culture; to collect books and send them to needy libraries, schools, and student organizations

in the United States and abroad. Compiles lists of books in print relating to Armenia and Armenians.
Publication: Kir ou Kirk, quarterly.

ARMENIAN NATIONAL EDUCATION COMMITTEE
138 East 39th Street
New York, New York 10016 (212) 689-7810
Mrs. Hourig Sahagian Founded 1962
President: Bishop Mesrob Ashjian

Coordinates the work of Armenian American education in day schools at primary and secondary educational levels. Develops language and cultural materials, and sponsors Student Festivals at which hundreds of Armenian school students gather.

ARMENIAN RENAISSANCE ASSOCIATION
87 Eileen Street
Yarmouth, Massachusetts 02675 (617) 362-3518
President: Ms. S.S. Saryan

ARMENIAN STUDENTS ASSOCIATION OF AMERICA
GPO Box 1557
New York, New York 10001 (212) 244-4818
President: Armen Enkababian Founded 1910

Provides scholarships and loans to college students of Armenian descent. Sponsors competitions; maintains speakers bureau. Presents awards in the fields of citizenship, humanities and science to notable Armenian-Americans.
Publications: News, quarterly; Convention Booklet, annual; Directory, annual.

EDUCATIONAL ASSOCIATION OF MALATIA
Post Office Box 387
Westside Station
Worcester, Massachusetts 01602
Secretary: Stepan Der Baghdasarian

FEDERATION OF ARMENIAN STUDENTS CLUBS OF AMERICA
1420 N Street, Northwest
Washington, D. C. 20005 (202) 332-3434
Coordinator: Laurens Ayvazian Founded 1980

Objectives are to provide services to the Armenian-American college student club community; to provide information and guidance to existing clubs while assisting in the establishment of new clubs; and to enhance participation of Armenian-Americans in campus community activities. Maintains Intern Placement Service which offers first-hand experience in congressional offices, federal agencies and in business law and journalism establishments; also maintains Washington Job Placement Service for seniors and graduate students seeking full-time positions in the federal government. Operates computerized data bank based on demographic and academic information provided by each FASCA club. Provides news of club activities, faculty appointments, information on scholarships, and grant opportunities. Affiliated with the Armenian Assembly Charitable Trust.
Publication: Newsletter, bimonthly.

NATIONAL ASSOCIATION FOR ARMENIAN STUDIES AND RESEARCH
175 Mount Auburn Street
Cambridge, Massachusetts 02138 (617) 876-7630
Chairman: Manoog S. Young Founded 1955

Fosters the study of Armenian history, culture, and language on an active, scholarly and continuous basis in America, particularly through American institutions of higher education and through a multifaceted program in support of research, scholarship and publications. Has established centers of learning, research and training at Harvard University and the University of California at Los Angeles by endowing permanent Chairs of Armenian Studies and has supported programs of Armenian Studies at Columbia University, the University of Massachusetts and other universities. Has established a permanent endowment fund for Armenian Studies to support research grants, fellowships, publications, libraries, conferences and other programs and activities. Houses an Armenian information and education center. Maintains a reference and research library of over 8,000 volumes on various aspects of Armenian history, culture, language, literature, music, architecture, art, church history, archaeology and related subjects. Operates an Armenian Book Clearinghouse of primarily English-language books; approximately 400 titles are available on Armenian and related subjects; discounts available to members, schools, libraries and retailers. Has established Armenian Heritage Press for the publication of both popular and scholarly works as well as translations. Sponsors conferences, institutes, seminars, lecture series, scholar-in-residence program, bookfairs, exhibits and heritage tours.
Publications: Newsletter, quarterly; Journal of Armenian Studies, semiannual; Books on Armenia and the Armenians, 1-2 per year.

SOCIETY FOR ARMENIAN STUDIES
6 Divinity Avenue, Room 103
Cambridge, Massachusetts 02138
President: Kevork Bardakjian Founded 1974

Organized to serve those who make contributions to Armenian studies through scholarship and teaching.

TEKEYAN CULTURAL ASSOCIATION
755 Mount Auburn
Watertown, Massachusetts 02172 (617) 924-4420
President: Dr. H. Arzoumian Founded 1965

Founded to assist educational institutions which teach Armenian language, religion, arts and sciences. Awards scholarships, sponsors cultural projects, translates Armenian works into English, and assists Armenian authors, editors, scholars and musicians.

Foundations

ARAKELIAN FOUNDATION
56372 Road 200
O'Neals, California 93645
Donor: Krikor Arakelian
President: Aram Arakelian Founded 1943

Has established student loan funds at five institutions of higher learning; gives grants to hospitals, health agencies, community funds, educational and youth agencies, primarily in California.

BEN H. AND GLADYS ARKELIAN FOUNDATION
1107 Truxtun Avenue
Post Office Box 1825
Bakersfield, California 93303 (805) 324-9801
President: Henry C. Mack Established 1959

Grants emphasize higher education, youth agencies, hospitals and the aged.

ARMENIAN EDUCATIONAL FOUNDATION
5301 Laurel Canyon Boulevard, #211
North Hollywood, California 91607 (213) 763-8512
Director: Norair Bahlavouni Founded 1950

Renders financial assistance to Armenian schools in the United States and countries friendly to the United States. Has built schools in Athens, Greece, Beirut, Lebanon, and Pico Rivera, California. Supports other schools and youth activities; makes scholarship grants; organizes cultural, literary, and musical events.

GULLABI GULBENKIAN FOUNDATION, INCORPORATED
c/o Golbert and Epstein
66 South Tyson Avenue
Floral Park, New York 11001 (516) 328-3800
Donors: Gullabi, Seroupe and Vergine Gulbenkian Incorporated 1920
President: Gould R. Kardashian

Charitable and educational grants primarily in the Middle East, with emphasis on a cathedral building fund and higher education.

KAZANJIAN ECONOMICS FOUNDATION, INCORPORATED
Post Office Box 1110
Waterbury, Connecticut 06720 Incorporated 1947
Donor: Calvin K. Kazanjian
President: Mrs. Lloyd W. Elston

To increase man's understanding of economics through research and to disseminate knowledge utilizing the media. Particular emphasis on education through the provision of classroom materials.

KAZANJIAN FOUNDATION
332 North Rodeo Drive
Beverly Hills, California 90210 (213) 276-8480
Executive Director: Michael J. Kazanjian
President: Carl S. Denzel

Provides scholarships and charitable grants.

KEVORKIAN FUND
1411 Third Avenue (212) 988-9304
New York, New York 10028 Established 1950
Donor: Hagop Kevorkian Incorporated 1951
President: Miss Marjorie Kevorkian

Promotes interest in Near and Middle Eastern art through exhibitions and through scholarships and fellowships for research and study in this field. Formerly called the Kevorkian Foundation.

ALEX AND MARIE MANOOGIAN FOUNDATION
500 Stephenson Highway, Suite 410 (313) 588-2000
Troy, Michigan 48084 Incorporated 1942
Donors: Alex and Marie Manoogian
Secretary: H.S. Derderian

Gives support primarily for Armenian welfare funds and religious institutions, higher and secondary education, with emphasis on music and the arts.

MARDIGIAN FOUNDATION
1525 Tottenham Street
Birmingham, Michigan 48009 (313) 939-9410
Donors: Edward and Helen Mardigan, Mardigian Corporation, Marco Manufacturing Corporation Incorporated 1955
Director: Edward Mardigian

Grants largely for Armenian church support, religious associations and welfare funds.

THE MUGAR FOUNDATION
29 Commonwealth Avenue
Boston, Massachusetts 02116 (617) 262-2161
Donors: Stephen P. and Carolyn J. Mugar
Director: David G. Mugar

Gifts to Armenian religious and charitable groups.

TOWER LAKES FOUNDATION
111 West Monroe Street
Chicago, Illinois 60603 Incorporated 1954
Donors: Nazareth and Rose A. Barsumian
President: G.A. Goshgarian

Gives aid to Armenian refugees and immigrants coming to the United States as well as to Armenian churches and missions.

Charitable Organizations

AMERICAN NATIONAL COMMITTEE TO AID HOMELESS ARMENIANS
160 Sansome Street, Room 900
San Francisco, California 94104 (415) 433-0440
President and Founder: S.M. Saroyan Founded 1948

488 Graphic Boulevard
New Milford, New Jersey 07646
Eastern Chairman: Ms. Arpi Papazian

Seeks to aid Armenian refugees throughout the world. Resettles many escapees from behind the Iron Curtain in the United States, Canada, South America and Australia.

ARMENIAN ASSEMBLY CHARITABLE TRUST
1420 N Street, Northwest, Suite 101
Washington, D.C. 20005 (202) 833-1367

4250 Wilshire Boulevard, Suite 212
Los Angeles, California 90010
Director: Ross Vartian

Persons of Armenian ancestry and those interested in the perpetuation and expansion of Armenian culture. Organized to serve as a forum for the promotion of communication, cooperation and coordination of activities within the Armenian-American community; to foster an awareness and appreciation of the Armenian cultural heritage and to promote the preservation of significant Armenian cultural materials and monuments; to advance research and data collection and to disseminate accurate information regarding the Armenian people. Has prepared a union catalog of all books about Armenians in major American libraries. Conducts seminars with representatives of major Armenian-American organizations to discuss problems of current interest. Conducts professional training symposia. Maintains library and information service for Armenian history and culture. Offers placement service for applicants for congressional intership positions. Compiles statistics; bestows awards; maintains biographical archives. The Assembly also coordinates ongoing programs commemorating the Armenian genocide with the United States Holocaust Memorial Council.
Publications: Washington Briefing, monthly; Newsletter, quarterly; Airlie Assembly Reports, biennial; Directory of Armenian-American Scholars, biennial.

ARMENIAN EVANGELICAL SOCIAL SERVICE CENTER
5250 Santa Monica Boulevard
Suite 201 (213) 664-1137
Los Angeles, California 90029
Director: Hratch Baliozian

ARMENIAN GENERAL BENEVOLENT UNION OF AMERICA
585 Saddle River Road
Saddle Brook, New Jersey 07662 (201) 797-7600
Executive Director: Haig Messerlian Founded 1906

589 North Larchmont Road
Los Angeles, California 90004 (213) 467-2428

Charitable and educational organization established to promote Armenian culture. Sponsors competitions; maintains placement service; owns and operates three day schools. Administers the Hovnaniau Fellowship Fund.
Publications: Hoosharar, semimonthly; Ararat, quarterly.

ARMENIAN RELIEF SOCIETY
212 Stuart Street (617) 542-0528
Boston, Massachusetts 02116 Founded 1910
Executive Secretary: Ms. Arpie Balian

108A North Brand Boulevard
Glendale, California 91203 (213) 241-7533

Armenian women and men throughout the world. Raises and distributes money for relief of Armenian people and for advancement of educational and cultural activities. Awards scholarships to needy students. Helps support and operate 30 Armenian language classes in America. Sends students abroad to study at Armenian education centers. Supports Armenian day schools in North America and abroad; clinics; concerts, lectures and dramatic programs; fresh air camps; orphanages and sanitoria; "Plate of Food" program abroad. Formerly called Armenian Red Cross.
Publications: Hai Sird (Armenian Heart), annual; also publishes bulletins, ethnic heritage materials and slides and tapes for bilingual studies.

ARMENIAN WOMEN'S WELFARE ASSOCIATION
431 Pond Street (617) 522-2600
Jamaica Plain, Massachusetts 02130 Founded 1934
President: Anne T. Hintlian

Women interested in helping with charitable work. Maintains a nursing home to care for the aged.

KARAGHEUSIAN COMMEMORATIVE CORPORATION
79 Madison Avenue, Room 904 (212) 725-0973
New York, New York 10016 Incorporated
Director: Walter Bandazian 1921

Promotes child welfare, public health services and relief programs in the Armenian refugee communities in Greece, the Lebanon, and Syria.

UNITED ARMENIAN CHARITIES
One Park Avenue, Room 414
New York, New York 10016 Incorporated
President: Artin Aslanian 1951

Aids Armenian religious and cultural institutions in the United States and elsewhere. Grants are made largely to support churches and education.

Religious Organizations

ARMENIAN APOSTOLIC CHURCH OF AMERICA
Eastern Diocese
630 Second Avenue
New York, New York 10016 (212) 686-0710
Primate: Archbishop Torkom Manoogian

Western Diocese
1201 North Vine Street (213) 466-5265
Hollywood, California 90038
Primate: Archibishop Vatche Hovsepian

Eastern Prelacy
138 East 39th Street (212) 689-7810
New York, New York 10016
Prelate: Bishop Mesrob Ashjian

Western Prelacy
4401 Russell Avenue (213) 466-5265
Los Angeles, California 90027
Prelate: Bishop Yeprem Tabakian

Functions as one church in dogma and liturgy despite the existence of a Western Diocese in California and on Eastern Diocese excluding California.
Publications: The Armenian Church, monthly; Outreach, monthly; Bema, monthly; Keghart, quarterly.

ARMENIAN CATHOLIC COMMUNITY
100 Mount Auburn Street
Cambridge, Massachusetts 02138 (617) 547-2122
Father Luke Arakelian

ARMENIAN CHURCH YOUTH ORGANIZATION OF AMERICA
630 Second Avenue
New York, New York 10016 (212) 686-0710
Director: James Magarian Founded 1946

440 Ladera
Monterey Park, California 91754
Chairman: Greg Shamlian

Young people who are members of the Armenian Church. Conducts religious, educational, cultural, service, social and recreational programs; sponsors religious conferences, retreats, study and mission programs; also holds national sports weekend; gives scholarships.
Publications: Keghard, quarterly; Directory of Chapter Executives, annual; also publishes educational pamphlets and guidebooks.

ARMENIAN EVANGELICAL STUDENTS ASSOCIATION OF AMERICA
140 Forest Avenue
Paramus, New Jersey 07652

422 Mount Auburn
Watertown, Massachusetts 02172 (617) 923-9182
President: John Baboian

ARMENIAN EVANGELICAL UNION
140 Forest Avenue
Paramus, New Jersey 07652

c/o United Armenian Congregation Church
3480 Cahuenga Boulevard
Hollywood, California 90068 (213) 851-5265
Chairman: Reverend Vartas Kassouni

Union of all Armenian Protestant denominations.

ARMENIAN MISSIONARY ASSOCIATION OF AMERICA
140 Forest Avenue
Paramus, New Jersey 07652 (201) 265-2607
Executive Director: Dr. Giragos H. Chopourian Founded 1918

Ministers and laymen of Armenian Churches in the United States and others interested in missions. Administers Child Education Sponsorship Program in five overseas countries. Owns and administers through local Board of Managers Haigazian College in Beirut, Lebanon. Maintains library of 500 volumes.
Publications: News, bimonthly; Annual Report; also publishes books in English and Armenian.

Research Centers and Special Institutes

ARMENIAN STUDIES PROGRAM
American Armenian International College
1950 Third Street
Box 667
La Verne, California (714) 593-0432
Directors: George Bournutian
Srbouk Hairapetian

ARMENIAN STUDIES PROGRAM
California State University
Fresno, California 93740 (209) 487-2832
Director: Dr. Dickran Kouymjian Founded 1977

The language, history, literature and art of Armenia and the Armenian people are taught as a service to the area's very large Armenian population. Offers an Armenian Studies Minor as preparation for graduate work in Armenian studies at Harvard, Columbia, University of Pennsylvania, University of Michigan or University of California Los Angeles, all of which have Chairs of Armenian Studies. The program is the largest Armenian Studies Program in the United States and is the only program in Armenian art and architecture outside of Soviet Armenia. Sponsors the establishment of the Armenian National Museum and Cultural Center to be built on the Fresno campus.
Publications: Index of Armenian Art, fascicles issued irregularly.

CHAIR OF ARMENIAN STUDIES
Columbia University
Department of Middle East Languages and Cultures
New York, New York 10027
Chair currently held by Professor Nina Garsoian

CHAIR OF ARMENIAN STUDIES
Harvard University
College of Arts and Sciences
Cambridge, Massachusetts 02138
Chair currently held by Professor Robert Thomson

CHAIR OF ARMENIAN STUDIES
University of California at Los Angeles
Department of Near Eastern Languages
405 Hilyard Avenue
Los Angeles, California 90024
Chair currently held by Professor Avedis Sanjian

CHAIR OF ARMENIAN STUDIES
University of Michigan
Modern Languages Building
Ann Arbor, Michigan 48109
Chair currently held by Professor Ronald Suny

CHAIR OF ARMENIAN STUDIES
University of Pennsylvania
College of Arts and Sciences
Philadelphia, Pennsylvania 19179
Chair currently held by Professor Vahe Oshagan

Museums

ARMENIAN LIBRARY AND MUSEUM OF AMERICA
Post Office Box 147
Belmont, Massachusetts 02178 (617) 643-1700
Director: Dr. Paul Barsam Founded 1971

Founded for the purpose of accumulating books, artifacts and other materials with a view to construction of a permanent library and museum.

Special Libraries and Subject Collections

ARMENIAN ASSEMBLY CHARITABLE TRUST - LIBRARY AND INFORMATION CENTER
522 21st Street, Northwest
Washington, D.C. 20006 (202) 332-3434
Director: Ross Vartian Founded 1972

Subjects: Armenian history, culture, genocide, political evolution. Holdings: Books, 50 pamphlets (cataloged); clippings; AV material; oral history archives. Subscriptions: Journals and other serials. Services: Copying; library open to public with permission of director.
Publications: Directory of Armenian Scholars; Participation in the Democratic Process; Directory of Armenian Lawyers; Newsletter, quarterly.

ARMENIAN NATIONAL ARCHIVES
212 Stuart Street
Boston, Massachusetts 02116

Documentation of materials from the foundation of the Armenian Republic 1918-1920.

NATIONAL ASSOCIATION FOR ARMENIAN STUDIES AND RESEARCH
175 Mount Auburn Street
Cambridge, Massachusetts 02138 (617) 876-7630

Subjects: Armenian history, culture, language, literature, music, architecture, art, church history, archeaology. Holdings: A reference and research library of more than 8,000 volumes. Services: Armenian Book Clearinghouse.

TOPALIAN LIBRARY
Armenian Cultural Center
441 Mystic (617) 646-1579
Arlington, Massachusetts 02174

UNIVERSITY OF CALIFORNIA AT LOS ANGELES - LIBRARY
Los Angeles, California 90024

Maintains one of the largest American collections of publications in Armenian and about Armenia.

Newspapers and Newsletters

AMAA NEWS. 1967-. Bimonthly. Editor: G.H. Chopourian. Publisher: Armenian Missionary Association of America, 140 Forest Avenue, Paramus, New Jersey 07652. In English.

Carries news of the missionary association and of Armenian people outside their homeland, with profiles of outstanding persons and articles on significant places and events. Reinforces national and ethnic dignity and identity. Includes book reviews and announcements of available publications, reports from district committees and associated churches, obituary items, inspirational material, and two pages written in Armenian. Combines the former AMAA Newsletter and the Armenian/American Outlook, September 1976.

ARMENIAN ASSEMBLY NEWSLETTER. 1968-. Quarterly. Editor: Susan Carlin. Publisher: The Armenian Assembly Charitable Trust, 1420 N Street, Northwest, Washington, D.C. 20005. In English.

Describes the work of the assembly in aiding Armenian people in the United States and throughout the world and in promoting Armenian educational and cultural programs. Some issues deal with a single topic, and regular features include a schedule of activities and news of research in progress.

ARMENIAN HORIZON. 1981-. Monthly. Editor: Mark Malkasian. Publisher: UCLA Armenian Students Association and UCLA Armenian Studies Program, 1023 Hilgard Avenue, Los Angeles, California 90024. In English.

University local and national news of interest to Armenian community.

THE ARMENIAN MIRROR-SPECTATOR. 1934-. Weekly. Editor: Barbara Merguerian. Publisher: Baikar Association, Incorporated, 755 Mount Auburn Street, Watertown, Massachusetts 02172. In English.

Publishes general news and news of Armenian cultural and religious activities.

ARMENIAN OBSERVER. 1970-. Weekly. Editor: Osheen Keshishian. Publisher: 6646 Hollywood Boulevard, Suite 207, Los Angeles, California 90028. In English.

National and regional Armenian news.

THE ARMENIAN REPORTER. 1967-. Weekly. Editor: Edward K. Boghosian. Publisher: The Armenian Reporter, Incorporated, Post Office Box 488, 5300 Santa Monica Boulevard, Los Angeles, California 90029. In English.

Reports on various social, cultural, religious, and other activities of Armenian communities in the United States and abroad. Special features include profiles of successful Armenian personalities.

THE ARMENIAN WEEKLY. 1933-. Weekly. Managing Editor: Ohannes Balian. Publisher: Hairenik Association, Incorporated, 212 Stuart Street, Boston, Massachusetts 02116. In English.

Publishes materials of a social, cultural, political, and historical nature which are of interest to people of Armenian background. Includes sections on national and international news, and translations from the Armenian language press.

ASBAREZ ARENA. 1908-. Semiweekly. Editors: Kristapor Pakradouni (Armenian), Serge Samoniantz (English). Publisher: Asbarez Publishing Company, Incorporated, 1501 Venice Boulevard, Los Angeles, California 90006. In Armenian and English.

Covers international, national, cultural, and scientific affairs; political commentaries; and topics relating to Armenian communities.

BAIKAR (Struggle). 1922-. Daily. Editor: Dr. Nubar Berberian. Publisher: Baikar Association, Incorporated, 755 Mount Auburn Street, Watertown, Massachusetts 02172. In Armenian.

Official publication of the Armenian Democratic Liberal Party. Includes news of international, national, and local events of special interest to Armenians.

BARI LOUR (Good News). 1958-. Monthly. Editor: Reverend Shahe Semerdjyan. Publisher: St. Peter Armenian Apostolic Church, 17231 Sherman Way, Van Nuys, California 91406. In Armenian and English.

BEMA (Diocesan Chronicle). 1980-. Monthly. Editor: Very Reverend Ghevont Samoorian, Box 79, Chelmsford, Massachusetts 01824.

Acts as the voice of the Diocese of the Armenian Church. Provides commentaries and presents the Church's stand on current issues; keeps the community informed on religious events and other Church related activities.

BULLETIN OF THE ARMENIAN SCIENTIFIC ASSOCIATION OF AMERICA. 1968-. Semiannual. Publisher: Armenian Scientific Association of America, 30 Half Moon Lane, Irvington, New York 10533. In English.

Carries news of the activities of the Association.

THE CALIFORNIA COURIER. 1958-. Weekly. Editor and publisher: George Mason, Post Office Box 966, Fresno, California 93714. In English.

ERITASSARD HAYASTAN (Young Armenia). 1903-. Monthly. Editor: Mr. Jereghian. Publisher: Hunchakian Party of America, Post Office Box 742, or 353 Forest Avenue, Paramus, New Jersey 07652. In Armenian.

General news and political articles. A publication of the Social Democratic Armenian Party.

FASCA NEWSLETTER. Bimonthly. Editor: Laurens Ayvazian. Publisher: Federation of Armenian Student Clubs of America, 1420 N Street, Northwest, Washington, D.C. 20005. In English.

HAIRENIK (Fatherland). 1899-. Daily. Editor: Kevork Donabedian. Publisher: Hairenik Association, Incorporated, 212 Stuart Street, Boston, Massachusetts 02116. Sponsor: Armenian Revolutionary Federation of America. In Armenian.

Oldest Armenian daily in the United States. Covers national, international, local, and group news of interest to Armenians. An Armenian weekly is published in English under the same title (1933-).

HOOSHARAR (The Prompter). 1915-. Monthly except July and August. Editor: Antrania Poladian. Publisher: Armenian General Benevolent Union of America, 585 Saddle River Road, Saddle Brook, New Jersey 07622. In Armenian.

Official organ of the Armenian General Benevolent Union of America. Carries cultural and philanthropic news.

HOOSHARAR (Reminder). 1929-. Monthly except July and August. Editor: Terry Chisholm. Publisher: Armenian General Benevolent Union, 585 Saddle River Road, Saddle Brook, New Jersey 07662.

HYE SHARZHOOM (Armenian Action). 1978-. Quarterly. Editors: Flora Tchaderjian and Cynthia Avakian. Publisher: Armenian Students Organization, California State University, Fresno, California.

Publishes political and cultural news of national and local interest. Reviews books and articles.

KIR-OU-KIRK (Letter and Book). 1956-. Semiannual. Editor: K. N. Magarian. Publisher: Armenian Literary Society, New York, Incorporated, 114 First Street, Yonkers, New York 10704. In Armenian and English.

Covers the world of Armenian literature, past and contemporary. Reports on the meetings, programs, and activities of the Armenian Literary Society.

LOUSAVORICH (Illuminator). 1938-. Irregular. Editor: Reverend Arsen Hagopian. Publisher: St. Gregory Illuminator Church of Armenia, 221 East 27th Street, New York, New York. In Armenian and English.

Reports on news related to church and parish affairs. Also includes religious and spiritual articles.

LRAPER (Herald). 1937-. Weekly. Editor: L. Tabakian. Publisher: Post Office Box 38821, Los Angeles, California 90038. Sponsor: Armenian Progressive League of America. In Armenian and English.

Covers international, national, local, and group news. Emphasizes issues of special interest to Armenians.

MAIR YEGEGHETZI (Mother Church). 1940-. Monthly. Editor: Reverend Moushegh Der Kaloustian. Publisher: St. Illuminator's Armenian Apostolic Cathedral, 221 East 27th Street, New York, New York 10016. In Armenian and English.

Publishes news of church affairs, special services, and the activities of various church-affiliated groups.

THE MONTHLY BULLETIN (Amsat'ert'ik). 1912-. Monthly. Publisher: The Armenian Evangelical Church of New York, 152 East 34th Street, New York, New York 10016. In Armenian and English.

NOR GYANK (New Life). 1978-. Weekly. Editor: Leon Fermanian. Publisher: Nor Gyank, 111 East Broadway, Suite 20, Glendale, California 91203. In English and Armenian.

Serves as a forum for the exchange of thoughts and attitudes in the American Armenian community. Brings cultural and political news and book reviews.

NOR OR (New Day). 1922-. Semiweekly. Editor: Assadour Devedian. Publisher: Nor Or Publishers Association, Incorporated, 7466 West Beverly Boulevard, Suite 101, Los Angeles, California 90036. In Armenian.

OUTREACH. 1978-. Monthly. Armenian Editor: Very Reverend K. Hagopian. Acting Editor: Iris Papazian. Publisher: Prelacy of the Armenian Apostolic Church of America, 138 East 39th Street, New York, New York 10016.

Church, cultural and political news of interest to the Armenian community. Calendar of events.

P'AROS (Lighthouse). 1958-. Monthly. Editor: Hayk Quaha Tonikyan. Publisher: S. Sahak and S. Mesrop Armenian Apostolic Church, 70 Jefferson Street, Providence, Rhode Island 02908. In Armenian and English.

SHOGHAKAT' (Radiance). 1955-. Quarterly. Publisher: S. Grigor Lousavoritch Armenian Apostolic Church, 2215 East Colorado Boulevard, Pasadena, California 91107. In Armenian.

SHOGHAKAT' (Radiance). 1962-. Editor: Asoghik Kelejian. Publisher: St. Sargis Armenian Apostolic Church, 42nd Avenue and 213th Street, Bayside, New York 11361. In English and Armenian.

SOCIETY OF ARMENIAN STUDIES - NEWSLETTER. Editor: Dr. Gerard Libaridian, 33 Montgomery Street, Cambridge, Massachusetts 02140.

Brings news of the Society and of research in progress.

Magazines

ARARAT. 1960-. Quarterly. Editor: Leo Hamalian. Publisher: Armenian General Benevolent Union of America, Incorporated, 585 Saddle River Road, Saddle Brook, New Jersey 07662. In English.

Provides a vehicle for writers of Armenian ancestry, although authorship is not limited to Armenian writers. Contents include articles, short stories, poetry, plays, and book reviews. Topics include Armenian history and culture, problems of assimilation and acculturation of the Armenian community in the United States religion, education, and social sciences.

THE ARMENIAN REVIEW. 1947-. Quarterly. Editor: James H. Tashjian. Publisher: Hairenik Association, Incorporated, 212 Stuart Street, Boston, Massachusetts 02116. In English.

Publishes historical articles, memoirs, political studies, commentaries, short stories, poetry, editorials, book reviews, and translations from Armenian language materials. Supports the Armenian quest for an independent, free, united democratic Armenian State.

JOURNAL OF THE SOCIETY FOR ARMENIAN STUDIES. 1982-. Annual. Editor: Avedis K. Sanjian. Department of Near Eastern Languages and Cultures, University of California, Los Angeles, California 90024.

Publishes scholarly articles.

KEGHARD. Quarterly. Publisher: Diocese of the Armenian Apostolic Church, 630 Second Avenue, New York, New York 10016. Contact Person: James Magarian.

Publication of the Armenian Church Youth Organization of America of the Diocese of the Armenian Apostolic Church. Informs the youth of the Armenian Church about Armenian culture, religion, and history; offers commentaries and articles as well as listings of significant religious, cultural and social events.

KERMANIK. 1930-. Quarterly. Editor: Ara Kalaydjian. Publisher: Union of Marash Armenians, Central Committee, Post Office Box 95 New Town Branch, Boston, Massachusetts 02258. In Armenian and English.

Radio Programs

California - Dinuba

KRDU - 597 North Alta Avenue, Dinuba, California 93618, (209) 591-1130. Armenian programs, 1/2 hour weekly.

California - Fresno

KVPR(FM) - 1515 Van Ness, Fresno, California 93721, (209) 486-7710. Armenian programs, 1 hour weekly.

California - Inglewood

KTYM - 6803 West Boulevard, Inglewood, California 90302, (213) 678-3731. Armenian programs, 3 hours weekly.

California - Pasadena

KPCC(FM) - 1570 East Colorado, Pasadena, California 91106, (213) 578-7231. Armenian programs, 1 hour weekly.

California - San Francisco

KBRG(FM) - 1355 Market Street, San Francisco, California 94103, (415) 626-1053. Armenian programs, 1 hour weekly.

Illinois - Chicago

WNIB(FM) - 12 East Delaware Place, Chicago, Illinois 60611. Armenian programs, 1 hour weekly.

Massachusetts - Boston

WUNR - 275 Tremont Street, Boston, Massachusetts 02116, (617) 357-8677. Armenian programs, 1/2 hour weekly.

Massachusetts - Waltham

WCRB(FM) - 750 South Street, Waltham, Massachusetts 02154, (617) 893-7080. Armenian programs, 1 hour weekly.

Michigan - Detroit

WDET(FM) - 655 Merrick, Detroit, Michigan 48202, (313) 577-4204. Armenian programs, 1 hour weekly.

WMZK - 2050 City National Bank Building, Detroit, Michigan 48226, (313) 965-2000. Armenian programs, 2 hours weekly.

Michigan - Garden City

WCAR - 32500 Park Lane, Garden City, Michigan 48226, (313) 525-1111. Armenian programs, 1 1/2 hours weekly.

New Jersey - South Orange

WSOU(FM) - 400 South Orange Avenue, South Orange, New Jersey 07079, (201) 762-8950. Armenian programs, 2 hours weekly.

New York - New York

WHBI - 80 Riverside Drive, New York, New York 10024, (212) 799-8000. Armenian programs.

Pennsylvania - Philadelphia

WTEL - 4140 Old York Road, Philadelphia, Pennsylvania 19140 (215) 455-9200. Armenian programs, 1 hour weekly.

Rhode Island - Providence

WHJJ - 115 Eastern Avenue, Providence, Rhode Island 02914, (401) 438-6110. Armenian programs, 1 hour weekly.

Wisconsin - Racine

WRJN - 4201 Victory Avenue, Racine, Wisconsin 53405, (414) 634-3311. Armenian programs, 1 hour weekly.

Television Programs

California - Corona-Los Angeles

KBSC-TV - 1139 Grand Central Avenue, Glendale, California 91201, (213) 956-8611. Armenian programs, 1 hour weekly.

Festivals, Fairs, and Celebrations

ARMENIAN MARTYRS' DAY

Held annually in April in many locations throughout the country.

Contact: Armenian Assembly of America, 1420 N Street, Northwest, Washington, D.C. 20005, (202) 332-3434.

Massachusetts - Boston

OLYMPICS
Armenian Youth Federation
212 Stuart Street
Boston, Massachusetts 02116 (617) 926-3860

Olympic games are held in various locations across the country, sponsored by regional organizations belonging to the Federation.

New York - New York

NATIONAL SPORTS WEEKEND
Location changes from year to year

Contact: Armenian Church Youth Organization of America, 630 Second Avenue, New York, New York 10016, (212) 686-0710.

ONE WORLD FESTIVAL STREET FAIR
St. Vartan's Armenian Church
New York, New York

Two day festival featuring Armenian music, dance, traditional crafts and food. Held annually in September.
Contact: New York Convention Center and Visitors Bureau, 90 East 42nd Street, New York, New York 10017, (212) 687-1300.

Bookdealers and Publishers' Representatives

ARTHUR GORDON
Box 64
Leonia, New Jersey 07605

MARK A. KALUSTIAN
259 Pleasant Street
Arlington, Massachusetts 02174 (617) 648-3437

NATIONAL ASSOCIATION FOR ARMENIAN STUDIES AND RESEARCH
175 Mount Auburn Street
Boston, Massachusetts 02138

NEW AGE PUBLISHERS
Post Office Box 883
Plandome, New York 11030

Books and Pamphlets

ARMENIAN AMERICANS

ARMENIAN COMMUNITY: THE HISTORICAL DEVELOPMENT OF A SOCIAL AND IDEOLOGICAL CONFLICT. By Sarkis Atamin. New York, 1955.

The political conflict within the American Armenian community related to acknowledging how the Soviet Armenian is treated from the Tashnag perspective.

THE ARMENIANS IN AMERICA. By Arra S. Avakian. Minneapolis, Lerner Publications, 1977.

A book intended for younger readers giving an historical overview of more than three thousand years of Armenian history, telling about Armenian immigration to the United States and how the Armenians live in America today. Illustrated with black and white photographs.

THE ARMENIANS IN AMERICA. By M. Vartan Malcolm. Boston, Pilgrim Press, 1919. Reprint R&E Research Associates, 1969.

Portrays the Armenians' historical background, their immigration to America from colonial times to 1917, their social and economic conditions in the United States.

THE ARMENIANS IN MASSACHUSETTS. Boston, WPA Writers Project, 1937.

THE ARMENIANS OF THE UNITED STATES AND CANADA. By James H. Tashjian. Boston, Hairenik Press, 1947. Reprint R&E Research Associates, 1970.

Part I deals with three waves of immigration of Armenians to America: during the colonial period; from 1834 to 1894 under the influence of missionaries; and from 1895 to 1914 as a result of Armenian massacres in Turkey. Part II discusses Armenian life in America, including occupations, organizations, religion, publications, education, and contributions of groups and individuals.

CULTURAL PERSISTENCE AND SOCIO-ECONOMIC MOBILITY: A COMPARATIVE STUDY AMONG ARMENIANS AND JAPANESE IN LOS ANGELES. By Sheila E. Henry, San Francisco, R&E Research Associates, 1978.

DIRECTORY OF ARMENIAN-AMERICAN SCHOLARS. Washington, D.C., Armenian Assembly Charitable Trust, 1976.

Lists individuals of Armenian heritage in America concerned with the study and preservation of the Armenian culture giving name, address, title and affiliation; educational, personal, and career data; areas of study. Arrangement: Alphabetical. Frequency: Latest edition 1976; new edition planned. Price: Single copies free.

FRESNO ARMENIANS TO 1919. By Wilson D. Wallis. Lawrence, Kansas, 1965.

HISTORY OF THE ARMENIANS IN CALIFORNIA. By Charles Mahakian. San Francisco, 1974.

PASSAGE TO ARARAT. By Michael Arlen. New York, Farrar, Straus and Giroux, 1975.

The author, of Armenian descent, visits the land of Armenia, retells its history and recounts his experiences.

Audiovisual Material

FILMS

THE ARMENIAN CASE. 16mm. Color and sound. 43 minutes. By Michael Hagopian. Atlantis Production, Incorporated, Thousand Oaks, California.

Presents the evidence for the mass deaths of Armenians at the hands of the Turks after the First World War.

THE FORGOTTEN GENOCIDE. 16mm. Color and sound. 28 minutes. By Michael Hagopian. Atlantis Productions, Incorporated, Thousand Oaks, California.

A shorter version of The Armenian Case.

THE HEART OF A NATION. 16mm. Color and sound. 30 minutes. By Toukhanian. Armenian Relief Society, Boston, 1971.

Describes the founding, development, and present-day activities of the Armenian Relief Society.

SIGHTS AND SOUNDS OF ARMENIA. Audio-cassette. Produced by the Armenian Relief Society, Boston, Massachusetts.

ASIANS
(Includes BUDDHISTS)
See also: Individual Asian Peoples

Fraternal Organizations

PAN PACIFIC AND SOUTHEAST ASIA WOMEN'S ASSOCIATION OF THE U.S.A.
Two Times Square
New York, New York 10036 (212) 944-0045
President: Barbara Tuber Founded 1928

To further international understanding and friendship among the women of Asia, the Pacific and women of the United States of America. Provides hospitality to temporary residents and visitors from Pacific and Asian areas. Offers assistance with study and travel programs to such visitors when referred by United States Department of State, Missions to the United Nations and Consulates General. Fosters international friendships. Conducts classes in English, French and Japanese conversation, American history and other subjects. Operates Asian and Pacific Women's Center. Formerly: (1955) Pan Pacific Women's Association of U.S.A.
Publications: Newsletter, quarterly.

Professional Organizations

ACUPUNCTURE INTERNATIONAL ASSOCIATION
2330 South Brentwood Boulevard
Saint Louis, Missouri 63144
Executive Officer: Dr. Robert X. Adams (314) 961-9826
Founded 1949

Doctors of medicine, chiropractic and osteopathy who practice acupuncture. Conducts professional education and public health programs and seminars. Maintains library of 686 volumes. Bestows awards and conducts charitable programs. Publishes newsletters, bulletins, proceedings and abstracts.

ASIAN/PACIFIC AMERICAN LIBRARIANS ASSOCIATION
c/o Kingsborough Community College Library
Oriental Boulevard
Brooklyn, New York 11235
President: Dr. Sharad Karkhanis Founded 1980

Librarians and information specialists of Asian Pacific descent working in the United States; other interested persons. Seeks to provide a forum for discussing problems and concerns; to support and encourage library services to Asian Pacific communities; to recruit and support Asian Pacific Americans in the library and information science professions. Offers placement service.
Publications: Newsletter, quarterly; Membership Directory, annual.

ASIAN POLITICAL SCIENTISTS GROUP IN USA
c/o Dr. Chun-Tu Hsueh
Department of Politics
University of Maryland
College Park, Maryland 20742
Chairman, Executive Committee: Chun-Tu Hsueh (301) 454-6706
Founded 1973

Political scientists of Asian descent in the United States. Purpose is to promote the professional and ethnic interests of the group. Activities include organization of panels for the annual meeting of the American Political Science Association. Maintains placement service. Publishes books.

ASSOCIATION OF ASIAN/PACIFIC AMERICAN ARTISTS
6546 Hollywood Boulevard, Suite 201
Hollywood, California 90028 (213) 464-8381
President: Sumi Haru Founded 1975

Active members are individuals in the entertainment industry, including performers, producers, designers, directors, technicians, and writers. Supporting members include students, indivuals and organizations. Encourages equal employment opportunities in all aspects of the entertainment industry in order to assure realistic images and portrayals of Asian/Pacific peoples as they exist in real life and in the mainstream of America. Speaks with decision makers in the industry to fulfill goals. Sponsors business and professional seminars with industry leaders to expand members' knowledge of theatre, motion pictures and television. Maintains library; offers specialized education.
Publications: Newsletter, quarterly.

INDEPENDENT SCHOLARS OF ASIA
260 Stephen Hall
University of California
Berkeley, California 94720
National Director: Dr. Ruth-Inge Heinze (415) 849-3791
Founded 1981

Independent scholars and students of Asia; institutions of higher learning. To aid independent scholars of Asia by focusing on changing roles of Asian scholars, discussing career alternatives, teaching survival techniques and making the expertise of members known. Conducts lectures, workshop series and outreach programs through international institutes, public libraries and other institutions. Is organizing task forces and pressure groups to maintain contact with institutions of higher learning, corporations, mass media, and other agencies. Maintains information bank, speakers bureau, consultant rosters, and placement service. Sponsors fund-raising drives and state-of-the-field workshops to assist in career planning. Compiles statistics. Affiliated with Association for Asian Studies.
Publications: Newsletter, quarterly; also publishes International Directory of Independent Scholars.

INTERNATIONAL ASSOCIATION OF HISTORIANS OF ASIA
c/o Serafin Quiason
National Library of the Philippines
T.M. Kalaw Street
Manila, Philippines Founded 1961

Historians throughout the world who have an interest in East, Southeast or South Asia. Executive committee, comprised of group's president and five members from various countries, arranged triennial conferences at which papers are presented, historical concepts discussed and personal contacts promoted among historians with similar interests. Association is operated by representatives of Asian countries; organizational structure includes national committees of two or three persons, with Professor Van Niel and Professor Allen B. Cole of Tufts University, Medford, Massachusetts, as United States representatives.
Publications: Philippine Historical Review, annual.

PAN-PACIFIC SURGICAL ASSOCIATION
Post Office Box 553
Honolulu, Hawaii 96809 (808) 536-4911
Chairman: Kazuo Teruya, M.D. Founded 1929

Professional, international surgical association.
Publications: Newsletter, quarterly; also publishes program.

INTERNATIONAL ASSOCIATION OF ORIENTALIST LIBRARIANS
National Library Building, Room 405
T. M. Kalaw Street
Manila, Philippines
Secretary-Treasurer: Rosa M. Vallejo (808) 948-7853
Founded 1967

To promote better communication between Orientalist librarians and libraries throughout the world; to provide a forum for the discussion of problems of common concern; to improve international cooperation among institutions holding research resources for Oriental studies. Affiliated with International Federation of Library Associations. Address changes with contact person.
Publications: Bulletin, semiannual; Proceedings of Conference, triennial.

PACIFIC ASIAN AMERICAN WOMEN WRITERS WEST

Originally formed in 1978 as a workshop for Asian-American women who wished to develop their writing talent. Members plan to write and produce a six-part drama for television about Asian-American women. Present projects include exposing a larger public to Asian literature and emphasizing the talent in the Asian Pacific community which is now mostly confined to stereotypical roles.

Public Affairs Organizations

ASIAN AMERICAN FREE LABOR INSTITUTE
1125 15th Street, Northwest
Washington, D.C. 20005 (202) 737-3000
Executive Director: Morris Paladino Founded 1968

An auxiliary of the AFL-CIO created to promote the growth of free and effective trade unions in Asia and the Middle East. Through the Institute, Asian trade unions in 14 countries receive technical assistance in the fields of labor education, community projects, cooperatives, and related fields.
Publications: News, 10 times a year; also publishes various booklets and a handbook on labor.

ASIAN AMERICAN LEGAL DEFENSE AND EDUCATION FUND
350 Broadway, Suite 308 (212) 966-5932
New York, New York 10013 Founded 1976

Attorneys, legal workers and members of the community who seek to employ legal and educational methods to attack critical problems in Asian-American communities. Provides bilingual legal counseling and representation for people who cannot obtain access to legal assistance. Litigates cases that have the potential of improving the quality of life in the community. Conducts workshops, seminars and training sessions to inform community workers and residents of their rights and benefits before legal problems arise. To offset a shortage of Asian attorneys, seeks to train paralegals and community workers in unemployment law, immigration and housing. Sponsors Employment-Labor program to assist workers in service occupations such as restaurants and garment factories, a law student internship project and legal services for the Asian elderly. Publishes pamphlets which are geared towards Asian-Americans and are produced in Chinese, Korean and Japanese.

ASIAN-AMERICAN WOMEN'S POLITICAL CAUCUS
c/o Dr. Tin Myaing Thein
11650 Iberia Place, Suite 8
San Diego, California 92128
Executive Officer: Dr. Tin Myaing Thein

Purpose is to promote the involvement of Asian-American women in politics. Conducts training seminars; provides information on women in politics; offers referral services.

ASIAN CULTURAL FORUM ON DEVELOPMENT
501 South Main Street
Normal, Illinois 61761
Representative: Michael G. Matejka (309) 452-5046
Founded 1975

Concerned individuals and religious, agricultural and labor organizations working toward integral human development in Asia. Promotes international understanding of the Asian situation; defines effects of United States political and economic developments on Asia. Offers speakers and presentations.
Publications: Asian Action, irregular; also publishes pamphlets and booklets.

ASIAN PACIFIC WOMEN'S NETWORK
c/o Irene Hirano
6720 Sherbourne Drive
Los Angeles, California 90056 (213) 295-6571
Executive Officer: Irene Hirano Founded 1980

Purpose is to promote the involvement of Asian-American women in all aspects of life. Conducts training seminars; provides information on women in politics; offers referral services.

CHURCH COMMITTEE ON HUMAN RIGHTS IN ASIA
5700 South Woodlawn Avenue
Chicago, Illinois 60637 (312) 643-7111
Coordinator: Linda Jones Founded 1973

Coalition of groups whose purpose is to act on behalf of persons struggling for human rights in South Korea and the Philippines. Focuses attention on United States foreign policy and carries the needs and concerns expressed by Asian Christians to United States legislators and policymakers. Challenges locally-based corporate interests with subsidiaries in Asia to abide by decent wage and living standards for Asian workers. Provides programs and resources for local study/action groups and works with the local media to publicize human rights violations in Asia. Maintains speakers bureau; offers films and slide programs. Conducts research on corporate interests and working conditions in Asia; sponsors educational programs on Asian human rights.
Publications: Asian Rights Advocate, monthly; also publishes Human Rights Study Packet and pamphlets.

COALITION FOR ASIAN PEACE AND SECURITY
1015 18th Street, Northwest, Suite 805
Washington, D.C. 20036 (202) 223-8596
President: Ray S. Cline Founded 1979

To provide educational written and oral material on developments in Asia and the Western Pacific; and to identify real or potential threats to the security of nations in that area. Plans to sponsor writings and lectures on Asian peace and security.

COALITION OF ASIANS TO NIX CHARLIE CHAN
c/o 737A Grant Avenue
San Francisco, California 94108 (415) 986-9055
Chairman: Forrest Gok Founded 1980

Individuals and local community organizations devoted to monitoring and improving media images of Asian Americans. Established to protest the perpetuation of stereotypes in the proposed filming of "Charlie Chan and the Curse of the Dragon Lady." Is currently forming speakers bureau and media presentations as part of an educational outreach program.

ORGANIZATION OF PAN ASIAN-AMERICAN WOMEN
915 15th Street, Northwest
Suite 600
Washington, D.C. 20005
President: Joseph Vehara (202) 737-1377

To provide a voice for the concerns of Asian-American women and to encourage their full participation in all aspects of American society with particular emphasis on employment. Seeks to promote an accurate and realistic image of Asian women in America; develop the leadership skills and increase the occupational mobility of these women; and maintain a national communications network. Sponsors seminars, workshops, lectures and presentations by leaders of major national women's groups.

Publications: Newsletter, bimonthly; Membership Directory, annual.

SOCIETY FOR THE PROTECTION OF EAST ASIAN'S HUMAN RIGHTS
Post Office Box 1212
New York, New York 10025 (212) 222-9012
President: James D. Seymour Founded 1977

Individuals united to promote human rights (as defined by the UN's Universal Declaration of Human Rights) and nonviolence in East Asia (China, Taiwan, North and South Korea, Mongolia and Hong Kong) and among Asian minorities in the Soviet Union. Compiles and disseminates information concerning human rights problems in these countries; plans to organize educational programs. Conducts research programs and bibliographical services. Maintains files of research material, and data bank.
Publications: SPEAHRhead (bulletin), quarterly.

U.S. - TIBET COMMITTEE (Tibetan)
c/o Office of Tibet
801 Second Avenue
New York, New York 10017 (212) 867-8720
Director: Francis Thargay Founded 1978

Tibetans, Americans of Tibetan origins and other interested persons. Purpose is to uphold the human rights of Tibetans. Specifically, seeks to correct "the Chinese violations of human rights in Tibet by taking steps to open communication between Tibetans in the United States and their parents and relatives in Tibet"; to create a better awareness and understanding of Tibet by organizing cultural events, and making literature on Tibet more accessible to the public; to correct "misinformation in the press about Tibet and Tibetans by organizing individuals to write responses." (The Epistolare Circle, a sub-group, performs this function.) Commemorates the anniversary of the March 10 uprising of the Tibetan people by organizing rallies annually; contacts organizations with human rights divisions and solicits their support; seeks active support and advice from Dharma centers in the United States; arranges legal advice and services for Tibetans in the United States having visa or residence difficulties. Holds seminars.
Publications: Epistolary Circle Mailing, bimonthly; Proceedings of Seminars, annual.

U.S.-ASIA INSTITUTE
1015 20th Street, Northwest, Suite 200
Washington, D.C. 20036
Executive Director: Esther G. Kee (202) 466-6124
Founded 1979

Members are Americans of Asian descent, individuals with an interest in United States-Asia relations, United States companies doing business with Asia, and Asian companies doing business with the United States. Purpose is to strengthen ties between the East and the West, fostering cooperation, communication, and cultural exchange between the United States and the 2.5 billion people of Asia. Places special emphasis on the "unique capabilities" of Asian-Americans to assist in this process, and on the contribution of Asian-Americans to the cultural, social and economic mainstream of American life. Seeks to promote a firm understanding of the issues important to the development of American domestic and foreign policies through research, symposiums and special programs. Sponsors the Tom Chan Future Leader Award competition in which college students can earn an internship with the Institute. Presents USAI Achievement Awards, given annually to Asian-Americans who have made outstanding contributions to America in their individuals fields; also bestows the Kay Sugahara Awards for the contributions of young United States Asians.
Publications: Asian/Pacific American National Leadership Conference Journal, annual; U.S.-Asia Economic Relations: Policies and Proposals (journal), annual; also publishes An Asian/Pacific American Perspective: Future Directions of U.S. Immigration and Refugee Policy, booklets and brochures.

Cultural and Educational Organizations

ACUPUNCTURE RESEARCH INSTITUTE
313 West Andrix Street
Monterey Park, California 91754 (213) 722-7353
Secretary: Louis Gasper, Ph.D. Founded 1973

Medical doctors, dentists, physical therapists, nurses, acupuncturists and persons associated with the medical professions. To investigate the validity and American application of acupuncture; to establish a means of exchange of information and experience, and to provide basic study courses in acupuncture concerning theory and methods leading to an acupuncture degree. Maintains library on acupuncture and homeopathy. Offers placement service.
Publications: Meridian (newsletter), quarterly.

AMERICAN-ASIAN EDUCATIONAL EXCHANGE
Professional Building 555 Lake Avenue
Saint James, New York 11780 (212) 662-8610
President: William Henderson Founded 1957

Provides for "the exchange of information, literature and personnel for the purposes of creating a broader understanding between the peoples of the United States and the independent nations of Asia." Maintains international educational program in two categories: publication, circulation and translation of printed materials; liaison and cooperation between the Exchange and similar organizations and academic groups in Asia and the United States. Formerly: (1967) American Afro-Asian Educational Exchange.
Publications: Asian Affairs, An American Review, bimonthly; also publishes monograph series.

AMERICAN COMMITTEE FOR SOUTH ASIAN ART
c/o Professor Sara L. Schastok
Department of Fine Arts
Fayerweather Hall
Amherst College
Amherst, Massachusetts 01002 (413) 542-2123
President: Sara L. Schastok Founded 1966

Scholars, collectors, students, university departments, museums and other institutions with holdings or programs in South Asian art. Supports advancement of knowledge and understanding of the art and archaeology of South Asia and related areas by providing research and teaching materials and disseminating information about scholarly and public activity in the field. Holds scholarly panels annually.
Publications: Slide Sets on India, 5 times a year; Newsletter, semiannual; Bibliography on South Asian Art, annual; Microfiche Archive of Art, irregular; also publishes a list of museums with South Asian art.

AMERICAN ORIENTAL SOCIETY
329 Sterling Memorial Library
New Haven, Connecticut 06520
Secretary-Treasurer: Stanley Insler (203) 436-1040
Founded 1842

Professional and amateur Orientalists. To promote research in Oriental languages, history and civilizations. Maintains library of 20,0000 periodicals and monographs dealing with various aspects of oriental culture. Grants scholarships for the study of Chinese art. Affiliated with: American Council of Learned Societies.
Publications: Journal of the AOS, quarterly; American Oriental Series (Monograph Series), irregular; American Oriental Series Essays, irregular.

AMERICAN SCHOOLS OF ORIENTAL RESEARCH
126 Inman Street
Cambridge, Massachusetts 02139
Executive Director: Dr. Thomas Beale (617) 547-9780
Founded 1900

Colleges, universities, theological seminaries and research institutes; scholars working in archaeological, historical and especially Biblical fields and interested laymen. "To promote the study and teaching and to extend the knowledge of Biblical literature and of geography, history, archaeology, and ancient and modern languages and literatures of Palestine, Mesopotamia and other Oriental countries, by affording educational opportunities to graduates of American colleges and universities and to other qualified students and by the prosecution of original research, excavation and exploration." Conducts research programs.
Publications: Newsletter, 8 times a year; Bulletin, quarterly; Biblical Archaeologist, quarterly; Journal of Cuneiform Studies, quarterly; The Annual (Monograph Series); also publishes reports, books and series.

AMHERST ASIAN AMERICAN EDUCATION COMMITTEE
Post Office Box 370
North Amherst, Massachusetts 01059 (413) 549-6627

Advocates multi-cultural education and conducts workshops on the Asian American experience.
Publications: Multi-Cultural Workshop Resource Packet on Asian Americans.

ASIA HOUSE
725 Park Avenue
New York, New York 10021

A center for cultural interchange between individuals and organizations of the United States and Asia. Located in New York City, Asia House maintains an art gallery, library, formal garden and auditorium.

ASIA SOCIETY
725 Park Avenue
New York, New York 10021
President: Dr. Robert B. Oxnam (212) 288-6400
Founded 1956

Aims are: to deepen American understanding of Asia and to stimulate thoughtful trans-Pacific intellectual discourse. Serves as consultants on curriculum development and multimedia materials; offers services to educators to help strengthen school resources on Asian peoples and cultures; sponsors student group visits to Asia House Gallery. Sponsors Country Councils on 16 Asian countries, composed of Asia Society members with interest in or professional knowledge of a particular area. Conducts research on development problems in Southeast Asia. Maintains 2,000 volume library on Asia. Maintains Asia House

Gallery for exhibitions of Asian art. Conducts national program on Asian performing arts. Has office in Washington, D.C. Absorbed: Conference on Asian Affairs; Chinese Art Society of America. Publications: Asia (magazine), bimonthly; Annual Report; Archives of Asian Art, annual; also publishes performing arts monographs, books, seadag reports, educational guides and catalogs of Asia House Gallery exhibitions.

ASIA SOCIETY/HOUSTON
3417 Milam
Houston, Texas 77002 (713) 520-7771
Director: Patricia M. Young Founded 1979

Houston branch of the Asia Society. Sponsors lecture series on the political and historical background of the major Asia regions and the classical arts of Asia; organizes seminars and concerts. Collaborates with the New York and Washington departments of the Asia Society and with other civic and academic organizations.
Publications: Newsletter.

ASIAN BENEVOLENT CORPS
2142 F Street, Northwest
Washington, D.C. 20037 (202) 331-0129
President: Alfred H. Liu Founded 1963

Organized for artistic, cultural, educational and community service activities. Supports Gallery Amerasia and Amerasian Center.
Publications: ABC Newsletter, monthly; Asian Voice (magazine), quarterly. Also publishes monographs and occasional papers.

ASIAN CULTURAL EXCHANGE FOUNDATION
c/o Paul J. Wisdom
Development Office
Towson State University
Towson, Maryland 21204 (301) 321-2235
Executive Officer: Paul G. Wisdom Founded 1952

To promote interest in the peoples of Asia through Asian arts and crafts. Collections of typical Asian art and crafts are given to schools, colleges and libraries. Arranges for special exhibits.

ASIAN FOLKLORE STUDIES GROUP
260 Stephens Hall
University of California
Berkeley, California 94720
President: Dr. Ruth-Inge Heinze (415) 849-3791
Founded 1977

Institutions of higher learning and scholars of anthropology, geography, history, linguistics, psychology, religon, and social sciences interested in the study of Asian folklore. To promote and study Asian folklore through team research, standardized collection of data and analysis. Organizes local, state, national, and international workshops and seminars. Maintains archive of folklore items and biographical files on Asian folklore scholars. Affiliated with Association for Asian Studies.
Publications: Journal, semiannual; Newsletter, semiannual; Directory, triennial.

ASIAN LITERATURE DIVISION
c/o Don Schojai
3546 Millikan Avenue
San Diego, California 92122
Executive Officer: Don Schojai Founded 1953

Scholars, teachers and others interested in the teaching of non-Western literatures in English translation in the colleges of the United States. Affiliated with: Modern Language Association of America. Formerly: (1976) Conference on Oriental-Western Literary Relations.
Publications: Literature East and West, quarterly.

ASSOCIATION FOR ASIAN STUDIES
One Lane Hall
University of Michigan
Ann Arbor, Michigan 48109
Secretary-Treasurer: Rhoads Murphey (313) 665-2490
Founded 1941

Educators, students, government officials and others interested in the study of Asia. Publishes scholarly research and other materials designed to promote Asian studies; sponsors research through conferences; administers special projects. Maintains placement service. Has councils on China and Inner Asia; Northeast Asia; South Asia; Southeast Asia. Formerly: (1957) Far Eastern Association
Publications: Newsletter, 5 times a year; Journal of Asian Studies, quarterly; Bibliography of Asian Studies, annual; also publishes monograph series and membership directory.

COMMITTEE ON RESEARCH MATERIALS ON SOUTHEAST ASIA
Box 6A
Yale Station
New Haven, Connecticut 06520
Chairman: Charles R. Bryant Founded 1969

A committee of the Southeast Asia Council of the Association for Asian Studies. Programs and objectives include: supporting research for bibliographical and other reference aids for Southeast Asian studies; proposing changes in basic cataloging procedures for the management of Southeast Asian language materials; working with national and international organizations in developing research materials on microfilm. Formerly Committee on American Library Resources on South Asia; Committee on American Library Resources. Publications: CORMOSEA Bulletin, semiannual.

CONFERENCE ON ASIAN HISTORY
c/o Department of History
University of Kansas
Lawrence, Kansas 66045 (913) 864-3108
Chairman: Grant K. Goodman Founded 1953

Asian historians at American universities and colleges. Dedicated to the exchange of information on Asia. Sponsors luncheon and panel discussions on Asian history during American Historical Association meeting.

CULTURAL INTEGRATION FELLOWSHIP
3494 21st Street
San Francisco, California 94110 (415) 648-6777
President: Mrs. Bina Chaudhuri Founded 1951

Individuals interested in the concepts of universal religion, cultural harmony and creative self-fulfillment. Promotes intercultural understanding between Asia and America; emphasizes the "spiritual oneness of the human race"; and applies fundamental spiritual principles in daily living. Activities include weekly lectures and study groups, a summer seminar on Oriental philosophy and a student essay contest. Maintains a Sunday school; operates a bookstore. Publications: Ashram Bulletin, quarterly; Special Cultural Events, quarterly; also sponsors and publishes books and monographs.

EAST-WEST CULTURAL CENTER
2865 West Nineth Street
Los Angeles, California 90006 (213) 480-8325
Acting President: Robert Dane Founded 1953

Seeks to relate and integrate the cultural and spiritual values of the East (primarily India) with those of Western civilization. Sponsors study groups and college classes based on the teachings of Sri Aurobindo, an Indian mystic. Offers classes in Sanskrit, Yoga and Oriental religion, philosophy and literature. Maintains a 2,000 volume library which covers Eastern religion, philosophy, language and culture. Has published First Lessons in Sanskrit Grammar and Reading and The Language of the Gods. Sponsors the work at Auroville, the "City of Human Unity" being built in Madras State, India.

INDO-PACIFIC PREHISTORY ASSOCIATION
Department of Prehistory and Anthropology
Australian National University
Box 4 P.O.
Canberra, A.C.T. 2600 Australia
President: Jack Golson Founded 1953

Archaeologists, anthropologists, and professionals in related fields; registered students in archaeology or anthropology; others interested in the area. To provide a channel of communication for people active in the field or in research on the prehistory of the Far East and Oceania; area covered extends from Northeast Asia (Siberia) to Australia and New Zealand, Easter Island to India and Pakistan, plus Madagascar. Arranges symposia, and international meetings; provides help in making contacts for persons wishing to do field work in the area of coverage. Presidency rotates from one country to another. Formerly (1976) Far-Eastern Pre-history Association. Affiliated with Archaeological Institute of America. Publications: Bulletin, annual; Newsletter, irregular.

INSTITUTE FOR ADVANCED RESEARCH IN ASIAN SCIENCE AND MEDICINE
Post Office Box 555
Garden City, New York 11530 (212) 270-1164
Director: Frederick F. Kao Founded 1979

Purpose is to advance international understanding between Asia and the West in the areas of science, medical systems and health care delivery. Provides clearinghouse for international scholarly efforts in the comparative study of science and medicine. Provides consultation services and mediation of scientific and biomedical exchange with Asian countries. Assists in generating innovative curricula in medical education; translates contemporary and classical Asian scientific and medical literature; offers research fellowships for the humanistic study of Asian scientific and medical traditions; gives grants for scientific research in comparative physiology and medicine. Organizes international conferences. Publications: American Journal of Chinese Medicine, quarterly; also publishes monographs series on Asian Science and Medicine.

MONGOLIA SOCIETY
Post Office Box 606
Bloomington, Indiana 47402
Executive Director: John G. Hangin (812) 337-1566
Founded 1961

Individuals, libraries and other organizations interested in furthering the study of Mongolia and adjacent areas of Inner Asia. Sponsors films, lectures and exhibits. Presents scholarships. Maintains small

library including Mongolian newspapers and periodicals.
Publications: Mongolian Studies, annual; Occasional Papers, irregular; Special Papers (in Mongolian), irregular; also publishes dictionaries and textbook of Mongolian language.

PERMANENT INTERNATIONAL ALTAISTIC CONFERENCE
Goodbody Hall 101
Indiana University
Bloomington, Indiana 47401
Secretary General: Professor Denis Sinor
(812) 337-2233
Founded 1957

Scholars interested in Altaic or Inner Asian studies. Provides a forum for the reading of scholarly papers and the exchange of information of common interest. Awards gold medal of the Indiana University Prize for Altaic Studies.
Publications: Newsletter, irregular.

SOCIETY FOR ASIAN AND COMPARATIVE PHILOSOPHY
Department of Philosophy
Box 329, Baruch College, CUNY
17 Lexington Avenue
New York, New York 10010
Secretary-Treasurer: Robert A. McDermott
(212) 725-7155
Founded 1968

Professors, graduate students and Asian scholars. To advance the development of Asian and comparative philosophies and to bring Asian and Western philosophers together for a mutual beneficial exchange of ideas. Sponsors panels and workshops in themes of both scholarly and topical interest.
Publication: Monograph Series, annual.

SOCIETY FOR ASIAN ART
Asian Art Museum
Golden Gate Park
San Francisco, California 94118
(415) 387-5675
Secretary: Marge Dodge
Founded 1958

Persons interested in Asian art; membership concentrated on West Coast.

SOCIETY FOR ASIAN MUSIC
Center for Near Eastern Studies
50 Washington Square South
New York University
New York, New York 10003
(212) 769-1900
President: Pat Kennedy
Founded 1959

Encourages appreciation and performance of Asian music (October through May) covering Middle East to Far East.
Publications: Asian Music (journal), semiannual.

SUMI-E SOCIETY OF AMERICA (Art)
4200 Kings Mill Lane
Annandale, Virginia 22003
Corresponding Secretary: Margaret McAdams
Founded 1962

Artists and others interested in oriental brush-paintings. Encourages display of oriental brush-paintings in private or public art galleries; conducts annual competition and exhibition. Compiles bibliography of books on oriental brush-painting; disseminates information on location of artworks in museums and private collections. Presents awards.
Publications: Sumi-e-Notes, quarterly; Catalogue, annual; also publishes membership lists, book lists and reviews.

TIBET SOCIETY
Post Office Box 1968
Bloomington, Indiana 47402
(812) 337-4339
Founder: Mr. Thubten J. Norbu
Founded 1966

Scholars, students, researchers; libraries, institutes and organizations having an interest in the languages, history, religion and other aspects of life in Tibet and Central Asia. Serves as a forum and center of research information on Tibetan studies and affairs. Planned activities include films, lectures, discussions and panels. Affiliated with Mongolia Society (sister group, but administered separately).
Publications: Journal, semiannual; Newsletter, irregular.

WASHINGTON CENTER OF THE ASIA SOCIETY
1785 Massachusetts Avenue
Washington, D.C. 20036
President: Honorable William Gleysteen
(202) 387-6500
Founded 1970

Seeks to offer fresh perspectives on Asian cultural, economic, political and strategic affairs and on Asian-American relations. Serves as forum for views presented by Asian and American officials, journalists, business people, scholars, educators and artists. Organizes briefings, colloquia, conferences, films, lectures, panels and workshops; provides information on Asia-related resources in the Washington area; publishes resource materials.
Publication: Asia in Washington, (calendar of events), monthly.

Foundations

AGRICULTURAL DEVELOPMENT COUNCIL
1290 Avenue of the Americas
New York, New York 10019
Secretary-Treasurer: James Dillard — (212) 765-3500 — Founded 1953

Foundation to support teaching and research in the social sciences relating to agricultural development, with primary attention to Agricultural Economics, Rural Sociology, Extension Education in Asia. Provides for graduate fellowships at the M.S. level in Asia and at the Ph.D. level in the United States. Supports pilot research projects: an interregional program in Asia to enable social scientists to work together on common problems; book and equipment grants. Formerly (1963) Council on Economic and Cultural Affairs.
Publications: Newsletter, quarterly; Directory of Fellows, triennial; ADC Papers, irregular; ADC Reprints, irregular; also publishes books and monographs.

AMERICAN-NEPAL EDUCATION FOUNDATION
Box ANEF
Oceanside, Oregon 97134 — (503) 842-4024
Executive Secretary: Hugh B. Wood — Founded 1956

To provide scholarships and other educational facilities for Nepal and acquaint Americans with Nepal's educational problems. Conducts research on Nepal's educational system. Publishes books and pamphlets. Prepares bibliography on Nepal. Maintains library of 2,000 volumes of reference material pertaining to Nepal.

ASIA FOUNDATION
Post Office Box 3223
San Francisco, California 94119 — (415) 982-4640

2301 E Street, Northwest
Washington, D.C. — (202) 223-5268
President: Haydn Williams — Founded 1954

Supported by United States government grants and private contributions. To strengthen Asian economic and social development with private American assistance. Emphasis is on human resources development, assistance to Asian institutions engaged in national development, facilitating of professional exchanges and promotion of intra-Asian cooperation. Fields of interest include rural and community development; food and nutrition; population and community health; law and justice; communication, books and libraries; management, employment and economic development; and exchange for Asian-American understanding. Books for Asia project has distributed over 18 million books and journals to more than 30,000 institutions in 19 Asian countries. Maintains library on current Asian affairs. Has offices in San Francisco, California, and Washington, D.C. and maintains programs in 15 Asian nations.
Publications: Asia Foundation News, bimonthly; President's Review (annual report).

DE RANCE, INCORPORATED
7700 West Blue Mound Road
Milwaukee, Wisconsin 53213 — (414) 475-7700
President: Harry G. John — Inc. in 1946

Among other grant areas, the foundation supports educational and social development programs in Asia.

GRIGGS (MARY LIVINGSTON) AND MARY GRIGGS BURKE FOUNDATION
1400 Northwestern National Bank Building
55 East Fifth Street
Saint Paul, Minnesota 55101
Donor: Mary L. Griggs — Estab. 1966

Gives grants primarily in Minnesota and New York, with emphasis on higher and secondary education, Asian cultural societies, museums, historic preservation, conservation, and local community funds.

HARVARD YENCHING INSTITUTE
Two Divinity Avenue
Cambridge, Massachusetts 02138 — (617) 495-3369
Director: Albert M. Craig — Inc. in 1928

Goal is to aid the development of higher education in eastern and southern Asia. Gives grants primarily for certain universities in Asia to support teaching, research, and study by Asians in the humanities and social sciences relating to Asian cultures and offers support for inter-Asian personnel exchange in these fields. Sponsors fellowships at Harvard University for research, or scholarships for graduate study, by younger faculty members of selected Asian institutions. Contributes to the Harvard-Yenching Library, which became an integral part of Harvard University on July 1, 1976. Areas of concern confined to Japan, East and Southeast Asia, and, under a special fund, to one institution at Allahabad, India.

THE JDR 3RD FUND, INCORPORATED
30 Rockefeller Plaza, Room 5432
New York, New York 10112
President: Mrs. John D. Rockefeller, 3rd — (212) 765-2323 — Inc. in 1963

Asian Cultural Program now established as a new organization known as the Asian Cultural Council and will operate under comparable guidelines as the Program.

THE HENRY LUCE FOUNDATION, INCORPORATED
111 West 50th Street
New York, New York 10020
President: Henry Luce, III
Program Director: Robert E. Armstrong — (212) 489-7700 — Inc. in 1936

Awards grants for specific projects in the broad areas of public affairs (including minority relations and urban programs), East/West relations, and theology. The Foundation has several programs. The Luce Scholars Program, giving a select group of young American professionals, not Asian specialists, a year's work/study experience in the Far East. The Henry R. Luce Professorship Program, providing five- or eight-year support for a limited number of integrative academic programs in the humanities and social sciences at private colleges and universities. The Luce Fund for Asian Studies, offering support for projects in the area of Asian-American relations at ten designated university centers. Its international activities are confined to East and Southeast Asia.

THE MEMTON FUND, INCORPORATED
One East 75th Street
New York, New York 10021
President: Samuel R. Milbank — Inc. in 1936

Charitable purposes; in practice makes grants in those fields in which the founders were interested, with emphasis on higher education, Asian studies and cultural relations, community funds, health agencies, youth agencies, and child welfare.

STANDARD FRUIT CHARITIES, INCORPORATED
50 California Street
San Francisco, California 94111
President: D. J. Kirchhoft — Inc. in 1945

Grants for education, including scholarship funds, hospitals, child welfare, and church support in Costa Rica, Honduras, Ecuador, Philippines, Nicaragua, and Thailand.

TIBETAN FOUNDATION
801 Second Avenue
New York, New York 10017
Chairman of Board: Dr. Alfredo C. Bartholomew — (212) 867-8720 — Founded 1968

To help Tibetan refugees from the Chinese Communists establish themselves in their new homes. Supports schools, child care facilities, health services, handicraft centers and farm programs. Supports Tibet House (museum and library) for the preservation of Tibetan culture and literature and Tibetan National Library in Dharamsala, India.

Charitable Organizations

BUDDHIST COUNCIL FOR REFUGEE RESCUE AND RESETTLEMENT
City of 10,000 Buddhas
Box 217
Talmage, California 95481
Executive Co-Director: Douglas Powers — (707) 462-0939

Voluntary agency, composed of Buddhist organizations and Asian-American civic associations in the United States, which resettles Indochinese refugees. Operates an English language and acculturation training program for newly arrived refugees.

NATIONAL PACIFIC/ASIAN RESOURCE CENTER ON AGING
811 First Avenue, Suite 210
Seattle, Washington 98104
Director: Louise M. Kamikawa — (206) 622-5124 — Founded 1979

Group comprised of Pacific/Asian service providers, professors, policymakers, consumers, researchers and other persons of similar professions. Goals are to ensure and improve the delivery of health and social services to elderly Pacific/Asians; to increase the capabilities of community-based services by expanding their information base and to include Pacific/Asians in planning and organizational activities, thus maintaining a strong link between the Center and the community. Maintains library of 150 volumes. Publications: Update (newsletter), bimonthly; National Community Service Directory: Pacific/Asian Elderly, biennial; National Consultation Resource Roster, biennial; also publishes Pacific/Asian Elderly: Bibliography.

PAN PACIFIC CENTERS
Box 742
Pacific Palisades, California 90272
Director Emeritus: Mary Ellen Saunders
(213) 459-4524
Founded 1950

Objectives are: orientation of international students from all countries on arrival; limited scholarship aid; assistance to orphans in Korea, Hong Kong, Taiwan and India. Formerly (1950) American Oriental Friendship Association.

REFUGEES INTERNATIONAL
19175 Doewood, Box T
Monument, Colorado
President: Susan H. Morton
Founded 1979

To provide educational information, coordination and media outreach to further the understanding of and assistance to refugees around the globe. Through voluntary action, seeks alternative means of handling refugee migration and permanent resettlement. Hopes to empty the refugee camps in Cambodia, Thailand, Malaysia and Indonesia; find new homelands for these refugees and provide food and supplies to help rebuild Cambodia. Long term goal is to buy 200 square miles of land so that up to two million refugees from around the world can build a new society. Facilitates the primary care work of on-site voluntary agencies and international organizations working with refugees. Current focus is on coordinating the work of World Relief Corporation which maintains a staff in Southeast Asia. Is also involved in designing sanitation facilities and temporary shelters for refugee camps. Seeks voluntary support in the form of funds, sponsorship of refugee families, letters urging governmental support, and medical services. Develops grant proposals.

TIBETAN AID PROJECT
2425 Hillside Avenue
Berkeley, California 94704
President: Tarthang Tulku
(415) 548-5407
Founded 1974

A project of the Tibetan Nyingma Relief Foundation. Offers assistance to Tibetan refugees in India, Nepal, Bhutan and Sikkima. Conducts Tibetan Pen Friend Program. Sponsors relief distribution to communities for support of religious and community activities. Organizes benefits of all types, including seminars on Tibetan meditation and physical yoga. Maintains speakers bureau. Publishes brochures and booklets; plans to publish a book.

VOLUNTEERS IN ASIA
Box 4543
Stanford, California 94305
Executive Director: Dwight D. Clark
(415) 497-3228
Founded 1963

Provides volunteers to Asian institutions. Volunteers are drawn mostly from Stanford University and University of California, Santa Cruz and serve either a 6-month or 1-2 year term. Assignments range from teaching to development reportage and basic village technology. The volunteer's education is as much an objective as any serivce which he/she can provide. Provides cross-cultural training resources to other educational organizations.
Publications: VIAlogue, quarterly; also publishes Health Handbook, Transcultural Study Guide, Appropriate Technology Sourcebook, On Your Own Guide to Asia and other books.

Religious Organizations

AMERICAN BUDDHIST ACADEMY
331 Riverside Drive
New York, New York 10025
Buddhist Minister: Reverend Hozen Seki
(212) 678-9213
Founded 1938

Buddhists and others interested in the religion. Activities include a Sunday religious service, lecture and classes in Buddhist studies. Maintains library of 9,000 Buddhist books.
Publications: Buddhist Sangha, monthly.

AMERICAN BUDDHIST ASSOCIATION
1151 West Leland Avenue
Chicago, Illinois 60640
President: Richard Davison
(312) 334-4661
Founded 1955

"To study, publish and make known the principles of Buddhism and to encourage the understanding and application of these principles." Holds study classes, discussion groups, lectures and retreats.
Publications: Onceness, 3 times a year.

AMERICAN MISSION TO THE CHINESE AND ASIANS
c/o Reverend Peter P. S. Ching, D.D.
144-25 Roosevelt Avenue
Flushing, New York 11354
President: Reverend Peter P. S. Ching
(212) 461-5756
Founded 1945

Interdenominational organization founded by Americans "to spread the Gospel among the Chinese." Sponsors mission work in Hong Kong-Kowloon-Macao, and other Asian areas including India, Philippines, Indonesia, Singapore and Madagascar; supports medical and educational institutions and distributes donated funds, clothing, food and medicine for Asian and Chinese refugees in the Far East; provides relief and adoption services for refugee children and orphans. Promotes United States sale of products handmade by refugees, in order to increase employment in Hong Kong. Maintains employment, legal, immigration and marriage counseling services in the United States; conducts educational, agricultural, medical and scientific exchange, Christian education training programs and research studies of southeastern Asian economic and social problems. Sponsors Chinese Culture Institute of International College of Art and Science. Formerly: (1954) Far Eastern Refugee Service; (1976) American Mission to the Chinese.
Publications: Bulletin, monthly; Evangel Refugee, annual.

BUDDHIST CHURCHES OF AMERICA
1710 Octavia Street
San Francisco, California 94109
Bishop: Rt. Reverend Kenryu Tsuji — Founded 1899

Founded in 1899, organized in 1914 as the Buddhist Mission of North America, this body was incorporated in 1942 under the present name and represents the Jodo Shinshu Sect of Buddhism in this country. It is a school of Buddhism which believes in salvation by faith in the wisdom and compassion of Amida Buddha. Affiliates are Western Adult Buddhist League, National Young Buddhist Association; National Buddhist Women's Association; Federation of Western Buddhist Sunday School Teachers; and Institute of Buddhist Studies.

BUDDHIST PEACE FELLOWSHIP
Post Office Box 4650
Berkeley, California 94704
Coordinator: Robert Aitken — Founded 1979

American Buddhists devoted to the cultivation of worldwide peace, social justice and non-violence. Objectives include witnessing to the Buddhist commitment to nonviolence as a means of achieving peace and promotion of national and international Buddhist peace projects. Sponsors Chittagong Hill Tracts Project to save the people in that area of Bangladesh from persecution. Affiliated with Fellowship of Reconciliation.
Publications: Newsletter, quarterly; plans to publish English text on the historical and scriptural roots of Buddhist activism.

BUDDHIST VIHARA SOCIETY, INCORPORATED
5017 16th Street, Northwest
Washington, D.C. 20011
Honorable General Secretary: Mahathera H. Gunaratana — (202) 723-0773 — Founded 1966

"To provide a religious and educational center to present Buddhist thought, practice and culture and more broadly, to aid cross-cultural communication and understanding - prerequisites for a peaceful world." Formed by the Most Venerable Madihe Pannaseeha, Maha Nayaka Thera, of Sri Lanka, who noted a serious and growing interest in Buddhism in the United States after he visited this country in 1964. The Society offers the perspective of Theravada Buddhism which it claims is "the oldest continuous school of Buddhism that today characterizes the cultures of Burma, Laos, Cambodia, Sri Lanka and Thailand." Conducts Sunday services, operates a bookstore and mail order service, holds discussions, provides lectures, conducts classes on meditation for adults and children, and on Buddhism. Sanskrit and Sinhalese and organizes celebrations on days of special Buddhist significance. The Society is headquartered in the Washington Buddhist Vihara (Temple) which also houses a shrine room, a meditation room, a library of 3,000 volumes on Buddhism and related subjects, a garden and the bookstore.
Publications: Washington Buddhist (newsletter), quarterly; also publishes the Vihara Papers (an essay series), brochures and a devotional handbook.

"EVANGELIZE CHINA" FELLOWSHIP
Post Office Box 418
Pasadena, California 91102
Executive Officer: Dr. Paul C. Szeto — (213) 793-5444 — Founded 1947

Carries on a program of education, relief and religious work in Hong Kong, Macao, Thailand, Malaya, Singapore, Indonesia and Taiwan. Conducts its education programs in 69 schools, orphanages and churches.
Publications: News, quarterly.

FIRST ZEN INSTITUTE OF AMERICA
113 East 30th Street
New York, New York 10016 — (212) 684-9487
Secretary: Mary Farkas — Founded 1930

Carries on program of daily life, with meditation practice in the Rinzai tradition.
Publications: Zen Notes, 10 times a year.

INTERNATIONAL BUDDHIST MEDITATION CENTER
2835 West Olympic Boulevard
Los Angeles, California 90006 (213) 384-0850
Abbess: Reverend Dr. Thich An-Tn Founded 1970

Religious congregation whose goals are to provide instruction in Oriental culture and Buddhist religion, philosophy, and meditation and to develop social and charitable activities. Offers regular lectures, meditation practices, seminars and retreats; performs ordination ceremonies; acts as training institute for both American and foreign monks and nuns. Maintains library of 5,000 volumes.
Publications: Schedule, monthly; Lotus in the West, biennial.

NATIONAL BUDDHIST WOMEN'S ASSOCIATIONS
c/o Buddhist Churches of America
1710 Octavia Street
San Francisco, California 94109
Bishop: Seigen H. Yamaoka Founded 1952

Women members of Buddhist churches of Jodo Shinshu faith. Promotes American Buddhism through publications, community service, fund raising and recreational and educational programs.

NATIONAL YOUNG BUDDHIST ASSOCIATION
c/o Buddhist Churches of America
1710 Octavia Street
San Francisco, California 94109 (415) 776-5600
Executive Secretary: Steve Taketa Founded 1948

Buddhist youths from 15 to 25 years of age. Coordinates activities of young Buddhists of Jodo Shinshu denomination in the continental United States.
Publications: College Directory.

UNITED BOARD FOR CHRISTIAN HIGHER EDUCATION IN ASIA
475 Riverside Drive
New York, New York 10027
Executive Director: Dr. Paul T. Lauby (212) 870-2608
Founded 1932

To aid indigenous Christian universities and associations of universities in East and Southeast Asia. Formerly (1945) Associated Boards for Christian Colleges in China; (1955) United Board for Christian Colleges in China.
Publications: New Horizons, 3 times a year; Annual Report.

WESTERN YOUNG BUDDHIST LEAGUE
c/o Youth Department, BCA
1710 Octavia Street
San Francisco, California 94109
Executive Secretary: Steve Taketa (415) 776-5600

Young people (ages 13-25) of Jodo Shinshu Buddhist faith. Promotes Buddhism; provides unity and fellowship; conducts charitable and social activities; offers scholarships.
Publications: Newsletter; Directory.

ZEN STUDIES SOCIETY
Dai Bosatsu Zendo, Kongo-Ji
Beecher Lake, Star Rte.
Livingston Manor, New York 12758 (914) 439-4566
Roshi (Abbot): Eido Tai Shimano Founded 1965

For Zen Buddhist training, practice and retreats. Maintains Temple (New York Zendo), Lay Mountain Monastery (Dai Bosatsu Zendo) in New York state. Also maintains 1,200 volume library on Zen Buddhism and related subjects.
Publications: Namu Dai Bosa, quarterly; also produces books and cassettes.

Research Centers and Special Institutes

AMERICAN ACADEMY OF ASIAN STUDIES
2842 Buchanan
San Francisco, California 94132 (415) 921-6028
President: Dr. Edszen N. Landrum Founded 1951

Evening adult graduate school specializing in Asian studies and languages; offers M.A. and Ph.D. degrees. Seeks to integrate philosophies and cultures of the East and West. Teaches (over a five-year cycle) more than 90 courses. Subjects of courses include: Bhagavad Gita, Urdu, Hebrew, Sanskrit, calligraphy, Indian dances, psychology of Zen, Yoga Bhakti, Indian theism, Yoga exercises, Vedanta in the original, philosophy of Taoism. Sponsors special lectures for the public. Maintains 10,000 volume library on Asian countries and countries in the northern part of Africa. Presently inactive.

ASIAN LANGUAGES AND LITERATURE
225 Gowen Hall, DO-21
University of Washington
Seattle, Washington 98195 (206) 543-4996
Chairman: Frederick P. Brandauer Founded 1969

Research and teaching of Chinese, Japanese, Korean, South Asian (Hindi, Sanskrit, and Tamil), Tibetan, Turkic, Thai, and Tagelog.

ASIAN STUDIES
University of Florida
Director's Office
404 Little Hall
Gainesville, Florida 32611
Director: Dr. Irmgard Johnson (904) 392-1581

Offers an interdisciplinary major and minor in Asian Studies with studies in art, religion, history, philosophy, government and politics.

ASIAN STUDIES CENTER
Michigan State University
College of Social Science
East Lansing, Michigan 48823
Director: Dr. William T. Ross Founded 1962

Aims to further knowledge of countries of Asia, with concentration on India and Pakistan in South Asia and China and Japan in Far East. Pursues curriculum development and advancement of instruction in Hindi, Urdu, Bengali, Marathi, Sanskrit, Chinese and Japanese, both at the University and as a tool for field research. Also facilitates research by faculty members and students in Asian countries and assists faculty members and graduate students in obtaining financial support for both on-campus and overseas research concerning Asia.

ASIAN STUDIES COMMITTEE
Towson State University
Towson, Maryland 21204 (301) 321-2913
Director: Edwin Hirschmann Founded 1974

An interdisciplinary program, consisting of faculty members who have teaching or research interests in Asia. Disciplines represented are art, economics, history, geography, political science, philosophy and languages.

ASIAN STUDIES COMMITTEE
University of Tennessee at Knoxville
Knoxville, Tennessee 37916 (615) 974-5406
Director: Professor Eric J. Gangloff Founded 1971

Studies the rich and diversified civilizations both ancient and modern of the Islamic world, India, China and Japan. Offers language training and work in history, sociology, literature, art, music, philosophy and religion. Sponsors lectures, films, concerts, seminars and conferences to create awareness of traditional culture and current topics of interest. A major and minor are available.

ASIAN STUDIES PROGRAM
California State University, Hayward
Hayward, California 94542
Director: William W. Van Groenou, Ph.D. (415) 881-3852
Founded 1963

The program is principally oriented to the realities in East, South-East and South Asia, but also relates to an increasing extent to the immigrant communities from Asia, with the aim of creating fellow-feeling in American schools for Asian culture and people, and of understanding the impact of Asian economics on the American situation.

ASIAN STUDIES PROGRAM
Dartmouth College, Bartlett Hall
Hanover, New Hampshire 03755 (603) 646-2861
Chairman: Gene R. Garthwaite Founded 1973

An undergraduate education program, emphasizing Chinese language and literature, Asian culture, geography, religion, political science, and history (China, Japan, India, Middle East, Israel, Southeast Asia).

ASIAN STUDIES PROGRAM
East Carolina University
Greenville, North Carolina 27834 (919) 757-6193
Director: Dr. Avtar Singh Founded 1967

The program mainly involves teaching. Whenever available, "Field Study in Asia" is offered under the leadership of a professor from East Carolina University.

ASIAN STUDIES PROGRAM
School of Advanced International Studies
1740 Massachusetts Avenue, Northwest
Washington, D.C. 20036
Director: Nathaniel B. Thayer (202) 785-6200

ASIAN STUDIES PROGRAM
State University of New York,
College at New Paltz
New Paltz, New York 12561 (914) 257-2365
Director: Ronald G. Knapp Founded 1977

An interdisciplinary program including art history, geography, political science, history, philosophy, economics, literature and language of major Asian geographical areas (China, India, Japan). Also sponsors films, concerts, lectures, and special events. An exchange program with Beijing University brings visiting scholars and students as well as giving Americans the chance to study in China.

ASIAN STUDIES PROGRAM
University of Pittsburgh
4E05 Forbes Quad
Pittsburgh, Pennsylvania 15260
Director: Dr. Edward M. Anthony
(412) 624-5566
Founded 1960

Conducts research and classes in Japanese anthropology; Chinese and Japanese literature and linguistics; Japanese drama; Chinese economics; Chinese; Japanese and Inner Asian art history; Chinese and Southeast Asian geography; Chinese and Japanese history; Chinese sociology; Chinese, Japanese, Southeast Asian and Indian politics; Indian religion; Chinese music; Chinese law.

ASIAN STUDIES PROGRAM
Wake Forest University
Box 7547, Reynolds Station
Winston-Salem, North Carolina 27109
Director: Balkrisha G. Gokhale
(919) 725-9711
Founded 1960

Research in the history and politics of Asia and Far East, including Korea, through studies in history, political science, sociology, anthropology, literature and art. Also provides graduate and undergraduate instruction in Asian civilization and special training for high school teachers in courses and seminars at the University. Holds weekly graduate student seminars, monthly faculty seminars and a summer institute and seminars for high school teachers. Maintains a library of 5,000 volumes on Asian history, culture and politics.
Publications: Research results published in books and professional journals.

ASIAN STUDIES RESEARCH INSTITUTE
Indiana University
Goodbody Hall
Bloomington, Indiana 47401
Director: Professor Denis Sinor
(812) 337-2398
Founded 1967

Integral unit of Indiana University, but with its own board of control. Supported by parent institution and outside funding. Utilizes various members of University faculty, plus supporting nonprofessional staff. Focus is on Inner Asia, including central Asia, Siberia, Mongolia and Tibet; also prepares and publishes teaching aids for study of inner Asia. Maintains Antoinette K. Gordon Collection of Tibetan Art and a Turkish folklore archive, also a punchcard catalog of Chinese frontier tribes. Maintains a reference library.
Publications: Journal of Asian History, 2 times a year; Oriental Series; Reprint Series; Occasional Papers and Teaching Aids for the Study of Inner Asia.

CALIFORNIA INSTITUTE OF ASIAN STUDIES
3494 21st Street
San Francisco, California 94110
(415) 648-1488

Evening graduate school in San Francisco, California specializing in Asian culture and civilization.
The Institute cooperates with the Cultural Integration Fellowship and is dedicated to "East-West international understanding and original research in universal humanistic values." Accredited toward M.A. and Ph.D. degrees.

CENTER FOR ASIAN STUDIES
Arizona State University
Social Science Building
Tempe, Arizona 85281
Director: Dr. Yung-Hwan Jo
(602) 965-7184
Founded 1966

Studies Asian history, political science, economics, geography, anthropology, sociology and languages. Also encourages development of Asian studies at both undergraduate and graduate levels at the University. Research results published in occasional papers and project reports. (Holds a symposium every other year).

CENTER FOR ASIAN STUDIES
California State University, Long Beach
6101 East Seventh Street
Long Beach, California 90840
Director: Dr. Charlotte Furth
(213) 498-5493
Founded 1971

Research spans east, southeast and south Asian areas and disciplines. Also coordinates undergraduate studies in those areas and disciplines at the University, as well as an interdisciplinary program in Asian studies at master's level, and participates in Japan and China seminars.

CENTER FOR ASIAN STUDIES
San Diego State University
College of Arts and Letters
San Diego, California 92182
Director: Professor Alvin D. Coox

Interdisciplinary research and instructional unit in College of Arts and Letters at San Diego State University, drawing upon faculty members from many areas of the University. Secures and administers grants and other support for research and development in Asian studies. Coordinates and publicizes activities of faculty members engaged in Asian-centered studies. Develops and administers Asian studies program and relevant curricula at undergraduate and graduate levels. Responds to campus and community requests for information and services and fosters campus and community interest in Asian studies. Maintains a reading room and study facility containing Asian periodicals, books, pamphlets, dictionaries and maps.

CENTER FOR ASIAN STUDIES
University of Illinois
1208 West California
Urbana, Illinois 61801 (217) 333-4850
Director: Dr. Peter Schran Founded 1964

Studies social, economic and political change in contemporary Asian societies, historical development of Asian societies and Asian linguistics. Also participates in research and exchange project at Keio University in Tokyo and research project at University of Tehran. Holds interdisciplinary seminars on economic development and comparative research on changing east Asian states and societies. Maintains a library of 100,000 volumes in vernacular languages on China, Japan, Southeast Asia, south Asia and Middle East.
Publications: New Books on Asian Studies Announced for Publication in the Soviet Union, annually.

CENTER FOR ASIAN STUDIES
University of Texas
Speech Building 310
Austin, Texas 78712
Director: Dr. F. Tomasson Jannuzi (512) 471-1191
Founded 1959

Research conducted in aspects of ancient and modern South Asian, Chinese and Japanese arts; political science; geography; economics; education; history; anthropology; philosophy; languages and linguistics, including Hindi, Telugu, Tamil, Sanskrit, Urdu, Kannada, Malayalam, classical and modern Chinese and Japanese; policies of finance and trade in China and Japan. Intensive studies have been devoted to politics and social change in Kerala, India; agrarian reform programs in various regions of India; history of women's education and political activity in India; entrepreneurship in engineering industry of an Indian city; Chinese in Texas, Manchu court at end of Ch'ing Dynasty; syntax of classical Chinese, especially particles of negation; acquisition of sociolinguistic rules in Japanese; language acquisition and development in Japanese and grammatical interference in Japanese. Also conducts a special program of community outreach in a program on educational resources in Asia. Holds seminars and lectures on various aspects of south and east Asian life and thought, also current political and social situations. Maintains a library collection including 100,000 volumes of South Asian materials, 20,000 volumes of Japanese materials and 5,000 of Chinese materials.
Publications: journals, books and graduate student dissertations.

CENTER FOR ASIAN STUDIES
Saint John's University
Grand Central and Utopia Parkways
Jamaica, New York 11439 (212) 969-8000
Director: Dr. Paul K. T. Sih Founded 1959

Integral unit of Graduate School of Arts and Sciences at Saint John's University; previously known as Institute of Asian Studies. Supported by parent institution. Principal field of research: Historical development of major nations in Asia. Also translates Asian classical works into English and compiles texts and teaching materials for advanced instruction in Chinese language.
Publication: Asia in the Modern World, a monograph series.

CENTER FOR DEVELOPMENT STUDIES
Social Science Research Institute
University of Hawaii
Honolulu, Hawaii 96822
Director: Dr. Burnham O. Campbell Founded 1978

Integral unit of recently reorganized and renamed Social Science Research Institute in Research Division of Graduate School of University of Hawaii on its Manoa campus. Supported by parent institution, foundations and foreign agencies. Investigates problems associated with developing countries of Pacific area and Asia in all aspects of development, but currently restricted to economic and demographic studies with emphasis on east and southeast Asia, all involving collaboration with research organization in Asia and some outside funding.

CENTER FOR EDUCATION IN ASIA
Columbia University
525 West 120th Street
New York, New York 10027 (212) 870-4065
Director: Professor C. T. Hu Founded 1967

A part of the Institute of International Studies at Teachers College which engages in research on the history of Asian education, with particular emphasis on China in modern times and stressing educational part of modernization process, including social, cultural and educational developments since Communist accession to power, also collection and analysis of historical data on modern Chinese education and comparative study of education and cultural change in China, India and Japan. Also in collaboration with East Asian Institute at the University provides graduate instruction and research training on education in modern China and provides assistance to secondary school teachers in coverage of Asia. Research results published in professional journals, books and graduate student theses and dissertations. Holds occasional conferences on special topics. Maintains a special collection of books and journals on Asian education.

CENTER FOR SOUTH PACIFIC STUDIES
University of California at Santa Cruz
Santa Cruz, California 95060 (408) 429-2191
Director: Dr. Bryan H. Farrell Founded 1967

Explores the potential of South Pacific area for controlled comparative study of anthropological, biological, humanistic, ecological, political and linguistic developments, especially in Oceania, Australia, New Zealand and insular southeast Asia, including interdisciplinary studies of social change, impact of tourism, Pacific migrants in an urban setting, nutrition and health. Also provides instruction, field research and interaction with distinguished Pacific residents on campus and through faculty exchange program. Holds periodic seminars and workshops on contemporary Pacific anthropological, political and economic problems. Utilizes developing Pacific collection in the University's McHenry Library.
Publications: Research results published in series of monographs.

COMMITTEE ON ASIAN STUDIES
180 College Avenue
New Brunswick, New Jersey 08903 (201) 932-7637
Director: Dr. Ching-I Tu Founded 1969

Research and teaching conducted in Asian languages, literatures, political science, history and other fields relating to Asian studies.

DEPARTMENT OF ASIAN LANGUAGES AND LITERATURE/PROGRAM IN ASIAN STUDIES
The University of Iowa
314 Gilmore Hall
Iowa City, Iowa 52242
Chairman: Professor Marleigh G. Ryan (319) 353-4262
Founded 1972

Research and teaching in Japanese literature, anthropology and linguistics; Chinese literature, philosophy, drama, modern and ancient linguistics; Sanskrit and Indian literature; and related studies in other departments. Offers an undergraduate major in Asian languages and literature and a M.A. in Asian civilization.

DEPARTMENT OF ASIAN STUDIES
Seton Hall University
South Orange, New Jersey 07079 (201) 762-9000
Chairman: Dr. Barry B. Blakeley Founded 1958

Concentrates on three major geographical and cultural areas: China, Japan and India. In each area work is done in pre-modern and modern history, religion and such disciplines as language and literature, politics, anthropology, philosophy and art. Undergraduate majors and an M.A. in Asian Studies with a Chinese or Japanese concentration as well as a M.A. in general Asian Studies are offered. There are also Chinese and Japanese language programs for undergraduate and graduate fields of concentration.

EAST-WEST CENTER
University of Hawaii
1777 East-West Road
Honolulu, Hawaii 96822
President: Dr. Everett Kleinjans (808) 948-8955
Founded 1970

Nonprofit organization, formally known as Center for Cultural and Technical Interchange between East and West, originally established in 1960 by United States Congress "to promote relations and understanding between the United States and nations of Asia and the Pacific through cooperative study, training and research," located on University of Hawaii campus but separated from the University's administration in 1975 when Hawaii state legislature chartered a nonprofit, educational corporation governed by an international board to operate the Center under agreement with the U.S. Department of State. Supported by United States Government and cooperating Asian/Pacific governments and agencies.

EAST-WEST CULTURE LEARNING INSTITUTE
1777 East-West Road
Honolulu, Hawaii 9684
Director: Dr. Verner C. Bickley Founded 1970

Integral unit of East-West Center, formally known as Center for Cultural and Technical Interchange between East and West, originally established by United States Congress in 1960 in cooperation with University of Hawaii, became problem-oriented in 1970 and a corporate structure separated from the University's administration in 1975. Conducts research in the differences and similarities between cultures and subcultures, also changes that occur when an individual moves from one culture to another, including studies concerned with cultural identity, role of language in culture, transcultural education, international uses of the English language, transnational organizations, and cultural aspects of treaty negotiation. Also provides graduate instruction and facilities for professional development of new knowledge gained through its research.

EAST-WEST ENVIRONMENT AND POLICY INSTITUTE
1777 East-West Road
Honolulu, Hawaii 96844

Recently established problem-oriented unit of East-West Center conducting research and other programs of the Center in close and cooperative relation with the University of Hawaii and utilizing its facilities.

EAST-WEST RESOURCE SYSTEMS INSTITUTE
1777 East-West Road
Honolulu, Hawaii 96848 (808) 948-8694
Director: Dr. Harrison Brown Founded 1977

Problem-oriented integral unit of East-West Center conducting research and other programs of the Center in close and cooperative relation with University of Hawaii and utilizing its facilities. Supported by parent institution, United States Government and various other research grants. Studies resource systems and their interrelation with emphasis on food systems, energy systems and raw materials systems. Includes interdisciplinary studies of how nations can maintain adequate, equitable and reliable access to such resources and exploration of feasibility, advantages and costs of moving resource systems of East-West area toward greater stability and resilience, stressing interrelationship of these problems in both local and international terms in Asian and Pacific regions. Research results published in project-generated books, monographs, professional and scientific journals and workshop and conference reports. Holds international workshops and conferences each year.
Publication: RSI Newsletter (quarterly)

INSTITUTE OF ASIATIC AFFAIRS
University of Oklahoma
Norman, Oklahoma 73069 (405) 534-2797
Director: Dr. Sidney D. Brown Founded 1952

Performs historical, cultural, economic and political studies on countries of the Orient, with a view to stimulating interest and providing information on oriental affairs in the University, the state and the Southwest. Also secures for the University books, magazines, pamphlets and primary research materials in English, Chinese and Japanese as background for its research efforts, to which are also being added Hindi, Urdu and Korean language material.
Publications: Research results published in professional and popular journals, monographs and newspapers.

PACIFIC AND ASIAN LINGUISTICS INSTITUTE
2635 South King Street
Honolulu, Hawaii 96822
Director: Professor Donald M. Topping (808) 944-8930
Founded 1965

Research is devoted to general theory and specific problems of lexicography, structural semantics and grammatical theory and description of languages and linguistics of the Pacific and adjacent areas, including studies of seven Austronesian languages, contrast of pidgin Hawaiian with a standard variety of English, phonological algorithms needed to convert Korean morphophonemic orthography into phonetic representation, Japanese syntax and computerizable models of language change and linguistic comparison, also preparation of pedagogical materials for courses in linguistic theory and in languages of the Pacific and of a dictionary and comparative linguistic materials for languages of the Pacific.
Publication: Oceanic Linguistics, semiannual.

EAST ASIA

ASIAN STUDIES PROGRAM
University of Notre Dame
Notre Dame, Indiana 46556 283-6377
Director: Peter Moody Founded 1973

Conducts research and teaching in Chinese and Japanese History, Politics, Japanese Language and Literature.

ASIAN STUDIES PROGRAM
University of Pittsburgh
4E05 Forbes Quadrangle
Pittsburgh, Pennsylvania 15260 (412) 624-5566
Director: Dr. Keith Brown Founded 1960

Studies Chinese and Japanese culture, including interdisciplinary language and area studies in anthropology, economics, fine arts, geography, history, linguistics, philosophy, political science and sociology. Also provides instruction in East Asian studies at the University. Formerly known as East Asian Center.

Holds series of research seminars and lectures by visiting scholars. Maintains a library of over 86,500 volumes on Chinese, Japanese and Korean classics, history and literature, plus 1,210 titles of current Chinese and Japanese periodicals and 7,255 volumes of bound journals in Chinese, Japanese and Korean. Publications: Research results published in professional journals and books.

CENTER FOR EAST ASIAN STUDIES
Stanford University
Stanford, California 94305 (415) 497-3362
Director: Professor Peter Duus Founded 1957

Research carried out in history, cultures, social sciences and languages of East Asia, with emphasis on China and Japan, including a number of independent interdisciplinary projects and a variety of public education programs in cooperation with secondary schools, local colleges, civic groups and businesses. Also provides graduate instruction and research training in these fields. Holds weekly colloquia on a wide variety of topics and periodic ongoing problem-centered workshops. Utilizes East Asian collection of 200,000 titles and 2,000 periodicals in Hoover Institution on War, Revolution and Peace. Publications: Research results published in professional journals and books.

CENTER FOR EAST ASIAN STUDIES
University of Kansas
Lawrence, Kansas 66044
Co-Directors: Chae J. Lee and Cameron Hurst (913) 864-3849
Founded 1958

Concentrates on East Asian countries, including studies on modern China, modern Korea especially since 1945, Japanese in the Pacific Islands 1916-45 and Philippine voting behavior. Also coordinates faculty research, graduate and undergraduate instruction and other programs relating to East Asia at the University. Maintains a library of 55,000 volumes on Chinese communism, Japanese left wing movements and Japan in the Pacific, including many in Chinese, Japanese and Korean. Publications: Research results published in monographs and books.

CENTER FOR FAR EASTERN STUDIES
Kelly Hall 403
5848 University Avenue
Chicago, Illinois 60637 (312) 753-2632
Director: William L. Parish Founded 1959

Faculty research on China and Japan includes studies in the humanities (languages and literature), political science, sociology, history, comparative religions, library science, geography, linguistics, art history and business administration. Publications: Newsletter; also publishes selected papers from the Center for Far Eastern Studies and a Resource Guide on China and Japan for Teachers in the Chicago Area.

CENTER FOR ASIAN STUDIES
University of Rochester
555 Rush Rhees Library
Rochester, New York 14627
Director: Professor Robert B. Hall, Jr. (716) 275-2521
Founded 1965

Research centers primarily on the cultures of East Asia; also some studies on South Asia. Maintains a library of 27,000 volumes on South Asia in various languages. Formed by the East Asian Language and Area Center and the South Asian Language and Area Center. Publications: Research results published in professional journals.

COUNCIL ON EAST ASIAN STUDIES
Yale University, Box 13A
New Haven, Connecticut 06520
Director: Professor Edwin McClellan (203) 436-0627

Field of research are those fields covered by faculty in East Asian Studies: Anthropology, East Asian Languages and Literatures (Japanese, Chinese and some Korean), Economics, History, History of Art, Political Science, Religious Studies and Sociology. Administers M.A. Program in East Asian Studies as well as an undergraduate major.

EAST ASIA JOURNALISM PROGRAM
Graduate School of Journalism
Journalism Building
Columbia University
New York, New York 10027 (212) 280-3844
Director: Dr. Frederick T. C. Yu Founded 1967

A three-year study program sponsored jointly by the Graduate School of Journalism and the East Asian Institute of Columbia University leading to a Master of Science degree in journalism and the certificate of the East Asian Institute. Objective is to "produce competent foreign correspondents who combine the arts and skills of a journalist with the knowledge and discipline of an East Asia specialist." Involves intensive study of Chinese or Japanese language and culture with journalism graduate courses.

EAST ASIAN INSTITUTE
Columbia University
420 West 118th Street
New York, New York 10027 (212) 280-2591
Director: Dr. Gerald L. Curtis Founded 1949

Integral unit of School of International Affairs at Columbia University. Principal fields of research concentrate on modern and contemporary conditions in east Asia, with emphasis on social sciences, including studies on contemporary China, Japan and Korea and on United States-East Asian relations, and a Chinese oral history project. Also serves as a graduate teaching body preparing specialists for college and university teaching, government service and careers in public life related to east Asia. Holds occasional conferences with specially invited participants, special lectures and seminars for graduate students. Maintains documentation centers on Japan and China, collecting materials on contemporary social sciences in addition to a library of 295,000 volumes in all fields relating to China, Japan and Korea except natural sciences.
Publications: East Asian Institute Studies Series.

EAST ASIA LANGUAGE AND AREA CENTER
Randall Hall, University of Virginia
Charlottesville, Virginia 22903
Co-Directors: John Israel and William Speidel (804) 924-3303
Founded 1975

Research performed in Chinese History, Chinese Language, literature and linguistics both classical and modern, Chinese Government and Politics; Japanese Government and Politics; Chinese and Japanese Art History, Buddhism and Chinese Religions; East Asian Architecture, Philosophy and Education.

EAST ASIAN LEGAL STUDIES PROGRAM
Harvard University
Cambridge, Massachusetts 02138 (617) 495-3117
Assistant Dean: David N. Smith Founded 1954

A part of the International Legal Studies Program. Studies the legal and institutional bases of economic development, tax systems, and the legal framework for international trade and investment.

EAST ASIAN RESEARCH CENTER
Harvard University
1737 Cambridge Street
Cambridge, Massachusetts 02138 (617) 495-4046
Director: Professor Ezra F. Vogel Founded 1955

Integral unit of Harvard University; formerly called Center for East Asian Studies. Research conducted in East Asia, including economic, political, history, social and legal studies of People's Republic of China, Korea, Vietnam and Japan, also studies on Chinese cultural heritage and foreign relations, including Sino-Russian relations and diplomatic history. Also provides editorial and bibliographical assistance for publications of research based on Chinese, Japanese, Korean, Vietnamese and Russian sources. Holds conferences, colloquia, seminars and meetings with visiting scholars. Maintains a small reading and research collection, mainly in western languages and in language of People's Republic of China.
Publications: Annual Report; Harvard East Asian Series; Harvard East Asian Monographs; Asia News Bulletin.

EAST ASIAN STUDIES
Wittenberg University
Springfield, Ohio 45501 (513) 327-7433
Director: Eugene R. Swanger Founded 1970

Publications: Oracle Bones of Shang Dynasty; History of the Japanese Press; Japanese Folk Religions.

EAST ASIAN STUDIES CENTER
University of Southern California
University Park
Los Angeles, California 90007 (213) 741-5080
Director: Sumako Kimizuka Founded 1958

Studies art, religion, education, politics, history, linguistics, language and literature with particular reference to Asian countries, including studies of Chinese and Japanese literature, Chinese communism, Sino-Soviet relations and methods of teaching Chinese and Japanese languages, also development of teaching materials for secondary schools. Research results published in books and professional journals.

EAST ASIAN STUDIES PROGRAM
Indiana University
Goodbody Hall 248
Bloomington, Indiana 47401
Department Chairman: Professor Irving Y. Lo (812) 337-1992
Founded 1963

Research and teaching activity of Department of East Asian Languages and Cultures at Indiana University conducted under supervision of an interdepartmental faculty. Supported by public and private funds. Staff drawn from various disciplines at the University. Principal fields of research: Chinese and Japanese classical and modern language and literature, East

Asian history, government, anthropology, fine arts, economics, folklore, religions and law, comparative study of literature, and literary relationships. Also provides degree programs on both undergraduate and graduate level. Research results published in professional journals, books and student theses.

EAST ASIAN STUDIES PROGRAM
University of Wisconsin
1440 Van Hise Hall
Madison, Wisconsin 53706
Chairman: Professor Edward Friedman (608) 262-3643
Founded 1961

Research centers on East Asia, including studies in anthropology, history, Buddhism, political science, economics, communications, geography, business, sociology, history of science, comparative literature and languages, labor, theatre, cinema, language, literature. Also provides instruction in East Asian area studies and languages at the University. Maintains a growing library on East Asian countries and their literature, including well over 130,000 volumes in Chinese and Japanese.
Publications: Wen Lin; Chinese Literature.

INSTITUTE OF EAST ASIAN STUDIES
460 Stephens Hall
Berkeley, California 94720
Director: Professor Robert A. Scalapino (415) 642-2809
Founded 1978

Research in the principal social sciences and humanities fields pertaining to East Asian affairs.
Publications: Asian Survey; Early China; China Research Monograph series; Korean Research Monograph series; Japan Research Monograph series; Research Papers and Policy Studies Series; Faculty Reprint Series.

INSTITUTE OF FAR EASTERN STUDIES
Seton Hall University
South Orange, New Jersey 07079 (201) 762-9000
Director: Dr. John B. Bsu
Founded 1951

Research arm of the Department of Asian Studies and Non-Western Civilization, operating under primary control of an advisory board consisting of international scholars. Principal fields of research are in oriental culture and philosophy, including studies on scientific manpower of modern China and preparation of Chinese textbooks and dictionaries, also Chinese and Japanese languages. Also provides graduate and undergraduate instruction in Chinese and Japanese linguistics and area studies. Holds conferences on teaching of Japanese in secondary schools and seminars on Chinese and Japanese linguistics, also summer language institute for high school teachers. Maintains a library of 30,000 volumes on Chinese and Japanese languages, history, philosophy, political sciences and literature. Research results published in professional journals, monographs and books.

PROGRAM FOR THE STUDY OF EAST ASIAN CULTURE
Department of History
University of California at Davis
Davis, California 95616 (916) 752-0776
Director: K. C. Liu
Founded 1979

History, art, religion, politics, literature, economics of China and Japan.

PROGRAM IN EAST ASIAN STUDIES
211 Jones Hall, Princeton University
Princeton, New Jersey 08540
Director: Professor Marion J. Levy, Jr. (609) 452-4276
Founded 1963

Interdepartmental research and training activity at Princeton University. Concerned with language, history and contemporary problems of one or more of the peoples of Asia, with particular focus on civilization and societies of East Asia, their art, history, religion, politics and sociology. Also coordinates undergraduate and graduate instruction in East Asian studies at the University. Utilizes Gest Oriental Library of Princeton University. Research results published in professional journals and monographs.

PROJECT ON ASIAN STUDIES IN EDUCATION
300 Lane Hall
University of Michigan
Ann Arbor, Michigan
Director: Donald Munro

Aims to provide help to teachers and others wishing to know about Asian peoples, particularly China and Japan. Coordinates a speakers' bureau and a resource center; sponsors seminars, workshops and conference centers; prepares resource guides for teaching about China and Japan.

SOUTH AND SOUTHEAST ASIA

CENTER FOR SOUTH AND SOUTHEAST ASIAN STUDIES
2420 Bowditch
Berkeley, California 94720 (415) 642-3608
Director: George F. Dales
Founded 1969

Research unit at University of California located on its Berkeley campus, resulting from merger of Center for South Asia Studies and Center for Southeast Asia Studies. Principal fields of research are in anthropology, art, history, linguistics, philosophy, political science, sociology, languages and literature of south and southeast Asian countries, usually through support of research projects of individual faculty members of the University. Maintains a south and southeast Asia reading room providing bibliographic services and featuring periodicals, newspapers and reference materials in Western and indigenous languages. Holds periodic colloquia and seminars bringing together faculty members and students from various disciplines for exchange of ideas and information and often involving visiting scholars.
Publications: Research Monograph Series; Occasional Papers Series.

CENTER FOR SOUTH AND SOUTHEAST ASIAN STUDIES
University of Michigan
130 Lane Hall
Ann Arbor, Michigan 48109
Directors: Professor Madhar M. Deshpande and Avam A. Yengoyan — (313) 764-0352 — Founded 1961

Studies aspects of social, economic and political modernization in southeast Asia and cultures, including art, music, drama, literature and languages, of South and Southeast Asia. Also directs a studies program, with principal responsibilities for stimulating and facilitating training and research activities dealing with important areas of Southeast Asia and the Indian subcontinent in various departments and schools in the University and provides an organized focus for area and language programs and research interests of faculty and graduate students. Holds both lecture courses and graduate seminars in various schools and departments of the University. Maintains specialized library collections on South and Southeast Asia.

CENTER FOR SOUTH ASIAN STUDIES
Randall Hall, University of Virginia
Charlottesville, Virginia 22903 — (804) 924-3173
Director: Richard B. Barnett — Founded 1976

Growing out of the South Asia Area Studies Committee established in 1962, the Center supports and coordinates curriculum and degree programs at the University which may lead to a B.A. in Asian Studies. Masters and Ph.D. degrees with South Asian concentration are available in Anthropology, Government and Foreign Affairs, History, Religious Studies, Sociology and Education. The Center does not itself confer degrees. Language training is offered in Hindi-Urdu, Persian, Arabic, Sanskrit, Pali, Buddhist Hybrid Sanskrit and Tibetan. Cooperates with the Division of Parapsychology in research related to South Asian reincarnation phenomena. Other activities of the Center include maintaining a film lending library for use by other institutions and individuals; obtaining and allocating funds for projects related to the study of South Asia; arranging for guest speakers at inter-disciplinary South Asia Seminars, held biweekly throughout the academic year; performing outreach functions such as teachers' workshops, curriculum review for member institutions of the Virginia Consortium for Asian Studies, and exchange teaching programs; aiding in library acquisitions; sponsoring cultural events that are open to the general public, such as concerts by Nikhil Banerjee and Yamini Krishnamurti, and public lectures by His Holiness the Dalai Lama; inviting distinguished visiting professors; and coordinating interdisciplinary projects with the School of Medicine and the School of Architecture. The Center has a collection of 300,000 volumes of South Asian published materials, many relevant periodicals, journals, newspapers and reference works available at Alderman Library.

CENTER FOR SOUTHEAST ASIAN STUDIES
Northern Illinois University
Dekalb, Illinois 60115 — (815) 753-1771
Director: Dr. Donn V. Hart — Founded 1963

Research in social science and humanities topics dealing with Southeast Asia, including studies in anthropology, ethnomusicology, art history, geography, history, sociology, political science, linguistics and southeast Asian languages. Also coordinates southeast Asian studies offered by various departments of the University, develops specialized library and research facilities, facilitates research by graduate students and faculty members, promotes exchange programs with universities in southeast Asia and provides consultation to colleges desiring assistance in development of Asian studies programs. Maintains a special collection of 25,000 volumes on Southeast Asia in University library.
Publications: Special Reports and Occasional Papers (both serially as monographs).

CENTER FOR SOUTHEAST ASIAN STUDIES
4113 Helen C. White Hall
600 North Park Street
Madison, Wisconsin 53706 — (608) 263-1755
Director: Daniel F. Doeppers — Founded 1966

Promotes and coordinates activities of faculty and students having teaching and/or research interests in Southeast Asia (specifically Indonesia, Malaysia, Thailand, the Philippines, Vietnam, Singapore, Burma, and Cambodia.) The Center does not offer courses or award degrees, but advises students with interests in Southeast Asia and facilitates the development of

interdisciplinary programs. Students with a concentration in Southeast Asia are enrolled in degree programs in various departments such as: History, Anthropology, South Asian Studies, Linguistics, Political Science, and Library Science. The academic program is enriched by a series of lunchtime speakers, both local and visiting, who report on current research and cultural activities.
Publications: Wisconsin Papers on Southeast Asia; Bibliographical Series; Monograph Series.

COMMITTEE ON SOUTHERN ASIA STUDIES
University of Chicago
1130 East 59th Street
Chicago, Illinois 60637
Chairman: Professor Edward C. Dimock (312) 753-4350
Founded 1959

Integral unit of University of Chicago, but with its own board of control. Research concentrates on south and southeast Asia, ranging from classical culture of Indian subcontinent through modern Asian demography and including history, art, anthropology and a dozen other disciplines in humanities and social sciences with reference to area comprised of India, Bangladesh, Pakistan, Sri Lanka, Nepal, Sikkim and Bhutan. Also provides instruction in these fields in various degree-granting departments of the University. Holds periodic seminar programs. Maintains a library of more than 100,000 volumes and bound serials relating to South Asia in various collections in the University's library system, all listed in general catalog of Regenstein Library. Formerly called South Asia Language and Area Center.

DEPARTMENT OF SOUTH ASIA REGIONAL STUDIES
University of Pennsylvania
820 Williams Hall
Philadelphia, Pennsylvania 19174 (215) 594-7475
Chairman: Dr. Richard D. Lambert Founded 1948

Studies anthropology, art, economics, geography, political and cultural history, linguistics, literature, philosophy, public health, political science, religion, music, dance, theatre, sociology and archaeology of India, Pakistan, Bangladesh, Sri Lanka, Afghanistan and Nepal, also language studies of Bengali, Gujarati, Hindi, Malayalam, Maranthi, Nepali, Pali, Persian, Prakrit, Sanskrit, Sinhalese, Tamil, Telugu, and Urdu. Holds a weekly South Asia seminar for faculty members and advanced graduate students of the University and an annual summer school program. Maintains a library of 250,000 volumes on South Asia.

PROGRAM IN COMPARATIVE STUDIES ON SOUTHERN ASIA
Duke University
Center for International Studies
Durham, North Carolina 27706
Chairman: Professor Bruce B. Lawrence
Founded 1961

Research facility and training program for graduate students at Duke University. Research in the political and economic development of southern Asia. Also provides systematic training of graduate students in anthropology, economics, education, history, political science, religion and sociology, with special emphasis on Commonwealth countries of southern Asia (India, Pakistan, Ceylon, Malaysia, Singapore and Brunei), and an area and language training center for Hindi, Urdu and the vernaculars. Utilizes facilities of Duke University Library, which has 12,000 holdings in Hindi, Urdu and Bengali and substantial collections of 19th and early 20th Century newspapers, pamphlets and public documents drawn from major archival research collections in London and India. Research results published in monographs and occasional papers.

SOUTH ASIA PROGRAM
Cornell University
130-A Uris Hall
Ithaca, New York 14853
Director: Professor Kenneth A. R. Kennedy (607) 256-4958
Founded 1951

Research activity of Department of Asian Studies at Cornell University; formerly known as India Program. Principal fields of research are in economics, anthropology, government, tribal peoples, language, change and development in South Asia. Also supports course work and graduate training in South Asian studies. Research results published in professional journals, books and monographs.

SOUTH ASIA PROGRAM
Syracuse University
823 East Raynor Avenue
Syracuse, New York 13210 (315) 476-5541
Director: Dr. Robert I. Crane Founded 1963

Research activity of Maxwell Graduate School of Citizenship and Public Affairs at Syracuse University. Does research on south Asia, especially India, Pakistan and Ceylon, including studies on development, urbanism and metropolitan problems. In collaboration with Departments of Anthropology, Geography, History, Political Science, Religion and Sociology also provides graduate instruction in these fields and in South Asian languages and linguistics at the University. Holds annual symposia and monthly colloquia on some major aspect of South Asian studies and, in the summer, special training programs at the University and study-tour programs in India for selected high school teachers. Maintains a library of 35,000 volumes on modern South Asia. Research results published in professional journals and books.

SOUTH ASIAN CENTER
Kansas State University
Manhattan, Kansas 66502
Director: Dr. Kenneth W. Jones Founded 1967

Conducts research in South Asian culture, history, politics and sociology, including studies on history of Panjab, princely state politics in India and Indian village culture. Also provides South Asian language and area instruction. Holds periodic colloquia on diverse South Asian subjects, for faculty members and interested graduate students. Maintains a library of 1,000 South Asian language books, also Indian periodicals. Research results published in professional journals and books.

SOUTH ASIAN STUDIES CENTER
University of Wisconsin
1242 Van Hise Hall
Madison, Wisconsin 53706
Director: Professor M. K. Verma (608) 262-3012
Founded 1960

Integral unit of Department of South Asian Studies at University of Wisconsin; previously known as Indian Language and Area Center. Studies anthropology, ancient, medieval and modern history, linguistics, languages and literatures, philosophy, political science, religion and sociology of South Asia. Holds annual conferences on South Asia. Maintains a special collection of 20,000 volumes on Indian languages, history and religion in humanities section of University's Memorial Library. Research results published in professional journals, general periodicals and books.

SOUTHEAST ASIA PROGRAM
Cornell University
120 Uris Hall
Ithaca, New York 14850
Director: Dr. Stanley J. O'Conner (607) 256-2378
Founded 1951

Research activity of Department of Asian Studies at Cornell University. Investigates social and political conditions in countries of southeast Asia, their history and cultures, including Brunei, Burma, Democratic Kampuchea, Indonesia, Laos, Malaysia, Philippines, Singapore, Thailand and Vietnam; their cultural stability and change, especially consequences of modern Western influences; political behavior and political organization; international relations between southeast Asia and the Chinas, India, Soviet Union and United States, economic development; economic nationalism; comparative linguistics of southeast Asia ; organization and role of major Asian minorities in the region; and tribal peoples and their acculturation. Is preparing Indonesian-English, Cebuano, Yao-English, Akha-English and White-Meo-English dictionaries, Thai cultural readers, A.U.A. Thai lessons and Indonesian lessons and tapes. Also provides instruction and graduate research training in southeast Asia language and area studies at the University. Holds annual series of area-focused and problem seminars and intensive summer language programs. Maintains a library on southeast Asia (catalog of holdings published in spring 1976). Research results published in professional journals, monographs, books and data papers.

SOUTHEAST ASIA STUDIES PROGRAM
Ohio University
56 East Union Street
Athens, Ohio 45701
Director: Dr. Donald Jordan

Integral unit of Center for International Studies at Ohio University. Principal fields of research: Anthropology, sociology, economics, history, political science and languages of various countries of southeast Asia. Also provides instruction in this field at the University. Utilizes major southeast Asia library collection maintained as part of the University collection.

SOUTHERN ASIAN INSTITUTE
Columbia University
622 West 113th Street
New York, New York 10025 (212) 280-4662
Director: Ainslie T. Embree Founded 1966

Integral unit of School of International Affairs at Columbia University. Performs general social science studies relating to south and southeast Asia, including Afghanistan, India, Pakistan, Nepal, Sri Lanka, Malaysia and Indonesia. Also provides support for individual scholarly work, directs and administers larger projects and coordinates departmental programs at the University as they bear on southern Asia. In 1970 reactivated a Pakistan center for research and scholarly exchange. Research results published in a series of southern Asian books. Holds monthly seminars.

ASIAN AMERICANS

ASIAN AMERICAN BILINGUAL CENTER
Berkeley Unified School District
2168 Shattuck Avenue
Berkeley, California 94704
Director: Linda Wing (415) 848-3199

Prepares curriculum material for Chinese, Japanese, Korean and Filipino languages.

ASIAN AMERICAN EDUCATION PROGRAM
University of Colorado, Denver
1100 Fourteenth Street
Denver, Colorado 80202 (303) 629-2578
Director: Frederick Hom Dow Founded 1972

The program is responsible for the Asian American Studies program which is under the Department of Ethnic Studies. Offers classes in the History and Sociology of Asian-Pacific American minority communities. Administers admission, financial aid and academic support services for Asian-Pacific American students who are permanent residents or citizens of the United States.

ASIAN AMERICAN EDUCATIONAL OPPORTUNITY PROGRAM
Campus Box 136, University of Colorado
Boulder, Colorado 80309 (303) 492-8461
Director: Phil Hays Founded 1970

Engages in research (based on own work experience and data as well as published material) on the subject of Asian/Pacific American needs in higher education, especially as it relates to personal/social/cultural adjustment and developing. Counsels Asian/Pacific Americans in higher education. Establishes admissions and retention parameters, especially in regard to immigrant and refugee students.

ASIAN AMERICAN STUDIES/ASIAN LANGUAGES (CHINESE AND JAPANESE) PROGRAMS
California State University Long Beach
1250 Bellflower Boulevard
Long Beach, California 90840 (213) 498-4821
Acting Director: Lloyd Inui Founded 1970

An ethnic studies program emphasizing Asian Americans, Chinese, Indochinese, Japanese, Koreans, Filipinos and Pacific Islanders. Also administers the Chinese and Japanese language programs.
Publications: Echoes From Gold Mountain.

ASIAN AMERICAN STUDIES CENTER
University of California at Los Angeles
3232 Campbell Hall
Los Angeles, California 90024
Director: Professor Lucie Cheng Hirata (213) 825-2974
Founded 1965

Principal field of research is in Asian Americans and their characteristics and problems. Also responsible for stimulation, coordination and assistance of faculty research into history, culture, conditions, problems and potentialities of its subject ethnic group. Assists departments of the University in recruiting and attracting capable scholars. Enhances library holdings and other needed research resources. Stimulates course innovation through appropriate departments, schools and colleges of the University and by interdisciplinary curriculum development and provides assistance to the community by making available expertise of its staff for solution of problems identified and studied by them. Holds weekly seminars on critical issues in Asian American studies and exploration of current research in various social sciences related to Asians and Asian-Americans. Maintains a library on history and current experience of five major Asian-American groups: Chinese, Japanese, Korean, Filipino and Samoan.
Publication: Amerasia Journal, semiannual.

ASIAN AMERICAN STUDIES PROGRAM
School of Social Sciences
California State University, Fresno
Fresno, California 93740 (209) 487-1002
Director: Dr. Franklin Ng Founded 1969

Centers on Asian Americans and Pacific Islanders. Also offers courses.

ASIAN BILINGUAL CROSS CULTURAL DEVELOPMENT CENTER
615 Grant Avenue, 2nd Floor
San Francisco, California 94108
Director: George Woo (415) 781-2472

Chinese and Filipino language and cultural studies are conducted.

ASIAN BILINGUAL CURRICULUM DEVELOPMENT CENTER
Seton Hall University
Parrish House
162 South Orange Avenue
South Orange, New Jersey 07079
Director: Byounghye Chang (201) 762-4382

Chinese, Japanese and Korean educational materials are researched and prepared for schools.

ASIAN STUDIES DEPARTMENT
Ethnic Studies Division
City College of the City University of New York
138th Street and Convent Avenue
New York, New York 10031 (212) 690-8267
Director: Professor Betty Lee Sung Founded 1971

Conducts research on Asians in America - their history, communities, contemporary problems, political participation and laws pertaining to them. Principal publications have been centered on the Chinese in the United States.

ETHNIC STUDIES PROGRAM, UNIVERSITY OF HAWAII-MANOA
East-West Road 4, Room 4D
Honolulu, Hawaii 96822 (808) 948-8086
Director: Dr. Franklin S. Odo Founded 1970

Focuses on the historical and contemporary contributions and experiences of Hawaii's multi-ethnic people as viewed from their perspective. The aim is to encourage students to understand and appreciate their unique ethnic heritage and roots as well as those of other ethnic groups in the community. Ethnic groups covered are Japanese, Chinese, Filipinos, Caucasians, Blacks, Hawaiians, Koreans and American Indians. Is carrying out an Oral History Project.
Publications: Ethnic Studies Newsletter (Ka Maka'-Ainana); Waialua & Haleiwa: The People Tell Their Story: Life Histories of Native Hawaiians; The 1924 Filipino Strike on Kauai; Women Workers in Hawaii's Pineapple Industry; Uchinanchu: A History of Okinawans in Hawaii.

NATIONAL ASIAN CENTER FOR BILINGUAL EDUCATION
10801 National Boulevard, Suite 102
Los Angeles, California 90064
Director: Mieko S. Han (213) 474-7173

Specializes in Chinese, Japanese, Korean, Vietnamese, Cambodian and Laotian studies pertaining to problems of education. Prepares curriculum materials.

NATIONAL MULTILINGUAL/MULTICULTURAL MATERIALS DEVELOPMENT CENTER
California State Polytechnic University
Building 55
3801 West Temple Avenue
Pomona, California 91768
Director: Roberto Ortiz (714) 598-4991

Korean and Vietnamese educational curricula and materials are researched and prepared for dissemination.

PACIFIC/ASIAN-AMERICAN MENTAL HEALTH CENTER
1640 West Roosevelt Road
Chicago, Illinois 60608 (312) 226-0117
Director: Dr. William T. Liu Founded 1974

Separately incorporated nonprofit organization independently affiliated with University of Illinois at its Chicago Circle campus, with its own board of control and a community advisory board. Concerned with identifying, understanding and helping to solve problems encountered by Americans of Asian and Pacific Island backgrounds, including a four-year follow-up study of refugees from Vietnam and social structure of a Samoan community in a west coast city. Also serves as a consultant to regional and local organizations who are developing research projects and maintains a scholar-in-residence program that brings other community-knowledgeable researchers into the Center's activities. Holds a summer research workshop for individuals involved in research in related areas. Maintains a constantly expanding documentation center on Pacific/Asian-American population, a file of Asian-American mental health professionals interested in learning about employment opportunities and a comprehensive Asian/Pacific-American Mental Health Directory which lists several thousand persons and their professional affiliations.
Publications: P/AAMHRC Newsletter, quarterly. Also publishes a monograph series, bibliographies and occasional papers.

U.S. Government Programs

ASIAN/PACIFIC AMERICAN CONCERNS STAFF
United States Department of Education
400 Maryland Avenue, Southwest
Room 501, Reporter's Building
Washington, D.C. 20202 (202) 472-4646
Director: Stephen Thom Founded 1977

Promotes equal educational opportunity in both public and non-public educational institutions; works to ensure equal access to policy development, regulatory processes, employment counseling and guidance, grants and programs.

EAST-WEST CENTER
1777 East-West Road
Honolulu, Hawaii 96848 (808) 944-7111
President: Victor Haoli Founded 1960

Established by Congress as a national educational institution to promote better relations and understanding among the nations and peoples of Asia, the Pacific and the United States through cooperative study,

training and research. Multidisciplinary, problem-oriented projects conducted through the center's East-West Communication Institute, East-West Culture Learning Institute, East-West Environment and Policy Institute, East-West Population Institute, East-West Resource Systems Institute and Open Grants. Provides awards to scholars, researchers, graduate students and professionals in business and government at a ratio of one American to two Asian/Pacific. Funded by congressional appropriation, cost-sharing with countries, research grants and contributions by Asian-Pacific governments. Holds seminars, conferences and workshops in conjunction with long-term research projects. Also known as Center for Cultural and Technical Interchange Between East and West.
Publications: Asia-Pacific Census Newsletter, quarterly; East-West Culture Learning Institute Report, quarterly; East-West Perspectives, (magazine), quarterly; Environment and Policy Newsletter, quarterly; Language Planning Newsletter, quarterly; Resource Systems Institute Newsletter, quarterly; Catalog of Program Activities, annual; Communication Institute Newsletter, irregular; also publishes occasional reprints, working papers, newsletters and books.

Museums

ASIA HOUSE GALLERY (OF THE ASIA SOCIETY, INCORPORATED)
725 Park Avenue
New York, New York 10021 (212) 751-3210
Director: Allen Wardwell Founded 1956

Collection formed around the Mrs. John D. Rockefeller 3rd Collection of Asian Art. Also has many loan exhibitions of paintings, sculpture, graphics, decorative arts and archaeology. Maintains a 1,600 volume library of books and journals on Asian art and archaeology. Services include tape-recorded guide tours, films, TV and radio programs, loan and traveling exhibitions.

ASIAN ART MUSEUM OF SAN FRANCISCO, THE AVERY BRUNDAGE COLLECTION
Golden Gate Park
San Francisco, California 94118
Director and Chief Curator: (415) 558-2993
Rene-Yvon Lefebvre d'Argence Founded 1969

Collections include nearly 10,000 objects of Asian art, including the Avery Brundage Collection and the Roy C. Leventritt Collection. Conducts research in the arts of Asia, with emphasis on China, Korea, Japan, India, Nepal, Tibet, Southeast Asia and Iran. Maintains over 12,000 volume library on Oriental art and related subjects available for use on premises; conservation laboratory; photography laboratory; auditorium. Services include guided tours; lectures; films; intern program for graduate students; docent council; docent training programs available to public; inter-museum loan, permanent, temporary and traveling exhibitions. Museum sponsors: docent tours for the deaf.
Publications: Handbooks; catalog on museum collections and traveling shows; slides; photographs.

BREEZEWOOD FOUNDATION
3722 Hess Road
Monkton, Maryland 21111 (301) 771-4485
President: Alexander B. Griswold Founded 1955

Primarily a sculpture museum whose collections center around Buddhist art and Southeast Asian art and history. Also maintains an oriental garden.

CRAFT AND FOLK ART MUSEUM
5814 Wilshire Boulevard
Los Angeles, California 90036 (213) 937-5544
Director: Edith R. Wyle Founded 1976

Collections of arts and crafts of the Far East including Japanese folk art, East Indian crafts, folk paintings, sculpture and decorated household artifacts. Offers educational programs and lectures, special exhibitions and workshops.
Publications: Newsletter, quarterly; also publishes exhibition catalogs.

FREER GALLERY OF ART
12th and Jefferson Drive, Southwest
Washington, D.C. 20560 (202) 357-2104
Director: Dr. Thomas Lawton Founded 1906

The art gallery is a part of the Smithsonian Institution. Its collections range over Far Eastern, Indian, Indo-Chinese and Near Eastern bronze, jade, sculpture, painting, lacquer, pottery, porcelain, manuscripts, metalwork and glass. Also owns works by 19th and early 20th century American artists including James McNeill Whistler. Maintains more than 30,000 volume library of books, pamphlets and periodicals half of which are in Chinese and Japanese pertaining to collection available for research in reading room; 40,000 slides and 8,000 study photographs for research purposes; 325 seat auditorium; publications; slides, prints, postcards, reproductions for sale, guided tours lectures, educational programs for graduate students; periodicals, half of which are in Chinese and Japanese pertaining to collections available for research in reading room; slides and study photographs for research purposes;

auditorium and museum shop which sells publications, slides, prints, postcards and reproductions. Services include guided tours; lectures; formally organized education programs for graduate students affiliated with University of Michigan; gallery talks; permanent and temporary exhibitions.
Publications: Ars Orientalis; 2 series of monographs, Freer Gallery of Art Oriental Studies; Freer Gallery of Art Occasional Papers; various booklets and pamphlets.

FOGG ART MUSEUM
Quincy and Broadway
Cambridge, Massachusetts 02138 (617) 495-7768

Collections range through most of Asian art, India, Central Asia, South East Asia, Indonesia, China, Japan as well as other parts of the cultural map. Facilities include tours, films, lectures, workshops and a museum shop. Maintains Rubel Asiatic Research Library.

JACQUES MARCHAIS CENTER OF TIBETAN ARTS
338 Lighthouse Avenue
Staten Island, New York 10306 (212) 987-3478
Director: Joyce T. Cini Founded 1946

A collection of Tibetan and Buddhist art. Facilities include 1,100 volume library of philosophy and Eastern religions available on the premises; reading room; exhibit space; garden. Sponsors lectures; permanent exhibitions; concerts; oriental dancing; poetry readings; Tibetan mystery play; demonstrations; classes and lecture series; Tibetan Harvest Festival; Night in Tibet.

PACIFIC ASIA MUSEUM
46 North Los Robles Avenue
Pasadena, California 91101 (213) 449-2742
Director: David Kamansky Founded 1971

The museum is housed in the Grace Nicholson Building, built in the style of the Chinese Imperial Palace. Its collections include Chinese and Japanese textiles, scrolls, screens, toys, ceramics and other art objects. Research is conducted in the arts related to specific areas of interest including the Pacific and Pacific Basin Countries. Maintains 1,500 volume library of material relating to Oriental Arts, available for research to members and scholars by appointment only. Offers guided tours; lectures; films; gallery talks; concerts; dance recitals; arts festivals; study clubs; hobby workshops; formally organized education programs for adults; docent program; permanent, temporary and loan exhibits and a museum shop which sells books and Oriental art objects.

Special Libraries and Subject Collections

AMERICAN ACADEMY OF ASIAN STUDIES - LIBRARY
134-140 Church Street
San Francisco, California 94114

Subjects: Asia and North Africa. Holdings: Books; bound periodical volumes.

AMERICAN ORIENTAL SOCIETY LIBRARY - YALE UNIVERSITY
Sterling Memorial Library, Room 329
New Haven, Connecticut 06520
Librarian: Rutherford D. Rogers Founded 1843

Subjects: Oriental civilizations - language, literature, history, culture. Holdings: Books, journals and other serials. Services: Collection open only to members of the Society, Yale University personnel, and visiting scholars on application.

ASIA FOUNDATION/LIBRARY
550 Kearny Street
San Francisco, California 94119 (415) 982-4640
Librarian: Amelia Trippe Founded 1951

Subjects: Current Asian affairs - Northeast, South and Southeast Asia. Holdings: Books; drawers of pamphlets; Asian organization material; American and international organization materials; journals and other serials; newspapers. Services: Interlibrary loans; library open to graduate students and others with professional interest in Asia. Mailing Address: Box 3223, San Francisco, California 94119.

ASIA SOCIETY - LIBRARY
725 Park Avenue
New York, New York 10021
Librarian Assistant: Mary Anne Cartelli (212) 288-6400
Founded 1956

Subjects: Literature, religion, politics, geography, other aspects of Asia. Special Collections: Education Library. Holdings: Books and periodicals. Services: Library open to public for reference use only.

ASIAN ART MUSEUM OF SAN FRANCISCO - AVERY BRUNDAGE COLLECTION
Golden Gate Park
San Francisco, California 94118 (415) 558-2993
Librarian: Fred A. Cline, Jr. Founded 1967

Subjects: Oriental art including titles in Oriental languages. Holdings: Books; bound periodical volumes; microfiche; microfilm; pamphlet file, journals and other serials. Services: Copying; library open to public. Special Indexes: Index to sales catalogs; Indexes to Chinese and Japanese paintings in books.

ASIAN CULTURAL EXCHANGE FOUNDATION - LIBRARY
c/o Institutional Development
Towson State University (301) 321-2235
Towson, Maryland 21204 Founded 1952

Subjects: Oriental art and culture. Holdings: Books, reports and manuscripts. Services: Reference and exhibit items available. Remarks: Library was formerly located in Washington, D.C.

CALIFORNIA INSTITUTE OF ASIAN STUDIES - LIBRARY
3494 21st Street
San Francisco, California 94110 (415) 648-1489
Librarian Director: Vern Haddick Founded 1955

Subjects: Philosophy, psychology, religion, Hindu and Buddhist literature, Yoga and Zen discipline, art, Asian languages, counseling. Special Collections: Works of Sri Aurobindo, Gandhi, Nehru, Sivananda, Vivekananda, Raman Maharishi, Haridas Chandhuri. Holdings: Books; dissertations, philosophy and psychology tapes; journals and other serials. Services: Interlibrary loans; library serves the Institute Community.

FREER GALLERY OF ART - LIBRARY, SMITHSONIAN INSTITUTION
Twelfth and Jefferson Drive, Southwest
Washington, D.C. 20560 (202) 357-2091
Librarian: Priscilla P. Smith Founded 1923

Subjects: Art and cultures of the Far East, Near East, and South Asia; history and civilization; art and art history; archaeology, pottery, painting. Special Collections: Washington Biblical manuscripts. Holdings: Books and bound periodical volumes (both Western and Oriental languages); rubbings from Chinese monuments; maps; study photographs; slides. Services: Interlibrary loans; library open to public for reference use only on a limited schedule. Special Indexes: Index to KOKKA and Index to sales catalogs.

INSTITUTE FOR ADVANCED STUDIES OF WORLD RELIGIONS - LIBRARY
Melville Memorial Library, 5th Floor
SUNY at Stony Brook
Stony Brook, New York 11794 (516) 246-8366
President/Librarian: C. T. Shen Founded 1972

Subjects: Buddhism and related subjects in history, philosophy and culture; other Asian religions; Indology; Western religions. Special Collections: Richard A. Gard Collection of Buddhist and Related Studies; Ngiam Hoo-pang Collection of Chinese Buddhist Texts; Christopher S. George Rare Nepalese Manuscript Collection; Galen Eugene Sargent Collection on Asian Studies; D.D. Crescenzo, Dubois LeFevre and John P. Mitton Collections on Pastoral Theology. Holdings: Books; bound periodical volumes; maps (cataloged); Buddhist Canon; Chinese, Tibetan and Pali versions; Tibetan PL 480 (SFC) materials, hardbound and microform; Buddhist Sanskrit manuscripts, microform; pamphlets, offprints and typed manuscripts; journals and other serials. Services: Copying; SDI; library open to public for reference use only. Computerized cataloging; multi-lingual technical term index development. Special Catalogs: Descriptive Catalog of Buddhist Sanskrit Manuscripts in the IASWR Microform Collection; catalog cards for Tibetan PL 480 (SFC) books. (The Institute aims to preserve religious literature which has not received adequate attention from scholars and translators, especially Buddhist material in Chinese and Tibetan. IASWR seeks to provide bibliographic information, as well as publish important religious materials in various languages and the translation of selected texts into English. In addition to the use of microforms, the Institute is developing new, computer-based research tools). Publications: List of publications - available on request.

INSTITUTE OF BUDDHISTS STUDIES - LIBRARY
2717 Haste Street
Berkeley, California 94704
Director: Haruyoshi Kusada (415) 849-2383

Subjects: Buddhism; Japanese religion; oriental philosophy; Japanese in United States; Shin sect. Holdings: Books; bound periodical volumes; clippings; realia budistica; journals and other serials. Services: Interlibrary loans; copying; library open to serious researchers by appointment.

LIBRARY OF CONGRESS - ASIAN DIVISION
John Adams Building, Room 1024
Washington, D.C. 20540
Acting Chief: Dr. Richard C. Howard (202) 287-5420

Subjects: Asian Division contains more than a million volumes in Asian languages. Chinese, especially strong in Ch'ing period (1644-1911); Japanese: especially strong in social sciences and modern history; Korean: with emphasis on historical works and current publications; Southern Asia, literature from Pakistan to Philippines, especially Bengali, Marathi, Hindu, Urdu, Nepali, Indonesian, Vietnamese, Thai, Burmese.

LIBRARY OF CONGRESS - FAR EASTERN LAW DIVISION - LAW LIBRARY
James Madison Memorial Building
Room 235
Washington, D.C. 20540
Chief: Tao-Tai Hsia (202) 287-5085

Subjects: Legal materials on all subjects covering the nations of East and Southeast Asia, including Communist China, Nationalist China, Indonesia, Japan, Korea, Thailand, and former British and French possessions in the area. Holdings: Books, monographs and serials.

MCLAUGHLIN LIBRARY - SETON HALL
405 South Orange Avenue
South Orange, New Jersey 07079
Acting University Librarian:
Reverend James C. Sharp (201) 762-9000

Special Collection: Oriental Collection.

NEW YORK PUBLIC LIBRARY - ORIENTAL DIVISION
Fifth Avenue and 42nd Street
Room 219
New York, New York 10018
Division Chief: E. Christian Filstrup (212) 930-0716
Founded 1897

Subjects: Oriental languages and literature; archaeology of the Ancient East. Special Collections: Arabic manuscripts; Japanese technical periodicals. Holdings: Books; bound periodical volumes; pamphlets. Services: Open to public for reference use only.

PACIFIC HOUSE LIBRARY - PACIFIC AND ASIAN AFFAIRS COUNCIL
2004 University Avenue (808) 941-5355
Honolulu, Hawaii 96816 Founded 1925

Subjects: International affairs, Asia and the Pacific, futuristics, foreign policy, Pacific and Asian foreign policy. Holdings: Books; journals and other serials; newspapers. Services: Interlibrary loans; library open to public.

RESEARCH INSTITUTE FOR INNER ASIAN STUDIES - LIBRARY - INDIANA UNIVERSITY
Goodbody Hall 157
Bloomington, Indiana 47405
Director: Professor Stephen Halkovic (812) 337-1605
Founded 1967

Subjects: Inner Asian history; Inner Asian civilization; Inner Asian linguistics studies. Holdings: Books; journals and other serials. Library open to public.

RUBEL ASIATIC RESEARCH LIBRARY - FOGG ART MUSEUM - HARVARD UNIVERSITY
Quincy and Broadway
Cambridge, Massachusetts 02138
Librarian: Mrs. Yen-Shew Lynn Chao (617) 495-2391
Founded 1932

Subjects: Fine arts of the Far East - India, Central Asia, South East Asia, Indonesia, China, Japan. Holdings: Books and bound periodical volumes; mounted and documented photographs; journals and other serials. Services: Interlibrary loans; library open to public for reference use only on request.

TRINITY UNIVERSITY - LIBRARY
715 Stadium Drive, Box 56
San Antonio, Texas 78284
Library Director: Robert A. Houze (512) 736-8121
Founded 1903

Special Collection: Asian Studies Collection.

UNIVERSITY OF ARIZONA - ORIENTAL STUDIES COLLECTION
University Library
Tucson, Arizona 85721 (602) 626-3695
Head Librarian: Riaz Ahmad Founded 1964

Subjects: Social studies and humanities of China, Japan, South Asia, Middle East; vernacular language materials - Chinese, Japanese, Arabic, Hindi, Urdu, Persian, Turkish. Holdings: Books and bound periodical volumes; microfilm; journals and other serials; newspapers. Services: Interlibrary loans; copying; library open to public by permission.

UNIVERSITY OF HAWAII - ASIA COLLECTION
Hamilton Library, 2550 The Mall
Honolulu, Hawaii 96822 (808) 948-8116
Head: Joyce Wright Founded 1962

Subjects: East, Southeast and South Asia. Holdings: Books; microfilm; microfiche; uncataloged monographs. Services: Interlibrary loans; copying;

library open to public.
Publications: Selected Acquisitions of the Asia Collection.

UNIVERSITY OF SOUTHERN CALIFORNIA - VON KLEINSMID LIBRARY
University Park
Los Angeles, California 90007
Librarian: Mr. Lynn Sipe (213) 743-7347

Subjects: Social sciences, humanities. Holdings: Books; journals and other serials. Services: Interlibrary loans; copying; library open to public for reference use only.

EAST ASIAN

ASIA LIBRARY - UNIVERSITY OF MICHIGAN
Hatcher Graduate Library, 4th Floor
Ann Arbor, Michigan 48109 (313) 764-0406
Head: Weiying Wan Founded 1947

Subjects: East Asian humanities and the social sciences, including anthropology, archaeology, calligraphy, communism, drama, theatre, economics, education, ethics, fine arts, geography, history, journalism, linguistics, phonology, library science, military history, military science, music, political science, religion, sociology. Special Collections: Union Research Institute Classified Files on China; Red Guards materials, classified files in the Cultural Revolution; rare editions of Chinese fiction in Japanese collections; Ming local gazetteers and literary collections; National Peking Library Rare Book Collection on microfilm; British Public Record Office Archives on China; non-Buddhist Tun-huang materials from the British Museum and the Bibliotheque Nationale; Japanese local history; materials on the Occupation of Japan; Japanese literature; Japanese Diet Proceedings; Bartlett Collection of Botanical Works and Materia Medica; Kamada Collection of Pre-War Japanese Works. Holdings: Books in Chinese, Japanese and Korean; microfilm and microfiche in Chinese; microfilm and microfiche in Japanese; journals and other serials; newspapers. Services: Interlibrary loans; copying.
Publications: Selective List of New Acquisitions, bimonthly.

ASIAN COLLECTION - SAINT JOHN'S UNIVERSITY
Grand Central and Utopia Parkways
Jamaica, New York 11439
Assistant Librarian: Hou Ran Ferng (212) 990-6161
Founded 1966

Subjects: Chinese and Japanese literature, history, philosophy, religions, arts. Special Collections: Taoism; Buddhism; Serial bound periodical volumes; Survey of China mainland press since 1958; selections from China mainland magazines since 1960; Mainichi Daily News (Japanese daily newspaper on microfilm, 1960-1973; current background since 1958; journals and other serials; newspapers. Services: Interlibrary loans; copying; library open to public with restrictions.

EAST ASIA LIBRARY - UNIVERSITY OF WASHINGTON
Gowen Hall, DO-27
Seattle, Washington 98195
Head, Asiatic Collection: Karl Lo (206) 543-4490
Founded 1947

Subjects: Social sciences, humanities, natural sciences. Special Collections: Works in Indonesian, Chinese, Japanese, Korean, Mongolian, Thai, Tibetan, Vietnamese. Holdings: Books and bound periodical volumes; microfilm, microfiche; pamphlets; journals and other serials; newspapers. Services: Interlibrary loans; copying; library open to public for reference use only.

RUTGERS UNIVERSITY, THE STATE UNIVERSITY OF NEW JERSEY - ALEXANDER LIBRARY - EAST ASIAN LIBRARY
College Avenue
New Brunswick, New Jersey 08903 (201) 932-7161
Librarian: Dr. Nelson Chou Founded 1970

Subjects: China - language, literature, history, philosophy, religion, arts and sciences; Japanese history; Korean history. Special Collections: Complete microfilm collection of the rare books in the National Central Library, Taiwan; Pamphlet Collection of Tiao-yu-t'ai Problems. Holdings: Books and bound periodical volumes; cataloged items; pamphlets; journals and other serials; newspapers.
Publications: Serial Holding List, irregular - distributed on request.

EAST ASIAN LIBRARY - UNIVERSITY OF KANSAS
Libraries
Lawrence, Kansas 66045 (913) 864-4669
Librarian: Eugene Carvalho Founded 1964

Subjects: Chinese and Japanese history, literature, language, culture; contemporary China; contemporary Japan. Materials primarily in East Asian languages. Holdings: Books and bound periodical volumes; microforms; journals and other serials; newspapers. Services: Interlibrary loans; copying; library open to public.

EAST ASIAN LIBRARY - UNIVERSITY OF MINNESOTA
Wilson Library, S-30
309 19th Avenue, South
Minneapolis, Minnesota 55455
Acting Head: Richard Wang (612) 373-3737

Subjects: Chinese literature and history; Asian art history; Japanese literature and history; Asian bibliography; Sinology. Holdings: Books; journals and other serials. Services: Interlibrary loans; copying; library open to public.

EAST ASIAN LIBRARY - UNIVERSITY OF PITTSBURGH
234 Hillman Library
Pittsburgh, Pennsylvania 15260 (412) 624-4457
Head Librarian: Dr. Thomas Kuo Founded 1960

Subjects: Chinese, Japanese and Korean humanities and social sciences. Special Collections: Complete Sets of KuChin T'u Shu Chi Ch'eng - 1934 photo-lithographic edition of 1728 original collection; Yuan Chien Lei Han (Imperial Palace Block print edition of 1710); Shigaku Zasshi, 1889-present and Rekishi-Gaku Kenkyu, 1928-present. Holdings: Books; bound periodical volumes; microfilm (cataloged); journals and other serials; newspapers. Services: Interlibrary loans; copying; library open to public with patron card. Special Catalogs: East Asian Periodicals and Serials (1970); Catalog of Microfilms of the East Asian Library of the University of Pittsburgh (1971).
Publications: A Selected List of Outstanding New Acquisitions, quarterly.

EAST ASIAN LIBRARY - WASHINGTON UNIVERSITY
Saint Louis, Missouri 63130 (314) 889-5155
Librarian: Ernest J. Tsai Founded 1964

Subjects: Chinese and Japanese materials. Special Collections: Rare Book collection; Robert S. Elegant Collection. Holdings: Books; microfilm; drawers of archival materials; journals and other serials; newspapers. Services: Interlibrary loans; library open to public.
Publications: Guide to Library Resources for Chinese Studies, 1978; Resource Sources for Chinese and Japanese Studies; List of Serials related to Chinese and Japanese Studies, 1973.

JOHN K. FAIRBANK CENTER FOR EAST ASIAN RESEARCH - LIBRARY - HARVARD UNIVERSITY
1737 Cambridge Street
Cambridge, Massachusetts 02138
Librarian: Nancy Hearst (617) 495-5753

Subjects: Post-1949 China, Post-WWII Japan. Holdings: Books; volumes of translation services of the United States Consulate General; journals and other serials. Services: Library open to public with restrictions.
Publications: New Acquisitions: I, China; II, Japan, quarterly.

FAR EASTERN LIBRARY - UNIVERSITY OF CHICAGO
Regenstein Library
1100 East 57th Street
Chicago, Illinois 60637 (312) 753-4116
Curator: James K. M. Cheng Founded 1936

Subjects: Chinese classics, philosophy, history, archaeology, biography, social sciences, literature and art; Japanese history, social sciences, and literature. Special Collections: Chinese classics; Chinese local gazetteers, rare books. Holdings: Books in Chinese, Japanese, Korean, Tibetan, Mongol, Manchu and other Far Eastern languages; as well as Western languages; pamphlets; microforms; journals and other serials. Services: Interlibrary loans; copying; library open to qualified visitors. Special Catalogs: Author-title catalog of Chinese Collection; Author-title catalog of Japanese Collection; classified catalog and subject index of the Chinese and Japanese Collections, 1974; First Supplement to above catalogs, 1979.
Publications: Reference List: Chinese local histories, 1969; Far Eastern serials, 1976.

FAR EASTERN LIBRARY - UNIVERSITY OF ILLINOIS
227 Main Library
Urbana, Illinois 61801
East Asian Librarian: (217) 333-1501
Sheh Wong Founded 1965

Subjects: China and Japan - history, literature, linguistics, economics, sociology; Koreanalia. Special Collection: Japanese rare books. Holdings: Books; journals and other serials. Services: Interlibrary loans; copying; library open to public.

FEMAS TRADE LIBRARY - FAR EAST MERCHANTS ASSOCIATION
1597 Curtis Street
Berkeley, California 94702 (415) 527-3455
Librarian: Ruth R. Goodman Founded 1932

Subjects: Trade with Far Eastern countries, especially China, Japan, Philippine Islands and Singapore. Holdings: Books; bound periodical volumes; pamphlets; journals and other serials. Services: Interlibrary loans; copying; library not open to public. Remarks: Formerly located in Flushing, New York.

FIELD MUSEUM OF NATURAL HISTORY - LIBRARY
Roosevelt Road and Lake Shore Drive
Chicago, Illinois 60605
Head Librarian: W. Peyton Fawcett (312) 922-9410
Founded 1894

Special Collections: East Asian Library (book collection on the Far East); Tibetan xylographs. Services: Interlibrary loans; copying; library open to public. Formerly: Chicago Natural History Museum.

HARVARD YENCHING INSTITUTE - LIBRARY
Harvard University
2 Divinity Avenue
Cambridge, Massachusetts 02138
Librarian: Eugene Wu (617) 495-2756

Subjects: Humanities and social sciences relating to China, Japan, and Korea. Special Collections: Rare Chinese books and manuscripts; rubs from Chinese monumental inscriptions; Tibetan religious book in wood-block print. Holdings: Books; microfilms; journals and other serials. Services: Interlibrary loans; copying.
Publications: Occasional Reference Notes.

INDIANA UNIVERSITY - EAST ASIAN COLLECTION
Bloomington, Indiana 47405
Librarian: Shizue Matsuda (812) 337-9695

Subjects: East Asian (Chinese, Japanese and Korean) humanities, social sciences, history. Special Collections: Ebara Bunko Literature Collection on microfilm. Holdings: Books and bound periodical volumes; microfilms of Chinese newspapers, serials and books; journals and other serials; newspapers. Services: Interlibrary loans; copying; collection open to public.

OHIO STATE UNIVERSITY - EAST ASIAN COLLECTION
1858 Neil Avenue Mall
Columbus, Ohio 43210
Bibliographer: David Y. Hu (614) 422-3520

Subjects: Chinese and Japanese studies. Holdings: Books and bound periodical volumes; journals and other serials; newspapers. Services: Interlibrary loans; library open to public.

ORIENTAL LIBRARY - UNIVERSITY OF CALIFORNIA, LOS ANGELES
21617 University Research Library
Los Angeles, California 90024 (213) 825-4836
Head: Mr. Ik-Sam Kim
Founded 1948

Subjects: Books on art, archeology, history, literature, Buddhism, linguistics, political science, religion and sociology of East Asia in the Chinese, Japanese and Korean languages. Holdings: Books and bound periodical volumes; microfilm; journals and other serials; newspapers. Services: Interlibrary loans; copying; library open to public for reference use only.

ROBERT ALLERTON LIBRARY - HONOLULU ACADEMY OF ARTS
900 South Beretania Street
Honolulu, Hawaii 98614 (808) 538-3693
Librarian: Anne I. Seaman
Founded 1927

Subjects: Art history, especially Chinese and Japanese art. Special Collections: Michigan archives of the Palace Museum, Taiwan. Holdings: Books; bound periodical volumes; pamphlets (cataloged); clippings and announcements; microfilm; journals and other serials. Services: Interlibrary loans; copying; library open to members.

UNIVERSITY OF MARYLAND, COLLEGE PARK - EAST ASIA COLLECTION
College Park, Maryland 20742 (301) 454-5459
Head: Frank Joseph Shulman
Founded 1963

Subjects: Social sciences (Japanese and Chinese languages); modern Japanese and Chinese history and literature; World War II (Pacific area). Special Collections: Gordon W. Prang Collection: Allied Occupation of Japan, 1945-1952. Holdings: Books; bound periodical volumes; microfilm (cataloged); United States Army Allied Translator and Interpreter Service documents and transcripts of International Military Tribunal for the Far East; photograph albums relating to Japanese history and naval affairs; United States Office of Strategic Bombing Survey materials on the interrogation of Japanese officials; journals and other serials; newspapers. Services: Interlibrary loans; library open to public with permission of the Head Librarian. Special Catalogs: Newspapers and periodicals from period of Allied Occupation of Japan - card file.

YALE UNIVERSITY - EAST ASIAN COLLECTION
Sterling Memorial Library
New Haven, Connecticut 06520
Curator: Hideo Kaneko (203) 436-4810

Subjects: East Asian languages and literature, history, art, politics, government, economics, law, social conditions, religion, education, humanities and social sciences. Holdings: Books in Chinese, Japanese and Korean; microfilm. Services: Interlibrary loans; copying; collection open to qualified outside users.

SOUTH AND SOUTHEAST ASIAN

CLEVELAND PUBLIC LIBRARY - JOHN G. WHITE COLLECTION OF FOLKLORE, ORIENTALIA AND CHESS

325 Superior Avenue
Cleveland, Ohio 44114 (216) 623-2818
Head: Alice N. Loranth Founded 1869

Subjects: Orientalia; folklore; chess. Special Collections: Melville papers and papers of the East India Company (manuscripts on British India); India and Southeast Asia; Sanskrit literature; Arabic and Persian literature; Omar Khayyam; Arabian Nights; Tibet; Judaica; Madagascar; Oriental manuscript catalogs.

INTERNATIONAL LIBRARY - MICHIGAN STATE UNIVERSITY

W309-316 University Library
East Lansing, Michigan 48824
Head Professor: Dr. Eugene De Benko (517) 355-2366
Founded 1964

Special Collections: South and Southeast Asia.

KANSAS STATE UNIVERSITY - SOUTH ASIA COLLECTION

Farrell Library
Manhattan, Kansas 66506 (913) 532-6516
Librarian: Sylvia J. Blanding Founded 1968

Subjects: South Asia - history, economics, sociology, politics, languages, literature, religion, philosophy; children's books. Special Collections: Pre-1900 History of India Collection. Holdings: Books; bound periodical volumes; microfiche of Indian Census, 1881-1951; microfilm including South Asian newspapers in English; AV materials; journals and other serials; newspapers. Services: Interlibrary loans; library open to public.

SOUTH AND WEST ASIA LIBRARY - UNIVERSITY OF ILLINOIS

225B Main Library
Urbana, Illinois 61801
South Asian Librarian: Narindar K. Aggarwal (217) 333-2492
Founded 1964

Subjects: South and West Asia - languages, literature, history, culture. Holdings: Books; bound periodical volumes. Services: Interlibrary loans; library open to public.

ASIAN AMERICANS

ASIAN AMERICAN RESOURCE CENTER

c/o Basement Workshop
199 Lafayette Street, Seventh Floor
New York, New York 10012 (212) 925-3258
Director: Jack Tchen Founded 1971

Subjects: History of Asian Americans. Holdings: Books; periodicals, audiovisual materials, archives and oral history.

ASIAN AMERICAN STUDIES LIBRARY - UNIVERSITY OF CALIFORNIA

3407 Dwinelle Hall
Berkeley, California 94720
Head Librarian: Mrs. Wei Chi Poon (415) 642-2218
Founded 1970

Subjects: Asians in the United States past and present; Asia. Holdings: Books; microforms; videotapes; films; journals and other serials and newspapers. Services: Library open to public for reference use only. Publications: Asian American Review, annual. Serves as a support unit for the Oakland Public Library - Asian Community Library.

ASIAN LIBRARY - OAKLAND PUBLIC LIBRARY

449 Ninth Street
Oakland, California 94612 (415) 273-3400
Librarian: Judy Yung Founded 1975

Subjects: Asian-American experience; Asian language and literature - Chinese, Tagalog, Japanese, Korean, Vietnamese. Holdings: Books; clippings; historical pictures; Asian language phonograph records and cassettes; films; filmstrips; journals and other serials; newspapers. Services: Interlibrary loans; copying; library open to public.

Newspapers and Newsletters

ASIA FOUNDATION NEWS. 1976-. Bimonthly. Publisher: The Asia Foundation, Post Office Box 3223, San Francisco, California 94119, (415) 982-4640. In English.

Publishes articles about the Foundation's program in Asia.

ASIA IN WASHINGTON. Monthly. Editor: Liz Nichols. Publisher: Washington Center of the Asia Society and China Council, 1785 Massachusetts Avenue, Northwest, Washington, D.C. 20036. In English.

Gives an overview of events and meetings of interest to residents of the Washington, D.C. area.

THE ASIA LETTER. 1964-. Weekly. Editor: Arthur C. Miller. Publisher: The Asia Letter, Limited, Post Office Box 54149, Los Angeles, California 90054. In English.

Provides an analysis of economic, political, and social developments and trends in the Asian region.

ASIA RECORD. 1980-. Monthly. Editor: Buzz Thompson. Publisher: Asia Pacific Affairs Associates, Incorporated, 580 College Avenue, Palo Alto, California 94306. In English.

Prints articles on current events in East and Southeast Asia.

ASIAN-AMERICAN JOURNEY. Publisher: Agape Fellowship, 332 South Virgil Avenue, Los Angeles, California 90020. In English.

Concentrates on news of interest to Asian American women.

ASIAN FAMILY AFFAIR. 1972-. Monthly. Editor: Kathy Tagawa. Publisher: Asian Family Affair, Incorporated, Box 3445 International Branch, Seattle, Washington 98114. In English.

Speaks to Asian interests in the United States.

THE ASIAN STUDENT. 1952-. Biweekly, September through May. Editor: C. Y. Hsu. Publisher: The Asia Foundation, 550 Kearny Street, San Francisco, California 94108. In English.

Directed toward Asian and Asian American students.

ASIAN STUDIES NEWSLETTER. 1955-. Five times a year. Publisher: Association for Asian Studies, Incorporated, 1 Lane Hall, University of Michigan, Ann Arbor, Michigan 48109. In English.

Provides news of the association, of conferences and meetings, study programs, exhibits, grants and fellowships in Asian Studies. Includes a professional personnel registry and announcements of new publications on Asian studies and related subjects.

ASIAN VOICE. 1974-. Quarterly. Editors: Dr. Dwan Tai and Alfred Liu. Publisher: Asian Benevolent Corps, 2142 F Street, Northwest, Washington, D.C. 20037.

Provides cultural, community service and legal news as well as information about social events.

ASIAN WEEK. 1979-. Weekly. Editor: Patrick Andersen. Publisher: Asian Week, 811 Sacramento Street, San Francisco, California 94108. In English.

Published for Asian Americans in the United States with news of interest on the national, international and local scene.

BRIDGE (NEW YORK); An Asian American Perspective. 1971-. Quarterly. Editors: William P. Wang and N. T. Yung. Publisher: Asian American Perspectives, Box 477, Canal Street Station, New York, New York 10013. In English.

BULLETIN OF CONCERNED ASIAN SCHOLARS. 1969-. Quarterly. Publisher: Bryant Avery, Post Office Box W, Charelemont, Massachusetts 01339, (413) 625-2714. In English.

Newsletter for Asian studies specialists.

BULLETIN OF THE AMERICAN SCHOOL OF ORIENTAL RESEARCH. 1921-. Quarterly. Editor: Dr. William Dever. Publisher: American Schools of Oriental, 1053 LS&A Building, University of Michigan, Ann Arbor, Michigan 48109. In English.

Prints articles on archaeological studies.

CLIPPINGS. Publisher: National Association for Asian and Pacific American Education, 1414 Walnut Street, Room 9, Berkeley, California 94709. In English.

Newsletter of the association.

NEWSLETTER OF PACIFIC ASIAN AMERICANS. MENTAL HEALTH RESEARCH CENTER. Publisher: Pacific Asian American Mental Health Research Center, 1640 West Roosevelt Road, Chicago, Illinois 60608. In English.

ORIENT TIMES. Weekly. Editor: Rodney Bicknell. Publisher: In Yu Wei, Orient Times Publications, 211 East 42nd Street, New York, New York 10017.

Provides news from the Orient particularly financial, cultural, touristic and political as well as coverage of the local Asian Community.

PACIFIC-ASIA REPORT. 1970-. Biweekly. Editor: David W. Carr. Publisher: National Foreign Trade Council, 10 Rockefeller Plaza, New York, New York 10020.

Covers "significant government actions affecting foreign trade and investment climates and major industrial and mineral projects in the Pacific Asia region."

SOUTHEAST ASIA CHRONICLE. 1971-. Six times a year. Publisher: Southeast Asia Resource Center, Post Office Box 4000-D, Berkeley, California 94704. In English.

Prints articles on current events, cultural and historical features for readers interested in Southeast Asia.

WESTERN BODHI. 1963-. Editor: Ven. Dr. H. H. Priebe. Publisher: Universal Buddhist Fellowship, Post Office Box 1079, Ojai, California 93023. In English.

Provides a personal commentary by the president of the fellowship or a contributed article from a member on current events significant to those of the Buddhist faith.

WILL OF DHARMA. 1977-. Monthly. Editor: Elson Snow. Publisher: Buddhist Churches of America, 1710 Octavia Street, San Francisco, California 94109. In English and Japanese.

Official organ of the Buddhist Churches of America.

ZEN BOW NEWSLETTER. 1967-. Quarterly. Publisher: Zen Center, 7 Arnold Park, Rochester, New York 14607.

Magazines

AMERICAN BUDDHIST

ASIA MAGAZINE. 1978-. Six times a year. Editor: Joan Freseman. Publisher: The Asia Society, 725 Park Avenue, New York, New York 10021. In English.

A beautifully illustrated magazine with special feature articles on art, history and culture from various Asian countries. Includes book reviews and commentary. Brings news of the Society and its activities.

ASIAN AFFAIRS, AN AMERICAN REVIEW. 1973-. Bimonthly. Editor: William Henderson, III. Publisher: American-Asian Educational Exchange, Incorporated, 88 Morningside Drive, New York, New York 10027. In English.

A journal of international relations with particular reference to Asia.

ASIAN SURVEY. 1961-. Monthly. Editor: R. A. Scalapino and Leo Rose. Publisher: University of California Press, University of California, Berkeley, California 94720. In English.

Reviews current Asian affairs.

JADE. 1974-. Quarterly. Editor: Gerald Jann. Publisher: Dan Louie Morrison, 3932 Wilshire Boulevard, Suite 208, Los Angeles, California 90010. In English.

Published for Asian Americans with articles showing the variety of living experiences which forms their identify.

JOURNAL OF THE AMERICAN ORIENTAL SOCIETY. 1842-. Quarterly. Editor: Professor Ernest Bender. Publisher: American Oriental Society, 329 Sterling Memorial Library, Yale University, New Haven, Connecticut 06520.

MODERN ASIA. 1967-. Eleven times a year. Editor: Martha Downing. Publisher: Johnston International Publishing Corporation, 386 Park Avenue, South, New York, New York 10016.

Devoted to business analysis and background reports.

Radio Programs

California - Santa Cruz

KUSP - Box 423, Santa Cruz, California 95061, (408) 476-2800. Asian programs, 15 hours weekly.

Massachusetts - Lowell

WJUL (FM) - 1 University Avenue, Lowell, Massachusetts 01854, (617) 459-0579. Asian programs, 1 hour weekly.

Commercial and Trade Organizations

ASSOCIATION OF ASIAN-AMERICAN CHAMBERS OF COMMERCE
Post Office Box 1933
Washington, D.C. 20013
Associate Executive Director: Norman A. Curon — (202) 638-5595
Founded 1965

Maintains speakers bureau, conducts specialized education. Absorbed: Korean-American Chamber of Commerce (founded 1964); Malaysian-American Chamber of Commerce; Chinese-American Chamber of Commerce; and Indonesian-American Chamber of Commerce.
Publications: Asian-American Newsletter, monthly; Asian-American Journal of Commerce, monthly.

FAR EAST-AMERICA COUNCIL OF COMMERCE AND INDUSTRY
475 Park Avenue South
New York, New York 10016
Executive Director: June D. Mayer — (212) 683-4677
Founded 1942

Promotes sound economic relations and the expansion of trade between the countries of Asia and the United States. Conducts meetings, conferences and forums for American and Far Eastern business men and government officials. Formerly: (1949) China-America Council of Commerce and Industry.

FAR EAST CONFERENCE
40 Rector Street, Room 1610
New York, New York 10006
Chairman: Gerald J. Flynn — (212) 269-9073

Rate and rule making organization for steamship lines operating from United States ports on the Atlantic Ocean and Gulf of Mexico to ports in Japan, Korea, Taiwan, Hong Kong, Philippine Islands, Vietnam, Cambodia, Laos, People's Republic of China and Siberia. Publishes Far East Conference Tariff.

HONG KONG TRADE DEVELOPMENT COUNCIL
548 Fifth Avenue
New York, New York 10036
Sr. Representative, U.S.A. Andrew Ma — (212) 582-6610
Founded 1966

Quasi-governmental body responsible for promoting Hong Kong products and creating a favorable image for Hong Kong as a trading partner and manufacturing center. Sponsors trade missions around the world.
Publications: Enterprise - HK, monthly; Hong Kong Cable, monthly; HK Trader, bimonthly; Industrial Investment, annual; Toys, annual; Apparel, biennial.

Bookdealers and Publishers' Representatives

CHRISTOPHER ACKERMAN (Oriental Languages)
180 East Inlet Drive
Palm Beach, Florida 33480

THE ASIAN AMERICAN MATERIALS CENTRE
(materials relating to Asian Americans; also antiquarian)
165 West 66th Street
New York, New York 10023 — (212) 787-7954

RON BEVER (Oriental Art)
Route 3, Box 243 B
Edmond, Oklahoma 73034 — (405) 478-0125

BUDDHIST BOOKSTORE
1710 Octavia Street
San Francisco, California 94109 (415) 776-7877

THE CELLAR BOOKSHOP
(books from Asia, Australia, New Zealand)
18090 Wyoming
Detroit, Michigan 48221 (313) 861-1776

HENRY A. CLAUSEN
(Asian art books)
224 North Tejon Street
Colorado Springs, Colorado 80902 (303) 634-1193

DAR AL KUTUB WAL NASHRAT AL ISLAMIYYA
(books from Africa, Asia, Middle East)
Post Office Box 207
New Brunswick, New Jersey 08901 (201) 249-6961

JEAN E. DOBBS
(oriental art)
Schooley's Mountain, New Jersey
07870 (201) 852-7337

THE EAST AND WEST SHOP
(books on Asia)
4 Appleblossom Lane
Newtown, Connecticut 06470 (203) 426-0661

ET CETERA
(Orientalia)
107 West Locust
San Antonio, Texas 78212 (512) 732-1389

THE GATEWAY BOOKSHOP
(Buddhism and other Eastern religions)
Ferndale, Pennsylvania 18921 (215) 346-7416

GORDON GLADMAN
(Asian art)
441 Desnoyer Avenue
Saint Paul, Minnesota 55104 (612) 644-3564

HAN LIN ORIENTAL BOOK EMPORIUM
Post Office Box 858
Grand Central Station
New York, New York 10017

HUTCHINS ORIENTAL BOOKS
1034 Mission Street
South Pasadena, California 91030 (213) 799-5774

MARK A. KALUSTIAN
(books on Asia)
259 Pleasant Street
Arlington, Massachusetts 02174 (617) 648-3437

E. LANGSTAFF - BOOKS
(United States District Orient Culture Service)
(anthropological and sociological materials on Asia)
919 Fremont Avenue South
Pasadena, California 91030 (213) 441-3233

J. JAMES LEWIS, BOOKSELLERS
(books on Asia)
416 South Benton Way
Los Angeles, California 90057 (213) 383-6507

MOE'S BOOKS
(Asian studies materials)
2484 Telegraph Avenue
Berkeley, California 94704 (415) 849-2087

MISSOURI BOOKSHELF
(books on Karma)
Old Highway 66
Pacific, Missouri 63069 (314) 257-BOOK

NAROPA INSTITUTE BOOKSTORE
2034 14th Street
Boulder, Colorado 80302 (303) 449-6219

JAMES NORMILE, BOOKS
(Asian art)
6888 Alta Loma Terrace
Los Angeles, California 90068 (213) 874-8434

PARAGON BOOK GALLERY LIMITED
14 East 38th Street
New York, New York 10016 (212) 532-4920

A. PARKER'S BOOKS
1465 Main Street
Sarasota, Florida 33577 (813) 366-2898

RICHARD C. RAMER, Old & Rare Books
(Portuguese Asia)
225 East 70th Street
New York, New York 10021 (212) 737-0222

RISING SUN BOOKS
(oriental art)
228 Ray Street
Manchester, New Hampshire 03104 (603) 668-6929

CECIL ARCHER RUSH
(history and culture of Tibet; antiquarian)
1410 Northgate Road
Baltimore, Maryland 21218 (301) 323-7767

ARTHUR SCHARF, TRAVEL BOOKS
(travel in Asia)
5040 Carolyn Drive
Pittsburgh, Pennsylvania 15236 (412) 653-4402

KURT L. SCHWARZ, FINE AND RARE BOOKS
738 South Bristol Avenue
Los Angeles, California (213) 828-7927

SEBASTOPOL BOOK SHOP
(Orientalia)
133 North Main Street
Sabastopol, California 95472 (707) 823-9788

JERROLD G. STANOFF, RARE ORIENTAL BOOK-SELLER
Box 1599
Aptos, California 95003

SAMUEL WEISER, INCORPORATED
740 Broadway
New York, New York 10003 (212) 777-6363

ZEN CENTER OF LOS ANGELES BOOKSTORE
(Japanese)
905 South Normandic Avenue
Los Angeles, California 90006 (213) 387-2357

Books and Pamphlets

ASIA; A Core Collection. Compiled by G. Raymond Nunn. Ann Arbor, Michigan, University Microfilms, 1973. In English.

A listing of 1,000 entries of materials regardless of availability. Excludes reference works, periodical articles and periodicals. Entries are annotated and graded.

ASIA, REFERENCE WORKS: A SELECT ANNOTATED GUIDE. By G. Raymond Nunn. London, Mansell, 1980.

An annotated listing of reference materials in Western languages focusing on the countries of Asia.

ASIAN BIBLIOGRAPHY. By Milton Meyer. Los Angeles, 1967.

A simple listing of books and periodicals on China, Asia (in general), northeast Asia, southeast Asia and south Asia.

ASIAN SOCIAL SCIENCE BIBLIOGRAPHY. Edited by N. K. Goil. Delhi, Vikas Publishing House, 1974.

A listing of books and articles published in 1967 that deal with social science literature on Asia. The majority of the materials has been published in English.

ASSOCIATION FOR ASIAN STUDIES - MEMBERSHIP DIRECTORY. Ann Arbor, University of Michigan, Association for Asian Studies, 1977.

Entries include name, address, primary discipline, primary occupation, country or region of greatest interest, regional conference of greatest participatory interest. Supporting member listings show name and address only.

BIBLIOGRAPHY OF ASIAN STUDIES, 1941. Ann Arbor, Michigan, Association for Asian Studies, Incorporated.

This basic reference work appears annually; latest issue for 1975. Books and periodical articles in Western languages arranged by region, then country, then subject, with an author index.

A BIBLIOGRAPHY OF THE GEOGRAPHICAL LITERATURE ON SOUTHEAST ASIA, 1920-. By Alvar Carlson. Monticello, Illinois, Council of Planning Librarians, 1974.

A listing of articles, reports, books, pamphlets and unpublished masters' theses and doctoral dissertations, written in English and written by geographers or published in geographical periodicals on the geography of Southeast Asia.

BIBLIOGRAPHY OF THE PEOPLES AND CULTURES OF MAINLAND SOUTHEAST ASIA. By John F. Embree and Lillian Ota Dotson. New Haven, Yale University, Southeast Asia Studies, 1950.

Includes four page list of bibliographies. Lists both books and periodical articles. For the most part, arranged by country, then by ethnic group.

BIBLIOGRAPHY ON BUDDHISM. By Shinsho Harayama. Tokyo, Hokuseido Press, 1961.

A comprehensive listing of books and articles on Buddhism in Western languages. Arranged alphabetically by author's name.

BOOKS ON ASIA FROM THE NEAR EAST TO THE FAR EAST; A Guide for the General Reader. By Eleanor Birnbaum. Toronto, University of Toronto Press, 1971.

An annotated listing of works on Asia, its heritage and status at the time. This bibliography, including only English and French books, is divided into four main parts: Asia as a whole; the Islamic world; India, South and Southeast Asia; and the Far East.

BOOKS ON BUDDHISM: AN ANNOTATED SUBJECT GUIDE. By Yushin Yoo. Metuchen, New Jersey, Scarecrow Press, 1976.

Begins with a biographical sketch of Buddha; lists reference works, anthologies and books on various categories such as art, doctrine, fiction, lamaism, missions, monasticism, mythology, inter-faith relations, rituals, school of Buddhism, and yoga, to name but a few. An author, editor, translator index as well as a title index are included.

BOOKS ON SOUTHEAST ASIA: A SELECT BIBLIOGRAPHY. American Institute of Pacific Relations, New York, 1960.

BUDDHISM: A SUBJECT INDEX TO PERIODICAL ARTICLES IN ENGLISH, 1728-1971. By Yushin Yoo. Metuchen, New Jersey, Scarecrow Press, 1973.

Articles are listed topically under such headings as art, biography, civilization, doctrines, education, ethnics, history, literature, missions, mythology, nirvana, Pali Canon, psychology, scriptures, sociology, etc. Included are international directory of Buddhist association, a periodicals list as well as title and author/subject index.

CUMULATIVE BIBLIOGRAPHY OF ASIAN STUDIES, 1941-1965. 8 volumes. Boston, G. H. Hall, 1969-1970.

CUMULATIVE BIBLIOGRAPHY OF ASIAN STUDIES, 1966-70. 8 volumes. Boston, G. H. Hall, 1971-1972.

Each set of eight volumes has listings by authors and by subjects. This bibliography is exhaustive in scope and detail.

DIRECTORY OF ASIAN AND AFRICAN LIBRARIANS IN NORTH AMERICA. Edited by Henry Scholberg. Chicago, American Library Association, Association of College and Research Libraries, 1978.

Covers about 460 librarians active in library services concerned with Asia and Africa (special language capabilities, cataloging, collection development, acquisitions, instruction, etc.) or members of the Asian and African Section of ALA. Entries include name, title, address and are arranged alphabetically.

DIRECTORY OF EAST ASIAN COLLECTIONS IN NORTH AMERICAN LIBRARIES. Edited by Hideo Kaneko. New Haven, Connecticut, Committee on East Asian Libraries, Association for Asian Studies, 1982.

Covers about 90 library collections in the United States and Canada concerned with China, Japan, Korea, and Vietnam. Entries include collection name, institution name, address, names and titles of personnel arranged alphabetically.

A GUIDE TO REFERENCE MATERIALS ON SOUTHEAST ASIA. By Donald Johnson. New Haven, Yale University Press, 1970.

A listing of reference sources dealing with Southeast Asia that can be found in either the Yale University or Cornell University libraries, or both.

INTERNATIONAL DIRECTORY OF CENTERS FOR ASIAN STUDIES. Edited by Nelson Leung. Hong Kong Asian Research Service, 1980.

Entries include center name, address, phone, year established, area of research, name of director, number and names of staff, publications, universities or organizations with which affiliated. Arranged geographically. Includes an alphabetical index.

INTRODUCTION TO ASIA; A Selective Guide to Background Reading. By Lau-King Quan. Washington, D.C., Library of Congress, Reference Department, 1955.

A listing of works that deal with the problems and aspirations of Asia, their causes, historical growth, cultural background and the area's relations to the West. Includes lengthy annotations.

PAPERBOUND BOOKS ON ASIA. Compiled by Cynthia T. Morehouse. Ann Arbor, 5th revised edition, 1963.

This is a checklist for paperbound books on Asia mostly published in the United States and a few selected publications from abroad.

SOUTHEAST ASIA; A Critical Bibliography. By Kennedy G. Tregonning. Tucson, University of Arizona Press, 1969.

A selected, annotated and graded list of works, in English, that deal with traditional and modern Southeast Asia. Arranged by subject and then by authoritativeness and accessibility.

SOUTHEAST ASIA AND THE PACIFIC: A SELECT BIBLIOGRAPHY, 1947-1977. By Attar Chand. New Delhi, Sterling, 1979.

A list of the most significant books and periodical articles that have been published from 1947-1977. The bibliography is divided into countries.

SOUTHEAST ASIAN HISTORY: A BIBLIOGRAPHIC GUIDE. Edited by Stephen Hay. New York, Praeger, 1962.

An annotated listing of literature on the history of Southeast Asia. Majority of the entries are in English and a few in French.

A WORLD BIBLIOGRAPHY OF ORIENTAL BIBLIOGRAPHIES. By Theodore Besterman. Totowa, New Jersey, Rowman and Littlefield, 1975.

A collection of bibliographies from around the world that deal with Asian and Oceanic countries. Arranged geographically.

ZEN BUDDHISM; A Bibliography of Books and Articles in English, 1892-1975. By Patricia A. Vessie. Ann Arbor, University Microfilms International, 1976.

Lists general works, books and articles on its historical development, texts and commentaries and Zen Sects. The remainder of the bibliography lists works on Zen and various other subjects, such as Zen and the arts, Zen and science, etc. A list of Zen periodicals is included.

ASIAN AMERICANS

THE ALIEN AND THE ASIATIC IN AMERICAN LAW. By Milton Konvitz. Ithaca, Cornell University Press, 1946.

This book discusses how the United States Supreme Court has reacted to problems relating to the alien and to the American citizen of Asiatic descent plus a look at the legal status of these groups before and during this time.

AMERICANS IN PROCESS. By William Carlson Smith. Ann Arbor, Michigan, Edwards Brothers, 1937.

This book is a study of the second generation Oriental in Hawaii and how his attitudes and adjustment were influenced by social environmental factors and not inborn racial traits.

ASIA IN NEW YORK CITY. New York, Asia Society, 1981.

A guidebook to information about Asian resources in metropolitan New York. Includes museums, exhibits, performing arts, outdoor events, restaurants, craft shops etc.

THE ASIAN AMERICAN: THE HISTORICAL EXPERIENCE: ESSAYS. By Roger Daniels. Santa Barbara, California, Cito Books, 1976.

A collection of eight essays dealing with the experiences of Asia American residents - Chinese, Japanese, Filipinos, Koreans and East Indians.

ASIAN AMERICAN REFERENCE DATA DIRECTORY. By Division of Asian American Affairs, Health, Education, and Welfare Department, Washington, Government Printing Office, 1977.

A bibliography containing full abstracts of some 480 of the "major reference materials related to the health, education, and social welfare characteristics of Asian Americans."

ASIAN AMERICANS: AN ANNOTATED BIBLIOGRAPHY. By Harry L. Kitano et al. Los Angeles, University of California, Asian American Studies Center, 1971.

Describes materials available at the Asian American Studies Center, and in so doing gives an overview of the field.

ASIAN AMERICANS: AN ANNOTATED BIBLIOGRAPHY FOR PUBLIC LIBRARIES. Compiled by the Bibliography Committee. Chicago, Office for Library Service to the Disadvantaged, ALA, 1977.

An annotated listing of Asian American titles for public libraries. Included are adult and children's titles covering the Asian American groups; Chinese Americans, Japanese Americans, Korean Americans, and Filipino Americans.

ASIAN AMERICANS: A STUDY GUIDE AND SOURCE BOOK. San Francisco, R & E Research Associates, 1975.

A study guide and source book on Asian Americans that treats three themes: identity, conflict and integration. It is part of a four volume series on American minorities.

ASIAN-AMERICANS: PSYCHOLOGICAL PERSPECTIVES. Edited by Stanley Sue and Ben Lomond. California, Science and Behavior Books, 1973 and 80.

A two volume set (one published in 1973 and the other in 1980) that contains articles about Asian American from various social science aspects. Written to provide literature on a minority group aspect that has not been researched extensively.

THE ASIAN IN NORTH AMERICA. Edited by Stanford M. Lyman. Santa Barbara, California, ABC-Clio Books, 1977.

Contains articles and essays on the Chinese Americans and Japanese Americans. Also includes numerous reviews of publications and an interview with the editor.

ASIAN WHO? IN AMERICA. Compiled and edited by Samuel Lo. Roseland, New Jersey, East-West Who, 1971.

A biographical dictionary of persons of Asian extraction, residing in America who have contributed significantly to society or organizations.

ASIANS IN AMERICA: A BIBLIOGRAPHY. By William Wong Lum. Davis, California, University of California at Davis, 1969.

Arranged topically. Includes periodical literature.

ASIANS IN AMERICA: A BIBLIOGRAPHY OF MASTER'S THESES AND DISSERTATIONS. Compiled by William Wong Lum. California, University of California at Davis, 1970.

A listing of 750 dissertations and theses on subjects relevant to Asian experience in America. Includes occasional annotations.

ASIANS IN AMERICA: A SELECTED BIBLIOGRAPHY. By Isao Fugimoto et al. Davis, California, Asian American Research Project, University of California at Davis, 1971.

ASIANS IN AMERICA; A Selected Bibliography for Use in Social Work Education. Compiled by Harry Kitano. New York, Council on Social Work Education, 1971.

An annotated bibliography of works concerning the Chinese, Japanese, Filipinos, and Koreans with emphasis on social science literature in the areas of Psychology-Personality and Sociology-Social work.

ASIANS IN AMERICA: FILIPINOS, KOREANS, AND EAST INDIANS. By H. Brett Melendy. Boston, Twayne Publishers, 1977. (Immigrant Heritage of America Series).

An examination of the Filipinos, Koreans, and East Indians to understand what motivated them to migrate and what their experiences were when first living in America. Includes a selected bibliography.

THE ASIANS IN THE WEST. By Stanford M. Lyman. Reno, Nevada, Desert Research Institute, University of Nevada System, 1970.

The author uses sociological methodology to compare assimilation and acculturation in two groups of Asian settlers, the Chinese and the Japanese.

ASIANS IN THE WEST. By Edwin P. Hoyt. Nashville, T. Nelson, 1974.

A history of the immigration of Asians to the United States - the Chinese, Japanese and Indians. The appendix includes the basic laws and rules governing the immigration of Orientals into the United States.

BUDDHISM IN AMERICA: THE SOCIAL ORGANIZATION OF AN ETHNIC RELIGIOUS INSTITUTION. By Tetsuden Kashime. Westport, Connecticut, Greenwood Press, 1977.

The Buddhist Churches of America, representing the Jodo Shinshu branch of Buddhism has been an extremely important institution in helping the Japanese American community retain its religious beliefs and practices and obtain community cohesion. The author traces the evolution of Buddhism in America and its role in ethnic adjustment. Appendices, bibliography, glossary and index are included.

CALIFORNIA AND THE ORIENTAL: JAPANESE, CHINESE AND HINDUS. State Board of Control, Sacramento, California, State Printing Office, 1922. Reprint, San Francisco, R and E Research Associates, 1970.

A reprint of the State Board of Control of California's report on oriental immigration, population and land ownership to Governor Stephens of California.

CIVIL RIGHTS ISSUES OF ASIAN AND PACIFIC AMERICANS: MYTHS AND REALITIES: MAY 8-9, 1979. Washington, D.C. A Consultation. Washington, D.C. The Commission on Civil Rights Issues of Asian and Pacific Americans, 1980.

The papers and transcript of the proceedings of the consultation on civil rights issues of Asian and Pacific Americans comprise this volume.

COUNTERPOINT: PERSPECTIVES ON ASIAN AMERICANS. Edited by Emma Gee. Los Angeles, University of California, Asian American Studies Center, 1976.

An anthology that presents works which explore racial and economic conflicts and analyzes the impact of international politics. It is divided into three parts: critical perspectives, contemporary issues and literature.

DISCRIMINATION, INCOME, HUMAN CAPITAL INVESTMENT, AND ASIAN-AMERICANS. By Jared J. Young. San Francisco, R and E Research Associates, 1977.

This book studies the manner and process through which Asian-Americans have responded to the American capitalistic system within a discriminatory framework and the success they have achieved by responding in the way they did.

ETHNIC CONFLICT IN CALIFORNIA HISTORY. Edited by Charles Wollenberg. Los Angeles, Finnon-Brown, 1970, not in MK Catalog.

A collection of essays by various authors centering around the problems of discrimination and prejudice towards Asian Americans.

ORIENTAL CRIME IN CALIFORNIA. By Walter G. Beach. Palo Alto, Stanford University Press, 1932.

This book looks at what crimes Chinese and Japanese residents in California have committed and analyzes contributory reasons and conditions.

ORIENTALS AND THEIR CULTURAL ADJUSTMENT. Nashville, Tennessee, Social Science Institute, Fisk University, 1946.

This book provides realistic accounts of the conflicts and adjustments which members of the second and third generations of Orientals are confronting in America.

ORIENTALS IN AMERICAN LIFE. By Albert W. Palmer. New York, Friendship Press, 1934. Reprint San Francisco, R & E Research Associates, 1972.

This book tries to present a picture of the Chinese, Japanese and Filipinos, to make people understand that they are human beings like everybody else. Includes an annotated list of books.

OUR ORIENTAL AMERICANS. Edited by Ed Ritter. H. Ritter and S. Spector. Saint Louis, Missouri, McGraw-Hill, 1965.

OUT OF THE FAR EAST. By Allan A. Hunter. New York, Friendship Press, 1934. Reprint, San Francisco, R & E Research Associates, 1972.

This book takes a look at young people of Oriental origin and the problems they have faced due to their heritage.

RESIDENT ORIENTALS ON THE AMERICAN PACIFIC COAST: THEIR LEGAL AND ECONOMIC STATUS. By Elliot G. Mears. Chicago, University of Chicago Press, 1928.

This is a study of the operation and effects of the laws, regulations, and judicial decisions affecting resident Chinese and Japanese on the Pacific Coast. Includes a chronology, tables, charts and documents.

ROOTS: AN ASIAN AMERICAN READER. Edited by Amy Tachiki. Los Angeles, Continental Graphics, 1971.

A variety of materials presented from several perspectives on the experiences of Asian Americans within the context of the human condition. The selections are arranged under three headings: identity, history and community.

THE SECOND GENERATION ORIENTAL IN AMERICA. By William Carlson Smith. Honolulu, Institute of Pacific Relations, 1927. Reprint San Francisco, R and E Research Associates, 1971.

A look at the world through the eyes of second generation Japanese and Chinese Americans. Data was obtained from life histories.

THESES AND DISSERTATIONS ON ASIANS IN THE UNITED STATES WITH SELECTED REFERENCES TO OTHER OVERSEAS ASIANS. Compiled by Paul M. Ong. Asian American Studies, Department of Applied Behavioral Sciences, University of California, 1974.

This is a major revision and expansion of "Asians in America: A Bibliography of Master's Theses and Doctoral Dissertations", compiled by William Wong Lum.

TOPICAL BIBLIOGRAPHY OF THE ASIAN EXPERIENCE IN THE UNITED STATES. By T. Jesse Kwoh. Monticello, Illinois, Council of Planning Librarians Exchange Bibliography, 1974.

A listing of materials at Cornell University on the Asian experience in the United States.

WHEN THE EAST IS WEST. By Maude W. Madden. Reprint, San Francisco, R & R Research Associates, 1971. London, Fleming Revell Company, 1923.

A group of stories by the author that reflect her life as an Oriental while she was teaching at the Eugene Bible University. Valuable as a first hand account.

Audiovisual Material

ANCIENT CIVILIZATIONS: THE ORIENT. Super 8 mm. Color. Silent. 4 minutes. By Coronet Instructional Media, 1974.

Traces the development of the Hindu and Buddhist religions and describes the ideas of Oriental philosophers such as Confucius and Lao-Tse. With captions.

HONG KONG: A STORY OF HUMAN FREEDOM AND PROGRESS. 16 mm. Color and sound. 28 minutes. By Liberty Fund, Incorporated. Available from Modern Talking Picture Service.

In one generation, Hong Kong has transformed itself from a modest trading area into a modern industrial economy through reliance on the market, rather than central planning or government direction. It shows how opportunities available in the market economy enabled millions of refugees to lift themselves out of poverty on the basis of their own efforts.

INSTANT REFUGEES. 16 mm. Color and sound. 30 minutes. By Catholic Relief Services. Available from Modern Talking Picture Service.

Displaced Kampucheans, Laotians and Thais receive emergency aid and resettlement assistance from Catholic Relief Services. This film shows three stages of refugee life: feeding along the Kampuchea-Thailand border, day to day existence in a refugee camp, and the heartbreak-exhilaration of resettlement. A CINE Golden Eagle Award Winner.

SOUTHEAST ASIA: A CULTURE HISTORY. 16 mm. Color and sound. 16 minutes. By Sigma Educational Films. Released by Film Communicators, 1970.

A study of the history, culture, and peoples of Southeast Asia - Viet Nam, Laos, Cambodia and Thailand.

SOUTHEAST ASIA - LANDS AND PEOPLES. 16 mm. Color and sound. 14 minutes. Coronet Instructional Media, Chicago, 1976.

Examines the cultural, physical, and economic geography of the countries of Southeast Asia. Shows how the people, through their emergence from colonial status to independent nations, have used their lands to produce such products as rubber, oil, tin, teak, and rice.

AUSTRALIANS

Embassy and Consulates

EMBASSY OF AUSTRALIA
1601 Massachusetts Avenue, Northwest
Washington, D.C. 20036 (202) 797-3000

Commercial Office (202) 797-3440

Scientific Counselor (202) 797-3259

Press Office (202) 797-3176

CONSULATES GENERAL

111 East Wacker Drive
Chicago, Illinois 60601 (312) 329-1740

1000 Bishop Street
Honolulu, Hawaii 96813 (808) 524-5050

1990 South Post Oak Road
Three Post Oak Central
Eighth Floor
Houston, Texas 77056 (713) 877-8100

3550 Wilshire Boulevard
17th Floor
Los Angeles, California
90010 (213) 380-0980

636 Fifth Avenue
New York, New York 10111 (212) 245-4000

360 Post Street
San Francisco, California
94108 (415) 362-6160

Mission to the United Nations

AUSTRALIAN MISSION
1 Dag Hammarskjold Plaza
New York, New York 10017 (212) 421-6910

Information Offices

AUSTRALIAN INFORMATION SERVICE
636 Fifth Avenue
New York, New York 10111 (212) 245-4079

AUSTRALIAN TOURIST COMMISSION

3550 Wilshire Boulevard, #1740
Los Angeles, California 90010 (213) 380-6060

1270 Avenue of the Americas
New York, New York 10020 (212) 489-7550

Fraternal Organizations

AUSTRALASIAN CLUB AT HARVARD
c/o Student Association Office
Harvard Business School
Boston, Massachusetts 02163

A social group which caters to people in the Boston area interested in Australia and New Zealand. Most of the members are of Australian and New Zealand nationality.

AUSTRALIA KANGAROO CLUB
Post Office Box 4230 (714) 552-0175
Irvine, California 92716 Founded 1971

Founded to promote travel; membership open to Australians, New Zealanders, Americans, and other interested persons.

AUSTRALIA NEW ZEALAND AMERICA CLUB
Post Office Box 178204 (714) 561-5352
San Diego, California 92117 Founded 1977

Persons interested in creating a closer relationship between Australia, New Zealand, and America. Functions as a social club with special interests in sports, cultural activities, and business.

AUSTRALIA-NEW ZEALAND SOCIETY OF BOSTON, INCORPORATED
78 Woodbine Street
Auburndale, Boston, Massachusetts 02166
Membership Chairman:
Clyde Dyson

Persons interested in creating a closer relationship between America, Australia, and New Zealand.

AUSTRALIAN-NEW ZEALAND SOCIETY OF NEW YORK
41 East 42nd Street, Room 700
New York, New York 10017 (212) 986-1457
President: Mrs. A. Guy Grimaldi Founded 1939

Persons interested in creating a closer relationship between America, Australia and New Zealand. Sponsors students to the United States and American students to Australia and New Zealand through American Field Service International programs. Sponsors exchange school teachers from Australia to live and work in the United States for one-year periods. Also sponsors group flights to Australia and New Zealand. Formerly called the Australian Society of New York.
Publication: Bulletin.

COMMONWEALTH SOCIETY OF NORTH AMERICA
2201 Wilson Boulevard, Room 202
Arlington, Virginia 22201
President: Peter McLaughlin (703) 524-3121

A social club founded to promote and maintain the traditions of the Commonwealth nations. Membership open to former residents of the United Kingdom, Canada, Australia, and New Zealand.

DOWN UNDER CLUB OF NORTH CENTRAL USA
Box 3143 (612) 376-4056
Saint Paul, Minnesota 55165 Founded 1972

A social and travel club open to persons interested in Australia and New Zealand.

SOUTHERN CROSS CLUB
Post Office Box 19243 (703) 256-6549
Washington, D.C. 20036 Founded 1946

A social club for Australians, New Zealanders, and persons who have resided in either country.

Cultural and Educational Organizations

SOCIETY OF AUSTRALASIAN SPECIALISTS/OCEANIA
Box 82643
San Diego, California 92138
Financial Secretary: David Proctor (714) 225-7095
Founded 1978

Collectors who specialize in the stamps, stationery and postal history of Australia, Australian states, New Zealand, New Zealand dependencies and other Oceanic islands. Operates sales department. Maintains library of books, catalogs, handbooks, and other materials pertaining to Australian postal history. Functions primarily through correspondence, except in larger cities where informal meetings are held. Plans to hold periodic auctions of Australian items and to operate a film library. Awards gold, silver and bronze medals to notable stamp exhibits in the Pacific area. Associated with similar philatelic clubs in New South Wales and in Great Britain. Formed by the merger of the Society of Australasian Specialists (founded 1936) and Oceania Philatelic Society (founded 1967 and formerly Australian Commonwealth Collectors Circle-U.S.A.; American Society of Australian Philatelists; Oceania, Incorporated).
Publications: The Australasian Informer, monthly.

Research Centers and Special Institutes

CENTER FOR SOUTH PACIFIC STUDIES
University of California at Santa Cruz
Santa Cruz, California 95060 (408) 429-2191
Director: Dr. Bryan H. Farrell Founded 1967

Integral unit of University of California at Santa Cruz. Principal field of research: Exploration of potential of South Pacific area for controlled comparative study of anthropological, biological, humanistic, ecological, political and linguistic developments, especially in Oceania, Australia, New Zealand and insular southeast Asia, including interdisciplinary studies of social change, impact of tourism, Pacific migrants in an urban setting, nutrition and health. Also provides instruction, field research and interaction with distinguished Pacific residents on campus and through faculty exchange program. Research results published in series of monographs. Holds periodic seminars and workshops on contemporary Pacific anthropological, political and economic problems. Utilizes developing Pacific collection in the University's McHenry library.

Special Libraries and Subject Collections

AUSTRALIAN EMBASSY - LIBRARY
1601 Massachusetts Avenue
Washington, D.C. 20036
Librarian: Christine Cooze (202) 797-3166

Subjects: Australian reference material. Holdings: Books; bound periodical volumes; annual reports of Australian government departments and statutory corporations; press releases of Australian government departments; journals and other serials; newspapers. Services: Interlibrary loans; library open to public.

AUSTRALIAN INFORMATION SERVICE - REFERENCE LIBRARY/INFORMATION SERVICE
636 Fifth Avenue
New York, New York 10020
Director Information Services:
H. Hurst (212) 245-4000

Subjects: Australian reference material. Holdings: Books, periodicals, newspapers, pamphlets, reports, photographs, movie sound films and maps. Open to public. A.I.S. NY is the central office which services the other Australian Consulates-General throughout the United States. Formerly located in San Francisco, California.

UNIVERSITY OF CALIFORNIA, SANTA CRUZ - DEAN E. MC HENRY LIBRARY
Santa Cruz, California 95064
University Librarian: Allan J.
Dyson (408) 429-2801

Collection contains books, journals, and other material on the South Pacific area, especially Oceania, Australia, New Zealand, and insular southeast Asia.

Newspapers and Newsletters

THE AUSTRALASIAN INFORMER. Monthly. Publisher: Society of Australasian Specialists/ Oceania, Box 82643, San Diego, California 92138, (714) 225-7095.

Publishes philatelic news and activities of the Society.

AUSTRALIA NEWSLETTER. 1971-. Monthly. Editor: Brian Pilbern. Publisher: Sydney Morrell & Company, Incorporated, 152 East 78th Street, New York, New York 10021, (212) 249-7255.

AUSTRALIAN-NEW ZEALAND SOCIETY OF NEW YORK BULLETIN. Publisher: Australian-New Zealand Society, 41 East 42nd Street, New York, New York 10017, (212) 986-1457.

AUSTRALIAN TRADING NEWS. Quarterly. Publisher: Australian Trade Commission, 636 Fifth Avenue, New York, New York 10111, (212) 245-4000.

Radio Programs

RADIO AUSTRALIA

1 Rockefeller Plaza
Suite 1700
New York, New York 10020 (212) 757-1177

1147 20th Street, Northwest
Washington, D.C. 20036 (202) 466-8575

Radio Australia, the overseas service of the Australian Broadcasting Commission, transmits shortwave programs daily from Australia to the United States.

Bank Branches in the U.S.

AUSTRALIA AND NEW ZEALAND BANKING GROUP, LIMITED

63 Wall Street
New York, New York 10005 (212) 825-0700

Suite 4350
707 Wilshire Boulevard
Los Angeles, California 90017 (213) 620-0413

BANK OF NEW SOUTH WALES

200 Park Avenue
Suite 2412
New York, New York 10166 (212) 949-9830

3100, One California Street
San Francisco, California 94111 (415) 986-4222

COMMERCIAL BANK OF AUSTRALIA LIMITED
9 West 57th Street, 39th Floor
New York, New York 10019 (212) 593-9696

COMMERCIAL BANKING COMPANY OF SYDNEY, LIMITED
200 Park Avenue, Suite 2922
New York, New York 10166 (212) 972-1881

NATIONAL BANK OF AUSTRALASIA, LIMITED

299 Park Avenue, 25th Floor
New York, New York 10171 (212) 750-0120

707 Wilshire Boulevard
Los Angeles, California 90017 (213) 626-3434

Commercial and Trade Organizations

AMERICAN AUSTRALIAN ASSOCIATION
1251 Avenue of the Americas
New York, New York 10020 (212) 489-0939
Treasurer: Peter M. St. Germain Founded 1948

Acts as an advisory body in the area of business and cultural affairs; handles public relations activities for Australian business and political figures visiting the United States.

AUSTRALIAN-AMERICAN ASSOCIATION
Post Office Box 3450 (415) 772-9409
San Francisco, California 94119 Founded 1950

Purpose is to promote business between Australia and America. Membership open to Americans and Australians.

AUSTRALIAN TRADE COMMISSION
636 Fifth Avenue
New York, New York 10111
Commissioner: R. J. Barcham, Sr. (212) 245-4000

Objective is the promotion of trade between the United States and Australia. Compiles statistics; maintains speakers bureau.
Publication: Australian Trading News, quarterly.

Airline Offices

QANTAS AIRWAYS, LIMITED
North American Headquarters
360 Post Street
San Francisco, California 94108 (415) 445-6546

Operates from San Francisco, Los Angeles, and Honolulu to points in Australia. Other offices in the United States:

Illinois Center, Suite 1414
111 East Wacker Drive
Chicago, Illinois 60601 (312) 565-0740

Waikiki Trade Center
2255 Kuhio Avenue #1001
Honolulu, Hawaii 96815 (808) 923-5731

3550 Wilshire Boulevard
Suite 1038
Los Angeles, California 90010 (213) 417-20017

542 Fifth Avenue
New York, New York 10036 (212) 764-0214

Suite 1210
1825 K Street, Northwest
Washington, D.C. 20006 (202) 223-3033

Ship Lines

FARRELL LINE
One Whitehall Street
New York, New York 10004 (212) 440-4200

Operates from New York to Australia (Brisbane) via the Panama Canal and the South Pacific. Sailings twice a month, taking approximately 21 days - 12 passengers.

PRINCESS CRUISES/P & O
2029 Century Park East
Los Angeles, California 90067 (800) 252-0158
(rest of United States) (800) 421-0522

Offers cruises from North America to Australia via the South Pacific on an irregular basis.

ROYAL VIKING LINE
One Embarcadero Center
San Francisco, California 94111 (800) 792-2970
(rest of United States) (800) 227-4246

Offers cruises from North America to Australia via the South Pacific on an irregular basis.

Bookdealers and Publishers' Representatives

AUSTRALIAN BOOK CENTER
Post Office Box 634
New Rochelle, New York 10802 (914) 235-2347

THE CELLAR BOOKSHOP
18090 Wyoming
Detroit, Michigan 48221 (313) 861-1776

F & I BOOKS
Post Office Box 1900
Santa Monica, California 90406 (213) 394-7886

GRAEME VANDERSTOEL
Post Office Box 599
El Cerrito, California 94530 (415) 527-2882

INTERNATIONAL SCHOLARLY BOOK SERVICES, INCORPORATED
2130 Pacific Avenue
Forest Grove, Oregon 97116 (503) 357-7192

OLD MILL BOOKS
Post Office Box 77
Stillwater, New Jersey 07875 (201) 786-5344

PENNYWHEEL PRESS
Route 2
Poultney, Vermont 05764 (802) 287-4050

Books and Pamphlets

AMERICAN CHAMBER OF COMMERCE IN AUSTRALIA-DIRECTORY. Sydney, Australia, American Chamber of Commerce in Australia, 1982.

An annual publication that lists Australian and American businesses interested in developing trade and investment within and between the two countries.

AUSTRALIA HANDBOOK, 1981-82. By the Australian Information Service. Canberra, Australian Government Publishing Service, 1981.

Offers a comprehensive view of Australia's progress and development, economic, social, cultural, and scientific achievements.

AUSTRALIA IN BRIEF. By the Australian Information Service. Canberra, 1981.

A comprehensive view of Australia in summarized form. This information is available in greater detail in Australia Handbook.

THE AUSTRALIAN ABORIGINALS. Australian Information Service Publication, 1980.

A reference paper dealing with the native Australians and their descendants, government policies and responsibilities for them, their health, housing, employment, land, and legal status.

AUSTRALIAN-AMERICAN BUSINESS REVIEW/DIRECTORY. Edited by Barry V. Conforte. New York, Motivational Communications, Incorporated, 1979.

An alphabetical listing of import/export firms, manufacturers, and national agencies (United States and Australia) concerned with commerce between the two countries and recognized by the Australian Government Trade Commission.

AUSTRALIAN BIBLIOGRAPHY: A GUIDE TO PRINTED SOURCES OF INFORMATION. Compiled by Dietrich Hans Borchardt. Third edition. Rushcutter's Bay, N.S.W.; Pergamon Press, 1976.

A detailed bibliography with sources of information having paragraph-length evaluations. Scope of the work is restricted to mainland Australia and Tasmania.

THE AUSTRALIAN CATALOGUE: A REFERENCE INDEX TO THE BOOKS AND PERIODICALS PUBLISHED AND STILL CURRENT IN THE COMMONWEALTH OF AUSTRALIA. Compiled by Albert Broadbent Foxcroft. London, Pordes, 1961.

AUSTRALIAN LITERATURE, A BIBLIOGRAPHY TO 1938, EXTENDED TO 1950. Compiled by Edmund Morris Miller. Sydney, Angus and Robertson, 1956.

This bibliography begins with a historical outline, which points out the various writers that were of importance in the fields of poetry, fiction, essays, criticism, descriptive works, drama and anthologies. This outline is followed by an alphabetical listing by author of literature works.

AUSTRALIAN LITERATURE: A REFERENCE GUIDE. 2nd edition. By Fred Lock. Melbourne, New York, Oxford University Press, 1980.

Describes and evaluates the reference works most useful for the study of Australian literature. Includes a list of library collections at various universities and state libraries.

AUSTRALIAN LITERATURE TO 1900: A GUIDE TO INFORMATION SOURCES. By Barry G. Andrews. Detroit, Gale Research Company, 1980.

This is an annotated guide to the literature that emerged from the Australian colonial experience between 1788 and 1900. Part one is a listing of works about Australian literature, part two deals with sixty-six authors and part three deals with nonfiction prose.

AUSTRALIANS IN THE PENNSYLVANIA STATE UNIVERSITY LIBRARIES. By Bruce Sutherland. University Park, Pennsylvania State University Libraries, 1969.

A listing of materials contained in the collections of the Pennsylvania State University Libraries that deal with some aspect of Australia.

BIBLIOGRAPHY OF AUSTRALIA. Compiled by John Alexander Ferguson. Sydney, London, Angus and Robertson, 1941-1969.

A seven volume set that covers materials about Australia published during the years 1839-1900. Includes only materials published in Australia.

ILLUSTRATED ATLAS OF AUSTRALIA. Australian Information Service Publication, 1974.

Includes detailed maps of the six states of Australia, and also special maps showing the physical features, mineral deposits, vegetation, and rainfall of Australia.

SOCIAL POLICY AND ITS ADMINISTRATION: A SURVEY OF THE AUSTRALIAN LITERATURE, 1950-1975. By Joanna Monie. Rushcutter's Bay (Australia), Pergamon Press, 1977.

A bibliographic survey that covers Australian social policy thinking from 1950-1975. It is restricted to monograph and report literature and reference to series.

SOUTH AUSTRALIAN HISTORY: A SURVEY FOR RESEARCH STUDENTS. By Francis Crowley. Adelaide, Libraries Board of South Australia, 1966.

This book lists historical writings about South Australia that can be used by students doing research on South Australia. Each chapter begins with an introduction to the subject followed by materials that can be used for research.

AUSTRALIAN AMERICANS

AUSTRALIANS AND THE GOLD RUSH: CALIFORNIA AND DOWN UNDER 1849-1854. By Jay Monaghan. Berkeley, California, University of California Press, 1966.

Discusses the immigration of Australians to California during the Gold Rush. Includes extensive bibliography.

AUSTRALIANS IN AMERICA, 1876-1976. Edited by John Hammond Moore. Saint Lucia, Queensland: University of Queensland Press, 1977.

An anthology of comments by Australian travellers on the United States during 1876-1976. Contributors to the book are from all walks of life (professional writers, educators, reformers, tourists, etc.)

COMMITTEE OF VIGILANCE: REVOLUTION IN SAN FRANCISCO, 1851. By George R. Stewart. Boston, Houghton Mifflin, 1964.

An account of the hundred days in 1851 when certain San Francisco citizens undertook the suppression of the criminal activities of the Sydney ducks.

GOLD FLEET FOR CALIFORNIA: FORTY-NINERS FROM AUSTRALIA AND NEW ZEALAND. By Charles Bateson. East Lansing, Michigan State University Press, 1964.

Gives an account of the part played by Australians and New Zealanders in the mass migration to California after discovery there of gold in 1848. Tells of their passage on sailing vessels, their business ventures, and their experiences after reaching California.

HARRY BRIDGES: THE RISE AND FALL OF RADICAL LABOR IN THE UNITED STATES. By Charles P. Larrowe. New York, 1972.

Documents the life of Harry Bridges, the Australian immigrant who was active as a union organizer in San Francisco during the 1920's and 1930's.

Audiovisual Material

ALICE SPRINGS - RED HEART, BLUE CENTRE. 16 mm. Color and sound. 17 minutes. Film Australia, Sydney, 1974. Released in the United States by Australian Information Service, 1975.

Takes a look at the town and people of Alice Springs, located in the heart of the Australian outback. Shows some of its important attractions for visitors, including desert wildflowers, camel races and Ayers Rock.

AUSTRALIA. 16 mm. Color and sound. 14 minutes. Toronto, Film Arts, 1977.

Discusses the history, geography, nature, people, economics, sports, animals, and vegetation of Australia.

AUSTRALIA-DOWN UNDER AND OUTBACK. Videorecording or 16 mm. Color and sound. 25 minutes. National Geographic Society, Washington, The Society, 1973.

Examines the lives of people in the Australian outback, where existence is a struggle against heat, poison weeds, drought, and economic difficulties. With teacher's guide and collateral materials.

AUSTRALIA, THE TIMELESS LAND. Videorecording or 16 mm. Color and sound. 52 minutes. National Geographic Society. Washington, The Society, c.1969.

Explores the people and modes of living in Australia's outback. Visits a sheep ranch, an isolated cattle ranch, and Coober Pedy, a town where opal miners escape the heat by living and working underground.

AUSTRALIAN REPORT. 16 mm. Color and sound. 20 minutes. Australian Information Service, 1973. Made by Film Australia. Released in the United States, 1973.

A report on contemporary Australia, surveying its history, industry, and tourist attractions. Shows the life of the Australian people - in the growing cities, in traditional rural industries, and in the new mining developments in the outback.

THE AUSTRALIANS. 16 mm. Color and sound. 50 minutes. Toronto, CTV Television Network, 1976.

Presents a television special from the CTV program Olympiad, which shows the achievements of Australian athletes in various Olympic competitions. Notes that few nations on a comparative per capita basis have produced as many outstanding Olympic medal winners as Australia.

AUSTRALIA'S NORTHWEST. 16 mm. Color and sound. 11 minutes. Australian Information Service, 1972. Made by Film Australia. Released in the United States, 1972.

Shows how new irrigation schemes, mineral discoveries, and cattle breeding methods are contributing to the development of Australia's northwest coast.

AUTUMN OF A MINING TOWN. 16 mm. Color and sound. 9 minutes. Australian Information Service, 1972. Made by Film Australia. Released in the United States, 1973.

Presents the atmosphere and history of the Australian rural city of Ballarat, once a boom town of the gold rush days.

A DAY IN PERTH. 16 mm. Color and sound. 10 minutes. Australian Information Service, 1972. Made by Film Australia. Released in the United States, 1973.

Presents glimpses of the way of life in the Australian city of Perth.

EXPLORATION 1770 - REVIEWED 1970. 16 mm. Color and sound. 10 minutes. Australian News and Information Bureau, 1970. Made by Australian Commonwealth Film Unit. Released in the United States, 1970.

Commemorates the 200th anniversary of the discovery of Australia by Captain James Cook by contrasting the land he saw in 1770 with the Australia of 1970 as seen by Queen Elizabeth II on her visit.

INDUSTRIAL CITY. 16 mm. Color and sound. 14 minutes. Australian Information Service, 1972. Made by Film Australia. Released in the United States, 1973.

A study of an industrial city, focusing on Newcastle, Australia. Shows each activity in the city in its relationship to the whole city complex.

KATHERINE - AIR-CONDITIONED FRONTIER. 16 mm. Color and sound. 17 minutes. Film Australia, Sydney, 1974. Released in the United States by Australian Information Service, 1975.

Explores life in the northern Australian town of Katherine. Shows ranching activities in the surrounding area and follows tourists as they see the cliffs of an inland river gorge.

LARWARI AND WALKARA. 16 mm. Color and sound. 45 minutes. Australian Institute of Aboriginal Studies. Berkeley, University of California Extension Media Center, 1977.

Documents an aboriginal rite performed in 1972 by men of the Walbiri tribe in the Northern Territory, Australia. Also provides insight into the problems facing contemporary aborigines who wish to preserve and maintain their traditional customs and ceremonies.

MICHAEL. 16 mm. Color and sound. 31 minutes. Film Australia. White Plains, New York, Wombat Productions, 1973, made 1971.

Considers problems involved in the process of growth from dependence to independence experienced by young people with the story of a young Australian man, engaged to a middle class girl and with a secure job, who is drawn to the world of the counterculture and radicalism. Includes study guide.

OUR LAND AUSTRALIA. 16 mm. Color and sound. 12 minutes. Australian Information Service, 1972. Made by Film Australia. Released in the United States, 1973.

Presents a collage of Australian scenes, giving a brief, overall view of the country and its people.

PATTERNS OF TIME AND DISTANCE. 16 mm. Color and sound. 19 minutes. Australian Information Service, 1972. Made by Film Australia. Released in the United States, 1973.

Traces the overall pattern of Australia's development from primitive isolation to modern urbanized society.

PEARLS IN THE NORTH. 16 mm. Color and sound. 14 minutes. Australian Information Service, 1972. Made by Film Australia. Released in the United States, 1973.

Highlights the renewal of the pearling industry off Australia's northwest coast.

TENNANT CREEK IN PASSING. 16 mm. Color and sound. 7 minutes. Film Australia, Sydney, 1974. Released in the United States by Australian Information Service, 1975.

Presents impressions of life in Tennant Creek, a small town in the Australian outback.

TRAVELLIN ROUND. 16 mm. Color and sound. 31 minutes. Australian Tourist Commission. Made by Film Australia. New York, Australian Information Service, 1975, made 1974.

Details the adventures of three young Australians as they travel around Australia by landrover and motorbike. Starting from Sydney, they travel to the Great Barrier Reef, Darwin, Perth, and Adelaide. On the return route, one of them detours to the island State of Tasmania.

UNKNOWN LAND. 16 mm. Color and sound. 28 minutes. Australian Information Service, 1972. Made by Film Australia. Released in the United States, 1973.

Records the changes made in Australia's sparsely-populated northwest by new development projects.

Approximately 200 additional films made by Film Australia, composed primarily of recent short documentaries, feature Australian aborigines, armed forces, arts, architecture, music, development, education, environment, geography, the handicapped and health, history, marine life, sports, recreation, and wildlife. Of special interest are fiction and documentary compilation films with footage dating back to 1896. One series of films was produced by the Australians in cooperation with the government of Thailand, Malaysia, Indonesia, and India. There are individual films on World War I, film history from 1896 to 1929, jazz, the Namatjira, urban life, and the architecture of the Victoria Gallery and the Sydney Opera House.

For further information, contact:

Australian Information Service
Australian Consulate General
636 Fifth Avenue
New York, New York 10111 (212) 245-4000

AUSTRIANS
See also: GERMANS

Embassy and Consulates

EMBASSY OF AUSTRIA
2343 Massachusetts Avenue, Northwest
Washington, D.C. 20008 (202) 483-4474

CONSULATES GENERAL

410 North Michigan Avenue, Suite 672
Chicago, Illinois 60611 (312) 222-1515

3440 Wilshire Boulevard
Los Angeles, California 90010 (213) 380-7550

31 East 69th Street
New York, New York 10021 (212) 737-6400

CONSULATES

6075 Roswell Road, Northeast
Atlanta, Georgia 30328 (404) 252-7920

225 Franklin Street
Boston, Massachusetts 02110 (617) 542-2429

888 Statler Building
Buffalo, New York 14202 (716) 852-7000

55 Public Square, Suite 1630
Cleveland, Ohio 44113

911 West Big Beaver Road, Suite 404
Troy, Michigan 48048 (313) 362-2449
(Detroit)

Texas Commerce Bank N.A.
717 Travis Street
Post Office Box 2558
Houston, Texas 77001 (713) 236-5696

5388 Poola Street
Honolulu, Hawaii 96821 (808) 373-1234

Suite 20, Republic Building
1454 Northwest 17th Avenue
Miami, Florida 33125 (305) 325-1561

4700 One Shell Square
New Orleans, Louisiana 70139 (504) 581-5141

3 Parkway, 20th Floor
Philadelphia, Pennsylvania
19102 (215) 563-0650

1007 Northwest 24th Avenue
Portland, Oregon 97210 (503) 224-6000

370 Minnesota Street
Suite 1000 - Tenth Floor
Saint Paul, Minnesota 55101 (612) 298-6283

256 Sutter Street, Sixth Floor
San Francisco, California
94108 (415) 986-4040

201 Calle del Cristo
San Juan, Puerto Rico 00901 (809) 722-2136

4030 First National Bank Building
1001 Fourth Avenue
Seattle, Washington 98154 (206) 624-3450

Mission to the United Nations

AUSTRIAN MISSION
809 United Nations Plaza, 7th Floor
New York, New York 10017 (212) 949-1840

Information Offices

AUSTRIAN PRESS AND INFORMATION SERVICE
31 East 69th Street
New York, New York 10021 (212) 535-4295

Tourist and Travel Offices

AUSTRIAN NATIONAL TOURIST OFFICE

Standard Oil Building, Suite 7023
200 East Randolph Drive
Chicago, Illinois 60601 (312) 861-0100

3340 Wilshire Boulevard
Tishman Plaza #901
Los Angeles, California
90010 (213) 380-7990

545 Fifth Avenue
New York, New York 10017 (212) 697-0651

1007 Northwest 24th Avenue
Portland, Oregon 97210 (503) 224-6000

Fraternal Organizations

AMERICAN AUSTRIAN SOCIETY
c/o Monroe Karasik
1156 Fifteenth Street, Northwest
Washington, D.C. 20005
President: Lt. Col. William A. Vogel (301) 656-5254
Founded 1954

Persons interested in the promotion of cultural and social relations between the United States and Austria. Activities include: film showings of life in Austria; musical evenings; annual Christmas and spring parties; small group discussions; receptions for and lectures by distinguished visitors from Austria. Affiliated with the Austro-American Society, Vienna, Austria.
Publications: Newsletter, monthly; American Austrian Society directory, annual.

AMERICAN AUSTRIAN SOCIETY OF THE MIDWEST
121 South Mwyer
Arlington Heights, Illinois 60005
President: Joe Schneller

AMERICAN FRIENDS OF AUSTRIA
180 East Pearson, #3800
Chicago, Illinois 60611
President: Robert Lock

AUSTRIA CLUB SEATTLE
7335 Northeast 141st Street
Bothell, Washington 98020
President: Jerry Gertschitz

AUSTRIA CLUB TACOMA
Post Office Box 733
Steilacoom, Washington 98388
President: Mary Hoffmann

AUSTRIAN-AMERICAN ASSOCIATION
423 East Rivo Alto Drive
Rivo Alto Island
Miami Beach, Florida 33139
President: Professor Dr. Hans Hannau

AUSTRIAN ASSOCIATION OF PATTERSON & VICINITY, INCORPORATED
99 Catherine Avenue
Saddle Brook, New York 07662
President: Mrs. Bibi Ann Hevner

AUSTRIAN-AMERICAN FEDERATION, INCORPORATED
31 East 69th Street
New York, New York 10021
President: Dr. Clementine Zernik (212) 535-3261

AUSTRIAN-AMERICAN SOCIETY
3708 Orchard Avenue, North
Minneapolis, Minnesota 53422
President: Mrs. Gertrud Warsser

AUSTRIAN-AMERICAN SOCIETY OF WILMINGTON
2203 The Sweep
Arden-Wilmington, Delaware
President: Mrs. Charlotte Shedd

AUSTRIAN BENEFIT SOCIETY
12618 Shaw Avenue
East Cleveland, Ohio 44108
President: Georg Skieber

AUSTRIAN-HAWAII ASSOCIATION
Post Office Box 2200
Honolulu, Hawaii 96822
President: Otto Orenstein

AUSTRIAN SEA COAST BENEFICIAL ASSOCIATION
2644 East Huntingdon Street
Philadelphia, Pennsylvania 19125

AUSTRIAN SOCIETY OF DETROIT
26 Sangeen Avenue
Chatham, Ontario, N7M 554
Canada
President: Leo Polleiner

AUSTRIAN SOCIETY OF THE PACIFIC NORTHWEST
c/o Mr. Henry J. Bloch
1007 Northwest 24th Street
Portland, Oregon 97210

THE AUSTRIANS SOCIAL CLUB
6031 North Navarre Avenue
Chicago, Illinois 60631
President: Walter E. Pomper

AUSTRO-AMERICAN ASSOCIATION OF BOSTON, INCORPORATED
88 Marlborough Street
Boston, Massachusetts 02116
President: Dr. Martha Brunner-Orne

AUSTRO-AMERICAN SOCIETY OF PHILADELPHIA
6133 North Eighth Street
Philadelphia, Pennsylvania 19120

BROTHERHOOD OF THE BURGENLAENDER
Castle Harbor Casino
1118 Havemeyer Avenue
Bronx, New York 10062
President: Alois Zach

BUFFALO AMERICAN BENEVOLENT SOCIETY, INCORPORATED
600 East North Street
Buffalo, New York 14201

BURGENLAENDER-AMERICAN BENEFIT SOCIETY
24 Dayton Avenue
Passaic, New Jersey 07055
President: Joseph Klucsaries

BURGENLANDISCHE GEMEINSCHAFT
c/o Mr. Joe Baumann
1642 Second Avenue
New York, New York 10028

BURGENLANDISCHE GEMEINSCHAFT, AUSSENSTELLE
3158 West 93rd Street
Evergreen Park, Illinois 60642
President: Frank Radostits

CONTINENTAL CLUB
7601 Southeast 27th
Mercer Island, Washington 98040

CONTINENTAL FRIENDSHIP CLUB
Hibiscus Temple (Lodge Mason)
Alton Road
Miami Beach, Florida 33139
President: Mr. William Weisz

EDELWEISSFRAUEN
Moser's Cafe
3140 West Lisbon Avenue
Milwaukee, Wisconsin 52208
President: Mrs. Mary Mueller

FIRST BURGENLANDER SICK & DEATH BENEFIT SOCIETY
Castle Harbour Casino
1118 Havemayer Avenue
Bronx, New York 10062
Director: Mr. John Wukisevits

FRIENDS OF AUSTRIA
105 Montgomery Street
San Francisco, California 94104

GEBIRGSTRACHTENVEREIN "ALMENRAUSCH"
6133 North Eighth Street
Philadelphia, Pennsylvania 19120
President: Mr. Bernhard Friedel

GOTTSCHEER DEUTSCHER VEREIN
1741 West Fletcher Street
Chicago, Illinois 60657
President: Hans Loy

JOLLY BURGENLANDER
14319 Minerva Drive
869 Oakwood Drive
Frankfort, Illinois 60423
President: Sharon Wolf

KAFKA SOCIETY OF AMERICA
c/o Maria Luise Caputo-Mayr
Department of Germanic and Slavic Languages
Humanities Building, Room 339
Temple University
Philadelphia, Pennsylvania 19122
Executive Officer: Professor Maria Luise Caputo-Mayr (215) 787-8270
Founded 1975

Students, teachers, scholars and departments of modern literature, readers of Franz Kafka's works, psychologists, and academic and other libraries with holdings in modern literature. Presents and publishes papers on Kafka (1883-1924), Austrian poet and writer, and encourages bibliographical studies. Informs members of on-going research and events concerning Kafka, such as exhibitions, meetings and congresses. Affiliated with: Modern Language Association of America.
Publication: Newsletter, semiannual.

KARNTNER KLUB "KOSCHAT"
4831 Prospect, Norridge
Chicago, Illinois 60656
President: Willi Wedam

OESTERREICHER VEREIN
1307 Bennington Avenue
Pittsburgh, Pennsylvania 15217
President: Professor Gerhard Werner

ROSEGGER-STEIRER CLUB
3149 Duluth Avenue
Highland, Indiana 46322
President: Mr. Carl Rossner

STEIRER KLUB VON CHICAGO
7361 Jonquil Terrace
Hanover Park, Illinois 60703
President: Josef Wilfinger

TIROLER STERBEVERSICHERUNGSVEREIN
(Tiroler Beneficial Society)
4829 Rising Sun Avenue
Philadelphia, Pennsylvania 19120
President: Joseph Mirth

VEREIN OSTERREICH, INCORPORATED
6127 Harwood Avenue
Oakland, California 96618
President: Louis A. Reinthaler

Professional Organizations

AMERICAN ASSOCIATION OF FORMER AUSTRIAN JURISTS
244 East 86th Street
New York, New York 10028
President: Dr. Joseph Heim

COMMITTEE OF FORMER AUSTRIAN BANK EMPLOYEES
104-60 Queens Boulevard, Apartment 15K
Forest Hills, New York 11375
President: Dr. Otto Mandl

Public Affairs Organizations

AMERICAN FRIENDS OF AUSTRIAN LABOR
242 East 19th Street
New York, New York 10003
President: Dr. Richard Berczeller

Cultural and Educational Organizations

AUSTRIA PHILATELIC SOCIETY OF NEW YORK
120 East Cedar Street
Livingston, New Jersey 07039 (201) 992-5279
Secretary: Richard Green Founded 1948

Collectors of Austrian stamps and related philatelic materials. Sponsors exhibits and lectures. Maintains expertizing service and exchange circuit.
Publication: Bulletin, quarterly.

AUSTRIAN FORUM
c/o Margaret Bush
305 West End Avenue
New York, New York 10023 (212) 873-2858
President: Margaret Bush Founded 1942

Seeks to increase understanding and cultural ties between the United States and Austria through various programs, publications, exchange activities, and cooperation with other organizations, institutes, and individuals. Arranges lectures and performances on literature, music, art, science, economics, social science, cultural and public relations.

AUSTRIAN INSTITUTE
Cultural Affairs Section
Austrian Consulate General
11 East 52nd Street
New York, New York 10022 (212) 759-5165
Director: Dr. Fritz Cocron Founded 1962

Not a membership organization. Austrian government agency responsible for cultural and science relations between America and Austria. Maintains a reference library.
Publications: Newsletter, bimonthly; also publishes other material on Austrian cultural life.

BRUCKNER SOCIETY OF AMERICA
Post Office Box 2570
Iowa City, Iowa 52244 (319) 338-0313
President: Charles L. Eble Founded 1932

Persons interested in the music of Gustav Mahler (1863-1911), Austrian composer and conductor, and Anton Bruckner (1824-96), Austrian composer. Presents Bruckner Medal of Honor and Mahler Medal of Honor annually to persons or organizations making significant contributions in furthering the music of Bruckner or Mahler.
Publication: Chord and Discord, irregular.

BURGENLANDER MANNERCHOR
9221 South Kedzie
Evergreen Park, Illinois 60642
President: Georg Wiesler

COMMITTEE TO PROMOTE THE STUDY OF AUSTRIAN HISTORY
University of Minnesota
Center for Austrian Studies
715 Social Sciences Building
267 19th Avenue South
Minneapolis, Minnesota 55455 (612) 373-4670
Editor: Professor John Rath Founded 1957

Persons doing research in Austrian history.
Publication: Austrian History Yearbook.

FEDERATION OF ALPINE AND SCHUHPLATTLER CLUBS IN NORTH AMERICA
54 Cathedral Lane
Cheektowaga, New York 14225 (716) 892-4119
President: Walter R. Wieand Founded 1966

Local groups from varied professions. To foster and promote Bavarian and Austrian culture and dance. Sponsors competitions; conducts charitable program and service for children. Offers specialized education. Sponsors biennial Schuhplattler Group Competitive Dancing; bestows trophy. Compiles statistics. Also known as: Gauverband Nordamerika.
Publications: Trachten Kalender (directory), annual.

INTERNATIONAL ARTHUR SCHNITZLER RESEARCH ASSOCIATION
Department of Literatures and Languages
University of California at Riverside
Riverside, California 92521
President: Professor Donald G. Daviau (714) 787-5603

Persons interested in Austrian literature, particularly in Arthur Schnitzler (1862-1931), Austrian playwright and novelist, and in his contemporaries. Encourages and facilitates research on Schnitzler, his works, and related subjects, and aids in rendering his writings more generally known and better understood. Aids Schnitzler scholars through exchange of information, coordination of research projects, research grants, and archive materials. IASRA Schnitzler Archive located at the University of California at Riverside, contains microfilms of Schnitzler's posthumous papers, as well as published writings by and about Schnitzler.
Publication: Modern Austrian Literature, quarterly (includes annual directory).

MILWAUKEE ZITHER CLUB
2952 North 48th Street
Milwaukee, Wisconsin 53210
President: Hans Gassner

PRO MOZART SOCIETY OF GREATER DETROIT
14511 Rosemary
Oakpark, Michigan 48237
President: Professor Marguerite Kozenn-Chajes

PRO MOZART SOCIETY OF GREATER MIAMI
12300 Old Cutler Road
Miami, Florida 33156
President: Dr. Sanel Beer

STEIRER DAMENCHOR
1402 West North Shore
Chicago, Illinois 60626
President: Eleanore Weers

UNITED STATES COMMITTEE TO PROMOTE STUDIES OF THE HISTORY OF THE HABSBURG MONARCHY
c/o Professor George Barany
Department of History
University of Denver
Denver, Colorado 80208
Executive Secretary: George Barany Founded 1957

Scholars interested in Central European history. Presents annual grant by the Austrian Ministry for Science and Research for research and study in Austrian history. Affiliated with the Conference Group for Central European History of American Historical Association.
Publication: Austrian History Yearbook.

VIENNESE CULTURE CLUB
Studio City, California 91604
President: Dona Pegita

Religious Organizations

AMERICAN CONGREGATION OF JEWS FROM AUSTRIA
118 West 95th Street
New York, New York 10025

Executive Secretary: (212) 663-1920
J. H. Hall Founded 1945

Conducts religious services

PFARRE SAINT STEPHAN
3705 Woodlawn Avenue
Los Angeles, California 90011

Research Centers and Special Institutes

CENTER FOR AUSTRIAN STUDIES
715 Social Sciences Building
267 Nineteenth Avenue, South
Minneapolis, Minnesota 55455 (612) 373-4670
Director: Professor John Rath Founded 1957

Special Libraries and Subject Collections

AUSTRIAN INFORMATION SERVICE
31 East 69th Street
New York, New York 10021 (212) 737-6400
Director: Erich Fenkart Founded 1948

Subjects: Austrian affairs. Holdings: Books; current Austrian newspapers and periodicals. Services: General educational and cultural information supplied; service not open to public. Merged with library of the Austrian Consulate General.

AUSTRIAN INSTITUTE
11 East 52nd Street
New York, New York 10022 (212) 759-5165
Librarian: Friederike Zeitlhofer Founded 1962

Subjects: Austrian history, fine arts, theatre, philosophy, psychology, geography and fiction. Holdings: Books; current Austrian newspapers; photographs and a poster/graphics collection. Services: Open to the public for reference.

Newspapers and Newsletters

NEWS AND EVENTS. 1973-. Bimonthly. Editor: Dr. Fritz Cocran. Publisher: Austrian Institute, 11 East 52nd Street, New York, New York 10022. In English.

Reports on news of cultural activities in the arts, fine arts, science and research on events concerning Austrian organizations and people in the United States.

Magazines

AUSTRIAN INFORMATION. Ten times a year. Publisher: Austrian Press and Information Service, 31 East 69th Street, New York, New York 10021. In English.

A news magazine which publishes general news from Austria and comprehensive articles about Austria's economy, history, culture and politics.

ENCOUNTER AUSTRIA. Editor: Margaret Zellers. Publisher: Oesterreichische Freurdenverkehrswerburg, Vienna. In English.

Written with the tourist in mind and describing the capital city of Vienna as well as Salzburg, Innsbruck, Bregenz, Graz, Klagenfurt, Luiz and Eisenstadt, the mountain areas, folklore, music, food, shopping, youth travel and vacation activities.

Radio Programs

New York - Bronx

WFUV - Third Avenue and East Fordham Road, Bronx, New York 10458, (212) 365-8050. Austrian program "Nachrichten aus Oesterreich," a weekly summary of Austrian news, 1/2 hour weekly.

Austria - Vienna

ORF - Auslandsdienst, Post Office Box 700, A-1041, Vienna, Austria. Transmits shortwave radio programs daily in German from Vienna to the United States.

"Welcome to Austria"; bimonthly program (30 minutes) in English with music, interviews and news from Austria. Distributed nationwide by the Broadcasting Foundation of America.

Additional information on all radio programs available from the Austrian Press- and Information Service, 31 East 69th Street, New York, New York 10021.

Bank Branches in the U.S.

AUSTRIAN LAENDERBANK
11 Broadway
New York, New York 10004 (212) 344-7090

CREDITANSTALT-BANKVEREIN
United States Affiliate:
European and American Banking Corporation
10 Hanover Square
New York, New York 10005 (212) 623-3600

GZB/VIENNA
630 Fifth Avenue, Suite 3550
New York, New York 10020 (212) 586-8274

Commercial and Trade Organizations

AUSTRIAN CHAMBER OF COMMERCE, INCORPORATED
Post Office Box 12010
Seattle, Washington 98112
Director: Franz Schneighofer

AUSTRIAN TRADE COMMISSION

845 Third Avenue, 21st Floor
New York, New York 10022 (212) 421-5250

Standard Oil Building, Suite 5130
200 East Randolph Drive
Chicago, Illinois 60601 (312) 681-0100

3440 Wilshire Boulevard
Los Angeles, California 90010 (213) 380-7990

U.S. AUSTRIAN CHAMBER OF COMMERCE
165 West 46th Street
New York, New York 10036 (212) 757-0117
President: John E. Leslie Founded 1949

Hosts receptions and luncheons. Sponsors the Viennese Opera Ball.
Publication: Austrian Business, bimonthly.

AUSTRIAN WINE INSTITUTE
845 Third Avenue
New York, New York 10022 (212) 759-6500

Airline Offices

AUSTRIAN AIRLINES
North American Headquarters:
608 Fifth Avenue, Suite 507
New York, New York 10020 (212) 265-6350

Flies from Austria to most Western European countries, to the Middle East, and Moscow. Offers extensive services in Eastern Europe.

MONTANA AUSTRIA AIRLINE
1 World Trade Center, Suite 8519
New York, New York 10048 (212) 775-1347

Operates direct flights between New York and Vienna.

Books and Pamphlets

AUSTRIA. Vienna, Federal Press Service, 1979.

A small book in German, English, French and Italian showing the glories of Austria from the aspects of its mountains, its rivers, its agricultural areas, its churches and other architecture and its iron industry. Richly illustrated with scenic, folkloristic and human interest photographs.

AUSTRIA AS A COUNTRY OF ASYLUM. Vienna, Federal Press Service, 1981.

Due to its geographical position and its own historical experience, Austria has become one of the most important transit points for refugees and emigrants since the end of the Second World War. This booklet tells about the institutions, both public and voluntary, which have arisen to deal with refugees, discusses some of the problems of aid and gives statistical descriptions of the work.

AUSTRIA - AT THE HEART OF EUROPE. Vienna, Federal Press Service.

A brochure with short descriptions of Austria's economic system and performance, the various ethnic groups within the country, history, Austria's position in the world, education, culture, welfare and political system. Includes a map and statistical information.

AUSTRIA - CONSERVATION, PRESERVATION. Vienna, Federal Press Service.

A brochure showing restoration projects from important castles and churches to farmhouses and wayside shrines. Tells about the techniques of conservation. Has many illustrations.

AUSTRIA: FACTS AND FIGURES. Vienna, Federal Press Service, 1979.

Discusses the country's history and geography, government and politics, economy, social services, sports, education, and culture.

AUSTRIA - MODERN ARCHITECTURE. Vienna, Federal Press Service.

Against a historic tradition of fine architecture the Austrian modernists developed a tradition of innovation which is described and illustrated in this brochure. Architects such as Adolf Loos, Richard Neutra, Gustav Peichl, Carl Auboeck and Johann Staber are touched upon.

AUSTRIA - MODERN GRAPHIC ART. Vienna, Federal Press Service.

Names such as Kokoschka, Schiele, Klimt, Kubin, Thony and Boeckl are represented in this brochure which also tells about the younger generation of graphic artists, Flora, Melcher, Hrdlicka, Frohner, to name but a few. Illustrations are in black and white.

AUSTRIA - MODERN LITERATURE. Vienna, Federal Press Service.

Tells about Austria's modern masters, Kafka, Rulke, Hofmannsthal, Schnitzler, Zweig, Kraus, Roth, Musil, Broch, Canetti, Celan as well as the best known of the contemporary generation Handke, Bernard, Jandl and many others. Illustrated in black and white.

AUSTRIA - MODERN PAINTING. Vienna, Federal Press Service.

Austrian painters have tended to draw upon nature and to put the sensual before the abstract, to put color before graphic expression. Representative works of several dozen artists are reproduced in color.

AUSTRIA - MODERN SCULPTURE. Vienna, Federal Press Service.

The many directions taken by Austrian sculpturers are described and illustrated in this brochure.

AUSTRIAN HISTORICAL BIBLIOGRAPHY, 1966. Edited by Eric H. Boehm and Fritz Fellner. Santa Barbara, California, Clio Press, 1969.

Provides comprehensive bibliographical coverage of Austrian historical studies. Includes books, periodical articles, festschriften, and dissertations in a classified arrangement. Materials published in Austria on the history of other countries are also included. Contains an author index.

INNSBRUCK. Innsbruck, Fremdenverkehrsverband, 1980.

Printed in both summer and winter versions, showing winter sports and summer hiking and cultural activities and sights. A map of the city is laid in.

SALZBURG, THE BEAUTIFUL CITY. Salzburg, Stadtverkehrsburo.

A city famous for its musical life, home of the world-renowned Salzburg Festival, it is also a city of outstanding architectural harmony and charm located in a beautiful scenic region. Folder includes a small map of the town and pictures of its sights.

TIROL. Innsbruck, Tiroler Fremdenverkehrswerbung, 1982.

Includes several topographic maps of the Alps in the areas around Innsbruck, Landeck, Kitzbuhel, Kufstein, Schwaz and Lienz and pictures of typical Tyrolian scenes. An outline map is also provided.

WIEN-VIENNA-VIENNE-VIENA. Vienna, Vienna Tourist Board.

Magazine format abundantly illustrated in color and with a centerfold map of the city as well as one of the inner city, showing major buildings, this publication tells about the history of the city, its international institutions, parks, palaces, architecture, shopping, museums, music, theater, the Vienna Woods, Prater. Gives several pages of useful information for the visitor.

AUSTRIAN AMERICANS

AUSTRIAN AID TO AMERICAN CATHOLICS, 1830-1860. By Reverend Benjamin J. Blied. Milwaukee, Wisconsin, 1944.

Gives an account of the activities of Austrian clergymen in various regions of the United States in the years before the American Civil War. This period coincided with the most active period of the Leopoldine Society, whose sole objective was to help the Catholic missions in America.

AUSTRIAN EMIGRATION: 1936-1945. By Franz Goldner. Translated by Edith Simons. New York, F. Ungar Publishing Company, 1979.

Austrian emigration just prior to and during the Second World War was primarily motivated by Germany's Anschluss of Austria and the anti-Semitic, anti-socialist, anti-intellectual policies of the Hitler regime. The author treats groups and individuals who were a part of this exodus, shows how they were driven out and what became of them.

AUSTRIAN WRITERS IN THE UNITED STATES, 1938-1968. New York, Austrian Institute, 1969.

A catalogue prepared for an exhibition of exiled and emigre writers which includes both biography and bibliography for sixty-two authors.

DETAILED REPORTS OF THE SALZBERGER EMIGRANTS WHO SETTLED IN AMERICA. Edited by Samuel Urlsperger. Athens, Georgia, University of Georgia Press, 1968.

Translations of letters and diaries with comment and annotation by George Fenwick Jones.

FROM THE DANUBE TO THE HUDSON; U. S. Ministerial and Consular Dispatches on Immigration from the Habsburg Monarchy, 1850-1900. By Zoltan Kramar. Atlanta, Georgia, Hungarian Cultural Foundation, 1978.

A collection of dispatches of officials from the former Hapsburg Empire that shows the official views of the emigration, motives for emigration, description of the emigrants and the "bad faith" immigrants.

GUIDE TO THE ARCHIVAL MATERIALS OF THE GERMAN-SPEAKING EMIGRATION TO THE UNITED STATES AFTER 1933. By Jon M. Spalek. Charlottesville, Publishing for the Bibliographical Society of the University of Virginia by the University Press of Virginia, 1978.

An alphabetical arrangement of individuals who are of some importance in their professions and may have collections on them. Each individual has listed below their name; the location of materials and descriptive paragraphs (call numbers, restrictions, history of the collection).

PILGRIMS OF '48: ONE MAN'S PART IN THE AUSTRIAN REVOLUTION OF 1848, AND A FAMILY MIGRATION TO AMERICA. By Josephine Clara Goldmark. New Haven, Yale University Press, 1930.

THE QUIET INVADERS; The Story of the Austrian Impact upon America. By E. Wilder Spaulding. Vienna, Osterreichischer Bundesverlag fur Unterricht, Wissenschaft und Kunst, 1968.

Discusses Austrian immigrants to America, their historical background, the occupations they pursued, and their contributions in music, science, art, literature, medicine, and other fields.

Audiovisual Material

MAP

AUSTRIA; At the Heart of Europe. Vienna, Federal Press Service, 1981.

A detailed map of Austria showing roads, railroads, airports, political divisions, and other information. On the verso are brief overviews of Austria's position in the world, government, history, social conditions, culture, science, education, economic system, and statistical data. In color. Approximately 19 by 24 inches.

FILMS

AUSTRIA AND THE LIPIZZANER HORSES. 16 mm. Color and sound. 17 minutes. By Paul Hoefler Productions. Mar/Chuck Film Industries, Mount Prospect, Illinois, 1972.

Shows the spectacular scenery of Austria and some of the country's talented artisans. In Vienna women are shown working petit point designs, at Augarten Palace workers create fine porcelain, and in the alpine village of Piber the famed Lipizzaner horses perform.

AUSTRIA TODAY. 16 mm. Color and sound. 27 minutes.

Shows the achievements Austria has made since World War II, the main characteristics of life and work in Austria today, and the beautiful Austrian landscape.

AUSTRIA - CRADLE OF MUSIC. 16 mm. Color and sound. 30 minutes.

Discusses the music and lives of great Austrian composers: Haydn, Mozart, Beethoven, Schubert, Bruckner. The film shows documents written by the composers, while playing their music and showing the Austrian landscape and places where they lived.

MONTAGE OF PLEASURE. 16 mm. Color and sound. 23 minutes.

This award-winning picture presents an impressionistic sequence from all over Austria, grouped by themes (music, castles, sports, etc.) rather than geographically. Without narration, the film scores its impact through the rapid, modern style of editing, in harmony with the musical background.

THE NAZI STRIKE. Videorecording. Black and white. Sound. 41 minutes. By United States Office of War Information, Domestic Branch. Distributed by National Audiovisual Center, Washington, D.C., 1979.

A documentary film record of Germany's preparation for war, the conquest of Austria and Czechoslovakia and the attack upon Poland.

NEW HORIZONS - A JOURNEY THROUGH AUSTRIA. 16 mm. Color and sound. 20 minutes.

Shows the landscape of Austria and the beauties of Vienna, as well as the possibilities of gourmet dining in Austrian restaurants.

Additional information on printed and audiovisual material available from the Austrian Press and Information Service, 31 East 69th Street, New York, New York 10021.

BASQUES

Fraternal Organizations

BASQUE CLUB, INCORPORATED
Post Office Box 27021
San Francisco, California 94127

Holds a picnic the first Sunday in June at which a mass is held and special foods and Basque dancing are featured. Sponsors a "klinka" or Basque musical band.

CHINO BASQUE CLUB
Post Office Box 1080
Chino, California 91710

On Labor Day weekend the club puts on its annual picnic with mass and Basque dancers on Sunday and handball games on Monday.

ELKO BASQUE CLUB
Post Office Box 1321
Elko, Nevada 89801

Hosts the National Basques games on the Fourth of July weekend. The games bring together the best from all the Basque associations for contests in weight-lifting, wood-chopping and tug-of-war. There is a parade with colorful costumes, a dance for the public as well as Basque dancing. On Sunday, mass is celebrated.

ELY BASQUE CLUB
Post Office Box 1014
Ely, Nevada

Holds an annual festival the third weekend in July with Basque games, consisting of weight-carrying, wood-chopping and a tug-of-war, a parade and public dancing. On Sunday a mass is celebrated, followed by lunch and Basque dance exhibitions.

EUZKALDUNAK DANAK BAT
c/o Kathleen Ceranguena
Box 70
Winnemucca, Nevada 89445

Sponsors a Basque weekend in mid-July with a parade, Basque games, dancing and a mass.

EUZKALDUNAK, INCORPORATED
Post Office Box 2613
Boise, Idaho 83701

On the last weekend in July the Basques of the Boise area gather to celebrate mass together and have a pot-luck picnic. The night before there is a dance.

EUZKALDUNAK OF CALDWELL, INCORPORATED
220 East Logan Street
Caldwell, Idaho 83605

FRESNO BASQUE CLUB
Post Office Box 406
Fresno, California 93708

Father's Day is the date when the members of the club have their annual reunion and picnic. The festivities are preceded by a mass.

KERN COUNTY BASQUE CLUB
Post Office Box 416
Bakersfield, California 93308

The highlight of the year's activities is a meeting on Memorial Day weekend with dancing on Saturday evening, mass on Sunday followed by a barbeque and Basque dancers in performance and joined by the public.

LOS ANGELES OBERENA
2801 Leonis Boulevard
Vernon, California 90058

LOS BANOS BASQUE CLUB
Post Office Box 123
Los Banos, California 95365

Holds an annual get-together the third Sunday in May which begins with a religious service followed by a picnic at which Basque dancers perform and the entire group joins in. Music is both Basque and American.

NORTH AMERICAN BASQUE ORGANIZATIONS, INCORPORATED
1125 West Plumb Lane
Reno, Nevada 89509
Vice President: Janet Inda Founded 1973

Umbrella organization for the Basque Clubs in the western part of the United States. Sponsors classes in the Basque language and traditional dances. Runs a summer camp where young people may learn and experience their Basque heritage.

ONTARIO BASQUE CLUB, INCORPORATED
Post Office Box 823
Ontario, Oregon 97914

Celebrates the Basque heritage on Father's Day with a communal mass followed by a lunch featuring Basque delicacies.

UTAH BASQUE CLUB
c/o Claudia Bilbao
1334 East Fairoaks Way
Sandy, Utah 84070

WESTERN SLOPES BASQUE ASSOCIATION
c/o Jean Gorrino
789 22nd Road
Grand Junction, Colorado 81501

ZAZPIAK-BAT CLUB, INCORPORATED
Post Office Box 7382
Menlo Park, California 94025

ZOZPIAK-BAT BASQUE CLUB
Post Office Box 7771
Reno, Nevada 89510

On the second Saturday in August the Basques of Reno gather for mass, an afternoon of Basque games, a barbeque followed by ethnic and other dancing.

Professional Organizations

NATIONAL ASSOCIATION OF JAI ALAI FRONTONS
9999 North East Second Avenue
Miami Shores, Florida 33138
Executive Director: J. Patrick McCann — (305) 758-2524
Founded 1977

Jai alai fronton (arena) operators. Purposes are: to promote the development and acceptance of jai alai and to provide a forum for the exchange of ideas, information and methods of operation among fronton operators. Promotes high standards of conduct for jai alai contests.
Publications: NAJF Notes, quarterly.

Cultural and Educational Organizations

OINKARI BASQUE DANCERS
1615 Pomander Road
Boise, Idaho 83705
President: Cindy Shaffeld — Founded 1950

A civic, non-profit group of ethnic dancers.

UNITED STATES AMATEUR JAI ALAI PLAYERS ASSOCIATION
c/o Jacques Unhassobiscay
30 Altura Way
Larkspur, California 94939
Executive Director: Jacques Unhassobiscay — (305) 377-3333
Founded 1966

Persons who participate in playing Jai Alai. Aims to develop the ancient Basque sport of Jai Alai in the United States, to attend world tournaments and to send United States teams to these tournaments. The Association sent a team to the Olympics in Mexico in 1968.
Publications: Bulletin, irregular.

Research Centers and Special Institutes

BASQUE STUDIES PROGRAM
University of Nevada
Getchell Library, Room 274
Reno, Nevada 89557
Coordinator: Dr. William A. Douglass — (702) 784-4854
Founded 1967

Pursues research on Basques in America, including studies on the history of Basque immigration in the New World, ethnicity maintenance among Basque Americans, social anthropology of Old World Basque society, Basque structural linguistics, and currently the nature of rural-urban ties in Old World Basque society. Research results are published in professional journals and the Basque Book Series of the University of Nevada Press. Holds a summer session abroad every third year in the Basque area of Europe. Maintains a Basque collection of 12,000 volumes on Basque history, politics, literature, and ethnology.
Publication: Newsletter, biannual.

Museums

NORTHEASTERN NEVADA MUSEUM
1515 Idaho Street
Elko, Nevada 89801
Mailing Address:
Post Office Box 503
Elk, Nevada 89801 (702) 738-3418
Director: Howard Hickson Founded 1968

Collections include materials relating to Basque settlers in the area.

Special Libraries and Subject Collections

BASQUE STUDIES PROGRAM
Room 274, Getchell Literary
University of Nevada
Reno, Nevada 89557 (702) 782-4854

Subjects: Basque materials both European and American. Holdings: Books, periodicals, audiovisual materials, artifacts, archives, oral history. Services: Copying facilities, tours, lectures, and other presentations for schools, radio and television.

Newspapers and Newsletters

THE BASQUE STUDIES PROGRAM--NEWSLETTER. 1968-. Semiannual. Editor: William A. Douglass. Publisher: Basque Studies Program, University of Nevada Library, Reno, Nevada 89557.

Covers highlights of the Basque Studies Program and Basque-related news, articles about Basques in old and new worlds, announcements of interest on this subject, status of research in Basque studies. Includes notices of books and films, program activities.

Radio Programs

Idaho - Boise

KBOI - Box 1280, Boise, Idaho 83701, (208) 336-3670. Basque programs, 1/2 hour weekly.

Nevada - Elko

KELK - Box 790, Elko, Nevada 89801, (702) 738-7118. Basque programs, 2 hours weekly.

Festivals, Fairs, and Celebrations

Idaho - Sun Valley

BASQUE BENEFIT
Trail Creek Cabin, Sun Valley Village
Sun Valley, Idaho

A spectacular Basque festival in this major resort area. Features shows by the colorful Oinkari Dancers and contests in weightlifting and wood-chopping as brawny men test their strength. There is a lamb barbeque as well as a sheep auction, raffle and prizes. Held in mid-July.
Contact James W. Ball, Ketchum - Sun Valley Chamber of Commerce, Box 465, Ketchem, Idaho 83340 or Jack Brown, Sun Valley, Idaho 83353.

Nevada - Elko

NATIONAL BASQUE FESTIVAL
Elko, Nevada

The ancient European heritage of the Basque people is celebrated with dancing, music, authentic costumes, handcrafts, a parade and feasting. Basques from all over the western states convene at Elko and try their skill at sheepherding and shearing contests, competitive games, and mountaineer skills. Held the first weekend in July.
Contact: Elko Euzkaldunak Club, Post Office Box 1321, Elko, Nevada 89801.

Utah - Snowbird

BASQUE FESTIVAL
Snowbird, Utah

Colorful Basque costumes, exhibition dancers and Basque music highlight the festival held the first week of June.
Contact: Snowbird Chamber of Commerce, Snowbird, Utah 84092.

Books and Pamphlets

BASQUE AMERICANS

AMERIKANUAK: BASQUES IN THE NEW WORLD. By William A. Douglass and Jon Bilbao. Reno, University of Nevada Press, 1975.

After collecting oral histories, personal observations, questionnaires, examination of official records, and analyzing newspaper files, the authors have presented a history of Basque activities in the New World.

ANGLO-AMERICAN CONTRIBUTIONS TO BASQUE STUDIES: ESSAYS IN HONOR OF JON BILBAO. Edited by William A. Douglass. Reno, Nevada; Desert Research Institute, 1977.

This collection of essays is divided into three sections: the first deals with the Old World Basque experience, the second looks at the Basques as an immigrant ethnic group in the New World, and the last section deals with the language of the Basques.

BASQUE-AMERICANS AND A SEQUENTIAL THEORY OF MIGRATION AND ADAPTATION. By Grant McCall. San Francisco College, 1968. Reprint San Francisco, R and E Research Associates, 1973.

This thesis explores the regularities and common patterns to be found in the phenomena of acculturation, urbanization and immigration and shows how the Basques fit into those phenomena.

SWEET PROMISED LAND. By Robert Laxalt. New York, 1957.

Biography of a Basque sheepman in the western part of America written by his son.

Audiovisual Material

FILMS

BASQUE COUNTRY. 16 mm. Color and sound. 14 minutes.

Shows the Basque country in France which offers sea, mountains and countryside in a radius of 50 kilometers. The Basque people have preserved their original way of life so well adapted to the variety of the geography.

EL PAIS VASCO. 16 mm. Color and sound. 16 minutes. Chicago, International Film Bureau, 1969.

Shows the Basque region of Spain, with scenes of Bilbao, Fuenterribia, San Sebastian, and the Cantabrian Coast. Uses a narrative technique for presenting vocabulary and grammatical structure for first year Spanish students.

SEASONS OF THE BASQUE. 16 mm. Color and sound. 30 minutes. By Basque Studies Program, University of Nevada.

Documentation of the Basque sheepherding cycle in the American West. Funded by National Endowment for the Arts.

SLIDES

EUSKALERRIA: HOMELAND OF THE BASQUES. 30 minutes. (Accompanied by a cassette tape). By North American Basque Organizations, Incorporated, Reno, Nevada.

EUSKALDUNAK: BASQUES OF THE AMERICAN WEST. 30 minutes. (Accompanied by a cassette tape). By North American Basque Organizations, Incorporated, Reno, Nevada.

PHOTOGRAPHS

BASQUE SHEEPHERDERS: END OF AN ERA. By Richard Lane. 37 framed color photographs.

Depicts Basque involvement in sheepherding in the American West.

BELGIANS
(Includes FLEMISH)
See also: FRENCH-SPEAKING PEOPLES

Embassy and Consulates

BELGIAN EMBASSY
3330 Garfield Street, Northwest
Washington, D.C. 20008 (202) 333-6900

CONSULATES GENERAL

Suite 2306
Peachtree Center
Cain Tower
229 Peachtree Street, Northeast
Atlanta, Georgia 30303 (404) 659-2150

333 North Michigan Avenue,
Room 2000
Chicago, Illinois 60601 (312) 263-6624

2001 Kirby Drive, Suite 314
Houston, Texas 77019 (713) 526-0242

3921 Wilshire Boulevard, Suite 600
Los Angeles, California 90010 (213) 385-8116

50 Rockefeller Plaza,
Room 1104
New York, New York 10020 (212) 586-5110

100 Bush Street, 14th Floor
San Francisco, California
94104 (415) 986-2883

HONORARY CONSULATES

28 State Street
Boston, Massachusetts 02109 (617) 523-7493

2231 Northeast 192nd Street
Miami, Florida 33160 (305) 932-4263

Honorary Consulates are also located in Mobile, Alabama; Anchorage, Alaska; Phoenix, Arizona; San Diego, California; Denver, Colorado; Tampa, Florida; Honolulu, Hawaii; Moline, Illinois; Mishawaka, Indiana; Des Moines, Iowa; Louisville, Kentucky; New Orleans, Louisiana; Baltimore, Maryland; Detroit, Michigan; Minneapolis, Minnesota; Kansas City and Saint Louis, Missouri; Cleveland, Ohio; Oklahoma City, Oklahoma; Portland, Oregon; Philadelphia and Pittsburgh, Pennsylvania; San Juan, Puerto Rico; Dallas and El Paso, Texas; Norfolk, Virginia; Seattle, Washington; Milwaukee, Wisconsin.

Mission to the United Nations

BELGIAN MISSION
809 United Nations Plaza, 2nd Floor
New York, New York 10017 (212) 599-5250

Information Offices

BELGIAN INDUSTRIAL INFORMATION SERVICE
50 Rockefeller Plaza
New York, New York 10020 (212) 586-5110

Tourist and Travel Offices

BELGIAN NATIONAL TOURIST OFFICE
720 Fifth Avenue
New York, New York 10019 (212) 758-8130

Fraternal Organizations

BELGIAN AMERICAN CLUB
3839 North Janssens
Chicago, Illinois 60613
President: Arnold Van Puymbroeck

BELGIAN-AMERICAN CLUB OF TEXAS
2706 Northland
San Antonio, Texas 78217
President: Albert DeWinne

BELGIAN AMERICAN RIK VAN LOOY CLUB
6214 Bissell Street
Huntington Park, California 90255
Chairman: Frank Smets

BROEDERKRING CLUB
B. K. Hall
721 South West Street
Mishawaka, Indiana 46544
President: Andre Verstraete

FLEMISH AMERICAN CLUB
932 Cole Street
Kewanee, Illinois 61443
President: Cyriel Van Daele

UNITED BELGIAN AMERICAN SOCIETIES
20623 Country Club Drive
Harper Woods, Michigan 48225
President: Oscar Haezebrouck

Cultural and Educational Organizations

CENTER FOR BELGIAN CULTURE OF WESTERN ILLINOIS
712 - 18th Avenue
Moline, Illinois 61265 (309) 762-0167
Director: Arthur Holevoet Founded 1963

Provides lectures, art presentations, films, and craft classes. Maintains a library with books and audio-visual materials, archives for the organization and for Belgian ethnic culture in the United States. Publications: Newsletter (monthly); also publishes brochures on Belgian life in America.

Foundations

BELGIAN AMERICAN EDUCATIONAL FOUNDATION
420 Lexington Avenue
New York, New York 10017 (212) 683-1496
President: Emile L. Boulpaep Founded 1920

Promotes closer relations and the exchange of intellectual ideas between Belgium and the United States through fellowships granted to graduate students of one country for study and research in the other. Assists higher education and scientific research. Commemorates the work of the Commission for Relief in Belgium and associated organizations during the First World War, 1914-1918. Not a membership organization.

BELGIAN ART FOUNDATION IN THE UNITED STATES, INCORPORATED
521 Fifth Avenue
New York, New York 10017 (212) 687-6327

THE ROBERT BRUNNER FOUNDATION
63 Wall Street, Suite 1903
New York, New York 10005 (212) 344-0050
President: John M. Bruderman Incorporated 1949

Grants for Roman Catholic institutions in the United States and Belgium, but principally for educational and religious organizations founded by the donor. No grants to individuals or for building or endowment funds.

Religious Organizations

BELGIAN BUREAU
Archdiocese of New York
502 West 41st Street
New York, New York
Director: Father Adhemar de Pauw (212) 594-0130

Provides religious and charitable assistance to Belgian communicants.

Research Centers and Special Institutes

CENTER FOR FLEMISH ART AND CULTURE
University of Kansas
Spencer Art Museum
Lawrence, Kansas 66045 (913) 864-4710
Director: Professor Erik Larsen Founded 1970

An integral unit of the University of Kansas supported by the parent institution. Pursues research in the fields of Flemish art, literature, history, musicology, and theatre.

Special Libraries and Subject Collections

BELGIAN CONSULATE GENERAL - LIBRARY
50 Rockefeller Plaza (212) 586-5110
New York, New York 10020 Founded 1941

Subjects: Belgian history, art, cultures, and other aspects of Belgian life; Belgian literature in French, Dutch, and English translation. Holdings: Books; journals and other serials; newspapers; clippings; reports; documents; pamphlets; photographs; records. Services: Library is open to public for reference use only. Formerly known as the Belgian Government Information Center.

BLACK HAWK COLLEGE - LEARNING RESOURCES CENTER
6600 34th Avenue
Moline, Illinois 61265 (309) 755-1311
Director: Donald C. Rowland Founded 1946

Subjects: Belgian history and culture. Holdings: Books; tape recordings; magnetic tapes. Services: Interlibrary loans; copying; library is open to outside users with restrictions.

UNIVERSITY OF WISCONSIN AT GREEN BAY - LIBRARY
Green Bay, Wisconsin 54302

Repository of the Belgian-American Resources Collection.

Newspapers and Newsletters

BELGIAN AMERICAN TRADE REVIEW. 1927-. Monthly. Editor: Gustave Pairoux. Publisher: Belgian American Chamber of Commerce in United States, 50 Rockefeller Plaza, Room 1003, New York, New York 10020.

GAZETTE VAN DETROIT (Detroit Gazette). 1914-. Weekly. Editors: Mrs. Godelieve B. Van Reybrouck and Frans du Pont. Publisher: Belgian Publishing Company, 18740 Thirteen Mile Road, Roseville, Michigan 48066. In Flemish.

Publishes general news and reports on the activities of Flemish groups and individuals.

Bank Branches in the U.S.

BANQUE BRUXELLES LAMBERT, S.A.
New York Representative:
630 Fifth Avenue
New York, New York 10111 (212) 765-8285

Formed by a recent merger of the Banque de Bruxelles and the Banque Lambert.

KREDIETBANK, N.V.
450 Park Avenue
New York, New York 10022 (212) 832-7200

SOCIETE GENERALE DE BANQUE, S.A.
United States Affiliate:
499 Park Avenue
New York, New York 10022 (212) 980-9480

Commercial and Trade Organizations

BELGIAN AMERICAN CHAMBER OF COMMERCE IN THE UNITED STATES
50 Rockefeller Plaza
New York, New York 10020
Executive Secretary: Gastave E. Pairoux (212) 247-7613
Founded 1925

Formerly called the Belgian Chamber of Commerce in the United States.
Publications: Belgian Trade Review, ten times a year; Belgian American Trade Directory, triennial.

BELGIAN ENDIVES MARKETING BOARD
888 Seventh Avenue
New York, New York 10106 (212) 582-7373
Director: Mr. Weiner Founded 1980

BELGIAN LINEN ASSOCIATION
280 Madison Avenue
New York, New York 10016
U.S. Promotion Director: Pauline V. Delli-Carpini (212) 685-0424
Founded 1955

Belgian linen mills and flax processors in and near Kortrijk, Belgium. Promotes and advertises Belgian linen in the United States and Europe. Distributes booklets and pamphlets describing production of Belgian flax and spinning and weaving of linen.

BELGIAN TRADE OFFICE
150 Southeast Second Avenue
Miami, Florida 33131 (305) 358-5150

Festivals, Fairs, and Celebrations

BELGIAN AMERICAN DAY
Ghent, Minnesota

Events for the day includa a parade, queen coronation, and the Belgian national sport of prysbolling (like lawn bowling). Belgian cookies and waffles are available. Held in mid-August.
Contact: Department of Economic Development, 480 Cedar Street, Saint Paul, Minnesota 55101.

Airline Offices

SABENA AIRLINES
(Belgian World Airlines)

North American Headquarters:
Lake Success Business Park
125 Community Drive
Great Neck, New York 11021 (516) 466-6100

New York Office:
720 Fifth Avenue
New York, New York 10019 (212) 247-8880

Washington Office:
1725 K Street, Northwest
Washington, D.C. 20006 (202) 833-9600

Flies intercontinental routes to: the United States, Canada, Mexico, and Central America; to India, Southeast Asia, and Japan; to the Near East; to 24 cities throughout Africa; and to about 40 cities throughout Europe. Other offices in the United States: Anchorage (Alaska), Atlanta, Baltimore, Boston, Buffalo, Chicago, Cincinnati, Cleveland, Dallas, Detroit, Hartford, Kansas City, Los Angeles, Miami, Milwaukee, Minneapolis, Newark, New York, Philadelphia, Pittsburgh, San Francisco, and Washington.

Ship Lines

BELGIAN LINE
BELGIAN AFRICAN LINE
5 World Trade Center
New York, New York 10007 (212) 432-9050

Books and Pamphlets

BELGIUM. Brussels, Belgian Information and Documentation Institute, 1980.

A brochure telling about various aspects of Belgian life and institutions. Also gives a brief history of the country and its cultural tradition. Small maps are provided.

BELGIUM AT THE HEART OF EUROPE. Directed and revised by P. De Prins. Brussels, Belgian Information and Documentation Institute, 1977 13th ed.

A small book telling about the country of Belgium. It gives a geographical survey, takes a brief look at the past and at Belgians in the world. Describes institutions and authorities, Belgium's participation in international organizations, its intellectual life, trade and industry, social affairs, art and literature, and gives useful addresses. The informative text is accompanied by pictures and maps.

BELGIUM: FACTS AND FIGURES. 8th edition. Brussels, Belgian Information and Documentation Institute, 1981.

Presents statistical tables concerning the land, people, health, education, elections, labor, standard of living, social security, production, trade, finance, and related topics.

BELGIUM. Historic Cities. Brussels, Belgian National Tourist Office, 1982.

Several pages in this booklet are devoted to each of several well-known towns such as the city of Antwerp, Bruges, Brussels, Ghent, Liege, but there are also descriptions and pictures of lesser-known places of interest such as Arlon, Binche, Bouillon, Damme, Diest, Dinant, Huy, Ypres, Louvain, Mons, Namur, Oudenaarde etc. City maps are provided for the major towns and sometimes for the smaller ones as well.

BELGIUM. Where to go, What to see. Brussels, Belgian National Tourist Office, 1982.

A booklet for the tourist which gives short descriptions of Brussels, the cities and towns of Flanders and their treasures, the coastal holiday towns, the towns and cities of Wallonia, the Ardenne-et-Meuse, suggested routes for touring by car, by train, special festivals and folklore, sports activities, shopping, gastronomy and entertainment. General tourist information as well as several maps and many pictures make this an excellent introduction for the visitor.

GENT. Ghent, Stedelijke Dient voor Toerisme, 1973.

Presents detailed maps, many color photographs, and descriptions of places of interest in the city of Ghent. The text of the brochure is in four languages, including English.

A SELECTIVE BIBLIOGRAPHY OF BOOKS ON SUBJECTS RELATED TO BELGIUM AND BY BELGIAN AUTHORS, AND OF BOOKS ON BELGIUM'S POETRY REGARDING THE CONGO; Published in the United States, New York, Belgian Government Information Center.

A series of bibliographies published during the 1960's, each supplementing the other, of materials on Belgium written by Belgian authors.

WEST FLANDERS, BELGIUM. Brussels, Belgian National Tourist Office.

A tourist and travel brochure with many color photographs and brief descriptions of vacation activities and sights of interest in the seaside province of Flanders.

BELGIAN AMERICANS

THE BELGIANS: FIRST SETTLERS IN NEW YORK. By Henry G. Bayer. New York, Devin-Adair Company, 1925.

Gives an historical account of the very first Belgians in America.

BELGIANS IN AMERICA. By Philemon D. Sabbe. Thielt, Belgium, Lannoo, 1960.

A description of Belgians from the Wallonian section in American history and society.

THE CONTRIBUTION OF BELGIUM TO THE CATHOLIC CHURCH IN AMERICA (1523-1857). By Joseph A. Griffin. New York, AMS Press, 1974.

A dissertation on Belgium's contribution to the foundation of the American College at Louvain, which marks the beginning of an effort to train and send missionaries to America.

Audiovisual Material

MAPS

ATLAS OF BELGIUM. Brussels, Belgian Information and Documentation Institute, 1980.

A portfolio of maps each showing an aspect of Belgium, its position in Europe, political structure, population, agriculture, metallurgical industry, chemical and textile industry, energy, road network, railways and inland waterways.

TOURIST MAP OF BELGIUM. Brussels, Cartography Girault-Gilbert and Belgian National Tourist Office, 1981.

A road map of the country which also shows provincial borders and some typographical features. On the verso maps of Brussels, Bruges, Liege, Antwerp and Ghent. An explanation of traffic signs is given. Approximately 24 x 28 inches.

FILMS

BELGIAN SUITE. 16 mm. Color and sound. 20 minutes. Directed by Lucien Deroisy.

Surveys the country of Belgium to the accompaniment of a musical suite in four movements: land, water, air, and fire. Shows the countryside and cities from the North Sea to the East. Follows brooks, streams, and rivers on their way to the sea. Presents sighing wind, shimmering light, and church towers thrusting into the air. Shows the rhythm and delight of festivals, fairs, and carnivals.

BELGIUM SEEN FROM THE SKIES. 16 mm. Color and sound. 25 minutes. Embassy of Belgium, 1979.

A succession of aerial views of Belgium's varied countryside from the sea coast to the forests of the Ardenne from medieval cities and villages to the modern metropolis. Accompanied by a musical score.

BELGIUM TODAY, TECHNOLOGY FOR TOMORROW. 16 mm. Color and sound. 25 minutes. Embassy of Belgium, 1980.

Gives an overview of some of Belgium's more interesting technological discoveries and innovations in such areas as engineering and the diamond industry.

BELGIUM'S MAGNIFICENT SEVEN. 16 mm. Color and sound. 12 minutes. By Unicorn Films. Embassy of Belgium, 1977.

The seven most famous chiefs d'oeuvres of Belgium, for example Ruben's Descent from the Cross in Antwerp, Breughel's Fall of Icarus in Brussels, Memling's Shrine of Saint Ursula in Bruges, the Baptismal Font by Renier de Huy in Liege, the Adoration of the Mystical Lamb by the Van Eyck brothers in Ghent and the Treasure of Oignies Priory in Namur.

BELGIUM'S NATURE RESERVES. 16 mm. Color and sound. 33 minutes. Embassy of Belgium, 1979.

Nature reserves in the polders, the coast, the forests and plains are toured on foot to show the great variety of fauna and flora.

BRUEGHEL. 16 mm. Color and sound. 55 minutes. Directed by Paul Haesaerts.

Explores the many-faceted character of Pieter Brueghel, the remarkable variety of his paintings, and the way he saw the age in which he lived.

BRUGES. 16 mm. Color and sound. 12 minutes. Embassy of Belgium, 1970.

A short visit to Belgium's loveliest town, medieval Bruges,with its canals and lace-makers.

BRUGES' LIVING PAST. 16 mm. Color and sound. 26 minutes. Embassy of Belgium, 1977.

The former port of Bruges, now inland, is shown with its beautiful old structures and canals along with more modern developments.

BRUGES: THE STORY OF A MEDIEVAL CITY. 16 mm. Color and sound. 60 minutes. Embassy of Belgium, 1978.

A lingering look at the city of art treasures, churches, canals, lovely old residences and fine food.

CARNIVAL IN MALMEDY. 16 mm. Color and sound. 40 minutes. Embassy of Belgium, 1971.

Forty minutes of gaiety, music, fun and folklore.

CASTLES AND ABBEYS OF BELGIUM. 16 mm. Color and sound. 10 minutes. Directed by Jean Pichonnier.

A wide-ranging air tour shows fortresses, castles, and abbeys dating from feudal times.

THE FAGNES UPLANDS. 16 mm. Color and sound. 45 minutes. In French with English subtitles. Embassy of Belgium.

A tour of the Ardenne countryside.

FLEMISH SEASCAPES. 16 mm. Color and sound. 18 minutes. Embassy of Belgium.

The coast line of Belgium in Flanders is like a series of paintings. The many tiny villages and holiday resorts are shown.

THE HEART OF THE WESTERN WORLD. 16 mm. Color and sound. 15 minutes. Embassy of Belgium, 1966.

Not just Belgium's geographical location, but also its place in history earns for it the appelation "Heart of Europe." This film is an introduction to Belgium's contribution to Europe as a whole.

KNIGHTS OF BRUGES. 16 mm. Color and sound. 20 minutes. Embassy of Belgium, 1975.

Each year the town of Bruges commemorates the historic entry of the Duke of Burgundy into the city in 1331 by reenacting the procession of nobility, courtiers and jesters. A jousting tournament is also held. Members of the Belgian aristocracy take the roles of their forefathers.

MARKET SQUARE IN BRUSSELS. 16 mm. Color and sound. 28 minutes. Embassy of Belgium, 1975.

The Market Square in Brussels is one of the showpieces of Europe with its wealth of beautiful aristocratic and patrician edifices. The film describes the origin of the buildings and their histories, shows restoration efforts and details that the visitor cannot see from the ground.

THE PALETTE OF THE STAINED GLASS MAKER. 16 mm. Color and sound. 18 minutes. Directed by Karel Demesmaeker.

Shows the different stages in the creation of stained glass windows according to medieval methods of manufacture, still taught at the Antwerp Academy of Fine Arts.

PROMENADE IN THE ARDENNES. 16 mm. Color and sound. 11 minutes. Embassy of Belgium, 1977.

A walk through the scenery of the southern part of Belgium from Liege to Luxembourg. Musical accompaniment to establish an impressionistic mood.

VAL - SAINT LAMBERT. 16 mm. Color and sound. 20 minutes. Embassy of Belgium, 1962.

An older film showing the glass industry and art which has made Belgian glass a hallmark for quality.

VIOLENCE AND VISION. 16 mm. Color and sound. Embassy of Belgium.

Gives a history of Expressionism from fresco to folklore and shows Belgium's place in this movement.

THE VOICE OF BRONZE. 16 mm. Color and sound. 16 minutes. Directed by Charles Conrad.

Presents a history and tour of the carillons of Belgium. Tells about how church bells were made, their uses, mechanization, and the development of the art of bell ringing.

(For information concerning the borrowing or purchase of films listed above, write to the Cultural Services of the Belgian Embassy.)

INTRODUCING BELGIUM. 16 mm. Black and white. Sound. 29 minutes. Also available as videorecording. By Ytzen Brusse. Brussels, NATO, Washington, D.C. Distributed by National Audiovisual Center, 1979.

Describes the country and people of Belgium, including geographical features, historical development and achievements, economic life, occupations of the people, and social customs. Explains briefly the role of Belgium in the North Atlantic Treaty Organization.

A PLAY ON BELGIUM. 16 mm. Color and sound. 26 minutes. Film and Television Communications, McDonnell Douglas Corporation for Belgium National Tourist Office and Sabena World Airlines, Long Beach, California. Film and Television Communications, 1978.

Highlights cities and sights of Belgium in a promotional travelog that includes visits to Brussels, Bruges, Liege, Ghent, Antwerp, Dinant, and the war memorial at Bastogne.

TWO WORLDS, TWENTY YEARS. Videorecording. By North Atlantic Treaty Organization, Brussels. Distributed by National Audiovisual Center, Washington, 1979.

Contrasts the economic development of Belgium and Czechoslovakia in the post-World War II era. Points out that Belgium, aided under the Marshall plan and protected by NATO, has prospered under a free economy, while Czechoslovakia, deprived of this aid by the USSR, has not.

BOLIVIANS
See also: SPANISH-SPEAKING PEOPLES

Embassy and Consulates

EMBASSY OF BOLIVIA
3014 Massachusetts Avenue
Washington, D.C. 20008 (202) 483-4410

Permanent Mission to the OAS
818 18th Street, Northwest
Suite 1000
Washington, D.C. 20006 (202) 785-0219

CONSULATES GENERAL

1337 International Trade Mart
New Orleans, Louisiana 70130 (504) 523-7488

10 Rockefeller Plaza #616
New York, New York 10020 (212) 586-1607

870 Market Street
San Francisco, California 94103 (415) 495-5173

CONSULATE
25 Southeast Second Avenue
Coral Gables, Florida 33134 (305) 358-3450

Mission to the United Nations

BOLIVIAN MISSION
211 East 43rd Street, 11th Floor
New York, New York 10017 (212) 682-8132

Cultural and Educational Organizations

BOLIVARIAN SOCIETY OF THE UNITED STATES
680 Park Avenue
New York, New York 10021
Executive Secretary: Pola Schijman (212) 628-9400
Founded 1941

Businessmen, college faculty and students and others interested in the contributions of Simon Bolivar (1783-1830) to independence and unity in the Americas. Maintains library.

Airline Offices

LAB (Lloyd Bolivian Airlines)
225 Southeast First Street
Miami, Florida 33131 (800) 327-3098

Books and Pamphlets

BIBLIOGRAPHY OF THE ANDEAN COUNTRIES. By Richard Wilbur Patch. New York, American Universities Field Staff, 1958.

The subtitle describes this bibliography as a selected, current, annotated bibliography relating to Peru, Bolivia and Ecuador, drawn from reasonably accessible works published in English and Spanish.

BOLIVIA: AGRICULTURA, ECONOMICA Y POLITICA-A BIBLIOGRAPHY. Compiled by Theresa J. Anderson. Madison, Wisconsin: Land Tenure Center Library, University of Wisconsin, 1968.

Lists holdings at the University of Wisconsin Steenbook Memorial Library.

BOLIVIA MAGICA: ENCYCLOPEDIC GUIDE. By Hugo Rojo. La Paz, Los Amigos del Libro, Casilla 4415, 1975.

A comprehensive guide to Bolivia giving history and pre-history, geography and geology of Bolivia. Discusses the Indian culture, folklore, painting, literature, cinema, music and wildlife. Furnishes general tourist information, tells about the various monuments and sights, the landscape, lakes, mineral deposits, food, recreation and accommodations. Illustrated in black and white and color.

HISTORICAL DICTIONARY OF BOLIVIA. By Dwight B. Heath. Metuchen, New Jersey, Scarecrow Press, 1972.

Sourcebook of historical and contemporary facts and statistics about persons, places, events, geography and political organizations. Includes a bibliography.

IMAGE OF BOLIVIA. By the Department of Information and Public Affairs of the General Secretariat of the Organization of American States in conjunction with Americas monthly magazine. Washington, 1973.

A booklet presenting detailed information about the geographical features, history, political organization, people, culture, cities and landscapes, economic and social development of Bolivia. Beautifully illustrated with photographs and map. Issued in English, Spanish, and Portuguese.

Audiovisual Material

FILMS

BOLIVIA, PERU, AND ECUADOR. 16mm. Color and sound. 19 minutes. By William Claiborne, Inc. Latin America series: A Focus on People. New York, Sterling Educational Films, 1973.

Analyzes the far reaching social reforms, political changes, and achievements in frontier areas which are happening in Bolivia, Peru, and Ecuador. Discusses the mixed influence of the Indian and Hispanic cultures.

CASIMIRO, AN ANDEAN JOURNEY. 16mm. Color and sound. 30 minutes. By Asterisk Productions. Oxfam-America, Newton, Massachusetts, 1975.

Presents the life of a Bolivian peasant in the context of general problems in this developing country.

COUNTRIES OF THE ANDES. 16mm. Color and sound. 11 minutes. Coronet Instructional Media, Chicago, Illinois, 1977.

Describes the people, culture, cities, and rural areas of Bolivia, Ecuador, Peru, and Chile. Compares and contrasts the people of each country, points out their cultural achievements, and identifies important factors in their economic growth.

THE CRY OF THE PEOPLE. 16mm. Color and sound. 65 minutes. Grupo Tercer Cine, Buenos Aires. Released in the United States by Tricontinental Film Center, 1972.

Presents social and political factors in Bolivia, 1900-1971. English version of the motion picture entitled Al grito de este pueblo.

BRAZILIANS
See also: PORTUGUESE

Embassy and Consulates

BRAZILIAN EMBASSY
3006 Massachusetts Avenue, Northwest
Washington, D.C. 20008 (202) 797-0100

Commercial Section (202) 797-0266

Consular Section (202) 797-0200

Information Section (202) 797-0212

Scientific Attache (202) 797-0240

Permanent Mission to the OAS
2600 Virginia Avenue, Northwest,
Suite 412 (202) 333-4224
Washington, D.C. 20037 333-4226

CONSULATES GENERAL

20 North Wacker Drive, Suite 500
Chicago, Illinois 60606 (312) 372-2176

5900 Wilshire Boulevard, Suite 650
Los Angeles, California 90036 (213) 937-5166

2 Canal Street
1306 International Trade Mart
New Orleans, Louisiana 70130 (504) 588-9187

630 Fifth Avenue, Room 2720
New York, New York 10020 (212) 757-3080

CONSULATES

229 Peachtree Street, Northeast,
Suite 2420
Atlanta, Georgia 30303 (404) 659-0660

World Trade Center, Suite 174
Dallas, Texas 75258 (214) 651-1854

1333 West Loop South, Suite 1100
Houston, Texas 77027 (713) 961-3063

100 North Biscayne Boulevard,
Suite 2113
Miami, Florida 33132 (305) 377-1734

300 Montgomery, Suite 1160
San Francisco, California 94104 (415) 981-8170

Honorary Consulates are located in New Bedford, Massachusetts; Norfolk, Virginia; and Savannah, Georgia.

Mission to the United Nations

BRAZILIAN MISSION
747 Third Avenue, 9th Floor
New York, New York 10017 (212) 832-6868

Information Offices

EMBRATUR
Brazilian Government Tourist Office
230 Park Avenue, Suite 824
New York, New York 10169 (212) 286-9600
Manager: Marlene Schwartz (800) 221-1054

Fraternal Organizations

BRAZILIAN-AMERICAN CULTURAL CENTER
20 West 46th Street, 2nd Floor (212) 730-0515
New York, New York 10036 (800) 223-2182
President: Joao de Matos Founded 1974

Brazilians and others interested in Brazil. Promotes friendship and understanding between Brazilians and Americans. Sponsors various cultural, educational, and social activities, conducts Portuguese and English classes, and maintains a library of Brazilian books on many subjects. Sponsors Miss Brazil-America contest. Charters flights to Brazil. Publications: Carnival in Rio Booklet, annual; Brazilian-American Bulletin, monthly.

BRAZILIAN CULTURAL FOUNDATION
201 East 87th Street
New York, New York 10028
Administrative Assistant: Holly W. Maurer (212) 860-4300
Founded 1977

Dedicated to increasing national awareness in the United States of the cultural heritage and dynamic activity of the arts in Brazil today. Organizes exhibitions of Brazilian arts and crafts, sponsors tours of outstanding Brazilian performers and composers, promotes translations of classic and contemporary Brazial authors, holds poetry readings and panel discussions, presents Brazilian films and has also produced cultural films on Brazil.

Cultural and Educational Organizations

BRAZIL PHILATELIC ASSOCIATION
170 Steeplechase Road
Devon, Pennsylvania 19333 (215) 688-7686
President: David C. Stump

United to develop and distribute to members information relating to philatelic topics of Brazil, including stamps, postal stationery and postal history. Publications: Bulls Eyes (bulletin), quarterly.

BRAZILIAN AMERICAN CULTURAL INSTITUTE
4201 Connecticut Avenue, Northwest, Suite 211
Washington, D.C. 20008
Executive Director: Jose Neistein (202) 362-8334
Founded 1964

Persons interested in fostering understanding between Brazil and the United States through cultural exchange. Offers courses in Portuguese language and Brazilian literature. Maintains an art gallery for American and Brazilian works with frequent art exhibits. Sponsors annual seminars of Brazilian studies. Presents movies, lectures, and concerts. Has a library of fiction and non-fiction in Portuguese and some English, with several titles in French, Spanish, and German translations. Maintains collections of photos, slides, records, and tape recordings. Publishes books

BRAZILIAN INSTITUTE OF LANGUAGES, INCORPORATED
500 Fifth Avenue, Suite 5222
New York, New York 10036 (212) 279-9027
Director: Professor Cesar Yazigi Founded 1975

Supplies translations from Portuguese into English and from English into Portuguese. Offers private lessons in Portuguese. Promotes the Portuguese language (language of Brazil) in the United States. Publications: Course of Conversational Portuguese; Portuguese Grammar; Brazil Highlights.

BRAZILIAN PROMOTION CENTER, INCORPORATED
37 West 46th Street
New York, New York 10036 (212) 719-4045
Executive Director: Jota Alves Founded 1972

Promotes the interests of Brazil in the United States. Arranges travel opportunities for its members, Brazilians and Americans. Plans cultural and social events, including the biggest carnival ball outside Brazil, held at the Waldorf Astoria Hotel. Distributes Brazilian newspapers and magazines. Publishes The Brasilians, the only newspaper in the United States concerned with Brazil. Supplies information on trade, culture, climate, translations, etc. to Americans interested in Brazil. Other branches are located in Newark, New Jersey, and Center Falls, Rhode Island.
Publication: The Brasilians, monthly.

Religious Organizations

BRAZILIAN CATHOLIC CENTER
Religious of the Eucharist
2907 Ellicott Terrace, Northwest
Washington, D.C. 20008 (202) 966-3111

Masses are held in the Portuguese language.

Research Centers and Special Institutes

Brazilian Studies are often carried out in the framework of Latin American studies which are listed in the Spanish-speaking section. A few of the programs whose offerings are particularly strong in Brazilian studies are listed below. The Brazilian Embassy issues an up-to-date survey of courses at institutions of higher learning in the United States.

CENTER FOR LATIN AMERICAN AND CARIBBEAN STUDIES
University of Illinois
Urbana, Illinois 61801

CENTER FOR LATIN AMERICAN AND CARIBBEAN STUDIES
New York University
24 Waverly Place, Room 566
New York, New York 10003

IBERO-AMERICAN STUDIES CENTER
University of Wisconsin
1470 Van Hise Hall
Madison, Wisconsin 53706
Director: Professor Robert T. Aubey (608) 262-2811
Founded 1930

LATIN AMERICAN DEPARTMENT
University of California
Los Angeles, California 90024

LATIN AMERICAN DEPARTMENT
University of California
Santa Barbara, California 93106

LATIN AMERICAN DEPARTMENT
University of Florida
Gainesville, Florida 32601

LATIN AMERICAN DEPARTMENT
Indiana University
Bloomington, Indiana 47401

LUSO-BRAZILIAN STUDIES
Queens College of the City University of New York
Flushing, New York 11367

PORTUGUESE AND BRAZILIAN STUDIES
University of North Carolina
Chapel Hill, North Carolina 21614

Special Libraries and Subject Collections

OLIVEIRA LIMA LIBRARY
Catholic University of America
Washington, D.C. 20064 (202) 635-5059
Curator: Manoel Cardozo Founded 1916

Subjects: Brazilian and Portuguese history, Brazilian and Portuguese literature, Portuguese and Brazilian church history, Portuguese colonial expansion, Portuguese diplomatic history, Brazilian travel. Special Collections: Lima Family papers; Tracts on the Portuguese Inquisition; Collection of pamphlets on 19th century Portuguese liberalism; Dutch pamphlets on 17th century Brazil; Portuguese Restoration; Society of Jesus. Holdings: Books; journals and other serials; historical manuscripts. Services: Copying; library open to public with restrictions. Special Catalogs: Catalog of the Oliveira Lima Library, 2 volumes, 1970. Publications: Conspectus of the Oliveira Library and its Holdings; Newsletter.

Newspapers and Newsletters

BOLETIM ESPECIAL. Irregular. Publisher: Embassy of Brazil, 3006 Massachusetts Avenue, Northwest, Washington, D.C. 20008. In Portuguese.

A newsletter presenting general news of events and people in Brazil, including political, industrial, economic, agricultural, financial, judicial, transportation, and recreational developments.

THE BRASILIANS. Monthly. Editor and Publisher: Jota Alves, 37 West 46th Street, New York, New York 10036. In English and Portuguese.

A newspaper sponsored by the Brazilian Promotion Center, Incorporated, to promote the interests of Brazil in the United States and to provide general news of people and current events concerned with Brazil.

BRAZIL TODAY. Irregular. Publisher: Embassy of Brazil, 3006 Massachusetts Avenue, Northwest, Washington, D.C. 20008. In English.

A newsletter containing current data on Brazilian and Latin American issues culled from a wide variety of sources, both private and governmental.

BRAZILIAN-AMERICAN CHAMBER OF COMMERCE NEWS BULLETIN. 1970-. Biweekly. Publisher: Brazilian-American Chamber of Commerce, 22 West 48th Street, New York, New York 10036.

A resume of current events related to business life in Brazil, with material organized in categories: Finance, energy, import/export, agriculture. Culls Brazilian and English-language press for relevant news. Includes a significant feature story in each issue.

Magazines

BRAZIL BUSINESS. Annual. Editor: Barry V. Conforte. Publisher: Motivational Communications, Incorporated, 175 Fifth Avenue, New York, New York 10010.

Covers import and export firms, manufacturers, and federal agencies in the United States and Brazil concerned with commerce between the two countries. Entries include company name, address, phone, and products or services.

LUSO-BRAZILIAN REVIEW. Biennial. Publisher: Ibero-American Studies Center, 1470 Van Hise Hall, University of Wisconsin, Madison, Wisconsin 53706.

Radio Programs

New York - New York

WKCR(FM) - 208 Ferris Booth Hall, New York, New York 10027, (212) 280-5223. Brazilian programs, 2 hours weekly.

Bank Branches in the U.S.

BANCO DO BRASIL, S.A.
(Bank of Brazil)
New York Branch:
550 Fifth Avenue
New York, New York 10036 (212) 730-6700

BANCO DO BRASIL CENTRAL AND NORTH AMERICAN DIVISION
1919 Pennsylvania Avenue
Washington, D.C. 20006 (202) 857-0651

BANCO DO COMMERCIO E INDUSTRIA DE SAO PAULO, S.A.
299 Park Avenue
New York, New York 10022 (212) 223-1200

BANCO DO ESTADO DE SAO PAULO, S.A.
(Bank of the State of Sao Paulo)
153 East 53rd
New York, New York 10022 (212) 888-9550

BANCO ESTADO RIO DE JANEIRO
(Bank of the State of Rio de Janeiro)
680 Fifth Avenue
New York, New York 10019 (212) 586-7990

BANCO MERCANTIL DE SAO PAULO, S.A.
One Wall Street
New York, New York (212) 422-9700

BANCO REAL, S.A.
(Brazilian Bank)
New York Office:
680 Fifth Avenue, 20th and 21st Floors
New York, New York 10019 (212) 489-0100

Washington Office:
1707 H Street, Northwest, Suite 707
Washington, D.C. 20433 (202) 965-4520

Commercial and Trade Organizations

BRAZIL-CALIFORNIA TRADE ASSOCIATION
350 South Figueroa Street, Suite 226
Los Angeles, California 90071 (213) 627-0634

BRAZILIAN AMERICAN CHAMBER OF COMMERCE
22 West 48th Street
New York, New York 10036
Executive Director: Suzanne K. Barner (212) 575-9030

Corporations, partnerships, financial institutions, and individuals either in the United States or Brazil interested in fostering two-way trade and investment between both countries. Presents "Man of the Year" awards annually to a Brazilian and to an American who have rendered outstanding services to the cause of furthering Brazilian-American business ties. Compiles statistics and provides special mailings, press releases, information, certifications, and business contacts. Sponsors discussion groups and socials. Maintains a reference library. Formerly called the American Brazilian Association.
Publications: News Bulletin, bimonthly; Brazilian-American Business Review Directory, annual.

BRAZILIAN COFFEE INSTITUTE
767 Fifth Avenue, 39th Floor
New York, New York 10022
Representative: Caesar A. Gomes (212) 421-4422

Represents the Instituto Brasileiro do Cafe, an executive agency of the Brazilian government in charge of coffee matters. Promotes the use of Brazilian coffee.

BRAZILIAN GOVERNMENT TRADE BUREAU
551 Fifth Avenue, Suite 210
New York, New York 10017
Director: Renato Prado Guimaraes (212) 922-1133
Founded 1941

Commercial department of the Consulate General of Brazil in New York. Provides economic and tourist information on Brazil; helps in establishing trade contacts between United States and Brazilian firms. Maintains a library of books and other publications on Brazil.
Publications: Brazilian Bulletin, monthly; also publishes tourist folders and information on Brazilian laws and decrees relevant to the economy of Brazil.

BRAZILIAN PETROLEUM COMPANY (PETROBRAS)
(Petroleo Brasileiro, S.A.)
1221 Avenue of the Americas, 9th Floor
New York, New York 10020 (212) 869-3100

A Brazilian government organization for the petroleum industry.

BRAZILIAN TRADE CENTER
350 South Figueroa, Suite 240
Los Angeles, California 90071 (213) 628-7291

A part of the Brazilian consulate in Los Angeles at a separate location.

Airline Offices

VARIG, S.A.
(Viacao Aerea Rio-Grandense)
North American Headquarters:
622 Third Avenue
New York, New York 10017 (212) 340-0200

Provides intercontinental services from Brazil to Europe, North America, South America, and Japan. Other offices in the United States: Atlanta, Chicago, Dallas, Detroit, Houston, Los Angeles, Miami, New Orleans, Philadelphia, San Francisco, and Washington.

Ship Lines

LLOYD BRASILEIRO STEAMSHIP LINE
(Companhia de Navegacao Lloyd Brasileiro)
17 Battery Place, Suite 2026
New York, New York 10004 (212) 943-9339

Bookdealers and Publishers' Representatives

ALZOFON BOOKS
2662 Glenmawr Avenue
Columbus, Ohio 43202
Proprietor: Sammy Alzofon (614) 263-3013

BRAZILIAN AMERICAN CULTURAL INSTITUTE, INCORPORATED
4201 Connecticut Avenue, Northwest
Suite 211
Washington, D.C. 20008 (202) 362-8334

ROBERT E. CALVIN
Post Office Box 2201
Station "A"
Champaign, Illinois 61820 (217) 357-7100

EDITORIA ABRIL, LIMITED
444 Madison Avenue, Room 2201
New York, New York 10022 (212) 688-0530

WOLFGANG SCHIEFER FINE OLD BOOKS
Box 474
New Haven, Connecticut 06502 (203) 787-9902

Books and Pamphlets

AGRARIAN REFORM IN BRAZIL: A BIBLIOGRAPHY. Part I. Compiled by Teresa Anderson. Madison, University of Wisconsin Land Tenure Center Library, 1972.

AGRARIAN REFORM IN BRAZIL: A BIBLIOGRAPHY. Part II, Regional Development. Compiled by Teresa Anderson. Madison, University of Wisconsin Land Tenure Center Library, 1972.

A BIBLIOGRAPHY OF BRAZILIAN BIBLIOGRAPHIES. By Bruno Basseches. Detroit, B. Ethridge, 1978.

The introductory matter is given in English although the bibliography itself is in Portuguese.

BRASIL: NORTHEAST REGION. By the Brazilian Ministry of Industry and Commerce. Rio de Janeiro, 1973.

A guide to states, cities, hotels, restaurants, and

services in the Northeast region of Brazil is enclosed in a booklet with many beautiful color photographs of the region.

BRASIL: SOUTH REGION. By the Ministry of Industry and Commerce. Rio de Janeiro, 1973.

A guide to states, cities, airports, excursions, hotels, restaurants, and services in the South of Brazil is enclosed in a booklet illustrated with lovely color photographs showing outstanding scenic views of the region.

BRAZIL BOOKS; A Guide to Contemporary Works. By Anthony Knopp. New York, Center for Inter-american Relations, 1970.

BRAZIL: CHALLENGE AND PROGRESS. By the Brazilian Embassy, 32 Green Street, London W1, England. Available from the Brazilian Embassy in Washington, D.C.

A detailed presentation of Brazil's history, people, culture, science and technology, economy, social welfare and geography. Generously illustrated in black and white. Includes a select bibliography in English.

BRAZIL, PORTUGAL AND OTHER PORTUGUESE-SPEAKING LANDS; A List of Books Primarily in English. By Francis M. Rogers and David T. Haberly. Cambridge, Massachusetts, Harvard University Press, 1968.

A publication of the Department of Romance Languages and Literature at Harvard University.

CATALOG OF BRAZILIAN ACQUISITIONS OF THE LIBRARY OF CONGRESS 1964-1974. Compiled by William V. Jackson. Boston, Massachusetts, G.K. Hall, 1977.

CATALOG OF LUSO-BRAZILIAN MATERIAL IN THE UNIVERSITY OF NEW MEXICO LIBRARIES. Compiled by Theresa Gillett and Helen McIntyre. Metuchen, New Jersey, Scarecrow Press, 1970.

GET TO KNOW BRAZIL. By Rene Lecler. Rio de Janeiro, Brazilian Tourist Authority.

An introduction to the geography, ethnic composition, history and visual arts of Brazil. Sections on the major cities and geographical regions. Black and white as well as many colored illustrations.

IMAGE OF BRAZIL: ORDER AND PROGRESS. By Guillermo de Zendegui, Cultural Department of the Ministry of External Relations. Available from the sales and circulation unit of the General Secretariat of the Organization of American States, Washington, D.C., 1975.

A short survey of Brazilian development, profusely illustrated. One of the series on the culture, history, art and development of the member states of the Organization of American States.

LIBRARY GUIDE FOR BRAZILIAN STUDIES. By William Vernon Jackson. Pittsburgh, Pennsylvania, University of Pittsburgh Book Centers, 1964.

Surveys the holdings in 1963-64 on Brazilian studies in major research collections in the United States. Separate chapters cover general materials, humanities, social sciences, science, and technology. Includes a bibliography of published catalogs, guides, and descriptions of specific collections, also a union list of Brazilian periodicals.

A SURVEY OF COURSES IN THE PORTUGUESE LANGUAGE, LUSO BRAZILIAN, AND LATIN AMERICAN AREA STUDIES OFFERED IN INSTITUTIONS OF HIGHER LEARNING IN THE UNITED STATES. By the Brazilian Embassy, Washington, D.C.

Periodically updated roster of courses of interest to the student of Brazilian culture.

A WORKING BIBLIOGRAPHY OF BRAZILIAN LITERATURE. By Jose Manuel Topete. Gainesville, University of Florida Press, 1957.

Brings together major writers and critical works, and contemporary authors. A supplement to the author's Working Bibliography of Latin American Literature, which omitted Brazil.

Audiovisual Material

MAP

MAP OF BRAZIL. Rio de Janeiro, Brazilian Institute of Geography and Statistics.

A political map of Brazil in color showing provinces,

major cities and highways and rivers. An inset designates the greater regional divisions. On the verso information on population, economic and social development, transportation, education, agriculture, mining, manufacturing, media, foreign trade, physical aspects and tourism, accompanied by statistical data. About 14-1/2 by 18.

FILMS

AMAZON. 16mm. Color and sound. 25 minutes. Natural Environment Series. Made by Wilf Gray Productions. Journal Films, Evanston, Illinois, 1980.

Focuses on the Amazon, an integrated system of rivers and jungle. Identifies the South American region through which the Amazon travels, showing the plants and animals unique to the region and the people who inhabit it.

THE AWAKENING GIANT. 16mm. Color and sound. 25 minutes. Eye of the Beholder Series. By Carole Ann Michael. RCP Destination Films, Toronto, 1972. Released in the United States by Viacom International.

Shows how Brazil is rapidly moving from being a large, poor South American country to being one of the world's great powers.

BAHIA. 16mm. Color and sound. 18 minutes. Embratur, Brazilian Tourism Authority, 1981.

An interesting short film on one of the provinces of Brazil. Includes historical and nature shots.

BRAZIL. 16mm. Color and sound. 10 minutes. Geography of South America Series. Coronet Instructional Media, Chicago, 1977.

Offers a look at Brazil and its people. Focuses on geographic regions, economic activities, and major cities.

BRAZIL: NO TIME FOR TEARS. 16mm. Black and white. Sound. 40 minutes. By Pedro Chaskel and Luis Alberto Sanz. Film Department, University of Chile, Santiago, 1971. Released in the United States by Tricontinental Film Center.

Nine recently released Brazilian political prisoners recount their ordeals under torture.

BRAZIL, SOUTH AMERICA'S GIANT. 16mm. Color and sound. 18 minutes. By Andrew Nemes. BFA Educational Media, Santa Monica, California, 1979.

Focuses on Brazil by highlighting its history, geography, economy, and culture. Explains that it is a nation of vast size and natural resources and states that it is beginning to assume an important economic position in the world.

A BRAZILIAN FAMILY. 16mm. Color and sound. 20 minutes. By Vladimir Bibic. International Film Foundation, New York, 1978.

Focuses on an upper middle-class Brazilian family. Shows, through the jobs, working conditions, and lifestyles of the family members, some of the political, economic, and social problems confronting Brazil.

CARLOS OF BRAZIL. 16mm. Color and sound. 22 minutes. Made by Filmedia for American Lutheran Church. Released by Augsburg Publishing House Film Department, 1975.

Demonstrates the self-help philosophy of the American Lutheran Church Division of World Missions through the experiences of a young Brazilian boy who is confronted with the problems of his country which is in the midst of economic change.

CARNIVAL. 35mm. Color and sound. 18 minutes. Noe and Seremetef, Clarkston, Michigan, 1975.

A documentary on the annual Carnival in Rio de Janeiro. Portuguese version also issued.

EYE OF THE GODS. 16mm. Color and sound. 33 minutes. American Sportsman Series. ABC Sports, New York, 1979.

Follows an expedition which ascends a 2,000-foot rock cliff in the heart of the Amazon.

FROM THIS GARDEN. 16mm. Color and sound. 12 minutes. New York Botanical Garden. Made by Vision Associates, Bronx, New York, 1977.

Shows an expedition carried out by the Botanical Garden in the Amazon.

MANABU MABE PAINTS A PICTURE. 16mm. Color and sound. 13 minutes. Also available on video cassette. Museum of Modern Art of Latin America, Washington, D.C., 1965.

Japanese-Brazilian artist Mabe is shown creating an abstract painting.

MR. LUDWIG'S TROPICAL DREAMLAND. 16mm. Color and sound. 57 minutes. Also available as video recording. Made by BBC-TV, WGBH. Released by Time-Life Video, New York, 1980.

A documentary focusing on Daniel Ludwig, an American billionaire who is attempting to transform three million acres of Amazon rain forest into a profitable lumber industry.

OURO PRETO (City of Today and Tomorrow). 16mm. Color and sound. 30 minutes. Embratur, Brazilian Tourism Authority.

A travelogue about a famous Brazilian village, abundant in Colonial art.

THE PEOPLE OF BRAZIL. 16mm. Color and sound. 23 minutes. Made by The Filmakers. 3M Company, 1974.

Looks at the life of Brazilians in the cities, on the waterways and the plantations, in the marketplaces, including views of the people at work, at prayer, and at play.

VIAGEM PELO BRAZIL. Videocassette. Color and sound. 30 minutes. Embratur, Brazilian Tourism Authority, New York.

Covers all of Brazil, its cities, landscapes and people.

VIVA RIO. Super 8mm. Color and sound. Embratur, Brazilian Tourism Authority, New York.

Shows highlights of the life and beauty of Rio.

ZECA. 16mm. Color and sound. 19 minutes. Made by George R. Sluizer, Amsterdam. Released in the United States by Phoenix Films, 1974.

Traces the professional, social, and family life of Zeca, a cowherd from the northeast of Brazil.

BRITISH
(Includes CORNISH; ENGLISH; MANX)
See also: IRISH; SCOTS; WELSH

Embassy and Consulates

BRITISH EMBASSY
3100 Massachusetts Avenue, Northwest
Washington, D.C. 20008 (202) 462-1340

CONSULATES GENERAL

225 Peachtree Street, Northeast
Suite 912
Atlanta, Georgia 30303 (404) 524-5856

Prudential Tower, Suite 4740
Boston, Massachusetts 02199 (617) 261-3060

33 North Dearborn Street
Chicago, Illinois 60602 (312) 346-1810

55 Public Square
1828 Illuminating Building
Cleveland, Ohio 44113 (216) 621-7674

2200 Detroit Bank and Trust Building
211 Fort Street, West
Detroit, Michigan 48226 (313) 962-4776

601 Jefferson, Suite 2250
Houston, Texas 77002 (713) 659-6270

Ahmanson Center East Building
Suite 312
3701 Wilshire Boulevard
Los Angeles, California 90010 (213) 385-7381

150 East 58th Street
New York, New York 10022 (212) 593-2258

12 South 12th Street
Philadelphia, Pennsylvania 19107 (215) 925-2430

Gateway Tower, Suite 700
1 Memorial Drive
Saint Louis, Missouri 63102 (314) 621-4688

Equitable Building, 9th Floor
120 Montgomery Street
San Francisco, California 94104 (415) 981-3030

GPO Box 2157
Banco Popular
Center Hato Rey
San Juan, Puerto Rico 00936 (809) 767-4435

1216 Norton Building
Second Avenue and Columbia Street
Seattle, Washington 98104 (206) 622-9253

3100 Massachusetts Avenue, Northwest
Washington, D.C. 20008 (202) 462-1340

CONSULATE

813 Stemmons Tower West
2730 Stemmons Freeway
Dallas, Texas 75207 (214) 637-3600

Mission to the United Nations

UNITED KINGDOM MISSION
845 Third Avenue, Tenth Floor
New York, New York 10022 (212) 752-8400

Information Offices

BRITISH INFORMATION SERVICES
845 Third Avenue
New York, New York 10022 (212) 752-5747

Tourist and Travel Offices

BRITISH TOURIST AUTHORITY

680 Fifth Avenue
New York, New York 10019 (202) 581-4700

875 North Michigan Avenue
#2450
Chicago, Illinois 60611 (312) 787-0490

1712 Commerce Street
Empire Life Building #2115
Dallas, Texas 75201 (214) 748-2279

612 South Flower Street
Los Angeles, California 90017 (213) 623-8196

BRITRAIL TRAVEL INTERNATIONAL
630 Fifth Avenue
New York, New York (212) 599-5407

An office of British Railways.

Fraternal Organizations

ASSOCIATION OF AMERICAN RHODES SCHOLARS
c/o J. B. Justice
1100 Philadelphia National Bank Building
Philadelphia, Pennsylvania 19107
Secretary: J. B. Justice Founded 1907

Former Rhodes scholars living in the United States, or elected to their scholarships from the United States.
Publication: American Oxonian, quarterly.

BRITISH WAR VETERANS OF AMERICA
c/o Anthony Li-Cansi
133-22 117th Street
South Ozone Park, New York 11420 (212) 843-7217
President: Eric H. Taylor, M.B.E. Founded 1919

Veterans of the armed forces of the British Commonwealth and persons of British birth who served with Allied Forces. Sponsors annual remembrance service. Maintains fund for burial of Commonwealth Veterans. Formerly called British Great War Veterans of America.
Publication: Bulletin, monthly.

THE COUNCIL OF BRITISH SOCIETIES IN SOUTHERN CALIFORNIA
11950 San Vicente Boulevard
Post Office Box 49804 (213) 826-4985
Los Angeles, California 90049 Founded 1932

Conducts its affairs on a non-profit, non-political, and non-sectarian basis. Co-ordinates the functions and activities of British organizations with a purpose and activities similar to those of the Council, and furthers their mutual interests. Promotes and establishes friendly relations between citizens of the British Commonwealth and the United States. Sponsors charter flights between Great Britain and Commonwealth countries and the United States for its members.

ENGLISH-SPEAKING UNION OF THE UNITED STATES
16 East 69th Street
New York, New York 10021
Executive Director: John D. Walker (212) 879-6800
Founded 1920

Fosters mutual understanding and friendship among people of the United States and the British Commonwealth and enlarges channels of communication. Administers travel grants and scholarships, information programs and English in Action programs. Bestows book award to a writer who is published in English but who is not a native speaker of English. Maintains 8,000 volume library. Affiliated with the English-Speaking Union of the Commonwealth (sister society).
Publications: English-Speaking Union News, quarterly; English Around the World, semiannual.

GENERAL SOCIETY OF MAYFLOWER DESCENDANTS
Four Winslow Street
Plymouth, Massachusetts 02360
Secretary General: Mildred Ramos (617) 746-3188
Founded 1897

Persons descended from a passenger on the Mayflower on the voyage which terminated at Plymouth, Massachusetts, December, 1620. Conducts research into descendants of the Mayflower Pilgrims through the fifth generation. Maintains library on Pilgrim history and genealogy.
Publications: Mayflower Quarterly; also publishes Mayflower Families Through Five Generations in several volumes.

JAMESTOWNE SOCIETY
Post Office Box 7389
Richmond, Virginia 23221
Executive Secretary: Mrs. C.A. Ramstetter Founded 1936

Lineal descendants of early settlers of Jamestown, Virginia.

NATIONAL SOCIETY COLONIAL DAMES XVII CENTURY
1300 New Hampshire Avenue, Northwest
Washington, D.C. 20036

President-General: Mrs. Frank P. Copeland, Jr. Founded 1915

American women who are lineal descendants of persons who rendered various civil or military service and lived in one of the British Colonies in the United States before 1701 as a colonist or a descendant of one. Aids in preservation of records and historical shrines and fosters interests in historical colonial research. Gives scholarships and awards. Maintains museum collection and library dealing with lineage, birth and cemetery records and county histories.

NATIONAL SOCIETY, DAUGHTERS OF THE BARONS OF RUNNEMEDE
4530 Connecticut Avenue, Northwest
Washington, D.C. 20008 (202) 244-6525
President: Catherine D. Callahan Founded 1921

Descendants of barons who forced King John to sign the Magna Carta in 1215. Promotes genealogical and historical research and encourages appreciation of the English background of its members. Restores and preserves records of genealogical value.
Publications: Yearbook.

NORTH AMERICAN MANX ASSOCIATION
Box 716
William Street
Liverpool, Nova Scotia
Canada BOT 1KO (902) 354-3015
President: George Curphy Founded 1928

Individuals with proven Manx birth, marriage or descent and Manx men and women and their descendants who do not live in areas served by independent Manx societies. Formed by independent Manx ethnic self-help and relief associations founded in the United States and Canada throughout the nineteenth century by immigrants from the Isle of Man. Promotes mutual benefit and social welfare of the Manx paople and their descendants; works to establish a closer union of all Manx people and those of Manx origins in North America and to stimulate ties with the Isle of Man through the World Manx Association. Bestows Heritage Award to honor Manx youth for outstanding achievement in Manx language, music, and arts and crafts. Presidency alternates from the United States to Canada.
Publications: Bulletin, quarterly; Convention Yearbook, biennial; Directory, irregular; Factsheets, irregular.

ORDER OF FIRST FAMILIES OF VIRGINIA, 1607-1625
c/o Mrs. Charles Marbury Seaman
5055 Seminary Road
Alexandria, Virginia 22311
Corres. Secretary: Mrs. Charles M. Seaman, Sr. Founded 1912

Descendants of men and women who assisted in establishing the Colony of Virginia under the regime of the Virginia Company of London, 1607-1624/5. To encourage research concerning the history of the founding of the country. To establish lineages of founder families and to publish such proven lineages.
Publications: Newsletter, annual; Membership Roster, every 3-5 years; also publishes book.

ROYAL NAVAL OFFICERS CLUB
c/o New York Yacht Club
37 West 44th Street
New York, New York 10036 (516) 543-0200
President: David G. Pacy Founded 1954

Ex-officers of the (British) Royal navies and associates. Founded to make and maintain friendships, and to arrange sailing excursions and contests.

TRANSATLANTIC BRIDES AND PARENTS ASSOCIATION
1610 Second Street
Peru, Illinois 61354
United States Secretary: Joan Castner (815) 224-2221
Founded 1946

United Kingdom Division includes British persons whose sons or daughters are residents of the United States or Canada, as well as the sons or daughters, brothers and sisters (including those relationships by marriage or adoption) of these British persons. Also includes British immigrants, born in the United Kingdom, their husbands or wives, their children, and their children's husbands or wives. Promotes fellowship among the relatives in Britain and in Northern Ireland. Assists in problems arising between parents in the United Kingdom and their daughters or sons and their families in the United States and Canada. Operates charter and group flight programs for qualified members to visit their relatives.
Publication: Together Again, monthly.

Professional Organizations

ANCIENT AND HONOURABLE ORDER OF SMALL CASTLE OWNERS OF GREAT BRITAIN
c/o Hollis M. Baker
220 Lyon Northwest
Grand Rapids, Michigan 49503 (616) 458-1464
Secretary: Hollis M. Baker

Owners of ancient edifices in Great Britain, many of whom are Americans. A tongue-in-cheek organization, whose stationery shows a wine bottle, wine glass and radiator surrounding a castle. The radiator represents the castle owners' biggest headache, the heating problem. Motto is "Tax Vobiscum" (Tax be with you).

BRITISH HERITAGE SOCIETY
509 Madison Avenue, Suite 412
New York, New York 10022
Executive Director: Jeannette R. Radley (212) 838-9215
Founded 1978

Professional men and women of British descent engaged in the arts, business, law and medicine. Objectives are to assist members in furthering their goals and careers; promote understanding of the American way of life by encouraging temporary international exchanges. Seeks to strengthen ties with British counterparts and uphold British traditions; serves as a point of contact for visiting British men and women. Familiarizes members and the public in general with the achievements of the British and opportunities open in the United States.

Public Affairs Organizations

BRITISH-NORTH AMERICAN COMMITTEE
c/o National Planning Association
1606 New Hampshire Avenue, Northwest
Washington, D.C. 20009 (202) 265-7685
Director: Sperry Lea Founded 1969

American, British and Canadian leaders in business, organized labor, agriculture and the professions. Analyzes the key international and domestic issues facing the three countries, and provides the opportunity for an exchange of views. Members discuss current concerns with high officials and experts, consider presentations, and meet in groups and task forces to develop projects for committee action. Publishes research studies on trade, investment, international monetary issues, raw materials issues, and relations between developed and developing countries.

PILGRIMS OF THE UNITED STATES
74 Trinity Place
New York, New York 10006 (212) 943-0635
President: Hugh Bullock Founded 1903

"To promote Angle-American relations through speeches of prominent English and Americans to clarify problems arising between the two countries." An incoming British ambassador to the United States has, traditionally, made his first speech at a United States Pilgrim dinner. Affiliated with the English Organization, Pilgrims of Great Britain.

Cultural and Educational Organizations

AMERICAN BLAKE FOUNDATION
Department of English
Memphis State University
Memphis, Tennessee 38152
Executive Secretary: Kay Parkhurst Easson (901) 454-2653
Founded 1970

Not a public membership organization. Has advisory board of scholars and executive board of directors. To publish high-quality facsimiles of Blake materials at prices within reach of students; to create a research library; to award research grants to graduate students and scholars, and to hold national symposia devoted to the study of William Blake (1757-1827), English romantic poet, painter, printer and mystic. Maintains library of 1,400 volumes.
Publications: Materials for the Study of William Blake: A Facsimile Series for the General Reader, semiannual; has also published William Blake: Book Illustrator (3 volumes).

AMERICAN BRITISH CAB SOCIETY
Post Office Box 904
Stamford, Connecticut 06904 (203) 322-9332
Director: Gerald L. Vincent Founded 1973

American hobbyists and car enthusiasts who own taxicabs which were designed for and retired from use in London. Purposes are: to foster and maintain interest in English taxicabs; to encourage preservation and restoration of such vehicles. Serves as clearinghouse for information on history, parts and service, resales and rentals. Activities include parades, auto shows, exchange of services, maintenance and restoration information.
Publications: Newsletter, quarterly.

AMERICAN GUILD OF ENGLISH HANDBELL RINGERS
703 Compton Road
Cincinnati, Ohio 45231 (513) 521-7369
President: David R. Davidson Founded 1954

Church and school groups and individual musicians interested in the art of English handbell ringing. Encourages participation in area and national festivals. Holds workshops.
Publications: Overtones, bimonthly; Newsletter, quarterly; Roster, annual; Handbell Music.

ANGLO-AMERICAN ASSOCIATES
117 East 35th Street
New York, New York 10016 (212) 684-4528
Executive Secretary: Ruth Emery Founded 1964

Scholars in the field of British studies in history, literature, and fine arts. Seeks to establish stronger lines of communication between scholars on both sides of the Atlantic in the field of British studies. Secures lectures for visiting British scholars.
Publications: British Studies Monitor, three times a year; Research in Progress in British Studies, triennial.

AUGUSTAN REPRINT SOCIETY
William Andrews Clark Memorial Library
2520 Cimarron Street
Los Angeles, California 90018
Corres. Secretary: Beverly J. Olney (213) 731-8529
Founded 1946

Individuals and institutions interested in seventeenth and eighteenth century English literary history. Publishes reprints (usually facsimile reproductions) of rare works.

BERTRAND RUSSELL SOCIETY
1500 Johns Road
Augusta, Georgia 30904
Board Chairman: Peter G. Cranford (404) 736-3514
Founded 1974

Seeks to promote the views and causes championed by Bertrand Russell (1872-1970), British mathematician, philosopher and social activist. According to the Society, Bertrand Russell was "a man passionately devoted to rationality, freedom and equality, who hated hypocrisy, injustice, tyranny, superstition and H-bombs." The Society also notes that he is "probably the most influential philosopher of modern times and has the most books in print (over 70) of all the philosophers since Aristotle. Presents annual award to individual representing a cause or idea advocated by Russell, also bestows annual cash scholarship to a doctoral candidate. Maintains library.
Publications: Russell Society News, quarterly.

BRITISH AMERICAN ARTS ASSOCIATION
49 Wellington Street
London WC2E 7BN, England
Director: Jennifer Williams Founded 1979

Information service and clearinghouse for exchange between the United States and Great Britain in all fields including music, dance, theater and literature. Counsels artists, administrators, organizations and sponsors on promotion and touring opportunities; conducts seminars and conferences on topics of British and American arts. Maintains 250 volume library of reference books designed to aid artists planning American and British tours.

BRITISH NORTH AMERICA PHILATELIC SOCIETY
c/o Edward J. Whiting
25 Kings Circle
Malvern, Pennsylvania 19355 (215) 644-7838
Secretary: Edward J. Whiting Founded 1943

Individuals interested in various branches of specialization in Canadian stamps united for collection and dissemination of knowledge in the field. Maintains library. Sponsors study groups on various facets of Canadian philately.
Publications: BNA Topics, bimonthly; Membership Handbook and Directory, biennial.

BRITISH SCHOOLS AND UNIVERSITIES CLUB OF NEW YORK
c/o The Williams Club
24 East 39th Street
New York, New York 10016
Honorary Secretary: Dr. Thomas M. Noone (212) 697-5300
Founded 1895

Graduates of British schools and universities. Occasionally sponsors lectures.

BRONTE SOCIETY
335 Grove Street
Oradell, New Jersey 07649
Honorary American Representative:
Katherine M. Reise Founded 1893

Individuals, universities, and libraries. Brings together people throughout the world who are interested in the lives and works of the Bronte sisters (Charlotte, 1816-1855; Emily Jane, 1818-1848; Anne, 1820-1849); all of whom were English novelists. Acts as guardian of Bronte memorabilia; maintains the Bronte Parsonage Museum; sponsors lectures, guided tours, and excursions. Maintains a library pertaining to the Bronte sisters, including their complete works, many in foreign languages. Awards an annual prize for an essay on a subject connected with the Brontes. Publications: Transactions, annual; Newsletter, irregular (sent to American members); also publishes occasional booklets, guides, and catalogs.

BROWNING INSTITUTE
Post Office Box 2983
Grand Central Station
New York, New York 10163
Executive Secretary: Peter N. Heydon
(212) 473-3468
Founded 1971

Founded to acquire the apartment occupied by Elizabeth Barrett (1806-1861) and Robert Browning (1812-1889) in Florence, Italy, "Casa Guidi." Restoration work to preserve the apartment as a fitting memorial to the two poets is nearly complete. Principal rooms to be refurnished as when the Brownings lived there in the mid-19th century. Also plans to establish library and study facilities there. Publications: Browning Institute Studies, annual; Through Casa Guidi Windows (bulletin), irregular; also publishes book every two years.

BYRON SOCIETY
259 New Jersey Avenue
Collingswood, New Jersey 08108
Executive Director: Marsha M. Manns
(609) 858-0514
Founded 1971

University professors of romantic literature; graduate students studying romantic literature; public and university libraries and persons interested in the works of George Gordon, Lord Byron (1788-1824), English romantic poet. Conducts annual international seminar focusing on aspects of Byron's poetry and influence and an annual tour of a country or literary association connected with Byron. National committees develop lecture series, dramatic readings and concerts. Affiliated with the Modern Language Association of America.
Publications: Journal, annual; Newsletter, every 18 months.

CONFERENCE ON BRITISH STUDIES
c/o J. M. Price
University of Michigan
Department of History
Ann Arbor, Michigan 48109
Executive Secretary: J. M. Price
(313) 764-6353
Founded 1951

American scholars specializing in British studies, including history, literature, and political science. Offers a triennial prize for the best book published in English on Commonwealth history by an American or Canadian scholar (must be the author's first book). Affiliated with the American Historical Association. Publications: Albion, quarterly; Journal of British Studies, semiannual; Bibliography of Current Research in British History in U.S. and Canada, quadrennial; also publishes bibliographical handbooks, British biographies series and studies in British History and Culture.

COUNTRY DANCE AND SONG SOCIETY OF AMERICA
505 Eighth Avenue, Room 2500
New York, New York 10018
Executive Director: Bertha Hatvary
(212) 594-8833
Founded 1915

Promotes present day use of English and American folk dances, songs, music. Studies folklore and historical background. Maintains 2,000 volume library. Sponsors adult and family camps. Publications: Newsletter, monthly; Country Dance and Song, annual; also publishes books containing dance descriptions and tunes; issues records and films.

DESCENDANTS OF THE ILLEGITIMATE SONS AND DAUGHTERS OF THE KINGS OF BRITAIN
c/o Herman Nickerson, Jr.
107 Lake Lane Rock Creek
Jacksonville, North Carolina 28540
Secretary: Herman Nickerson, Jr.
(919) 324-4954
Founded 1950

Persons who "can show acceptable proof of descent from an illegitimate son or daughter of a royal prince of Britain." The aim of the group, according to its president, is "to encourage high quality in genealogical research rather than the slipshod work so common in the past in hereditary societies." The group also refers to itself as "Royal Bastards." Publications: Directory, annual; also publishes a loose-leaf lineage book of the members.

D. H. LAWRENCE SOCIETY OF NORTH AMERICA
204 Memorial Hall
English Department
University of Delaware
Newark, Delaware 19711
President: Professor L.D. Clark
(302) 454-1480
Founded 1975

Persons interested in studying the works of D. H. Lawrence (1885-1930), English novelist. Sponsors conferences, symposia and meetings concerned with the literature of D. H. Lawrence.
Publications: Newsletter, semiannual.

DICKENS SOCIETY
Department of English
Villanova University
Villanova, Pennsylvania 19085
Secretary-Treasurer: Deborah A. Thomas — (215) 645-4653
Founded 1970

Individuals interested in the life and work of Charles Dickens (1812-1870), English novelist. Purpose is to conduct, encourage, further and support research, publication, instruction and general interest in the life, times, and literature of Charles Dickens.
Publication: Dickens Studies Newsletter, quarterly.

ELIZABETHAN CLUB OF YALE UNIVERSITY
459 College Street
New Haven, Connecticut 06510 — (203) 432-3777
Librarian: Stephen R. Parks — Founded 1911

Promotion of appreciation of things literary, aesthetic and intellectual. Possesses an "outstanding collection" of Elizabethan books. Occasionally underwrites publication of scholarly books.

EVELYN WAUGH SOCIETY
English Department
Nassau Community College
State University of New York
Garden City, New York 11530 — (516) 222-7187
President: Paul A. Doyle — Founded 1967

College and high school teachers, librarians, book collectors, literature specialists, and others interested in the life and writings of Evelyn Waugh (1903-1966), English novelist and critic. Serves as a forum for members; gathers bibliographies and other data about Waugh; provides information on library materials, sources, Waugh research, etc. Maintains a collection of books, journals, off-prints and other material by and about Evelyn Waugh.
Publications: Newsletter, three times a year; Year's Work in Waugh Studies, annual.

FRANCIS GROSE SOCIETY
2005 Columbia Pike, No. 134
Arlington, Virginia 22204 — (703) 979-9383
Director: Dan J. Cragg — Founded 1976

Persons interested in literature, history and military affairs. Organization is named after Francis Grose 1731-1791), 18th-century British antiquary and humorist. Stages informal and convivial gatherings modeled after those attended by Grose and his friends at the King's Arms Tavern in Holborn and the Feathers Tavern in Leicester Square, London. Publishes reprint, The Mirror's Image.

GILBERT AND SULLIVAN SOCIETY
c/o Mrs. Vivian Denison
137 Riverside Drive, Apartment 1E
New York, New York 10024
Corres. Secretary: Mrs. Vivian Denison — (212) 873-5010
Founded 1936

Persons interested in Gilbert and Sullivan operas. Brings Gilbert and Sullivan fans together, and encourages the production of the operas in a traditional manner. Its collection of more than 100 volumes (including biographies of Sullivan, various editions of operas, plays by Gilbert, etc.) has been donated to the library of the General Society of Mechanics and Tradesmen and the Walter Hampden Memorial Library, both in New York City. Branches of the Society also exist in Los Angeles, Minneapolis, Philadelphia, Shreveport, Louisiana, Norfolk, Virginia, and other parts of the English-speaking world. The parent organization is the Gilbert and Sullivan Society, 273 Northfield Avenue, London W5, England.
Publication: The Palace Peeper, ten times a year; G and S Journal, semiannual.

JANE AUSTEN SOCIETY OF NORTH AMERICA
400 West 34th Street, No. 44M
New York, New York 10036 — (212) 594-1507
President: J. David Grey — Founded 1979

Individuals interested in the life and works of Jane Austen (1775-1817), English novelist. To encourage interest in Jane Austen and to publish and distribute materials pertaining to her life. Activities include: regional meetings and a drive to restore and maintain Jane Austen's church, St. Nicholas, in Steventon, England. Maintains library of 1,000 volumes, including recordings, tapes, slides and memorabilia.
Publications: Persuasions (journal), annual; also publishes newsletter.

THE JOHNSONIANS
c/o S. R. Parks
1914 Yale Station
New Haven, Connecticut 06520 — (203) 436-8535
Secretary: S. R. Parks — Founded 1946

A club having as its primary function the annual celebration of the birthday of Dr. Samuel Johnson (1709-1784), English lexicographer, essayist and author.
Publications: Keepsakes, annual.

JOSEPH CONRAD SOCIETY OF AMERICA
English Department
State University of New York
New Paltz, New York 12562 (914) 257-2595
President: Dr. Adam Gillon Founded 1974

Professors of English and graduate students; college and university libraries and "Conrad lovers everywhere." Promotes interest in and knowledge of the life, times and work of Joseph Conrad (1857-1924), English novelist born in Poland.
Publications: Joseph Conrad Today (newsletter), quarterly.

KATE GREENAWAY SOCIETY
3709 Gradyville Road
Newton Square, Pennsylvania 19073 (215) 353-1689
Director: James L. Lowe Founded 1971

Collectors, librarians, and archivists interested in the life and work of Kate Greenaway (1846-1901), illustrator and author of children's literature. Promotes interest in Kate Greenaway collecting. Currently conducting research in several areas, results of which are to be published in the organization's journal or in handbook form.
Publication: Under The Window, quarterly.

KEATS-SHELLEY ASSOCIATION OF AMERICA
41 East 42nd Street, Room 815
New York, New York 10017
Treasurer: Dr. Donald H. Reiman (212) 697-7217
Founded 1948

Publication: Keats-Shelley Journal, annual.

KIPLING SOCIETY
420 Riverside Drive, No. 7D
New York, New York 10025
Secretary for U.S.: J. R. Dulap Founded 1932

Persons interested in the writings of Rudyard Kipling. International headquarters located in London, England.
Publication: Kipling Journal.

LEWIS CARROLL SOCIETY OF NORTH AMERICA
617 Rockford Road
Silver Spring, Maryland 20902 (301) 593-7077
President: David H. Schaefer Founded 1974

Collectors, authors, publishers, rare book dealers and others interested in the life and works of Charles Lutwidge Dodgson (1832-1898), who wrote under the pen name of Lewis Carroll. Purpose is to encourage study of the life, work, times and influence of Charles Lutwidge Dodgson; to publish journals and books to advance that study and to become the center for Carroll Studies.
Publications: Knight Letter (newsletter), quarterly; also publishes Chapbook Series and books.

MILTON SOCIETY OF AMERICA
Duquesne University
Pittsburgh, Pennsylvania 15219 (412) 434-6420
Secretary: Albert Labriola Founded 1948

Professors, graduate students, and others interested in the study of John Milton, the English poet (1608-1674). Occasionally honors an outstanding Milton scholar. Affiliated with the Modern Language Association.
Publications: Bulletin, annual; also partially supports quarterly magazines, 17th Century News, and Milton Quarterly.

NEW YORK BROWNING SOCIETY
54 Old Fort Road
Bernardsville, New Jersey 07924 (201) 766-1648
President: Donald R. Pepper Founded 1907

Persons interested in the study of Robert Browning (1812-1889) and his poetry. The New York Browning Society is one of more than twenty such associations in the United States and abroad. Though the Society's scope is mainly local, it records members from California, Texas, Michigan, Florida, and even Saudi Arabia. Seeks to cultivate among members an interest in the life and works of Robert Browning and in the highest forms of literature, music and art, and to work for the intellectual development of its members. Conducts research and arranges literary programs. Successfully completed a compaign to preserve Casa Guidi, the historic residence of Robert and Elizabeth Browning in Florence, Italy; ownership is now vested in the Browning Institute, Incorporated.

NEW YORK C. S. LEWIS SOCIETY
c/o Eugene McGovern
32 Park Drive
Ossining, New York 10562 (914) 762-0549
Editor: Eugene McGovern Founded 1969

Individuals united to foster and share an enthusiasm for the works of C. S. Lewis (1898-1963), English novelist and essayist. Although its name implies otherwise, the organization is an international group which publishes articles and reviews concerning the life and works of Lewis.
Publications: Bulletin, monthly.

PILGRIM SOCIETY
Pilgrim Hall Museum
Plymouth, Massachusetts 02360 (617) 746-1620
Director: Laurence R. Pizer Founded 1820

To collect and preserve artifacts and written and photographic records relating to the Pilgrims, Plymouth Colony and the Town of Plymouth; to encourage research in these areas; to maintain Coles Hill, Forefathers Monument and Pilgrim Hall. Maintains museum and library of more than 10,000 volumes and 5,000 manuscripts.
Publications: Annual Report; Pilgrim Society Notes, irregular; also publishes Pilgrim Society News.

RENAISSANCE ENGLISH TEXT SOCIETY
c/o James M. Wells
The Newberry Library
Chicago, Illinois 60610
Secretary-Treasurer: James M. Wells (312) 943-9090
Founded 1959

Founded to publish scarce literary texts, chiefly non-dramatic, of the period 1475-1660. Two volumes of texts are normally issued in each series either in photographic facsimile or in type. Six volumes, three published with the University of Chicago Press, and two with the University of South Carolina Press, have appeared to date.

RICHARD III SOCIETY
207 Carpenter Avenue
Sea Cliff, New York 11579 (516) 676-2374
Vice Chairman: William Hogarth Founded 1924

Teachers, historians, students and others interested in historical research into the life and times of Richard III (1452-1485, King of England 1483-1485). Seeks "to secure a reassessment of the historical material relating to this period and of the role in English history of this monarch," especially in regard to the fate of the two young "Princes in the Tower" and the character of their uncle, Richard, who was accused of murdering his nephews to claim the throne. Headquarters in London, England, with branches in the United States, Australia and Canada. Writes letters and prepares articles to correct "misinformation" about Richard III; conducts research; publishes annual memorial notices in the New York Times and London Times; sponsors occasional essay contests in schools; American branch sponsors annual matching grant Scholarship Fund for graduate study assistance. In England, maintains several memorials and historic sites and conducts expeditions to places of interest connected with Richard III. English parent society planning to erect a life-size sculpture of Richard III by noted British sculptor James Butler, RA, at Leicester, city nearest Bosworth Field, where Richard died in battle. Maintains collection of published and unpublished materials, including articles, speeches, plays and excerpts from documents. Also known as The Fellowship of the White Boar (emblem of Richard III). Formerly Fellowship of the White Boar. Absorbed Friends of Richard III, Incorporated.
Publications: Ricardian Register (American Newsletter), quarterly.

SAMUEL BUTLER SOCIETY
c/o James A. Donovan, Jr.
4100 Cathedral Avenue, Northwest
Washington, D.C. 20016 (202) 362-6276
Editor: James A. Donovan, Jr. Founded 1978

Individuals interested in the life and writings of Samuel Butler (1835-1902), English satirist and author of The Way of All Flesh.
Publications: Newsletter, semiannual.

SHAKESPEARE ASSOCIATION OF AMERICA
Administrative Offices
Box 6328, Station B
Nashville, Tennessee 37235
Executive Secretary: Ann Jennalie Cook (615) 383-8058
Founded 1972

Scholars and teachers of Shakespeare, actors, directors and other interested persons. Provides members with an opportunity for the discussion of all aspects of Shakespeare: his life, his plays, and his poems. Through development or continuation of appropriate projects, the Association hopes to forward research, criticism, teaching, and the production of Shakespearean as well as other Renaissance drama. Supersedes the original Shakespeare Association of America (founded 1932; dissolved 1972). Before final arrangements were made with the older Association's former trustees, the present Association was known for a short time as the Shakespeare Council of America.

SHAKESPEARE OXFORD SOCIETY
110 Glen Argyle Road
Baltimore, Maryland 21212
Executive Vice President: Gordon C. Cyr (301) 377-2958
Founded 1957

Persons interested in the humanities, especially research into the history of the Elizabethan period of English literature. Explores and attempts to verify evidence bearing on the authorship of the Shakespearean works, particularly evidence indicating that Edward de Vere, the 17th Earl of Oxford, was their author. Searches for original manuscripts in England to support its theories.
Publications: News-Letter, quarterly; also publishes occasional pamphlets and brochures.

SHAKESPEARE SOCIETY OF AMERICA
1107 North Kings Road
West Hollywood, California 90069 (213) 654-9100
President: R. Thad Taylor Founded 1967

Persons interested in promoting and advancing the works of William Shakespeare. Plans to travel all over the United States and the world presenting Shakespeare's plays. Eventually hopes to construct a Shakespearean Center with two theaters, The Globe and Blackfriars, a Boar's Head Inn, Mermaid Tavern, and the New Place Library and Museum. Maintains a Rare Book Library of first editions.
Publications: Hamlet's Proclamation, quarterly; Shakespeare's Proclamation, quarterly.

SIR THOMAS BEECHAM SOCIETY
664 South Irena Avenue
Redondo Beach, California 90277
Executive Secretary: Stanley H. Mayes (213) 374-0865
Founded 1964

Record collectors, music lovers, interested individuals. Objectives are: to preserve the memory of Sir Thomas Beecham; to support the music of Frederick Delius; to act as a "pressure group" to seek the release of new commercial recordings or the reissuance of recordings no longer in the catalog and to attempt to prevent deletions from the catalog of recordings presently available; to preserve the memory of other giants of the past, such as Arturo Toscanini, Serge Koussevitzky, Bruno Walter, Wilhelm Furtwangler and others; to support the cause of opera (which, like the music of Delius, was close to the heart of Sir Thomas). Maintains sound archive to collect and preserve as many of Sir Thomas' recordings as possible. Has issued private recordings, including several discs and sets, to members. Also maintains films archive including several films with music conducted by Beecham.
Publications: Newsletter, bimonthly; LeGrand Baton (journal), quarterly; Bulletin, semiannual; Directory; has also published complete discography (list) of Beecham's recordings.

STONEHENGE STUDY GROUP
2821 DeLaVina Street
Santa Barbara, California 93105 (805) 687-9350
Editor: Donald L. Cyr Founded 1970

Individuals interested in astronomy, geology, archaeology and related arts and sciences. Activities include: expeditions to megalithic sites such as Stonehenge, Avebury, Newgrange, Callanish and Carnac where stone circles are available for study; local lectures and study groups covering archaeo-astronomy, Druids, legends and bibical interpretations. Maintains library of 4,000 volumes. Conducts biennial expeditions.
Publications: Stonehenge Viewpoint, 6 times a year; also makes available copies of Annular Newsletter, Vail's Annular World Magazine and The Earth's Annular System.

THOMAS HARDY SOCIETY OF AMERICA
Department of English
New York University
19 University Plaza
New York, New York 10003
President: Kevin Z. Moore Founded 1979

Persons interested in the study and criticism of the works of Thomas Hardy (1840-1928), English novelist and poet. Presents scholarly papers at forums and symposia; sponsors competitions.
Publications: Newsletter, quarterly.

VIRGINIA WOOLF SOCIETY
c/o Professor Morris Beja
English Department
Ohio State University
Columbus, Ohio 43210
Executive Secretary: Morris Beja (614) 422-8369
Founded 1975

Critics, scholars, teachers, readers and students. Purpose is to foster and encourage the study of, critical attention to, and general interest in the work and career of Virginia Woolf (1882-1941), English author. Conducts university conferences; holds seminars at conventions.
Publications: Newsletter, semiannual; Directory, irregular.

WILLIAM MORRIS SOCIETY
North American Branch
c/o J. R. Dunlap
420 Riverside Drive, 12G
New York, New York 10025
North American Secretary: (212) 222-3375
J. R. Dunlap Founded 1956

Persons interested in the life, activities, ideas and influence of William Morris (1834-1896), Englishman known through his varied work as a poet, writer, designer, craftsman, printer, pioneer and socialist. Seeks to deepen understanding and stimulate a wider appreciation of Morris, his friends and their work. Affiliated with the William Morris Society and Kelmscott Fellowship.
Publications: News from Anywhere, annual; also publishes collections of essays.

WINSTON S. CHURCHILL ASSOCIATION
549 Baughman Avenue
Claremont, California 91711 (714) 626-0516
President: Harry V. Jaffa Founded 1969

Founded to commemorate the famous words and deeds of Sir Winston Leonard Spencer Churchill (1874-1965), and encourage research and study of his life and works. Held a Centennial Celebration on Churchill's one hundreth birthday.
Publications: Studies in Statesmanship, a monograph series.

P. G. WODEHOUSE SOCIETY
530 Georgina Avenue
Santa Monica, California 90402
President: Jeremy H. Thompson Founded 1979

Persons interested in the writings of Pelham Grenville Wodehouse (1881-1975), English humorous novelist. Facilitates the exchange of information on Wodehouse and his writings and encourages the tracing and exchange of Wodehouse works. Sponsors private exhibits.
Publications: The Perennial Plum, quarterly.

WORDSWORTH-COLERIDGE ASSOCIATION
c/o Bishop C. Hunt
College of Charleston
Charleston, South Carolina 29401
President: Bishop C. Hunt Founded 1970

Persons interested in the life and work of the English poets William Wordsworth (1770-1850) and Samuel Taylor Coleridge (1772-1834).

Foundations

AMERICAN FRIENDS OF CAMBRIDGE UNIVERSITY
1611 35th Street, Northwest
Washington, D.C. 20007 (202) 338-5641
President: Gordon Williams Founded 1967

Individuals who contribute and who seek contributions to help fund grants made to Cambridge University (England), its colleges and institutions.
Publications: Annual Report.

BRITISH-AMERICAN EDUCATIONAL FOUNDATION
426 East 89th Street
New York, New York 10028
Executive Director: Mrs. Frederick
V. P. Bryan (212) 722-3196

Offers carefully selected American secondary-school graduates an opportunity to spend a year at a school in Great Britain before going on to college in America. Primary purpose is to "develop leadership abilities among young Americans by challenging them with the unique educational and social environment of the British Public Schools."

BRITISH SCHOOLS AND UNIVERSITIES FOUNDATION
c/o Bank of New York
530 Fifth Avenue
New York, New York 10036
President: Bruce Harvey (203) 869-5835

Attempts to strengthen understanding between the United States and the British Commonwealth by promoting, fostering and assisting the education and academic work of British scholars and students in American educational institutions and American scholars and students in British educational institutions. Makes donations, gifts, contributions and loans without interest to schools, colleges and universities, and other educational, scientific or literary institutions.

THE COMMONWEALTH FUND
One East 75th Street
New York, New York 10021 (212) 535-0400
Chairman: C. Sims Farr Incorporated 1918

One of the grant activities of the Fund is to award Harkness Fellowships to young potential leaders from the United Kingdom, Australia and New Zealand for study and travel in the United States. Also active in health care services.

FRANCIS BACON FOUNDATION
655 North Dartmouth Avenue
Claremont, California 91711 (714) 624-6305
President: Elizabeth S. Wrigley Founded 1938

Educational and research institution affiliated with the Claremont Colleges. Promotes study in science, literature, religion, history, and philosophy, with special reference to the works of Francis Bacon, his character, and his life, and his influence on his own and succeeding times. (Bacon, 1561-1626, was an English philosopher, essayist, and statesman.) Maintains a rare book library on the campus of the Claremont Colleges, open to faculty, students, and the public. The library contains books by and about Francis Bacon, Elizabethan and Jacobean background material, on early cryptography collection, an early Rosicrucian collection, an early to modern Dante collection, anti-Shakespeareana, an 18th century collection in American Political Theory, and 16th and 17th century emblem literature. The Foundation makes grants to private colleges and universities to enable them to hire outstanding scholars as visiting professors and lecturers and occasionally assists in publication of their lectures. Provides bibliographies and reading lists for persons engaged in research in fields covered by the Foundation library.
Publications: Annual Report; also publishes bibliographies of the library collections.

WINSTON CHURCHILL FOUNDATION
Post Office Box 1240, Gracie Station
New York, New York 10028
Executive Director: Harold Epstein (212) 546-7364
Founded 1959

Finances several overseas Fellows annually appointed by Churchill College, Cambridge University, England, from the teaching staffs of United States universities or from the research units in American industry. Also awards about ten annual scholarships to United States graduate students to do advanced work in the sciences, engineering and mathematics at Churchill College. The Foundation's operation is intended to help step up the training of top-level American men and women, to encourage Anglo-American academic and scientific cooperation and to serve as a tribute to the late Sir Winston Churchill, who sparked the founding of the science-oriented College in 1959 and served as honorary chairman of its board. Formerly called the United States Churchill Foundation.

Charitable Organizations

NATIONAL SOCIETY, DAUGHTERS OF THE BRITISH EMPIRE IN THE UNITED STATES OF AMERICA
11820 Southeast 154th Avenue
Portland, Oregon 97236
National President: Mrs. John T. Mitchell Founded 1909

Women of British birth; daughters and granddaughters of British subjects. Maintains homes for aged British men and women. Formerly known as the Imperial Order Daughters of the British Empire in the United States of America. Affiliated with the Imperial Order Daughters of the Empire (Canadian).
Publication: The Organizer, quarterly.

SAINT GEORGE'S SOCIETY OF NEW YORK
71 West 23rd Street, Room 1609
New York, New York 10010 (212) 924-1434
President: Roger C. Norwood Founded 1770

Men of British or Commonwealth birth or descent. Engages solely in charitable activities.

Research Centers and Special Institutes

CENTER FOR BRITISH ART AND BRITISH STUDIES
Box 2120, Yale Station
New Haven, Connecticut 06520 (203) 432-4594
Director: Edmund P. Pillsbury Founded 1968

An integral unit of Yale University, includes an art gallery, library, seminar rooms, and lecture hall, pursues research on British art and British studies. Provides research fellowships and active participation in graduate and undergraduate programs in British studies at the University. Houses the Mellon collection of British art and rare books. The entire collection will be available for special research purposes. Also associated with the Paul Mellon Foundation for British Art in London. Presently maintains a library of about 20,000 volumes on British art.

CENTER FOR COMMONWEALTH AND COMPARATIVE STUDIES
Duke University
Durham, North Carolina 27706
Director: Dean A. Kenneth Pyle (919) 684-2446

An integral unit of Duke University operating under the supervision of a Committee on Commonwealth Studies. Formerly known as the Center for Commonwealth Studies. Supported by the parent institution and foundations. Carries out collaborative studies on political, social, economic, and legal developments and phenomena relating to the British Commonwealth of Nations. Also assists graduate students from Commonwealth countries in their study and research in economics, history, and political science at the University. Publishes research results in books and professional journals. Conducts a joint seminar each spring for graduate students and faculty of the University and occasional special conferences on the Commonwealth.
Publication: Commonwealth Studies Series, irregular.

EARLY MODERN ENGLISH DICTIONARY PROJECT
University of Michigan
7609 Haven Hall
Ann Arbor, Michigan 48104
Director: Dr. R. Bailey

Project completed by Department of English in College of Literature, Science and the Arts at University of Michigan which produced a historical dictionary of Early Modern English.

FRANCIS BACON FOUNDATION
655 North Dartmouth Avenue
Claremont, California 91711
President: Mrs. Elizabeth S. Wrigley
(714) 624-6305
Founded 1938

See Foundations.

MIDDLE ENGLISH DICTIONARY PROJECT
University of Michigan
5208 Angell Hall
Ann Arbor, Michigan 48104
Editor: Dr. S. M. Kuhn

Research and publication activity of College of Literature, Science and the Arts at University of Michigan, operating under its administrative and interdepartmental Advisory Committees on Dictionaries and supported by parent institution, special funds and recent grant from Mellon Foundation, to compile a scholars' dictionary of Middle English, covering the English language from 1100 to 1500, with quotations from Middle English texts supporting each definition. Research results published in 128-page fascicles at irregular intervals, 1 to 3 per year.

Museums

COLONIAL WILLIAMSBURG
Goodwin Building
Williamsburg, Virginia 23185
Director of Museum Operations: Peter A. G. Brown
(804) 229-1000
Founded 1926

On site preservation of the former capital of Virginia Colony includes 88 restored or preserved buildings whose construction dates are from 1693 to 1837, and 50 reconstructed buildings of the eighteenth century. Collections include archeological artifacts, paintings, sculpture, graphic art, decorative arts, costumes, folk art, military artifacts, music and textiles. Services offered are guided tours, films, lectures, concerts, permanent and temporary exhibitions, educational programs for adults and children, museum shops, archival materials and interlibrary loan.

FORT FREDERICA NATIONAL MONUMENT
Route 4
Saint Simons Island, Georgia 31522
Superintendent: Ellen Britton
(912) 638-3639
Founded 1945

The site includes the ruins of an eighteenth century English barracks, fort and houses. There are study collections of artifacts found at Fort Frederica and in the town of Frederica. A 25-minute film, tours, historical publications and a museum shop are maintained.

JAMESTOWN MUSEUM
Jamestown, Virginia
Mailing Address:
Colonial National Historical Park
Post Office Box 210
Yorktown, Virginia 23690
Superintendent: James R. Sullivan
(804) 898-3400
Founded 1930

Exhibits seventeenth century artifacts and glass. Offers guided tours, lectures, films, educational programs for children and a museum shop.

JAMESTOWN NATIONAL HISTORIC SITE
Jamestown, Virginia 23081
Executive Director: Robert A. Murdock
Founded 1607

The site of the first permanent English settlement in America has interpretive markers, monuments and memorials, seventeenth century artifacts and oil paintings.

PENDARVIS
Shake Rag Street (608) 987-2122
Mineral Point, Wisconsin 53565 Founded 1935

Mineral Point is an early settlement of miners from Cornwall. Many of the original houses are still being occupied. Pendarvis is open to the public as a museum exhibiting household furnishings from the mid-nineteenth century. There is a small library and a museum shop.

PENNSBURY MANOR
Route 9
Morrisville, Pennsylvania 19067
Historic Site Administrator: (215) 946-0400
Nancy D. Kolb Founded 1939

Residence of William Penn built in 1683 exhibits seventeenth century English furnishings and accessories. Research is performed in early Pennsylvania history, Quaker cultural life and all matters pertaining to William Penn. There is a small library, an auditorium, period garden and museum shop. The Museum offers guided tours, concerts, and educational programs. Sponsors Spring Seminar in May and Americana Forum in September.

THE PILGRIM SOCIETY
75 Court Street
Plymouth, Massachusetts 02360 (617) 746-1620
Director: Laurence R. Pizer Founded 1820

Collections include fine and decorative arts; furniture; manuscripts; books; archeological artifacts. Research is conducted in pilgrim history; Plymouth Colony and the Town of Plymouth. The Society offers tours, lectures, permanent and temporary exhibitions and internships.
Publications: Pilgrim Society Notes; Pilgrim Society News; books and pamphlets.

PLIMOUTH PLANTATION, INCORPORATED
Warren Avenue
Plymouth, Massachusetts 02360
Mailing Address:
Box 1620 (617) 746-1622
Plymouth, Massachusetts 02360 Founded 1947

An outdoor, living history museum exhibiting seventeenth century English and native American artifacts, house furnishings, tools, arms and armor, replicas of the Mayflower ship which brought the Pilgrims to America and Pilgrim village which has a seventeenth century barn, post-hole houses, a fort-meeting house and period costumes. There is a 3,000 volume library of imprints and manuscripts, theater, cafeteria and museum shop. Guided tours as well as films and lectures and educational programs for adults and children are offered.
Publications: Of Plimouth Plantation, newsletter; Annual Report; occasional papers.

ST. GEORGE'S UNITED METHODIST CHURCH
235 North Fourth Street (215) 925-7788
Philadelphia, Pennsylvania 19106 Founded 1767

Religious Museum which is housed in 1763, St. George's United Methodist Church, built of British brick and located on the original site of construction. Collections include original John Wesley Chalice Cup sent from England to Francis Asbury in 1784; Frances Asbury's personal Bible brought with him from England in 1771; Asbury watch. A library concentrating on British and American Methodist church history and an archives of closed churches are maintained.

SILVERADO MUSEUM
Post Office Box 409
St. Helena, California 94574 (707) 963-3757
Chairman: Dr. Norman H. Strouse Founded 1969

Independent nonprofit research center operating under grants from Vailima Foundation. Principal field of research is in the life and works of Robert Louis Stevenson, mainly through use of its collection of books, manuscripts and other Stevenson memorabilia by authorized Stevenson scholars. Maintains a library of 2,000 volumes relating to Robert Louis Stevenson, as well as original manuscripts and first editions of his writings.

YALE CENTER FOR BRITISH ART
Box 2120, Yale Station
New Haven, Connecticut 06520 (203) 432-4594
Director: Edmund P. Pillsbury Founded 1977

A collection of British art including 1,300 paintings, 10,000 drawings, 20,000 prints and 20,000 rare books from the 16th through 19th centuries. The Center maintains a 13,000 volume library of reference books, as well as photographic collection of British art. Facilities include a reading room, auditorium, guided tours, lectures, films, gallery talks, concerts, Resident Fellow program, symposia, colloquia and a museum shop.

Special Libraries and Subject Collections

AMERICAN BLAKE FOUNDATION - RESEARCH LIBRARY
Memphis State University
Department of English
Memphis, Tennessee 38152
Executive Director: Dr. Roger R. Easson (901) 454-2653
Founded 1970

Subjects: Blake - his art, editions of his works, biography, bibliography, original engravings, his followers, auction catalogs, poetry criticism. Holdings: books; unpublished essays and catalogs; prints and slides; journals and other serials. Services: Copying; library open to public with written permission. Remarks: This is a public Research Library consisting mainly of rare materials. Persons wishing to use the library should direct their inquiries in writing to the American Blake Foundation.
Publications: Blake Studies, semiannual; William Blake: Book Illustrator, 3 volumes.

ARMSTRONG BROWNING LIBRARY
Baylor University
Post Office Box 6336
Waco, Texas 76706 (817) 755-3566
Director: Dr. Jack W. Herring Founded 1918

Carries out research on material associated with Robert and Elizabeth Browning, including the collection, preservation, and cataloging of such material. Research results are published in monographs and professional journals. Maintains a library of Browning's works and extensive original source materials.
Publications: Baylor Browning Interests, yearly; Studies in Browning and His Circle, semiannual.

BOSTON COLLEGE LIBRARY - FRANCIS THOMPSON COLLECTION
Chestnut Hill, Massachusetts 02167
Special Coll. Librarian: Frank J. Seegraber (617) 969-0100

Subjects: Francis Thompson. Special Collections: Coventry Patmore; Wilfred and Alice Meynell. Holdings: books; manuscripts, notebooks and complete separate manuscripts of Francis Thompson. Services: Interlibrary loans; copying; collection open to public for reference use only.

BRITISH CONSULATE-GENERAL - LIBRARY
120 Montgomery Street
San Francisco, California 94104 (415) 981-3030
Librarian: Vera Skaar Founded 1946

Subjects: British education, economy, journals, social services, trade statistics, newspapers, and history. Holdings: Books; reference pamphlets; Government Command Papers. Services: Interlibrary loans; library not open to public.

BRITISH INFORMATION SERVICES - LIBRARY
845 Third Avenue
New York, New York 10022 (212) 752-8400
Librarian: Margaret J. Gale Founded 1942

Subjects: British affairs (economics, education, foreign affairs, industry and trade, research, social services, law, World War II); colonial development and welfare; Commonwealth relations. Holdings: About 2,000 books. Library not open to the public.

ENGLISH-SPEAKING UNION OF THE U.S.A. - BOOKS ACROSS THE SEA LIBRARY
16 East 69th Street
New York, New York 10021
Library Consultant: Mary Ellen Moll (212) 879-6800
Founded 1942

Subjects: Books for all ages descriptive of life, thought, history, and institutions in Britain and the other Commonwealth countries. Holdings: Books, journals, and other serials. Services: Lending services to schools, libraries, and colleges; library open to public for research and study.

ENGLISH-SPEAKING UNION OF THE U.S.A.- WASHINGTON D.C. BRANCH LIBRARY
2131 S Street, Northwest
Washington, D.C. 20008
Librarian: Eleanor Johnson (202) 234-4602

Subjects: English history, biography, travel, historical novels, aspects of Commonwealth life. Special Collections: Works of Churchill. Holdings: books and periodicals. Services: Interlibrary loans; library open to public for reference use only on request.

FOLGER SHAKESPEARE LIBRARY
201 East Capitol Street
Washington, D.C. 20003
Director: Dr. O. B. Hardison, Jr. (202) 544-4600
Founded 1932

An independent, nonprofit research organization administered by the Trustees of Amherst College. Supported by income from endowment. Principal fields of research: British civilization of Tudor and Stuart periods, Continental Renaissance, theatrical history, and Shakespeare. Sponsors an Institute of Renaissance and Eighteenth Century Studies in cooperation with eleven colleges and universities. Awards annual research fellowships, maintains a publication program, and supplies photoduplications of material in collections. Publishes research results in books. Holds colloquia and symposia on research in progress and frequent lectures, plays, poetry, readings and concerts. Maintains a library of 300,000 volumes on Shakespeare, drama, and British history of the Tudor and Stuart periods as well as an extensive manuscript collection.
Publications: Newsletter; Folger Documents of Tudor and Stuart Civilization; Folger Monographs of Tudor and Stuart Civilization; Folger Booklets on Tudor and Stuart Civilization.

LIBRARY OF CONGRESS - LAW LIBRARY - AMERICAN-BRITISH LAW DIVISION
James Madison Memorial Building
Room 235
Washington, D.C. 20540
Chief: Marlene C. McGuirl (202) 287-5077

Subjects: American federal and state law; British Commonwealth law. Special Collections: International and comparative law; American colonial and early state law. United States court records and briefs; early British law; American and English trials; United States legislative publications. Remarks: This division administers three law reading rooms: Anglo-American Law Reading Room; Law Library Gallery (congressional documents collection); Law Library in the Capitol (reserved for Congressional use only).

SAINT MARK'S LIBRARY - GENERAL THEOLOGICAL SEMINARY OF THE PROTESTANT EPISCOPAL CHURCH IN THE U.S.A.
175 Nineth Avenue
New York, New York 10011 (212) 243-5150
Librarian: Anne-Marie Salgat Founded 1817

Special Collections: Early English Theology Collection (6,600 titles printed before 1701 on the Church of England). Holdings: books; manuscripts, clippings, microfilms, journals and other serials. Services: Interlibrary loans; copying; library open to public for reference use only.
Publications: New Book List, monthly; Annual Report; Library Guidebook; descriptive pamphlets on the collections.

YALE CENTER FOR BRITISH ART - RARE BOOK COLLECTION - YALE UNIVERSITY
2120 Yale Station
New Haven, Connecticut 06520
Cur. of Rare Books: Joan M. Friedman (203) 432-4099

Subjects: British art and typography, graphic arts, printing history. Special Collections: Photograph archive of British art. Holdings: Rare and reference books; paintings; prints and drawings; journals and other serials. Services: Copying; Center open to public. Automated Operations: Computerized cataloging of art objects and photograph collection. Special Indexes: Current Research in British Art (computer-based file).

Newspapers and Newsletters

ALBION. 1969. Quarterly. Editor: Michael Moore. Publisher: Conference on British Studies, University of Michigan, Department of History, Ann Arbor, Michigan 48109.

Publishes scholarly articles and addresses on British history, politics and culture.

BRITISH-AMERICAN TRADE NEWS. 1965-. 9 times a year. Publisher: The British-American Chamber of Commerce, 10 East 40th Street, New York, New York 10016.

Intended "to provide regular communication with corporate members and their staffs and with associates, government employees, and trade associations on both sides of the Atlantic who are concerned with Anglo-American industry and commerce." Offers "selected items of authoritative information on international trade matters." Provides accounts and pictures of chamber functions. Lists new members.

BRITISH STUDIES INTELLIGENCER. 1959-. 3 times a year. Editor: Lamar Hill. Publisher: University of California, Department of History, Irvine, California 92717.

Centers on British history, literature, and culture, especially the scholarship in these fields and the development of new literature and academic projects. Includes British Empire and Commonwealth fields. Supplies news of developments and of activities of related scholarly bodies and groups, as well as of the Conference on British Studies and its officers. Recurring Features: Includes announcements of scholarly meetings, reports of meetings held, notices of new programs of study, seminars, scholarship and fellowship opportunities, items on new literary works in the field and new reference works useful to scholars. First Published: 1952 (original series); 1970 (current series).

BRITISH STUDIES MONITOR. 1970-. Three times a year. Editor: Howard Leichman. Publisher: Anglo-American Associates, 117 East 35th Street, New York, New York 10016.

ENGLISH-SPEAKING UNION NEWS. 1952-. Quarterly. Editor: Natalie Beck. Publisher: English-Speaking Union of the United States, 16 East 69th Street, New York, New York 10021.

Newsletter for all chapters of the English-Speaking Union.

Magazines

IN BRITAIN. Monthly. Editor: Bryn Frank. Publisher: British Tourist Authority, 680 Fifth Avenue, New York, New York 10019.

Contains up-to-date information on events and activities for tourists and others interested in Britain and the British people. Features a varied assortment of articles about the British scene, past and present, and an abundance of scenic, architectural, and action photographs.

JOURNAL OF BRITISH STUDIES. 1961-. Semiannual. Editor: Bentley Gilbert. Publisher: Conference on British Studies, University of Michigan, Department of History, Ann Arbor, Michigan 48109.

A scholarly journal for British history, literature, arts and economics.

Radio Programs

BRITISH BROADCASTING CORPORATION (BBC)
630 Fifth Avenue
New York, New York 10020 (212) 581-7100

Broadcasts shortwave radio programs from London to the United States and to countries in all parts of the world. A program guide, London Calling, may be obtained by writing to the BBC.

Washington - Seattle

KXA - 1307 Second Avenue, Seattle, Washington 98101, (206) 682-9033. British programming, 1 hour weekly.

Bank Branches in the U.S.

BARCLAYS BANK INTERNATIONAL, LIMITED
(Controlled by Barclays Bank, Limited)

United States Subsidiaries:
Barclays Bank of New York
200 Park Avenue
New York, New York 10017 (212) 687-8030

Barclays Bank of California
111 Pine Street
San Francisco, California
94111 (415) 981-8090

United States Branches
100 Water Street
New York, New York 10005 (212) 530-0100

J. F. Kennedy International Airport
New York, New York 11830 (212) 656-6656

110 Tremont Street
Boston, Massachusetts 02108 (617) 423-1775

208 South La Salle Street
Chicago, Illinois 60604 (312) 621-9300

First Atlanta Tower
2 Peachtree Street, Southwest
Atlanta, Georgia 30303 (404) 588-0437

1 Oliver Plaza
Pittsburgh, Pennsylvania (412) 562-9200

KLEINWORT, BENSON

United States Subsidiaries:
Kleinwort, Benson North America Corporation
100 Wall Street
New York, New York 10005 (212) 797-1330

Sharps Pixley, Incorporated
100 Wall Street
New York, New York 10005 (212) 248-5060

LLOYD'S BANK, LIMITED
New York Office:
95 Wall Street
New York, New York 10005 (212) 825-4900

MIDLAND BANK LIMITED

United States Affiliates:
European-American Banking Corporation
10 Hanover Square
New York, New York 10005 (212) 437-4300

NATIONAL WESTMINSTER BANK, LIMITED

New York Branch:
100 Wall Street
New York, New York 10005 (212) 943-6000

San Francisco Branch:
44 Montgomery Street
San Francisco, California 94104 (415) 956-8300

Chicago Branch:
33 North Dearborn
Chicago, Illinois (312) 621-1500

SCHRODERS, INCORPORATED
New York Office:
1 State Street
New York, New York 10004 (212) 269-6500

STANDARD CHARTERED BANK, LIMITED

New York Offices:
160 Water Street
New York, New York 10005 (212) 269-3100

Rockefeller Center
10 West 49th Street
New York, New York 10020 (212) 581-1680

San Francisco Office:
465 California Street
San Francisco, California 94104 (415) 434-1023

WILLIAMS AND GLYN'S BANK, LIMITED

New York Representative:
G. C. Brooks
63 Wall Street
New York, New York 10005 (212) 943-2050

Commercial and Trade Organizations

BRITISH-AMERICAN CHAMBER OF COMMERCE
10 East 40th Street
New York, New York 10016
Executive Director: Arthur H. Phelan (212) 889-0680
Founded 1920

International group of American and British corporations interested in fostering trade between the United States and Great Britain. Maintains a library of 1,000 volumes on United States and British trade, including directories, statistics, reports, periodicals.
Publications: British-American Trade News, monthly; Classified Membership Directory, annual.

BRITISH-AMERICAN CHAMBER OF COMMERCE AND TRADE CENTER OF THE PACIFIC SOUTHWEST
Suite 562
350 South Figueroa Street
Los Angeles, California 90071 (213) 622-7124

BRITISH TRADE DEVELOPMENT OFFICE
150 East 58th Street
New York, New York 10155
Director: J. L. Beaven (212) 593-2258

Not a membership organization. British government group which promotes trade with the United States; assists British companies selling in the United States; and aids American companies which wish to import goods from Britain. Maintains a library of trade directories and commercial reference books.

Festivals, Fairs, and Celebrations

California - Agoura

RENAISSANCE PLEASURE FAIR AND SPRINGTIME MARKET
Old Paramount Ranch
Agoura, California

Re-creates the atmosphere of a county fair in Elizabethan England with pageantry, games, music, good, crafts and varied entertainment. Held in late April and early May for six weekends.
Contact: Chamber of Commerce, Post Office Box 208, Agoura, California 91301.

California - San Francisco

BRITISH WEEK FESTIVAL
San Francisco, California

Highlights British imports, art, history, and music. A "Pub" is set up in Union Square. Held in early October for 9 days.
Contact: Redwood Empire Association, Visitor's Information Bureau, 476 Post Street, San Francisco, California 94102.

California - San Rafael

RENAISSANCE PLEASURE FAIRE
San Rafael, California

Re-creates north of San Francisco, Queen Elizabeth's merry olde England. Presents giants and jesters, music and mummery, pageants and plays, jugglers, fire-eaters, and puppet shows. Features ale and wine gardens, a great variety of gourmet foods, and handcrafted wares. Provides an opportunity to try various crafts and rustic games, such as pitch-the-hay and tug-o-war. Held annually since 1963 from late August through September for six weekends.
Contact: Renaissance Faire, Post Office Box 18104, San Francisco, California 94118. (415) 922-9600.

Florida - Jacksonville

DELIUS FESTIVAL
Jacksonville, Florida

The English composer, Frederick Delius, who once lived near Jacksonville, is honored each year by the city's musical and civic groups the week before and after his birthday on January 29. His musical works are featured in concerts, and the public library arranges a special Delius exhibit.
Contact: Delius Association of Florida, 3305 Saint Johns Avenue, Jacksonville, Florida 32202 or Delius House, Jacksonville University, Jacksonville, Florida 32211.

Illinois - Brinfield

JUBILEE COLLEGE, OLD ENGLISH FAIRE
Jubilee College State Park
Brinfield, Illinois

Presents strolling troubadors, colorful pageants, traditional English plays, hot air ballooning, and other activities at the site of the first Episcopal institution of higher learning in the midwest. The Jubilee College Fair is held in late June.
Contact: Director of Parks and Memorials Division, Program Services Section, 605 State Office Building, Springfield, Illinois 62706.

Indiana - Evansville

MADRIGAL DINNERS
Forum Room
Indiana State University
Evansville, Indiana

Trumpet fanfare heralds the arrival of strolling minstrels, court jesters, and a steaming bowl of wassail as a regal Yuletide feast is celebrated in sixteenth century English manor tradition. Court rituals are re-enacted. The Mid-America Singers, costumed in elegant brocades and lace of authentic Renaissance vintage, perform a gay round of madrigals as the flaming pudding is served. The banquets are held in early December.
Contact: Indiana State University, 8600 University Boulevard, Evansville, Indiana 47712.

Kansas - Liberal

INTERNATIONAL PANCAKE DAY RACE
Liberal, Kansas

Housewives in Olney, England and Liberal, Kansas, compete simultaneously in running a half-mile with a pancake in a skillet and tossing it twice while running. Started in Liberal in 1950 after the Jaycee president saw a picture of the pancake race in Olney. The winner gets the traditional "Kiss of Peace". Pancake racing began around 500 years ago when the story goes it was customary to use up accumulated cooking grease by making pancakes. One housewife was so engrossed as to forget the time. When the church bells rang, she ran to church still in her apron and carrying the pancakes in her skillet. In the course of the Liberal celebration, there are also pancake eating contests, beauty pageants, parades, children's races, and musical performances.
Contact: Rod Wilson, Chamber of Commerce, Box 676, Liberal, Kansas 67901.

Minnesota - Chaska

RENAISSANCE FESTIVAL
Highway 169
Chaska, Minnesota

A sixteenth century fair including music, dancers, actors, mime artists, gourmet menus, engineering competition, gypsy dance caravan, jousting, horse races, contests, parades, arts and crafts festival, period costuming, jugglers, players of ancient instruments, magicians, jesters, puppeteers, and tumblers all reminiscent of Elizabethan England. Begun in 1971. Held four weekends in August and September. Contact: Renaissance Festivals, Incorporated, Route 1, Post Office Box 125, Chaska, Minnesota 55318.

New York - New York

SPRING FESTIVAL OF ENGLISH AND AMERICAN DANCE
New York, New York

Features music and traiditional dance. Held in April.
Contact: Country Dance and Song Society, 505 Eighth Avenue, New York, New York 10018. (212) 594-8833.

Ohio - Akron

ENGLISH FAIRE
Stan Hywet Hall
Akron, Ohio

Visitors are invited to join the revelry in costume and enter into a traditional English village celebration. A village is set up in Manor Auditorium with a pub wine cellar, tea room and craft shops. The Carriage House offers games: skittles, darts, dunk-the-wench, fortune-telling and apple bobbing. Held for two days in February.
Contact: Director of Public Relations, Stan Hywet Hall Foundation, 714 North Portage Path, Akron, Ohio 44303.

Oregon - Ashland

OREGON SHAKESPEAREAN FESTIVAL
Ashland, Oregon

America's oldest Shakespearean Festival presents four plays in nightly rotation in an outdoor theater patterned after the Fortune Theater of 1599 London. The plays are presented as they were in Shakespeare's Day - without scene breaks or intermissions. Prior to show time, Dancing on the Green features Elizabethan-era dancing and singing. The educational division of the festival is the Institute of Renaissance Studies. Held annually June through August.
Contact: Oregon Shakespearean Festival, Ashland, Oregon 97520.

South Carolina - Charleston

ENGLISH EMPHASIS FESTIVAL
Charleston, South Carolina

Part of the Founders' Festivals, a continuing series of month-long festivals centering on the ethnic groups which were instrumental in the founding and growth of Charleston. Special exhibits in the Gibbes Art Gallery and Charleston Museum, special ethnic foods in local restaurants, and two or three major events. Held during the month of November.
Contact: Mr. James B. Bagwell, Jr., 313 Pitt Street, Mount Pleasant, South Carolina 29464.

Virginia - Charlottesville

MERRIE OLD ENGLAND CHRISTMAS CELEBRATION
Charlottesville, Virginia

A medieval celebration featuring costumed performers, old carols and madrigals, musical tumblers, jugglers, and a conjurer. Court dancers, mummers, musicians playing medieval instruments, fireworks, and a bonfire add to the festivities. Held Christmas week.
Contact: Boar's Head Inn, Ednam Forest, Charlottesville, Virginia 23903. (804) 296-2181

MERRIE OLD ENGLAND SUMMER FESTIVAL AND VILLAGE FAIR OF ARTS AND HANDICRAFTS
Charlottesville, Virginia

Features crafts exhibits, pageantry, early English dancing, archery, and jousing tournaments, festival feasts, and special entertainments. Held a weekend in late July.
Contact: Boar's Head Inn, Ednam Forest, Charlottesville, Virginia 23903. (804) 296-2181.

Washington - Fall City

FALLSHIRE RENAISSANCE FAIRE
Fall City, Washington

Re-creates the sights, sounds, and spirit of medieval English fairs. In costumes of the times, troubadours, mummers, dancers, musicians, actors, and magicians perform for visitors. Artists and craftsmen display their fine jewelry, woodcrafts, pots, woven fabrics and clothes, candles, and batik wares. Fencing and jousting tournaments. Sponsored by the Society for Creative Anachronism. Held on four successive weekends in August and early September.
Contact: Snoqualmie Falls Forest Theater, 14240 Southeast Allen Road, Bellevue, Washington 98006.

Airline Offices

BRITISH AIRWAYS - BOAC
United States Headquarters:
245 Park Avenue
New York, New York 10017 (212) 878-4500

Flies the North Atlantic to link six United Kingdom cities with ten American and eight Canadian cities. Also flies to Australia with stops in New York, Los Angeles, and Honolulu. Other offices in the United States: Anchorage (Alaska), Atlanta, Boston, Chicago, Cleveland, Detroit, Hartford, Honolulu, Houston, Los Angeles, Miami, Minneapolis, Philadelphia, Pittsburgh, Rochester, Saint Louis, San Diego, San Francisco, Union (New Jersey), and Washington.

BRITISH CALEDONIAN AIRWAYS
North American Headquarters
415 Madison Avenue
New York, New York 10017 (212) 935-9550

Flights link New York with Gatwick, Manchester, and Prestwick, Scotland. Schedules international service to 25 countries in Europe, Africa, North and South America. Other offices in the United States: Atlanta, Cincinnati, Hartford, Houston, Los Angeles, and Washington.

Ship Lines

CUNARD LINE LIMITED
555 Fifth Avenue
New York, New York 10017 (212) 880-7500

Ships leave New York for cruises to the Caribbean, South America, or around the world. Air/sea Caribbean cruises depart by air from Los Angeles or San Diego and by sea from San Juan, Puerto Rico.

P & O/THE BRITISH CRUISE LINE
c/o P & O Straph Services
17 Battery Place
New York, New York 10004 (212) 747-3300

Sails from Port Everglades, Florida, for the Caribbean, California, Hawaii, and England. Sails from Los Angeles, San Francisco, and Honolulu for Australia or to the Bahamas, Florida, and England.

Bookdealers and Publishers' Representatives

ARNOLDS OF MICHIGAN
(antiquarian)
511 South Union Street
Traverse City, Michigan 49684 (616) 946-9212

BOOKPHIL
(antiquarian)
Post Office Box 5628
Columbus, Ohio 43221 (614) 268-2272

BRITISH BOOK CENTRE
395 Saw Mill River Road
Elmsford, New York 10523 (914) 592-7700

BRITISH PUBLICATIONS, INCORPORATED
(posters and books)
11-03 Forty-Sixth Avenue
Long Island City, New York 11101 (212) 937-4606

BRITISH TRAVEL BOOKSHOP
(posters and books)
680 Fifth Avenue
New York, New York 10019 (212) 581-4700

THE CHURCHILLIANA COMPANY
4629 Sunset Drive
Sacramento, California 95822 (916) 448-7053

CROSS HILL BOOKS
Post Office Box 798
866 Washington Street
Bath, Maine 04530 (207) 443-5652

CUMBERLAND LITERARY AGENCY
Belle Meade Station Box 50331
Nashville, Tennessee 37205 (615) 794-7253

HAROLD B. DIAMOND, BOOKSELLER
(antiquarian 19th century)
Box 1193
Burbank, California 91507 (213) 846-0342

DUFOUR EDITIONS, INCORPORATED
(antiquarian 18th century)
53 Byers Road
Chester Springs, Pennsylvania 19425 (215) 458-5005

PAULETTE GREENE, RARE BOOKS
(antiquarian 19th century)
140 Princeton Road
Rockville Centre, New York 11570 (516) 766-8602

HARTFIELD BOOKS
(antiquarian 19th century)
117 Dixboro Road
Ann Arbor, Michigan 48105 (313) 662-6035

HOUSE OF BOOKS INCORPORATED
Post Office Box 231
Kearny, New Jersey 07032

HOUSE OF DAVID
(Jewish books from United Kingdom)
12826 Victory Boulevard
North Hollywood, California 91606 (213) 763-2070

INTERNATIONAL PUBLICATIONS SERVICE
114 East 32nd Street
New York, New York 10016 (212) 685-9351

JITCO SPECIALIZED BOOK DISTRIBUTORS
1776 South Jefferson Street
Rockville, Maryland 20852 (301) 881-2305

WILLIAM S. JOHNSON, BOOKS
829 East Drive Woodruff Place
Indianapolis, Indiana 46201 (317) 639-1256

LEGACY BOOKS
(English folklore)
Post Office Box 494
Hatboro, Pennsylvania 19040

THE LONDON BOOKSHOP
(history and literature)
79 West Monroe Street, Suite 1122
Chicago, Illinois 60603

JOHN WILLIAM MARTIN - BOOKSELLER
(18th and 19th centuries)
436 South Seventh Avenue
La Grange, Illinois 60525 (312) 352-8115

H. J. MOLLOY
(antiquarian; English medieval history and literature)
Post Office Box 5267
San Francisco, California 94101

J & J O'DONOGHUE
1927 Second Avenue South
Anoka, Minnesota 55303

PALINURUS - ANTIQUARIAN BOOKS
RD #1
Box 257
Stockton, New Jersey 08559 (609) 397-1831

PAN AMERICAN BOOKS
Box 270
Cazenovia, New York 13035 (315) OL 5-9654

PENDRAGON HOUSE, INCORPORATED
(British Government Publications)
2595 East Bayshore Road
Palo Alto, California 94303 (415) 327-5631

PENDRAGON HOUSE OF CONNECTICUT, INCORPORATED
(British Government Publications)
Post Office Box 221
Old Mystic, Connecticut 06372 (203) 536-1163

PENNYWHEEL PRESS
Route 2
Poultney, Vermont 05764 (802) 287-4050

SCOTCH HOUSE
187 Post Street
San Francisco, California 94108 (415) 391-1264

SKY BOOKS INTERNATIONAL INCORPORATED
48 East 50th Street
New York, New York 10022 (212) 688-5086

SONS OF LIBERTY - BOOKS
Post Office Box 452
Manchester, New Hampshire 03105 (603) 622-5853

SUPERSNIPE COMIC BOOK EUPHORIUM & ART GALLERY
1617 Second Avenue
New York, New York 10028 (212) 879-9628

TRANSATLANTIC ARTS, INCORPORATED
88 Bridge Road
Central Islip, New York 11722 (516) 234-0055

TRANSATLANTIC BOOKS
Post Office Box 44
Matawan, New Jersey 07747 (201) 566-8689

UNIVERSAL DISTRIBUTORS COMPANY
54 West 13th Street
New York, New York 10011 (212) 243-4317

WOODEN SHOE BOOKS & RECORDS
112 South 20th Street
Philadelphia, Pennsylvania 19103 (215) 569-2477

Books and Pamphlets

ANNUAL BIBLIOGRAPHY OF BRITISH AND IRISH HISTORY. 1975-. Harvester Press; Atlantic Hylands, New Jersey; Humanities Press.

An annual publication that lists materials published in London on British and Irish history. Arranged by sections whose headings may change from publication to publication. Includes an author and subject index followed by other works in chronological order. Also includes an index of authors and a guide to subjects.

BIBLIOGRAPHY OF BRITISH HISTORY, 1851-1914. Edited by H. J. Hanham. Oxford; Clarendon Press, 1976.

List the major works of literature published before 1973 that deal with British history during the time period 1851-1914. Materials have been grouped by categories such as external relations, the churches and local history. Contains both English and American publications.

BIBLIOGRAPHY OF BRITISH HISTORY, 1789-1851. Edited by Lucy M. Brown. Oxford; Clarendon Press, 1977.

Includes a wide variety of materials; books, pamphlets, essays and journals which are arranged by subjects such as political history, legal history and cultural history. Majority of the books listed in this bibliography can be found in the British Library or other specialist libraries in London.

BOOKS ON THE BRITISH EMPIRE AND COMMONWEALTH: A GUIDE FOR STUDENTS. By John E. Flint. London; Royal Commonwealth Society, 1968.

A guide to descriptive, geographic, economic, literary works and most of all, historical and political literature on the British Empire and Commonwealth. Includes important books published since 1940. An update of "Best Books on the British Empire."

BRITAIN IN BRIEF. New York, British Information Services, 1982.

A booklet presenting a brief overview of Great Britain, its people, government, legal system, armed forces, economy, industry, scientific advances, agriculture, finance, trade, social services, housing, culture, religion, and communications network.

BRITAIN 1981; An Official Handbook. By the British Central Office of Information, London. Palo Alto, California, Pendragon House.

An annual volume covering many topics concerning the British land and people, their government, laws, defense system, housing, religion, economy, transportation, communication, recreation, and social services. Illustrated with photographs, maps, and diagrams.

BRITAIN - THE WEST COUNTRY. London, British Tourist Authority, 1982.

A pamphlet introducing the counties of Avon, Cornwall, Dorset, Somerset, Wiltshire and the Isles of Scilly. Includes colored pictures, a map and a listing of hotels and other accomodations.

BRITAIN'S OVERSEAS RELATIONS. London, Central Office of Information, Research Division, 1980.

A booklet outlining the main features of Britain's overseas relations such as British membership in the European Community and in the Commonwealth, the United Nations, development cooperation and international peace and security. Includes a reading list.

BRITISH ECONOMIC AND SOCIAL HISTORY: A BIBLIOGRAPHICAL GUIDE. Compiled by W. H. Chalvner. Manchester; Manchester University Press, 1976.

A select bibliography to the literature of British economic and social history from 1066 to 1970. The guide is divided chronologically at 1300, 1500 and at 1700 and then arranged by subject within the different periods. Also includes an index of authors and editors.

BRITISH HISTORY SINCE 1760: A SELECT BIBLIOGRAPHY. By Ian R. Christie. London, Historical Association, 1970.

Provides guidance to the standard works covering this period, collections of printed source material and articles in periodicals are excluded. Divided into five sections; bibliography and periodicals, general series and general works, later Hanoverian Age, Victorian Britain and the Twentieth Century. Each of these sections may be divided into subsections. Occasional annotations.

DISSERTATIONS ON BRITISH HISTORY, 1815-1914; An Index to British and American Theses. Compiled by S. Peter Bell. Metuchen, New Jersey; Scarecrow Press, 1974.

Listing of some 2,300 British and American titles which discuss the history of Great Britain and Ireland. Arranged by five subjects: political history, economic history, social history, ecclesiastical history and history of education. Includes author, person, place and subject indexes.

EAST ANGLIA. London, Central Office of Information, 1976.

One of a series describing English regions. East Anglia comprises the counties of Cambridgeshire, Norfolk and Suffolk and is the least populous of the English regions. The booklet describes geology and scenery, history, today's economy, administration, planning and development, education and research and the amenities for leisure and tourism. Maps and illustrations as well as a reading list are included.

EDUCATION IN BRITAIN. London, Central Office of Information, Reference Division, 1979.

A booklet which discusses all levels of education in Britain including nursery and primary schools, secondary schools, post-school education at universities, polytechnics and adult education, international programs and youth services. A reading list for further information is included.

ENGLISH HISTORY, 1815-1914. By R. K. Webb. Washington, D.C., Service Center for Teachers of History, 1967.

A bibliographic essay on English history with emphasis on politics (structure and substance), the transformation of English society, the spread of industrialism and the Victorian intellect.

THE ENGLISH LEGAL SYSTEM. By the British Central Office of Information, London. New York, British Information Services, 1976.

A pamphlet discussing origins of English law, branches of the law, the court system, legal personnel, administration of justice, judicial procedures, legal aid and law reform. Includes a reading list. One in a series of many reference pamphlets on British institutions and activities.

FACT SHEETS ON BRITAIN. London, Central Office of Information.

A series of reference sheets on specific topics of interest.

FROM HERE TO THE WHITE HOUSE. Belfast, Ulster, Northern Ireland Tourist Board, 1981.

Beautifully illustrated booklet on Northern Ireland from the point of view of its connections with American presidents and other prominent men in American history.

GOVERNMENT AND PARLIAMENT IN BRITAIN: A BIBLIOGRAPHY. By John Palmer - 2nd edition. rev. London; Hansard Society for Parliamentary Government, 1964.

A briefly annotated bibliography of materials (excluding legal works, books on political theory, historical works and periodical articles) which describe how government and Parliament are organized. Arranged under various headings like The Crown, The Constitution, and Political Parties.

A GUIDE TO THE PRINTED MATERIALS FOR ENGLISH SOCIAL AND ECONOMIC HISTORY, 1750-1850. By Judith Williams. New York; Columbia University Press, 1926.

Two volume selective guide to materials on the social and economic history of England, with emphasis on the Industrial Revolution, and economic and social effects of the Napoleonic wars. Each section begins with an introduction followed by bibliographies, official publications and periodical publications.

HEALTH SERVICES IN BRITAIN. By the British Central Office of Information, London. New York, British Information Services, 1974.

A pamphlet covering various types of British health services: public health, primary health care, hospital services, maternal and child care, care of the elderly and disabled, mental illness, occupational health, medical research, and professional training. Discusses health services in England, Scotland, Wales, and Northern Ireland. Includes a reading list, special appendices, and photographs of health service activities.

THE HISTORIOGRAPHY OF THE BRITISH EMPIRE - COMMONWEALTH; Trends, Interpretations and Resources. Edited by Robin W. Winks. Durham, North Carolina; Duke University Press, 1966.

A collection of bibliographical essays that inform the user on what literature is available about the British Empire and Commonwealth and how this literature developed in the way that it did. Covers only literature published through 1963.

HOW TO FIND OUT ABOUT THE VICTORIAN PERIOD; A Guide to Sources of Information. By Lionel Madden. Oxford, New York, Pergamon Press, 1970.

THE LAND OF BRITAIN. London, Central Office of Information, 1978.

A folder of separate pages each with descriptions and pictures of an aspect of British life such as government, economy, industry, agriculture, transportation and communications, environmental planning, home and community, sports and recreation, health and social services, education, science and technology, the arts and international relations.

LONDON IS . . . London, British Tourist Authority, 1981.

Description of various points of interest and special events in London. Accompanied by colored pictures and maps of parts of London. Includes hotel information.

MODERN ENGLAND, 1901- 1970. By Alfred F. Havighurst (Conference on British Studies Bibliographical Handbooks). New York; Cambridge University Press, 1976.

A bibliographical handbook of published material (primary and secondary sources) covering the periods 1901-1970 in British history. Includes historical literature published before 1974.

THE MONARCHY IN BRITAIN. By the British Central Office of Information, London. New York, British Information Services, 1977.

A pamphlet tracing the evolution and present status of the monarchy, including its titles, customs, functions, income, royal household, royal arms, regalia, and modes of traveling. Includes a list of additional reading materials.

NINETEENTH-CENTURY BRITAIN, 1815-1914. By David Nicholls. (Critical Bibliographies in Modern History). Hamden, Connecticut; Archon Books, 1978.

A bibliography of the books on nineteenth-century Britain in the English language that are available and suitable for the average history student. An introduction to each section presents a review of current trends in that branch of history.

THE NORTH WEST. London, Central Office of Information, 1975.

The counties of Cheshire and Lancashire, Greater Manchester and Merseyside are the most densely populated industrial areas in England. The geography and geology, history and industrial development, today's economy and cultural resources are described. Maps and illustrations as well as a reading list are provided.

NORTHERN IRELAND. Belfast, Ulster, Northern Ireland Tourist Board, 1981.

A booklet illustrated in color showing the beauties of the Causeway Coast, the Ard Peninsula, The County Down Coast, the inland areas and the Lake District.

NORTHERN IRELAND. London, Central Office of Information, 1981.

Informational booklet about Ulster, the northern part of Ireland which is a part of the United Kingdom. Describes its origins, civil disturbances, reform program and constitutional change, human rights, emergency powers, prisons, police, administration, relations with the United Kingdom Parliament and with the Irish Republic, geography, economy and social affairs. Illustrations in color, a map, a list of addresses and a reading list are included.

NORTHERN IRELAND, 1921-1974, A SELECT BIBLIOGRAPHY. By Richard Deutsch, New York, Garland Publishing, 1975.

A select bibliography of books and pamphlets as an introduction to the Northern crisis. There are three sections to the book- non-fiction, fiction and index of authors. Also includes a chronology.

PARLIAMENTARY ELECTIONS IN BRITAIN. London, Central Office of Information, Research Division, 1978.

A booklet describing the history of parliamentary elections, the extension of the franchise, the present constituencies, voters and candidates and the electoral procedure. A reading list is included.

RACE RELATIONS IN BRITAIN. London, Central Office of Information, 1977.

A booklet dealing with recent immigration to Britain from New Commonwealth Countries and Pakistan, outlining the numbers and distribution of ethnic minorities, race relations legislation, the housing, health and social service, educational and employment opportunities and media and police relations with the various groups. Includes appendices and a reading list.

READER'S GUIDE TO GREAT BRITAIN: A BIBLIOGRAPHY. By Bruce Stevenson. London; National Book League; British Council, 1977.

A revised and enlarged edition of the booklist British Civilization and Institutions published by the League in 1945. This bibliography covers the language, literature, life and customs of the British people. Arrangement follows the Dewey Decimal Classification and contains books published before May 1976.

SOCIAL SECURITY IN BRITAIN. By the British Central Office of Information, London. New York, British Information Services, 1973.

A pamphlet discussing the growth of the British social security system and provisions for family allowances, attendance allowances, national insurance, industrial injuries insurance, war pensions, and supplementary benefits. Includes appendices and a reading list.

THE SOUTH WEST. London, Central Office of Information, 1978.

A booklet about the seven counties of Avon, Cornwall, Devon, Dorset, Gloucestershire, Somerset and Wiltshire describing geology, scenery and climate, history, aspects of the economy and administration and amenities for leisure and tourism. Pictures, maps and a reading list are included.

STONEHENGE. By Leonard Smith. Salisbury, England; Salisbury District Office, Publicity Office.

Gives the neo-lithic history of Stonehenge, a discussion of the probable uses to which various ancient peoples put the monument, a description of the astronomical alignments and tells of other interesting sites in the immediate vicinity. Includes pictures, maps and a chronology of restoration and research at Stonehenge.

VICTORIAN ENGLAND 1837-1901. By Josef Altholz. Cambridge, Cambridge University Press, 1970. (Conference on British Studies Bibliographical Handbooks).

A bibliographical handbook on the various aspects of the history of Victorian England. Materials arranged under 14 headings, political history, science and technology and history of the fine arts to name a few.

A YEAR BOOK OF THE COMMONWEALTH, 1980. London, Her Majesty's Stationery Office.

An annual publication containing essential information about all the countries constituting the Commonwealth today, including member nations, associated states, and dependencies. Provides background information on the constitutional development of the Commonwealth and countries comprising it, on Commonwealth trade, and on British government relations with other Commonwealth countries. The yearbook is revised and updated each year from official sources.

BRITISH AMERICANS

AMERICA'S BRITISH HERITAGE. London, British Tourist Authority, 1978.

Places in England, Wales, Scotland and Northern Ireland which are associated with America's heritage are listed alphabetically and described briefly. Maps for each area are embellished with portraits of the important people who lived there.

BRITISH AND CANADIAN IMMIGRATION TO THE UNITED STATES SINCE 1920. By Kenneth Lines. San Francisco, R and E Research Associates, 1978.

A study interpreting British and Canadian immigration to the United States in the decades after the First World War. Data was obtained from experiences of British and Canadian immigrants residing in four states; California, Hawaii, Oregon and Washington.

THE BRITISH AND IRISH IN OKLAHOMA. By Patrick J. Blessing. Norman, University of Oklahoma Press, 1980. (Newcomers to a New Land).

Analyzes the role of the British and Irish and how they have contributed to the history of Oklahoma.

BRITISH CHARTISTS IN AMERICA, 1830-1900. By Ray Boston. Totowa, New Jersey. Rowman and Littlefield, 1971.

Deals with a particular group of English immigrants.

BRITISH EMIGRATION TO NORTH AMERICA; Projects and Opinions in the Early Victorian Period. By Wilbur S. Shepperson. Minneapolis, University of Minnesota Press, 1957.

Particularly useful for nineteenth century emigration patterns.

BRITISH IMMIGRANTS IN INDUSTRIAL AMERICA, 1790-1950. By Rowland Tappan Berthoff, 1953. Reprint 1968. New York, Russell & Russell (Atheneum House).

Documents the easy integration of British immigrants into the economic and social life of the United States, supporting the assumption that they enjoyed a place in nineteenth century America unlike that of other foreigners. Part I: The Economic Adjustment; Part II: The Cultural Adjustment.

THE BRITISH IN AMERICA, 1578-1970; A Chronology & Fact Book. Compiled and edited by Howard B. Furer. Ethnic Chronology Series, no. 7. Dobbs Ferry, Oceana Publications, 1972.

Presents a chronology of events concerning English, Scotch-Irish, Scottish, and Welsh immigration in the United States in the first section. The second section consists of selected documents chosen to give a varied picture of the British experience in America.

THE BRITISH IN IOWA. By Jacob Van der Zee. Iowa City, State Historical Society of Iowa, 1922.

Consists of two essays: one discusses British emigrants to Iowa; the other tells of the British invasion of Northwestern Iowa. The first essay surveys the English, Irish, Scottish, and Welsh components in the population of Iowa. The second essay relates to the settlement of several hundreds of Britons in north-western Iowa near Le Mars during the nineteenth century.

THE BRITISH REGIME IN WISCONSIN AND THE NORTHWEST. By Louise P. Kellogg. Madison, State Historical Society of Wisconsin, 1935.

Discusses the British occupation or regime of Wisconsin from 1760 (after the departure of the French) to 1815.

BRITONS IN AMERICAN LABOR; A History of the Influence of the United Kingdom Immigrants on American Labor, 1820-1914. By Clifton K. Yearley, Jr. Baltimore, The Johns Hopkins Press, 1957.

Inquires into the impact of men and ideas from the United Kingdom upon early labor and labor reform movements in the United States. Emphasis is on English, Scottish, and Welsh immigrants.

COLONISTS IN BONDAGE. By Abbot Emerson Smith. Chapel Hill, North Carolina, University of North Carolina Press, 1947. Reprint Gloucester, Massachusetts, P. Smith, 1965. Reprint New York, 1971.

A study sponsored by the Institute of Early American History and Culture at Williamsburg which deals with immigrants from England who paid for their passage by agreeing to become indentured servants for a certain length of time. Also discusses convict labor. Covers the period 1607-1776.

CONFLICT AND CONCORD: THE ANGLO-AMERICAN RELATIONSHIP SINCE 1783. By Harry C. Allen. New York, Saint Martin's Press, 1959.

Discusses American attitudes toward England and the English and the role of immigrants from England in forming these attitudes.

THE CORNISH MINER IN AMERICA. By Arthur C. Todd. Glendale, California, Clark, 1967.

The importance of Cornish immigrants in recovering America's mineral resources is discussed.

THE COUNSIN JACKS: THE CORNISH IN AMERICA. By A. L. Rowse. New York, Scribner, 1969.

Though many of the Cornish immigrants were miners and justly important in settling the West, many were farmers or sailors. The patterns of emigration, settlement and acculturation are presented in a very readable form and the contribution of the Cornish to America are discussed.

THE ELIZABETHANS' AMERICA; A Collection of Early Reports by Englishmen on the New World. By Louis B. Wright. Cambridge, Harvard University Press, 1965.

The second volume of a library on Elizabethan and Jacobean life and literature. Begins with an introduction on the wonders and mysteries of Trans-Atlantic lands, followed by documents by Englishmen on America.

EMIGRATION & DISENCHANTMENT; Portraits of Englishmen Repatriated from the United States. By Wilbur S. Shepperson. Norman, Oklahoma, University of Oklahoma Press, 1965.

Investigates the magnitude and significance of the return movement to England of people who emigrated to the United States until 1854. Includes brief sketches of 75 returnees and the personal circumstances which led them to leave America, as examples of similar situations among other disenchanted Englishmen.

ENGLISH FAMILY RESEARCH. Edited by John Konrad. Munroe Falls, Summit Publications, Ohio, 1979.

Publication includes hereditary and patriotic organizations for the Colonial and Revolutionary periods, federal archives, and genealogical societies and other sources in England. Entries include name and address.

THE ENGLISH ON THE DELAWARE: 1610-1682. By C. A. Weslager. New Brunswick, New Jersey, Rutgers University Press, 1967.

Presents the sequence of historic events in the Delaware Valley from the English point of view, in contrast to the part played by the Dutch and Swedes. Deals with the discovery of Delaware Bay in 1610, the history of settlements in the region, their subjugation by the English, and conveyance of the region to William Penn in 1682.

EXPECTATIONS WESTWARD. By Philip A. M. Taylor. Ithaca, New York, Cornell University Press, 1966.

Discusses the recruitment of Mormons from England.

GOING TO AMERICA. By Terry Coleman. New York, Pantheon Books (Random House), 1972.

Tells the story of the millions of emigrants who left Great Britain and Ireland for America in 1846 through 1855. Explains who they were, why they left home and how, and what happened to them in America.

THE HARD-ROCK MEN: CORNISH IMMIGRANTS AND THE NORTH AMERICAN MINING FRONTIER. By John Rowe. New York, Barnes and Noble Books, 1974.

A HISTORY OF EMIGRATION FROM THE UNITED KINGDOM TO NORTH AMERICA, 1762-1912. By Stanley C. Johnson. Reprint 1913, New York, A. M. Kelley, 1966.

An early and still useful study which talks about the background of emigration for many different reasons, the experience of sailing to the North American continent, settling and forming communities.

IMAGINING AMERICA. By Peter Conrad. New York, Oxford University Press, 1980.

Different aspects of America (Institutional America, Primitive America plus seven others) are discussed by British writers (H. G. Wells, Aldous Huxley and more) as seen through their eyes and writings.

INVISIBLE IMMIGRANTS; The Adaptation of English and Scottish Immigrants in Nineteenth-Century America. By Charlotte Erickson. Coral Gables, Florida, University of Miami Press, 1972.

Letters written by English and Scottish immigrants are arranged in three parts with introductory material on motives for emigration, networks of migration, economic and social adjustment. Part I deals with immigrants in agriculture; Part II with immigrants in industry; and Part III with immigrants in professional, commercial, and clerical occupations.

THE KING'S FRIENDS. By Wallace Brown. Providence, Rhode Island, Brown University Press, 1965.

Prior to and during the War of Independence, many English settlers took the side of Great Britain. This book discusses the Loyalists and their part in making American history.

THE LONG WINTER ENDS. By Newton G. Thomas. New York, Macmillan, 1941.

A regional description of Cornish life in Michigan.

PRAIRIE ALBION; An English Settlement in Pioneer Illinois. By Charles Boewe. Carbondale, Southern Illinois University Press, 1962.

Excerpts from books, pamphlets, and articles of the period tell the story of a trek from the Virginia coast to Illinois territory and the settlement founded at Albion by a group of Englishmen. Gives a vivid, firsthand view of the colonists' adventures from 1817 on through the early years of the settlement.

THOMAS KELLY AND FAMILY'S JOURNALS. London, Times Press, 1965.

This diary documents the experiences of an early settler from the Isle of Man in Ohio and is one of the few glimpses into the Manx emigration to America.

Audiovisual Material

FILMS

ANGLO-SAXON ENGLAND. 16 mm. Color and sound. 22 minutes. By D. C. Chipperfield for Boulton-Hawker Films, Hadleigh, England. Released in the United States by International Film Bureau, Chicago, 1971.

Presents an outline of English history from the end of Roman rule around 410 A.D. to the Norman conquest in 1066. Reports on the various raids and migrations which changed the English country. Examines the settlements of Anglo-Saxons as shown by recent excavations at Cadbury, West Stow, and Winchester. Shows the growth of monasteries in England.

THE BATTLE OF BRITAIN. Videorecording. Black and white. Sound. 55 minutes. By United States War Department. Distributed by National Audiovisual Center, 1979.

Presents a documentary film record of the bombing of England by the German Luftwaffe in 1940 and the defense offered by the Royal Air Force.

BRITAIN, WHO SHOT THE WOODCOCK? 16 mm. Color and sound. 50 minutes. By CTV Television Network, Toronto, 1976.

Examines Britain in terms of recent political and economic developments, and tries to determine historical factors that contributed to weakening the country's power and influence.

THE CHANGING WORLD OF CHARLES DICKENS. 16 mm. Color and sound. 28 minutes. By John Irvin for Allan King Associates, London. Released by Learning Corporation of America, New York, 1970.

The events and characters of Dickens' novels show the turmoil and conflict rampant in nineteenth century England.

CHURCHILL AND BRITISH HISTORY, 1874-1918. Black and white. Sound. 29 minutes. By Chatsworth Film Distributors Limited, Lawrence, Kansas, Centron Educational Films, 1977.

Presents, through the use of still and newsreel film, a biography of Churchill's early years, from his school days through World War I and his activities in the British Cabinet. Covers major influences in Churchill's life and political figures and crises of the period. Narrated by Michael Redgrave.

ELIZABETH: THE QUEEN WHO SHAPED AN AGE. 16 mm. Color and sound. 26 minutes. By John H. Secondari Productions. Released by Learning Corporation of America, New York, 1971.

Discusses the character of Queen Elizabeth I and its effect on the Elizabethan Era. Describes how she made England the richest and most powerful nation in the world through her handling of the problem of religious divisiveness, the conflict between Spain and England, and the question of Mary, Queen of Scots.

FAMILIES OF THE WORLD - GREAT BRITAIN. 16 mm. Color and sound. 10 minutes. By Goldberg/ Werrenrath Productions, Journal Films, Evanston, Illinois, 1977.

Presents insight into the history, culture, and family life of the British people by focusing on some of the activities of a family from Leeds, England.

FOREIGNERS. 16 mm. Color and sound. 29 minutes. Canadian Film-Makers' Distribution Centre, Toronto, 1974.

A documentary showing two North Americans hitch-hiking around England and France.

INDUSTRIAL BRITAIN. 16 mm. Black and white. Sound. 21 minutes. By Empire Marketing Board Film Unit, London, 1933. Released in the United States by Pyramid Films, 1975.

Documents work in Britain's factories and mines during the early 1930's.

THE INDUSTRIAL REVOLUTION. 16 mm. Color and sound. 23 minutes. Also issued as video recording. By Hugh Baddeley Productions, International Film Bureau, Chicago, 1980.

Traces the developments in England during the 1700's that lead to the Industrial revolution, telling how one invention or improvement inspired another, enabling persons to produce more goods.

INTRODUCING THE UNITED KINGDOM. Videorecording. Black and white. Sound. 22 minutes. By World Mirror Productions, Brussels, NATO. Distributed by National Audiovisual Center, Washington, 1979.

Describes the country and people of the United Kingdom, including geographical features, historical development and achievements, economic life, occupations of the people, and social customs. Explains briefly the role of the United Kingdom in the North Atlantic Treaty Organization.

THE MANXMEN. 16 mm. Color and sound. 25 minutes. By RCP Destination Films, Toronto. Released by Viacom International, 1974.

A documentary on the Isle of Man, a little known island set in the midst of the Irish Sea. Points out that it is all that remains of an ancient Norse Kingdom, and yet, it contains a fascinating wealth of stories.

A MUCH MALIGNED MONARCH. 16 mm. Color and sound. 29 minutes. By European Color Productions, Xerox Films, Middletown, Connecticut, 1977.

Presents a conversation between Prince Charles of Wales and British historian Alistair Cooke on the subject of King George III, who ruled Great Britain from 1762 to 1830. Prince Charles points out that King George was misunderstood by the people of his day and that external factors beyond his control created problems in England which predisposed the American Revolution.

OH,TO BE IN ENGLAND: The American Trail. 16 mm. Color and sound. 25 minutes. Also issued as videocassette. By BBC-TV, Time-Life Multimedia, New York, 1978.

Follows a group of Americans on a sightseeing tour of England, covering sites such as Windsor Castle, Canterbury, King's School, and the home of Winston Churchill.

A PHOTOGRAPHER'S BRITAIN. 16 mm. Color and sound. 5 minutes. By Insight Productions, Toronto. Released by Harry Smith and Sons, 1973.

Presents a study of Britain as shown in still photographs filmed and set to music and effects.

SCOTLAND YARD. 16 mm. Color and sound. 51 minutes. New York, National Broadcasting Company Educational Enterprises, 1971.

Examines the history of Scotland Yard and reports on some of the methods used in dealing with modern police problems, such as working with demonstrations, drug abuse, and interracial relations.

THE SECOND BATTLE OF BRITAIN. 16 mm. Color and sound. 49 minutes. By John Tiffin, CBS News. Carousel Films, New York, 1976, made 1975.

Examines causes for Great Britain's economic decline and explains the plight of the middle class Englishman in supporting the poor and the Government. Includes interviews with Malcolm Muggeridge, Claud Cockburn, and others concerning their views on these conditions.

SHAKESPEARE OF STRATFORD AND LONDON. 16 mm. Color and sound. 32 minutes. Also issued as videorecording. By National Geographic Society, in association with WQED Pittsburgh, Washington, 1978.

Deals with the life of William Shakespeare, including footage showing Stratford-upon-Avon, the Warwickshire country-side, and 16th century London. Produced with the cooperation of Shakespeare Birthplace Trust, Stratford-upon-Avon.

THE TIME IS OUT OF JOINT. 16 mm. Color and sound. 20 minutes. Also issued as videorecording. By National Geographic Society, in association with WQED Pittsburgh, Washington, 1978.

Explores the reasons why William Shakespeare chose a medieval setting for his play Hamlet, with special emphasis on the political and social situation in England at the time. Produced with the cooperation of Shakespeare Birthplace Trust, Stratford-upon-Avon.

WILL THERE ALWAYS BE AN ENGLAND? 16 mm. Color and sound. 24 minutes. By CBS News, Carousel Films, New York, 1977.

Outlines the social and economic decline of Great Britain within the past few years and suggests that this fact may threaten her existence as a democratic nation.

Several different American distributors handle British classic documentaries, travel films, documentaries, and theatrical films. For a list write:
Embassy of Great Britain
3100 Massachusetts Avenue, Northwest
Washington, D.C. 20008
(202) 462-1340

BULGARIANS
See also: SLAVIC PEOPLES

Embassy and Consulates

EMBASSY OF BULGARIA
1621 22nd Street, Northwest
Washington, D. C. 20008 (202) 387-7969

Office of Commercial Counselor
121 East 62nd Street
New York, New York 10021 (212) 935-4646

Mission to the United Nations

BULGARIAN MISSION
11 East 84th Street
New York, New York 10028 (202) 737-1791

Tourist and Travel Offices

BULGARIAN TOURIST OFFICE
161 East 86th Street, 2nd Floor
New York, New York 10028 (212) 722-1110

Fraternal Organizations

AMERICAN BULGARIAN LEAGUE
35 Sutton Place
New York, New York 10022 (212) 755-8480
President: Dr. George Obreshkow Founded 1944

Persons of Bulgarian birth or descent in the United States and Canada.
Publication: American Bulgarian Review, irregular.

Public Affairs Organizations

BULGARIAN NATIONAL FRONT
Post Office Box 1204, Grand Central Station
New York, New York 10017 (212) 362-7266
President: Dr. Ivan Docheff Founded 1948

Americans of Bulgarian origin and American friends of Bulgaria. Advocates the right of the people of Bulgaria, enslaved by Communists today, to regain their freedom and independence. Works to make known in America the culture and history of Bulgaria for establishing in the future friendly relations between the United States and Free Bulgaria. Sponsors seminars, and plans to open a museum.
Publication: Borba, monthly.

MACEDONIAN PATRIOTIC ORGANIZATION OF U. S. AND CANADA
c/o Macedonian Tribune
542 South Meridian Street
Indianapolis, Indiana 46225 (317) 635-2157
Founded 1922

Americans and Canadians of Macedonian origin (mostly the Slav or Bulgarian element). Conducts cultural and social activities. Promotes idea of political autonomy for Macedonia. Formerly (1952) Union of Macedonian Political Organizations.
Publication: Makedonska Tribuna (Macedonian Tribune), weekly.

Cultural and Educational Organizations

BULGARIAN-AMERICAN CULTURAL AND EDUCATIONAL SOCIETY
1530 North Vermont Avenue
Los Angeles, California 90027 (213) 666-9123

BULGARIAN STUDIES ASSOCIATION
Department of Slavic Languages
State University of New York at Albany
1400 Washington Avenue
Albany, New York 12222
President: James F. Clarke
Secretary-Treasurer: Ernest A. Seatton

Devoted to the promotion of Bulgarian studies and to the exchange of information among those interested in the field. Affiliated with American Association for the Advancement of Slavic Studies and the American Association for Southeast European Studies.
Publication: Newsletter, three times a year.

MACGAHAN AMERICAN-BULGARIAN FOUNDATION
Post Office Box 641
New Lexington, Ohio 43764
Chairman Professor: James F. Clark
Founded 1978

1581 West Market Street
Akron, Ohio 44313
Executive Director: Dr. George Tabakov

Aims to assist young Americans study the impact the Americans made on the Balkans in the nineteenth century; establish a museum and library in the MacGahan homestead.
Publications: Newsletter, bimonthly; also publishes books and brochures.

Religious Organizations

BULGARIAN EASTERN ORTHODOX CHURCH
1953 Stockbridge Road
Akron, Ohio 44313
Administrator: Bishop Dometian

312 West 101st Street
New York, New York 10025
Metropolitan: Bishop Joseph

The First Bulgarian Orthodox church was built in Madison, Illinois, in 1907 by Bulgarian immigrants. The diocese was established as an Episcopate in 1938. A decision of the Holy Synod in 1972 divided the Bulgarian Eastern Orthodox Church into the New York and Akron Dioceses.

Research Centers and Special Institutes

CENTRE FOR SLAVIC AND EAST EUROPEAN STUDIES
Ohio State University
Dulles Hall
Columbus, Ohio 43210
Director: Professor Leon I. Twarog

Especially strong in Russian, Yugoslav and Bulgarian studies.

TAMBURITZANS INSTITUTE OF FOLK ART
1801 Boulevard of Allies
Pittsburgh, Pennsylvania 15219

Active in the fields of Bulgarian literature and folklore.

Newspapers and Newsletters

BULGARIAN STUDIES ASSOCIATION NEWSLETTER. Editor: Frederick B. Chary, Department of History and Philosophy, Tamarack Hall F20, Indiana University Northwest, 3400 Broadway, Gary, Indiana 46408.

Brings news of the Association, reviews books and research.

MAKEDONSKA TRIBUNA (Macedonian Tribune). 1927-. Weekly. Editor: Anton N. Popov. Publisher: Macedonian Patriotic Organization of the U.S.A. and Canada, 542 South Meridian Street, Indianapolis, Indiana 46225. In Bulgarian and English.

Deals primarily with news concerning the Balkans. Includes editorial comments on national and international issues. A section of the newspaper is devoted to social and cultural activities of Bulgarians in America. Seeks to preserve the cultural and religious heritage of Macedonian-Bulgarians and to work for the creation of a united and independent state of Macedonia.

NARODNA VOLYA (People's Will). 1940-. Semi-monthly. Editor: Bocho Mircheff. Publisher: Co-operative Publishing Company, 5856 Chene Street, Detroit, Michigan 48211. In Bulgarian and English.

Covers general news of special interest to Bulgarians. Also includes news items concerning the activities of various Bulgarian groups and individuals in the United States.

SOFIA NEWS. 1970-. Weekly. Publisher: Sofia Press Agency, Sofia, Bulgaria. In English.

Publishes international and national news concerning Bulgaria, feature articles, sports news, a calendar of events, and guide to places of interest in the Sofia area.

Magazines

BULGARIA TODAY. 1973-. Monthly. Editor: Nikola Zahariev. Publisher: Sofia Press Agency.

A government sponsored publication carrying political news about Bulgaria, Bulgaria's participation in international affairs, cultural news and features, economic, scientific and medical information, and book reviews.

NEWS FROM BULGARIA. Weekly. Publisher: Sofia Press Agency, Ninth of September Square, Sofia, Bulgaria.

Each issue devoted to a particular topic of social or cultural importance.

OBZOR. A BULGARIAN QUARTERLY REVIEW OF LITERATURE AND ARTS. 1977-. Quarterly. Editor: Lilyana Stephanova. Publisher: Obzor, 39 Dondukov Boulevard, 1080 Sofia, Post Office Box 392, Bulgaria. In English, French, Spanish and Russian.

Reproductions of art works, reports on writers' conferences, poems, short stories, criticism, news from the musical world, cinema, theater and dance, book reviews on Bulgarian books and comments on Bulgarian authors abroad comprise this journal.

Bookdealers and Publishers' Representatives

FAM BOOK SERVICE
69 Fifth Avenue
New York, New York 10003

IMPORTED PUBLICATIONS, INCORPORATED
320 West Ohio Street
Chicago, Illinois 60610 (312) 787-9017

SLAVICA PUBLISHING COMPANY
Post Office Box 14388
Columbus, Ohio 43214 (614) 268-4002

TEC-BOOKS LIMITED (Librairie De Documentation Technique SA)
41 William
Pittsburgh, Pennsylvania 12901 (518) 561-0005

Books and Pamphlets

THE BOYANA CHURCH. By Johanna Genova. Sofia, Photostat, 1974.

A folder containing ten beautiful reproductions of the architecture and art treasures of the Boyana Church in the foothills eight kilometers from Sofia. This artistic and religious monument of the thirteenth century is also described in an essay accompanying the pictures.

BULGARIA: A BIBLIOGRAPHIC GUIDE. By Marin V. Pundeff. Washington, U. S. Library of Congress Reference Department, Slavic and Central European Division, 1965.

The first part contains a bibliographic survey of major sources grouped into seven subject categories: general reference works, land and people, language and literature, history, politics, government and law, economy and social conditions, and intellectual and artistic life. The second part lists alphabetically over 1,200 sources discussed in the first section.

BULGARIA IN THIRTEEN CENTURIES. By Vasil A. Vasilev. Sofia, Sofia Press, 1979.

A booklet describing the earliest history of the Bulgarian nation, its Golden Age and recent political history.

BULGARIA-RILA MONASTERY. Sofia, State Committee for Tourism.

Many colored illustrations adorn this brochure about the famous Rila Monastery, founded in 865 in the mountains south of Sofia. Its architecture, works of art and library are described. Accommodations for tourists are listed.

BULGARIA-THE VALLEY OF ROSES. Sofia, State Committee of Tourism.

A tourist brochure illustrated in color about the Kazanluk valley reknowned for its roses and for the distilleries of attar of roses, as well as for traditional picturesque villages.

BULGARIAN PRINTS OF THE NATIONAL REVIVAL PERIOD. By Evtim Tomov. Sofia, Bulgarski Houdozhnik, 1979.

After centuries of Ottoman rule, Bulgarian national feeling found expression in the religious subjects of the Bulgarian church. The graphic works produced primarily during the nineteenth century as mementos for pilgrims to monasteries document the religious image as a part of nationalistic revival. An art historical essay accompanies the twenty-four full page reproductions.

FORMATION OF THE BULGARIAN NATION. By Dimiter Angelov. Sofia, Sofia Press, 1978.

A booklet giving a historic account of Bulgaria's formation in the nineth through fourteenth centuries. Thracian, Slavic and Proto-Bulgarian contributions resulted in 881 in the founding of Bulgaria with the Slavs predominating. Important formative forces were the beginning of literacy with the official language of Old Bulgarian (Slavonic) instead of Greek and the adoption of the name Bulgaria, although this element was less numerous than the Slavs. After two centuries of Byzantine rule, the Bulgarian nation was restored in 1185 and remained independent and one of the culturally most advanced nations in Medieval Europe until conquered by the Ottoman Turks at the end of the fourteenth century.

ICONS FROM BULGARIA. By Svetlin Bossiklov. Sofia, The Bulgarski Houdozhnik Publishing House, 1979.

An art historical essay describing the tradition of icon painting in Bulgaria accompanies the twelve full-color full page reproductions. Black and white illustrations are also included in the text.

A JOURNEY THROUGH THE AGES. By Bogomil Nonev. Sofia, Sofia Press, 1978.

Pre-historic culture, Thracian, early Byzantine and early medieval artifacts and settlements, as well as Roman influences gave way to the predominance of Constantinople at the end of the fourth century. The ninth century is regarded as the Golden Age of the first Bulgarian state, a time of outstanding Bulgarian statesmanship, building and artistic achievement which coincided with the adoption of Christianity and the advent of literacy. This booklet is devoted to a history of Bulgaria's national classic heritage.

MEDIAEVAL BULGARIAN CIVILIZATION. Sofia, Sofia Press.

A collection of essays designed to accompany an exhibition of Old Bulgarian culture of the seventh through fourteenth centuries.

MODERN BULGARIA. HISTORY, POLICY, ECONOMY, CULTURE. Edited by Georgi Bokov. Sofia, Sofia Press, 1981.

Official handbook on today's Bulgaria includes chapters on early history and the national revival in the nineteenth century, the victory of socialism, Bulgaria's communist party, labor and economic policy, the organization of the government, social policy, culture and art, science and education, geography, international relations, sport and tourism. Each chapter written by an expert in the field. Photographs, some in color, accompany the text. Published as a hard-bound volume to celebrate Bulgaria's thirteen hundred years of existence.

NEW BULGARIA. By Stefan Efremov. Sofia, Sofia Press, 1980.

A booklet explaining the policy of Bulgaria's socialist state as it applies to production, employment, income, consumption, culture and the socialist way of life.

PAMPOROVA, BULGARIA. Sofia, State Committee for Tourism.

A tourist brochure describing the Rhodope mountain resort in winter and in summer. Illustrated in color.

THE RILA MONASTERY. Sofia, Photostat, 1974.

A folder containing beautiful reproductions of the architecture and art treasures of Bulgaria's famous monastery which was founded in the tenth century and was important in the First and Second Bulgarian Kingdoms. A brief explanation of the history of the monastery is included.

THIRTEENTH CENTENNIAL OF THE FOUNDATION OF THE BULGARIAN STATE. Sofia, Sofia Press, 1981.

A colored catalogue for an official exhibition commemorating Bulgaria's thirteen centuries of national history. Strong emphasis on the last thirty-five years of socialistic change.

BULGARIAN AMERICANS

THE BULGARIAN-AMERICANS. By Nickolay Altankov. San Carlos, California, 1979.

The first full length study of the Bulgarians in America.

THE EAGLE AND THE STORK; AN AMERICAN MEMOIR. By Stoyan Christowe. New York, 1976.

The memories of the life of a Bulgarian immigrant.

HOMESTEAD: THE HOUSEHOLDS OF A MILL TOWN. By Margaret Byington. First published 1910; Reprint Pittsburgh, 1974.

An early sociological study of a Pennsylvania mill town and the Bulgarian contribution.

MY AMERICAN PILGRIMAGE. By Stoyan Christowe. Boston, Little, Brown, 1947.

Autobiographical fiction account of the experiences of a Bulgarian immigrant.

PETER MENIKOFF, THE STORY OF A BULGARIAN BOY IN THE GREAT AMERICAN MELTING POT. By Peter D. Yankoff. Nashville, Tennessee, 1928.

Shows life in Bulgaria as a background to the author's account of his experiences as an immigrant.

SON OF THE DANUBE. By Boris George Petroff. New York, 1940.

An autobiographical account of immigration.

THIS IS MY COUNTRY: AN AUTOBIOGRAPHY. By Stoyan Christowe. New York, Carrick and Evans, 1938.

The author who attained importance in his new country tells about life in Bulgaria, the experiences of immigration and acclimation.

Audiovisual Material

MAP

PEOPLES REPUBLIC OF BULGARIA. Sofia, Institute for Cartographic Investigation and Projection, 1981.

Shows topological features as well as major cities and roads. Approximately 8 x 12.

BURMESE
See also: ASIANS

Embassy and Consulates

EMBASSY OF THE SOCIALIST REPUBLIC
OF THE UNION OF BURMA
2300 S Street, Northwest
Washington, D.C. 20008 (202) 332-9044

Office of the Military, Naval and Air Attache
2300 California Street, Northwest
Washington, D.C. 20008 (202) 332-1938

CONSULATE GENERAL
10 East 77th Street
New York, New York 10021 (212) 535-1310

Mission to the United Nations

BURMESE MISSION
10 East 77th Street
New York, New York 10021 (212) 535-1310

Fraternal Organizations

BURMESE AMERICAN ASSOCIATION (Capital Area)
c/o Maung Maung Tin
14010 Crest Hill Lane (301) 384-0691
Silver Spring, Maryland 20904 Founded 1983

Organized to promote cultural, educational and social activities. Does not engage in political or religious activities.

CHINA-BURMA-INDIA HUMP PILOTS ASSOCIATION
917 Pine Boulevard
Poplar Bluff, Missouri 63901 (314) 785-2420
Executive Secretary: Jan Thies Founded 1945

Association of air crew veterans who fought in the China-Burma-India theater of World War II. Maintains library of World War II memorabilia. Bestows awards. Maintains museum and biographical archives.
Publications: Newsletter, quarterly; also publishes roster and China Airlift - The Hump (book).

MERRILL'S MARAUDERS ASSOCIATION
c/o David Hurwitt
10828 Painted Tree
Pineville, North Carolina 28134
Executive Aide and Liaison: (704) 542-0819
David Hurwitt Founded 1947

Men who served in Merrill's Marauders during World War II. The Marauders were composed of soldiers who volunteered for a "dangerous and hazardous mission" and subsequently fought behind Japanese lines in Burma. To perpetuate the traditions and heritage of this unusual combat unit. In 1969 the name "Merrill's Marauders" was reactivated by the Army for the 75th Infantry Rangers. Presents awards annually.
Publications: Bulletin, three or four per year; Directory, annual.

Religious Organizations

BURMA AMERICAN BUDDHIST ASSOCIATION
1708 Powder Mill Road (301) 439-4035
Silver Spring, Maryland 20903 Founded 1980
President: U Tunwai

Individuals interested in the philosophic and cultural environment of Buddhism. Serves as a religious, educational and cultural resource center to promote Buddhist (Theravada) thought, beliefs and practices. Encourages the practice of insight meditation (Vipassana), "discipline to develop mindfulness, to provide an opportunity to find oneself, and see the truth." Conducts seminars on Buddhism, meditation sessions, Sunday services, religious counseling services and educational programs. Sponsors various cultural activities, bazaars and community charity services. Maintains library of 1,000 volumes on Buddhist subject matter.
Publication: Newsletter, monthly.

Ship Lines

BURMA FIVE STAR LINE
71 Broadway
New York, New York 10006 (212) 440-0100

Books and Pamphlets

ANNOTATED BIBLIOGRAPHY OF BURMA. New York University, Burma Research Project. New Haven, Human Relations Area Files, 1956.

This bibliography consists of a consecutive listing of sources divided into four groups: bibliographies; books, pamphlets, and other separates; periodical articles; and selected publications by the Government of Burma. Also includes the listing of sources in a topical bibliography.

A BIBLIOGRAPHY ON LAND, PEASANTS, AND POLITICS FOR BURMA AND THAILAND. Compiled by James C. Scott. Madison, Wisconsin, University of Wisconsin, Land Tenure Center, 1972.

BURMA: A SELECTED AND ANNOTATED BIBLIOGRAPHY. Compiled by Frank N. Trager. New Haven, Connecticut, Human Relations Area Files Press, 1973.

Eight chapters divide over 2,000 entries into bibliographies, books and other separates, journal articles, documents, English language serials, samples of Burmese language materials, materials in Russian and East European languages, and dissertations. Provides annotations for many of the entires. Includes author and topical indexes.

BURMESE CUSTOMS. Washington, D.C., Embassy of Burma.

An introduction to the Burmese way of life centering on the family and communal unit. Tells about the naming ceremony, adolescent initiation, both religious and secular, marriage customs, offering breakfast to Monks, the Burmese water festival "Thingyan" which precedes the New Year and features parades, satirical skits, dancing and getting wet as much as possible, and the Thadingyat to celebrate the end of the rainy season.

HISTORICAL BACKGROUND OF BURMA. Washington, D.C., Embassy of the Socialist Republic of the Union of Burma.

Gives a general overview of the course of history in Burma, discussing the pre-historic period, the Pagan Taungoo and Konbaung Dynastyes, British colonial times, the war years, independence and development since then.

MANDALAY. Rangoon, Tourist Burma.

Illustrated brochure showing the city's beautiful pagodas, monasteries and ruins.

PAGAN: THE ANCIENT CITY OF BURMA. Rangoon, Tourist Burma.

The most impressive and well-preserved architectural relics of ancient Burma are in Pagan which is known as the city of four million pagodas. Most were built in the eleventh to thirteenth centuries. This brochure shows views from the air, examples of frescos and architectural details from such sites as Ananda, Schwezigon and Thatbyinnyu.

Audiovisual Material

MAP

BURMA. Embassy of the Socialist Republic of the Union of Burma.

An outline map of Burma showing states and major towns, roads and railways.

FILM

SOUTHEAST ASIA: BURMA AND THAILAND. 16mm. Color and sound. 14 minutes. Chicago, Coronet Instructional Media, 1973.

Presents a geographical overview of Burma and Thailand. Shows social, economic, and political changes that are taking place there.

BYELORUSSIANS
See also: RUSSIANS; SLAVIC PEOPLES

Mission to the United Nations

MISSION OF THE BYELORUSSIAN SOVIET SOCIALIST REPUBLIC
136 East 67th Street
New York, New York (212) 535-3420

Represents Byelorussians in the Soviet Union.

Fraternal Organizations

BIELARUSSIAN COORDINATING COMMITTEE OF CHICAGO
Post Office Box 30079
Chicago, Illinois 60630 (312) 384-7886
Chairman: William Puntus
Secretary: Mrs. Vera Ramuk

Fraternal and political organization which promotes Byelorussian culture and the ideas of Byelorussian Independent State. Participates in all ethnic and political activities of the city of Chicago. Maintains large archives in various organizations including two Byelorussian Churches-the Eastern Rite Catholic Church of Christ the Redeemer, 3107 West Fullerton Avenue and the Eastern Orthodox Byelorussian Church of St. George, 1500 North Maplewood Avenue. Supports Byelorussian Sunday School and various youth groups including a dance group and a choir. The organization takes a very active participation in Chicago's International Festivals and Annual Christmas Exhibitions at the Chicago Museum of Science and Industry. Includes the following member organizations:

- Byelorussian American National Council of Chicago: the oldest Byelorussian organization in U.S., established in 1941.
- Byelorussian American Association in Illinois: established in 1953.
- Bielarussian American Youth Organization in Illinois, 1960.

Publications: Church of Christ the Redeemer, weekly church bulletin, English and Byelorussian.

BYELORUSSIAN-AMERICAN ASSOCIATION IN THE U. S. A.
166-34 Gothic Drive
Jamaica, New York 11432
President: Anton Shukeloyts Founded 1949

Made up of Americans of Byelorussion descent. Aims to coordinate and intensify Byelorussian-American participation in the peace efforts of the U.S.A. and to strengthen and propagate the American way of life; to support the Byelorussian people in their struggle for freedom and independence; to help the Byelorussians in their native land to receive fair and equal treatment with other nations, as a free member in the family of other nations. Maintains library of 4,000 volumes; promotes lectures about American and Byelorussian history and culture; organizes commemorations and celebrations, political meetings and demonstrations; opposes communism. Has branches in California, District of Columbia, Maine, Maryland, New Jersey and Ohio.
Publications: Bielarus, monthly.

BYELORUSSIAN-AMERICAN CENTER
South Whitehead Avenue
South River, New Jersey 08882 (201) 257-8431
President: George Naumchyk Founded 1972

Sponsors active youth programs, maintains library and archives.

BYELORUSSIAN-AMERICAN VETERAN ASSOCIATION
9 River Road
Highland Park, New Jersey 08904 (313) 779-8984
Executive Officer: Dr. Joseph S. Sazyc

Former soldiers of American and other military units with a common goal of promoting the ideas of Byelorussian independence.

BYELORUSSIAN-AMERICAN UNION
104-29 Atlantic Avenue
Richmond Hill, New York 11418 (212) 441-8053
President: Constant Mierlak Founded 1965

Goals are to promote the Byelorussian cultural heritage and the idea of a Byelorussian Independent state. Maintains archives and a small library.

BYELORUSSIAN-AMERICAN WOMEN ASSOCIATION
166-34 Gothic Drive
Jamaica, New York 11432 Founded 1956

Women of Byelorussian birth or descent and those related by marriage to Byelorussian-Americans. Aim is to preserve national identity, cultural heritage and traditions. Organizes and supports school programs of Byelorussian supplementary schools. Also organizes shows and exhibitions of fine arts and ethnic crafts. Offers Byelorussian language classes. Publishes Woman's Page in Belarus (Byelorussian newspaper). Affiliated with the Byelorussian-American Association.

BYELORUSSIAN-AMERICAN YOUTH ORGANIZATION
166-34 Gothic Drive
Jamaica, New York 11432
President: George Azarko Founded 1950

Made up of young people 15-35 years old of Byelorussian descent. Attempts to preserve Byelorussia's rich and diverse culture for its youth. Informs Byelorussian youth and others about the plight of the Byelorussian people in the USSR. Encourages its members to learn the Byelorussian language and obtain higher education. Participates in international festivals; sponsors Vasilok, a Byelorussian folk dancing group at the Garden State Arts Center in Holmdel, New Jersey. Formerly (1967) Byelorussian Youth Association of America.
Publications: Byelorussian Youth, quarterly; also publishes Byelorussian Youth Almanac.

BYELORUSSIAN COMMUNITY CENTER "POLACAK"
11022 Webster Road
Strongsville, Ohio 44136 (216) 238-3842
President: Serge Karnilovich Founded 1965

Extensive archives on Byelorussian organizations and activities in Ohio. Sponsors conferences and extensive youth programs. Cooperates with the Cleveland Public Library on development of Byelorussian reference and circulation collections of the Cleveland Public Library.

BYELORUSSIAN CONGRESS COMMITTEE OF AMERICA
2128 West Cortez Street
Chicago, Illinois 60622 (212) 817-0719
Executive Officer: John J. Kosiak Founded 1949

Organizations of Americans of Byelorussian birth or descent. Provides information about Byelorussia and Americans of Byelorussian descent; supports "desires of the Byelorussian people for liberation from occupation by Soviet Russia." Formerly, 1973 Whiteruthenian (Byelorussian) Congress Committee of America.

RELIGIOUS RECREATION CENTER BELAIR-MIENSK, GLEN SPEY, NEW YORK
109-31 Lefferts Boulevard
Richmond Hill, New York 11419 (212) VI8-9512
(mailing address) Founded 1963

Summer resort for the Byelorussian community on the East coast. Various cultural programs, library, summer camp.

Public Affairs Organizations

BYELORUSSIAN LIBERATION FRONT
c/o John Shimchik
6526 Anita Drive
Cleveland, Ohio 44130 (216) 845-6425
Chairman: John Shimchik Founded 1957

Americans of Byelorussian birth or descent including war veterans and youth. Works toward the aim of "liberation of Byelorussia".
Publications: Baracba (Struggle).

Cultural and Educational Organizations

BYELORUSSIAN CHARITABLE EDUCATIONAL FUND, INCORPORATED
1716 Northeast Seventh Terrace
Gainesville, Florida 32601 Founded 1976

Scholarly organization, the purpose of which is to promote brotherhood, liberty and equality among all people and to promote classic cultural achievements among Byelorussians. Publishes an annual bulletin (bilingual) and series of monographs on Greek Classics.

BYELORUSSIAN CULTURAL AND RELIGIOUS CENTER
3107 West Fullerton Avenue
Chicago, Illinois 60647 (312) 227-0029
Director: Rev. Uladzimir Tarasevich, O.S.B. Founded 1959

Develops extensive cultural programs and sponsors conferences on various aspects of Byelorussian culture and Byelorussian heritage. Extensive library and archives on Byelorussians in U. S.

BYELORUSSIAN CULTURAL SOCIETY
South Whitehead Avenue
South River, New Jersey 08882 (201) 254-9594
President: Anton Danilovich Founded 1973

The Society maintains library, archives and museum. The emphasis is on the representation of Byelorussian culture in the United States. Organizes an annual exhibition on Byelorussian arts and crafts, usually in March-April. Co-sponsors an annual publication "Byelorussian Thought".

BYELORUSSIAN INSTITUTE OF ARTS AND SCIENCES, INCORPORATED
3441 Tibbett Avenue
Bronx, New York 10463 (212) 549-5395
President: Dr. Vitaut Tumash Founded 1950

Promotes Byelorussian culture, literature, arts and Byelorussian-American heritage. Helps Byelorussian scholars in the United States and abroad. The Institute maintains an extensive library. Sponsors topical conferences, bi-annual. Participates in National Conferences of various Slavic and non-Slavic scholarly organizations and societies. Organizes annual exhibitions of Byelorussion painters, most frequently in New York City.
Publications: Zapisy, annual, articles in Byelorussian and summaries in English; also publishes monographs.

BYELORUSSIAN WOMEN'S CHOIR "KALINA"
28 Herman Street
South River, New Jersey 08882 (201) 254-5058
Founder and Director: Xavery Borisovets Founded 1963

Cultivates Byelorussian musical heritage and gives public performances.

BYELORUSSIAN WOMEN'S ENSEMBLE, VASILKI
11022 Webster Road
Strongsville, Ohio 44136 (216) 238-3842
Director: Konstantin Kalosha Founded 1956

FRANCIS SKARYNA BYELORUSSIAN SOCIETY OF ARTS AND SCIENCES, USA
107 Boulevard
Mountain Lake, New Jersey 07046 (201) 334-0785
Secretary: Mrs. Mary Stankievich Founded 1947

To study Byelorussian linguistics and history. (Founded in Germany in 1947. Moved to the USA in 1949).
Publication: "Vieda" mostly in Byelorussian, irregular.

VASILOK, BYELORUSSIAN AMERICAN YOUTH DANCE GROUP
9 River Road
Highland Park, New Jersey 08904 (516) 627-6491
Director: Dr. Ala Orsa Romano Founded 1958

Charitable Organizations

WHITERUTHENIAN AMERICAN RELIEF
c/o Byelorussian Autocephal Orthodox Church
401 Atlantic Avenue
Brooklyn, New York 11217 (212) 858-4560
Founded 1958

Persons interested in aiding needy Whiteruthenians (Byelorussians) outside the U. S.

Special Libraries and Subject Collections

ALL BYELORUSSIAN ARCHIVES
464 46th Street
New York, New York 11220 (212) 492-8109
Director: Mikola Pankou Founded 1952

Subjects: History and cultural tradition of the Byelorussians. Holdings: Books, Periodicals, documents and other records.

BYELORUSSIAN INSTITUTE OF ARTS AND SCIENCES, INCORPORATED
3441 Tibbett Avenue
Bronx, New York 10463 (212) 549-5395

Subjects: Byelorussian history, language and culture. Special Collections: Bibliographic file of materials on Byelorussians in the western languages; publications related to Dr. Francishak Skaryna, pioneer of Byelorussian printing. Holdings: Books, newspapers, clippings, special files and indexes.

Newspapers and Newsletters

BIELARUS (Byelorussian). 1950-. Monthly. Editor: Dr. Jan Zaprudnik. Publisher: Byelorussian-American Association, Incorporated, 166-34 Gothic Drive, Jamaica, New York 11431. In Byelorussian, and English.

The oldest and most widely distributed Byelorussian newspaper in the free world. Covers such topics as: Byelorussian social, economic, and cultural life in the United States; Byelorussian problems in the U.S.S.R.; and United States policy toward the Soviet Union.

CARKOUNY SVIETAC (The Church's Light). 1951-. Semiannual. Editor: Rev. Sviataslau Kous. Publisher: Byelorussian Orthodox Church in South River, South Whitehead Avenue, South River, New Jersey 08882. In English and Byelorussian.

Contains articles on religious, cultural, and historical developments in Byelorussian communities in the United States and other countries.

VIECA (The Council). 1970-. Monthly. Editor: Dr. P. Markowski. Publisher: The Whiteruthenian Press, 204 State Highway 18, East Brunswick, New Jersey 08816. In Byelorussian and English.

Publishes news of Byelorussian political activities and activities of Byelorussian organizations and people in the United States.

Magazines

BIELARUSKAJA DUMKA (Byelorussian Thought). 1959-. Editor: Antony Danilovich. Publisher: Byelorussian-American Relief Committee, 34 Richter Avenue, Milltown, New Jersey 08850. In Byelorussian.

Reports on Byelorussian political life in the United States and abroad and activities of Byelorussian organizations in the United States. Includes features on literature and the arts.

THE BYELORUSSIAN TIMES. 1965-. Quarterly. Editor: Dr. Roger Horoshko, 9-06 Parsons Boulevard, Flushing, New York 11357. In Byelorussian and English.

Concentrates on Byelorussian political interests.

BYELORUSSIAN WORLD. 1971-. Quarterly. Editor: Mikola Prusky. Publisher: Byelorussian World, 1086 Forest Hills Avenue, Southeast, Grand Rapids, Michigan 49506. In Byelorussian.

Devoted to literature and humor.

BYELORUSSIAN YOUTH. 1959-. Quarterly. Editor: Ms. Raisa Stankievich. Publisher: Byelorussian-American Youth Organization, 166-34 Gothic Drive, Jamaica, New York 11431. In Byelorussian and English.

Publishes materials of general interest to the younger Byelorussian community. Profusely illustrated.

ZAPISY. 1965-. Annual. Editor: Dr. Vitaut Tumash. Publisher: Byelorussian Institute of Arts and Sciences, 3441 Tibbett Avenue, Bronx, New York 10463.

Scholarly journal devoted to all aspects of Byelorussian history, arts, culture and literature. Has very wide circulation and is easily accessible in many academic and special libraries.

Radio Programs

Illinois - Chicago

WEDC - 5475 North Milwaukee Avenue, Chicago, Illinois, (312) 631-0700. Byelorussian programs.

Festivals, Fairs, and Celebrations

New Jersey - Holmdel

BYELORUSSIAN HERITAGE FOUNDATION
Garden State Arts Center
Holmdel, New Jersey

The festival includes popular dancing, singing, skits, and comedy. The festival attracts Byelorussians from all over the country and Canada. Prior to the stage performance, on the mall there are exhibitions of Byelorussian arts and crafts, fine art shows, sports and food stands. A major attraction is the parade of costumes from various parts of Byelorussia. In addition there is also a talent show of Byelorussian American Youth for which different Sunday Schools prepare programs. Held annually Labor Day Weekend.
Contact: Dr. Vitaut Kipel, 230 Springfield Avenue, Rutherford, New Jersey 07070.

Books and Pamphlets

BELORUSSIA AND THE BELORUSSIANS. By Jan Zaprudnik. In Handbook of Major Soviet Nationalities. New York, Free Press, 1975.

Focuses on the more recent history and political developments in Soviet Byelorussia.

BELORUSSIA: THE MAKING OF A NATION. By Nicholas Vakar. Cambridge, Massachusetts, 1956.

A cultural and political history of the Byelorussian homeland.

BELORUSSIA UNDER SOVIET RULE, 1917 - 1957. By Ivan Lubachko. Lexington, The University Press of Kentucky, 1972.

Traces the development of Soviet Byelorussia and the Stalinist purges.

BYELORUSSIAN COMMUNITY IN CLEVELAND. By Vitaut Kipel. Cleveland, Cleveland State University, 1982.

An updated study of the cohesion of a major Byelorussian ethnic group.

BYELORUSSIAN HERITAGE. New York Byelorussian American Association, Incorporated.

A pamphlet describing Byelorussia's thousand year history, the Golden Age of Byelorussian culture and Byelorussians in the United States.

BYELORUSSIAN INDEPENDENCE DAY IN AMERICA'S BICENTENNIAL YEAR. By Jan Zaprudnik. New York, Byelorussian American Association, 1977.

A survey of Byelorussian participation in America's Bicentennial.

BYELORUSSIANS IN NEW JERSEY. By Vitaut Kipel. In The New Jersey Ethnic Experience, edited by Barbara Cunningham, Union City, New Jersey, William H. Wise and Company, 1977.

A comprehensive study of one of the major Byelorussian settlements in the United States.

CANADIANS
See also: FRENCH-SPEAKING PEOPLES

Embassy and Consulates

CANADIAN EMBASSY
1746 Massachusetts Avenue, Northwest
Washington, D.C. 20036 (202) 785-1400

Office of Information
1771 N Street, Northwest
Washington, D.C. 20036 (202) 785-1400

CONSULATES GENERAL

900 Coastal States Building
260 Peachtree Street
Atlanta, Georgia 30303 (404) 577-6810

500 Boylston Street, 5th Floor
Boston, Massachusetts 02116 (617) 262-3760

1 Marine Midland Center, Suite 3550
Buffalo, New York 14203 (716) 852-1247

310 South Michigan Avenue,
Suite 2000
Chicago, Illinois 60604 (312) 427-1031

Illuminating Building
55 Public Square
Cleveland, Ohio 44113 (216) 861-1660

2001 Bryan Tower, Suite 1600
Dallas, Texas 75201 (214) 742-8031

1920 First Federal Building
1001 Woodward Avenue
Detroit, Michigan 48226 (313) 965-2811

510 West Sixth Street
Los Angeles, California 90014 (213) 627-9511

Chamber of Commerce Building
15 South Fifth Street
Minneapolis, Minnesota 55402 (612) 336-4641

International Trade Mart
2 Canal Street, Suite 2110
New Orleans, Louisiana 70130 (504) 525-2136

1251 Avenue of the Americas
New York, New York 10020 (212) 586-2400

3 Parkway Building, Suite 1310
Philadelphia, Pennsylvania 19102 (215) 561-1750

1 Maritime Plaza, 11th Floor
Golden Gateway Center
San Francisco, California 94111 (415) 981-2670

412 Plaza 600
Sixth and Stewart Streets
Seattle, Washington 98101 (206) 487-3800

Mission to the United Nations

CANADIAN MISSION
866 United Nations Plaza, Suite 250
New York, New York 10017 (212) 751-5600

Tourist and Travel Offices

CANADIAN GOVERNMENT OFFICE OF TOURISM
Office de tourisme du Canada

1771 N Street, Northwest
Washington, D.C. 20036 (202) 785-1400

Province of Alberta

Tourism Alberta
703 - 510 West 6th Street
Los Angeles, California 90014 (213) 624-6371

Province of British Columbia

Tourism British Columbia
3303 Wilshire Boulevard
Suite 52
Los Angeles, California 90010 (213) 380-9171

100 Bush Street, Suite 400
San Francisco, California 94104 (405) 981-4780

Pier 69
2700 Alaskan Way
Seattle, Washington 98121

Province of Nova Scotia and Atlantic Canada

Atlantic Canada/Nova Scotia
129 Commercial Street
Portland, Maine 04101 (207) 772-0017
(in operation only Mid April - end July)

Province of Ontario

Government of Ontario, Ministry of Industry and Tourism
Suite 1816, 208 LaSalle Street
Chicago, Illinois 60604 (312) 782-8688

Suite 1420, 700 South Flower Street
Los Angeles, California 90017 (213) 622-4302

Suite 1080, 1251 Avenue of the Americas
New York, New York 10020 (212) 247-2744

Province of Quebec

Delegation du Quebec
Suite 1501
Peachtree Center Tower
230 Peachtree Street, Northwest
Atlanta, Georgia 30303 (404) 581-0488

100 Franklin Street, Fourth Floor
Park Square Building, Suite 409
Boston, Massachusetts 02110 (617) 426-2660

35 East Wacker Street, Suite 2052
Chicago, Illinois 60601 (313) 726-0681

Adolphus Tower, Suite 900
1412 Main Street (214) 742-9663
Dallas, Texas 75202 (214) 742-6095

American Bank Building, Box 4011
905 Jefferson Street, Suite 406
Lafayette, Louisiana 70502 (318) 232-8080

700 South Flower Street,
Suite 1520
Los Angeles, California 90017

Quebec Government House
17 West 50th Street
New York, New York 10020 (212) 397-0226

Quebec Tourism
1300 19th Street (202) 659-8990
Washington, D.C. 20036 (202) 659-8991

Fraternal Organizations

CANADIAN-AMERICAN CLUB, INCORPORATED
202 Arlington
Boston, Massachusetts 02170 (617) 924-9827

CANADIAN CLUB OF CALIFORNIA, INCORPORATED
Post Office Box 3993
Anaheim, California 92803 (714) 537-7560

CANADIAN CLUB OF CHICAGO
6 East Monroe Street
Chicago, Illinois 60603 (312) 346-3456
President: George G. Copeland Founded 1930

Seeks to promote and increase friendship and goodwill between the people of Canada and the United States.
Publication: Annual Roster of Members.

CANADIAN CLUB OF NEW YORK
One East 60th Street
New York, New York 10022 (212) 753-6162
President: Reid Lighton Founded 1903

Canadian social club.
Publication: Maple Leaf, quarterly.

COMMONWEALTH SOCIETY OF NORTH AMERICA
2201 Wilson Boulevard, Room 202
Arlington, Virginia 22201 (703) 524-3121
President: Peter McLaughlin

A social club founded to promote and maintain the traditions of the commonwealth nations. Membership open to former residents of the United Kingdom, Canada, Australia, and New Zealand.

Public Affairs Organizations

BRITISH-NORTH AMERICAN COMMITTEE
c/o National Planning Association
1606 New Hampshire Avenue, Northwest
Washington, D.C. 20009
United States Research Director: (202) 265-7685
Sperry Lea Founded 1969

American, British and Canadian leaders in business, organized labor, agriculture and the professions. Analyzes the key international and domestic issues facing the three countries, and provides the opportunity for an exchange of views. Members discuss current concerns with high officials and experts, consider presentations, and meet in groups and task forces to develop projects for committee action. Publishes research studies on trade, investment, international monetary issues, raw materials issues, and relations between developed and developing countries.

CANADA-UNITED STATES ENVIRONMENTAL COUNCIL
c/o Defenders of Wildlife
1244 19th Street, Northwest
Washington, D.C. 20036 (202) 659-9510
Co-Chairman: James G. Deane Founded 1974

National and regional environmental and conservation groups. To facilitate interchange of information and cooperative action on current environmental issues such as acid precipitation, Great Lakes pollution, protection of arctic wildlife habitat , and the future of the Antarctic and the oceans. Serves as a forum to discuss ideas, approve resolutions and establish contacts.

CANADIAN-AMERICAN COMMITTEE
c/o National Planning Association
1606 New Hampshire Avenue, Northwest
Washington, D.C. 20009
United States Research Director: Peter Morici (202) 265-7685
Founded 1957

Canadian and American leaders from major segments of the private economy including agriculture, business, labor, and the professions. Jointly sponsored by the National Planning Association (in the United States) and the C. D. Howe Research Institute (in Canada). Studies long-range problems arising from growing interdependence between Canada and the United States in order to expand areas of agreement and narrow areas of conflict. Publishes research studies written by qualified experts of both countries; issues policy statements signed by members based on these studies and discussions at meetings. Subjects of current research include: new approaches to trade policy; investment flows between the two countries in terms of their economic effects; acid rain; improving bilateral consultation on economic issues. Canadian office: c/o C. D. Howe Research Institute, 1155 Metcalfe Street, Suite 2064, Montreal PQ, Canada H3B2X7.

Cultural and Educational Organizations

AMERICAN-CANADIAN GENEALOGICAL SOCIETY
Post Office Box 668
Manchester, New Hampshire 03105 (603) 356-3009
President: Richard L. Fortin Founded 1973

Genealogists interested in ancestries of Canadian origin. Serves as a resource center for the collection, preservation and dissemination of American-Canadian genealogical information. Acquires and purchases repertories, genealogies, notarial records, indexes, histories, biographies, journals, census records and other pertinent data. Encourages the gathering of personal and public data such as is found in Bibles, newspapers, directories, histories, and photographs; promotes the gathering of civil and church records for publication and/or genealogical research; encourages individual members to research their family lineage and contribute a duplicate to the library. Conducts genealogical workshops; sponsores speakers bureau. Maintains library of 600 volumes.
Publication: The Genealogist, semiannual.

ASSOCIATION FOR CANADIAN STUDIES IN THE UNITED STATES
1776 Massachusetts Avenue, Northwest
Room 210
Washington, D.C. 20036 (202) 452-0606
Secretary: Rufus Z. Smith Founded 1971

Individuals and institutions including librarians, professors, publishers, students, teachers, and government, business and corporation officials with an educational interest in Canada. Purpose is to promote scholarly activities including study, research, teaching and publication about Canada at all educational levels and in all disciplines in the United States. Holds regional conferences and symposia; attempts to assist those interested in structuring courses and programs on Canada. Bestows awards; maintains library.
Publications: American Review of Canadian Studies, semiannual; Membership Directory, two times a year; also publishes newsletters and special reprints.

BRITISH NORTH AMERICA PHILATIC SOCIETY
c/o Edward J. Whiting
25 Kings Circle
Malvern, Pennsylvania 19355 (215) 644-7838
Secretary: Edward J. Whiting Founded 1943

Individuals interested in various branches of specialization in Canadian stamps united for collection and dissemination of knowledge in the field. Maintains library. Sponsors study groups on various facets of Canadian philately.
Publications: BNA Topics, bimonthly; Membership Handbook and Directory, biennial.

CANADIAN AIR MAIL COLLECTORS CLUB
Post Office Box 269
Brookfield, Illinois 60513
Executive Director: Fred L. Wellman — (312) 485-1109
Founded 1941

Philatelists and historians of Canadian aviation. Bestows awards; maintains speakers bureau; sponsors competitions. Maintains 250 volume library.
Publication: Canada Air Notes, quarterly.

NORTHEAST FOLKLORE SOCIETY
University of Maine
Orono, Maine 04473 — (207) 581-7466

Promotes an interest in folk music and oral history. Focus is on the traditions of New England and the Atlantic Provinces of Canada.
Publication: Newsletter, 4 to 6 times a year.

Charitable Organization

GRENFELL ASSOCIATION OF AMERICA
c/o Davis, Polk and Wardwell
Nine West 57th Street, 11th Floor
New York, New York 10019 — (212) 593-8725
President: Dr. Robert T. Potter — Founded 1905

To promote medical and social service work in Northern Newfoundland and Labrador. Supports hospitals, nursing stations, and other medical facilities in the area.
Publication: Among the Deep Sea Fishers, quarterly.

Foundation

DONNER (THE WILLIAM H.) FOUNDATION, INCORPORATED
630 Fifth Avenue
New York, New York 10020
Donor: William D. Donner — (212) 765-1695
President: Donald S. Rickerd — Founded 1961

Promotes projects in the United States relating to Canada in order to foster an awareness of Canadian history, current problems and achievements, cultural interests, and relations with the United States.

Research Centers and Special Institutes

CANADIAN STUDIES CENTER
Duke University
2101 Campus Drive
Durham, North Carolina 27706
Director: Dr. Richard Preston

Conducts research activities relating to Canada.

Special Libraries and Subject Collections

CANADIAN CONSULATE GENERAL - CHICAGO LIBRARY
310 South Michigan Avenue
Chicago, Illinois 60604
Librarian: Elizabeth A. Bibby — (312) 427-1031

Subjects: Canada - literature, business, history, arts, social sciences. Holdings: books; Canadian films; pamphlets and clippings; journals and other serials; newspapers. Services: Interlibrary loans; library open to public with restrictions.

CANADIAN CONSULATE GENERAL - LIBRARY
1251 Avenue of the Americas
New York, New York 10020
Head Librarian: Sheila M. Purse — (212) 586-2400

Subjects: Canadian government and politics, business, industry, trade, history, geography, literature, art, education, law, Canada-United States relations. Special Collections: Parliamentary Papers (beginning 1875); Canadian Government Publications (selective depository); Statistics Canada (full depository); Canada Treaty Series. Holdings: Books, periodicals, government documents, news clippings and pamphlet files, newspapers, microforms. Services: Interlibrary loans, copying, library open to the public by appointment only.

CANADIAN EMBASSY - LIBRARY
1771 N Street, Northwest
Washington, D.C. 20036 — (202) 785-1400
Librarian: Merle G. Fabian — Founded 1947

Subjects: Canadiana; economics; biography; international affairs; Canada - United States relations. Holdings: Books; journals and other serials; newspapers; vertical file drawers of material on Canadian subjects. Services: Inter-library loans; copying (limited); library open to public.

CANADIAN TRAVEL FILM LIBRARY
111 East Wacker Drive, Suite 915
Chicago, Illinois 60601
Manager: R. A. Searle (312) 565-0200

Subjects: Travelogues set in Canada. Holdings: cataloged 16mm sound films. Services: library open to public by application.

CLEVELAND PUBLIC LIBRARY - JOHN G. WHITE COLLECTION OF FOLKLORE, ORIENTALIA, CHESS, AND RARE BOOKS
325 Superior Avenue
Cleveland, Ohio 44114
Head Librarian: Alice N. Loranth (216) 623-2818
Founded 1869

Subjects: Orientalia; folklore; chess. Special Collections: Melville papers and papers of the East India Company (manuscripts on British India); India and Southeast Asia; Sanskrit literature; Arabic and Persian literature; Omar Khayyam; Arabian Nights; Tibet; Judaica; Madagascar; Oriental manuscript catalogs; proverb collection; ballads; Robin Hood; gypsies; Chapbooks; occultism; medieval literature; Celtic and Icelandic languages and literature; Derrydale Press; Rabelais; Castiglione; Vida; all aspects of chess literature; Margaret Klipple Memorial Archives of African folktales; Newbell Niles Puckett Memorial Archives of "Ohio Superstitions and Popular Beliefs", "Negro Names", "Religious Beliefs of the Southern Negro", "Canadian Lumberjack Songs"; Cleveland Author Collection; Cleveland Imprint Collection; Prostitution Collection; Children's Books and Juvenilia. Holdings: Books, manuscripts, clippings, pictorial material, tapes; microfilm reels, journals and other serials. Services: Interlibrary loans; copying; programs; exhibits; lectures.

SUNY - COLLEGE AT PLATTSBURGH
Benjamin F. Feinberg Library
Plattsburgh, New York 12901 (518) 564-3180
Director: Dr. Bruce Stark Founded 1961

Subjects: History of Upstate New York and Vermont; Canadiana; folklore of Adirondacks and Champlain Valley; recent environmental, industrial and demographic studies of the region; Rockwell Kent; University archives. Special Collections: Marjorie Lansing Porter Folklore Collection (original discs and tapes); Kent-Delord papers; William Bailey papers; Truesdell Print Collection; Signor/Langlois Collection of architectural drawings and maps; Rockwell Kent Collection; Feinberg Collection; 1980 Lake Placid Olympics. Holdings: Books, manuscripts; maps and atlases; photographs; microfilm; recordings; pamphlets; clippings; journals and other serials. Services: Copying; center open to public.

Newspapers and Newsletters

BNA TOPICS. Bimonthly. Publisher: British North American Philatelic Society, c/o Edward J. Whiting, 25 Kings Circle, Malvern, Pennsylvania 19355 (215) 644-7838.

Publishes news of Canadian philately and activities of the Society.

CANADA AIR NOTES. Quarterly. Publisher: Canadian Air Mail Collectors Club, Post Office Box 269, Brookfield, New Jersey 60513 (312) 485-1109.

Publishes items relating to Canadian aviation philately and activities of the club.

MAPLE LEAF. Quarterly. Publisher: Canadian Club of New York, One East 60th Street, New York, New York 10022 (212) 753-6162.

Covers the activities of the club and its members.

NORTHEAST FOLKLORE SOCIETY - NEWSLETTER. 1958 -. Four to six times a year. Editor: Florence E. Ireland. Publisher: Northeast Folklore Society, Room B, South Stevens Hall, University of Maine, Orono, Maine 04473.

Announces and discusses events, meetings, publications, records relating to folk music and oral history. Focus is on the traditions of New England and the Atlantic Provinces of Canada.

Magazines

AMERICAN REVIEW OF CANADIAN STUDIES. Semiannual. Publisher: Association for Canadian Studies in the United States, 1776 Massachusetts

Avenue, Northwest, Room 210, Washington, D.C. 20036 (202) 452-0606.

A scholarly journal that reviews Canadian studies in all disciplines in the United States.

CANADA TODAY/D'AUJOURD'HUI. 1970-. Monthly. Publisher: Canadian Embassy, Office of Information, 1771 N Street, Northwest, Washington, D.C. 20036. In English.

Presents short articles concerned with Canadian trends, cities, regions, people, and events. Also includes international issues, such as peacekeeping, which involve Canada. Each month a different theme is chosen for the issue.

THE GENEALOGIST. Semiannual. Publisher: American - Canadian Genealogical Society, Post Office Box 668, Manchester, New Hampshire 03105 (603) 356-3009.

Publishes items of interest to genealogists concerned with ancestries of Canadian origin.

Radio Programs

Massachusetts - Cambridge

WMBR (FM) - 3 Ames Street, Cambridge, Massachusetts 02142 (617) 253-4000. Canadian Maritime, 1 1/2 hours weekly.

Bank Branches in the U.S.

BANK OF BRITISH COLUMBIA
300 Montgomery Street
San Francisco, California 94104 (415) 788-7373

BANK OF MONTREAL

30 North La Salle Street
Chicago, Illinois 60602 (312) 726-7766

One Houston Center, Suite 1106
Houston, Texas 77010 (713) 223-2600

811 Wilshire Boulevard
Los Angeles, California 90071 (213) 624-0255

Subsidiary Banks

Bank of Montreal Trust Company
Two Wall Street
New York, New York 10005 (212) 964-1100

Bank of Montreal (California)
425 California Street
San Francisco, California 94120 (415) 391-8060

BANK OF NOVA SCOTIA

Suite 909, Two Peachtree Street, Northwest
Atlanta, Georgia 30303 (404) 581-0807

111 Franklin Street
Box 2799
Boston, Massachusetts 02208 (617) 451-5500

55 West Monroe
Chicago, Illinois 60603 (312) 346-5520

Suite 1006, 1300 East Ninth Street
Cleveland, Ohio 44114 (216) 579-1400

2430 Two Shell Plaza
Houston, Texas 77002 (713) 224-5624

Suite 837, 523 West Sixth Street
Los Angeles, California 90027 (213) 624-1883

Suite 1600, Two South Biscayne Boulevard
Miami, Florida 33131 (305) 358-4920

67 Wall Street
New York, New York 10005 (212) 825-2400

56 Southwest Salmon Street
Portland, Oregon 97204 (503) 222-4396

44 Market Street
San Francisco, California 94111 (415) 986-1100

CANADIAN IMPERIAL BANK OF COMMERCE

Two Peachtree Street, Northwest
Atlanta, Georgia 30303 (404) 577-1628

3425 Southwest Cedar Hills Boulevard
Post Office Box 22
Beaverton, Oregon 97005 (503) 242-9276

135 South LaSalle Street, Suite 4100
Chicago, Illinois 60603 (312) 726-8858

One Main Place, Suite 818
Dallas, Texas 75250 (214) 748-5187

245 Park Avenue
New York, New York 10017 (212) 490-9200

22 William Street
Box 181
New York, New York 10005 (212) 825-7000

504 Southwest Sixth Avenue, Drawer 69
Portland, Oregon 97207 (503) 242-9241

1600 Southwest Fourth Avenue
Box 944
Portland, Oregon 97207 (503) 242-9288

Ninth and Halsey
Box 12025
Portland, Oregon 97212 (503) 287-8511

801 Second Avenue
Post Office Box 100
Seattle, Washington 98111 (206) 223-7951

Subsidiary Banks

California Canadian Bank

100 West San Fernando
Campbell, California 95008 (408) 275-1830

700 South Flower Street
Los Angeles, California 90017 (213) 612-4500

3301 Wilshire Boulevard
Los Angeles, California 90010 (213) 612-4600

4699 Jamboree Boulevard
Newport Beach, California 92660
(714) 752-6042

501 South Main Street
Post Office Box 1608
Orange, California 92668 (714) 558-3741

3902 Middlefield Road
Palo Alto, California 94303 (415) 494-3100

One Twin Dolphin Drive
Redwood City, California 94065
(415) 592-9320

515 L Street
Sacramento, California 95814 (916) 444-6940

770 B Street
Post Office Box 2392
San Diego, California 92101 (619) 233-6162

344 Pine Street
San Francisco, California 94104
(415) 362-5210

100 West San Fernando Street
San Jose, California 95113 (408) 275-1830

100 South Ellsworth Avenue
San Mateo, California 94401 (415) 347-2363

1202 East Arques Avenue
Post Office Box 62128
Sunnyvale, California 94086 (408) 738-2112

Canadian Bank of Commerce Trust Company
20 Exchange Place
New York, New York 10005 (212) 825-7000

MERCANTILE BANK OF CANADA
515 South Flower Street
Los Angeles, California 90017 (213) 488-0166

NATIONAL BANK OF CANADA

650 Fifth Avenue
New York, New York 10019 (212) 397-0770

535 Madison Avenue
New York, New York 10022 (212) 605-8800

ROYAL BANK OF CANADA

33 North Dearborn Street
Chicago, Illinois 60602 (312) 372-4404

333 North Saint Paul Street
Republic National Bank Tower
Dallas, Texas 75201 (214) 741-1169

510 West Sixth Street
Los Angeles, California 90014 (213) 623-2371

68 William Street
New York, New York 10038 (212) 363-6000

1515 Southwest Fifth Avenue
Portland, Oregon 97201 (503) 224-2282

560 California Street
San Francisco, California 94104 (415) 986-1700

ROYAL TRUSTCO LIMITED

2001 49th Street, South
Gulfport, Florida 33737 (813) 321-2000

9225 Baymeadows Road
Jacksonville, Florida 32216 (904) 731-4600

18545 Biscayne Boulevard, North
Miami, Florida 33180 (305) 935-0897

940 Ives Dairy Road
Maimi, Florida 33179 (305) 653-0713

7200 Northwest 19th Avenue
Miami, Florida 33147 (305) 591-2562

627 Southwest 27th Avenue
Miami, Florida 33135 (305) 642-7800

5620 Southwest 137th Avenue
Miami, Florida 33183 (305) 387-7505

7950 South Orange Blossom Trail
Orlando, Florida 32809 (305) 859-1776

411 South County Road
Palm Beach, Florida 33480 (305) 655-3900

5404 Silver Star Road
Pine Hills, Florida 32808 (305) 293-7027

4710 Eisenhower Boulevard
Tampa, Florida 33614 (813) 884-2751

TORONTO DOMINION BANK

1600 Peachtree Center South Tower
Atlanta, Georgia 30303 (404) 522-9360

9430 Wilshire Boulevard
Beverly Hills, California 90212 (213) 278-6010

Three First National Plaza
Chicago, Illinois 60603 (312) 346-4628

Suite 1115, 811 Rusk Avenue
Houston, Texas 77002 (713) 227-6181

888 West South Street
Los Angeles, California 90017 (213) 489-3080

600 Grant Street
Pittsburgh, Pennsylvania 15219 (412) 562-9100

Subsidiary Banks

Toronto Dominion Bank of California

114 Sansome Street (415) 989-4900
San Francisco, California 94104

100 Sansome Street (415) 989-4900
San Francisco, California 94104

Toronto Dominion Bank Trust Company
45 Wall Street
New York, New York 10005 (212) 820-2000

Commercial and Trade Organizations

CANADIAN-AMERICAN MOTOR CARRIERS ASSOCIATION
1730 M Street, Northwest #501
Washington, D.C. 20016
Director: Paul L. Martinson Founded 1978

Motor carriers in the United States and Canada which operate between those countries in single-line or joint-line service. Will attempt to bring together United States and Canadian regulators to establish a single period for the effectiveness of rates on international movements between the two countries. Seeks to improve interim authority procedures in the United States and Canada on international movements. Has offered to cooperate with all other motor carrier associations and to assist Canadian and United States regulatory bodies on problems unique to international transportation between the United States and Canada.

COMMITTEE ON CANADA-UNITED STATES RELATIONS
c/o Chamber of Commerce of the United States
1615 H Street, Northwest
Washington, D.C. 20062
Executive Secretary: Dr. Roger Frank Swanson (202) 463-5489
Founded 1933

Committee jointly sponsored by the Chamber of Commerce of the United States and the Canadian Chamber of Commerce. Consists of two sections, one for each country, of 25 members each. Investigates mutual problems of the two countries, especially in the fields of trade and investment. Formerly called the Canada-United States Committee.

Festivals, Fairs, and Celebrations

California - Desert Hot Springs

CANADIAN DAY
Desert Hot Springs, California

A salute to Canadians, with events including a golf tournament, a picnic, games, and celebrations. Held each year in early February. Contact: Southern California Visitors Council, 705 West Seventh Street, Los Angeles, California 90017, (213) 628-3101; or Chamber of Commerce, Desert Hot Springs, California 92240.

Florida - Daytona Beach Shores

CANADIAN WEEKEND
Daytona Beach Shores, Florida

Reflecting a theme of "Hands of Friendship across the Border," the celebration honors Canadian visitors to the area. Special guests, arriving by jet, are honored in various activities. On Sunday a joint worship service between the community's Drive-In Christian Church and the Carmen United Church in Toronto is conducted by a special telephone hookup. Held the last weekend of January each year. Contact: Rev. Wallace Pomplun, Drive-In Christian Church, 3812 Emilia Drive, Daytona Beach, Florida 32019. (904) 767-8761.

Florida - Lake Buena Vista

CANADIAN FESTIVAL
Walt Disney World
Lake Buena Vista, Florida

A week-long salute to Canada highlighted by special Magic Kingdom concerts, ceremonies, parades, decorations, and guest appearances by Canadian entertainers. Held annually in January. Contact: Publicity Office, Post Office Box 40, Lake Buena Vista, Florida 32830. (305) 824-2222.

Michigan - Detroit

DETROIT/WINDSOR INTERNATIONAL FREEDOM FESTIVAL
Detroit, Michigan

Since 1959, the neighboring cities of Detroit and Windsor, Canada, which are connected by a bridge and tunnel and share an unfortified border, have held a week-long celebration coinciding with the Fourth of July holiday. This festival celebrates the unique friendship and harmony between the United States and Canada. Attractions include river parades, air show, hydroplane and Grand Prix races, concerts, sporting tournaments, dancing, bike-along, fireworks, and a Children's Day. Contact: J. Joyce Cusmano or Dawn A. Lynch; phone: (313) 259-8064 or Detroit Chamber of Commerce, 150 Michigan Avenue, Detroit, Michigan 48226 (313) 964-4000.

South Carolina - Myrtle Beach

CANADIAN-AMERICAN DAYS
Grand Stand
Myrtle Beach, South Carolina

Honors Canadian visitors with special events and activities, including square dancing, parades, tours of historic sites, sand-castle building contests, fishing tourney, receptions, amusement parks, kids' day, and golfing. Held annually since 1962 in mid-March over a nine-day period. At approximately the same time, a one-day Canadian-American Folk Festival is held in Myrtle Beach, featuring concerts, workshops, folklore, and arts and crafts displays by Canadian and American artists. Contact: Greater Myrtle Beach Chamber of Commerce, Post Office Box 1326, Myrtle Beach, South Carolina 29577. (803) 448-5135.

Airline Offices

AIR CANADA
United States Headquarters
1166 Avenue of the Americas, 25th Floor
New York, New York 10036 (212) 869-1900

Provides extensive domestic services, as well as many short-haul services to gateway cities in the United States. Flies North Atlantic routes to France, Germany, Great Britain, and Switzerland. Also flies to Bermuda, the Bahamas, Florida, and the Caribbean. Other offices in the United States: Boston, Chicago, Cleveland, Dallas, Houston, Los Angeles, Miami, San Francisco, Seattle, and Washington.

CP AIR
Canadian Pacific Airlines
489 Fifth Avenue, Suite 2602 (212) 697-6308
New York, New York 10017 (800) 426-7000

Flies routes from Montreal to Ottawa, Toronto, Winnipeg, Calgary, Vancouver, Victoria; Vancouver to San Francisco; to Los Angeles; to Yukon, Northwest Territories, and Western Canada; Toronto/ Montreal to Halifax, Amsterdam; to Lisbon, Milan and Rome; Vancouver, Edmonton, and Calgary over the Polar Route to Amsterdam; Vancouver to Tokyo, Hong Kong; Toronto to Honolulu, Sydney; Vancouver to Honolulu, Fiji, Sydney; and Toronto to Lima, Santiago, Buenos Aires. Other offices in the United States: Boston, Buffalo, Chicago, Cleveland, Detroit, Los Angeles, Miami, Philadelphia, Portland, San Francisco, Seattle, Spokane, and Washington, D.C.

NORDAIR, LIMITED
Pittsburgh Office
430 Market Square
Pittsburgh, Pennsylvania 15222 (412) 391-2107

Schedules flights between Pittsburgh and Hamilton, Ontario. Offers domestic services throughout eastern Canada, including charter services.

Bookdealers and Publishers' Representatives

FAMILY BOOK SHOP
4951 Glacier Drive
Los Angeles, California 90041
Proprietor: Dan Moore (213) 257-3069

Carries books on Canada.

DOUGLAS N. HARDING
35 East Pearl Street
Box 361
Nashua, New Hampshire 03061
Proprietor: D. N. Harding (603) 883-4882

Specializes in Canadiana.

JACQUES NOEL JACOBSEN, JR.
60 Manor Road
Staten Island, New York 10310
Proprietor: J. N. Jacobson, Jr. (212) 981-0973

Carries Canadiana materials, also antiquarian.

THE LOOKING GLASS SEARCH SERVICE
5584 Morning Street
Worthington, Ohio 43085
Proprietor: N. C. Strohl (614) 885-4800

Specializes in antiquarian books on Canada and Canadian literature.

R. M. WEATHERFORD - BOOKS
10902 Woods Creek Road
Monroe, Washington 98272
Proprietor: R. M. Weatherford

Lists books on Canadiana for mail order.

MARK WEISS
Sand Hill Road
Peterborough, New Hampshire 03458
Proprietor: Mark Weiss (603) 924-6467

Specializes in Canadiana.

YANKEE PEDDLER BOOKSHOP
94 Mill Street
Pultneyville, New York 14538
Proprietors: John, Janet and Douglass Westerberg (315) 589-2063

Carries Canadiana books.

Books and Pamphlets

BIBLIOGRAPHIA CANADIANA. By Claude Thibault. Don Mills, Ontario, Longman Canada, 1973.

A classified bibliography of over 25,000 books, periodical articles, and documents on the history of Canada. Arranged under three main chronological headings: The French Colonial Regime; British North America, 1713-1867; and the Dominion of Canada, 1867-1967. Omits genealogical, biographical, local, or provincial works.

BIBLIOGRAPHY OF CANADIAN BIBLIOGRAPHIES. By Ramond Tanghe. Toronto, University of Toronto Press, 1960.

Includes nearly 1,700 items classified under 29 headings. Annotations are in English or in French, according to the language of the title. Indexed by authors, compilers, and subjects. Supplements issued by the Bibliographical Society of Canada.

A BIBLIOGRAPHY OF THE PRAIRIE PROVINCES TO 1953, WITH BIOGRAPHICAL INDEX. By Bruce B. Peel. Toronto, University of Toronto Press, 1973.

A BIBLIOGRAPHY OF WORKS ON CANADIAN FOREIGN RELATIONS, 1971-1975. By Donald M. Page. Toronto, Canadian Institute of International Affairs, 1977.

Contains selections written about Canadian foreign relations plus writings of important Canadians on international affairs when the writings help to understand Canada's foreign policy. Also provides a chronological list of statements and speeches issued by the Department of External Affairs.

CANADA HANDBOOK; HANDBOOK OF PRESENT CONDITIONS AND RECENT PROGRESS. 49th edition. Ottawa, Statistics Canada, 1981.

Presents information about the land and people of Canada and a summary of recent government activities, economic, social, and cultural developments. The yearbook is illustrated with numerous photographs, many in color. Issued biennially.

CANADA; PAST AND PRESENT. By John Saywell. Toronto, Clarke, Irwin and Company Limited, 1975.

Offers a succinct history of Canada and a discussion of its development as a nation. Includes picture essays on: The Conquest of New France; Winning the West; Cartoonists' Political History; and Canadian Life.

CANADA SINCE 1867; A BIBLIOGRAPHIC GUIDE. Edited by J. L. Granatstein and Paul Stevens. Toronto; Hakkert, 1977.

A guide to materials written on Canadian history, government and politics. Materials are arranged under these subject headings: national politics; foreign and defense policy; business and economic history; social and intellectual history; the west; Ontario; Quebec, and Atlantic Canada.

CANADIAN GENEALOGICAL HANDBOOK. Edited by Eric Jonasson. Winnipeg, Wheatfield Press, 1981.

About 1,800 government departments, societies, etcetera, useful in genealogical research in Canada are listed geographically, then by type of record or repository. Entires include: source name, address; many listings include additional information.

A CANADIAN INDIAN BIBLIOGRAPHY, 1969-1970. By Thomas S. Abler, Douglas Sanders, and Sally M. Weaver. Toronto and Buffalo, University of Toronto Press, 1974.

A comprehensive bibliography listing about 3,000 entries on Canadian Indians and Metis. The first part presents a topical arrangement of books, monographs, articles, dissertations, and reports. The second part, Case Law Digest, includes case law related to Indian legal questions since 1867. Covers English and French publications.

CANADIAN POLITICS, 1950-1975: A SELECTED RESEARCH BIBLIOGRAPHY. By John Dreijmaris. Monticello, Illinois, Council of Planning Librarians, 1976.

A listing of scholarly books on the following subjects: civil liberties and the constitution; the electoral system and voting; Federalism and Nationalism; foreign policy; governmental institutions; political leaders; political parties and pressure groups; provincial and local politics; public administration, bureaucracy, and finance; and public opinion and the mass media.

CANADIAN REFERENCE SOURCES: A SELECTIVE GUIDE. Edited by Dorothy Ryder. Ottowa, Canadian Library Association, 1973. Supplement in 1975.

An annotated listing of Canadian works of reference that covers Canada in general, the ten provinces, the territories and three cities - Ottawa, Montreal, and Toronto. The guide is based on the National Library Collection.

CANADIAN RURAL SOCIOLOGY BIBLIOGRAPHY. By Meg Richeson. Monticello, Illinois, Council of Planning Librarians, 1971.

This bibliography includes items on demography, levels of rural living, rural history, rual and regional development, rural poverty, rural institutions and rural organizations.

A CHECKLIST OF CANADIAN LITERATURE AND BACKGROUND MATERIALS, 1628 - 1960. By Reginald Watters, Toronto, Buffalo, University of Toronto Press, 1972.

Part I contains titles in the forms of poetry, fiction and drama that were produced by English speaking Canadians and Part II contains books by

Canadians on the literature or culture of Canada

ECONOMIC HISTORY OF CANADA: A GUIDE TO INFORMATION SOURCES. By Trevor Dick, Detroit, Gale Research Company, 1978.

An annotated bibliography of published works that have made a significant contribution to the literature of economic history in Canada. The bibliography is organized partly chronologically and partly topically.

HOW TO FIND OUT ABOUT CANADA. By Henry Campbell. Oxford, New York; Pergamon Press, 1967.

A detailed introduction to sources that provide information about Canada. Most of the works are described in English. Covers Canada in 15 areas.

ONTARIO AND THE CANADIAN NORTH. By William F. Morley. Toronto, University of Toronto Press, 1978.

This bibliography is volume 3 of the series entitled Canadian Local Histories to 1950.

A PRACTICAL GUIDE TO CANADIAN POLITICAL ECONOMY. By Wallace Clement. Toronto: J. Coriner, 1978.

A listing of 1,500 materials that deal with Canadian political economy. Revised edition of the Canadian State, Political Economy and Political Power. Begins with an essay, "Rediscovering Canadian Political Economy."

LA PROVINCE DE QUEBEC. By Andre Beaulieu and William F. E. Morley. Toronto, University of Toronto Press, 1971.

This bibliography is volume 2 to the series entitled Canadian Local Histories to 1950.

SOURCES OF INFORMATION FOR RESEARCH IN CANADIAN POLITICAL SCIENCE AND PUBLIC ADMINISTRATION. Ottawa, Carleton University, 1964.

An annotated bibliography useful for those preparing a thesis or research essay. All materials listed are in the Carleton Library Collection, Carleton University, Ottawa.

UNION LIST OF CANADIAN NEWSPAPERS HELD BY CANADIAN LIBRARIES. Ottawa, National Library of Canada, 1977.

This bibliography contains holdings data on nearly 5,000 newspapers in inkprint as well as in microform held by libraries throughout Canada.

WINNIPEG: A CENTENNIAL BIBLIOGRAPHY: A Centennial Project of the Manitoba Library Association. Winnipeg, Manitoba Library Association, 1974.

Contains over 1,400 entries arranged under 15 categories, including history, politics and government, city planning, economics, transportation, sports and recreation, etcetera. Based on bibliographical data submitted by participating libraries from their holdings.

CANADIAN AMERICANS

BRITISH AND CANADIAN IMMIGRATION TO THE UNITED STATES SINCE 1920. By Kenneth Lines. San Francisco; R and E Research Associates, 1978.

A study of British and Canadian immigration after resumption of immigration after the world war. Data for the study were obtained from government records, and a questionnaire and interview survey. The study concentrated on the Pacific Coast states and Hawaii, where a large number of immigrants had settled.

THE CANADIAN BORN IN THE UNITED STATES; An Analysis of the Canadian Element in the Population of the United States, 1850 to 1930. By Leon E. Truesdell. New Haven, Yale University Press, 1943.

Written by the Chief Statistician for Population, United States Bureau of the Census, this volume presents statistical cross sections of the intermingling populations of the United States and Canada, spaced at ten-year intervals from 1850 to 1930. Shows the net results of the movements and changes which took place in various areas of the United States. Tabulates and discusses the characteristics of Canadian born persons according to color, sex, age, marital status, literacy, economic status, and size of family.

L'EMIGRATION DES CANADIENS AUX ETATS-UNIS AVANT 1930; mesure du phenomene. By Yolande Lavoie. Montreal, Presses de l'Universite de Montreal, 1972.

This book, written in French, discusses the emigration of Canadians to the United States up to 1930.

L'EMIGRATION DES QUEBECOIS AUX ETATS-UNIS DE 1840 a 1930. By Yolande Lavoie. Quebec, Conseil de la langue francaise, 1979.

Discusses the emigration of the Quebecois from Canada to the United States during the period 1840 to 1930. In French.

THE MINGLING OF THE CANADIAN AND AMERICAN PEOPLES. Volume I. Historical. By Marcus Lee Hansen. New Haven, Yale University Press, 1940.

Discusses and documents the interplay between Americans moving to Canada and Canadians settling in the United States during various periods from 1604 to 1938. Explains the causes leading to immigration and the activities of the immigrants intermingling with the inhabitants of each country.

Audiovisual Material

MAPS

CANADA HIGHWAY MAP. Ottawa, Canadian Government Office of Tourism.

A road map of the provinces of Canada as well as adjacent parts of the United States. Inset maps show Newfoundland, the Yukon and the Northeast Territories. In color. Approximately 27 by 38 inches.

FILMS

ALIAS SILAS HUCKLEBACK. 16mm. Color and sound. 30 minutes. Toronto, Canadian Broadcasting Corporation, 1973.

Presents a profile of a fast-vanishing breed of Canadian, the prairie pioneer.

THE BEST OF TIMES ... THE WORST OF TIMES. 16mm. Color and sound with black and white sequences. 60 minutes. Toronto, Canadian Broadcasting Corporation, 1973.

Presents the personalities and events that contributed to Canada's development as a nation during the first half of the depressed thirties. Traces as well the life and career of R. B. Bennett, Canada's eleventh prime minister.

THE BIBLE BELT; A CBC WHITE PAPER: THE POLITICS OF THE SECOND COMING. 16mm. Color and sound. 90 minutes. Canadian Broadcasting Corporation, 1972.

Examines the rise of the fundamentalist Protestant sects in Western Canada during the 1920's and 1930's and shows their influence on Canadian politics then and now.

BIELER. 16mm. Color and sound. 19 minutes. Quarry Films, Kingston, Ontario. Released by Department of Film Studies, Queen's University, Kingston, Ontario, 1973.

Explores the interaction between the artist and his community by presenting Andre Bieler in his studio, in his home, and in conversation.

CANADA FOR THE FUN OF IT. 16mm. Color and sound. 60 minutes. Toronto, Canadian Broadcasting Corporation, 1972.

Presents a musical trip through Canada, showing how Canadians enjoy their winter activities.

CANADA IMPRESSIONS. 16mm. Color and sound. 12 minutes. Toronto, Moreland-Latchford Productions. Released in the United States by Canadian Travel Film Library, 1972.

Mixes music, sound effects, and scenes of the Canadian outdoors from the Pacific to the Atlantic to provide an impression of the variety of Canada's land and people during all seasons of the year. Without narration. French version released under the same title.

CANADA, OUR NORTHERN NEIGHBOR. 16mm. Color and sound. 17 minutes. Santa Monica, California. BFA Educational Media, 1978.

Deals with the geography, history, and economy of Canada and the variety of lifestyles in its five regions. Includes teacher's guide.

CANADA - THE LAND. 16mm and 35mm. Color and sound. 8 minutes. National Film Board of Canada, 1969.

Reveals Canada's scenic and industrial features from the vantage point of a low-flying aircraft, contrasting the immensity of the Canadian wilderness with the dams and highways of Canadian industry. French version released under the title Canada Pays Vaste.

CANADA, THE NORTHERN GIANT. 16mm. Color and sound. 90 minutes. Calgary, Alta. Great West Productions, 1976, made 1973-1975.

A travelog on Canada from the Atlantic Coast to the Pacific Coast. Visits nine provinces plus the Yukon Territory. Includes script.

CANADA'S ATLANTIC PROVINCES. 16mm. Color and sound. 14 minutes. Coronet Instructional Media, 1973.

Provides a geographic introduction to the Canadian Atlantic Provinces, including a look at the ethnic and national backgrounds of their people, and the economic role played by fishing, shipping, lumbering, and mining. With teacher's guide.

CANADA'S CENTRAL PROVINCES. 16mm. Color and sound. 14 minutes. Coronet Instructional Media, 1973.

Provides a geographic introduction to the Canadian central Provinces, including a look at the ethnic backgrounds of their people, and the contrasts between rural and urban life. With teacher's guide.

CANADA'S PACIFIC PROVINCE AND NORTHLAND. 16mm. Color and sound. 14 minutes. Coronet Instructional Media, 1973.

Provides a geographic introduction to the Canadian Pacific Province of British Columbia and Canadian northlands, including a look at the historical back-ground of their people and land. With teacher's guide.

CANADA'S PRAIRIE PROVINCES. 16mm. Color and sound. 14 minutes. Coronet Instructional Media, 1973.

Provides a geographic introduction to the Canadian prairie Provinces, including a look at the historic and ethnic backgrounds of their people, and the traditional occupations of farming, cattle raising, and lumbering. With teacher's guide.

CANADA'S PROVINCES AND PEOPLE. 16mm. Color and sound. 14 minutes. Coronet Instructional Media, 1973.

Offers a geographic overview of Canada's people, land, resources, and industrial potential for the future. With teacher's guide. Second edition of the 1956 motion picture entitled Canada: Geography of the Americas.

THE CANADIANS. 16mm. Color and sound. 2 films, 20 minutes each. Toronto, Visual Educational Centre, and Encyclopaedia Britannica Educational Corporation, 1973.

Takes a documentary look using real people, at Canada and Canadians. Part 1: How Canadians live in cities; Part 2: How Canadians live in the country.

THE CANADIANS: THEIR CITIES. 16mm. Color and sound. 16 minutes. Toronto, Visual Education Centre, 1973. Released in the United States by Encyclopaedia Britannica Educational Corporation, 1974.

A film for juveniles that examines life in five of the largest cities of Canada. With teacher's guide.

THE CANADIANS: THEIR LAND. 16mm. Color and sound. 16 minutes. Toronto, Visual Education Centre, 1973. Released in the United States by Encyclopaedia Britannica Educational Corporation, 1974.

A film for juveniles that explores several different regions of Canada, showing how each contributes to the Canadian economy and way of life. With teacher's guide.

A CAPITAL FOR CANADIANS. 16mm. Color and sound. 27 minutes. National Capital Commission, made by D. McIntosh. Montreal, Modern Talking Picture Service, 1975.

Shows the National Capital Commission's area of responsibility including Ottawa and Hull. French version released under title: La capitale pour Canadiens.

CENTRAL REGION. 16mm. Color and sound. 180 minutes. Montreal, Canadian Film Development Corporation. Released by Canadian Film-Makers' Distribution Centre, Toronto, 1971.

Uses a specially designed camera mount in order to provide a new perspective on the scenery of the wilderness of northern Quebec. French version released under the title La region centrale.

COLOURS. 16mm. Color and sound. 4 minutes. Communicaet Film Productions, 1972.

Deals with west coast Canadiana.

THE CONQUERED DREAM (CANADA, PAST AND PRESENT). 16mm. Color and sound. 52 minutes. British Broadcasting Corporation, London, and National Film Board of Canada. 1971. Released in the United States by Centron Educational Films, 1973.

Offers a broad view of the significant events of Canada's life and history, including the early explorations, the Klondike gold rush, the search for the Northwest Passage, and the art and legends of the Eskimo. With leader's guide by H. Lewis McKinney. Issued in two parts.

THE CRAFT OF HISTORY. 16mm. Color and sound. 60 minutes. Canadian Broadcasting Corporation, Toronto, 1972.

Three of Canada's senior historians comment on Canada's past and reflect on the future.

A DREAM OF FREEDOM. 16mm. Color and sound. 52 minutes. Montreal, BBC, National Film Board of Canada: The Board, 1976.

Documents the history of immigration to Canada from the United Kingdom.

THE DRYLANDERS. 16mm. Black and white. Sound. 60 minutes. National Film Board of Canada, 1963.

Presents the epic story of the opening of the Canadian west and describes the drought that brought depression in the thirties. Cast: Frances Hyland, James Douglas, Mary Savage, and Don Francks.

FACES WEST. 16mm. Color and sound. 18 minutes. Montreal, CN Audio Visual Communications: Modern Talking Picture Service, 1975.

A travelog of a tour of western Canada by train, from Winnipeg to Vancouver.

THE FIRST YEAR. 16mm. Color and sound. 37 minutes. Montreal, National Film Board of Canada.

Traces training and careers of new Royal Canadian Mounted Police recruits.

HERE IS CANADA. 35mm. Color and sound. 28 minutes. Ottawa, Department of External Affairs, 1972. Made by National Film Board of Canada.

Describes Canada for viewers outside the country. Contrasts the various types of terrain, occupations, and cultures found there.

GRAVITY IS NOT SAD, BUT GLAD. 16mm. Color and sound. 130 minutes. Toronto, Canadian Film-Makers' Distribution Centre, 1975.

Deals with Canada, religion, language, tearing things apart that are together, and putting things together that are apart.

HERE IS CANADA. 16mm and 35mm. Color and sound. 28 minutes. New York, National Film Board of Canada, 1972.

Contrasts mountains, plains, sea coasts; the life of cities; the industries and manufacturing that have grown from the abundance of natural resources and the challenges of space and distance; varied cultures and traditions, and individuals who have contributed to the Canadian mosaic.

HEROIC BEGINNINGS. 16mm. Color and sound. 60 minutes. Toronto, Canadian Broadcasting Corporation, 1972.

Explores eleven historical sites in Canada from Newfoundland to the Pacific.

I'VE HAD IT. 35mm. Color and sound. 90 minutes. Kit Films, Productions mutuelles, Cinevideo, Kangourou Films, and Canadian Film Development Corporation, Canada. Released by Films mutuels, Montreal, 1972.

Show how the Cartier family take a trailer trip to Vancouver, British Columbia, and experience various adventures on the road, discovering that Canada is not as bilingual and bi-cultural as they thought. Cast: Dominque Michel, Jean Lefebvre, Rene Simard, Francis Blanche, Yvan Ducharme.

A LOOK AT THIS LAND. 16mm. Color and sound. 30 minutes. Toronto, Canadian Broadcasting Corporation, 1972.

Explores the Canadian landscape from the Maritimes to the West Coast as seen through eyes of an old man.

THE MACKENZIE ROAD. 16mm. Color and sound. 30 minutes. Toronto, Canadian Broadcasting Corporation, 1972.

Takes a look at the proposed route of the Mackenzie Highway.

THE MANY FACES OF WINNIPEG. 16mm. Color and sound. 28 minutes. Manitoba Department of Tourism, Recreation and Cultural Affairs; made by Western Films, 1975.

A look at the cultural mix of Winnipeg as displayed in the annual Folklorama celebrations. Shorter version released under title: Folklorama Winnipeg.

THE MAPLE LEAF FOREVER. 16mm. Color and sound. 10 minutes. Evanston, Illinois, Film Works. Journal Films, 1977.

Uses authentic costumes, buildings, and language to re-create the life of a small Canadian town in the middle of the 19th century, the time of the celebration of that country's nationhood. Includes teacher's guide.

MONTREAL - OLYMPIC CITY. 16mm and 35mm. Color and sound. 11 minutes. BP Canada Limited, made by Onyx Films, Montreal, BP Canada, 1976.

A promotional film about Montreal.

MORE THAN A RED COAT. 16mm. Color and sound. 30 minutes. Great-West Life Assurance Company, Winnipeg. Made and released by Onyx Films, Montreal, 1973.

Traces the history of Canada's Royal Canadian Mounted Police.

NEW BRUNSWICK PROMENADE. 16mm. Color and sound. 14 minutes. Province of New Brunswick. Made by Fiddlehead Film Productions, Canada. Released by Canadian Travel Film Library, Ottawa, 1973.

Shows various scenic tourist delights in New Brunswick, Canada.

NORTH OF 60 EAST. 16mm. Color and sound. 28 minutes. Royal Canadian Mounted Police, Ottawa. Made and released by National Film Board of Canada, 1970.

Follows a Royal Canadian Mounted Policeman through a tour of duty in the Canadian Arctic above the 60th parallel, providing examples of the kind of life and work found in the Canadian Arctic.

THE OTHER SIDE OF THE LEDGER. 16mm. Color and sound. 42 minutes. National Film Board of Canada, 1972.

Presents an articulate denial of many facets of the white man's version of Canadian history.

PAWAGANAK. 16mm. Color and sound. 20 minutes. Ottawa, Canada Council; The Council, 1975.

Shows young people traveling in Canada in search of themselves and their role as adults.

PICTURE CANADA. 16mm. Color and sound. 27 minutes. Kodak Canada, Canada. Made by Crawley Films, Montreal. Released by Canadian Travel Film Library, Montreal, 1973.

Presents a look at the character and mood of Canada in the work of 15 photographers.

SEARCH OF THE WESTERN SEA. 16mm. Color and sound. 29 minutes. New York, Devonian Group of Charitable Foundations; McGraw-Hill Films, 1978.

The epic story of Alexander Mackenzie's expedition to the Pacific coast. Includes teacher's guide. Made in Canada.

SONGS OF THE WEST. 16mm. Color and sound. 6 minutes. Toronto, Film Arts, 1974.

Uses pictures and songs to trace the early history of the farming pioneers that settled on the Canadian prairies. Cast: Stan Endersby.

STRUGGLE FOR A BORDER: CANADA'S RELATIONS WITH THE UNITED STATES. 16mm. Black and white. Sound. 58 minutes each film. New York, National Film Board of Canada.

Series of nine films: New England and New France (1490-1763); Canada and the American Revolution (1763-1783); The War of 1812 (1783-1818); Dangerous Decades (1818-1846); The New Equation; Annexation and Reciprocity (1840-1860); The Friendly Fifties and the Sinister Sixties (1850-1863); The Triumphant Union and the Canadian Confederation (1863-1867); The Border Confirmed; The Treaty of Washington (1867-1871); and A Second Transcontinental Nation (1872).

Explores the economic, political, military, diplomatic, social, and geographic forces that created and confirmed the United States-Canada border. The resources of hundreds of archives in North America and Europe provided material to chronicle, dramatize, and clarify the complex story. Illustrations are frequently in the form of contemporary political cartoons, incisive in their wit, giving edge and immediacy to the issues of the day.

SUMMER CELEBRATIONS. 16mm. Black and white. Sound. 7 minutes. National Film Board of Canada, 1961.

A screen magazine film showing: brisk boats, views of an international regatta of home-built boats in the Thousand Islands waterway - Flin Flon fun, views of summer festival time in Flin Flon, Manitoba - The stampede is on. Highlights of the round-up at the Calgary Stampede.

SUMMER FISHING DREAMLAND. 16mm. Color and sound. 26 minutes. Regina, Department of Toursim and Renewable Resources of Saskatchewan, Extension Services Branch, 1975.

Shows the beauty of the wilderness in northern Saskatchewan.

SUMMER IN CANADA. 35mm. Color and sound. 12 minutes. Toronto, Canadian Government Travel Bureau, made by MacLaren Advertising Company, Canadian Government Travel Bureau; Columbia Pictures of Canada, 1975.

A travelog on Canada from coast to coast.

TO THE PRAIRIES! 16mm. Color and sound. 28 minutes. Toronto, Ontario Educational Communications Authority, 1972.

Presents impressions of the immigration to the Canadian West using pictures, documents, and reminiscences from an exhibition held at the Canadian National Archives.

WHO ARE WE? 16mm. Color and sound. 10 minutes. Montreal, National Film Board of Canada, 1974.

An animated film on Canada and her people.

Approximately 300 additional films are available from the Embassy of Canada. Most of these films are documentaries on the arts, history, industry, science, sports and people of Canada. Of special interest is a group of experimental films by Norman McLaren and others. Both English language and French language films are included. There are short biographical films of celebrated Canadians including Norman Bethune, Leonard Cohen, John Grieson, Norman Jewison and others. A nine-part series explores Canadian-United States relations using extensive archival material. Other compilations use much archival motion picture footage. The life of the Netsilik Eskimos is explored in a two-part documentary and a thirteen-part series for children. Other topics include Jane Jacobs, Castleguard Cave, Cree Indians, Blissymbols, early film history, aviation history, the Yukon gold rush, restoration, explorers, salmon fisheries, the Northwest Passage, arctic oil, space telecommunication, wheat, wildlife, mental retardation, skiing, gliding, snowmobiles, skating, hockey. For further information, contact:

Canadian Embassy
Public Affairs Division
1771 N Street, Northwest
Washington, D.C. 20036 (202) 785-1400

CHILEANS
See also: SPANISH-SPEAKING PEOPLES

Embassy

EMBASSY OF CHILE
1732 Massachusetts Avenue, Northwest
Washington, D.C. 20036 (202) 785-1746

Permanent Mission to the OAS
2101 L Street, Northwest,
Suite 401 (202) 223-4027
Washington, D.C. 20037 223-4029

CONSULATES GENERAL

619 South Olive
Los Angeles, California 90014 (213) 624-6357

25 Southeast Avenue, Suite 1234
Miami, Florida 33131 (305) 373-8623

688 Second Avenue, Suite 501 (212) 628-8808
New York, New York 10017 628-8807

870 Market Street, Suite 1062
San Francisco, California 94102 (415) 982-7662

Mission to the United Nations

CHILEAN MISSION
809 United Nations Plaza, 4th Floor
New York, New York 10017 (212) 687-7547

Tourist and Travel Offices

Each of the above listed Consulates General provides information and tourist services.

Public Affairs Organizations

CHILE LEGISLATIVE CENTER
201 Massachusetts Avenue, Northeast,
Suite 102
Washington, D.C. 20002
Director: Reverend Charles Buody (202) 889-4670
Founded 1976

Involved in legislative work concerning Chile. Objectives are to cut off all military and economic aid to Chile; to work on behalf of political prisoners there; and to disseminate information on current legislation affecting that country. Affiliated with the National Chile Center. Publishes Update and Action Memos (keyed to Congressional activities).

NATIONAL COORDINATING CENTER IN SOLIDARITY WITH CHILE
(National Chile Center)
7 East 15th Street, Suite 408
New York, New York 10003
National Coordinator: Lewis M. Moroze (212) 989-0085
Founded 1974

Comprised of local Chile solidarity committees, ecumenical Committees of Concern for Chile, trade union and student groups, peace organizations, political parties and community organizations. Ojective is to help in the struggle to restore democratic and human rights in Chile. Activities include campaigning to release political prisoners in Chile; campaigning to adopt a Chilean political prisoner; congressional lobbying seeking to cut all economic and military aid to Chile; disseminating information on the current situation in Chile; arranging and supporting speaking tours by prominent Chilean exiles; collecting biographies of Chilean political prisoners; fund raising.
Publications: Chile Vencera (Chile Will Win), irregular; also publishes monographs, booklets, films, documents and information packets.

NON-INTERVENTION IN CHILE
Post Office Box 800 (415) 835-0810
Berkeley, California 94701 Founded 1972

Conducts activities aimed at the economic and political isolation of the military junta in Chile. Conducts research.
Publications: Chile Newsletter, bimonthly; Political Prisoners Bulletin, bimonthly.

Cultural and Educational Organizations

COMMITTEE FOR CHILE
International Fund for Monuments, Incorporated
3624 Legation Avenue, Northwest
Washington, D.C. 20015 (202) 726-5225

The Fund supports an extensive program of archaeological, restoration, and preservation of Easter Island's gigantic stone figures, temples, towers, and petroglyphs. The Island has 180 km^2 (112 square miles) located in the Pacific Ocean, 2,000 nautical miles from the continent. Also known in the native language as Te Pito o Te Henua (the center of the world), Matakiterangi (eyes that look up at the sky), Rapa-Nui (great island).

Newsletters

CHILE NEWSLETTER. Bimonthly. Publisher: Non-Intervention in Chile, Post Office Box 800, Berkeley, California 94701.

Publishes current information about anti-government activities in Chile and in other countries.

CHILE TODAY. Monthly. Publisher: Press Department, Embassy of Chile, 1732 Massachusetts Avenue, Northwest, Washington, D.C. 20036. In English.

Publishes poiitical, economic, industrial, financial, and foreign news concerning Chile.

Magazines

CHILE NOW. Monthly. Publisher: Ministry for Foreign Affairs, Santiago, Chile.

Publishes political, economic, industrial, financial and foreign affairs news concerning Chile. In English.

Commercial and Trade Organizations

CHILEAN TRADING CORPORATION
One World Trade Center
New York, New York 10048 (212) 938-0550

CORFO
One World Trade Center, Room 5151
New York, New York 10048 (212) 558-4144

NORTH AMERICAN-CHILEAN CHAMBER OF COMMERCE, INCORPORATED
220 East 81st Street
New York, New York 10028 (212) 288-5691

PRO-CHILE
230 Park Avenue, Suite 1430
New York, New York 10017 (212) 466-1026

Economic and Commercial office for the Chilean government.

Airline Offices

LAN-CHILE AIRLINES
North American Headquarters:
150 Southeast Second Avenue, 4th Floor
Miami, Florida 33131 (305) 377-4721

630 Fifth Avenue
New York, New York 10020 (212) 582-3250

Provides international services to Central America, Miami, and New York; to Europe; and to Easter Island and Tahiti. Other offices in the United States: Boston, Chicago, Los Angeles, New York, and Washington.

Ship Lines

CHILEAN LINE

1 World Trade Center, Suite 2073
New York, New York 10048 (212) 775-0111

1730 Rhode Island Avenue, Northwest
Washington, D.C. 20036 (202) 293-2250

Carries freight and a limited number of passengers between Valparaiso, Chile, and Baltimore, Philadelphia, and New York.

Books and Pamphlets

CHILE. By Mario Correa. Washington, D.C., The Cultural Department of the Embassy of Chile.

This tourist publication contains information on each region of Chile. Also a glossary of the principal dishes and beverages. Available from the Cultural Affairs Department of the Embassy of Chile, 1732 Massachusetts Avenue, Northwest, Washington, D.C. 20036.

CHILE: THE CHALLENGE. Odeplan Document, series Auriga. Santiago, Dinex, the information service of the Chilean Ministry of Foreign Affairs, 1974.

Discusses political and economic situations and policies, industries, agriculture, and the Foreign Investment Statute. The text is bilingual, in Spanish and English.

CHILEAN CULTURAL PANORAMA. By Mario Correa, Washington, D.C., The Cultural Department of the Embassy of Chile. In English.

Presently available issues Number 1, National Emblems, Amusements and Games; Number 3, Chilean Antarctica, Easter Island and Juan Fernandez Archipelago; Number 4, Mistral Neruda, Huidobro, Three Figures in Chilean Literature; and Number 5, Chilean Painting.

CHILEAN LITERATURE: A WORKING BIBLIOGRAPHY OF SECONDARY SOURCES. By David W. Foster. Boston, G.K. Hall, 1978.

CHILE'S AGRICULTURAL ECONOMY: A BIBLIOGRAPHY. Compiled by Teresa Anderson. Madison, Wisconsin, University of Wisconsin Land Tenure Center Library, 1970. Supplement 1, 1971; Supplement 2, 1973.

HISTORICAL DICTIONARY OF CHILE. By Salvatore Bizzaro. Metuchen, New Jersey, Scarecrow Press, 1972.

A sourcebook of historical and contemporary facts about persons, places, events, geography and political organization. Includes bibliography.

REPORT ON CHILEAN UNIVERSITY LIFE. By Mario Correa. Washington, D.C., The Cultural Department, Embassy of Chile. In English.

Regularly updated review of Chilean academic programs available free of charge from the Cultural Department of the Embassy of Chile.

SAN MARTIN, LIBERATOR OF ARGENTINA, CHILE AND PERU. By John Crane. Washington, American Historical Series, 1948.

A booklet concerning the life of Jose de San Martin and his struggle to free the colonies of Spanish America. Discusses San Martin's crossing of the Andes, his campaigns against Spanish Royalists, and his work for the independence of Argentina, Chile, and Peru. Illustrated with reproductions of paintings and engravings.

A SELECTED ANNOTATED BIBLIOGRAPHY OF ENVIRONMENTAL STUDIES OF ARGENTINA, CHILE, AND URUGUAY. Compiled by Vincent J. Creasi. Washington, U.S. Air Force Environmental Technical Applications Center, 1970.

An annotated bibliography available from the National Technical Information Service in Springfield, Virginia.

CHILEAN AMERICANS

CHILE, PERU, AND THE CALIFORNIA GOLD RUSH OF 1849. By Jay Monaghan. Berkeley, University of California Press, 1973.

Tells about the rush of Chileans and Peruvians to the California gold fields and their experiences after arriving. An epilogue assesses the long-term effects of the migration.

CHILENOS IN CALIFORNIA: A STUDY OF THE 1850, 1852 and 1860 CENSUS. By Carlos U. Lopez. San Francisco, 1973.

An investigation of early Chilean immigration.

Audiovisual Material

FILMS

CAMPAMENTO. 16mm. Color and sound. 29 minutes. By Amram Nowak Associates for Maryknoll Fathers. Released by World Horizon Films, 1972.

Examines the struggles of a group of slum dwellers in Chile to educate themselves, to build houses, schools, and roads, and to develop a new consciousness of their role in Chile and in their society.

CAMPAMENTO. 16mm. Color and sound. 26 minutes. By Amram Nowak Associates for Maryknoll Missioners. Released by Carousel Films, 1972.

A documentary on Chilean peasants who have recently become politically conscious and banded together in a struggle for equal rights. The leaders of the nonviolent movement explain - in Spanish with English subtitles - the reasons for the revolution and what it has accomplished so far.

CHILE AND ARGENTINA. 16mm and Super 8mm. Color and sound. 19 minutes. Latin American Series: A Focus on People. William Claiborne, Incorporated. Released by Sterling Educational Films, 1973.

Analyzes the social and political structure of Chile and Argentina, discussing the non-Spanish background of half the population, the European aspects of life, the problems in Argentina arising from high expectations and low productivity, and the crises in Chile resulting from Marxist government and nationalization of industry.

CHILE NUEVO. 16mm. Color and sound. 23 minutes. Ontario Educational Communications Authority, Toronto, and Allen Rogers Productions, Toronto, 1972.

Examines the problems of squatters who have occupied areas on the outskirts of Santiago, Chile, and who now claim squatter's rights.

CHILE, WHERE THE EARTH BEGAN. 16mm. Color and sound. 30 minutes. Cultural Department, Embassy of Chile, Washington, D.C.

COUNTRIES OF THE ANDES. 16mm. Color and sound. 11 minutes. Geography of South America Series. Coronet Instructional Media, 1977.

Describes the people, culture, cities, and rural areas of Bolivia, Ecuador, Peru, and Chile. Compares and contrasts the people of each country, points out their cultural achievements, and identifies important factors in their economic growth.

EASTER ISLAND. 16mm. Color and sound. 25 minutes. Also available as video cassette. Museum of Modern Art of Latin America, Washington, D.C., 1968.

Shows the mysterious monolithic stone figures of Easter Island with English and Spanish narration.

FAMILIES OF THE WORLD - CHILE. 16mm. Color and sound. 19 minutes. United Nations Children's Fund. Journal Films, Evanston, Illinois, 1976.

Examines family life in Chile. Explores through the eyes of two young boys, one wealthy and the other poor, the climate, geography, school, and culture of Chile.

THE JACKAL OF NAHUELTORO. 16mm and 35mm. Black and white with sound. 95 minutes. By Miguel Littin. Cine Experimental, University of Chile, Santiago, and Cinematografica Tercer Mundo, Chile, 1969. Released in the United States by Tricontinental Film Center.

A reenactment of a famous Chilean murder case that took place in 1963. Reveals the social conditions which led to the tragedy.

POET OF HIS PEOPLE, PABLO NERUDA. 16mm. Color and sound. 13 minutes. Lilyan Productions, Watchung, New Jersey, 1978.

Uses still footage and computer images in offering a symbolic representation of the life of Chilean poet Pablo Neruda as portrayed and narrated in his poem entitled la barcarola.

SKY IN CHILE. 16mm. Color and sound. 30 minutes. Cultural Department, Embassy of Chile, Washington, D.C.

VOYAGE TO THE BOTTOM OF THE WORLD. 16mm. Color and sound. 24 minutes. Hayden Productions, Dublin, California, 1977.

A promotional film for Prudential Lines' sea cruise from Buenos Aires through the Strait of Magellan to Valparaiso. Also issued in Portuguese and Spanish.

WHEN THE PEOPLE AWAKE. 16mm. Color and sound. 60 minutes. Tricontinental Film Center, 1973.

Examines the historical development of Chile's social structure from the turn of the century to 1970.

CHINESE
See also: ASIANS

Embassy and Consulates

EMBASSY OF THE PEOPLE'S REPUBLIC OF CHINA
2300 Connecticut Avenue
Washington, D.C. 20008 (202) 328-2500

CONSULATES GENERAL

1450 Laguna Street
San Francisco, California
94115 (415) 563-4885

520 Twelfth Avenue
New York, New York 10036 (212) 279-4275

3417 Montrose Boulevard
Houston, Texas 77006 (713) 524-0780

COORDINATION COUNCIL OF THE REPUBLIC OF CHINA FOR NORTH AMERICAN AFFAIRS
Offices in the U.S.A.
5161 River Road
Bethesda, Maryland 20816 (301) 657-2130

Suite 1602, Peachtree Center
Cain Tower
229 Peachtree Street, Northeast
Atlanta, Georgia 30303 (404) 522-0182

20 North Clark Street
19th Floor
Chicago, Illinois 60602 (312) 372-1213

2746 Pali Highway
Honolulu, Hawaii 96817 (808) 595-6347

11 Green Way Plaza
Suite 2006
Houston, Texas 77046 (713) 626-7445

3660 Wilshire Boulevard
Suite 1050
Los Angeles, California 90010 (213) 389-1215

801 Second Avenue
New York, New York 10017 (212) 697-1250

300 Montgomery Street, Suite 535
San Francisco, California
94104 (415) 362-7680

24th Floor, Westin Building
2001 Sixth Avenue
Seattle, Washington 98121 (206) 682-4967

Mission to the United Nations

MISSION OF THE PEOPLE'S REPUBLIC OF CHINA
155 West 66th Street
New York, New York 10023 (212) 787-3838

Information Office

CHINESE CULTURAL CENTER
159 Lexington Avenue
New York, New York 10016
Acting Director: T. C. Chiang (212) 725-4950
Founded 1941

Government agency of the Republic of China. Provides informational materials on China to interested groups or individuals. Maintains library of 10,000 volumes in Chinese and English. Formerly (1966) Chinese News Service; (1979) Chinese Information Service.
Publications: Free China Weekly; Free China Review, monthly; Vista, quarterly; China Yearbook; Background on China, irregular; also issues books and pamphlets on Chinese culture, leaders, politics and Taiwan.

Tourist and Travel Offices

CHINA INTERNATIONAL TOURIST SERVICE, INCORPORATED
60 East 42nd Street
Suite 465
New York, New York 10065 (212) 867-0271

Official tourist center of the People's Republic of China.

REPUBLIC OF CHINA TOURISM BUREAU
210 Post Street, Room 705
San Francisco, California 94108 (415) 563-4885

Fraternal Organizations

CHINESE AMERICAN CITIZENS ALLIANCE

415 Bamboo Lane
Los Angeles, California 90012
President: Baldwin Tom (213) 628-8015

1044 Stockton
San Francisco, California 94108 (415) 982-4618

Persons of Chinese birth or ancestry. Seeks to practice good citizenship and to know and understand the United States. Conducts essay contest and specialized education programs. Bestows three scholarships annually. Maintains speakers bureau.
Publications: Bulletin, monthly; Directory, biennial.

CHINESE AMERICAN CIVIC COUNCIL
2249 South Wentworth, 2nd Floor
Chicago, Illinois 60616
Executive Secretary: Helen Wong Jean (312) 225-0234
Founded 1951

Goals are to become better American citizens and to take an active part in the American way of life. Works to provide a means for Chinese Americans to participate in and contribute to American culture. Seeks to improve housing, business, and educational standards, and to develop parental responsibility and responsible behavior among youth. Sponsors a girl scout troop; conducts lectures; bestows awards to outgoing presidents.

CHINESE CONSOLIDATED BENEVOLENT ASSOCIATION

62 Mott Street
New York, New York 10013 (212) 267-5780
President: Ping Kee Chan Founded 1880

843 Stockton
San Francisco, California 94108 (415) 982-6000

Promotes cultural understanding through educational, charitable, social, and recreational activities.

CHINESE WOMEN'S ASSOCIATION
13541 Emperor Drive
Santa Ana, California 92705 (714) 838-2620
Secretary: Ruth R. Goodman Founded 1932

Founded to promote, stimulate, and maintain better understanding of the Chinese and their customs, history, and problems. Renders practical services toward the welfare of Free China and that of the overseas Chinese in the United States. Maintains a library of about 3,800 volumes.
Publication: Chinese Woman, quarterly.

CHINESE WOMEN'S BENEVOLENT ASSOCIATION
22 Pell Street
New York, New York 10013
President: Mrs. Louis F.S. Hong (212) 267-4764

Chinese women who volunteer in fund raising drives, aid students, and conduct other philanthropic activities. Provides interpreting and translating services when needed. Activities centered in New York City area.

FEDERAL CHINESE STUDENTS ASSOCIATION
41-54 74th Street
Elmhurst, New York 11373 (212) 446-4880

REPUBLIC OF CHINA STUDENTS ASSOCIATION OF WASHINGTON
Post Office Box 407
College Park, Maryland 20740
President: Jing-Yih Hsyu (301) 454-4699

SINO-AMERICAN AMITY FUND
86 Riverside Drive
New York, New York 10024 (212) 787-6969
President: Rev. Msgr. John Mao Founded 1951

To promote better understanding and friendly relations between the Americans and Chinese Nationalists through cultural, social, educational, and religious programs. Conducts welfare program for Chinese college students.

TAIWANESE ASSOCIATION OF AMERICA
Post Office Box 94514
Schaumburg, Illinois 60194
President: Mark Chen Founded 1970

Promotes friendship and welfare among Taiwanese-Americans and those concerned with Taiwanese human rights. Encourages Taiwanese to participate and contribute actively in sharing the diverse ethnic and cultural heritage of America. Conducts seminars; maintains library. Sponsors charitable programs, placement services and children's services; compiles statistics. Formerly (1978) Formosan Club of America.
Publications: Mayflower (in Taiwanese), monthly; also publishes directories and other materials at local levels.

WORLD FEDERATION OF TAIWANESE ASSOCIATIONS
Post Office Box 2461
Springfield, Virginia
President: Mark Chen Founded 1974

Individuals interested in Taiwan and those who consider Taiwan their homeland. Promotes friendship and Taiwanese culture. Affiliated with Taiwanese Association of America.

Professional Organizations

AMERICAN CHINESE MEDICAL SOCIETY
c/o Dr. Hsueh-hwa Wang
281 Edgewood Avenue
Teaneck, New Jersey 07666
President: Hsueh-hwa Wang, M.D. Founded 1963

Physicians of Chinese origin residing in the United States and Canada. Purposes are: to advance medical knowledge, scientific research and interchange of information among members; to establish scholarship and endowments in medical schools and hospitals of good standing; to hold periodic meetings for professional purposes. Conducts educational meetings; supports research. Grants annual scientific award to member with highest scholastic achievements. Maintains placement service. Sponsors limited charitable program.
Publications: Bulletin, quarterly; Membership Directory, biennial.

CHINESE-AMERICAN LIBRARIANS ASSOCIATION
Post Office Box 444
Oak Park, Illinois 60303
Executive Director: Tze-Chung Li Founded 1973

Purposes are to promote better communication among Chinese-American librarians in the United States, serving as a forum for the discussion of mutual problems, and to support the development and promotion of librarianship. Maintains placement referral service. Affiliated with: American Library Association. Formerly: Mid-West Chinese American Librarians Association.
Publications: Newsletter, three times a year; Journal of Library and Information Science, semiannual; has also published Directory of Chinese-American Librarians in the United States.

CHINESE AMERICAN RESTAURANT ASSOCIATION
173 Canal Street
New York, New York 10013 (212) 966-5747
President: George Law Founded 1935

Owners of Chinese restaurants. Membership concentrated in New York City.

CHINESE GARMENT MAKERS ASSOCIATION
220 Canal Street
New York, New York 10013 (212) 349-3941

CHINESE HAND LAUNDRY ASSOCIATION
149 Canal Street (212) 966-7765
New York, New York 10013 Founded 1932

Retail hand laundry operators in the New York City area; membership primarily persons of Chinese descent.

CHINESE INSTITUTE OF ENGINEERS - U.S.A.
c/o Vincent Chu
1310 Woodland Circle
Bethlehem, Pennsylvania 18017 (215) 867-0909
Director: Vincent Chu Founded 1953

Professional engineers and scientists. Scientific and educational organization which promotes communication among engineers and scientists who are interested in the well-being of the Chinese engineering community in the United States and abroad. Engages in on-site visits of factories and plants in Taiwan, Republic of China as part of a program to encourage the modernization of Taiwan's industry; hopes to develop a similar program with Singapore. Holds special computer training sessions; sponsors scholarships; bestows awards. Maintains a library. Originally founded in 1917 as the Chinese Institute of Engineers, which moved to China; was reactivated as a separate organization in 1953. Formerly (1977) Chinese Institute of Engineers, New York.
Publications: Communication, quarterly; Convention Journal, annual; also publishes Operation Manual, Directory of Members and booklet.

CHINESE LIBRARIANS ASSOCIATION
Post Office Box 2688
Stanford, California 94305 (714) 265-6715
Executive Officer: Susana Liu Founded 1974

Librarians of Chinese descent; supportive individuals; students of library science. Objectives are: to enhance the abilities of Chinese librarians to contribute towards the development of librarianship; to further their common interests. Programs and activities include: periodic meetings; workshops and conferences; research

in library and information services; cultural exhibitions; book fairs; publications work.
Publications: Newsletter, quarterly.

Public Affairs Organizations

CHINESE FOR AFFIRMATIVE ACTION
121 Waverly Place
San Francisco, California 94108 (415) 398-8212
Executive Director: Henry Der Founded 1969

Individuals and corporations which seek equal opportunity and civil rights for Chinese Americans. Works with the Chinese-American community to help insure fair treatment under the law in matters dealing with employment; has cooperated with state and local governmental agencies to help develop bilingual materials to aid Asian American job applicants; encourages the appointment and participation of Chinese Americans on public boards and commissions that influence the welfare of Chinese Americans. Works to secure a fair share of public resources for the Chinese American; induces broadcast stations to produce public affairs programming and to present accurate portrayals of Chinese Americans. Provides counseling information on legal rights and makes referrals to sources of additional assistance; assists employers in meeting affirmative action goals. Trains Asian Americans to be public speakers and community spokesmen. Maintains library of video and audio tapes on Asian/Chinese Americans. Provides speakers and guests for public and private institutions and radio and television shows. Produced children's television series.
Publications: Newsletter, monthly; also publishes "Practical English" books and tapes, and Citizenship Made Easy.

COMMITTEE FOR A FREE CHINA
1015 18th Street, Northwest
Suite 805
Washington, D.C. 20036 (202) 223-8596
President: Dr. Ray S. Cline Founded 1972

To support and encourage freedom and peace in Asia by the establishment of full relations with free China. The Committee's immediate task is to ensure continuation and growth of the Republic of China's economic strength, adequate increase of its defense capabilities, and improvement of its relations with the United States. Serves as a national clearinghouse for information about Communist China and Free China. Supports Chinese refugee leaders on United States speaking tours. Offers financial assistance to mainland China refugees in Hong Kong. Supersedes: Committee of One Million (founded 1953).
Publications: The China Letter, monthly; also publishes brochures and reprints of articles and speeches.

INTERNATIONAL COMMITTEE FOR HUMAN RIGHTS IN TAIWAN
Post Office Box 5205
Seattle, Washington 98105 (206) 723-0062
U.S. Coordinator: G. VanDerWess Founded 1976

Individuals and organizations interested in human rights violations in Taiwan. Collects and disseminates information; campaigns for the release of political prisoners. Supports establishment of a free and democratic political system in Taiwan. Occasionally organizes lectures on political developments. Submits testimony to Congressional hearings.
Publications: Taiwan Communique, monthly.

NATIONAL COMMITTEE ON UNITED STATES-CHINA RELATIONS
777 United Nations Plaza
Room 9B
New York, New York 10017 (212) 682-6848
President: Arthur H. Rosen Founded 1966

Nonpartisan educational and exchange organization which encourages public interest and understanding of China and United States-China relations. Membership is by invitation. Does not adopt or advocate policy proposals, but has encouraged a national dialogue on China through public symposia, seminars for opinion leaders in business, education, journalism, academia and a speakers bureau service. Has become active in the areas of cultural, educational, civic, sports and performing arts exchanges with China. Administered the United States visit of the Table Tennis team from the People's Republic of China in April, 1972. Since that time it has sponsored reciprocal visits of acrobatic, sports and performing arts delegations; visits of leaders of world affairs, civic affairs and educational organizations. Seeks to facilitate such exchanges through consultation, referrals and direct staff support. Prepares specialized briefing kits on China. Has produced "China Conversations," a series of audiotaped interviews with China specialists.
Publications: Notes, quarterly; also publishes books and reports of delegations.

ORGANIZATION FOR THE SUPPORT OF DEMOCRATIC MOVEMENT OF TAIWAN
Post Office Box 53447
Chicago, Illinois 60615 (312) 752-1355
President: Peter Chen Founded 1979

Professionals and students from Taiwan involved in promoting the country's democratic movement. Sponsors lectures and discussions. Maintains 1,000 volume library of books and periodicals from Taiwan and other United States organizations. Supersedes: Committee to Stop Secret Execution of Political Prisoners in Taiwan (founded in 1979).
Publications: Democratic Taiwan (in Chinese), bimonthly; also publishes Taiwan KMT Spy Activities on United States University Campuses (pamphlet).

ORGANIZATION OF CHINESE AMERICAN WOMEN
956 North Monroe Street
Arlington, Virginia 22201 (703) 522-6721
President: Pauline W. Tsui Founded 1977

To advance the cause of Chinese American women in the United States and to foster public awareness of their special needs and concerns. Seeks to integrate Chinese American women into the mainstream of women's activities and programs. Addresses issues such as: equal employment opportunities at both the professional and non-professional levels; overcoming of stereotypes; racial discrimination and restrictive traditional beliefs; assistance to poverty striken recent immigrants; access to leadership and policy-making positions. Develops training models for Chinese and Asian American women. Affiliated with Federation of Organizations for Professional Women and Organization of Chinese-Americans.
Publications: OCAW Speaks (newsletter), bimonthly; also publishes bibliography of Asian American women in education and employment.

ORGANIZATION OF CHINESE AMERICANS
2025 Eye Street, Northwest
Suite 926
Washington, D.C. 20006 (202) 223-5500
Executive Director: Laura Chin Founded 1973

United States citizens and permanent residents over age 18, most of whom are Chinese Americans. Objectives are: to advance the cause and foster public awareness of the needs and concerns of Chinese Americans in the United States; to promote participation through advancement of equal rights, responsibilities and opportunities; to promote cultural awareness; and to unite Chinese Americans. Activities include: eradicating negative stereotypes and advocating special needs (such as those of refugees); creating closer ties between industry and Chinese Americans; sponsoring cultural exhibitions and festivals. Is currently producing a textbook on the Chinese in America. Sponsors organizational, cultural, educational and political seminars and charitable programs such as aid to Indochinese refugees. Bestows awards to distinguished Chinese Americans. Maintains speakers bureau and biographical archives. Conducts research programs; compiles statistics.
Publications: Image (newsletter), bimonthly; Convention Proceedings, semiannual; Membership Directory, semiannual; also publishes chapter newsletters and advocacy alerts.

U.S.-CHINA PEOPLES FRIENDSHIP ASSOCIATION
635 South Westlake
Room 202
Los Angeles, California 90057 (213) 483-5810
President: Unita Blackwell Founded 1974

Individuals united to build active and lasting friendship based on mutual understanding between the people of the United States and the people of China. Works to develop cultural, academic and commercial relations between the two countries. Assists other organizations in developing ties with the People's Republic of China. Arranges study tours to China, and hosts visiting China delegations. Promotes the exchange of visitors. Operates Center for Teaching about China.
Publications: U.S.-China Review (magazine), bimonthly; Teaching about China (newsletter), quarterly; also publishes pamphlets resource catalogs, films and photo exhibits and curriculum material for American schools.

Cultural and Educational Organizations

AMERICAN ASSOCIATION FOR CHINESE STUDIES
Sun Yat Sen Hall
Saint John's University
Jamaica, New York 11439
Executive Secretary: Abraham P. Ho (212) 969-8000
Founded 1958

Scholars engaged in teaching Chinese language and/or Chinese cultural subjects in American colleges and universities, and persons interested in Chinese culture. Promotes cooperation among its members, especially in pedagogical matters. Conducts research in teaching of Chinese language and culture; compiles statistics. Formerly American Association of Teachers of Chinese Language and Culture.
Publications: Newsletter, semiannual; Directory of Members, irregular; also publishes monographs and teaching aids.

CENTER FOR CHINESE RESEARCH MATERIALS
Association of Research Libraries
1527 New Hampshire Avenue, Northwest
Washington, D.C. 20036 (202) 387-7172
Director: P. K. Yu Founded 1967

Established in an effort to fill gaps in the study of contemporary China by attempting to maintain complete records of Chinese language publications and by helping libraries and scholars strengthen collections of Chinese monographs, periodicals and newspapers. Established because the flow of publications from mainland China has been erratic and intermittent since the late 1930's, resulting in deficiencies in libraries which support extensive study and research programs on China. Policy guidance is provided by an advisory committee of three professors in Chinese studies and three librarians. Funded by the Mellon Foundation and the National Endowment for the Humanities.
Publication: Newsletter, irregular.

CENTER FOR TEACHING ABOUT CHINA
c/o U.S.-China Peoples Friendship Association
407 South Dearborn, Suite 945
Chicago, Illinois 60605 (312) 663-9608
Director: Mary Kay Hobbs Founded 1977

Teachers at all levels; Asian outreach personnel; interested individuals. A national clearinghouse for instructional materials on China. Offers assistance and consultation in developing classroom programs, courses and materials on China; keeps abreast of and evaluates new classroom materials. Supplies display material and conducts workshops for local, regional and national educational conferences. Sponsors a tour program to enable teachers to visit China. Affiliated with U.S.-China Peoples Friendship Association (parent).
Publications: Teaching About China (newsletter), quarterly; China in the Classroom (resource catalog), annual, with supplements; also publishes China Study Series of pamphlets on different subject areas concerning China.

CHINA COUNCIL OF THE ASIA SOCIETY
1785 Massachusetts Avenue, Northwest
Washington, D.C. 20036 (202) 387-6500
Program Director: Robert B. Oxnam Founded 1975

An educational organization seeking fresh approaches to American public education about China. Develops adult educational materials on major themes concerning traditional and contemporary Chinese affairs as well as United States - China relations. Provides briefing material and consultation for the American print and broadcast media. Sponsors lectures by specialists on Chinese affairs.
Publication: China Council Report, quarterly.

CHINA INSTITUTE IN AMERICA
125 East 65th Street
New York, New York 10021 (212) 744-8181
President: F. Richard Hsu Founded 1926

To promote better understanding between the American and Chinese peoples and to serve the Chinese ethnic minority in the United States. School of Chinese Studies offers a full curriculum dealing with Chinese language and culture. Academic courses include art history, the Chinese-American heritage, contemporary China, folklore, geography, history, language (both Mandarin and Cantonese dialect), literature, philosophy, religion and Sino-American relations. Studio courses include calligraphy, cooking and nutrition, dance, music, painting and Taichichuan. China House Gallery presents semiannual exhibitions of unusual facets of classical Chinese art. The Center for Community Study and Service investigates and develops programs in areas of interest and concern to the Chinese community in the United States. Maintains a research library of books, pamphlets and other materials relating to the Chinese experience in America.
Publications: Exhibition Catalogs, semiannual; also publishes School Catalog.

CHINA PHILATELIC STUDY GROUP
Box 630, North Avenue
Millbrook, New York 12545
Executive Officer: Eugene Klein (914) 677-3950
Founded 1978

Individuals interested in the study of Chinese postal history. Conducts local and international exhibitions of stamps and coins. Maintains library which specializes in China and its postal history. Sponsors competitions; bestows awards; conducts charitable program.
Publications: China (bulletin), four times a year; China Trader (newsletter), four times a year.

CHINA STAMP SOCIETY (Philatelic)
c/o Frederik C. J. DeRidder
100 Font Boulevard - Parkmerced
San Francisco, California 94132
Secretary: Frederik C. J. DeRidder (415) 334-8506
Founded 1936

Individuals who collect stamps and study postal history of China and related areas such as Hong Kong, Shanghai, and treaty ports, Tibet, Formosa, Taiwan, Korea, Mongolia, Macao, and Manchukuo. To create a

spirit of fraternity among members, to encourage research through mutual exchange of information and assistance, and to promote interest in this branch of philately. Maintains library; bestows annual award for outstanding literary contributions and exhibits.
Publications: China Clipper, bimonthly; Membership Directory, annual.

CHINESE-AMERICAN CULTURAL ASSOCIATION
8122 Mayfield Road
Chesterland, Ohio 44026 (216) 729-9937

An organization aimed at preserving Chinese culture in the United States by offering courses, developing a library and publishing a journal.
Publications: Pamir, monthly (1973-).

CHINESE CULTURAL ASSOCIATION
Post Office Box 1272
Palo Alto, California 94302
Board Director: Professor P.F. Tao (415) 948-2251
Founded 1966

Professors, scientists, engineers, artists, physicians, and businessmen. Founded to promote communication between the members and mutual understanding between the Chinese and people of other countries. Sponsors social meetings, lectures, concerts, painting, and dancing exhibitions, films, seminars, and discussions.
Publications: Journal, two or three times a year; Newsletter, four or five times a year.

CHINESE-ENGLISH TRANSLATION ASSISTANCE GROUP
Box 400
9811 Connecticut Avenue
Kensington, Maryland 20795
Executive Secretary: Jim Mathias (301) 946-7006
Founded 1971

Chinese language and computer specialists from academia, government and business. Participatory cooperative organization designed to improve computer-stored and printed Chinese-English dictionaries. Currently developing Chinese-English dictionaries of general terms and scientific and technical terms. All dictionaries and bibliographies are computer stored, computer revised and computer printed. Also specializes in research and dissemination of information on Chinese language characteristics relevant to translation; assessment of current systems of machine-aided translation, optical character reading and computer input/output. Maintains 300 volume library of Chinese dictionaries.
Publications: Bulletin, irregular; also publishes research papers, Modern Chinese Colloquial Dictionary and Bibliography of 2,000 Chinese Dictionaries.

CHINESE HISTORICAL SOCIETY OF AMERICA
17 Adler Place
San Francisco, California 94133 (415) 391-1188
President: Ernest Chan Founded 1963

Persons interested in studying and preserving manuscripts, books, works of art or their facsimiles, and other artifacts which have a bearing on the history of the Chinese living in the United States. Promotes knowledge of the contributions the Chinese have made to America. Established a small museum and a collection of documents and clippings.
Publications: Bulletin, monthly; also published anniversary bulletin of articles on Chinese immigrants to the United States; also publishes The Chinese in America (catalog), books and a syllabus.

CHINESE LANGUAGE COMPUTER SOCIETY
c/o Professor S. K. Chang
Department of Information Engineering
Box 4348
University of Illinois - Chicago
Chicago, Illinois 60680 (312) 996-5490
President: Dr. Tien Chi Chen Founded 1976

Data processing, scientific and engineering professionals interested in Chinese language processing. To advance the study, design, development, construction and application of modern computer systems for general information processing in Chinese as well as other languages such as Japanese and Korean. Promotes the free exchange of information about Chinese language information processing; sponsors and co-sponsors conferences. Addresses such issues as the problem of automatic understanding of Chinese and whether it can be solved by faster, more current hardware or by new techniques in encoding, programming and heuristics (exploratory problem solving techniques utilizing self-education).
Publications: Newsletter, three times a year; also publishes conference proceedings.

CHINESE LANGUAGE TEACHERS ASSOCIATION
Institute of Far Eastern Studies
Seton Hall University
South Orange, New Jersey 07079
Secretary-Treasurer: Professor John Young (201) 761-9447
Founded 1963

Teachers and scholars of the Chinese language in colleges and schools. Promotes the study of Chinese language, linguistics, and literature. Organizes panels on Chinese language and literature. Maintains a placement service. Affiliated with Modern Language Association; Association for Asian Studies; American Council on the Teaching of Foreign Languages.
Publications: Journal, three times a year; Newsletter, three times a year; Directory, annual.

CHINESE MUSIC SOCIETY OF NORTH AMERICA
2329 Charmingfare
Woodridge, Illinois 60515 (312) 985-1600
President: Sin-Yan Shen Founded 1976

Individuals interested in increasing their knowledge of theoretical and applied Chinese music. Sponsors lectures and concerts to heighten understanding and appreciation of Chinese music by the public. Coordinates field projects and conferences which enable members to interact with experts in Chinese music on an international scale. Maintains library of scores, books and music consulting service which guides members in selecting recordings, books and other materials concerning Chinese music.
Publications: Chinese Music (journal), quarterly; also publishes educational materials and music recordings.

CHINESE MUSICAL AND THEATRICAL ASSOCIATION
181 Canal Street
New York, New York 10013
Executive Chairman: Stanley Chiu (212) 226-8744
Founded 1934

Founded to perpetuate Chinese culture and customs; to disseminate Chinese music and art.

COMMITTEE ON SCHOLARLY COMMUNICATIONS WITH MAINLAND CHINA
c/o National Research Council
National Academy of Sciences
2101 Constitution Avenue
Washington, D.C. 20418 (202) 334-2000

CONFERENCE FOR CHINESE ORAL AND PERFORMING LITERATURE
China-Japan Program
140 Uris Hall, Cornell University
Ithaca, New York 14853
Secretary-Editor: Harold Shadick (607) 256-6222
Founded 1969

To foster knowledge of Chinese oral and performing literature; to provide a written and/or taped record of such literature and of papers written concerning it. Conducts research programs and specialized education.
Publications: CHINOPERL Papers, annual.

FRIENDS OF FREE CHINA
1629 K Street, Northwest
Washington, D.C. 20006
Executive Director: Jack E. Buttram (202) 356-0706
Founded 1973

Individuals interested in promoting understanding and appreciation of Chinese achievements, culture and society. Attempts to show Americans a factual picture of various aspects of life in China. Sponsors discussions, cultural events, annual tour of the Republic of China, and high school speech and essay contest. Bestows awards; provides speakers.
Publications: Newsletter, every six weeks.

HAWAII CHINESE HISTORY CENTER
111 North King Street
Room 410
Honolulu, Hawaii 96817 (808) 521-5948

Promotes interest in the cultural and historical aspects of the Chinese in Hawaii.
Publications: Newsletter; also publishes pamphlets and books.

INSTITUTE OF CHINESE CULTURE
86 Riverside Drive
New York, New York 10024
Executive Officer: Dr. Liang-Chien Cha (212) 787-6969
Founded 1944

Scholars, community leaders and others who are interested in China. Purpose is to further cultural relations between the United States and the Republic of China and to promote cultural and educational programs and activities among the American and Chinese people. Sponsors Chinese Forum, art exhibits; holds cultural classes in Chinese art and in the Chinese language; offers lecturing service. Presents awards for scholarly achivements.

INTERNATIONAL CHINESE SNUFF BOTTLE SOCIETY
2601 North Charles Street
Baltimore, Maryland 21218
Vice President and Secretary: John G. Ford (301) 467-9400
Founded 1968

Collectors interested in snuff bottles. The bottles, which were made only in China toward the beginning of the Ch'ing Dynasty (middle 17th Century), are generally two to four inches in height and have been rendered in many kinds of materials; they may be inlaid, enameled, carved, painted or otherwise finished. Promotes scholarship regarding the nature and sources of snuff bottles; holds exhibits. Sponsors competitions and presents awards. Formerly (1975) Chinese Snuff Bottle Society.
Publications: Chinese Snuff Bottle Journal, quarterly; Directory, biennial.

SINO-AMERICAN CULTURAL SOCIETY
Van Ness Center
4301 Connecticut Avenue, Northwest
Suite 131
Washington, D.C. 20008 (202) 686-1638
President: Dr. William G. Carr Founded 1958

Educational organization formed to arrange educational and cultural programs related to China and the United States. Encourages the performance of Chinese music, drama, and opera. Holds art exhibits. Edits pamphlets and other publications on Sino-American culture and education. Assists Chinese educational leaders visiting Washington, D.C. Organizes Sino-American social functions. Awards two P.W. Kuo Scholarships in Taiwan each year.

SOCIETY FOR CH'ING STUDIES
c/o Mary Rankin
1614 44th Street, Northwest
Washington, D.C. 20007
Co-Editor: Mary Rankin Founded 1965

Purpose is to bring scholarly works dealing with Ch'ing dynasty China (17th to early 20th centuries) to libraries and scholars around the world.
Publication: Ch'ing-shih wen-t'i, semiannual.

SOCIETY FOR THE STUDY OF EARLY CHINA
c/o Department of History
University of California
Berkeley, California 94720 (415) 642-2503
Secretary: David N. Keightley Founded 1975

Professors, graduate students and scholars. Publishes articles and information about the study of early Chinese culture, promotes scholarship in the field. Formerly (1975) Society for the Study of Pre-Han China.
Publications: Early China, annual.

UNITED STATES - CHINA EDUCATIONAL INSTITUTE
1144 Pacific Avenue
San Francisco, California 94133 (415) 775-1151
President: G. Hanmin Liu Founded 1978

Board members and advisers who are health professionals, scientists, social scientists, cultural anthropologists, and writers; members represent institutional participation. Objectives are to promote the exchange of scientific and cultural knowledge and improve relations between people and institutions in the United States and the People's Republic of China; to facilitate the exchange of professionals, practitioners, and scholars in order to encourage communication and information exchange; and to promote research in medicine, biology, information science, communications, and learning theories and methods. Sponsors Scientific Education Exchange and an orientation program for scholars going to China or coming to the United States. Operates Scientific Education Clearinghouse, which acts as resource network among American and Chinese researchers and practitioners in science and technology. Plans to sponsor United States-China House Program which will develop cultural resources in such areas as Chinese and English languages, history, political science, economics, social sciences, and philosophy. Promotes research on combining Chinese and Western medicine and conducts seminars on Chinese medical education and traditional Chinese medicine. Offers colloquia and workshops.
Publications: Newsletter, quarterly.

YALE-CHINA ASSOCIATION
442 Temple Street
New Haven, Connecticut 06511
Executive Director: John Bryan Starr (203) 436-4422
Founded 1901

Yale alumni, foundations and other individuals seeking to educate Americans about China and to assist Chinese in obtaining advanced education. Provides financial support for New Asia College (of the Chinese University of Hong Kong); awards 65 scholarships and work-study grants each year to Chinese students attending the Chinese University of Hong Kong. Operates the Yale "Bachelor" program, which selects recent Yale graduates on the basis of outstanding academic and personal achievement, to undertake two-year teaching assignments at the Chinese University of Hong Kong, Hunan Medical College and Wuhan University. The program was initiated in 1910, in Hunan Province in Mainland China, but was suspended for political reasons in 1950, and was reinstituted in 1980. The Hong Kong program has been continuous since 1953. Operates a contemporary Chinese Studies Program at its New Haven offices; and is recruiting agent for North America for the International Asian Studies Program at the Chinese University of Hong Kong. Formerly(1975) Yale-in-China Association.
Publications: China Update (newsletter), quarterly; Newsletter, semiannual; Annual Report; has also published Yale-in-China - The Mainland, 1901-1950; and Hsiang-Ya Journal.

Foundations

CHINESE-AMERICAN EDUCATIONAL FOUNDATION
1609 East Peachtree
Arlington Heights, Illinois 60004 (312) 398-0325
Secretary: Sheila Hung Founded 1965

Supported by individuals, churches, and corporations interested in aiding youth for higher education. Grants scholarships for college students in Taiwan, and Youth Awards to American high school graduates of Chinese descent.
Publications: Letter to Members, irregular; also published A List of Doctoral Dissertations by Chinese Students in the United States, 1961-64.

CHINESE CULTURE FOUNDATION OF SAN FRANCISCO
750 Kearny Street
San Francisco, California 94108
Executive Director: Rolland C. Lowe (415) 982-1822
Founded 1965

Members include individuals from the Chinese communities of the San Francisco Bay area, including Mandarin, Cantonese and English speaking people of all ages, residents of inner-city Chinatown and suburban areas, new immigrants, American-born Chinese and the general public. A neighborhood Arts Program of the San Francisco Arts Commission facilitates the activities of over thirty community groups year round. Promotes understanding and appreciation of Chinese and Chinese-American culture and history in the United States. Offers educational and cultural programs including art exhibitions, lecture and film series, workshops in the performing arts, classes, research projects, Chinatown Walks. Also sponsors events in conjunction with academic and cultural organizations in the Bay Area to expand resources and offerings and to promote cooperation among the various groups and individuals interested in Chinese and Chinese-American culture and history.

JOINT COMMITTEE ON CONTEMPORARY CHINA
Social Science Research Council
605 Third Avenue
New York, New York 10016 (212) 557-9500

Sponsored by Social Science Research Council and American Council of Learned Societies (see separate entries). Awards dissertation grants to social scientists and humanists doing research on modern and pre-modern China. Offers post-doctoral awards for scholars doing research on post-1911 China.

Charitable Organizations

AMERICAN BUREAU FOR MEDICAL ADVANCEMENT IN CHINA
Two East 103rd Street
New York, New York 10029
Executive Director: John R. Watt (216) 860-1990
Founded 1937

Cooperates with medical and health personnel in the support of a broad program of medical and health services for the Chinese people. Provides consultants for development projects and visiting professors for longer term teaching and clinical assignments in Taiwan. Sponsors fellowships for study, research and observation in the United States. Organizes research projects for treatment of diseases prevalent in Southeast Asia. Provides medical equipment, supplies and publications. Maintains biographical archives. Formerly (1978) American Bureau for Medical Aid to China.
Publications: Bulletin, quarterly; Annual Report.

CHINA MEDICAL BOARD OF NEW YORK
622 Third Avenue
New York, New York 10017
President: Patrick A. Ongley, M.D. (212) 682-8000
Founded 1928

Purpose is to support programs of medical, nursing and public health education and research. Assists local institutions in improving the health levels and services in Asian Societies. Seeks to improve the quality and increase the numbers of appropriate health practitioners in these societies. Has programs in Korea, Taiwan, Hong Kong, the Philippines, Thailand, Malaysia, Singapore, Indonesia and China. Endowed by the Rockefeller Foundation and controlled by an independent board of trustees, who serve without compensation. Formerly devoted entire income to support of Peking Union Medical College, nationalized in 1951 by Peoples Republic of China. Reports published annually. Formerly (1955) China Medical Board.

CHINESE AMERICAN WELFARE ASSOCIATION
151 Canal Street
New York, New York (212) 431-6314

CHINESE DEVELOPMENT COUNCIL
5 Division Street
New York, New York 10002 (212) 966-6340
Executive Director: David Ho Founded 1968

Immigrants and youth groups, including high school clubs and youth gangs. Established to meet the pressing problems of immigrants in New York's Chinatown. Begun by volunteers, CDC conducts a Manpower Training and Referral Program to train unemployed and refer underemployed to better paying jobs. Also offers sewing classes, educational counseling, a food stamp program, English language classes, typing, bookkeeping, restaurant management class, and recreation activities. Presents the annual Exxon Community Leadership Award. Formerly called the Chinese Youth Council.

Religious Organizations

AMERICAN MISSION TO THE CHINESE AND ASIAN
144-25 Roosevelt Avenue
Flushing, New York 11354
President: Rev. Dr. Peter P. S. Ching — (212) 461-5756
Founded 1945

Interdenominational organization founded by Americans to spread the Gospel among the Chinese. Sponsors mission work in Hong Kong-Kowloon-Macao, Mainland China and other Asian areas, including India, Philippines, Indonesia, Singapore and Madagascar. Supports medical and educational institutions and distributes donated funds, clothing, food, and medicine for Asian and Chinese refugees in the Far East. Provides relief and adoption services for refugee children and orphans. Promotes the sale in the United States of products handmade by refugees, in order to increase employment in Hong Kong. Maintains employment, legal, immigration, and marriage counseling services in the United States. Conducts educational, agricultural, medical, and scientific exchange, Christian education training programs, and research studies of southeastern Asian economic and social problems. Sponsors the Chinese Culture Institute of the International College of Art and Science. Formerly called the Far Eastern Refugee Service, American Mission to the Chinese.
Publications: Bulletin, monthly; Evangel Refugee, annual.

CHINESE APOSTOLATE ARCHDIOCESE OF NEW YORK
105 Park Avenue
New York, New York — (212) 619-0875

EVANGELIZE CHINA FELLOWSHIP
Post Office Box 418
Pasadena, California 91102
General Director: Dr. Paul C. C. Szeto — (213) 793-5444
Founded 1947

Carries on a program of education, relief, and religious work in Hong Kong, Macao, Thailand, Malaya, Singapore, Indonesia, and Taiwan. Conducts its educational programs in schools, orphanages, and churches.
Publication: News, quarterly.

SINO-AMERICAN BUDDHIST ASSOCIATION
Gold Mountain Dhyana Monastery
1731 Fifteenth Street — (415) 861-9672
San Francisco, California 94103 — Founded 1971

Activities include nightly Sutra lectures by members of the Sangha, daily recreation and meditation periods, Dharma Realm Buddhist University Extension classes, meditation sessions. Affiliated with Gold Wheel Temple, the International Institute for the Translation of Buddhist Texts and the City of Ten Thousand Buddhas.

VOICE OF CHINA AND ASIA MISSIONARY SOCIETY
Post Office Box 15-M
Pasadena, California 91102
President: Reverend Robert B. Hammond — (213) 796-3117
Founded 1946

To proclaim the gospel of Christ throughout Asia, the Far East and the world, through missionaries, literature, evangelism, and radio broadcasts. Sponsors medical clinics and hospitals in Asia and supports medical care units for lepers in Korea, Taiwan and India. Gives aid to homes for the needy, handicapped, widowed and elderly. Holds conferences for Bible study and sponsors youth camps for the training of future Christian leaders and for youth evangelism. Has established schools and churches worldwide. Supersedes: China Peniel Missionary Society (founded 1939).
Publications: Flashlight (booklet), monthly.

Research Centers and Special Institutes

CENTER FOR CHINESE STUDIES
University of California
12 Barrows Hall
Berkeley, California 94720 (415) 642-6510
Chairman: Dr. Lowell Dittmer Founded 1957

Conducts research on economics, law, international relations, military affairs, social welfare, organization, politics, anthropology, sociology, and history of Communist China. Also provides limited support for graduate students and visiting scholars in the social sciences specializing in Communist China. Research results are published in books, monographs, and professional journals. Holds occasional seminars, regional seminars, and colloquia. Maintains a library of more than 23,000 volumes on social sciences about Communist China.
Publications: Studies in Communist Chinese Terminology; China Research Monograph Series; also sponsors a series of books on China published by the University of California Press.

CENTER FOR CHINESE STUDIES
University of Michigan
104 Lane Hall
Ann Arbor, Michigan 48104 (313) 764-6308
Acting Director: Allen S. Whitney Founded 1961

An integral unit of the College of Literature, Science and the Arts at the University of Michigan. Pursues research on the economic history and social structure of modern China, the economy of communist China, Chinese communist law, Chinese history, colloquial literature, linguistics, and painting. Also promotes and supports research in social sciences and humanities relating to China by faculty members, graduate students, and associates of the Center. Coordinates teaching and research programs at the University in those areas. Publishes research results in professional journals, books, and occasional papers. Holds public lectures and research colloquia on China during the academic year and weekly luncheon seminars for staff members, students, and visitors. Maintains a library of over 100,000 units of Chinese language materials in social sciences and humanities, also Chinese language periodicals.
Publications: Michigan Papers in Chinese Studies; and reprint series.

CHINA-JAPAN PROGRAM
Cornell University
Ithaca, New York 14853 (607) 256-6222
Director: Dr. Tsu-Lin Mei Founded 1950

Research program of the Department of Asian Studies at Cornell University but with its own board of control. Originally known as the China Program. Principal fields of research: History, government, sociology, literature, fine arts, anthropology, and linguistics of China and Japan, with major concentration on social science research on China. Collaborates closely with South Asia and Southeast Asia Programs of the Department. Research results are published in books and professional journals. Maintains an extensive library of Chinese and Japanese language books, monographs, and journals on China, particularly strong on nineteenth century history and modern China.

CHINA PROGRAM
School of International Studies
DR-05
University of Washington
Seattle, Washington
Chairman: Jack L. Dull (206) 543-4391

Provides interdisciplinary studies in economics, geography, history, literature, poetry, linguistics, philosophy, anthropology, political science, art, music and psychiatry on undergraduate and master's level leading to degrees in international studies with a concentration in China regional studies.
Publications: Parega (occasional papers).

CHINESE LANGUAGE INFORMATION CENTER
Seton Hall University
South Orange, New Jersey 07079 (201) 762-9000
Head: Professor Winston Yang Founded 1964

An integral unit of the Department of Asian Studies at Seton Hall University, but with its own board of control. Conducts research on the teaching of Chinese and Japanese languages, including the collection of teaching and research materials, creation of audiovisual teaching aids, furnishing information to the profession and issuing annotated bibliographies. Maintains a reference library.

INSTITUTE FOR SINO-SOVIET STUDIES
George Washington University
Washington, D.C. 20052 (202) 676-6340
Director: Dr. Gaston Sigur Founded 1962

A unit of the School of Public and International Affairs at George Washington University. Pursues research programs on the historical, political, economic, sociological, psychological, cultural, geographic, legal, ideological, and military aspects of Communist China, Soviet Union and Eastern Europe, communism in the new states, and the role of the communist bloc in international relations. Also offers a graduate program of interdisciplinary studies of communist affairs at the University, including specialized courses based on research in progress and on contemporary events. Publishes research results in books, monographs, and articles. Holds weekly colloquia and presents lectures by prominent visitors.

INSTITUTE OF POLITICAL PSYCHOLOGY
Brooklyn College
Brooklyn, New York 11210 (212) 780-5031
Director: Dr. Ivan D. London Founded 1961

Integral unit of Department of Psychology at Brooklyn College, a division of City University of New York. Principal research concerns the political psychology of communist nations, particularly China, including empirical studies. Research results published in books, professional journals and monographs.

INTERNATIONAL INSTITUTE FOR THE TRANSLATION OF BUDDHIST TEXTS
3636 Washington Street
San Francisco, California 94103

Translates the Buddhist Canon into English and other major Western languages and trains translators using a combination of traditional and up-to-date scientific methods. Currently engaged in preparing a translation of the 100-volume Tripitika. Institute also provides residential quarters for bhiksunis and lay women connected with the Sino-American Buddhist Association, a library and research facilities and a Buddhahall.

RESEARCH INSTITUTE ON THE SINO-SOVIET BLOC
131 Intervale Road
Chestnut Hill, Massachusetts 02167
Executive Director: Professor Peter S. H. Tang (617) 969-6778
Founded 1959

Academic institution dedicated to the study of the world communist movement, with particular emphasis on the roles of the U.S.S.R. and People's Republic of China. Through its research facilities, seeks to cooperate with scholars in the field and other research institutions, nationally and internationally, in advancing world knowledge and understanding of current problems integrally connected with communism. Current research interests include: Sino-Soviet relations; communist ideology; government and politics of the countries of the Sino-Soviet bloc, and communist movement in Africa, Asia and Latin America. Maintains library of 85,000 volumes including books, periodicals, newspapers, translation series on Communist bloc countries and Yugoslavia and material on international communist movement in general. Publishes book series, monograph series, pamphlet series and reprint series.

Museums

CHINA HOUSE GALLERY
125 East 65th Street
New York, New York 10021 (212) 744-8181
Director: F. Richard Hsu Founded 1966

The gallery is affiliated with the China Institute in America and exhibits loan collections of Chinese art. Offers guided tours, lectures, and gallery talks.

CHINESE ART GALLERY
3522 Southeast Hawthorne Boulevard
Portland, Oregon 97402 (503) 235-1064

CHINESE CULTURE CENTER GALLERY
750 Kearny Street
San Francisco, California 94108 (415) 986-1822
Acting Director: Vivian Chiang Founded 1965

Museum collections include photographs pertaining to the Chinese American historical experience, Chinese art, folk art and crafts. Maintains a library and auditorium. Offers tours, lectures, seminars, classes, films, TV and radio programs, docent program and traveling exhibition. Museum shop sells Chinese folk art and crafts, works by Chinese and Chinese American artists.

CHINESE HISTORICAL SOCIETY OF AMERICA
17 Adler Place (415) 391-1188
San Francisco, California 94133 Founded 1963

Located in the San Francisco Public Library. Collections include art, artifacts and archival materials of importance in the history of Chinese Americans.

CHINESE MUSEUM
Box 12
Fiddletown, California 95629
President, Fiddletown Preservation Society: Marie Scofield (209) 296-4519
Founded 1968

The museum is housed in a rammed earth adobe joss house dating from 1850 and exhibits Chinese and early California artifacts. Research centers on Chinese history in Fiddletown.

CHINESE MUSEUM AND CHINESE DRAGON
8 Mott Street
New York, New York 10013 (212) 964-1542

MUSEUM OF THE AMERICAN CHINA TRADE
215 Adams Street
Milton, Massachusetts 02186 (617) 696-1815

Collections included artifacts and memorabilia of the New England China trade. The Museum maintains a library and archive on America-China trade, Chinese history and art with special collections of journals and documents relating to specific China traders such as Robert Bennet Forbes and Samuel Shaw.

NEW ENGLAND CENTER FOR CONTEMPORARY ART
Route 169
Brooklyn, Connecticut 06234 (203) 774-8899
Director: Henry Riseman Founded 1975

Collections include an important woodblock print collection from the People's Republic of China as well as a print collection from Russia. Research centers primarily on contemporary Chinese art from the People's Republic.

OROVILLE CHINESE TEMPLE
1500 Broderick Street
Oroville, California 95965
Director of Parks: Jim P. Carpenter (916) 533-1496
Founded 1863

A preserved and restored Chinese Temple dating from 1863, including religious figures, tapestries, writings, screens, altars. Museum maintains a library and gift shop. Guided tours are available.

VIRGINIA CITY CHINATOWN CORPORATION
Union and "I" Streets, Box 6
Virginia City, Nevada 89440 (702) 847-0645
President: Gwendolyn B. Lynch Founded 1976

Shows the life of Chinese miners who brought their culture and traditions to Nevada's mining frontier. There are eleven buildings reconstructed on the museum site, including an opium den, Tong Hall and various Chinese businesses.

WEAVERVILLE JOSS HOUSE STATE HISTORICAL MONUMENT
State Historic Park (916) 623-5284
Weaverville, California 96093 Founded 1956

Historic Joss House, a Chinese temple of worship, was constructed by Chinese gold miners in 1874 and has been in continuous use since then. The furnishings were brought over from China in 1874. Contains objects depicting the role of the Chinese in the history of California, and articles relating to the function of a Taoist temple of worship. Tours are provided.

WING LUKE MEMORIAL MUSEUM
414 Eighth Avenue, South
Seattle, Washington 98104 (206) 623-5124
Director: Margaret Marshall Founded 1966

The museum is named for Seattle's first City Councilman of Chinese descent. Collections center on Asian Americans and especially the Chinese in the history of Seattle and the Pacific Northwest. They include folk art and artifacts of daily life, clothing, photographs and documents. The museum offers guided tours, educational programs in art, calligraphy, language and herbal medicine, and traveling exhibition. Maintains a Chinese-language library.

Special Libraries and Subject Collections

CENTER FOR CHINESE RESEARCH MATERIALS
1527 New Hampshire Avenue, Northwest
Washington, D.C. 20036 (202) 387-7172
Director: P. K. Yu Founded 1968

The library maintained by the Center includes books, monographs, serials and microfilm for research purposes. In addition, materials generated by the Center's research staff are sold.

CENTER FOR CHINESE STUDIES - LIBRARY
University of California, Berkeley
Barrows Hall, Room 64
Berkeley, California 94720 (415) 642-6510
Head: Chi-Peng Chen Founded 1959

Subjects: China since 1949 (social sciences and humanities of Peoples' Republic of China); Chinese Communist movement. Special Collections: Chen, Hatano, Kei-o and Yushodo Collection (microfilm holdings); Union Research Institute Classified File on Mainland China (reels of microfilm). Holdings: Books; journals and other serials; maps; reels of microfilm; pamphlets; sound recordings. Services: Interlibrary loans; copying; library open to outside users for reference only.

CHATHAM SQUARE BRANCH
The New York Public Library
33 East Broadway
New York, New York 10002
Librarian: Virginia Swift (212) 964-6598

Subjects: New York's Chinatown; Chinese in the United States; Chinese language; local Chinese newspapers; Chinese popular and classical music. Holdings: Books, vertical files, newspapers, phonodiscs. Facilities: Photocopying.

CHINA INSTITUTE IN AMERICA LIBRARY
125 East 65th Street
New York, New York 10021 (212) 744-8181
President: F. Richard Hsu Founded 1926

Subjects: Chinese immigration, heritage and contribution to America. Holdings: Books, periodicals, newspapers, archival materials, films. Facilities: Films, lectures, photocopying.

CHINATOWN BRANCH
Chicago Public Library
3214 South Wentworth Avenue (312) 326-4255
Chicago, Illinois 60616 Founded 1972

Subjects: Chinese interest and history, Chinese Americans. Holdings: Books, periodicals, audiovisual materials, works of art. Library is located in the Chinatown area of Chicago.

CHINATOWN BRANCH
Los Angeles Public Library
536 West College Street
Los Angeles, California 90012 (213) 620-0925
Librarian: Juliana Cheng Founded 1977

Subjects: Chinese history and culture; Chinese Americans. Holdings: Books, periodicals, audiovisual materials.

CHINESE AMERICAN CULTURAL ASSOCIATION LIBRARY
8122 Mayfield
Chesterland, Ohio 44026 (216) 729-9937
Director: Peter Wang Founded 1963

Subjects: Chinese American heritage and history.
Holdings: Books, periodicals, manuscripts.
Services: Lectures, speaker's bureau, special programs.

CHINESE CONSOLIDATED BENEVOLENT ASSOCIATION
62 Mott Street
New York, New York 10013
Director: Chung Ping Tom (212) 267-5781

Subjects: Chinese literature and history; New York's Chinatown; Chinese immigration. Holdings: Books, photographs, vertical files, documents and letters.

CHINESE CULTURAL CENTER - INFORMATIONAL AND COMMUNICATION DIVISION - LIBRARY
159 Lexington Avenue
New York, New York 10016 (212) 725-4950
Librarian: David C. Liu Founded 1972

Subjects: Political, economic, cultural, and social developments of the Republic of China; Chinese history, language, literature, art, philosophy, religion and related subjects; Chinese and international communism; foreign relations. Holdings: Books; journals and other serials; newspapers. Services: Library is open to outside users; photocopy facilities are available.
Publications: News from China (daily news reports, separate English and Chinese editions).

CHINESE CULTURE FOUNDATION OF SAN FRANCISCO - LIBRARY
750 Kearny Street
San Francisco, California 94108
Executive Director: Dr. Shirley Sun (415) 986-1822
Founded 1965

Subjects: Chinese American history and culture. Holdings: Books, periodicals, audiovisual materials, art and artifacts, oral history archive. Services: Lectures, films, seminars, classes, exhibitions, reading room.

CHINESE WOMEN'S ASSOCIATION - LIBRARY
13541 Emperor Drive
Santa Ana, California 92705 (714) 838-2620
Librarian: Ruth R. Goodman Founded 1932

Subjects: Chinese history, culture, and customs; Chinese in America. Holdings: Books; journals and other serials.

EAST ASIATIC LIBRARY
University of California, Berkeley
208 Durant Hall
Berkeley, California 94720 (415) 642-2556
Acting Head: Richard S. Cooper Founded 1947

Subjects: Publications in Chinese, Korean and Japanese languages, primarily in literature, history, social sciences and art. Holdings: Books, manuscripts, Chinese rubbings, maps, microfilms, prints and photographs, journals and other serials, newspapers. Services: Interlibrary loans; copying; library open to public for reference use only.

FAR EASTERN LIBRARY
University of Chicago
Regenstein Library
1100 East 57th Street
Chicago, Illinois 60637 (312) 753-4116
Curator: James K. M. Cheng Founded 1936

Subjects: Chinese classics, philosophy, history, archaeology, biography, social sciences, literature and art; Japanese history, social sciences, and literature. Special Collections: Chinese classics; Chinese local gazetteers, rare books. Holdings: Books, pamphlets, microfilms, journals and other serials. Services: Interlibrary loans; copying; library open to qualified visitors. Special Catalogs: Author-title catalog of Chinese Collection (8 volumes); Author-title catalog of Japanese Collection (4 volumes); classified catalog and subject index of the Chinese and Japanese Collections (6 volumes), 1974; supplements to above catalogs.
Publications: Reference List; Chinese local histories, 1969; Far Eastern serials, 1976.

GEST ORIENTAL LIBRARY AND EAST ASIAN COLLECTIONS
Princeton University
317 Palmer Hall
Princeton, New Jersey 08544 (609) 452-3183
Curator: Kang-i Sun Chang Founded 1926

Subjects: Chinese classics, philosophy, and religion; historical sciences; social sciences; language and literature; fine and recreative arts. Special Collections: Books on Buddhism; books on Chinese medicine and materia medica; books printed in the Ming dynasty, 1368-1644. Holdings: Books; journals and other serials; manuscripts; microfilms; newspapers. Services: Interlibrary loans; reference work and information service for outside inquirers on questions of general interest relating to China, Japan, and Korea.

HARVARD YENCHING INSTITUTE - LIBRARY
Harvard University
2 Divinity Avenue
Cambridge, Massachusetts 02138
Librarian: Eugene Wu (617) 495-2756

Subjects: Humanities and social sciences relating to China, Japan, and Korea. Special Collections: Rare Chinese books and manuscripts; rubs from Chinese monumental inscriptions; Tibetan religious book in wood-block print. Holdings: Books, microfilms, journals and other serials. Services: Interlibrary loans; copying.
Publications: Occasional Reference Notes.

HAWAII CHINESE HISTORY CENTER
111 North King Street
No. 410
Honolulu, Hawaii 96817 (808) 521-5948
Head Librarian: Violet L. Lai Founded 1970

Subjects: Chinese in Hawaii. Holdings: Books, monographs, periodicals, artifacts, oral history archive. Services: Lectures, films, workshops.
Publications: Hawaii Chinese History Center Newsletter, quarterly; also publishes monographs, bibliographies, catalog, annual report.

SAINT JOHN'S UNIVERSITY - ASIAN COLLECTION
Grand Central and Utopia Parkways
Jamaica, New York 11439
Librarian: Hou Ran Ferng (212) 990-6161

Subjects: Chinese literature, history, philosophy, and religions. Holdings: Books; journals and other serials; newspapers. Services: Interlibrary loans; copying; library open to public.

WASON COLLECTION ON CHINA AND THE CHINESE
Cornell University
Olin Library
Ithaca, New York 14853
Curator: Diana E. Perushek (607) 256-4357

Subjects: China and the Chinese; Far East. Holdings: Books; journals and other serials; newspapers; manuscripts; reels of microfilm. Services: Interlibrary loans; copying.

Newspapers and Newsletters

ABMAC BULLETIN. 1938-. Bimonthly. Editor: B. A. Garside. Publisher: American Bureau for Medical Aid to China, Incorporated, 1790 Broadway, New York, New York 10019. In English.

Concerned with medical and health conditions and related matters on Taiwan, and activities in the United States in support of the programs there. Covers training of doctors and nurses, postgraduate fellowships, applied research and experimentation, rehabilitation of handicapped, public health services. Features biographical sketches of ABMAC leaders, reports on meetings and speeches at annual dinners held in the United States.

BULLETIN OF THE CHINESE HISTORICAL SOCIETY OF AMERICA. 1966-. Monthly. Editor: Thomas W. Chinn. Publisher: Chinese Historical Society of America, 17 Adler Place, San Francisco, California 94133. In English.

Carries articles on topics dealing with the history of the Chinese in America and related subjects. Restricted to members of the Chinese Historical Society of America, and to other historical organizations on an exchange basis.

CENTER FOR CHINESE RESEARCH MATERIALS--NEWSLETTER, 1968-. Editor: P. K. Yu. Publisher: Association of Research Libraries, 1527 New Hampshire Avenue, Northwest, Washington, D.C. 20036. In English.

Deals with 20th century China and bibliographic materials on it, including books and collections of books, journals, archival holdings; government reports, yearbooks, handbooks, newspapers, and other periodicals. Announces new materials published and other materials reproduced and made available by the Center. Intended for scholars. Carries articles and news items on matters affecting scholarship on contemporary China.

CHINA DAILY. Semiweekly. Editor: James Lee. Publisher: China Daily News, Incorporated, 30 Market Street, New York, New York 10002. In English.

THE CHINA LETTER. 1971-. Monthly. Editor: Arthur C. Miller. Publisher: The Asia Letter, Limited, Post Office Box 54149, Los Angeles, California 90054. In English.

Provides commentary and analysis of economic, trade, political, and social developments and trends in the People's Republic of China.

CHINA POST. Daily. Editor: Jeng Shyh-rong. Publisher: Concourse Publishing Corporation, 133 Canal Street, New York, New York 10002.

CHINA TRIBUNE. 1943-. Daily. Editor: T. S. Loh. Publisher: Chinese American Cultural Corporation, 85 Walker, New York, New York 10013. In English.

CHINA UPDATE. Six times a year. Editor: The Hannaford Company, Incorporated, 1225 19th Street, Northwest, Washington, D.C. 20036. Publisher: China Update, 10960 Wilshire Boulevard, Suite 422, Los Angeles, California 90024. In English.

Prints news and news excerpts as well as commentary from the media on events in the Republic of China. Includes business and political news, special interest coverage and comment on relations with the Chinese mainland.

C A A NEWSLETTER. 1969-. Monthly. Publisher: Chinese for Affirmative Action, 950 Stockton Street, No. 3-F, San Francisco, California 94108.

Brings news of the Association's public affairs efforts and activities.

CHINESE LIBRARIANS ASSOCIATION--NEWSLETTER. 1975-. Quarterly. Editors: George Huang and Mark Tam. Publisher: Chinese Librarian Association, Post Office Box 2688, Stanford, California 94305. In English and Chinese.

Provides information of interest to Chinese librarians including bibliographies, book reviews, and listings of job opportunities. Includes schedules of activities. Publishes cumulative index every five years.

CHINESE PACIFIC WEEKLY. 1946-. Weekly. Editor: Gordon Lew. Publisher: Chinese Pacific Publishing Company, Incorporated, 838 Grant Street, San Francisco, California 94108. In Chinese.

Publishes commentaries and special news reports, as well as feature articles dealing with the ethnic situation, events in China, and national and local affairs.

CHINESE TIMES (Jin Shan Shyr Pao). 1924-. Daily. Editor: Kuang P. Yeh. Publisher: The Chinese Times Publishing Company, Incorporated, 686 Sacramento Street, San Francisco, California 94111. In Chinese.

Carries news items on domestic, foreign, and Chinese group affairs and events. Also prints medical information, editorials, stories, and poetry.

FREE CHINA WEEKLY. 1959-. Weekly. Editor: Yin Lai. Publisher: Sung Tzu-li, Kwang Hwa Publishing Company, 3-1, Chung Hsiao East Road, Sec. 1 Taipei, Taiwan 100, Republic of China. In English.

Provides news from Taiwan on politics, the economy and community topics.

NEW CHINA DAILY PRESS (Hsin Chung Kuo Jih Pao). 1900-. Daily. Editor: Yick Kam Leong. Publisher: Sun Chung Kwock Bo, Limited, 1124 Smith Street, Honolulu, Hawaii 96806. In Chinese.

Publishes news items on international, national, local, and group affairs. Includes feature articles on Chinese personalities.

PEIMEI NEWS. 1968-. Daily except Sunday. Editor: Ying Chan. Publisher: Peimei News Company, Post Office Box 799, New York, New York 10013 or 7-8 Chatham Square, 2nd Floor, New York, New York 10038. In Chinese.

Formerly called Singtaojih Pao, since 1978 the Peimei News.

SANPAN. Monthly. Publisher: CACA Multiservice Center, 18 Oxford Street, Boston, Massachusetts 02111. In Chinese.

A monthly newspaper summarizing latest developments in national, international and local news of interest to Chinese Americans.

SING TAO JIH PAO (Star Island Daily). 1910-. Daily. Editor: Valerie Kong. Publisher: Sing Tao Jih Pao, 625 Kearny, San Francisco, California 94108. In Chinese.

Prints international and national news, news from Asia in general, and items concerning the Chinese community in Hong Kong.

UNITED CHINESE PRESS. 1951-. Daily. Editor: Kam Fui. Publisher: United Chinese Press, Limited, 170 North King Street, Honolulu, Hawaii 96806. In English.

Publishes international, national, and general news of interest to Chinese.

THE UNITED JOURNAL. 1952-. Daily. Editor: Yuk Tsun Wang. Publisher: Chin Fu Woo, Chinese-American Press, Incorporated, 199 Canal Street, New York, New York 10013. In English.

WORLD JOURNAL. 1976-. Daily except Sunday. Editor: Jacob Ma. Publisher: World Journal, 135-16 39th Avenue, Flushing, New York 11354. In Chinese.

THE YOUNG CHINA DAILY (Shao Nien Chung Kuo Ch'en Pao). 1910-. Daily. Editors: Johnson Lee, Yueh-hua Lee, Gordon S. K. Mah. Publisher: Ta Chuan Fong, Young China Daily Publishing Company, 51 Hang Ah Street, San Francisco, California 94108. In Chinese.

Covers national, international, and local news.

Magazines

AMERICAN CHINESE NEWS. Weekly. Editor: Yin Po Lin. Publisher: American Chinese News Company, 737 South San Pedro, Los Angeles, California 90014. In English.

BEIJING REVIEW. 1957-. Weekly. Publisher: Beijing Review, 24 Baiwanzhuang Road, Beijing, China. Distributed by China Publications Center, Post Office Box 399, Beijing, China. In English, French, Spanish, Japanese or German.

News articles report on domestic events and programs, international politics, the economy, culture and science. Editorial views are presented and there is a section for letters to the editors.

CHINA BUSINESS REVIEW. 1974-. Bimonthly. Editor: Nicholas H. Ludlow. Publisher: National Council for U.S.-China Trade, 1050 17th Street, Northwest, Washington, D.C. 20036. In English.

CHINA PICTORIAL. Monthly. Publisher: China Pictorial, Huayuancun, Beijing, 28, China. Distributed by Guoji Shudian, Post Office Box 399, Beijing, China. In Chinese, Mongolian, Tibetan, Uygyr, Kazak, Korean, Russian, English, German, French, Japanese, Hindi, Spanish, Arabic, Swedish, Swahili, Italian, Urdu or Romanian.

A large-format magazine with beautiful photography showing cultural, artistic and economic achievements, scenic splendors and significant people. Articles are short accompaniments to the pictures.

CHINA RECONSTRUCTS. 1951-. Monthly. Publisher: China Reconstructs, Wai Wen Building, Beijing, China. Distributed by China Publications Center, Post Office Box 399, Beijing, China. In English, Spanish, French, Arabic, German, Portuguese or Chinese.

Regular sections are devoted to the economy, culture and art, science and medicine, social issues, sports, national friendships, archaeology, human interest stories in China, humor, cookery, language and literature. A few pages of colored photographs are included. Other photographs are in black and white.

CHINA SPORTS. Monthly. Distributed by Guoji Shudian, Post Office Box 399, Beijing, China. In English.

Reports on the development and popularization of sports in China; the promotion of traditional Chinese sports; the life and training of Chinese athletes; local, national and international competitions; Chinese sports history; and traditional Chinese medical practices applied to contemporary health and fitness research. Illustrated with color photos, charts and tables.

CHINESE AMERICAN PROGRESS. 1951-. Irregular. Editor: Jerri Lee. Publisher: Chinese American Civic Council, 2249 Wentworth Avenue, Chicago, Illinois 60619. In Chinese and English.

Carries news of the Chinese American Civic Council and articles promoting good citizenship, progress, and intergroup understanding.

EAST/WEST (Tung Hsi Pao). 1967-. Weekly. Editor: Gordon Lew. Publisher: East/West Publishing Company, 838 Grant Avenue, Suite 307, San Francisco, California 94108. In English and Chinese.

Covers topics on civil rights, youth movements, welfare, housing problems, working conditions, etc. to serve the Chinese community in this country and to serve as a link between the Chinese and English speaking worlds.

FREE CHINA REVIEW. Monthly. Editor: James Wei. Publisher: China Publishing Company, 159 Lexington Avenue, New York, New York 10016. In English.

GETTING TOGETHER. 1970-. Monthly. Publisher: I Wor Kuen, 24 Maricet Street, New York, New York 10002. In English and Chinese.

A political publication containing articles on Chinese-American and Chinese history, community news, the war, and liberation struggles. Discusses the nature of fascism in the United States and revolutionary alternatives.

MODERN CHINA. 1975-. Quarterly. Editor: Philip C. Huang. Publisher: Sage Publications, Incorporated, 275 South Beverly Drive, Beverly Hills, California 90212. In English.

Articles treat Chinese society, modern history and social sciences.

NEW CHINA. 1974-. Quarterly. Editor: Robin Platt. Publisher: US China Peoples Friendship Association, 41 Union Square, West, Room 721, New York, New York 10003. In English.

Presents mainland Chinese society to American readers to promote friendship between the two peoples.

PAMIR MAGAZINE/PA MI ERH ZAZHI. 1964-. Monthly. Editor: Peter Chieh Wang. Publisher: Chinese-American Cultural Association, Incorporated, 8122 Mayfield Road, Chesterland, Ohio 44026. In Chinese and English.

Articles are concerned with Chinese culture in the United States.

SINORAMA. Monthly. Publisher: Kwang Publishing Company, 3-1, Chung Hsiao East Road, Sec. 1, Taipei, Taiwan 100, Republic of China. In English.

A bilingual pictorial monthly on Taiwan today.

SOVIET-EAST EUROPEAN-CHINA BUSINESS & TRADE. 1974-. Semimonthly. Editor: Lisa Freeman. Publisher: Leo B. Wilt, 1511 K Street, Northwest, Suite 316, Washington, D.C. 20005.

TRUTH SEMI-WEEKLY (Cheng Yen Pao). 1967-. Biweekly. Editor: Frank Y. S. Wong. Publisher: Truth Semi-Weekly Publishing Company, 809 Sacramento Street, San Francisco, California 94108. In Chinese.

Publishes general news on international, national, and group events, including activities within Chinatown and topics of special interest to Chinese in the United States.

TSU KUO I CHOU (Fatherland Weekly). Weekly. Editor: James Wei. Publisher: China Publishing Company, c/o Chinese Cultural Center, 159 Lexington Avenue, New York, New York 10016. In Chinese.

Condenses and reprints most important news from local Chinese newspapers in Taiwan.

VISTA. Bimonthly. Editor: James Wei. Publisher: China Publishing Company, c/o Chinese Cultural Center, 159 Lexington Avenue, New York, New York 10016. In English.

Pictorial magazine on various aspects of the Republic of China.

WOMEN OF CHINA. Monthly. Publisher: Women of China, 50 Deng Shi Kou, Beijing, China. Distributed by China Publications Centre, Post Office Box 399, Beijing, China. In English.

A magazine devoted to women's interests and including sections on friendship, women who have achieved success, marriage and family, society, arts and literature, children, sports, history and legend and Chinese cooking. Written in a direct style, illustrated with black and white and colored photographs.

Radio Programs

California - San Francisco

KALW (FM) - 2905 21st Street, San Francisco, California 94110, (415) 648-1177. Chinese programs, 8 hours weekly.

KUSF (FM) - 2130 Fulton Street, San Francisco, California 94117, (415) 666-6206. Cantonese programs, 5 hours weekly.

Illinois - Chicago

WUIC (FM) - Box 4348, Chicago, Illinois 60680, (312) 996-2720. Chinese programs, 1 1/2 hours weekly.

New York - New York

WKCR (FM) - 208 Ferris Booth Hall, New York, New York 10027, (212) 280-5223. Chinese programs, 3 hours weekly.

New York - Stony Brook

WUSB (FM) - State University of New York, Stony Brook, New York 11794, (516) 246-7900. Chinese programs, 1 hour weekly.

New York - Troy

WRPI (FM) - Troy, New York 12181, (518) 270-6248. Chinese programs, 3 hours weekly.

Texas - Dallas

KVTT (FM) - 8300 Douglas Avenue, Dallas, Texas 75225, (214) 361-5599. Chinese programs, 1 hour weekly.

Television Programs

California - Los Angeles

KWHY-TV - 5545 Sunset Boulevard, Los Angeles, California 90028, (213) 466-5441. Chinese programs.

California - Oakland-San Francisco

KTVU-TV - One Jack London Square, Oakland, California 94607, (415) 834-2000. Chinese programs, 1 hour weekly.

California - San Francisco

KTSF-TV - 185 Berry Street, San Francisco, California 94107, (415) 495-4995. Chinese programs.

Hawaii - Honolulu

KHET - Studio 2350 Dole Street, Honolulu, Hawaii 96822, (808) 955-7878. Chinese programs, 1-1/2 hours weekly.

KIKU-TV - 150-B Puuhale Road, Honolulu, Hawaii 96819, (808) 847-1178. Chinese programs.

New York - New York-Newark, New Jersey

WWHT - 416 Eagle Rock Avenue, West Orange, New Jersey 07052, (201) 731-9024. Chinese programs.

Bank Branches in the U.S.

BANK OF CHINA
415 Madison Avenue
New York, New York 10017 (212) 935-3101

American branch of the mainland Bank of China.

BANK SINE
360 East 72nd Street
New York, New York 10021 (212) 628-2659

HONG KONG AND SHANGHAI BANKING CORPORATION
New York Branch:
Five World Trade Center
New York, New York 10048 (212) 938-3100

San Francisco Branch:
180 Samsome Street
San Francisco, California 94104 (415) 421-3077

INTERNATIONAL COMMERCIAL BANK OF CHINA (Republic of China)
New York Agency:
40 Wall Street
New York, New York 10005 (212) 943-5000

Chicago Branch:
208 South LaSalle Street
Chicago, Illinois 60604 (312) 332-4014

Houston Representative:
1200 Milam
Suite 3425
Houston, Texas 77002 (713) 650-1849

Commercial and Trade Organizations

CHINESE CHAMBER OF COMMERCE
42 North King Street
Honolulu, Hawaii 96817
Executive Vice President: (808) 533-3181
Welton W. T. Won Founded 1911

Publications: Lantern (newsletter), monthly; Narcissus Festival Program, annual.

CHINESE CHAMBER OF COMMERCE OF NEW YORK
Room C03
Confucius Plaza
33rd Bowery
New York, New York 10002 (212) 226-2795

CHINESE CHAMBER OF COMMERCE OF SAN FRANCISCO
730 Sacramento Street
San Francisco, California 94108 (415) 982-3000

CHINESE MERCHANTS ASSOCIATION
83 Mott Street
New York, New York 10013
Secretary: Jimmy Eng (212) 962-3734

CETDC BRANCH OFFICE IN NEW YORK
14th Floor, New York Merchandise Mart
41 Madison Avenue
New York, New York 10010
Director: Daniel H.C. Lyn (212) 532-7055

COORDINATION COUNCIL FOR NORTH AMERICAN AFFAIRS
Economic Division:
4301 Connecticut Avenue, Northwest
Suite 420
Washington, D.C. 20008
Acting Director: Martin Wang

Investment and Trade Office:
515 Madison Avenue, Suite 1212
New York, New York 10022
Director: M. T. Wu (212) 752-2340

FAR EAST TRADE SERVICE, INCORPORATED
Branch Office in Chicago:
Suite 272, The Merchandise Mart
Chicago, Illinois 60654
Director: Joseph Lin (312) 321-9338

Dallas Branch Office:
World Trade Center Dallas
Post Office Box 58007
Dallas, Texas 75258
Director: Gregory S. L. Hang (214) 744-0568

Branch Office in Los Angeles:
Suite 279, Los Angeles World Trade Center
350 South Figueroa Street
Los Angeles, California 90071
Director: Charles C. L. Hsu (213) 628-8761

Representative in San Francisco:
604 Commercial Street
San Francisco, California 94111
Representative: David Wang (415) 362-6882

Liaison Center of the General Chamber of Commerce of the Republic of China:
Suite 1046, 870 Market Street
San Francisco, California 94102
Director: Augustine C. T. Wu (415) 981-5387

NATIONAL COUNCIL FOR U.S.-CHINA TRADE
1050 17th Street, Northwest, Suite 350
Washington, D.C. 20036 (202) 331-0290
President: Christopher H. Phillips Founded 1973

American companies involved in exporting to and importing from the People's Republic of China (PRC). Established to facilitate the development of Sino-U.S. commerce. Provides representation, practical assistance and up-to-date information to American companies in developing and continuing their trade with the PRC. Hosts delegations to and from the PRC. Acts as a contact point for reciprocal exhibitions in the two countries. Provides importer and exporter advisory services; sponsors conferences and speakers on China trade subjects. Maintains reference library on topics relating to China's trade and economy.
Publications: China Business Review, bimonthly; also publishes numerous special reports, market surveys and directories.

USA - REPUBLIC OF CHINA ECONOMIC COUNCIL
200 Main Street
Crystal Lake, Illinois 60014 (815) 459-5875
President: William N. Morell, Jr. Founded 1976

United States firms engaged in business activity with the Republic of China on Taiwan. Seeks to promote business relations between the United States and Taiwan. Holds business conferences and seminars to promote understanding of business opportunities, government policies, laws and regulations and means for achieving technological transfer. Acts to improve regulations; aids in business communications and contacts and the resolution of business disputes. Serves as a liaison between business and government. Maintains basic files of background material on Taiwan of importance to United States business.
Publications: Conference Reports, annual; Taiwan Economic News, irregular; also publishes laws and regulations of the Republic of China on Taiwan, membership list and a brochure; disseminates a variety of Taiwan business publications.

Festivals, Fairs, and Celebrations

California - Marysville

BOK KAI FESTIVAL
Marysville, California

This Bomb Day Festival features street entertainment, a gala parade, lion dancers, and Chinese opera. As a special highlight of the festival, Lucky Bombs are fired. Held in late February or early March.
Contact: Greater Yuba City - Marysville Chamber of Commerce, Post Office Box 1429, Marysville, California 95901.

California - San Francisco

CHINESE NEW YEAR CELEBRATION
Chinatown
San Francisco, California

Opens with a pageant and traditional Chinese ceremonial lion dancers. The nine-day celebration features a "Miss Chinatown USA" coronation ceremony, festival tours of Chinatown, a carnival, fashion show, Chinese opera, folk dancing, music, films, special exhibits and demonstrations. An exotic parade with dragons, lions, Oriental deities, floats, mythical birds and beasts, the festival queen and her court, and troupes of elaborately costumed musicians and lantern bearers winds up the festivities. Celebrated each year on varying dates from the end of January to mid-February to welcome the lunar New Year.
Contact: Chinese Chamber of Commerce, 730 Sacramento Street, San Francisco, California 94108 or San Francisco Convention and Visitors Bureau, Fox Plaza, San Francisco, California 94102, (415) 626-5500.

Hawaii - Honolulu

NARCISSUS FESTIVAL
Honolulu International Center
Honolulu, Hawaii

"A night in Chinatown" with dancing in the streets, firework display, queen contest, and coronation ball. Rampaging lion, dances, dinners, art, fashion, garden shows and traditional tea ceremony, historical pageant, floral display, and demonstration of Chinese cooking. The first three days are traditionally dedicated to family reunions and visits to friends. The third day - prayers are offered to the God of Wealth, then for the next ten days the birthdays of different animals and grains are celebrated. A parade with the beating of gongs and cymbals and a Chinese Village Fair, herald the arrival of the Chinese New Year. Held in late January or early February.
Contact: Hawaii Visitors Bureau, Suite 801, Waikiki Business Plaza, 2270 Kalakaua Avenue, Honolulu, Hawaii 96815, (808) 923-1811.

Massachusetts - Boston

CHINESE NEW YEAR
Chinatown
Boston, Massachusetts

The picturesque celebration begins with a dragon dance held in Chinatown. Includes special programs of Chinese entertainment such as folk singing, classical dancing, and the dramatization of a Chinese play. Traditional costumes and Chinese foods add to the colorful, flavorful festivities.
Contact: Greater Boston Chamber of Commerce, 125 High Street, Boston, Massachusetts 02110, (617) 426-1250.

FESTIVAL OF THE AUGUST MOON
Chinatown
Boston, Massachusetts

A street celebration with parade, special foods and costumes.
Contact: Greater Boston Chamber of Commerce, 125 High Street, Boston, Massachusetts 02110, (617) 426-1250.

New York - New York

CHINESE NEW YEAR
Chinatown
New York, New York

Celebrated with lion dances, a parade with many floats and colorful costumes, fireworks, feasts, music, and merriment. Held in late January or early February at the beginning of the new lunar year.
Contact: New York Convention and Visitors Bureau, Incorporated, 90 East 42nd Street, New York, New York 10017, (212) 687-1300.

Pennsylvania - Philadelphia

CHINESE NEW YEAR
Chinatown
Philadelphia, Pennsylvania

Celebrated with parades, fire dragons, fireworks, and special programs in Chinatown. The celebration is held annually in late January or early February.
Contact: Philadelphia Convention and Visitors Bureau, 1525 John F. Kennedy Boulevard, Philadelphia, Pennsylvania 19102, (215) 864-1976.

Wyoming - Evanston

CELEBRATION IN EVANSTON'S CHINATOWN
Evanston, Wyoming
Events include a tour, festival, exhibit, fair, ceremony, parade, and performance. Held for six days in late January.
Contact: Evanston Chamber of Commerce, Box 365, Evanston, Wyoming 82930.

Airline Offices

CHINA AIRLINES, LIMITED (CAL)
North American Headquarters:
391 Sutter Street, 2nd Floor
San Francisco, California 94108 (415) 391-3950

Schedules flights on a trans-Pacific route linking Taipei (Taiwan) with San Francisco and Los Angeles via Tokyo and Honolulu. Offers far eastern regional services. Other offices in the United States: Chicago, Honolulu, Houston, Los Angeles, New York, and Washington

CAAC (Civil Aviation Authority of China)
477 Madison Avenue
New York, New York

51 Grant Avenue
San Francisco, California 94108 (415) 392-2156

2500 Wilshire Boulevard
Los Angeles, California 90057 (213) 384-2703

Bookdealers and Publishers' Representatives

CHRISTOPHER ACKERMAN
(China and other Asian regions)
180 East Inlet Drive
Palm Beach, Florida 33480 (305) 842-6096

THE ASIAN AMERICAN MATERIALS CENTER
(Chinese in America)
165 West 66th Street
New York, New York 10023 (212) 787-7954

BOOKS AND THINGS
Schooley's Mount, New Jersey
07870 (201) 852-7337

BOOKS NEW CHINA
53 East Broadway
New York, New York 10002 (212) 233-6565

C & T COMPANY (Cheng & Tsui Company)
Post Office Box 328
Cambridge, Massachusetts 02139 (619) 277-1769

WILLIAM C. CHAN
37 Elizabeth Street
New York, New York 10013 (212) CA6-0255

CHINA BOOKS & CRAFTS
101 Cherry
Seattle, Washington 98104 (206) 622-2800

CHINA BOOKS AND PERIODICALS

174 Randolph Street
Chicago, Illinois 60601 (312) 782-6004

125 Fifth Avenue
New York, New York 10003 (212) 677-2650

2929 24th Street
San Francisco, California
94110 (415) 282-2994

CHINA CULTURAL CENTER
970 North Broadway
Suite 210
Los Angeles, California 90012 (213) 489-3827

CHINESE AMERICAN COMPANY INCORPORATED
81-83 Harrison Avenue
Boston, Massachusetts 02111 (617) 423-2264

CHINESE BOOKS & RECORDS
943 North Hill
Los Angeles, California 90012 (213) 629-3966

CHINESE FOR CHRIST BOOKSTORE & LIBRARY
Post Office Box 29126
Los Angeles, California 90029

CHINESE MATERIALS CENTER, INCORPORATED
809 Taraval Street
San Francisco, California 94116 (415) 665-0952

THE CLOTHES HORSE
(China, Japan and Korea)
217 West Read Street
Baltimore, Maryland 21201 (301) 728-3818

CO-OP BOOKS
(political)
Post Office Box 2436
Tallahassee, Florida 32304 (904) 222-6677

JEAN E. DOBBS
(Chinese art)
Schooley's Mountain, New Jersey
07870 (201) 852-7337

DRAGON GATE BOOKSTORE
(Chinese)
Post Office Box 27143
Honolulu, Hawaii 96827 (808) 533-7147

THE EAST AND WEST SHOP
(Chinese and Asian)
4 Appleblossom Lane
Newtown, Connecticut 06470 (203) 426-0661

J. S. EDGREN
(Chinese, Japanese and Korean)
Post Office Box 326
Carmel, California 93921 (408) 625-2575

EVERYBODY'S BOOKSTORE
(Chinese)
17 Brenham Place
San Francisco, California 94108 (415) 781-4989

F & I BOOKS
(antiquarian materials pertaining to Chinese)
Post Office Box 1900
Santa Monica, California 90406 (213) 394-7886

IACONI BOOK IMPORTS
300 Pennsylvania Avenue
San Francisco, California 94107 (415) 285-7393

E. LANGSTAFF - BOOKS
U. S. District Orient Culture Service
910 Fremont Avenue
South Pasadena, California 91030 (213) 441-3233

J. JAMES LEWIS - BOOKSELLERS
(Missionary movement in China)
416 South Benton Way
Los Angeles, California 90057 (213) 383-6507

LI MIN BOOKS & CHINESE PRODUCTS
(Chinese books and specialties)
969 North Hill Street
Los Angeles, California 90012 (213) 687-9817

LIBERATION BOOKSTORE
(political publications in Chinese, Persian and Spanish)
1828 Broadway
Seattle, Washington 98122 (206) 323-9222

SAMUEL L. LOWE, JR., ANTIQUES, INCORPORATED
(antiquarian books concerning the China trade)
80 Charles Street
Boston, Massachusetts 02114 (617) 742-0845

MAY DAY BOOKS & PUBLICATIONS
(political publications in Arabic, Chinese, Persian and Spanish)
3134 East Davison
Detroit, Michigan 48212 (313) 893-0523

MCBLAIN BOOKS
(antiquarian books on China)
Post Office Box 971
Des Moines, Iowa 50304

MIDDLEBURY COLLEGE STORE
5 Hillcrest Road
Middlebury, Vermont 05753 (802) 388-7722

PARAGON BOOK GALLERY LIMITED
14 East 38th Street
New York, New York 10016 (212) 532-4920

RED BOOK, INCORPORATED
(political publications in Chinese, Russian and Spanish)
135 River Street
Cambridge, Massachusetts 02139 (617) 491-6930

RISING SUN BOOKS
(China and other Asian regions)
228 Ray Street
Manchester, New Hampshire 03104 (603) 668-6929

SINO AMERICAN LIBRARY & INFORMATION SERVICES
(Chinese and Chinese-American)
1814 Pepper Street
Alhambra, California 91801 (213) 282-4314

J. STANOFF
Rare Oriental Bookseller
Box 1599
Aptos, California 95003

TEC-BOOKS LIMITED (Librairie De Documentation Technique SA)
(technical books in Chinese)
41 William
Pittsburgh, Pennsylvania 12901 (518) 561-0005

WAH KUE COMPANY
58 Mott Street
New York, New York 10013 (212) 226-1494

EDWARD T. WALLACE
(Chinese mail order)
Box 165
Ridgefield, New Jersey 07657

Books and Pamphlets

BIBLIOGRAPHY OF CHINESE HUMANITIES, 1941-1972: STUDIES ON CHINESE PHILOSOPHY, RELIGION, HISTORY, GEOGRAPHY, BIOGRAPHY ART AND LANGUAGE AND LITERATURE. By Scott Ling. Taipei, Liberal Arts Press, 1975.

Includes material such as books, periodicals, articles, theses, and dissertations written in many languages and published from 1941-1972.

BIBLIOGRAPHY ON CHINESE SOCIAL HISTORY; A Selected and Critical List of Chinese Periodical Sources. By E-tu (Zen) Sun. New Haven, Institute of Far Eastern Languages, Yale University, 1952.

This is a listing of important articles on the social history of traditional China which have appeared in Chinese scholarly journals from 1930 to 1950.

A CHECKLIST OF CHINESE LOCAL HISTORIES. Stanford, California, Joint East Asia Center, 1980. (East Asia Library Series).

CHINA; A Critical Bibliography. By Charles Hucker. Tucson, University of Arizona Press, 1962.

This work is an annotated list of books, articles and individual chapters or sections of books that deal with the lands and people, history, intellectual and aesthetic patterns, political patterns, social patterns and economic patterns of China.

CHINA-A GENERAL SURVEY. By Qi Wen. Beijing, China, Foreign Languages Press, 1979.

Chapters are devoted to geography, history, politics, economy and culture. There is a map showing China's administrative divisions, a chronology of Chinese dynasties and some visitor information. The book is an official government publication.

CHINA: A RESOURCE AND CURRICULUM GUIDE. By Arlene Fosner. 2nd edition, Chicago, University of Chicago Press, 1976.

This guide provides a listing of materials available to the public and offering views of the social, economic, political and cultural aspects of China's society and international relations. Divided into three parts: essays on teaching about China; materials on China; and materials from the People's Republic of China.

CHINA: AN ANALYTICAL SURVEY OF LITERATURE. By Headquarters, Department of the Army, Washington, D.C., United States Government Printing Office, 1978.

This book, fourth in a series, contains abstracts of books, periodical articles, studies and documents, that present a picture of China (Mainland and Taiwan). This edition covers the period 1971-1976 and information is supported by charts, tables and maps.

CHINA: AN ANNOTATED BIBLIOGRAPHY OF BIBLIOGRAPHIES, COMPILED BY TSUEN-HSUIN TSIEN. Boston, G. K. Hall, 1978.

An annotated list of over 2,500 bibliographies concerning China, mainly in English, Chinese and Japanese. It contains separate works, bibliographies in periodicals, bibliographic essays, surveys of literature on specific fields or periods and listings of bibliographies in monographs, published up to December 1977.

CHINA AND AMERICA: A BIBLIOGRAPHY OF INTERACTIONS, FOREIGN AND DOMESTIC. Compiled by James M. McCutcheon. Honolulu, University Press of Hawaii, 1972.

Bibliographical items are arranged under 12 topics, such as China and American Missions, China and American Education, and China and the Arts. Contains books, articles, and dissertations written in English and published before Spring, 1971.

CHINA: FACTS AND FIGURES. Beijing, Foreign Languages Press, 1982.

Factsheets giving information on specialized subjects: education, energy resources and their exploitation, Chinese arts and crafts, communications and transport, the land and the people, China's 4,000 year history.

CHINA HANDBOOK SERIES. Beijing, Foreign Languages Press.

Each handbook is devoted to a separate aspect of life in China today: geography, history, politics, economy, education and science, art and literature, sports and public health, culture, life and lifestyle, tourism.

CHINA HANDBOOK, 1975. 6th edition. Taipei, Taiwan, Chung Hwa Information Service, 1982.

Presents a summary of the geography, history and culture, philosophy and religion, arts and crafts, government, economics, education and sports, social conditions, and communications in the Republic of China.

CHINA IN BOOKS: A BASIC BIBLIOGRAPHY IN WESTERN LANGUAGES. By Norman E. Tanis. Greenwich, Connecticut, Jai Press, 1979.

This book is a listing of 4,000 books about China and its people which are divided into twenty-one general topics. The majority of the works listed are in the English language.

CHINA TODAY. Volume 1. POPULATION AND OTHER PROBLEMS. Edited by Su Wenming. Beijing, China, 1981.

The first in a series of books describing China in the process of modernizing its agriculture, industry, defense and science, this booklet deals with problems associated with population, family planning, housing, employment and juvenile reform. Includes tables and photographs.

CHINA YEARBOOK. Taipei, Taiwan, Kwang Hwa Publishing Company, 1982.

Standard reference book on Republic of China. Contains chronology, who's who, maps, charts, tables, photographs and an index.

CHINESE AGRICULTURE AND RURAL SOCIETY. Edited by K. P. Broadbent, (Farnham Royal). Commonwealth Agricultural Bureau, 1974.

A bibliography of studies on Chinese agriculture and rural society which were published between 1970 - 1973. It is based on the World Agricultural Economics and Rural Sociology Abstracts.

CHINESE CULTURAL SERIES. Taipei, Taiwan, Kwang Hwa Publishing Company.

Illustrated folders mostly in color and published in several languages. Topics include the Chinese language, bronzes , ceramics, calligraphy, festivals, music, painting, Confucius, jade, accupuncture, opera, silk, stamps, books.

CHINESE HISTORIOGRAPHY ON THE REVOLUTION OF 1911: A CRITICAL SURVEY AND A SELECTED BIBLIOGRAPHY. By Winston Hsieh. Stanford, California, Hoover Institution Press, Stanford University, 1975.

A bibliographic essay of related series of major events, movements, phases, or problems in the development of China's history, especially the Revolution of 1911.

CHINESE HISTORY. Taipei, Taiwan, Kwang Hwa Publishing Company.

Illustrated booklet tracing Chinese history from prehistoric times. Appendix correlates dates of Chinese and world history from 3,000 B.C. to the present.

CHINESE HISTORY: SELECTED WORKS IN ENGLISH; A Preliminary Bibliography. By Chi Wang. Washington, D.C., Department of History, Georgetown University, 1970.

This is a selected list of books and pamphlets in English relating to Chinese history. It is based on a survey of the Library of Congress and Library of the Georgetown University collections.

CHINESE STUDIES IN PAPERBACK. By David L. Weitzman. Berkeley, California, McCutchan Publishing Company, 1968. c.1967.

An annotated listing of materials, in paperback, on Chinese history and China in general.

COMMUNIST CHINA: A BIBLIOGRAPHIC SURVEY. By United States Department of the Army, Washington, D.C.; Superintendent of Documents, United States Government Printing Office, 1971.

This book contains 800 abstracts of periodical articles, books, studies, and reports on Communist China. Information appearing in the abstracts is supported by appendices of charts, tables and 17 maps of military, political, economic and sociological nature.

CONTEMPORARY CHINA. (Bibliography). Compiled by Charles White. Washington, D.C. Howard University Founders Library, 1972.

CONTEMPORARY CHINA; A Bibliography of Reports on China Published by the United States Joint Publications Research Service. By Richard Sorich. Prepared for the Joint Committee on Contemporary China of the American Council of Learned Societies and the Social Science Research Council. New York, Reader Microprint Corporation, 1961.

This is a bibliography of all the reports on China published by the Joint Publications Research Service from late 1957 - July 1960. It is divided into three parts: part one is the bibliography; part two is a list of abbreviations for Chinese and non-Chinese serials appearing in citations of part one; and part three is a subject index.

CONTEMPORARY CHINA; A Research Guide. By Peter Berton. Stanford, California, Hoover Institution on War, Revolution, and Peace, 1967.

A guide to bibliographical and reference works, selected documentary compilations, series, dissertations and theses on contemporary China (post-1949 Mainland China and post-1945 Taiwan). Emphasis is on the humanities and social sciences.

THE CULTURAL REVOLUTION IN CHINA: AN ANNOTATED BIBLIOGRAPHY. By James Wang. New York, Garland Publishing, 1976.

An annotated listing of books, monographs, and journal articles in English on the cultural Revolution.

DEVELOPMENT IN THE PEOPLE'S REPUBLIC OF CHINA: A SELECTED BIBLIOGRAPHY. By Patricia Blair. Washington, D.C., Overseas Development Council, 1976.

Begins with an essay on the political and social context of the development in the People's Republic of China followed by a selected bibliography. Includes categories of development strategy, economic and social performance and political and social conditions.

ECONOMIC AND SOCIAL DEVELOPMENT OF MODERN CHINA: A BIBLIOGRAPHICAL GUIDE. By T'ung-li Yuan. New Haven, Human Relations Area Files, 1956.

A listing of monographs and pamphlets published in English, French and German from the beginning of the 20th century to the end of 1955 dealing with the aspects of social and economic development in China.

FOREIGN TRADE DEVELOPMENT IN THE REPUBLIC OF CHINA. Edited by Fountain and Youth Company, Limited. Taipei, Taiwan, Board of Foreign Trade, Chinese Ministry of Economic Affairs, 1974.

Describes industrialization in Taiwan, foreign trade development, export and import commodities, tourism, and investment opportunities. A booklet illustrated with numerous color photographs.

A GUIDE TO LIBRARY RESOURCES FOR CHINESE STUDIES. By Ernest J. Tsai. Saint Louis, Missouri, Washington University Libraries, 1978.

This is a guide to materials, in Chinese and English related to Chinese studies, and available in the Washington University collections. Call number and library location is given.

INDEX SINICUS: A CATALOGUE OF ARTICLES RELATING TO CHINA IN PERIODICALS AND OTHER COLLECTIVE PUBLICATIONS, 1920-1955. By John Lust. Cambridge, England, W. Heffer, 1964.

This is an index to articles dealing with China in periodicals, memorial volumes, symposia and proceedings of conferences published between 1920 and 1955, in western languages only.

AN INTRODUCTION TO THE SOURCES OF MING HISTORY. By Wolfgang Franke. Kuala Lumpur, University of Malaya Press. Distributed by Oxford University Press, London, 1968.

A bibliography of the historical sources available on Ming history. Includes a list of the emperors of the Ming Dynasty and reigns.

MODERN CHINA; A Bibliographical Guide to Chinese Works, 1898-1937. By John Fairbanks. Cambridge, Harvard University Press, 1961, c.1950.

A listing of works from the Chinese-Japanese Library at Harvard University covering the era of Reform and Revolution.

MODERN CHINESE SOCIETY: AN ANALYTICAL BIBLIOGRAPHY. Edited by G. William Skinner and others. Stanford, California, Stanford University Press, 1973.

A comprehensive bibliography divided into three volumes on the basis of language: Volume 1, publications in Western languages; Volume 2, publications in Chinese; and Volume 3, publications in Japanese. About 31,500 entries cover the modern period of Chinese history from 1644 on.

PEOPLE'S REPUBLIC OF CHINA: A BIBLIOGRAPHY OF RESEARCH AND PRIMARY SOURCES IN ENGLISH. By Yeen-mei Wu Chang. Seattle, University of Washington Libraries, 1979.

A bibliography of materials about the People's Republic of China that are available in the University of Washington Libraries, collections. Call numbers and library location are given.

PICTORIAL CHINA. Beijing, China, Foreign Language Printing House, 1982.

A series of brochures published by the magazine of the same name, each one of which treats a particular subject such as the life expectancy of Shanghai residents, the Gezhouba Project, the truck industry, rockets, agriculture, the origin of man, mainland-Taiwan friendship, sports, shipbuilding.

PREMODERN CHINA; A Bibliographical Introduction. By Ch'un-shu Chang. Ann Arbor, Michigan, University of Michigan, Center for Chinese Studies, 1971.

This book is an introductory bibliography of western language works on premodern China from prehistoric times to the early nineteenth century. The bibliography is divided into three groups: the first part is an introduction to the field of Chinese studies, the second part contains lists of western language reference works and the third part is a bibliography of western language sources of the history and civilization of China.

THE PROVINCES OF THE PEOPLE'S REPUBLIC OF CHINA: A POLITICAL AND ECONOMIC BIBLIOGRAPHY. By John Emerson. United States Department of Commerce, Bureau of Economic Analysis. United States Government Printing Office, 1976.

This bibliography is a listing of major sources on political and economic developments in the provinces of the People's Republic of China which can be found in Chinese newspapers, periodicals, and other publications in the United States.

QUESTIONS AND ANSWERS ABOUT THE REPUBLIC OF CHINA. Taipei, Taiwan, Republic of China, Government Information Office, 1981.

Introduces the people and way of life of the Republic of China on Taiwan, describing the government, education, arts and crafts, economy, agriculture, industry, transportation and communications, cities and urban development, social security, mass communications, tourism, history and international relations. Uses a question and answer format. Illustrated in color.

RESEARCH MATERIALS ON TWENTIETH-CENTURY CHINA: AN ANNOTATED LIST OF CCRM PRODUCTIONS. Washington, D.C., Association of Research Libraries. Center for Chinese Research Materials, 1975.

A listing of all of the available publications on 20th century China published by the Center for Chinese Research Materials.

SCIENCE AND TECHNOLOGY IN THE DEVELOPMENT OF MODERN CHINA: AN ANNOTATED BIBLIOGRAPHY. By Genevieve C. Dean. London, Mansell Information, 1974.

Covers almost 1,000 books, articles, dissertations, reports, and documents dealing with economic growth as related to scientific and technological knowledge in contemporary China. Coverage is international, but does not include works written in the People's Republic of China. Annotated entries are arranged under five major headings: technology and economic growth, technology policy, science policy, scientific activities, and technology in China.

A SELECTED AND ANNOTATED GUIDE TO THE GOVERNMENT AND POLITICS OF CHINA. By Robert Harmon. Monticello, Illinois, Council of Planning Librarians, 1976.

A basic, annotated guide to literature on Chinese political structures and functions.

STUDIES OF CHINESE RELIGION: A COMPREHENSIVE AND CLASSIFIED BIBLIOGRAPHY OF PUBLICATIONS IN ENGLISH, FRENCH AND GERMAN THROUGH 1970. By Laurence Thompson. Encino, California, Dickenson Publishing Company, 1976.

This bibliography of Chinese religion is divided into three parts: bibliography and general studies; Chinese religion exclusive of Buddhism; and Chinese Buddhism.

STUDIES ON CHINESE EXTERNAL AFFAIRS: AN INSTRUCTIONAL BIBLIOGRAPHY OF COMMONWEALTH AND AMERICAN LITERATURE. By Roger Dial. Halifax, N.S. Centre for Foreign Policy Studies, Department of Political Science, Dalhousie University, 1973.

A listing of analytic studies of Chinese politics and foreign policy which may be used by students doing research in these two fields.

TAIWAN - ISLAND PROVINCE OF CHINA. Taipei, Taiwan, Tourism Bureau, Ministry of Communications.

Provides general information for the visitor including an outline map. Pictures show scenic and architectural highlights.

THE T. L. YUAN BIBLIOGRAPHY OF WESTERN WRITINGS ON CHINESE ART AND ARCHAEOLOGY. By Tung Yuan. London, Mansell, 1975.

This bibliography lists books and reviews, catalogs of exhibitions, journal articles and other material on Chinese art and archaeology in western languages published between 1920 and 1965.

CHINESE AMERICANS

ACCULTURATION OF THE CHINESE IN THE UNITED STATES. By David Cheng. Philadelphia, University of Pennsylvania Press, 1948.

Contrasts Chinese life in the Province of Kwangtung with that of Chinatown in Philadelphia.

THE ANTI-CHINESE MOVEMENT. By Elmer Sandmeyer. Urbana, University of Illinois Press, 1973.

This study traces the development of the movement against the Chinese in California: what conditions caused the movement, which groups were involved, the obstacles the groups encountered and the methods employed by the group.

ASIAN AMERICA. Edited by Victor and Brett Nee. San Francisco, Bulletin of Concerned Asian Scholars, 1972.

A special issue of the Bulletin of Concerned Asian Scholars that contains excerpts from books, articles, book reviews, and poetry dealing with the subject of Chinese-Americans.

THE BAMBOO PATH. By Tin-Yuke Char. Honolulu, Hawaii Chinese History Center, 1977.

Several essays on Chinese-Hawaiians.

BIBLIOGRAPHY OF THE CHINESE QUESTION IN THE UNITED STATES. By Robert Cowan. San Francisco, A. M. Robertson, 1909. Reprint San Francisco, California, R and E Research Associates, 1970.

A reprint of a 1909 bibliography of books, pamphlets and other publications on the literature of Chinese immigration and its various phases.

BITTER STRENGTH; A History of the Chinese in the United States, 1850-1870. By Gunther Barth. Cambridge, Massachusetts, Harvard University Press, 1964.

Explores the background, arrival, and life in the United States of Chinese immigrants in California during the mid-nineteenth century. Explains the developments leading to the first restrictive laws on immigration.

CATHAY IN ELDORADO: THE CHINESE IN CALIFORNIA. Introduction by Oscar Lewis. San Francisco, Book Club of California, 1972.

Eleven selections which focus on the history of the Chinese in California. This is the Book Club of California 1972 Keepsake Series.

A CENTURY OF AMERICAN IMMIGRATION POLICY TOWARD CHINA. By I-Yao Shen. Washington, D.C., American Foreign Service Association, 1974.

This is a reprint of an article published in the Foreign Service Journal on the various government policies implemented concerning the immigration of Chinese to America.

THE CHALLENGE OF THE AMERICAN DREAM: THE CHINESE IN THE UNITED STATES. By Francis Hsu. Belmont, California, Wadsworth Publishing Company, 1971. (Minorities in American Life Series).

A sociological study of the contact and conflict between the Chinese and Americans, its effect on behavior patterns and infrastructure of the Chinese and attempts to indicate what lies ahead for these two groups. Includes numerous photographs.

CHINA MEN. By Maxine Kingston. New York, Knopf, 1980.

Each chapter portrays Chinese men from earliest times (411 A.D.) to the Vietnam War.

CHINAMAN'S CHANCE. By No Yong Park. Boston, Meador Press, 1940.

An autobiographical account of a Chinese who rushes to become as American as possible and then returns to his Chinese tradition. Although told in a light tone it reveals the kinds of prejudice the author had to confront.

CHINATOWN FAMILY. By Lin Yutang. New York, John Day, 1948.

The characters in this book illustrate the extremes in assimilation of western values, from almost total rejection to acceptance of the very worst of America, and, happily, the several gradations in between.

CHINATOWN, NEW YORK: LABOR AND POLITICS, 1930-1950. By Peter Kway. New York, Monthly Review Press, 1979.

The history of the labor movement in New York's Chinatown during the mid-1930 s to the early 1950 s is dealt with in this book. Depicts the story of activism and struggle in the labor movement.

CHINATOWN, U.S.A. By Calvin Lee. Garden City, New York, Doubleday and Company, 1965.

Explodes stereotyped images of the Chinese in America by providing insight into the social structure, domestic life, business, finance, traditions, customs, religious beliefs, and festivals of Chinese people in various Chinatowns in the United States. Illustrated with photographs from the California Historical Society in San Francisco.

THE CHINESE-AMERICAN GIRL; A Study in Cultural Conflicts. By Florence Brugger. New York, New York University, 1935.

This study analyzes cultural conflict situations in the lives of Chinese-American girls, especially the socio-psychological factors which cause the conflicts. Data was obtained from interviews with eight Chinese-American girls.

CHINESE AMERICANS. By Stanford Lyman. New York, Random House, 1974. (Ethnic Groups in Comparative Perspective.)

The author endeavors to answer questions about the Chinese diaspora, the background of communal organizations, the anti-Chinese movement, the class structure of the Chinese-Americans and their internal social problems and ways of coping with them.

CHINESE-AMERICANS: SCHOOL AND COMMUNITY PROBLEMS. Chicago, Integrated Education Associates, 1972.

A collection of essays depicting the problems Chinese-Americans face in their communities and their schools. Includes selected references on Asia-American school and community affairs.

THE CHINESE AND THE CHINESE QUESTION. By James Whitney. 2nd edition. New York, Tibbals Book Company, 1888. Reprint San Francisco, R and E Research Associates, 1970.

Covers the Chinese, their work, institutions and character as people; the Chinese's modern relations with the nations of the West; their migration to America; and the methods dictated by policy and law for the restriction and exclusion from America. An early discussion of the subject matter, interesting as a contemporaneous account.

THE CHINESE AT HOME AND ABROAD. By Willard Farwen. A. L. Bancroft and Company, 1885; reprint, San Francisco, R and E Research Associates, 1970.

Divided into two parts, part one looks at the question of Chinese immigration and the second part is a reprint of the Report of Special Committee of Board of Supervisors of San Francisco. Document of an anti-Chinese view current at the time.

THE CHINESE COMMUNITY IN NEW YORK: A STUDY IN THEIR CULTURAL ADJUSTMENT, 1920-1940. By Julia J. Hsuan Chen. American University, Washington, 1941. Reprint San Francisco, R and E Research Associates, 1974.

A general study of the life and activities of New York's Chinatown, its philosophy and behavior, its social, educational and religious institutions and its relationship to America and the white community.

CHINESE EXCLUSION VERSUS THE OPEN DOOR POLICY, 1900-1906: CLASHES OVER CHINA POLICY IN THE ROOSEVELT ERA. By Delber McKee. Detroit, Wayne State University Press, 1977.

Investigates the exclusion law and the effect it had on foreign relations between China and the United States. This book also shows the role of Chinese American during this time.

THE CHINESE HELPED BUILD AMERICA. By Dorothy and Joseph Dowdell. New York, Messner, 1972.

A book for children showing the contributions made by Chinese Americans.

CHINESE IMMIGRANT CHILDREN. By Rose Chao. New York, Department of Asian Studies, City College of New York, 1977.

CHINESE IMMIGRATION. By Mary Coolidge. New York, Holt and Company, 1909. Reprint New York, Arno Press, 1969.

Presents the history of immigration from the free immigration (1848-1882), restriction and exclusion to competition and assimilation. Focuses on the legislative actions taken during this history of immigration. Considered a classic study in the field.

THE CHINESE IN AMERICA. By Betty Lee Sung. New York, Macmillan, 1973.

Written to explain to children the extremely hard labor and social conditions with which the Chinese immigrants were confronted and how their courage and perserverance helped them to rise up from these beginnings.

THE CHINESE IN AMERICA. By Ruthanne Lum McCunn. Washington, D.C., National Center for Urban Ethnic Affairs.

This publication paints a vivid picture of the Chinese in America. It tells of Chinese immigrants who labored in mines and worked on railroads. It relates the Chinese struggle for survival, their grouping together in Chinatowns and fighting unfair legislation through the American court system. Finally, the book is illustrated with drawings and old photographs, many of which are published for the first time.

THE CHINESE IN AMERICA, 1820-1973: A CHRONOLOGY AND FACT BOOK. Ethnic Chronology Series Number 14. Dobbs Ferry, New York, Oceana Publications, 1974.

Gives brief chronological entires grouped under four main periods: free immigration period, 1820-1882; period of discriminatory restrictions, 1882-1904; period of absolute exclusion, 1904-1943; and the era of gradual liberalization, 1943-. In the second section, selected documents are arranged chronologically under the categories: federal and state laws affecting the Chinese; treaties between the United States and China; and judicial decisions relating to the immigration status of the Chinese. Also contains a bibliography in two parts: Official Publications and Materials; and Books, Pamphlets and Articles.

CHINESE IN AMERICAN LIFE: SOME ASPECTS OF THEIR HISTORY, STATUS, PROBLEMS, AND CONTRIBUTIONS. By Shien-woo Kung. Seattle, Washington, University of Washington Press, 1962.

A general book on Chinese immigrants and Americans of Chinese ancestry. The text is supported by numerous tables and a bibliography.

THE CHINESE IN BUTTE COUNTY, CALIFORNIA, 1860-1920. By Susan Book. San Francisco, R and E Research Associates, 1976.

Study focuses on the settlement patterns of the Chinese in Butte County, California, as early as the Gold Rush days. Explains the life of the Chinese in Butte County and how they were forced to leave because of decrease in gold and prejudice by the white residents.

THE CHINESE IN EL PASO. By Nancy Farrar. Southwestern Studies Monograph No. 33. El Paso, Texas Western Press, 1972.

Documents the history of the Chinese community in El Paso, Texas, starting with the arrival of the Southern Pacific Railroad in 1881 and its Chinese workers. Describes in detail many different facets of Chinese life, drawing primarily on contemporary newspaper articles.

THE CHINESE IN HAWAII: AN ANNOTATED BIBLIOGRAPHY. By Nancy Foon Young. Honolulu, Social Science Research Institute, University of Hawaii. Distributed by University Press of Hawaii, Honolulu, 1973.

Books, periodical articles, and pamphlets on many aspects of the Chinese experience in Hawaii are arranged alphabetically by author or title. Entries provide a bibliographical citation, a descriptive annotation, and locations of the materials. Includes a subject index.

THE CHINESE IN HAWAII: A BIBLIOGRAPHIC SURVEY. By Chuan-hua Lowe. Taipei, China Print, 1972.

THE CHINESE IN HAWAII: A CHECKLIST OF CHINESE MATERIALS IN THE ASIAN AND HAWAIIAN COLLECTIONS OF THE UNIVERSITY OF HAWAII LIBRARY. By Chau-mun Lau. Honolulu, University of Hawaii Library, 1975.

THE CHINESE IN THE CALIFORNIA MINES, 1848-1860. By Stephen Williams, Stanford, California, 1930. Reprint San Francisco, R and E Research Associates, 1971.

A discussion of the Chinese movement into California, Chinese life at the mines and the effect of the anti-Chinese movement at the mines. Includes a bibliography.

THE CHINESE IN THE UNITED STATES OF AMERICA. By Rose Hum Lee. Hong Kong, Hong Kong University Press, 1960.

A sociological study which investigates the social, economic, occupational, institutional and associational life of the Chinese in America. Appendices include Chinese students and alumni services, Chinese institutions and associations and a glossary.

THE CHINESE IN THE UNITED STATES: SOCIAL MOBILITY AND ASSIMILATION. By Mely Tan. Taipei Orient Cultural Service, 1973, c.1968.

This book presents evidence of social mobility among the Chinese in the United States based on an analysis of the social structure of the Chinese community in San Francisco and asks whether social mobility among the Chinese leads to structural assimilation.

CHINESE LABOR IN CALIFORNIA, 1850-1880: AN ECONOMIC STUDY. By Ping Chiu. Madison, Wisconsin, 1963.

The Chinese were employed in the mines, railroads, agriculture and some industries. This book is a detailed study of their employment situation during the second half of the last century.

THE CHINESE OF AMERICA. By Jack Chen. San Francisco, Harper and Row, 1980.

The story of the immigrant Chinese as told in three distinct parts: the coming, 1785-1882; exclusion, 1882-1943 and integration, 1943-1980. The appendix includes a discussion on Chinatowns and Chinese American communities in the United States.

THE CHINESE PROBLEM. By L. T. Townsend. Boston, Lee and Shepard Publishers, 1876. Reprinted 1970 by R and E Associates, San Francisco.

A contemporary account, based on the author's travels along the Pacific Coast in 1875, of hostility toward early Chinese settlers in California. Refutes derogatory charges against the Chinese, attributes the charges to economic competition, urges an end to discrimination against the Chinese, and advocates their conversion to Christianity.

THE CHINESE SIX COMPANIES. By William Hoy. San Francisco, Chinese Consolidated Benevolent Association, 1942.

Tells about the importance of these groups in Chinese American social organizations.

"CHINK!" A Documentary History of Anti-Chinese Prejudice in America. Edited by Cheng-Tsu Wu. New York, World Publishing Company, 1972.

Documents the history of racial prejudice against the Chinese in the United States. Discusses discriminatory laws passed in the nineteenth century, economic and social discrimination, individual acts of brutality and injustice, and changing attitudes toward the Chinese. Also deals with prejudice from the Chinese community.

DOUBLE TEN; Captain O'Banion's Story of the Chinese Rebellion. By Carl Glick. New York, Whittlesey House (McGraw-Hill), 1945.

Recounts the part played by Captain O'Banion and Americans of Chinese descent in the Chinese Revolution of 1911, which toppled a corrupt empress from her throne. Tells about the plotting and planning and sacrifices made to bring about democracy in China.

EAT A BOWL OF TEA. By Louis Chu. New York, Lyle Stuart, 1961.

A novel set in a realistic setting of Chinatown.

FATHER AND GLORIOUS DESCENDENT. By Pardee Lowe. Boston, Little, Brown & Company, 1943.

An autobiographical account of a young Chinese growing up to become an American.

FIFTH CHINESE DAUGHTER. By Jade Snow Wong. New York, Harper and Brothers, 1945.

An autobiography of an American Chinese girl's first twenty-four years. Describes her life in San Francisco, the Chinese customs and attitudes of her family, her school and work experiences.

FUSANG, THE CHINESE WHO BUILT AMERICA. By Stanley Steiner. New York, Harper and Row, 1979.

Stories of the Chinese who discovered America, and played such an essential part in developing it, are presented in this book.

HANDBOOK OF CHINESE IN AMERICA. By Ju-chou Chen. New York, The People's Foreign Relations Association of China, 1946.

A kind of "Who's Who" with entries in English and Chinese.

THE HATCHET MEN; The Story of the Tong Wars in San Francisco's Chinatown. By Richard H. Dillon. New York, Coward-McCann, 1962.

Covers a lurid, violent chapter in San Francisco's history. Describes the origin and activities of the Chinese criminal gangs that ruled Chinatown from the 1880 s to the earthquake of 1906.

HISTORY OF CHINESE-AMERICANS IN BALTIMORE. By Leslie Chin. Baltimore, Greater Baltimore Chinese-American Bicentennial Committee, 1976.

This book accomplishes its purpose by compiling and condensing all written materials, personal interviews and pictures into a short history of the Chinese Americans in Baltimore. It presents Chinese culture as it existed in the 1970 s and provides a bibliography.

THE INDISPENSABLE ENEMY: LABOR AND THE ANTI-CHINESE MOVEMENT IN CALIFORNIA. By Alexander Saxton. Berkeley, University of California Press, 1971.

Chinese labor was crucial in the building of the California economy, yet the presence of the Chinese gave rise to bitter prejudice.

LONGTIME CALIFORN': A DOCUMENTARY STUDY OF AN AMERICAN CHINATOWN. By Victor Nee. New York, Pantheon Books, 1973.

This book portrays Chinatown's past and present through interviews of residents of Chinatown. Discusses the three societies that have evolved: bachelor society, family society and working class society.

THE MISSISSIPPI CHINESE; Between Black and White. By James W. Loewen. Cambridge, Massachusetts, Harvard University Press, 1971.

This book focuses on the causes of the change in the Chinese's status (from being referred to as negro to white status), the processes by which it came about and the opposition it engendered. Includes appendices (tables, resolutions, labor contracts) and a glossary.

MOUNTAIN OF GOLD; The Story of the Chinese in America. By Betty Lee Sung. New York, Macmillan Company, 1967.

Chronicles the history of Chinese people in the United States from gold rush days to modern times. Dispels old, unfavorable cliches. Discusses problems of assimilation, prejudice, Chinatowns, family life, occupations, and contributions of Chinese-Americans in many fields. Paperback edition is entitled "The Story of the Chinese in America."

MUST THE CHINESE GO? By Esther Baldwin. New York, Issued from the Press of H. B. Elkins, 1890. Reprint San Francisco, R and E Research Associates, 1970.

Originally a pamphlet defending the Chinese at a time when prejudice against them was rampant. Attacks the government for passing anti-Chinese laws.

OCCUPATIONAL MOBILITY AND KINSHIP ASSISTANCE: A STUDY OF CHINESE IMMIGRANTS IN CHICAGO. By Peter S. Li. San Francisco, R and E Research Associates, 1978. c.1977.

Analyzes the occupational changes of Chinese immigrants in Chicago. The author provides answers to two questions: how mobile are the Chinese occupationally in terms of upward and downward movements and what factors determine success or failure.

ORIENTALS AND THEIR CULTURAL ADJUSTMENT; Interviews, Life Histories, and Social Adjustment Experience of Chinese and Japanese; Backgrounds and Length of Residence in the United States. Fisk University, Nashville, Tennessee, Social Science Institute, Fisk University, 1946.

This book provides realistic accounts of the conflicts and adjustments which the members of the second and third generations of orientals are confronting in America.

OUTLINES: HISTORY OF THE CHINESE IN AMERICA. By H. M. Lai and Philip P. Choy. San Francisco, Chinese-American Studies Planning Group, 1973.

A chronology in outline form of the important events pertaining to the Chinese in America.

PASSAGE TO THE GOLDEN GATE; A History of the Chinese in America to 1910. By Daniel Chu and Samuel Chu. Garden City, New York, Doubleday and Company, 1967.

A colorful, illustrated story of China clipper ships, the rush of Chinese to California to find gold, their toil building the first railroad across the West, discrimination and hardship, life in Chinatown, and the destructive San Francisco earthquake of 1906.

PIGTAILS AND GOLD DUST; A Panorama of Chinese Life in Early California. By Alexander McLeod. Caldwell, Idaho, Caxton Printers, 1948.

Describes the way of life of the Chinese in California from gold rush days to the earthquake of 1906. A detailed study of their economic and social conditions, leisure pursuits, local governing organization, religious beliefs, customs and superstitutions.

PRESTIGE WITH LIMITATIONS: REALITIES OF THE CHINESE-AMERICAN ELITE. By Dean Lan. San Francisco, R and E Research Associates, 1976.

This study focuses on the discrepancies between the Chinese image and the reality in American society.

THE REAL CHINESE IN AMERICA. By J. S. Tow. New York, Academy Press, 1923. Reprint San Francisco, R and E Research Associates, 1970.

Gives information concerning the lives, character, business, and organizations of Chinese people in the United States from the viewpoint of a Chinese observer.

THE REEMERGENCE OF AN INNER CITY: THE PIVOT OF CHINESE SETTLEMENT IN THE EAST BAY REGION OF THE SAN FRANCISCO BAY AREA. By Willard T. Chow, San Francisco, R & E Research Associates, 1977.

Looks at the Chinese settlement and how its foundations were set up as well as the racial constraints on the structure, but mainly shows how an inner city reemerged.

SAN FRANCISCO'S CHINATOWN: HOW CHINESE A TOWN? By Christopher L. Salter. San Francisco, R and E Research Associates, 1978.

A look at the origins, visual and functional morphology and cultural isolation of San Francisco's Chinatown.

THE SANDALWOOD MOUNTAINS: READINGS AND STORIES OF THE EARLY CHINESE IN HAWAII. Compiled and edited by Tin-Yuke Char. Honolulu, University Press of Hawaii, 1975.

Included in this collection of readings about the Chinese in Hawaii are excerpts of printed articles, extractions from books, government documents and a few news stories.

SOCIAL AND POLITICAL CHANGE IN NEW YROK'S CHINATOWN: THE ROLE OF VOLUNTARY ASSOCIATIONS. By Chia-ling Kuo. New York, Praeger, 1977.

This book examines the role of voluntary associations in the recent social and political changes in New York's Chinatown and traces the evolution of traditional into modern voluntary associations.

SOJOURNERS AND SETTLERS, CHINESE MIGRANTS IN HAWAII. By Clarence Glick. Honolulu, University Press of Hawaii, 1980.

The first section of this book deals with the Chinese who immigrated to America. The later chapters discuss the movement of the migrants and families into the economic mainstream of Hawaii, the opposition they met and the organizations they developed to help them cope with the opposition.

A SURVEY OF CHINESE-AMERICAN MANPOWER AND EMPLOYMENT. By Betty Lee Sung. New York, Praeger, 1976.

This book provides a look at Chinese-American manpower and employment characteristics. Includes patterns of Chinese immigration, geographical dispersion, demographic characteristics, educational level, occupational pattern, working women, unions, income, unemployment and underemployment and cultural differences.

THE UNWELCOME IMMIGRANT: THE AMERICAN IMAGE OF THE CHINESE, 1785-1822. By Stuart Miller. Berkeley, University of California Press, 1969.

This book shows that anti-Chinese attitudes were national not regional and reflected a clash of confronting cultures and values.

VALLEY CITY: A CHINESE COMMUNITY IN AMERICA. By Melford S. Weiss. Cambridge, Massachusetts. Schenkman Publishing Company. Distributed by General Learning Press, Morristown, New Jersey, 1974.

This book examines the community of Valley City, California and its Chinese American residents and discusses the era of the traditional Chinatown (1850-1900), the time of transition (1900-1940); and the contemporary scene.

WRITINGS ON THE CHINESE IN CALIFORNIA. By Pearl Ng, 1939. Reprint, San Francisco, R and E Research Associates, 1972.

Part one contains four writings on the Chinese in California and part two is a bibliography of writings on the Chinese. Includes books, pamphlets and periodical articles.

THE WOMAN WARRIOR: MEMOIRS OF A GIRLHOOD AMONG GHOSTS. By Maxine Hong Kingston. New York, 1976.

An autobiography of a young Chinese American woman.

Audiovisual Material

FILMS

ABSTRACTING. 16 mm. Color and sound. 4 minutes. By University of Southern California, Division of Cinema/TV, Los Angeles, 1979.

An introduction to Chinese calligraphy and its relation to Chinese philosophy and culture.

THE ANCIENT CHINESE. 16 mm. Color and sound. 24 Minutes. By Julien Bryan. New York, International Film Foundation, 1974.

Shows highlights from the major dynasties in Chinese history. Discusses eminent achievements in each period up to the present time. Explains the influence of ancient Chinese traditions on contemporary life styles in China.

ANCIENT CHINESE PAINTINGS. 16 mm. Color and sound. 26 minutes. By China Art Film Limited, 1978.

As early as 2,000 years ago, Chinese painting had achieved excellence in both technique and inspiration. Introducing the unique concepts and character of Chinese painting, this film presents a number of the finest works from the collection of the National Palace Museum in Taipei. The master-pieces shown include four from the Tang dynasty (618-907), three from the Sung dynasty (960-1280), three from the Yuan dynasty (1280-1368), five from the Ming dynasty (1368-1644), and two from the Ching dynasty (1644-1911).

BAREFOOT LITTLE LEAGUERS. 16 mm. Color. 10 minutes. By Kwang Hwa Film Syndicate, 1979.

Dealing with the fast growth of baseball in the Republic of China, especially among primary and high school boys, this film explores the reason why teams from Taiwan have for many years won the titles in the Little League, Senior League and Big League world series, sometimes by lop-sided scores, and on occasion by no-hitter. The film recalls that only a decade or so ago, boys in Taiwan used bamboo sticks as bats and rubber balls as baseballs. Traditional Chinese diligence and a nine-year free education system are the main factors contributing to this remarkable achievement.

THE BATTLE OF CHINA. Videorecording. Black and white and sound. 67 minutes. By United States War Department, Washington. Distributed by National Audiovisual Center, 1979.

Depicts Japanese aggression against China during World War II and describes Japan's plans for world conquest. Recalls Chinese development of the compass, printing, astronomy, gunpowder, and porcelain. Originally a motion picture issued in 1944.

THE BEAUTIFUL BAIT. 16 mm. Color. 15 minutes. By Taiwan Film Studio, 1966.

This is a short documentary film showing the features of Chinese opera. The story is about a heroine of some 1,000 years ago, who sacrificed herself for the sake of nation by serving as a beautiful bait in assassination of a crafty and traitorous prime minister. Performers of this story are students of the Foo Hsing School of Dramatic Arts in Taipei. The stylized singing and dancing as features of Chinese opera are fully demonstrated in this film which is marked with synchronized recording of sound and music, together with superb color.

THE BONANZA FROM SLOPELANDS: SLOPELAND DEVELOPMENT IN TAIWAN. 16 mm. Color. 28 minutes. By China Art Film Limited, 1977.

Taiwan is a small island with a large population. Proper land utilization is, therefore, of great importance. The government has carried out a number of projects to use hill areas for industry, agriculture, forestry, animal husbandry, community development, recreation and tourism. This film introduces these projects and progress to date. Reclamation of slopeland is a complex task, involving scientific surveys and special techniques, and above all, the strenuous efforts of all concerned. This film illustrates the unwavering spirit of the Chinese people.

THE BUFFALO REVOLUTION. 16 mm. Color. 27 minutes. By China Art Film Limited, 1977.

The population of water buffalo, long used in China as a farm draft animal, is declining replaced as power tillers are increasingly being used in Taiwan's paddy fields. Other factors contributing to the success of agricultural programs in Taiwan include wide use of fertilizers and pesticides, increased irrigation, hybrid seeds, intensive planting, and rotation of crops. The successful completion of a land reform movement, which has featured the reduction of farm rentals, sale of public lands, and implementation of a land-to-the-tiller program, has made the biggest contribution of all.

BUILDING FOR THE FUTURE. 16 mm. Color. 43 minutes. By China Art Film, Limited, 1976.

Between 1973 and 1979, the government of the Republic of China successfully completed 10 major construction projects, involving a total investment of US $8 billion. The projects are: the North-South Freeway (now called the Sun Yat-sen Freeway), railroad electrification, North Link Railroad, Taoyuan International Airport (now called the Chiang Kai-shek International Airport), Taichung Harbor, Suao Port, the integrated steel mill, the Kaohsiung shipyard, petrochemical complexes, and nuclear power plants. This film, made in 1976, shows the construction projects during the early stages of implementation.

CHINA. 16 mm. Color and sound. 50 minutes. By BBC-TV, New York, Time-Life Multimedia, 1971.

A documentary film about contemporary life and politics in China. Portrays China as a completely monolithic society in which agriculture is flourishing, industry is making great strides, and the people are well-fed, well-housed, well-clothed, and literate.

CHINA, A CLASS BY ITSELF. 16 mm. Color and sound. 51 minutes. Also available as videorecording. By NBC, Films, Incorporated, Wilmette, Illinois, 1979.

An inside look at China working towards the goal of becoming a superpower by the year 2000 via education as the key to modernization. Filmed in Peking on a rural commune in central China, and in the industrial northeast region, Jack Reynolds interviews Vice Premier Fang Yi and the president of Peking University, as well as students, workers, and peasants.

CHINA: A HOLE IN THE BAMBOO CURTAIN. 16 mm. Color and sound. 28 minutes. New York, Carousel Films, 1973.

Evaluates life in modern mainland China as compared with the political and economic standard of living in the United States. Shows scenes in Shenyang, Peking, Shanghai, and Canton, including China's historic sites and medical advances through accupuncture.

CHINA - A NETWORK OF COMMUNES. 16 mm. Color and sound. 15 minutes. By Encyclopaedia Britannica Educational Corporation, Chicago, 1977.

Shows communes in China engaged in various kinds of production activities. Investigates the Chinese concept of the farm-factory in which communes are encouraged to become self-sufficient and to mass-produce. Edited from the modern picture issued in 1973 under title, The awakening giant - China.

CHINA, AN EMERGING GIANT. 16 mm. Color and sound. 25 minutes. Also available as videorecording. By National Geographic Society, Washington, The Society, 1978.

Deals with industrial aspects of contemporary China, including the nation's energy resources and the lives of the workers.

CHINA: AN END TO ISOLATION. 16 mm. Color and sound. 23 minutes. By Filmfact Educational Production Company. Released by ACI Films, 1972.

Takes a look at life in the People's Republic of China. Examines the country's agricultural, economic, and industrial accomplishments and links the everyday life of the people with the teachings of Chairman Mao.

CHINA: AN OPEN DOOR. 16 mm. Color with black and white sequences. Sound. 20 minutes for each of the three parts. By Mizlou Productions. New York, Associated Press, 1972.

Part 1: The Awakening Giant, describes the rise of Communism and the revolutionary government of Mao Tse-Tung in order to give a better understanding of China today. Part 2: The Past in Prologue, gives insight into the major internal struggles of China including the civil war between the Nationalists and the Communists and the role of the Red Guard in the Great Prolitarian Cultural Revolution. Part 3: Today . . . and Tomorrow, deals with China as she opens the door to the Western World. Focuses on political and cultural aspects of the country, the entrance of the People's Republic of China into the United Nations, and President Nixon's visit to Peking.

CHINA AND THE WORLD. 16 mm. Black and white. Sound. 20 minutes. Also issued as videorecording. By BBC-TV, New York, Time Life Multimedia, 1970.

Discusses the 19th century invasions and defeats of China by foreign powers. Explains the effect of the Japanese war and the seizure of Taiwan, Korea, and Manchuria, including China's reactions toward restored dignity in Korea and the deterioration of her relations with the Soviet Union.

CHINA, COMING OF THE WEST. 16 mm. Color and sound. 20 minutes. Also available as videocassette. Chinese History Series. By China Institude in America, Incorporated, University Audio-Visual Center, Bloomington, Indiana, 1977, c.1976.

Highlights the confrontation between modern Western civilization and ancient Chinese civilization from the 16th to 20th century.

CHINA: COMMUNIST TRIUMPH AND CONSOLIDATION, 1945-1971. 16 mm. Black and white. Sound. 29 minutes. By Metromedia Producers Corporation. Edited and released by Films Incorporated, 1972.

Shows that even though the allies support Chiang Kai-sheck, United States confidence fades as he loses out to the Communists. Describes his retreats to Formosa with his Nationalists, surrounded by symbols of an ancient China. Explains that in two decades Mao Tse-tung has gained full control of the mainland of China and has created a new tyranny. Edited from the motion pictures entitled China: roots of madness and Rise of Communist power, 1941-1967.

CHINA-EDUCATION FOR A NEW SOCIETY. 16 mm. Color and sound. 15 minutes. By Jens Bjerre, Chicago, Encyclopaedia Britannica Educational Corporation, 1976.

Discusses the philosophy of education and its relation to political ideology in the People's Republic of China.

CHINA: HER PEOPLE TODAY. 16 mm. Color and sound. 17 minutes. Los Angeles, Shaw Productions, 1972.

Presents a study of how Communist Chinese live today. Shows family life, farming methods, the ballet and other recreation, motivation through propaganda, the revival of old crafts and skills, communal life, the role of women, and how children are indoctrinated. Includes scenes in Shanghai and Peking of old and new buildings and methods of transportation.

CHINA, HUNDRED SCHOOLS TO ONE. 16 mm. Color and sound. 19 minutes. Also available as videocassette. Chinese History Series. By China Institute in America, Incorporated, Bloomington, Indiana University Audio-Visual Center, 1977. c. 1976.

Focuses on the period of Chinese history between 475 B.C. and 221 B.C. marked by the warring between states and the technological and agricultural revolution which led to the formation of the Ch'in empire.

CHINA, THE AGE OF MATURITY. 16 mm. Color and sound. 23 minutes. Also available as videocassette. Chinese History Series. By China Institute in America, Incorporated, Bloomington, Indiana University Audio-Visual Center, 1977, c.1976.

Focuses on the period of Chinese history between A.D. 907 and A.D. 1279, marked by the Sung dynasty.

CHINA, THE BEGINNINGS. 16 mm. Color and sound. 19 minutes. Also issued as videocassette. Chinese History Series. By China Institute in America, Incorporated, Bloomington, Indiana University, Audio-Visual Center, 1977.

Uses anthropological findings in exploring the origin of the Chinese people and their civilization up to 1100 B.C.

CHINA: THE EAST IS RED. 16 mm and Super 8 mm. Color and sound. 20 minutes. By Asahi TV News, Tokyo, 1967. Released in the United States by Doubleday Multimedia, 1969.

A study of the economic and cultural problems of present-day China. Traces the development of these problems from the social and political traditions of the past.

CHINA, THE ENDURING HERITAGE. 16 mm. Color and sound. 19 minutes. Also available as videocassette. Chinese History Series. By China Institute in America, Incorporated, Bloomington, Indiana University, Audio-Visual Center, 1977.

Highlights events and cultural achievements in China's history from earliest times to 1911.

CHINA, THE FIRST EMPIRES. 16 mm. Color and sound. 19 minutes. Also issued as videocassette. Chinese History Series. By China Institute in America, Incorporated, Bloomington, Indiana University Audio-Visual Center, 1977, c.1976.

Focuses on the period of Chinese history between 221 B.C. and A.D. 220, marked by the advent of China's imperial age with Ch'in and the expansion of the empire under Han.

CHINA, THE GOLDEN AGE. 16 mm. Color and sound. 23 minutes. Also available as videocassette. Chinese History Series. By China Institute in America, Incorporated, Bloomington, Indiana University, Audio-Visual Center, 1977.

Focuses on the expansion of a reunited China under the rules of the Sui and T'ang Dynasties.

CHINA, THE GREAT CULTURAL MIX. 16 mm. Color and sound. 17 minutes. Also available as videocassette. Chinese History Series. By China Institute in America, Incorporated, Bloomington, Indiana University Audio-Visual Center, 1977, c.1976.

Focuses on the period of Chinese history between A.D. 220 and A.D. 581, marked by the disintegration of the Han empire, the formation of new dynasties, and developments in religion and art.

CHINA, THE HEAVENLY KHAN. 16 mm. Color and sound. 22 minutes. Also available as videocassette. Chinese History Series. By China Institute in America, Incorporated, Bloomington, Indiana University Audio-Visual Center, 1977, c.1976.

Focuses on the period of Chinese history from A.D. 618 to A.D. 907, marked by cultural exchanges between China and other countries.

CHINA, THE MAKING OF A CIVILIZATION. 16 mm. Color and sound. 18 minutes. Also available as videocassette. Chinese History Series. By China Institute in America, Incorporated, Bloomington, Indiana University Audio-Visual Center, 1977, c. 1976.

Highlights the political, social, and religious characteristics of the period in Chinese history from 1100 B.C. to 475 B.C.

CHINA, THE MANCHU RULE. 16 mm. Color and sound. 19 minutes. Also available as videocassette. Chinese History Series. By China Institute in America, Incorporated, Bloomington, Indiana University Audio-Visual Center, 1977.

Focuses on the period of Chinese history from 1644 to 1911, which was characterized by secure borders and peace in the 17th century, peasant uprisings in the late 18th century, the Opium War with the British in the first half of the 19th century, and defeat of the Ch'ing dynasty at the end of the 19th century.

CHINA: THE RED SONS. 16 mm. Color and sound. 52 minutes. By Roger Whittaker Productions, Sydney, Australia. Released in the United States by Contemporary Films/McGraw-Hill, New York, 1970.

A documentary film made by two Australian students. Describes what it is like to travel in China and meet its ordinary citizens. Includes interviews with Red

Guard students and workers, who tell about their lives and the meaning of the thoughts of Mao Tse-Tung.

CHINA, THE RESTORATION. 16 mm. Color and sound. 22 minutes. Also available as videocassette. By China Institute in America, Incorporated, Bloomington, Indiana University Audio-Visual Center, 1977.

Focuses on the period of Chinese history between 1368 and 1644, which was marked by recovery from foreign rule and the rise and fall of the Ming dynasty.

CHINA TODAY. 16 mm. Color and sound. 22 minutes. By NBC News. Released by NBC Educational Enterprises, 1972.

Explores some of the aspects of present-day China. Shows how the Chinese Government stresses participation rather than efficiency in its work in building the nation's economic, agricultural, educational, and medical capabilities, and tells how China's future leaders and bureaucrats are trained to use their hands in manual labor in helping build the nation.

CHINA, UNDER THE MONGOLS. 16 mm. Color and sound. 18 minutes. Also available as videocassette. Chinese History Series. By China Institute in America, Incorporated, Bloomington, Indiana University Audio-Visual Center, 1977.

Focuses on the period of Chinese history between A.D. 1279 and A.D. 1368, which was marked by Mongol domination and the return to native rule with the advent of the Ming dynasty.

CHINA'S CHANGING FACE. 16 mm. Color and sound. 25 minutes. Also available as videorecording. By National Geographic Society, Washington, 1978.

Uses still photographs and historical footage to reveal what China was like before the founding of the People's Republic. Then shows what China is like today, with the commune as the basic organizational unit, and examines China's educational system and medicine, as well as its industry and agriculture.

CHINESE CHILDREN'S GAMES. 16 mm. Color and sound. Kwang Hwa Film Syndicate, 1982.

CHINESE COSTUMES - AN EVOLUTIONARY STORY. 16 mm. Color. 26 minutes. By Free China Film Syndicate, 1971.

This film provides a graphic illustration of the evolution of fashion in China over the past 4,000 years. The history of clothes is told in a fascinating way by a girl student at the College of Home Economics in Taipei, who majored in dress design. After explaining the development of costumes in detail with the aid of models, the film ends with shots from the Miss Tourism contest held in Taipei. All the garments were styled and made in Taiwan with Taiwan-made materials.

CHINESE FOLK ARTS. 16 mm. Color. 24 minutes. By China Art Film Limited, 1976.

Employing the new and effective technique of montage, this film introduces seven major traditional Chinese folk arts: Shadow puppetry, embroidery, paper cutting, kite flying lanterns, puppet show, and lion dances. Emphasis is placed on the fact that the free Chinese manage to maintain their cultural traditions while modernizing society. Folk arts may flourish only in a land where people are free to develop their talents.

CHINESE JOURNEY. 16 mm. Color and sound. 25 minutes. By BBC-TV, London, and Odyssey Productions, 1968. Released in the United States by Time-Life Films.

Explores China from Shanghai up the Yangtse River to Peking. Shows the Mongolian capital of Ulan Bator. Includes scenes of the Gobi desert, showing Mongols who live in nomadic life. Narrated by Lowell Thomas.

CHINESE MUSIC AND MUSICAL INSTRUMENTS. 16 mm. Color. 23 minutes. By China Art Film Limited, 1968.

China has a very old civilization. As early as 5,000 years ago, Fu Hsi-shih invented several musical instruments, sowing the first seeds of formal Chinese music. Ancient instruments were divided into eight categories based on the material used, such as metal, stone and bamboo. The principal function of music in early time was to educate. Today music has an important place in the daily life of the people. This film illustrates the special character of Chinese music and musical instruments. It also describes the development and improvement of Chinese music in the social and educational fields.

CHINESE NEW YEAR. 16 mm. Color. 13 minutes. By China Art Film Limited, 1964.

This film shows traditional customs of the Lunar New Year season in China. Included are colorful scenes from a farewell party for the Kitchen God, children receiving red envelopes containing money, dragon and lion dances, a wedding, and a family dinner. The Lunar New Year is the most important festival in China when everybody goes home to enjoy family reunions. This tradition holds just as strongly today as in the past even though industry has replaced agriculture as the basis of the economy.

CHINESE PORCELAIN. 16 mm. Color. 21 minutes. By China Art Film Limited, 1969.

The unparalleled beauty of Chinese porcelain was first revealed to the outside world when Chang Chien went West to Asia Minor as a Chinese envoy in 135 B.C. In the 2,000 years that followed, many changes occurred in the design of Chinese porcelain. The use of the word china, to categorize fine porcelain, is the best indication of its country of origin. This film shows how the Chinese art of porcelain making was started, developed and reached its peak, with the help of illustrations of masterpieces kept in the National Palace Museum. The film also illustrates improvements being made to pottery techniques in the Republic of China today.

A CITY OF CATHAY. 16 mm. Color. 28-1/2 minutes. By China Art Film Limited, 1960.

This is a photographic representation of a famous Chinese scroll painting which depicts the people and everyday activities in the Sung dynasty (960-1279) in the riverside capital of Kaifeng during the spring festival. The scroll is 37 feet long and only one foot high. Within its horizontal purview, more than 4,000 human figures, each only half an inch tall, are shown performing daily activities in much the same way as they have throughout history. One of the greatest Chinese art works, the scroll is kept in the National Palace Museum in the Republic of China.

CONFUCIUS. 16 mm. Color. 28 minutes. By Mass Communications, Incorporated, 1975.

Confucius, whose philosophy emphasizes the importance of ethical relations and the dignity of man, is the greatest teacher in Chinese history, who has been respected in all ages. Through interpretations by contemporary scholars, this film illustrates the sage's thinking and its impact on the Chinese view and way of life. An important Confucian concept is that when personal life is cultivated, family life is regulated; when family life is regulated, national life is orderly; when national life is orderly, there is peace in the world.

EDUCATION IN THE REPUBLIC OF CHINA. 16 mm. Color. 25 minutes. By Free China Film Syndicate, 1979.

Education in the Republic of China stresses national morality, cultural traditions, scientific knowledge and the ability to work and contribute to the community. Depicting various student activities, this film also stresses that education in the Republic of China is based on the Three Principles of the People which embody traditional Chinese culture and the Confucian spirit of education without discrimination. On a wider level, the Principles advocate national independence, democracy and social well-being, and finally the establishment of a Great Commonwealth of Nations.

EIGHT OR NINE IN THE MORNING. 16 mm. Color and sound. 25 minutes. Also available as videorecording. By Felix Greene. New York, Time-Life Multimedia, 1973.

Examines the educational system in China and shows how new ideas conceived during the cultural revolution are being applied.

FRIENDSHIP FIRST, COMPETITION SECOND. 16 mm. Color and sound. 25 minutes. Also available as videorecording. By Felix Greene. New York, Time-Life Multimedia, 1973.

Focuses on sports in China, showing the Chinese enthusiasm for many sports adopted from the West, such as table tennis, as well as their own traditional entertainments, including acrobatics, juggling, and gymnastics.

FROM WAR TO REVOLUTION. 16 mm. Black and white. Sound. 20 minutes. Also available as videorecording. By BBC-TV, New York, Time-Life Multimedia, 1970.

Analyzes social, economic, and political conditions in China in the 19th century. Discusses the establishment of the Chinese Republic and its collapse, the civil war, Chiang Kai-shek's takeover of the Nationalists Party in 1926, the Japanese invasion, and the defeat of Chiang Kai-shek by Mao Tse-tung in 1949.

GOLDEN HERITAGE GOLDEN HARVEST. 16 mm. Color. 28 minutes. By Mass Communications, Incorporated, 1974.

The people of the Republic of China cherish their traditions, particularly the Confucian philosophy, which is more a way of life than a religion. This philosophy stresses a harmonious human relationship through mutual support such as consideration for others, and fulfilling individual obligations. While preserving this heritage, the Chinese people in Taiwan have created an economic miracle which has enabled them to enjoy lives of unprecedented prosperity. They have also shared their experience of progress with people in developing countries in Africa and Latin America. This film gives an insight into this progress.

HARVEST FROM THE SEA. 16 mm. Color. 29 minutes. Free China Film Syndicate, 1977.

Taiwan's subtropical location makes it ideal for the development of the fishing industry. This film describes how fishermen use modern techniques to increase production of deep-sea, inshore and coastal resources, as well as expand fish culture. Government assistance, in the form of construction and expansion of fishing ports, provision of low-interest loans, and the introduction of modern techniques has been helpful in fishery development. Many developing countries have turned to Taiwan for technical assistance in the field.

HERE COMES THE CHAIRMAN. 16 mm. Color and sound. 5 minutes. Curtis Choy, 1973.

Contrasts old and new China. Expresses different qualities of life in different times as personified by Chinese leaders.

HERITAGE OF CHINESE OPERA. 16 mm. Color. 31 minutes. By Chinese Art Films, Incorporated, 1978.

Chinese Opera has a history of more than 13 centuries, beginning with the court ballet of the early Tang dynasty. It differs from Western opera in that it combines singing, reciting, acting and dancing. The distinguishing features of Chinese opera include: (1) paucity of stage props, (2) falsetto singing, (3) symbolism in gait and gesture, (4) face painting, which is used to reveal character, (5) acrobatics, (6) stylized and colorful costumes, and (7) accompaniment by a small orchestra. This film illustrates all these features in detail.

IMPRESSIONS OF CHINA. 16 mm. Color and sound. 22 minutes. Marlin Motion Pictures, Port Credit, Ontario, 1974.

Follows a group of Canadian high school students on their tour of the People's Republic of China.

IT'S ALWAYS SO IN THE WORLD. 16 mm. Color and sound. 28 minutes. By Film Australia. New York, Learning Corporation of America, 1979, made 1978.

Shows the day-to-day life of a Chinese family at work and at leisure.

THE KINGDOM OF BUTTERFLIES. 16 mm. Color and sound. Kwang Hwa Film Syndicate, 1982.

KINMEN: OUTPOST OF FREEDOM. 16 mm. Color. 16 minutes. By Free China Film Syndicate, 1975.

Kinmen, also known as Quemoy, is an offshore island within sight and sound of the Communist-controlled mainland. In 1958, the Chinese Communist artillery bombarded this outpost of freedom with half a million shells in 44 days, but the island stood fast, and was hailed by many as "the strongest fortress of free China." Depicting life on the island, this film is a treatise on the importance of freedom. It won high honors for its richness in local color and human interest at the Asian Film Festival in 1975.

LI MAO-TSUNG'S POTTERY. 16 mm. Color. 7 minutes. By Free China Film Syndicate, 1973.

This film tells the story of a young Chinese potter, Li Mao-tsung. Long restricted by the hard creative process by which he learned the art, Li finally breaks out of the traditional pattern of pottery-making and establishes his own style. In his works one may find a distinctive mingling of ancient Chinese and modern ceramic art. Through rubbing, molding, trimming and glazing, Li produces pottery invested with the soul of ancient Chinese, but as modern as tomorrow. Li has incorporated the Chinese qualities of sincerity and determination into his works.

LIFE IN NORTH CHINA. 16 mm. Color and sound. 18 minutes. By Public Media. Released by Films Incorporated, Wilmette, Illinois, 1971.

Shows how commune workers from the country join city workers of North China (formerly Manchuria) to celebrate National Liberation Day. Includes scenes of Chinese thronging through the city to watch the parade.

MAHAYANA BUDDHISM. 16 mm. Color and sound. 12 minutes. By Lew Ayres. Irvine, California, Doubleday Multimedia, 1976, made 1975.

Examines the differing interpretations of Buddhist teachings. Includes ceremonies of Chinese nuns, a brief introduction to Confucianism, and the principles of Taoism.

MAO - ORGANISED CHAOS. 16 mm. Color and sound. 24 minutes. By Nielsen-Ferns International. New York, Learning Corporation of America, 1979, made 1978.

Points out China's difficulties, both at home and abroad, after Mao Tse-tung came to power. Examines strained relations with the U.S.S.R. and the United States and shows how the cultural revolution brought China near the brink of disaster.

MASTERPIECES OF CHINESE ART. 16 mm. Color. 28 minutes. By Mass Communications, Incorporated, 1973.

The finest and largest collection of Chinese art treasures in the world is housed in the National Palace Museum in the suburbs of Taipei. Since its formal opening on November 12, 1965, the 100th birthday anniversary of Dr. Sun Yat-sen, founding father of the Republic of China, the museum has attracted visitors from all over the world at an average annual rate of 1.3 million.

MEDICINE IN CHINA. 16 mm. Color and sound. 25 minutes. Also available as videorecording. By Felix Greene. New York, Time-Life Multimedia, 1973.

Documents the revolution in Chinese medicine, showing how the Chinese have succeeded in bringing medicine to every corner of their nation. Includes a demonstration of acupuncture treatment.

MISSION TO YENAN. 16 mm, 8 mm, and 35 mm. Color and sound. 32 minutes. By Joseph DeCola. Released by Films Incorporated, 1972.

Provides a historical reevaluation of America's policy towards China.

MORNING IN TAIPEI. 16 mm. Color. 21 minutes. By China Art Film Limited, 1973.

A Chinese proverb says spring is the best time to start the year's work, and morning the best time to start the day's work. This film entitled Morning in Taipei, tells how people in Taipei, the temporary capital of the Republic of China, fully utilize the best time of the day. With a population of two million, Taipei is fast becoming a major world metropolis. This presentation shows how two brothers start one of their busy days against the background of morning in Taipei.

THE NEW CHINA. 16 mm. Black and white. Sound. 20 minutes. By BBC-TV, London, 1969. Released in the United States by Time-Life Films, 1970.

Follows the restructuring of China's social and economic order during the rule of Mao Tse-Tung, including the establishment of farm cooperatives, achievement of social equality for women, and the Red Guard inquisitions of 1966-67.

NEW FRONTIER. 16 mm. Color and sound. Kwang Hwa Film Syndicate, 1982.

OLD TRADITIONS & NEW TECHNOLOGIES. 16 mm. Color. 33 minutes. By Kwang Hwa Film Syndicate, 1979.

The goal of the Republic of China is to give Taiwan an industrialized economy with a high standard of living and rich high quality of life. Through years of strenuous effort, a traditional agricultural society has been transformed into a modern industrial one. The people are proud of the achievements of China's past, and confident in facing the challenge of the future. Shown in this film are such recently started projects as the manufacture of electric cars, processing pineapple bagasse into paper and making artificial reefs. Also shown are such activities as the application of acupuncture in the cure of asthma and preservation of old Chinese paintings.

OLD TREASURES FROM NEW CHINA. 16 mm. Color and sound. 55 minutes. By Shirley Sun. Berkeley, University of California Extension Media Center, 1977, made 1976.

Portrays China's evolution from primitive society through the Yuan dynasty by telling the story of her technological and artistic achievements as well as her contributions to world civilization. Selections from the 1975 archaeological exhibit from the People's Republic of China are shown.

OLD WORLD NEW WOMEN. 16 mm. Color. 28 minutes. By Mass Communications, Incorporated, 1975.

The status of Chinese women has improved steadily since the birth of the Republic of China in 1912. Equality is guaranteed by the Constitution. While upholding the virtues inherited from the past, the women of the Republic of China are today playing an important role in the nation's modernization. They work in government organizations, serve in the armed forces, engage in social work and enter the professions. This film shows the accomplishments of women in free China today in all walks of life, working in the spirit of equality and fair competition.

ONE NATION, MANY PEOPLES. 16 mm. Color and sound. 25 minutes. Also available as videorecording. By Felix Greene. New York, Time-Life Multimedia, 1973.

Conveys the diversity of China's many ethnic groups, showing the colorful lifestyles, music, dance, and dress of the different nationalities. Examines the relationship between Chinese authorities and the ethnic groups.

THE OTHER FACES OF TAIWAN. 16 mm. Color. 23 minutes. By China Art Film Limited, 1976.

In recent years, international tourists have increasingly been including Taiwan in their itineraries as they realize it is the only place in the world where genuine Chinese culture has been preserved. This film, however, presents another face of Taiwan - the natural beauty of the island. In addition to such popular scenic spots as Alishan and Sun Moon Lake, the film introduces such lesser known attractions as the coral reefs at Hengechun, the sea of clouds over Yushan, the flower season at Yangmingshan, and the aboriginal settlements on Orchid Island.

THE OTHER HALF OF THE SKY: A CHINA MEMOIR. 16 mm. Color and sound. 74 minutes. By Shirley MacLaine and Claudia Weill. Franklin Lakes, New Jersey, New Day Films, 1976.

Depicts life in the People's Republic of China as seen by a delegation of eight American women who visited there in 1973. Includes glimpses of a Peking family's apartment, visits to schools, nurseries, and recreational centers, and interviews with Chinese citizens who discuss their own and American lifestyles.

PAINTINGS BY HO HUAI-SHAO. 16 mm. Color. 11 minutes. By Free China Film Syndicate, 1976.

Chinese painting techniques reached maturity in the Sung and Yuan dynasties between the 10th and the 13th centuries. Each dynasty has its own typical works, but most painters did not reach out beyond conventional styles. Today, however, the young painters of the Republic of China are breathing new life into a time-honored traditions. They are trying out new concepts and techniques in their efforts to formulate a fresh style based on the past. The paintings of Ho Huai-shao, one of the leaders of this new wave, show complex feelings which combine intimacy with a sense of alienation.

THE PEOPLE OF THE PEOPLE'S REPUBLIC OF CHINA. 16 mm. Color and sound. 52 minutes. By ABC News. Released by Xerox Films, 1974.

Uses interviews with several citizens from the People's Republic of China in order to show living conditions in their country and to provide insight into their everyday lives and feeling.

THE PEOPLE'S ARMY. 16 mm. Color and sound. 25 minutes. Also available as videorecording. By Felix Greene. New York, Time-Life Multimedia, 1973.

Focuses on the Chinese army as a school of politics, engineering, agriculture, and fighting techniques. Shows soldiers working in the rice paddies, sweeping village streets, digging canals, undergoing military exercises and instruction, and interrelating with officers.

THE PEOPLE'S COMMUNES. 16 mm. Color and sound. 25 minutes. Also available as videorecording. By Felix Greene. New York, Time-Life Multimedia, 1973.

Shows how China reached self-sufficiency in agriculture through massive decentralization of authority. Examines the Chinese peasants' life on the communes, portraying their homes, shops, meetings, and capacity for hard work.

RED CHINA. 16 mm. Color and sound. 50 minutes. By the British Broadcasting Company, London. Released in the United States by Time-Life Films, New York, 1971.

A documentary film concerning life and politics in China. Portrays Red China as a monolithic society with one mind, one direction, and one omniscient leader.

REPORT ON ACUPUNCTURE. 16 mm. Color. 27 minutes. By Leo Seltzer Associates, Incorporated, 1973.

Acupuncture has been practiced as a therapy in China for more than a thousand years. Through interpretations by contemporary practitioners, this film illustrates how acupuncture is applied in the treatment of diseases and scientific research currently under way in the Republic of China. In recent years many foreigners have come to Taiwan to learn the techniques of acupuncture. This film shows them during their studies and the facilities available in Taiwan. It also provides an insight into the mysteries of acupuncture, and analyzes its value in medical treatment.

REPUBLIC OF CHINA, NEW FACE. 16 mm. Color and sound. Kwang Hwa Film Syndicate, 1982.

A documentary film showing recent programs and changes in Chinese society on Taiwan.

SELF-RELIANCE. 16 mm. Color and sound. 25 minutes. Also available as videorecording. By Felix Greene. New York, Time-Life Multimedia, 1973.

Shows how China is working toward industrialization through decentralization of industry and the encouragement of local small-scale enterprises.

SEVEN CHINESE FESTIVALS. 16 mm. Color. 24 minutes. By Echo Production, 1972. Presented by Tourism Bureau, Ministry of Communications.

This film depicts the Chinese way of life as it is manifested in seven major festivals: Lunar New Year, the Lantern Festival, the Ching Ming Festival, the Birthday Anniversary of Matsu, the Dragon Boat Festival, the Birthday of Confucius, and the Moon Festival.

THE STORY OF BAMBOO. 16 mm. Color. 26 minutes. By China Art Film Limited, 1977.

Bamboo plays a central role in every aspect of Chinese life. Before the invention of paper, it was used as a medium to record historical events. Chinese scholars regard the bamboo as characterizing the personality of a dignified gentleman. For more than 2,000 years, the Chinese have used bamboo widely as a material for making furniture, utensils, chopsticks, musical instruments, boats and even houses. This film shows how the Chinese make full use of bamboo and how it is esteemed as a symbol of Chinese customs and philosophy.

TAINAN-TAIWAN'S CULTURAL CAPITAL. 16 mm. Color. 28 minutes. By Free China Film Syndicate, 1978.

Taiwan's old capital of Tainan was the first place on the island to be settled by emigrants from the Chinese mainland. From this base, the pioneers gradually developed Taiwan into a land of abundance and prosperity. In the early days, Tainan was the military, political, cultural and commercial center of Taiwan. The city's early importance is shown by the saying, "First Tainan, second Lukang and third Wanhua." Though it can be said to be the cradle of Chinese culture in Taiwan. Tainan today is fully modernized and industrialized, and the third largest city on the island.

TAIWAN-WESTERN DRAGON OF CHINA. 16 mm. Color. 54 minutes. By Niles International, 1973.

This film comprises an extensive familiarization course on the people of the Republic of China. It shows that though the people of Taiwan have experienced all manner of hardships, they have transformed their bastion of freedom into an impregnable fortress and built a strong foundation for national recovery. They are confident that they are prepared to make the ultimate effort to win victory in the struggle against Communism.

TEA IN TAIWAN. 16 mm. Color. 15 minutes. By Free China Film Syndicate, 1978.

The Chinese knew the existence of tea plants some 5,000 years ago. In the 7th to 3rd century B.C. during the Chinese dynasties of Han and Tang, drinking tea was already a favorite among the people, considered as a source of living interest. To Chinese, tea is not merely a beverage, but also a means to promote health and friendship as well as a glass that cheers on the road to wisdom. This film shows how Taiwan farmers have improved the technique of growing and harvesting tea and some ideas about its proper preparation. Tea exports from Taiwan are also seen in the film.

THIS LAND, THIS PEOPLE. 16 mm. Color. 23 minutes. By China Art Film Limited, 1975.

This film tells how and why the people of free China are not dispirited and are firm in dignity, self-reliance and vigor, during a time of adversity. Consisting of a general description of the Republic of China in the mid-1970 s, this documentary takes note of economic development, cultural rejuvenation, and the safeguarding of democracy. A narrator in the film points out: "If you were to measure our Republic against the millennia of Chinese civilization, it was only established recently. But that doesn't mean freedom's lessons haven't taken root. They have. And that's why we've fought so hard, against such odds, to preserve freedom."

THREE DECADES TO THE MIRACLE. 16 mm. Color. 29 minutes. By Kwang Hwa Film Syndicate, 1979.

This documentary film describes how the Republic of China in the last 30 years has turned Taiwan into a model province of the Three Principles of the People as advocated by Dr. Sun Yat-sen, the nation's founding father. The film shows that the existence of the Republic of China not only safeguards the 17 million free Chinese people on Taiwan, who are continuing to enjoy a free, equitable and prosperous life, but also guarantees the sacred mission of terminating Communist tyrannical rule in a common struggle with the Chinese people on the mainland.

THREE FACES OF THE CHINESE DANCE. 16 mm. Color. 23 minutes. By China Art Film Limited, 1968.

Confucius was writing about the dance and prescribing its form and ritual 2,500 years ago. Dance in China therefore has a long history. This cultural heritage has been handed down to modern times as a part of the Chinese national drama that the West knows as Chinese opera. This film centers around three different types of Chinese dance. "Two Maids in a Garden" illustrates the gentleness, delicacy and grace of Chinese women; "Ten Thousand Cuts for the Foe" depicts the unique character of military dance and music; and "Yin, Yang" reflects the mystery of life.

TREE AND LIFE. 16 mm. Color. 23 minutes. By China Art Film Limited, 1974.

Trees play an important role in the life of man. This cinematic exposition also demonstrates how much they contribute to the beauty of Taiwan. The cameraman explores Taiwan's forests and reveals the endless uses of wood and its by-products. On every March 12, the people of Taiwan fan out across the countryside to plant thousands of saplings. The celebration of Arbor Day shows the great importance attached to trees in the Republic of China.

THE TWO FACES OF CHINA. 16 mm. Color and sound. 50 minutes. By BBC-TV, London. Released in the United States by Pictura Films.

Shows Chinese people working in fields and factories, and explains how Imperialist China has influenced Communist China. Uses examples from daily rural and urban life to describe how traditional beliefs have survived the blow of political change in China.

VOICE OF ANGELS. 16 mm. Color. 25 minutes. By Kwang Hwa Film Syndicate, 1980.

This is a film showing the activities of children in the Republic of China, who are loved, looked after, and treasured. The children are made to know how important they are. The resulting happiness can be seen in their faces and heard in their songs. The Chinese have always been famous for the respect they pay to their elders. But the traditional works as well the other way around. For they also feel a deep affection for the young. This linking of love for youth and age makes the family strong.

WASTE LAND TO WEALTH. 16 mm. Color. 23 minutes. By China Art Film, Limited, 1975.

On many seacoasts all over the world, the tides deposit silt which eventually builds up into new land. Taiwan has succeeded in turning such tidal lands of sand and mud into paddy fields, sugarcane plantations, salt fields, fish ponds, industrial parks, and residential areas. In showing the process of transformation, this film illustrates the Chinese saying that "Man's efforts may change nature." The people of Taiwan feel sure that through their wisdom and diligence, they may turn nothing into plenty, and make the desert bloom.

A WOMAN, A FAMILY. 16 mm. Color and sound. 108 minutes. Also available as videorecording. By Capi Films, New York, Cinema Perspectives, 1979, made 1978.

Using direct cinema techniques and dubbed conversations, offers a personal study of contemporary life in the People's Republic of China. Shows scenes of daily routines of a young factory worker living in the suburbs as contrasted with scenes of bustling Peking streets. Emphasizes how the cultural revolution has positively affected living conditions, men's and women's roles, and work relationships.

FILMS ABOUT CHINESE AMERICANS

THE CHINESE AMERICAN - THE EARLY IMMIGRANTS. 16 mm. Color and sound. 20 minutes. Americana Series, no. 13. Hollywood, California, Handel Film Corporation, 1973.

Traces the early history of Chinese immigration to the United States. Explores the role played by Chinese in the California gold rush, the construction of the transcontinental railroad, and their later persecution and exclusion from the United States.

THE CHINESE AMERICAN - THE TWENTIETH CENTURY. 16 mm. Color and sound. 20 minutes. Americana Series, no. 14. Hollywood, California, Handel Film Corporation, 1973.

Examines the history of Chinese Americans during the twentieth century. Deals with the special problems created by America's often hostile relations with the People's Republic of China.

DIANE LI. Color and sound. 30 minutes. By Karil Daniels and Diane Friedman. San Francisco, Daniels, 1979.

Features Diane Li, a Chinese-American filmmaker, along with clips of her films. She tells how she aims at dispelling the cliched image of look-alike Chinese and explores the myths and symbols of a celebration which is indigenous to Chinese culture.

THE DRAGON WORE TENNIS SHOES. 16 mm. Color and sound. 10 minutes. Stanford, California, Diane Li Productions, 1975.

Shows how children and adults from the San Francisco Bay area and Chinatown dress in elaborate costumes for an exciting evening of firecrackers, gongs, and the music of American marching bands: the Chinese New Year's parade, featuring the 120-foot Golden Dragon.

ETHNIC CITY. 16 mm. Color and sound. 28 minutes. By Robert Radycki, 1974.

Presents the cultural diversity and civic unity of Chicago with unnarrated views of multinational participation in a parade in the Chinese community.

IN TRANSIT - THE CHINESE IN CALIFORNIA. 16 mm. Color and sound. 26 minutes. By Lilian Wu. Los Angeles, Wu, 1977, made 1976.

A short history of the Chinese in California from 1848 to the present day.

INSIDE CHINATOWN. 16 mm. Color and sound. 45 minutes. By Michael Chin and David Goldstein. New York, Phoenix Films, 1977.

Offers a look at San Francisco's Chinatown, presents its people, and examines the issues affecting the lives of Chinese-Americans today.

JADE SNOW WONG. 16 mm. Color and sound. 28 minutes. Also available as videocassette. By WNET/13, Wilmette, Illinois, Films Incorporated, 1977, made 1976.

The Chinese-American success story of Jade Snow Wong who rejected the traditional Chinese role of female subservience to her father and brother and became an accomplished author and ceramist.

JUNG SAI, CHINESE AMERICAN. 16 mm. Color and sound. 29 minutes. By Saul Rubin and Elaine Attia, National Communications Foundation, 1975. Mount Vernon, New York, Macmillan Films, 1977.

A young Chinese American journalist seeks her ethnic origins by traveling through the West Coast Chinese community interviewing people on the coolie labor immigrations, work in railroads and mines, and contributions made by Chinese to American culture.

MEL WONG: WHO SHALL I BE? 16 mm. Color and sound. 18 minutes. By Michael Ahnemann. Released by Learning Corporation of America, 1971.

A study of one of the ethnic groups of American society. Describes a family conflict which arises when a Chinese girl wishes to study ballet after school and her father wishes her to continue to study Chinese. For elementary grades.

PAMELA WONG'S BIRTHDAY FOR GRANDMA.
16 mm. Color and sound. 8 minutes. By Lifestyle Productions; in cooperation with Saint Theresa's School, 1976, Chicago. Encyclopaedia Britannica Educational Corporation, 1977.

Depicts a special event in the life of a Chinese-American family, and shows various aspects of life in Chicago's Chinatown. Also encourages discussions of responsibility and participation of children in family events. For elementary grades.

COLOMBIANS
See also: SPANISH-SPEAKING PEOPLES

Embassy

EMBASSY OF COLOMBIA
2118 Leroy Place
Washington, D. C. 20008 (202) 387-8338

Office of the Commercial Counselor
140 East 57th Street
New York, New York 10022 (212) 758-4772

Office of the Economic Attache
140 East 57th Street
New York, New York 10022 (212) 758-4773

Permanent Mission to the OAS
1609 22nd Street, Northwest (202) 667-6007
Washington, D.C. 20008 667-6411

CONSULATES GENERAL

2990 Richmond Avenue, Suite 544
Houston, Texas 77098 (713) 527-8919

3255 Wilshire Boulevard (213) 382-1136
Los Angeles, California 90010 382-1137

14 Northeast First Avenue
507 Ainsley Building (305) 373-3087
Miami, Florida 33132 373-3188

1844 International Trade Mart
New Orleans, Louisiana 70130 (504) 525-5580

10 East 46th Street (212) 949-9898
New York, New York 10017 949-9878

870 Market Street, Suite 509
San Francisco, California 94105 (415) 362-0080

605 Avenida El Condado, Suite 503
Condominio San Alberto
San Juan, Puerto Rico 00907 (809) 722-3562

CONSULATES

816 Munsey Building
Calvert and Fayette Streets
Baltimore, Maryland 21202 (301) 244-0011

604 Statler Office Building
Boston, Massachusetts 02116 (617) 423-9714

37 South Wabash Avenue
Chicago, Illinois 60603 (312) 372-1298

125 Hidden Oak Drive
Longwood, Florida 32750 (305) 862-1306

1015 Chestnut Street
Philadelphia, Pennsylvania
19107 (215) 922-1927

310 North Snelling
Saint Paul, Minnesota 55104 (612) 647-0201

1399 Ninth Avenue, Suite 1307
San Diego, California 92101 (714) 235-4480

17000 West Eight Mile Road,
Suite 227
Southfield, Michigan 48075 (313) 569-1847

1211 North Westshore Boulevard
A.D.P. Building, Suite 411
Tampa, Florida 33607 (813) 879-6614

Mission to the United Nations

COLOMBIAN MISSION
140 East 57th Street, 5th Floor
New York, New York 10022 (212) 355-7776

Tourist and Travel Offices

COLOMBIA INFORMATION SERVICE AND
TOURIST OFFICE
140 East 57th Street
New York, New York 10022 (212) 688-0151
Director: Mr. Luis Toro Founded 1957

New York City and United States office for the Corporacion Nacional de Turismo in Bogota, Colombia. Includes representatives of the Colombian government organizations directly connected with the development of the tourist industry in Colombia. Conducts public relations and advertising campaign in United States consumer and trade publications. Publishes tourist promotion brochures and information sheets. Formerly called the National Tourist Corporation of Colombia.

Newsletters

COLOMBIA TODAY. 1966-. Monthly. Publisher: Colombia Information Service, Colombian Center, 140 East 57th Street, New York, New York 10022. In English.

Presents economic, industrial, and other news concerning Colombia and its development, trade, and foreign relations.

COLOMBIAN NEWSLETTER. Monthly. Publisher: Colombian-American Association, 115 Broadway, New York, New York 10006.

Bank Branches in the U.S. ates

BANCO DE BOGOTA
375 Park Avenue
New York, New York 10022 (212) 826-0250

Commercial and Trade Organizations

COLOMBIAN-AMERICAN ASSOCIATION
115 Broadway, Room 1110
New York, New York 10006
Executive Secretary: Paul E. Calvet (212) 233-7776
Founded 1927

Formerly called Colombian-American Chamber of Commerce.
Publication: Colombian Newsletter, monthly.

COLOMBIAN COFFEE BUREAU
140 East 57th Street
New York, New York 10022 (212) 421-8300

COLOMBIAN DEVELOPMENT CORPORATION
366 Madison Avenue
New York, New York 10017 (212) 986-7838

COLOMBIAN GOVERNMENT TRADE BUREAU
140 East 57th Street
New York, New York 10022 (212) 758-4772

Airline Offices

AVIANCA
(Aerovias Nacionales de Colombia, S.A.)
North American Headquarters:
6 West 49th Street (212) 399-0800
New York, New York 10020 246-7825

Connects North American and European cities with extensive routes in South America and a domestic route system centered in Bogota, Colombia. Other offices are located in the following cities in the United States: Boston, Chicago, Hartford, Houston, Los Angeles, Miami, Philadelphia, San Francisco, and Washington.

Books and Pamphlets

COLOMBIA. By Carla Hunt. New York, Colombia Government Tourist Office, 1981.

Although intended as a tourist sales planning guide, contains much useful information about the country in general and about the various regions of Colombia: La Sierra, La Costa, La Selva, and San Agustin. Illustrated in color.

COLOMBIA: BACKGROUND AND TRENDS: A BIBLIOGRAPHY. Compiled by Teresa Anderson. Madison, Wisconsin, University of Wisconsin Land Tenure Center Library, 1969. Supplement 1, 1971; Supplement 2, 1972.

COLOMBIA - BARRANQUILLA. New York, Colombia Government Tourist Office.

A pamphlet describing the port city of Barranquilla, sightseeing, hotels and restaurants and recreation. Includes small city map.

COLOMBIA - BOGOTA. New York, Colombia Government Tourist Office.

A pamphlet with map of the capitol city describing the museums, monuments and other places of interest. Gives a walking tour, shopping suggestions and other information useful to the visitor.

COLOMBIA - CARTAGENA. New York, Colombia Government Tourist Office.

A pamphlet telling about the sights and vacation possibilities of this former Spanish colonial port city. Includes a map.

COLOMBIA, ECUADOR AND VENEZUELA; An Annotated Guide to Reference Materials in the Humanities and Social Sciences. By Gayle Hudgens Watson. Metuchen, New Jersey, Scarecrow Press, 1971.

A bibliographic guide to 894 works, emphasizing monographs and government publications. A bibliographical essay discussing major information sources precedes a listing of items in classified arrangement with descriptive annotations. Contains a main entry index.

COLOMBIA - LETICIA. New York, Colombia Government Tourist Office.

A pamphlet describing the small frontier town of Leticia located in the Amazon jungle where Brazil, Peru and Colombia come together. Wildlife and primitive culture are featured.

COLOMBIA - SAN ANDRES. New York, Colombia Government Tourist Office.

The recreational aspects of the Colombian island of San Andres lying off the coast of Nicaragua are described in this pamphlet.

COLOMBIA - SANTA MARTA. New York, Colombia Government Tourist Office.

A pamphlet describing the natural beauty and entertainment found in the popular resort town of Santa Marta and its environs.

HISTORICAL DICTIONARY OF COLOMBIA. By Robert H. Davis. Metuchen, New Jersey, Scarecrow Press, 1977.

One of a series of historical dictionaries on Latin America.

IMAGE OF COLOMBIA. Washington, General Secretariat of the Organization of American States, 1977.

Discusses the land, history and political development, culture, principal cities, social and economic development of Colombia. A booklet illustrated with many photographs, some in color.

Audiovisual Material

MAP

COLOMBIA. Bogota, Colombian Corporacion Nacional de Turismo, 1974.

An outline map of the country with colorful, whimsical illustrations of tourist attractions and captions describing places of interest. Approximately 20 by 27 inches.

FILMS

ALEJANDRO OBREGON PAINTS A FRESCO. 16mm. Color and sound. 21 minutes. Also available on video cassette. Museum of Modern Art of Latin America, Washington, D.C., 1970.

Colombian painter Alejandro Obregon demonstrates techniques he uses when painting a fresco.

COLOMBIA: A JOY OF EXPECTATIONS. 16mm. Color and sound. 26 minutes. By Welebit Productions. Avianca Airlines, New York, 1978.

Looks at the old, the traditional, and the unchanged in the country of Colombia, which in some ways have inspired the new. Visits Conquistador-built fortress walls in Cartagena, ageless Colombian monoliths in St. Augustin, etc., in encouraging travel to this South American country.

DAVID MANZUR PAINTS A PICTURE. 16mm. Color and sound. 13 minutes. Museum of Modern Latin American Art, Washington, 1966.

Demonstration of painting by the Colombian painter Manzur.

FAMILY OF THE VALLEY: THE FAMILY COFFEE FARM. 16mm. Color and sound. 11 minutes. By Vision Associates for McGraw-Hill and Pan American World Airways. Released by McGraw-Hill, New York, 1971.

Portrays life on a coffee farm in Colombia. Shows a family picking ripe coffee beans, using a machine to separate them from the skin, spreading them in the sun to dry, and sorting the beans. Also shows a mother and daughter cooking and serving meals and doing the family shopping at an outdoor market.

FIVE NORTHERN COUNTRIES. 16mm. Color and sound. 11 minutes. Geography of South America Series. Coronet Instructional Media, Chicago, Illinois, 1977.

Describes the varying geographic features of Colombia, Venezuela, Guyana, Surinam, and French Guiana. Compares and contrasts the people, lands, and culture of Colombia and Venezuela with the three smaller nations.

A LONG HOUR'S WALK. 16mm. Color and sound. 26 minutes. National Council of Churches, Westport, Connecticut. Released by Mass Communications, 1974.

Depicts the poverty of 85 percent of the population of a typical South American country, Colombia. Shows scenes in the country and city. Points out that it takes school children an hour to walk to elementary school in parts of rural Colombia.

THE NEW COLOMBIA. 16mm. Color and sound. 15 minutes. By Gemini Productions. Released by Colombia Government Tourist Office, New York, 1977.

A travel film on Colombia featuring the major cities of Bogota, Medellin, Santa Marta, Cartagena, and Cali. Emphasizes the numerous golf and tennis clubs available for tourists. In English or Spanish.

A PROBLEM OF POWER. 16mm. Color and sound. 45 minutes. By the Center for Mass Communication, Columbia University Press. New York, National Council of Churches, 1970.

Using Colombia as a representative nation, the film describes the general social and economic situation in Latin America. Shows views of the agrarian culture, the urban poor, and individuals working to achieve change in Latin American conditions.

QUIEN SABE? 16mm. Color and sound. 60 minutes. Canadian Broadcasting Corporation, Toronto, 1972.

Explores the Republic of Colombia and examines the life of its people.

THE ROAR OF THE GODS. 16mm. Color and sound. 20 minutes. Also available on video cassette. Museum of Modern Art of Latin America, Washington, 1976.

Examines various pre-Columbian stone monoliths found in the area of San Agustin, Colombia, and explains their anthropological meaning.

COSTA RICANS
See also: SPANISH-SPEAKING PEOPLES

Embassy

EMBASSY OF COSTA RICA
and Permanent Mission to the OAS
2112 S Street, Northwest
Washington, D.C. 20008 (202) 234-2945

CONSULATES GENERAL

919 North Michigan Avenue,
Suite 2102
Chicago, Illinois 60611 (312) 621-8091

7331 Harwin, Suite 205
Houston, Texas 77036 (713) 972-1369

3807 Wilshire Boulevard,
Suite 1026
Los Angeles, California 90010 (213) 462-7718

200 Southeast First Street,
Suite 400
Miami, Florida 33131 (305) 377-4242

1610 International Trade Mart
New Orleans, Louisiana 70130 (504) 525-5445

211 East 43rd Street, #606
New York, New York 10017 (212) 867-3922

861 Sixth Avenue, Suite 522
San Diego, California 92102 (714) 232-1806

870 Market Street, #452
San Francisco, California 94102 (415) 392-8488

Mission to the United Nations

COSTA RICAN MISSION
211 East 43rd Street, Room 2002
New York, New York 10017 (212) 986-6373

Tourist and Travel Offices

COSTA RICA TOURIST BOARD
200 Southeast First Street (305) 358-2150
Miami, Florida 33131 (800) 327-7033

630 Fifth Avenue
New York, New York 10022 (212) 245-6370

Cultural and Educational Organizations

SOCIETY OF COSTA RICA COLLECTORS
Route 4, Box 472
Marble Falls, Texas 78654 (512) 267-1306
Secretary: J.W. Sauber Founded 1963

Collectors of the stamps and postal history of Costa Rica and other Central American countries. Promotes the philately of these countries by means of publications and sales of members' material to other members. Offers expert service on Costa Rican philately to members. Maintains library of books and periodicals on Latin American philately. Affiliated with American Philatelic Society. Publications: The Oxcart, quarterly; also publishes Index of Costa Rican Philatelic Literature and Specialized Catalog of the Stamps of Costa Rica.

Commercial and Trade Organizations

COSTA RICA EXPORT AND INVESTMENT
PROMOTION CENTER
200 Southeast First Street, Suite 400
Miami, Florida 33131 (305) 358-1891

COSTA RICAN BOARD OF TRADE
108 East 66th Street
New York, New York 10021 (212) 988-5190

Airline Offices

LACSA
(Lineas Aereas Constarricenses, S.A.)
North American Headquarters:
42 Northwest 27th Avenue
Miami, Florida 33125 (305) 643-4221

630 Fifth Avenue
New York, New York 10022 (212) 245-6370

Provides domestic services plus international flights

to Miami and to cities in Colombia, El Salvador, Grand Cayman, Mexico, and Venezuela.

Books and Pamphlets

COSTA RICA. San Jose, Costa Rica, Costa Rican Tourist Board.

Tourist promotion brochure with many photographs in color showing the various landscapes and activities of Costa Rica.

COSTA RICA: GETTING ITS OWN IMAGE. By Derek Bamber. Euromoney, 1980. Bound separately and distributed by the Central Bank of Costa Rica.

In depth discussion of the Costa Rican economy in several articles pertaining to various aspects such as banking, energy, finance, exports and imports.

FOREIGN INVESTMENT IN COSTA RICA. By Humberto Pacheco A. Coral Gables, Florida, Lawyer of the Americas, n.d. Reprinted and distributed by the Costa Rican Tourist Board.

Gives the legal framework for foreign investors and gives background information on taxation, banking and government incentives.

GETTING TO KNOW COSTA RICA. Miami, Costa Rican Tourist Board.

Illustrated tourist brochure telling about the country, customs, traditions and legends, and climate and giving useful tourist information.

HISTORICAL DICTIONARY OF COSTA RICA. By Theodore S. Creedmann. Metuchen, New Jersey, Scarecrow Press, 1977.

A sourcebook of historical and contemporary facts about people, places, events, geography and political organization. Includes a bibliography.

IMAGE OF COSTA RICA. By the General Secretariat, Organization of American States. Washington, 1973.

A booklet giving an overall view of Costa Rica, the country's historical and political development, culture, regions and cities, economic and social development, including education, health, transportation and communications, and tourism. Illustrated with many photographs, some in color. A centerfold map has symbols showing areas featuring colonial and Indian relics, various sports, folk arts, unusual fauna and flora, and pirate headquarters for treasure hunting.

Audiovisual Material

FILMS

COSTA RICA: MY COUNTRY. 16mm. Color and sound. 14 minutes. By Hector J. Lemieux in association with Eric Wrate and Charlotte Hacker, Toronto, 1973. Released in the United States by Encyclopaedia Britannica Educational Corporation, Chicago, 1974.

Discusses the culture, people, geography, and economy of Costa Rica.

EDUCATION IN COSTA RICA. 16mm. Color and sound. 20 minutes. By the Instituto Costarricense de Turismo, San Jose, Costa Rica.

FAMILIES OF THE WORLD - COSTA RICA. 16mm. Color and sound. 20 minutes. United Nations Children's Fund. Journal Films, Evanston, Illinois, 1976.

Examines family life in Costa Rica. Focuses on a family during harvesting time on a coffee plantation. Shows traditional roles of the parents as they relate to each other and to the children. Also examines the climate, customs, diet, economy, and culture of the country.

POINT OF CONVERGENCE. 16mm. Color and sound. 15 minutes. By Museum of Modern Art of Latin America. Released by Pan American Development Foundation, Washington, 1973.

Examines the cultures and artifacts of three early pre-Columbian civilizations in Costa Rica. A Spanish version is issued also.

POPULATION TIME-BOMB. 16mm. Color and sound. 28 minutes. By Cousteau Society. Educational Media Corporation, Los Angeles, 1977, made 1976.

Compares and contrasts the response of El Salvador and Costa Rica to their overpopulation problems.

CUBANS
See also: SPANISH-SPEAKING PEOPLES

Embassy

CUBAN INTERESTS SECTION
2630 and 2639 Sixteenth Street, Northwest
Washington, D.C. 20009 (202) 797-8609

Mission to the United Nations

PERMANENT MISSION OF CUBA
315 Lexington Avenue
New York, New York 10016 (212) 689-7215

Fraternal Organizations

MIDWEST CUBAN FEDERATION
c/o Dr. Lincoln S. Mendez
42 Buttermilk Park Pike
Lakeside Park, Kentucky 41017
Secretary: Dr. Lincoln S. Mendez (606) 341-0477
Founded 1967

Purposes are: to coordinate the activities of associations of Cubans in the Midwest and create new ones; to create and foster a spirit of generous consideration among free countries, especially the United States and nations in the Americas, with special emphasis on the reinstatement of a free and representative regime in Cuba; to help Cuban refugees to start a new life in this country; to provide a forum for the full discussion of all matters concerning the dangers that the Castro regime constitutes for the safety of and liberty in the United States and other countries in this hemisphere; to take an active interest in the study of the language, culture, history, and traditions of the Cuban people before Castro. Maintains a library regarding history and economic conditions of the United States and Cuba. Presents awards. Compiles statistics; maintains a placement service; conducts charitable programs.
Publications: Boletin, quarterly.

Professional Organizations

ASSOCIATION OF CUBAN ARCHITECTS IN EXILE ASSOCIATION
Post Office Box 35-186
Miami, Florida 33135
President: Santiago Jorge Ventura (305) 545-7385
Founded 1934

Members of the Colegio de Arquitectos de Cuba up to January 17, 1961, new architects and students of architecture. Seeks "the restoration of a democratic regime in Cuba based on the principles set forth by the Cuban Constitution of 1940." Encourages members to maintain the highest professional skills while in the United States. Conducts research programs in architecture, social welfare and town planning. Presents awards; sponsors exhibits. Formerly College of Architects of Cuba in Exile. Also known as Asociacion "Colegio de Arquitectos de Cuba" en el Exilio.
Publications: Informative Bulletin, monthly; Newsletter, monthly; also publishes Architecture in Exile.

Public Affairs Organizations

ALPHA-66
1530 36th Street
Miami, Florida 33125
National Chairman: Eloy Guitierrez Manoyo (305) 633-5842
Founded 1961

Cuban exiles in the United States and their sympathizers in Cuba. Objective is to "liberate Cuba from the communists" and to bring to the island a democratic, free enterprise system modeled on the United States. Trains and has sent commandos to Cuba to fight Premier Fidel Castro's troops. The group's general assembly, comprised of delegates from throughout the United States, functions as a government in exile and has formulated Ideological Principles, which it hopes to see implemented upon overthrow of the present government. Sponsors nightly radio broadcasts to Cuba.
Publications: Alpha-66 (newsletter), monthly.

CUBA RESOURCE CENTER
11 John Street, Room 506
New York, New York 10038 (212) 964-6214
Coordinator: Nariana Gaston
Founded 1970

People who have visited Cuba and conducted research on Cuba. Promotes communication and seeks to enhance friendship between United States and Cuba.
Publications: Cubatimes, quarterly.

CUBAN NATIONAL PLANNING COUNCIL
300 Southwest Twelfth Avenue, Third Floor
Miami, Florida 33130 (305) 642-3484
Founded 1972

Aim is to identify the socio-economic needs of the Cuban communities in the United States and to promote the necessary human services to resolve them. Assists the Cuban community in its interaction with government officials and members of Congress. Provides support in obtaining federal, state and local funds for needed services. Services include: information about public welfare; housing; youth; vocational training; employment opportunities; old age; legal aid; individual and family counseling and guidance; education; and mental health. Conducts annual Southeast Hispanic Conference on Human Services.
Publications: Noticiero, quarterly; also publishes The Cuban Community in the U.S.: Preliminary Report and Final Report.

CUBAN REPRESENTATION OF EXILES
1784 West Flagler Street, Room 21
Miami, Florida 33135
Executive Officer: George Mas (305) 642-3236

Organization of Cuban exiles living in the United States and other countries, united in support of the liberation of Cuba. Purposes are to raise the necessary funds to carry out the liberation efforts; to integrate the efforts of all Cubans pursuing the patriotic goal of liberating Cuba; to demand from the Organization of American States immediate compliance with the treaties and regional agreements in force, which make it mandatory to reject the intervention of communist power in Cuba and the hemisphere; to organize and direct the most effective information campaign to divulge the Cuban tragedy; and to request the cooperation and identification by the governments and peoples of the Free World with the cause of Cuban liberty. Also known as Representacion Cubana del Exilo (RECE).
Publication: RECE (newspaper), monthly.

FREE CUBA PATRIOTIC MOVEMENT
1635 Southwest 98th Court
Miami, Florida 33165
General Delegate: Carlos Marquez Sterling
Founded 1963

Cuban citizens seeking the liberation of Cuba from communism. Works with 51 other Cuban exile groups for a Cuban Democratic Republic. Conducts an educational program. Maintains a library of books by Cuban authors and volumes on Latin America. Also known as the Movimiento Patriotico Cuba Libre. Absorbed (1976) Liberation Committee of Cuba.

MOVEMENT FOR AN INDEPENDENT AND DEMOCRATIC CUBA
10000 Southwest 37th Terrace
Miami, Florida 33165
Secretary General: Commander Huber Matos (305) 551-0271
Founded 1980

According to an advertisement in the New York Times, August 23, 1981, the Movement was organized to "denounce the aggressive nature of Castro's satellite government, and to establish the need for a joint strategy which will prevent the large majorities of the peoples of the Americas from succumbing to minority groups directed from Havana and Moscow." Objectives are defined by the Movement's five "ideological-programmatical points"; national independence, political democracy, economic democracy, social justice and Latin American integration. Maintains that at the "end of Soviet occupation and the Castro dictatorship we will see the rebirth of Cuban democracy." Urges support from other democratic forces of the continent and the western world.

OF HUMAN RIGHTS
Box 868, East Campus
Georgetown University
Washington, D.C. 20057 (202) 466-3583
Chairman: Elena M. Gonzalez Founded 1975

Individuals concerned about human rights in Cuba. Monitors violations of human rights; conducts research on Cuban political prisoners, religious repression, censorship and repression of Cuba's labor movement. Passes information received from Cuban political prisoners on to appropriate bodies. Sponsors lectures and seminars.
Publications: Of Human Rights, annual.

Cultural and Educational Organizations

CENTER FOR CUBAN STUDIES
220 East 23rd Street
New York, New York 10010
Executive Director: Sandra Levinson (212) 685-9038
Founded 1972

Individuals and institutions united to provide to educational and cultural institutions a wide range of Cuban resource materials. Sponsors film showings, lectures and seminars. Conducts concerts, Spanish language classes and classes on revolutionary Cuba. Maintains library of 3,000 volumes and reading room containing Cuban books, photographic archives, research material, magazines and newspapers with emphasis on the post-1959 period.
Publications: Cuba Update, bimonthly; Canto Libre, quarterly; Bilingual Books and Document Series, biennial; also publishes Cuba in Focus, educational pamphlets and informational packets.

CIRCULO DE CULTURA CUBANA, INCORPORATED
G.P.O. 2174
New York, New York 10116 (212) 594-6739
Director: Marifeli Perez-Stable Founded 1979

Founded by Cubans living abroad to promote cultural and educational exchanges with those living in Cuba. Believes that knowledge of cultural life in Cuba must be maintained by those Cubans living outside of the country and also recognizes that Cubans living abroad have manifested Cuban culture in a different setting. Seeks to disseminate knowledge of Cuban culture among other Latinos living in the United States and Puerto Rico. Sponsors exhibitions, conferences and seminars. Organizes specialized trips to Cuba.
Publication: Boletin del Circulo de Cultura Cubana.

Foundation

CINTAS FOUNDATION, INCORPORATED
140 Broadway, Room 4500
New York, New York 10005 (212) 344-8000
President: Ethan D. Alyea Incorporated 1957

Fosters and encourages art within Cuba and art created by persons of Cuban citizenship or lineage within or outside of Cuba. Present activities restricted to fostering art and granting fellowships to those in the above categories living outside of Cuba who show professional achievement in music, literature, or the arts; students pursuing academic programs are not eligible.

Charitable Organizations

CENTRO HISPANO CATOLICO
130 Northeast Second Street
Miami, Florida 33132
Executive Officer: Sister Suzanne Simo (305) 371-5657
Founded 1959

Roman Catholic center established to aid Spanish-speaking immigrants, particularly Cuban refugees and to facilitate their integration into the Miami community. Provides spiritual, intellectual and physical assistance, senior citizens programs, as well as social activities; maintains medical and dental clinic and day nursery; provides clothing, food and infant layettes; helps individuals obtain employment. Also known as Catholic Spanish Center.

NATIONAL VOLUNTEER AGENCIES INVOLVED IN THE RESETTLEMENT OF CUBAN ENTRANTS. (These agencies are assisted by contracts from the Office of Refugee Resettlement, U.S. Department of Health and Human Services).

AMERICAN COUNCIL OF VOLUNTARY AGENCIES FOR FOREIGN SERVICE, INCORPORATED
Committee on Migration and Refugee Affairs
200 Park Avenue South
New York, New York 10003 (212) 777-8210
Contact: Catherine McElroy Founded 1945

Provides national voluntary agencies listed in this section with a forum for information exchange, planning and joint action in consultation with the United States government, the United Nations and other organizations active in relief, development and refugee assistance. Participates in the allocation of refugees who are to be resettled.

AMERICAN COUNCIL FOR NATIONALITIES SERVICE
20 West 40th Street
New York, New York 10018
Contact: Frank Sharry (212) 777-8210

CHURCH WORLD SERVICE
Migration and Refugee Program
475 Riverside Drive, Room 666
New York, New York 10027
Contact: Desma Holcum (212) 870-2164

5250 Santa Monica Boulevard
Suite 311
Los Angeles, California 90029 (213) 666-2708

INTERNATIONAL RESCUE COMMITTEE
386 Park Avenue South
New York, New York 10016
Contact: Charles Sternberg (212) 679-0010

1732 "Eye" Street, Northwest
Washington, D.C. 20006 (202) 333-6814

LUTHERAN IMMIGRATION AND REFUGEE SERVICE
Lutheran Council in the U.S.A.
360 Park Avenue South
New York, New York 10010 (800) 223-7656
Contact: Zdenka Seiner (212) 532-6350

PRESIDING BISHOPS FUND FOR WORLD RELIEF
Episcopal Center
815 Second Avenue
New York, New York 10017
Contact: Marnie Dawson (202) 867-8400

UNITED STATES CATHOLIC CONFERENCE
Migration and Refugee Services
1312 Massachusetts Avenue, Northwest
Washington, D.C. 20005
Contact: Gerry Wynn (202) 659-6625

1250 Broadway
New York, New York 10001 (212) 563-4300

WORLD RELIEF REFUGEE SERVICES
National Association of Evangelicals
Post Office Box WRC
Nyack, New York 10960
Contact: Winston Johnston (914) 353-1444

A description of the services rendered by these agencies will be found in the listing in the Indochinese section.

Other agencies cooperating with the Office of Refugee Resettlement, United States Department of Health and Human Services in resettling Cuban entrants.

CUBAN NATIONAL PLANNING COUNCIL
300 Southwest 12th Avenue, Third Floor
Miami, Florida 33130
Contact: Guarione Diaz or
David Perez (305) 649-6660

CUBAN REFUGEE RESETTLEMENT OF WASHINGTON
11740 Aurora Avenue North
Seattle, Washington 98133
Contact: Thomas Brothers (206) 364-4888

DISMAS HOUSE
3110 Flora
Kansas City, Missouri
Director: Reverend Thornton (816) 923-1644

ECLECTIC COMMUNICATIONS, INCORPORATED
307 Matilija #H
Ojai, California 93023
Director: Arthur McDonald (805) 646-7229

FELLOWSHIP HOUSE FARM, INCORPORATED
R.D. 3, Sanatoga Road
Pottstown, Pennsylvania 19464
Contact: David Tulin (215) 248-3343

LITTLE HAVANA ACTIVITIES AND NUTRITION CENTER
819 Southwest 12th Avenue
Miami, Florida 33130
Director: Josephina Carbonell (305) 541-7511

Project: 936 Saint Charles
New Orleans, Louisiana
Project Director:
Dr. Curbelo (504) 568-9622

MARCUS GARVEY MEMORIAL BLACK SOLIDARITY
12-14 Hoeltzer Street
Rochester, New York 14621
Director: Amefika Geuka (716) 325-6900

METROPOLITAN DEVELOPMENT COUNCIL
2302 Sixth Avenue
Tacoma, Washington 98403
Contact: Don Bryce (206) 383-3921

U.S. Government Programs

CUBAN/HAITIAN ENTRANT PROGRAM
Department of Health and Human Services
Office of Refugee Resettlement
330 C Street, Southwest
Switzer Building
Washington, D.C. 20201
Chief: Deni Blackburn (202) 245-0979

In 1980 the Cuban/Haitian Task Force was merged with the Office of Refugee Resettlement in the Department of Health and Human Service. Programs of assistance to entrants administered from this office under block grants to states include cash assistance, aid to families with dependent children, supplemental security income, medical assistance and social services. These may include an outreach program; English-as-a-Second-Language instruction; vocational assistance in career counseling, job orientation, job placement and follow-up, and assessment; vocational training; skills recertification; day care and transportation necessary for participation in an employability or social service plan; social adjustment services, (information and referral, emergency services, health (including mental health) related services, home management services, orientation services); and transportation and interpreter services. The ORR also maintains a data systems and analysis program and hotlines in Miami (800-327-3463) and Washington (800-424-9304) to provide information and referral services in the areas of health, employment, legal and housing assistance and other social services. Hotline staff speak Spanish, Creole and English.

OFFICE OF BILINGUAL EDUCATION AND MINORITY LANGUAGES AFFAIRS
Refugee Children Assistance Programs
Department of Education
Reporters Building - Room 505
400 Maryland Avenue, Southwest
Washington, D.C. 20202
Chief: James H. Lockhart (202) 472-3520

Provides supplementary educational assistance to meet the special educational needs of Cuban and Haitian entrant children who are enrolled in public and non-profit elementary and secondary schools. Program is operated through grants.

OFFICE OF REFUGEE HEALTH AFFAIRS
Room 18A-30, Parklawn Building
5600 Fisher's Lane
Rockville, Maryland 20857
Director: Robert F. Knouss, M.D. (301) 443-4130

Coordinates all Public Health Service-supported health programs for Cuban and Haitian entrants. These include medical screening and the services of community health centers, maternal and child health programs, and community mental health centers.

Subject Collections

UNIVERSITY OF MIAMI LIBRARY
Post Office Box 8214
Coral Gables, Florida 33124
Director of Libraries: Archie L. McNeal

Features a special collection of Cuban materials.

UNIVERSITY OF PITTSBURGH LIBRARIES
Hillman Library
Pittsburgh, Pennsylvania 15213

Contains a collection of Cuban books, pamphlets, and periodicals. Emphasis is on material published in Cuba from 1959 on and publications concerning Revolutionary Cuba.

Newspapers and Newsletters

BOLETIN. Quarterly. Editor: Dr. Lincoln S. Mendez. Publisher: Midwest Cuban Federation, 42 Buttermilk Park, Fort Mitchell, Kentucky 41017. In English.

Newsletter of the organization.

BOLETIN DE CIRCULO DE CULTURA CUBANA. 1979-. Publisher: Circulo de Cultura Cubana, Incorporated, G.P.O. 2174, New York, New York 10116. In Spanish.

Newsletter which reports on publications and activities of the association.

CUBA UPDATE. Bimonthly. Publisher: Center for Cuban Studies, 220 East 23rd Street, New York, New York 10010. In English.

Brings political and cultural news of contemporary Cuba and tells of the Center's activities.

CUBATIMES. Quarterly. Publisher: Cuba Resource Center, 11 John Street, New York, New York 10038. In English.

Prints articles about Cuba for persons interested in the modern changes in the country.

NOTICIERO. 1980-. Quarterly. Publisher: Cuban National Planning Council, 300 Southwest Twelfth Avenue, Miami, Florida 33130.

Brings news of interest to the Cuban communities in the United States.

RECE. Monthly. Publisher: Cuban Representation of Exiles, 1784 West Flagler Street, Room 21, Miami, Florida 33135.

Publishes news of interest to Cubans living in the United States and working towards the liberation of Cuba.

Magazines

AREITO. 1974-. Quarterly. Editor: Marifeli Perez Stable. Publisher: Ediciones Vitral, Incorporated, GPO Box 1913, New York, New York 10001. In Spanish.

CANTO LIBRE. 1974-. Quarterly. Editor: Susan Ortega. Publisher: Center for Cuban Studies, 220 East 23rd Street, New York, New York 10010. In Spanish and English.

A magazine devoted to Cuban and Latin American art.

CUBAN STUDIES/ESTUDIOS CUBANOS. 1970-. Biannually. Editor: Carmelo Mesa-Lago. Publisher: Center for Latin American Studies, University of Pittsburgh, Pittsburgh, Pennsylvania 15260. In Spanish and English.

Publishes scholarly articles on contemporary Cuba, book reviews and a topically arranged bibliography.

Radio Programs

Connecticut - Hamden

WQAQ (FM) - 555 New Road, Quinnipiac College, Hamden, Connecticut 06518, (203) 281-0011. Cuban programs, 2 hours weekly.

Bookdealers

CUBAN BOY'S SPANISH BOOKS
1225 West 18th Street
Chicago, Illinois 60608 (312) 243-5911

Books and Pamphlets

CUBAN ACQUISITIONS AND BIBLIOGRAPHY: PROCEEDINGS AND WORKING PAPERS OF AN INTERNATIONAL CONFERENCE HELD AT THE LIBRARY OF CONGRESS, APRIL 13-15, 1970. Edited by Earl J. Pariseau. Washington, D.C., Library of Congress, 1970.

CUBAN CRISIS - BAY OF PIGS. Compiled by Marvin Soloman. Edwardsville, Illinois, Southern Illinois University, Lovejoy Library, 1972.

An annotated bibliography.

THE CUBAN REVOLUTION: A DOCUMENTARY BIBLIOGRAPHY, 1952-1968. By Jaime Suchlicki. Coral Gables, Florida, Research Institute for Cuba and the Caribbean, University of Miami, 1968.

An annotated guide to speeches, editorials, manifestos and communiques available on the Revolution.

THE CUBAN REVOLUTION: A RESEARCH-STUDY GUIDE, 1959-1969. By Nelson P. Valdes and Edwin Lieuwen. Albuquerque, University of New Mexico Press, 1971.

Materials are classified and grouped according to topics such as politics, international relations, economy, education, religion, society, culture, and the revolution in general. Each category is divided into subtopics. Some entries have short annotations. Includes publications from all parts of the world, but mainly Cuban or American. Contains an author index.

THE CUBAN REVOLUTION OF FIDEL CASTRO VIEWED FROM ABROAD: AN ANNOTATED BIBLIOGRAPHY. Compiled by Gilberto V. Fort. Lawrence, University of Kansas Libraries, 1969.

Both English and Spanish materials are annotated. Contains an index.

REVOLUTIONARY CUBA; A Bibliographical Guide. Coral Gables, Florida, University of Miami Press, 1970.

An annual bibliographical guide on Cuba. Only publications in English and Spanish are included. Also has a few annotations.

CUBAN AMERICANS

ANNOTATED BIBLIOGRAPHY ON CUBANS IN THE UNITED STATES, 1960-1976. Compiled by Esther Gonzalez, Miami, Florida, 1977.

An interdisciplinary inventory of bibliographical sources and material in Cuban American studies. Includes periodical literature, reports, theses, dissertations, monographic material, congressional hearing and occasional government publications. Topical division into Cuban refugee resettlement, cultural and occupational adjustment, Cubans in Miami and refugee needs and program services.

THE ASSIMILATION OF CUBAN EXILES: THE ROLE OF COMMUNITY AND CLASS. By Eleanor Meyer Rogg. New York, Aberdeen Press, 1974.

Investigates the adjustment of middle and upper class Cuban people in the West New York and Union City, New Jersey as a comparison to the mostly poorer settlers from Puerto Rico to determine the relative influence of language barriers and social class in case of assimilation.

BILINGUAL SCHOOLS FOR A BICULTURAL COMMUNITY: MIAMI'S ADAPTATION TO THE CUBAN REFUGEES. By William Mackey. Rowley, Massachusetts, Newbury House Publishers, 1977.

CUBAN AMERICANS: MASTERS OF SURVIVAL. By Jose Llanos. Cambridge, Massachusetts, Abt Books, 1982.

THE CUBAN COMMUNITY OF WASHINGTON HEIGHTS IN NEW YORK CITY. Edited by M. Cohn. Brooklyn, New York, Brooklyn Children's Museum, 1967.

More than 250 people were interviewed in the course of this study.

THE CUBAN IMMIGRATION, 1959-1966, AND ITS IMPACT ON MIAMI-DADE COUNTY, FLORIDA. Coral Gables, Florida, Research Institute for Cuba and the Caribbean, Center for Advanced International Studies, University of Miami, 1967.

Discusses the nature of the refugee problem, refugee assistance, economic impact, education and training, and sociological impact, for the area most intimately involved in receiving Cuban refugees in America. Includes charts, figures and appendices.

THE CUBAN MINORITY IN THE U.S.: FINAL REPORT ON NEED IDENTIFICATION AND PROGRAM EVALUATION. Edited by Andres R. Hernandez. Washington, D.C., Cuban National Planning Council, 1974.

THE CUBAN MINORITY IN THE U.S.: PRELIMINARY REPORT ON NEED IDENTIFICATION AND PROGRAM EVALUATION, FINAL REPORT FOR FISCAL YEAR 1973. 2nd ed. Rev. Edited by Rafael J. Prohlas. Washington, D.C., Cuban National Planning Council, 1974.

A very thorough scholarly study which includes tables, statistics and an annotated bibliography of Spanish and English materials.

CUBAN REFUGEE PROGRAMS. Edited by Carlos Cortes. New York, Arno Press, 1980.

Examines the Cuban refugee programs through documents and studies. The studies focus on the problems faced by unaccompanied Cuban children and the efforts of government and private agencies to solve the problems.

CUBANS IN EXILE: DISAFFECTION AND THE REVOLUTION. By Richard R. Fagen, Richard A. Brody and Thomas J. O'Leary. Palo Alto, California, Stanford University Press, 1968.

Concerned with the distribution, attitudes, political participation, and the Cuban background and revolution of the refugees who entered the United States from the fall of Batista (end of 1958) until the discontinuation of air flights from Cuba to Miami (October, 1962).

ELDERLY CUBANS IN EXILE. By Manolo J. Reyes. Washington, D.C., United States Government Printing Office, 1971.

A pamphlet dealing with the special problems faced by older immigrants.

NEW FACES IN AMERICAN CITIES: THE CUBAN EXILES. Miami Beach, Florida, 78th Annual Convention of the American Psychological Association, 1970.

Papers and speeches concerned with the influx of Cuban refugees.

A STUDY OF THE EFFECTS OF ENVIRONMENTAL CHANGE ON HUMAN CAPITAL AMONG SELECTED SKILLED CUBANS. By Raul Moncarz. Washington, D.C., 1976.

Treats economic adjustment among Cubans in the United States.

WORKING-CLASS EMIGRES FROM CUBA. By Geoffrey Fox. Palo Alto, California, R & E Research Associates, 1979.

This book attempts to show the structure of the counterrevolutionary consciousness of the emigres and to also show how their personal experiences of Cuba contributed to its formation. Data was derived from personal interviews with emigres.

Audiovisual Material

FILMS

CUBA: ART AND REVOLUTION. 16 mm. Color and sound. 46 minutes. By the British Broadcasting Corporation, London. Released in the United States by Time-Life Films, New York, 1971.

Documents the effect of revolution on the cultural life of Cuba, including films, ballet, and the theater. Presents interviews with prima ballerina Alicia Alonso and with leading Cuban writers on the role played by the artist in Castro's revolution and the amount of freedom possible under communism.

CUBA AND FIDEL. 16 mm. Color and sound. 24 minutes. By Focal Point Films. Released by Churchill Films, 1976.

A documentary on Fidel Castro and Cuba. Shows some changes which have taken place since relations were severed with the United States and points out areas which have not changed. Castro, in interviews, expresses himself on Cuba's revolution, social systems, freedom, and relations with the United States.

CUBA - THE CASTRO GENERATION. 16 mm. Color and sound. 49 minutes. By American Broadcasting Company. McGraw-Hill Films, New York, 1977.

Looks at the life and thoughts of the generation of Cubans raised under communism, concentrating on the average citizen and how he copes with everyday problems such as food rationing and shortages of consumer goods.

ESCAPE FROM CUBA. 16 mm. Color. Silent. 3 minutes. Joyce Motion Picture Company, Northridge, California, 1975, made 1973.

Presents in American sign language a true story of the escape of two teenagers from Cuba to America. Signed by Jack Burns.

TROUBLED NEIGHBORS - CUBA AND THE UNITED STATES. 16 mm. Color and sound. 15 minutes. Hearst Metrotone News, New York, 1975.

An analysis of the changing nature of Cuban-American relations since Fidel Castro's seizure of power in 1959.

WAITING FOR FIDEL. 16 mm. Color and sound. 58 minutes. By National Film Board of Canada, Montreal, 1974.

Documents a trip to Cuba by former Premier of Newfoundland, Joey Smallwood. Shows a country trying to be Communist.

CZECHOSLOVAKIANS
(Includes SLOVAKS)
See also: SLAVIC PEOPLES

Embassy

EMBASSY OF CZECHOSLOVAKIA
3900 Linnean Avenue, Northwest
Washington, D. C. 20008 (202) 363-6315

Commercial Section (202) 363-6307

Visa Section (202) 363-6308

Office of Commercial Counselor
292 Madison Avenue
New York, New York 10017 (212) 535-8814

Mission to the United Nations

CZECHOSLOVAKIAN MISSION
1109-1111 Madison Avenue
New York, New York 10028 (212) 535-8814

Tourist and Travel Office

CEDOK
Czechoslovak Travel Bureau
10 East 40th Street
New York, New York 10016 (212) 689-9720

CZECHOSLOVAK CENTRAL TRAVEL BUREAU
1365 Fifth Avenue
New York, New York (212) 988-8080

Fraternal Organizations

AMERICAN SOKOL EDUCATIONAL AND PHYSICAL CULTURE ORGANIZATION
6426 West Cermak Road
Berwyn, Illinois 60402 (312) 795-6671
Secretary: Ellan Jeanne Schnabl Founded 1865

Physical fitness organization for children and adults from age 3 to 65 and over. Sponsors gymnastic meets and competitions, clinics, workshops, and schools. Conducts educational activities. Offers lectures and films. Compiles statistics on gymnasts and members. Maintains a library. Affiliated with the Slovak Gymnastic Union Sokol.
Publication: American Sokol, monthly.

CATHOLIC WORKMAN
New Prague, Minnesota 56071 (612) 758-2229
Secretary: S. F. Wagner Founded 1891

Fraternal benefit life insurance organization of practicing Catholics. Absorbed the Western Bohemian Catholic Union and the Daughters of Columbus. Formerly known as the Katolicky Delnik.
Publication: Catholic Workman, monthly.

CZECH-AMERICAN HERITAGE CENTER
2657 South Lawnsdale Avenue
Chicago, Illinois 60623 (212) 762-2044

CZECH CATHOLIC UNION
5349 Dolloff Road
Cleveland, Ohio 44127 (216) 341-0444
Founded 1879

Fraternal benefit life insurance society for persons of Catholic faith. Makes annual donation to the Holy Family Cancer Home. Educates a young man to the priesthood at St. Procopius Abbey. Bestows awards; offers children's services; participates in various civic and cultural programs on the local level.
Publications: Posel (messenger), quarterly.

CZECHOSLOVAK SOCIETY OF AMERICA
2701 South Harlem Avenue
Berwyn, Illinois 60402 (312) 795-5800
President: Frank J. Vodrazka Founded 1854

Fraternal benefit life insurance society. Sponsors competitions; maintains museum, biographical archives, and library of magazines and Czech books dating back to the 1870's. Absorbed (1977) Unity of Czech Ladies and Men.
Publications: Journal, monthly.

NATIONAL COUNCIL OF WOMEN OF FREE CZECHOSLOVAKIA
Post Office Box 121
Newark, New Jersey 07104 (201) 484-1591
President: Mrs. Jan Papanek Founded 1951

Women of Czechoslovak origin or background. Carries on the democratic program of the National Council of Women of Czechoslovakia disbanded by the communists. Activities include cultural, educational, welfare (helping Czechoslovak refugees) activities, as well as exhibits of art and handcrafts. Affiliated with the National Council of Women of the United States.
Publication: Bulletin, three times a year.

WESTERN FRATERNAL LIFE ASSOCIATION
1900 First Avenue, Northeast
Cedar Rapids, Iowa 52402
National President: Elmer F. Karasek (319) 363-2653
Founded 1897

Fraternal benefit life insurance society primarily for persons of Czechoslovakian descent.
Publication: Fraternal Herald, monthly.

SLOVAKS

FIRST CATHOLIC SLOVAK LADIES ASSOCIATION
24950 Chagrin Boulevard
Beachwood, Ohio 44122 (216) 464-8015
President: Louise M. Yash Founded 1892

Fraternal benefit life insurance society. Owns a home for the aged, "Villa Sancta Anna," in Beachwood, Ohio. Formerly called the First Catholic Slovak Ladies Union. Absorbed the Catholic Slovak Brotherhood.
Publication: Fraternally Yours, monthly.

FIRST CATHOLIC SLOVAK UNION OF THE U.S.A. AND CANADA
3289 East 55th Street
Cleveland, Ohio 44127 (216) 341-3355
Executive Secretary: Stephen F. Ungvarsky Founded 1890

Fraternal benefit life insurance society for Catholic Americans of Slovak descent. Also known as Prva Katolicka Slovenska Jednota.
Publications: Jednota, weekly; Almanac, annual.

JUNIOR SLOVAK CATHOLIC SOKOL
205 Madison Street
Passaic, New Jersey 07055

Publication: Priatel Dietok (The Children's Friend), ten times a year.

NATIONAL SLOVAK SOCIETY OF THE UNITED STATES OF AMERICA
2325 East Carson Street
Pittsburgh, Pennsylvania 15203 (412) 281-5728
President: Joseph Stefka Founded 1890

Fraternal benefit life insurance society for men and women of Slovak descent and their families in the United States and Canada. Offers aid to orphans, widows, aged and disabled persons. Holds citizenship classes. Sponsors athletic and cultural programs. Maintains a 1,000 volume library of Slovak history, culture, literature. Conducts research in cooperation with university and college students. Is in the process of opening a museum of Slovak artifacts. Bestows scholarships and awards.
Publications: Narodne Noviny (National News), monthly; Kalendar (almanac), annual; Convention Journal, quadrennial.

SLOVAK CATHOLIC SOKOL
205 Madison Street
Passaic, New Jersey 07055 (201) 777-2605
Supreme Secretary: Tibor T. Kovalovsky Founded 1905

Americans of Slovak or Slav descent. Sponsors gymnastic and athletic activities such as a biennial National Track and Field Meet. Presents Slovak Catholic Sokol Scholarship Grant Awards. Maintains a library. Sponsors Junior Slovak Catholic Sokol groups for children.
Publications: Katolicky Sokol (The Falcon, English supplement of Katolicky Sokol), weekly; Children's Friend (Priatel Dietok - Slovak supplement to Children's Friend), monthly; also publishes Slovak Catholic Sokol Cook Book, and Slovak-English Dictionary.

SLOVAK LEAGUE OF AMERICA
870 Rifle Camp Road
West Patterson, New Jersey 07424 (201) 256-1687
Secretary: John A. Holy Founded 1907

Cultural and civic federation of Slovak American organizations. Supports freedom and political independence for Slovakia, the oldest Christian nation in Central Europe. Promotes better understanding and appreciation of the Slovak nation,

its history, culture, traditions, and desires. Makes America better known to Slovakia and Slovakia better known to America in the interests of world peace, freedom, and security. Sponsors a scholarship program.
Publication: Slovakia, annual.

SLOVAK LEAGUE OF AMERICA HERITAGE FOUNDATION
178 Elliott Street
Stratford, Connecticut 06497
Secretary: John A. Holy Founded 1978

Dedicated to preserving the Slovak culture and heritage in the U. S. Seeks to expand institutions concerned with Slovak culture, including archives, libraries and the Slovak Institute in Cleveland, Ohio. Affiliated with Slovak League of America.

SOKOL U.S.A.
276 Prospect Street
Post Office Box 189
East Orange, New Jersey 07017 (201) 676-0280
Secretary: John Sopoci Founded 1896

Fraternal benefit life insurance society. Promotes physical fitness through gymnastic competitions and exhibitions. Maintains camps and halls in several states. Awards scholarships to members. Also known as the Slovak Gymnastic Union Sokol of the U.S.A.
Publication: Sokol Times, biweekly.

Public Affairs Organizations

COUNCIL OF FREE CZECHOSLOVAKIA
420 East 71st Street
New York, New York 10021 (212) 543-8661
Secretary General: Jiri Horak Founded 1949

Established to work for the return of a democratic government in Czechoslovakia. Opposes the communist regime and the suppression of civil and human rights.
Publications: Czechoslovak Newsletter, monthly (in English and French).

CZECHOSLOVAK CHRISTIAN-DEMOCRACY
247 South Street
Hartford, Connecticut 06114
U. S. Representative: Rudolph Krempl (203) 524-5741
Founded 1957

Czechs, Slovaks, and Ruthenians living in exile as political refugees. Members may be naturalized citizens of the United States or of other countries. Works for a Free Czechoslovakia; informs the free world about communism; helps political refugees. Sponsors debates and meetings. Prepares articles and letters to publications opposing communism and commenting on political activity throughout the world. Maintains a library of some 800 Czech, Slovak, English, and German books on political, historical, cultural, and literary aspects of Czechoslovakia. Headquarters is in Munich, Germany. Formerly Movement of Czechoslovak Christian-Democrats in Exile.
Publications: Demokracia v Exilu (Democracy in Exile), bimonthly; The Ambassador (newsletter in English), irregular.

CZECHOSLOVAK NATIONAL COUNCIL OF AMERICA
2137 South Lombard Avenue, Room 202
Cicero, Illinois 60650 (312) 656-1117
Founded 1918

Monitors violations of human rights in Czechoslovakia, and reports these violations to the U. S. State Department and to the Commission of Security and Cooperation in Europe. Maintains a regional office in Washington, D. C. Assists in relocating Czechoslovak refugees in the U. S.
Publications: American Bulletin, monthly; Vestnik, monthly.

Cultural and Educational Organizations

COMENIUS WORLD COUNCIL
c/o Rudolph Ch. Krempl
247 South Street
Hartford, Connecticut 06114 (203) 524-5741
Secretary: Rudolph Ch. Krempl Founded 1974

Students of the teachings of Comenius (1592-1670), Czech theologian and educator. Comenianism (trinitarian humanism) concerns the three fundamental relations to man: society, nature and God. Freedom in all three relations expresses the true freedom of man, created to the image of God. Applies ideas of Comenius in the contemporary world movement for democratization, liberalization and unification of all mankind. Participates in international seminars and workshops, symposia, conferences and congresses dealing with the problems of man in the atomic age.
Publication: Newsletter.

CZECHOSLOVAK SOCIETY OF ARTS AND SCIENCES
3200 Holly Berry Court
Falls Church, Virginia 22042 (703) 573-0517
Secretary General: Blanka Glos Founded 1958

College professors, writers, artists and scientists interested in Czech or Slovak matters. Activities are conducted in cultural, educational, literary, artistic and scientific fields through lectures, concerts, and exhibitions. Bestows awards. Also Known As Spolecnost pro Vedy a Umeni. Formerly (1979) Czechoslovak Society of Arts and Sciences in America.
Publications: Zpravy SVU, biennial; Promeny, quarterly; also publishes books and Biographical Directory.

SOCIETY FOR CZECHOSLOVAK PHILATELY
427 King Street
Woodbury, New Jersey 08096 (609) 845-1040
Secretary: Edward J. Sabol Founded 1939

Collectors of philatelic items and postal issues of Czechoslovakia. Conducts stamp exchange service. Maintains 150-volume library on Czechoslovakian postal issues. Affiliated with the American Philatelic Society. Formerly (1973) Czechoslovak Philatelic Society.
Publications: The Czechoslovak Specialist, monthly.

SLOVAKS

SLOVAK-AMERICAN CULTURAL CENTER
Post Office Box 291
New York, New York 10008 (212) 461-7789
Executive Vice President: Joseph Ihnat Founded: 1967

Slovaks and others interested in Slovak culture. Wishes to maintain and extend Slovak national and cultural history. Sponsors cultural programs in music and art in addition to social and sports events. Bestows awards.
Publications: Slovak Press Digest and Slobodna Tribuna

SLOVAK WRITERS AND ARTISTS ASSOCIATION
2900 East Boulevard
Cleveland, Ohio 44104 (216) 521-7288
Secretary: Nicholas Sprinc Founded 1954

Persons of Slovak birth or descent who are authors, intellectuals, journalists, painters, editors, composers, or musicians. Promotes free Christian Slovak culture abroad by publishing the works of Slovak authors and helping them in their creative efforts. Maintains the Slovak Institute in Cleveland, Ohio, which contains a library on Slovak history, art and literature and the cultural achievements of Americans of Slovak ancestry.
Publication: Most (Bridge), quarterly.

Charitable Organizations

AMERICAN FUND FOR CZECHOSLOVAK REFUGEES
1790 Broadway, Room 513
New York, New York 10019 (212) 265-1919
President: Dr. Jan Papanek Founded 1948

Helps Czechoslovak refugees with temporary housing, material aid, counseling and processing for emigration to countries of the free world. Refugees who come to the United States, are met, housed temporarily, and placed in employment. Has field offices in Munich, Vienna, Rome, and Paris.

SLOVAKS

SLOVAK RELIEF FUND
c/o National Committee for Liberation of Slovakia
1065 National Press Building
Washington, D. C. 20004 (202) 347-7362
President: V. Stephen Krajcovic Founded 1953

Assists Slovaks throughout the world.

Religious Organizations

NATIONAL ALLIANCE OF CZECH CATHOLICS
2657-59 South Lawndale Avenue
Chicago, Illinois 60623 (312) 522-7575
Executive Officer: Vaciav Hyvnar Founded 1917

Founded to unite Czech-American Catholics for religious, civic, charitable, and educational activities.

SLOVAKS

SLOVAK CATHOLIC FEDERATION
c/o Rev. Joseph V. Adamec
1515 Cass Avenue
Bay City, Michigan 48606
President: Rev. Joseph V. Adamec Founded 1911

Parishes, societies, sodalities, and individuals interested in Catholic action and aid for exiled and persecuted Slovaks in Slovakia and other parts of the world. Supports the Institute of Sts. Cyril and Methodius in educating refugee boys for the priesthood in Rome, Italy. Publishes books and other literature for Americans of Slovak descent. Presents Sts. Cyril and Methodius Award for defense of faith, morals, and advancement of the Slovak people.
Publication: Dobry Pastier (Good Shepherd), bimonthly.

Museums

CLARKSON HISTORICAL MUSEUM
Clarkson, Nebraska 68629 (402) 892-3812
Director: Mrs. Henry Hamernik Founded 1967

Has artifacts from early Czech and German settlement of the area as well as a collection of Czech books and old Bibles. Offers guided tours, lectures, library exhibitions. Participation in the Czech Festival held annually in late June.

THE OLD BOHEMIA HISTORICAL SOCIETY, INCORPORATED
Post Office Box 61
Warwick, Maryland 21912 (609) 299-0582
President: Frank W. Krastel Founded 1953

This ethnic historical society is housed in old Bohemia Rectory 1792-1797, located on the site of St. Francis Xavier Mission founded 1704. Its collections include old furniture and church related articles; farm equipment, tools and a library. The principal aim is the restoration and maintenance of the old Bohemia Shrine. Guided tours are offered.

RACINE COUNTY HISTORICAL MUSEUM
701 South Main Street
Racine, Wisconsin 53403 (414) 637-8585
Director: Gilbert D. Stieg Founded 1962

Sponsors maintenance of a restored 1888 Bohemian schoolhouse.

SLAVONIC BENEVOLENT ORDER OF THE STATE OF TEXAS
520 North Main
Temple, Texas 76501 (817) 773-1575
Curator: Otto Hanus Founded 1971

Collections include artifacts and articles of early pioneer Czech-Texas settlers; housewares; musical instruments, agriculture implements; medical displays. Researches the customs and way of life of Czech pioneers in Texas as well as the history of the Slavonic Benevolent Order. Maintains a 17,500 volume library mostly of Czech imprints. Offers guided tours, study groups, lectures and films.

WILBER CZECH MUSEUM
Box 253
Wilber, Nebraska 68465 (402) 821-2485
President: Irma Ourecky Founded 1962

Devoted to the Czech history of Wilbur, the museum displays textiles; glass; agricultural implements; paintings; costumes; decorative arts; guns; antiques and medical tools. The museum provides guided tours, lectures, loans to schools and a museum shop. Participates in the annual Czech Festival.

Special Libraries and Subject Collections

CZECH HERITAGE COLLECTION
303 Love Library
University of Nebraska
Lincoln, Nebraska 68588 (402) 472-2531
Librarian: Joseph G. Svoboda

Subject: The Czechs in Nebraska. Holdings: Books, audiotapes, pictures

FIRST CATHOLIC SLOVAK UNION OF THE U.S.A. AND CANADA LIBRARY
3289 East 55th Street
Cleveland, Ohio 44127 (216) 341-3355
Executive Secretary: Stephen F. Ungvarsky

Subjects: Slovakia. Special Collections: Books by Slovak authors. Remarks: Publications for this organization are handled by Joseph C. Krajsa, Editor and Manager, JEDNOTA Printery, Box 150, Middletown, Pennsylvania 17057. The phone number is (717) 944-0461

MASARYK-BENES LIBRARY
University of California
Berkeley, California 94720
Librarian: Rudolf Lednicky

Subjects: Czechoslovak and European history. Special collections: writings by and about Tomas and Jan

Masaryk and Benes. Holdings: books, monographs, periodical articles, reprints, newspapers.

SLAVONIC BENEVOLENT ORDER OF THE STATE OF TEXAS - LIBRARY, ARCHIVES, MUSEUM
520 North Main Street
Temple, Texas 76501 (817) 773-1575
Librarian and Curator: Otto Hanus

Subjects: Education, medicine, religion, history, music. Special Collections: Czech plays. Holdings: 16,000 volumes (mostly in Czech language). Services: Interlibrary loans; copying; library open to public. Special Catalogs: Catalog of books; will ship to interested patrons.

SLOVAK INSTITUTE - SLOVAK WRITERS AND ARTISTS ASSOCIATION LIBRARY
St. Andrew's Abbey, 2900 East Boulevard
Cleveland, Ohio 44104 (216) 521-7288
Secretary: Nicholas Sprinc

Subjects: Slovak history, Slovak art, Slovak literature, cultural achievements of Americans of Slovak ancestry. Holdings: Books. Services: Library open to public for reference use only by special arrangement.

Newspapers and Newsletters

AMBASSADOR. Irregular. Publisher: Czechoslovak Christian Democracy, 247 South Street, Hartford, Connecticut 06114.

Newsletter of the organization.

AMERICKE LISTY (American Letters). 1962-. Weekly. Editor: Josef Martinek. Publisher: University Press Company, 283 Oak Street, Perth Amboy, New Jersey 08861. In Czech.

Publishes news on political, cultural, and social topics of interest to the Czech community.

BULLETIN SVU. 1979-. Quarterly. Editors: Zdenke Fishmann and Michael Heim. Publisher: Czechoslovak Society of Arts and Sciences in America, Box 134, Corona, California 91720. In English.

Informational articles and announcements pertaining to the Society.

THE CZECHOSLOVAK SPECIALIST. 1938-. Monthly. Society for Czechoslovak Philately, Incorporated, Harlan W. Miller Press, 821 Vermont Street, Lawrence, Kansas. Editor: Mrs. Joseph Sterba.

Provides discussions of all phases of Czechoslovakian philately: covers, stamps, cancellations, forgeries, post marks, stamp shows, new issues. Includes information on the occupations under the Austro-Hungarian Empire and Hitler. Includes reports of mail auctions and special sales, news of research in progress, statistics, calendars of events. Indexed approximately every 5 years.

DEMOKRACIA V EXILU. Bimonthly. Publisher: Czechoslav Christian Democracy, 247 South Street, Hartford, Connecticut 06114. In Czech and Slovak.

DENNI HLASATEL (The Daily Herald). 1891-. Daily. Editor: Josef Kucera. Publisher: Denni Hlasatel Printing and Publishing Company, 6426 Cermak Road, Berwyn, Illinois 60402. In Czech.

Covers general, international, and national news of interest to Czechs in the United States.

HLAS NOVODA (Voice of the People). 1893-. Weekly. Editor: Rev. Vojtech Vit, O.S.B. Publisher: Benedictine Abbey Press, 2657 South Lawndale Avenue, Chicago, Illinois 60623. In Czech.

Like Katolik, this paper is published by the Bohemian Benedictine Order and its contents are similar to those of Katolik. Part one is published in the Czech language as a Saturday edition, while Part two is published in English as a Sunday edition. Narod was a daily until 1956.

HLASATEL (The Herald). 1892-. Weekly. Editor: Anton S. Jurcik. Publisher: Volclav Zolman, 5234 West 25th Street, Cicero, Illinois 60650. In Czech and English.

KATOLIK (The Catholic). 1893-. Weekly. Editor: Very Reverend Alex Machacek. Publisher: Benedictine Abbey Press, 2657 South Lawndale Avenue, Chicago, Illinois 60623. In Czech.

Carries articles concerned with international, national, regional, and local news. Emphasis is on the Catholic Church and church activities. Includes articles on the origin of the Czechs, their life in America, and their contributions to the United States.

NASINEC (Fellow Countryman). 1914-. Weekly. Editor: Joe Maresh, Sr. Publisher: Czech Roman Catholic Union of Texas, East Davila Street, Post Office Box 158, Granger, Texas 76530. In Czech.

NATIONAL COUNCIL OF WOMEN OF FREE CZECHOSLOVAKIA BULLETIN. 3 times per year. Publisher: National Council of Women of Free Czechoslovakia, Post Office Box 121, Newark, New Jersey 07104.

NOVY SVET (The New World). 1950-. Weekly. Editor: Miloslava Hyvnar. Publisher: Novy Svet Printing and Publishing Company, 4732 Broadway, Cleveland, Ohio 44127. In Czech.

Publishes general, international, national and local news.

SOKOL TIMES. Biweekly. Publisher: Sokol USA, 276 Prospect Street, East Orange, New Jersey 07017.

Newsletter covers insurance and physical education news of interest to its members.

VESTNIK (Herald). 1916-. Weekly. Editor: Nick A. Morris. Publisher: Slavonic Benevolent Order of Texas, Oak Street, West, Post Office Box 85, Texas 76691. In Czech and English.

Covers fraternal news.

SLOVAKS

JEDNOTA (Union). 1893-. Weekly. Editor: Joseph C. Krajsa. Publisher: First Catholic Slovak Union, 1655 West Harrisburg Pike, Post Office Box 150, Middletown, Pennsylvania 17057. In Slovak and English.

The official organ of the First Catholic Slovak Union, a fraternal life insurance company. Founded to promote and preserve the Catholic faith of the Slovac people, their language, and identity.

KATOLICKY SOKOL (Catholic Falcon). 1911-. Weekly. Editor: John C. Sciranka. Publisher: Slovak Catholic Sokol, 205 Madison Street, Passaic, New Jersey 07055. In Slovak and English.

A fraternal publication.

LUDOVE NOVINY (People's News). 1905-. Weekly. Editor: John Zuskar. Publisher: People's News, Incorporated, 1510 West 18th Street, Chicago, Illinois 60608. In Slovak.

Covers general news of special interest to Slovaks.

NARODNE NOVINY (National News). 1910-. Semimonthly. Editor: Edward Kovac. Publisher: National Slovak Society, 516 Court Place, Pittsburgh, Pennsylvania 15063. In Slovak and English.

Publishes news concerning the events and activities of the fraternal organization.

NASE SNAHY (Our Trends). 1965-. Bimonthly. Publisher: Permanent Conference of Slovak Democratic Exiles, 4014 North Le Claire Avenue, Chicago, Illinois 60641.

NEW YORSKY DENIK (New York Daily). 1912-. Weekly. Editor: Karol Bednar. Publisher: Universum Sokol Publications, 283 Oak Street, Perth Amboy, New Jersey 08861. In Slovak.

Articles on politics, culture and economics.

SLOVAK V AMERIKE (Slovak in America). 1889-. Weekly. Editor: Michael J. Krajsa. Publisher: Joseph Pauco, Post Office Box 150, Middletown, Pennsylvania 17057. In Slovak.

Covers national, international and local news of special concern to Slovak readers.

SLOVENSKY SOKOL (Sokol Times). 1905-. Weekly. Editor: Karol Bednar. Publisher: Slovak Gymnastic Union Sokol of U.S.A., 276 Prospect Street, East Orange, New Jersey 07019. In English and Slovak.

Presents articles on the history and program of the Sokol movement, gymnastics, and sports. Official publication of the fraternal and physical education organization.

UNITED LUTHERAN. 1893-. Monthly. Editor: Daniel M. Zornan. Publisher: United Lutheran Society, 223 East Main Street, Ligonier, Pennsylvania 15658. In Slovak and English.

Official organ of the United Lutheran Society.

ZORNICKA (Morning Star). 1941-. Weekly. Editor: Edward Kovac, Jr. Publisher: Ladies Pennsylvania Slovak Catholic Union, 315 Oak Hill Drive, Post Office Box 168, Middletown, Pennsylvania 17057. In Slovak.

Covers general news and news about events and activities of the Union.

Magazines

AMERICAN BULLETIN. 1957-. Monthly. Editor: Vlasta Vraz. Publisher: Czechoslovak National Council of America, 2137 South Lombard, Room 202, Cicero, Illinois 60650. In English.

AMERICAN SOKOL (American Falcon). 1885-. Monthly. Editor: Jackie Kourim. Publisher: American Sokol Organization, 6426 West Cermak Road, Berwyn, Illinois 60402. In Czech.

A fraternal publication featuring materials on physical education.

BESIDKA SOKOLSKA (Sokol News). 1892-. Monthly. Editor: W. E. Dolezal. Publisher: Czechoslovak Workingmen's Gymnastic Association, 29-19 24th Avenue, Astoria, New York 11102. In Czech and English.

Presents articles about current events within the Czechoslovak Workingmen's Gymnastic Association. Most of the news items deal with sports and physical fitness.

BRATRSKE-LISTY (The Brethren Journal). 1902-. Monthly. Editor: Reverend Jesse E. Skrivanek. Publisher: Unity of the Brethren in Texas, 5905 Carleen Drive, Austin, Texas 78731. In English and Czech.

Publishes information concerning religious interests and the activities of the Unity of the Brethren Organication.

BRATRSKY VESTNIK (Fraternal Herald). 1897-. Monthly. Editor: Henrietta Shutt. Publisher: Western Bohemian Fraternal Association, 1900 First Avenue, Northeast, Cedar Rapids, Iowa 52402. In English and Czech.

Reports on various activities of affiliated lodges of the Association. Includes articles pertaining to Czech or Slovak history and political matters.

C.S.A. JOURNAL. 1892-. Monthly. Editor: William R. Cicovsky. Publisher: Czechoslovak Society of America, 2701 South Harlem Avenue, Berwyn, Illinois 60402. In English and Czech.

CZECHOSLOVAK LIFE. Monthly. Editor: Karel Beba. Publisher: Orbis Publishing House, Praha 2, Vlnohradska 46, Czechoslovakia. In English, Russian, German, French, or Italian.

Carries news articles on people, places, and events in Czechoslovakia. Illustrated with photographs, including a color reproduction each month of a painting by a national artist. Has a children's page.

FOR YOU FROM CZECHOSLOVAKIA. Quarterly. Prague, Rapid Publishing Offices.

Publishes articles on cultural and social topics with beautiful colored illustrations. Includes a large section on Czechoslovakia products and their production, for example, pipes, furs, glass,accordions, timber and wood products.

HLAS JEDNOTY (Voice of the Unity). 1894-. Quarterly. Editor: R. J. Heukal. Publisher: Czechoslovak Society of America, 2701 South Harlem Avenue, Berwyn, Illinois 60402. In Czech and English.

Prints articles on matters pertaining to Fraternal Life Insurance. Includes letters from lodge officers reporting on fraternal activities, short articles on various subjects, and editorials.

HOSPODAR (The Farmer). 1889-. Semimonthly. Editor: Jerome Kopecky. Publisher: Czechoslovak Publishing Company, 214 West Oak, Post Office Box 38, West, Texas 76691. In Czech.

Features articles on agricultural topics, general news, and other subjects of interest to the Czech community.

KATOLICKY DELNIK (Catholic Workman). 1907-. Monthly. Editor: Pauline O'Brien. Publisher: Catholic Workmen's Fraternal Association, 112-1/2 East Main Street, Post Office Box 47, New Prague, Minnesota 56071. In English and Czech.

Publishes news of the Association, including decisions of the Supreme Executive reports of State Executive Council, and news from branches. Reprints editors' comments and articles from other fraternal magazines.

KJZT NEWS. 1955-. Monthly. Editor: Mrs. Benita Pavlu. Publisher: Catholic Women's Fraternal of Texas, Post Office Box 1884, Austin, Texas 78767. In English and Czech.

Prints items on events and activities of the Fraternal Benefit Society, the KJZT.

KOSMAS. Journal of Czechoslovak and Central European Studies. 1982-. Biennial. Editor: John F. Bradley. Publisher: Czechoslovak Society of Arts and Sciences in America, 3200 Holly Berry Court, Falls Church, Virginia 22042. In English.

An interdisciplinary cultural forum for scholars and scientists which publishes articles on literature, history, politics, the arts.

LEADER-NEWS. 1885-. Weekly. Editor: Herschiel L. Hunt, Post Office Box 907, El Campo, Texas 77437. In Czech and English.

POSEL (The Messenger). 1926-. Quarterly. Editor: Elsie Filous. Publisher: The Czech Catholic Union, 5349 Dolloff Road, Cleveland, Ohio 44127. In Czech.

PRAVDA A SLAVNA NADEJE (Truth and Glorious Hope). 1919-. Monthly. Editor: Reverend J. P. Piroch. Publisher: Czechoslovak Baptist Convention of United States and Canada, 316 South Park Street, Westmont, Illinois 60559. In Czech and Slovak.

PROMENY (Metamorphoses). 1964-. Quarterly. Editor: Josef Stasa. Publisher: Czechoslovak Society of Arts and Sciences in America, Harvard University Planning Office, 900 Holyoke Center, Cambridge, Massachusetts 02138. In Czech and Slovak.

A literary quarterly containing scholarly articles on philosophy, economics, political science, history, art and other fields in the humanities and the social sciences. Also includes short stories, poetry, and critical book reviews.

SOKOL TYRS NEWSLETTER. Monthly. Editor: Sandra A. Srsen. Publisher: American Sokol Gymnastic Organization, 20110 Harvard Avenue, Cleveland, Ohio 44122. In Czech and English.

A fraternal magazine featuring sports news.

SPJST VESTNIK (SPJST Herald). 1897-. Weekly. Editor: Nick A. Morris. Publisher: Slavonic Benevolent Order of the State of Texas, Oak Street, West, Texas 76691. In English and Czech.

This fraternal publication includes news of members, reports from the various lodges, and a section devoted to youth activities.

SVOBODNA SKOLA (Free Thinking School). 1893-. Bimonthly. Editor: Frances Hrdlicka. Publisher: Bohemian Free Thinking School Society, 1904 South 61st Avenue, Cicero, Illinois 60650. In Czech.

SVOBODNE CESKOSLOVENSKO (Free Czechoslovakia). 1943-. Monthly. Editor: Mrs. Bela Kotrsal. Publisher: Czech American National Alliance, 4029 West 25th Place, Chicago, Illinois 60623. In Czech.

This monthly publishes political news and articles.

VESTNIK (Herald). 1954-. Monthly. Editor: Vlasta Vraz. Publisher: Czechoslovak National Council of America, 2137 South Lombard Avenue, Cicero, Illinois 60650. In Czech.

Contains reports on the activities of the Czech and Slovak communities in the United States, articles on current events in Czechoslovakia and in the United States from the standpoint of Czech-Slovak American citizens, and articles on Czechoslovak culture.

WELCOME TO CZECHOSLOVAKIA. Quarterly. Editor: Petra Frankeova. Publisher: Czech Government Committee for Tourism, 12000 Prague, Vinohradska 46, Hastalska 14, Czechoslovakia.

Contains feature articles written in English and abundantly illustrated with color photography. Describes places of interest in various cities and regions of the country, including their historical background, as well as reporting on activities appealing to vacationers.

ZPRAVODAJ (Reporter). 1969-. Monthly. Publisher: Alliance of Czechoslovak Exiles in Chicago, 2619 South Lawndale Avenue, Chicago, Illinois 60623. In Czech.

ZPRAVY SVU (Bulletin of the Czechoslovak Society of Arts and Sciences in America). 1959-. Bimonthly. Editor: Hana Demetz. Publisher: Czechoslovak Society of Arts and Sciences in America, 283 Greene Street, New Haven, Connecticut 06510. In Czech and Slovak.

Includes announcements of the Society, reports on activities of local chapters, news items concerning the arts and sciences, book reviews, and biographic items.

SLOVAKS

AVE MARIA. 1916-. Monthly. Editor: Reverend Andrew Pier. Publisher: Slovak Benedictine Fathers, 2900 East Boulevard, Cleveland, Ohio 44104. In Slovak.

BRATSTVO (Brotherhood). 1898-. Monthly. Editor: Stephen J. Kavulich. Publisher: Pennsylvania Slovak Catholic Union, 173 North Main Street, Wilkes Barre, Pennsylvania 18702. In Slovak and English.

A fraternal publication providing general news of interest to the Slovak community, as well as reports of Union activities.

DEDICSTVO SLOVAKOV (Slovak Heritage). 1975-. Monthly. Editor and Publisher: Jan Beliansky, 9939 St. Marys Street, Detroit, Michigan 48227.

DOBRY PASTIER (Good Shepherd). 1926-. Monthly. Editor: Reverend John Sciranka. Publisher: Slovak Catholic Federation of America, 605 Ninth Avenue, Munhall, Pennsylvania 15120. In Slovak.

FLORIDSKY SLOVAK (Floridian Slovak). 1952-. Quarterly. Editor: Charles Belohlavek, Route 1, Box 39, Maitland, Florida 32751. In Slovak and English.

Publishes news of special interest to retired Slovaks, especially articles on Slovak culture.

FRATERNALLY YOURS. 1913-. Monthly. Editor: Mrs. Anne Fusillo. Publisher: First Catholic Slovak Ladies Association, 24950 Chagrin Boulevard, Beachwood, Ohio 44122. In Slovak and English.

Publishes articles on the activities of the Association, Slovak culture, and Slovak leaders. Formerly called Zenska Jednota.

LISTY SVATEHO FRANTISKA (Leaflets of St. Francis). 1926-. Monthly. Editor: Reverend Rudolf Dilong, O.F.M. Publisher: Slovak Catholic Sokol, 232 South Home Avenue, Pittsburgh, Pennsylvania 15202. In Slovak.

Primarily religious and spiritual content, although some educational materials are published.

MOST (Bridge). 1954-. Quarterly. Editor: Nicholas Sprinc. Publisher: The Slovak Institute, 2900 East Boulevard, Cleveland, Ohio 44104. In Slovak.

This cultural and literary quarterly features articles on Slovak literature, fine arts, history, social sciences, and philosophy by Slovak authors outside Slovakia.

PRIATEL DIETOK (The Children's Friend). 1913-. Ten times a year. Editor: John C. Sciranka. Publisher: Junior Slovak Catholic Sokol, 205 Madison Street, Passaic, New Jersey 07055. In Slovak and English.

A children's magazine.

SION (Zion). 1929-. Monthly. Editor: Reverend John Kovacik. Publisher: Slovak Zion Synod, 342 Boulevard of the Allies, Pittsburgh, Pennsylvania 15222. In Slovak.

A religious magazine.

SLOVAK PRESS DIGEST. 1968-. Irregular. Editor: Jozef Ihnat. Publisher: Slovak-American Cultural Center, Box 291, New York, New York 10008. In English.

Publishes news digests, translations and book reviews.

SLOVAKIA. 1951-. Irregular. Editor: Joseph Pauco. Publisher: Slovak League of America, 313 Ridge Avenue, Middletown, Pennsylvania 17057. In English.

Publishes scholarly articles on Slovak history, culture, politics, and related topics. Contains a book review section.

SLOVENSKA OBRANA (Slovak Defense). 1913-. Weekly. Editor: Edward Kovac, Jr. Publisher: Bosak Publications, Box 150, Middletown, Pennsylvania 17057. In Slovak.

Covers general, national, and local news, and feature articles on Slovak activities and organizations in the United States.

SVEDOK (The Witness). 1906-. Monthly. Editor: Jaroslav Pelikan, Sr. Publisher: Synod of Evangelical Lutheran Churches, 342 Boulevard of the Allies, Pittsburgh, Pennsylvania 15222. In Slovak.

A religious magazine for Lutheran Slovaks.

SVORNOST (Harmony). 1912-. Bimonthly. Editor: Reverend Thomas Harnyak. Publisher: Catholic Slovak Brotherhood, 342 Boulevard of the Allies, Pittsburgh, Pennsylvania 15222. In Slovak.

A fraternal religious magazine.

ZIVENA. 1908-. Monthly. Editor: John Cieker. Publisher: Zivena Beneficial Society, 157 McNielly Road, Pittsburgh, Pennsylvania 15226. In Slovak and English.

A fraternal publication.

Radio Programs

Alabama - Foley

WHEP - Box F, Foley, Alabama 36535, (205) 943-7131. Czech programs, 1 hour weekly.

Iowa - Cedar Rapids

KCRG - Second Avenue at Fifth Street, Southeast, Cedar Rapids, Iowa 52401, (319) 398-8422, TWX (910) 525-1341. Czech programs, 4 hours weekly.

New York - New York

WPOW - 1111 Woodrow Road, Staten Island, New York, New York 10312, (212) 984-4600. Czech programs, 2 hours weekly.

Ohio - Bellaire

WOMP - Box 448, Route 214, Bellaire, Ohio 43906, (614) 676-5661. Czech programs, 2 hours weekly.

Ohio - Cleveland

WERE - 1500 Chester Avenue, Cleveland, Ohio 44114, (216) 696-1300. Czech programs, 1/2 hour weekly.

Texas - Cameron

KMIL - Drawer 832, Cameron, Texas 76520, (817) 697-6633. Czech programs, 8 hours weekly.

Texas - Dallas

KSKY - Stoneleigh Terrace, 2927 Maple Avenue, Dallas, Texas 75201, (214) 742-6193. Czech musical programs, 1 hour weekly.

Texas - Grandbury

KPAR - 425 St. George Street, Grandbury, Texas 78629, (512) 672-3631. Czech programs, 18 hours weekly.

Texas - Hallettsville

KRJH - 111 North Main Street, Hallettsville, Texas 77964, (512) 798-4333. Czech programs, 3 hours weekly.

Texas - Hillsboro

KHBR - Box 569, Hillsboro, Texas 76645, (817) 582-3431. Czech programs, 2 hours weekly.

Texas - La Grange

KVLG - Drawer K, La Grange, Texas 78945, (713) 968-3173. Czech - German programs, 8 hours weekly.

Texas - Rosenberg-Richmond

KFRD - 1501 Radio Lane, Rosenberg-Richmond, Texas 77471, (713) 342-6601. Czech programs, 12 hours weekly.

Texas - Temple

KTEM - Box 1230, Temple, Texas 76501, (817) 773-5252. Czech programs, 3 hours weekly.

Wisconsin - Kewaunee

WAUN(FM) - Box 224A, Route 3, Kewaunee, Wisconsin 54216, (414) 388-4852. Czech programs, 1 hour weekly.

SLOVAK

Illinois - Chicago

WSBC - 4949 West Belmont Avenue, Chicago, Illinois 60641, (312) 777-1700. Slovak programs, 1 hour weekly.

WAUP(FM) - 302 East Buchtel Avenue, Chicago, Illinois 44325, (216) 375-7105. Slovak programs, 1 hour weekly.

Ohio - Cleveland

WERE - 1500 Chester Avenue, Cleveland, Ohio 44114, (216) 696-1300. Slovak programs, 1 hour weekly.

Pennsylvania - Pittsburgh

WPIT-FM - 200 Gateway Towers, Pittsburgh, Pennsylvania 15222. Slovak programs, 1 hour weekly.

Festivals, Fairs, and Celebrations

Florida - Masaryktown

CZECHOSLOVAKIAN INDEPENDENCE DAY CELEBRATION
Masaryktown, Florida

Settled in the mid-1920's by Czechoslovakians who made it the egg capital of the world, this community north of Tampa annually celebrates the traditions of the homeland. The folk festival includes dinner, dancing, and a performance by the Beseda Dancers, a group of local young people in native Czech costumes performing national dances. Staged on the Sunday nearest October 28 each year.
Contact: Vera Buchton, Route 1, Box 242, Masaryktown, Florida 33512. (904) 796-4145.

Illinois - Cicero

CICERO INTERNATIONAL HOUBY FESTIVAL
Cermak Road
Cicero, Illinois

The two-day celebration features a houby parade, (houby is the Czech word for mushrooms), arts and crafts, green pageant, sports and games, and Czech foods. Held in early October.
Contact: Norm, (312) 863-2104.

Kansas - Wilson

AFTER HARVEST CZECH FESTIVAL
Wilson, Kansas

Features Czech dancers, a parade with colorful floats, Czech dinners, dances, and musical attractions each year the last part of July. Kolaches (pastries) and jaternize (sausages) are sold. Also includes arts and crafts exhibits, horseshoe pitching contests, and tractor pulls. The festival usually runs two days.
Contact: Chamber of Commerce, Wilson, Kansas 67490.

Minnesota - Montgomery

KOLACKY DAY
Montgomery, Minnesota

The kolacky, a Bohemian bun, is celebrated by this Czech town on a full day of activities, including a parade, slow pitch softball tournament, midway, and king and queen coronation. The king qualifies by the number of kolackies he can consume. Held in early September. Begun around 1935.
Contact: Chamber of Commerce, Montgomery, Minnesota 56069. (612) 364-5286.

Nebraska - Clarkson

CLARKSON CZECH FESTIVAL
Clarkson, Nebraska

A three-day festival with ethnic music and dance throughout the community. Crafts and Czech food are featured. Held in June.
Contact: Ron Vavrina, 511 Maple, Clarkson, Nebraska 68629, (402) 892-3444.

Nebraska - Verdigre

KOLACH DAYS
Verdigre, Nebraska

Features special Czech pastries filled with delicious assorted fruits. Visitors watch the crowning of the Kolach Queen, Czech dancers performing intricate steps to fast-paced musical accompaniment, and a magnificent parade. Held in early June for two days.
Contact: Improvement Club, Verdigre, Nebraska 68783.

Nebraska - Wilber

CZECH FESTIVAL
Wilber, Nebraska

A gay two-day festival celebrates this little town's Czechoslovakian heritage. A rich array of ethnic dishes prepared especially for the event, abundant displays of Czech handicrafts, and a parade down Wilber's quaint streets highlight the festivities. Held in early August. Began around 1960.
Contact: Milo T. Jelinek, President, Nebraska Czechs of Wilber, Incorporated, Wilber, Nebraska 68465.

Ohio - Dillonvale

CZECH DAYS
Co-op Picnic Grounds
Rhodes Street
Dillonvale, Ohio 43917

Czech music and dance, food and handcrafts, are in the spotlight during this two-day festival in August.
Contact: Mary Pospisil, RFD #1, Dillonvale, Ohio 43917.

Oklahoma - Prague

KOLACHE FESTIVAL
Prague, Oklahoma

At the community's Czechoslovakian festival, kolaches (sweet rolls with fruit and other fillings) are served by the thousands. Features a parade, rodeo, folk dancing, and a beauty pageant. Held annually in early May.
Contact: Prague Chamber of Commerce, Post Office Box 223, Prague, Oklahoma 74864. (405) 567-3196.

Oklahoma - Yukon

CZECH FESTIVAL
Yukon, Oklahoma

Features strolling polka bands, ethnic costumes, native country dances, a parade, and beauty contest. Czech food specialties, such as kolaches and kholbasy, are served. Held annually in early October.
Contact: Director, Czech Festival, Route 2, Box 106, El Reno, Oklahoma 73036.

Oregon - Cottage Grove

BOHEMIA MINING DAYS
Cottage Grove, Oregon

Contact: Chamber of Commerce, Cottage Grove, Oregon 97424, (503) 942-2411.

South Dakota - Tabor

CZECH DAYS FESTIVAL
Tabor, South Dakota

A gala celebration in honor of the town's Czechoslovakian heritage. Features singing, dancing, oom-pa-pa bands, parades, colorful costumes, and good food. Spontaneous street dancing, yummy kolaches (fruit-filled pastries), and a queen contest add to the festivities. Held in mid-June annually since 1946.
Contact: Czech Days, Box 128, Tabor, South Dakota 57063.

Texas - Ennis

NATIONAL POLKA FESTIVAL
Ennis, Texas

Dedicated to enjoyment of polka music, rich food, and colorful Czech traditions. Dozen or more bands provide polkas, local cooks provide country style kolbase, dumplings and sauerkraut, barbeque, apple strudel and kolache. Visitors come from throughout the nation.

Texas - New Braunfels

CZECH FEST
New Braunfels, Texas

Features folk dancing, bright costumes, tasty Czech foods, and horse racing. The festival is held for two days in early June.
Contact: Chamber of Commerce, 390 South Sequin, Post Office Box 180, New Braunfels, Texas 78130.

Texas - West

ST. MARY'S ANNUAL HOMECOMING FESTIVAL
West, Texas

A church festival celebrating the Czech heritage with foods, games, arts and crafts, auctions, and Czech sausages. Held in June.
Contact: Reverend George Doskocil, Church of the Assumption, West, Texas 76691.

Airline Offices

CSA (CESKOSLOVENSKE AEROLINIE)
North American Headquarters
545 Fifth Avenue
New York, New York 10017 (212) 682-7541

Seabrook, Maryland 20706 (301) 577-4300

An extensive domestic network connects with world-wide routes to the Balkans and the Middle East; to North Africa; to Western Europe; to the United States and Canada; to Russia, India, Southeast Asia, and Australia.

Bookdealers

CZECHOSLOVAK STORE
1363 First Avenue
New York, New York 10021 (212) 249-7414

FAM BOOK SERVICE
69 Fifth Avenue
New York, New York 10003 (212) 243-3737

FOUR CONTINENT BOOK CORPORATION
149 Fifth Avenue
New York, New York 10010 (212) 533-0250

IMPORTED PUBLICATIONS, INCORPORATED
320 West Ohio Street
Chicago, Illinois 60610 (312) 787-9017

S & D BOOK STORE
16 South 11th Street
Indiana, Pennsylvania 15701 (412) 465-2795

Books and Pamphlets

BASIC INFORMATION ON TRAVEL TO SOCIALIST CZECHOSLOVAKIA. Government Committee for Tourism, Prague, 1975.

Gives general information about the country, its geographic and climatic conditions, spas, hunting and recreation.

BIBLIOGRAPHY OF SOCIAL SCIENCE PERIODICALS AND MONOGRAPHS: CZECHOSLAVAKIA 1948-63. Bureau of the Census, 1965.

Entries are in Czech with descriptive material in English.

THE CONSTITUTIONAL FOUNDATIONS OF THE CZECHOSLOVAK FEDERATION. Prague, Orbis Press Agency, 1978.

A translation of the Constitution into English as well as the Constitutional Act concerning the Federation and the Constitutional Act concerning the Status of Ethnic Groups, both amendments to the Constitution in 1968.

COUNCIL FOR MUTUAL ECONOMIC ASSISTANCE AND THE CZECHOSLOVAK SOCIALIST REPUBLIC. By Vladimir Wacker. Prague, Orbis Press Agency, 1979.

Description of the economic union of Socialist countries oriented toward the Soviet Union.

THE CZECHOSLOVAK AGRICULTURE. By the Czechoslovak Ministry of Agriculture and Nutrition. Prague, Czechoslovakia, 1974.

An attractive booklet with many color photographs and text in English explaining various aspects of Czechoslovakian agriculture, food processing, marketing and agricultural research.

CZECHOSLOVAK RESISTANCE TO THE INVASION AND OCCUPATION OF AUGUST, 1968. Compiled by Millicent Palmer. Edwardsville, Southern Illinois University, Lovejoy Library, 1972.

An annotated bibliography.

CZECHOSLOVAK SOCIALIST REPUBLIC. Prague, RAPID Czechoslovak Advertising Agency.

An information booklet illustrated with numerous color photographs. The text in English tells about the people and government, industries and agriculture, trade, social services, sports and culture of Czechoslovakia.

CZECHOSLOVAK SPARTAKIADES. By Julius Chvalny. Prague, Orbis Press Agency, 1980.

A book of colored photographs from the 1975 Spartakiade in Prague, a mammouth gymnastic meet whose origins are associated with the workers movement in Czechoslovakia and other Socialist states. Described as "a direct manifestation of the people for socialism, an expression of their faith in the policy of the Communist Party which successfully led Czechoslovakia out of the crisis and turbulence of 1968-69, an expression of friendship for the people of the Soviet Union whose sons, more than thirty years before, had returned freedom and peace to Czechoslovakia."

CZECHOSLOVAK STATE ENSEMBLE OF SONGS AND DANCES. Prague, CSESD and Kovo, 1975.

Magnificent colored photographs of the renowned folk dance groups which has revived ethnic dance from various parts of Czechoslovakia. An explanatory essay and captions are in English as well as in Russian, German and French.

CZECHOSLOVAKIA. Prague, Cedok Travel and Hotel Corporation.

A tourist brochure giving general travel information for the country and highlights of the various regions. Illustrated in color.

CZECHOSLOVAKIA: A BIBLIOGRAPHIC GUIDE. By Rudolf Sturm. Washington, D.C., U.S. Library of Congress, Slavic and Central European Division, 1967.

Covers publications issued after World War II and emphasizes materials in western languages, especially English. The first part consists of a narrative bibliographic survey, while the second part lists about 1,500 items in alphabetical order by main entry.

CZECHOSLOVAKIA 1968 - 1969. Chronology, Bibliography and Annotation. By Zdenek Hejzler and Vladimir Kusin. New York, Garland Publishers, 1975.

Gives a month by month chronology of the Prague uprising and a list of the main documents pertaining to the Prague Spring available in English translation. There are also bibliographies of Alexander Dubcek's speeches, articles and interviews, a selected list of newspapers and periodicals published in Czechoslavakia in 1968-69, a bibliography of Czech and Slovak articles pertaining to the Prague Spring 1968-1970, and of books published from 1968-74.

CZECHOSLOVAKIA ON THE THRESHOLD OF THE EIGHTIES. Prague, Orbis Press Agency, 1980.

Maps and tables and an abundance of colored photographs illustrating the political and social organization of the country, its economy, resources, industry and cultural establishment.

CZECHOSLOVAKIA: The Country of your Congress Meetings in the Heart of Europa. Prague, Cedok, 1978.

Promotional brochure with colored photographs showing the beauties of various cities and resorts in Czechoslovakia.

CZECHOSLOVAKIA WITH CEDOK IN PRAGUE. Prague, Cedok, 1979.

A detailed city map of Czechoslovakia's ancient capital city with many colored photographs and information about transportation, accommodations and nearby places of interest.

CZECH-POLISH RELATIONS 1918-1939. A selected and annotated bibliography. By C. M. Nowak. Stanford, California, Hoover Institute Press, 1976.

Lists bibliographies and research aids, published documents, diaries and memoirs, general works and writings specific to Czechoslovak-Polish relations in various periods and areas of conflict during the interwar period.

FRANTISKOVY LAZNE. Prague, Balnea, 1979.

A brochure about one of Czechoslovakia's famous therapeutic spas with colored illustrations.

THE 1968 CZECHOSLOVAK CRISIS: A BIBLIOGRAPHY, 1968-1970. By Michael Parrish. Santa Barbara, California, ABC Clio, 1971.

Includes books and periodical articles published from 1968 to 1970, mainly in the English language. Contains about 750 entries, without annotations. Does not cover the Soviet point of view.

PHOTO REPORTAGES FROM CZECHOSLOVAKIA. Prague, Orbis Press Agency, 1979.

A portfolio of large colored photographs showing aspects of Czechoslovakian agriculture and rural life.

POPULATION POLICY IN CZECHOSLOVAKIA. Second Edition, Prague, Orbis Press Agency, 1978.

Essays and tables on medical care, education and social policy.

SLOVAKIA - AN OASIS OF STILLNESS. By the Slovak National Council Committee for Tourism, Bratislava, Czechoslovakia.

A colorfully illustrated booklet with tripartite text in English, Czechoslovak, and German. Describes areas, activities, and tourist attractions in the eastern region of Czechoslovakia.

CZECHOSLOVAK AMERICANS

AMERICAN CZECHS IN PUBLIC OFFICE. By Thomas Capek. Omaha, Czech Historical Society of Nebraska 1940.

THE CECH (BOHEMIAN) COMMUNITY OF NEW YORK; With Introductory Remarks on the Czechoslovaks in the United States. By Thomas Capek. New York, America's Making, 1921. Reprinted by R and E Associates, San Francisco, 1969.

Part I deals with Czech immigrants, their distribution in America, occupations, press, politics, organizations, churches, and culture, focusing on New York City. Part II discusses similar topics concerning Slovak immigrants.

THE CECHS (BOHEMIANS) IN AMERICA; A Study of Their National, Cultural, Political, Social, Economic, and Religious Life. By Thomas Capek. Boston, Houghton Mifflin Company, 1920.

Deals briefly with seventeenth and eighteenth century Czech settlers, then concentrates on the tide of Czech immigration beginning in 1848. Discusses where and how the Czechs lived, their occupations, assimilation, culture, communication, education, religion, and social life.

CZECH-AMERICAN CATHOLICS, 1850-1920. By Joseph Cada. Lisle, Illinois, Center for Slav Culture, Saint Procopius College, 1964.

As the parish was often the center of the community, this study gives a good picture of Czech settlement during the earlier years of immigration.

CZECH CONTRIBUTIONS TO THE AMERICAN CULTURE. By Leroy F. Psencik. Austin, Texas: Texas Education Agency, 1970.

A bibliographic essay.

CZECH CONTRIBUTIONS TO THE GROWTH OF THE UNITED STATES. By Francis Dvornik. Chicago, Benedictine Abbey Press, 1962.

Famous as well as lesser-known individuals of Czech descent are introduced.

CZECH CULTURAL CONTRIBUTIONS. By Ernest Zizka. Chicago, 1937.

A sociological study of the Czech imput into American cultural life.

CZECH PIONEERS OF THE SOUTHWEST. By Estelle Hudson and H. R. Maresh. Dallas, Texas: Southwest, 1934.

CZECHOSLOVAK IMMIGRATION. By Thomas Capek. New York: Service Bureau for Intercultural Education, 1938.

THE CZECHO-SLOVAKS IN AMERICA. By K. Miller. New York, Doran, 1922.

CZECHS AND SLOVAKS IN AMERICA. By Joseph S. Roucek. Minneapolis, Lerner, 1957.

Written primarily for a younger reader but gives a good overview of Czech immigration, social organization, religious activity and participation in political life.

CZECHS AND SLOVAKS IN NORTH AMERICA. By Esther Jerabek. New York, 1977.

The best recent bibliography on Czechs in the United States and Canada.

THE CZECHS IN AMERICA, 1633-1977. A CHRONOLOGY AND FACT BOOK. Compiled and edited by Vera Laska. Dobbs Ferry, New York, Oceana Publications, 1978.

A history of Czechs in the United States in a chronology format with a selection of illustrative documents, appendices and a bibliography.

THE CZECHS IN OKLAHOMA. By Karel D. Bicha. Norman, Oklahoma, University of Oklahoma Press, 1980.

Following introductory material on the Czechs and the Czechs in America, the study focuses on Czech settlements in Oklahoma, their religious and social life, agriculture, family life and famous Czech Oklahomans.

CZECHS OF CLEVELAND. By Eleanor E. Ledbetter. Cleveland, Americanization Committee, 1919.

Although of an early date, this treatment is of interest for its regional focus.

EDUCATORS WITH CZECHOSLOVAK ROOTS: A U. S. AND CANADIAN FACULTY ROSTER. Edited by Mitoslav Rechcigl, Jr. Falls Church, Virginia, Czechoslovak Society of Arts and Sciences, 1981.

Covers about 1,500 persons with Czechoslovak roots (defined geographically) and persons who have resided or were educated in the region or have interests in Czechoslovak affairs. Entries include: Institution name, address, and name, department, and last known rank of persons coming within the scope of the book. The arrangement is geographical but there are indexes for names and academic discipline.

GENEALOGICAL RESEARCH FOR CZECH AND SLOVAK AMERICANS. Edited by Olga K. Miller, Detroit, Gale Research Company.

A comprehensive bibliographic research guide which covers the history and geography of Czechoslovakia and provides a detailed presentation of specific research procedures and problems. The guide lists the location and availability of vital records, parish registers, census returns, military records, and land records that are important to the genealogical researcher.

A HISTORY OF CZECHS (BOHEMIANS) IN NEBRASKA. By Rose Rosicky. Omaha, Czech Historical Society of Nebraska, 1929.

MY ANTONIA. By Willa Cather. Boston, Houghton Mifflin, 1918.

A novel about a Bohemian family settling in Nebraska and their difficulties in learning American ways.

OBSCURE DESTINIES. By Willa Cather. New York, Knopf, 1932.

Story centers around a Czech farmer in the prairie corn belt.

ONE HUNDRED YEARS OF CZECH POETRY IN AMERICA. By Jose F. Martinek. Chicago, Czechoslovak National Council of America, 1971.

PANORAMA: A HISTORICAL REVIEW OF CZECHS AND SLOVAKS IN THE UNITED STATES OF AMERICA. Cicero, Illinois, Czechoslovak National Council and Sczechoslovak Society of Arts and Sciences, 1970.

A collection of articles treating various aspects of the Czechoslovakian immigrant experience.

SAINTS AND TOMAHAWKS. By J. J. Sessler. New York: Pyramid, 1940.

A novel located in Bethlehem, Pennsylvania dealing with an early Moravian settlement.

THE STORY OF A BOHEMIAN-AMERICAN VILLAGE; A Study of Social Persistence and Change. By Robert I. Kutak. New York, Arno Press and the New York Times, 1970, c1933.

Discusses persistence and change in modes of behavior of Czech immigrants in a country environment as compared with their adjustment to a city environment. Covers their background in Bohemia, occupations, local politics, religion, education, home life, age differences, social activities, leisure-time interests, and community attitudes.

TIME AND TIDE. By Ruby R. Krider. Philadelphia: Dorrance, 1968.

A novel of frontier life in Minnesota, focusing on a Czech community.

TRACING YOUR CZECH AND SLOVAK ROOTS. By Maralyn A. Wellauer, Milwaukee, Wisconsin, 1980.

Publication includes: List of archives, libraries, organizations, and similar research sources in Europe and the United States useful in research into Czech and Slovak ancestry. Entries are arranged by type of source.

WINDSWEPT. By M. E. Chase, New York, Macmillan, 1941.

A novel set in Maine in which a Czech immigrant finds help and friendship from native residents.

SLOVAK AMERICANS

FLIGHT TO WONDERLAND. By Jozef Pauco. New York, Speller, 1963.

A novelistic account about a Slovak family as they emigrate to America and try to adjust to the new way of life.

A HISTORY OF THE SLOVAK EVANGELICAL LUTHERAN CHURCH IN THE UNITED STATES OF AMERICA, 1902-1927. By George Dolak. St. Louis, Missouri: Concordia, 1955.

A comprehensive analysis of the church history from its inception in America.

HUNKY. By Thames R. Williamson. St. Louis, Coward, 1929.

A novel dealing with the psychology of a Slovakian who works as a laborer in a flour mill.

HUNKY JOHNNY. By Edward Nicholas. Boston, Houghton Mifflin, 1945.

The fictionalized story of two brothers, one educated in the traditional Slovakian way, the other a gangster. The story is set in Chicago during the Depression and revolves around conflict in ethical values.

IN KRYSACK'S HOUSE. By Thames R. Williamson. New York, Harcourt, Brace, 1931.

The sequel to Hunky.

MILA NADAYA. By Michael Simko. Philadelphia, Dorrance, 1968.

A novel about a young woman facing economic difficulties and the problems of her own sexuality in the context of Slovakian family life in America.

OUR SLOVAK HERITAGE. By Joseph Cincik. Cleveland, Ohio: First Catholic Slovak Union, 1974.

A pamphlet celebrating Slovakian ethnicity.

OUT OF THIS FURNACE. By Thomas Bell. Boston: Little, Brown, 1941.

Set in the steel mills of western Pennsylvania, this story revolves around Slovak immigrants.

PEASANTS AND STRANGERS: ITALIANS, RUMANIANS AND SLOVAKS IN AN AMERICAN CITY 1890-1950. By Joseph J. Barton. Cambridge, Massachusetts, Harvard University Press, 1975.

A comparative study of three immigrant groups.

SLOVAK CHRISTMAS: A SYMPOSIUM OF SONGS, CUSTOMS AND PLAYS. Edited by Jozef Duris. Cleveland, 1960.

An anthology of Slovak American traditions.

SLOVAKS IN CHICAGO, 1872-1962. By Adam Padrivacky. Chicago, Slovak League of Chicago, 1962.

SLOVAKS OF CHICAGO. By Peter P. Hletho. Chicago, 1967. Reprinted in Slovakia. 1969.

Contains biographical material on prominent Slovaks in Chicago.

THE VALLEY OF DECISION. By Marcia Davenport. New York, Scribner's, 1943.

A novel about Slovaks in America.

Audiovisual Material

MAP

CZECHOSLOVAKIA. By Merkur Prague. Prague, Government Committee for Tourism in Czechoslovakia, 1974.

A large, full color map of Czechoslovakia surrounded by smaller specialized maps showing recreation areas, petrol pumps and repair garages, and airline routes. On the verso, tourist information is given about places of interest in the regions of Bohemia, Moravia and Slovakia. Approximately 26 by 38 inches.

FILMS

ALTAR OF ST. GEORGE. 16 mm. Color and sound.

Views and discussion of the famous altar.

ANTONIN DVORAK. 16 mm. Color and sound.

The story of the well-known Czech composer and the places he lived.

BALLAD OF ROSES. 16 mm. Color and sound.

Shows the city of Lidice which was completely destroyed in World War II.

CONCERTO GLASSICO. 16 mm. Color and sound.

Shows how Czechoslovak glass is made and some of the extraordinary results.

COUNTRYSIDE NEAR NACHOD. 16 mm. Color and sound.

Landscape and life near the city of Nachod.

CZECH BAROQUE. 16 mm. Color and sound.

In Prague and elsewhere in Czechoslovakia the Baroque period of architecture produced magnificent edifices as well as painting.

CZECHOSLOVAKIA: UNKNOWN COUNTRY. 16 mm. Color and sound.

A description and travel film about the country and people.

LYRIC VIEWS OF PRAGUE. 16 mm. Color and sound.

Shows scenes in the capital city.

MIDDLE AGES TOWNS IN SLOVAKIA. 16 mm. Color and sound.

Historical views of remains of the Middle Ages in Slovakia.

MORAVIAN GOTHIC. 16 mm. Color and sound.

In the Moravian part of Czechoslovakia there are still Gothic structures which are shown in this film.

MOUNTAINS IN CZECHOSLOVAKIA. 16 mm. Color and sound.

NOW SLOVAKIA. 16 mm. Color and sound.

Introduces Slovakia, the eastern region of Czechoslovakia.

OLD PAINTINGS IN SLOVAK CHURCHES. 16 mm. Color and sound.

PERSONAL DETOUR. 16 mm. Color and sound.

Views of Northern Moravia.

SUMMER IN SOUTH BOHEMIA. 16 mm. Color and sound.

Describes sunny days in the southern region of Bohemia.

TRANSFORMATIONS. 16 mm. Color and sound.

Filmic excursion in Eastern Bohemia.

TWO JEWELS OF GOTHIC ARCHITECTURE. 16 mm. Black and white. Sound.

Examines Gothic architecture preserved in Prague.

WHITE FACE OF SLOVAKIA. 16 mm. Color and sound.

Describes winter in Slovakia.

WINTER IN CZECHOSLOVAKIA. 16 mm. Color and sound.

Presents winter time scenes in various regions of Czechoslovakia.

VIA CENTRAL SLOVAKIA. 16 mm. Color and sound.

Describes the central region of Slovakia.

(For information about borrowing the films listed above and others, write to the Embassy of Czechoslovakia.)

CZECHOSLOVAKIA: THE LAND AND THE PEOPLE. 16 mm. Color and sound. 16 minutes. Coronet Instructional Films, Chicago, 1969.

Presents geographic views of Czechoslovakia. Points out the environmental factors that made the country a strong industrial and agricultural nation.

INVASION OF CZECHOSLOVAKIA, 1939. Super 8 mm. Black and White. Silent. 4 minutes. By Anargyros Film Library, 1973.

Describes the aggressive nature of a Fascist government by focusing on German activities prior to World War II, particularly the invasion of Czechoslovakia in 1939.

THE NAZI STRIKE. Videorecording. Black and white. Sound. 41 minutes. By United States War Department. United States Office of War Information, Domestic Branch, Washington, D.C. Distributed by National Audiovisual Center, 1979.

A documentary film record issued as a motion picture in 1943, of Germany's preparation for war, the conquest of Austria and Czechoslovakia, and the attack upon Poland.

SEVEN DAYS TO REMEMBER. 16 mm. Black and white. Sound. 56 minutes. By Peter R. D. MacKell, Canada. Released in the United States by Films Incorporated, Wilmette, Illinois, 1969.

Presents a chronology of events following the invasion of Czechoslovakia by the Soviets on August 20, 1968. Reports on the confrontation between the inhabitants and the powerful invader.

TWO WORLDS - TWENTY YEARS. 16 mm. Black and white. Sound. 29 minutes. Also available as videorecording, 1979. By North Atlantic Treaty Organization. Released by National Audiovisual Center, 1971.

Contrasts the economic development of Belgium and Czechoslovakia in the post-World War II era. Points out that Belgium aided under the Marshall plan and protected by NATO, has prospered under a free economy, while Czechoslovakia, deprived of this aid by the USSR, has not.

DANES
See also: SCANDINAVIANS

Embassy and Consulates

EMBASSY OF DENMARK
3200 Whitehaven Street, Northwest
Washington, D.C. 20008 (202) 234-4300

CONSULATES GENERAL

360 North Michigan Avenue
Chicago, Illinois 60601 (312) 329-9644

Two Post Oak Central
Suite 1710
1980 South Post Oak Road
Houston, Texas 77056 (713) 850-9520

3440 Wilshire Boulevard
Suite 904
Los Angeles, California
90010 (213) 387-4277

280 Park Avenue
New York, New York
10017 (212) 697-5101

CONSULATES

The Broadway Southwest
Coronado Center
Albuquerque, New Mexico
87110 (505) 883-2500

Alaska Mutual Bank Building
601 West Fifth Avenue
Suite 700
Anchorage, Alaska 99501 (970) 272-7401

225 Peachtree Street, Northeast
Suite 201
Atlanta, Georgia 30303 (404) 522-8811

33 South Gay Street
Post Office Box 1717
Baltimore, Maryland 21203 (301) 332-4872

28 State Street
Suite 1700
Boston, Massachusetts 02109 (617) 227-8716

607 Peoples Building
28 Broad Street
Post Office Box 993
Charleston, South Carolina
29402 (803) 577-4000

3200 National City Center
Cleveland, Ohio 44114 (216) 621-0200

4517 Baldwin Boulevard
Post Office Box 4585
Corpus Christi, Texas 78408 (512) 884-6344

717 North Harwood
Suite 2200
Dallas, Texas 75201 (214) 744-9300

3100 South Sheridan Boulevard
Suite 10
Denver, Colorado 80227 (303) 922-4545

222 Equitable Building
Des Moines, Iowa 50309 (515) 244-4201

4113 North Woodward Avenue
Royal Oak
Detroit, Michigan 48072 (313) 549-3666

Roger Street
Post Office Box 481
Gloucester, Massachusetts
01930 (617) 283-5745

Villa Professional Plaza
444 Hebron Lane, Suite 311
Honolulu, Hawaii 96815 (808) 955-1001

1510 Talleyrand Avenue
Post Office Box 88
Jacksonville, Florida 32201 (904) 353-1741

1700 West 12th Street
Post Office Box 4046
Kansas City, Missouri 64101 (816) 421-0633

1117 City National Bank Building
25 West Flagler Street
Miami, Florida 33130 (305) 373-7768

700 First National Bank Building
Minneapolis, Minnesota
55402 (612) 332-3941

302 Commerce Building
118 North Royal Street
Mobile, Alabama 36601 (205) 432-1397

421 Ellendale Drive
Nashville, Tennessee 37205 (615) 298-4744

735 Whilney Building
624 Common Street
New Orleans, Louisiana
70130 (504) 525-1018

1800 Virginia National Bank
Building
Norfolk, Virginia 23510 (804) 627-0611

1500 Woodmen Tower
Omaha, Nebraska 68102 (402) 344-0500

956 Public Ledger Building
Independence Square
Philadelphia, Pennsylvania
19106 (215) 625-9900

Trust Department
Valley National Bank of
Arizona
Post Office Box 71
Phoenix, Arizona 85001 (602) 261-1254

200 Market Building, #1790
200 Southwest Market Street
Portland, Oregon 97201 (503) 226-3876

c/o Roitman and Son,
Incorporated
161 South Main Street
Providence, Rhode Island
02903 (401) 861-6010

6515 Page Boulevard
Post Office Box 31
Saint Louis, Missouri 63133 (314) 725-1111

231 Edison Street
Salt Lake City, Utah 84111 (801) 355-2135

445 West Ash Street, Suite 1
San Diego, California 92101 (714) 232-3066

One Market Plaza
Steuart Street Tower
Suite 2510
San Francisco, California
94105 (415) 781-1309

900 Savannah Bank & Trust
Company Building
2 East Bryan Street
Post Office Box 9667
Savannah, Georgia 31402 (912) 234-6671

Seattle-King County Conventions
and Visitors Bureau
1815 Seventh Avenue
Seattle, Washington 98101 (206) 447-7220

c/o A.R. Savage and Son
203 Marion Street
Tampa, Florida 33602 (813) 223-1521

4500 South Garnett Road
Suite 1000
Tulsa, Oklahoma 74145 (918) 838-9881

Mission to the United Nations

DANISH MISSION
235 East 42nd Street, 32nd Floor
New York, New York 10017 (212) 867-1530

Tourist and Travel Offices

DANISH INFORMATION OFFICE
280 Park Avenue
New York, New York 10017 (212) 697-5107

DANISH NATIONAL TOURIST OFFICE
75 Rockefeller Plaza
New York, New York 10019 (212) 582-2802

DANISH TOURIST BOARD
Post Office Box 3240
Los Angeles, California 90053 (213) 906-0646

Fraternal Organizations

DANISH AMERICAN CENTER
4200 Cedar Avenue
Minneapolis, Minnesota 55407 (612) 729-3800

DANISH AMERICAN CLUB BYRAM
21 Division Street
Greenwich (Byram), Connecticut
06830 (203) 531-4567

DANISH BROTHERHOOD IN AMERICA
3717 Harney Street
Post Office Box 31748
Omaha, Nebraska 68131
Secretary-Treasurer: Howard Christensen — (402) 341-5049
Founded 1882

Fraternal organization of persons of Danish birth or descent, persons who have lived in Denmark six months or more or who speak Danish fluently, and persons who are friends, spouses or relatives of members. Encourages members to be faithful to the constitution and laws of the country in which they live; perpetuate memories and traditions from Denmark for the benefit of future generations; aids members and their dependents in illness, disability and death; assists unemployed members; conducts affairs as a fraternal benefit society. Maintains porfolio of family life insurance products. Presents four-year college scholarships, camp grants and essay awards to members. Sponsors monthly Hans and Greta coloring contest and creative writing contest. Individual lodges sponsor Danish heritage programs, civic awards, picnics, dances, parades and festivals.
Publications: American Dane Magazine, monthly; Harbor Highlights (newsletter), monthly; Directory of Lodges, annual.

DANISH CLUB OF DETROIT
22711 West Grand River
Detroit, Michigan 48219 — (313) 532-2790

DANISH CLUB OF WASHINGTON, D.C., INCORPORATED
6209 Wedgewood Road
Bethesda, Maryland 20034
Chairman of the Board of Directors: Erik J. Pedersen — (301) 229-6227
Founded 1931

Preserves and fosters Danish traditions and culture among its members. Promotes fellowship with Danes, persons of Danish ancestry, and anyone interested in Danish culture, history, subjects, and events. Renders financial and educational aid and assistance to Danes who have recently immigrated to the United States of America. Fosters and promotes cultural exchanges between the United States and Denmark. Receives gifts and grants of money and property of every kind and administers the same for charitable, educational, civic, and philanthropic uses.

SUPREME LODGE OF THE DANISH SISTERHOOD OF AMERICA
3438 North Opal Avenue
Chicago, Illinois 60634
National Secretary: Virginia A. Christensen — (312) 625-9031
Founded 1883

Women of or related to those of Danish birth, descent, or heritage, or married to a man of Danish descent. Bestows scholarships.
Publication: Danish Sisterhood News, monthly.

Professional Organizations

AMERICAN SOCIETY OF DANISH ENGINEERS
38 Old Farm Road
Darien, Connecticut 06820 — (203) 655-8537
President: Henrik S. Frolich — Founded 1930

Engineers of Danish birth or descent residing in the United States of America or Canada; awards scholarships.
Publications: Newsletter, 5 times a year; Membership Directory, annual.

Cultural and Educational Organizations

DANISH AMERICAN HERITAGE SOCIETY
29672 Dane Lane
Junction City, Oregon 97448 — (503) 998-6725
Contact: Arnold N. Bodtker — Founded 1977

Seeks to establish and/or support ethnic museums, libraries and archives in the United States.

Museum

HISTORIC TRUBE HOUSE
1627 Sealy Avenue
Galveston, Texas 77550 — (713) 763-5205
Owner: Mary D. Trube — Founded 1965

Trube Home built in 1890, is an exact copy of Denmark Castle. Collection includes Danish furnishings; furniture; glass; music; architecture. Offers guided tours; concerts; and lectures. Open to public by special appointment.

Special Libraries

DANA COLLEGE - C. A. DANE-LIFE LIBRARY
College Drive
Blair, Nebraska 68008
Library Director: Ronald D. Johnson — (402) 426-4101
Founded 1884

Subjects: Danish literature and language; history, humanities. Special Collections: Lauritz Melchior Memorial (records, scores, tapes, scrapbooks, artifacts, paintings). Holdings: Books; microfilm; records, pamphlets; journals and other serials; newspapers. Services: Interlibrary loans; copying; library not open to public. Library is said to be one of the best collections of Danish literature in translation and in the original language in the United States.

DANISH BAPTIST GENERAL CONFERENCE OF AMERICA - ARCHIVES
American Baptist Historical Society
1106 South Goodman Street
Rochester, New York 14620
Executive Director: William H. Brackney (716) 473-1740
Founded 1910

Subjects: Denominational history and records. Holdings: Annual reports, hymn books, tracts, devotional books, photographs. Archives have been in the care of the American Baptist Historical Society since 1958 when the Danish General Conference consolidated with the American Baptist Convention.

DANISH CONSULATE GENERAL INFORMATION OFFICE LIBRARY
280 Park Avenue
New York, New York 10017 (212) 697-5107
Secretary: Anette Essemann Founded 1945

Subjects: Denmark and Danish subjects. Special Collections: Danish authors in Danish. Holdings: About 2,000 books. Services: Office is open to the public. Formerly called Danish Information Office.

GRAND VIEW COLLEGE - ARCHIVES
1351 Grandview
Des Moines, Iowa 50316 (515) 266-2651
Archivist: Thorwald Hansen Founded 1896

Subjects: Danish-American church life 1871-1962; Danish-American culture; Danish literature, 18th to 20th century. Holdings: About 2,500 volumes. Services: Interlibrary loans; copying; archives open to public.

Newspapers and Newsletters

BIEN (The Bee). 1882-. Weekly. Editor: Sven A. Stribolt. Publisher: Bien Publishing Company, c/o Barbara R. Stribolt, 435 Duboce Avenue, San Francisco, California 94117. In Danish.

Offers national, international, and local news, plus coverage of group activities and events. Strives to maintain and support the Danish language and customs.

DER DANSKE PIONEER (The Danish Pioneer). 1872-. Biweekly. Editor: Hjalmar Bertelsen. Publisher: Bertelsen Publishing Company, 36 Conti Parkway, Elmwood Park, Illinois 60635. In Danish and English.

Publishes news of events in Denmark and the United States. Covers activities by Danish groups throughout the United States and prints feature articles on individuals and their accomplishments.

HARBOR HIGHLIGHTS. Monthly. Publisher: Danish Brotherhood in America, 3717 Harney Street, Post Office Box 31748, Omaha, Nebraska 68131. In English.

Newsletter covering activities of the Brotherhood and its members.

Magazines

AMERICAN DANE MAGAZINE. 1916-. Monthly. Editor: Howard Christensen. Publisher: Danish Brotherhood in America, 3717 Harney Street, Post Office Box 31748, Omaha, Nebraska 68131. In English.

Publication of the fraternal organization, Danish Brotherhood in America, featuring Danish ethnic articles, poetry, puzzles, and photographs.

THE DANA REVIEW. 1945-. Monthly. Editor: Kenneth Anderson. Sponsor: Dana College and Trinity Seminary, 2848 College Drive, Dana College, Blair, Nebraska 68008. In English.

DANISH BROTHERHOOD MAGAZINE. 1926-. Monthly. Editor: Einar Danielsen. Publisher: Danish Brotherhood in America, Post Office Box 155, Askov, Minnesota 55704. In English.

DANISH SISTERHOOD NEWS. 1947-. Monthly. Editor: Mrs. Virginia Christensen. Publisher: Danish Sisterhood of America, 3438 North Opal Avenue, Chicago, Illinois 60634. In English.

A fraternal publication providing information concerning its members and activities of lodges in the various states.

KIRKE OG FOLK. 1952-. Semimonthly. Editor: Dr. Johannes Kundsen. Publisher: Danish Special Interest Conference of the Lutheran Church in America, 1506 Thompson Avenue, Des Moines, Iowa 50316. In English and Danish.

Religious publication featuring articles on the religious and cultural heritage of the Danes.

Commercial and Trade Organizations

DANISH AMERICAN CHAMBER OF COMMERCE
75 Rockefeller Plaza, 11th Floor
New York, New York 10019
Chairman of the Board: E. W. Lichtenhagen

Danish-American business leaders; includes firms and institutions. Functions as an advisory board to support and promote commercial relations between the United States and Denmark, in either direction; makes itself available for consultation to the Danish Consulates General in the United States, and to the United States Department of Commerce, as well as trade groups and members in Denmark and the United States. Attempts to avoid duplication of governmental activities. Formed by merger of Danish Luncheon Club of New York (founded 1931) and Danish American Trade Council (founded 1964).

DENMARK CHEESE ASSOCIATION
570 Taxter Road
Elmsford, New York 10523
Managing Director: Jorgen Kolding
(914) 592-5277
Founded 1936

Service and promotional organization for Danish cheese in the United States. Participates in four to five trade shows and cheese seminars per year, giving demonstrations and multi-media presentations.
Publication: Danish Cheese News, 8-10 times a year.

Festivals, Fairs, and Celebrations

California - Solvang

DANISH DAYS
Copenhagen Square
Solvang, California

Townspeople dress in Danish costumes and revive Danish foods and traditions to celebrate Denmark's Independence Day. Danish band music, folk singing, dancing, story-telling. Aebleskiver breakfasts and other Danish food. Parade (sometimes torchlight). Held in late September for 2-3 days.
Contact: Chamber of Commerce, 515 Fourth Place, Post Office Box 465, Solvang, California 93463.

Michigan - Greenville

DANISH FESTIVAL
Greenville, Michigan

Danish folk dancers in native costumes, Danish food (smorgasbords), a grand parade, talent show, strolling bands, concerts, amusement rides, auto show, art fair, and antique show celebrate the Danish heritage in Michigan. Held annually since 1965 on the third weekend in August for three days.
Contact: Danish Festival, Incorporated, 302 South Lafayette Street, Greenville, Michigan 48838. (616) 754-6369.

Minnesota - Askov

RUTABAGA FESTIVAL AND DANISH DAYS
Askov, Minnesota

Festival events include a parade, folk dancing, exhibits, talent show for the locals, entertainment by the inmates from Sandstone prison, aebleskivers (Danish pancake delicacy), sports and rides. Held in late August for two days.
Contact: Chamber of Commerce, Askov, Minnesota 55704.

Minnesota - Minneapolis

DANISH CONSTITUTION DAY
Minnehaha Park
Minneapolis, Minnesota

Features a Danish "smorrebrod" lunch, folk dancing, music, clowns, and gymnasts on June 9, Danish Constitution Day. A Danish outdoor church service

is also conducted.
Contact: Greater Minneapolis Chamber of Commerce, 15 South Fifth Street, Minneapolis, Minnesota 55402.

Minnesota - Tyler

AEBLESKIVER DAYS
Tyler, Minnesota

Aebleskivers, Danish pancakes, are served throughout the two-day festival held in mid-June. The celebration includes a barbecue, queen contest, regional dairy days for local 4-H Clubs and a parade.
Contact: Department of Economic Development, 480 Cedar Street, Saint Paul, Minnesota 55101.

Nebraska - Minden

DANISH DAYS CELEBRATION
Minden, Nebraska

Danish descendants welcome visitors and offer special foods such as aebleskivers, a light, round-shaped pastry served with strawberry jam. A display of Danish handicrafts is set up. The festival features ethnic folk dancing and a parade. Held in mid-June for 2-3 days.
Contact: Chamber of Commerce, Box 375, Minden, Nebraska 68959.

South Dakota - Viborg

DANISH DAYS CELEBRATION
Viborg, South Dakota

A two-day celebration of Danish Independence Day and the town's Danish heritage. Features ethnic singing, dancing, and food. Held in early June.
Contact: Division of Tourism, State Office Building 2, Pierre, South Dakota 57501.

Ship Line

MOLLER STEAMSHIP COMPANY
1 World Trade Center, Suite 3527
New York, New York 10048 (212) 432-8200

Books and Pamphlets

DANIA POLYGLOTTA; Literature on Denmark in Languages Other than Danish and Books of Danish Interest Published Abroad. New Series. Copenhagen, The Royal Library.

An annual bibliography compiled by the Danish Department of the Royal Library based entirely on material in the Royal Library in Copenhagen. Titles are arranged in subject groups according to a Danish modification of the Dewey Decimal Classification System. Within subdivisions the titles are grouped by their language. Includes an alphabetical author and title index.

DANISH MUSEUMS. By Gudmund Boesen. Copenhagen, Committee for Danish Cultural Activities Abroad, 1966.

A book dealing primarily with museum materials in Copenhagen, and also with museum collections in Zealand, Funen, Jutland, and the Faroe Islands. Profusely illustrated with numerous black and white photographs.

DENMARK: LITERATURE, LANGUAGE, HISTORY, SOCIETY, EDUCATION, ARTS; A Select Bibliography of Books and Articles in the English Language. Copenhagen, Kongelige Bibliotek, Kobenhaven, The Royal Library, 1966.

This bibliography includes a selection of books and articles published between 1950 and 1965 on Denmark and Danish literature in English.

DENMARK--USA: 200 YEARS OF CLOSE RELATIONS. Copenhagen; Royal Danish Ministry of Foreign Affairs, 1976.

A special issue of the Danish Journal (magazine about Denmark) describing the relations between Denmark and the United States from 1776 to 1976. Contains numerous photographs and illustrations.

FACT SHEET, DENMARK. Copenhagen, Press and Cultural Relations Department of the Ministry of Foreign Affairs.

A series of brief fact sheets on specific topics within the following categories: Denmark in General; Government and Legislation; Economy; Social Activity; Education and Mass Media; Foreign Relations; and The Arts.

FACT SHEET, DENMARK: LITERATURE ON DENMARK. Compiled by Sven C. Jacobsen, Karsten Kromann, and Jan William Rasmussen. Copenhagen, Press and Cultural Relations Department of the Ministry of Foreign Affairs of Denmark, 1974.

A brief bibliographical list offering a selection of publications in English covering various aspects of Danish life and culture in a general, popular way. Authors and titles are arranged alphabetically under subject headings corresponding to the main groups of the Danish decimal classification system.

FLIGHT TO AMERICA: THE SOCIAL BACKGROUND OF 300,000 DANISH EMIGRANTS. By Kristian Hvidt. New York, Academic Press, 1975.

A comprehensive study of Danish emigration covering the period of 1868 to 1900.

A GUIDE TO DANISH BIBLIOGRAPHY. Compiled by Erland Munch-Petersen. Copenhagen, Royal School of Librarianship, 1965.

This guide is of value to those interested in finding the works of Danish authors or the literature on subjects relative to Denmark. Arranged by subject and then by title.

A HISTORY OF THE DANES IN AMERICA. By John H. Bille. San Francisco, R and E Research Associates, 1971. Reprint from the Transactions of the Wisconsin Academy of Sciences, Arts, and Letters, Vol. XI, 1896.

Begins with a brief discussion of the Danes in Denmark, then presents a short history of Danish settlements in America, churches and schools, and the society called the Dansk Folkesamfund.

A HISTORY OF THE DANES IN IOWA. By Thomas Peter Christensen. Solvang, California, 1952.

Summarizes Danish immigrant history and provides a definitive account of Danes in Iowa.

HOW A DANE BECAME AN AMERICAN, OR HITS AND MISSES OF MY LIFE. By T. M. Nielsen. Cedar Rapids, Iowa, Torch, 1935.

An autobiography of a Danish-American.

HOW THE DANES LIVE. Special Issue of the Danish Journal. Copenhagen, Royal Danish Ministry of Foreign Affairs, 1981.

A collection of articles on types of housing and architectural styles in Denmark, covering single-family housing, high-rises, institutions, and housing for special groups. Includes illustrations.

LIFE IN AN AMERICAN DENMARK. By Alfred C. Nielsen. Des Moines, Iowa, Grand View College, 1962.

Memories of the author's life among a community of Danes in Howard County, Nebraska.

THE MAKING OF AN AMERICAN. By Jacob Riis. New York, Macmillan, 1901.

An autobiography by a famous Danish-American newspaperman, author, and social reformer.

ROOK. By Johannes Knudsen. Askov, Minnesota, American, 1973.

A memoir recounting the experiences of growing up in Nebraska as the son of Danish immigrants.

DANISH AMERICANS

AN AMERICAN SAGA. By Carl Christian Jensen. Boston, Little, Brown, 1927.

An autobiography of a Danish-American social scientist and criminologist.

THE AMERICANIZATION OF THE DANISH LUTHERAN CHURCHES IN AMERICA. By Paul C. Nyholm. Copenhagen, Institute for Danish Church History. Distributed by Augsburg Publishing House, Minneapolis, 1963.

An abridgement of the author's dissertation, University of Chicago, 1952.

CIRCLE OF TREES. By Dana Faralla. Philadelphia, Lippincott, 1955.

A fictionalized account of two years in the lives of Danish immigrants on the Minnesota prairies in the 1880's.

DANES GO WEST: A BOOK ABOUT THE EMIGRATION TO AMERICA. By Kristian Hvidt. Rebild, Denmark, Rebild National Park Society, 1976.

An account of the Danish emigration from 1868 to 1900 written for the lay person. A sequel to the author's Flight to America.

DANISH-AMERICAN LIFE AND LITERATURE. By Enok Mortensen. Des Moines, Iowa, Committee on Publications of the Danish Evangelical Lutheran Church in America, 1945.

A bibliography that includes listings of pioneer materials in Danish.

THE DANISH LUTHERAN CHURCH IN AMERICA: THE HISTORY AND HERITAGE OF THE AMERICAN EVANGELICAL LUTHERAN CHURCH. By Enok Mortensen. Philadelphia, Board of Publication, Lutheran Church in America, 1967.

THE SALT OF THE EARTH; A History of Norwegian-Danish Methodism in America. By Arlow W. Andersen. Nashville, Parthenon Press, 1962.

Covers a century of immigrant and church history from the organization in 1843 of the first Methodist class in a Norwegian settlement in Illinois to the official termination of the Norwegian-Danish Conference a hundred years later. Tells about missionary work among Norwegian and Danish immigrants, the establishment of Norwegian and Danish districts and conferences, westward movement of the Methodists, and the accomplishments of individual church leaders.

TAKE ALL TO NEBRASKA. Mortgage Your Heart. This Passion Never Dies. By Sophus Winther. New York, Macmillan, 1936; 1937, 1938.

A trilogy of novels that focus on the assimilation of Peter Grimsen, a Danish immigrant farmer, and of his family.

THE VANISHING VILLAGE; A Danish Maritime Community. By Robert T. Anderson and Barbara Gallatin Anderson. Seattle, University of Washington Press, 1964.

Audiovisual Material

FILMS

AN ALTERNATIVE TO SUBURBIA OR HOW TO PLAY MUNICIPALITY. 16 mm. Color and sound. 24 minutes.

Gladsaxe - a suburb of Copenhagen with a population of 75,000 has in recent years become an alternative to suburbia, the way we normally perceive it. Gladsaxe's local government has tried to create a home town offering some of the facilities available in a modern Metropolis. This documentary describes Gladsaxe's cultural activities, its social services and some innovative experiments in education.

ANDERSEN, HANSEN AND JENSEN. 16 mm. Color and sound. 22 minutes.

A film about modern Danish agriculture - about the production machine behind the export of foodstuffs. The film is based on visits to three typical farms specializing in the production of cattle, pigs and poultry, respectively.

BJORN WIINBLAD. 16 mm. Color and sound. 14 minutes.

Bjorn Wiinblad has been called the merry flutist in the Danish handicraft's orchestra. The film reflects the abundance of his creative talent showing ceramics, porcelain, graphic posters, costumes for the theater, etc.

CARE AND ACTIVATION. 16 mm. Color and sound. 20 minutes.

Elderly people are still very much part of the society and this film shows what a capital city like Copenhagen does to brighten the life of its senior citizens by giving them opportunities to continue to lead an active life.

CARL NIELSEN 1865-1931. 16 mm. Color and sound. 50 minutes.

The film portrays the multi-faceted artistic and personal qualities of the world famous Danish composer Carl Nielsen. His instrumental music is exemplified by recordings of concerts and rehearsals in various countries, alternating with illustrations of his sources of inspiration.

COPENHAGEN. 16 mm. Color and sound. 15 minutes.

A very fast-moving film which gives a kaleidoscopic view of Copenhagen and its port, with many glimpses of the people and their everyday life.

DAIRY DENMARK BY VICTOR BORGE. 16 mm. Color and sound. 13 minutes.

Victor Borge enjoys a breakfast of Danish dairy products and introduces the audience to one of his Danish friends, the cow. From grazing cattle the film takes us to a Danish farm, then to the industrialized dairy plant and back to Victor Borge at breakfast.

A DANISH FARMER. 16 mm. Color and sound. 23 minutes.

In the film we meet a Danish farming family and through them we are introduced to Denmark, Danish agriculture and Danish food products.

DANISH FISH. 16 mm. Color, music only. 21 minutes.

With striking footage of fishermen working the seas around the island kingdom, this is the story of modern Danish fishing from the catch through processing to marketing and export. The film gives a diversified picture of this ancient trade in Denmark, also showing the elaborate control apparatus characteristic of Danish export industries in maintaining a high standard of quality.

DANISH HOUSES. 16 mm. Black/white and sound. 13 minutes.

A film about modern Danish architecture illustrated by recently designed buildings; a one-family house, a vacation home, a school, a church, a folk high school, a factory and an airport.

DANISH VILLAGE CHURCH. 16 mm. Black/white and sound. 14 minutes.

The history of Danish country church architecture is told by showing scenes from churches, beginning with the celebration of mass in a small and simple wooden church 800 years ago. The film is directed by Carl Th. Dreyer, who achieved worldwide fame for his movies.

THE DANISH WEATHER. 16 mm. Color and sound. 16 minutes.

Almost constantly changing, the Danish weather is and has always been a nice conversation piece for the Danes. This film is a lyrical tribute to Danish weather showing the landscape of the country through the changing seasons.

DEDICATED A POET. 16 mm. Color and sound. 12 minutes.

The focus of this biographical film is to illustrate Hans Christian Andersen's life via a tour of the Andersen Museum and the surrounding quarter. In addition to tracing the author's career, the film depicts the influences his birthplace (Odense) had upon the man and his subject matter.

DENMARK: A LOVING EMBRACE. 16 mm. Color and sound. 27 minutes.

Made by Comco Productions for the Danish National Tourist Office. New York, Tribune Films, 1972. Portrays Denmark through on-the-spot interviews with people who live, work, travel, or play there.

DENMARK BETWEEN DANES. 16 mm. Color and sound. 32 minutes.

A new general film on Denmark as seen by her own people. The film consists of a series of interviews, filmed all over the country. It conveys to the viewer an impression of themes, opinions and attitudes among Danes of various ages and from all walks of life. Denmark between Danes can only be recommended for all audiences having some prior knowledge of modern Denmark, for instance college and university students who have taken courses on Denmark or Scandinavia.

DENMARK PRESENTS. 16 mm. Color and sound. 2 minutes.

An introductory film which in short glimpses captures Denmark's red/white national colors.

DENMARK - THE SEA. 16 mm. Color and sound. 8 minutes.

No Dane lives more than 30 miles from the sea, and Denmark's long coastline has many contrasting features, from the quiet of the fjords to the roaring of the open sea. In a series of colorful pictures and with a musical score of traditional seamen's songs, the film captures the beauty of the sea which - since the Viking Age - has been a vital part of life in Denmark.

ELLEHAMMER - THE FLYING DANE. Black/white and sound. 14 minutes.

A film about Danish pioneer of aviation, J. C. Ellehammer. The incredible flying contraptions, the bowler hats, flying coattails and whiskers of the pioneers of aviation have an involuntary comic effect.

EMILIE FROM SARQAQ. 16 mm. Color and sound. 16 minutes.

A film about a young girl in Greenland, from the time she leaves her familiar surroundings in a fishing village, until she becomes a valued assistant in a production plant in a larger town. The film gives an insight into the condition of shrimp fishing and processing.

ERIK BRUHN - ARTIST OF THE BALLET. 16 mm. Color and sound. 21 minutes.

A portrait of the dancer Erik Bruhn tells of the development that made him become one of the world's most outstanding ballet dancers. Can only be recommended for audiences professionally interested in dance.

FOURTH OF JULY IN REBILD - 4,000 MILES FROM PHILADELPHIA. 16 mm. Color and sound. 15 minutes.

This film shows how, and why, the Danes are celebrating the Fourth of July.

FRESCOES IN DANISH CHURCHES. 16 mm. Black/white and sound. 12 minutes.

The film tells in pictures and music of the mediaeval frescoes in Danish village churches.

THE GREENLAND SEA. 16 mm. Color and sound. 12 minutes.

This film especially illustrates the development of fishing in Greenland. Trawling at sea has proven successful in providing raw materials to be utilized in the modern production facilities on shore. This way employment possibilities are provided for Greenlanders.

THE GRIPPING BEAST. 16 mm. Color and sound. 15 minutes.

An animated educational film dealing with the ornaments and art of the Viking Age.

HANDBALL, A JOINT LESSON WITH THE ALL-DENMARK TEAM. 16 mm. Color and sound. 22 minutes.

Handball was a Danish invention, but is now played throughout the world. This film gives theoretical information as to how team handball should be played.

HANS CHRISTIAN ANDERSEN AT THE PHOTOGRAPHERS. 16 mm. Color and sound. 13 minutes.

A film on Andersen by Jorgen Roos, produced in 1975 - the 100th year of the death of the poet. The film is made over existing photos, paintings, and drawings of Andersen designed to show the importance of Hans Christian Andersen as an author for a world audience.

MADE IN DENMARK. 16 mm. Color and sound. 15 minutes.

Made in Denmark gives a general introduction to the manufacturing industry concerning high level flexibility, quality, know-how and design. Danish industrial production covers many commodity groups. In spite of this, it is all characterized by specialization, quality and design.

MONARCHY AND DEMOCRACY. 16 mm. Color and sound. 26 minutes.

The Danes have an easygoing attitude towards their monarchy. They appreciate it because of its traditions and because its highest representative, Queen Margrethe II of Denmark, is performing the leading role with feeling, balance and skill. The 36 year old Monarch also plays the leading role in this film which shows the historical background of the Danish monarchy and in a relaxed, fabulating style, the daily functions and duties of Queen Margrethe II. The well known documentarist Jorgen Roos has directed and photographed.

NATHALIE KREBS. 16 mm. Color and sound. 12 minutes.

Camera follows Nathalie Krebs, chemical engineer and creator of unique stoneware glazes, in her workshop where the famous glazes are mixed according to her own secret formulas. Magnificent close-ups of glazed stoneware, reminiscent of the ancient Chinese ceramics, but inspired by nature's own shapes and colors.

ON THE SEVEN SEAS. 16 mm. Color and sound. 22 minutes.

The film describes the world-wide exchange of goods which make shipping an all-important factor in international trade and commerce and shows the importance of Danish shipping for the economy of the country. Glimpses from work in Danish shipyards, a brief mentioning of the training of Danish seamen and the working conditions of the merchant marine.

ON THE TRACK OF THE BOG PEOPLE. 16 mm. Color and sound. 35 minutes.

A film showing the method Danish archaeologists employ in tracing the habits and patterns of daily life of the people of the Iron age. The site is Lejre where intensive research into the life of ancient people takes place in original and recreated settings.

ONCE UPON A TIME AND TODAY. 16 mm. Color and sound. 28 minutes.

A film about the Danish royal castles: Amalienborg, Rosenborg, Fredensborg, Kronborg and Frederiksborg. Your guides are Queen Margrethe II of Denmark and her husband the Prince of Denmark. Being the resident of several of the castles, the Queen, who is a devout historian, lends a special perspective to the fascinating past and present history of these castles, one of which Shakespeare used as a model for Hamlet's castle.

RHYTHMICAL GYMNASTICS. 16 mm. Color and sound. 22 minutes.

The Danish pedagogue Liss Burmester's modern rhythmic gymnastics for women are based on clear and easily understood principles where balance, use of gravity and the body's elasticity are the main elements. An elite group from the Gymnastic club Elbe demonstrates some exercises in five series against changing Danish landscape backgrounds.

SAILING. 16 mm. Color and sound. 12 minutes.

Paul Elvstrom, world's top racing sailor, is shown sailing three different types of boats while explaining why sailing to him is such an important part of life.

17 MINUTES GREENLAND. 16 mm. Color and sound. 17 minutes. Directed by Jorgen Roos.

Where is Greenland situated? What does the country really look like? Who lives there? How is life there? This film attempts to answer these and similar questions by illustrating life and nature in various places in Greenland today, in the developing towns on the West Coast, and in the less developed settlements on the East Coast, and on the large Thule Base in the far North.

SHAKESPEARE AND KRONBORG. 16 mm. Black/white and sound. 10 minutes.

A series of pictures from Elsinore's famous Kronborg Castle shows the way Shakespeare probably would have seen the castle 300 years ago. Scenes from a Hamlet performance are played in the courtyard.

SIT DOWN - SIT DANISH. 16 mm. Color and sound. 14 minutes.

The audience is taken on a headlong drive from the furniture maker's warehouse into the everyday lives of people. A film about Danish furniture as a starting point for the way people live, work, rest, play and eat.

SLEDGE PATROL SIRIUS. 16 mm. Color and sound. 45 minutes.

A dogsledge patrol from the Danish armed forces patroling one of the most rugged and deserted areas on earth - Northeast Greenland.

THE STORY OF MY LIFE. (Hans Christian Andersen). 16 mm. Black/white and sound. 27 minutes. Directed by Jorgen Roos.

A biographical film of the late life of Hans Christian Andersen told in the famous Danish writer's own words and with a wealth of pictorial material of the actual period 1805-1875.

THORVALDSEN. 16 mm. Black/white and sound. 12 minutes.

This film shows some of the Danish sculptor Thorvaldsen's most famous works. Using the camera at different angles and with special lighting, the film attempts to make the statues come alive so that they will remain in the viewer's mind. Directed by Carl Th. Dreyer.

100,000-PIECE JIGSAW PUZZLE. 16 mm. Color and sound. 26 minutes.

A description of the painstaking care required to preserve and assemble the remnants of viking ships discovered a few years ago in Roskilde Fjord in Denmark. The wood had splintered and disintegrated after almost a thousand years' immersion. Infinite patience and ingenuity were required to restore the remnants to the original form in which they are now on display at the Viking Museum at Roskilde.

TIME FOR WORK AND TIME FOR PLAY. 16 mm. Color and sound. 15 minutes.

Denmark's transformation from an agricultural country into an industrial nation was accomplished largely over the past fifteen years. What factors made this revolution possible? And at what price? And why was the result not another Wirtschaftswunder? These are some of the questions raised in the film which deals with Denmark as an industrial country but also gives a broad impression of the Danish people in our day and age.

THE VIKING SHIPS OF ROSKILDE. 16 mm. Color and sound. 14 minutes.

A report of the very extensive excavations made after ships from the Viking period were found underwater in a channel in Roskilde Fjord. The special circumstances of the find presented scientists and technicians with many new problems that had to be solved before the fragments of the wrecks could be removed for conservation.

THE WEDDING OF PRINCESS MARGRETHE. 16 mm. Color and sound. 32 minutes.

Detailed coverage of the events preceding the wedding on June 10th, 1967 of Princess Margrethe - now Queen Margrethe II - to Prince Henrik.

WHAT MAKES THE FAROE ISLANDS? 16 mm. Color and sound. 28 minutes.

The Faroese society is changing. The small islands in the North Atlantic are becoming more and more industrialized. But there is a strong feeling that this development must be handled with caution in order to preserve the natural beauty of the islands and their cultural traditions. These problems and the islands relations with Denmark are the main themes of this new film, which gives an up-to-date picture of the inhabitants and the nature of the Faroe Islands.

(For information about borrowing the films listed above, contact the nearest office of the Royal Danish Consulate General in Chicago, Houston, Los Angeles or New York.)

DENMARK. 16 mm. Color and sound. 2 minutes. Victor Sarin, Canada, 1972

Presents various impressions of the country of Denmark.

DENMARK . . . A LOVING EMBRACE. 16 mm. Color and sound. 27 minutes. Danish National Tourist Office. Made by Comco Productions. Released by Tribune Films, 1972.

A study of Denmark as portrayed in on-the-spot interviews with the people who live, work, travel, or play there.

INTRODUCING DENMARK. Videocassette. Black and white. Sound. 20 minutes. North Atlantic Treaty Organization. Made by Nordisk film junior. Brussels: NATO: Washington, D.C., distributed by National Audiovisual Center, 1979.

Describes the country and people of Denmark, including geographical features, historical development and achievements, economic life, occupations of the people, and social customs. Explains briefly the role of Denmark in the North Atlantic Treaty Organization. Issued in 1955 as motion picture.

SLIDES

AGRICULTURAL DENMARK

80 color slides illustrating the development of Danish agriculture - one of the world's largest exporters of food products.

DANISH DESIGN TODAY.

80 slides showing modern Danish design, in a variety of products.

DENMARK IN PICTURES.

80 color slides divided in nine segments: Denmark from the Baltic to the Arctic; By sea, on land and in the air; investment in know-how; Denmark an industrial country; Specialists in all-round production; Denmark the great larder; A kingdom for 1,000 years; Both freedom and more common effort; Debate on the

social system and life-style. Especially suited for educational purposes up to college level.

GREENLAND - ARCTIC DENMARK.

80 color slides giving an impression of life and nature in Greenland, the world's largest island.

INDUSTRIAL DENMARK.

80 color slides showing the production facilities, products and design of Danish industry. Industry today accounts for the bulk of Danish exports and is by far the country's largest employer.

(For information about borrowing the slides listed above, contact the nearest office of the Royal Danish Consulate General in Chicago, Houston, Los Angeles, or New York.)

DOMINICANS
See also: SPANISH-SPEAKING PEOPLES

Embassy and Consulates

EMBASSY OF THE DOMINICAN REPUBLIC
and Permanent Mission to the OAS
1715 22nd Street, Northwest
Washington, D.C. 20008 (202) 332-6280

CONSULATES GENERAL

439 South La Cienega Boulevard,
Suite 220
Los Angeles, California 90048 (213) 273-4526

1038 Brickell Avenue
Miami, Florida 33131 (305) 373-4862

901 International Building
611 Gravier Street
New Orleans, Louisiana 70130 (504) 833-4782

1270 Sixth Avenue, Suite 300
New York, New York 10020 (212) 265-0630

1026 Fortuna Avenue
Park Ridge, Illinois 60068 (312) 825-8058

Lafayette Building Associates,
Room 422
Fifth and Chestnut
Philadelphia, Pennsylvania
19106 (215) 923-3006

CONSULATE

870 Market Street, Suite 982
San Francisco, California 94103 (415) 982-5144

Mission to the United Nations

DOMINICAN REPUBLIC MISSION
144 East 44th Street, 4th Floor
New York, New York 10017 (212) 867-0833

Tourist and Travel Offices

DOMINICAN REPUBLIC TOURIST OFFICE

485 Madison Avenue
New York, New York 10020 (212) 826-0750

1038 Brickell Avenue
Miami, Florida 33131 (305) 371-2813

Cultural and Educational Organization

DOMINICAN REPUBLIC STUDY GROUP
431 George Cross Drive
Norman, Oklahoma 73069 (405) 364-7718
Editor: James W. Smith Founded 1979

Established to promote the study and understanding of the various philatelic aspects of the stamps, covers and postal stationery of the Dominican Republic.
Publication: Bulletin, quarterly.

Commercial and Trade Organization

DOMINICAN REPUBLIC EXPORT PROMOTION
CENTER
One World Trade Center, Room 86065
New York, New York 10048 (212) 432-9498

Airline Offices

DOMINICANA AIRLINES
(Dominicana de Aviacion)
North American Headquarters:
1444 Biscayne Boulevard
Miami, Florida 33148 (305) 358-5355

64 West 50th Street
Rockefeller Center
New York, New York 10020 (212) 397-3411

Schedules flights to Santo Domingo from New York, Miami, San Juan, Haiti, Caracas, and Curacao.

Ship Lines

DOMINICANA SHIPPING COMPANY
1257 St. Nicholas Avenue
New York, New York 10032 (212) 781-3859

Books and Pamphlets

AMBER: OUR WONDERFUL TREASURE. By Joaquin R. Priego. Santo Domingo, Ministry of Tourism.

A booklet explaining the chemical composition and formation of this vegetable mineral, its history and uses and the recent discoveries of high quality amber in the Dominican Republic.

THE DOMINICAN REPUBLIC: CENTRAL HIGHLANDS AND NORTH COAST. Santo Domingo, Ministry of Tourism, 1980.

A tourist brochure illustrated in color for two of the major regions of the Dominican Republic. Hotel, restaurant, bank and travel information is provided for Santiago and Puerto Plata.

THE DOMINICAN REPUBLIC: SANTO DOMINGO. Santo Domingo, Ministry of Tourism, 1979.

A generously illustrated tourist brochure about the Dominican Republic's major city, its history and culture, accommodations and dining, night life, shopping and museums.

DOMINICAN REPUBLIC: VISITOR'S GUIDE. New York, Dominican Tourist Information Center, Incorporated, 1979.

Gives detailed information on entry requirements, transportation, currency, and hotels, as well as more general information on sightseeing, climate, history, economy, sports, shopping and language.

IMAGE OF THE DOMINICAN REPUBLIC. Washington, Department of Publications, General Secretariat of the Organization of American States in conjunction with America's monthly magazine, 1976.

Discusses the history and political development of the Dominican Republic, traditions and customs, cultural evolution, cities and regions, social and economic development. Many illustrations.

THE TREASURE TROVE OF THE CONCEPCION. By John Alexander. Reprinted from the September issue of Museum magazine by the First Investment Bank in the Dominican Republic.

The article tells the story of the voyage of the Concepcion in 1641, its wreck and the history of the attempts to locate it, culminating in 1978 with the success of Burt Webber and Seaquest.

DOMINICAN AMERICANS

THE DOMINICAN DIASPORA. By Glenn Hendricks. New York, 1974.

An anthropological study of the life of villagers from the Dominican Republic in New York City.

Audiovisual Material

MAP

THE DOMINICAN REPUBLIC - TOURIST MAP. Santo Domingo, Dominican Republic Ministry of Tourism, 1980.

Map of the country shows both political and physical features and indicates also points of interest to the visitor by means of symbols. On the verso there are street plans of Santo Domingo, and its colonial section, Puerto Plata and La Romana as well as general travel and motoring information. In color. Approximately 12 by 18.

FILMS

DOMINICAN REPUBLIC - CRADLE OF THE AMERICAS. 16mm. Color and sound. 25 minutes. Museum of Modern Latin American Art, Washington, D.C.

Folk-life, pre-Columbian art and cultural aspects of the oldest country in America are shown and narrated in English and Spanish.

LATIN AMERICA MINIATURE: THE DOMINICAN REPUBLIC. 16mm. Color and sound. 29 minutes. Sleeping Giant Films, Hamden, Connecticut, 1972.

Presents a brief history of the Dominican Republic. Shows how the geography and economy affect the people living there. Discusses elements of national life and the possibility of increased economic development.

DUTCH

Embassy and Consulates

EMBASSY OF THE NETHERLANDS
4200 Linnean Avenue, Northwest
Washington, D.C. 20008 (202) 244-5300

CONSULATES GENERAL

303 East Wacker Drive, Suite 410
Chicago, Illinois 60601 (312) 865-0110

2200 South Post Oak Boulevard
Suite 610
Post Oak Building
Houston, Texas 77056 (713) 622-8000

3460 Wilshire Boulevard
Suite 509
Los Angeles, California 90010 (213) 380-3440

HONORARY CONSULATES

646 West Fourth Avenue
Anchorage, Alaska 99501 (907) 265-3401

Suite 2710 Harris Tower
233 Peachtree Street, Northeast
Atlanta, Georgia 30303 (404) 525-4513

10 Light Street
Baltimore, Maryland 21203 (301) 244-6806

80 Boylston Street
Boston, Massachusetts 02116 (617) 542-8426

121 Reist Street
Buffalo, New York 14221 (716) 633-1818

7550 Independence Drive
Wilton Hills, Ohio 44146 (216) 232-5100

633 17th Street
Denver, Colorado 80217 (303) 893-2211

26555 Evergreen Road, Suite 505
Southfield
Detroit, Michigan 40076 (313) 353-7483

200 Monroe Avenue, Northwest
Grand Rapids, Michigan
49503 (616) 774-0076

2255 Kuhio Avenue
Suite 2100
Honolulu, Hawaii 96815 (808) 923-3344

43 A West Duval Street
Jacksonville, Florida 32202 (904) 356-7696

922 Walnut Street
Kansas City, Missouri 64106 (816) 234-2391

1111 South Bayshore Drive
Miami, Florida 33131 (305) 358-3830

416 Common Street
Room 101
New Orleans, Louisiana
70130 (504) 586-0666

300 East Main Street
Second Floor
Norfolk, Virginia 23510 (804) 623-6638

3 Girard Plaza
Philadelphia, Pennsylvania
19102 (215) 568-7118

Mellon Bank Building
Mellon Square
Pittsburgh, Pennsylvania
15230 (412) 391-2172

200 Market Building,
Suite 1470
Portland, Oregon 97201 (503) 222-3235

411 North Seventh Street,
Suite 808
Saint Louis, Missouri 63101 (314) 421-0882

E-1500 First National Bank
Building
Saint Paul, Minnesota 55101 (612) 291-9333

10 Wall Street
Seattle, Washington 98121 (206) 623-5300

c/o Uiterwyk Corporation
3105 West Waters Avenue
Tampa, Florida 33614 (813) 933-4045

Mission to the United Nations

NETHERLANDS MISSION
711 Third Avenue, 9th Floor
New York, New York 10017 (212) 697-5547

Tourist and Travel Offices

NETHERLANDS NATIONAL TOURIST OFFICE

576 Fifth Avenue
New York, New York 10036 (212) 245-5320

681 Market Street, Room 941
San Francisco, California 94105 (415) 781-3387

Netherlands Antilles

BONAIRE TOURIST INFORMATION OFFICE
685 Fifth Avenue
New York, New York 10022 (212) 838-1791

Disseminates travel information on the Dutch Antillean Island of Bonaire.

ST. MAARTEN, SABA AND ST. EUSTATIUS TOURIST INFORMATION OFFICE
445 Park Avenue
New York, New York 10022
Manager: Janet Myers (212) 688-8350

Provides travel information on the Netherlands Antilles Windward Islands of St. Maarten, Saba, and St. Eustatius. Formerly called the Netherlands Windward Islands Information Office.

Fraternal Organizations

DUTCH-AMERICAN SOCIETY OF MASSACHUSETTS, INCORPORATED
49 Rocky Hill Road
Oxford, Massachusetts 01540 (617) 987-8811
President: Maarten C. Tromp Founded 1967

An open, non-profit society whose members are Dutch or Dutch descent, who meet from time to time socially to preserve their Dutch language and heritage. Offers services and financial aid to new Dutch immigrants.
Publication: Vrijbuiter, quarterly.

DUTCH IMMIGRANT SOCIETY
1239 East Fulton
Grand Rapids, Michigan 49503
President: William Turkenburg (616) 451-2609

Serves and advances the spiritual and religious activities and interests of immigrants from the Netherlands. Promotes and maintains spiritual and cultural ties with the Netherlands. Promotes greater respect and interest in Dutch heritage and traditions. Gives aid and assistance wherever possible to immigrants from the Netherlands, in order that they may more quickly adjust themselves to the American way of life.
Publication: Dutch Immigrant Society Magazine, quarterly.

DUTCH SETTLERS SOCIETY OF ALBANY, NEW YORK
100 New Shaker Road
Albany, New York 12205
President: Richard H. Winne

EAST BAY HOLLAND CLUB
2535 Mason Street
Oakland, California 94605
President: A. Kopper-Drayer

HOLLAND AMERICA CLUB OF THE PACIFIC NORTHWEST, INCORPORATED
10051 Northeast 112th Street
Kirkland, Washington 98033 (206) 827-1969
Administrator: Mrs. Eta Gratama Founded 1956

Promotes contacts between Netherlanders, Americans of Dutch ancestry, and all other friends of the Netherlands. Gives moral and other support to immigrants. Maintains cultural and other contacts with the Netherlands for the benefit of the members and their American friends. Publishes the magazine, Ye Olde Dutch Mill, featuring news about the Club, its members, the Pacific Northwest, and the Netherlands.
Publication: Ye Olde Dutch Mill, six times a year.

HOLLAND SOCIETY OF NEW YORK
122 East 58th Street
New York, New York 10022
Executive Secretary: Mrs. Leon Stankowski (212) 758-1675
Founded 1885

Descendants in the direct male line of settlers in the Dutch Colonies in North America prior to 1675. Collects and preserves data on the early history of the Dutch Colonies and genealogy of descendants of early settlers. Has translated baptismal, marriage, and death records of early Dutch churches. Maintains a library of about 6,000 volumes and manuscripts relating to New Netherlands. Sponsors the Burgher Guard to participate in local patriotic and historical ceremonies.
Publication: de Halve Maen (Half Moon), quarterly.

NETHERLANDS AMERICAN SOCIETY
433 North June Street
Los Angeles, California 90004
President: Ben Lissauer

NETHERLANDS AMERICAN SOCIETY OF OHIO
5882 West Liberty Street
Vermillion, Ohio 44089
President: W. Nick Tazelaar

NETHERLANDS ASSOCIATION OF WASHINGTON, D.C.
1352 Q Street, Northwest
Washington, D.C.
President: Christian Dutilh

NETHERLAND CLUB OF NEW YORK
10 Rockefeller Plaza
New York, New York 10020 (212) 265-9500
Manager: Robert C. Sporre Founded 1903

Persons of Dutch birth or ancestry. Bestows Half Moon Trophy Award. Sponsors business luncheons and social affairs.
Publications: Annual Report; Membership List; also publishes Special Events Calendar.

NETHERLANDS SOCIETY OF PHILADELPHIA
210 Orchard Way
Wayne, Pennsylvania 19087
President: Herbert K. Zearfoss

NETHERLANDS SOCIETY OF SAINT LOUIS
562 North Woodlawn
Kirkwood, Missouri 63122
President: R. W. Lodge

SAINT NICHOLAS SOCIETY OF NEW YORK
122 East 58th Street
New York, New York 10022
President: Alexander Cannon

SOCIETY OF DAUGHTERS OF HOLLAND DAMES
c/o Mrs. William Conrad Kopper
Box 456
Ridgefield, Connecticut 06877
Registrar: Mrs. William Conrad Kopper (203) 438-3844
Founded 1895

Membership is limited to female descendants of founders of New Netherlands (New York) prior to 1674. Seeks to promote the principles and virtues of Dutch ancestors. Collects documents, genealogical and historical, relating to the Dutch in America.

VOOR ELK WAT WILS OF GRAND RAPIDS
1059 Cherrywood Lane
Grand Rapids, Michigan 49505
President: Lea P. Menko

Cultural and Educational Organizations

AMERICAN ASSOCIATION FOR NETHERLANDIC STUDIES
Department of Germanic and Slavic
University of Maryland
University Park, Maryland 20742 (301) 454-4301
Secretary: William H. Fletcher Founded 1971

Established to promote the study of the language, literature and culture of the Netherlandic language area (the Netherlands and northern Belgium) in the United States. Provides a contact organization among persons engaged in teaching and research in the field of Netherlandic studies. Maintains contacts with organizations in the United States and abroad whose goals are similar and complementary, such as the Canadian Association for the Advancement of Netherlandic Studies and the Association of Dutch Language Teachers in Great Britain, the Internationale Vereniging voor Neerlandistiek and the Dutch and Belgian Ministeries of Education and Culture, the Embassies and Consulates of the Netherlands and Belgium in the United States and the Modern Language Association. Encourages and assists the exchange of scholars and students between the United States and the Low Countries. Sponsors the Interdisciplinary Conference on Netherlandic Studies.
Publication: Newsletter, semiannual.

AMERICAN SOCIETY FOR NETHERLANDS PHILATELY
Post Office Box 555
Montclair, New Jersey 07042 (201) 744-6420
Editor: Paul E. VanReyen Founded 1975

Collectors of the stamps of the Netherlands and former colonies. Purpose is to encourage the collecting of such stamps and philatelic materials and to stimulate the study and knowledge of the postal history of the Dutch kingdom. Maintains library of 100 items (60% in Dutch).
Publications:' News, 8 times a year; Netherlands Philately, quarterly; Membership List, annual; plans to publish loose-leaf catalog of the stamps of Surinam and glossary of Dutch philatelic terms.

DUTCH-AMERICAN HISTORICAL COMMISSION
Netherlands Museum
8 East 12th Street
Holland, Michigan 49423
President: Peter Deklerk (616) 392-3129

Representatives of two colleges, two seminaries, and the Netherlands Museum in western Michigan. Founded to gather and preserve historical materials relating to western Michigan and to make them available to qualified scholars. The Commission is particularly concerned with materials on the Dutch, who settled in large numbers in western Michigan.
Publications: A Guide to the Archives of the Netherlands Museum; Guide to the Dutch-American Historical Collections of Western Michigan; The Manuscript and Archival Holdings of the Beardslee Library.

INTERDISCIPLINARY CONFERENCE ON NETHERLANDIC STUDIES
c/o Dr. William H. Fletcher
Department of Germanic and Slavic
University of Maryland
University Park, Maryland 20742

Promotes scholarly research on topics in Netherlandic Studies: art, music, history, contemporary civilization and politics and the history of the Dutch in North America.
Publication: Publication in Netherlandic Studies, biennial.

WILLEM MENGELBERG SOCIETY
2132 North 70th Street
Wauwatosa, Wisconsin 53213
Principal: Ronald Klett Founded 1970

Purpose is to spread interest and to increase knowledge of the Dutch orchestral conductor Willem Mengelberg (1871-1951) and to encourage the publication of his phonograph recordings. Disseminates information on all aspects of the life, recordings and concerts of Mengelberg.
Publication: Newsletter, quarterly.

Foundations

NETHERLANDS-AMERICA COMMUNITY ASSOCIATION
One Rockefeller Plaza
New York, New York 10020 (212) 246-1429
Executive Officer: Wanda Fleck Founded 1979

To advance educational, literary, artistic, scientific, historical and cultural relationships between the United States and the Netherlands; to financially aid and advise needy individuals of Netherlands birth or descent. Formed by Merger of: Netherland-America Foundation (founded 1921) and Netherland Benevolent Society of New York (founded 1908).
Publications: Annual Report.

NETHERLANDS AMERICAN AMITY TRUST
1725 De Sales Street, Northwest, Suite 304
Washington, D.C. 20036
Chairman: J. William Middendorf, II (202) 659-0697
Founded 1980

Originally founded to prepare for the celebration of 200 years of continuous diplomatic relationship between the Netherlands and the United States. Sponsored two major touring exhibitions of Dutch art and sent an American exhibition to the Netherlands. Arranged exchanged visits by two well-known symphony orchestras, sponsored trade shows, sports exchanges, lectures and conferences about Dutch-American history.

Religious Organizations

NETHERLANDS REFORMED CONGREGATIONS
Main Street, Box 42
East Norwich, Ontario N0J 1P0, Canada
President of Synod: Reverend A. M. Den Boer (616) 456-6323
Founded 1907

Formed from immigrants from the Netherlands who seceded from the State Church there. The doctrines are the Netherlands Confession, the Heidelberg Catechism, and the Canons of Dort. The Synod meets every two years (in even years).
Publication: The Banner of Truth, monthly.

REFORMED CHURCH IN AMERICA
475 Riverside Drive
New York, New York 10115 (212) 870-2841
President: Harry Buis Founded 1628

Established by early Dutch settlers in New York as the Reformed Protestant Dutch Church. It is the oldest Protestant denomination with a continuous ministry in North America. It is evangelical in theology and presbyterian in government.

Research Centers and Special Institutes

DUTCH STUDIES
Calvin College
Grand Rapids, Michigan 49509
Director: Walter Lagerwey

The program is centered around the study of the Dutch language, literature, history, economics and culture. The college has an endowed chair, the Princess Juliana Chair of Dutch Language, Literature and Culture.

DUTCH STUDIES
University of Texas
Austin, Texas 78712
Contact Person: Edgar Polome

DUTCH STUDIES
Department of Germanic Languages
University of California
Berkeley, California 94720
Director: Johan P. Snapper

The Queen Beatrix Chair of Dutch Language, Literature and Culture is located at Berkeley and is the nucleus of the program which takes in various aspects of Dutch culture.

DUTCH STUDIES
Department of Germanic Languages
Indiana University
Bloomington, Indiana 47405
Director: Dr. William Shetter

DUTCH STUDIES
Department of Germanic Languages
University of Michigan
Ann Arbor, Michigan 48109

Each year the program has a Dutch author in residence as well as a visiting teacher from the Netherlands.

DUTCH STUDIES
University of Minnesota
Department of Germanic Languages
Minneapolis, Minnesota 55455
Director: Ray Wakefield

A writer in residence from Holland is a part of each year's program.

DUTCH STUDIES
Department of Germanic Studies
University of California at Los Angeles
Los Angeles, California 90024
Director: Robert S. Kirsner

DUTCH STUDIES PROGRAM
University of Pennsylvania
Philadelphia, Pennsylvania 19104
Director: Dr. M. J. G. Reichenback

Dutch language and literature, history, politics, economy and art are combined in interdisciplinary study leading to a greater awareness of the Netherlands and its people.

Museums

CALVIN COLLEGE CENTER ART GALLERY
1801 East Beltline, Southeast
Grand Rapids, Michigan 49506
Director of Exhibitions: Timothy Van Laar (616) 949-4000
Founded 1974

Collections include seventeenth century Dutch paintings, nineteenth century Dutch drawings, twentieth century prints, drawings, paintings and sculpture. Maintains a library, theater and classrooms. Offers guided tours, lectures, films, permanent and loan exhibitions.
Publication: Catalogs.

COLUMBIA COUNTY HISTORICAL SOCIETY, INCORPORATED
16 Broad Street
Kinderhook, New York 12106 (518) 758-9265
President: William T. Appell Founded 1916

Maintains the 1737 Van Alex House and furnishings representative of New York Dutch colonial life.

DEKKER HUIS AND ZEELAND HISTORICAL MUSEUM
37 East Main Street
Zeeland, Michigan (617) 772-4079
Director: Mrs. Leon Voss Founded 1976

Historic Dutch house with collection of Dutch artifacts.

DYCKMAN HOUSE AND MUSEUM
204th Street and Broadway
New York, New York 10021
Mailing Address:
Arsenal Building
Central Park, New York 10053
Director Historic Parks, New York: Joseph Bresnan (212) 360-8172
Founded 1915

The historic Dyckman House, built in 1783 is an old Dutch farmhouse. Contains historical and military collections.

FORT CRAILO STATE HISTORIC SITE
9-1/2 Riverside Avenue
Rensselaer, New York 12144
Historic Site Manager: Christine Averill (518) 463-8738
Founded 1924

Museum is housed in Fort Crailo, a brick dwelling which once served as office of Van Rensselaer Manor and a fortified stronghold built about 1704. Collections include history; furnishings and artifacts relating to Dutch period. Research is carried out in eighteenth century Dutch culture in the Hudson River Valley and on Van Rensselaer family. Offers permanent and temporary exhibitions; film program for children; guided tours; lectures; gallery talks; special programs and demonstrations.

FORT KLOCK HISTORIC RESTORATION
Saint Johnsville, New York 13452
Mailing Address:
R.D. 1
Palatine Bridge, New York 13428
Director: Willis Barshied, Jr. Founded 1964

The Klock Homestead built in 1750 shows early Durch architecture and farmhouse furnishings. The restoration includes a little red schoolhouse and blacksmith shop.

NETHERLANDS MUSEUM
8 East 12th Street
Holland, Michigan 49423 (616) 392-3129
Director: Willard C. Wichers Founded 1937

Founded to perpetuate the memory of the pioneer founders of the Dutch-American communities of western Michigan and their heritage from the Netherlands. Housed in the 1889 residence of Dr. Kremer, an early physician in Holland. Maintains records and mementos pertaining to Dutch settlers. Has a replica of an early Dutch kitchen. Exhibitions also include crafts from Dutch colonial possessions. Operates a small souvenir stand specializing in articles imported from the Netherlands, such as wooden shoes, Delft pottery, and dolls in Dutch costumes. Formerly called the Netherlands Pioneer and Historical Foundation.

OLD DUTCH PARSONAGE
38 Washington Place
Somerville, New Jersey 08876
Interpreter: Tom Laverty (201) 725-1015

The old Dutch parsonage was built in 1751 and is the birthplace of Rutgers University and the New Brunswick Theological Seminary. It is furnished with colonial Dutch artifacts.

PELLA HISTORICAL VILLAGE
505 Franklin
Pella, Iowa 50219 (515) 628-4311
President: Bob Klein Founded 1965

A Dutch ethnic museum whose collections include authentic Dutch costumes and complete set of newspapers printed in Pella. It is responsible for maintaining several historic buildings: Wyatt Earp boyhood home, 1851; Pioneer log cabin, 1843; Van Spankeren store, 1853; Amsterdam School, 1874. A museum shop sells Netherlands souvenirs and brochures.

SCHUYLER MANSION STATE HISTORIC SITE
27 Clinton Street
Albany, New York 12202
Historic Site Manager: Christine Averill (518) 474-3953
Founded 1911

The home of General Philip Schuyler, prominent land owner and political leader, located on historic Schuyler property, The Pastures, which was built in 1761/62. It contains eighteenth century furnishings and decorative arts, including Schuyler family possessions; books; glass; silver. Research is conducted on General Schuyler; eighteenth century Dutch in New York; and American Revolution in New York State. There is an interpretation center for visitors.

VAN RIPER-HOPPER HOUSE-WAYNE MUSEUM
533 Berdan Avenue (201) 694-7192
Wayne, New Jersey 07470 Founded 1964

A restored 1786 Dutch colonial farm house containing furnishings from the Colonial period to 1860. Also includes the 1706 Van Duyne House. A small library on local history, an archaeology lab and nature center are associated with the museum. Offers guided tours, lectures, educational programs, films, concerts, school loan programs, a tinsel painting class and quilting demonstrations. Affiliated with the Township of Wayne, New Jersey.

VAN WYCK HOMESTEAD MUSEUM
Route 9
Fishkill, New York 12524
President and Museum Administrator: Louis J. Ahlbach (914) 896-9560
Founded 1971

Museum is housed in the Van Wyck Homestead, built in 1732, which was the site of the headquarters for the Supply Depot of Washington's Army in 1776-83. Its collections include early Dutch settler artifacts, Revolutionary War items and other displays in archaeology, agriculture and technology. Maintains a 400 volume library and reading room, as well as a museum shop with hand-made items. Offers guided tours, lectures, educational programs and a summer archaeological research project.
Publication: Newsletter, monthly.

WINDMILL ISLAND MUNICIPAL PARK
7th Street and Lincoln Avenue
Holland, Michigan 49423 (616) 396-5433
Director: Jacob R. de Blecourt Founded 1965

Housed in a restored 214 year old Dutch Windmill brought to the United States in 1965. Contains Little Netherlands Museum, containing panoramic exhibit of town and country in Old Holland. Offers a flower garden; Dutch carousel and draw bridge.

ZWAANENDAEL MUSEUM
King's Highway and Savannah Road (302) 645-9418
Lewes, Delaware Founded 1931

A state sponsored museum exhibiting Dutch artifacts from every Dutch settlements in the area. Also has Indian objects.

Special Libraries and Subject Collections

CALVIN LIBRARY
Colonial Origins Collection
Burton Street, Southeast
Grand Rapids, Michigan 49506

Collection of books, periodicals, audiovisual materials, manuscripts and personal papers, pictures and oral history materials pertaining to early Dutch settlers. Services: Copying, speakers' bureau.

CONSULATE GENERAL OF THE NETHERLANDS - PRESS AND CULTURAL SECTION
One Rockefeller Plaza
New York, New York 10020 (212) 246-1429

Subjects: Dutch history, economy, political system, geography and cultural life. Holdings: 3,000 volumes; pamphlets, photographs, films, and slides. Services: Library open to public.

HERRICK PUBLIC LIBRARY
300 River Avenue
Holland, Michigan 49423
Director: Hazel Hayes

Contains a collection of Dutch language and literature books.

HOLLAND SOCIETY OF NEW YORK - LIBRARY
122 East 58th Street
New York, New York 10022
President: Kenneth L. Demarest, Jr. (212) 759-1675

Specializes in New Netherland (New York, New Jersey and Delaware) history during the Dutch Period; materials on the Dutch Reformed Church; and Dutch-American family genealogy. Holdings: books, microfilm, journals and other serials.
Publications: de Halve Maen, quarterly.

NETHERLANDS EMBASSY REFERENCE ROOM
4200 Linnean Avenue, Northwest
Washington, D.C. 20008 (202) 244-5300

Subjects: Netherlands; United States. Services: Copying; library open to public.

NORTHWESTERN COLLEGE LIBRARY
Orange City, Iowa 51041
Curator: Nellie Kennedy (712) 737-4821

Collection of books pertaining to Dutch Americans, also periodicals, audiovisual materials, manuscripts, oral history and archives.

UNIVERSITY OF MICHIGAN GRADUATE LIBRARY
Ann Arbor, Michigan 48104

Contains a collection of more than 200 periodicals published in the Netherlands, as well as Dutch historical tracts for the sixteenth and seventeenth centuries.

Newspapers and Newsletters

THE BANNER. 1866-. Weekly. Editor: Dr. Andrew Kuyvenhoven. Publisher: Christian Reformed Publishing House, 2850 Kalamazoo Avenue, Southeast, Grand Rapids, Michigan 49508. In English.

Official organ of the Christian Reformed Church. The contents reflect spiritual aspects of life; however, articles dealing with topics relevant in today's world are also included.

FRISIAN NEWS ITEMS. Publisher: Frisian Information Bureau, 1229 Sylvan Avenue, Southeast, Grand Rapids, Michigan 49506. In English.

The sole Frisian interest publication in the United States.

HOLLAND HOME HORIZONS. 1912-. Monthly. Editor: Herman Nydam. Publisher: The Holland Union Benevolent Association, 1450 East Fulton Street, Grand Rapids, Michigan 49503. In English and Dutch.

Informs Association members of activities and current events which relate to the Association and its members. Includes articles on a variety of topics of special interest to members and their families.

HOLLAND NEWS. 1981-. Biweekly. Editor: John H. Wesseling. Publisher: Vista Publication Company, Post Office Box 1357, Bellflower, California 90706. In Dutch.

The largest Dutch newspaper in the United States. Publishes political, economic, cultural and sports news from the Netherlands and some Dutch-American features.

HOLLAND REPORT. 1961-. Weekly. Editor and Publisher: Marinus W.M. van der Steen, Jr., Post Office Box 42085, Los Angeles, California 90042. In Dutch and English.

Includes news from Holland and from the Dutch community in the United States. Tabloid format.

YE OLDE DUTCH MILL. 1957-. Bimonthly. Editor: Eta Gratama, 10051 Northeast 112th Street, Kirkland, Washington 98033. Publisher: Holland America Club of the Pacific Northwest, Incorporated. In English and Dutch.

Publishes club news and short articles of interest to Dutch Americans.

DE VRIJBUITER. Quarterly. Editor: Mrs. Peggy Gerit. Publisher: Dutch-American Society of Massachusetts, 49 Rocky Hill Road, Oxford, Massachusetts 01540.

Newsletter of the organization.

DE WACHTER (The Watchman). 1868-. Biweekly. Editor: Reverend William Haverkamp. Publisher: Christian Reformed Publishing House, 2850 Kalamazoo Avenue, Southeast, Grand Rapids, Michigan 49508. In Dutch.

An organ of the Christian Reformed Church containing religious news and articles on various aspects of the Church's activities and affairs.

WINDMILL HERALD. 1958-. Biweekly. Publisher: Albert Vanderheide, Vanderheide Publishing Company, Post Office Box 591, Lyndon, Washington 98264.

Publishes ethnic news for Dutch and Flemish groups as well as news from the Netherlands, Belgium and South Africa.

Magazines

DIS. 1970-. Quarterly. Editor: G. DenHollander. Publisher: Dutch Immigrant Society, 1239 East Fulton, Grand Rapids, Michigan 49503.

Serves not only as organ of the Dutch Immigrant Society but also prints articles on Dutch history and culture as related to the United States.

DE HALVE MAEN (The Half Moon). 1922-. Quarterly. Editor: Howard Hageman. Publisher: Holland Society of New York, 122 East 58th Street, New York, New York 10022. In English.

Publishes articles on the history of the early Dutch settlers in America (1609-1675), their contributions to American life, and the genealogy of Dutch families from the earliest times to date. Also carries news on the activities of the Society and its members.

HOLLAND HERALD. Editor: Ken Wilkie. US Editor: Ben van Meerendonck, Jr., 2 Pierreport Place, Brooklyn, New York 11201. Publisher: Roto Smeets International Publications, Weert, Netherlands. 110 Bank Street, New York, New York 10014. In English.

An illustrated news magazine about events, people, and places in the Netherlands and its overseas settlements. Includes childrens' section, book reviews, business news and a calendar of events.

NETHERLANDS-AMERICAN TRADE. Monthly. Editor: Monya M. Lange. Publisher: Nederlandse Kamer van Koophandel voor Amerika, Post Office Box 7643, The Hague, Netherlands. In English.

A trade magazine published by the Netherlands Chamber of Commerce for America. Contains articles on industries in the Netherlands, information about new products, trade opportunities, trade shows, and other news concerning industry and commerce.

Radio Programs

California - Pasadena

KMAX - 3844 East Foothill Boulevard, Pasadena, California, (213) 681-2486. Dutch programs, 1 hour weekly.

California - Long Beach

KLON - 1250 Bellflower, Long Beach, California, (213) 597-9441. Dutch music, 2 hours weekly.

California - Northridge

KCSN (FM) - 18111 Nordhoff Street, Northridge, California 91330, (213) 865-3090. Dutch programs, 3 hours weekly.

Illinois - Lansing

WLNR - 2915 Bernice Road, Lansing, Illinois, (312) 895-1400. Dutch programs, 1 hour weekly.

Pennsylvania - Red Lion

WGCB - Box 88, Red Lion, Pennsylvania 17356, (717) 244-5360. Dutch programs, 1 hour weekly.

Utah - Salt Lake City

KWHO - 329 East Second South, Salt Lake City, Utah 84111, (801) 534-4105. Dutch programs, 1 hour weekly.

Bank Branches in the U.S.

ALGEMENE BANK NEDERLAND N.V.

United States Affiliate:
General Bank of the Netherlands
84 William Street
New York, New York 10038 (212) 943-7900

301 Park Avenue
New York, New York 10022 (212) 944-5500

233 Peachtree Street, Northeast
Suite 401
Atlanta, Georgia 30303 (404) 688-4060

135 South LaSalle Street
Suite 1607
Chicago, Illinois 60603 (312) 443-2900

Corporate Service Office
Three Riverway
Suite 1600
Houston, Texas 77056 (713) 629-6666

555 South Flower Street
Los Angeles, California
90071 (213) 626-3401

5885 U. S. Steel Building
600 Grant Street
Pittsburgh, Pennsylvania
15219 (412) 566-2250

600 Montgomery Street
San Francisco, California
49111 (415) 397-7840

AMSTERDAM-ROTTERDAM BANK N.V.
(AMRO Bank)
United States Participation:
European-American Bank and Trust Company
10 Hanover Square
New York, New York 10005 (212) 437-4300

430 Park Avenue
New York, New York 10022 (212) 838-9550

NEDERLANDSCHE MIDDENSTANDSBANK N.V.
United States Affiliate:
450 Park Avenue
New York, New York 10022 (212) 758-0600

Commercial and Trade Organizations

HOLLAND CHEESE EXPORTERS ASSOCIATION
45 Rockefeller Plaza, Suite 2263
New York, New York 10020
Marketing Manager: Frans Donzelmann (212) 265-1512
Founded 1951

Producers and exporters of cheese in the Netherlands. Conducts public relations, sales promotion, and advertising campaigns.
Publication: Cheese of Holland News, irregular.

NETHERLANDS CHAMBER OF COMMERCE IN THE UNITED STATES
1 Rockefeller Plaza
New York, New York 10020
Executive Secretary: J. M. Bakels (212) 265-6460
Founded 1920

303 East Wacker Drive
Suite 412
Chicago, Illinois 60601 (312) 938-9050

Publication: Netherlands North American Trade, 11 times a year; Newsletter, 11 times a year.

NETHERLANDS FLOWER BULB INSTITUTE
90 West Street
New York, New York 10006 (212) 227-2106

NETHERLANDS INDUSTRIAL COMMISSIONER
1 Rockefeller Plaza, 11th Floor
New York, New York 10020 (212) 246-1434

Bank Building, Suite 610
2200 South Port Oak Boulevard
Houston, Texas 77056
Executive Secretary:
G.F.A.M. Vromak

601 California Street,
Suite 1805
San Francisco, California
94104
Executive Secretary: F. G. Hamelenk (415) 981-1468
Founded 1912

Affiliated with the Netherlands Chamber of Commerce in the United States.
Publication: Netherlands-American Trade, monthly.

Festivals, Fairs, and Celebrations

Illinois - Fulton

DUTCH DAYS
Fulton, Illinois

A community celebration held for three days in May. Contact: Fulton Chamber of Commerce, Box 253, Fulton, Illinois 61252, (815) 589-3864.

Iowa - Orange City

TULIP FESTIVAL
Orange City, Iowa

In preparation, the citizens follow an old world custom and scrub the streets before the dignitaries arrive. The scrubbers frequently get wet as well. In honor of their Dutch heritage, the celebrants dress in Dutch costumes and do wooden shoe dances in the streets. Tulips and marching bands, wooden shoe making, flower shows, tulip exhibit, coronation ceremonies, and drill demonstrations are featured. Parade includes floats. A Dutch museum in the main room of a reconstructed Dutch windmill is open for visitors. Started in 1936. Held annually in mid-May.
Contact: Orange City Chamber of Commerce, 125 Central Avenue, Southeast, Orange City, Iowa 51041.

Iowa - Pella

PELLA TULIP TIME FESTIVAL
Pella, Iowa

In honor of Dutch heritage citizens wear Dutch costumes and scrub the streets (an old custom preparatory to a visit by dignitaries). Tulip exhibitions, stage productions, music, folk dancing, foods, a parade with Dutch Street Organ, coronation of queen, and folk games are featured. There are conducted tours, visits to Pella Historical Village and Tulip Toren--a tower honoring the founding fathers, whom the festival also honors. Other events include a display of antiques and historic items, square dancing, Volks Parade, massed bands, and Parade of Provinces. There is also a Pella Tulip Time Festival Art Fair (3 days) in the Pella Historical Village. Started in 1936.

Michigan - Holland

TULIP TIME
Holland, Michigan

Klompen Dancers, a flower show, Tulip Time Market, and Festival Musicale celebrate the Dutch heritage. Street scrubbing, a Volksparade, tours of tulip fields and farms, and colorful costumes are other attractions. Held annually for four days since 1930 in mid-May.
Contact: Holland Tulip Festival, 150 West Eighth Street, Holland, Michigan 49423.

Minnesota - Edgerton

ANNUAL DUTCH FESTIVAL
Edgerton, Minnesota

Local residents dress in traditional Dutch attire for two days during the mid-July festival. Ball games, a parade, and special entertainment are featured. Began around 1950.
Contact: Edgerton Dutch Festival, Chamber of Commerce, Edgerton, Minnesota 56128, (507) 442-7861.

New York - Albany

ANNUAL TULIP FESTIVAL
Washington Park
Albany, New York

Founded by Henry Hudson, Albany hosts an annual festival featuring that famous Dutch flower, the tulip. Visitors see a magnificent flower-decked parade, watch the crowning of the Tulip Queen, and tour countless displays in the city park. Held in mid-May.
Contact: Chamber of Commerce, 510 Broadway, Albany, New York 12201.

South Dakota - Corsica

DUTCH SMORGASBORD AN KLOMPEN DANCE
Corsica, South Dakota

Events include a bountiful homecooked meal served in smorgasbord style and Klompen (wooden shoe) dances. Held in May.
Contact: Mrs. Margaret Mulder, Corsica, South Dakota 57328.

Texas - Nederland

HERITAGE FESTIVAL
Nederland, Texas

This southeast Texas community salutes its Dutch heritage during the festival, which features a queen contest, carnival, flea market, and arts and crafts show. Held for five days in March.
Contact: Chamber of Commerce, Post Office Box 891, Nederland, Texas 77627.

Washington - Oak Harbor

HOLLAND HAPPENING
Oak Harbor, Washington

A celebration of Dutch traditions held in early May.
Contact: Chamber of Commerce, Oak Harbor, Washington 98277.

Wisconsin - Cedar Grove

HOLLAND FESTIVAL
Cedar Grove, Wisconsin

Began in 1947, the Festival features events in keeping with authentic Dutch traditions such as street dancing in costume, Klompen Dancing, Dutch food and a wooden-shoe maker. A Dutch play is performed and there are Dutch handicrafts for sale. A parade and queen contest, an art fair and a folk fair are part of the festivities.
Contact: Cedar Grove Holland Festival, Chamber of Commerce, Cedar Grove, Wisconsin 53013.

Airline Offices

KLM - ROYAL DUTCH AIRLINES
(Koninklijke Luchtvaart Mattschappij)
North American Headquarters:
KLM Building
437 Madison Avenue
New York, New York 10022 (212) 759-2400

Flies international routes from Amsterdam to the United States, Canada, and Mexico; to Caribbean islands and Panama; to Argentina, Brazil, Chile, and Peru; to Africa; and to the Far East. Provides services to virtually all countries in Europe. Other offices in the United States: Anchorage (Alaska), Atlanta, Beverly Hills (California), Boston, Buffalo, Charlotte, Chicago, Cleveland, Dallas, Denver, Detroit, Hartford, Houston, Indianapolis, Los Angeles, Miami, Milwaukee, Minneapolis, New Orleans, Philadelphia, San Francisco, Seattle, Tampa, Tulsa, and Washington.

Ship Lines

HOLLAND-AMERICA CRUISES
2 Penn Plaza
New York, New York 10121 (212) 290-0100

Cruises to the Caribbean from New York City and from Miami and Port Everglades, Florida. Schedules trips to Alaska and the Orient from Vancouver, Canada. Around the World cruises depart from and return to New York City.

HOLLAND-AMERICA LINE
Biehl and Company, Incorporated, Agents
416 Common Street
New Orleans, Louisiana 70130 (504) 581-7788

Carries freight and some passengers from United States Gulf or South Atlantic ports to France, Belgium, and the Netherlands.

ROYAL NETHERLANDS STEAMSHIP COMPANY
5 World Trade Center
New York, New York 10048 (212) 938-9200

Accommodates 12 passengers on each yacht-like freighter sailing from New York via Aruba, Curacao, Venezuela, Trinidad, Georgetown, and Paramaribo to the first port of call in Holland. Sails from New Orleans to Caribbean ports, returning to New Orleans via Houston.

Bookdealers and Publishers' Representatives

AMERICAN ELSEVIER PUBLISHING COMPANY, INCORPORATED
2 Park Avenue
New York, New York 10016 (212) 725-1818

IACONI BOOK IMPORTS
300 Pennsylvania Avenue
San Francisco, California 94107 (415) 285-7393

MARTINUS NIJHOFF PUBLISHING
160 Old Derby Street
Hingham, Massachusetts 02043 (617) 749-3289

SKY BOOKS INTERNATIONAL, INCORPORATED
48 East 50th Street
New York, New York 10022 (212) 688-5086

TEC-BOOKS LIMITED
(Librairie De Documentation Technique SA)
41 William
Pittsburgh, Pennsylvania 12901 (518) 561-0005

UNITED DUTCH PUBLISHING COMPANIES, INCORPORATED
55 West 42nd Street
New York, New York 10036 (212) PE6-3595

VNU AMERICA INCORPORATED
101 College Road
Princeton, New Jersey (212) 986-2730

300 East 40th Street
New York, New York (212) 986-2730

25 West 33rd Street
New York, New York (212) 575-0100

Books and Pamphlets

COMPACT GEOGRAPHY OF THE NETHERLANDS. The Hague, Ministry of Foreign Affairs, 1979.

A booklet explaining the geographical features of the Netherlands such as land reclamation, polders, water control, the Zuyder Zee and Delta works, demography, the Randstad, economy, industry, agriculture, mineral production, major ports, etc. Each short chapter is accompanied by a full page map.

COSTUMES IN THE NETHERLANDS.

A small booklet picturing the costumes of the various regions of the Netherlands. Illustrated in color and black and white. In Dutch, English, German, French and Spanish.

GUIDE TO NETHERLANDIC STUDIES: BIBLIOGRAPHY. By Walter Lagerwey. Grand Rapids, Michigan. Calvin College, 1964.

A revised and augmented edition of GUIDE TO DUTCH STUDIES (Grand Rapids: Calvin College, 1961), this annotated bibliography has a short section called "The Dutch in the United States."

HOLLAND - A CENTURY OF FORM AND COLOR. By C. Broos. The Hague, Drukkerij Meijer Wormerveer b.v.

Reproduces paintings of some of Holland's foremost artists, van Gogh, Jongkind, Jacob and Willem Maris, Breitner, Robertson, Mondriaan, Van Dongen, Werkman, Kruyder, Chabot, Escher, Appel, Constant, Westerik, to name a few. The accompanying test describes the development of Dutch art during the last century.

I.D.G. BULLETIN 1980/81. By Drs. Henk Meijer. Utrecht/The Hague, Information and Documentation Centre for the Geography of the Netherlands, 1981.

A detailed examination of the region of the great rivers in the Netherlands. Many maps, diagrams, pictures and tables. One in a series concentrating on geographical regions or undertakings.

THE NETHERLANDS. The Hague, Ministry of Foreign Affairs, 1982.

A large folder with a map of the Netherlands, a poster showing many aspects of Dutch life and the landscape and explanations of each of the pictures.

THE NETHERLANDS, A WET COUNTRY SHORT OF WATER. The Hague, Ministry of Transport and Public Works, 1980.

Three larger and many smaller maps are included in this examination of Holland's struggle with the sea, with sources of sweet water, pollution and government management of water resources.

THE NETHERLANDS AND THE UNITED STATES. By Hans Koning. The Hague, Government Publishing Office, 1982.

Diplomatic relations were established between the Netherlands and the United States in 1782 and have never been interrupted. This handsome booklet, illustrated with old engravings and maps, tells the story of the fruitful encounters between the Dutch and the Americans from the explorer Henry Hudson and the settlement of New Amsterdam, to the settlement of Separatists in Michigan to the present.

THE NETHERLANDS IN BRIEF. By M.J.M. van Hezik and L. Verheijen. The Hague, Ministry of Foreign Affairs, 1980.

Tells about the history, government, administration, economy, industry, finance, trade, agriculture, arts, media and social institutions. Illustrated in color.

PICTORIAL ATLAS OF THE NETHERLANDS. The Hague, Ministry of Foreign Affairs, 1977.

Sections are devoted to the struggle against the water, land reclamation, water control, the Randstad, agriculture, horticulture, industry, foreign trade and traffic and the two cities of Amsterdam and Rotterdam. Each section has a small map and pictures.

WINDMILLS IN HOLLAND. New York, Netherlands Information Service, 1970.

Tells about polder mills which keep the land dry and industrial mills which grind grain, run sawmills or extract edible oils. Mills are also used to send messages by the angle of the sails. Illustrated.

SANTA CLAUS THE DUTCH WAY. The Hague, Albani.

Tells about the Feast of Saint Nicholas on December 6th when Sinterklaas brings gifts to young children accompanied by a whimsical poem. Also describes Christmas traditions such as the Midwinter Horn Blowing and New Year's Eve celebrations. Illustrated with photographs and children's paintings. Also includes recipes for holiday sweets.

ZUYDER ZEE. Lake Ijssel. By Drs. Henk Meijer. Utrecht/The Hague, Information and Documentation Center for the Geography of the Netherlands, third revised edition, 1981.

A detailed examination of the Zuyder Zee giving an explanation of its origin and development, its significance for the Netherlands and descriptions of its major areas. Includes excursion routes for those wishing to visit the area. Also has appendices, bibliography and maps.

DUTCH AMERICANS

ALBERTUS C. VAN RAALTE AND HIS DUTCH SETTLEMENTS IN THE UNITED STATES. By Albert Hyma. Grand Rapids, Michigan, W. B. Eerdmans Publishing Company, 1947.

A biography of the founder of Holland, Michigan. Gives the Dutch background for emigration and tells how land was purchased and financed, how the settlers maintained independent religious views and finally made their peace with the Dutch Reformed Church.

THE AMERICANIZATION OF A CONGREGATION. By Elton U. Bruins. Grand Rapids, Michigan, W. B. Eerdmans Publishing Company, 1970.

In the century between 1867 and 1967, the Dutch Reformed Church in Holland, Michigan, underwent changes which are illustrative of many other ethnically related churches.

AMERICANS FROM HOLLAND. By Arnold Mulder. The Peoples of America Series. Philadelphia, J. B. Lippincott Company, 1947.

Chronicles the history of the Dutch in America from the first colonists through later immigrations to the 1940's.

DUTCH AMERICANS. Edited by Linda Pegman Doezema. Detroit, Gale Research Company, 1979.

An annotated bibliography of books and articles concerned with the Dutch in America. Sections devoted to reference works, general works on various topics, the colonial period and the new immigration (1846 to present). Appendices list archives and libraries, retrospective and current newspapers and periodicals, as well as audiovisual materials. There are author, title and subject indices.

THE DUTCH & SWEDES ON THE DELAWARE 1609-64. By Christopher Ward. Philadelphia, University of Pennsylvania Press, 1930.

Tells the story of Dutch and Swedish settlements from the discovery of Delaware Bay in 1609 by Henry Hudson until the taking of New Amsterdam and the Delaware River territory by the English in 1664.

DUTCH EMIGRATION TO NORTH AMERICA, 1624-1860; A Short History. By Bertus Harry Wabeke. New York, Netherlands Information Bureau, 1944.

Investigates why and how Dutch emigrants came to America before the Civil War, and how they first adjusted to the new life here.

DUTCH IMMIGRANT MEMOIRS AND RELATED WRITINGS. 2 volumes. Edited by Henry S. Lucas. Assen, Netherlands, Van Gorcum, 1955.

THE DUTCH IN AMERICA: A BIBLIOGRAPHICAL GUIDE FOR STUDENTS. By Elton Bruins. Holland, Michigan, Hope College, 1975.

The compiler of this 332-item bibliography intended the work for the use of students who are interested in Dutch emigration to America, particularly the nineteenth century emigration, and who need to know the best available materials on the topic. The compiler has stressed English-language material and has included only those books, pamphlets, and articles useful and available to students. The last thirty to forty entries are Dutch-language materials. This bibliography was compiled from the bibliographical references of many of the major works concerning Dutch Americans: particularly the works of Wabeke, Lucas, and DeJong. The bibliography is one of the more complete listings on this topic.

THE DUTCH IN AMERICA, 1609-1970; A Chronology & Fact Book. Compiled and Edited by Pamela and J. W. Smit. Ethnic Chronology Series Number 5. Dobbs Ferry, New York, Oceana Publications, 1972.

The first section presents a chronology in three parts: I, The Original Wave of Dutch Immigration; II, Dutch Immigration to the United States of America; and III, The Dutch Immigrants' Cultural Experience and Contribution. The second section reprints documents pertaining to Dutch activities and experiences in America.

THE DUTCH IN AMERICA, 1609-1974. Gerald DeJong. Boston, Twayne Publishers, 1975.

A well researched general history which devotes great care to the Dutch colonial period.

THE DUTCH IN NEW NETHERLAND AND THE UNITED STATES. By the Netherland Chamber of Commerce in America, 1909. Reprint San Francisco, R and E Research Associates, 1970.

The first section, New Netherland, presents a concise account of exploration and settlement along the Hudson and Delaware Rivers. The second section, The United States, deals briefly with Dutch emigration to the Middle West and other areas after establishment of the United States as an independent nation.

THE EARLY DUTCH AND SWEDISH SETTLERS OF NEW JERSEY. By Adrian C. Leiby. The New Jersey Historical Series. Princeton, New Jersey, D. Van Nostrand Company, 1964.

Tells the story of Dutch colonists in New Jersey and their contributions to the American heritage.

THE GANSEVOORTS OF ALBANY: DUTCH PATRICIANS IN THE UPPER HUDSON VALLEY. By Alice P. Kenney. Syracuse, New York, Syracuse University Press, 1969.

In following the fortunes of the Gansevoort family, the author elucidates one of the patterns of early Dutch settlement, the urban settlement, where many native traditions and structures were maintained. The story begins in 1660 and is carried through the nineteenth century, when acculturation had blurred the clarity of these patterns.

GLIMPSES OF THE EARLY DUTCH SETTLEMENTS IN MICHIGAN. By Lewis George Vander Velde. Ann Arbor, University of Michigan, 1947.

Brief introductory information on the story of Dutch settlements in Holland and Kalmazoo, Michigan. The information derived from the personal papers of Albertus C. van Raalte and Paulus den Bleyker.

THE HOLLANDERS IN AMERICA; A Choice Collection of Books, Maps, and Pamphlets Relating to the Early Colonisation, Voyages, Exploration, etc. by the Hollanders in Different Parts of North and South America. By Martinus Nijhoff. The Hague, Martinus Nijhoff, 1925. (San Francisco, R and E Research Associates, 1972).

Alphabetical listing of both English and Dutch publications with some annotations.

THE HOLLANDERS IN IOWA. By Jacob Vander Zee. Iowa City, Iowa, State Historical Society of Iowa, 1912.

An early regional study of the origins of the principal Dutch settlements in Iowa and their condition at the beginning of this century.

HOLLANDERS WHO HELPED BUILD AMERICA. By Bernard H. M. Vlekke and Henry Beets. New York, American Biographical Company, 1942.

Part I surveys Dutch activities and influence in the United States from the beginnings of colonial history on through the American Revolution and "the winning of the West" to modern times. Offers detailed biographical information on Dutch Americans in Part II.

NARRATIVES OF NEW NETHERLAND, 1609-1664; Original Narratives of Early American History. Edited by J. Franklin Jameson. New York, Charles Scribner's Sons, 1909.

Presents translations of Dutch accounts of early exploration and settlement of Manhattan and nearby areas. Each narrative is preceded by an explanatory introduction.

NETHERLANDERS IN AMERICA; Dutch Immigration to the United States and Canada, 1789-1950. By Henry S. Lucas. Ann Arbor, University of Michigan Press, 1955.

Traces the history of Dutch settlements and immigrant experiences in different areas of the United States and Canada. Three sections cover: Early Settlement; Expansion and Dispersal; and The Dutch Character and Contribution.

PIETY AND PATRIOTISM: Bicentennial Studies of the Reformed Church in America, 1776-1976. Edited by James W. Van Hoeven. Grand Rapids, W. B. Eerdmans Publishing Company, 1976.

A collection of historical essays concerning the Reformed Church in its American setting. The Reformed Church and the American Revolution, the frontier, immigration, world mission, theology, social concerns and education and the role of women in nineteenth century missionary work are covered.

THE REVOLUTIONARY WAR IN THE HACKENSACK VALLEY; The Jersey Dutch and the Neutral Ground, 1775-1783. By Adrian C. Leiby. New Brunswick, New Jersey, Rutgers University Press, 1962.

Dutchmen living in Bergen County, New Jersey, during the American Revolution found themselves surrounded by British and opposing patriot forces, invaded by both, divided in their loyalties, and fighting with one another.

THE SCANDINAVIAN AND DUTCH RURAL SETTLEMENTS IN THE STILLAGUAMISH AND NOOSACK VALLEYS OF WESTERN WASHINGTON. By Burton L. Anderson. Ann Arbor, Michigan, University Microfilms, 1957.

SOME FACTORS INFLUENCING POSTWAR EMIGRATION FROM THE NETHERLANDS. By William Petersen. The Hague, Netherlands, M. Nighoff, 1952.

Population pressure in the Netherlands as well as psychological factors gave impetus to emigration in the post war period. The author examines statistics and governmental policies relevant to Dutch emigration to America as well as other countries.

STUBBORN FOR LIBERTY: THE DUTCH IN NEW YORK. By Alice P. Kenney. Syracuse, Published for the New York State American Revolution Bicentennial Commission, Syracuse University Press, 1975.

An account of the Hudson Valley Dutch; development of their way of life over three and a half centuries from their first settlements to the present.

A SWEET AND ALIEN LAND: THE STORY OF DUTCH NEW YORK. By Henri van der Zee, New York, Viking Press, 1978.

The history of the Dutch in New York during colonial times. Begins with a chronology of both the new world and the old world. Also includes a bibliography.

WILLIAM PENN AND THE DUTCH QUAKER MIGRATION TO PENNSYLVANIA. By William Hull. Baltimore, Genealogical Publishing Company, 1970.

This study of William Penn's relations with the Dutch Quakers looks at his journeys to Holland and Germany and the rise and progress of these congregations that he converted to Quakerism and invited to Pennsylvania.

Audiovisual Material

MAP

THE NETHERLANDS. The Hague. Cartoprint B.V.

A large colored map of the Netherlands showing land use areas in different colors, major roads and towns, rivers and railways. Inset maps show the country in relation to the rest of Europe and the Height above sea level of the parts of the Netherlands. Approximately 32-1/2 X 42.

FILMS

AMSTERDAM. 16 mm. Color and sound. 40 minutes. By BBC-TV, New York, Time-Life Multimedia, 1977.

A tour of the sights of Amsterdam, including the tulip gardens, the canals, Rembrandt's home, and the Rijksmuseum.

AMSTERDAM CONCERTO. 16 mm. Color and sound. 10 minutes. By Joop Geesink. Royal Netherlands Embassy, Cultural Section.

The Concertgebouw Orchestra has provided the musical background for this film about the past and present of Holland's capital city. Amsterdam, with its colorful history as a port and center of trade, is still today a scene of bustling activity. And big plans are being laid for the future, too. Where many work, many must dwell - in pleasant flats and houses. After a day's work, it's time for relaxation; in this city all tastes are catered for. Yes, Amsterdam throbs with life, twenty-four hours a day.

AND THERE WAS NO MORE SEA. 16 mm. Color and sound. 25 minutes. By Bert Haanstra. Royal Netherlands Embassy, Cultural Section.

The Zuyder Zee has become Lake IJssel and large parts of Lake IJssel have been reclaimed to provide living-space for thousands of Dutchmen. An inevitable consequence of this development is the gradual disappearance of the folklore and the ancient customs which were once observed in the little towns on the shores of this former sea. Although this is of course very much to be regretted, it is a logical outcome of the "modernization" of this area. The waves of the sea have had to give way to fields of waving corn; the old dies out as the new emerges.

AND THEY NAMED IT HOLLAND. 16 mm. Color and sound. 10 minutes. By Ger Raucamp.

Shot entirely from a helicopter, this film presents a condensed, panoramic view of the genesis of the Netherlands: the Ice Age, the low-lying delta area, the play of wind and water, the first plants and animals, the arrival of man, and the changes he has wrought in the course of the centuries. What he has achieved in his unremitting struggle with the elements is recorded in a series of poetic images.

CHILDREN'S WORLD: HOLLAND. 16 mm. Color and sound. 15 minutes. By John Tedford. Made by Lem Bailey Productions. Released by AV-ED Films, 1971.

Uses the experiences of two Dutch children and their guest from the United States to show that the children understand each other even though they do not speak each other's language. Shows how life in Holland compares to life in the United States. For elementary grades.

A COUNTRY FOR MY SON. 16 mm. Color and sound. 21 minutes. By Jan Wiegel.

In a small and densely populated country like Holland only planning on a nationwide scale can offer a satisfactory solution to the problem of the often conflicting interests of economic development, living conditions, and recreational needs. New industries are a threat to health in Holland, as anywhere else, if they are established indiscriminately.

A DAY AT THE ZUYDERSEA. 16 mm. Color and sound. 22 minutes. By Jan Wiegel. Royal Netherlands Embassy, Cultural Section.

Another film on the construction of dikes and polders? Well, of course you see that the work, started in the thirties, is still going on, but the idea of this picture is to show what happened after the closing of the dikes. It presents the people, their life in the new towns, on land that is still being prepared for cultivation, on the shores of the lakes in the new recreation areas, on former islands, all of which are part of the Zuydersea project. When a circus comes to the bottom of the sea, the people feel that they are really land dwellers.

DIRC BOUTS FROM HAARLEM. 16 mm. Color and sound. 16 minutes. Also issued as videorecording. By Bert van Dale. International Film Bureau, Chicago, 1979.

Examines the paintings of Dirc Bouts, the Flemish painter known as the successor to Van Eyck.

DUTCH MUSEUMS. 16 mm. Color and sound. 27 minutes. By Paul Huf. Royal Netherlands Embassy, Cultural Section.

The film, "Dutch Museums" reveals that, in addition to Rembrandt and his contemporaries, there is much more to be seen. In some 500 Dutch museums there are around 12 million objects preserved and displayed. And these are, by far, not all paintings. In one small museum you can see how 40% of the Netherlands would be under water if there were no dunes and dikes. In another place you seem to be standing on top of a dune with sea, shore beaches, dunes and hinterland all around you. In fact you stand on an artificial dune beyond which everything is a tremendous and a marvelously painted canvas in the round. The film "Dutch Museums" is a playful guided tour. A preview of what you will encounter in the museums of the Netherlands. The film also presents in a light-hearted way the landscape and cities of the Netherlands because, "don't we spend most of our lives outside the museum?"

FISHERMEN FROM URK. 16 mm. Color and sound. 23 minutes. By Krsto Papio. Royal Netherlands Embassy, Cultural Section.

There have never been many picture postcards of the fishing village of Urk, situated on what was an island of the same name in the former Zuyder Zee. Both village and harbor were even scheduled to be wiped off the map. The planners had decided that after the reclamation of the Zuyder Zee the inhabitants of Urk would exchange their fishing gear for the implements of agriculture and industry. But something happened that surprised all the planners: Urk's fishing fleet today is one of the biggest and best-equipped in Western Europe. The film tells the story of this astonishing development and follows one of the fishing families on their weekly voyages.

FRIESLAND IS YOURS. 16 mm. Color and sound. 21 minutes. By Jolijn Tichelaar. Royal Netherlands Embassy, Cultural Section.

This beautifully photographed tour of the Netherlands' northern-most province of Friesland tells the engaging and light-hearted story of one visiting family's growing affection for the countryside, the villages and the people of Friesland. After landing at Schiphol airport near Amsterdam, the family rents a car and drives north, across the long Afsluitdijk that seals off the IJsselmeer from the North Sea. Once in Friesland a few hours later, they discover charming old villages and historic monuments and churches, vast fields and expanses of water, learning that Friesland is a province with its own culture and traditions, its own language (Frisian), a province that has succeeded in preserving its own way of life while remaining a part of the modern mainstream of the Netherlands. As the family in the film and the viewer learn, Friesland - off the beaten track of international tourism - is one of the jewels of Europe.

GREAT GARDENS OF THE WORLD - HOLLAND. 16 mm. Color and sound. 27 minutes. By Walter Schenk. Royal Netherlands Embassy, Cultural Section.

The Netherlands has been called the flower garden of the world. In the spring this land behind the dunes comes to life. Hundreds of thousands of tourists come to visit the bulb fields in full bloom and the Keukenhof. This film goes into the history of the tulip and the significance for the Netherlands of the export of bulbs overseas, as well as the world's largest flower auction in Aalsmeer and the flower processions. Finally we come to Amsterdam: the front door to Europe.

THE HAGUE, A MONUMENT. 16 mm. Color and sound. 20 minutes. By Peter Moricke and Ronny Erends. Royal Netherlands Embassy, Cultural Section.

This film sets out to portray The Hague and at the same time to show what the citizens of The Hague are doing with their town and with their historic monuments. The monuments are being restored; not only the grander buildings but also ordinary houses, which are once more becoming habitable. All kinds of monuments have been given a new lease on life in The Hague, but what is happening there is also happening in many other Dutch towns and villages.

HOLD BACK THE SEA. 16 mm. Color and sound. 29 minutes. By George Sluizer. Royal Netherlands Embassy, Cultural Section.

The story of that remarkable tract of country called the Netherlands, of which Pliny the Elder said in 40 A.D.: "Here there is some doubt as to whether the ground belongs to the land or to the sea". The shape of the country has been constantly changed, at first, for millions of years, by Nature only, but for the last 2,000 years to an increasing degree by man. He declared war on the water, and made the Netherlands of today by building dykes and dams and by turning the marshes and lakes into fertile land.

HOLLAND AGAINST THE SEA. 16 mm. Color and sound. 52 minutes. By Bert Haanstra, National Geographic, Washington, D.C. Royal Netherlands Embassy, Cultural Section.

Never has the love-hate relationship between The Netherlands and the sea been shown better than in this film. The sea has brought wealth as well as disaster. Wealth when for centuries sailors and fishermen went overseas to bring back from far countries goods and spices. Disaster came when in 1953 the North Sea broke the thousand year old dikes and flooded a large part of the land, leaving behind victims and taking back land. Through canal-laced Amsterdam to tulip-tinted fields, windmills and the colossal Delta Project, designed to shut out the sea.

HOLLAND: DELTA PROJECT PHASE 1. 16 mm. 8 mm. or 35 mm. Color and sound. 20 minutes. By Netherlands Information Service, The Hague, 1972. Released in the United States by Films, Incorporated.

Explores the construction of four massive dams in the Dutch project to project delta lowlands from the sea.

HOLLAND HEARTBEAT. 16 mm. Color and sound. 25 minutes. By Sikorsky Aircraft, 1972.

Presents a one-day helicopter tour of the Netherlands, showing the combination of modern technology and medieval charm of that country.

HOLLAND TERRA AGRONOMICA. 16 mm. Color and sound. 19 minutes. By Ronny Erends. Royal Netherlands Embassy, Cultural Section.

The film gives an impression of the care which is lavished on Dutch agricultural, horticultural and fishery products. The special role of scientific research is obvious. Its center is at Wageningen, where there is an Agricultural University and many, many other institutes and laboratories which together guarantee the high quality of Dutch products.

HOLLAND TERRA FERTILIS. 16 mm. Color and sound. 10 minutes. By Ronnie Erends. Royal Netherlands Embassy, Cultural Section.

A mercurial, often unconventionally-made film introducing Dutch agricultural and horticultural products to the world's consumers. The light-hearted and often humorous way in which the various delicacies are served up ensures even the non-participant viewer's enjoyment of the feast.

HOLLAND: THE BOY FROM AMSTERDAM. 16 mm. Color and sound. 18 minutes. By Ontario Educational Communications Authority, Toronto, 1969. Released in the United States by NBC Educational Enterprises, 1972.

Deals with daily life of young people in Holland, focusing on a young Dutch boy who lives with his parents and younger brother in Amsterdam. Tells that in school he learns French, English, German and other subjects, and on Saturdays does household chores to earn spending money for his trips to downtown Amsterdam on his bicycle. For elementary grades.

INTO THE WIND'S EYE. 16 mm. Color and sound. 10 minutes. By Otto van Neyenhoff.

In the flat Low Countries where the wind never seems to stop blowing, the wind has for centuries been harnessed for many different purposes. Windmills pumped lakes dry and drained the polders. Windmills were used for grinding corn and pressing oil. Windmills helped to make paper. With a few exceptions all that work is now done by electrically driven machinery. There are many folkloristic customs associated with windmills, and they have played an important part in the life of the people ever since windmills were first built.

INTRODUCING THE NETHERLANDS. Videorecording. Black and white. Sound. 22 minutes. By Ytzen Brusse. Distributed by National Audiovisual Center, Washington, 1979.

Describes the country and people of the Netherlands, including geographical features, historical development and achievements, economic life, occupation of the people, and social customs. Explains briefly the role of the Netherlands in the North Atlantic Treaty Organization.

LIFE AROUND THE WORLD: DUTCH BARGE FAMILY. Super 8 mm. Color. Silent. 4 minutes. By Coronet Instructional Materials, 1972.

Portrays life on a barge in the Netherlands.

THE LIGHT OF EXPERIENCE. Videorecording. Color and sound. 52 minutes. By British Broadcasting Corporation, Time-Life Multimedia, New York, 1971.

Surveys the development of Western civilization during the 17th century. Points out that the works of such Dutch painters as Rembrandt, Frans Hals, Vermeer, and Saenredam show the revolutionary change in thought that replaced divine authority with experience, experiment and observation. A part of the "Civilization" series by Kenneth Clark.

PORTRAIT OF FRANS HALS. 16 mm. Color and sound. 18 minutes. By Frans Dupont.

The painter Frans Hals lived in Holland most of his life. He died in Haarlem in 1666, and it is this city that boasts a special Frans Hals Museum. The film shows the very remarkable manner in which Frans Hals developed into one of Holland's most famous painters.

REMBRANDT, PAINTER OF MAN. 16 mm. Color and sound. 20 minutes. By Bert Haanstra.

The life story of the great Rembrandt van Rijn is told through his paintings. They show the painter rising in the world, his first important commission, his marriage to Saskia van Uylenburgh, the birth of his son Titus, the death of Saskia, and his life with Hendrikje Stoffels. The film mounts to an emotional climax as a number of self-portraits are gradually merged together and the proud face of the young, successful, fashionable painter ages before our eyes.

SAILING. 16 mm. Color and sound. 13 minutes. By Hattum Hoving. Royal Netherlands Embassy, Cultural Section.

The film is a symphonic poem dedicated to wind and water and to the sport of yachting, intimately linked with these elements. The opening chords are like a largo in the early-morning stillness of the water; the bustle and activity as the boats are made ready are like an andante, which is then followed by the allegro of the sunny spectacle of summer yachting. The rising storm comes up like a tempestuoso, and the yachtsmen need all their skill to reach a safe harbor. Finally there is the largo a tranquillo of the evening over waters that are calm once again.

THE SPIRIT OF JOHN ADAMS IN THE NETHERLANDS. 16 mm. Color and sound. 25 minutes. By Juan Goudsmit. Royal Netherlands Embassy, Cultural Section.

The film shows, through documentary on-the-spot-investigations and historical reconstruction, the links between the rebelling American Colonies and one of the important European Powers of the 18th Century: The Republic of The Netherlands. One of America's Founding Fathers, John Adams, appears in the film through his letters and diaries, played by a Dutchman who looks remarkably like "His Rotundity" as Adams was called. The film doesn't dwell only on the two years Adams was in Holland but also deals with our own time and draws parallels in history. For example Adams' work in getting recognition of the USA and loans to sustain it finds its counterpart in the post-World-War-II-relations between Holland and America, but the other way around. The film was shot in Rotterdam, The Hague, Leiden, Haarlem, Amsterdam, Utrecht, Breukelen (equals Brooklyn!) along the scenic River Vecht . . . in fact on 27 different locations in Holland.

STEAMBOAT TO HOLLAND. 16 mm. Color and sound. 15 minutes. By Theo van Haren Noman. Royal Netherlands Embassy, Cultural Section.

For this film about Saint Nicolas, the legendary Spanish bishop and great friend of Dutch children, the producer used a large number of drawings made by the children themselves. They depicted not only the festive arrival of the Good Saint in Holland and the zest with which young and old celebrate his birthday on December 5th, but also his dangerous voyage through rough seas to Holland, and his life in sunny, colorful Spain. The film has the same serious and imaginative touch that so strongly characterizes the children's drawings.

TOUCH. 16 mm. Color and sound. 17 minutes. By Tom Tholen. Royal Netherlands Embassy, Cultural Section.

An unusual succession of personal impressions of the port of Rotterdam-Europoort, showing the pictorial beauty of ships, dockyards and cranes, at the same time emphasizing the rapidly increasing integration of shipping and industry, which particularly accounts for the ports' spectacular growth.

UNKNOWN HOLLAND. 16 mm. Color and sound. 22 minutes. By Joop Scheltens. Royal Netherlands Embassy, Cultural Section.

The Netherlands, today one of the most prosperous countries, once was a swampy delta, forbidding but in an exceptionally beautiful way. Those who - perhaps lured by that beauty - defied the odd chances and managed to survive, succeeded by seeking shelter behind handmade, primitive walls of clay, which successive generations of descendants have gradually fortified and shaped into tentacles with which they have grabbed increasingly large chunks of fertile soil from the sea. From behind their dikes the Dutch have defied the surrounding seas in yet another fashion; riding those waters in almost every direction by the beginning of the 17th century they had made the Low Countries a prosperous and powerful nation. Much man-made beauty was added in those times to the delta's natural beauty. Much of that beauty has been preserved even though perhaps less visible from the highways serving a modern industrial community of some 14 million as means of communication. Producer Scheltens has successfully traced much of that Unknown Holland.

UNMISTAKABLY HOLLAND. 16 mm. Color and sound. 23 minutes. By Ronny Erends. Royal Netherlands Embassy, Cultural Section.

The very first feet of the new Holland Promotion film "Unmistakably Holland" leave no one in any doubt as to what it is about: the Netherlands of today. The low-lying polder land where anything goes or - if it turns out that way - practically nothing - a country for the tourist and the hippy; a country where minority initiative resulted in the bold experiment of the White Cars - self-drive electrically operated taxis in Amsterdam. The environmentalist will appreciate the hundreds of natural beauty spots, the conservationist rejoice in the untouched corners of historic towns, all of them within a stone's throw of each other and reached with ease by a unique system of roads, railways, and waterways. "Unmistakably Holland" sees its country objectively through the cameraman's lens.

VINCENT VAN GOGH. 16 mm. Color and sound. 20 minutes. By Jan Hulsker.

The dramatic life of Vincent van Gogh is traced in his letters to his brother Theo. When he worked as a preacher among the miners in Belgium, Van Gogh painted landscapes and the workers and peasants he met in a sombre, realistic style. In 1886 he moved on to France where he made the acquaintance of the work of the impressionists. His style changed, particularly his color, which became light and radiant. During the last years of his life both his treatment of the subjects and his use of color expressed the violence of his inner turmoil.

VOICE OF THE WATER. 16 mm. Color and sound. 80 minutes. By Bert Haanstra.

The word "Water" has a lot of different meanings to the Dutch people. This film shows how they use it for aquatic sports and recreation, how they make a living out of it, but, above all, how they fight it grimly with dredgers, dykes, and lifeboats. They try to prevent their land from being engulfed and try to capture new land from the sea.

WADDENSEA, BIRDS' PARADISE. 16 mm. Color and sound. 28 minutes. By Jan van de Kam. Royal Netherlands Embassy, Cultural Section.

The Waddensea, off the northern coasts of Holland, is a unique wetland area, visited by thousands of birds for longer or shorter periods, their daily lives being governed by the rhythm of the tides. The film is an eloquent plea for preserving the area in its original state, for safe-guarding it against the drainage schemes which threaten it and against the further pollution of its waters.

ECUADORIANS
See also: SPANISH-SPEAKING PEOPLES

Embassy and Consulates

EMBASSY OF ECUADOR
and Permanent Mission to the OAS
2535 15th Street, Northwest
Washington, D.C. 20009 (202) 234-7200

Office of Commercial Counselor (202) 234-7426

CONSULATES GENERAL

427 West Fifth Street
Los Angeles, California 90013 (213) 628-3014

Ingrahan Building, #1130
25 South East Second Avenue
Miami, Florida 33131 (305) 371-8366

2 Canal Street, Room 1044
New Orleans, Louisiana 70130 (504) 523-7497

1270 Avenue of Americas, Room 2411
New York, New York 10020 (212) 245-5380

The Flood Building, Suite 858
870 Market Street
San Francisco, California 94102 (415) 391-4148

CONSULATES

2925 North Charles Street
Baltimore, Maryland 21218 (301) 889-4422

60 State Street
Boston, Massachusetts 02109 (617) 227-7200

612 North Michigan Avenue
Chicago, Illinois 60601 (312) 642-8579

6300 Richmond Avenue, Suite 313
Houston, Texas 77057 (713) 977-8750

24 Pear Tree Lane
Lafayette Hill, Pennsylvania
19106 (215) 825-5209

530 Broadway, Suite 618
San Diego, California 92101 (714) 233-8640

2535 15th Street, Northwest
Washington, D.C. 20009 (202) 234-7166

Mission to the United Nations

ECUADOR MISSION
820 Second Avenue, 15th Floor
New York, New York 10017 (212) 986-6670

Tourist and Travel Offices

ECUADOR NATIONAL TOURIST OFFICE
167 West 72nd Street
New York, New York 10023 (212) 873-0600

Religious Organizations

ECUADOR CONCERNS COMMITTEE
475 Riverside Drive, 16th Floor
New York, New York 10027 (212) 870-2833
Chairman: Reverend Jeffrey Utter Founded 1965

Sponsored by the United Methodist Church, Presbyterian Church in the United States, Church of the Brethren, United Church of Christ and United Presbyterian Church in the United States of America. Works in the Andes Mountain areas of Ecuador, South America to support the work of and maintain relations with the United Evangelical Church of Ecuador, an autonomous national church. Also supports the work of the United Brethren Foundations, an indigenous organization devoted to rural agricultural and community development, health care delivery, legal aid and the empowerment of women. The work of the Foundation is based on a Christian concept of mission, but is not itself of an evangelistic nature. Supersedes United Andean Indian Mission.

GABRIEL GARCIA MORENO MEMORIAL
ASSOCIATION
3610 Meadowbrook Avenue
Nashville, Tennessee 37205 (615) 292-9695
Director: John C. Moran Founded 1975

Purposes are to commemorate the martyrdom of and defend the memory of Dr. Garcia Moreno (1821-1875), president of Ecuador, and to work for his canonization. Also encourages and promotes Roman Catholic social and moral principles in the public order.

Subject Collection

HILLMAN LIBRARY
171 Hillman Library
Pittsburgh, Pennsylvania 15260 (412) 624-4425
Bibliographer: Eduardo Lozano

Contains a general collection of Latin American literature with strong holdings on Bolivian, Ecuadorian, and Cuban literature, especially contemporary literature.

Newsletter

ECUADOREAN NEWS DIGEST. Monthly.
Editor: Paul Calvet. Publisher: Ecuadorean American Association, Room 1110, 115 Broadway, New York, New York 10006.

Bank Branches in the U.S.

BANCO LA FILANTROPICA ECUADOR
667 Madison Avenue
New York, New York 10021 (212) 752-1060

Commercial and Trade Organizations

ECUADOREAN AMERICAN ASSOCIATION
115 Broadway
New York, New York 10006
President: Rene Valverde (212) 233-7776
Secretary: Paul Calvet Founded 1932

Established to intensify trade, investments, travel and cultural relations between Ecuador and the United States.
Publication: Ecuadorean News Digest, monthly.

ECUADOREAN PROMOTION CENTER
One World Trade Center, Suite 86095
New York, New York 10048 (212) 775-1180
President: Rene Valverde

Economic and Commercial Office for the Ecuadorean government.

Airline Offices

ECUATORIANA
(Compania Ecuatoriana de Aviacion, S.A.)
North American Headquarters:
Northwest 62nd Avenue, Building 1006
International Airport
Miami, Florida 33148 (305) 526-5864

1290 Avenue of the Americas (212) 247-8844
New York, New York (800) 327-1377

Offers domestic services plus international routes serving Miami, Mexico City, Panama City, Bogota, Cali, Guayaquil, Quito, and Lima. Other offices in the United States: Los Angeles, and Washington, D.C.

Ship Line

ECUADOREAN LINE, INCORPORATED
19 Rector
New York, New York (212) 425-8100

Books and Pamphlets

BIBLIOGRAPHY OF THE ANDEAN COUNTRIES. By Richard Wilbur Patch. New York, American Universities Field Staff, 1958.

Described in the subtitle as a "selected, current, annotated bibliography relating to Peru, Bolivia and Ecuador, drawn from reasonably accessible works published in English and Spanish."

COLOMBIA, ECUADOR AND VENEZUELA; An Annotated Guide to Reference Materials in the Humanities and Social Sciences. By Gayle Hudgens Watson. Metuchen, New Jersey, Scarecrow Press, 1971.

A bibliographic guide to 894 works, emphasizing monographs and government publications. A bibliographical essay discussing major information sources precedes a listing of items in a classified arrangement with descriptive annotations. Contains a main entry index.

CULTURAL PORTRAIT OF ECUADOR. By Jorge Carrera Andrade. Pittsburgh, Gulf Oil Corporation.

An essay by the Foreign Minister of Ecuador, a member of the Royal Academy of Language of Spain. Discusses the characteristics of Ecuadorians, their cultural history, and contributions made by individual poets, novelists, satirists, scientists, mathematicians, historians, biographers, and artists. The brochure is illustrated with reproductions of paintings, sculpture, and architecture and the text is trilingual in Spanish, English, and French.

ECONOMIC ASPECTS OF AGRICULTURAL DEVELOPMENT IN ECUADOR: A BIBLIOGRAPHY. Compiled by Teresa Anderson. Madison, Wisconsin, University of Wisconsin, Madison Land Tenure Center Library, 1972.

ECUADOR. Quito, Ecuador, Nacional de Turismo, 1974.

A booklet showing places of interest to tourists in Ecuador, outstanding examples of architecture, sculpture, sports and recreational activities, unusual animals and plants, arts and crafts, folklore, beaches, pre-Columbian relics, and people of Ecuador. A collection of lovely photographs in full color.

ECUADOR IN FIGURES. Quito, Central Bank of Ecuador, 1979.

A folder giving statistics on population, the gross national product, industrial production, international trade, public finances and the monetary system.

IMAGE OF ECUADOR. By the General Secretariat, Organization of American States. Washington, 1980.

Discusses the origins and historical development of Ecuador, the people and their culture, the cities and regions of Ecuador, and economic development. A booklet illustrated with maps and photographs, some in color.

INVEST IN ECUADOR. Quito. Central Bank of Ecuador.

A booklet outlining the Ecuadorean economic structure and the advantages for foreign investors. Beautifully illustrated with scenes of the landscape, people and wildlife.

THE INVESTMENT CLIMATE IN ECUADOR. Quito, Cendes, 1979.

A booklet outlining the current political economy and the outlook for development.

SYNTHESIS OF THE TREATMENT OF FOREIGN INVESTMENT IN ECUADOR. By Juan F. Casals. Technical Division, Central Bank of Ecuador, 1981.

A booklet explaining the implementation of the Cartagena Agreement, Decision 24, in Ecuadorean economic policy in regard to foreign investment in the country.

Audiovisual Material

FILMS

ALFONZO: A LONG WAY FROM HOME. 16mm. Color and sound. 19 minutes. Released by Journal Films, 1975.

Portrays the difficulties of an Ecuadorian weaver when he leaves his small community and moves into modern society.

BOLIVIA, PERU, AND ECUADOR. 16mm. Color and sound. 19 minutes. By William Clairborne, Incorporated. Latin America series: A Focus on People. Released by Sterling Educational Films, New York, 1973.

Analyzes the far-reaching social reforms, political changes, and achievements in frontier areas which are happening in Bolivia, Peru, and Ecuador. Discusses the mixed influence of the Indian and Hispanic cultures.

COUNTRIES OF THE ANDES. 16mm. Color and sound. 11 minutes. Coronet Instructional Media, Chicago, 1977.

Describes the people, culture, cities, and rural areas of Bolivia, Ecuador, Peru, and Chile. Compares and contrasts the people of each country, points out their cultural achievements, and identifies important factors in their economic growth.

DAWN OVER ECUADOR. 16mm. Color and sound. 29 minutes. By Directors Group Motion Pictures for Texaco. Released by Association-Sterling Films, New York, 1972.

Describes the human and natural resources of Ecuador as seen by a young teacher, his students, and a geologist. Shows how the discovery of petroleum in the Amazon and the building of an oil pipeline over the Andes to the Pacific Ocean are opening up new opportunities to the people of Ecuador.

THE ENCHANTED ISLANDS. 16mm. Color and sound. 1 hour.

A film about the Galapagos Islands situated in the Pacific Ocean about five hundred miles west of Ecuador. Discusses the history of the islands and shows the unusual animals, plants, and rock formations there.

(For information about borrowing the films listed above, write to the Embassy of Ecuador.)

OVER THE ANDES IN ECUADOR. 16mm. Color and sound. 18 minutes. By Public Media, Incorporated. Released by Films Incorporated, Wilmette, Illinois, 1969.

Deals with the transportation, industry, dress, and customs of the people of Ecuador.

THE ROADS TO THE SUN. 16mm. Color and sound. 30 minutes.

Introduces the land and people of Ecuador, their occupations, handicrafts, costumes, dances, and the various regions where they live.

EGYPTIANS
See also: ARABS

Embassy and Consulates

EMBASSY OF THE ARAB REPUBLIC OF EGYPT
Chancery Office
2310 Decatur Place, Northwest
Washington, D.C. 20008 (202) 232-5400

Agricultural Bureau
2300 Decatur Place, Northwest
Washington, D.C. 20008 (202) 232-5400

Commercial Office
2715 Connecticut Avenue, Northwest
Washington, D.C. 20008 (202) 234-1414

Cultural and Educational Bureau
2200 Kalorama Road, Northwest
Washington, D.C. 20008 (202) 265-6400

Military Office
2308 Tracy Place, Northwest
Washington, D.C. 20008 (202) 462-6561

Press and Information Office
1825 Connecticut Avenue, Northwest
Washington, D.C. 20009 (202) 667-3402

CONSULATES

Suite 4902
505 North Lakeshore Drive
Chicago, Illinois 60611 (312) 670-2633

2000 West Loop South
Suite 1750
Control Data Building
Houston, Texas 77027 (713) 961-4915

1110 Second Avenue
New York, New York 10022 (212) 759-7120

3001 Pacific Avenue
San Francisco, California
94115 (415) 346-9700

Mission to the United Nations

EGYPTIAN MISSION
36 East 67th Street
New York, New York 10021 (212) 879-6300

Tourist and Travel Offices

EGYPTIAN TOURIST OFFICE
630 Fifth Avenue
New York, New York 10020 (212) 246-6960

Cultural and Educational Organizations

AMERICAN COPTIC ASSOCIATION
Post Office Box 9119 G.L.S.
Jersey City, New Jersey 07304 (201) 435-3287
President: Dr. Shawky F. Karas Founded 1974

Copts (Christian Egyptians) who immigrated to the United States. Promotes Coptic culture and history; defends human rights of the Copts in Egypt; helps immigrants to the United States to be good and productive citizens. Sponsors lectures and conferences. Maintains library on psychology, sociology and history. Publications: The Copts (journal), quarterly; also publishes Census of the Copts in Egypt; Implications of Applying Islamic Rules in Egypt; Plight of the Copts in Egypt and other reports.

Religious Organization

COPTIC ORTHODOX CHURCH
1882 Grove Street
Ridgewood, New York 11227

Contact:
Archpriest Fr. Gabriel Abdelsayed
427 West Side Avenue
Jersey City, New Jersey 07304

This body is part of the ancient Coptic Orthodox Church of Egypt which is currently headed by His Holiness Pope Shenouda III. In the United States many parishes have been organized consisting of Egyptian immigrants to the United States. Copts exist outside of Egypt in Ethiopia, Europe, Asia, Australia, Canada, and the United States.

Research Centers and Special Institutes

AMERICAN RESEARCH CENTER IN EGYPT
20 Nassau Street
Princeton, New Jersey 08540
President: Professor John A. Wilson
(609) 921-3797
Founded 1948

Independent nonprofit research organization with centers both in Princeton and in Cairo, Egypt. Principal fields of research: Ancient and Islamic civilization in Egypt, including humanities and social studies in all periods. Archaeological projects include epigraphic survey of Medinet Habu by Oriental Institute at University of Chicago, reconstruction of part of Akhenaten Temple by University Museum at University of Pennsylvania and excavations at Gebel Adda, Fustat and Karnak. Maintains a small library in Cairo Center.
Publications: Journal, periodically; Newsletter, quarterly.

ANTHROPOLOGY RESEARCH CENTER
Southern Methodist University
Heroy Building
Dallas, Texas 75275
Director: Dr. Anthony Marks
(214) 692-2926
Founded 1963

Integral unit of Department of Anthropology at Southern Methodist University. Principal fields of research: Archaeology, human biology, ethnology, linguistics and medical anthropology, also archaeological investigations in Egypt, Ethiopia and Israel in the Old World; Belize, Mexico, New Mexico and Texas in the New World. Other work in progress in Mexico and United States through its archaeology research and medical anthropology programs. Maintains collections of Old World paleolithic artifacts and human relations area files.

INSTITUTE FOR ANTIQUITY AND CHRISTIANITY
Claremont Graduate School
831 North Dartmouth Avenue
Claremont, California 91711
Director: Dr. James M. Robinson
(714) 626-8511
Founded 1967

Integral unit of Claremont Graduate School, collaborating with School of Theology at Claremont and in association with the five undergraduate colleges in Claremont cluster, operating under a research council consisting of project directors and an advisory board composed of leaders in education, business and the professions. Principal field of research: Origins of Western civilization, embracing Ancient Near East from Mesopotamia to Egypt, classical Greece, Hellenistic and Roman worlds, Judaism and early Christianity and including projects on international Greek New Testament, Corpus Hellenisticum Novi Testamenti, Coptic Gnostic Library, Patmos Monastery Library, Ugaritic and Hebrew parallels and Dead Sea Scrolls. Also maintains a center for historic preservation, including research and teaching collections of basic artifacts such as papyri, pottery, sherds and clay tablets for training of future archaeologists and conservationists. Maintains a library of 400 volumes on Ancient Near East, philology and reference works; James Brashler, librarian.
Publication: Bulletin, quarterly.

Museums

KELSEY MUSEUM OF ANCIENT AND MEDIAEVAL ARCHAEOLOGY
University of Michigan
434 South State Street
Ann Arbor, Michigan 48104
Director: John G. Pedley
(313) 764-9304
Founded 1929

Displays collections on classical and Near Eastern archaeology, especially of Roman and Coptic Egypt. Display includes the results of excavations at three Roman sites in Egypt and at Seleucia on the Tigris River in Iraq.

ROSICRUCIAN EGYPTIAN MUSEUM AND ART GALLERY
Rosicrucian Park
San Jose, California 95191
Director: Ralph M. Lewis
(408) 287-9171
Founded 1929

Designed in the form of an ancient Egyptian temple, the museum contains materials on Egyptian, Babylonian, and Assyrian antiquities; sculpture; paintings; archaeology; coptic textiles; utensils; jewelry; scarabs; amulets; statuary. Offers guided tours, lectures, and films.
Publications: Newsletter, monthly; Egypt the Eternal - Guidebook; It Began in Egypt; About Mummies; Mesopotamia.

Special Libraries and Subject Collections

BROOKLYN MUSEUM - WILBOUR LIBRARY OF EGYPTOLOGY
188 Eastern Parkway
Brooklyn, New York 11238 (212) 638-5000
Librarian: Diane Guzman Founded 1934

Subjects: Ancient Egyptian art, archaeology, philology, travel in Egypt from antiquity to modern times.
Special Collections: Egyptological collections of Charles Edwin Wilbour, Carl Richard Lepsius and Georg Steindorff. Holdings: Books; bound periodical volumes; pamphlets (cataloged), journals and other serials. Services: Interlibrary loans; copying; library open to scholars and qualified researchers by appointment.
Publications: Egyptology Titles published in Cambridge, England by faculty of Oriental Studies, lists acquisitions of both institutions.

CLEVELAND PUBLIC LIBRARY - JOHN G. WHITE COLLECTION OF FOLKLORE, ORIENTALIA, AND CHESS
325 Superior Avenue
Cleveland, Ohio 44114
Head: Alice N. Loranth (216) 623-2818

Contains an extensive collection of books, manuscripts, pictures, and research material on Egyptian antiquities and philological studies, including excavation reports.

ROSICRUCIAN EGYPTIAN MUSEUM, ART GALLERY AND RESEARCH LIBRARY
Rosicrucian Park
San Jose, California 95191 (408) 287-9171
Curator: Curt Schild Founded 1929

Contains thousands of volumes on mysticism, philosophy, history, the arts and sciences. The collection is cataloged.

Newspapers and Newsletters

AMERICAN RESEARCH CENTER IN EGYPT NEWSLETTER. Quarterly. Publisher: American Research Center in Egypt, 20 Nassau Street, Princeton, New Jersey 08540. In English.

INSTITUTE FOR ANTIQUITY AND CHRISTIANITY BULLETIN. Quarterly. Publisher: Institute for Antiquity and Christianity, Claremont Graduate School, 831 North Dartmouth Avenue, Claremont, California 91711. In English.

ROSICRUCIAN EGYPTIAN MUSEUM AND ART CENTER NEWSLETTER. Monthly. Publisher: Rosicrucian Egyptian Museum and Art Center, Rosicrucian Park, San Jose, California 95191. In English.

SAOT MASR (Voice of Masr (Egypt)). 1972-. Monthly. Editor: William Elmirz. Publisher: Egyptian Community Center, 48 Prospect Street, Jersey City, New Jersey 07307. In Arabic and English.

News and items relating to Egypt and Egyptian immigrants.

Magazines

THE COPTS. Quarterly. Publisher: American Coptic Association, Post Office Box 9119 G.L.S., Jersey City, New Jersey 07304. In English.

A journal containing articles and news relating to Copts (Christian Egyptians) and Coptic culture and history.

EGYPTIAN AMERICAN BUSINESS REVIEW. Bimonthly. Publisher: Egyptian-American Chamber of Commerce, One World Trade Center, Suite 86041, New York, New York 10048. In English.

Contains news and advice on trade and business relations between the United States and Egypt.

Commercial and Trade Organizations

EGYPTIAN-AMERICAN CHAMBER OF COMMERCE
One World Trade Center, Suite 86041
New York, New York 10048 (212) 466-1866
Executive Director: Farouk Zaki Founded 1980

International trading, manufacturing, shipping and consulting companies; commercial and investment banks. Fosters trade and business relations between the United States and Egypt. Secures and disseminates information on laws, regulations, and statistics pertaining to trade, investment, industry, agriculture, construction, transportation, and tourism; responds to inquiries on trade and investment opportunities; provides and circulates information on tenders; compiles data and statistics; conducts liaison services; assists members in securing professional services in areas such as accounting, legal counseling, agency agreements, and shipping documents of goods exported to Egypt; provides news on fairs and exhibitions. Operates small library containing books, directories, statistical records, pamphlets, newspapers, and magazines dealing with investment and trade. Publications: Egyptian American Business Review, bimonthly; Membership Directory, quarterly.

Airline Office

EGYPTAIR
North American Headquarters:
720 Fifth Avenue, Room 604
New York, New York 10019 (212) 581-5600

Offers international flights to most European capitals; extensive Middle East and African service; and a Far East route to Bombay, Bangkok, Hong Kong, Manila, and Tokyo.

Bookdealers

ABACUS BOOKS
(carries antiquarian books on Egyptology)
145 East Jackson
Ripley, Tennessee 38063 (901) 635-1771

HYMAN & SONS
(lists rare books on Egyptian culture)
2315 Westwood Boulevard
Los Angeles, California 90025 (217) 474-8023

SAMUEL WEISER, INCORPORATED
(carries antiquarian Egyptian publications)
734 Broadway
New York, New York 10003 (212) 477-8453

Books and Pamphlets

ANCIENT EGYPT; Sources of Information in the New York Public Library. New York Public Library, 1925, New York, Kraus, 1969.

This bibliography lists and classifies the books and articles on the subject of Ancient Egypt that can be found in the New York Public Library. Coverage is up to the conquest of Egypt by the Arabs.

EGYPT. Cairo, Egyptian Ministry of Tourism, 1972.

Discusses aspects of Egyptian history, geography, archaeology, religion, and development. Takes the reader on a tour of various cities and reigons along the Nile River from Abu Simbel in the south to Alexandria at the mouth of the river. The booklet is illustrated with color photographs of ancient splendors and modern cities. Trilingual text in English, French, and German.

EGYPT TODAY: A VIBRANT HERITAGE OF CULTURE, CRAFTS, THE ARTS. Cairo, Egyptian State Information Service, 1981.

A collection of articles on Egypt's culture, crafts, and arts, reprinted from the magazine Cairo Today. The booklet also contains numerous photographs.

THE LITERATURE OF EGYPT AND THE SOUDAN FROM THE EARLIEST TIMES TO THE YEAR 1885 INCLUSIVE. By Prince Ibrahim Hilmy. London, Routledge and Kegan Paul, 1886, Nendelin, Lichtenstein, Kraus Reprint, 1966.

An alphabetical listing of books, articles, papers of societies, maps and charts, ancient papyri, manuscripts and drawings all relating to Egypt and the Soudan. A two-volume set.

MODERN EGYPT; A List of References to Material in the New York Public Library. New York, The New York Public Library, 1929. New York, Kraus, 1969.

This follow-up edition of Ancient Egypt contains the titles of all works in the New York Public Library's collection relating to Modern Egypt.

TOURISM. By Egyptian State Information Service. Cairo, Al-Ahram Press, 1981.

A booklet describing and illustrating the main sites of antiquities and other tourist attractions in Egypt.

TRAVEL INFORMATION ON EGYPT. New York, Egyptian Tourist Office, 1974.

A brochure containing information on visas, currency, customs regulations, transportation, driving, climate, clothing, and communications.

Audiovisual Material

FILMS

ANCIENT CIVILIZATIONS: EGYPT. Super 8 mm. Color. Silent with study guide. 4 minutes. By Coronet Instructional Media, Chicago, 1974.

Describes the development of agriculture, writing, and architecture in ancient Egypt. With captions.

ANCIENT EGYPT. Videocassette and 16 mm. Color and sound. 51 minutes. Time-Life Films. Producer: Brian Brake. New York, Time-Life Multimedia, 1971.

Shows examples of ancient Egyptian art and architecture while briefly outlining Egypt's history. Traces the development of Egyptology and includes interviews with Egyptologists and archaeologists currently working in Egypt.

ANCIENT EGYPT. 16 mm. Color and sound. 11 minutes. Consultants: Anita M. Walker, Elizabeth W. Ransom. Chicago, Coronet Instructional Media, 1977.

Traces Egypt's ancient past in North Africa's Nile Valley through the Pyramid Age and the Middle Kingdom to the empire's destruction by the Assyrians. Includes study guide. Revised version of the motion picture issued in 1952 under the same title.

ARTS OF EGYPT. Videocassette. Color and sound. 30 minutes. Stamford, Connecticut, Educational Dimensions Group, 1979.

Highlights the art, architecture, and crafts in Egypt throughout the ages.

EGYPT: LAND OF ANTIQUITY. 16 mm. Color and sound. 17 minutes. By Paul Hoefler Productions. Released by Bailey-Film Associates, Santa Monica, California, 1969.

Explores the Nile River valley and shows the ancient hieroglyphics carved into rock faces, mountains, temples, obelisks, and tombs. Describes the important part played by the Nile throughout the history of Egypt. Includes scenes of the Sphinx and the great pyramids.

EGYPT: PARTNERSHIP ALONG THE NILE. 16 mm. Color and sound. 28 minutes. Catholic Relief Services. Distributed by Modern Talking Pictures, 5000 Park Street North, Saint Petersburg, Florida 33709.

In a country symbolized by the timeless Nile River, the similarities and contrasts between the modern and the traditional methods of agriculture, marketing and construction are blatant. This program describes the Catholic Relief Services' efforts to help the needy of urban and rural Egypt move into the 1980's.

EGYPT: SABHA DISCOVERS THE PAST. 16 mm. Color and sound. 20 minutes. By Universal Education and Visual Arts, Universal City, California, 1967.

Portrays the daily experiences of a young Bedouin girl whose family has come from the Libyan desert to an Egyptian village in search of a better life.

EGYPT TODAY: THE UNITED ARAB REPUBLIC. 16 mm. Color and sound. 17 minutes. By Paul Hoefler Productions. Released by Bailey-Film Associates, Santa Monica, California, 1969.

Explores modern Egypt, including scenes of the old and new sections of Cairo and of the primitive farming practices carried on by the majority of the people.

EGYPT'S PYRAMIDS, HOUSES OF ETERNITY. Videocassette and 16 mm. Color and sound. 22 minutes. National Geographic Society, Washington, The Society, c. 1978.

Deals with the architectural evolution and historical background of Egyptian pyramids at Saqqara, Dahshur, Meidum, and Giza. Includes teacher's guide.

EGYPTIAN VILLAGERS. 16 mm. Color and sound. 14 minutes. Man and His World series. By Public Media, Incorporated. Released by Films Incorporated, Wilmette, Illinois, 1969.

Describes agricultural practices in an Egyptian village near the Nile. Shows three cotton crops being harvested and night-time irrigation being carried on with hand-operated waterwheels. Points out that village life is a mixture of old and new cultures. Includes scenes of modern schools, the government-sponsored health program, and the muezzin call for midnight prayer.

IN SEARCH OF PYRAMID SECRETS. Videocassette and 16 mm. Color and sound. 24 minutes. Alan Landsburg Productions, Narrator: Leonard Nimoy, Santa Monica, California, Pyramid Films, 1978.

Focuses on the pyramids of ancient Egypt, discussing their design and construction and presenting a closeup view of their surfaces and interiors. Also examines the Egyptians' burial practices and religious beliefs. Includes teacher's guide.

IN THE BEGINNING. Videocassette and 16 mm. Color and sound. 58 minutes. Reader's Digest Association, Santa Monica, California, Pyramid Films, 1975. Producer: Colin Clark; Director: Michael Gill; Writer: Kenneth Clark; Photographer: Walter Lassally.

Sir Kenneth Clark takes the viewer on a personal odyssey as he journeys through Egypt and the Nile Valley. Examines the beginnings and development of Egyptian civilization as expressed in its early art and architecture. Includes teacher's guide. Shorter version (27 minutes) also issued.

KING TUTANKHAMUN. Videocassette. Color and sound. 30 minutes. Agency for Instructional Television. Made by KCPQ-TV, Tacoma, Washington. Bloomington, Incorporated, The Agency, 1980, made 1978.

Dramatizations and archival photos depict the 1922 discovery of King Tut's tomb. Examines the treasures and relates the activities of Egyptians of that era to those of today. Contents: Part 1. Life; Part 2. Death.

A MATTER OF LIFE AND DEATH. 16 mm. Color and sound. 30 minutes. By British Broadcasting Corporation-TV, London. Writer and narrator: Robert Erskine. Released in the United States by Time-Life Films, New York, 1970.

Describes the everyday activities of the ancient Egyptians, using models, paintings, and reliefs found in their tombs.

NILE DESERT CROPS. 8 mm. Color. Silent. 3 minutes. Institut fur Film und Bild, Munich. Edited and released in the United States by Films Incorporated, 1972.

Gives a view of land near the Nile River. Shows the Aswan High Dam, and irrigation canals. Describes how man is able to cultivate ground and grow crops in the desert.

NILE RIVER JOURNEY. 8 mm. Color. Silent. 3 minutes. Institut fur Film und Bild, Munich. Edited and released in the United States by Films Incorporated, 1972.

Follows the journey of a passenger boat up the Nile River from Malakal to Juba.

OF TIME, TOMBS, AND TREASURES: THE TREASURES OF TUTANKHAMUN. 16 mm. Color and sound. 29 minutes. Exxon Corporation. Made by Charlie/Papa Productions, New York, Exxon, 1977.

Takes a close look at artifacts in the exhibit entitled The Treasures of Tutankhamun, seen in various cities in the United States beginning in 1976.

THE STORY OF MODERN EGYPT. Videocassette and 16 mm. Black and white. Sound. 20 minutes. BBC-TV, New York, Time-Life Multimedia, 1970.

Describes Egypt's occupation and rule by England until 1922 and her subsequent rule by King Faud, King Farouk, and Gamul Abdul Nasser. Discusses Nasser's pan-Arabic policies, the controversy over the nationalization of the Suez Canal, and the Arab-Israeli war of 1967. In Spanish.

THE THOUSAND YEAR WALK. 16 mm. Color and sound. 30 minutes. By British Broadcasting Corporation-TV, London. Released in the United States by Time-Life Films, New York, 1970.

Shows the reliefs and inscriptions which cover the Egyptian temple of Karnak, and points out that these reliefs and inscriptions are a recording of the political events of a thousand years of empire from 1800 B.C. Traces the history of the temple and its construction.

THE TREASURES OF KING TUT. 16 mm. Color and sound. 15 minutes. Stamford, Connecticut, Educational Dimensions Group, 1978.

Surveys the art objects, gold and jewels found in King Tut's tomb.

THE TREASURES OF KING TUT. Videocassette. Color and sound. 20 minutes. Stamford, Connecticut, Educational Dimensions Group, 1979.

Focuses on the moment of discovery as Lord Carnarvon and Howard Carter open the tomb of King Tut. Adapted from the filmstrip issued in 1978 under the same title.

TUT, THE BOY KING. 16 mm. Color and sound. 52 minutes. National Broadcasting Company, Wilmette, Illinois, Films Incorporated, 1977.

A tour of the Egyptian treasures taken from the tomb of King Tutankhamun. This program, which was taken from the television special of the same title, features Orson Welles in an on-screen narration of a traveling exhibition at the National Gallery of Art, Washington, D.C. Includes poster.

A collection of short documentaries depicting ancient and modern Egypt is available from the Embassy of Egypt. For further information, contact:

Press and Information Office
Embassy of Egypt
1825 Connecticut Avenue, Northwest
Washington, D.C. 20009 (202) 667-3402

ESTONIANS

Consulates

CONSULATE GENERAL
9 Rockefeller Plaza
New York, New York 10020 (212) 247-1450

CONSULATE
1053 North Vine Street
Los Angeles, California 90038 (213) 463-5542

Fraternal Organizations

BALTIC WOMEN'S COUNCIL
162 High Crest Drive
West Milford, New Jersey 07480
President: Aldona Pintsch Founded 1947

Estonian, Latvian and Lithuanian women's clubs in the United States and overseas. Unites the women of Estonian, Latvian and Lithuanian origin to preserve native culture; to struggle for restoration of the freedom and independence of their countries of birth; to promote the spirit of Baltic solidarity and friendship among the young generations. Sponsors literary, arts and musical events; also sponsors charitable activities to help Baltic refugees in Germany, Austria and other countries. Works for reunification of Baltic refugee families.

ESTONIAN HOUSE OF BALTIMORE
1932 Belair Road
Baltimore, Maryland 21213 (301) 327-7634

ESTONIAN HOUSE OF CHICAGO
Estonian Lane
Post Office Box 95
Prairie View, Illinois 60069 (312) 537-9585
Director: Oskar Kookla Founded 1964

Seeks to preserve and further Estonian culture and heritage in the mid-West. Activities include chorus singing, folk dancing, sports, gymnastics, theater, literature, art exhibits, religious services, Estonian language school, handicrafts, and overall exchange of Estonian and American cultural heritage.
Publication: Estonian House Monthly Program.

ESTONIAN HOUSE OF LAKEWOOD
Cross Street and New Egypt Road
Jackson, New Jersey 08527 (201) 363-9524

ESTONIAN HOUSE OF LOS ANGELES
1306 West 24th Street
Los Angeles, California 90007 (213) 732-4362

ESTONIAN HOUSE OF MIAMI
111 West 29th Street
Hialeah, Florida 33012 (305) 887-0887

ESTONIAN HOUSE OF NEW YORK
243 East 34th Street
New York, New York 10016 (212) 675-0825

ESTONIAN HOUSE OF SAN FRANCISCO
537 Brannan
San Francisco, California 94107 (415) 421-6670

ESTONIAN HOUSE OF SEABROOK
Post Office Box 116
Seabrook, New Jersey 08302 (609) 455-1660

ESTONIAN STUDENT ASSOCIATION IN THE UNITED STATES OF AMERICA
243 East 34th Street
New York, New York 10016
President: Victor V. Vinkman Founded 1949

University students primarily of Estonian ethnic origin. Seeks the preservation of Estonian culture. Promotes the study of Estonian language, literature, songs, folk art, and history. Sponsors lectures, symposia, and the reading of papers. Provides annual scholarships for graduate studies at Helsinki and Turku Universities in Finland. Maintains a library on Estonian literature, history, and international law. Maintains an alumnae cooperative which is semiactive.
Publications: Sonumitooja (newsletter), semiannual also publishes papers.

WORLD ASSOCIATION OF ESTONIANS
243 East 34th Street
New York, New York 10016
Secretary: Harald Raudsepp (212) 686-3356

Americans of Estonian descent and Estonions in other countries of the Free World. Founded to spread culture and friendship between the United States and Estonia and to gather information about communist atrocities in occupied Estonia and use the data in the fight against communism.
Publication: Meie Tee, monthly.

Public Affairs Organizations

BALTIC WORLD CONFERENCE
243 East 34th Street
New York, New York 10016 (212) 685-0776
President: Ilmar Pleer Founded 1972

Members of Baltic central global organizations, the Estonian World Council, the Supreme Committee for the Liberation of Lithuania and the World Federation of Free Latvians. Purposes are: to emphasize the friendship and harmony that have flourished throughout centuries among Lithuanians, Estonians and Latvians; by joint and mutually agreed action to help the Estonian, Latvian and Lithuanian nations free themselves from the Soviet Russian occupation that is threatening the very physical and cultural existence of the Baltic people; to work towards the restoration of independence of Latvia, Lithuania and Estonia so that the people of the Baltic States may exercise their rights of self-determination. Coordinates world-wide joint political actions; facilitates exchange of information. Is establishing a joint information center.

ESTONIAN AMERICAN NATIONAL COUNCIL
243 East 34th Street
New York, New York 10016 (212) 685-0776
President: Juhan Simonson

JOINT BALTIC AMERICAN NATIONAL COMMITTEE
Post Office Box 432
400 Hurley Avenue
Rockville, Maryland 20850 (301) 340-1954
Chairman: John B. Genys Founded 1961

Representatives of the American Latvian Association in the United States, the Lithuanian American Council and the Estonian American National Council. Coordinates the presentation to the United States Congress of issues relating to the Baltic States of Estonia, Latvia and Lithuania. Seeks the restoration of the independence of the Baltic States and their right to self-determination. Conducts summer internship program for interested students of Baltic/Soviet affairs. Maintains library of 500 volumes. Publishes periodic news releases. Affiliated with the Baltic World Conference. Formerly (1977) called Joint Baltic American Committee.

Cultural and Educational Organizations

ASSOCIATION FOR THE ADVANCEMENT OF BALTIC STUDIES
366 86th Street
Brooklyn, New York 11209
Director: Herbert Valdsaar

ESTONIAN ATHLETIC UNION IN U.S.A., INCORPORATED
43 Genesee Place
Lakewood, New Jersey 08701 (201) 363-4251
Chairman: Eda Treumuth

ESTONIAN EDUCATIONAL SOCIETY
243 East 34th Street
New York, New York 10016 (212) 684-0336
President: Linold Miles Founded 1929

Maintains school of Estonian language and history; maintains library of 3,000 volumes in Estonian.

ESTONIAN LEARNED SOCIETY OF AMERICA
Estonian House
243 East 34th Street
New York, New York 10016 (301) 454-5506
Secretary: Dr. T. Parming Founded 1950

Persons of Estonian descent with Masters and Doctoral degrees, or equivalent, who are interested in Estonian studies. To unite and assist scholars and scientists of Estonian descent, and to further the development of Estonian ethnic studies. Supports research and competitions; bestows awards.
Publications: Newsletter, semiannual; Yearbook, biennial.

Charitable Organizations

ESTONIAN AID
Post Office Box 357
Cooper Station
New York, New York 10003 (212) 675-0825
Executive Secretary: Erich Park Founded 1950

Americans of Estonian origin and refugee immigrants from Estonia. Activities include resettlement of Estonian refugees, assistance in immigration, general counseling, and overseas relief. Offers college scholarships for Estonian students. Maintains a library of about 1,500 books in the Estonian language and on Estonian history, culture, and literature.
Publication: Information Bulletins, irregular.

ESTONIAN RELIEF COMMITTEE
243 East 34th Street
New York, New York 10016 (212) 685-7467
Secretary-General Paul Saar Founded 1941

Founded to provide relief to distressed Estonians in any part of the world through funds for medicine, food, clothing, etc. Makes grants to Estonian Boy Scouts and Girl Scouts organizations in the United States for their activities. Cooperates with government authorities on immigration matters. Obtains employment and other assurances in accordance with regulations of the Immigration and Naturalization Act.

Religious Organizations

ESTONIAN EVANGELICAL LUTHERAN CHURCH
230 South Euclid Avenue
Oak Park, Illinois 60302 (612) 386-6274
Assistant to the Bishop: Dr. Arthur Voobus

Founded in 1917 in Estonia and reorganized in 1944 in Sweden. The North American Church is headed by a Bishop whose seat is in Ontario, Canada.

Research Centers

SUBCOMMITTEE ON URALIC LANGUAGES
Columbia University
404 Philosophy Hall
New York, New York 10027 (212) 280-3963
Chairman: Professor Robert Austerlitz Founded 1959

Principal fields of research: Uralic (Hungarian, Finnish, Estonian, etc.) languages, linguistics, folklore and other aspects of culture. Also provides graduate instruction in descriptive and comparative Uralic linguistics and germane fields. Maintains a library of 25,000 volumes dealing with Hungarian, Finnish, Estonian and other Uralic subjects; George Lowy, librarian. Research results published in books and professional journals.

URALIC AND ALTAIC STUDIES DEPARTMENT
Indiana University
Goodbody Hall
Bloomington, Indiana 47401 (812) 337-2233
Chairman: Professor Denis Sinor Founded 1949

Principal fields of research include Uralic (Hungarian, Finnish and Estonian) and Altaic and Inner Asian (Turkish, Uzbek, Mongolian, Korean, Manchu and Tibetan) language and area studies, also teaching of those languages. Research results published in books and professional journals.

Special Libraries and Subject Collections

ESTONIAN ARCHIVES IN THE UNITED STATES
607 East Seventh Street
Lakewood, New Jersey 08701 (201) 363-6523

ESTONIAN HOUSE LIBRARY
243 East 34th Street
New York, New York 10016 (212) 675-0825
Librarian: T. Peter Park Founded 1972

Subjects: Estonian literature, history and culture.
Holdings: Books, newspapers, pamphlets and photographs.

Newspaper

VABA EESTI SONA (Free Estonian Word). 1949-. Weekly. Editors: Erich Ernits and Harald Raudsepp. Publisher: Nordic Press, Incorporated, 243 East 34th Street, New York, New York 10016. In Estonian.

Offers general, international, and national news coverage.

Magazine

MEIE TEE (Our Path). 1931-. Bimonthly. Editor: Harald Raudsepp. Publisher: World Association of Estonians, Incorporated, 243 East

43rd Street, New York, New York 10016. In Estonian.

Discusses questions of a cultural and political nature of interest to Estonians. Presents a strong anti-communist view and a pro-American leaning.

Radio Program

Minnesota - Northfield

WCAL - St. Olaf College, Northfield, Minnesota 55057, (507) 663-3071. Estonian programs 1 hour biweekly.

Books and Pamphlets

A BIBLIOGRAPHY OF ENGLISH-LANGUAGE SOURCES ON ESTONIA: PERIODICALS, BIBLIOGRAPHIES, PAMPHLETS AND BOOKS. By Marju Rink Parming and Tonu Parming. New York, Estonian Learned Society in America, 1974.

Lists about 660 English language publications on Estonia and Estonians. Includes periodicals, reference books, general works, and publications on culture, history, economics, and other subjects. Arranged by topics. Includes an author and title index.

ESTO - 76. ESTONIAN SALUTE TO THE BI-CENTENNIAL. Baltimore, 1977.

A collection of media documents about the world-wide Estonian celebration of America's bicentennial which took place in Baltimore.

ESTONIA: A SELECTED BIBLIOGRAPHY. Compiled by Salme Kuri. Washington, D.C., United States Library of Congress, Slavic and Central European Division, 1958.

Most titles are in English, but other western European languages as well as Estonian, Finnish, Swedish and Hungarian are included. Arranged according to topics: general reference, the land, the people, history, religion, law, politics and government, economics, social conditions, intellectual life, language and literature.

ESTONIA; Highlights on History, Independence, and Soviet Occupation. New York, Estonian World Council.

A booklet outlining the history of Estonia, the struggle to gain and keep its independence, and its subjugation by the Soviet Union.

ESTONIAN OFFICIAL GUIDE. Baltimore, Baltimore Estonian Society, 1972.

Includes an English translation of the Estonian constitution. Other selections are in Estonian.

THE ESTONIANS IN AMERICA, 1627-1975: A CHRONOLOGY AND FACT BOOK. Compiled and edited by Jean Pennar in association with Tonu Parming and P. Peter Rebane. Dobbs Ferry, Oceana Publications, 1975.

Gives a chronology of Estonian immigration in the colonial period, the nineteenth and early twentieth centuries, the interwar years and the post-war refugee period. Reprints documents germane to Estonian immigration. Includes bibliographical aids and name index.

FILIPINOS
See also: ASIANS

Embassy and Consulates

EMBASSY OF THE PHILIPPINES
1617 Massachusetts Avenue, Northwest
Washington, D.C. 20036 (202) 483-1414

CONSULATES GENERAL

Guam International Center
Fourth Floor
Marine Drive
Tamuning, Guam
(Agana)

30 North Michigan Avenue
Suite 210
Chicago, Illinois 60602 (312) 332-6458

2433 Pali Highway
Honolulu, Hawaii 96817 (808) 595-6316

American General Tower Building
Eighth Floor
2727 Allen Parkway
Houston, Texas 77019 (713) 524-0234

2975 Wilshire Boulevard
Suite 450
Los Angeles, California 90010 (213) 387-5321

International Trade Mart
Suite 1440-43
2 Canal Street, Suite 1440
New Orleans, Louisiana 70130 (504) 524-2755

Philippine Center
556 Fifth Avenue
New York, New York 10036 (212) 764-1330

Philippine Center Building
6th Floor
447 Sutter Street
San Francisco, California 94108 (415) 433-6666

Center Building
Suites 422-430
810 Third Avenue
Seattle, Washington 98104 (206) 624-7703

Mission to the United Nations

PHILIPPINE MISSION
556 Fifth Avenue
New York, New York 10036 (212) 764-1300

Tourist and Travel Offices

PHILIPPINE TOURIST OFFICE

556 Fifth Avenue
New York, New York 10036 (212) 764-1330

445-447 Sutter Street
San Francisco, California 94108 (415) 433-6666

2975 Wilshire Boulevard
Los Angeles, California 90010 (213) 387-5321

Fraternal Organizations

COUNCIL OF UNITED FILIPINO ORGANIZATIONS, INCORPORATED
4208 Lookout Road
Virginia Beach, Virginia 23455
President: Dr. Manuel Hipol

FILIPINO AMERICAN COMMUNITY OF LOS ANGELES, INCORPORATED
1740 West Temple Street
Los Angeles, California 90026 (213) 483-1597
President: Remedios V. Geaga Founded 1945

A non-profit, charitable organization for persons of Filipino descent or affiliation by marriage. Awards scholarship grants to deserving and needy Filipinos. Protects legimate interests of all Filipinos. Preserves the national heritage. The cultural center is a nucleus for all community activities - civic, social, educational, and cultural. Administers funded programs for senior citizens, such as the senior citizens nutrition and multi-service programs.
Publication: Filipino American Community Bulletin, monthly.

THE FILIPINO COMMUNITY OF SAN FRANCISCO, INCORPORATED
2970 California Street
San Francisco, California 94115 (415) 346-7252

MILITARY ORDER OF THE CARABAO
4242 East-West Highway
Chevy Chase, Maryland 20015
Secretary-Treasurer: Ralph M. Bogart (301) 654-2277
Founded 1900

Commissioned officers of the United States armed services who have served in or adjacent to the Philippines in peace or war.

Professional Organizations

ASSOCIATION OF PHILIPPINE-AMERICAN NURSES
c/o Mrs. Fe Catama
10023 West Constable Court
Fairfax, Virginia 22032 (703) 323-9299

ASSOCIATION OF PHILIPPINE PRACTICING PHYSICIANS IN AMERICA
15666 Snow Road
Brook Park, Ohio 44142
Executive Secretary: Arturo S. Busa (216) 267-5060
Founded 1972

Individuals from the Philippines, who are licensed to practice medicine in the United States. Conducts medical research. Sponsors seminars and conventions offering creditation hours for physicians. Makes charitable contributions to render free medical care to indigent persons; to establish a continuing medical education program for physicians; to provide aid for education of physicians; and to support medical research.
Publications: APPPA News, quarterly; Directory, biennial; plans to publish Journal of Medicine.

PHILIPPINE LAWYERS ASSOCIATION
c/o Mr. Julio Macaranas, Jr.
9026 Parliament Drive
Burke, Virginia 22015 (703) 323-0448

SOCIETY OF FILIPINO ACCOUNTANTS
2010 Buckingham
Birmingham, Michigan 48008 (313) 649-5814
President: Milton White
Founded 1980

Filipino graduates of business accounting courses. Seeks to "enhance the Filipino accountant in the practice of his profession." Conducts seminars and professional training programs; operates job assistance and placement service. Maintains charitable program; compiles statistics. Is currently forming a library. Currently functions on state level only, but plans to expand to form a national society.
Publications: The Account - News and Views, monthly.

SOCIETY OF PHILIPPINE SURGEONS OF AMERICA
c/o Juan M. Montero, II
2147 Old Greenbriar Road
Chesapeake, Virginia 23320
Executive Secretary: Juan M. Montero, II, M.D. (804) 424-5485
Founded 1972

Offers annual continuing education in surgery. Organizes social and cultural activities including reunions.
Publications: Newsletter, quarterly; Directory (membership), annual.

Public Affairs Organizations

ALLIANCE FOR PHILIPPINE CONCERNS
Post Office Box 70
110 Maryland Avenue, Northeast
Washington, D.C. 20002 (202) 543-1094
Coordinator: Dante Simbulan
Founded 1982

Coordinates efforts and mobilizes support of organizations in opposition to the Marcos regime in the Philippines. Is currently directing its efforts towards opposition to the United States/Phillipine Extradition Treaty with a campaign that includes letter writing, petitioning, encouraging people to make their views known to legislators and the publication of a Primer on Extradition. Is particularly concerned with the human rights issue in the Philippines.

CHURCH COALITION FOR HUMAN RIGHTS IN THE PHILIPPINES
110 Maryland Avenue, Northeast
Suite 103
Washington, D.C. 20002
Executive Director: Dr. Dante C. Simbulan (202) 543-1094
Founded 1978

Individuals affiliated with religious organizations concerned about human rights in the Philippines. To share information about human rights violations in the Philippines and to suggest ways that American individuals and religious groups can work to enhance basic human rights for persons in the Philippines. Issues of concern include political prisoners, economic development policies and cultural minorities' rights. Conducts educational forums.

CONGRESS TASK FORCE
1322 18th Street, Northwest, No. 42
Washington, D.C. 20036
Co-Director: Dr. Walden Bello (202) 223-5611

A joint project of the Coalition Against the Marcos Dictatorship and the Friends of the Filipino People. Works to provide Congress, organizations, churches and individuals with information on violations of human rights in the Philippines and the results of foreign intervention. Campaigns for a reduction in United States aid to the Philippines.
Publications: Bulletin, semimonthly.

FRIENDS OF THE FILIPINO PEOPLE
Post Office Box 70
100 Maryland Avenue, Northeast
Washington, D.C. 20002
National Coordinator: Tim McGloin (202) 543-1094
Founded 1973

Persons interested in human rights and in a democratic and non-interventionist foreign policy for the United States. Purposes are "to cut off all United States support for the Marcos dictatorship; to withdraw United States bases from the Philippines and to prevent the export of unsafe nuclear technology to the Philippines." Supports Filipino people in their attempts "to secure full independence and freedom in their country and social and economic justice in the United States." Condemns "domination of the Philippine economy by United States corporations which has been a major cause of the continued poverty and underdevelopment of that nation." Makes available slide presentations and printed material. Maintains speakers bureau. Has sponsored and engaged in educational forums, public hearings, petition campaigns and congressional legislative activity.
Publications: Bulletin, quarterly; also publishes briefs and research papers.

INTERNATIONAL ASSOCIATION OF FILIPINO PATRIOTS
Post Office Box 64
Oakland, California 94668 (415) 548-2546
President: Geline Avila Founded 1976

Conducts educational programs, lectures, and workshops on current developments in the Philippines and on United States intervention in that country. Compiles articles and other resources on the Philippines.
Publications: Philippine Liberation Courier, monthly.

MOVEMENT FOR A FREE PHILIPPINES
National Press Building, Suite 804
Washington, D.C. 20045 (202) 638-0400
President: Raul S. Manglapus Founded 1973

Supports the militant democratic movement in the Philippines. Lobbies Congress to cut military assistance to the Marcos government. Maintains offices in 50 cities around the world. Publishes reports of human rights violations in the Philippines, and attempts to secure the release of political prisoners.
Publication: Free Philippines, monthly.

Cultural and Educational Organizations

FILIPINAS AMERICAS SCIENCE AND ART FOUNDATION
1209 Park Avenue
New York, New York 10028
Chairman: J. C. R. L. Villamaria, III (212) 427-6930
Founded 1976

Resource center and sponsor for activities designed to increase the appreciation for Philippine and other Asian cultures. Sponsors the Town House International School, a culturally diverse pre-school, kindergarten and elementary school. Sponsors art shows, seminars and competitions. Bestows awards. Conducts specialized education, children's services and charitable programs. Maintains library of 150 volumes on art and cultures. Publishes brochures.

JOSE RIZAL CENTER
1332 West Irving Park Road
Chicago, Illinois 60613 (312) 281-1210

PHILIPPINE CENTER
Managing Office
556 Fifth Avenue
New York, New York 10036 (212) 575-7920
Executive Director: Ernesto Llamas Founded 1974

The Center houses all of the official Philippine government offices in New York, the Consulate General, Mission to the United Nations, National Media Center, Tourism Office. Functions as a social and cultural center for Filipinos in the New York area. Also includes a restaurant.

PHILIPPINE CENTER
445 Sutter Street
San Francisco, California 94108 (415) 433-5345

Sponsors cultural and educational activities as well as serving as the official Philippine government office building.

PHILIPPINE CULTURAL AND TRADE CENTER, INCORPORATED
Post Office Box 844
San Francisco, California 94101
Secretary-Treasurer: Frank C. Mangrobang (415) 441-8072
Founded 1972

A private corporation registered in the State of California by a group of Filipinos who immigrated into the United States; some are Philippine citizens and a majority are United States citizens. Engaged in building a Philippine Cultural and Trade Center in the heart of San Francisco, funded by private contributions of shareholders and with loans from local sources. As the name indicates, it will promote the Philippine cultural heritage and products of the Philippines. It will maintain a Filipiniana library. Weekly and periodical social gatherings will be sponsored to enhance comradeship and family ties of the Filipinos. The center will provide apartments to house the needy, maintain commercial shops for Philippine goods and products, and an information center about the Philippines and its people.

PHILIPPINE CULTURAL CENTER FOUNDATION OF SANTA CLARA COUNTY, INCORPORATED
588 North Central Avenue (408) 377-4407
Campbell, California 95008 Founded 1973

Sponsors lectures, art exhibits and musical programs. Provides social and cultural activities. Engages in research on the Philippines. Maintains a library.

Research Center

PHILIPPINE STUDIES PROGRAM
University of Chicago
1126 East 59th Street
Chicago, Illinois 60637 (312) 753-4311
Director: Dr. Fred R. Eggan Founded 1953

A research activity of the Department of Anthropology at the University of Chicago, supported by the parent institution and foundations. Pursues research on Philippine society and culture, including translation of sixteenth and seventeenth century manuscripts regarding the Philippines. Maintains field and resident graduate student guidance liaisons with academic and scientific institutions and personnel in the Philippines. Holds annual seminars. Maintains a library of books, periodicals, and pamphlets on anthropology, sociology, geography, national resources, agriculture, economics, history, linguistics, art, literature, health and welfare. Research results are published in transcript and research report series.

Special Libraries and Subject Collections

PHILIPPINE ASSOCIATION LIBRARY
501 Madison Avenue
New York, New York 10022 (212) 688-2755

Collection concentrates on economics, law and government in the Philippines.

PHILIPPINE HERITAGE COLLECTION
Indiana University Library
Bloomington, Indiana 47401

Subjects: Colonial period in the Philippines; history of Filipino experience in the United States. Special Collections: Boxer and Mendel collections on Portuguese exploration in the Philippines and the Far East. Holdings: Books, archival materials, letters, documents. Publications: Filipinos in the United States Series, irregular.

UNIVERSITY OF MICHIGAN - DEPARTMENT OF RARE BOOKS AND SPECIAL COLLECTIONS
711 Hatcher Graduate Library
Ann Arbor, Michigan 48109
Acting Head: Jane G. Flener (313) 764-9377

Holdings: Books; bound periodical volumes, pamphlets, manuscripts and non-book materials. Services: Interlibrary loans (limited); copying (limited); collection open to qualified researchers.

Newspapers and Newsletters

ASIAN-AMERICAN ADVERTISER. Editor and Publisher: Eduardo G. Fernandez, 2011 West Irving Park Road, Chicago, Illinois 60618.

ASIAN AMERICAN NEWS. Editor and Publisher: David C. Martinez, 3050 West Seventh Street, Suite 101, Los Angeles, California 90005.

ASIAN PACIFIC NEWS. Editor and Publisher: Ernie Flores, Jr., 310 East Eighth Street, National City, California 92050. In English.

BAYANIHAN TRIBUNE. Editors and Publishers: D. V. Corsilles/Ely U. Orias, 524 South King, Seattle, Washington 98104.

FILIPINO-AMERICAN COMMUNITY BULLETIN. Monthly. Editor: Ted A. Villaganas. Publisher: Filipino American Community of Los Angeles, 1740 West Temple Street, Los Angeles, California 90026. In English.

Contains news of special interest to Filipino Americans, particularly in the Los Angeles area.

FILIPINO-AMERICAN. 1942-. Monthly. Editor and Publisher: Emiliano A. Francis, 508 Maynard Avenue, South, Seattle, Washington 98140. In English.

Prints news of interest to the Filipino American community, including stories about people and groups and a calendar of events.

FILIPINO CHRONICLE. 1931-. Bimonthly. Editor: Eduardo D. Caparas, 1410 N Street, Northwest, Washington, D.C. 20005. In English and Tagalog.

Prints articles of national, international and local scope of particular interest to the Filipino American community. A news round up from the Philippines is a regular feature as are recipes and human interest stories.

FILIPINO FORUM. 1928-. Monthly. Editor: Martin J. Sibonga, 4627 43rd Avenue South, Seattle, Washington 98119. In English.

Carries news and articles on the Filipino-American community and its ethnic heritage.

FILIPINO REPORTER. Editor and Publisher: Libertito Pelayo, 41 Union Square, Suite 325, New York, New York 10003.

FILIPINO TRIBUNE. Bimonthly. Editor and Publisher: Pedronio O. Ramos, 2404 West Lunt Avenue, Chicago, Illinois 60645.

HAWAII-FILIPINO NEWS. Monthly. Editor: Juan C. Dionisio. Publisher: HFN Corporation, 1149 Bethel Street, Suite 718, Honolulu, Hawaii 96813.

INTERNATIONAL EXAMINER. Ron Chow, 318 Sixth Avenue, South, Suite 123, Seattle, Washington 98104.

THE MABUHAY NEWSLETTER. The Mabuhay Newsletter, Incorporated, Post Office Box 751, Beaverton, Oregon 97075.

THE MABUHAY REPUBLIC. 1969-. Monthly. Editor: J. V. Esteva. Publisher: Philippine Service Company, 833 Market Street, Room 502, San Francisco, California 94103. In English.

Reports on the social and cultural life of the Filipino community in California. Includes articles on the contribution of individual Filipinos.

PHILIPPINE AMERICAN. Editor and Publisher: Ernie T. Bitong, Suite 2, 2741 Fruitride Road, Sacramento, California 95820. In English.

PHILIPPINE NEWS. Editor and Publisher: Alex A. Esclamado, 148 South Spruce Avenue, South, San Francisco, California 94118.

PHILIPPINE NEWS. Publisher: 5201 South Kimbark, Chicago, Illinois 60615.

PHILIPPINE PRESS. Frank L. Gonzales, 2252 West Beverly Boulevard, Suite 210, Los Angeles, California 90057.

THE PHILIPPINES MAIL. 1930-. Monthly. Editor: Delfin F. Cruz, Post Office Box 1783, Salinas, California 93901. In English.

Carries international, national, and local news, with emphasis on events concerning the Philippines and Filipino-American groups. Contains commentaries and articles on various issues and topics of special interest to Filipino communities in the United States.

THE SOUTHEAST ASIA RECORD. Jerry Underdal and Michael Shorrock, 580 College Avenue, Suite 6, Palo Alto, California.

Magazines

BALIKBAYAN MAGAZINE. 1982-. Monthly. Editor: Rodolfo T. Reyes. Publisher: Celebrity Publications, Incorporated, 912 Pasay Road, Makati, Metro Manila, Philippines. In English.

Each issue includes a calendar of events in the Philippines, articles on dining out, handcrafts, interesting people and weekend activities. Additionally there are feature articles on the Filipino identity, places of historic or cultural interest, international friendship and the economy.

MANILA TODAY. 1982-. Biweekly. Editor: Jose Luna Castro. Publisher: Philippines Journalists, Incorporated, 19th and Railroad Streets, Port Area, Manila, Philippines. American office, 605 14th Street, Suite 500, Washington, D.C. 20005. In English.

A news magazine containing editorial comment, news feature articles, people in the news and regular columns. Intended for overseas Filipinos and those interested in the politics and culture of the Philippines.

NINGAS MAGAZINE. 1971-. Monthly. Editor: Nelson Navarro. Publisher: Angel Cruz, 17 East 16th Street, 4th Floor, New York, New York 10011.

SAMPAUGITA. 1982-. Monthly. Editor: Elisa "Boots" Anson Roa. Publisher: Philippine Journalists, Incorporated, Westory Building, Suite 500, 605 14th Street, Northwest, Washington, D.C. 20005. In English.

A family oriented magazine for overseas Filipinos. Many of the articles feature the Filipino American experience whereas others discuss the cultural scene in the Philippines.

Radio Programs

Alaska - Kodiak

KMXT (FM) - Box 484, Kodiak, Alaska 99615, (907) 486-3181. Filipino programs, 2 hours weekly.

California - Delano

KCHJ - Box 1000, Delano, California 93216, (805) 725-8676 Filipino programs, 13 hours weekly.

California - Dinuba

KRDU - 597 North Alta Avenue, Dinuba, California 93618, (209) 591-1130. Filipino programs, 9 hours weekly.

KLTA (FM) - 597 North Alta Avenue, Dinuba, California 93618, (209) 591-1130. Filipino programs, 12 hours weekly.

California - El Cajon

KECR (FM) - 312 West Douglas, El Cajon, California 92020, (714) 442-4414. Filipino programs, 15 hours weekly.

California - Escondido

KOWN - Box 398, Escondido, California 92025, (714) 745-8511. Filipino programs, 2 hours weekly.

California - San Francisco

KEST - 1231 Market Street, San Francisco, California 94103, (415) 626-5585. Filipino programs.

California - Stockton

KSTN (FM) - 2171 Ralph Avenue, Stockton, California 95206, (209) 948-5784. Filipino programs.

Hawaii - Hilo

KHLO - Waiakea Resort Village, 400 Hualani, Hilo, Hawaii 96720, (808) 935-0091. Filipino programs, 5 hours weekly.

KIPA - Box 1602, Hilo, Hawaii 96720, (808) 935-6858. Filipino programs, 7 hours weekly.

Hawaii - Honolulu

KISA - 904 Kohou Street, Honolulu, Hawaii 96817, (808) 841-4555. All Filipino programs.

Hawaii - Kahului

KNUI - Box 35, Kahului, Hawaii 96732, (808) 877-5566. Filipino programs, 11 hours weekly.

Hawaii - Lihue

KIVM - Box 1748, Lihue, Hawaii 96766, (808) 245-4741. Filipino programs, 10 hours weekly.

Hawaii - Wailuku

KAOI (FM) - 1728 Kaahumanu Avenue, Wailuku, Hawaii 96793, (808) 244-9145. Filipino programs, 1 hour weekly.

KMVI - Box 550, Wailuku, Hawaii 96793, (808) 244-3982. Filipino programs, 7 hours weekly.

Hawaii - Waipahu

KDEO - Box 1007, Waipahu, Hawaii 96797, (808) 677-5667. Filipino programs, 7 hours weekly.

Guam - Agana

KUAM - Box 368, Agana, Guam 96910, 477-9861, TWX 721-6142. Tagalog programs, 5 hours weekly.

Television Programs

California - Los Angeles

KWHY-TV - 5545 Sunset Boulevard, Los Angeles, California 90028, (213) 466-5441. Filipino programs.

California - Oakland-San Francisco

KTVU - One Jack London Square, Oakland, California 94607, (415) 834-2000. Tagalog programs, 1 hour weekly.

Guam - Agana

KGTF - Guam Educational Telecommunications Corporation, Box 21449, Guam, Marianas Islands, Guam 96921. Tagalog programs.

Hawaii - Honolulu

KHON - Western Sun Incorporated, 1170 Auahi Street, Honolulu, Hawaii 96814. Filipino programs, 1-1/2 hours weekly.

KIKU - 150-B Puuhale Road, Honolulu, Hawaii 96819, (808) 847-1178. Filipino programs.

Illinois - Chicago

WCIU - Board of Trade Building, 141 West Jackson Boulevard, Chicago, Illinois 60604, (312) 663-0260. Filipino programs.

Bank Branches in the U.S.

PHILIPPINE BANK OF CALIFORNIA
455 Montgomery
San Francisco, California 94104 (415) 981-7070

PHILIPPINE COMMERCIAL AND INDUSTRIAL BANK
1 World Trade Center
New York, New York 10048 (212) 466-0960

PHILIPPINE NATIONAL BANK

5 World Trade Center
New York, New York 10048 (212) 466-6600

233 South Wacker Drive
Chicago, Illinois 60606 (312) 993-9880

700 South Flower
Los Angeles, California 90017 (213) 489-7210

Commercial and Trade Organizations

NORTH AMERICAN CHAMBER OF COMMERCE
8846 180th Street
Jamaica, New York 11432
Director: Evan Prado (212) 658-4380

PHILIPPINE-AMERICAN CHAMBER OF COMMERCE
565 Fifth Avenue
New York, New York 10017
Executive Secretary: Nenita O. Santiago (212) 972-9326
Founded 1920

Publication: Monthly Bulletins.

PHILIPPINE-AMERICAN CHAMBER OF COMMERCE
c/o Philippine Consulate
447 Sutter Street
San Francisco, California 94108 (415) 391-3655

PHILIPPINE ASSOCIATION
40 East 49th Street
New York, New York 10017
U.S. Director: George Peabody (212) 688-2755
Founded 1950

Industrial, financial, and business firms in the Philippines and in the United States. Founded to aid in the economic development of the Philippines. Headquarters in Manila. Maintains a library on Philippine economics and law.
Publications: Legislative Reports on Philippine Congress, weekly when in session; Philippine Weekly Economic Review; Philippine Mining Reports (including statistics), monthly.

PHILIPPINE SUGAR COMMISSION
1001 Connecticut Avenue, Northwest
Washington, D.C. 20036
General Counsel: John A. O'Donnell (202) 331-1041
Founded 1925

Association of mills processing sugar for local consumption and export. Represents the Philippine sugar industry before executive and legislative branches of the United States government. Studies common problems with United States domestic sugar producers and refiners and representatives of sugar industries of countries supplying the United States sugar market. Formerly called Philippine Sugar Association.
Publication: Philippine Sugar News, monthly.

PHILIPPINE TRADE OFFICES

c/o Philippine Center
556 Fifth Avenue
New York, New York 10036
Director: Paul Cunnion (212) 575-7920

c/o Philippine Consulate General
445-447 Sutter Street
San Francisco, California 94108 (415) 433-5345

c/o Philippine Embassy
1617 Massachusetts Avenue
Washington, D.C. 20036 (202) 387-2810

c/o Philippine Consulate General
30 North Michigan Avenue
Chicago, Illinois 60602 (312) 236-3676

Festivals, Fairs, and Celebrations

Hawaii - Honolulu

FIESTA FILIPINA
Honolulu International Center
Honolulu, Hawaii

Music, food, dancing, and pageantries of the Philippines. Queen pageant and coronation contests, games, songs, and dramas portraying the Philippino revolt against the Spanish. Terno Ball (terno is a Philippine dress), cooking and food show, Concert of the Stars, fashion show of Philippine fashions, Barrio Fiesta, and Santa Cruzan musical play. Begun around 1959. Held for one month in May and June.
Contact: United Filipino Council, 1834 Nweana Avenue, Honolulu, Hawaii 96817, or Jose Sanidad, Areco Travel, 1160 Nuuanu Avenue, Honolulu, Hawaii 96817.

SAMPAGUITA FESTIVAL
Honolulu, Hawaii

Music, dance, drama, art, and other Filipino ethnocultural traditions. Part of the Filipino Fiesta.
Contact: The State Foundation on Culture and the Arts, 250 South King Street, Room 310, Honolulu, Hawaii 96813.

Missouri - Kansas City

FIESTA FILIPINA
Crown Center Square
Kansas City, Missouri

The festival features music, dance, food, and entertainment from the Philippine Islands. Held for two days in mid-July.
Contact: Convention and Visitors Bureau of Greater Kansas City, 1221 Baltimore, Kansas City, Missouri 64105.

Airline Offices

PHILIPPINE AIRLINES, INCORPORATED
North American Headquarters:
166 Geary
San Francisco, California 94108 (415) 391-0270

Flies air routes from Manila to Honolulu and San Francisco; to Bangkok, Karachi, Rome, Frankfurt, and Amsterdam; to Sydney and Melbourne; to Hong Kong, Singapore, Taipei, and Tokyo. Other offices in the United States: Chicago, Dallas, Honolulu, Los Angeles, Miami, New York, Seattle, and Washington.

Bookdealers

EVERYBODY'S BOOKSTORE
17 Brenham Place
San Francisco, California 94108 (415) 781-4989

IACONI BOOK IMPORTS (books in Tagalog)
300 Pennsylvania Avenue
San Francisco, California 94107 (415) 285-7393

PHILIPPINE & ASIAN BOOK CENTER
611 Geary Street
San Francisco, California 94102 (415) 673-2660

Books and Pamphlets

A BIBLIOGRAPHY OF PHILIPPINE ANTHROPOLOGY. Edited by Mario D. Zamora and Jose Y. Arcellana. Baguro, University of the Philippines at Baguro, 1971.

A list of resources on the subject of Philippine anthropology primarily found in the University of Philippines Library. Arranged by eight subjects and within those subjects by author.

BIBLIOGRAPHY OF THE PHILIPPINE ISLANDS, PRINTED AND MANUSCRIPT, PRECEDED BY A DESCRIPTIVE ACCOUNT OF THE MOST IMPORTANT ARCHIVES AND COLLECTIONS CONTAINING PHILIPPINA. By James Robertson. Cleveland, A. H. Clark Company, 1908. Reprint New York, Kraus, 1970.

A bibliography of printed books and pamphlets dealing with the Philippine Islands. There are three sections: Philippine bibliographies and important bibliographical lists; other bibliographies, catalogs of public and private libraries and sales catalogs; and books, pamphlets, etc. containing bibliographical lists, notes, etc.

A BIBLIOGRAPHY ON LAND, PEASANTS, AND POLITICS FOR MALAYSIA, INDONESIA, AND THE PHILIPPINES. Compiled by James C. Scott and Howard Leichter, 1972.

Subdivided into fourteen topics, this bibliography emphasizes studies which deal with social structure and peasant politics. This bibliography would be most useful to scholars relating economic change to social structure and politics.

CALENDAR OF PHILIPPINE DOCUMENTS IN THE AYER COLLECTION OF THE NEWBERRY LIBRARIES. By Paul Lietz. Chicago, Newberry Library, 1956.

A list of all the Philippine documents that make up the Edward E. Ayer collection of the Newberry Library.

THE MARCOS ADMINISTRATION. Manila, National Media Production Center, 1982.

A booklet introducing the ministers and officers of the government, each of whom is pictured. Tells about the duties of each office.

PHILIPPINE BIBLIOGRAPHY. By Charles Houston. Manila, Philippines, University of Manila, 1960.

An annotated bibliography of Philippine bibliographies published since 1900 and before 1957. All bibliographies are in English.

PHILIPPINE BIBLIOGRAPHY, 1899-1946. Edited by Michael Onorato. Santa Barbara, California, American Bibliographical Center, 1968. (Bibliography and Reference Series, no. 10).

A critical bibliography of primary and secondary works plus a few government documents that deal with the Philippine Islands and the experience of the Philippine-American.

PHILIPPINE ETHNOGRAPHY: A CRITICALLY ANNOTATED AND SELECTED BIBLIOGRAPHY. By Shiro Saito. Honolulu, University Press of Hawaii, 1972.

Contains over 4,000 entries for books, journal articles, theses, and mimeographed documents. The first section includes material on the country as a whole classified by subject. The last three sections deal with three major geographic areas of the country, and the entries here are arranged by ethnic groups. Annotations and critical evaluations are provided, as well as a cultural-linguistic group index and author index.

PHILIPPINE RESEARCH MATERIALS AND LIBRARY RESOURCES: AN OVERVIEW. By Shiro Saito. Honolulu, Asian Studies Program, University of Hawaii Library, 1973.

A guide to basic bibliographies, indexes, and catalogs of Philippine materials in the Philippines and in the United States. Surveys major American collections of Filipiniana and describes research materials in the Philippines and indexes and catalogs for their use.

THE PHILIPPINES. Manila, National Media Production Center, 1982.

A portfolio of booklets each dealing with a single theme: Phillipine-American Relations; Land and People; the Economy; Social Development, 1973-82; Ferdinand E. Marcos; and Imelda Romualdez Marcos. Illustrated in color and black and white.

THE PHILIPPINES; A Review of Bibliographies. By Shiro Saito. Honolulu, East-West Center Library, East-West Center, 1966.

A bibliographical essay that describes those bibliographies published in the fields of the social sciences and humanities between 1900 and 1964 that deal with the Philippines.

THE PHILIPPINES IN PROFILE. Manila, National Economic and Development Authority, 1981.

A brochure presenting the land, people, government, legislature, education, labor, tourism, economy, export, import, balance of payments, foreign investments and government expenditures primarily by means of statistical tables.

THE PHILIPPINES IN WORLD WAR II AND TO INDEPENDENCE (DECEMBER 8, 1941-JULY 4, 1946): AN ANNOTATED BIBLIOGRAPHY. By Morton Netzorg. Ithaca, New York, Southeast Asia Program, Department of Asian Studies, Cornell University, 1977.

This annotated bibliography covers books, selections from books, theses and dissertations, published government documents and journal articles. Also provides information on newspapers and journals published in the Philippines during the time period covered in this bibliography.

THE PHILIPPINES. The Land and the People. By Carmen Guerrero Nakpil. Manila, National Media Production Center, 1978.

A booklet introducing the Philippines for the general reader.

PHILIPPINES. Where Asia Wears a Smile. Manila, Philippine Tourism Authority.

A booklet illustrated in color describing the islands of the Philippines: Luzon, Visayas and Mindanao. Includes an outline map.

SELECTED BIBLIOGRAPHY OF THE PHILIPPINES, TOPICALLY ARRANGED AND ANNOTATED. Philippine Studies Program, University of Chicago, New Haven, Human Relations Area Files, 1956.

This bibliography includes primarily those works consulted by the staff of the Philippine Studies Program in preparing the Area Handbook on the Philippines. The bibliography is organized according to the chapter outline in the Handbook.

FILIPINO AMERICANS

AMERICA IS IN THE HEART: A PERSONAL HISTORY. By Carlos Bulosan. New York, Harcourt, Brace, 1946. Reprint Seattle, University of Washington Press, 1973.

ASIANS IN AMERICA: FILIPINOS, KOREANS, AND EAST INDIANS. By Howard Melendy. Boston, Twayne Publishers, 1977. (The Immigrant Heritage of America Series).

Examines the three immigrant groups; their motivations for migrating, how they adapted economically to life in the United States, and their struggles for jobs, equality and citizenship.

THE ELDER FILIPINO. By Roberta Peterson. San Diego, Center on Aging, San Diego State University, 1978.

A study of Filipino old people in San Diego, California which would analyze their characteristic lifestyles and customs.

THE FILIPINO COMMUNITY IN LOS ANGELES. By Valentin Aquino. San Francisco, R and E Research Associates, 1974. (Reprint of Thesis, University of Southern California, 1952).

Concentrates on the occupational, religious, domestic, and social aspects of the cultural life of the Filipino community in Los Angeles. Includes appendices, maps, charts, bibliography and glossary.

THE FILIPINO IMMIGRANTS IN THE UNITED STATES. By Honorante Mariano. San Francisco, R and E Research Associates, 1972. (Reprint of Thesis, University of Oregon, 1933).

Gives a brief history of Filipino immigration to Hawaii and to the United States. Tells about the life of the Filipinos in the United States including description of anti-Filipino feelings and the battle for restriction and exclusion.

FILIPINO IMMIGRATION. By Bruno Losker. New York, Arno Press, 1969. (Reprint of Filipino Immigration to Continental United States and to Hawaii, published in 1931, America Immigration Collection).

The standard scholarly work covering historical, sociological, health and educational aspects of Filipino American life causes for immigration and the effects of discrimination are discussed.

THE FILIPINOS IN AMERICA, 1898-1974; A Chronology and Fact Book. Compiled by Hyung-chan Kim. Dobbs Ferry, New York, Oceana Publications, 1976. (Ethnic Chronology Series, no. 23).

A chronology of Filipinos in the United States and a selection of documents pertinent to their history.

THE FILIPINOS IN CALIFORNIA. By Sonia Wallovits. San Francisco, R and E Research Associates, 1972. (Reprint of Thesis, University of Southern California, 1966).

An attempt to trace the history of the Filipinos in California from their earliest arrival to the 60's and to show the similarities and differences among other minority groups such as the Mexicans, the Japanese, and the Chinese.

THE FILIPINOS IN HAWAII: A SURVEY OF THEIR ECONOMIC AND SOCIAL CONDITIONS. By Roman Cariaga. Honolulu, Filipino Public Relations Bureau, 1937. Reprint San Francisco, R and E Research Associates, 1974.

A survey of the Filipino's social and economic experience in Hawaii (modes of living, reaction to American society and what customs, ideas and beliefs have been carried on) are presented in this thesis.

I HAVE LIVED WITH THE AMERICAN PEOPLE. By Manual Buaken. Caldwell, Idaho, Caxton Printers, 1958.

A personal narrative of the experiences of a Filipino describes family life in the Philippines and how he came to America, his difficulties in finding work and a place to live. Particularly vivid in discussing prejudice in America against Filipinos. Also gives biographical sketches of successful Filipino Americans.

LETTERS IN EXILE: AN INTRODUCTORY READER ON THE HISTORY OF FILIPINOS IN AMERICA. Los Angeles, Asian American Studies Center, University of California, 1976.

An anthology which presents the Filipino experience of immigration and settlement in first-hand accounts.

OUT OF THIS STRUGGLE: THE FILIPINOS IN HAWAII. Edited by Luis V. Teodoro, Jr. Honolulu, University Press of Hawaii, 1981.

Written to celebrate the seventy-fifth anniversary of the arrival of the first Filipinos in Hawaii, this book gives an overview of Filipino experience in Hawaii.

PROFILES OF NOTABLE FILIPINOS IN THE U.S.A. By Precioso M. Nicanor. New York, Pre-Mer Publishing Company, 1963.

Presents brief biographies of ninety-one outstanding, successful Filipinos living in New York and New Jersey. Includes a photograph with each biographical sketch.

THE SOCIAL ADJUSTMENT OF FILIPINOS IN THE UNITED STATES. By Bernicio Catapusan. San Francisco, R and E Research Associates, 1972. (Reprint of Thesis, University of Southern California, 1940).

Provides various data related to the causes of immigration, the problems of adjustment and the efforts of programs to improve relations between the Filipino and native American.

A STUDY OF THE FILIPINO REPATRIATION MOVEMENT. By Casiano Pagchlao Coloma. San Francisco, R and E Research Associates, 1974. (Reprint of Thesis, University of Southern California, 1939).

Focuses on the cultural misunderstandings and relationships between the Filipinos and Americans. Also tries to discover how these misunderstandings affect the Filipino repatriation and the significance of the repatriation movement in relation to both Americans and Filipinos.

UNDERSTANDING THE FILIPINO-AMERICAN, 1900-1976: A SELECTIVE BIBLIOGRAPHY. By Irene Rockman. Monticello, Illinois, Council of Planning Librarians, 1976.

An introductory list of materials about the economic, political, and social life of the Filipino-American. Includes books, government documents, journal articles, theses and dissertations written in English.

VIOLENCE IN THE FIELDS: CALIFORNIA FILIPINO FARM LABOR UNIONIZATION DURING THE GREAT DEPRESSION. By Howard DeWitt. Saratoga, California, Century Twenty One Publishing, 1980.

Audiovisual Material

FILMS

ANG MAGBUBURDA. 16 mm. Color and sound. 8 minutes. Embassy of the Philippines.

A film showing the famous embroidery of the Philippines.

HOW LONG DOES IT TAKE A TREE TO GROW HERE? 16 mm. Color and sound. 26 minutes. Man Alive series. By Religious Television Associates. Released by the Canadian Broadcasting Corporation, Toronto, 1972.

Compares two social situations in the Philippines - the Mindanao Agricultural Settlement Agency and a village of urban poor surrounding Manila harbor.

KASAYSAYAN NG LAHI. 16 mm. Color and sound. 55 minutes. Embassy of the Philippines.

Presents Philippine history through dance, pageantry, costumes and song.

LIFE AROUND THE WORLD: ASIA-PHILIPPINE FARM. Super 8 mm. Color. Silent with study guide. 4 minutes. By Coronet Instructional Materials, Chicago, 1972.

Pictures life in the small villages of the Philippine Islands.

THE LURE OF EMPIRE: AMERICA DEBATES IMPERIALISM. 16 mm. Color and sound. 27 minutes. By Robert Saudek Associates. Released by Learning Corporation of America, New York, 1974.

Centers on the debate on the floor of Congress in 1898 for the islands gained by chance during the Spanish-American War undertaken to free Cuba. Also deals with the debate in the Philippines, where General Emilio Aguinaldo argues with the American military for the freedom promised his people by the United States for their cooperation in the war against Spain.

MAGIC HANDS. 16 mm. Color and sound. 8 minutes. Embassy of the Philippines.

A film showing some of the handicrafts of the Philippines.

PANDAYAN. 16 mm. Color and sound. 8 minutes. Embassy of the Philippines.

Shows the craft of bolo making.

PEASANT ECOLOGY IN THE RURAL PHILIPPINES. 16 mm. Color and sound. 26 minutes. By George M. Guthrie. Released by Psychological Cinema Register, Pennsylvania State University, 1971.

Illustrates wet rice cultivation from plowing to harvest, examines vegetable and fruit production, and shows housing and village industries of a rural tropical area in the Philippines. Shows how poor diets restrict growth and health of children and illustrates the complexity of relationships between culture patterns, physical environment, and limited technology.

PHILIPPINES: LAND AND PEOPLE. 16 mm. Color and sound. 25 minutes. Embassy of the Philippines.

A documentary and educational film showing the landscapes, cities and villages of the Philippine Islands and the activities of the people who live there.

PHILIPPINES: THE FURTHEST CROSS. 16 mm. Color and sound. 52 minutes. By Film Australia, Australian Broadcasting Commission and University of Queensland Press. Released by Australian Information Service, New York, 1977, made 1976.

Provides insight into the historical and cultural background of the Philippines, emphasizing the problem of identity: to be Asian or otherwise. Tells how the Philippines have been colonized twice, by the Spanish, who brought Christianity and a complex social structure, and by the Americans.

A REVOLUTION FROM THE CENTER. 16 mm. Color and sound. 28 minutes. Embassy of the Philippines.

A film depicting the achievements of the New Society.

SOUTHEAST ASIA: INTRODUCING THE PHILIPPINES AND THAILAND. 16 mm. Color and sound. 18 minutes. By the American Association of Colleges for Teacher Education, Washington, D.C., 1971.

Describes the life-style and customs of the people of the Philippines and Thailand, focusing on housing, religion, education, and the production of food and export products.

TOUCH A HUNGRY WORLD - PHILIPPINES. Audiocassette. Color and sound. 12 minutes. Made by Catholic Relief Services.

The Catholic Relief Service shows how it tries to meet the needs of the people of the Philippines from nutrition education to trade training.

FILIPINO AMERICANS

THE FILIPINO IMMIGRANTS. 16 mm. Color and sound. 32 minutes. Filipino Development Associates, 1974.

Documents the contemporary experience and struggle of Filipinos in America. Traces their problems from their journey to the United States to their efforts in overcoming unemployment, poor housing, cultural differences, and isolation.

FINNS
See also: SCANDINAVIANS

Embassy and Consulates

EMBASSY OF FINLAND
3216 New Mexico Avenue, Northwest
Washington, D.C. 20016 (202) 363-2430

CONSULATES GENERAL

Finland House
540 Madison Avenue
New York, New York 10022 (212) 832-6550

120 Montgomery Street
Suite 2175
San Francisco, California
94104 (415) 981-4656

CONSULATES

4200 Wisconsin Avenue, Northwest
Suite 419
Alexandria, Virginia 20016 (202) 362-6300

810 Stolt Lane
Anchorage, Alaska 99501 (907) 272-0951

1105 West 52nd Street
Ashtabula, Ohio 44004 (216) 998-0623

415 West Marine Drive
Astoria, Oregon 97103 (503) 325-0761

1 Dunwoody Park
Suite 130
Atlanta, Georgia 30338 (404) 394-6130

1 South Calvert Street
Baltimore, Maryland 21202 (301) 962-6512

77 Franklin Street
Boston, Massachusetts 02110 (617) 451-0818

6-10 First National Bank Building
Butte, Montana 59701 (406) 723-5411

35 East Wacker Street
Suite 1900
Chicago, Illinois 60601 (312) 346-1150

1 Public Square #1200
Cleveland, Ohio 44113 (216) 621-1113

Post Office Box 61208
Dallas, Texas 75261 (214) 556-0500

2315 East Seventh Avenue Parkway
Denver, Colorado 80206 (303) 377-0536

17631 Norborne Avenue
Detroit, Michigan 48240 (313) 533-8612

700 Lonsdale Building
Duluth, Minnesota 55802 (218) 727-8420

56 Elm Street
Fitchburg, Massachusetts 01420 (617) 342-6035

5000 Kahala Avenue
Honolulu, Hawaii 96816 (808) 737-8888

3000 Post Oak Boulevard
Suite 1350
Houston, Texas 77056 (713) 627-9700

Stevens Shipping & Terminal Company
2831 Talleyrand Avenue
Jacksonville, Florida 32206 (904) 354-0883

4800 Main Street, Suite 100
Kansas City, Missouri 64112 (816) 932-7200

508 Lucerne Avenue
Lake Worth, Florida 33460 (305) 585-6484

3600 Wilshire Boulevard
Suite 1720
Los Angeles, California 90010 (213) 385-1779

1400 West Avenue
Marquette, Michigan 49855 (906) 226-7913

224 Catalonia Avenue
Coral Gables
Miami, Florida 33134 (305) 448-4343

404 Minnesota Federal Building
607 Marquette Avenue
Minneapolis, Minnesota 55402 (612) 335-2259

6913 Cobblestone Way North
Mobile, Alabama 36608 (205) 433-6576

2100 International Trade Mart
New Orleans, Louisiana 70130 (504) 523-6431

C & O Terminal Building
Room 302
Newport News, Virginia 23607 (804) 247-6355

22 Shetucket Street
Norwich, Connecticut 06360 (203) 889-3321

112 Christian Street
Philadelphia, Pennsylvania 19147 (215) 465-5565

9744 West Bell Road
Phoenix, Arizona 85255 (602) 974-4444

1123 Southwest Washington
Portland, Oregon 97205 (503) 223-7355

79 South Main Street
Salt Lake City, Utah 84111 (801) 350-5456

530 Broadway
Suite 750
San Diego, California 92112 (714) 238-4433

515 Union Street
Seattle, Washington 98101 (206) 682-1959

Florida and Oak Avenue
Post Office Box 2349
Florida Citrus Exchange Building
Tampa, Florida 33602 (813) 223-6864

13th and Kidder Streets
Post Office Box 3175
Wilmington, North Carolina 28401 (919) 763-5451

Mission to the United Nations

FINNISH MISSION
866 United Nations Plaza, 2nd Floor
New York, New York 10017 (212) 355-2100

Tourist and Travel Offices

FINLAND NATIONAL TOURIST OFFICE

75 Rockefeller Plaza
New York, New York 10019 (212) 582-2802

3600 Wilshire Boulevard
Los Angeles, California 90010 (213) 387-7181

Fraternal Organizations

FINNISH AMERICAN LEAGUE FOR DEMOCRACY
147 Elm Street
Post Office Box 600
Fitchburg, Massachusetts 01420 (617) 343-3822
Executive Secretary: Savele Syrjala Founded 1904

Formerly called the Finnish Socialist Federation.
Publication: Raivaaja (The Pioneer), weekly.

LEAGUE OF FINNISH-AMERICAN SOCIETIES
Ms. Pia Green
c/o Erik B. Paulson
151 West 51st Street
Suite 200 (212) 582-3649
New York, New York 10019 Founded 1943

Based in Helsinki, Finland, with regional offices in the United States. Promotes cultural exchange between the United States and Finland. In cooperation with the American-Scandinavian Foundation in New York, Finlandia Foundation, Institute of International Education, People to People, Scandinavian Seminar, Thanks to Scandinavia, Sister Cities International (see separate entries), World Experience, Blue Lake International Exchange Program and Friendship Force. Sponsors a Scandinavian Trainee Program, scholarship programs, English teaching in Finland and travel between the United States and Finland. Formerly: Finnish-American Society.
Publications: Suomi-Finland U.S.A., bimonthly.

Cultural and Educational Organizations

FINNISH-AMERICAN CULTURAL SOCIETY OF BALTIMORE
5912 Shady Spring Avenue
Baltimore, Maryland 21237 (301) 866-4899
President: Ilmi Anderson Founded 1974

Founded to promote understanding and awareness of the history and culture of the Finnish people in the United States, including their contributions in music, literature, art, crafts, and in the labor movement.

FINNISH-AMERICAN HISTORICAL SOCIETY OF MICHIGAN
19885 Melrose
Southfield, Michigan 48075 (313) 354-1994
President: Felix V. Jackonen Founded 1945

Founded to preserve the culture and conduct research on the history of Finnish-Americans in Michigan. Maintains a library of books in the Finnish language.

FINNISH-AMERICAN HISTORICAL SOCIETY OF THE WEST
Post Office Box 5522
Portland, Oregon 97208 (503) 281-5439
President: Fred Soyring Founded 1962

People of Finnish ancestry and friends of Finland interested in discovering, collecting, and preserving material to establish and illustrate the history of persons of Finnish descent in the American West. Encourages research on the Finnish language, churches and migration.
Publications: FINNAM Newsletter, quarterly.

Foundation

FINLANDIA FOUNDATION
c/o Dr. Vaino A. Hoover
1433 San Vincente Boulevard
Santa Monica, California 90402 (213) 451-5147
President: Dr. Vaino A. Hoover Founded 1953

Founded to further cultural exchange between the United States and Finland and to preserve and cultivate the heritage and cultural interests of both Americans and Finns. Sponsors scholarship exchange program between Finland and the United States. Bestows awards; sponsors scholarships in music for study at Sibelius Academy in Helsinki, Finland.
Publication: Newsletter, annual.

Religious Organizations

APOSTALIC LUTHERAN CHURCH OF AMERICA
New York Mills, Minnesota 56567 (218) 385-2166
President: Reverend George Wilson Founded 1872

A Finnish body, organized under the name of Solomon Korteniemi Lutheran Society. In 1929 was incorporated as the Finnish Apostolic Lutheran Church of America. In 1962 the name was changed as above.
Publication: Christian Monthly.

SUOMI CONFERENCE OF THE LUTHERAN CHURCH IN AMERICA
516 Villa Verde
Rio Rancho, New Mexico 87124
President: Dr. Raymond Wargelin (505) 898-6673

Research Centers and Special Institutes

INDIANA UNIVERSITY
Uralic and Altaic Studies Department
Goodbody Hall
Bloomington, Indiana 47401 (812) 337-2233
Chairman: Professor Denis Sinor Founded 1949

Integral unit of Graduate School at Indiana University. Principal fields of research: Uralic (Hungarian, Finnish and Estonian) and Altaic and Inner Asian (Turkish, Uzbek, Mongolian, Korean, Manchu and Tibetan) language and area studies, also teaching of those languages.

Museums

PASADENA HISTORICAL SOCIETY MUSEUM
470 West Walnut Street
Pasadena, California 91103 (213) 577-1660
President: Robert R. McClellan Founded 1924

Pasadena home built in 1905 belonging to the Curtin-Paloheimo family, containing original furnishings, antiques, and paintings. Includes a sauna house and a collection of Finnish Folk Art.

PINE COUNTY HISTORICAL SOCIETY
Askov, Minnesota 55704
President: Ronald L. Nelson Founded 1948

Collection features folklore and agricultural items relating to the local Finnish settlers. Historic buildings dating from 1900 include: Great Northern Depot; Old Partbridge Store: Hinckly Memorial Fire Museum; Pine County Historic Rural School. Guided tours, lectures, and films are offered. Closed in winter.

THE SAINT LOUIS COUNTY HISTORICAL SOCIETY
506 West Michigan Street
Duluth, Minnesota 55802 (218) 722-8011
Director: Lawrence J. Sommer Founded 1922

Housed in restored Duluth Union Depot, the collection contains Eastman Johnson paintings; artifacts related to history of Northern Minnesota; books, photographs, manuscript, historical research material relating to mining, shipping, lumbering and settlement of Northeastern Minnesota history. A pioneer Finnish farmstead dating from 1907 has been restored.

SHELDON JACKSON MUSEUM
Box 479
Sitka, Alaska 99835 (907) 747-5228
Director/Curator: Peter L. Corey Founded 1888

Affiliated with Sheldon Jackson College, the museum is housed in the first cement building in the territory of Alaska, 1895. The collection features Haida slate carvings; Eskimo implements, ivory carvings, marks, skin clothing, baskets, kayaks, umiak; Athabascan birchbark canoes, skin clothing, implements; Tlingit relics, totems and totem poles, shaman charms, baskets, ceremonial equipment; Russian Orthodox and Finnish Lutheran religious objects and other historic pieces.

Special Libraries and Subject Collections

FINNISH-AMERICAN HISTORICAL ARCHIVES
Suomi College
Hancock, Michigan 49930 (906) 482-5300
President: Felix V. Jackonen Founded 1945

Subjects: Finnish history, culture, and religion; books in Finnish. Holdings: Books; archives, clippings and pamphlets; minutes to societies no longer functioning. Services: Copying; translation; archives not open to the public.

FITCHBURG HISTORICAL SOCIETY - LIBRARY
50 Grove Street
Box 953
Fitchburg, Massachusetts 01420
Curator of Museum: Eleanora F. West Founded 1892

Subjects: Education; special education; nursing; industrial arts; liberal arts. Special Collections: Finnish Collection, cataloged and maintained to support research on Finnish history, language and culture. Holdings: Books; journals and other serials; newspapers; pamphlets (cataloged); microfiche. Services: Interlibrary loans; library open to public for reference use only.

MINNESOTA HISTORICAL SOCIETY - REFERENCE LIBRARY
690 Cedar Street
Saint Paul, Minnesota 55101
Chief of Reference Library: Patricia C. Harpole (612) 296-2143
Founded 1849

Contains manuscripts and tape-recorded interviews with Finnish immigrants to the United States.

PINE COUNTY HISTORICAL SOCIETY - LIBRARY
Askov, Minnesota 55704
President: Ron Nelson

Contains books and manuscripts on English and Finnish culture, literature and history.

SUOMI CONFERENCE OF THE LUTHERAN CHURCH IN AMERICA
516 Villa Verde
Rio Rancho, New Mexico 87124 (505) 898-6673
Archivist: Ellen Rynanen Founded 1962

Collection contains manuscripts, correspondence, dissertations, documents, pictorial material, and oral history for the use of scholars conducting research on Finnish-Americans.

UNIVERSITY OF MINNESOTA - IMMIGRATION HISTORY RESEARCH CENTER
826 Berry Street
Saint Paul, Minnesota 55114
Director: Rudolph J. Vecoli (612) 373-5581

Newspapers and Newsletters

AMERIKAN UUTISET (American News). 1932-. Weekly. Editor: Topi A. Halonen. Publisher: Northwestern Publishing Company, Post Office Box 158, New York Mills, Minnesota 56567. In Finnish.

Contains international, national, and local news of general interest to the Finnish-American community.

FINLANDIA FOUNDATION NEWSLETTER. Annual. Publisher: Finlandia Foundation, 1433 San Vicente Boulevard, Santa Monica, California 90402.

FINNAM NEWSLETTER. 1962-. Quarterly. Publisher: Finnish-American Historical Society of the West, Post Office Box 5522, Portland, Oregon 97208. In English with occasional Finnish.

Contains promotional literature on Finns in the West, as well as articles on the various achievements of Finnish pioneers, particularly in the Northwest.

INDUSTRIALISTI (Industrialist). 1917-. Semiweekly. Editor: Jack Ujanen. Publisher: Workers Publishing Company, 106 East First Street, Duluth, Minnesota 55802. In Finnish and English.

NAISTEN VIIRI (Women's Banner). 1910-. Weekly. Editor: Helen Kruth. Publisher: Tyomies Society, 601 Tower Avenue, Superior, Wisconsin 54880. In Finnish.

Publishes news and articles of interest to Finnish-American women.

NEW YORKIN UUTISET (The Finnish New York News). 1906-. Weekly. Editor: Anita Valkama. Publisher: Finnish Newspaper Company, Incorporated, 4422 Eighth Avenue, Brooklyn, New York 11220. In Finnish and English.

Offers general news, as well as items on various cultural and social activities and events of interest to Finnish-Americans. Nonpolitical.

RAIVAAJA (The Pioneer). 1905-. Weekly. Editor: Savele Syrjala. Publisher: Finnish-American League for Democracy, 147 Elm Street, Post Office Box 600, Fitchburg, Massachusetts 01420. In Finnish.

Publishes general news.

TYOMIES-ETEENPAIN (Workingman-Forward). 1903-. Three times a week. Editor: T. Poropudas. Publisher: Tyomies Society, 601 Tower Avenue, Post Office Box 553, Superior, Wisconsin 54880. In Finnish.

Provides news and comments in the cultural, political, economic, and trade union fields of concern to Finnish Americans, as well as local news concerning people of Finnish extraction.

Magazines

CHRISTIAN MONTHLY. Monthly. Editor: Alvat Helmes, Route 2, Box 293, Rockford, Minnesota 55373. Publisher: Apostolic Lutheran Book Concern, Route 1, Box 150, New York Mills, Minnesota 56567.

A religious publication of the Apostolic Lutheran Church of America, formerly known as the Finnish Apostolic Lutheran Church of America.

LOOK AT FINLAND. Quarterly. Editor: Bengt Pihlstrom. Publishers: Finnish Tourist Board and the Ministry for Foreign Affairs, Post Office Box 10625 SF-00101 Helsinki 10, Finland. Distributed in the United States by the Consulate General, 540 Madison Avenue, New York, New York 10022. In English.

Presents articles about the country, people, and culture of Finland, health, environment, foods, recreation, industry, and other topics of general interest. A picture magazine attractively illustrated with many photographs, some in color.

SUOMI-FINLAND U.S.A. Bimonthly. Publisher: League of Finnish-American Societies, Mechelininkatu 10, SF-00100 Helsinki 10, Finland. Distributed in the United States by the regional office of the League; contact Ms. Pia Green, c/o Erik B. Paulson, 151 West 51st Street, Suite 200, New York, New York 10019. In English.

SUOMI-OPISTON VIESTI (Suomi College News). 1963-. Quarterly. Editor: E. Olaf Rankinen. Publisher: Suomi College, 601 Quincy Street, Hancock, Michigan 49930. In Finnish.

A college quarterly, this publication contains items related to the activities, events, and affairs of Suomi College.

Radio Programs

Florida - Palm Beach

WPBR - 3000 South Ocean Boulevard, Palm Beach, Florida 33480, (305) 582-7401. Finnish programs, 1-1/2 hours a week.

Massachusetts - Fitchburg

WEIM - Box 727, Fitchburg, Massachusetts 01420, (617) 343-3766. Finnish programs, 1 hour weekly.

Michigan - Ironwood

WJMS - 222 South Lawrence Street, Ironwood, Michigan 49938, (906) 932-2411. Finnish programs, 1 hour weekly.

Minnesota - Cloquet

WKLK - 15 South Tenth Street, Cloquet, Minnesota 55720, (218) 879-6725. Finnish programs, 1 hour weekly.

Minnesota - Eveleth

WEVE - Box 650, Eveleth, Minnesota 55734, (218) 741-5922. Finnish programs, 1 hour weekly.

Minnesota - Grand Rapids

KAXE (FM) - Box 719, Route 2, Grand Rapids, Minnesota 55744, (218) 326-1234. Finnish programs, 1 hour weekly.

New York - Baldwinsville

WBXL (FM) - East Oneida Street Complex, Baldwinsville, New York 13027, (315) 635-3949. Finnish programs, 2 hours weekly.

Television Programs

Michigan - Marquette

WLUC-TV - Post Office Box 460, Marquette, Michigan 49855, (906) 475-4161. Finnish programs, 1 hour weekly.

Bank Branches in the U.S.

NORDIC AMERICAN BANKING CORPORATION
600 Fifth Avenue
New York, New York 10020 (212) 765-4800

(Associated with Kansallis-Osake-Pankki, Helsinki, Finland).

Commercial and Trade Organizations

FINNISH-AMERICAN CHAMBER OF COMMERCE
540 Madison Avenue
New York, New York 10022 (212) 832-2588
Executive Secretary: Tor Sonntag Founded 1958

Publication: Newsletter, 8 times a year.

FINNISH-AMERICAN CHAMBER OF COMMERCE OF THE MIDWEST
35 East Wacker Drive
Suite 1900
Chicago, Illinois 60601
Executive Secretary: Antti Wuorenjuuri (312) 346-1150

FINNISH-AMERICAN CHAMBER OF COMMERCE OF THE ROCKY MOUNTAINS
Post Office Box 1556
Boulder, Colorado 80306
President: Walden Porter

FINNISH-AMERICAN CHAMBER OF COMMERCE OF THE WEST COAST
3600 Wilshire Boulevard
Suite 1720
Los Angeles, California 90010
President: Sven Lillquist

SAUNA SOCIETY OF AMERICA
1001 Connecticut Avenue
Washington, D.C. 20036
Executive Director: V. S. Choslowsky (202) 331-1365
Founded 1965

Importers, manufacturers, builders and suppliers of saunas; persons who operate saunas as a business. Purpose is to provide information to the general public about the construction and use of the authentic Finnish sauna. Conducts program in cooperation with the International Sauna Society in Helsinki, Finland to assist in medical documentation of the use and research into the sauna. Maintains information and referral service.
Publications: Newsletter, monthly.

Festivals, Fairs, and Celebrations

Minnesota - Saint Paul

SAINT PAUL FINNAFFAIR
Saint Paul, Minnesota

Begun in 1975, this annual two-day celebration held in early September features international folk dancing, Finnish crafts such as spinning and weaving, a folk concer, karkeldt, dart throwing, horseshoe pitching, and a Paavo Nurmi mini-marathon.
Contact: Ahvo Paavo Taipale, 765 Rose Avenue, Saint Paul, Minnesota 55106, (612) 774-2172 or 645-2443.

Airline Offices

FINNAIR
North American Headquarters:
10 East 40th Street
New York, New York 10016 (212) 689-9300

Flies the North Atlantic from New York, as well as international routes to Amsterdam, Copenhagen, and other European cities. Other offices in the United States: Boston, Chicago, Dallas, Detroit, Lake Worth, Los Angeles, Philadelphia, and Washington.

Ship Lines

FINNLINES, LIMITED
c/o Scandinavian Marketing Services, Incorporated
535 Broadhollow Road
Suite B34
Melville, New York 11747 (516) 752-9411

SILJA LINE
c/o Bergen Line
505 Fifth Avenue
New York, New York 10017 (212) 986-2711

VIKING LINE
c/o Scandinavian Express International
500 Fifth Avenue
New York, New York 10036 (212) 751-4572

Bookdealers

RED ROVER BOOK SHOP
24 South Tenth Street
Cloquet, Minnesota 55720 (218) 879-8530

SKY BOOKS INTERNATIONAL, INCORPORATED
48 East 50th Street
New York, New York 10022 (212) 688-5086

Books and Pamphlets

FACTS ABOUT FINLAND. Edited by Jyrki Leskinen. Helsinki, Otava Publishing Company, 1979.

Discusses the land and people of Finland, history, government, economy, social and educational policies, culture, sports, famous figures, and provides travel information. Includes illustrations and a bibliography.

FINLAND HANDBOOK, 1979. Helsinki, Finnish Tourist Board and other tourist organizations, 1980.

Contains information about the land and people of Finland, climate, helpful tips for travelers, tourist information on Finnish towns, transportation and tours, sports activities, and a listing of accommodations. A fold-out tourist map of Finland is attached to the back cover of this paperback book.

FINNISH AND BALTIC HISTORY AND LITERATURES; Classification Schedule, Classified Listing by Call Number, Chronological Listing, Author and Title Listing. By Harvard University Library. Cambridge, Massachusetts, Harvard University Press, 1972.

Provides bibliographic entries in shelflist order according to the classification schedule and call number. Also lists works chronologically by publication date. Includes an author and title listing. A volume in the Widener Library Shelflist series.

FINNISH BIBLIOGRAPHY. Hancock, Michigan, Suomi College Library, 1973.

FINNISH MUSEUMS. Edited by Kaisa Gronholm and Anja-Tuulikki Huovinen. Helsinki, Finnish Museums Association, 1973.

Information about the museums and their collections and publications is arranged alphabetically by geographic location. The pamphlet includes a classified index to historical, art, natural history, technical and industrial, and special museums. An illustrated appendix contains photographs of museums and items from their collections.

FOCUS ON FINLAND. Helsinki, Ministry for Foreign Affairs, 1977.

Illustrated booklet gives brief introduction to Finland.

FINNISH AMERICANS

THE AMERICANIZATION OF THE FINNS. By John Wargelin. Hancock, Michigan, The Finnish Lutheran Book Concern, 1924. Reprint San Francisco, R and E Research Associates, 1972.

Discusses what is meant by Americanization, gives background information about Finland and causes for emigration and tells about the distribution of Finns in America, their schools, press, church, societies and participation in political life.

CASE STUDIES OF CONSUMERS'COOPERATIVES; Successful Cooperatives Started by Finnish Groups in the U.S., Studies in Relation to their Social and Economic Environment. By Howard Turner. New York, Columbia University Press, 1941.

Two case studies of Finnish-American consumers' cooperatives (an enterprise or business that belongs to the people who use its services, the control of which rests equally with all the members and the gains are distributed to the members in proportion to the use which they make of its services) are presented in this book. Part I looks at a cooperative society in an industrial New England town (Maynard, Massachusetts), and Part II looks at a federation of 20 cooperative store societies (Lake Superior region). The author draws conclusions from these two studies and makes speculation on the future for consumers' cooperatives.

CONSUMERS' COOPERATIVES IN THE NORTH CENTRAL STATES. Edited by Roland Vaile. Minneapolis, University of Minnesota Press, 1941.

This book is a combination of three studies in consumers' cooperation. Divided into three parts, Parts I and II provide a general and specific analysis of the cooperative experience among Finnish-Americans in the North Central States and Part III contains eighteen case studies of consumers' cooperatives.

THE DELAWARE FINNS; Or, the First Permanent Settlements in Pennsylvania, Delaware, West New Jersey and Eastern Part of Maryland. By Evert Louhi. New York, Humanity Press, 1925.

A history of the Delaware Finns; from their motives that led them to America to the establishment of various settlements and churches.

THE FAITH OF THE FINNS: HISTORICAL PERSPECTIVES ON THE FINNISH LUTHERAN CHURCH IN AMERICA. Edited by Ralph J. Jalkanen. East Lansing, Michigan, Michigan State University Press, 1972.

A collection of essays discussing the Finnish Church in Finland, the early development of the American branch, how it met the challenges of change brought by American culture and church life and descriptions of life among Finnish Americans.

THE FINNISH EXPERIENCE IN THE WESTERN GREAT LAKES REGION: NEW PERSPECTIVES. Edited by Michael Karni, Matti Kaups, Douglas Gilila, Jr. Turku, Finland, Institute for Migration and Saint Paul, Immigration History Research Center, University of Minnesota, 1975.

Papers in this book, which examine how Finnish immigrants organized and worked to shape the cultural patterns of the Western Great Lakes region, were presented at a conference held at the University of Minnesota, Duluth. This conference was the first time scholars from both Finland and the United States shared the results of their research on Finnish-American culture.

FINNISH IMMIGRANTS IN AMERICA, 1880-1920. By A. William Hoglund. Madison, University of Wisconsin Press, 1960.

Discusses the Finnish heritage and how it was reshaped in America. Deals with occupations, associations, family life, politics, religion, and achievements of Finnish immigrants. Includes extensive notes and bibliography.

THE FINNS IN AMERICA: A BIBLIOGRAPHICAL GUIDE TO THEIR HISTORY. By John I. Kolehmainen. Hancock, Michigan, Finnish American Historical Library, Suomi College, 1947.

Includes sections on emigration, employment, economic, religious and social aspects.

THE FINNS IN AMERICA: A STUDENTS' GUIDE TO LOCALIZED HISTORY. By John I. Kolehmaimen. New York, Teachers College Press, 1968.

A bibliographical essay divided into the topics of emigration, settlement and employment, the immigrant's world and American influences.

FINNS IN NORTH AMERICA. By Eloise Engle. Annapolis, Leeward Publications, Incorporated, 1975.

After a brief review of the history of the Finnish people, the author discusses the great migrations and describes the only major concentrations of Finns in Delaware, Alaska, the Great Lakes area, and Canada and the process of their assimilation up to the present time. Contributions of the immigrants to the American heritage are also noted.

THE FINNS IN NORTH AMERICA; A Social Symposium. Edited by Ralph J. Jalkanen. Hancock, Michigan, Michigan State University Press, 1969.

Presents essays, grouped by topics, concerning Finnish origins and history; emigration to America; community life, newspapers, and Suomi College; Finnish-American culture; religious life; social problems and the ethnic heritage of Finns in America.

FINNS IN THE UNITED STATES: A BIBLIOGRAPHY OF ENGLISH AND FINNISH REFERENCES. Edited by Taisto J. Niemi. Kalamazoo, Michigan, Western Michigan College Library, 1947.

Bibliography of titles in English and in Finnish of which most titles have not been translated into English.

THE FINNS IN THE UNITED STATES: THE PROJECT ON FINNISH IMMIGRATION OF THE MICHIGAN HISTORICAL COLLECTIONS. By Keijo Bentley. Virtanen, Ann Arbor, Michigan Historical Collections, Historical Library, University of Michigan, 1975.

Contains immigrant letters sent by Michigan Finns to their homeland, which record not only adventures but the everyday experience of the people who came to America.

THE FINNS ON THE DELAWARE, 1638-1655; An Essay in American Colonial History. By John Wuorinen. New York, Columbia University Press, 1938.

Basic history of the Finns on the Delaware; how and when they came and how they adjusted and lived in the new land. The appendix contains numerous congressional resolutions and reports pertaining to the Finns on the Delaware.

FOR THE COMMON GOOD: FINNISH IMMIGRANTS AND THE RADICAL RESPONSE TO INDUSTRIAL AMERICA. Edited by Michael Karni and Douglas J. Ollila, Jr. Superior, Wisconsin, Tyomies Society, 1977.

A collection of seven essays which present the role of Finnish immigrants in the Labor Movement especially the radical political activities.

FROM LAKE ERIE'S SHORES TO THE MAHONING AND MONONGAHELA VALLEYS: A HISTORY OF THE FINNS IN OHIO, WESTERN PENNSYLVANIA AND WEST VIRGINIA. By John I. Kolehmainen. Painesville, Minnesota, Ohio Finnish-American Historical Society, 1977.

An updated version of the author's thesis. Discusses emigration and rural settlement, the temperance crusade, religious life, worker's movement, cooperative movement, press and libraries, organizational activities, home life and relations with Finland.

HAVEN IN THE WOODS; The Story of the Finns in Wisconsin. By John I. Kolemainen and George W. Hill. Madison, State Historical Society of Wisconsin, 1951.

The story of the Wisconsin Finns; why they left Finland, where they settled in Wisconsin, how they made a living farming, and their way of life. An appendix contains emigration statistics, statistics on foreign born Finns and a summary of institutional activity in Wisconsin.

HISTORY OF THE FINNS IN MINNESOTA. Edited by Hans R. Wasastjerna. Translated by Toivo Rosvall. Minneapolis, Finnish American Historical Society, 1967.

MAYNARD WEAVERS, THE STORY OF THE UNITED CO-OPERATIVE SOCIETY OF MAYNARD. By Frank Aaltonen. Maynard, Massachusetts, United Cooperative Society, 1941.

Tells the story of the Finnish American cooperative founded in 1906 to combat exploitation in the American employment market.

MIGRATION FROM FINLAND TO NORTH AMERICA IN THE YEARS BETWEEN THE UNITED STATES CIVIL WAR AND THE FIRST WORLD WAR. By Reino Kero. Turku, Finland, Turun Yliopisto, 1974.

A detailed scholarly study which looks at the geographical origin of emigration, cyclical phases, composition according to occupation, sex, age and whether individual or family, the competition for emigrants among shipping lines. Includes tables, appendices and a bibliography.

THE SWEDES AND FINNS IN NEW JERSEY. By Irene Fuhlbruegge, Federal Writers' Project, Bayonne, New Jersey, Jersey Printing, 1938.

Describes the settlement and development of a section of the Delaware River Valley in New Jersey by Swedish and Finnish immigrants and records the process of their assimilation. Includes history of New Sweden.

URBAN AND RURAL FINNISH COMMUNITIES IN CALIFORNIA: 1860-1960. By Jerry P. Schofer. San Francisco, R and E Research Associates, 1975.

A sociological study of Finns in northern California especially where they established strong group identities and an active ethnic tradition.

Audiovisual Material

FILMS

FASCINATING FINLAND. 35 mm. Color and sound. 9 minutes. By John Savage. Released by Paramount Pictures Corporation, New York, 1964.

A travelog picturing the rugged countryside of Finland, as well as the modern capital of Helsinki. Examines the peculiarities of the Finnish language and points out the popularity of the sauna bath.

FINLAND - LAND OF WOOD AND WATER. 16 mm. Black and white. Sound. 20 minutes. By Peggie Broadhead, British Broadcasting Corporation-TV, London. Released in the United States by Time-Life Films, New York, 1970.

Describes the population, location, and geography of Finland and points out that it is a leading producer and exporter of wood and paper products. Shows a large pulp and paper mill, a sawmill, and furniture and glass factories. Includes scenes of the winter activities of children.

FINLANDIA. 16 mm. Black and white. Sound. A Columbia Broadcasting System News Special Report. By CBS News and the Finnish Broadcasting Company, Helsinki, 1965.

Traces major events in the life of Jean Sibelius and describes the nature of his music. Performances of Finlandia and other works of Sibelius by the Radio Symphony Orchestra of Finland and the University of Helsinki Chorus pay tribute to Sibelius on the hundredth anniversary of his birth.

GREEN GOLD. 35 mm. Color and sound. 10 minutes. A Movietone Adventury. By Twentieth Century-Fox Film Corporation, New York, 1963.

Presents a tour of Finland, pointing out that two-thirds of the country is covered with rich forests. Shows scenes of Helsinki and describes the activities of Finland's Lapp population.

A TOUCH OF FINLAND. 16 mm. Color and sound. 28 minutes. Finland National Tourist Office, made by Film Authors, Incorporated, New York, The Office, 1978.

Pictures the beauty of a land ruled by nature and man, presenting a symphony of islands, lakes, architecture, art, and honesty that is called Finlandia.

Additional documentary films about Finland, with emphasis on the arts and architecture, may be obtained from:

Films of the Nations
7820 20th Avenue
Brooklyn, New York 11214 (212) 331-1045

FRENCH-SPEAKING PEOPLES
(Includes ARCADIANS; CAJUNS; FRENCH CANADIANS; HUGUENOTS)
See also: ALGERIANS; BELGIANS; HAITIANS; MOROCCANS; TUNISIANS

Embassy and Consulates

EMBASSY OF FRANCE
Chancery
2535 Belmont Road, Northwest
Washington, D.C. 20008 (202) 234-0990

Commercial Counselor's Office
2000 L Street, Northwest
Suite 715
Washington, D.C. 20036 (202) 223-6710

Financial Counselor's Office
2011 Eye Street, Northwest
Washington, D.C. 20006 (202) 296-1653

Transportation Attachè
1050 17th Street, Northwest
Suite 220
Washington, D.C. 20036 (202) 331-1669

Cultural Services
4400 Jenifer Street, Northwest
Room 325
Washington, D.C. 20015 (202) 363-6361

CONSULATES GENERAL

3 Commonwealth Avenue
Boston, Massachusetts 02116 (617) 266-1680

444 North Michigan Avenue
Suite 3140
Chicago, Illinois 60611 (312) 787-5359

100 Renaissance Center
Suite 2975
Detroit, Michigan 48243 (313) 568-0990

2727 Allen Parkway
Suite 867
Houston, Texas 77019 (713) 528-2181

Sunset Doheney Building
9255 Sunset Boulevard
Los Angeles, California 90069 (213) 272-5452

3305 Saint Charles Avenue
New Orleans, Louisiana 70115 (504) 897-6381

934 Fifth Avenue
New York, New York 10021 (212) 535-0100

2570 Jackson Street
San Francisco, California 94115 (415) 922-3255

CONSULATE
2129 Wyoming Avenue, Northwest
Washington, D.C. 20008 (202) 332-8400

Mission to the United Nations

FRENCH MISSION
One Dag Hammarskjold Plaza, 8th Floor
New York, New York 10017 (212) 753-9200

Tourist and Travel Offices

FRENCH GOVERNMENT TOURIST OFFICE

610 Fifth Avenue, No. 222
New York, New York 10020 (212) 757-1125

9401 Wilshire Boulevard, Suite 314
Beverly Hills, California 90212 (213) 272-2661

645 North Michigan Avenue
Chicago, Illinois 60611 (312) 337-6301

323 Geary Street
San Francisco, California
94102 (415) 986-4161

Fraternal Organizations

AMERICAN ORDER OF THE FRENCH CROIX DE GUERRE
159 West 33rd Street
New York, New York 10001
President: Lt. Col. Steven F. Kovach
Founded 1954

American holders of the French Croix de Guerre; French and other allied veterans living in the United States who are holders of the medal. The Croix de Guerre, or War Cross, is awarded by the French government for gallantry in combat. Encourages social exchange and fellowship. Seeks to preserve the traditions of French-American friendship. Cooperates with the Order of Lafayette in many of its activities and in the establishment of the Lafayette Museum in New York City. The United States counterpart of the Association Nationale des Croix de Guerre of France.

AMERICAN SOCIETY OF THE FRENCH LEGION OF HONOR
22 East 60th Street
New York, New York 10022 (212) 751-8537
President: Grayson Kirk Founded 1922

Founded to provide a social and fraternal medium for members of the French Order of the Legion of Honor residing in the United States. Promotes appreciation of French culture in the United States and American culture in France. Strengthens the traditional friendship and goodwill existing between the peoples of the two countries.
Publication: ASLH Magazine, three times a year.

ASSOCIATION CANADO AMERICAINE
52 Concord Street
Manchester, New Hampshire 03101 (603) 625-8577
President General: Gerald Robert Founded 1896

Fraternal benefit life insurance society of American and Canadian Roman Catholics of French descent. Maintains a library of about 25,000 volumes dealing with the French in North America, French classics, and modern French authors.
Publication: Le Canado-Americain, quarterly.

ASSOCIATION OF THE FREE FRENCH IN THE U.S.
40 Park Avenue
New York, New York 10007 (212) 679-8192
President: A. Tchenkell-Thamys Founded 1945

Fraternal society of former members of the Free French Forces, France Forever, or the American Field Service, who either served under General de Gaulle or participated in the liberation of Europe during World War II. Affiliated with the Association des Français Libres (Paris).
Publication: Bulletin, monthly.

COMMITTEE OF FRENCH SPEAKING SOCIETIES
Bureau 930
250 West 57th Street
New York, New York 10039 (212) 246-9397
President: Andre Maman Founded 1927

Federation of French and French-speaking societies. Sponsors celebrations of French holidays (Bastille Day, Armistice Day).

FEDERATION OF FRENCH ALLIANCES IN THE UNITED STATES
22 East 60th Street
New York, New York 10022 (212) 355-6100
Executive Director: Jean Vallier Founded 1902

Federation of local Alliance Française and Cercle Français groups interested in French language and culture, representing more than 19,000 persons. The majority of the groups are in colleges, universities, and high schools. Sponsors lectures in French and English. Helps groups in starting conversation and language programs in French. Provides prize books to be awarded to outstanding students of French in local groups. Awards certificates annually to best students of French in New York City. Presents an annual award to the American contributing most to the Franco-American cultural relations. Formerly known as the Federation of French Alliances in the United States and Canada.
Publication: Annual Report.

FEDERATION OF FRENCH WAR VETERANS
159 West 33rd Street
New York, New York 10001 (212) 695-5195
President: Bruno Kaiser Founded 1919

Veterans of World Wars I and II who are of French origin or descent.

ORDER OF LAFAYETTE
c/o Asa E. Phillips, Jr.
60 State Street
Boston, Massachusetts 02109 (617) 742-2590
President-General: Asa E. Phillips

Officers who served in France during World War I and II. To strengthen the traditional friendship of United States with France. Presents annual Freedom Award for distinguished leadership in combating communism.

UNION SAINT-JEAN-BAPTISTE
1 Social Street
Woonsocket, Rhode Island 02895 (401) 769-0520
President General: Edgar J. Martel Founded 1900

Fraternal benefit life insurance society of Roman Catholics of French origin. Sponsors the Order of Merit and Honor, to recognize outstanding members. Maintains a library of about 5,000 volumes.
Publication: L'Union, quarterly.

Professional Organizations

AMERICAN ASSOCIATION OF TEACHERS OF FRENCH
57 East Armory
Champaign, Illinois 61820
Executive Secretary: Fred M. Jenkins
(217) 333-2842
Founded 1927

Teachers of French in public and private elementary and secondary schools, colleges, and universities. Maintains a National Information Bureau, offering at cost maps, pictures, booklets, and songs in French. Conducts an annual French contest in elementary and secondary schools, giving scholarships to the winners. Awards annual summer study-abroad scholarships to teachers. Sponsors a placement bureau, and a high school honor society. Arranges flights to France. Furnishes traveling art exhibits. Provides a pen-pal agency for exchange letters between French and American boys and girls.
Publication: French Review, six times a year (directory included in May issue); National Bulletin, quarterly.

ASSOCIATION DES PROFESSEURS FRANCO-AMERICAINS
341 Fourth Street
Fall River, Massachusetts 02721
Executive Secretary: Francis J. Martineau
(617) 672-0408
Founded 1964

Founded to help members become better teachers of French. Conducts workshops. Maintains a small library; provides a placement service.

FRENCH ENGINEERS IN THE UNITED STATES
Post Office Box 734
Stuyvesant Station
New York, New York 10009
Secretary-Treasurer: Robert Gueydan
(516) 673-0068
Founded 1944

Professional engineers interested in technical developments in France or developments abroad influenced by French techniques. Founded to foster friendly relations between American and French engineers in all fields. Sponsors monthly lectures in New York City by prominent French and American engineers. Affiliated with the Societe des Ingenieurs Civils de France.
Publication: Newsletter, monthly; Sciences et Techniques (French), ten times a year.

SOCIETE DES PROFESSEURS FRANÇAIS EN AMERIQUE
22 East 60th Street
New York, New York 10022
President: Micheline Herz
(201) 359-3977
Founded 1904

French men and women teaching in American colleges and secondary schools, American and other foreigners teaching French at any level or any discipline relating to French cultures can be members. Sponsors an annual competition in the secondary schools of New York. Offers scholarships for study in Quebec and France. Maintains a placement service.
Publications: Bulletin de la Societe des Professeurs Français en Amerique (including directory), annual; Bulletin II, annual; and newsletters.

Public Affairs Organizations

SOCIETY FOR FRENCH-AMERICAN AFFAIRS
c/o Mr. Benjamin Protter
301 West 108th Street
New York, New York 10025
Secretary-General: Benjamin Protter
(212) 749-3843
Founded 1962

Individuals and university libraries interested in French-American political relations and in international affairs. Formed to study and disseminate information on related French and American political affairs and to work toward a better understanding between Americans and Frenchmen. Distributes French political and news publications to members. Sponsors receptions, dinners, and lectures by visiting French political dignitaries. Requested permission from French authorities to open an affiliate in Paris.
Publication: Today in France, bimonthly.

Cultural and Educational Organizations

AMERICAN-FRENCH GENEALOGICAL SOCIETY
Box 2113
Pawtucket, Rhode Island 02861
President: Robert J. Quintin
(401) 723-6797
Founded 1978

Maintains library of 2,000 volumes on family histories and genealogies.
Publications: Je Me Souviens, quarterly.

AMERICAN FRIENDS OF LAFAYETTE
c/o Robert G. Gennett
Lafayette College
Skillman Library
Easton, Pennsylvania 18042 (215) 253-6281
Secretary: Robert G. Gennett Founded 1932

Individuals, historical societies, universities, and colleges interested in the study of the Marquis de Lafayette (1757-1834), Frenchman who fought in the American Revolution. Promotes historical research relative to Lafayette through the collection of books, manuscripts, documents, and other associated material. Promotes the traditional friendship between the United States and France of which Lafayette is a symbol. Maintains a library that includes mementos, engravings, and original letters; also maintains a museum and a biographical archive.
Publication: Gazette, annual or bienniel.

AMERICAN TEILHARD ASSOCIATION FOR THE FUTURE OF MAN
Box 67
White Plains, New York 10604
President: Thomas Berry Founded 1964

Persons interested in the questions which the writings of Father Pierre Teilhard de Chardin (1881-1955) pose to the modern world. A distinguished French Jesuit paleontologist and one of the discoverers of the Peking man, Teilhard was exiled to field work in Asia and Africa, and forbidden by his order to teach or publish his nontechnical writing on evolution and theology. Twenty-three volumes of his works and letters have been published in the United States, including "The Phenomenon of Man" and "The Future of Man." Central belief of Teilhard's writings was that evolution has not stopped, but merely shifted its emphasis from the material to the spiritual. As evidenced in his work, his interests ranged from spiritual implications of the atomic age, to the biological basis of the democratic spirit, to the nature of Christian education. ATCA maintains a speakers bureau and a 670 volume reference and lending library of books, periodicals and other works by and about Teilhard. An international committee sponsors publication of his collected works. Formerly: (1975) American Teilhard de Chardin Association.
Publications: The Teilhard Review (in cooperation with the Teilhard Centre for the Future of Man in London), three times a year; Newsletter, two times a year; also publishes Teilhard Studies (monograph series) and a basic Teilhard bibliography and offers a cassette tape series on the thought of Teilhard de Chardin.

CONFERENCE GROUP ON FRENCH POLITICS AND SOCIETY
Institute of International Studies
University of South Carolina
Columbia, South Carolina 29208
Executive Secretary: D. Bruce Marshall (803) 777-8180
Founded 1974

Independent association of scholars concerned with the study of contemporary French political and social issues. Holds conferences on French problems in conjunction with other specialized groups. Awards prize for best doctoral dissertation on contemporary French politics and social problems submitted during the previous two years.
Publications: Newsletter, quarterly; Checklist of Current Books on French, irregular; Research and Teaching Register (includes directory), irregular.

CONFRERIE DES CHEVALIERS DU TASTEVIN
Commanderie D'Amerique
22 East 60th Street
New York, New York 10022 (212) 751-8576
President: S. T. Harris Founded 1934

Select social order of wine lovers and gourmands. Encourages use of products of Burgundy, particularly wines and regional cuisine; revival of Burgundian folklore; visits to Burgundy. Promotes viticultural and gastronomic education. Local groups sponsor occasional dinners at which a ceremonial "inspired by the common sense and the philosophy of Moliere and by the truculence and the optimism of Rabelais" is followed. Aims to restore the Bacchic rites of the past, especially those of a certain Ordre de la Boisson, founded in 1703. Headquarters: Chateau du Clos de Vougeot, Cote-d'Or, France.
Publications: Tastevin en Main (from France); Quoi de Neuf (from USA).

FACETS TOUR FRANCE
485 Madison Avenue
New York, New York 10022 (212) 838-9290
President: Dominque Decaudin Founded 1970

Created by the French Ministry of Education for the promotion and organization of student programs and educational travel in Europe. Sponsors summer study programs in Spain, Italy and France as well as year-round travel programs. Formerly: (1980) Franco American Committee for Educational Travel and Studies.
Publications: Brochure, semiannual.

FEDERATION OF FRANCO-AMERICAN GENEALOGICAL AND HISTORICAL SOCIETIES
Post Office Box 2113
Pawtucket, Rhode Island 02861 (603) 356-3009
President: Robert J. Quintin Founded 1981

Genealogical and historical societies that have collections of Franco-American resources helpful to researchers doing genealogical and local historical studies. Seeks to act as spokesman for its membership in dealing with various public and private agencies having appropriate genealogical and historical holdings, and to accumulate and disseminate information helpful to individuals and groups doing Franco-American research. Compiles statistics; maintains biographical archives.
Publications: Franco-American Genealogical Information Service, quarterly.

FRANCE AND COLONIES PHILATELIC SOCIETY
103 Spruce Street
Bloomfield, New Jersey 07003
Secretary: Walter E. Parshall Founded 1936

Collectors of the postage stamps of France, Monaco, and all the French colonies, past and present. Presents annual Gerard Gilbert Memorial Award for the best English publication related to French philately.
Publication: The France and Colonies Philatelist, quarterly. Also publishes Glossary for Collectors of France, indexes, keys and lists of postmarks, post offices and stamps.

FRENCH INSTITUTE - ALLIANCE FRANÇAISE DE NEW YORK
22 East 60th Street
New York, New York 10022
Executive Director: Jean Vallier (212) 355-6100
Founded 1971

Seeks to encourage the study of French language and culture, and foster friendly relations between French and American peoples. Offers classes in French, lectures, films, concerts, slide lectures, and special events. Administers a program of postgraduate study scholarships to French students in the United States and American students in France. Maintains a library of about 35,000 volumes (in French) on French literature, art, and history. Formed by the merger of the Alliance Française de New York and the French Institute in the United States.
Publications: French XX Bibliography, annual; Alliance (magazine) biennial.

HUGUENOT HISTORICAL SOCIETY
Post Office Box 339
New Paltz, New York 12561
President: Kenneth E. Hasbrouck (914) 255-1660
Founded 1894

Persons interested in the preservation of Huguenot history. Restored and maintains the stone houses and buildings of Huguenot Street, now a National Historic Site, at New Paltz, New York. The site now contains seven houses, a farm museum, two museums, a wildlife sanctuary, and a rebuilt French church dating from 1717. Maintains a library and biographical archive of about 4,000 books and manuscripts on Huguenot history, genealogy, and culture.
Publications: Letters, quarterly; Report, quarterly; Newsletter, quarterly; Yearbook, biennial.

INSTITUTE FOR AMERICAN UNIVERSITIES
27 Place De L'Universite
F-13625 Aix-En-Provence, France
President: Herbert Maza Founded 1957

Provides a program of study abroad for American undergraduates and graduate students from more than 450 United States universities. Provides French Civilization Program in Avignon, France; European Business Studies in Toulon, France; British Studies Centre in Canterbury, England. Conducts research and educational programs in areas of Mediterranean studies and European civilization. Maintains library of 18,000 volumes on European civilization, Mediterranean studies and French language and literature; a language laboratory; and microfilm archives.
Divisions: Advanced French Program; French Honors Program; Intaglio Printmaking; Mediterranean and European Area Studies; Studio Art.
Publications: Bulletin, annual; LaCigale, annual; Alumni Directory, quinquennial.

MALRAUX SOCIETY
3231 University Station
University of Wyoming
Laramie, Wyoming 82071
Executive Secretary: Walter G. Langlois (307) 766-4177
Founded 1969

Persons interested in the life and writings of Andre Malraux (1901-1976), French novelist and art critic. For many years, a minister of Charles de Gaulle, Malraux published in 1970 his reminiscences of the General, titled "Les Chenes qu'on abat." Coordinates research activities relating to Malraux, particularly theses; records sources of information and materials; facilitates exchange of information. Engaged in organizing a Malraux archive, primarily for original materials, via machine duplication, etc.

Publications: Melanges Malraux Miscellany, semi-annual; Serie Andre Malraux (Yearbook), annual.

MASSENET SOCIETY/AMERICAN BRANCH
Post Office Box 294
Old Greenwich, Connecticut 06870 (203) 874-7125
Secretary: Martin S. Lippman Founded 1977

People interested in operas; specifically, in the French repertoire and works of French composer Jules Massenet (1842-1912). Objective is to promote a greater knowledge and understanding of the life and works of Massenet by encouraging performances of his music and organizing cultural and social functions for members and the general public. Conducts quarterly lectures and concerts. Plans to publish compendium of detailed plot synopses for all of Massenet's published operas and oratorios, including stage production information.

NATIONAL HUGUENOT SOCIETY
9027 South Damen Avenue
Chicago, Illinois 60620
President General: Mrs. Luther D. Swanstrom

Individuals of Protestant faith over 18 years old and lineally descended from men and women called "Huguenots," who because of religious persecution in France emigrated to America or other countries or remained in France after the promulgation of the Edict of Toleration in 1787. Seeks to commemorate the events of Huguenot history; collect and preserve historical data and relics of Huguenot life, manners, and customs. Sponsors various patriotic, educational, charitable, and religious projects.
Publications: Cross of Languedoc (newsletter), biennial.

PAUL CLAUDEL SOCIETY
c/o Dr. Ann Bugliani
Loyola University
6525 North Sheridan Road
Chicago, Illinois 60626 (312) 274-3000
President: Ann Bugliani Founded 1968

College professors and high school teachers. Provides a forum for discussion. Encourages and supports critical studies. Provides research materials. Encourages the performance of dramatic works. Discusses related authors and works, and in general brings together those interested in the life and works of Paul Claudel (1868-1955), French diplomat, poet, and dramatist.
Publication: Claudel Studies, quarterly.

PERE MARQUETTE MEMORIAL ASSOCIATION
716 East Ludington Avenue
Ludington, Michigan 49431 (616) 843-4622
President: Eugene Christman Founded 1936

Maintains Memorial cross and markers near Ludington, Michigan, commemorating the death of Jacques Marquette (1637-1675), a French Jesuit priest and missionary (also known as Pere Marquette) who explored Canada and northern Michigan. Marquette is believed to have died south of Ludington on May 18, 1675 and the Association sponsors an annual pilgrimage to the death site. Promoted special recognition for him in 1975, the tercentenary of his death. Has published a booklet on the life of Pere Marquette.

PHENOMENON OF MAN PROJECT
Post Office Box 836
South Pasadena, California 91030
President: Robert L. Stowell Founded 1962

Founded to advance the thinking and writing of French Jesuit paleontologist and philosopher Pierre Teilhard de Chardin. Specifically focuses on The Phenomenon of Man, published in English in 1959, Teilhard's best known and most widely quoted book. The POM Project informs members of books, films, TV and radio broadcasts relating to Teilhard. Assists in organizing meetings, conferences, and lecture-seminars. Helps in organizing study groups. Provides illustrated lectures, study kits, and other aids for private study groups. Functions as an information center for the intercommunication of like-minded groups. Affiliated with the American Teilhard de Chardin Association.
Publication: Phenomena (newsletter), quarterly.

PROUST RESEARCH ASSOCIATION
Department of French and Italian
Lawrence, Kansas 66045 (913) 864-4728
Editor: J. Theodore Johnson Founded 1967

Scholars interested in the twentieth century French writer Marcel Proust (1871-1922). Provides a forum for problems relating to current research on Proust. Maintains loose contact with Proust groups in Europe.
Publication: Newsletter, semiannual (including bibliographic material).

SOCIETE HISTORIQUE ET FOLKLORIQUE FRANCAISE
56-52 203rd Street
Bayside, New York 11364 (212) 225-4453
President: Pierre Courtines Founded 1936

Teachers, historians, and others interested in French folklore and historical studies; includes libraries on a subscription basis. Promotes interest in Franco-American cultural and historical relations. Participates in anniversaries and other celebrations commemorating Franco-American events and national figures. Records aspects of French folklore and history. Also known as the French Folklore Society.
Publications: Bulletin of French Folklore Society, annual; occasionally prints materials on French dances, songs, etc.

SOCIETY FOR FRENCH AMERICAN CULTURAL SERVICES AND EDUCATIONAL AIDS
972 Fifth Avenue
New York, New York 10021
Executive Director: Anne Marie Marotte
(212) 570-4400
Founded 1955

Prepares and lends for a fee materials to schools, universities, libraries, museums, and educational organizations for use in French language and civilization, art, social studies, and science courses, and wherever France is the subject of study. Materials available for loan include films, slides and television series. Sells brochures and posters. Also known as FACSEA.
Publications: Newsletter, monthly; Documentation, annual; Short Film Catalogue, annual; also publishes long feature film catalogue and scientific and medical film catalogue.

SOCIETY FOR FRENCH HISTORICAL STUDIES
c/o Alexander Sedgwick
Department of History
Randall Hall, University of Virginia
Charlottesville, Virginia 22903
Executive Officer: Alexander Sedgwick
Founded 1955

Professional historians and people interested in French history. Seeks to further the study of French history in the United States and Canada. Affiliated with the Societe d'Histoire Moderne, Paris, France.
Publication: French Historical Studies, semiannual.

Foundations

FRENCH-AMERICAN FOUNDATION
680 Park Avenue
New York, New York 10021
Chairman: Arthur King Peters
(212) 734-7344
Founded 1977

To strengthen relations between the United States and France by initiating working contacts between French and American professionals who address problems of major concern to both societies and reducing the misperceptions which hinder each country's understanding of the other. Conducts projects which stimulate change including exchanges of specialists, internships, study tours, conferences, research fellowships, surveys and special studies. Sponsors Tocqueville Grant Program, Saint-John Perse Research Fellowship, seminars in Contemporary American Studies and a continuing Chair in American Civilization at a French university.
Publications: Project Reports, semiannual; President's Report, annual.

GEBHARD-GOURGAUD FOUNDATION
55 Liberty Street
New York, New York 10005
Donor: Eva B. Gebhard Gourgaud
Founded 1947

Provides grants in France and in New England and the Middle Atlantic states for historic preservation and related educational activities.

Charitable Organizations

ASSOCIATION POUR LE RETABLISSEMENT DES INSTITUTIONS ET OEUVRES ISRAELITES EN FRANCE
119 East 95th Street
New York, New York 10028
Secretary: Rabbi Simon Langer
(212) 876-1448
Founded 1943

To aid Jewish religious and cultural organizations in France.

COMMITTEE OF FRENCH AMERICAN WIVES
22 East 60th Street
New York, New York 10022
(212) 688-4949
Founded 1939

Founded to extend relief to destitute French children regardless of race or creed, and to render financial aid and assistance to organizations for charitable purposes.

Research Centers and Special Institutes

W. T. BANDY CENTER FOR BAUDELAIRE STUDIES
Box 1830, Station B
Vanderbilt University
Nashville, Tennessee 37235 (615) 322-2657
Director: Raymond P. Poggenburg Founded 1968

Scholarly research center for the study of the works of Charles Pierre Baudelaire (1821-1867), French poet. Maintains extensive holdings of materials by and about Baudelaire, including magazines and newspapers, first editions, a large file of magazine articles and thousands of volumes containing references to Baudelaire. Maintains 30,000 file card bibliography.
Publications: Bulletin Baudelairien, semiannual; Bibliography, annual.

INSTITUTE OF FRENCH STUDIES
New York University
15 Washington News
New York, New York 10003 (215) 598-2174
Director: Nicholas Wahl Founded 1978

Offers interdisciplinary programs of study on contemporary French society and culture. There are courses integrating the value orientations of the humanities with the empirical data of the social sciences as well as traditional courses in French history, politics, society and culture. Offers a Master's Degree in French Studies, a joint Master's Degree with Business Administration, a Doctor's Degree in French Studies and a joint Ph.D. with either history, politics or sociology. Also offers two professional Certificates of Achievement in French Studies. Affiliated with the University's Center for French Civilization and Culture which includes the Department of France, La Maison Francaise and New York University in France.
Publications: Liaison, (newsletter), quarterly.

NATIONAL MATERIALS DEVELOPMENT CENTER FOR FRENCH AND CREOLE
168 South River Road
Bedford, New Hampshire 03102 (603) 668-7198
Director: Norman Dube

Museums

ACADIAN HOUSE MUSEUM
Post Office Box 497 (318) 394-3754
St. Martinsville, Louisiana 70582 Founded 1926

The museum, housed in a 1765 structure of Acadian architecture is located in Longfellow-Evangeline State Park. Its collections include samples of old weaving art, palmetto artistry and basketry, a botanical garden. Offers guided tours, lectures and handicraft sales.

BOLDUC HOUSE
South Main Street
Ste. Genevieve, Missouri 63670
Mailing Address:
7 Sunningdale Drive
Saint Louis, Missouri 63124
Director: Vergie Stange (314) 883-3105

Museum consists of the Bolduc House (1770), the Bolduc Le Meilleur House (1820) and four additional houses. Open during Jour de Fete, which the museum sponsors. Period furnishings and a French colonial garden as well as exhibits concerning the preservation processes are featured.

FELIX-VALLE HOUSE, STATE HISTORIC SITE
Ste. Genevieve, Missouri 63670
Site Administrator: Susan Williams (314) 883-2472
Founded 1970

The Felix-Valle House (1818) contributes to the preservation of the French-American period in Southern Mississippi.

FRENCH AZILUM
R.D. 2
Towanda, Pennsylvania 18848
Mailing Address:
Box 266
Towanda, Pennsylvania 18848 (717) 265-3376

During the terror of the French Revolution, places were made for the evacuation of the French royal family to the wilderness of Pennsylvania. The Museum village has preserved some of the original structures, such as the Laporte House and displays. Collections: heirlooms of the emigrees; antique farm tools, blacksmith tools; carpenters' tools; spinning and weaving implements.

DE MORES HISTORIC SITE
Medora, North Dakota 58645 (701) 623-4355
Personnel: Cur., Norman Paulson Founded 1936

The 1883 home of the Marquis de Mores, a French nobleman contains original furnishings.

FORT DE BUADE MUSEUM, INCORPORATED
334 North State Street
St. Ignace, Michigan 49781 (906) 643-8686
Director: Donald E. Benson Founded 1975

Museum combines Indian artifacts and displays of French frontier life on the site of Fort de Buade built by the French in 1681.

FORT DE CHARTRES HISTORIC SITE MUSEUM
Fort de Chartres Historic Site
Prairie du Rocher, Illinois 62277 (618) 284-7230
Site Supt.: Darrell Duensing Founded 1917

The museum is located on the original site of the 18th century stone French Fort de Chartes built 1753-56. Collections include historical texts; French herb garden; archaeology; military; tools; weapons; utensils; artifacts; reconstructed period buildings. Research is carried out in archaeology; French, colonial and military life in North America during the 18th century. Services offered include a small research library, lectures, visitors center and the annual Traders' Rendezvous.

FORT LE BOEUF MUSEUM
123 South High Street (814) 796-4113
Waterford, Pennsylvania 16441 Founded 1929

Collections include period furniture; artifacts from French occupation; archives; and the 1820 historic house of Amos Judson located on the site of the 1753 French and 1760 British forts. A research library for reference is available as are guided tours and lectures.

HUGUENOT HISTORICAL SOCIETY
6 Broadhead Avenue
New Paltz, New York 12561
Director: Kenneth E. Hasbrouck, Sr. (914) 255-1660
Founded 1894

The museum is located on the oldest street in the United States. Its collections include 17th-18th century French and Dutch documents and manuscripts; 17th-18th century furnishings and several historic houses: Jean Hasbrouck House, 1692; DuBois Homestead, 1705; Deyo House, remodeled 1890, 1692; Bevier-Elting House, 1698; Hugo Freer House, 1694-1720; LeFevre House, 1799; Reconstructed French Church, 1717; Col. Josiah Hasbrouck Mansion, 1814; Terwilliger Homestead, 1738; Snyder Estate, carriage museum and barns, D & H canal site, old cement kilns. Research is conducted with 17th century documents and items of French Huguenot families. There is a 2,000 volume library of Huguenot history, genealogy, history and literature available by appointment for use on the premises; also a nature center; reading room; exhibit space; auditorium and museum shop. The society offers guided tours, lectures, formally organized education programs for children and adults, training programs for professional museum workers, temporary exhibitions and manuscript collections.
Publications: Huguenot Historical Society, biennial; also publishes family genealogies; guides; catalogue; booklets.

ISLESFORD MUSEUM
Acadia National Park
Route 1
Bar Harbor, Maine 04646 (207) 288-3338
Superintendent: W. Lowell White Founded 1929

Collections include artifacts from French and English colonization; tools; crafts and seafaring objects of early Maine; stone age and Indian antiquities. Other facilities include a 200 volume library of history books available for use by reservation, manuscript collection, visitor center, seashore, woodland and mountaintop nature walks; exhibits; slide talks.

LA NAPOULE ART FOUNDATION-HENRY CLEWS MEMORIAL
133 Bennett Hall
University of Pennsylvania
Philadelphia, Pennsylvania 19104 (215) 243-8911
President: Paul O. Gaddis Founded 1950

The edifice in which the sculpture and painting of Henry Clews, Jr. is housed in a reconstructed medieval fortress from the ninth and eleventh centuries, Chateau de la Napoule, from Alpes Maritime, France.

SAINTE MARIE DE GANNENTAHA
Onondaga Lake Park
Liverpool, New York 13088
Mailing Address:
Box 146
Liverpool, New York 13088 (315) 457-2990
Site Manager: Robert Mehlow Founded 1933

A memorial to French Jesuit mission community of 1656, first attempt to begin a permanent settlement among the Onondaga Indians as part of a peace settlement with the Iroquois. Collections consist of artifacts and documents pertaining to the history of the French experience in North America. Research is conducted in French Jesuit mission activity in New France and 17th century colonial building techniques. The pallisaded mission site includes exhibit area, craft and garden areas. In addition to the permanent exhibitions there are 17th century craft and farming demonstrations and guided tours.

VILLA LOUIS AND MUSEUM
Villa Road and Boilvin
Prairie du Chien, Wisconsin 53821 (608) 326-2721
Curator: Donald L. Munson Founded 1932

This history museum is housed in the 1870 Villa Louis home of family of fur trader Hercules Dousman, on the site of Fort Shelby (1814) and Fort Crawford (1816-29). A 3,500 volume library of history books and Dousman Family Collection are available on premises.

Special Libraries and Subject Collections

FRENCH EMBASSY - FRENCH CULTURAL SERVICES
972 Fifth Avenue
New York, New York 10021
Executive Director: Anne Marie Morrotte (212) 737-9700
Founded 1955

Subjects: French history and culture. Holdings: Cultural films, slides, and filmstrips; scientific films, radio programs; records. Services: Offers French language courses.
Publications: Catalogs for each department.

FRENCH INSTITUTE/ALLIANCE FRANCAISE - LIBRARY
22 East 60th Street
New York, New York 10022 (212) 355-6100
Librarian: Fred J. Gitner Founded 1911

Subjects: French literature, art, history, and civilization; Paris. Holdings: Books; journals and other serials; readers for students; phonograph records (cataloged). Services: Copying; books may be borrowed by mail; library is open to outside users for reference only.
Publication: Quarterly list of new accessions.

FRENCH LIBRARY IN BOSTON, INCORPORATED
53 Marlborough Street
Boston, Massachusetts 02116 (617) 266-4351
Executive Director: Mylo Housen Founded 1945

Subjects: Classical and contemporary French literature including criticism; French history, politics, social life; language and art; cinema, education, architecture; Canadian literature. Special Collections: La Petite Illustration (Serie-Theatre).
Holdings: books; French records; depository for films of Society for French American Cultural Services and Educational Aids (FACSEA) located at French Embassy in New York City. Journals and other serials. Services: Interlibrary loans; library open to public with restrictions.
Publications: Le Bibliophile, monthly newsletter, published October to July; bibliographies.

HUGUENOT HISTORICAL SOCIETY NEW PALTZ - LIBRARY
6 Broadhead Avenue
Box 339
New Paltz, New York 12561 (914) 255-1660
Curator: Kenneth E. Hasbrouck Founded 1894

Subjects: History and genealogy of Ulster and Orange counties; Huguenots; Civil War. Special Collections: Lincoln collection. Holdings: Books; journals and other serials; reports; manuscripts; documents. Services: Copying; library open to public for reference by appointment only.

HUGUENOT SOCIETY OF AMERICA - LIBRARY
122 East 58th Street
New York, New York 10022
Executive Secretary: W. Stephen Kratzen (212) 755-0592

Subjects: French Huguenot migration to America; Huguenot history in France and elsewhere; biography, genealogy. Holdings: books and bound periodical volumes; manuscripts; autograph letters. Services: Copying; library open to public with restrictions.

HUGUENOT SOCIETY OF SOUTH CAROLINA - LIBRARY
25 Chalmers Street
Charleston, South Carolina 29401 (803) 723-3235

Subjects: Genealogical data on Huguenots and allied families, especially French Huguenots.
Special Collections: Publications of the Huguenot Society of London (England); Gorssline collection on Huguenot subjects. Holdings: Genealogical data, books, journals and other serials. Services: Library open to public on a limited basis.

LAFAYETTE COLLEGE - AMERICAN FRIENDS OF LAFAYETTE COLLECTION
David Bishop Skillman Library
Easton, Pennsylvania 18042
Special Collection Librarian:
Robert G. Gennett (215) 253-6281

Subjects: Marquis de Lafayette, American Revolutionary War, George Washington. Special Collections: Hubbard Collection of Lafayette letters to Washington. Holdings: books and manuscripts; engravings of Lafayette. Services: Copying; library open to public by appointment.

UNION SAINT-JEAN-BAPTISTE-MALLET LIBRARY
One Social Street
Woonsocket, Rhode Island 02895 (401) 769-0520
Librarian: Brother Felician, S.C. Founded 1908

Subjects: Franco-Americans, history and civilization, biography, genealogy, literature, religion, social sciences. Special Collections: 600 letters, 500 of which are addressed to Major Edmond Mallet; Ephemerides. Holdings: books; bound periodical volumes; pamphlets; manuscript notes; maps; vertical file; dissertations; photographs; microfilms; newspapers. Services: Copying; library open to public with lending restrictions. Also known as Bibliotheque Mallet.

UNIVERSITY OF SOUTHWESTERN LOUISIANA - JEFFERSON CAFFERY LOUISIANA ROOM
Dupre Library
302 East St. Mary
Lafayette, Louisiana 70504 (318) 264-6031
Archv.: Dr. Frederick J. Stielow Founded 1962

Subjects: State and local history, description and travel, agriculture, education, politics and government, literature, local genealogy, folklore, French language in Louisiana. Special Collections: Acadiana; Louisiana State documents; Caffery Collection (rare books). Holdings: books and bound periodical volumes; VF drawers; clippings and pamphlets; theses; journals and other serials. Services: Copying; microfilming; library open to adults only.

Newspapers and Newsletters

AATF NATIONAL BULLETIN. 1975-. Quarterly. Editor: Stanley L. Shinall. Publisher: American Association of Teachers of French, 57 East Armory Avenue, Champaign, Illinois 61820. Text is partly in French.

Concerned with the French language and culture and the problems of teaching French in the United States. Carries short articles on France and other French-speaking countries, articles on teaching French as a foreign language, reports of commissions, as, for example, those on testing and teacher training. Includes association news and announcements of professional interest.

AMERICAN FRIENDS OF LAFAYETTE--GAZETTE. 1942-. Editor: Dr. M.M. Barr Koon. Publisher: Skillman Library, Lafayette College, Easton, Pennsylvania 18042.

Strives for continuing increase of Franco-American cooperation and the correction of a lack of basic information in Franco-American relations. Carries articles on the French statesman and officer, the Marquis de Lafayette (1757-1834), and the places he stayed or visited in the United States.

LE CANADO-AMERICAIN (The American Canadian). 1900-. Quarterly. Editor: Gerald Rober. Publisher: Association Canado-Americaine, 52 Concord Street, Manchester, New Hampshire 03101. In French.

Reports on fraternal activities of the Association Canado-Americaine, a fraternal insurance society.

FRANCE-AMERIQUE (America's French Weekly). 1941-Weekly. Editor: Mrs. Francoise D. Martin. Publisher: Trocadero Publishing, Incorporated, 1556 Third Avenue, New York, New York 10028. In French.

Emphasizes news from France and news about the French in the United States. Also includes international news and comments, short stories, interviews and various features. Continuation of Le Courrier Français des Etats - Unis first established in New York in 1827.

LA SALETTE. 1969-. Quarterly. Editor: Father Gilles Genest. Publisher: La Salette Center of Light, Enfield, New Hampshire 03748. In French and English.

A newsletter published in French and English editions containing news concerning the activities of the La Salette Fathers.

Magazines

ACADIANA PROFILE. 1969-. Bimonthly. Editor: Jim Bradshow. Publisher: Trent Angers, Acadiana Profile, Incorporated, 501 University, Lafayette, Louisiana 70503. In French and English.

Features stories of interest to the French ethnic community of Louisiana.

ALLIANCE. 1979-. Biennial. Editor: Jean-Jacques Sicard. Publisher: French Institute and Alliance Française de New York, 22 East 60th Street, New York, New York 10022. In French.

Publishes articles on French culture, literature, art and history, reviews noteworthy, books and films and reports on activities of the French Institute.

AMERICAN SOCIETY LEGION OF HONOR MAGAZINE. 1930-. 3 times a year. Editor: Sylviane Glad. Publisher: American Society of the French Legion of Honor, 22 East 60th Street, New York, New York 10022. In English.

Seeks to promote appreciation in the United States of French culture and to strengthen friendship between the people of the United States and France. Publishes articles on history, literature, music, art, and other subjects related to French and American culture.

LE CALIFORNIEN (The Californian). 1963-. Weekly. Editor: Pierre Idiart. Publisher: Le Californien Publishing Company, Le Californien Building, 1051 Divisadero Street, San Francisco, California 94115. In French.

Carries international news with emphasis on political and cultural events in France, and social and cultural activities among French-Americans in California and other states. Includes editorials and excerpts from Le Monde, Le Figaro, Paris Match, etc.

FRENCH-AMERICAN COMMERCE. 1896-. Quarterly. Editor: Bernard Friedrich. Publisher: French American Chamber of Commerce, 1350 Avenue of the Americas, New York, New York 10019.

Prints articles of interest to businessmen in France and America.

FRENCH FORUM. Three times a year. Box 5108, Lexington, Kentucky 40505. In English and French.

A journal of literary criticism.

JOURNAL FRANCAIS D'AMERIQUE. 1965-. Biweekly. Editor: Anne Perochon. Publisher: Marie Galanti, National Advertising Manager, 1051 Divisadero, San Francisco, California 94115. In French.

Conveys news from France. Has sections on food and wine.

L'UNION (The Union). 1902-. Quarterly. Editor: Joseph E. Gadbois. Publisher: Union Saint-Jean-Baptiste, 1 Social Street, Woonsocket, Rhode Island 02895. In French.

Official organ of the Union Saint-Jean-Baptiste, a mutual benefit fraternal society with 225 lodges.

MIEUX VIVRE (Better Living). 1917-. Monthly. Editor: Serve V. Collins. Publisher: Seventh Day Adventist Church, 1350 Villa Street, Mountain View, California 94040. In French.

Published by the Seventh Day Adventist Church for the French-speaking public. Contains religious news and articles on religious teachings.

REVUE DE LOUISIANE/LOUISIANA REVIEW. 1972-. Biennial. Editor: Adele St. Martin. Publisher: Center for Louisiana Studies, Box 4-0831 University of Southern Louisiana, Lafayette, Louisiana 70504. In English and French.

Carries cultural and historical essays on the French contribution to Louisiana.

REVUE D'HISTOIRE DE L'AMERIQUE FRANÇAISE. 1947-. Quarterly. Editor: Jacques Mathieu. Publisher: Institut d'Histoire de l'Amerique Française, 261 Avenue Bloomfield, Montreal, Quebec, H2V 3R6, Canada.

Prints articles on various aspects of the history of French civilization in North America.

ROMANIC REVIEW. 1910-. Quarterly. Editor: Professor Michael Riffaterre. Publisher: Columbia University, Department of French and Romance and Philology, New York, New York 10025. In English and French.

TODAY IN FRANCE. 1961-. Bimonthly. Editor: Benjamin Protter. Publisher: Society for French-American Affairs, Post Office Box 551, Cathedral Station, New York, New York 10025.

Covers current news concerning France for Americans interested in establishing greater understanding between the two countries. Analyzes certain events in international affairs and in the United States. Includes book reviews, signed articles, reprints of significant documents. Former Name: France Today, January 1962.

TRIBUNE DES FRANCOPHONES. 1976-. Biennial. Editors: Georges Planel and Jacqueline Millerand Planel. Publisher: Institute des Etudes Françaises, 937 Marilyn, Lafayette, Louisiana 70503. In French.

Contains articles on the language and cultures of French-speaking peoples throughout the world, literary contributions, word games and puzzles, book reviews, information about scholarships and programs of study.

Radio Programs

California - Berkeley

KALX (FM) - Eshleman Hall, University of California, Berkeley, California 94720, (415) 642-1111. French programs, 1 hour weekly.

California - San Francisco

KUSF (FM) - 2130 Fulton Street, San Francisco, California 94117, (415) 666-6206. French programs, 1 hour weekly.

Connecticut - Bristol

WBIS - 1021 Farmington Avenue, Bristol, Connecticut 06010, (203) 583-9265. French programs, 2 hours weekly.

Connecticut - Hartford

WCCC (FM) - 11 Asylum Street, Hartford, Connecticut 06103, (203) 549-3456. French programs, 2 hours weekly.

WRTC (FM) - Trinity College, Hartford, Connecticut 06106, (203) 527-0447. French programs, 2 hours weekly.

Connecticut - Putnam

WINY - 237 Kennedy Drive, Putnam, Connecticut 06260, (203) 928-2721. French programs, 1 hour weekly.

Connecticut - West Hartford

WMLB - 630 Oakwood Avenue, West Hartford, Connecticut 06110, (203) 521-1550. French programs, 1 hour weekly.

Florida - Boynton Beach

WHRS (FM) - 505 South Congress Avenue, Boynton Beach, Florida 33435, (305) 732-7850. French programs, 1 hour weekly.

Florida - Fort Lauderdale

WAVS - 2727 East Oakland Place, Fort Lauderdale, Florida 33306, (305) 561-1190. French programs, 1 hour weekly.

Florida - Miami

WDNA (FM) - Box WDNA, Ludlam Br., Miami, Florida 33155, (305) 264-9362. French programs, 2 hours weekly.

Florida - Pompano Beach

WCKO (FM) - 4431 Rock Island Road, Fort Lauderdale, Florida 33319, (305) 731-4800. French programs, 2 hours weekly.

Georgia - Athens

WCCD - Box 5860, Athens, Georgia 30604, (404) 549-1470. French programs, 3 hours weekly.

Georgia - Moultrie

WMGA - Box 1380, Moultrie, Georgia 31768, (912) 985-1130. French programs, 24 hours weekly.

Hawaii - Honolulu

KNDI - 1734 South King Street, Honolulu, Hawaii 96826, (808) 946-2844. French programs, 2 hours weekly.

Illinois - Chicago

WSSD (FM) - 1950 East 71st Street, Chicago, Illinois 60649. French programs.

Illinois - Galesburg

WVKC (FM) - Box 154, Knox College, Galesburg, Illinois 61401, (309) 343-8992. French programs, 1 hour weekly.

Illinois - Park Forest

WRHS (FM) - 300 Sauk Trail, Park Forest, Illinois 60466, (312) 747-0963. French programs, 1 hour weekly.

Illinois - Winnetka

WNTH (FM) - 385 Winnetka Avenue, Winnetka, Illinois 60093, (312) 446-7013. French programs, 2 hours weekly.

Indiana - New Albany

WNAS (FM) - 1020 Vincennes Street, New Albany, Indiana 47150, (812) 944-2216. French programs, 1 hour weekly.

Iowa - Waverly

KWAR (FM) - Wartburg College, Waverly, Iowa 50677, (319) 352-1200. French programs, 1 hour weekly.

Louisiana - Baton Rouge

WYNK - Box 2541, 854 Main Street, Baton Rouge, Louisiana 70821. (504) 343-8348. French programs, 1 hour weekly.

Louisiana - Crowley

KAJN - Box 1561, Crowley, Louisiana 70526, (318) 783-1560. French programs, 2 hours weekly.

KSIG - 320 North Parkerson Avenue, Crowley, Louisiana 70526, (318) 783-2520. French programs, 18 hours weekly.

Louisiana - Eunice

KEUN - Box 1049, Eunice, Louisiana 70535, (318) 457-3041. French programs, 6 hours weekly.

Louisiana - Golden Meadow

KLEB - Box 726, 1842 Henry Street, Golden Meadow, Louisiana 70357, (504) 475-5141. French programs, 12 hours weekly.

Louisiana - Houma

KHOM (FM) - 2306 West Main Street, Thibodaux, Louisiana 70360, (504) 876-5466. French programs, 9 hours weekly.

Louisiana - Jennings

KJEF - Drawer 1248, Jennings, Louisiana 70546, (318) 824-2934. French programs, 12 hours weekly.

Louisiana - Lafayette

KPEL - Box 52046, Lafayette, Louisiana 70505, (318) 233-7003. French programs, 1 hour weekly.

KRVS (FM) - Box 2171, USL Station, Lafayette, Louisiana 70504, (318) 234-9495. French programs, 10 hours weekly.

KVOL - 123 East Main Street, Box 3030, Lafayette, Louisiana 70502, (318) 234-5151. French programs, 1 hour weekly.

KXKW - Box J, Lafayette, Louisiana 70501, (318) 232-2632. French programs, 2 hours weekly.

Louisiana - Lake Charles

KAOK - Box S, Lake Charles, Louisiana 70602, (318) 436-7541. French programs, 1 hour weekly.

Louisiana - Lake Charles

KLCL - Box 3067, Lake Charles, Louisiana 70601, (318) 433-1641. French programs, 3 hours weekly.

Louisiana - Moreauville

KLIL (FM) - Box 365, Moreauville, Louisiana 71355, (318) 985-2929. French programs, 2 hours weekly.

Louisiana - New Orleans

WWNO (FM) - c/o University of New Orleans, New Orleans, Louisiana 70122, (504) 283-0315. French programs, 3 hours weekly.

Louisiana - New Roads

KQXL - 700 Olinde Street, New Roads, Louisiana 70760, (504) 638-9058. French programs, 3 hours weekly.

Louisiana - Opelousas

KSLO - Box 1150, Opelousas, Louisiana 70570, (318) 942-2633. French programs, 20 hours weekly.

Louisiana - Sulphur

KTQQ (FM) - Box 606, Lake Charles, Louisiana 70602, (318) 625-7777. French programs, 2 hours weekly.

Louisiana - Thibodaux

KTIB - Box 682, Thibodaux, Louisiana 70301, (504) 447-9006. French programs, 4 hours weekly.

Louisiana - Ville Platte

KVPI (AM & FM) - Drawer J, Ville Platte, Louisiana 70586, (318) 363-2124. French programs, 15 hours weekly.

Maine - Augusta

WFAU (AM & FM) - Box 307, 160 Bangor Street, Augusta, Maine 04330, (207) 623-3878. French programs, 1 hour weekly.

Maine - Gorham

WDCI - 28 School Street, Gorham, Maine 04038. French programs, 1 hour weekly.

Maine - Lewiston

WCOU - 129 Lisbon Street, Lewiston, Maine 04240, (207) 784-6921. French programs, 3 hours weekly.

WAYU (FM) - 129 Lisbon Street, Lewiston, Maine 04240, (207) 784-5786. French programs, 3 hours weekly.

WLAM - Box 929, Lewiston, Maine 04240, (207) 784-5401. French programs, 2 hours weekly.

Maine - Sanford

WSME - Box 1220, Sanford, Maine 04073, (207) 324-7271. French programs, 1 hour weekly.

Maine - Waterville

WMHB (FM) - Mayflower Hill Drive, Waterville, Maine 04901, (207) 872-8037. French programs, 3 hours weekly.

Maryland - Baltimore

WSPH (FM) - 7400 Old North Point Road, Baltimore, Maryland 21219, (301) 477-0750. French programs, 1 hour weekly.

Maryland - Bethesda

WHFS (FM) - 4853 Cordell Avenue, Bethesda, Maryland 20014, (301) 656-0600. French programs, 1 hour weekly.

Massachusetts - Amherst

WFCR (FM) - Five College Radio, Hampshire House, University of Massachusetts, Amherst, Massachusetts 01003, (413) 545-0100. French programs, 1 hour weekly.

Massachusetts - Fall River

WALE - Box 208, 130 Rock Street, Fall River, Massachusetts 02722, (617) 674-3535. French programs, 1 hour weekly.

Massachusetts - Gardner

WGAW - Box 87, Green Street, Gardner, Massachusetts 01440, (617) 632-1340. French programs, 1 hour weekly.

Massachusetts - Holyoke

WREB - Box 507, Dwight Street, Holyoke, Massachusetts 01040, (413) 536-3930. French programs, 5 hours weekly.

Massachusetts - Southbridge

WESO - 399 Main Street, Southbridge, Massachusetts 01550, (617) 764-4381. French programs, 1 hour weekly.

Massachusetts - Ware

WARE - 90 South Street, Ware, Massachusetts 01082, (413) 967-6231. French programs, 2 hours weekly.

Michigan - Beaverton

WGEO (FM) - Box 278, Beaverton, Michigan 48612, (517) 435-7797. French programs, 1 hour weekly.

Michigan - Garden City

WCAR - 32500 Park Lane, Garden City, Michigan 48135, (313) 525-1111. French programs, 1 hour weekly.

Mississippi - Canton

WMGO - Box 182, Canton, Mississippi 39046, (601) 859-2373. French programs, 1 hour weekly.

Mississippi - Laurel

WQIS - Box 2336, Laurel, Mississippi 39440, (601) 426-3182. French programs, 2 hours weekly.

Missouri - Columbia

KOPN (FM) - 915 East Broadway, Columbia, Missouri 65201, (314) 874-1139. French programs, 1 hour weekly.

New Hampshire - Berlin

WBRL - 40 Main Street, Berlin, New Hampshire 03570, (603) 752-4656. French programs, 1 hour weekly.

WMOU - 40 Main Street, Berlin, New Hampshire 03570, (603) 752-1230. French programs, 4 hours weekly.

New Hampshire - Claremont

WTSV - 221 Washington Street, Claremont, New Hampshire 03743, (603) 542-7735. French programs, 2 hours weekly.

New Hampshire - Manchester

WZID (FM) - 30 Riverfront Street, Manchester, New Hampshire 03102, (603) 669-5777. French programs, 3 hours weekly.

New Hampshire - Plymouth

WPNH - 2 High Street, Plymouth, New Hampshire 03264, (603) 536-2500. French programs, 2 hours weekly.

New York - Baldwinsville

WBXL (FM) - East Oneida Street Complex, Baldwinsville, New York 13027, (315) 635-3949. French programs, 2 hours weekly.

New York - Geneseo

WGSU (FM) - State University College, Geneseo, New York 14454, (716) 245-5586. French programs, 1/2 hour weekly.

New York - Hempstead

WVHC (FM) - 1000 Fulton Avenue, Hempstead, New York 11550, (516) 489-8870. French programs, 1/2 hour weekly.

New York - New York

WFUV (FM) - Fordham University, Bronx, New York 10458, (212) 933-2233. French programs, 3 hours weekly.

New York - New York

WKCR (FM) - 208 Ferris Booth Hall, New York, New York 10027, (212) 280-5223. French programs, 4 hours weekly.

Ohio - Cleveland

WZAK (FM) - 1303 Prospect Avenue, Cleveland, Ohio 44115, (216) 621-9300. French programs, 1/2 hour weekly.

Pennsylvania - Carlisle

WDCV (FM) - Box 640, Holland Union Building, Dickinson College, Carlisle, Pennsylvania 17013, (717) 245-1444. French programs, 3 hours weekly.

Pennsylvania - Pittsburgh

WYEP (FM) - 4 Cable Place, Pittsburgh, Pennsylvania 15213, (412) 687-0200. French programs, 1 hour weekly.

Rhode Island - West Warwick

WKRI - 1501 Main Street, West Warwick, Rhode Island 02893, (401) 821-6200. French programs, 1 hour weekly.

WWON - 98 Getchell Avenue, West Warwick, Rhode Island 02895, (401) 762-1240. French programs, 3 hours weekly.

South Carolina - Rock Hill

WNSC (FM) - Drawer L, Columbia, South Carolina 29250, (803) 758-7318. French programs, 1 hour weekly.

Tennessee - Lebanon

WFMQ (FM) - Box 609, Lebanon, Tennessee 37087, (615) 444-0305. French programs, 1 hour weekly.

Texas - Levelland

KLVT - Box 1230, Levelland, Texas, (805) 894-3134. French programs, 9 hours weekly.

Texas - Lubbock

KOHM (FM) - 3211 47th Street, Lubbock, Texas 79413, (806) 799-9035. French programs, 1 hour weekly.

Vermont - Burlington

WVMT - Box 12, Colchester, Burlington, Vermont 05446, (802) 655-1620. French programs, 1/2 hour weekly.

Washington - Bellevue

KASB (FM) - 1001 108th Avenue, Southeast, Bellevue, Washington 98004, (206) 455-6154. French programs, 2 hours weekly.

Washington - Ephrata

KULE - Box 1077, Ephrata, Washington 98823, (509) 754-4686. French programs, 6 hours weekly.

Wisconsin - Eau Claire

WUEC (FM) - University of Wisconsin-Eau Claire, Wisconsin 54701, (715) 886-4170. French programs, 1 hour weekly.

Wisconsin - Sheboygan

WSHS (FM) - 1042 School Avenue, Sheboygan, Wisconsin 53081, (414) 459-3610. French programs, 1 hour weekly.

Puerto Rico - Levittown

WJDZ (FM) - BM-5 Dr. Villalobos Street, Levittown, Puerto Rico 00632, (809) 784-2484. French programs, 1 hour weekly.

Virgin Islands - Saint Thomas

WIUJ (FM) - Box 7175, Saint Thomas, Virgin Islands 00801, (809) 774-2752. French programs, 1 hour weekly.

Television Programs

California - San Diego

KPBS-TV - San Diego State University, San Diego, California 92182, (714) 265-6415. French: unspecified.

Louisiana - Lafayette

KLFY-TV - 2410 Eraste Landry Road, Box 3687, Lafayette, Louisiana 70502, (318) 981-4823. French: 2-1/2 hours a week.

Louisiana - Lake Charles

KPLC-TV - 320 Division Street, Lake Charles, Louisiana 70601, (318) 439-9071. French: news segment.

Maine - Orono

WMEB-TV - Alumni Hall, University of Maine, Orono, Maine 04473, (207) 866-4493. French: 1 hour a week.

Massachusetts - Springfield

WGBY-TV - 44 Hampden Street, Springfield, Massachusetts 01103, (413) 781-2801. French: 1/2 hour a week.

Missouri - Springfield

KOZK - 1101 North Summit, Springfield, Missouri 65801, (417) 865-2100. French: unspecified.

New York - New York

WNYE-TV - 112 Tillary Street, Brooklyn, New York 11201, (212) 596-4425. French: unspecified.

Ohio - Lima-Bowling Green

WBGU-TV - Troup Avenue, Bowling Green, Ohio 43403, (419) 372-0121. French: 20 minutes a week.

Tennessee - Sneedville

WSJK-TV - 209 Communications Building, University of Tennessee, Knoxville, Tennessee 37916, (615) 974-5281. French: 40 minutes a week.

Washington - Tacoma

KTPS - 1101 South Yakima Avenue, Tacoma, Washington 98402, (206) 572-6262. French: unspecified.

Bank Branches in the U.S.

BANQUE FRANÇAISE & ITALIENNE POUR L'AMÉRIQUE DU SUD-SUDAMÉRIS
United States and Canada Representative:
280 Park Avenue
New York, New York 10017 (212) 661-6140

BANQUE NATIONALE DE PARIS

New York Branch:
499 Park Avenue
New York, New York 10022 (212) 750-1400

New York Representative:
40 Wall Street
New York, New York (212) 943-6055

Los Angeles Branch:
707 Wilshire Boulevard
Los Angeles, California 90017 (213) 488-9120

San Francisco Branch:
130 Montgomery
San Francisco, California 94104 (415) 765-4800

Chicago Branch:
33 North Dearborn Street
Chicago, Illinois 60602 (312) 977-2200

Houston Representative Office:
One Houston Center
Houston, Texas 77002 (713) 659-1707

CREDIT COMMERCIEL DE FRANCE SA

New York Branch:
450 Park Avenue
New York, New York 10022

CREDIT INDUSTRIEL ET COMMERCIEL

United States Representative
280 Park Avenue
New York, New York 10017 (212) 490-7373

CREDIT LYONNAIS S.A.

New York Branch:
95 Wall Street
New York, New York 10005 (212) 344-0500

San Francisco Branch:
Battery Street
San Francisco, California 94111

Los Angeles Branch:
515 South Flower Street
Los Angeles, California 90017

Chicago Branch:
55 East Monroe Street
Chicago, Illinois 60603

SOCIÉTÉ GÉNÉRALE - FRANCE

United States Subsidiary:
Hudson Securities, Incorporated
630 Fifth Avenue
New York, New York 10020 (212) 245-5015

United States Affiliates:
European-American Banking Corporation
European-American Bank and Trust Company
10 Hanover Square
New York, New York 10005 (212) 437-4300

New York Branch:
50 Rockefeller Plaza
New York, New York (212) 397-6000

Commercial and Trade Organizations

AMERICAN CHAMBER OF COMMERCE IN FRANCE
21 Avenue George V
F-75008 Paris, France
Executive Director: W. Barrett Dower Founded 1894

Affiliated with: Council of American Chambers of Commerce in Europe and the Mediterranean.
Publications: Commerce in France, bimonthly; Directory of Members, annual; also publishes List of American Branches and Subsidiaries in France and List of European Headquarters of United States Firms.

FOOD AND WINES FROM FRANCE
1350 Avenue of the Americas
New York, New York 10019 (212) 581-7270

Promotes agricultural and vinicultural products from France. Also serves as information center.

FRENCH-AMERICAN CHAMBER OF COMMERCE
1350 Avenue of the Americas
New York, New York 10019
General Manager: Bernard A. Friedrich (212) 581-4554
Founded 1896

Promotes trade between the United States and France. Formerly (1977) French Chamber of Commerce in the United States.
Publications: Newsletter, every 4 weeks; French American Commerce, 4 times a year; Roster, annual.

FRENCH COMMERCIAL COUNSELOR AND FRENCH TRADE INFORMATION SERVICE
40 West 57th Street
New York, New York 10019 (212) 541-6720

401 North Michigan Avenue
Suite 3040
Chicago, Illinois 60601 (302) 661-1880

2777 Allen Parkway
Suite 360
Houston, Texas 77019 (713) 522-8231

1801 Avenue of the Stars
Suite 921
Los Angeles, California 90067 (213) 879-1847

2040 International Trade Mart
2 Canal Street
New Orleans, Louisiana 70130 (504) 523-7953

400 Montgomery Street
Suite 908
San Francisco, California 94104 (415) 781-0986

First Federal Savings Building
Suite 709
Ponce de Leon Avenue, Stop 23
Santruce, Puerto Rico 00909 (809) 725-4279

FRENCH INDUSTRIAL DEVELOPMENT AGENCY
610 Fifth Avenue
New York, New York 10020 (212) 757-9340

INTERNATIONAL TRADE EXHIBITION IN FRANCE
1350 Avenue of the Americas
New York, New York 10019 (212) 869-1720

Provides information about international trade shows in France and artists' firms which want to participate.

ROQUEFORT ASSOCIATION
41 East 42nd Street
New York, New York 10017
President: Frank O. Fredericks (212) 682-0767

Promotes the sale of Roquefort cheese. To publicize and protect the name, Roquefort, on behalf of the community of Roquefort (France) and the producers of Roquefort cheese.

Festivals, Fairs, and Celebrations

Alabama - Mobile

MARDI GRAS
Mobile, Alabama

Festival originated in Mobile 200 years ago (before New Orleans festival). Bands, floats, gaily-colored costumes, minstrels, mummers, marching units, parades and balls, and Krew de Bienville Ball for visitors. Festival extends through the ten days prior to Lent. Mardi Gras day, Tuesday before Ash Wednesday - all day and night.
Contact: Mobile Area Chamber of Commerce, Post Office Box 2187, Mobile, Alabama 36601.

Illinois - Creve Coeur

FORT CREVECOEUR RENDEZVOUS
300 block of Lawnridge
Creve Coeur, Illinois

A celebration of the history of Creve Coeur featuring Indian and voyageur music, Indian and folk dance, story telling, crafts, French and Indian food, tomahawk and knife competition. Held in September.
Contact: Margaret Miller, 125 Sherwood Court, Creve Coeur, Illinois 61611; (309) 694-3193 or 699-5446; 9am-6pm.

Illinois - Nauvoo

GRAPE FESTIVAL
Banks of the Mississippi
Nauroo, Illinois

Re-enactment of an old French rite, Wedding of the Wine and Cheese, symbolic of the idea that the two are best when taken together. Festival honors early Mormon and French settlers. Held Labor Day weekend.
Contact: The Division of Tourism, Illinois Department of Business and Economic Development, 222 South College Street, Springfield, Illinois 62706.

Illinois - Prairie du Rocher

FORT DE CHARTRES RENDEZVOUS
Fort de Chartres State Park
Prairie du Rocher, Illinois

Re-creates the early French frontier era in Illinois. Period music by roving minstrel singers and the Tippecanoe Ancient Fife and Drum Corps, minuet dancing by Le Rochey Dansants, greased pole contests, and militia demonstrations take place within the partially reconstructed walls of the colonial fort. Traditional Rendezvous contests consist of flintlock shooting, a tug-of-war between frontiersmen and voyageurs, and birch-bark canoe races. Cultural demonstrations include French colonial cooking, blacksmithing, cooperage, soap making, tanning, carving, silversmithing, and weaving. French ox cart rides are available for children. Held annually in early June since 1970.
Contact: Special Events, Illinois Department of Conservation, 605 State Office Building, Springfield, Illinois 62706. (217) 782-3340.

Indiana - Fort Ouiatenon

FEAST OF THE HUNTER'S MOON
Fort Ouiatenon, Indiana

A reconstructed French fort dating from the mid-1700's, Fort Ouiatenon is the center of a re-creation each year of eighteenth century life. Canoes race up the Wabash. French traders and Indians gather to celebrate a bountiful harvest. Pioneer clad craftsmen revive the arts of spinning, candle-dipping, and blacksmithing. Music provided by fiddlers, fifes and drums. Buffalo stew, home-baked bread and fresh churned butter are provided. French folk music and dancing plus an eighteenth century French play.
Contact: Tippecanoe County Historical Association, Tenth and South Streets, Lafayette, Indiana 47901.

Louisiana - Abbeville

FRENCH ACADIAN MUSIC FESTIVAL
Comeaux Recreation Center
Abbeville, Louisiana

The festival commemorates the coming of the Acadians to Louisiana and is also intended to further the preservation of French customs and traditions. The program includes contests in singing, playing French folksongs, French skits, short stories and poems. This is followed by dance performances and contests, including the mazurka, polka, two-step, and the Lancer Dance, an ancient French dance. Acadian handicrafts are on sale. Begun around 1971. Held in late April.
Contact: Robert P. Prejean, 209 North Bailey Avenue, Abbeville, Louisiana 70510; or Louisiana Tourist Commission, Post Office Box 44291, Baton Rouge, Louisiana 70804.

Louisiana - Acadiana

MARDI GRAS
Acadiana, Louisiana

A band of grotesquely masked and garbed horsemen start out in the dawn hours and ride into the countryside under the leadership of "Le Capitaine", who rides a richly decked horse. The leader blows a cow horn at each farmhouse and inquires if anyone is in mourning. If yes, they ride on, if not the men (if welcomed) sing folk songs and cavort for the entertainment of the household. They then seek a gift to be used in making gumbo. The farmer may hand them rice, or let loose a chicken which they must catch. After they have been to all the farms, the booty is taken back to town and cooked by the women. The whole town feasts, after which there is revelry, music, dancing, and libations. Held on Shrove Tuesday.
Contact: Louisiana Tourist Commission, Post Office Box 44291, Baton Rouge, Louisiana 70804

Louisiana - Bridge City

GUMBO FESTIVAL
Bridge City, Louisiana

A huge 4,000 gallon gumbo pot, gumbo cooking and eating contests are special features of the festival. Other highlights include a parade, fireworks, an art exhibit, and continuous Cajun entertainment. Held in late October.
Contact: Reverend J. A. Luminais, 908 Wiegand Drive, Bridge City, Louisiana 70094. (504) 341-1641.

Louisiana - Chauvin

LAGNIAPPE ON THE BAYOU
Chauvin, Louisiana

An old-fashioned festival including a country store, seafood, games and street dances. There is a saloon with live entertainment, a replica of a shrimp drying platform, rides and country booths where the townspeople sell the items which they have been making for the past year. Cajun food such as pecan gralle and sweet-dough pie are served. The festival is an expression of Acadian culture. Held for three days in mid-October.
Contact: Louisiana Tourist Commission, Post Office Box 44291, Baton Rouge, Louisiana 70804.

Louisiana - Galliano

CAJUN FESTIVAL
South Lafourche High School
Galliano, Louisiana

Rides and games, formal opening and dedication ceremonies, Cajun street dance, potato dance contest, a waltzing contest, Cajun dress contest, displays, food, Cajun piroque race, air show, continuous Cajun music, auction, beauty contest, choir, airplane rides, beard contest, Cajun play, Cajun foods, bike race, quilting, and commercial exhibits. Held in mid-June for three days.
Contact: Dale Guidry, Post Office Drawer A, Galliano, Louisiana 70354.

Louisiana - Lafayette

FESTIVAL ACADIENS
Lafayette, Louisiana

Bayou food festival featuring Cajun music and dance, and native crafts. Held in September.
Contact: Festival Acadiens, Post Office Box 52066, Lafayette, Louisiana 70501.

LE FESTIVAL WILLIS F. DUCREST DES ARTS ACADIENS ET FRANÇAIS
Lafayette, Louisiana

Concerts, dramatic presentations, dances, vocalists, exhibits, and demonstrations by artisans, all oriented towards French or Acadian cultures. Music includes chamber music, vocal, impressionistic, spiritual, etc. Begun around 1973. Held for ten days in late October to early November.
Contact: Director, School of Music, University of Southwestern Louisiana, Lafayette, Louisiana 70501.

Louisiana - Larose

FRENCH FOOD FESTIVAL
Larose Regional Park
Highway 308
Larose, Louisiana

In addition to French and Cajun foods in great abundance, the festival holds special Cajun heritage events and games.
Contact: John Rabb, Post Office Box 602, Larose, Louisiana 70373. (504) 693-4567.

Louisiana - Napoleonville

MADEWOOD ARTS FESTIVAL
Madewood Plantation
Napoleonville, Louisiana

The Festival sponsors a vast array of cultural events in the home and on the grounds of this famous plantation. There are exhibits of regional arts and crafts for public viewing, and seminars by visiting artists as well as literary discussions initiated by several of Louisiana's outstanding writers. Musical programs include concerts of songs and arias, bands and orchestras, ballet, and a symphony orchestra concert. There is also an Acadian fair. Held over several days in mid-April.
Contact: Executive Director, Louisiana Tourist Commission, Post Office Box 44291, Baton Rouge, Louisiana 70804.

Louisiana - New Orleans

FRANCE LOUISIANA FESTIVAL
New Orleans, Louisiana

The festival commemorates the special association of Louisiana and France through joint commemoration of France's Bastille Day and America's Independence Day. Included in this festival is the New Orleans Food Festival. Events include special art displays and exhibits, Louisiana craft exhibits and demonstrations, etc. In addition there are concerts, ballets, children's chorale, films, jazz and gospel evening, comic opera, singers from Quebec, and fireworks display. Held for 11 days in early July.
Contact: France-Louisiana Festival, New Orleans Bicentennial Commission, 545 Saint Charles Avenue, New Orleans, Louisiana 70130.

MARDI GRAS
New Orleans, Louisiana

In this, perhaps the most famous of all the Mardi Gras festivals, revelers wear costumes, and mummers stroll through the streets throwing doubloons and trinkets. Parties and balls (at least five dozen private masked balls in the Municipal Auditorium) are frequent and lavish. Marching bands, animated paper mache figures and displays, and elaborate floats in the parades through the streets. Observers become participants, and the fun is infectious. Held annually for two weeks preceding Lent.
Contact: Louisiana Tourist Commission, Post Office Box 44291, Baton Rouge, Louisiana 70804.

Louisiana - Plaquemine

INTERNATIONAL ACADIAN FESTIVAL
Plaquemine, Louisiana

Celebrates the Acadian culture and the story of Evangeline. Street dances, Cajun costume contests, horse shows, and a rodeo are scheduled. Also features a boat parade, street parade, and a reenactment of Evangeline's journey, when French people were driven from Nova Scotia. Held annually in late October.
Sponsor: Plaquemine Council 970, Knights of Columbus.
Contact: Chamber of Commerce, Post Office Box 248, Plaquemine, Louisiana 70764.

Mississippi - Biloxi

MARDI GRAS
Biloxi, Mississippi

In continuation of the ancient French and Creole tradition, Biloxi celebrates Fat Tuesday with evening and afternoon parades and pageantry including lavish floats, costumed celebrants, carnival favors, and special balls. Held on Shrove Tuesday.
Contact: Travel/Tourism Department, Mississippi Agricultural and Industrial Board, Post Office Box 849, Jackson, Mississippi 39205.

Missouri - Saint Louis

FETE DE NORMANDIE
Pasadena Mall
Saint Louis, Missouri

Features a parade, entertainment, arts, crafts, booths, carnival games, food and refreshments with a French flair. Held in late September.
Contact: Saint Louis Regional Commerce and Growth Association, 10 Broadway, Saint Louis, Missouri 63102.

Missouri - Saint Louis

SOULARD SUNDAY
Soulard Market
Saint Louis, Missouri

This festival seeks to capture the French and pioneer spirit of the city's founders. Market dates back to 1779. French cuisine, international music, international dancing, tours of the area and refreshments. Held in mid-July.
Contact: Convention and Visitors Bureau of Greater Saint Louis, 500 Broadway Building, Saint Louis, Missouri 63102.

Missouri - Sainte Genevieve

JOUR DE FETE
Sainte Genevieve, Missouri

Sainte Genevieve honors its French heritage and celebrates its founding in 1735 as the first permanent settlement west of the Mississippi River. Tours include several homes dating back to the 1770's which have been preserved and restored. The festival features folk dancing, a pageant, parades, arts and crafts displays, international cuisine, French costumes, and a King's Ball. Held in early August.
Contact: Sainte Genevieve Chamber of Commerce, Post Office Box 166, Sainte Genevieve, Missouri 63670.

New York - Cape Vincent

ANNUAL FRENCH FESTIVAL
Cape Vincent, New York

Celebrates the French heritage of the Thousand Islands region with a parade, crowing of a French Festival Queen, awards to winning bands and floats, buffet dinner, fireworks, and other festivities. Gay carts line the streets offering French pastry, cheeses, nosegays, souvenirs, berets, balloons, and fancy work. Exhibits display historical French items, art work, handicrafts, dolls, antique muskets and ammunition. Band concerts, dancers, and film showings add to the festivities. Held annually since 1969 in mid-July.
Contact: Chamber of Commerce, William Street, Cape Vincent, New York 13618.

New York - New Paltz

ANNUAL HISTORIC HUGUENOT STREET STONE HOUSE DAY
New Paltz, New York

Contact: Huguenot Historical Society, Box 339, New Paltz, New York 12561. (914) 255-1660.

South Carolina - Charleston

FRENCH EMPHASIS FESTIVAL
Charleston, South Carolina

Part of Founders' Festivals, a continuing series of month-long festivals centering on the ethnic groups which were instrumental in the founding and growth of Charleston. Special exhibits in the Gibbes Art Gallery and Charleston Museum, special ethnic foods offered in local restaurants, and two or three major events. Held in February or March.
Contact: Mr. James B. Bagwell, Jr., 313 Pitt Street, Mount Pleasant, South Carolina 29464.

Texas - Castroville

SAINT LOUIS DAY CELEBRATION
Koenig Park on the banks of Medina River
Castroville, Texas

Descendants of Alsatian pioneers gather for annual homecoming. The festival atmosphere is brightened by traditional Alsace-style costumes, dances and rich foods of European heritage. A dance and tours of pioneer homes are other features. There is continuous entertainment throughout the day. Begun in 1889. Held in August.
Contact: Castroville Chamber of Commerce, Post Office Box 572, Castroville, Texas 78009; or Father Larry Steubben, Castroville, Texas 78009.

Texas - Port Arthur

TEXAS-LOUISIANA CAJUN FESTIVAL
Port Arthur, Texas

An ethnic celebration including the Monsieur and Madam Cajun contest, with a king and queen coronation. A cooking contest featuring the renowned creole cooking and French and rock music. Additional activities include a dune buggy parade, accordion contest, and baseball tournaments. Held in May.
Contact: Chamber of Commerce, Post Office Box 460, Port Arthur, Texas 77640.

Airline Offices

AIR FRANCE
(Compagnie Nationale Air France)
North American Headquarters:
1350 Avenue of the Americas
New York, New York 10019 (212) 841-7300

Schedules flights from Paris to: Canada, the United States, and Mexico; to Central and South America; to the Canary Islands and West Africa; to East Africa and Indian Ocean points; to Japan via India and Southeast Asia, via Russia, or via Alaska. Provides services to European countries and the Mediterranean Sea area. Also flies from the United States to Chile via the Caribbean and from Japan to South America via Tahiti. Regional sales offices in the United States: Chicago, Los Angeles, Miami, and Washington. Other sales offices in the United States: Anchorage, Atlanta, Boston, Cleveland, Dallas, Detroit, Hartford, Houston, Kansas City, Milwaukee, New Orleans, Philadelphia, Pittsburgh, San Francisco, and Seattle.

UTA
(Union de Transports Aeriens)
North American Headquarters:
9841 Airport Boulevard, Suite 1000
Los Angeles, California 90045 (213) 649-1810

Provides around-the-world services eastbound and westbound from Paris via Italy, Greece, Pakistan, Sri Lanka, Thailand, Cambodia, Malaysia, Indonesia, New Caledonia, Australia, Fiji, Tahiti, and the west coast of the United States. Flies from France, Switzerland, and Italy to more than 20 cities throughout Africa. Other offices in the United States: Chicago, Dallas, Detroit, Fort Lauderdale, Honolulu, Houston, New York, Saint Louis, San Francisco, Seattle, and Washington.

Ship Lines

FARRELL LINES, INCORPORATED
1 Whitehall
New York, New York 10004 (212) 420-4200

FRENCH LINE

Balfour, Guthrie and Company, Limited, General Agents
1 Maritime Plaza
San Francisco, California 94119 (415) 433-1550

530 West Sixth Street
Los Angeles, California 90014 (213) 627-9051

One World Trade Center
New York, New York 10048 (212) 524-0996

Carries freight and a few passengers from San Francisco and Los Angeles to various ports of the Pacific Northwest, including Vancouver.

PAQUET CRUISES
1370 Avenue of the Americas
New York, New York 10019 (212) 757-9050

Cruises from Port Everglades and Jacksonville, Florida, to the Caribbean, Central America, and Mexico.

Bookdealers and Publishers' Representatives

ADLER'S FOREIGN BOOKS, INCORPORATED
162 Fifth Avenue
New York, New York 10010 (212) 691-5151

ANGELESCU BOOK SERVICE
1800 Fairfield
Detroit, Michigan 48221 (313) 861-5342

THE BOOK COLLECTION OF DR. E. R. MEYER
Post Office Box 815
Rochester, New York 14603 (716) 271-1024

BRODT MUSIC COMPANY
Post Office Box 9345
Charlotte, North Carolina 28299 (704) 332-2177

LA CITE DES LIVRES (new and antiquarian)
2306 Westwood Boulevard
Los Angeles, California 90064 (213) 475-0658

CONTINENTAL BOOK COMPANY
11-03 46th Avenue
Long Island City, New York 11101 (212) 937-4868

DAR AL KUTUB WAL NASHRAT AL ISLAMIYYA
Post Office Box 207
New Brunswick, New Jersey 08901 (201) 249-6961

HAROLD B. DIAMOND, BOOKSELLER
Box 1193
Burbank, California 91507 (213) 846-0342

EUROPA BOOKSTORE
3229 North Clark
Chicago, Illinois 60657 (312) 922-1836

EUROPEAN BOOK COMPANY
925 Larkin Street
San Francisco, California 94109 (415) 474-0626

EUROPEAN PUBLISHERS REPRESENTATIVES
11-03 46th Avenue
Long Island City, New York 11101 (212) 937-4606

LEONARD FOX, LIMITED (antiquarian)
667 Madison Avenue
New York, New York 10021 (212) 888-5480

FRENCH AND EUROPEAN PUBLICATIONS, INCORPORATED (LIBRAIRIE DE FRANCE)
610 Fifth Avenue
New York, New York 10020 (212) 581-8810

FRENCH & SPANISH BOOK CORPORATION
652 South Olive Street
Los Angeles, California 90014 (213) 489-7963

FRENCH BOOK GUILD, CERCLE DU LIVRE DE FRANCE
11-03 46th Avenue
Long Island City, New York 11101 (212) 937-4868

FRENCH BOOK HOUSE (LIBRAIRIE LIPTON)
813 Lexington Avenue
New York, New York 10021 (212) 838-8538

FRENCH BOOKS INTERNATIONAL
500 Sutter
San Francisco, California 94102

FRENCH INSTITUTE AND ALLIANCE FRANCAISE BOOKSTORE
22 East 60th Street
New York, New York 10022 (212) 355-6100

GARNER AND SMITH BOOK STORE
2116 Guadalupe
Austin, Texas 78705 (512) 477-9725

D.O. & G.M. GILFILLAN (history)
1361 Blewett Avenue
San Jose, California 95125 (408) 288-7668

GLOBE BOOK SHOP
1700 Pennsylvania Avenue
Washington, D.C. 20006 (202) 393-1490

GOLDEN GRIFFIN BOOKSHOP
Post Office Box 5292 FDR Station
New York, New York 10150 (212) EL5-3353

LUCIEN GOLDSCHMIDT (rare books, prints, manuscripts)
1117 Madison Avenue
New York, New York 10028 (212) 879-0070

GREAT EXPECTATIONS
911 Foster
Evanston, Illinois 60201 (312) 864-3881

HAMMER MOUNTAIN BOOK HALLS, ABAA (antiquarian)
771 State Street
Schenectady, New York 12307 (518) 393-5266

HATHAWAY HOUSE BOOKSHOP
103 Central Street
Wellesley, Massachusetts 02181 (617) 235-2830

J. N. HERLIN, INCORPORATED
(antiquarian)
68 Thompson Street
New York, New York 10012 (212) 431-8732

IACONI BOOK IMPORTS
300 Pennsylvania Avenue
San Francisco, California 94107 (415) 285-7393

IMPORTED BOOKS
Post Office Box 4414
Dallas, Texas 75208 (214) 941-6497

INSTITUTE OF MODERN LANGUAGES BOOKSTORE
Post Office Box 1087
Silver Spring, Maryland 20910 (301) 565-2580

JUILLIARD SCHOOL BOOKSTORE
Lincoln Center
New York, New York 10023 (212) 799-5000

KINOKUNIYA BOOKSTORES OF AMERICA COMPANY, LIMITED
1581 Webster Street
San Francisco, California 94115 (415) 567-7625

LAROUSSE AND COMPANY
572 Fifth Avenue
New York, New York 10036 (212) 575-9515

Specializes in French and Spanish publications.

R. E. LEWIS, INCORPORATED
Post Office Box 1108
San Rafael, California 94902 (415) 461-4161

LA LIBRAIRIE POPULAIRE
356 Meadow Road
Lowell, Massachusetts 01854 (617) 459-9456

LING'S INTERNATIONAL BOOKS
Post Office Box 82684
San Diego, California 92138 (714) 292-8104

LIPTON BOOKSTORE CORPORATION
813 Lexington Avenue
New York, New York 10021 (212) 838-8538

LE MARAIS: FOREIGN LANGUAGE BOOKS
1700 Shattuck Avenue
Berkeley, California 94709 (415) 849-3683

LOUIS MARTEL & FILS
(antiquarian)
104 Brodge Street
Box 390
Manchester, New Hampshire 03105 (603) 669-1849

MIDDLEBURY COLLEGE STORE
5 Hillcrest Road
Middlebury, Vermont 05753 (802) 388-7722

MIDWEST EUROPEAN PUBLICATIONS, INCORPORATED
915 Foster Street
Evanston, Illinois 60201 (312) 866-6262

MILES
48 Winter Street
Boston, Massachusetts 02108 (617) 482-0751

MODERN LANGUAGE BOOK STORE
3160 O Street, Northwest
Washington, D.C. 20007 (202) 338-8963

OWL AND THE PUSSYCAT
321 South Ashland Avenue
Lexington, Kentucky 40502 (606) 266-7121

PENDRAGON HOUSE, INCORPORATED
2595 East Bayshore Road
Palo Alto, California 94303 (415) 327-5631

PENDRAGON HOUSE OF CONNECTICUT, INCORPORATED
Post Office Box 225
Old Mystic, Connecticut 06372 (203) 536-1163

PENNYWHEEL PRESS
Route 2
Poultney, Vermont 05764 (802) 287-4050

RIZZOLI INTERNATIONAL BOOKSTORE
712 Fifth Avenue
New York, New York 10019 (212) 397-3700

MARY S. ROSENBERG, INCORPORATED
17 West 60th Street
New York, New York 10023 (212) 362-4873

LEONA ROSTENBERG
Box 188
Gracie Station
New York, New York 10026 (212) 831-6628

SCHOENHOF'S FOREIGN BOOKS, INCORPORATED
1280 Massachusetts Avenue
Cambridge, Massachusetts 02138 (617) 547-8855

F.A.O. SCHWARZ
745 Fifth Avenue
New York, New York 10022 (212) 644-9400

SCIENTIFIC AND MEDICAL PUBLICATIONS OF FRANCE CORPORATION
14 East 60th Street
New York, New York 10022 (212) 688-5060

SHERMAN'S
332 Park Avenue
Baltimore, Maryland 21201 (301) 837-3363

SKY BOOKS INTERNATIONAL, INCORPORATED
48 East 50th Street
New York, New York 10022 (212) 688-5086

STAVER BOOKSELLERS
1301 East 57th Street
Chicago, Illinois 60637 (312) 667-3227

TEC-BOOKS LIMITED (Librairie De Documentation TECHNIQUE SA)
41 William
Pittsburgh, Pennsylvania 12901 (518) 561-0005

UNIVERSAL BOOK STORE
5458 North Fifth Street
Philadelphia, Pennsylvania 19120 (215) 549-2897

UNIVERSITY BOOKSTORE
850 West Cross Street
Ypsilanti, Michigan 48197 (313) 487-1000

YALE COOPERATIVE CORPORATION
77 Broadway
New Haven, Connecticut 06520 (203) 772-0670

Books and Pamphlets

THE CITY OF PARIS. Twenty Centuries Young. New York, French Embassy Press and Information Services.

A booklet describing the climate, population, history, administration, economy, public services, media, intellectual and artistic life, and urban planning of France's capital city. Illustrated in black and white.

FRANCE. By Frances Chambers. Oxford and Santa Barbara, California, Clio Press, 1980. (World Bibliographical series)

Annotated entries on works dealing with France's history, geography, economy and politics, as well as its people, their culture, customs, religion and social organizations.

FRENCH LANGUAGE AND LITERATURE: SELECTED REFERENCE MATERIALS. New Haven, Connecticut, Yale University Library, 1971.

FRENCH LANGUAGE AND LITERATURE SERIALS IN SYRACUSE UNIVERSITY LIBRARIES. Compiled by Savita Sharma and Janet Graham. Syracuse, New York, Syracuse University's E.S. Bird Library, 1973.

HOW TO FIND OUT ABOUT FRANCE; A GUIDE TO SOURCES OF INFORMATION. By John Pemberton. Oxford and New York, Pergamon Press, 1966.

Sources of information relevant to various major subject fields are described. Coverage is not restricted to works of French origin.

INTRODUCTION A LA FRANCE. New York, French Cultural Services.

Discusses French ethnic backgrounds, geopolitical elements, population, religion, education, cultural life, science, economics, and industry. A brochure illustrated with many photographs.

A SELECTED, ANNOTATED BIBLIOGRAPHY OF FRENCH LANGUAGE AND LITERATURE OF TITLES AVAILABLE IN THE UNIVERSITY OF MICHIGAN LIBRARIES. Compiled by Connie R. Dunlap. Ann Arbor, Michigan, University of Michigan Library, 1973.

FRENCH-SPEAKING AMERICANS

AMERICA AND FRENCH CULTURE, 1750-1848. By Howard Mumford Jones. Chapel Hill, North Carolina Press, 1927.

Discusses the influence of French politics, religion, language, artistic tradition and customs on American cultural life.

AMERICAN AND FRENCH CULTURE. 1800-1900. By Henry Blumenthal. Baton Rouge, Louisiana, LA State University Press, 1976.

Discusses interchanges in art, science, literature and manners during the nineteenth century.

A BRIEF HISTORY OF THE ACADIANS. By Harry Lewis Griffin. Grand Coteau, Louisiana, College of the Sacred Heart, 1952.

A useful pamphlet.

CAJUN SKETCHES FROM THE PRAIRIES OF SOUTH-WEST LOUISIANA. By Lauren Post, LA State University, 1962.

Tells about the country and people, their traditions and values with stress on Acadian life.

THE CAJUNS; ESSAYS ON THEIR HISTORY AND CULTURE. Edited by Glenn Conrad. 2nd edition. Lafayette, Center for Louisiana Studies, University of Southwestern Louisiana, 1978.

Twelve essays that tell the story of the Cajuns from the time of their exile from Nova Scotia to 1978 and how they had a role in shaping contemporary Louisiana.

THE CAJUNS: FROM ACADIA TO LOUISIANA. By William Raston. New York, Farrar Straus Giroux, 1979.

Combination of history and social customs or way of life (music, cooking, etc.) of the Cajuns. Includes a chronology, numerous illustrations and short play.

CAJUNS ON THE BAYOUS. By Carolyn Ramsey. New York, Hastings House, 1957.

Author's story of her search for the true Cajun of Evangeline's land (Louisiana).

CHURCH AND STATE IN FRENCH COLONIAL LOUISIANA POLICY AND POLITICS TO 1732. By Charles Edwards O'Neill. New Haven, Yale University Press, 1966.

Uses documents of the times to examine the relations between civil and religious politics.

A COMPARATIVE VIEW OF FRENCH LOUISIANA, 1699 and 1762: THE JOURNALS OF PIERRE LE MOYNE D'IBERVILLE AND JEAN-JACQUES-BLAISE D'ABBADIE. Edited by Carl Brasseaux, Lafayette, Louisiana, Center for Louisiana Studies, University of Southwestern Louisiana, 1979.

Iberville's journal gives his account of the journey to and exploration of the Mississippi River and D'Abbadie's journal is an account of Louisiana's development during the aftermath of the Seven Years' War.

ÉMIGRÉS IN THE WILDERNESS. By Thomas Wood Clarke. New York, Macmillan, 1941.

During the terror of the French Revolution supporters of the royal house as well as of Napoleon sought asylum in the New World. They were active in establishing colonies in Pennsylvania and New York. One of their number, Eleazar Williams, claimed to be the lost Dauphin of the house of Bourbon.

AN ETHNIC SURVEY OF WOONSOCKET, RHODE ISLAND. By Bessie Wessel. Chicago, Illinois, University of Chicago Press, 1931.

The results of a survey conducted among the children and the families represented in the public schools. It describes the ethnic and regional derivation of the population, ethnic changes which were taking place and the cultural situations which existed there at the time.

EVANGELINE AND THE ACADIANS. By Robert Tallant. New York, Random House, 1957.

Juvenile book depicting the history of the Acadians in Louisiana.

FRANCE AND ENGLAND IN NORTH AMERICA - BEING A COMPREHENSIVE HISTORY. 16 volumes. By Francis Parkman. Boston, Little, Brown, 1851-1892.

Standard work and still of great value although superceded in many aspects. The fundamental question is why France lost out to England in the struggle for the North American continent. Parkman asserts that the exhaustion of France's monarchy, feudalistic system and Roman Catholic Church could not adequately meet the challenge of England's more liberal politics and reformed church. Volumes 1-2 Pioneers of France in the New World (1865); Volume 5 La Salle and the Discovery of the Great West (1879; originally The Discovery of the Great West, 1869); Volumes 6-7 The Old Regime in Canada (1874);

Volume 8 Count Frontenac and New France Under Louis XIV (1877); Volumes 9-10 A Half-Century of Conflict (1892); Volumes 11-13 (Montcalm and Wolfe (1884); Volumes 14-15 The Conspiracy of Pontiac (1851). A one-volume edition of the series was published in 1902 under the title "The Struggle for a Continent."

FRANCE AND RHODE ISLAND, 1686-1800. By Mary Ellen Loughrey. New York, King's Crown Press, 1944.

A study of the relations between France and Rhode Island mostly dealing with political and military history.

FRANCE IN AMERICA. By William John Eccles. New American Nation series. New York, Harper, 1972.

Takes issue with Parkman's thesis that France failed to maintain its North American possessions because of internal political and social weakness. Blames the bad military tactics before Quebec. Includes descriptive bibliography.

FRANCE IN AMERICA. By Reuben Gold Thwaites, 1497-1763. Volume 7 of the American Nation: A History. Edited by Albert B. Hart. New York, York and London: Harper, 1905; rpt, New York: Cooper Square, 1968; rpt. New York: Haskel House, 1969; rpt. Westport, Connecticut: Greenwood, 1970.

History of the French in Canada, the Old Northwest and Louisiana, and their relations with the neighboring English colonies.

THE FRANCO-TEXAN LAND COMPANY. By Virginia Taylor. Austin, University of Texas Press, 1969.

Story of the Franco-Texan Land Company, a company that gained control of acres of Texas land due to bonds they held.

FRENCH ACTIVITIES IN CALIFORNIA; AN ARCHIVAL CALENDAR-GUIDE. By Abraham Nasatir. Stanford University, California, Stanford University Press, London, H. Milford, Oxford University Press, 1945.

Part one consists of French activities in California prior to statehood and part 2 is a calendar guide of the materials relating to California in the Archives of France.

THE FRENCH AND BRITISH IN THE OLD NORTHWEST. By Henry Putney Beers. Detroit, Michigan, Wayne State University Press, 1964.

Essays on the acquisition, preservation, and publication of the French and British officials in the old Northwest. Followed by an extensive bibliographical list.

FRENCH CATHOLIC MISSIONARIES IN THE PRESENT UNITED STATES (1604-1791). By Sister Mary Mulvey. Washington, Catholic University of America, 1936. (New York, AMS Press, 1974).

The story of the French missionaries in America based on published source collections and secondary works. Also includes a selective bibliography.

FRENCH COLONISTS AND EXILES IN THE UNITED STATES. By J. G. Rosengarten. Philadelphia, J. B. Lippincott Company, 1907.

Discusses the prominent part played by French settlers in the United States from colonial times through the nineteenth century. Deals with early French settlements, origins, and characteristics of various types of settlers, principal regions of settlement, and outstanding Frenchmen who came to the United States. Appendix A contains a bibliography; Appendix B lists French place names in the United States and their origins.

FRENCH ÉMIGRÉ PRIESTS IN THE UNITED STATES (1791-1815). By Leo Ruskowski. Washington, Catholic University of America Press, 1940. (New York, AMS Press, 1974).

Tells the story of the French priests who came to America after the outbreak of the French Revolution and continued to come up to the Bourbon restoration in 1815.

THE FRENCH FOUNDATIONS, 1680-1693. Edited by Theodore C. Pease and Raymond C. Werner. Springfield, Illinois, Illinois State Historical Library, 1934.

The role of the French in what later became Illinois is presented in the relevant documents accompanied by an explanatory historical essay.

THE FRENCH IN AMERICA. By Virginia Brainerd Kunz. New York, Lerner, 1966.

Part of the In America Series. Suitable for children.

THE FRENCH IN AMERICA, 1488-1974: A CHRONOLOGY AND FACTBOOK. By James Pula. Cobbs Ferry, New York, Oceana Publications, 1975. (Ethnic Chronology Series, No. 20).

A brief introduction to French influences on American life, that tries to cover a broad range of topics; politics, military affairs, education, sports, music, etc. Also includes various documents and a bibliography.

THE FRENCH IN NORTH AMERICA; A BIBLIOGRAPHICAL GUIDE TO FRENCH ARCHIVES, REPRODUCTIONS, AND RESEARCH MISSIONS. By Henry Beers, Baton Rouge, Louisiana State University Press, 1957.

A history of the activities of American and Canadian institutions, historians and others connected with reproductions of archives and manuscript collections pertaining to the French in America. An extensive bibliography is included.

THE FRENCH IN THE HEART OF AMERICA. By John Finley. New York, Charles Scribner's Sons, 1916.

Tells the story of French exploration and settlement from Labrador to the Great Lakes and south to the Gulf of Mexico. Discusses the development of western cities and towns from French forts and portage paths, and the struggle for dominion over the Mississippi Valley region. Based on a series of lectures at the Sorbonne in Paris.

THE FRENCH IN THE MISSISSIPPI VALLEY. Edited by John Francis McDermott. Urbana, University of Illinois Press, 1965.

Describes the early history of Saint Louis, Missouri, and activities of French explorers, traders, naturalists, and settlers in the Mississippi Valley. The fourteen papers included were presented originally at a conference observing the 200th anniversary of the founding of Saint Louis.

THE FRENCH IN THE MISSISSIPPI VALLEY, 1740-1750. By Norman Ward Caldwell. Urbana, Illinois, University of Illinois Press, 1941; rpt. Philadelphia, Porcupine, 1974.

Examines the governmental system of New France, and its weaknesses, population and industry in the western country, fur trade and Anglo-French rivalry, and Indian affairs. Based on primary documents, many of which, like the Vaudreuil manuscripts are here used for the first time.

FRENCH-INDIAN RELATIONS ON THE SOUTHERN FRONTIER, 1699-1762. By Patricia Woods. Ann Arbor, Michigan, UMI Research Press, 1980.

A doctoral thesis originally published under the title: "The Relations between the French of Colonial Louisiana and the Choctaw, Chickasaw and Natchez Indians, 1699-1762."

A FRENCH JOURNALIST IN THE CALIFORNIA GOLD RUSH; THE LETTERS OF ÉTIENNE DERBEC. By Etienne Derbec. Edited by A. P. Nasatir. Georgetown, California, Talisman Press, 1964.

Book begins with a short narrative of Derbec's life followed by translations of his letters.

THE FRENCH OF CANADA AND NEW ENGLAND, A NEWCOMEN SOCIETY IN NORTH AMERICA. By Olivier Maurault. Newcomen Society in North America, 1950.

THE FRENCH PRESENCE IN MARYLAND, 1524-1800. By Gregory Wood. Baltimore, Gateway Press, 1978.

A three century account of French presence in Maryland, divided into periods 1524 to French and Indian War, 1755 to 1775 and 1776 to 1800.

THE FRENCH REGIME IN WISCONSIN AND THE NORTHWEST. By Louise Phelps Kellogg. Madison, Wisconsin, State Historical Society of Madison, 1925; rpt. Washington, D.C.: Cooper Square, 1968.

Useful history, though derived from printed sources only.

FRENCH REFUGEE LIFE IN THE UNITED STATES, 1790-1800. By Frances S. Child. Baltimore, 1940.

Examines the complex relations between America and France after the American Revolution and during the French Revolution.

THE FRENCH TRADITION IN AMERICA. By Yves F. Zoltvany. New York, Harper, 1969; Columbia, South Carolina, University of South Carolina Press, 1969.

Reprints primary documents illustrative of the French presence in America, each introduced by a short historical sketch and suggestions for further reading.

General introductory essay is a good historical overview.

FRENCHMEN AND FRENCH WAYS IN THE MISSISSIPPI VALLEY, CONFERENCE ON THE FRENCH IN THE MISSISSIPPI VALLEY. Urbana, University of Illinois Press, 1969.

A variety of papers on political, military, architectural, social, scientific and cultural aspects of the history of the French in the Mississippi Valley.

FROM QUEBEC TO NEW ORLEANS; The Story of the French in America. By J. H. Schlarman. Belleville, Illinois, Buechler Publishing Company, 1929.

Describes the adventures of French explorers, missionaries, and settlers and their struggle to dominate and keep the lands from Quebec to New Orleans. Ends with the American Revolution and the capture of Vincennes in 1779.

HISTORY OF THE FRENCH PROTESTANT REFUGEES, FROM THE REVOCATION OF THE EDICT OF NANTES TO OUR OWN DAYS. By M. Charles Weiss. New York, Stringer and Townsend, 1854.

A two volume set that studies the destiny of those exiles who left their country to come to America.

HISTORY OF THE HUGUENOT EMIGRATION TO AMERICA. By Charles Baird. New York, Dodd, Mead and Company, 1885. Baltimore Regional Publishing Company, 1968.

A two volume set that narrates the emigration of the persecuted Protestants of France to the New World after the Edict of Nantes had been revoked. Volume one deals with before the revocation of the Edict and volume two deals with settlement in America.

THE HUGUENOT; The Story of the Huguenot Emigrations, Particularly to New England, in Which is Included the Early Life of Apollos Rivoire, the Father of Paul Revere. By Donald Douglas. New York, E. P. Dutton and Company, 1954.

Narrates the story of Apollos Rivoire as a type and example of the French Huguenot immigrant in New England. Presents the customs, habits, beliefs, and qualities of early Huguenot settlers and their contributions to the civilization and culture of New England, New York, Pennsylvania, and southern colonies. The first section deals with the Old World, and the second section with life in the New World.

A HUGUENOT EXILE IN VIRGINIA; OR VOYAGES OF A FRENCHMAN EXILED FOR HIS RELIGION. Durand, New York, Press of the Pioneers, 1934.

Book contains an account of the measures taken against the Protestants after the Revocation of the Edict of Nantes and the flight of a Dauphin nobleman.

THE HUGUENOTS OF COLONIAL SOUTH CAROLINA. By Arthur Hirsch. Durham, North Carolina, Duke University Press, 1928.

This book presents the contributions made in South Carolina by the French Protestants. Includes a bibliography.

THE INFLUENCE OF FRENCH IMMIGRATION ON THE POLITICAL HISTORY OF THE UNITED STATES. By Elizabeth H. Avery. Reprinted from the American Historical Review, 1925. San Francisco, R and E Research Associates, 1972.

Evaluates the influence exerted by two groups of French settlers: the French Protestants in the Atlantic colonies, and the French Catholics in the Mississippi Valley and the "old Northwest." Examines their influence on the outcome of the American Revolution, on the formation of state constitutions, on the national Constitution, during the early period of the Constitution, and after the Louisiana Purchase.

MEMOIR CONCERNING THE FRENCH SETTLEMENTS AND FRENCH SETTLERS IN THE COLONY OF RHODE ISLAND. By Elisha Potter. Providence, Rhode Island, Rider, 1879. Reprint: Baltimore, Genealogical Publishing Company, 1968.

Relates the story of the settlement of French town in 1689 and what happened to it later. Follows a few prominent French families of Rhode Island.

MEMOIRS OF A HUGUENOT FAMILY. By Jacques Fontaine. Baltimore, Genealogical Publishing Company, 1967.

Drawn from family manuscripts, this book is a history of a Huguenot family. Appendix contains various documents and a translation of the Edict of Nantes.

MEMORIALS OF THE HUGUENOTS IN AMERICA, WITH SPECIAL REFERENCE TO THEIR EMIGRATION TO PENNSYLVANIA. By Ammon Stapleton. Baltimore, Genealogical Publishing Company, 1964.

THE MISSISSIPPI VALLEY FRONTIER; The Age of French Exploration and Settlement. By John Anthony Caruso. Indianapolis, Bobbs-Merrill Company, 1966.

Narrates a social history of the French voyageurs, missionaries, explorers, and settlers who mapped out trade routes, founded settlements, and established contact with Indian cultures.

THE NAPOLEONIC EXILES IN AMERICA; A Study in American Diplomatic History, 1815-1819. By Jesse Reeves. Baltimore, John Hopkins Press, 1905.

This study of the Napoleonic exiles who fled to America after the monarchy was re-established in France centers about the colonial enterprise called Champ d'Asile on the banks of the Trinity River in Texas.

OLD MOBILE: FORT LOUIS DE LA LOUISIANA, 1702-1711. By Jay Higginbotham. Mobile, Alabama, Museum of the City of Mobile, 1977.

A history of the personalities and events surrounding the establishment and life of the now extinct town, Old Mobile.

PEOPLE OF THE BAYOU: CAJUN LIFE IN LOST AMERICA. By Christopher Hallowell. New York, Dutton, 1979.

Story of the Cajuns and the environment they live in, one that never ceases influencing their lives.

THE RISE AND FALL OF NEW FRANCE. Two volumes. By George M. Wrong. New York, Macmillan, 1928.

Comprehensive general history. Wrong sees conflict between France and England in America as essentially a conflict between absolutism and liberty.

THE SHADOWS OF THE TREES. The Story of the French Canadians in New England. By Jacques Ducharme. New York, Harper, 1943.

Illustrates the cultural impact and interaction of French Canadians living in New England.

THE TRUE STORY OF THE ACADIANS. By Dudley LeBlanc. Lafayette, Louisiana, 1932.

Depicts the events of Acadian history from their exile to the settlement in Louisiana.

Audiovisual Material

MAP

MAP OF FRANCE. Paris, Ministry for Youth, Sport and Leisure, 1980.

A road map of France with the eastern part of the country on one side and the western part on the other. An insert enlarges the area around Paris. Information is given for tourists on the formalities of entering France, catagories of hotels, information bureaus, traveling by train or car. Short descriptions of major regions are given.

FILMS

ADD PENICILLIN, STIR WELL. (Videorecording). Color and sound. 30 minutes. By BBC-TV. Released by Time-Life Multimedia, New York, 1978.

Depicts the rustic lifestyle of a region in southwestern France where the production of Roquefort cheese, made from a unique fungus found in local caves, is a major occupation.

AN AGE OF REVOLUTIONS. 16 mm. Color and sound. 26 minutes. Also issued as videorecording. By Polonius Film Services. Released by International Film Bureau, Chicago, 1976.

Explores fundamental changes in Western civilization which occurred as a result of industrialization and the French Revolution.

ALL ABOUT BRITTANY. 16 mm. Color and sound. 20 minutes. By Armor Film. Available from F.A.C. S.E.A., New York. In French or English.

Life in Brittany: fishing sardines and tuna fish, collecting seaweeds, building small fishing boats, making lace and Quimper pottery. Women in their folk costumes, shipyards in St. Nazaire and Brest. Visits to St. Malo, Dinan, Concarneau, Locronan, La Baule and the menhirs.

ALLONS EN FRANCE. 16 mm. Color and sound. 26 minutes. By Creation and Information. Available from F.A.C.S.E.A., New York. In French and English. Beautiful travel film on the green holiday resorts. Shows forgotten sites, landscapes, vacation villages, river tourism, especially in Brittany, the south of France and the valley of the Loire.

ALSACE. 16 mm. Color and sound. 12 minutes. By S.M. Productions, 1971. Available from F.A.C. S.E.A., New York. In French and English.

A flight over a picturesque province which has kept its own character despite its remarkable development since the creation of the Common Market. Strasbourg, Colmar, Riquewihr are treasures of local architecture. The ever-present Rhine is the soul of the region.

". . . AND I AM FRENCH". 16 mm. Color and sound. 27 minutes. By French Ministry of Foreign Affairs. Released by Association Films, New York, 1979.

In a visual tour of the Alsace, Brittany and Basque regions, this film treats a theme common to a modern man: the preservation of his cultural and ethnic identity. The film highlights regional languages, which far from tempering the national spirit, serve to strengthen it. The little-known characteristics peculiar to each French region now receive the support of the central government. "Yes, we speak Basque . . . but we are French . . ."; against the backdrop of beautiful countryside, this statement sums up the profound feeling of the inhabitants of the French Provinces who are proud to be . . . French above all.

CHANZEAUX-PARIS: TWO FRENCH FAMILIES. 16 mm. Color and sound. 28 minutes. By French Ministry of Foreign Affairs. Released by Association Films, New York, 1979.

"Two French Families" takes a look at the lifestyles of a traditional large farming family in western France and a young urban couple with one child in Paris. The film is narrated by Dr. Laurence Wylie, a Harvard anthropologist and author of numerous works on France. It shows that despite growing differences in their lifestyles, French families, whether traditional or modern, remain strongly attached to the same basic principles. By describing two models of family life in France, the film attempts to provide a deeper insight into this time-honored institution and the significance it has in French national life.

A CHOCOLATE SANDWICH? 16 mm. Color and sound. 17 minutes. By Films/West. Released by FilmFair Communications, Studio City, California, 1976.

Uses a chocolate sandwich to introduce French culture and customs. Shows the importance of bread and neighborhood bakeries in the daily life of a French family.

CONFLUENT SANS ÂGE. 16 mm. Color and sound. 18 minutes. By Films Caravelle. Available from F.A.C.S.E.A., New York. In French or English.

The city of Lyon's two thousand years are written into the stones which witnessed a glorious past. Culture and activity show continuity from Gaul until modern times at this ageless meeting-place of rivers.

EN FRANCE. 16 mm. Color. 30 minutes. By Creation 9 Information S.A., 1973. Available from F.A.C.S.E.A., New York.

A panoramic view of France. The film includes views of Versailles, Alsace, the Camargue, Paris, etc.

ENTRE MARNE ET SEINE. 16 mm. Color and sound. 17 minutes. By Atlantic Films. Available from F.A.C.S.E.A., New York. In French and English.

At approximately one half-hour's journey from Paris one can find all the charm of spring, the calm of the river, the gentle quietness of winter in the forest. One is reminded of Bossuet, Proust, Gerard de Nerval. The film takes us from Meaux to Guermantes, from Vaux-le-Vicomte to Fountainebleau, places often of glorious memory.

DE PARIS AUX CHATEAUX DE LA LOIRE. 16 mm. Color and sound. 25 minutes. By Lucien Censier. Available from F.A.C.S.E.A., New York. In English.

A very lively visit to the chateaux; each portrait comes to life and we tour the castle with its original owner.

FAMILIES OF THE WORLD - FRANCE. 16 mm. Color and sound. 19 minutes. By Goldberg/Werrenrath Productions. Journal Films, Evanston, Illinois, 1979.

Presents insight into the history, culture, and life-style of the French people by focusing on some of the activities of a family living in a suburb of Paris.

THE FOREIGN LEGION. 16 mm. Color and sound. 60 minutes. By Bomi Productions, Canada, 1972.

A documentary about the French Foreign Legion today.

FRANCE. 16 mm. Color and sound. 25 minutes. Screenscope, Arlington, Virginia, 1978.

Presents an intimate portrait of France through visits to five different families living in different areas of France.

FRANCE, MOMENTS IN HISTORY. 16 mm. Color and sound. 17 minutes. By Ernest Kleinberg Films, Santa Barbara, California, 1979.

Traces the evolution of France beginning in the pre-Christian era through the French Revolution.

FRANCE, THE CHANGING SCENE. 16 mm. Color and sound. 20 minutes. Ernest Kleinberg Films, Santa Barbara, California, 1979.

Presents a view of contemporary life in France and shows that France remains strongly attached to traditions and institutions from the past while at the same time embracing the technological advancements of the future.

FRANCE TODAY: PATTERNS OF PROGRESS. 16 mm. Color and sound. By the French Ministry of Foreign Affairs, 1972.

France is famed for its 18th-century democratic revolution, but its more recent industrial revolution has made it one of the world's economic leaders as well. This film shows the industrial face of France from the ancient industries such as glass and textiles to ultra modern transportation and communications. In this fast-paced film, France shows its other revolution.

FRENCH VILLAGE. 16 mm. Color and sound. 22 minutes. By Juniper Films. International Film Foundation, New York, 1979.

Portrays the daily continuity of activities in the small French village of Saint-Alvere. Captures picturesque routines of existence, along with scenes of festive celebrations which are part of the tradition and culture of the village. Without narration.

FRENCHMAN'S HOLIDAY. 16 mm. Color and sound. 30 minutes. Also issued as videocassette. By BBC-TV. Released by Time-Life Multimedia, New York, 1978.

Explores the region of the Dordogne River and the Auvergne Mountains in southwestern France, which serves as a playground for vacationing Frenchmen.

HIGH IN THE MOUNTAINS. 16 mm. Color and sound. 26 minutes. By French Ministry of Foreign Affairs, 1977. In French and English.

In the shadow of Mont Blanc, the Chamonix mountain guides are busy. Chamonix is a unique town which commands a certain way of life. The Maurienne mountain medics share the hardy life of farmers and artisans. And then there are the toilers of the mountain, building aerial cable cars in the most perilous conditions.

IN THE NAME OF FRANCE. 16 mm. Black and white. Sound. 40 minutes. Also issued as video-recording. By BBC-TV. Released by Time-Life Multimedia, New York, 1971.

Tells the story of the French men and women who resisted and of those who collaborated with the Nazis during World War II.

INTRODUCING FRANCE. Videorecording. Black and white. Sound. 20 minutes. By Madeleine Films for North Atlantic Treaty Organization. Distributed by National Audiovisual Center, 1979.

Describes the country and the people of France, including geographical features, historical development and achievements, economic life, occupations of the people, and social customs. Explains briefly the role of France in the North Atlantic Treaty Organization.

INVASION OF SOUTHERN FRANCE. Videorecording. Black and white. Sound. 19 minutes. By United States Department of the Army, Washington. Distributed by National Audiovisual Center, Washington, 1980.

Portrays the World War II invasion of southern France by the 7th U.S. Army and its subsequent juncture with the 3d Army in northern France.

PARIS. 16 mm. Color and sound. 15 minutes. By M. Productions, 1972. Available from F.A.C.S.E.A., New York. In English or French.

A flight over Paris in a helicopter.

PARIS JAMAIS VU. 16 mm. Color and sound. By Films Montsouris, 1968. Available from F.A.C.S.E.A., New York. In French or English.

Paris seen from a helicopter with good background music.

PALACE TEMPLE OF THE SUN KING. 16 mm. Color and sound. By Knosos France Films, 1975. Available from F.A.C.S.E.A., New York. In French or English.

The film approaches Versailles from a brand new angle: it is the one of the "solar myth", which means that following the ancient traditions, the orientation of a place is not an arbitrary act. It sets a place in line with the sun. It opens it to the sky--it puts it in harmony with the order of the universe. Providentially preserved, Versailles, mankind's last solar temple, lies open to the heavens. Now as ever, Versailles belongs to eternity.

LE PAYS D'ARLES. 16 mm. Color and sound. 21 minutes. By Les Films Jean Leherissey. Available from F.A.C.S.E.A., New York. In French and English.

The Arles country is, in itself, a perfect synthesis of Provence. It is a land of history, art, poetry and tradition. This film depicts Arles, Roman and Romanesque city, the Abbeys of Montmajour and Fontvielle with the memory of Alphonse Daudet; the Alpilles with les Baux; Saint-Remy evoking Van Gogh, Nostradamus and Gounod; the antiques and the evocations of Glanum; the Camargue region with the Vaccares reservation, the salt works, the culture of rice, the life of wild cattle and the pilgrimage to Saintes-Maries.

LES PRISONNIERES. 16 mm. Color and sound. 44 minutes. Released by General Conference of Seventh-Day Adventists, Department of Public Affairs and Religious Liberty, Washington, D.C., 1979. By Burt Martin Associates, Incorporated.

A 15-year old American girl discovers her Huguenot heritage while attending school in France. She also learns about the experiences of Marie Durand who was imprisoned for 38 years because of her beliefs.

THE PROMISE OF GREENER DAYS. 16 mm. Color and sound. 27 minutes. By French Ministry of Foreign Affairs, 1977.

This film will capture the interest of anyone concerned about the environment. Its subject is the river Seine, which gives Paris so much charm. Winding its way through northern France, the Seine flows through centuries-old villages whose beauty must be preserved, and into fishing communities whose livelihoods depend upon it. Much more than a dialogue, it is an outstanding visual study of this vital issue in a modern industrial society. This film won a "Silver Screen" at the International Industrial Film Festival in Chicago, April 1979.

LA PROVINCE DE PARIS. 16 mm. Color and sound. 16 minutes. By S. M. Productions, 1972. Available from F.A.C.S.E.A., New York.

A flight over the Île-de-France. An insight into this area's historical past as evoked by its cathedrals (Senlis, Chartres, Orleans), its ancient towns (Provins, Dreux, Moret-sur-Loina) and its chateaux (Fountainebleaux, Chantilly, Versailles). A description of Île-de-France touristic attractions (lakes, forests, sites) and economic resources.

THE RISE OF NATIONS IN EUROPE. 16 mm. Color and sound. 13 minutes. By Coronet Instructional Media, Chicago, 1977.

Tells how and why the countries of Western Europe, particularly France, developed from groups of independent states to strong national governments.

THEN TURN NOT PALE, BELOVED SNAIL. Videorecording. Color and sound. 30 minutes. By BBC-TV. Released by Time-Life Multimedia, New York, 1978.

Visits a picturesque village in southwestern France and observes a typical French wedding ceremony and the festivities that continue for two days.

FILMS ABOUT CAJUNS

ALLONS Á LOUISIANA. Cajun Country! 16 mm. Color and sound. 29 minutes. By Carolyn Ramsey Films, Baton Rouge, Louisiana for the Louisiana Travel Promotion Association, 1975.

Gives an account of dispossessed Acadian exiles who made their home in the Louisiana bayou country over 200 years ago. Shows the land, settlements and personality of these people.

LOUISIANA BUSS CHAMP. 16 mm. Color and sound. 25 minutes. Charlotte, North Carolina, Victory Film Productions, 1978.

Focuses on the Atchafalaya Basin in Louisiana discussing its early settlement by French Canadians and showing the various types of wildlife found in the area.

SPEND IT ALL. Videorecording. Color and sound. 41 minutes. By Flower Films, El Cerrito, California, 1979.

Presents the history, dances, leisure, people, and places of Louisiana's Cajun country. Captures the bravado and vitality of the Cajun people in various social and cultural activities, along with the music of the Balfa Brothers, More Avoy, Nathan Abshire and others.

FILMS ABOUT FRENCH CANADIANS

THE BALLAD OF JOE CARIBOU. 16 mm. Color and sound. 19 minutes. By ITT Films and Broadcast. Released by Schoenfeld Film Distributing Corporation, 1973. Also available in French.

Tells 100 years of history of Quebec's north shore through the story of one family. Presents songs and dances to describe French Canadian culture.

THE FRENCH. 16 mm. Color and sound. 50 minutes. CTV Television Network, 1976.

Examines France's contribution to Canada. Traces the settlement of the French in Canada up to the present. Points out problems of French Canadians today, who regard themselves as an endangered cultural group.

THE INVISIBLE FRENCH? 16 mm. Color and sound. 40 minutes. By York. University Department of Instructional Aid Resources, Toronto, 1972.

Takes a look at the nonvisible group of the Toronto French community through the eyes of the French themselves.

A RIDICULOUS KIND OF COUNTRY. 16 mm. Black and white. Sound. 117 minutes. By National Film Board of Canada, 1970.

In French with voice-over English translation of the titles and dialog. French Canadians metaphorically explore their own identity in a bilingual country.

WE SING MORE THAN WE CRY. 16 mm. Color and sound. 16 minutes. By National Film Board of Canada, Montreal, 1975.

A documentary on Acadia in word, song, and music, in which young and old offer personal expressions of their Acadian identity.

GERMANS
(Includes MENNONITES; MORAVIANS; PENNSYLVANIA DUTCH)

Embassy and Consulates

EMBASSY OF THE FEDERAL REPUBLIC OF GERMANY (West Germany)
4645 Reservoir Road, Northwest
Washington, D. C. 20007 (202) 298-4000

CONSULATES GENERAL

229 Peachtree Street Northeast, Suite 909
Atlanta, Georgia 30303 (404) 659-4760

535 Boylston Street
Boston, Massachusetts 02116 (617) 536-4414

104 South Michigan Avenue
Chicago, Illinois 60603 (312) 263-0850

2200 Book Building
1249 Washington Boulevard
Detroit, Michigan 48226 (313) 962-6526

1900 Yorktown
San Felipe Professional Building, Suite 405
Houston, Texas 77056 (713) 627-7770

6435 Wilshire Boulevard
Los Angeles, California 90048 (213) 852-0441

100 North Biscayne Boulevard
Miami, Florida 33132 (305) 358-0290

2 Canal Street
2834 International Trade Mart
New Orleans, Louisiana 70130 (504) 524-6560

460 Park Avenue
New York, New York 10022 (212) 940-9200

601 California Street, 6th Floor
San Francisco, California 94108 (415) 981-4250

1200 Fifth Avenue
1617 IBM Building
Seattle, Washington 98101 (206) 682-4313

EMBASSY OF THE GERMAN DEMOCRATIC REPUBLIC (East Germany)
1717 Massachusetts Avenue, Northwest
Washington, D. C. 20036 (202) 232-3134

Mission to the United Nations

FEDERAL REPUBLIC OF GERMANY MISSION (West Germany)
600 Third Avenue
New York, New York 10016 (212) 949-9200

GERMAN DEMOCRATIC REPUBLIC MISSION (East Germany)
58 Park Avenue
New York, New York 10016 (212) 686-2596

Tourist and Travel Offices

GERMAN INFORMATION CENTER
410 Park Avenue
New York, New York 10022 (212) 752-5020

GERMAN NATIONAL TOURIST OFFICE
630 Fifth Avenue
New York, New York (212) 757-8570

11 South La Salle Street
Chicago, Illinois 60603 (312) 263-2958

700 South Flower Street #1714
Los Angeles, California 90017 (213) 688-7332

Fraternal Organizations

ALLIANCE OF TRANSYLVANIAN SAXONS
5393 Pearl Road
Cleveland, Ohio 44129 (216) 842-0333
President: Edward R. Schneider Founded 1902

Fraternal benefit life insurance society. Maintains museum and biographical archives; sponsors competitions. Committees: National; Orphan Fund. Formerly: (1966) Central Verband der Siebenburger Sachsen of the U. S.
Publications: Saxon News VolkBlatt, weekly; Annual Report; Yearbook.

AMERICAN COUNCIL ON GERMANY
680 Fifth Avenue
New York, New York 10019 (212) 397-0076
Executive Director: David Klein Founded 1952

To promote understanding between the U. S. and the Federal Republic of Germany. Provides opportunities for the exchange of ideas and experiences between leading nationals of the two countries. Initiates a variety of programs not duplicated by governmental or private groups to achieve these purposes. Recently dealt with the problems of nuclear energy, international economic and monetary policy, and the relations of the developed industrial states with the threshold countries of the developing world. Supports efforts by other organizations which promise political, economic, or social benefits to both the U.S. and the Federal Republic. Publications on German problems issued from time to time.

CORPS BRANDENBURGIA
2950 Warrensville Center Road
Shaker Heights, Ohio 44122 (216) 752-9927
Secretary: Edward M. Grala Founded 1937

Koesener League of Germanic (Germany, Austria and Switzerland) dueling corps at the various universities of the corresponding lands. "Conducts traditional corps activities of so-called dueling program (Schlaeger-Mensur), 'Kneipen,' 'Kommerse,' and literary-lecture program" Maintains 400 volume library.
Publications: Corpszeitung (bulletin), annual.

COSMOPOLITAN SOCCER LEAGUE
Post Office Box 1117
Secaucus, New Jersey 07094 (201) 338-7403
General Secretary: Fritz L. Marth Founded 1923

Soccer clubs comprising about 250 teams with about 5,000 active members. Founded to play and promote the sport of soccer football and to promote soccer among junior players. Sponsors an annual (usually May) goodwill tour of the United States by a German soccer team. Affiliated with the United States Soccer Football Association.
Formerly: German-American Football Association.

GERMAN-AMERICAN NATIONAL CONGRESS
999 Elmhurst Road, Suite 33
Mt. Prospect, Illinois 60056 (312) 870-7666
President: Willy Scharpenberg Founded 1958

Americans of German ancestry (noncitizens may join if willing to become United States citizens). A non-partisan, politically and culturally interested civic organization which seeks to maintain German culture, art, and customs. Works for the extended promotion and dissemination of the German language in educational institutions in the United States. Promotes friendly relations between the United States and Germany. Seeks to counter through suitable means anti-German agitation and propaganda. Maintains Arthur Koegel Library of German Literature. Also known as Deutsch-Amerikanischer National-Kongress. Absorbed Federation of American Citizens of German Descent.
Publication: Der Deutsch-Amerikaner, monthly.

GERMAN ORDER OF HARUGARI
c/o Viola Hartz
124 Plattsburg Avenue
Burlington, Vermont 05401 (802) 864-6598
Supreme Grand Secretary: Viola Hartz Founded 1847

Fraternal benefit life insurance society of German-Americans. Also known as: Deutscher Orden der Harugari.

GERMANS-FROM-RUSSIA HERITAGE SOCIETY
Box 1671
Bismarck, North Dakota 58501 (701) 223-6167

Dedicated to preserving the ethnic heritage of Germans from Russia. Maintains archives and a library. Publishes books, pamphlets and audiovisual materials.
Publication: Heritage Review, quarterly.

SCHLARAFFIA NORD-AMERIKA
35 Ojibway Road
Randallstown, Maryland 21133 (301) 655-8451
National Secretary: H. C. Palm Founded 1859

German-American cultural and social organization for professional and business men.
Publications: Membership Roster, annual.

STEUBEN SOCIETY OF AMERICA
6705 Fresh Pond Road
Ridgewood, New York 11385 (212) 381-0900
National Secretary: William K. Muschler Founded 1919

American citizens of Germanic extraction. Named after General Frederick William von Steuben (1730-1794) who came from Germany to fight in the American Revolution.
Publication: Steuben News, monthly.

Professional Organizations

AMERICAN ASSOCIATION OF TEACHERS OF GERMAN
523 Building, Suite 201
Route 38
Cherry Hill, New Jersey 08034 (609) 663-5264
Executive Director: R. Govier Founded 1926

Professional and educational society of teachers of German at all levels. Bestows awards to outstanding high school students of German. Maintains Placement Information Center to assist teachers of German in locating employment.
Publications: German Quarterly; Newsletter, quarterly; Unterrichtspraxis, semiannual.

ASSOCIATION OF GERMAN BROADCASTERS
45 Rockefeller Plaza, Suite 554
New York, New York 10111 (212) 757-7911
Executive Officer: David Berger Founded 1955

Regionally organized noncommercial radio and TV networks in the Federal Republic of Germany. Maintains a United States office to distribute radio programs of German origin in the United States in order to acquaint the American public with cultural trends in Germany and with the work of the German networks in the musical field.

Public Affairs Organizations

AKON/USA
Post Office Box 1057
Trenton, New Jersey 08608
Executive Officer: Mrs. Ingeborg Winkler Founded 1964

"Authoritarian organization opposed to all totalitarian groups including the Nazi party and Zionists." Purposes are reunification of the German Reich into one nation with a common language - German; removal of all occupation troops from German soil; exposure of all crimes against Germans before, during and after World War II; ending "Holocaust" payments to Israel and demanding "real self-government for the Reich of all Germans." Opposes "liberalism and race mixing." Publishes books and flyers. Affiliated with: National States Rights Party.

CONFERENCE GROUP ON GERMAN POLITICS
Post Office Box 345
Durham, New Hampshire 03824 (207) 748-0942
Secretary: Professor G. K. Romoser Founded 1968

Political scientists, historians, sociologists, economists, and other scholars conducting research on German politics and other topics related to contemporary ideas and European affairs. Encourages contact among members and between members and German academicians and political leaders. Conducts conferences in the United States and Europe; sponsors an intern program for students in European government agencies.
Publications: Newsletter, annual; Directory of Current Research, triennial.

NATIONAL COMMITTEE FOR AMISH RELIGIOUS FREEDOM
30650 Six Mile Road
Livonia, Michigan 48152 (313) 427-1414
Chairman: Reverend William C. Lindholm Founded 1966

Professors, clergymen, attorneys and others interested in "legal defense in behalf of minority groups' religious and educational liberty." The Committee supplies legal defense, since the Amish have religious scruples against defending themselves or seeking court action. Sponsors conferences and lectures and a speakers' bureau.

NSDAP AUSLANDS UND AUFBAUORGANISATION
Box 6414
Lincoln, Nebraska 68506

Non-Jewish white adults, primarily in Germany, working for the reformation of the NSDAP (National Socialist German Workers - NAZI Party) as a legal political party, with the ultimate goal "the creation of a National Socialist state in a sovereign and united German Reich." Exists as an underground movement in Germany, with headquarters and publishing facilities in the United States.
Publications: The New Order (in English), monthly; NS Kampfruf (in German), bimonthly; also publishes assorted leaflets, stickers, posters and various other materials in several languages. Formerly: (1979) NSDAP Auslands Organisation.

WORLD ASSOCIATION OF UPPER SILESIANS
c/o Karol Sitko
R.D. No. 2
Dalton, Pennsylvania 18414
President: Mr. Karol H. Sitko Founded 1948

Persons from or interested in, the area known as Upper Silesia and who wish to promote Polish-German reconciliation. (Silesia is a region of some 20,000 square miles in east central Europe divided between north central Czechoslovakia and southwest Poland; it was formerly a province of Prussia and a crownland of Austria.) Cooperates with Upper Silesian organizations throughout the Western world, representing a total membership of over 1,800,000. Conducts specialized education and research programs. Maintains museum and biographical archives. Compiles statistics. Committees: American-European Cooperation; International. Councils: Heritage Group. Publications: Der-Oberschlesier, monthly; The New Approach, monthly.

Cultural and Educational Organizations

ALBRECHT DÜRER STUDY UNIT
Box 399, R.D. 1
Beckers Road
Temple, Pennsylvania 19560 Founded 1978
Secretary-Treasurer: Mrs. Ursel E. Kissinger

A unit of the American Topical Association. Philatelists interested in stamps and other philatelic items depicting Albrecht Dürer (1471-1528), German painter and engraver. Encourages the study of Dürer's life and works through member participation by mail or personal contact. Plans to present awards to encourage exhibitions of collections and is compiling a handbook/catalog of Dürer's works.
Publications: Dürer Journal (newsletter), quarterly.

AMERICAN HISTORICAL SOCIETY OF GERMANS FROM RUSSIA
631 D Street
Lincoln, Nebraska 68502 (402) 477-4524
Executive Director: Ruth M. Amen Founded 1968

Individuals who are of Russian German heritage; researchers, historians, libraries, genealogical societies, historical societies. Purposes are to record the history of Germans from Russia, encourage research, assist with genealogical research. Conducts annual workshops in folklore, genealogy, religious history, translations, research and bibliography; maintains library, museum and biographical archives in Greeley, Colorado.
Publications: Journal, 3/year; Newsletter, 3/year; Clues (genealogical resource), semiannual; also publishes books and maps.

AMERICAN ORFF-SCHULWERK ASSOCIATION
Department of Music
Cleveland State University
Cleveland, Ohio 44115 (216) 543-5366
Executive Secretary: Cindi Wobig Founded 1968

Music educators and church choir directors united to promote and encourage the philosophy of Carl Orff's (German composer, 1895-) Schulwerk (Music for Children) in America. Sponsors Scholarship Fund. Distributes information relevant to the activities and growth of Orff Schulwerk in America.
Publications: Orff Echo, quarterly; Directory, annual; also issues supplementary bulletins.

AMERICAN SOCIETY FOR GERMAN LITERATURE OF THE 16th AND 17th CENTURIES
Department of Foreign Languages
University of Nevada
Las Vegas, Nevada 89154
Executive Director: Professor John D. Lindberg Founded 1970

American and Canadian scholars active in the Renaissance and Baroque fields; other interested scholars. To promote the study of German literature of the 16th and 17th centuries.
Publications: Argenis, annual; Newsletter, irregular.

AMERICAN SOCIETY FOR REFORMATION RESEARCH
c/o Foundation for Reformation Research
6477 San Bonita
Saint Louis, Missouri 63105 (314) 727-6655
Administrative Secretary: Flora B. Klinck Founded 1947

Professors of history, church history, and religion; research libraries; publishers; graduate students, and others with a special interest in the history of the Reformation. Fosters historical research and promotes the writing of scholarly articles and monographs in the field of the Reformation. Encourages the translation into English of significant documents, books, and articles. Facilitates exchanges of ideas among its members and with similar groups in other countries.
Publications: Archive for Reformation History (in cooperation with the German Verein fuer Reformationsgeschichte), annual; Literature Supplement, annual.

COUNCIL OF MENNONITE COLLEGES
Eastern Mennonite College
Harrisonburg, Virginia 22801 (703) 433-2771
Chairman: Myron S. Augsburger Founded 1942

Mennonite institutions offering two or more years of college work. Promotes understanding and cooperation among member institutions and jointly sponsors projects and related activities. Sponsors an intercollegiate peace fellowship. In 1965, established International Educational Services as a committee of the Council, to develop international programs for students in Mennonite colleges abroad, for international students on Mennonite college campuses in the United States and for technical assistance programs by the U. S. colleges abroad. Cooperates with Brethren Colleges Abroad Programs to offer seminars and study for students during the summer and the academic years.

ERNST TOLLER MEMORIAL SOCIETY
Box 210-57, Campus Station
University of Cincinnati
Cincinnati, Ohio 45221 (513) 961-8865
Founder: Eva Lachman-Kalitzki Founded 1979

Persons interested in the life and works of Ernst Toller (1893-1939), German poet, playwright and politician. To promote literary, historical and political study and research concerning the life, work and times of Ernst Toller and other German expressionists. To further study of twentieth century German history and literature, and to promote studies concerning antifascism and exile.

GERMAN ACADEMIC EXCHANGE SERVICE
535 Fifth Avenue, Suite 1107
New York, New York 10017 (212) 599-0464
Director: Dr. Arnold Ebel

Offers information on the German educational system and administers German Government grants for graduate study or research in Germany.

GERMAN COLONIES COLLECTORS GROUP
c/o Col. Wilbur E. Davis
3313 Heritage Drive, Westminister
Wilmington, Delaware 19808 (302) 994-6777
Director: Col. Wilbur E. Davis Founded 1972

Study unit of the Germany Philatelic Society. Stamp collectors who specialize in the German colonies and offices abroad. Exchanges ideas, observations and information on related philatelic material. Operates semiannual auctions by mail. Renders translations of the (German) Friedemann Handbook.
Publications: Vorläufer, bimonthly; Index of Vorläufer Issues, annual.

GERMAN SOCIETY OF PENNSYLVANIA
611 Spring Garden Street
Philadelphia, Pennsylvania 19123 (215) 627-4365
President: Dr. George J. Beichl Founded 1764

Oldest German society in America. The objectives are to assist needy persons, maintain a public library, pursue educational and literary work, and conduct social activities among the members. Arranges lectures, exhibits, and concerts emphasizing German culture. Awards scholarships. Offers courses in the German language based on the method developed by the Goethe Institute of Munich. Bestows awards to high school students for proficiency in German. Maintains a 80,000 volume library, 85 percent of which is in German on German literature and German and American history.

GERMAN TEXAN HERITAGE SOCIETY
Southwest Texas State University
Department of Modern Languages
San Marcos, Texas 78666
President: Dona Reeves

Dedicated to preserving the German tradition in Texas.

GERMANY PHILATELIC SOCIETY
Post Office Box 563
Westminister, Maryland 21157
Secretary-Treasurer: Frederick Behrendt Founded 1949

Philatelists interested in collecting and studying postal issues and postal history of the old German states, Germany, its former colonies, offices abroad, plebiscites, and occupied and kindred areas. Maintains a library of over 400 volumes covering the postal history of Germany from medieval times to the present. Maintains an expertizing service for members. Presents medals at stamp exhibitions. Has received two different Silver awards for the German Postal Specialist in literature competition at two International stamp exhibitions in 1973.
Publications: The German Postal Specialist, monthly; Reference Manual of Forgeries, quarterly; Directory, triennial; also publishes Library Handbook Series and maps of Germany since 1849, and German-English Philatelic Dictionary.

GOETHE HOUSE
1014 Fifth Avenue
New York, New York 10028 (212) 744-8310

GOETHE HOUSE NEW YORK AT THE UNIVERSITY OF CINCINNATI
270 Calhoun Street
Cincinnati, Ohio 45219 (513) 475-2583

GOETHE INSTITUTE ATLANTA
400 Colony Square
Atlanta, Georgia 30361 (404) 892-2226

GOETHE INSTITUTE BOSTON
170 Beacon Street
Boston, Massachusetts 02116 (617) 262-6050
Founded 1966

GOETHE INSTITUTE CHICAGO
German Cultural Center
401 North Michigan Avenue
Chicago, Illinois 60611 (312) 329-0915
Director: Dr. Wolfgang Ule

GOETHE INSTITUTE HOUSTON
German Cultural Center
3400 Montrose Boulevard, Suite 808
Houston, Texas 77006
Director: Dr. R. Thoma

GOETH INSTITUTE SAN FRANCISCO
530 Bush Street
San Francisco, California 94108 (415) 391-0370

A branch of the Goethe Institute in Munich, Germany. Promotes international cultural cooperation through sponsorship of lectures in English and German, films, concerts and exhibits. Serves as language information center for teachers of German. Runs GAPP (German-American Partnership Program). Maintains library of 16,000 volumes of books, records and magazines in German and English, mainly by German authors covering all aspects of German civilization with emphasis on literature. Six other branches of the Institute in the U.S. are Boston, Massachusetts, Atlanta, Georgia, Chicago, Illinois, San Francisco, California, Houston, Texas and Cincinnati, Ohio.

HEGEL SOCIETY OF AMERICA
Department of Philosophy
Villanova University
Villanova, Pennsylvania 19085
Treasurer: Lawrence S. Stepelevich Founded 1969

Persons who are students of the philosophy of Georg Wilhelm Fredrich Hegel (1770-1831), the German philosopher. Purposes are "to promote the study of the philosophy of Hegel, its place in the history of thought, its relation to social, political and cultural movements since his time and its relevance to contemporary issues and fields of knowledge and to promote the furtherance of original philosophic thought which has its basis in the philosophy of Hegel or which treats issues in the style, manner or method of Hegel."
Publications: The Owl of Minerva, quarterly; also publishes the proceedings of symposia.

HISTORICAL COMMITTEE OF THE MENNONITE CHURCH
1700 South Main Street
Goshen, Indiana 46526 (219) 533-3161
Executive Secretary: Dr. Leonard Gross Founded 1911

Coordinates the Mennonite Church program of historical research and interpretation. Studies are centered in the 16th century Anabaptist period and the post-16th century Mennonite and Peace Church areas. Seeks to ensure chronicling of the Church history in an ongoing manner, interpreting Church heritage for new generations. Conducts research; maintains 31,000 volume library. Also maintains archives containing 700 personal collections and official Church records dating to the 16th century.
Publications: Mennonite Historical Bulletin, quarterly; Mennonite Quarterly Review; Studies in Anabaptist and Mennonite History (monograph series), irregular.

HROSWITHA CLUB
820 Fifth Avenue
New York, New York 10021 (212) 838-0032
President: Mrs. Sherman P. Haight Founded 1946

Private book collectors and bibliophiles interested in the collection of rare books by and about Hroswitha (c. 935-c. 1000), German poetess, dramatist, and chronicler. In 1965 the Club published Hroswitha of Gandersheim (her life, times, and works, with a comprehensive bibliography). Maintains a library of about 100 volumes by and about Hroswitha, which is under the custodianship of the Pierport Morgan Library.

IMPERIAL GERMAN MILITARY COLLECTOR'S ASSOCIATION
Post Office Box 1361
Dallas, Texas 75221 (214) 341-4196
Secretary: William E. Hamelman Founded 1970

Individuals, museums, and libraries in the United States and Europe who are interested in research on pre-1918 German militaria. Objectives are the

wider transmission of information and making available of previous non-English materials to English-speaking readers. Research programs currently consist of series publications of material on headgear, orders and decorations, regimental steins, German colonial research and Imperial German swords and sidearms. Maintains biographical archives. Compiles statistics.
Publication: Kaiserzeit, quarterly.

INTERNATIONAL BACH SOCIETY
173 Riverside Drive
New York, New York 10024 (212) 873-3551
Director: Rosalyn Tureck Founded 1966

Music teachers associations and music libraries; professional musicians, musicologists, music teachers, students, and laymen. Seeks to raise the standards of performance in all areas of the music of Johann Sebastian Bach (1685-1750), German organist, composer, and master contrapuntist. Awards study grants to professional musicians and gifted students for advanced study in Bach's style. Provides auditing opportunities for teachers, students, and laymen. Conducts classes on special problems in Bach performance on the clavier. Sponsors the Cantata Collegium for voice and orchestral instruments.
Publication: Report to Members, semiannual.

INTERNATIONAL BRECHT SOCIETY
c/o John Fuegi
Department of Comparative Literature
University of Maryland
College Park, Maryland 20742 (301) 454-2685
Founded 1968

Persons working in theater and filmmaking, university teachers and graduate students, editors, writers and libraries. Encourages free and open discussion on the relationship of the arts to the contemporary world. Emphasis is placed on the work of Bertolt Brecht (1898-1956), German playwright and poet. Members stage forms of Brecht's texts as well as political theater, film and radio in general.
Publications: Communications (newsletter), 3/year; Brecht Yearbook (also published in German as Brecht Jahrbuch).

INTERNATIONAL HEINRICH SCHÜTZ SOCIETY
35 Kassel-Wilhelmshohe
Henrich Schutz-Allee 35
Hessen, West Germany
President: Professor Kurt Gudewill Founded 1930

Individuals, groups, institutions and libraries interested in research in and the performance of the music of Heinrich Schütz and his contemporaries and the promotion of sacred music of the present day. Heinrich Schütz (1585-1672) is regarded as the composer of Musica Sacra. Holds festivals.
Publications: Acta Sagittariana, annual; Jahrbuch, annual.

LESSING SOCIETY
German Department
University of Cincinnati
Cincinnati, Ohio 45221 (513) 475-2752
Secretary-Treasurer: Richard E. Schade Founded 1966

Individuals interested in the life and work of Gotthold Ephraim Lessing (1729-1781), German dramatist and author of numerous critical and theological writings and active in the literature, philosophy and aesthetics of the 18th Century. "Encourages research on Lessing in order to stimulate a reappraisal of the pertinence of his thought in modern times; sponsors lectures; develops research facilities; reemphasizes Lessing's cosmopolitan humanism and his continuing importance throughout the world." Formerly: (1974) American Lessing Society.
Publications: Notes and Notices (newsletter), semiannual; Lessing Yearbook; also publishes Proceedings of International Lessing Conference.

MORAVIAN HISTORICAL SOCIETY
214 East Center
Nazareth, Pennsylvania 18064 (215) 759-0292
Curator: E. B. Clewell Founded 1857

Operates a museum pertaining to Moravian Church history and American colonial life, including religious paintings, musical instruments, household equipment, clothing and textiles, building materials, Indian and foreign mission artifacts. Maintains a library of old manuscripts and rare books.
Publication: Transactions, biennial.

NATIONAL CARL SCHURZ ASSOCIATION
339 Walnut Street
Philadelphia, Pennsylvania 19106 (215) 922-2036
Executive Director: Hans-Werner Deeken Founded 1930

Seeks to promote cultural relations between the United States and the German-speaking peoples. Named after Carl Schurz (1829-1906), German-American statesman.
Publications: NFSG Rundschau, eight times a year; NCSA/AATG Service Center Catalogue, annual.

NATIONAL FEDERATION OF STUDENTS OF GERMAN
339 Walnut Street
Philadelphia, Pennsylvania 19106 (215) 922-2036
Founded 1968

Founded to promote interest in the study of German language and culture. Conducts trips to Germany; awards scholarships. Affiliated with the National Carl Schurz Association.
Publication: Rundschau, monthly.

NORTHEASTERN SAENGERBUND OF AMERICA (Music)
c/o John Becker
21 A Independence Parkway
Crestwood Village
Whiting, New Jersey 08759
President: John Becker Founded 1850

Male and female singers primarily from the eastern states seeking to "cultivate and promote the singing of German songs, the German language, customs and sociability."

PENNSYLVANIA GERMAN SOCIETY
Box 97
Breinigsville, Pennsylvania 18031
President: Richard Druckenbrot Founded 1891

Descendants of German and Swiss pioneers who settled in Pennsylvania and other states and others interested in collecting and preserving landmarks and records of the genealogy and history of the Pennsylvania Germans (sometimes referred to as Pennsylvania Dutch). Sponsors trips to the areas in Germany and Switzerland from which the original settlers came. Presents awards; maintains library of 1000 volumes.
Publications: Der Reggeboge (The Rainbow), quarterly; annual volumes, published since 1891, on various aspects of the culture; also publishes a sources and document series based on primary source material.
Absorbed: (1966) Pennsylvania German Folklore Society.

POST WORLD WAR II STUDY AND RESEARCH GROUP OF THE GERMANY PHILATELIC SOCIETY
c/o Alfred Heinz
One Circle Drive
Sunset Village
Flemington, New Jersey 08822 (201) 782-4610
Director: Alfred Heinz Founded 1957

Stamp collectors specializing in Germany's post-World War II period. Conducts research on topics such as impounded mail, cork marks, courier mail, stampless mail, occupation-authority issues, and local and postal district issues. Presents slide shows at seminars and conventions; sponsors competitions; compiles statistics. Maintains four sub-study groups, such as the Allied Military Government Series, dedicated to specific subjects. Resources include small library of slides and articles. Affiliated with Germany Philatelic Society (parent).
Publications: Bulletin, four times a year; Handbooks, one - two times a year; Membership List (published in Bulletin), annual.

SOCIETY FOR THE DEVELOPMENT OF GERMAN IN TEXAS
8 Mission Drive
New Braunfels, Texas 78131
President: Hildegard Suhr

SOCIETY FOR GERMAN-AMERICAN STUDIES
c/o Dr. LaVern J. Rippley
St. Olaf College
Northfield, Minnesota 55057 (507) 663-3233
President: Dr. LaVern J. Rippley Founded 1976

Professors, teachers, students and organizations interested in German-American studies. Objectives are: to study history, linguistics, folklore, genealogy, literature, theatre, music and creative art forms as they apply to the cross-cultural relations between German-speaking lands and the Americas; to improve cross-cultural relations; and to assist interested individuals with their research. Conducts research on the development of immigration from German-speaking countries to North America and publishes findings. Bestows awards.
Publications: Journal of German-American Studies, quarterly; Newsletter, quarterly; also publishes occasional papers series.

SOCIETY FOR THE HISTORY OF THE GERMANS IN MARYLAND
231 Saint Paul Place
Baltimore, Maryland 21202
Secretary: Dr. Morgan H. Prichett Founded 1886

Individuals interested in German-American relations and in the preservation and publication of historical material relative to the activities of Americans of German descent in Maryland and other states.
Publication: Report, triennial.

THIRD REICH STUDY GROUP
Post Office Box 283
Needham Heights, Massachusetts 02194
Director: Myron Fox — Founded 1962

A study group of the Germany Philatelic Society. Persons interested in the postal history of Germany from 1933 to 1945. Conducts research on the German Military Mail Systems; offers Fieldpost identification inquiry service. Awards plaque for the best Third Reich postal history exhibit; sponsors bimonthly auction.
Publications: Bulletin, bimonthly; Membership Directory, annual; also publishes monographs, catalogs, research articles and notes on auction scheme, literature reviews, abstracts of foreign publications and survey articles.

WESTERN ASSOCIATION FOR GERMAN STUDIES
Arizona State University
Tempe, Arizona 85281
President: Dr. Gerald R. Kleinfeld

Publication: German Studies Review.

Foundations

GERMAN MARSHALL FUND OF THE UNITED STATES
11 Dupont Circle, Northwest
Suite 900
Washington, D. C. 20036 — (202) 797-6430
President: Frank Loy — Incorporated in 1972

Purpose and Activities: To contribute to the better understanding and resolution of significant, contemporary, or emerging common problems of industrial societies, internally and in their relations with each other and with developing societies, by facilitating and supporting sustained working relationships, studies, cooperation, and contacts by and between persons with shared interests and responsibilities in the United States, Europe and elsewhere. Fund program areas include common problems, international relations, and European/American comparative studies of industrial societies. Research fellowship program on the problems of industrial societies. Sponsored by the Federal Republic of Germany.

LIEDERKRANZ FOUNDATION
6 East 87th Street
New York, New York 10028 — (212) 534-0880
Vice President: Professor Edward Weiss — Founded 1947

Founded to help achieve and maintain high musical standards in America by giving recognition and encouragement to talented young artists. Finances and administers cultural, musical and educational programs of The Liederkranz, a musical society founded in New York City in 1847 by German-Americans to give as many people as possible an opportunity to hear and participate in fine music and to further close cultural ties between the United States and the German-speaking countries. In the past century, Liederkranz choral groups and the Liederkranz Orchestra have participated in numerous concerts and musical events. The Foundation encourages amateur and professional participation in choral groups, stages professionally coached plays and operettas and sponsors a variety of concerts. Has established a sholarship fund for young singers, instrumentalists, and composers to enable them to attend accredited music schools and conservatories or to study privately. Conducts specialized education and sponsors competitions.
Publication: LK, bimonthly.

MORAVIAN MUSIC FOUNDATION
20 Cascade Avenue, Salem Station
Winston-Salem, North Carolina 27108 — (919) 725-0651
Director: Karl Kroeger — Founded 1956

Founded to advance early American Moravian music and complementary music through research, publications, and education. The Foundation holds copyrights to the music collections of the Moravian Church in America, publishes literary and musical editions, and makes available its musical and documentary materials to accredited scholars and graduate students. Organizes workshops and seminars for church musicians; assists in, and occasionally presents, concerts of Moravian music. Supported by contributions from church congregations and others. Maintains a library of about 6,000 volumes on hymnology, church music, Americana, and Moraviana.
Publications: Bulletin, semiannual; also publishes bibliographical-historical reprints on the music of the American Moravians and catalogs of manuscript and early printed music; issues phonograph recordings.

Charitable Organizations

GERMAN SEAMEN'S MISSION
6612 Canal Boulevard
New Orleans, Louisiana 70124
Chaplain: H. Neumann

GERMAN SOCIETY OF THE CITY OF NEW YORK
150 Fifth Avenue
New York, New York 10011 (212) 989-2040
Executive Director: Wolfgang Hamel
Founded 1784

Individuals and firms interested in assisting German immigrants. Provides German families and individuals with welfare services, medical care, employment, and professional counseling.
Publication: Annual Report.

MENNONITE CENTRAL COMMITTEE
21 South 12th Street
Akron, Pennsylvania 17501 (717) 859-1151
Executive Secretary: William T. Snyder
Founded 1920

Official relief and service agency of North American Mennonite and Brethren in Christ churches. Administers and participates in programs of agricultural and economic development, education, medicine, self-help, relief, peace and disaster service. Approximately 722 volunteers serve in 46 countries in Africa, Asia, Europe, South America and North America.
Publications: News Service, weekly; Contact, monthly; Intercom, monthly; Peace Section Newsletter, bimonthly; Washington Memo, bimonthly; Women's Task Force Report, bimonthly; also publishes development monographs.

MENNONITE DISASTER SERVICE
21 South 12th Street
Akron, Pennsylvania 17501 (717) 859-1151
Executive Coordinator: Nelson Hostetter
Founded 1952

Local units are coordinated by Mennonite Central Committee (organization that coordinates relief and service for 14 Mennonite and Brethren in Christ bodies). Responds, through local units, with personal services in time of natural or manmade disasters. When need in a specific disaster is too large for a local unit, other units within the region assist. Also participates in non-disaster types of programs, such as supplying blood for local clinics and helping in home building in ghetto areas and rural poverty pockets.
Publications: Newsletter, quarterly.

MENNONITE HEALTH ASSEMBLY
Box 370
Elkhart, Indiana 46515 (219) 294-7523
Executive Secretary: Luke Birky
Founded 1952

Health and welfare institutions (hospitals, homes for the aging, retirement communities, child welfare homes, psychiatric centers). To give health and welfare services with strong Christian emphasis.
Affiliated with: Protestant Health and Welfare Assembly.
Publications: Mennonite Medical Messenger, bimonthly.

Religious Organizations

AMANA CHURCH SOCIETY
Amana, Iowa 52203
President of Board of Trustees: Charles L. Selzer

Founded as the Community of True Inspiration in Hessen, Germany, in 1714, the group emigrated to the United States in 1844 because of persecution. After settling at Ebenezer near Buffalo, New York, the group moved to Amana, Iowa, in 1854, where they located in seven villages. Members lived in communal society until a reorganization in 1932. The Elders of the church conduct church services.

BEACHY AMISH MENNONITE CHURCHES
c/o Ervin N. Hershberger
R. D. 1
Meyersdale, Pennsylvania 15552 (814) 662-2483

This group originates mostly from the Old Order Amish Mennonite Church. Two congregations were formed as early as 1927, but the others have all been organized since 1938.

Worship is held in meeting houses. Nearly all have Sunday schools, most congregations have prayer meetings and many have Christian day schools. They sponsor evangelical missions at home and abroad.
Publication: Calvary Mission, monthly.

CHURCH OF GOD IN CHRIST (MENNONITE)
420 North Wedel Street
Moundridge, Kansas 67107 (316) 345-2532
Moderator: Norman Koehn

A section of the Mennonite body organized in 1859, in Ohio, for the reestablishment of the order and discipline of the Church.
Publication: Messenger of Truth, biweekly.

EVANGELICAL MENNONITE BRETHREN CONFERENCE
5800 South 14th Street
Omaha, Nebraska 68107 (402) 731-4800
President: Reverend Jerry Franz

Formerly known as the Defenseless Mennonite Brethren in Christ of North America, this body emanates from the Russian immigration of Mennonites into the United States in 1873-74.
Publication: Gospel Tidings.

EVANGELICAL MENNONITE CHURCH, INCORPORATED
1420 Kerrway Court
Fort Wayne, Indiana 46805
President: Reverend Andrew Rupp

The Evangelical Mennonite Church traces its heritage directly to the early reformation period of the 16th century to a group known as Swiss Brethren, who believed that salvation could come only by repentance for sin and faith in Jesus Christ; that baptism was only for believers; and, that the church should be separate from controls of the state. These Swiss Brethren became known as Anabaptists. As the Anabaptist movement spread to other countries, a Dutch priest; Menno Simons, left the Catholic priesthood and became one of its leaders. Much of the Anabaptist movement became identified with the name of Menno Simons, and in the course of time the group became known as Mennonites. Around 1700 a Mennonite minister named Jacob Ammon led a division which came to be known as the Amish. Both the Mennonites and the Amish were much persecuted in some areas of Europe. Migrations to America took place in the early 1700's and at later times. Out of these, in the middle 1800's, emerged a minister of an Amish congregation in Indiana by the name of Henry Egly. After a deep spiritual renewal in his own life, he strongly emphasized the need of being "born again" as a prerequisite to baptism and church membership. This led to his separation from the group in 1865 and the beginning of what is now the Evangelical Mennonite Church, with congregations in Michigan, Ohio, Indiana, Illinois and Kansas.
Publications: Build, quarterly; Headquarters Communique, monthly.

GENERAL CONFERENCE OF MENNONITE BRETHREN CHURCHES
1362 L Street
Reedley, California 93654
Chairperson: Henry H. Dick

An immigration of Mennonite Brethren from Russia in the year 1874. (In 1960, the Krimmer Mennonite Brethren Conference merged with this body.)
Publications: Christian Leader, biweekly; Mennonite Brethren Herald.

MENNONITE BOARD OF EDUCATION
Box 1142
Elkhart, Indiana 46515 (219) 294-7531
Executive Secretary and Director: Founded 1905
Albert J. Meyer

Responsible for churchwide educational planning and development; coordination of planning and evaluation at three colleges and two seminaries; consultation with church high schools and congregations. Operates two colleges and one seminary.
Publications: Mennonite College Enrollments, annual; Mennonite High School Enrollments, annual; Mennonite Youth Census, annual; Mennonite Educator, irregular.

MENNONITE CHURCH
528 East Madison Street
Lombard, Illinois 60148
General Secretary: Ivan Kauffmann (312) 620-7802

The largest group of Mennonites, who first arrived in the United States in 1683 and settled in Germantown, Pennsylvania. Their name derives from their outstanding leader, Menno Sims, born in 1496.
Publications: Builder, monthly; Christian Living, monthly; Gospel Herald, weekly; Mennonite Quarterly Review, quarterly; Mennonite Yearbook, annual; On the Line, weekly; Purpose, weekly; Rejoice, quarterly; Story Friends, weekly; With, monthly; Sent, bimonthly; Sharing, semi-annual.

MENNONITE CHURCH, THE GENERAL CONFERENCE
722 Main
Newton, Kansas 67114 (316) 283-5100
President: Jacob Tilitsky

One of the oldest Mennonite conferences in the United States. The present denominational organization dates from 1860 (in Iowa).
Publications: The Mennonite, weekly; Builder, monthly; Window to Mission, quarterly; Der Bote, weekly.

MORAVIAN CHURCH IN AMERICA (Unitas Fratrum)
Northern Provincial Synod:
69 West Church Street, Post Office Box 1245
Bethlehem, Pennsylvania 18018
Treasurer: John F. Ziegler (215) 867-7566

Southern Provincial Synod:
459 South Church Street
Winston-Salem, North Carolina 27108
Treasurer: Ronald R. Hendrix (919) 725-5811

Moravian missionaries of the pre-Reformation faith of John Hus came to Georgia in 1735, to Pennsylvania in 1740, and to North Carolina in 1753. They established the Moravian Church, which is broadly evangelical, liturgical, and with an episcopacy as a spiritual office.
Publication: The North American Moravian, monthly.

OLD GERMAN BAPTIST BRETHREN
Route 1, Box 140
Bringhurst, Indiana 46913
Foreman: Elder Clement Skiles

A group which separated in 1881 from the Church of the Brethren (formerly called German Baptist Brethren) as a protest against a liberalizing tendency.
Publication: The Vindicator.

OLD ORDER AMISH CHURCH
c/o Raber's Book Store
Baltic, Ohio 43804

The congregations of this Old Order Amish group have no annual conference. They worship in private homes. They adhere to the older forms of worship and attire. This body has bishops, ministers, and deacons.

OLD ORDER (WISLER) MENNONITE CHURCH
c/o Henry W. Riehl
Route 1
Columbiana, Ohio 44408 (216) 482-4832

This body arose from a separation of Mennonites dated 1870, under Jacob Wisler, in opposition to what were thought to be innovations. At present, this group is located in the Eastern United States and Canada. There are approximately 8400 members and 60 congregations, with 19 bishops, 76 ministers, and 48 deacons. Each state, or district, has its own organization or government and holds a yearly conference.

SCHWENKFELDER CHURCH
Pennsburg, Pennsylvania 18073
Moderator: Andrew A. Anders

Founded by descendants of a German migration from Silesia from Pennsylvania in 1734. The migrants were followers of a Reformation leader, Caspar Schwenkfeld von Ossig.
Publication: The Schwenkfeldian, quarterly.

UNITY OF THE BRETHREN
2513 Revere
Pasadena, Texas 77502
President: Marvin Chlapek

Established by Czech and Moravian immigrants in Texas beginning about 1855. Formerly known as the Evangelical Unity of the Czech-Moravian Brethren in North America.
Publication: Brethren Journal, monthly.

Research Centers and Special Institutes

CONCORDIA HISTORICAL INSTITUTE
801 DuMun Avenue
St. Louis, Missouri 63105 (314) 721-5934
Director: Dr. Aug. R. Suelflow Founded 1847

Specializes in Lutheranism in America and the history of German-Americans. Maintains a museum and a 58,000 volume library of books, pamphlets and periodicals as well as a manuscript collection. Housed in the Historical Saxon Lutheran Memorial, Frohna, Missouri.
Publications: Concordia Historical Institute, quarterly; newsletter three times annually.

INSTITUTE FOR BASIC GERMAN
University of Pittsburgh
125 Loeffler Building
Pittsburgh, Pennsylvania 15260 (412) 621-3500
Director: Dr. J. Alan Pfeffer Founded 1960

Pursues research on basic spoken and written German, including preparation of basic German word lists, a semantic index, a basic spoken German idiom list, a basic structure list, a dictionary of basic German, and a study on evolution of basic German. Research results are published in monographs and books.

INSTITUTE OF GERMAN STUDIES
Indiana University
Ballantine Hall 666
Bloomington, Indiana 47401 (812) 337-1640
Director: Dr. Eberhard Reichmann Founded 1968

An integral part of Indiana University, supported by the parent institution and Volkswagen Foundation of West Germany. Carries out studies on cultural, economic, political, and social aspects of postwar West and East Germany and other German-speaking areas in Central Europe. Develops interdisciplinary bibliographies and archives. Offers courses on modern Germany and provides consulting and information services.

Maintains a library of about 3000 volumes on West and East Germany.
Publication: German Studies Notes, irregular. Also publishes research results in bound and paperback books.

Museums

BUSCH-REISINGER MUSEUM
Harvard University
29 Kirkland Street
Cambridge, Massachusetts 02138 (617) 495-2317
Curator: Dr. Charles Haxthausen Founded 1901

Originally known as the Germanic Museum. Associated with Harvard University. Carries out research on Germanic and Netherlands art in all media, dating from the Middle Ages to the present. Maintains extensive collections of twentieth century German paintings, sculpture, and drawings, as well as medieval objects, especially from the late Gothic period, and Baroque and Rococo art ranging from monumental ecclesiastical sculpture to miniature porcelain decorative figures. Maintains archives on the Bauhaus, Walter Gropius and Lyonel Feininger. Publishes research results in books and catalogs.

DEUTSCHHEIM STATE HISTORIC SITE
109 West Second Street
Herman, Missouri 65041 (314) 486-2200
Administrator: Martin E. Shay Founded 1979

Collections include period furnishings and decorative arts; furniture; books, and household items of 19th century German immigrants in mid-Missouri. The historic site includes the Pommer Gentner House built in 1841 and the Stehly House and Tavern built in 1842. Research is performed in German immigration and settlement.

EPHRATA CLOISTER
632 West Main Street
Ephrata, Pennsylvania 17522 (717) 733-6600
Administrator: John L. Kraft Founded 1732

Comprises twelve mid-18th century buildings of medieval Germanic architectural style, located on original site of communal celibate religious society. Collections include books printed on property in 18th and early 19th centuries; furniture produced by 18th century society, and buildings representative of unique architectural significance. Maintains a small library pertaining to the history of Ephrata Cloister. Performs a historic drama during the season.

FRANKENMUTH HISTORICAL MUSEUM
613 South Main
Frankenmuth, Michigan 48734 (517) 652-9701
Director: Carl R. Hansen Founded 1963

Collections center around German immigrant artifacts from the 19th century. Maintains a small library of German books and periodicals.

GERMANTOWN HISTORICAL SOCIETY
5214 Germantown Avenue
Philadelphia, Pennsylvania 19144 (215) 844-0514
President: Frederick C. Fiechter, Jr. Founded 1900

The Society maintains several branches located in houses of 18th century Germantown. Collections include 18th and 19th century artifacts relating to early Germantown; furniture; crystal; china, needlework; coverlets; toys; hardware; crafts. The Society has a 3,000 volume library of local historical books. It offers guided tours; lectures; monthly meetings; seminars.
Publication: Germantowne Crier, quarterly.

HERKIMER HOUSE STATE HISTORIC SITE
Route 169
Little Falls, New York 13365 (518) 823-0398
Manager: William Watkins Founded 1913

Museum located in the 1760 home of Nicholas Herkimer, well-to-do farmer, landowner, trader and leader of the militia in the American Revolution and includes period furnishings, and personal belongings. Research is performed on the Palatine German immigration in America.

HIGH PLAINS MUSEUM
423 Norris Avenue
McCook, Nebraska 69001 (308) 345-3661
Director: Dina McDonald Kanowicz Founded 1969

Collection includes paintings done by German prisoners of war done on camp walls.

HISTORIC BETHABARA
2147 Bethabara Road
Winston-Salem, North Carolina 27106 (919) 924-8191
Director: Mrs. Daniel R. Taylor Founded 1970

Museum is housed in Bethabara Brewer's House, 1803, on the site of the first Moravian settlement in North Carolina. Other historic buildings include the Potter's House, 1782; Bethabara Church and Gemeinhaus.

HISTORIC BETHLEHEM INCORPORATED
516 Main Street
Bethlehem, Pennsylvania 18018 (215) 868-6311
Director: Joan L. Ward Founded 1957

A Moravian settlement in the 18th century is the major emphasis with various restored community buildings: tannery, waterworks, grist mill, miller's house and the reconstructed springhouse.

HISTORIC HERMANN MUSEUM
Fourth and Schiller Streets
Hermann, Missouri 65041 (314) 486-2017
President: A. A. Schweighauser Founded 1956

Contains items portraying life in a German settlement, as well as Missouri River lore. Housed in a German school building built in 1871, the museum contains a library of books on German history and religion.

HISTORIC SCHAEFFERSTOWN, INCORPORATED
North Market Street
Schaefferstown, Pennsylvania 17088
President: John Miller Founded 1966

Portrays 19th century Pennsylvania German village life and culture. The Alexander Schaeffer Farm Museum exhibits tools and implements and illustrates agricultural practices of the Pennsylvania Germans. The Thomas R. Brendle Memorial Library has a 700 volume collection on Pennsylvania history, folklore and folklife of the Pennsylvania Germans.
Publications: Historic Schaefferstown Record, quarterly.

KAUFFMAN MUSEUM
East 27th Street
North Newton, Kansas 67117 (316) 283-2500
Director: Dr. Oswald Goering Founded 1940

Museum maintained by Bethel College and contains exhibits of Centennial of Coming of Mennonites to Plain States and their introduction of hard winter wheat.

MENNONITE IMMIGRANT HISTORICAL FOUNDATION
202 Poplar
Goessel, Kansas 67053 (316) 367-8200
President: Otto D. Unruh Founded 1974

Collection includes clothing, household goods and farm machinery related to the wheat industry in this German Russian Mennonite settlement.

MORAVIAN HISTORICAL SOCIETY
214 East Center Street
Nazareth, Pennsylvania 18064 (215) 759-0291
Curator: E. B. Clewell Founded 1857

Collection of art and artifacts related to the history of the Moravian Church.

MORAVIAN MUSEUM OF BETHLEHEM
66 West Church Street
Bethlehem, Pennsylvania 18018 (215) 867-0173
President: Mrs. Charles K. Zug, Jr. Founded 1938

Religious and secular objects reflecting the life of early Moravian settlers include furniture, clocks, silver, musical instruments, art and needlework of the Moravian Seminary, kitchen implements and tools.

MUSEUM OF AMERICAN HISTORICAL SOCIETY OF GERMANS FROM RUSSIA
631 D Street
Lincoln, Nebraska 68502 (402) 477-4524
Executive Director: Ruth M. Amen Founded 1973

Museum is located in area of city known as South Bottom, which served as the center of a German-Russian settlement at the turn of the century. Collections include memorabilia brought from Russia by the Germans from Russia and items used in their lives as pioneers in the area.

THE NEW BERLIN HISTORICAL SOCIETY
19765 West National Avenue
New Berlin, Wisconsin 53151 (414) 679-1722
President: Ethel Martin Founded 1965

The early settlers of New Berlin maintained many German traditions which are reflected in the farm and house collections of the Society, housed in 1870 Winton-Sprengel House.
Publication: New Berlin Almanack, annual.

OLD SALEM, INCORPORATED
Drawer F, Salem Station
Winston-Salem, North Carolina 27108 (919) 723-3688
President: R. Arthur Spaugh, Jr. Founded 1950

Many of the buildings of this Moravian congregation town have been restored: Single Brothers House, 1769-1786; Miksch Tobacco Shop, 1771; Salem Tavern, 1784; Boys School, 1794; Winkler Bakery, 1800; Yierling House, 1802; Market Fire House, 1803; John Vogler House, 1819; Shultz Shoemaker Shop, 1827. Collections show 18th and early 19th century Moravian artifacts, arts, furnishings and tools. There is a 1700 volume library, museum shop and

restaurant. Guided tours as well as lectures, films, concerts and classes are offered.
Publication: The Old Salem Gleamer.

PENNSYLVANIA DUTCH FOLK CULTURE SOCIETY, INCORPORATED
Lenhartsville, Pennsylvania 19534 (215) 562-4803
President: Florence Baver Founded 1965

Collections preserve the everyday life and customs, dialect, arts and agricultural practices of the Pennsylvania Germans. Five buildings of historic significance are a part of the museum. Services include guided tours, lectures, educational programs, demonstrations and a museum shop.
Publication: Pennsylvania Dutch News and Views, semiannual.

PENNSYLVANIA FARM MUSEUM OF LANDIS VALLEY
2451 Kissel Hill Road
Lancaster, Pennsylvania 17601 (717) 299-7556
Director: Robert N. Sieber Founded 1925

The collections are housed in historic buildings of the 18th and 19th century and include decorative arts, folk culture, textiles and agricultural methods. Research is done in agricultural, Pennsylvania Dutch oral history and material culture. A 12,000 volume library of agricultural books and journals is maintained. The museum offers guided tours, a museum shop, lectures, films, classes and workshop in addition to exhibitions.

PERRY COUNTY LUTHERAN HISTORICAL SOCIETY
Altenburg, Missouri 63732 (314) 824-5542
President: Leonard A. Kuehnert Founded 1912

A religious museum located on the site of the principal settlement of Saxon immigrants in 1839 which was the center for the Missouri Synod Lutheran Church. Collection includes religious books and Bibles, sermon books and old pictures.

SOPHIENBURG MUSEUM
401 West Coll Street
New Braunfels, Texas 78130 (512) 629-1572
President: Louise D. Woodward Founded 1932
Director: Mrs. Margaret Fields

A history museum, housed in fieldstone veneer building on site of headquarters of original German colony of 1845 in Republic of Texas. Collections include historical materials; furniture; household goods typical of period and people involved in colonization. Maintains a 250 volume historical library with reference to German immigration to Texas.

WINEDALE HISTORICAL CENTER
Post Office Box 11
Round Top, Texas 78954 (713) 278-3530
Interim Director: Wayne Bell Founded 1967

Collections include decorative arts, folk art, furniture, tools and agricultural implements pertaining to German settlement of Texas as well as historic houses complete with 1850's furnishings. Research is done in Texas-German cultural history; agricultural history; American social history; cabinetmaking; textiles and slavery in Central Texas. Services include guided tours; lectures; workshops; permanent and temporary exhibits; conference facility; 2 restored period buildings; 3 out-buildings; Spring festival; craft fair; plays; museum and library seminars; craft seminars; weekend farmers seminar.
Publication: Quid Nunc, quarterly newsletter.

ZOAR STATE MEMORIAL
Zoah, Ohio 44697 (216) 874-3011
Curator: Kathleen M. Fernandez

A village museum consisting of seven restored buildings of 1817 German religious sect village. Collections include folk Germanic-American arts and crafts and tools. Guided tours are available.

Special Libraries and Subject Collections

AMERICAN HISTORICAL SOCIETY OF GERMANS FROM RUSSIA - GREELEY PUBLIC LIBRARY
City Complex Building
Greeley, Colorado 80631 (303) 353-6123
Archiv./Director: Ester Fromm

Subjects: History, genealogy, personal reminiscences. Special Collections: German-Russian collection. Holdings: Books; tapes; maps, newspapers on microfilm. Services: Interlibrary loans; copying; library open to public with identification card.

ARCHIVES OF THE MENNONITE CHURCH
Historical Committee of the Mennonite Church
Goshen College
Goshen, Indiana 46526 (219) 533-3161
Arch.: Leonard Gross Founded 1937

Subjects: Official records of the Mennonite Church, its boards, committees, agencies and institutions; peace collections; archives collection of the Mennonite Central Committee; private papers of 500 Church leaders. Special Collections: J. F. Funk and H. S. Bender. Collections of manuscripts and papers. Holdings: More than three million items. Services: Copying; archives open to public. Publications: Mennonite Historical Bulletin, quarterly - subscription.

CARVER COUNTY HISTORICAL SOCIETY LIBRARY
119 South Cherry Street
Waconia, Minnesota 55387 (612) 442-4234
President: Francis Klein Founded 1940

Subjects: Carber County pioneer life. Special Collection: Early 1860 library of Swedes and Germans in the locality. Services: Library and museum open to public.

FREDERICK W. CRUMB MEMORIAL LIBRARY
State University of New York at Potsdam
Pierrepont Avenue
Potsdam, New York 13676 (315) 268-4991
Director: Dr. Thomas M. Peischl Founded 1880

Subjects: Music; education and curriculum materials; art; nineteenth and twentieth century German history; social history; northern New York State history. Special Collections: Snell Collection of public and private papers; College Archives. Holdings: Books; journals and other serials; newspapers; government documents, public school syllabi and public school tests; pamphlets; phonorecords; microfilm; microfiche; microcards; filmstrips; slides; maps and charts; college catalogs; music scores. Services: Interlibrary loans; copying; library open to public. Publications: Subject bibliographies and library guides, irregular.

EASTERN PENNSYLVANIA MENNONITE LIBRARY
1000 Forty Foot Road
Lansdale, Pennsylvania 19446 (215) 362-2675
Administrator: Joseph S. Miller

Subjects: Church history. Special Collections: Jacob B. Mench collection. Holdings: Books; bound periodical volumes; manuscripts. Publications: MHEP Newsletter, monthly - by subscription.

GERMAN INFORMATION CENTER - FEDERAL REPUBLIC OF GERMANY
410 Park Avenue
New York, New York 10022 (212) 888-9840
Founded 1961

Subjects: General information on the Federal Republic of Germany. Services: Center open to public.

GERMANS FROM RUSSIA PROJECT
Colorado State University Library
History Department
Fort Collins, Colorado 80523 (303) 491-6854
Project Archv.: John Newman

Subjects: Germans from Russia. Holdings: Books; bound periodical volumes; manuscripts. Services: Interlibrary loans; copying; library open to public with prior arrangement. Special Catalogs: Germans from Russia in Colorado by Sidney Heitman, University Microfilms, 1978, Ann Arbor.

GOETHE HOUSE LIBRARY
1014 Fifth Avenue
New York, New York 10028 (212) 744-8310
Librarian: Freya Jeschke Founded 1957

Subjects: German publications with special emphasis on German literature, art, history, and politics. Special Collections: Collected works of Goethe and other famous German poets. Holdings: Books; journals and other serials; newspapers; reports on Germany and German affairs. Services: Interlibrary loans; library open to outside users.

GOETHE INSTITUTE ATLANTA - LIBRARY
German Cultural Center
400 Colony Square
Atlanta, Georgia 30361 (404) 892-2226
Librarian: Margit Rostock Founded 1977

Subjects: Germany - contemporary literature, social science, geography, history. Holdings: Books; tapes, and slides; journals and other serials; newspapers. Services: Interlibrary loans; library open to public. Remarks: This institute is the German Cultural Center for the Southeastern United States. It is a branch of the Goethe Institute Munich.

GOETHE INSTITUTE BOSTON - LIBRARY
170 Beacon Street
Boston, Massachusetts 02116 (617) 262-6050
Director: Dorothy Burney Founded 1966

Subjects: Germany: literature, language, geography, customs, fine arts, history and politics, sociology, philosophy, theology and psychology. Holdings: Books; journals and other serials; newspapers. This is the German Cultural Center for New England. The holdings are in German with about 20% English translation. Services: Interlibrary loans; copying; library open to public.

GOETHE INSTITUTE SAN FRANCISCO - LIBRARY
530 Bush Street
San Francisco, California 94108 (415) 391-0370
Librarian: Helmi Schlueter Founded 1970

Subjects: Germany - contemporary literature, classics, history, political science, art, economics, education. Holdings: Books; bound periodical volumes; slides, tapes and phonograph records; journals and other serials; newspapers. Services: Interlibrary loans; library open to public.
Publications: Recent acquisitions, quarterly - to readers. 90% of books are in German; 10% are translations from German to English.

JOHN A. W. HAAS LIBRARY
Muhlenberg College
Allentown, Pennsylvania 18104 (215) 433-3191
Director of Librarians: Patricia Ann Sacks

JOSEPH HORNER MEMORIAL LIBRARY
German Society of Pennsylvania
611 Spring Garden Street
Philadelphia, Pennsylvania 19123 (215) 627-4365
Librarian: Christine E. Richardson Founded 1817

Subjects: All subjects with special emphasis on history, biography, literature (85% in German language), juvenile literature. Special Collections: German works printed in America. Holdings: Books, journals and other serials; archives (cataloged).

LANCASTER MENNONITE CONFERENCE HISTORICAL SOCIETY - LIBRARY
2215 Millstream Road
Lancaster, Pennsylvania 17602 (717) 393-9745
Director: Carolyn C. Wenger Founded 1958

Subjects: Theology; history - local and denominational; genealogy, especially Pennsylvania Dutch. Special Collections: Mennonitica; Amishana. Holdings: Books and bound periodical volumes; archive boxes; vital statistics cards; maps; pamphlets; journals and other serials. Services: Copying; translation; library open to public.
Publications: Pennsylvania Mennonite Heritage, quarterly. Mirror, bimonthly; Used Book Sales, Brochure, bimonthly - subscription.

MENNO SIMONS HISTORICAL LIBRARY AND ARCHIVES
Eastern Mennonite College
Harrisonburg, Virginia 22801 (703) 433-2771
Librarian: Grace Showalter Founded 1943

Subjects: Anabaptist and Mennonite history; German culture in the Eastern United States; history of the Shenandoah Valley; genealogy. Holdings: Books; journals and other serials; newspapers; microfilm; magnetic tape; manuscript and archival material. Services: Interlibrary loans; copying; library open to public for reference use only.

MENNONITE HISTORICAL LIBRARY
Bluffton College
Bluffton, Ohio 45817 (419) 358-8015
Librarian: Delbert Gratz Founded 1937

Subjects: Mennonite history, Amish history, Anabaptist History, Hutterian Brethren history, Apostolic Christian history, genealogy, peace. Holdings: Books; bound periodical volumes; boxes of letters and manuscripts; microfilm; theses, dissertations, pictures, maps and miscellaneous papers; journals and other serials; newspapers. Services: Interlibrary loans; library open to public by appointment. Special Indexes: Index to family histories relating to Mennonite and Amish families; Index to periodical articles in non-Mennonite periodicals relating to the Amish and Mennonites.

MENNONITE LIBRARY AND ARCHIVES
Bethel College
North Newton, Kansas 67117 (316) 283-2500
Director: Robert Kreider Founded 1935

Subjects: Anabaptists; Mennonites in Europe, America, Latin America and Asia; peace; Kansas. Special Collections: Anabaptist and Mennonite manuscript collection; General Conference Church Archives; rare Anabaptist books; 2000 Mennonite hymnbooks; Mennonite art collection including 17th century Dutch art. Holdings: Books; bound periodicals; microfilm (cataloged); audiotape (cataloged); maps; journals and other serials; newspapers. Services: Interlibrary loans; copying; translation; library open to public.
Publications: Mennonite Life, quarterly.

MORAVIAN ARCHIVES
Moravian Church in America - Northern Province
41 West Locust Street
Bethlehem, Pennsylvania 18018 (215) 866-3255
Archv.: Vernon H. Nelson Founded 1751

Subjects: Moravian Church history - general and American; history of Bethlehem and area; biography; hymnody; missions (Moravian). Holdings: Books; bound periodical volumes; manuscripts and documents; journals and other serials. Services: Library open to public; manuscripts may be consulted by special arrangement.

MORAVIAN ARCHIVES
Moravian Church in America - Southern Province
Drawer M, Salem Station
Winston-Salem, North Carolina 27108 (919) 722-1742
Archv.: Mary Creech Founded 1913

Subjects: Moravian Church history, Moravian missions, North Carolina. Holdings: Manuscripts, 1753 to present, relating chiefly to the Moravian settlement in North Carolina (known as Wachovia). Services: Copying(limited); library open to public by appointment, with fee for services of Archivist.

MORAVIAN MUSIC FOUNDATION, INCORPORATED - LIBRARY
20 Cascade Avenue
Winston-Salem, North Carolina 27108 (919) 725-0651
Director: James Boeringer Founded 1956

Subjects: Sacred anthems and arias; hymnological materials and books; American music of 18th and 19th centuries; symphonies and music of 18th and 19th centuries; music and religious history and biography. Special Collections: Irving Lowens Musical Americana Collection; Peter Memorial Library. Holdings: Books; manuscripts and early printed music editions; American and European manuscripts of 18th and 19th centuries; tape recordings of Moravian music; journals and other serials. Services: Copying (restricted); reference service by mail; music lending restricted to Moravian Churches; library open to public by application. Publications: Bulletin, semiannual - free upon request.

OLD SALEM, INCORPORATED - LIBRARY
Drawer F, Salem Station
Winston-Salem, North Carolina 27108 (919) 723-3688
Director, Department of Education:
Gene T. Capps

Subjects: Moravians in North Carolina; North Carolina history; traditional American crafts; historic preservation. Holdings: Books; VF drawers of Moraviana, preservation, crafts, interpretation clippings; VF drawers of items on life in early Salem, North Carolina, and restoration of Old Salem; journals and other serials. Services: Library open to public with restrictions.

REINHARDT ARCHIVE
State University of New York at Binghamton
Binghamton, New York 13901 (607) 798-4844
Founded 1966

Subjects: Max Reinhardt and the Theater of his Time; 19th and 20th century Theater. Services: Archive open to public by appointment.

RIFKIND COLLECTION - LIBRARY
9454 Wilshire Boulevard
Beverly Hills, California 90212 (213) 278-0970
Curator: Karin Brever Founded 1971

Subjects: German art of the 20th century. Special Collections: German-Expressionist art exhibition catalogs; monographs; original editions; "oeuvre" catalogs; graphics, drawings. Holdings: 2500 volumes. Services: Library open to authorized persons by appointment only.

Newspapers and Newsletters

AATG NEWSLETTER. 1966-. Quarterly. Editor: Dr. Louis F. Helbig. Publisher: American Association of Teachers of German, Incorporated, 339 Walnut Street, Philadelphia, Pennsylvania 19106.

Supplies information "for all those interested in the language, literature, and culture of the German-speaking countries," especially reports of interest to members of the association, chapter reports, and other announcements.

ABENDPOST (Eveningpost). 1889-. Daily, Tuesday-Friday. Editor: Ludwig Gehrken. Publisher: The Abendpost Company, 223 West Washington Street, Chicago, Illinois 60606. In German.

Provides international and national news, as well as news concerning activities and developments in Germany and events occurring in German-American communities in the United States.

AMERICAN TURNER TOPICS. 1885-. Bimonthly. Editor: William O. Huth. Publisher: American Turners, 1550 Clinton Avenue, North, Rochester, New York 14621. In English.

Presents general news and recreational and sports articles.

AMERIKA-WOCHE. (America-Weekly). 1972-. Weekly. Editor: Werner Baroni. Publisher: Courier Press, USA, Limited, 4740 North Western Avenue, Chicago, Illinois 60625. In German.

Now combined with the America Herold und Sonntags-post - Lincoln Freie Presse (1873; Nebraska), Buffalo Volksfreund (1868), California Freie Presse (1949), Cincinnati Kurier (1964), Milwaukee Herold (1854), Sonntagspost (1873), Volkszeitung Tribune (1875),

Weltpost (1916). A special edition is printed for California. Covers international, national and regional news of interest to the German American community.

AUFBAU (Reconstruction). 1934-. Weekly. Editor: Dr. Hans Steinitz. Publisher: New World Club, Incorporated, 2121 Broadway, New York, New York 10023. In German and English.

Created to represent the interests and viewpoints of refugees, mostly Jewish, from Hitler's Germany. Emphasizes the cultural German background, Jewish faith and traditions, and loyalty to the United States. Reports on life in Germany and Israel and cultural activities.

DER BOTE. 1924-. Weekly. Editor: Gerhard Ens. Publisher: Mennonite Church, 722 Main Street, Box 347, Newton, Kansas 67114. In English.

BULLETIN. INFORMATION FROM THE GDR. Monthly. Publisher: Panorama DDR, Wilhelm Pieck Strass 49, 1054 Berlin, GDR.

Short articles of topical interest about cultural events in the German Democratic Republic.

CALIFORNIA STAATS-ZEITUNG (California State Journal). 1890-. Weekly. Editor: Albert Ebert. Publisher: Peter Teichmann, 315 West Sixth Street, Los Angeles, California 90014. In German.

CONFERENCE GROUP ON GERMAN POLITICS--NEWSLETTER. 1968-. Semiannual. Editor: Dr. David Conradt. Publisher: Conference Group on German Politics, Box 345, Durham, New Hampshire 03824.

Publishes information on developments in German social science and humanities and activities by American scholars dealing with German affairs. Includes news items on the group, and announcements of grants available in the field.

CORPSZEITUNG (Corps Bulletin). 1946-. Annual. Editor: Edward Baron von Magnus. Publisher: Corps Brandenburgia-Berlin zu Cleveland, 2950 Warrensville Center Road, Shaker Heights, Ohio 44122. In German.

Prints general cultural articles, reports on corps activities and news of members.

DEUTSCHE WELT USA. 1979-. Monthly. Editor: L. Babin. Publisher: Lenora Enterprises, Incorporated, Post Office Box 35831, Houston, Texas 77035.

DETROITER ABEND-POST (Detroit Evening-Post). 1854-. Semiweekly. Editors: Berthold Vogt and Adelgund Fuchs. Publisher: Detroit Abend-Post Publishing Company, 1436 Brush Street, Detroit, Michigan 48226. In German.

Covers political, social, cultural, sports, and other news for German-Americans. Includes a women's page and a financial section.

DER DEUTSCH-AMERIKANER (The German-American). 1959-. Monthly. Editor: Werner Baroni. Publisher: German American National Congress, Incorporated, 4740 North Western Avenue, Chicago, Illinois 60625. In German and English.

Presents organizational news concerning the German-American National Congress.

EINTRACHT (Harmony). 1923-. Weekly. Editors and Publishers: Klaus and Werner Jüngling, 9456 North Lawler Avenue, Skokie, Illinois 60076. In German.

Publishes news about Germany, Austria, and German-American organizations in the Chicago area. The sports section emphasizes soccer-football.

DAS FREIE WORT (Voice of Freedom). 1932-. Monthly. Editor: Paul A. Kaufmann. Publisher: Freie Gemeinde, 2617 West Fond du Lac Avenue, Milwaukee, Wisconsin 54935. In German.

News of interest to the denominational community.

GERMAN-AMERICAN. 1941-. Bimonthly. Publisher: German American, Incorporated, 130 East 16th Street, New York, New York 10003.

Articles on political, cultural and historical subjects concerning the relationship between Germans and German Americans.

GERMAN-AMERICAN GENEALOGIST. 1975-. Quarterly. Publisher: Institute for German-American Studies, 7204 Langerford Drive, Cleveland, Ohio 44129.

GERMAN-AMERICAN WORLD. 1968-. Monthly. Publisher: Gak-Law Communications Media, Incorporated. 529-A-Central Avenue, Jersey City, New Jersey 07307, (201) 420-0159.

GERMAN PRESS REVIEW. Publisher: Press Office of the Embassy of the Federal Republic of Germany, 4645 Reservoir Road, Washington, D. C. In English.

Presents summaries of commentaries published in the Federal Republic of German on current events. Published irregularly but frequently and distributed by the Press Office though it does not necessarily represent the views of the German government.

GERMAN TRIBUNE. 1962-. Weekly. Editor: Otto Heinz. English language Editors: Alexander Anthony and Simon Burnett. Publisher: Friedrich Reinecke Verlag, GmbH, 23 Schone Aussicht, Hamburg 76, Germany. In English.

Prints commentaries which have appeared in the German press on world events, domestic political and economic affairs and cultural news.

GOSPEL HERALD. 1908-. Weekly. Editor: Daniel Hertzler, Publisher: Mennonite Publishing House, 616 Walnut, Scottsdale, Pennsylvania 15683, (412) 887-8500.

A Mennonite religious publication.

DER HARUGARI. Publisher: German Order of Harugari, 124 Plattsburg Avenue, Burlington, Vermont 05401.

Publishes fraternal benefit insurance organization news.

INTERCOM. 1957-. Monthly. Editor: Sarah Ann Eby. Publisher: Mennonite Central Committee, 21 South 12th Street, Akron, Pennsylvania 17501.

Carries news of Mennonite relief programs around the world, with items on persons serving with the Mennonite Central Committee and information on resources that may be helpful to them. Discusses ideas and opinions on community development, education, social services, medical services, agriculture, and other subjects useful for volunteers and other readers.

LK. Bimonthly. Publisher: Liederkranz Foundation, 6 East 87th Street, New York, New York 10028.

Publication of the Liederkranz Foundation, a musical society.

THE MENNONITE. 1885-. Weekly. Editor: Larry Kehler. Publisher: General Conference Mennonite Church, 722 Main Street, Box 347, Newton, Kansas 67114. In English.

Provides news, comment, and discussion on church and world affairs of interest to Mennonites.

MENNONITE HISTORICAL BULLETIN. Quarterly. Publisher: Historical Committee of the Mennonite Church, 1700 South Main Street, Goshen, Indiana 46526.

Publishes news of the Society and its activities, research in progress and historical articles about the church.

MILWAUKEE DEUTSCHE ZEITUNG (Milwaukee German Journal). 1890-. Daily, Tuesday-Friday. Editor: Ludwig Gehrken. Publisher: Abendpost Company, 223 West Washington Street, Chicago, Illinois 60606. In German.

DAS MITTEILUNGSBLATT (Information Bulletin). 3 times a year. Editor: Don Heinrich Rolzmann. Publisher: Association of German Language Authors in America, 2545 Harrison Avenue, Cincinnati, Ohio 45211. In German.

NACHRICHTEN DER DONAUSCHWABEN IN AMERIKA (News of the Danube Swabians in America). 1955-. Monthly. Editor: Jacob Awender. Publisher: Society of the Donau Swabians of the U. S., 4219 North Lincoln Avenue, Chicago, Illinois 60618. In German.

NEUE ZEITUNG (American European Weekly). 1967-. Weekly. Editor: Heinz Otto Jurisch. Publisher: German-American League, Incorporated, 9471 Hidden Valley Place, Beverly Hills, California 90210. In German.

Presents European political news and articles on commerce and travel.

NEW APPROACH. Monthly. Publisher: World Association of Upper Silesians, Dalton, Pennsylvania, 18414.

NEW JERSEY FREIE ZEITUNG (New Jersey Free Newspaper). 1856-. Weekly. Editor: Eberhard Schweizer. Publisher: New Jersey Freie Zeitung, Incorporated, 500 South 31st Street, Kenilworth, New Jersey 07033.

NEW YORKER STAATS-ZEITUNG UND HEROLD (New York State Journal and Herald). 1834-. Daily. Editor: Dr. Frederick Lachman. Publisher: Erwin Steuer, 3630 37th Street, Long Island City, New York 11101. In German.

Presents international, national, and regional news with emphasis on German events and the German-speaking community. Florida and Philadelphia editions of this influential German daily are also published.

DER OBERSCHLESIER (The Upper Silesian). Monthly. Publisher: World Association of Upper Silesians, Dalton, Pennsylvania 18414.

OSTFRIESEN ZEITUNG (East Frisia News). 1882-. Monthly. Editor: D. B. Aden, Breda, Iowa 51436. In German.

PALATINE IMMIGRANT. 1976-. Quarterly. Editor: Charles Hall. Publisher: Palatines to America, 157 North State Street, Salt Lake City, Utah 84103.

Newsletter for German immigrants from the Palatine.

PENNSYLVANIA DUTCH NEWS AND VIEWS. 1965-. Biennial. Editor: Florence Baver. Publisher: Pennsylvania Dutch Folk Culture Society, Incorporated, Lenhartsville, Pennsylvania 19534.

Newsletter of the Society carrying news of activities and features on Pennsylvania Dutch folk life.

PENNSYLVANIA MENNONITE HERITAGE. Quarterly. Publisher: Lancaster Mennonite Historical Society, 2215 Millstream Road, Lancaster, Pennsylvania 17602. In English.

Newsletter of the library centering on local and denominational history of the Pennsylvania Dutch Mennonites and Amish.

PHILADELPHIA GAZETTE-DEMOKRAT. 1890-. Weekly. Editor: Dr. Frederick Lachman. Publisher: Erwin Stewer, Staatszeitung und Herold Corporation, 3630 37th Street, Long Island City, New York 11101. In German.

Publishes news, commentary, and analysis of national, international, and local events with special emphasis on Germany and German Americans.

PLATTDEUTSCHE POST (Platt-German Post). 1934-. Weekly. Editor: Stefan Deubel. Publisher: Plattdeutsche Post, Incorporated, 4164 Lorain Avenue, Cleveland, Ohio 44113. In German.

Carries general and local news published in North German dialect.

SAENGER ZEITUNG (Journal for Singers). 1924-. Monthly. Editor: Harold W. Tausch. Publisher: Federation of Workers' Singing Societies of America, 1729 Springfield Avenue, Maplewood, New Jersey 07040. In German and English.

Official publication of the Federation of Workers' Singing Societies of the United States. Promotes song festivals and presents news of the affiliated singing societies.

SAXON NEWS VOLKSBLATT. 1905-. Weekly. Editor: Stefan Deubel. Publisher: Alliance of Transylvania Saxons, 5293 Pearl Road, Cleveland, Ohio 44129. In English and German.

Newly named newsletter for the Transylvania Saxons. Formerly called Siebenbürgisches Amerikanisches Volksblatt.

SONNTAGSBLATT STAATS-ZEITUNG. 1834-. Weekly. Editor: Dr. Frederick Lachman. Publisher: New Yorker Staats-Zeitung und Herold, 3630 37th Street, Long Island City, New York 11101.

Weekend edition of the New Yorker Staats-Zeitung und Herold. Prints news summaries and special feature articles.

SONNTAGPOST. 1889-. Weekly. Editor: Ludwig Gehrken. Publisher: Abendpost Company, Publisher, 223 West Washington Street, Chicago, Illinois 60606. In German.

Weekend edition of the Abendpost.

STEUBEN NEWS. 1928-. Bimonthly. Editor: Henry F. Heinlein. Publisher: Steuben Society of America, 6705 Fresh Pond Road, Ridgewood, New York 11385. In English.

Carries general, national, and local news, as well as news of the Steuben Society. Articles about European affairs are written by European correspondents.

TROY FREIE PRESSE (Troy Free Press). 1870-. Weekly. Editor: George F. Birkmayer, 193 River Street, Troy, New York 12180. In German.

Carries general news and local features of interest to the German American community.

WAECHTER UND ANZEIGER (Observer and Announcer). 1852-. Weekly. Editor: Stefan Deubel. Publisher: Waechter und Anzeiger Publishing Company, 4164 Lorain Avenue, Cleveland, Ohio 44113. In German.

Reports on international, national, and local news.

WASHINGTON JOURNAL. 1859-. Weekly. Editor: Gerald R. Kainz. Publisher: Washington Journal, Incorporated, 844 National Press Building, Washington, D. C. 20004. In German.

Publishes feature articles on Germany and news items on the activities of German Americans, as well as international, national, and local news.

THE WEEK IN GERMANY. 1970-. Weekly. Editors: G. Merton, P. Flory, P. Freedman, F. Helitzer. Publisher: German Information Center, 410 Park Avenue, New York, New York 10022. In English.

A digest of political, economic and cultural news from Germany.

WOCHENBLATT. 1980-. Weekly. Editors and Publishers: Margrit and Arthur F. Maasch, 4227 North 63rd Drive, Phoenix, Arizona 85033. In German.

DIE ZEIT (Times). 1945-. Editor: Dr. Karsten Plog. Publisher: Western Printers Association, Limited, 455 Spadina Avenue, Toronto, Ontario, Canada. In German.

North American edition of the German weekly. International and German national news coverage as well as economic and political analysis, literature and culture.

Magazines

BAHN FREI (Clear Track). 1883-. Monthly. Editor: S. A. Buttweiler. Publisher: New York Turn Verein, 152 East 85th Street, New York, New York 10028. In German and English.

A fraternal magazine reporting activities of the sponsoring organization, New York Turnverein.

CHRISTIAN LIVING. 1954-. Monthly. Editor: J. Lorne Peachey. Publisher: Mennonite Publishing House, 616 Walnut Avenue, Pittsburgh, Pennsylvania 15683. In English.

EUROPEAN MAGAZIN. 1969-. Monthly. Editor and Publisher, Post Office Box 14545, Phoenix, Arizona 85063. In German and English.

Features articles on European culture, food and travel.

EVANGELIUMS POSAUNE (Gospel Trumpet). 1895-. Weekly. Editor: Reverend Fritz Lenk. Publisher: Christian Unity Press, 4912 Northwestern Avenue, Racine, Wisconsin 53406. In German.

FILMHEFTE (Film Magazine). 1975. Biennial. Editor and Publisher: Herbert Linder, 140 East 28th Street, New York, New York 10016. In German.

FREIE ARBEITER STIMME (Free Voice of Labor). 1890-. Monthly. Editor: P. Constan. Publisher: c/o Frannie Breslaw, 290 Ninth Avenue, New York, New York 10001. In German.

A publication of the Libertarian Socialists.

G.B.U. REPORTER. 1892-. Monthly. Editor: Kathy Lee Barabas. Publisher: Greater Beneficial Union of Pittsburgh, 4254 Clairton Boulevard, Pittsburgh, Pennsylvania 15227. In English and German.

A fraternal magazine reporting on news and activities of the Greater Benevolent Union.

GDR REVIEW. 1961-. Monthly. Editor: Lena Smolny. Publisher: International Friendship League of the German Democratic Republic, Thalmannplatz 8-9, 1086 Berlin, GDR. In English, Danish, Dutch, Finnish, French, German, Italian and Swedish.

A public relations magazine which prints feature stories on various cultural and social aspects of the German Democratic Republic and articles on Russia's and East Germany's love of peace compared with the United States' and NATO's arms build up and militaristic policies. Lavishly illustrated.

GERMAN AMERICAN TRADE NEWS. 1955-. 10 times a year. Editors: Richard Jacob and Peter Goldman. Publisher: German American Chamber of Commerce, 666 Fifth Avenue, New York, New York 10019. In English.

Provides information on all aspects of German-American trade, with primary emphasis upon interpretation of the German economy and business trends to the American business community.

GERMAN QUARTERLY. 1927-. Quarterly. Editor: Ruth K. Angress. Publisher: American Association of Teachers of German, 523 Building, Suite 201, Route 38, Cherry Hill, New Jersey 08034. In German and English.

GERMAN STUDIES REVIEW. 1977-. 3 times a year. Editor: Gerald R. Kleinfeld. Publisher: Western Association for German studies, Arizona State University, Tempe, Arizona 85281.

THE GERMANIC REVIEW. 1925-. Quarterly. Editor: Joseph Bauke. Publisher: Cornelius W. Vahle, Jr., 4000 Albemarle Street, Northwest, Washington, D. C. 20016. In English and German.

Specializes in articles on Germanic languages and literature.

GOSPEL HERALD. Weekly. Editor: Daniel Hertzler, Scottsdale, Pennsylvania 15683. Publisher: Mennonite Church, 528 East Madison Street, Lombard, Illinois 60148.

A weekly church publication for the Mennonite faith.

DIE HAUSFRAU (The Housewife). 1904-. Monthly. Editor: J. Edelmann. Publisher: Die Hausfrau, Incorporated, 1517 West Fullerton Avenue, Chicago, Illinois 60614. In German.

A general interest magazine for the housewife and the whole family.

HERITAGE REVIEW. 1971. 3 times a year. Publisher: Germans from Russia Heritage Society, Box 1671, 107-1/2 North Fourth Street, Bismarck, North Dakota 58501. In English and German.

Publishes articles concerning the Germans from Russia, their history and the activities of the group in America.

HEROLD DER WAHRHEIT (Herald of Truth). 1912-. Monthly. Editors: Lester B. Miller and Jonas J. Beachy. Publisher: Amish-Mennonite Publishing Association, Route 2, Kalona, Iowa 52247. In German and English.

A religious journal published for and about the Amish Mennonite Churches.

INTERNATIONAL MONTHLY. 1959-. Monthly. Editor: Ute Lorenz. Publisher: International Monthly, Post Office Box 8522, San Jose, California 95125. In German and English.

Reviews the German press and world affairs. Presents cultural and historical articles, commentaries, trade and travel news.

INTERNATIONALE BIBEL-LEKTIONEN (International Bible Lessons). 1920-. Quarterly. Editor: Reverend Fritz Lenk. Publisher: Christian Unity Press, 4912 Northwestern Avenue, Racine, Wisconsin 53406. In German.

Promotes the teaching of the Bible as interpreted by the Church of God.

JOURNAL OF GERMAN-AMERICAN HISTORY. 1887-. 3 times a year. Editor: Klaus Wust, 350 Bleecker Street, New York, New York, 10014. Publisher: Society for the History of Germans in Maryland, 231 Saint Paul Place, Baltimore, Maryland 21202.

Articles on German American immigration history and the contributions of German Americans locally, regionally and nationally.

JOURNAL OF GERMAN AMERICAN STUDIES. 1965-. Quarterly. Editor: Robert E. Ward. Publisher: German-American Publishing Company, 21010 Mastick Road, Cleveland, Ohio 44126. In English.

A journal of history, literature, biography and genealogy.

KAISERZEIT. Bimonthly. Publisher: Imperial German Military Collectors' Association, Box 651, Shawnee Mission, Kansas 66201.

Features articles on historic artifacts from Imperial Germany as well as news of the Association.

KATHOLISCHER JUGENDFREUND (Catholic Young People's Friend). 1877-. Monthly. Editor: John S. West. Publisher: Angel Guardian Orphanage, 2001 Devon Avenue, Chicago, Illinois 60645. In German.

A Roman Catholic youth journal.

KIRCHLICHES MONATSBLATT FUR LUTHERISCHE GEMEINDEN (Church Monthly for the Lutheran Congregations). 1943-. Monthly. Editor: Reverend Karl Schild. Publisher: German Interest Conference of the Lutheran Church in America, 584 East Geneva Avenue, Philadelphia, Pennsylvania 19120. In German.

Publishes church news of special interest for the German-speaking congregations, as well as religious poetry, devotional material, and missionary news.

KOLPING BANNER. 1929-. Monthly. Editor: Herbert T. Bauer. Publisher: Catholic Kolping Society of America, 125 Stratton Lane, Mount Prospect, Illinois 60056. In English.

A fraternal monthly and official organ of the Society.

KONTAKT. 1942-. Bimonthly. Editor: Horst Doehler. Publisher: German-American, Incorporated, 130 East 16th Street, New York, New York 10003. In German.

News and articles of interest to German Americans.

KONTINENT. 1964-. Monthly. Editor: J. Hartmann. Publisher: Transatlantik Publishing Corporation, 601 West 26th Street, New York, New York 10001. In German.

News summaries and commentary.

DER LUTHERANER (The Lutheran). 1844-. Bimonthly. Editor: Reverend Herman A. Mayer. Publisher: Concordia Publishing House, 3558 South Jefferson Avenue, Saint Louis, Missouri 63118. In German.

Official organ of the Evangelical Lutheran Church, Missouri Synod. Covers news of church activities and presents religious and devotional material.

MENNONITE QUARTERLY REVIEW. Quarterly. Editor: John S. Oyer. Publisher: Mennonite Church, Goshen, Indiana 46526.

Official publication of the Mennonite Church with articles on church history and present activities.

MONATSHEFTE (Monthly News). 1899-. Quarterly. Editor: Reinhold Grimm. Publisher: University of Wisconsin Press, 114 North Murray Street, Madison, Wisconsin 53715. In English and German.

Scholarly articles on German literature and literary criticism.

NACHRICHTEN (News). 1952-. Monthly. Editors: Dr. Jacob Awender. Publisher: Society of the Danube Swabians of the United States, 4219 North Lincoln Avenue, Chicago, Illinois 60618. In German.

A publication promoting the social life, culture, economy, and progress of Danube Swabians. Carries information on the various activities of Danube Swabians in the United States.

PENNSYLVANIA GERMAN SOCIETY JOURNAL. Quarterly. Publisher: Fackenthal Library, Franklin and Marshall College, Lancaster, Pennsylvania 17604.

PRISMA. A Quarterly Digest from the GDR. Quarterly. Editor: Madelon Frank-Weiland. Publisher: Panorama DDR Redaktion "Prisma", Wilhelm Pieck Strasse 49, 1054 Berlin, GDR. In English.

Translations and interviews from the press in the German Democratic Republic on political, social, educational, cultural and scientific topics. Illustrated in color and black and white.

DER REGGEBOGE (The Rainbow). 1967-. Editor: Frederick S. Weiser. Publisher: Pennsylvania German Society, Rd 1, Box 469, Breinigsville, Pennsylvania 18031.

RUNDBRIEF (Round Robin). 1927-. Monthly. Editor and Publisher: Gilbert Derleberg, 357 Tom Hunter Road, Fort Lee, New Jersey 07024. In German.

A youth magazine with short stories and poems, general articles and travel reports.

SAINT JOSEPH'S BLATT (Saint Joseph's Page). 1887-. Semimonthly. Editor and Publisher: Manfred F. Ellenberger, Mount Angel Abbey, Saint Benedict, Oregon 97373. In German.

A Catholic religious magazine.

SCALA. Monthly. Editor: Werner Wirthle. Publisher: Frankfurter Societdts-Druckerei, 6000 Frankfurt am Main, Postfach 2929, Frankenallee 71-81, Germany. In English.

A pictorial magazine from the Federal Republic of Germany with editions in German, English, French, Spanish and Portuguese. Contains articles about various aspects of life in West Germany - city and country life, government, industry, arts, education, communication, and transportation. Illustrated with numerous photographs, many in color.

THE SCHWENKFELDIAN. 1903-. Quarterly. Editor: Jack R. Rothenberger. Publisher: Board of Publication of the Schwenkfelder Church, 1 Seminary Street, Pennsburg, Pennsylvania 18073. In English.

Publishes news concerning the various Schwenkfelder churches and religious material on church-related issues.

DER SENDBOTE (The Messenger). 1852-. Monthly. Editor: Reinhold J. Kerstan. Publisher: North American Baptist General Conference (Roger Williams Press,) 7308 Madison Street, Forest Park, Illinois 60130. In German.

Offers religious materials and denominational news.

SOLIDARITY. 1906-. Monthly. Editor: Jack Hengerson. Publisher: Workmen's Benefit Fund of the U.S.A., 714 Seneca Avenue, Ridgewood (Brooklyn), New York 11227. In English.

Presents articles on economic security, social problems, health, and international affairs. The German edition was discontinued after December, 1968.

TÄGLICHE ANDACHTEN (Daily Devotions). 1937-. Bimonthly. Editor: Louis J. Kohm. Publisher: Concordia Publishing House, 3558 South Jefferson Avenue, Saint Louis, Missouri 63118. In German.

Features daily devotional material taken from Biblical texts.

THE VINDICATOR. Publisher: Old German Baptist Brethren, RD 4, Delphi, Indiana 46923. In English and German.

VOICE OF AMERICANS OF GERMAN DESCENT. 1949-. Monthly. Editor: Gertrude Barron. Publisher: German American National Congress, 5917 Palmetto Street, Ridgewood, New York 11227.

THE WANDERER. 1867-. Weekly. Editor: Alphonse J. Matt. Publisher: Wanderer Printing Company, 128 East Tenth Street, Saint Paul, Minnesota 55101. In English.

Contains material on topics of interest to the German Catholic community.

ZEICHEN DER ZEIT (Signs of the Times). 1874-. Monthly. Editor: Lawrence Maxwell. Distributer: Pacific Press Publishing Association, 1350 Villa Street, Mountain View, California 94040. In German.

Presents religious material including interpretation of Biblical texts. Interprets world events in the light of prophecy. A fundamentalist, Bible-based publication.

Radio Programs

Alabama - Huntsville

WLRH (FM) - 222 Holmes Avenue, Huntsville, Alabama 35801, (205) 539-9405. German programs, 1 hour weekly.

Arizona - Sierra Vista

KSVA - 5200 East Highway 90, Box 2050, Sierra Vista, Arizona 85635, (602) 459-1470. German programs, 1/2 hour weekly.

Arkansas - Conway

KHDX (FM) - Hendrix College, Conway, Arkansas 72032, (501) 327-2600. German programs, 3 hours weekly.

California - Inglewood

KTYM - 6803 West Boulevard, Inglewood, California 90302, (213) 678-3731. German programs, 2 hours weekly.

California - Mission Viejo

KSBR (FM) - 28000 Marguerite Parkway, Mission Viejo, California 92691, (714) 831-5727. German programs, 2 hours weekly.

California - Northridge

KCSN (FM) - 18111 Nordhoff Street, Northridge, California 91330, (213) 885-3090. German programs, 3 hours weekly.

California - Pasadena

KPCC (FM) - 1570 East Colorado, Pasadena, California 91106, (213) 578-7231. German programs, 4 hours weekly.

California - Petaluma

KTOB - 58 East Washington Street, Petaluma, California 94952, (707) 763-1505. German programs, 1 hour weekly.

California - San Francisco

KALW (FM) - 2905 21st Street, San Francisco, California 94110, (415) 648-1177. German programs, 1 hour weekly.

KEST - 1231 Market Street, San Francisco, California 94103, (415) 626-5585. German programs.

Colorado - Colorado Springs

KRCC (FM) - Colorado College, Colorado Springs, Colorado 80903, (303) 473-4801. German programs, 3 hours weekly.

Colorado - Denver

KADX (FM) - 9805 East Lliff, Denver, Colorado 80231, (303) 755-1213. German programs, 3 hours weekly.

KFML - 1602 South Parker Road, Denver, Colorado 80231, (303) 751-1390. German programs, 1 hour weekly.

KPOF - 3455 West 83rd Avenue, Denver, Colorado 80030, (303) 428-0910. German programs, 1 hour weekly.

Colorado - Pueblo

KFEL - 4411 Goodnight Avenue, Pueblo, Colorado 81005, (303) 561-4884. German programs, 1 hour weekly.

Connecticut - Ansonia

WADS - Ansonia Mall, Ansonia, Connecticut 06401, (203) 735-4606. German programs, 2 hours weekly.

Connecticut - Norwalk

WNLK - Box 1350, Norwalk, Connecticut 06852, (203) 838-5566. German programs, 1 hour weekly.

Connecticut - Willimantic

WNOU (FM) - Box 98, Willimantic, Connecticut 06226, (203) 456-2251. German programs, 2 hours weekly.

Florida - Boynton Beach

WHRS (FM) - 505 South Congress Avenue, Boynton Beach, Florida 33435, (305) 732-7850. German programs, 1 hour weekly.

Florida - Miami

WDNA (FM) - Box WDNA, Ludlam Br, Miami, Florida 33155, (305) 264-9362. German programs, 1 hour weekly.

Florida - Pine Castle-Sky Lake

WHHL - 8421 South Orange Blossom Trail, Orlando, Florida 32809, (305) 859-4350. German programs, 2 hours weekly.

Florida - Tampa

WSOL - 1711 West Kennedy Boulevard, Tampa, Florida 33606, (813) 253-0135. German programs, 4 hours weekly.

Georgia - Athens

WCCD - Box 5860, Athens, Georgia 30604, (404) 549-1470. German programs, 3 hours weekly.

Georgia - Atlanta

WGKA - 100 Colony Square, Suite 421, Atlanta, Georgia 30361, (404) 892-1190. German programs, 1 hour weekly.

Hawaii - Honolulu

KNDI - 1734 South King Street, Honolulu, Hawaii 96826, (808) 946-2844. German programs, 2 hours weekly.

Illinois - Chicago

WSSD (FM) - 1950 East 71st Street, Chicago, Illinois 60649. German programs.

WUIC (FM) - Box 4348, Chicago, Illinois 60680, (312) 996-2720. German programs, 1 hour weekly.

Illinois - Cicero

WCEV - 5356 West Belmont Avenue, Cicero, Illinois 60641, (312) 282-6700. German programs, 1 hour weekly.

Illinois - Columbia

WCBW (FM) - Box 147, Columbia, Illinois 62235, (618) 281-5031. German programs, 9 hours weekly.

Illinois - Galesburg

WVKC (FM) - Box 154, Knox College, Galesburg, Illinois 61401, (309) 343-8992. German programs, 1 hour weekly.

Illinois - Geneva

WGSB - 1215 Fern Avenue, St. Charles, Illinois 60174, (312) 584-1480. German programs, 3 hours weekly.

Illinois - Harvard

WMCW - Box 306, Harvard, Illinois 60033, (815) 943-3100. German programs, 1 hour weekly.

Illinois - Highland

WINU - Box 303, Highland, Illinois 62249, (618) 654-7521. German programs, 2 hours weekly.

Illinois - Highland Park

WVVX (FM) - 210 Skokie Valley Road, Highland Park, Illinois 60035, (312) 831-5250. German programs, 14 hours weekly.

Illinois - La Grange

WTAQ - 9355 West Joliet Road, La Grange, Illinois 60525, (312) 352-1300. German programs, 5 hours weekly.

Indiana - Gary

WLTH - 3669 Broadway, Gary, Indiana 46409, (219) 884-9409. German programs, 1-1/2 hours weekly.

Indiana - Greenfield

WIKS (FM) - 1634 West Main Street, Greenfield, Indiana 46140, (317) 924-9457. German programs, 1 hour weekly.

Indiana - Indianapolis

WAJC (FM) - 46th and Sunset, Indianapolis, Indiana 46208, (317) 283-9292. German programs, 1-1/2 hours weekly.

Indiana - New Albany

WNAS (FM) - 1020 Vincennes Street, New Albany, Indiana 47150, (812) 944-2216. German programs, 1 hour weekly.

Iowa - Davenport

KWNT - 1019 Mound Street, Davenport, Iowa 52803, (319) 326-4407. German programs, 1/2 hour weekly.

Iowa - Waverly

KWAR (FM) - Wartburg College, Waverly, Iowa 50677, (319) 352-1200. German programs, 1 hour weekly.

Louisiana - Many

KWLV (FM) - Box 1005, Many, Louisiana 71449, (318) 256-5924. German programs, 9 hours weekly.

Maryland - Baltimore

WBMD - 5200 Moravia Road, Baltimore, Maryland 21206, (301) 485-2400. German programs, 1 hour weekly.

WSPH (FM) - 7400 Old North Point Road, Baltimore, Maryland 21219, (301) 477-0750. German programs, 1 hour weekly.

Maryland - Bethesda

WHFS (FM) - 4853 Cordell Avenue, Bethesda, Maryland 20014, (301) 656-0600. German programs, 1 hour weekly.

Massachusetts - Pittsfield

WBEC - 211 Jason Street, Pittsfield, Massachusetts 01201, (413) 499-3333. German programs, 1/2 hour weekly.

Massachusetts - Springfield

WMAS - 101 West Street, Springfield, Massachusetts 01104, (413) 737-1414. German programs, 2 hours weekly.

Massachusetts - Ware

WARE - 90 South Street, Ware, Massachusetts 01082, (413) 967-6231. German programs, 2 hours weekly.

Michigan - Alpena

WATZ - Alpena, Michigan 49707, (517) 354-8400. German programs, 2 hours weekly.

Michigan - Beaverton

WGEO (FM) - Box 278, Beaverton, Michigan 48612, (517) 435-7797. German programs, 1 hour weekly.

Michigan - Benton Harbor

WHFB - Box 608, Benton Harbor, Michigan 49022, (616) 927-3581. German programs, 2 hours weekly.

Michigan - Garden City

WCAR - 32500 Park Lane, Garden City, Michigan 48135, (313) 525-1111. German programs, 2 hours weekly.

Michigan - Grand Rapids

WEHB (FM) - 1514 Wealthy, Southeast, Grand Rapids, Michigan 49506. German programs, 1 hour weekly.

Michigan - Newberry

WNBY - Box 1, Newberry, Michigan 49868, (906) 293-3221. German programs, 5 hours weekly.

Minnesota - Albany

KASM - Albany, Minnesota 56307, (612) 845-2184. German programs, 1 hour weekly.

Minnesota - Minneapolis-St. Paul

KBEM (FM) - 1101 Third Avenue, South, Minneapolis, Minnesota 55404, (612) 348-4888. German programs, 1 hour weekly.

Minnesota - New Ulm

KNUJ - 510 1/2 Third Street North, New Ulm, Minnesota 56073, (507) 359-2921. German programs, 5 hours weekly.

Minnesota - Northfield

WCAL - Northfield, Minnesota 55057, (507) 663-3071. German programs, 1 hour weekly.

Minnesota - Shakopee

KSMM - 421 East First Avenue, Box 66, Shakopee, Minnesota 55379, (612) 445-1866. German programs, 2 hours weekly.

Minnesota - Stillwater

WAVN - Box C, Stillwater, Minnesota 55082, (612) 439-1220. German programs, 1-1/2 hours weekly.

Minnesota - Winona

KQAL (FM) - Winona State University, Winona, Minnesota 55987, (507) 457-2900. German programs, 1/2 hour weekly.

Missouri - Columbia

KOPN (FM) - 915 East Broadway, Columbia, Missouri 65201, (314) 874-1139. German programs, 1 hour weekly.

Nebraska - Omaha

KIOS (FM) - 3219 Cuming Street, Omaha, Nebraska 68131, (402) 556-2770. German programs, 1 hour weekly.

New Jersey - Trenton

WTTM - 333 West State Street, Trenton, New Jersey 08618, (609) 695-8515. German programs, 1-1/2 hours weekly.

New York - Baldwinsville

WBXL (FM) - East Oneida Street Complex, Baldwinsville, New York 13027, (315) 635-3949. German programs, 5 hours weekly.

WSEN (AM & FM) - Box 1050, Baldwinsville, New York 13027, (315) 635-3971. German programs, 2 hours weekly.

New York - Ellenville

WELV (AM & FM) - North Main Street, 309, Ellenville, New York 12428, (914) 626-0123. German programs, 2 hours weekly.

New York - Hempstead

WVHC (FM) - 1000 Fulton Avenue, Hempstead, New York 11550, (516) 489-8870. German programs, 1/2 hour weekly.

New York - Hyde Park

WWWI - Box 95, Hyde Park, New York 12538, (914) 471-9500. German programs, 2 hours weekly.

New York - Kingston

WGHQ - Box 1880, Kingston, New York 12401, (914) 331-8200. German programs, 1 hour weekly.

WKNY - 212 Fair Street, Kingston, New York 12401, (914) 331-1490. German programs, 1 hour weekly.

New York - Little Falls

WLFH - 341 South Second Street, Little Falls, New York 13365, (315) 823-1230. German programs, 2 hours weekly.

New York - Mineola

WTHE - 266 Maple Place, Mineola, New York 11501, (516) 742-1520. German programs, 1 hour weekly.

New York - New Rochelle

WVOX - One Broadcast Forum, New Rochelle, New York 10801, (914) 636-1460. German programs, 4 hours weekly.

New York - New York

WFUV (FM) - Fordham U. Bronx, New York 10458, (212) 933-2233. German programs, 1 hour weekly.

New York - Poughkeepsie

WEOK - Box 416, Poughkeepsie, New York 12602, (914) 471-1500. German programs, 1 hour weekly.

New York - Rensselaer

WQBK - Box 1300, Albany, New York 12201, (518) 462-5555. German programs, 1 hour weekly.

New York - Utica

WBVM - Box 1550, Utica, New York 13503, (315) 797-0803. German programs, 2 hours weekly.

Ohio - Cincinnati

WAIF (FM) - 2525 Victory Parkway, Cincinnati, Ohio 45206, (513) 961-8900. German programs, 2 hours weekly.

Ohio - Cleveland

WCSB (FM) - Cleveland State University, Cleveland, Ohio 44115, (216) 687-3523. German programs, 1 hour weekly.

WZAK (FM) - 1303 Prospect Avenue, Cleveland, Ohio 44115, (216) 621-9300. German programs, 8-1/2 hours weekly.

Ohio - Columbus

WRMZ (FM) - Southern Hotel, Columbus, Ohio 43215, (614) 221-1354. German programs, 2 hours weekly.

Ohio - Dayton

WCXL (FM) - 5554 West Third Street, Dayton, Ohio 45401, (513) 268-5293. German programs, 1 hour weekly.

Ohio - Mansfield

WMAN - 1400 Radio Lane, Box 8, Mansfield, Ohio 44901, (419) 524-2211. German programs, 1 hour weekly.

Ohio - Middletown

WPBF (FM) - 4505 Central Avenue, Middletown, Ohio 45042, (513) 422-3625. German programs, 8 hours weekly.

Ohio - Napoleon

WNDH (FM) - Box 111, Napoleon, Ohio 43545, (419) 592-8060. German programs, 13 hours weekly.

Ohio - Toledo

WIOT (FM) - 604 Jackson Street, Toledo, Ohio 43604. German programs, 1 hour weekly.

WGOR - 6695 Jackman Road, Toledo, Ohio 43612, (419) 243-7088. German programs, 2 hours weekly.

Ohio - Youngstown

WGFT - One Federal Plaza, West, Youngstown, Ohio 44503, (216) 744-5115. German programs, 1 hour weekly.

Oklahoma - Lawton

KCCO - Box 1050, 1525 South Flower Mound Road, Lawton, Oklahoma 73502, (405) 355-1050. German programs, 1 hour weekly.

Pennsylvania - Ephrata

WIOV (FM) - 44 Bethany Road, Ephrata, Pennsylvania 17522, (717) 738-1191. German programs, 1 hour weekly.

Pennsylvania - Greencastle

WKSL (FM) - Box 10, Greencastle, Pennsylvania 17225, (717) 597-7151. German programs, 5 hours weekly.

Pennsylvania - Jenkintown

WIBF (FM) - The Benson East, Jenkintown, Pennsylvania 19046, (215) 886-2000. German programs, 1 hour weekly.

Pennsylvania - Philadelphia

WTEL - 4140 Old York Road, Philadelphia, Pennsylvania 19140, (215) 455-9200. German programs, 6 hours weekly.

Pennsylvania - Pittsburgh

WPIT - 200 Gateway Towers, Pittsburgh, Pennsylvania 15222, (412) 281-1900. German programs, 1 hour weekly.

Pennsylvania - Stroudsburg

WVPO - 22 South Sixth Street, Stroudsburg, Pennsylvania 18360, (717) 421-2100. German programs, 2 hours weekly.

Texas - Columbus

KULM (FM) - 325 Radio Lane, Columbus, Texas 78934, (713) 732-5766. German programs, 5 hours weekly.

Texas - Dallas

KERA (FM) - 3000 Harry Hines, Dallas, Texas 75201, (214) 744-9010. German programs, 1-1/2 hours weekly.

Texas - El Paso

KTEP (FM) - University of Texas at El Paso, El Paso, Texas 79968, (915) 747-5152. German programs 1 hour weekly.

Texas - Fredericksburg

KNAF - 210 Woodcrest, Fredericksburg, Texas 78624, (512) 997-2197. German programs, 7 hours weekly.

Texas - Hallettsville

KRJH - 111 North Main Street, Hallettsville, Texas 77964, (512) 798-4333. German programs, 3 hours weekly.

Texas - Hamilton

KCLW - Box 592, Hamilton, Texas 76531, (817) 386-5259. German programs, 1 hour weekly.

Texas - Houston

KPFT (FM) - 419 Lovett Boulevard, Houston, Texas 77006, (713) 526-4000. German programs, 3 hours weekly.

Texas - La Grange

KVLG - Drawer K, La Grange, Texas 78945, (713) 968-3173. Czech-German programs, 8 hours weekly.

Texas - Lubbock

KOHM (FM) - 3211 47th Street, Lubbock, Texas 79413, (806) 799-9035. German programs, 1 hour weekly.

Texas - New Braunfels

KNBT (FM) - Loop 337 North, New Braunfels, Texas 78130, (512) 625-7311. German programs, 4 hours weekly.

Texas - Seminole

KIKZ - 120 Southeast Avenue B, Seminole, Texas 79360, (915) 758-5788. German programs, 1/2 hour weekly.

Utah - Cedar City

KGSU (FM) - Southern Utah State College, Cedar City, Utah 84720, (801) 586-4411. German programs, 4 hours weekly.

Utah - Salt Lake City

KWHO - 329 East 2nd South, Salt Lake City, Utah 84111, (801) 534-4105. German programs, 1 hour weekly.

Virginia - Newport News

WGH (FM) - Box 9347, Hampton, Virginia 23670, (804) 826-1310. German programs, 1 hour weekly.

Washington - Bellevue

KASB (FM) - 601 108th Avenue, Southeast, Bellevue, Washington 98004, (206) 455-6154. German programs, 1 hour weekly.

Washington - Blaine

KARI - Box X, Blaine, Washington 98230, (206) 332-5500. German programs, 5 hours weekly.

Washington - Puyallup

KRPM - Box 577, Puyallup, Washington 98371, (206) 848-5588. German programs, 1 hour weekly.

Washington - Seattle

KXA - 1307 53rd Avenue, Seattle, Washington 98101, (206) 682-9033. German programs, 1 hour weekly.

Washington - Tacoma

KRPM (FM) - Box 5497, Tacoma, Washington 98405, (206) 627-3137. German programs, 1 hour weekly.

Wisconsin - Eagle River

WERL - Box 309, Eagle River, Wisconsin 54521, (715) 479-4451. German programs, 2 hours weekly.

Wisconsin - Eau Claire

WUEC (FM) - University of Wisconsin-Eau Claire, Eau Claire, Wisconsin 54701, (715) 886-4170. German programs, 1 hour weekly.

Wisconsin - Hartford

WTKM - Box 216, Hartford, Wisconsin 53027, (414) 673-3550. German programs, 3 hours weekly.

Wisconsin - Jackson

WYLO - 2330 Highland Road, Jackson, Wisconsin 53037, (414) 353-5300. German programs, 12-1/2 hours weekly.

Wisconsin - Kenosha

WGTD (FM) - 3520 30th Avenue, Kenosha, Wisconsin 53141, (414) 552 9483. German programs, 1 hour weekly.

Wisconsin - Kewaunee

WAUN (FM) - Box 224A, Route 3, Kewaunee, Wisconsin 54216, (414) 388-4852. German programs, 1 hour weekly.

Wisconsin - Marshfield

WDLB - 1710 North Central Avenue, Marshfield, Wisconsin 54449, (715) 384-2191. German programs, 1 hour weekly.

Wisconsin - Merrill

WJMT - 120 South Mill Street, Merrill, Wisconsin 54452, (715) 536-6262. German programs, 1 hour weekly.

Wisconsin - Port Washington

WGLB (AM & FM) - Box 347, Port Washington, Wisconsin 53074, (414) 284-2666. German programs, 12 hours weekly.

Wisconsin - Sheboygan

WHBL - Box 27, Sheboygan, Wisconsin 53081, (414) 458-2107. German programs, 1 hour weekly.

WSHS (FM) - 1042 School Avenue, Sheboygan, Wisconsin 53081, (414) 459-3610. German programs, 1 hour weekly.

Wisconsin - West Bend

WBKV (FM) - Box 60, West Bend, Wisconsin 53095, (414) 334-2344. German programs, 3 hours weekly.

PENNSYLVANIA DUTCH

Pennsylvania - Boyertown

WBYO (FM) - Box 177, Boyertown, Pennsylvania 19512, (215) 369-1075. Pennsylvania Dutch programs, 1 hour weekly.

Pennsylvania - Ephrata

WGSA - 44 Bethany Road, Ephrata, Pennsylvania 17522, (717) 738-1191. Pennsylvania Dutch programs, 1 hour weekly.

Television Programs

California - San Diego

KPBS-TV - San Diego State University, San Diego, California 92182, (714) 265-6415. German unspecified.

California - San Francisco

KTSF-TV - Lincoln Television Incorporated, 185 Berry Street, San Francisco, California 94107, (415) 495-4995. German unspecified.

Kansas - Wichita-Hutchinson

KPTS - 352 North Broadway, Wichita, Kansas 67202, (316) 262-4461. German unspecified.

Minnesota - Duluth (Superior, Wisconsin)

WDSE-TV - 1202 East University Circle, Duluth, Minnesota 55811, (218) 724-8568. German unspecified.

Missouri - Springfield

KOZK - 1101 North Summit, Springfield, Missouri 65801, (417) 865-2100. German unspecified.

New Mexico - Portales

KENW - South Avenue North and West 17th Street, Eastern N.M.U. Campus, Portales, New Mexico, (505) 562-3112. German unspecified.

New York - Garden City

WLIW - Channel 21 Drive, Plainview, New York 11803, (516) 454-8866. German programs, 1 hour weekly.

New York - New York

WNYE-TV - 112 Tillary Street, Brooklyn, New York 11201, (212) 596-4425. German unspecified.

Ohio - Lima-Bowling Green

WBGU-TV - Troup Avenue, Bowling Green, Ohio 43403, (419) 372-0121. German programs, 75 minutes weekly.

Oregon - Corvallis

KOAC-TV - Oregon State University Campus, Corvallis, Oregon 97331, (503) 754-4311. German programs.

Oregon - Medford

KSYS - Channel 8, Southern Oregon Educational Company, 34 Fir Street, Medford, Oregon 975011.

Oregon - Portland

KOAP-TV - 2828 Southwest Front Avenue, Portland, Oregon 97201, (503) 229-4892. German unspecified.

Utah - Provo

KBYU-TV - Harris Fine Arts Center, Brigham Young University, Provo, Utah 84602, (801) 378-3551. German unspecified.

Washington - Tacoma

KTPS - 1101 South Yakima Avenue, (206) 572-6262. German unspecified.

Bank Branches in the U.S.

BAYERISCHE VEREINSBANK
New York Branch:
430 Park Avenue
New York, New York 10022 (212) 758-4604

Atlanta Office:
2 Peachtree Street, Northwest
Suite 2125
Atlanta, Georgia 30383 (404) 522-2636

Cleveland Office:
Ohio Savings Plaza
Suite 1030
1801 East Nineth Street
Cleveland, Ohio 44114 (216) 566-8055

Chicago Branch:
One First National Plaza
Suite 3131
Chicago, Illinois 60603 (312) 782-9225

Los Angeles Branch:
707 Wilshire Boulevard
Suite 4660
Los Angeles, California 90017 (213) 629-1821

COMMERZBANK, A. G.
New York Branch:
55 Broad Street
New York, New York 10004 (212) 248-1400

Chicago Branch:
55 East Monroe Street
Chicago, Illinois 60603 (312) 977-0400

Atlanta Agency:
2 Peachtree Street
Atlanta, Georgia 30303 (404) 524-0665

DEUTSCHE BANK, A. G.

New York Branch:
9 West 57th Street
New York, New York 10019 (212) 940-8000

DEUTSCHE GENOSSENSCHAFTSBANK
630 Fifth Avenue
New York, New York (212) 246-6000

DRESDNER BANK, A.G.

New York Branch:
60 Broad Street
New York, New York 10004 (212) 425-4640

California Branch:
445 South Figueroa Street
Los Angeles, California 90017 (213) 489-5720

Chicago Branch:
141 West Jackson
Chicago, Illinois 60604 (312) 922-8964

Houston Branch:
2100 Milam
Houston, Texas 77002 (713) 759-0130

WESTDEUTSCHE LANDESBANK GIROZENTRALE
New York Branch:
450 Park Avenue
New York, New York 10022 (212) 754-9600

Commercial and Trade Organizations

FEDERATION OF GERMAN INDUSTRIES
666 Fifth Avenue
New York, New York 10019 (212) 582-7788
Director: Werner Walbrol

Organization representing 37 associations which in turn represent 95 percent of private industry in Germany.

GERMAN AGRICULTURAL MARKETING BOARD
950 Third Avenue
New York, New York 10022 (212) 753-5900
Managing Director: Werner J. Gneiting Founded 1969

Persons involved in Germany's food and beverage industry, agriculture and forestry. Promotes German foods, beverages and agricultural products in the U. S. and Canada through advertising, public relations programs and promotional campaigns with supermarket chains and individual retailers. Conducts research; compiles statistics.

GERMAN AMERICAN CHAMBER OF COMMERCE
666 Fifth Avenue
New York, New York 10019 (212) 582-7788
Executive Director: Werner Waldbrof Founded 1947

Publications: German Business Weekly; German American Trade News, monthly; American Subsidiaries of German Firms, annual; United States-German Economic Survey, annual.

German-American Chamber of Commerce of Chicago
77 East Monroe Street
Chicago, Illinois 60603 (312) 782-8557

German-American Chamber of Commerce of Los Angeles, Incorporated
Suite 2212
One Park Plaza Building
3250 Wilshire Boulevard
Los Angeles, California 90010 (213) 381-2236

German-American Chamber of Commerce of the Pacific Coast, Incorporated
Suite 910
465 California Street
San Francisco, California 94104 (415) 392-2262

German-American Chamber of Commerce
Suite 606
One Farragut Square South
Washington, D. C. 20006 (202) 347-0247

GERMAN CONVENTION BUREAU
1640 Hempstead Turnpike
East Meadow, New York 11554 (516) 794-1632
Director: Horst Schwarte Founded 1973

Airlines, national tourist offices, federal railroads, cities, convention centers, hotels, car rental companies, travel agencies, city visitor's and convention bureaus interested in the promotion of the Federal Republic of Germany and West Berlin as sites for conventions, meetings, seminars and incentive travel. Conducts study tours and workshops. Publishes Convention Planner's Guide.

Festivals, Fairs, and Celebrations

Alabama - Montgomery

GERMAN FOLK FESTIVAL
Jasmine Hill
Montgomery, Alabama

Authentic German foods and outdoor performance by German folk dancers and musicians. A part of the Smithsonian Institution's "Old Ways in a New World". Held in July.
Contact: Jim T. Inscoe, Jasmine Hill, Post Office Box 6001, Montgomery, Alabama 36106.

Alaska - Fairbanks

OKTOBERFEST
Gold Dome in Alaskaland
Fairbanks, Alaska

A traditional Old World celebration with a German band, dancing, beer drinking, and German foods. Held in late September.
Contact: Alaska Travel Division, Pouch E, Juneau, Alaska 99801.

Arkansas - Wiederkehr Village

MAYFEST
Highway 186
Wiederkehr Village, Arkansas

A wine festival with German band music, polkas and other dances, crafts and German food. Held at the beginning of May.
Contact: Lois Turner, Route 1, Box 9, Wiederkehr Village, Arkansas 72871, (501) 468-2611.

Arkansas - Wiederkehr Village

OCTOBERFEST
Highway 186
Wiederkehr Village, Arkansas

Contact: Lois Turner, Route 1, Box 9, Wiederkehr Village, Arkansas 72871, (501) 468-2611.

California - Auburn

OCTOBERFEST
Auburn, California

Traditional Octoberfest activities including beer drinking contests, German food and music. Held in early October.
Contact: California Chamber of Commerce, 455 Capitol Mall, Sacramento, California 95814.

California - Big Bear Lake

OKTOBERFEST
Gold Mine Ski Area
Big Bear Lake, California

Tyrolian dancers, bands, contests (including pretzel eating and beer drinking), German and Bavarian food, dancing and music. Held for three days in early October.
Contact: California Chamber of Commerce, 455 Capitol Mall, Sacramento, California 95814.

California - La Mesa

OKTOBERFEST
La Mesa, California

A community celebration featuring a Bavarian Beer Garden Band, German folk dances, contests and German food.
Contact: Gordon Austin, 8155 University Avenue, La Mesa, California 92041, (714) 465-7700.

California - Los Angeles

OKTOBERFEST
Busch Gardens
Los Angeles, California

Features German bands, dancers, entertainment, and foods of Bavaria. The park is decorated like Oktoberfest in Munich. Held for two weeks in late September and early October.
Contact: Southern California Visitors Council, 705 West Seventh Street, Los Angeles, California 90017.

California - Rancho Bernardo

OCTOBERFEST
The Mercado
Rancho Bernardo, California

Entertainment includes the music of German bands and dancing. Held in Mid-October.
Contact: Southern California Visitors Council, 705 West Seventh Street, Los Angeles, California 90017.

California - Santa Rosa

OKTOBERFEST
Sonoma County Fairgrounds
Santa Rosa, California

Traditional German entertainment, food, and beer. Held annually in October.
Contact: Santa Rosa Jaycees, Post Office Box 1025, Santa Rosa, California 95402.

California - Torrance

GERMAN DAY
Alpine Village
Torrance, California

Entertainment features a German brass band, Bavarian dance band, singing and dancing. Held in early September.
Contact: Southern California Visitors Council, 705 West Seventh Street, Los Angeles, California 90017.

GERMAN DAY
Alpine Village
Torrance, California

The celebrations feature German culinary specialties, drinks, German dancing and bands. Held each Sunday in May.
Contact: Southern California Visitors Council, 705 West Seventh Street, Los Angeles, California 90017; or Torrance Area Chamber of Commerce, 1510 Cravens Avenue, Torrance, California 90501.

OKTOBERFEST
Alpine Village
Torrance, California

Events include beer drinking, yodeling, wood chopping, pretzel eating, beer stein carrying contests, and entertainment by a twelve man brass band from Bavaria. Held for a month from late September to late October.
Contact: Southern California Visitors Council, 705 West Seventh Street, Los Angeles, California 90017.

TYROLEAN FESTIVAL
Alpine Village
Torrance, California

A German and Austrian ethnic festival with German food and entertainment and Austrian singing, dancing and music. Held from mid-July to late August for a month and a half.
Contact: Torrance Area Chamber of Commerce, 1510 Cravens Avenue, Torrance, California 90501.

WURST FESTIVAL
Alpine Village
Torrance, California

Sausage from the continent on sale. Entertainment includes brass band from Germany. Held in June.
Contact: Southern California Visitors Council, 705 West Seventh Street, Los Angeles, California 90017.

Colorado - Georgetown

FASCHING
Georgetown, Colorado

A German festival fun-filled with singing and dancing, special foods, and good fellowship. Held for nine days in mid-February.
Contact: Chamber of Commerce, Post Office Box 655, Georgetown, Colorado 80444.

Delaware - Newark

OCTOBERFEST
49 Salem Church Road
Newark, Delaware

Contact: Delaware Saengerbund, 49 Salem Church Road, Newark, Delaware 19711.

Florida - Cape Coral

MARDI GRAS CARNIVAL
Cape Coral, Florida

Sponsored by German-American Social Club and patterned after European festivals, people dress in costumes; Prince Carnival and his Princess rule over Carnivalia; Prince Carnival reads a proclamation committing his subjects to unrestricted gaity, dancing and revelry. Annually on two Saturdays in February.
Contact: Jack FitzMaurice, 5246 Tower Drive, Cape Coral, Florida 33904.

OKTOBERFEST
Cape Coral, Florida

This Harvest Festival, the Florida counterpart of the famed Munich Beer Festival, is presented the first and third Saturdays in October each year. Sponsored by the German-American Social Club, the event features traditional costumes of the Old and New Worlds. German foods, dancing, music, an abundance of beer ceremoniously rolled out, and the Bavarian spirit of Gemuetlichkeit (good fellowship) promote an infectious mood of merriment.
Contact: Jack Fitz Maurice, German-American Social Club, Post Office Box 902, Cape Coral, Florida 33904. (813) 542-2642.

Georgia - Helen

BAVARIAN OKTOBERFEST
Helen, Georgia

Yodeling contests, summer stock theater, and spirited German music enliven the Oktoberfest in this recreated Bavarian village. Starts the first weekend in September and is held each weekend through the first weekend in October. Music, dancing, food and drinks.
Contact: Oktoberfest, Helen Chamber of Commerce, Helen, Georgia 30545.

Illinois - Belleville

DEUTSCHFEST
Moose Park
Belleville, Illinois

Festival with German atmosphere, bands, food, dancing, rides, and recreational events. Held for 2 days in late June.
Contact: The Division of Tourism, Illinois Department of Business and Economic Development, 222 South College Street, Springfield, Illinois 62706.

Illinois - Elgin

OKTOBERFEST
Elgin, Illinois

In addition to German beer and food, the festival held for two days in early October features Lederhosen and leaping Bavarian slap-dancers.
Contact: Elgin Chamber of Commerce, Elgin, Illinois

Illinois - Galena

OKTOBERFEST
Turner Hall
US 20 and SR 84
Galena, Illinois

The Oktoberfest offers folk dancing, polka bands, German food and beer. It is held in mid-October celebrating Galena's German and lead mining heritage.
Contact: Galena Chamber of Commerce, 101 Bouthillier Street, Galena, Illinois 61036, (815) 777-0203.

Illinois - Urbana

OKTOBERFEST
Lincoln Square Mall
US 45
Urbana, Illinois

Since 1978, Galena has celebrated its German heritage for three days in mid-October. The festival offers cultural demonstrations, German food and drink, folk dances and free translation.
Contact: Oktoberfest, Lincoln Square Mall, Post Office Box 327, Urbana, Illinois 61801, (217) 367-4092.

Indiana - Batesville

OKTOBERFEST
Liberty Park
South Park Avenue
Batesville, Indiana

Sauerkraut and sausage, German singing, dancing, and beer draw visitors to Liberty Park to celebrate the area's Old World heritage. Held in late September.
Contact: Dennis M. Harmeyer, Rural Route 3, Batesville, Indiana 47006. (812) 934-3616.

Indiana - Goshen

MICHIANA MENNONITE RELIEF SALE
Elkhart County Fairgrounds
County Road 34
Goshen, Indiana

The festival has been held since 1968 to raise money for the world's needy and features quilt and antique auctions. Food such as applebutter, swiss crumpets, cheese, sausage and barbequed chicken are sold. Grandfather clocks are also sold. Held at the end of September.
Contact: Leon Farmwald, Nappanee, Indiana, 46550, (219) 773-4995.

Indiana - Jasper

STRASSENFEST
Jasper, Indiana

This German settlement celebrates its German ethnic heritage each year for 4 days at the end of August. German music and food are main attractions.
Contact: Jasper Chamber of Commerce, 710 Newton Street, Jasper, Indiana 47546, (812) 482-6866.

Indiana - Nappanee

PLETCHER VILLAGE ART FESTIVAL
Amish Acres
Nappanee, Indiana

Held at an Amish farmland, the festival features quilting, threshing demonstrations, puppet shows as well as arts and crafts: paintings, ceramics, sculpture, jewelry, leather work and weaving. Held for four days in early August.
Contact: Richard Pletcher, 1600 West Market Street, Nappanee, Indiana 46550.

Indiana - Newburgh

OKTOBERFEST
Newburgh, Indiana

Recreates a lively Bavarian atmosphere with German music and dancing, a beer hall, and traditional German foods. A gala parade with floats highlights the festival. Held in late September for three days.
Contact: Newburgh Council of Clubs, Newburgh, Indiana 47630.

Indiana - Saint Henry

HEINRICHSDORF FEST
Saint Henry, Indiana

A germanic festival with beer gardens serving country sausage and Saint Henry style barbeque ribs and chicken, while oom-pah-pah music plays. Held for two days in late May.
Contact: Dennis L. Durcholtz, Rural Route 1, Box 42-a, Ferdinand, Indiana 47532.

Indiana - Seymour

OKTOBERFEST
Seymour, Indiana

Over 75 booths line the downtown streets, offering folk objects and special foods to celebrate a hearty German heritage. Bands and beer gardens provide lively accompaniment to crafts, antiques, and carnival rides. Held in early October for three days.
Contact: Larry Krukewitt, 224 South Chestnut, Post Office Box 312, Seymour, Indiana 47274. (812) 522-3681.

Indiana - Terre Haute

OKTOBERFEST
Wabash Valley Fairgrounds
Terre Haute, Indiana

Visitors tap the Oktoberfest keg in the Biergarten, dance to the music of Bavarian bands, and sample a variety of German foods and customs at the Wabash Valley Fairgrounds. Other activities include amusement rides, a muzzle-loading rifle shoot, and helicopter rides. Held in late September for two days.
Contact: Lee Phifer, Terre Haute German Oberlandler Club, Incorporated, 1937 Clay Avenue, Terre Haute, Indiana 47805, (812) 466-1415.

Iowa - Amana Colonies

OKTOBERFEST
Amana Colonies, Iowa

Authentic German food, wines and beer, costumes and music abound as the German heritage of the seven Amana Colonies is celebrated. The wineries, Amana Refrigeration Plant, woolen mills, and cloak and furniture factories are open to visitors. Held annually in early October or late September.
Contact: Oktoberfest, South Amana, Iowa 52334 or Amana Colonies Travel Council, Amana, Iowa 52203.

Iowa - Durant

POLKA FEST
Durant, Iowa

A large number of bands, German food such as bratworst, German potato salad, sauerkraut, and beer. There is bingo and dancing in the streets. Began in 1973. Held the first weekend after Labor Day.
Contact: Mr. Ron Alpen, Chairman-Polka Fest, Durant, Iowa 52747.

Kansas - North Newton

BETHEL COLLEGE FALL FESTIVAL
Campus
27th and College Avenue
North Newton, Kansas

Mennonite cultural activities are at the center of the festival. German and Swiss food are featured. Held in early October.
Contact: Monica Gross, Bethel College, North Newton, Kansas 67117, (316) 283-2500.

Kentucky - Covington

MAIFEST
Covington, Kentucky

Held at the end of May.
Contact: Main Strasse Fest Association, North Kentucky Convention Bureau, 605 Philadelphia Street, Covington, Kentucky 41011, (606) 261-4677.

MAIN STRASSE FALL FESTIVAL
Covington, Kentucky

Held at the beginning of September.
Contact: Main Strasse Fest Association, North Kentucky Convention Bureau, 605 Philadelphia Street, Covington, Kentucky 41011, (606) 261-4677.

Kentucky - Grand Rivers

SEPTEMBERFEST
Grand River, Kentucky

Held for a week at the end of September.
Contact: Kentucky Western Waterland, Route 1, Grand Rivers, Kentucky 42045, (502) 362-4282.

Maine - Waterville

OKTOBERFEST
Waterville, Maine

An annual German-style dance provides a fun-filled evening of pretzels, beer, music, and colorful German costumes. German dinners are served. Sponsored by the Waterville Area Chamber of Commerce in late September or early October.
Contact: Waterville Area Chamber of Commerce, 82 Common Street, Waterville, Maine 04901.

Maryland - Baltimore

OKTOBERFEST
Fifth Regiment Armory
Baltimore, Maryland

Baltimore's German community heralds autumn with music and dancing, culinary, cultural, and folk art presentations. Held annually since 1968 in mid-October.
Contact: Kurt Kuenzel, 1215 Hillside Road, Pasadena, Maryland 21228, (301) 437-2068.

Maryland - Bowie

OKTOBERFEST
Bowie Race Course
Bowie, Maryland

Presents Bavarian cultural and folk life in the manner of the Munich original, with traditional music and dancing, special foods and beer. Held annually since 1968 in late October.
Contact: Terry Weber, Recreation and Arts Office, Bowie, Maryland 20715, (301) 262-1200.

Maryland - Grantsville

SPRINGS FOLK FESTIVAL
Grantsville, Maryland

"Pioneer Days", crafts, farm demonstrations and area tours of Amish and Mennonite settlements. Ladies quilt, dip candles, bake bread and make spotza. Men and women press aples into cider and make apple butter. Shingles and axe handles are shaved on a "schnitzelbank". Pennsylvania Dutch style meals are served. Held annually for two days in early October. Co-sponsored by the Penn Alps, Incorporated and Springs, Pennsylvania Historical Society. Begun around 1960.

Michigan - Big Rapids

OKTOBERFEST
Micosta County Fairgrounds
Highway 131
Big Rapids, Michigan

Begun in 1972, the Octoberfest celebrates the area's German heritage with specialty foods and beer, polka bands and contests. Other features include a special children's program with contests, an air show, fireworks display, parade, hot air baloons and arts and crafts. Held annually in early October.
Contact: Big Rapids Chamber of Commerce, 246 North State Street, Big Rapids, Michigan 49307, (616) 796-7649.

Michigan - Detroit

Octoberfest
German-American Cultural Center
5251 East Outer Drive
Detroit, Michigan 48234

A traditional German fall festival with German food, music, arts and crafts. Held annually in September for ten days.
Contact: German-American Cultural Center, 5251 East Outer Drive, Detroit, Michigan 48234.

Michigan - Frankenmuth

BAVARIAN FESTIVAL
Heritage Park Festival Grounds
Weiss Road
Frankenmuth, Michigan

Authentically costumed German bands provide music for singing and dancing. A big parade features colorful floats and marching bands. Craftspeople create their specialized art products. Bavarian foods tempt the appetite - bratwurst, knackwurst, and metwurst, German bread, beer, and homemade pretzels. Polka bands compete for prizes, and a drum and bugle competition takes place. Held annually since 1959 the second week in June.
Contact: Chamber of Commerce, 635 South Main Street, Frankenmuth, Michigan 48734.

Michigan - Kalamazoo

BACH FESTIVAL
Kalamazoo College
1200 Academy Street
Kalamazoo, Michigan

Presents major orchestral and choral works of the German composer Johann Sebastian Bach. In addition to major concerts, there is a chamber music program and young artists programs.
Contact: Dr. Russell Hammar, Musical Director, 1200 Academy Street, Kalamazoo, Michigan 49007, (616) 349-2948 or 342-8270.

OKTOBERFEST
Angell Field
Kalamazoo College
Kalamazoo, Michigan

Bratwurst, beer and German bands provide the background for the annual fall festival held in mid-October.
Contact: Kalamazoo Chamber of Commerce, Kalamazoo, Michigan 49007.

Michigan - Sturgis

GEMÜTLICHKEITS - ABEND
Sturgis Armory
Sturgis, Michigan

A German ethnic festival held in May.
Contact: Mrs. Doris W. Reichard, Box 165, Sturgis, Michigan 40901.

Minnesota - Mountain Lake

UTSCHTALLUNG
Heritage House
Mountain Lake, Minnesota

A Mennonite fair featuring ethnic foods and crafts held in September.
Contact: Henry Kliewer, Heritage House, Mountain Lake, Minnesota 56159.

Minnesota - New Ulm

HERITAGE FEST
Pageant Hermannstraum
Brown County Fairgrounds
New Ulm, Minnesota

The German heritage of New Ulm is celebrated with German bands from West Germany, ethnic foods and folk art. Held in mid-July.
Contact: Leo Berg, 1412 Heinen Hill, New Ulm, Minnesota 56073. (507) 354-5893.

Minnesota - Young America

STIFTUNGFEST CELEBRATION
Young America, Minnesota

This German festival, started in 1861, is the oldest continuous celebration in Minnesota. Originally a musical celebration, it still features a beer garden and polka dancing, as well as a carnival, barbeque, and softball games. Held in late August.
Contact: Chamber of Commerce, Young America, Minnesota 55397.

Missouri - Hermann

MAIFEST
Hermann, Missouri

Events include tours of historic homes; visit to a local winery; German costumes, food, music, beer, biergarten; arts and crafts; children's events; dancing; tours of museum; church suppers; and parade. The purpose of the festival is to preserve German arts and culture brought over by the early settlers, and to encourage the restoration and preservation of old buildings. Begun around 1951. Held for two days in mid-May.
Contact: Chamber of Commerce, 312 Schiller Street, Hermann, Missouri 65041.

Missouri - Saint Louis

BADENFEST
8200 North Broadway
Saint Louis, Missouri

Features German foods, music, and dancing. Displays showing the German heritage and culture are arranged. A children's area offers rides and games. Held in early September. Dining rooms for dinners of sauerbraten, bratwurst, etc., wine gardens, beer gardens and handmade souvenirs.
Contact: Saint Louis Regional Commerce and Growth Association, 10 Broadway, Saint Louis, Missouri 63102.

BEVO DAY
Bevo Mill Area
Saint Louis, Missouri

Four stages provide continuous entertainment with German bands and dancing. Authentic German foods are served. Cultural activities include an art show, crafts, and music. Games and rides provide fun for young and old. Held in mid-September.
Contact: Convention and Visitors Bureau of Greater Saint Louis, 500 Broadway Building, Saint Louis, Missouri 63102.

DUTCHTOWN OKTOBERFEST
Marquette Park
Saint Louis, Missouri

A festival emphasizing the German-Slavic heritage of the Dutchtown area features the exuberance of tamburitza, the German Brass Band, drinking, dining, and polka dancing at a giant tent near the center of Marquette Park. Arts, crafts, and games are found in all directions nearby. Held in late September.
Contact: Convention and Visitors Bureau of Greater Saint Louis, 500 Broadway Building, Saint Louis, Missouri 63102.

STRASSENFEST
12th Street, 15th Street, Market Street, Olive Street, Memorial Plaza
Saint Louis, Missouri

This authentic German street festival features German food, folk songs, costumes, and entertainment. Visitors may enjoy scores of fine German dishes, polka around the dance floor, and tour interesting exhibits on display. Held in mid-July.
Contact: Convention and Visitors Bureau of Greater Saint Louis, 500 Broadway Building, Saint Louis, Missouri 63102, (314) 421-1023.

Montana - Laurel

HERBSTFEST
Laurel, Montana

A harvest festival with a German theme. Participants frequently wear costumes identical to those traditional in the region of Germany from which their ancestors came. The activities include parades and pageants. Started in 1973. Held in the last week of September.
Contact: Chamber of Commerce, Box 395, Laurel, Montana 59044.

Nebraska - McCook

GERMAN HERITAGE DAYS
McCook, Nebraska

Celebrates the rich German heritage of McCook's early residents. Bouncy German polka banda play favorite tunes. An abundance of bratwurst, sauerkraut, and other special German dishes are served. A parade and demonstrations of German ethnic folk dances take place. There are ethnic arts and crafts and children's events. Held in early May.

Contact: Lester Harsh, 2205 Norris, McCook, Nebraska 69001.

New Hampshire - Manchester

OCTOBERFEST
Manchester, New Hampshire

German music, food, and minstrels highlight the events of this traditional fall gathering. Held in mid-October.
Contact: New Hampshire Division of Economic Development, Concord, New Hampshire 03301.

New Hampshire - Waterville

OKTOBERFEST LOWENBRAU BEER FEST
Waterville, New Hampshire

At fall foliage time, German food and beer, music and dancing highlight the October festival. Held annually the first Saturday in October.
Contact: Waterville Valley, Incorporated, Waterville, New Hampshire 03223, (603) 236-8311.

New Jersey - Holmdel

GERMAN-AMERICAN FESTIVAL
Garden State Arts Center
Telegraph Hill Park
Holmdel, New Jersey

A demonstration of the treasured traditions of Germans in America and their meaning to the American way of life. The various German-American societies show what they are doing. There are singers, turners, Bavarian and Burgenlaender folkdancers, children from the German language schools, German folk theater, soccer games, presentation of banners, mass chorus, bands, German food and souvenirs. Begun in 1974. Held in early September.
Contact: German-American Festival, New Jersey Highway Authority, Garden State Parkway, Woodbridge, New Jersey 07095.

New York - Canandaigua

OKTOBERFEST
Bristol Mountain Ski Lodge
Canandaigua, New York

A German buffet, dance and campout with an ox roast and a German band. Entertainment includes a bicycle race and chair lift rides. Held in mid-October.
Contact: Finger Lakes Association, Incorporated, 309 Lake Street, Penn Yan, New York 14527.

New York - Hunter

GERMAN ALPS FESTIVAL IN THE CATSKILLS
Hunter Mountain Ski Bowl
Hunter, New York 12442

A Bavarian-style festival with oom-pah-pah bands, folk dancing and crafts. Held for three weeks in July.
Contact: German Alps Festival, Main Street, Hunter, New York 12442, (518) 263-4141.

New York - Phelps

SAUERKRAUT FESTIVAL
Phelps, New York

Held annually in Early August to celebrate the community's German heritage.
Contact: Geraldine Ver Straete, Ontario Street, Phelps, New York 14532, (315) 548-4221.

New York - Purling

GERMAN ALPS FESTIVAL
Bavarian Manor
Purling, New York

An old-style German festival with oom-pah-pah band music, singing waiters, and wine cellar. Features German food, an outdoor beer garden, German folk dancers, much music and merriment. Held for nine days in mid-August.
Contact: Director, German Alps Festival, 329 East Fifth Street, New York, New York 10003, (212) 673-6290.

New York - Rochester

OKTOBERFEST
East Avenue to Genesee River area
Rochester, New York

German food and entertainment, farmers market, bicycle race, parade, art and crafts sale, and a flea market highlight the festival events. Held in late September.
Contact: Finger Lakes Association, Incorporated, 309 Lake Street, Penn Yan, New York 14527.

New York - Webster

GERMAN-AMERICAN DAY
Firemen's Field
Webster, New York

Celebrates the local German heritage with ethnic music and dancing, special foods and folk arts.
Contact: Howard Tausch, 5 Main Street, Webster, New York 14580, (716) 872-2181.

North Carolina - Winston-Salem

CHRISTMAS IN OLD SALEM
Winston-Salem, North Carolina

A re-creation of the old Moravian town as it was in 1800. Moravian bands play traditional carols and chorales. Men in early Moravian dress ride horses along the streets, and a night watchman announces the hours by blowing a conch shell and singing eighteenth century chants. In Salem Square children play eighteenth century games and watch demonstrations, such as roasting a pig over an open fire. In the restored buildings visitors may watch activities typical of 1800 - baking, coffee roasting, needlework, tinsmithing, joinery, gunsmithing, and pottery.
Music of the period is performed by a chorus, organist, vocal soloists, flutists, and string quartet. Held annually the second week in December.
Contact: Director of Information, Old Salem, Incorporated, Drawer F, Salem Station, Winston-Salem, North Carolina 27108.

North Dakota - Edgeley

POLKA DAY
Edgeley, North Dakota

Features German music, cooking, and polka dancing, along with annual variations like turtle races.
Occurs in late August.
Contact: North Dakota Highway Department, Highway Building, Capitol Grounds, Bismarck, North Dakota 58505.

North Dakota - New Leipzig

OKTOBERFEST
New Leipzig, North Dakota

Festival activities include polka music and dancing, and feasting on traditional German cuisine. Held in late September to early October.
Contact: North Dakota State Highway Department, Capitol Grounds, Bismarck, North Dakota 58505.

North Dakota - Wishek

SAUERKRAUT DAY
Wishek, North Dakota

German descendants of the region celebrate a fun-filled festival featuring ethnic music, folk dancing, and foods, especially sauerkraut. Held in mid-October.
Contact: North Dakota Highway Department, Highway Building, Capitol Grounds, Bismarck, North Dakota 58505.

Ohio - Berea

BEREA BACH FESTIVAL
Baldwin-Wallace College
Conservatory of Music

First held in 1932, this music festival pays tribute to the German composer Johann Sebastian Bach.
Contact: Dr. Warren A. Schaf, Baldwin-Wallace College, Berea, Ohio 44017, (216) 826-2361.

Ohio - Bremen

OKTOBERFEST
Bremen, Ohio

Celebrates the German heritage of the Bremen community with a parade, live entertainment, foot race, food and craft sales.
Contact: Dale Shaw, 532 Highland Boulevard, Bremen, Ohio 43107, (614) 569-4131.

Ohio - Bucyrus

BRATWURST FESTIVAL
Bucyrus, Ohio

A German celebration with parades featuring bands, floats, drill teams, and a festival queen. Hundreds of thousands of roasted bratwurst links are consumed. Continuous free entertainment, craft show, art and photo exhibits are offered, as well as rides, contests, and games. Held in mid-August.
Contact: Mike Halms, Bratwurst Fest, Incorporated, 1545 Hopley Avenue, Bucyrus, Ohio 44820.

Ohio - Cincinnati

SAINT BERNARD GERMAN LUAU
Vine Street near I-175
Cincinnati, Ohio

The German community celebrates with a "day at the races", a pig roast and parade.
Contact: Joseph A. Schmidlin, 521 Church Street, Cincinnati, Ohio 45217, (513) 641-3075.

Ohio - Columbus

HAUS UND GARTEN TOUR
German Village
Columbus, Ohio

A tour of restored houses and gardens, shops, restaurants, and churches in German Village. Special German foods are served at restaurants and refreshment stands. Colorfully costumed Whetstone Dancers perform, the Harmonaires provide Music in the Air, and a German band, the Lederhosen Five, roves through the village. Activities include special art and publications exhibits and a painting contest. Held each year since 1960 on the last Sunday in June.
Contact: The German Village Society, 624 South Third Street, Columbus, Ohio 43216, (614) 221-8888.

OKTOBERFEST
German Village
Ohio State Fairgrounds
Columbus, Ohio

Celebrated with a parade, German foods and beer, arts and crafts show, and special entertainment at the Ohio State Fairgrounds. Held in for four days and early October.
Contact: Columbus Area Chamber of Commerce, 50 West Broad Street, Post Office Box 1527, Columbus, Ohio 43216.

Ohio - Eaton

HUMMEL FESTIVAL
Preble County Fairgrounds
Eaton, Ohio

Brings together collectors of Hummel figurines for seminars, auction, Hummel look-alike contest, German music and dancing.
Contact: Bob Miller, Hummel Festival, Post Office Box 210, Eaton, Ohio 45320, (513) 456-4151.

Ohio - Maumee

GERMAN-AMERICAN FESTIVAL
Lucas County Recreation Center
Maumee, Ohio

Patterned after the Oktoberfest held in Germany every fall. Features German sausage, potato salad, and beer, Bavarian costumes, polka music and dancing. The Lake Area District Cultural Exhibit displays imported crafts and handiwork made by the German people. Held in late August.
Sponsor: GAF Society. Chairman: Lee Weber, 2614 Chestnut Street, Toledo, Ohio 43608, (419) 244-9710.

Ohio - Middlefield

SWISS CHEESE FESTIVAL
Middlefield, Ohio

The event offers guided tours of Amish farm areas and the cheese plant. Good food is offered, including Amish homemade bread, trail bologna, cheese, barbequed chicken, and a cake display and demonstration. There is a flea market, flower show, rides, entertainment, a parade, and square and street dancing. Begun around 1959.

Ohio - Waynesville

OHIO SAUERKRAUT FESTIVAL
Waynesville, Ohio

A German folk-festival with German delicacies, including of course, sauerkraut. There is continuous entertainment, folk music and dancing. Craftsmen display and demonstrate, and the village is full of antique shops to browse in. There is a large antique car display. Held in mid-October.
Contact: Chamber of Commerce, 581 North Street, Post Office Box 588, Waynesville, Ohio 45068.

Oregon - Mount Angel

OKTOBERFEST
Mount Angel, Oregon

A harvest festival similar to the famed Munich festival, featuring harvest displays, a parade, street dancing, art shows, German food and beer garden. Held annually in mid or late September.
Contact: Oktoberfest Association, Mount Angel, Oregon 97362, (503) 845-2970.

Oregon - Verboort

KRAUT AND SAUSAGE FEED
Verboort, Oregon

Contact: Chamber of Commerce, Box 394, Hillsboro, Oregon 97123.

Pennsylvania - Adamstown

GEMÜTLICHKEIT BIERFEST
Black Angus Mall
Adamstown, Pennsylvania

German and Pennsylvania Dutch cultural activities are the focus of this festival held annually in August. Contact: Edward Stoudt, Route 272, Adamstown, Pennsylvania 19501, (215) 484-4655.

Pennsylvania - Ambridge

KUNSTFEST
Old Economy Village
Ambridge, Pennsylvania

Held at a beautifully restored village founded by the Harmonists, a celibate society of Germans devoted to work and prayer. Features demonstrations of early nineteenth century cabinet making, candle making, cooking, doughnut baking, shoemaking, spinning, weaving, sewing, lace making, and other crafts. Held in early June.
Contact: Harmonic Associates, Incorporated, Court House, Beaver Falls, Pennsylvania 15009, (412) 775-8600.

Pennsylvania - Barnesville

BAVARIAN SUMMER FESTIVAL
Lakewood Park
Barnesville, Pennsylvania

Non-stop music and dancing take place in the big German Beer Hall to many different German oom-pah bands. Entertainment is offered by the Schuhplattlers (German ethnic folk dancers) and by Alpine Horn Players and bellringers. Amusement rides, arts and crafts demonstrations, horse pulling, soccer games, and an animal nursery-land are other attractions. German foods and beer in abundance. Held in late June and early July.
Contact: Kermit A. Deitrich, Rural Delivery 2, Kempton, Pennsylvania 19529, (215) 756-3000.

Pennsylvania - East Greenville

GOSCHENHOPPEN FOLK FESTIVAL
East Greenville, Pennsylvania

Crafts, foods, and presentations depicting the life-style of the Pennsylvania Dutch. Held for three days in mid-August.
Contact: Montgomery County Convention and Visitors Bureau, One Montgomery Plaza, Suite 207, Norristown, Pennsylvania 19401.

Pennsylvania - Hershey

PENNSYLVANIA DUTCH DAYS
Hershey Park Avenue
Hershey, Pennsylvania

Working crafts and displays in the Hershey Park arena, feature pottery making, coopering, flax breaking, spinning and weaving, wood carving, glass blowing, fraktur art, leather craft, broom making, candle dipping and other early handicrafts. One highlight is a gigantic display of handmade quilts sewn at quilting parties of area Churches of the Brethren. In the Formerama area are found an old-time threshing rig in action, the village blacksmith, farming implements, and the famous "Schnitzelbank" or cutting bench. Special Pennsylvania Dutch motion pictures and seminars are presented, and ethnic foods are served. Held the last part of July.
Contact: Roger Connor, Hershey Estates, Hershey, Pennsylvania 17033, (717) 534-3172.

Pennsylvania - Kempton

PENNSYLVANIA DUTCH FARM FESTIVAL
Farm Museum
Kempton, Pennsylvania

Demonstrates authentic home and farm crafts still practiced by the Amish and Mennonites of Pennsylvania, such as the making of tar. Exhibits old farm tools, steam-powered tractors, and other contraptions. Children can romp in the hay and ride on the hay wagon. Home-cooked Pennsylvania Dutch foods are available, such as scrapple, chow-chow, and funnel cakes. Held early in September.
Contact: Don Conover, 329 East Fifth Street, New York, New York 10003, (212) 673-6290.

Pennsylvania - Kutztown

KUTZTOWN FOLK FESTIVAL
Fairgrounds
Kutztown, Pennsylvania

An exhibition of Pennsylvania Dutch arts, crafts, folkways, fun, and food. Features Amish pageantry: a barn raising, a quaint "Plain Dutch" wedding, and a hanging. German foods like ponhaws and brodwarsht (sausages), schnitz un knepp, chicken and dumplings, chow-chow, and shoo-fly pie are served. Crafts are demonstrated, such as hex art, tinsmithing, pewter making, basket weaving, spinning, wood carving, glass blowing, fraktur and block printing. Held annually late June or early July since 1949.
Contact: Peg Zecher, 717 Swarthmore Avenue, Swarthmore, Pennsylvania 17081, (215) 543-7124.

Pennsylvania - Lancaster

DUTCH FAMILY FESTIVAL
Lancaster, Pennsylvania

Mennonite and Amish craftsmen exhibit and demonstrate their skills. The Pennsylvania Dutch inhabitants offer a Plain People Pageant. Held on Route 30, six miles east of Lancaster from late June through late August.
Contact: Chamber of Commerce, Lancaster, Pennsylvania 17604.

Pennsylvania - Lenhart

PENNSYLVANIA DUTCH FOLK FAIR
Lenhartsville, Pennsylvania

Celebrated with a weekend of folk songs, bands, colorful costumes, arts and crafts demonstrations, and special Pennsylvania Dutch foods. Held the third weekend in July.
Contact: Chamber of Commerce, Hamburg, Pennsylvania 19526.

Pennsylvania - Macungie

DAS AWKSCHT FESCHT
Macungie Memorial Park
Macungie, Pennsylvania

A rural festival in Pennsylvania Dutch country featuring arts, crafts, customs, and foods dating back ten centuries. Includes antique and classic car shows, a sports car show, antique car flea market, and horse shows. Entertainment is provided in the park's outdoor theatre with comedy and music. Held annually for more than a decade in early August.
Contact: Allentown-Lehigh County Chamber of Commerce, Fifth and Walnut Streets, Allentown, Pennsylvania 18105.

Pennsylvania - Richfield

DUTCH DAYS FESTIVAL
Richfield, Pennsylvania

Country store, crafts, Penn-Dutch cooking, chicken barbeque, nightly entertainment, games, and parades. Held annually for four days in mid-July.
Contact: Russell Kratzer, Richfield, Pennsylvania 17086.

Rhode Island - Jamestown

OKTOBERFEST
Fort Getty
Jamestown, Rhode Island

German bands and dancing are included in the festive events. Held in mid-October.
Contact: Rhode Island Department of Economic Development, Tourist Promotion Division, One Weybosset Hill, Providence, Rhode Island 02903.

South Carolina - Charleston

GERMAN EMPHASIS FESTIVAL (GERMAN HERITAGE FESTIVAL)
Charleston, South Carolina

Part of the Founders' Festivals, a continuing series of month-long festivals centering on the ethnic groups which were instrumental in the founding and growth of Charleston. Special exhibits in the Gibbes Art Gallery and Charleston Museum, special ethnic food in local restaurants and two or three major events. Held for one month in October.
Contact: Mr. James B. Bagwell, Jr., 313 Pitt Street, Mount Pleasant, South Carolina 29464.

OKTOBERFEST
Geodesic Dome
Charleston Landing
1500 Old Town Road
Charleston, South Carolina

A festival to welcome the harvest festival featuring Bavarian music and German food.
Contact: Oktoberfest, 1500 Old Town Road, Charleston, South Carolina 29407, (803) 556-4450.

South Carolina - Spartanburg

OKTOBERFEST
Spartanburg, South Carolina

Contact: Chamber of Commerce, Spartanburg, South Carolina.

South Dakota - Freeman

SCHMECKFEST
Freeman, South Dakota

A three-day festival of tasting featuring the culinary arts of the Mennonite, Low German and Hutterite settlements. It is also a display of pioneer life with

demonstrations of sausage making, noodle making, basket weaving, rug braiding, quilting, and a host of other tasks and hobbies. There is always a student theater production. Held annually in early April or late March.
Contact: Chamber of Commerce, Freeman, South Dakota 57029.

Texas - Boerne

BERGES FEST
Boerne, Texas

A two-day "Feast of the Hills" with parade, games, queen coronation, German oom-pah music, food and beverage stands, German costumes, jumping frog contests, and turtle races. The town of Boerne, north of San Antonio, was settled by Germans in the 1800's. Celebrated in mid-June.
Contact: Chamber of Commerce, Post Office Box 429, Boerne, Texas 78006.

Texas - Brenham

MAIFEST
Brenham, Texas

A traditional German Volksfest dating from 1874. The entire town joins in two days of festival dances, feasts, and parades. Held annually in May.
Contact: Chamber of Commerce, Post Office Box 810, Brenham, Texas 77833.

Texas - Fredericksburg

CHRISTKINDL MARKT
Fredericksburg, Texas

A pre-Christmas celebration featuring traditional food of the season, music, dancing and handcrafts. Held annually in December.
Contact: Chamber of Commerce, Fredericksburg, Texas 78624.

Texas - New Braunfels

WURSTFEST
Landa Park, Landa Park Drive
New Braunfels, Texas

Rich in German heritage accented with plents of polka music and gemuetlichkeit (good fellowship). Features singing societies, traditional German bands, dancing groups, and sausages of every description. Sausage king and queen are crowned; a "sausage" dog show with dachshunds; a sausage golf tourney; and oom-pah music, all in honor of the sausage, for which the town is known. Held in early November for ten days.
Contact: Chamber of Commerce, 390 South Sequin, Post Office Box 180, New Braunfels, Texas 78130.

Texas - Schulenberg

ANNUAL FESTIVAL
Schulenburg, Texas

Local residents honor their German heritage with a festive parade, barbecue, horse show, art show, and beer garden. Held in August.
Contact: Bill Klesel, Schulenberg, Texas 78956.

Utah - Snowbird

OKTOBERFEST
Snowbird Plaza
Snowbird, Utah

The event features German specialties and entertainment. Begun in 1974. Held on Labor Day weekend.

Vermont - Stowe

OKTOBERFEST
Stowe, Vermont

A recapturing of the German Octoberfest with German music and foods.
Contact: Oktoberfest, Stowe, Vermont, (802) 253-7321.

Washington - Leavenworth

CHRISTMAS LIGHTING CEREMONY
Leavenworth, Washington

Christmas lights are turned on to illuminate and decorate buildings in this Bavarian style village. The weekend festivities include performances by the Edelweiss Dancers, several choirs and choruses, snowmobile rides, and dog sled demonstrations. Held annually since 1969 the first weekend in December.
Contact: Chamber of Commerce, Leavenworth, Washington 98826, (509) 548-8562.

MAIFEST
Downtown Leavenworth
Leavenworth, Washington

German ethnic culture as expressed in music, dance, folk art and food in the center of this annual Spring festival.
Contact: Lee West, Post Office Box 313, Leavenworth, Washington 98826, (509) 548-7914.

Washington - Odessa

DEUTSCHES FEST
Odessa, Washington

Features a German band, dancing, entertainment, and native costumes. German church services, a parade, football game, and German movies are part of the festivities. Booths are set up with German food and beer. Held annually since 1971 on the third weekend in September.
Secretary: Odessa Chamber of Commerce, 9 East First Avenue, Odessa, Washington 99159, (509) 982-2672.

Wisconsin - Milwaukee

BAVARIAN FOLK FESTIVAL
Old Heidelberg Park
700 West Lexington, Glendale
Milwaukee, Wisconsin

Old Bavarian GemUtlichkeit has been celebrated annually every July since 1931 with Bavarian folk dancing, German brass bands, singing, yodeling, a children's parade, beer drinking contest, authentic German food and Bavarian comedy.
Contact: George Enders, 2773 North 55th Street, Milwaukee, Wisconsin 53210, (414) 873-2885.

OKTOBERFEST
Old Heidelberg Park
700 West Lexington, Glendale
Milwaukee, Wisconsin

A long-standing annual festival held in the Glendale section of Milwaukee to keep alive the German traditions of the area. Special Bavarian food includes Spanferkel (suckling pig roasted over open coals) and pastries. There are Bavarian folk dancers, German brass bands, singing, dancing, yodeling and a green contest called Munchener Kindl.
Contact: George Enders, 2773 North 55th Street, Milwaukee, Wisconsin 53210, (404) 873-2885.

Wisconsin - LaCrosse

OKTOBERFEST
LaCrosse, Wisconsin

An Old World ethnic night features German bands and a costume contest. A Festmaster's Ball, where a festmaster is chosen, opens the festivities. A Miss Oktoberfest and Mrs. Oktoberfest are selected at other contests. Other highlights include a Maple Leaf Parade and Torchlight Parade. Held in early October.
Contact: Greater LaCrosse Chamber of Commerce, 710 Main Street, Post Office Box 842, LaCrosse, Wisconsin 54601; or Managing Director, 224 South Seventh Street, Box 1063, LaCrosse, Wisconsin 54601.

Wyoming - Worland

OKTOBERFEST
Worland, Wyoming

Wurst, Wienerschnitzel, oom-pah bands, and "Deutsche Bierstube" bring back the old German heritage at an authentic Oktoberfest in the tradition of the Munich celebration. The Bürgermeister leads a parade with a color guard, horse patrols, marching bands, Festhall participants decked out in Bavarian costumes, and elaborate wagons designed in European fashion and drawn by massive draft horses. Held annually in late September.
Contact: Wyoming Travel Commission, 2320 Capitol Avenue, Cheyenne, Wyoming 82002, (307) 777-7777, or Walt Jorgenson, 824 South 14th, Worland, Wyoming 82401.

Airline Offices

LUFTHANSA GERMAN AIRLINES
(Deutsche Lufthansa Aktiengesellschaft)
North American Headquarters:
1640 Hempstead Turnpike
East Meadow, New York 11554 (516) 489-2020

Seattle Office:
Skinner Building
Seattle, Washington 98011 (206) 624-6244

Provides direct North American flights to New York, Chicago, Los Angeles, Philadelphia, Montreal, and Mexico City. Follows routes to 69 countries in all five continents, as well as intensive European and domestic West German routes. Other offices in the United States: Albany, Anchorage, Atlanta,

Beverly Hills, Boston, Buffalo, Charlotte, Chicago, Cincinnati, Cleveland, Dallas, Denver, Detroit, Hartford, Houston, Indianapolis, Kansas City, Los Angeles, Miami, Milwaukee, Minneapolis, New Orleans, New York, Philadelphia, Pittsburgh, Saint Louis, San Diego, San Francisco, Seattle, and Washington.

Ship Lines

HAPAG-LLOYD A. G.
North German Lloyd Passenger Agency, Incorporated
277 Park Avenue
New York, New York 10017 (212) 371-4700

Sails from Miami to Caribbean and South American ports as part of a cruise originating in Lisbon. Freighters carry a few passengers from United States Gulf and South Atlantic ports to Europe.

SCHLUSSEL REEDEREI
Sea and Land Shipping, Incorporated
305 North Morgan Street
Tampa, Florida 33602 (813) 229-7284

Accommodates up to 12 passengers on freighters sailing from Tampa, Florida, to Holland.

Bookdealers and Publishers' Representatives

ADLER'S FOREIGN BOOKS
169 Fifth Avenue
New York, New York 10010 (212) 691-5151

FRANZ BADER, INCORPORATED
2001 Eye Street, Northwest
Washington, D. C. 20006 (202) 337-5440

THE BOOK COLLECTION OF DR. E. R. MEYER
Post Office Box 815
Rochester, New York 14603 (716) 271-1024

THE BOOK SHOP
2272 West Holcomb
Houston, Texas 77030 (713) 668-0075

BRODT MUSIC COMPANY
Post Office Box 9345
Charlotte, North Carolina 28299 (704) 332-2177

DER BUCHWURM
Box 3831
Thousand Oaks, California 91359 (805) 492-2393

CONTINENTAL BOOK COMPANY
11-03 46th Avenue
Long Island City, New York 11101 (212) 937-4868

DAR AL KUTUB WAL NASHRAT AL ISLAMIYYA
Post Office Box 207
New Brunswick, New Jersey 08901 (201) 249-6961

HAROLD B. DIAMOND BOOKSELLER
Box 1193
Burbank, California 91507 (213) 846-0342

EUROPA BOOKSTORE
3229 North Clark
Chicago, Illinois 60657 (312) 922-1836

EUROPE UNIE BOOKS
60 Reynolds Street
Staten Island, New York 10305 (212) 273-0475

EUROPEAN BOOK COMPANY
925 Larkin Street
San Francisco, California 94109 (415) 474-0626

EUROPEAN PUBLISHERS REPRESENTATIVES
11-03 46th Avenue
Long Island City, New York 11101 (212) 937-4606

FAM BOOK SERVICE
69 Fifth Avenue
New York, New York 10003

PETER THOMAS FISHER
41 Union Square, West
New York, New York 10003 (212) 255-6789

FRENCH BOOK GUILD
11-03 46th Avenue
Long Island, New York 11101 (212) 838-8538

LEONARD FOX, LIMITED
667 Madison Avenue
New York, New York 10021 (212) 888-5480

GERARD J. FUCHS, IMPORTED BOOKS
1841 Broadway
New York, New York 10023 (212) 757-6075

GARNER & SMITH BOOK STORE
2116 Guadalupe
Austin, Texas 78705 (512) 477-9725

GENERAL THEOLOGICAL SEMINARY BOOKSTORE
175 Nineth Avenue
New York, New York 10011 (212) 255-1324

GERMAN AND INTERNATIONAL BOOKSTORE
1767 North Vermont Avenue
Los Angeles, California 90027 (213) 660-0313

GERMAN BOOK STORE
1767 North Vermont
Los Angeles, California 90027 (213) 660-0313

GERMAN NEWS COMPANY INCORPORATED
220 East 86th Street
New York, New York 10028 (212) 288-5500

GLOBE INTERNATIONAL
DIVISION OF REVERE SUPPLY COMPANY
607 West 29th Street
New York, New York 10001 (212) 565-2660

GOLDEN GRIFFIN BOOKSHOP
32 East 58th Street
New York, New York 10022 (212) EL5-3353

GREAT EXPECTATIONS
909 Foster
Evanston, Illinois 60201 (312) 864-3881

HAMMER MOUNTAIN BOOK HALLS
771 State Street
Schenectady, New York 12307 (518) 393-5266

HATHAWAY HOUSE BOOKSHOP
103 Central Street
Wellesley, Massachusetts 02181 (617) 235-2830

LEW HAYMANN
Box 6448
Carmel, California 93921 (408) 624-3303

IACONI BOOK IMPORTS
300 Pennsylvania Avenue
San Francisco, California 94107 (415) 285-7393

IMPORTED BOOKS
Post Office Box 4414
Dallas, Texas 75208 (214) 941-6497

IMPORTED PUBLICATIONS, INCORPORATED
320 West Ohio Street
Chicago, Illinois 60610 (312) 787-9017

INSTITUTE OF MODERN LANGUAGES BOOK STORE
2125 S Street, Northwest
Washington, D. C. 20009 (202) 565-2580

JUILLIARD SCHOOL BOOKSTORE
Lincoln Center
New York, New York 10028 (212) 799-5000

KEREKES BROTHERS INCORPORATED
177 East 87th Street
New York, New York 10028 (212) 289-2020

LA GALERIA DE LOS ARTESANOS, ON THE PLAZA
Box 1657
Las Vegas, New Mexico 87701 (505) 425-8331

R. E. LEWIS, INCORPORATED
Post Office Box 1108
San Rafael, California 94902 (415) 461-4161

LE MARAIS: FOREIGN LANGUAGE BOOKS
1700 Shattuck Avenue
Berkeley, California 94709 (415) 849-3683

KURT B. MERLANDER
626 North Valley Street
Burbank, California 91505 (213) 849-2863

MIDDLEBURY COLLEGE STORE
5 Hillcrest Road
Middlebury, Vermont 05753 (802) 388-7722

MIDWEST EUROPEAN PUBLICATIONS, INCORPORATED
915 Foster Street
Evanston, Illinois 60201 (312) 866-6262

MILES
48 Winter Street
Boston, Massachusetts 02108 (617) 482-0751

MODERN LANGUAGE BOOK & RECORD STORE
3160 O Street, Northwest
Washington, D. C. 20007 (202) 338-8963

OWL & THE PUSSYCAT
321 South Ashland Avenue
Lexington, Kentucky 40502 (606) 266-7121

PENDRAGON HOUSE, INCORPORATED
2595 East Bayshore Road
Palo Alto, California 94303 (415) 327-5631

PENDRAGON HOUSE OF CONNECTICUT, INCORPORATED
Post Office Box 225
Old Mystic, Connecticut 06372 (203) 536-1163

RIZZOLI INTERNATIONAL BOOKSTORE
712 Fifth Avenue
New York, New York 10019 (212) 397-3700

MARY S. ROSENBERG, INCORPORATED
17 West 60th Street
New York, New York 10023 (212) 362-4873

S & D BOOK STORE
16 South 11th Street
Indiana, Pennsylvania 15701 (412) 465-2795

SANTA MONICA BOOK CENTER
2026 Pico Boulevard
Santa Monica, California 90405

WOLFGANG SCHIEFER FINE OLD BOOKS
Box 474
New Haven, Connecticut 06502 (203) 787-9902

SCHOENHOF'S FOREIGN BOOKS, INCORPORATED
1280 Massachusetts Avenue
Cambridge, Massachusetts 02138 (617) 547-8855

F.A.O. SCHWARZ
745 Fifth Avenue
New York, New York 10022 (212) 371-6500

SHERMAN'S
332 Park Avenue
Baltimore, Maryland 21201 (301) 837-3363

SKY BOOKS INTERNATIONAL INCORPORATED
48 East 50th Street
New York, New York 10022 (212) 688-5086

SPAUDA BOOKSTORE
10 John Street
Waterbury, Connecticut 06708 (203) 756-5173

SPECIALIZED BOOK SERVICE INCORPORATED
100 North Street
Burlington, Vermont 05401 (802) 863-2807

STAVER BOOKSELLERS
1301 East 57th Street
Chicago, Illinois 60637 (312) 667-3227

TEE-BOOKS LIMITED (Librairie De Documentation Technique SA)
41 William
Pittsburgh, Pennsylvania 12901 (518) 561-0005

PETER TUMARKIN FINE BOOKS INCORPORATED
1370 Lexington Avenue
New York, New York 10028 (212) 348-8187

UNIVERSAL BOOKSTORE
5458 Fifth Street
Philadelphia, Pennsylvania 19120 (215) 549-2897

UNIVERSITY BOOKSTORE
850 West Cross Street
Ypsilanti, Michigan 48197 (313) 487-1000

UNIVERSAL DISTRIBUTORS COMPANY
54 West 13th Street
New York, New York 10011 (212) 243-4317

YALE COOPERATIVE SERVICE
77 Broadway
New Haven, Connecticut 06520 (203) 772-0670

PENNSYLVANIA - DUTCH

JEAN'S BOOK SERVICE
Box 264
Hatfield, Pennsylvania 19440 (215) 362-0732

TAN BARK BOOKS
Box 217
Williamsville, New York 14221

Books and Pamphlets

AFTER HITLER GERMANY, 1945-1963. Compiled by Helen Kehr. London, Vallentine, Mitchell, 1963.

Listing of books, mainly German, of literature on Germany in the immediate postwar period.

A BIBLIOGRAPHY OF GERMAN STUDIES, 1945-1971; Germany under Allied Occupation, Federal Republic of Germany, German Democratic Republic. By Gisela Hersch. Bloomington, Indiana University Press, 1972.

Selected interdisciplinary bibliography which covers the occupation period and both West and East Germany after they became separate states.

THE CONSTITUTION OF THE GERMAN DEMOCRATIC REPUBLIC. Dresden, Staatsverlag der Deutschen Demokratischen Republik, 1974.

DOCUMENTATION. Berlin, East Germany, Panorama DDR, Auslandspresseagentur GmbH.

A series of reports issued irregularly, each issue devoted to a single theme such as housing in the GGR, social security, economic strategy, vocational training, the United Nations, democracy and socialism, women in the GGR.

EAST GERMANY, A SELECTED BIBLIOGRAPHY. By Arnold Hereward Priee. Washington, D.C.: Library of Congress, 1967.

Introductory bibliographical information on this country. Emphasis is placed on works published since 1958 and most titles are in German.

EAST GERMANY: A SELECTED BIBLIOGRAPHY. Compiled by Fritz T. Epstein. Washington, D. C. 1959.

Highly selective guide to general background sources on East Germany published between 1947 and 1958. Contains both English and German materials.

FACTS ABOUT GERMANY: THE FEDERAL REPUBLIC OF GERMANY. Edited by Karl Romer. Gütersloh, Lexikon-Institut Bertelsmann, 1979.

A book distributed by the Press and Information Office of the Federal Republic of Germany giving a brief history of Germany up to 1945 and then describing the Federal Republic, its constitution, the legal system, political purties, planning, public finance and service, foreign policy; its economic organization, society, welfare and leisure; and the educational, scientific and cultural areas. Updated periodically.

FEDERAL REPUBLIC OF GERMANY: A DIRECTORY FOR TEACHERS AND STUDENTS. By the German Information Center. New York, 1980.

Presents information about educational associations in the United States and Germany concerned with German studies. Also discusses scholarships, exchange programs for students and teachers, living conditions and travel in Germany.

THE FEDERAL REPUBLIC OF GERMANY; A Selected Bibliography of English-Language Publications with an Emphasis on the Social Sciences. Compiled by Arnold Herewold Price, Second Edition, Washington, D. C., U.S. Library of Congress, Washington, 1978.

Bibliography of materials on the Federal Republic of Germany covering areas of politics and government, foreign affairs, economy, culture. Includes a chapter on Berlin.

THE FEDERAL REPUBLIC OF GERMANY AT A GLANCE. Bonn, Press and Information Office of the Federal Republic of Germany, 1981.

An information brochure giving brief descriptions of the various regions of West Germany, and short summaries of its constitution and government, employment, social security, education and training, foreign policy, economy and foreign trade, transportation and tourism, the media, cultural life and West Germany's role in Europe. Includes a map.

FIRST HAND INFORMATION. Berlin, East Germany, Auslandspresseagentur Panorama DDR.

A series of booklets on various subjects concerning the German Democratic Republic. Titles include Learning for Living, Women and Socialism, Science and Society, Law and Justice in the GDR, the Role of the Trade Unions, to name but a few. These appear in German, English, French, Spanish, Italian, Arabic, Swedish and Finnish.

FIVE IMAGES OF GERMANY: HALF A CENTURY OF AMERICAN VIEWS ON GERMAN HISTORY. By Henry Cord Mayer, 2nd edition, Washington, D. C. Service Center for Teachers of History, 1960.

Bibliographic essay on Germany history.

GDR. Facts and Figures. Berlin, East Germany, Panorama DDR, Auslandspresseagentur GmbH, 1981.

A descriptive booklet about the German Democratic Republic, describing its socialistic form of government, its foreign policy goals, the economy and the unfolding of the socialist personality through right to work polities, equal educational opportunities, art and culture, health care, recreation and sport.

GDR. Government by the People. Democracy under Socialism. Berlin, East Germany, Panorama DDR, Auslandspresseagentur GmbH, 1981.

A booklet explaining participation in the political and economic programs in the German Democratic Republic.

THE GERMAN DEMOCRATIC REPUBLIC. Berlin, East Germany, Panorama DDR, Auslandspresseagentur GmbH, 1981.

A book illustrated with colored photographs and tables and graphs concerning the history of the German Democratic Republic from its founding in 1949, its social and administrative system, foreign policy, national economy, industry, agriculture, foreign trade, education, the cultural scene, health and social services, recreation and leisure, sport and geographical divisions.

GERMAN FOREIGN POLICY, 1890-1914 AND COLONIAL POLICY TO 1914; A HANDBOOK AND ANNOTATED BIBLIOGRAPHY. By Andrew R. Carlson, Metuchen, New Jersey, Scarecrow Press, 1970.

First four sections deal with the type of government in Germany and the formulation of its foreign and cultural policy, other sections include a listing of persons who helped shape the foreign and colonial policy, events affecting Germany and an annotated bibliography.

GERMAN HISTORY AND CIVILIZATION, 1806-1914; A BIBLIOGRAPHY OF SCHOLARLY PERIODICAL LITERATURE. By John C. Fout, Metuchen, New Jersey, Scarecrow Press, 1974.

Lengthy list of articles from scholarly journals in English, German and French.

HAPPY DAYS IN GERMANY. Frankfurt, Germany, German National Tourist Board, 1980.

A booklet about the cities and landscape of West Germany, its heritage of art works, tourist and travel information, food specialties, health resorts, hobby centers, festivals, cultural events, winter sports, and other attractions. Beautifully illustrated with color photographs. Contains a large centerfold map of West Germany and the Berlin area.

IN BRIEF BERLIN. Edited by Wolfgang Kruse. Berlin, Press and Information Office of Land Berlin, 1979.

A booklet giving the history of Berlin from its founding to its present unique situation as a divided city. Tells about the political and social organization, the economic, artistic, educational, religious and tourist features of West Berlin.

A MANDATE FOR DEMOCRACY. By Hans Kepper and Hans Walter Kettenbach. Bonn, Federal Press and Information Office, 1980.

Part One deals with the historical antecedents of the Federal Republic such as the beginning of the constitutional movement in the 19th century, the First World War and the Weimar Republic, the economic crisis and rise of Hitler and the birth of the Federal Republic out of the ruins of the Second World War. Part Two describes institutions and policies of the Federal Republic as it exists today. Abundantly illustrated with archival material, photographs and graphs.

MEET GERMANY. 15th revised edition. Edited by Irmgard Burmeister. Hamburg, Atlantik-Brucke, 1974.

Introduces West Germany in articles by authorities in various fields. Deals with the history, government, foreign policy, political parties, relationship between East and West Germany, economy, social security system, business and labor, education, communications media, cultural scene, and statistics concerning the Federal Republic of Germany. Illustrated with tables, graphs, and photographs.

MODERN GERMANY: THE RESEARCH COLLECTIONS OF BALL STATE UNIVERSITY. By Richard Wires. Muncie, Indiana; Ball State University, 1980.

Annotated guide of more than 2,250 source materials found on the Ball State University campus covering the period from 1815 to the present.

POLITICS, ECONOMICS, AND SOCIETY IN THE TWO GERMANIES, 1945-75: A BIBLIOGRAPHY OF ENGLISH-LANGUAGE WORKS. Compiled by Anna J. Merritt. Urbana, University of Illinois Press, 1978.

Listing of 8,548 books, periodicals, government publications and other materials dealing with postwar German politics, economics and society. Very comprehensive.

QUESTIONS AND ANSWERS. Life in the GDR. Berlin, East Germany, Panorama DDR, Auslandspress-eagentur GmbH, 1981.

A small book organized around questions which might be asked about East Germany. These are arranged in chapters on history; education, culture and sport; the economy and science; social policy; freedom and democracy; parties and trade unions; families, women and youth; health, the way of life and the environment; and foreign policy, trade and integration.

A SELECTED AND ANNOTATED GUIDE TO THE GOVERNMENT AND POLITICS OF GERMANY. By Robert B. Harmon. Monticello, Illinois, Council of Planning Librarians, 1978.

Outline and bibliography that will provide a starting point in obtaining knowledge on the government and politics of Germany.

GERMAN AMERICANS

BIBLIOGRAPHY OF GERMAN CULTURE IN AMERICA TO 1940. Edited by Henry A. Pochmann and Arthur R. Schultz. Madison, University of Wisconsin Press, 1953.

Lists more than 12,000 items in an abbreviated form. Includes a general index.

BONDS OF LOYALTY: GERMAN-AMERICANS AND WORLD WAR I. By Frederick C. Luebke. Dekalb, Northern Illinois University Press, 1974.

Explores the impact of World War I on every phase of German-American life.

BUCKET BOY, A MILWAUKEE LEGEND. By Ernest L. Meyer. New York, Hastings House, 1947.

Tells a personal tale of a German-American family and community in Milwaukee from about 1880, when the father escaped as a youth from Germany. He worked on a German-American newspaper, where the "bucket boy" who brought in the beer was a German in his sixties with varied experiences to recount.

BUILDERS, BURGHERS, BREWERS. By Dale Wirsing. 1950 South State Street, Tacoma, Washington 98411, 1976.

Published 1976 as a contribution towards the U.S. Bicentennial celebration; concentrates on German immigrants in the state of Washington. New edition is being prepared for publication in 1983 - celebrating 300 years of German immigration - and including other Pacific Northwest areas.

THE CATHOLIC CHURCH AND GERMAN-AMERICANS. By Colman J. Barry. Milwaukee, Bruce, 1953.

THE CONSERVATIVE REFORMERS; German-American Catholics and the Social Order. By Philip Gleason. Notre Dame, Indiana, University of Notre Dame Press, 1968.

Presents an organizational history of the Roman Catholic Central-Verein, established in 1855 as a federation of German-American Catholic mutual aid societies. After 1900 its activities broadened to include active propagandizing for social justice. Shows how an immigrant group and its organizations undergo changes and develop during the process of assimilation.

THE EARLY GERMANS OF NEW JERSEY; Their History, Churches, and Genealogies. By Theodore F. Chambers. Baltimore, Genealogical Publishing Company, 1969.

ENCYCLOPEDIA OF GERMAN-AMERICAN GENEALOGICAL RESEARCH. Edited by Clifford Neal Smith and Anna Piszczan-Czaja Smith. R. R. Bowker Company, New York, New York, 1976.

Publication includes chapters on both European and United States sources, such as church, occupational, military, naturalization, and other records; German Jewish records are included.

THE FORTY-EIGHTERS; Political Refugees of the German Revolution of 1848. Edited by A. E. Zucker. New York, Columbia University Press, 1950. Reprint New York, Russell and Russell, 1967.

Discusses the group of German idealists who fought to establish a liberal, unified Germany, then came to the United States as political refugees. Chapters by prominant Germanists and other scholars cover the European background of the refugees; the situation in America; assimilation to American ways; German-American organizations; political participation; radical ideas of the refugees; their role in the Civil War; and the career of Carl Schurz. Includes a biographical lexicon of several hundred names.

GENEALOGICAL HANDBOOK OF GERMAN RESEARCH. By Larry O. Jensen. Everton Publishers, Incorporated, Logan, Utah.

Publication includes a list of record repositories, genealogical and family organizations, and other sources in Germany of possible help to American genealogists. Entries include name of source, address, other details. Also includes general research guidance with respect to names, localities, correspondence, useful printed sources, etc.

GERMAN-AMERICAN PIONEERS IN WISCONSIN AND MICHIGAN: THE FRANK KERLER LETTERS, 1849-1864. By Louis F. Frank. Milwaukee, Wisconsin, 1971.

GERMAN-AMERICANA: A BIBLIOGRAPHY. Compiled by Don Heinrich Tolzmann. Metuchen, New Jersey, Scarecrow Press, 1975.

A guide listing books, pamphlets, records, photograph collections, dissertations, government documents, newspaper and journal articles concerned with German Americans. Covers immigration, settlement, ethnic characteristics, state history, politics, language and literature, religion, education, customs, folklore, music, theater, arts, business and industry, biography and genealogy. Includes American, German-American, and German publications through 1973.

THE GERMAN-AMERICANS; An Informal History. By Richard O'Connor. Boston, Little, Brown and Company, 1968.

Book I, Settlers and Citizens, discusses immigration, settlements, and activities of German-Americans from the 1600's through the end of the nineteenth century. Book II, Citizens and Dissidents, deals with westward movement of Germans in the nineteenth century, their accumulation of wealth and distinction in various fields, their customs and social conditions, political dissidents, World War I and Nazi repercussions, and other twentieth century events and problems.

GERMAN-AMERICANS AND THE WORLD WAR. By Carl Frederick Wittke. Columbus, Ohio, The Ohio State Archaeological and Historical Society, 1936.

Conclusions are drawn from the German press and other newspapers in Ohio which had the largest number of German publications.

THE GERMAN-AMERICANS IN POLITICS, 1914-1917. By Clifton James Child. Madison, University of Wisconsin Press, 1939.

Deals with the German's reactions to the war in Europe, their neutrality at home and their political activities and relations to national issues.

GERMAN CULTURE IN AMERICA; Philosophical and Literary Influences, 1600-1900. By Henry A. Pochmann. Madison, University of Wisconsin Press, 1961.

Appraises the impact of German philosophy, religion, education, and literature on American culture from colonial times to 1900. Book One deals with German Thought in America, while Book Two discusses German Literary Influence.

THE GERMAN ELEMENT IN THE UNITED STATES WITH SPECIAL REFERENCE TO ITS POLITICAL, MORAL, SOCIAL AND EDUCATIONAL INFLUENCE. By Albert B. Faust. 2 volumes. New York, The Steuben Society of America, 1927. Reprint New York, Arno Press, 1969.

A history in two volumes of the migration of Germans to the United States in the seventeenth, eighteenth, and early nineteenth centuries. Discusses the location, distribution, and general characteristics of German migrants and their influence on political, moral, social, and educational developments in the United States.

GERMAN EXILE LITERATURE IN AMERICA, 1933-1950: A HISTORY OF THE FREE GERMAN PRESS AND BOOK TRADE. By Robert Cazden. Chicago, American Library Association, 1969.

A bibliography on German works published in the United States during the period of exile.

GERMAN INTEREST IN CALIFORNIA BEFORE 1850. By George Peter Hammon. San Francisco, Rand E. Research Associates, 1971.

A study of the causes of German emigration to California.

GERMAN LANGUAGE PRESS IN AMERICA. By Carl Frederick Wittke. Lexington, Kentucky, University of Kentucky Press, 1957.

Presents a history of the founding, development, period of influential success, and subsidence of the German-language newspapers in the United States. Starts with the Philadelphische Zeitung founded by Benjamin Franklin in 1732 and ends with the 1950's.

GERMAN LITERATURE IN EXILE: THE CONCERN OF THE POETS. By William Pfeiler. Lincoln, Nebraska, University of Nebraska Press, 1957.

A description of the German literary community in North America and the literature it produced.

GERMAN PIONEERS IN EARLY CALIFORNIA. By Erwin Gustav Gudde. Hoboken, New Jersey, Concord Society, 1927. Reprint San Francisco, Rand E Research Associates, 1970.

An account of the part played by Germans and German-Americans in the pioneer stages of the history of California.

GERMAN POLITICAL REFUGEES IN THE UNITED STATES DURING THE PERIOD FROM 1815-1860. By Ernest Bruncken. Reprinted from the Deutsch-Amerikanische Geschichtsblätter, 1904. Reprint San Francisco, R and E Research Associates, 1970.

Seeking refuge from political absolutism and the failed Revolution of 1848, the German immigrants of this period were a special group who played an active part in American history. Deals with their role in German-American communities and their influence on social, political, and religious institutions in the United States during the short period of their ascendancy. Includes a discussion of the part played by German Americans during the struggle against slavery and the influence of German-American organizations and newspapers. German sources are also given.

GERMAN SEED IN TEXAS SOIL; Immigrant Farmers in Nineteenth Century Texas. By Terry G. Jordon. Austin, University of Texas Press, 1966.

German settlers had different agricultural methods which distinguished them from other pioneers. Also discussed social activities among the Germans.

THE GERMAN SOLDIER IN THE WARS OF THE UNITED STATES. By J. G. Rosengarten. Philadelphia, J. B. Lippincott Company, 1886. Reprinted by R and E Associates, San Francisco, 1972.

Recounts the history of German Americans' participation in the French and Indian War, the American Revolution, the Mexican War, and the Civil War.

GERMANIA, USA; Social Change in New Ulm, Minnesota. By Noel Iverson. Minneapolis, University of Minnesota Press, 1966.

Shows how German-American members of the Turnverein, a society of liberal thinkers, became an Americanized upper status group. Contrasts two generations of Turners with two corresponding generations of non-Turners. Analyzes four aspects of sociological change: class, status, power, and assimilation.

THE GERMANIC INFLUENCE IN THE MAKING OF MICHIGAN. By John Andrew Russell. Detroit, University of Detroit, 1927.

Discusses German settlements in Michigan from the 1800's on and contributions of Germans during war and peace. Covers their achievements in education, science, art, music, religion, medicine, law, engineering, architecture, journalism, commerce and industry, banking, politics, and community life.

THE GERMANIC PEOPLES IN THE AMERICAS. By Victor Wolfgang. Von Hagen, Norman; University of Oklahoma Press, 1976.

Based on the author's Der Ruf der Neuen Welt, which deals with the migration of Germans to the Americas and their role in the history of the Americas.

THE GERMANS IN AMERICA. By Theodore Huebener. Philadelphia, Chilton Company, 1962.

Tells the story of German settlers in America from early colonial times to the 1960's. Discusses their role in the American Revolution, in westward expansion, in later wars, and in an industrialized nation. Gives brief biographical sketches of eminent German immigrants, including their contributions to the material and cultural development of the United States.

THE GERMANS IN AMERICA, 1607-1970; A Chronology & Fact Book. Compiled and edited by Howard B. Furer. Ethnic Chronology Series Number 8. Dobbs Ferry, New York, Oceana Publications, 1973.

The first section gives a chronology of German immigration through 1970. The second section presents documents describing experiences of German settlers in various areas of the United States during different time periods. A third section contains a bibliography concerning Germans in the United States.

THE GERMANS IN COLONIAL TIMES. By Lucy Forney Bittinger. Philadelphia and London, Lippincott, 1901. Reprint. New York, Russell and Russell, 1968.

Especially valuable for information on the various German pietistic sects. Includes a map of German settlements in the thirteen colonies and a chronological table of German migration from 1683 to 1783.

THE GERMANS IN LOS ANGELES COUNTY, CALIFORNIA, 1850-1900. By Lamberta Margarette Vogeth. San Francisco, Rand E Research Associates, 1968.

Thesis discovers the early history, including industrial, social and religious life of the Germans of Los Angeles.

THE GERMANS IN TEXAS; A Study in Immigration. By Gilbert Giddings Benjamin, New York, Appleton 1910. Reprint San Francisco, R and E Research Associates, 1970.

Study of German immigration to Texas and its influences in forming the local culture.

HISTORY OF THE GERMAN ELEMENT IN THE STATE OF COLORADO. By Mildred Sherwood MacArthur. Chicago, German-American Historical Society of Illinois, 1917. Reprint San Francisco, R and E Research Associates, 1972.

Gives a brief historical sketch of the Germans in Colorado and their religious, educational, political and social growth of the state.

THE HISTORY OF THE GERMAN SETTLEMENTS IN TEXAS, 1831-1861. By Rudolph Leopold Biesele. Austin, Texas, Press of Von Boeckmann-Jures, 1930.

Study on how and why Germans left Germany to settle in Texas. Discusses settlements found in Texas, mainly the town of New Braunfels.

A HISTORY OF THE GERMAN SOCIETY OF PENNSYLVANIA, FOUNDED 1764. By Harry W. Pfund. 2nd edition. Philadelphia, Pennsylvania, The German Society of Pennsylvania, 1964.

Presents the evolution of one society and the work it does. Contains a list of prominent members and officials of the Society.

IMMIGRANTS AND POLITICS; The Germans of Nebraska, 1880-1900. By Frederick C. Luebke. Lincoln, Nebraska, University of Nebraska Press, 1969.

A study of the Germans who came to Nebraska from 1880 to 1900 in terms of their political participation in the political life of Nebraska.

THE MARYLAND GERMANS; A History. By Dieter Cunz. Princeton, New Jersey, Princeton University Press, 1948.

A history of immigration, settlements, outstanding individuals, and problems of Americanization of generations of German people in Maryland. Part One covers The Colonial Period, 1640-1790; Part Two considers The Middle Ages of Immigration, 1790-1865; and Part Three discusses The Last Generations, 1865-1940.

MUSEUMS, SITES AND COLLECTIONS OF GERMANIC CULTURE IN NORTH AMERICA: AN ANNOTATED DIRECTORY OF GERMAN IMMIGRANT CULTURE IN THE UNITED STATES AND CANADA. Compiled by Margaret Hobbie. Westport, Connecticut, Greenwood, 1980.

Chapter I gives descriptions of 152 repositories of materials relating to German-American and German-Canadian culture, listed alphabetically by state and province, city and name. Chapter 2 lists 103 historic sites including houses and farms, neighborhoods, museum villages, archeological sites, monuments and memorials and describes location and major features. Chapter 3 gives a selected list of European collections that have information about German immigrants. There is an appendix listing cultural attaches in America and Canada from Austria, East and West Germany, Luxembourg and Switzerland. Both a name index and general index are included.

OF GERMAN WAYS. By La Vern Rippley, Minneapolis, Dillon Press, 1970.

Tells of German customs in both the Old and New World.

REFUGEES OF REVOLUTION; The German Forty-Eighters in America. By Carl Wittke. Philadelphia, University of Pennsylvania Press, 1952.

Examines the importance of the political and cultural leadership provided in America by refugees from the German Revolutions of 1848 and 1849. Discusses their impact on foreign policy, the slavery issue, the early labor movement, the rise of the Republican Party, the Civil War, and post-war politics. Also explains their influence in religion, music, journalism, medicine, art, education, invention, crafts, professions, and German-American organizations.

REPORT ABOUT AND FROM AMERICA. By J. G. Hacker. Translated by Richard B. O'Connell. Memphis, John Willard Brister Library, Memphis State University, 1970.

Document written by the author to persuade Germans emigrating to the U.S., that they should settle in Morgan County, Tennessee.

THE SERENE CINCINNATIANS. By Alvin F. Harlow, New York: Dutton, 1950.

The German section of Cincinnati was important in German American histories. Emphasizes sound German imperturbability as a Cincinnati characteristic.

THE SETTLEMENT OF THE GERMAN COAST OF LOUISIANA AND THE CREOLES OF GERMAN DESCENT. By John Hanno Deiler. Philadelphia, German American Historical Society, 1909. Reprint Baltimore, Genealogical Publishing Company, 1969.

History of the first Germans who settled in Louisiana the people and their problems.

TEXAS POLITICS, 1906-1944; With Special Reference to the German Counties. By Seth S. McKay. Lubbock, Texas, Texas Tech Press, 1952.

TRACING YOUR GERMAN ROOTS. By Maralyn A. Wellauer. Milwaukee, Wisconsin, 1978.

Publication includes lists of publishers of German genealogical periodicals and books, and of genealogical societies in Germany. Also includes material on American records for determining immigrant ancestor's place of origin.

THE TRAGEDY OF GERMAN-AMERICA; The Germans in the United States of America during the Nineteenth Century - and After. By John A. Hawgood. New York, G. P. Putnam's Sons, 1940. Reprint New York, Arno Press, 1970.

The study concentrates on German immigrants settling in the United States in the early 1800's up to 1870, and attempting to remain separate in the American setting, maintaining their own press, social groups and special churches. Part I, The German as a Settler in the United States, deals with characteristics of the German settlers, their origins and destinations. Part II describes attempts to found new Germanies on American soil in Missouri, Texas, and Wisconsin by mass settlements of Germans in concentrated areas with their own culture and language. Part III explains the significance of the hyphenated term, German-Americans, and how the German-American point of view persisted until the hyphen was shaken loose during World War I. Includes first-hand accounts.

THE VIRGINIA GERMANS. By Klaus G. Wust. Charlottesville, University Press of Virginia, 1969.

Very thorough discussion of the Germans in Virginia, including maps.

AMISH, MENNONITES, MORAVIANS AND PENNSYLVANIA DUTCH

AMISH SOCIETY. By John A. Hostetler. 3rd edition. Baltimore, John Hopkins University Press, 1980.

Purpose of the book is to communicate a knowledge of Amish life to inquiring people. Explains origins, values, social relationships, problems and conflicts of being Amish.

THE AMISH TODAY: AN ANALYSIS OF THEIR BELIEFS, BEHAVIOR AND CONTEMPORARY PROBLEMS. By Elmer Lewis. Allentown, Pennsylvania, Pennsylvania German Folklore Society, 1960.

A sociological study citing the solidity of family structure as the most important factor in permitting the Amish their separate cultural identification.

ANNOTATED BIBLIOGRAPHY ON THE AMISH (Old Order Amish Mennonites). By John A. Hostetler. Scottdale, Pennsylvania: Mennonite, Publishers, 1951.

Bibliography is gathered from both published and unpublished sources and covers the history, sociology, religious beliefs and genealogy of the Amish up to 1950.

A BIBLIOGRAPHY OF ANABAPTISM, 1520-1680, A SEQUEL, 1962-1974. By Hans Joachim Hillerbrand. Saint Louis Center for Reformation Research, 1975.

Comprehensive listing of the literature about and emerging from sixteenth-century Anabaptism.

BIBLIOGRAPHY ON GERMAN SETTLEMENTS IN COLONIAL NORTH AMERICA, ESPECIALLY ON THE PENNSYLVANIA GERMANS AND THEIR DESCENDANTS 1683-1933. By Emil Meynen. Leipzig: Harrassowitz, 1937. Reprint, Detroit, Michigan: Gale, 1966.

Very important work; annotations given for the most important entries. About 8,000 titles are included, arranged topically.

BLUE HILLS AND SHOOFLY PIE IN PENNSYLVANIA DUTCHLAND. By Ann Hark. Philadelphia, J. B. Lippincott Company, 1952.

Tells about the author's personal experiences with people of German descent in the area near Lancaster, Pennsylvania. Discusses the customs, religion, history, and way of life of Amish, Mennonite, Dunker, and Moravian people of the region.

A CATALOGUE OF MUSIC BY AMERICAN MORAVIANS, 1742-1842, FROM THE ARCHIVES OF THE MORAVIAN CHURCH AT BETHLEHEM, PENNSYLVANIA. Compiled by Albert George Rau. New York, Ams Press, 1970.

List of anthems composed in America by musicians belonging to the Moravian church.

CHILDREN IN AMISH SOCIETY. By John A. Hostetler and Gertrude E. Huntington. New York, Holt, Rinehart and Winston, 1971.

Gives an account of the education and socialization of Amish children.

COMPULSORY EDUCATION AND THE AMISH. By Albert Keim. Boston, Beacon Press, 1975.

EDUCATIONAL ACHIEVEMENTS: ACHIEVEMENT AND LIFE STYLES IN A TRADITIONAL SOCIETY: THE OLD ORDER AMISH. By John A. Hostetler. Washington, D.C.: United States Department of Health, Education and Welfare, Office of Education, Bureau of Research, 1968.

FROM THE FIREY STAKES OF EUROPE TO THE FEDERAL COURTS OF AMERICA. By Elizabeth Miller. New York, Vantage, 1963.

Because the German Anabaptists including Amish, Mennonites, Moravians, Hutterites, etc. reject worldly government and violence they have been victims of political and social persecution from the beginning. A personal account.

THE GENTLE PEOPLE; A Portrait of the Amish. By James A. Warner. Soudersburg, Pennsylvania. Mill Bridge Museum in cooperation with Grossman, New York, 1969.

Collection of photographs depicting the life of the Amish. Bible quotes and basic information are interdispersed throughout the book.

THE GERMAN AND SWISS SETTLEMENTS OF COLONIAL PENNSYLVANIA: A STUDY OF THE SO-CALLED PENNSYLVANIA DUTCH. By Levi Oscar Kuhns. New York, Holt, 1901; Reprint, Harrisburg, Pennsylvania: Aurand, 1945.

An early study pointing out the unique characteristics of the 18th century German farmer in farming methods, customs and manners. Explains what German names mean and how they were Americanized.

GERMAN RELIGIOUS LIFE IN COLONIAL TIMES. By Lucy Bittinger. Philadelphia, Lippincott, 1906.

Especially valuable for discussion of the various religious sects which established themselves in America.

HISTORY AND CUSTOMS OF THE AMISH PEOPLE. By Harry Martin John Klein. York, Pennsylvania: Maple Press Company, 1946.

Narrative of the history and customs of the Amish people. Illustrations were sketched on an Amish farm.

THE HOUSE OF THE MILLER AT MILLBACH; THE ARCHITECTURE, ARTS AND CRAFTS OF THE PENNSYLVANIA GERMANS. By Joseph Downs. Philadelphia, Franklin Printing Company, 1929.

Illustrations and description of the furnishings and construction of a Pennsylvania Dutch house.

INTIMATE GLIMPSES OF THE PENNSYLVANIA GERMANS. Edited by Homer Rosenberger. Waynesboro, Pennsylvania, (Rose Hill Seminar), 1966.

Contains various papers presented at the Third Rose Hill Seminar on such topics as church matters, life and customs, politics, humor and literature.

MENNONITE BUSINESS AND PROFESSIONAL PEOPLE'S DIRECTORY. Edited by J. J. Hostetler. Mennonite Industry and Business Associates, Goshen, Indiana, 1982.

Covers 7,500 Mennonite business, professional and management people in United States and Canada. Entries include name, address and a code indicating type of business. Arrangement is geographical and by vocation; identical information in each part. Updated biennially.

MENNONITE ENCYCLOPEDIA: A COMPREHENSIVE REFERENCE WORK ON THE ANABAPTIST MOVEMENT. 4 volumes. Edited by C. Henry Smith and Harold S. Bender. Scottsdale, Pennsylvania, Mennonite Publishing House; Hillsboro, Kansas, Mennonite Brethren Publishing House; Newton, Kansas, Mennonite Publishing Office, 1955-1959.

A definitive work.

MENNONITE HISTORY AND THE MENNONITE CHURCH IN AMERICA. By John C. Wenger. Scottsdale, Pennsylvania, Herald Press, 1966.

Good general information source for the Mennonites in America.

THE MENNONITES IN INDIANA AND MICHIGAN. By John Christian Wenger. Scottdale, Pennsylvania. Herald Press, 1961.

THE MORAVIANS IN GEORGIA, 1735-1740. By Adelaide Lisetta Fries. Baltimore, Genealogical Publishing Company, 1967.

Focuses on the history of the Moravian settlement in Georgia and its effect on the establishment of the Moravian church and Methodist denomination.

MORAVIANS IN TWO WORLDS; A STUDY OF CHANGING COMMUNITIES. By Gillian Lindt Collin. New York, Columbia University Press, 1967.

A study that describes the changes in the value systems and social structures of two Moravian settlements; Herrenhut, East Germany and Bethlehem, Pennsylvania.

OUR AMISH NEIGHBORS. By William Ildephonse Schreiber. Chicago, University of Chicago Press, 1962.

Takes a look at the Amish way of life seen through the eyes of the author who was a neighbor of Amish people.

A PECULIAR PEOPLE; Iowa's Old Order Amish. By Elmer Schwieder. Ames: Iowa State University Press, 1975.

THE PENNSYLVANIA DUTCH. By Frederic Klees. New York: Macmillian, 1950.

A very detailed personal account which finds the basis of Pennsylvania Dutch culture in religion.

THE PENNSYLVANIA DUTCH: A PERSISTENT MINORITY. By William T. Parsons. Boston: Twayne, 1976.

THE PENNSYLVANIA DUTCH AND THEIR FURNITURE. By John Gerald Shea. New York, Van Nostrand Reinhold Company, 1980.

Focuses on the designs, construction and painting and decorating of Pennsylvania Dutch furniture. Contains chapters of hex sign designs and measured drawings of furniture designs, for reproductions.

THE PENNSYLVANIA-GERMAN IN THE SETTLEMENT OF MARYLAND. By Daniel Wunderlich Nead, Lancaster, Pennsylvania, Press of the New Era Printing Company, 1914.

Even though relatively old, still useful for information on the 18th century Mennonite and Palatine settlements in Maryland.

IN PENNSYLVANIA-GERMAN LAND, 1928-29. By Jesse Leonard Rosenberger. Chicago, Illinois, University of Chicago Press, 1929.

An array of information obtained by the author in the "Pennsylvania-German Land"; its people, buildings, churches and schools, farming and county fairs. Illustrations are reproductions of photographs taken by the author.

PENNSYLVANIA GERMAN LITERATURE: CHANGING TRENDS FROM 1683-1942. By Earl Robacker. Philadelphia, University of Pennsylvania Press, 1943.

The categories covered in this history include works in High German and English as well as the so called Pennsylvania Dutch dialect. Samples of characteristic literature are included.

THE PENNSYLVANIA GERMANS. Edited by Ralph Wood. Princeton, New Jersey: Princeton University Press, 1942.

A collection of very useful essays: "Pennsylvania, the Colonial Melting Pot", A. D. Graeff; "The Pennsylvania German Farmer," W. M. Kollmorgen, "The Sects, Apostles of Peace," G. P. Musselman; "Lutheran and Reformed, Pennsylvania German Style," Ralph Wood; "The Pennsylvania Germans and the School," C. S. Stine; "Journalism Among the Pennsylvania Germans," Ralph Wood; "Pennsylvania German Literature," H. H. Reichard; "The Pennsylvania German as Soldiers," A. D. Graeff; "The Pennsylvania Germans as Seen by the Historian," R. H. Shryock; and "The Pennsylvania German Dialect," A. F. Buffington.

THE PENNSYLVANIA GERMANS; A Sketch of their History and Life of the Mennonites, and of Side Lights from the Rosenberger Family. By Jesse Leonard Rosenberger. Chicago, University of Chicago Press, 1923.
Written by a Pennsylvania German primarily about his immediate family.

A PEOPLE OF TWO KINGDOMS: THE POLITICAL ACCULTURATION OF THE KANSAS MENNONITES. By James C. Juhnke. Newton, Kansas, Faith and Life Press, 1975.

A history of the Mennonites in America and how they came to terms with Kansan and American society.

THE PLAIN PEOPLE. By Phebe Earle Gibbons. Witmer, Applied Arts, 1963.

A reprinted and retitled group of essays, originally published in the nineteenth century on the aspects of Pennsylvania Dutch tradition. Includes sections on the Pennsylvania Dutch, an Amish meeting, Swiss exiles, the Dunker love-feast, Ephrata, Bethlehem and the Moravians, the Schwenkfelders, and the Pennsylvania German dialect.

THE QUIET PEOPLE OF THE LAND: A STORY OF THE NORTH CAROLINA MORAVIANS IN REVOLUTIONARY TIMES. By Hinder James. Chapel Hill: University of North Carolina Press, 1976.

History of the Moravians who came from Pennsylvania and Europe to settle in North Carolina.

ROSANNA OF THE AMISH. By Joseph W. Yoder. Scottsdale, Pennsylvania. Herald Press, 1940.

True story written by an Amish person who knew Rosanna and her family.

SKETCHES AND CHRONICLES: THE REFLECTIONS OF A NINETEENTH CENTURY PENNSYLVANIA GERMAN FOLK ARTIST. By Lewis Miller. York, Pennsylvania, 1966.

Reproductions of watercolor drawings of the time.

TWO CENTURIES OF AMERICAN MENNONITE LITERATURE; A Bibliography of Mennonitica Americana, 1727-1928. Edited by Harold Bender. Goshen, Indiana. The Mennonite Historical Society, 1929.

Bibliography of all books, pamphlets, and periodicals by Mennonites in the U.S. and Canada from the time of the first settlement until the end of the year 1928.

Audiovisual Material

FILMS

AROUND AND ABOUT THE MARIENPLATZ IN MUNICH. 16 mm. Color and sound. 5 minutes. By Bavarian Radio in cooperation with the Goethe Institute. Ministry of Foreign Affairs of the Federal Republic of Germany. Chicago: Distributed by International Film Bureau, 1973.

Explores the history and economy of Munich, one of the most famous of Germany's state capitals.

THE AUER DULT IN MUNICH. 16 mm. Color and sound. 5 minutes. By Bavarian Radio in cooperation with the Goethe Institute. Ministry of Foreign Affairs of the Federal Republic of Germany. Chicago: Distributed by International Film Bureau, 1973.

A study of the Munich Auer Dult (the colloquial term for folkfest).

BADEN-BADEN. 16 mm. Color and sound. 5 minutes. By Bavarian Radio in cooperation with the Goethe Institute. Ministry of Foreign Affairs of the Federal Republic of Germany. Distributed by International Film Bureau, Chicago, 1973.

Shows Baden-Baden near the Black Forest which has always been famous for its healthy air, mineral springs and mondain life.

BAUMA, THE BUILDING EQUIPMENT FAIR. 16 mm. Color and sound. 5 minutes. By Bavarian Radio in cooperation with the Goethe Institute. Ministry of Foreign Affairs of the Federal Republic of Germany. Distributed by International Film Bureau, Chicago, 1973.

Describes Bauma, a biannual Munich exhibition of construction equipment and heavy trucks from around the world.

BAVARIA - IMPRESSIONS OF GERMANY'S SOUTH. 16 mm. Color and sound. 29 minutes. By Bavarian Radio in cooperation with the Goethe Institute. Ministry of Foreign Affairs of the Federal Republic of Germany.

Bavaria, generally thought of as mountains, beer, tradition and, of course, ancient art and history. Pictured are the Oktoberfest, skiing in the mountains, carneval, easter customs and famous tourist attractions, such as the renown Wieskirche and the Castles Amalienburg in Munich and Linderhof.

BERLIN - WIEDERSEHEN MIT EINER STADT. (Reunion with a City). 16 mm. Color and sound. 16 minutes. By Ministry of Foreign Affairs of the Federal Republic of Germany. Distributed by Modern Talking Picture Service, Incorporated, Washington, D.C., 1973.

The journalist Paul Anderson talks about Berlin in the Thirties which he knew as a student. 40 years later he makes comparisons with today and concludes that modern Berlin is again a metropolis with a future.

BERLINER (Berliners). 16 mm. Color and sound. 28 minutes. By Ministry of Foreign Affairs of the Federal Republic of Germany. Distributed by Modern Talking Picture Service, Incorporated, Washington, D. C., 1975.

Berliners - a special species so they say; natives and migrants. The commentary gives an insight into the life in West Berlin and its political, economic and cultural situation.

BEYOND THE WALL. 16 mm. Color and sound. 52 minutes. By BBC-TV. Distributed by Time-Life Multimedia, New York, 1971.

Depicts life in East Germany today and examines the role of East Germany in contemporary Eastern European affairs. Sketches the career of German Communist Walter Ulbricht who governed East Germany from the end of World War II to his death in 1973.

BISMARCK: GERMANY FROM BLOOD AND IRON. 16 mm. Color and sound. 30 minutes. By Learning Corporation of America, 1976.

Traces the step-by-step creation of modern Germany and suggests its implications for the rest of the world. Presents a dramatized interview with Otto von Bismarck, who recollects the steps which led to Germany's unification, as told in a series of flash-backs.

THE BLACK FOREST. 16 mm. Color and sound. 17 minutes. By Ministry of Foreign Affairs of the Federal Republic of Germany. Distributed by Modern Talking Picture Service, Incorporated, Washington, D. C., 1973.

The largest expanse of mountain forest in Germany is shown developing from a basic agricultural to an industrial structure, also becoming an important holiday resort.

BOMBING OF GERMANY. Super 8 mm. Black and white. 4 minutes. By Anargyros Film Library, 1974.

Documents the aerial bombings of Germany by the Allied forces during World War II.

BREMEN - AROUND THE CLOCK. 16 mm. Color and sound. 10 minutes. By Ministry of Foreign Affairs of the Federal Republic of Germany. Distributed by Modern Talking Picture Service, Incorporated, Washington, D.C., 1967.

A documentary about everyday life in the Hanseatic City of Bremen.

BURGEN UND SCHLÖSSER AN DER SAALE (Castles and Palaces Along the Saale). 16 mm. Color and sound. 25 minutes. Distributed by the Embassy of the German Democratic Republic, Washington, D.C.

The castles and palaces on the Saale river in the GDR are interesting witnesses of the past. A visit there gives impressions of their history and our present. What is done to preserve these buildings? How are they used today?

CARNIVAL IN THE ALEMANNIC REGION. 16 mm. Color and sound. 5 minutes. By Bavarian Radio in cooperation with the Goethe Institute. Ministry of Foreign Affairs of the Federal Republic of Germany. Distributed by International Film Bureau, Chicago, 1973.

Traces the pre-Christian origins and describes the present-day celebration of the Pre-Lenten Spring festival.

DIE DDR (The German Democratic Republic). 16 mm. Color and sound. 35 minutes. Distributed by the Embassy of the German Democratic Republic, Washington, D. C.

Information about the country and people, political geography, social conditions, industry, agriculture and much more.

DORTMUND BEER. 16 mm. Color and sound. 5 minutes. By Bavarian Radio in cooperation with the Goethe Institute. Ministry of Foreign Affairs of the Federal Republic of Germany. Distributed by International Film Bureau, Chicago, 1973.

Describes the processes involved in the manufacture of various types of beer.

DRESDEN, SKIZZEN DES ELBEBEZIRKS (Sketches of the Elbe Region). 16 mm. Color and sound. 20 minutes. Distributed by the Embassy of the German Democratic Republic, Washington, D.C.

Drawings of the county on the Elbe River - this documentary film gives a large variety of impressions from the Elbe River region. Dresden is shown as the center of economy, science and art.

EAST GERMANY: A NATION IN TRANSITION. 16 mm. Color and sound. 17 minutes. By McGraw-Hill, 1972. Made in collaboration with Minerva Films.

Evaluates the rapid industrial growth of East Germany from the post-war period to the present, outlining the importance of the system of state partnership with private business, and evaluating its growth in terms of human and natural resources.

EICHSTÄTT, A SMALL TOWN IN BAVARIA. 16 mm. Color and sound. 5 minutes. By Bavarian Radio in cooperation with the Goethe Institute. Ministry of Foreign Affairs of the Federal Republic of Germany. Distributed by International Film Bureau, Chicago, 1973.

Describes the history of Eichstatt over the last 1200 years and shows surviving architecture and other artistic works.

EUROPA OHNE GRENZEN (Europe without Borders). 16 mm. Color and sound. 70 minutes. By Ministry of Foreign Affairs of the Federal Republic of Germany. Distributed by Modern Talking Picture Service, Incorporated, Washington, D.C., 1965.

Colorful outline of different folklore festivals in West European countries. Also shown are East Europeans including East Germans in exile, demonstrating their native folk dances.

EVERYDAY GERMANY. 16 mm. Color and sound. 26 minutes. By Ministry of Foreign Affairs of the Federal Republic of Germany. Distributed by Modern Talking Picture Service, Incorporated, Washington, D.C., 1964.

A trip from the North Sea through the industrial district of the Ruhr, along the Rhine to the Alps showing the everyday life in Germany.

FIVE ASPECTS OF BONN. 16 mm. Color and sound. 30 minutes. By Ministry of Foreign Affairs of the Federal Republic of Germany. Distributed by Modern Talking Picture Service, Incorporated, Washington, D.C., 1970.

An attempt to characterize the city of Bonn: The citizens, the politicans, the students and the tourists.

FOLLOWING THE RHINE. 16 mm. Color and sound. 58 minutes. By Ministry of Foreign Affairs of the Federal Republic of Germany. Distributed by Modern Talking Picture Service, Incorporated, Washington, D.C.

Part I shows the upper Rhine from Lake Constance to Mainz following through fertile farmlands and historic sites and cities. The film emphasizes the importance of the Rhine as a European shipping route. 24 minutes. Part II follows the middle Rhine from Mainz to Bonn, showing the most beautiful region of the Rhine with its numerous castles and vineyards. 17 minutes. Part III views the lower Rhine from Bonn to Emmerich of the Dutch border. World-renowned industrial and cultural centers characterize the areas on both sides of this part of the Rhine. 17 minutes.

FROM THE ISLAND OF HELGOLAND TO THE PEAK OF THE ZUGSPITZE. 16 mm. Color and sound. 114 minutes. By Ministry of Foreign Affairs of the Federal Republic of Germany. Distributed by Modern Talking Picture Service, Incorporated, Washington, D. C.

A three-part series, depicting three areas of Germany, from the north to the south.

FROM TAUBERGRUND TO THE RIES - OLD TOWNS ALONG THE ROMANTIC ROAD. 16 mm. Color and sound. 20 minutes. By Ministry of Foreign Affairs of the Federal Republic of Germany. Distributed by Modern Talking Picture Service, Incorporated, Washington, D. C.

This is "Old Franconia", the area between the River Main and the Danube. The main portion of the film focuses on the "romantic" stretch of the area with its small and picturesque villages and towns who up to present days have maintained their medieval impressions.

GERMANY. 16 mm. Color and sound. 25 minutes. By Screenscope. Arlington, Virginia, 1980.

Introduces the people and history of Germany. Shows scenes of historical importance, providing a basis for a better understanding and evaluation of the history of this century.

GERMANY - DADA. 16 mm. Color and sound. 55 minutes. By Helmut Herbst, 1968. Released by Universal Education and Visual Arts, 1973.

Deals with aims and activities of the revolutionary group of artists and writers who made up the Dadaist movement in Germany.

GERMANY: KINDER KARNEVAL. 16 mm. Color and sound. 18 minutes. By Ontario Educational Communications Authority, Toronto, 1970. Released in the U.S. by NBC Educational Enterprises, 1972.

Deals with daily life of young people in Germany. Shows a brother and sister from Cologne as they study at school from morning until early evening, learning German, reading and mathematics. Tells that they enjoy winter sports, especially the children's Karneval, held each year during the week before Lent. For elementary grades.

GERMANY - THE ROAD OF RETURN. 16 mm. Color and sound. 30 minutes. By Ernest Kleinberg Films, 1974.

Traces the development of divided Germany from the end of World War II to the present day, showing implications for the future. Designed to contribute to an understanding of the German people.

THE GREEN ROAD. 16 mm. Color and sound. 30 minutes. By Ministry of Foreign Affairs of the Federal Republic of Germany. Distributed by Modern Talking Picture Service, Incorporated, Washington, D. C., 1972.

Scenic travelog of the region between Lake Constance and Domremy, Alsace, France.

GUTEN TAG BERLIN (Hello Berlin). 16 mm. Color and sound. 25 minutes. By the Embassy of the German Democratic Republic, Washington, D.C.

Shows the neighborhoods and government buildings of the capital city of the GDR (East Berlin).

HAMBURG HARBOUR. 16 mm. Color and sound. 5 minutes. By Bavarian Radio in cooperation with the Goethe Institute. Ministry of Foreign Affairs of the Federal Republic of Germany. Distributed by International Film Bureau, Chicago, 1973.

HEIDELBERG. 16mm. Color and sound. 15 minutes. By Ministry of Foreign Affairs of the Federal Republic of Germany. Distributed by Modern Talking Picture Service, Incorporated, Washington, D.C., 1967.

The sites of the city and its surroundings are presented in the form of a discussion on what a film about Heidelberg should be like.

EIN HIMMEL, DRIN DIE TAUBE FLIEGT (A Heaven in Which the Dove Flies). 16mm. Color and sound. 30 minutes. By the Embassy of the German Democratic Republic, Washington, D.C.

Shows social conditions in East Germany for living in security.

HITLER - THE ROAD TO REVENGE. 16mm. Color and sound. 58 minutes. By Nielsen-Ferns International. Learning Corporation of America, New York, 1980, made 1978, c1979.

A film in two parts of 24 minutes. The first part traces the rise to power of Adolf Hitler as dictator of Germany, from a young corporal in the Kaiser's Army who was appalled by the terms of the Treaty of Versailles, bent upon avenging the humiliation of his country, to the realization of his dream and the surrender of France.

The second part tells how, from the fall of France, Hitler's dream gradually turns to nightmare as German fortunes are checked and then reversed in the Battle of Britain, Operation Barbarosa, and the entry of the United States into the war. In 1945 Hitler commits suicide amid the ruins of the Third Reich.

HITLER'S WAR. 16 mm. Black and white with sound. 20 minutes. Also available on video recording. By BBC-TV. Time-Life Multimedia, New York, 1970.

Deals with Hitler's plan to crush Western Europe, his failure to conquer England, and his attack on the Soviet Union which led to the defeat and surrender of Germany in 1945.

INZELL, CENTRE OF ICE SPORT. 16 mm. Color and sound. 5 minutes. By Bavarian Radio in cooperation with the Goethe Institute. Ministry of Foreign Affairs of the Federal Republic of Germany. Distributed by International Film Bureau, Chicago, 1973.

Describes Inzell, a Bavarian village which is famous for its winter sports facilities.

ISLANDS IN LAKE CONSTANCE. 16 mm. Color and sound. 5 minutes. By Bavarian Radio in cooperation with the Goethe Institute. Ministry of Foreign Affairs of the Federal Republic of Germany. Distributed by International Film Bureau, Chicago, 1973.

Describes the historical and cultural attractions of the Lake Constance islands, particularly Mainau and Reichnau.

JUNGE ALTE STADTE (Young Old Cities). 16 mm. Color and sound. 20 minutes. By the Embassy of the German Democratic Republic, Washington, D.C.

Demonstrates the importance of restorations for the preservation of several towns in the GDR.

THE KIEL CANAL. 16 mm. Color and sound. 5 minutes. By Bavarian Radio in cooperation with the Goethe Institute. Ministry of Foreign Affairs of the Federal Republic of Germany. Distributed by International Film Bureau, Chicago, 1973.

Describes the importance and operation of the Kiel Canal, the shortest connection between the North and Baltic Seas.

KIRCHE IN DER DDR (The Church in the GDR). 16 mm. Color and sound. 25 minutes. By the Embassy of the German Democratic Republic, Washington, D.C.

With this film an attempt is made to give a glimpse of the manifold ecclesiastical life in the GDR. On which basis does it work in a socialist country and which historical elements have formed today's relation between state and church? How do believes and marxists work together?

KUNST UND KÜNSTLER (Art and Artists). 16 mm. Color and sound. 35 minutes. By the Embassy of the German Democratic Republic, Washington, D.C.

Discusses the effect of art and artists on the development of the country. The authors Kant, Noll and the painter Sitte speak about the role of their work in society. A very interesting film on culture in the GDR.

LAKE CONSTANCE. 16 mm. Color and sound. 19 minutes. By Ministry of Foreign Affairs of the Federal Republic of Germany. Distributed by Modern Talking Picture Service, Incorporated, Washington, D.C., 1965.

This geographical film in the form of a lively report on the areas surrounding Lake Constance offers a mosaic of scenes from various walks of life.

LEIPZIG. 16 mm. Color and sound. 25 minutes. By the Embassy of the German Democratic Republic, Washington, D.C.

Shows the sights, history and present-day importance of the city of Leipzig.

THE NATIONAL SCHILLER MUSEUM IN MARBACH. 16 mm. Color and sound. 5 minutes. By Bavarian Radio in cooperation with the Goethe Institute. Ministry of Foreign Affairs of the Federal Republic of Germany. Distributed by International Film Bureau, Chicago, 1973.

Gives a description of Marbach, Germany and of the museum erected there to the memory of Friederich Schiller, containing the archives of many of Germany's most famous literary figures.

NAZI CONCENTRATION CAMPS. 16 mm. Black and white with sound. 59 minutes. Also issued as video cassette. By United States Counsel for the Prosecution of Axis Criminality. Distributed by National Audiovisual Center, Washington, D.C. 1945.

The official film record of the Nazi death camps as photographed by Allied forces advancing into Germany. Shows surviving prisoners, victims of medical experiments, gas chambers and open mass graves.

THE NAZI STRIKE. Videorecording. Black and white with sound. 41 minutes. By United States War Department. United States Office of War Information, Domestic Branch. Distributed by National Audiovisual Center, Washington, D.C., 1979.

A documentary film record of Germany's preparation for war, the conquest of Austria and Czechoslovakia, and the attack upon Poland. Issued in 1943 as a motion picture.

THE ODENWALD. A Land of Handicrafts and Traditions. 16 mm. Color and sound. 13 minutes. By Ministry of Foreign Affairs of Federal Republic of Germany. Distributed by Modern Talking Picture Service, Incorporated, Washington, D. C.

Shows the scenery, the history and life of the Odenwald region in which many of the places associated with the Nibelungen Saga are found.

RHEINBERG, A SMALL TOWN ON THE OUTSKIRTS OF THE RUHR. 16 mm. Color and sound. 5 minutes. By Bavarian Radio in cooperation with the Goethe Institute. Ministry of Foreign Affairs of the Federal Republic of Germany. Distributed by International Film Bureau, Chicago, 1973.

Gives a brief history of the Rheinberg area, and shows how its longstanding tranquility is being threatened by its own economic success.

THE RHINE: GEOGRAPHY, HISTORY AND LEGEND. 16 mm. Color and sound. 14 minutes. By Ernest Kleinberg Films. Released by Oxford Films, 1972.

Traces the history of the Rhine River from the time of Caesar's Roman Rhine fleet to the storming of the bridge at Remagen near the end of World War II. Explains the role of the Rhine in the destiny of the people of its six surrounding nations with a description of the river's geography and references to folklore of the region.

THE RHINE TODAY. 16 mm. Color and sound. 14 minutes. By Ernest Kleinberg Films. Released by Oxford Films, 1972.

Studies the effect which the Rhine River has had on the culture, ethnic development, and political interaction of the six nations which border it. Examines the relationship between the river and the large merchant fleet, the dense network of canals and waterways, riverside industry, pollution and the Common Market.

RHINE TUGBOAT. Super 8 mm. 3 minutes. By Institut für Film und Bild, Munich. Edited and released in the U.S. by Films Incorporated, 1972.

Follows a tugboat, Braunkohle, from Cologne, as it passes other kinds of vessels heading up the Rhine at Mainz.

THE RISE AND FALL OF THE THIRD REICH. PART I: RISE OF HITLER. 16 mm. Black and white with sound. 28 minutes. Metro-Goldwyn-Mayer. Released by Films Incorporated, 1972.

Traces the career of Adolf Hitler from birth to his assumption of power in Germany. Describes the role that economic stress can play in bringing totalitarianism to a modern industrial state and provides insights into how a minority, using terror and modern propaganda techniques can overcome the will of the majority.

THE RISE AND FALL OF THE THIRD REICH. PART 2: NAZI GERMANY - YEARS OF TRIUMPH. 16 mm. Black and white with sound. 28 minutes. Metro-Goldwyn-Mayer. Released by Films Incorporated, 1972.

Traces the expansion of Nazi Germany from Hitler's accession as Chancellor to the fall of France. Shows how terror and propaganda can transform a democratic government into an absolute dictatorship and examines the goals and ideals of the Nazi state.

THE RISE AND FALL OF THE THIRD REICH. PART 3: GOTTERDÄMMERUNG - COLLAPSE OF THE THIRD REICH. 16 mm. Black and white with sound. 28 minutes. Metro-Goldwyn-Mayer. Released by Films Incorporated, 1972.

Traces the collapse of the Hitler reign from the invasion of Russia in 1941 to his suicide in Berlin in 1945. Shows the extent of Nazi evil in the concentration camp system which was extended all over Europe and examines the external and internal reasons for the collapse of the Nazi army.

THE RISE OF HITLER. 16 mm. Black and white with sound. 20 minutes. Also issued as video recording. By BBC-TV, New York: Time-Life Multimedia, 1970.

Surveys the background of Europe prior to World War II, beginning with the Versailles peace settlement of 1919 and continuing to Hitler's attack on Poland in 1939.

ROSTOCK - DER OSTSEEBEZIRK (Rostock - The Baltic Region). 16 mm. Color and sound. 25 minutes. By the Embassy of the German Democratic Republic, Washington, D. C.

This film gives a review of the development of this former backward region towards a developed agricultural and industrial district. It describes life and achievements of the working population and gives impressions of this landscape's beauties.

SCHWÄBISCH HALL. 16 mm. Color and sound. 24 minutes. By Ministry of Foreign Affairs of the Federal Republic of Germany. Distributed by Modern Talking Picture Service, Incorporated, Washington, D. C.

Schwäbisch Hall exemplifies medieval architecture in Germany, a place where Swabia and Franconia border on each other.

SKETCHES FROM GERMANY. 16 mm. Color and sound. Each of seven parts 12 minutes. By Ministry of Foreign Affairs of the Federal Republic of Germany. Distributed by Modern Talking Picture Service, Incorporated, Washington, D.C.

A seven-part updated informative film on modern Germany including the following parts: I-The Federal Republic of Germany; II-The State and its Capital on the Rhine; III-From the North Sea to the Alps; IV-The Industrial State; V-The Old Germany; VI-Building for Tomorrow and the Day After; VII-The World Metropolis.

SWABIA - A GERMAN COUNTRYSIDE. 16 mm. Color and sound. 37 minutes. By Ministry of Foreign Affairs of the Federal Republic of Germany. Distributed by Modern Talking Picture Service, Incorporated, Washington, D.C., 1960.

Swabia, situated between the Danube and the Alps, is full of testimonies of the past, such as well-preserved castles, churches and monasteries.

SWABIA'S GENTLE HILLS. 16 mm. Color and sound. 17 minutes. By Ministry of Foreign Affairs of the Federal Republic of Germany. Distributed by Modern Talking Picture Service, Incorporated, Washington, D.C., 1961.

Fortresses, castles, monasteries, and old cities that have retained their medieval character provide a strange contrast to the modern roads connecting them.

STREIFZUG DURCH DEN BEZIRK LEIPZIG (Excursion through the Leipzig Region). 16 mm. Color and sound. 20 minutes. By the Embassy of the German Democratic Republic, Washington, D. C.

Shows several towns in the vicinity of Leipzig.

34 YEARS AFTER HITLER. 16 mm. Color and sound. 19 minutes. Also issued as video recording. CBS News, Carousel Films, New York, 1979.

A report about the ways the Hitler legacy lives on in Germany and is supported through an American operation in Lincoln, Nebraska. Tells of neo-Nazi groups in Germany today that have been known to destroy Jewish cemeteries, paint swastikas on the street, and distribute anti-semitic propaganda.

TOURISTS IN HEIDELBERG. 16 mm. Color and sound. 5 minutes. By Bavarian Radio in cooperation with the Goethe Institute. Ministry of Foreign Affairs of the Federal Republic of Germany. Distributed by International Film Bureau, Chicago, 1973.

Delineates history and tourist attractions of Heidelberg, Germany's oldest university city.

TOYS FROM NUREMBERG. 16 mm. Color and sound. 5 minutes. By Bavarian Radio in cooperation with the Goethe Institute. Ministry of Foreign Affairs of the Federal Republic of Germany. Distributed by International Film Bureau, Chicago, 1973.

Shows Nuremberg as a toy-producing center where many operations are still carried out by hand.

TRIER, ROMAN IMPERIAL CITY. 16 mm. Color and sound. 5 minutes. By Bavarian Radio in cooperation with the Goethe Institute. Ministry of Foreign Affairs of the Federal Republic of Germany. Distributed by International Film Bureau, Chicago, 1973.

Explains the development of Trier under nearly 500 years of ancient Roman rule.

TWENTY YEARS - A REPORT ABOUT HAMBURG. 16 mm. Black and white with sound. 32 minutes. By Ministry of Foreign Affairs of the Federal Republic of Germany. Distributed by Modern Talking Picture Service, Incorporated, Washington, D.C., 1965.

Shows the reconstruction of Hamburg from 1945 to 1965.

WEST GERMANY BECOMES A DEMOCRACY: 1945. Super 8 mm. Black and white. 4 minutes. By Anargyros Film Library, 1974.

Traces the formation of a democratic German state from the ashes of a fascist empire.

THE WORK OF THE GOETHE INSTITUTE IN GERMANY. 16 mm. Color and sound. 5 minutes. By Bavarian Radio in cooperation with the Goethe Institute. Ministry of Foreign Affairs of the Federal Republic of Germany. Distributed by International Film Bureau, Chicago, 1973.

Describes the work of the Goethe Institute which aims at fostering appreciation of the German language and culture.

(For information concerning the borrowing of these and other films about Germany, and tapes, records, slide series, and German language feature films, write to the nearest Consulate General or the Embassy of the Federal Republic of Germany or the Embassy of the German Democratic Republic.)

FILMS ABOUT GERMAN AMERICANS

AMERICANS FROM GERMANY. 16 mm. Color and sound. 30 minutes. By the Ministry of Foreign Affairs of the Federal Republic of Germany. Distributed by Modern Talking Picture Service, Incorporated, Washington, D. C.

A German-made film in English about the life of German immigrants in the United States.

THE AMISH: A PEOPLE OF PRESERVATION. 16 mm. Color and sound. 52 minutes. By Heritage Productions, 1975.

Discusses various aspects of the Amish community, including its history, the world view beliefs of the Amish and the simplicity of their lifestyle. Shows various activities of the family.

CANDLE IN THE WILDERNESS. 16 mm. Color and sound. 26 minutes. By WBTV Creative Services, Charlotte, North Carolina, 1975.

Traces the history of Moravian settlers in the United States in the 1700's as presented in the diary of an 18th century Moravian woman named Anna Catharina Ernst.

DUTCH WONDERLAND. 16 mm. Color and sound. 27 minutes. By Berghman's & Roberts Productions. Modern Talking Picture Service, New York, 1976.

Depicts the simple life of the Amish farmers and the recreational and educational facilities within the Lancaster, Pennsylvania area which is the theme of the Dutch Wonderland amusement part at Lancaster, Pennsylvania.

HAND IN HAND. 16 mm. Color and sound. 16 minutes. Released by the Eastern Mennonite Board of Missions and Charities, 1978. By Burt Martin Associates, Incorporated, Salunga, Pennsylvania.

Presents interviews with missionaries and Mennonite church leaders from around the world. Filmed at the 1978 Mennonite World Conference.

MENNO'S REINS. 16 mm. Color and sound. 50 minutes. By Dueck Productions. Released by the Crosstown Credit Union of Winnepeg, 1975.

Takes a look at the heritage of the Mennonites.

A MORNING SONG. 16 mm. Color and sound. 23 minutes. By Burt Martin Associates, Incorporated, Salunga, Pennsylvania: The Board, 1978. Released by the Eastern Mennonite Board of Missions and Charities, 1978.

Focuses on a farmer and his family near Lancaster, Pennsylvania in order to portray life as a Mennonite, history and beliefs of the Mennonites, and problems caused by the changing world around them.

PENNSYLVANIA COUNTRY COOKING. 16 mm. Color and sound. 20 minutes. Made and released by American Gas Association and Gas Appliance Manufacturers Association, 1964.

Portrays the Pennsylvania Dutch heritage as evidenced in their cuisine and their customs. Includes scenes of decorated barns, the Kutztown Fair, the Farmers' Market at Lancaster, and famous Dutch dishes, such as shoofly pie and funnel cake. Demonstrates the features of modern gas ranges.

SEEING GOD AT CHRISTMAS. 16 mm. Color and sound. 18 minutes. By Family Films, 1974.

Shows a variety of Christmas customs as practiced in the Moravian community in Bethlehem, Pennsylvania.

GREEKS
(Includes CRETANS)

Embassy and Consulates

EMBASSY OF GREECE
2221 Massachusetts Avenue, Northwest
Washington, D.C. 20008 (202) 667-3168

Commercial Counselor's Office
2211 Massachusetts Avenue, Northwest
Washington, D.C. 20008 (202) 332-2844

Economic Minister's Office
211 Massachusetts Avenue, Northwest
Washington, D.C. 20008 (202) 234-5800

Press and Information Office
2211 Massachusetts Avenue, Northwest
Washington, D.C. 20008 (202) 234-5800

Press and Information Office
2211 Massachusetts Avenue, Northwest
Washington, D.C. 20008 (202) 332-2727

Office of the Defense Attache
2228 Massachusetts Avenue, Northwest
Washington, D.C. 20008 (202) 234-5695

Office of the Naval Attache
2228 Massachusetts Avenue, Northwest
Washington, D.C. 20008 (202) 332-8222

Office of the Air Attache
2228 Massachusetts Avenue, Northwest
Washington, D.C. 20008 (202) 234-0561

CONSULATES GENERAL

168 North Michigan Avenue
Chicago, Illinois 60601 (312) 372-5356

69 East 79th Street
New York, New York 10021 (212) 988-5500

2441 Gough Street
San Francisco, California 94123 (415) 775-2102

CONSULATES

Park Square Building
31 Saint James Avenue
Boston, Massachusetts 02116 (617) 542-3240

2318 International Trade Mart
New Orleans, Louisiana 70130 (504) 523-1167

2211 Massachusetts Avenue, Northwest
Washington, D.C. 20008 (202) 232-8222

Mission to the United Nations

GREEK MISSION
69 East 79th Street
New York, New York 10021 (212) 744-4062

Tourist and Travel Offices

GREEK TOURIST ORGANIZATION
Olympic Tower
645 Fifth Avenue
New York, New York 10022

168 North Michigan Avenue
Chicago, Illinois 60601 (312) 782-1084

611 West Sixth Street, Suite 1998
Los Angeles, California 90017 (213) 626-6696

OFFICE OF PRESS AND INFORMATION
2211 Massachusetts Avenue, Northwest
Washington, D.C. 20008 (202) 332-2727

601 Fifth Avenue
New York, New York 10017 (212) 751-8788

878 Market Street, Suite 849
San Francisco, California 94102 (415) 398-1513

Fraternal Organizations

ATHENIAN FEDERATION OF UNITED STATES OF AMERICA AND CANADA
Post Office Box 6052
Long Island City, New York 11105
Offices and Athenian Clubs
35-10 Broadway
Long Island City, New York 11105
President: George Hatjigiannis

ATHENIANS' SOCIETY
25-18 Broadway
Astoria, New York 11106
President: George Manos

CRETANS' ASSOCIATION OMONOIA
32-33 31st Street
Astoria, New York 11105 (212) 278-8098

CYPRUS FEDERATION OF AMERICA
23-15 31st Street
Astoria, New York 11105

DAUGHTERS OF EVRYTANIA
121 Greenwich Road
Charlotte, North Carolina 28211 (704) 366-6571
Secretary: Margaret Nixon Founded 1948

Women with an interest in the province of Evrytania, Greece, especially in helping the schools and hospitals of the area. Affiliated with the Evrytanian Association of America (ladies' auxiliary).

DAUGHTERS OF PENELOPE
1422 K Street, Northwest
Washington, D.C. 20005
National Secretary: Irene M. Wallingford (202) 737-7638 Founded 1929

Women's fraternal organization. Awards Helen Karagiannis Scholarship and other scholarships to girls of Greek descent. Participates in other philanthropic activities. Affiliated with the Order of Ahepa.

EVRYTANIAN ASSOCIATION OF AMERICA
121 Greenwich Road
Charlotte, North Carolina 28211 (704) 366-6571
Secretary: Sam B. Nikopoulous Founded 1944

Men and women coming to the United States from the Greek province of Evrytania. Provides medical and educational facilities to the people of Evrytania. Sponsors a scholarship program for students in Greece and in the United States. Affiliated with the Daughters of Evrytania; Youth of Evrytania.
Publications: Velouchi Bulletin, quarterly; Membership Book, biennial.

FEDERATION OF HELLENIC AMERICAN SOCIETIES OF GREATER NEW YORK
23-53 31st Street
Astoria, New York 11105
President: George Vrotsos (212) 932-4197

Federation of local clubs in metropolitan New York of persons of Greek birth or descent.

GREEK AMERICAN PROGRESSIVE ASSOCIATION
3600 Fifth Avenue
Pittsburgh, Pennsylvania 15213
Supreme Secretary: Stavros Kalaras (412) 621-4676 Founded 1923

Persons of Greek ancestry or birth.
Publication: Tribune of GAPA, quarterly.

GREEK CATHOLIC UNION OF THE U.S.A.
502 East Eighth Avenue
Munhall, Pennsylvania 15120
National President: George Batyko (412) 462-9800 Founded 1892

Fraternal benefit life insurance society.

MACEDONIAN PATRIOTIC ORGANIZATION OF U.S. AND CANADA
542 South Meridian Street (317) 635-2157
Indianapolis, Indiana 46225 Founded 1922

Americans and Canadians of Macedonian origin (mostly the Slav or Bulgarian element). Conducts cultural and social activities. Promotes the idea of political autonomy for Macedonia.
Publication: Makedonska Tribuna (Macedonian Tribune), weekly.

MAIDS OF ATHENS
c/o Daughters of Penelope
1422 K Street, Northwest
Washington, D.C. 20005
National Secretary: Irene M. Wallingford (202) 237-7638 Founded 1930

Junior auxiliary of the Daughters of Penelope; affiliated with Order of Ahepa (American Hellenic Education Progressive Association). Strives to build character, to guide and prepare young women to lead socially productive lives. Engages in numerous charitable and service activities.

NATIONAL DODECANESIAN COUNCIL OF AMERICA
1730 K Street, Northwest,
Suite 903
Washington, D.C. 20006
President: Mayor George Athanson

NAXOS SOCIETY
116 Pinehurst Avenue
New York, New York 10033
President: Zannis Marmarinos (212) 927-7968

Fraternal organization of Greek Americans who were born on the Island of Naxos or are descended from such persons.

ORDER OF AHEPA
1422 K Street, Northwest
Washington, D.C. 20005
Executive Director: Timothy J. Maniatis (202) 628-4974
Founded 1922

Fraternal organization primarily for persons of Greek birth or descent. United States citizenship (or declared intention to achieve citizenship) is required. Conducts charitable and social activities in the United States, Australia, and Canada. Makes some 500 scholarships available to worthy students each year. Contributes financial aid to the people of Greece through organizations and institutions, such as Greek War Relief; aids hospitals in Athens and Thessaloniki; American Books for Greece; and CARE. Maintains library of books and articles on early Americans of Greek descent and Greek history. Also known as the American Hellenic Educational Progressive Association. Affiliated with the Maids of Athens (junior girls); Sons of Pericles (young men); Daughters of Penelope (women).
Publication: The Ahepan, bi-monthly.

PANCRETAN ASSOCIATION OF AMERICA
2521 Acorn Lane
Ceres, California 95307 (209) 537-2789
President: Gus S. Pallios Founded 1929

Fraternal organization of Greek Americans born on the island of Crete or descended from persons born there. Sponsors visits to Crete; awards scholarships.
Publication: Crete, monthly.

PANDODECANESIAN ASSOCIATION OF AMERICA
"Xanthos O Philikos"
12201 Saint James Road
Potomac, Maryland 20854
President: Louis Hajimihalis (301) 588-4680

Fraternal Order of Greek Americans whose roots are in the Dodicanese Islands.

PANIACONIAN FEDERATION OF THE USA AND CANADA
8506 Montpellier Drive
Laurel, Maryland 20811
President: Mr. William Campas

PANICARIAN BROTHERHOOD "ICAROS"
2682 Fairview Place
Cuyahoga Falls, Ohio 44221
President: Peter Zizes (216) 929-0368

Fraternal brotherhood of Greek Americans whose origins are on the Island of Icaria.

PANLEMNIAN SOCIETY "HYFESTOS"
35-20 28th Street
Astoria, New York 11106
President: Nick Giannopoulos

Fraternal association of Greek Americans from the Island of Lemnos.

PANLESVIAN SOCIETY OF AMERICA
144 Bently Avenue
Jersey City, New Jersey 07304
President: John Argiris

Fraternal order of Greeks in America whose origins are on the Island of Lesbos.

PAN-MACEDONIAN ASSOCIATION
370 Seventh Avenue
New York, New York 10001
Supreme Secretary: Andrew Manthos (212) 279-2821
Founded 1947

United States and Canadian citizens and residents who emigrated from Macedonia, Greece, or descendants of such persons. Works to advance cultural and friendly relations between the American and Greek peoples; promote the social welfare, public hygiene, and educational advancement of the inhabitants of Macedonia; and collect and distribute information on the land and people of Macedonia by publications, lectures, and exhibitions. Maintains library and bestows awards. Publications: Macedonia (in Greek and English), bimonthly; Convention Journal, annual.

PAN-RHODIAN SOCIETY OF AMERICA APOLLON
401 South Garfield Street
Arlington, Virginia 22204 (703) 892-2424
Secretary: E. Athanas Founded 1926

An association of Greek Americans from Rhodes. Conducts educational and philanthropic activities. Publication: Rodos (in Greek), quarterly.

PANSAMIAN FEDERATION
Post Office Box 02290
Cleveland, Ohio 44102
President: Mr. Xenophon Papageorge

Fraternal order of Greek Americans whose origins are on the Island of Samos.

PANTHESSALIAN FEDERATION
2411 First Street
Fort Lee, New Jersey 07027
President: Theodore Diamantopoulos (201) 886-2835

PHALANX OF GREEK VETERANS OF AMERICA
824 West Chicago Avenue
Chicago, Illinois 60606
President: Harry Mitsakopoulos
Mailing address:
Mr. Anthony Roumanos
4923 North Nashville
Chicago, Illinois 06056

PIRAEUS BENEVOLENT SOCIETY
140 East 103rd Street
New York, New York 10029
President: Prokopios Macedon

PONTION SOCIETY "KOMNINOI"
31-25 23rd Avenue
Astoria, New York 11105
President: Savvas Konstantinidis

SAMOS SOCIETY "PYTHAGORAS"
23-53 31st Street
Astoria, New York 11105
President: George Vrotsos

SKOPELITON SOCIETY "AGIOS RIGINOS"
58 East 86th Street
New York, New York 10028
President: Rigas Lambrou-Feraios

SOCIETY OF KASTORIANS "OMONIA"
246 Eighth Avenue
New York, New York 10011
Executive Secretary: Andrew Manthos (212) 242-1930
Founded 1910

Persons born in Kastoria (a commune in Macedonia, northern Greece) or of Kastorian descent. Promotes Greek-American relations. Assists in bettering conditions in Kastoria. Maintains scholarship and hospitalization funds. Operates a clubhouse. Affiliated with the Pan-Macedonian Association.

SPARTA BROTHERHOOD
2907 West Gregory
Chicago, Illinois 60625
President: Peter Panagoulias (312) 275-9106

SPARTA FRATERNITY
70 Locustwood Boulevard
Elmont, New York 11003
President: Louis Nikolopoulos

UNITED CHIOS SOCIETY OF AMERICA
12850 Evergreen Road
Detroit, Michigan 48223
President: John Madias

UNITED CYPRIANS OF AMERICA
28-16 Astoria Boulevard
Astoria, New York 11102
President: Socrates Katsiamidis

UNITED HELLENIC AMERICAN CONGRESS
112 South Michigan Avenue, Room 514
Chicago, Illinois 60603
Chairman: Andrew Athens

UNITED SOCIETIES OF THE UNITED STATES OF AMERICA
613 Sinclair Street
McKeesport, Pennsylvania 15132
National Secretary: Rev. William G. Levkulic (412) 672-3196
Founded 1903

Fraternal benefit life insurance society.

Formerly: United Societies of Greek Catholic Religion of United States.
Publication: Enlightenment, monthly.

Professional Organizations

HELLENIC BAR ASSOCIATION
c/o Assistant General Counsel
Montgomery Ward
Montgomery Ward Plaza
Chicago, Illinois 60071
President: Chris Michas

HELLENIC MEDICAL SOCIETY
30-02 30th Drive
Astoria, New York 11102
President: Dr. George Kokotakis

HELLENIC PROFESSIONAL SOCIETY OF ILLINOIS
35 Cour Deauville
Palos Hills, Illinois 60465
President: Anastasia Usher

HELLENIC TECHNOLOGICAL SOCIETY
5121 West Addison
Chicago, Illinois 60634
President: Panayiotes G. Danos

NATIONAL FORUM OF GREEK ORTHODOX CHURCH MUSICIANS
4030 South Hudson Way
Englewood, Colorado 80110
National Chairman: George T. Demos, M.D. Founded 1976

To advance and perpetuate the musical heritage of the Greek Orthodox Church in the Americas. Bestows awards; sponsors competitions; compiles statistics.
Publications: Liturgical Guidebook, annual.

PANHELLENIC SEAMENS ASSOCIATION
11 Broadway, Suite 1563
New York, New York 10004
President: Spyros Varras

PAN HELLENIC SOCIETY INVENTORS OF GREECE IN U.S.A.
2053 Narwood Avenue
South Merrick, New York 11566 (516) 223-5958
Executive Director: Dr. Kimon M. Louvaris Founded 1969

Inventors of Greek-American descent whose inventions are patented in both the United States and Greece; individuals with patents pending in the United States, South America, or in Athens, Greece. To assist the Greek-American individual with the patenting, protection, and marketing of his/her invention; to promote the marketing of inventions which contribute to health. In Athens, maintains data bank concerning inventions from the era of Plato, Archimedes, Aristotle and Socrates also maintains biographical archives and museum. Conducts triennial seminars in Athens.
Publications: Newsletter, monthly; also publishes Inventors Greek-English Guide and technical books.

Public Affairs Organizations

AMERICAN COMMITTEE FOR DEMOCRACY AND FREEDOM IN GREECE
303 West 42nd Street
New York, New York 10018 (212) 247-4397
Secretary: Nicholas D. Noulas Founded 1967

A non-partisan organization of individuals opposed to the military junta which took control of Greece in April, 1967. Its objective was to keep the problem before the American public and the political parties in the United States. The Committee has been inactive since the restoration of democracy in Greece in July, 1974.

AMERICAN HELLENIC CONGRESS
c/o Peter Chumbris
4200 Cathedral Avenue, Northwest
Washington, D.C. 20016 (202) 363-7607
Secretary: Peter N. Chumbris Founded 1960

Federation of national Hellenic organizations in the United States. Acts as a representative voice for Americans of Greek descent. Appears before Congressional and other legislative committees on issues affecting the American Hellenic family. Seeks to preserve the democratic tradition through public service, philanthropy, and civic responsibility. Compiles and distributes statistical information of national interest.

PAN AMERICAN COUNCIL FOR THE PRESERVATION OF THE HELLENIC ORTHODOX CHURCH AND THE HELLENIC LANGUAGE
Post Office Box 65
Oak Park, Illinois 60303 (312) 725-1960
General Secretary: N. Eliopoulos Founded 1970

Members of the Greek Orthodox Church. Purpose is to "accuse Iakovos, alias Demetrios Koukouzes, Archbishop of America North and South, of apostasy and heresy, of transgression against the Holy Writ and the Holy Cannons, of the denial of the 'Symbol of Faith' (also known as the Nicene Creed), of the deliberate denial of God the Trinity, that is to say, of the denial of the Revealed Word of God." Asks that "Iakovos Koukouzes be summoned to answer the cited accusations and that examiners be appointed in order to verify the accusations and that Iakovos Koukouzes be brought to trial before the appropriate ecclesiastical court." Has written letters to this effect to officials of all the Orthodox Christian Churches and has published a letter in the New York Times. Also seeks to keep in use the original Hellenic language of the Gospels. Bestows awards; compiles statistics; sponsors speakers bureau and research programs.
Publication: pamphlet, monthly.

Cultural and Educational Organizations

AMERICAN SOCIETY FOR NEO-HELLENIC STUDIES
Rural Delivery I, Box 107, Clay Road
Ulster Park, New York 12487
Executive Vice President: (914) 331-2154
Constantine N. Tsirpanlis Founded 1967

Professors, authors, students, and intellectuals. Seeks to promote knowledge and scholarly research concerning modern Greek language, literature, history, theology, philosophy, art, science, and folklore. Sponsors a monthly lecture on modern Greek immigrants to the United States.
Publication: Newsletter, quarterly.

CENTER FOR NEO-HELLENIC STUDIES
1010 West 22nd Street
Austin, Texas 78705 (512) 477-5526
Director: George G. Arnakis Founded 1965

Scholars and authors actively engaged in research and writing on various aspects of modern Greek history and culture. Promotes interest in Greek language, literature, history, theology, philosophy, art, history of art, folklore, and social and economic studies from the year 1204 A.D. to the twentieth century. Presents the Archbishop Iakovos Prize for Greek-American Studies, the Max Manus Award for Greek literature in the United States, and the Arthur Sockler Prize for Byzantine and Modern Greek Studies. Maintains the GraecoAmerican Collection, books and periodicals in Greek published in the United States and Canada.
Publications: Bulletin, annual; Neo-Hellenika (journal), annual; is preparing to publish two series; Americans in the Greek Revolution (1821-1830) and American Interest in the Cretan Struggle 1866-1869, as well as other literary studies.

HELLENIC PHILATELIC SOCIETY OF AMERICA
262 Central Park, West
New York, New York 10024
Secretary Treasury: Maurice R. Friend, M.D. (212) 362-7541
Founded 1942

Collectors interested in philatelic knowledge of classic Hermes heads, modern Greek stamps, covers, postal history of Greece and material of related countries. Acts as a clearinghouse on Hellenic philately. Participates in stamp exhibitions.
Publications: News Bulletin, bimonthly; Membership List, annual.

MODERN GREEK STUDIES ASSOCIATION
Post Office Box 337, Harvard Square Branch
Cambridge, Massachusetts 02138 (617) 876-8230
President: Edmund Keeley Founded 1968

Scholars and students of Modern Greek studies; friends of Greece; institutions and libraries. Aim is to foster and advance Modern Greek studies, assist in the establishment of chairs and departments of Modern Greek studies and serve as a center for dissemination of literature in the field and information about professional opportunities. Organizes symposia; maintains biographical archives and speakers bureau. Conducts research programs; compiles statistics. Maintains library of books and archival material on modern greek literature, history and culture.
Publications: (1) Bulletin, semiannual; (2) Byzantine and Modern Greek Studies, annual; also publishes Proceedings of Symposia.

SOCIETY FOR ANCIENT GREEK PHILOSOPHY
c/o John P. Anton
Department of Philosophy
Emory University
Atlanta, Georgia 30322
Secretary-Treasurer: John P. Anton (404) 329-4316
Founded 1953

Persons, mostly from universities, interested in ancient philosophy. Promotes closer coordination between philosophers and classical scholars. Has published book, "Essays in Ancient Greek Philosophy".

U. S. NATIONAL COMMITTEE FOR BYZANTINE STUDIES
c/o Alice-Mary M. Talbot
2995 Coleridge Road
Cleveland Heights, Ohio 44118 (216) 321-0527
Chairman: Alice-Mary Talbot Founded 1962

Members of the academic profession, institutions of higher learning, research institutions and museums who devote half or more of their professional activity to the study of and writing on, Byzantine history, art history, literature, theology and other disciplines constituting Byzantinology. Works for exchange of information between members and through affiliation with Association Internationale des Etudes Byzantines in Athens, Greece. Publishes ad hoc circulars.

Foundations

DEMOS FOUNDATION, INCORPORATED
c/o The Northern Trust Company
50 South La Salle Street
Chicago, Illinois 60690
Donor: Nicholas Demos
President: William H. McNeill Incorporated 1964

Bestows grants primarily for education and child welfare in Greece.

NORTHEAST ORTHODOX FOUNDATION
2120 Pacific Building
Third Avenue and Columbia
Seattle, Washington 98104
Executive Director: Rev. E. Anthony Tomaras (206) 272-0466

Especially concerned with projects related to the Greek Orthodox Church. Sponsors the Patriarch Athenagoras Retreat Center in Wyoming.

RAPTELIS FOUNDATION
c/o The First National Bank of Boston
100 Federal Street
Boston, Massachusetts 02110
Donor: Demosthenis Raptelis Founded 1972

Provides scholarship assistance for students from the island of Lesbos, Greece, and aids charitable organizations on the island.

SAINT NICHOLAS BROTHERHOOD FOUNDATION
7819 North Willow
Cloris, California 93612
Director: Rev. John Bakas (209) 298-8678

Sponsors the Saint Nicholas Ranch and Retreat Center near Fresno, California.

Charitable Organizations

GREEK-AMERICAN COUNSELOR CENTER OF GREECE IN U.S.A.
2053 Narwood Avenue
Merrick, New York 11566
Executive Director: Kimon M. Louvaris, M.D. (516) 223-5958
Founded 1972

Greek-American counseling and therapy centers. Purpose is to assist Greek-Americans to attain and/or maintain mental health. Aids individuals who have difficulty speaking and understanding English during the process of absorption into their new society. Works mainly with severely ill individuals. Seeks to relieve depression and alleviate self-destructive actions. Operates an emergency hot-line telephone therapy service for marital, personal and sexual difficulties. Conducts research and educational programs for newcomers. Maintains charitable program. Formerly known as Greek-American Psychological Center of Greece in U.S.A.

GREEK ORTHODOX LADIES PHILOPTOCHOS SOCIETY
Eight East 79th Street
New York, New York 10021 (212) 570-3500
Executive President: His Eminence Archbishop Iakoros Ext. 524
Founded 1894

A philanthropic organization which engages in helping immigrants and the poor as well as in educational concerns. Was instrumental in founding the Holy Cross Seminary in Pomfret, Connecticut and Saint Basil's Academy in Garrison, New York, a children's home and school.

UNITED GREEK ORTHODOX CHARITIES
60 East 42nd Street, Suite 453
New York, New York 10017 (212) 661-4565
Director: Mrs. Kakia Livanos Founded 1966

Holds an annual national fund solicitation drive and local fund-earning events. Provides philanthropic support to educational institutions, cultural activities, youth programs, and health and welfare activities. Affiliated with the Greek Orthodox Archdiocese of North and South America.

Religious Organizations

AMG International
6815 Shallowford Road
Chattanooga, Tennessee 34421 (615) 894-6062
President: Spiros Zodhiates Founded 1942

An interdenominational faith mission, world-wide in scope, but working particularly in Greece. Seeks to spread the Gospel to the Greeks around the world. Engages in a program of relief in instituting and supporting orphanages, schools, hospitals, and food and clothing centers for Greeks and others. Provides relief for individuals and families. Maintains a library of about 20,000 theological volumes. AMG also stands for Advancing the Message of the Gospel worldwide through newspaper evangelism, relief ministries, children's services and ministries to local churches. Formerly known as American Mission to Greeks.
Publications: News, monthly; Voice of the Gospel (in Greek), monthly; Pulpit Helps (newspaper), monthly.

BYZANTINE FELLOWSHIP
Third and Bedford Streets
Stamford, Connecticut 06905
Executive Officer: George Poulos (203) 348-2108
Founded 1958

Sponsored by the Greek Archdiocese of North and South America, headquartered in New York City, primarily for persons of Greek Orthodox faith. Conducts educational, travel, and service activities. Organizes pilgrimages to Greece and the Patriarchate at Istanbul, Turkey.

GREEK ORTHODOX ARCHDIOCESE OF NORTH AND SOUTH AMERICA
8-10 East 79th Street
New York, New York 10021
President: His Eminence Archbishop Iakovos (212) 570-3500
Founded 1864

This religious body is under the jurisdiction of the Ecumenical Patriarchate of Constantinople in Istanbul. It has parishes in the United States, Canada, Central and South America.
Publication: The Orthodox Observer, bimonthly.

GREEK ORTHODOX LADIES PHILOPTOCHOS SOCIETY
Eight East 79th Street
New York, New York 10021
National Director: Stella Coumantaros (212) 744-4390
Founded 1931

Women 18 years or older of the Greek Orthodox faith. Aim is to preserve the sacredness of the Orthodox family, perpetuate and promote the charitable and philanthropic purposes of the Greek Orthodox Archdiocese of North and South America. (The word "Philoptochos" is derived from "philo" meaning friend, and "ptochos" meaning poor; hence, "friend of the poor.") Seeks to aid the poor, destitute, aged, sick, unemployed, handicapped and to undertake the burial of impoverished persons. Supports educational institutions and offers scholarships and awards to needy and meritorious students of Greek birth or descent, or those of the Greek Orthodox faith. Encourages wider religious activity and participation in the communal aspects of the church, especially among young people. Conducts seminars.

GREEK ORTHODOX YOUTH OF AMERICA
Ten East 79th Street
New York, New York 10021
Director: Rev. Constantine L. Sitaras (212) 628-2500
Founded 1951

Greek Orthodox youth throughout the Americas. Conducts leadership and religious education workshops, athletic tournaments, summer camps, and other activities to assist the church program locally and nationally. Produces and distributes religious films. Maintains a Trading Post for religious medals and icons.
Publications: Challenge, monthly; Young Adult League Manual, annual; also publishes brochures, educational series and produces films.

ORDER OF SAINT ANDREW THE APOSTLE
Eight East 79th Street
New York, New York 10021
National Commander: Dr. Anthony G. Borden (212) 570-3500
Founded 1966

Greek Orthodox laymen who have been honored by the Ecumenical Patriarchate of Constantinople with Byzantine titles and offices of church and state. Objectives are: to support the Ecumenical Patriarchate of Constantinople and its philanthropic institutions; to assist the Ecumenical Patriarchate in furthering the ecumenical leadership of the mother church of Constantinople; and to uphold and defend the historical status of the Ecumenical

Patriarchate. Contributes to the support and maintenance of philanthropic and educational institutions in the United States. Bestows titles annually. Sponsors charities for Greek Orthodox people in Istanbul and children's home and camp. Has produced album "Archon" of members' biographies.
Publications: The Archon (newsletter), quarterly; Banquet Addresses, annual; Greek Orthodox Archdiocese Yearbook; also publishes pamphlets. Formerly known as (1980) Knights of Saint Andrew.

Research Centers and Special Institutes

CENTER FOR BYZANTINE AND MODERN GREEK STUDIES
153-06 61st Road
Queens College
Flushing, New York 11367 (212) 520-7035
Director: Harry Psomiades Founded 1974

Research is carried out in modern Greek language, literature, history, economics and culture, Byzantine art, and the Greek American community in the United States. Offers a minor in Modern Greek Studies. Research results are published in professional journals.

CENTER FOR HELLENIC STUDIES
3100 Whitehaven Street
Washington, D.C. 20008
Director: Dr. Bernard M. W. Knox (202) 234-3738
Founded 1962

International research center administered by Trustees for Harvard University. Supported by income from endowment. Research performed by 8 resident postdoctoral research fellows in ancient Greek literature, philosophy and history. Maintains a library of 30,000 volumes on ancient Greek literature, history and philosophy; Dr. Jeno Platthey, librarian.

CENTER FOR NEO-HELLENIC STUDIES
1010 West 22nd Street
Austin, Texas 78705 (512) 477-5526
Acting Director: E. G. Arnakis Founded 1965

Indpendent nonprofit research organization located at University of Texas but with its own board of trustees. Supported by patrons, benefactors and trustees.

Principal fields of research are in Greek history and culture from thirteenth to twentieth century, including studies in modern Greek literature and translation of literary works, also publication of old travel books and writings of Americans who took part in Greek War of Independence. Awards annual prizes for modern Greek literature in the United States and studies on modern Greece and the Greek-American community.
Publications: Bulletin; Neo-Hellenika.
Research results also published in professional journals and monographs.

HELLENIC COLLEGE AND HOLY CROSS GREEK ORTHODOX SCHOOL OF THEOLOGY
50 Goddard Avenue
Brookline, Massachusetts 02146 (617) 731-3500
President: Dr. Thomas C. Lelon Founded 1937

Hellenic College provides a four-year program in the liberal arts with fields of concentration in Pre-Theology, Greek Studies, Business Management, Human Development Teacher Education, and Communication. All programs emphasize Orthodox Christian faith and the Greek cultural heritage. Holy Cross is the graduate school of Hellenic College and offers Masters Degrees in Divinity, Theological Studies or Church Service (for lay persons).

SOCIAL STUDIES MATERIALS DEVELOPMENT CENTER FOR GREEK-SPEAKING STUDENTS
302 Education Building
Tallahassee, Florida 32306
Director: Byron G. Massialas (904) 644-5038

Pursues projects designed for the development of instructional materials for elementary and secondary schools. Deals with Greek Americans and their contribution to the American society in three areas: social, cultural, and political. The purpose of the project is to provide teachers with a variety of materials for teaching ethnic studies. Produces bilingual social studies materials for grades 1-6.

Museums

SAINT PHOTOS NATIONAL SHRINE
41 Saint George Street
Post Office Drawer AF
Saint Augustine, Florida 32084-0924
Executive Director: James G. Couchell (904) 829-8205
Dedicated 1982

The first Greeks to arrive in the New World established the colony of New Smyrna in 1768, eighty miles south of Saint Augustine. Survivors of this colony made their way north to Saint Augustine in 1777. One of the buildings used by these early settlers still stands in Saint Augustine and has been restored to commemorate these early Greek Americans. There are exhibit areas, audio-visual facilities and a chapel.

Special Libraries and Subject Collections

CENTER FOR HELLENIC STUDIES LIBRARY
Harvard University
3100 Whitehaven Street, Northwest
Washington, D.C. 20008
Librarian: Jeno Platthy (617) 234-3738

Subjects: Greek history and civilization. Holdings: Books; journals and other serials; and pamphlets. Services: Interlibrary loans; library is open to qualified scholars.

COTSIDAS-TONNA LIBRARY
Hellenic College and Holy Cross Greek Orthodox School of Theology
50 Goddard Avenue
Brookline, Massachusetts 02146
Acting Director of Libraries: Diane Paterakis (617) 731-3500
Founded 1954

Subjects: Modern Greek literature; Greek Orthodox theology; Byzantine history and culture; patristic literature; Orthodox liturgics; Byzantine music. Holdings: Books; newspapers, journals and other serials. Services: Interlibrary loans; library is open to public for reference use only.

JOHN MILLER BURNAM CLASSICAL LIBRARY
University of Cincinnati
671 Blegen
Cincinnati, Ohio 45221
Classics Librarian: Jean Susorney Wellington (513) 475-6724
Founded 1900

Subjects: Classical and bronze age archaeology; Greek and Latin languages and literatures; Greek and Latin paleography and epigraphy; Byzantine and modern Greece; modern Greek language and literature; ancient history and epigraphy. Special Collections: Paleography Collection; Modern Greek Collection. Holdings: Books; journals and other serials; foreign dissertations. Services: Interlibrary loans; copying; library is open to outside users for reference only.

Newspapers and Newsletters

ARCHON. 1977-. Quarterly. Editor: Rev. Dr. Miltiades B. Efthimiou. Publisher: Order of Saint Andrew the Apostle, Eight East 79th Street, New York, New York 10021. In English.

Newsletters of the order.

BYZANTIUM. Quarterly. Publisher: Byzantine Fellowship, Third and Bedford Streets, Stamford, Connecticut 06904. In English.

CAMBANA. Semimonthly. Editor and publisher: Costas Athansasiades, 600 West 188th Street, New York, New York 10040.

Prints news from Greece and about Greeks abroad as well as community events.

CHALLENGE. 1967-. Monthly. Editor: P.J. Gazouleas. Publisher: Greek Orthodox Youth of America, Ten East 79th Street, New York, New York 10021. In English.

THE CHICAGO PNYX. 1939-. Semimonthly. Editor: Peter N. Mantzoros. Publisher: PNYX Publishing Company, 301 Spruce Street, Post Office Box 67, Glenview, Illinois 60025. In English.

Covers national and local news and news about the Order of Ahepa. Also provides informative materials on Greece.

DAWN. 1976-. Publisher: Diocese of the South/OCA, 1180 Northwest 99th Street, Miami, Florida 33150. In English.

A diocesan newsletter.

ELLENIKOS-ASTER (The Greek Star). 1904-. Weekly. Editor: Andrew Fasseas. Publisher: Greek Star Publishing Company, 4731 North Western Avenue, Chicago, Illinois 60625. In English and Greek.

Publishes general news of interest to the Greek-American community.

ELLENIKOS TYPOS (The Greek Press). 1903-. Weekly. Editor: Aris Angelopoulos. Publisher: The Greek Star-Press Publishing Company, 168 North Michigan Avenue, Chicago, Illinois 60601. In Greek and English.

Provides political, social, cultural, and educational news concerning the Greek community, including news from Greece.

ELLINIKOS KOSMOS (Greek World). Editor and Publisher: Panos Kokkinos, 28-35 35th Street, Long Island City, New York 11103. In Greek.

G.O.Y.A. BULLETIN. Bimonthly. Editor: Mrs. Priscilla Carcales. Publisher: Greek Orthodox Youth of America, 8 East 79th Street, New York, New York 10021. In English.

THE HELLENIC CHRONICLE. 1950-. Weekly. Editor: Peter Agris. Publisher: Hellenic Publishing Corporation, 324 Newbury Street, Boston, Massachusetts 02115. In English.

Publishes international, national, and local news of concern to Greek Americans.

HELLENIC JOURNAL. 1975-. Biweekly. Editor and publisher: Frank P. Agnost, 527 Commercial Street, San Francisco, California 94111. In English and Greek.

Provides international, national, and local news coverage of interest to Greek Americans. Formerly called Western Hellenic Journal.

HELLENIC TIMES. Weekly. Editor: Harry Stathos, 229 Eighth Avenue, New York, New York 10001. In English.

HELLENIC TRIBUNE NEWS. 1981. Biweekly. Editor: Nick Therapos. Publisher: Hellenic Tribune News, 3107 West Irving Park Road, Chicago, Illinois 60618. In Green and English.

Publishes international and national news concerning Greeks and also provides local coverage of the Greek American community.

HELLENIC VOICE. Biweekly. Editor and Publisher: Mike Zapiti, 22-74 31st Street, Astoria, New York 11105

KATHEMERINA NEA (Sunday News). Daily. Editor: Stavros Marmarinos. Publisher: Jessy Stellas, 22-55 31st Street, Long Island City, New York 11105. In Greek.

KYPIA KATIKA NEA (Greek Sunday News). 1944-. Weekly. Editor and Publisher: William A. Harris, 231 Harrison Avenue, Boston, Massachusetts 02111. In Greek and English.

LEADER. 1907-. Weekly. Editor and Publisher: Frank E. Nixon, 11 East Orange Street, Tarpon Springs, Florida 33589. In Greek and English.

LIGHT OF LIFE. 1982-. Publisher: Diocese of the West, Post Office Box 28291, San Diego, California 92128.

A diocesan newsletter.

MAKEDONIA (Macedonia). 1953-. Bimonthly. Editor: Andrew Manthos. Publisher: Pan-Macedonian Association, 370 Seventh Avenue, Room 216, New York, New York 10001. In Greek and English.

Covers national and local Greek news especially on the land and people of Macedonia.

NATIONAL HERALD (Ethnikos Kerix). 1915-. Daily. Editor: Anthony Diamataris. Publisher: National Herald, Incorporated, 257 Park Avenue, New York, New York 10010. In Greek and English.

Publishes international, national, and local news with a special English section in the Sunday edition.

NATIONAL TRIBUNE. Weekly. Editor: Alexander N. Damianakos, 1472 Broadway, New York, New York 10036

NEA KALIFORNIA (New California). 1910-. Weekly. Editor and Publisher: Ted Kaplanis, 600 - 18th Avenue, San Francisco, California 94121. In Greek and English.

Carries general, national, and local news, mainly in Greek.

NEWSLETTER - DIOCESE OF NEW YORK AND NEW JERSEY. 1980-. Editor: Very Reverend Dimitri Oselinsky, 29 Huron Avenue, Clifton, New Jersey 07013.

A church publication.

OLOGOS (The Logos). 1950-. Bimonthly. Editor: Reverend G. Mastrantonis. Publisher: Orthodox Lore of the Gospel of Our Saviour, Post Office Box 5333, Saint Louis, Missouri 63115. In English.

OMOGENIA EPIKERA (Greek American News). Publisher: Greek American News, 21-34 Broadway, Astoria, New York 11106. In Greek.

Concentrates especially on local news of interest to Greek Americans.

ONE - Orthodox New England. 1981. Publisher: Orthodox New England, 305 Washington Street, New Britain, Connecticut 06051.

A church publication also available to persons outside the diocese.

THE ORTHODOX CHURCH. Monthly. Editor: Very Rev. John Meyendorf. Publisher: Metropolitan Council of the Orthodox Church in America, Post Office Box 675, Route 25-A, Syosset, New York 11791. In English.

Reports on the various branches of Orthodoxy in America and their activities throughout the world.

ORTHODOX OBSERVER. 1934-. Biweekly. Editor: P. J. Gazouleas. Publisher: Greek Orthodox Archdiocese Press, 8 East 79th Street, New York, New York 10021. Sponsor: Greek Orthodox Archdiocese of North and South America. In English and Greek.

Presents Greek Orthodox Church news and religious articles.

PANARKADIKI ECHO. Editor: John Athanasopoulos, 9901 South 87th Avenue, Palos Hills, Illinois 60465. In Greek and English.

Publication of the association.

PAN-EPIROTIKOS AGON. Editor: Menelaus Tselios, 25-14 Broadway, Long Island City, New York 11106.

The official publication of the association.

PHOS (The Light). 1970-. Monthly. Editor and Publisher: Eftihios Papagregorakis, 26-80 30th Street, Astoria, New York 11102. In Greek.

PROINI. Daily. Editors: George Licomitros (Greek) and Doris Tsiantar (English). Publisher: Fani Petalidou, 911 East 37th Street (Ninth Floor), New York, New York 10016. In Greek and English.

ROUMELI PRESS. 1964-. Monthly. Editor: Efthimios Thomopoulos, 34-37 33rd Street, Long Island City, New York 11106. In Greek and English.

THE VIGIL. 1981. Bimonthly. Publisher: Diocesan Council of the Diocese of the Midwest, Diocesan Center, 8200 South County Line Road, Hinsdale, Illinois 60521. In English and Greek.

Newsletter for the diocese.

THE VOICE (I PHONI). Biweekly. Editor and Publisher: Harry P. Papouras, 5512 Memphis Avenue, Cleveland, Ohio 44144. In English and Greek.

Magazines

THE AHEPA MESSENGER. 1931-. Monthly. Editor: Angelos G. Chaoush. Publisher: Metropolitan Chapter of Ahepa, 409 West 44th Street, New York, New York 10017. In English.

A fraternal publication issued by the American Hellenic Educational Progressive Association.

AHEPAN. 1927-. Quarterly. Editor: Elias Vlanton. Publisher: The Order of Ahepa, 1422 K Street, Northwest, Washington, D.C. 20005. In English.

A fraternal publication.

ENLIGHTENMENT. Monthly. Publisher: United Societies of the United States of America, 613 Sinclair Street, McKeesport, Pennsylvania 15132.

A fraternal publication.

GLEANINGS. Irregular. Publisher: New Skete Monastery, Cambridge, New York 12816.

Contains stories about the monastic community, poetry, photographs, accounts of journeys to Orthodox lands.

GREECE. Quarterly. Publisher: Greek Press and Information Service, 2211 Massachusetts Avenue, Northwest, Washington, D.C. 20008. In English.

A quarterly presenting articles on international issues and developments in Greece.

GREEK ACCENT. 1979. Monthly. Editor: Anthony Diamataris. Publisher: National Herald Incorporated, 257 Park Avenue, New York, New York 10010.

Prints articles about places and traditions in Greece, sports, food, politics and also about Greek American communities.

THE GREEK ORTHODOX THEOLOGICAL REVIEW. 1954. Biennial. Editor: Fr. N. M. Vaporis. Publisher: Holy Cross Greek Orthodox Theological School, Hellenic College, 50 Goddard Avenue, Brookline, Massachusetts 02146. In English.

Presents scholarly articles and reviews in the fields of Biblical studies, church history, orthodox theology, and related subjects.

HELLENIC CALENDAR. Editor: Steven Dean Pastis, Post Office Box 50, South Pasadena, California 91030. In English.

Provides coverage of the regional Greek American community and its activities.

ILLUMINATOR. Editor and Publisher: Niki Stephanopoulos, 31500 Fairview Avenue, Chagrin Falls, Ohio.

A religious publication.

JOURNAL OF THE HELLENIC DIASPORA. 1973-. Quarterly. Publisher: Hellenic American Society, Pella Publishing Company, 461 Eighth Avenue, New York, New York 10001.

Articles are concerned with political, historical and cultural matters.

KRITI (Crete). 1928-. Monthly. Editor: George H. Terezakis. Publisher: Pancretan Association of America, 263 West 30th Street, New York, New York 10001 or 30-43 36th Street, Astoria, New York 11103. In Greek and English.

NEO HELLENIKA. Annual. Editor: George G. Arnakis. Publisher: Center for Neo-Hellinic Studies, 1010 West 22nd Street, Austin, Texas 78705.

Publishes articles concerned with modern-day Greek culture and history.

NEW YORK. 1957-. Monthly. Editor and Publisher: Peter Makrias, Post Office Box 675, Grand Central Station, New York, New York 10163. In English and Greek.

Publishes articles about events and activities of the Greek community in the New York area.

ORTHODOX EDUCATOR MAGAZINE. 1981-. Three times a year. Circulation Manager: Arlene Kallaur, 88 Jean Avenue, Hempstead, New York 11550. Publisher: Orthodox Church of America, Department of Religious Education, New York, New York.

For lay people as well as clergy and church school teachers. Contains articles on Christian parenting, movie and book reviews, and Bible study suggestions.

ORTHODOX PEOPLE. 1981-. Quarterly. Publisher: Orthodox Christian Writers' Guild of North America, 71 Manville Hill Road, Cumberland, Rhode Island.

Pan-Orthodox views of cultural and social issues

are represented in this magazine.

PILGRIMAGE. 1975-. Monthly magazine for Greeks everywhere. Editor: John Daskalakis. Publisher: Daskalakis Publishing, 1112 East Elm Street, Wheaton, Illinois 60187. In Greek and English.

RODOS. 1930-. Quarterly. Editor: E. Athanas, 401 Garfield Street, Arlington, Virginia 22204. In Greek.

Magazine sponsored by the Panrhodian Society which publishes articles on Greek Orthodoxy and the special traditions of Rhodes.

THE SAINT GEORGE HERALD. Monthly. Publisher: Greek Orthodox Church of Saint George, 7701 Bradley Boulevard, Bethesda, Maryland 20034. In English.

Contains religious articles and church news.

THE TRIBUNE OF G.A.P.A. Five times a year. Publisher: Greek-American Progressive Association, 32 Oregon Trail, Bethel Park, Pennsylvania 15102. In Greek and English.

This is a fraternal publication.

VELOUCHI BULLETIN. Quarterly. Editor: Sam B. Nikopoulos, 121 Greenwich Road, Charlotte, North Carolina 28211.

Official publication of the Evrytanian Association.

THE VOICE OF THE GOSPEL (I Fone Tou Evangeliou). 1941-. Monthly. Editor: Spiros Zodhiates. Publisher: American Mission to Greeks, 801 Broad Avenue, Ridgefield, New Jersey 07657. In Greek.

A monthly exposition featuring religious articles, sermons, and missionary news.

Radio Programs

Arizona - Phoenix

KXEG - 719 North Third Street, Phoenix, Arizona 85004, (602) 254-5001. Greek programs, 1-1/2 hours weekly.

Arkansas - Hot Springs

KGUS-FM - Box 1089, 208-1/2 Broadway, Hot Springs, Arkansas 71901, (501) 624-5425. Greek programs, 1 hour weekly.

California - Los Altos

KFJC-FM - 12345 El Monte Road, Los Altos Hills, Los Altos, California 94022, (415) 948-8590 ext. 260. Greek programs, 2 hours weekly.

California - Los Gatos

KRVE-FM - 227 North Santa Cruz Avenue, Los Gatos, California 95030, (408) 354-6622. Greek Programs, 1 hour weekly.

California - Pasadena

KPCC-FM - 1570 East Colorado, Pasadena, California 91106, (213) 578-7231. Greek Programs, 2 hours weekly.

California - Santa Cruz

KUSP-FM - Box 423, Santa Cruz, California 95061, (408) 476-2800. Greek Programs, 2 hours weekly.

California - Stockton

KSJC-FM - 5151 Pacific Avenue, Stockton, California 95207, (209) 951-6023. Greek Programs, 1/2 hour weekly.

Connecticut - New Britain

WRYM - 1056 Willard Avenue, Newington, Connecticut 06111, (203) 666-5646. Greek Programs, 1 hour weekly.

Florida - Dunedin

WWQT - 2633 Enterprise Road, Dunedin, Florida 33515, (813) 796-9495. Greek Programs, 3 hours weekly.

Georgia - Atlanta

100 Colony Square, Suite 421, Atlanta, Georgia

30361, (404) 892-1190. Greek programs, 1 hour weekly.

Illinois - Chicago

WCRW - 2756 Pine Grove Avenue, Chicago, Illinois 60614, (312) 327-6860. Greek and Spanish format.

WEDC - 5475 North Milwaukee Avenue, Chicago, Illinois 60630, (312) 631-0700. Greek programs, 1 hour weekly.

Illinois - Cicero

WCEV - 5356 West Belmont Avenue, Cicero, Illinois 60641, (312) 282-6700. Greek programs, 1 hour weekly.

Illinois - East Saint Louis

WMRY-FM - Route 15, Belleville, Illinois 62223, (618) 397-6700. Greek programs, 1 hour weekly.

Indiana - Hammond

WJOB - 6405 Olcott, Hammond, Indiana 46320, (219) 844-1230. Greek programs, 1 hour weekly.

Maryland - Baltimore

WBMD - 5200 Moravia Road, Baltimore, Maryland 21206, (301) 485-2400. Greek programs, 2 hours weekly.

Maryland - Laurel

WLMD - Box 42, Laurel, Maryland 20810, (301) 953-2332. Greek programs, 2 hours weekly.

Massachusetts - Brookline

WUNR - 275 Tremont Street, Boston, Massachusetts 02116, (617) 357-8677. Greek programs, 12 hours weekly.

Massachusetts - Chicopee

WACE - Box One, Springfield, Massachusetts 01101, (413) 781-2240. Greek programs, 1 hour weekly.

Massachusetts - Lynn

WLYN-FM - Box 631, Lynn, Massachusetts 01903, (617) 595-6200. Greek programs, 17 hours weekly.

Massachusetts - Newton

WNTN - 143 Rumford Avenue, Newton, Massachusetts 02166, (617) 969-1550. Greek programs, 5 hours weekly.

Massachusetts - Southbridge

WESO - 399 Main Street, Southbridge, Massachusetts 01550, (617) 764-4381. Greek programs, 1 hour weekly.

Massachusetts - Springfield

WMAS - 101 West Street, Springfield, Massachusetts 01104, (413) 737-1414. Greek programs, 2 hours weekly.

Massachusetts - Westfield

WLDM - 249 Union Street, Westfield, Massachusetts 01085, (413) 568-8643. Greek programs, 1 hour weekly.

Massachusetts - Worcester

WNEB - 236 Worcester Center, Worcester, Massachusetts 01608, (617) 756-4672. Greek programs, 1 hour weekly.

WORC - Eight Portland Street, Worcester, Massachusetts 01608, (617) 799-0581. Greek programs, 2 hours weekly.

Michigan - Ann Arbor

WAAM - 4230 Packard Road, Ann Arbor, Michigan 48104 (313) 971-1600. Greek programs, 1 hour weekly.

Michigan - Garden City

WCAR - 32500 Park Lane, Garden City, Michigan 48135, (313) 525-1111. Greek programs, 2 hours weekly.

New Hampshire - Manchester

WFEA - Box 5300, Manchester, New Hampshire 03108, (603) 625-5491. Greek programs, 1 hour weekly.

New Hampshire - Nashua

WOTW - Box 448, Nashua, New Hampshire 03061, (603) 883-9090. Greek programs, 4 hours weekly.

New Jersey - New Brunswick

WRSU-FM - 126 College Avenue, New Brunswick, New Jersey 08903, (201) 937-7800. Greek programs, 1 hour weekly.

New Jersey - Vineland

WKQV-FM - 632 Maurice Boulevard, Box 457, Vineland, New Jersey 08360, (609) 691-9292. Greek programs, 1 hour weekly.

New York - Binghamton

WKOP - 32 West State Street, Binghamton, New York 13901, (607) 722-3437. Greek programs, 1 hour weekly.

New York - New York

WPOW - 1111 Woodrow Road, Staten Island, New York 10312, (212) 984-4600. Greek programs, 1 hour weekly.

Ohio - Akron

WAUD-FM - 302 East Buchtel Avenue, Akron, Ohio 44325, (216) 375-7105. Greek programs, 2 hours weekly.

Ohio - Canton

WNYN - 1515 Cleveland, Northwest, Canton, Ohio 44703, (216) 456-8396. Greek programs, 2 hours weekly.

Ohio - Cleveland

WBOE-FM - 10600 Quincy Avenue, Cleveland, Ohio 44106, (216) 421-7373. Greek programs, 1 hour weekly.

WCSB-FM - Cleveland State University, Cleveland, Ohio 44115, (216) 687-3523. Greek programs, 1 hour weekly.

WZAK-FM - 1303 Prospect Avenue, Cleveland, Ohio 44115, (216) 621-9300. Greek programs, 4-1/2 hours weekly.

Ohio - Reading

WRCJ-FM - 810 East Columbia Avenue, Reading, Ohio 45215, (513) 733-4887. Greek programs, 2 hours weekly.

Ohio - Warren

WHHH - 108 Main Street, Southwest, Warren, Ohio 44481, (216) 392-2529. Greek programs, 1 hour weekly.

WTCL - 1295 Lane West Road, Southwest, Warren, Ohio 44481, (216) 373-1570. Greek programs, 2 hours weekly.

Pennsylvania - Chester

WDNR-FM - Box 1000 Widener University, Chester, Pennsylvania 19013, (215) 499-4437. Greek programs, 2 hours weekly.

Pennsylvania - Erie

WERG-FM - Box 236 Gannon University, Erie, Pennsylvania 16541, (814) 871-7325. Greek programs, 2 hours weekly.

Pennsylvania - Jenkintown

WIBF-FM - The Benson East, Jenkintown, Pennsylvania 19046, (215) 886-2000. Greek programs, 3 hours weekly.

Pennsylvania - McKeesport

WEDO - 414 Fifth Avenue, Midtown Plaza Mall, McKeesport, Pennsylvania 15132, (412) 462-9922. Greek programs, 1 hour weekly.

Pennsylvania - Pittsburgh

WPIT - 200 Gateway Towers, Pittsburgh, Pennsylvania 15222, (412) 281-1900. Greek programs, 1 hour weekly.

Rhode Island - Providence

WRIB - 200 Water Street, East Providence, Rhode Island, (401) 434-0406. Greek programs, 3 hours weekly.

South Carolina - Summerville

WWWZ-FM - Box 30669, Charleston, South Carolina 29407, (803) 556-9132. Greek programs, 1 hour weekly.

Tennessee - Nashville

WRVU-FM - Box 6303, Station B, Nashville, Tennessee 37235, (615) 322-7625. Greek programs, 1 hour weekly.

Texas - Dallas

KNON-FM - 4415 San Jacinto, Dallas, Texas 75204, (214) 823-7490. Greek programs, 1 hour weekly.

Virginia - Falls Church

WFAX - 161-B, Hillwood Avenue, Tower Square, Falls Church, Virginia 22046, (703) 532-1220. Greek programs, 1 hour weekly.

Washington - Seattle

KRAB-FM - 2212 South Jackson, Seattle, Washington 98144, (206) 325-5110. Greek programs, 1 hour weekly.

KXA - 1307 Second Avenue, Seattle, Washington 98101, (206) 682-9033. Greek programs, 1 hour weekly.

West Virginia - Weirton

WEIR - 3578 Pennsylvania Avenue, Weirton, West Virginia 26062, (304) 723-1430. Greek programs, 1 hour weekly.

Wisconsin - Milwaukee

WNOV - 3815 North Tentonia Avenue, Milwaukee, Wisconsin 53206, (414) 445-1986. Greek programs, 1 hour weekly.

Television Programs

Illinois - Chicago

WCIU-TV - Board of Trade Building, 141 West Jackson Boulevard, Chicago, Illinois 60604, (312) 663-0260. Greek: unspecified.

Massachusetts - Boston

WQTV - 390 Commonwealth Avenue, Boston, Massachusetts 02215, (617) 267-1530. Greek: 2 hours a week.

New York, New York - Newark, New Jersey

WNJU-TV - Symphony Hall, 1020 Broad Street, Newark, New Jersey, (201) 643-9100. Greek: unspecified.

WWHT - 416 Eagle Rock Avenue, West Orange, New Jersey 07052, (201) 731-9024. Greek: unspecified.

Bank Branches in the U.S.

NATIONAL BANK OF GREECE

71 West 35th Street
New York, New York (212) 947-7735

168 North Michigan Avenue
Chicago, Illinois 60601 (312) 641-6600

33 State Street
Boston, Massachusetts 02109 (617) 367-2200

Commercial and Trade Organizations

AMERICAN HELLENIC INSTITUTE
1730 K Street, Northwest
Washington, D.C. 20006 (202) 785-8430
Chairman: Leon P. Stavrou Founded 1974

An information center which seeks to strengthen trade and commerce between the United States and Greece, between the United States and Cyprus, and within the American Hellenic community. Plans to publish a looseleaf business guide with periodic updates on the legal, financial and commercial aspects of doing business in Greece. A guide for Cyprus is also planned.

GREEK TRADE CENTERS
2211 Massachusetts Avenue, Northwest
Washington, D.C. 20008 (202) 332-2844

150 East 58th Street
New York, New York 10022 (212) 751-2406

168 North Michigan Avenue, Suite 804
Chicago, Illinois 60601 (312) 332-1716

HELLENIC-AMERICAN CHAMBER OF COMMERCE
25 Broadway
New York, New York 10004 (212) 943-8594

Publications: Newsletter, bimonthly; Journal, annual.

HELLENIC ORGANIZATION OF INDUSTRIES AND HANDICRAFTS
150 East 58th Street
New York, New York 10022 (212) 371-1425

Information Center sponsored by the Greek Embassy.

Festivals, Fairs, and Celebrations

California - San Rafael

GREEK FESTIVAL
San Rafael, California

Contact: (415) 479-4493

California - Stockton

GREEK FOOD FESTIVAL
Stockton, California

Dance, songs, displays, and of course, all varieties of Greek foods. Held annually for two days in mid October.
Contact: California Chamber of Commerce, 455 Capitol Mall, Sacramento, California 95814.

California - Torrance

GREEK FESTIVAL
Torrance Recreation Center
Torrance and Madrona Boulevards
Torrance, California

Features Hellenic dance groups, continuous live music and entertainment, authentic Greek food and exotic pastries. Grecian exhibits and displays, as well as children's booths, are set up. Held annually the first weekend in October.
Sponsor: St. Katherine's Greek Orthodox Church, 722 Knob Hill Avenue, Redondo Beach, California 90277.

Delaware - Wilmington

GREEK FESTIVAL
Holy Trinity Greek Orthodox Church
Wilmington, Delaware

Greek foods and pastries as well as displays of Greek handicrafts, books and a bazaar highlight this annual festival in June.
Contact: Holy Trinity Greek Orthodox Church, 808 North Broom Street, Wilmington, Delaware 19806.

District of Columbia

FOLK FESTIVAL
Saints Constantine and Helen Greek Orthodox Church
Washington, D.C.

Events include clowns, pony rides, Greek dance group performances with audience participation, native food, arts and crafts booths, and white elephant sale. Held annually for one weekend in September.
Contact: Saints Constantine and Helen Greek Orthodox Church, 4115 16th Street Northwest, Washington, D.C. 20011.

Florida - Jacksonville

GRECIAN FESTIVAL
Jacksonville, Florida

Contact: Maria Condaxis, 3850 Atlantic Boulevard, Jacksonville, Florida 32207. (904) 724-5405

Florida - Pensacola

GREEK FESTIVAL BAZAAR
Hellenic Center
1720 West Garden Street
Pensacola, Florida

Greek music and dance, food and crafts are featured in this annual festival held in November. Contact: Bill Mathers, 803 North Palafox Street, Pensacola, Florida 32501. (904) 433-3065.

Florida - Tarpon Springs

INTERNATIONAL GLENDI
Sponge Exchange on the Docks
Tarpon Springs, Florida

Delicious Greek food, ethnic dances and costumes as well as displays of ethnic handicrafts, are the center of this annual celebration in November. Contact: Tarpon Springs Chamber of Commerce, 112 South Pinellas Avenue, Tarpon Springs, Florida 33589. (813) 937-6109.

GREEK CROSS DAY
(Epiphany Celebration)
Tarpon Springs, Florida

The Greek community commemorates the baptism of Christ with an Epiphany observance, preceded the day before by the blessing of the sponge fleet and a Greek dinner dance. A colorful "diving for the cross" ceremony takes place at Spring Bayou. Good fortune is believed to follow the lucky youth who retrieves the cross, blessed and cast into the water by the bishop. A Greek festival follows the ceremony. Held each January 6.
Contact: Father Elias Kalariotes, Post Office Box 248, Tarpon Springs, Florida 33589. (813) 937-3540.

Georgia - Atlanta

ATLANTA GREEK FESTIVAL
Greek Orthodox Cathedral
2500 Clairmont Road, Northeast
Atlanta, Georgia

Presents an array of authentic Greek foods, music, and dancers. Also features a Greek Wine Cellar, handicraft and art work, records and tapes, posters, jewelry, clothing, and other items. Continuous films on Greece and the Greek Islands are shown in a movie room. Held in early October.
Contact: Georgia Department of Community Development, Post Office Box 38097, Atlanta, Georgia 30334.

Illinois - East Moline

GREEK FESTIVAL
U. A. W. Hall
East Moline, Illinois

Ethnic music and dances highlight this one day celebration of Greek heritage. Held in mid August.
Contact: The Division of Tourism, Illinois Department of Business and Economic Development, 222 South College Street, Springfield, Illinois 62706.

Illinois - Elgin

ELGIN GREEK FESTIVAL
Eagles Country Home
Elgin, Illinois

A Greek taverna and booths with ethnic foods provide sustenance for body and spirit. Greek dancing by special groups as well as festical participants, ethnic displays and craft booths are also featured. Held in mid July.
Contact: Elgin Chamber of Commerce, Elgin, Illinois.

Indiana - Merrillville

GRECIAN FESTIVAL
Cathedral Grounds
US 30 at Madison Street
Merrillville, Indiana

An outdoor taverna featuring saganaki (flaming cheese), broiled squid, smelt, gyros and other Greek specialties, booths selling Greek pastries, roast lamb, shish-ka-bob and chicken provide authentic tastes and fragrances. In addition there are wine tasting and Greek dancing, tours of the Greek Orthodox Cathedral, drawings for large prizes and the sale of handicrafts and icons. Held annually in July since 1969.
Contact: Michael G. Kapnas, Suite 700, Twin Towers North, Merrillville, Indiana 46410. (219) 769-6601.

Massachusetts - Ipswich

GREEK LOBSTER AND DANCE FESTIVAL
Hellenic Center
Ipswich, Massachusetts

Specialties from the sea, cooked in the Greek fashion, ethnic dances and entertainment, and crafts displays are featured in this annual festival held in July.
Contact: Chamber of Commerce, Lynn Five Cents Savings Bank, High Street, Ipswich, Massachusetts 01938. (617) 356-7333.

Missouri - Kansas City

GREEK PLAKA
Crown Center Square
Kansas City, Missouri

Greek food, music and dancing highlight this gala festival. Held annually in late June for three days. Begun around 1973.
Contact: Convention and Visitors Bureau of Greater Kansas City, 1221 Baltimore, Kansas City, Missouri 64105.

Nebraska - Omaha

GREEK FESTIVAL
Saint Johns Greek Orthodox Church
602 Park Avenue
Omaha, Nebraska

Crafts, liturgical objects and delicious Greek food cooked by parishioners highlight this annual two-day festival held in mid-August.
Contact: Saint Johns Greek Orthodox Church, 602 Park Avenue, Omaha, Nebraska 68105.

New Jersey - Holmdel

GRECIAN ARTS FESTIVAL
Garden State Arts Center
Holmdel, New Jersey

Morning folk festivities include art exhibits, folk dancing, and Greek drama. Greek foods and delicacies and other refreshments are available. An afternoon stage program features Greek concert singers, musicians, dancers, and the Metropolitan Greek Chorale. Begun in 1974. Held in late September.
Contact: Grecian Arts Festival, New Jersey Highway Authority, Garden State Parkway, Woodbridge, New Jersey 07095. (201) 442-8600.

New York - New York

DELPHIC FESTIVAL
One Sheridan Square (old Cafe Society)
New York, New York

Presented by the Greek Art Theater, the festival is a presentation in English of ancient and modern Greek plays and other ethnic cultural activities such as concerts and national dancers. The theater also plans to serve as a training studio and library. Lasts throughout the year (40 weeks).
Contact: Greek Art Theater, Incorporated, One Sheridan Square, New York, New York 10014.

Ohio - Toledo

GREEK-AMERICAN FAMILY FESTIVAL
Church of the Holy Trinity
Toledo, Ohio

Three orchestras provide live entertainment, and instructions are given to those who want to learn Greek dances. Women of the church prepare authentic foods, such as shish kebab, mousaka, grape leaves, meatballs, and Greek bakaclava. A dakaliko (gourmet shop) offers bread, olives, and cheese, while the agora (marketplace) displays gifts for sale. There is a wine garden, and also game booths for the children. Tours are conducted through the Greek Orthodox church. Held in early September.
Sponsor: Church of the Holy Trinity, 740 Superior Street, Toledo, Ohio 43604.

Pennsylvania - Media

GREEK FESTIVAL
Rose Tree County Park
Media, Pennsylvania

Greek festival with food, dancing, games and festivities. Takes place in late July for two days.
Contact: Delaware County Commission, Toal Building, Second and Orange Streets, Media, Pennsylvania 19063.

Rhode Island - Pawtucket

APPLE FESTIVAL
Greek Orthodox Church
Pawtucket, Rhode Island

The parish and ethnic community celebrate the apple harvest with a two-day festival featuring authentic Greek foods and pastries, dancing and

handicrafts.
Contact: Greek Orthodox Church, 97 Walcott Street, Pawtucket, Rhode Island 02860

South Carolina - Charleston

GREEK EMPHASIS FESTIVAL (GREEK HERITAGE FESTIVAL)
Charleston, South Carolina

Part of Founders' Festivals, a continuing series of month-long festivals centering on the ethnic groups which were instrumental in the founding and growth of Charleston. Special exhibits in the Gibbes Art Gallery and Charleston Museum, special ethnic foods offered in local restaurants, and two or there major events. Held for one month, usually May.
Contact: Mr. James B. Bagwell, Jr., 313 Pitt Street, Mount Pleasant, South Carolina 29464.

GREEK SPRING FESTIVAL
Middleton Place
Charleston, South Carolina

A Greek Orthodox service takes place at noon, then the celebration of spring begins. The festival features bazoukia music, Greek folk dancing for experts and novices, and such famous Greek foods as baklava, feta cheese, stuffed grape leaves, and shish kebab. Held in mid-May.
Contact: Alan Powell, Middleton Place Gardens and Plantation Stableyards, Route 4, Charleston, South Carolina 29407. (803) 556-6020.

Texas - Houston

GREEK FESTIVAL
Greek Orthodox Cathedral
3511 Yoakum Boulevard
Houston, Texas

Features authentic Greek foods and pastries, native Greek dances and music, travel films and literature, and religious tours and icon display. An agora (marketplace) displays imported foods and wines, Greek novelties, antique brass and copperware, jewelry, records, books, and pottery. Held annually in mid-October.
Contact: S. Paul Voinis, Post Office Box 13089, Houston, Texas 77019. (713) 528-8361.

Texas - San Antonio

GREEK FUNSTIVAL
San Antonio, Texas

A festival saluting the Greek heritage. Held in October.
Contact: Saint Sophia Greek Orthodox Church, 2504 South Saint Mary's Street, San Antonio, Texas 78210. (512) 735-5051.

Utah - Salt Lake City

GREEK FESTIVAL
Holy Trinity Greek Orthodox Church
Salt Lake City, Utah

A three-day festival held in mid-September features ethnic music and dancing as well as handicrafts and Greek culinary specialties.
Contact: William Kandas, 279 South 300 West, Salt Lake City, Utah 84101. (801) 328-9681.

Airline Offices

OLYMPIC AIRWAYS, S.A.
North American Headquarters
647 Fifth Avenue
New York, New York 10022 (212) 750-7900

Flies intercontinental routes west to Canada and the United States; east to Siam, Singapore, and Australia; and south to Kenya and South Africa. Provides international service to European capitals and to cities bordering the eastern Mediterranean. Domestic flights from Athens provide service throughout the mainland and to the Greek islands. Other offices in the United States: Atlanta, Boston, Chicago, Cleveland, Dallas, Hartford, Houston, Los Angeles, Miami, Philadelphia, San Francisco, and Washington.

Ship Lines

CHANDRIS, INCORPORATED

701 Southeast 24th
Fort Lauderdale, Florida 33316 (305) 947-7523

665 Fifth Avenue
New York, New York 10022 (212) 586-8370

9570 Wilshire Boulevard
Beverly Hills, California 90212 (213) 272-2141

Sails from New York, Norfolk, Baltimore, and Boston to Bermuda. Air/sea Caribbean cruises depart by air from Los Angeles, San Diego, and San Francisco and by sea from San Juan, Puerto Rico, for cruises to Caribbean ports.

HELLENIC LINES LIMITED

39 Broadway
New York, New York 10006 (212) 480-0950

1133 International Trade Mart
2 Canal Street
New Orleans, Louisiana 70130 (504) 581-2825

605 College Street
Houston, Texas 77005 (713) 941-5184

Transports freight and a few passengers from New York to Mediterranean ports; to South Africa, East Africa, and Red Sea ports; to the Arabian Gulf, Pakistan, Ceylon, and India. From New Orleans or Houston modern Greek freighters sail to the Mediterranean; or to the Arabian Gulf, Pakistan, Ceylon, and India.

ROYAL CRUISE LINE (USA), INCORPORATED
One Maritime Plaza, Suite 2540
San Francisco, California 94111 (415) 956-7200

Air/sea Mediterranean cruises start with air departure from Los Angeles. Cruises leave Athens for eastern Mediterranean ports.

SUN LINE
One Rockefeller Plaza
New York, New York 10020 (212) 397-6400
(800) 223-5567
toll free

Sails from Port Everglades, Florida, to Caribbean ports. Offers air/sea cruises from Maimi, Florida, to Central America, the Galapagos Islands, and Mexico; and to South America.

Bookdealers and Publishers' Representatives

THE BIBLIOPHILE
83 East Avenue
Norwalk, Connecticut 06851 (203) 853-1203

BIBLIOPHILOS - EUROPEAN PUBLICATIONS SERVICE
83 Trowbridge Street
Cambridge, Massachusetts 02138 (617) 876-1746

CARATZAS BROTHERS
481 Main Street
New Rochelle, New York 10801 (212) 823-6665

INTERNATIONAL PUBLICATIONS SERVICE
114 East 32nd Street
New York, New York 10016 (212) 685-9351

PELLA PUBLISHING COMPANY
461 Eighth Avenue
New York, New York 10001 (212) 279-9586

E. K. SCHREIBER
Post Office Box 144
Kingsbridge Station
Bronx, New York 10463 (212) 884-9139

SOURCE BOOK STORE
305 West Second Street
Davenport, Iowa 52801 (319) 324-8941

TEC-BOOKS LIMITED (Librairie De Documentation Technique SA)
41 William
Pittsburgh, Pennsylvania 12901 (518) 561-0005

Books and Pamphlets

AN ANNOTATED BIBLIOGRAPHY OF GREEK MIGRATION. By Evangelos C. Vlachos, Athens, Greece, Social Sciences Centre, 1966.

Bibliography includes entries in four categories: the study of migration, Greek emigration, Greeks abroad (excluding United States), and Greeks in the United States. Part I is a bibliographic essay in English. Part II lists works in all languages alphabetically.

FACTS ABOUT GREECE. Athens, General Information, 1980.

Explains the administration, physical geography, population statistics, social programs, education and sports, aspects of the economy including banking, agriculture, mining, manufacturing, foreign trade, transportation, as well as tourism and communications media.

GENERAL INFORMATION ABOUT GREECE. Athens, Greek National Tourist Organization, 1980.

A useful booklet for the visitor to Greece which gives an introduction about Greece in general and its history and describes formalities for entering, places to stay and how to travel within the country. Several tours are suggested and the most famous museums and archeological sites are described. Additional sections are devoted to sports, caves, artistic events and local festivities.

GREECE. Athens, National Tourist Organization, 1978.

This informational booklet describes in some detail the various parts of Greece: Attica and the Saronic Isles, Central Greece, Northern Greece, The Northeastern Aegean Islands, The Cyclades Islands, the Dodecanese Island, Crete, The Peloponnese and Western Greece. Each section has its own detailed map and is beautifully illustrated in color.

GREECE. By Mary Jo Clogg, (World Bibliographies, 17), Oxford, England; Santa Barbara, California, Clio Press, 1980.

Annotated entries on works dealing with Greece's history, geography, economy and politics, as well as, with its people, their culture, customs, religion and social organizations.

GREECE. A PORTRAIT. Athens, Research and Publicity Center Kede Limited, 1979.

Has chapters on the state, the international position of Greece, its economy, modern Greek culture including folk tradition, fine arts, literature, theater and music, festivals, museums and libraries, religion, education and science, the press and Greeks around the world. At the end of each section the reader will find additional information and useful addresses. Illustrated with charts and pictures and a map.

GREECE THROUGH THE AGES. Athens, Greek National Tourist Organization, 1978.

A beautifully illustrated description of many historic sites and archeological excavations important to ancient Greece, Byzantine Greece, and Medieval Greece. A map shows the location of these sites.

GREECE: USEFUL INFORMATION. By S. Zervos for the National Tourist Organisation of Greece. Athens, ARMOS General Advertising, 1979.

A booklet presenting useful information on traveling in Greece, including organized tours, places to stay, restaurants, museums, sports, festivals, maps, and seasonal events of interest to tourist.

A LIST OF MODERN GREEK SECTIONS AT AMERICAN UNIVERSITITES BROUGHT IN CONTACT WITH THE CULTURAL RELATIONS DIVISION. By the Greek Ministry of Culture and Sciences. Athens, 1975.

A circular listing names and addresses of universities and names of professors of Greek in the United States.

MODERN GREEK CULTURE: A SELECTED BIBLIOGRAPHY. 4th rev. edition. By C. Th. Dimaras, C. Koumarianou, and L. Droulia. Athens, Greece, National Hellenic Committee of the International Association for South Eastern European Studies, 1974.

Entries are arranged by topics (geography, history, language, literature, and texts) within the main sections: A. General Reference on Modern Greece; B. Authors; C. Supplement. The supplement includes works inspired by Greece and periodicals. Covers books in Greek, as well as translation into English, French, German, and Italian.

SELECTED RECIPES OF GREEK COOKING. New York, Greek National Tourist Organization.

A booklet of recipes suggested for a Greek buffet supper menu. Includes sources of Greek food products in New York City.

GREEK AMERICANS

THE ASSIMILATION OF GREEKS IN THE UNITED STATES: WITH SPECIAL REFERENCE TO THE GREEK COMMUNITY OF ANDERSON, INDIANA. By Evangelos Constantine Vlachos, Athens, Greece, Publications of the National Centre of Social Researches, 2, 1968.

In the assimilation of American mores, the traditional Greek culture brought by immigrants produced distinctive new Greek American cultural patterns. This phenomenan is studied in Greek American communities across America but using the one in

Anderson, Indiana, as a model. Particular emphasis is given to third-generation affinity to these patterns.

A BIBLIOGRAPHICAL GUIDE TO MATERIALS ON GREEKS IN THE UNITED STATES, 1890-1968. Compiled by Michael N. Cutsumbis. Staten Island, New York, Center for Migration Studies, 1970.

Sections 1-6 are arranged chronologically and 7-11 alphabetically. Lists books and articles, unpublished materials, directories and serials concerning Greeks in the United States as well as the Greek Orthodox Church.

COMMUNICATIONS DIRECTORY. 1982-1984. Edited by Mary Danakis. New York. Greek Orthodox Archdiocese, 1972.

Contains the names, addresses, telephone numbers, and professional affiliation of nearly one thousand Greek Americans in the media.

THE EVOLUTION OF THE GREEK ORTHODOX CHURCH IN AMERICA AND ITS PRESENT PROBLEMS. By Peter Kourides. New York, Cosmos Greek Publishing Company, 1959.

Useful in understanding the strong role of the Church in the experience of the Greek American.

FAMILY AND MOBILITY AMONG GREEK AMERICANS. By Nicholas Tavuchis. Athens, 1972.

FROM MARS TO MANHATTAN: THE GREEK ORTHODOX CHURCH IN AMERICA UNDER PATRIARCH ATHENAGORAS. By George Papiannou. Minneapolis, 1976.

GO NAKED IN THE WORLD. By Tom Chamales. New York, Scribner's, 1959.

A novel dealing with the divided loyalty of a Greek American.

GOLD IN THE STREETS. By Mary Vardoulakis. New York, Dodd, Mead Company, 1945.

The Americanization of Greeks is treated humorously.

GREEK AMERICANS, STRUGGLE AND SUCCESS. By Charles C. Moskos, Jr., (Ethnic groups in American life series). Englewood Cliffs, New Jersey, Prentice-Hall, 1980.

A descriptive history of the Greek experience in America.

GREEK IMMIGRATION TO THE UNITED STATES. By Henry Pratt Fairchild. New Haven, Yale University Press, 1911.

Shows that the major cause for emigration was economic, but depicts the Greek immigrant as less desirable than earlier immigrants.

GREEK ORTHODOX ARCHDIOCESE OF NORTH AND SOUTH AMERICA YEARBOOK, 1982. Edited by Dmitri Gemelos and Rev. Kosmas Karavellas. New York, 1982.

Contains information concerning the organization of the Archdiocese and its institutions; calendars and pictorial records of events; directories of parishes, priests, publications, radio and TV producers, organizations, Greek Embassies and Consular offices.

GREEKS IN AMERICA. By Thomas Burgess. The American Immigration Collection. Boston, Sherman, French and Company, 1913. Reprinted by Arno Press and The New York Times, New York, 1970.

Discusses immigration of Greeks to America starting in 1882, their occupations, institutions, celebrations, religion, life in cities and towns, and contributions of famous Greek Americans.

THE GREEKS IN AMERICA. By J. P. Xenides. New York, George H. Doran Company, 1922. Reprinted by R and E Associates, San Francisco, 1972.

Examines the European background and the experiences of Greek immigrants in America. Describes economic and social conditions, recreation, family life, education, assimulation, war service, religion (especially contacts between Greek Orthodox and Protestant Churches), literature, and special problems and recommendations.

THE GREEKS IN AMERICA, 1528-1977: A CHRONOLOGY AND FACT BOOK. Edited by Melvin Hecker and Heike Fenton. Dobbs Ferry, New

York, Oceana Publications, 1978.

Part One, the chronology, has selected key dates and events to indicate the progress of the Greeks in America and Part Two, the documents section, provides a deeper look at various significant events referred to in the chronology.

THE GREEKS IN THE UNITED STATES. By Theodore Saloutos. Cambridge, Massachusetts, Harvard University Press, 1964.

Presents a study of the impact of the Old Country on Greek immigrants; the early years of immigration from 1880 on; social, community, and religious life in America; political views; World War 1; Americanization of Greek immigrants; business activities; second generation Greek Americans; depression years; World War II, and the "era of respectability."

HISTORY OF THE ORDER OF AHEPA, 1922-1972. By George Leber. Washington, D.C. 1972.

The Order of Ahepa has played a seminal part in the life of Greek Americans. This account of its activities is particularly crucial to understanding the Greek experience in America.

IF . . . IT'S ALL GREEK TO YOU - THE GREEKS HAVE A WORD FOR IT . . By Peter S. Lambros. Milwaukee, Wisconsin, Cureo Press, 1946.

A book that analyzes Greek-English words, topics and anecdotes.

LION AT MY HEART. By Harry Mark Petrakis. Boston, Little, Brown, 1959.

Fictional setting for the very real conflict between love for Greece and love for America experienced by many Greek immigrants and their families.

MY NEW FOUND LAND. By Dean Brelis. Boston, Houghton, Myflin, 1963.

The story of a young Greek American boy trying to balance his sentiment for this Greek heritage with his allegiance to America during the decade of the 1930's.

NEW SMYRNA; An Eighteenth Century Greek Odyssey. By E. P. Panagopoulos. Gainesville, University of Florida Press, 1966.

Recounts the history of an ill-fated migration of Greeks, Italians, Minorcans, and Corsicans to New Smyrna, Florida, in 1768 under the leadership of their colonizer, Dr. Andrew Turnbull. Chronicles a tale of frustration, suffering, oppression, revolt, and death in creating a new, productive life in a swampy, mosquito-ridden wilderness. Based on examination of the pertinent documents and manuscripts.

SELECTIVE BIBLIOGRAPHY FOR THE SOCIOLOGICAL STUDY OF GREEK-AMERICANS. Compiled by Michael N. Cutsumbis. Lancaster, Pennsylvania, 1967.

STRANGERS AT ITHACA: THE STORY OF THE SPONGERS OF TARPON SPRINGS. By George T. Frantsis, St. Petersburg, Florida: Great Outdoors, 1962.

The important Greek settlement of sponge fishermen in Florida is the setting for this historical account.

THEY REMEMBER AMERICA; THE STORY OF THE REPATRIATED GREEK- AMERICANS. By Theodore Saloutos. Berkeley, University of California Press, 1956.

Covers the period from 1908 to 1924 and stresses the years immediately before and after World War I when many Greeks returned to their homeland. Includes a bibliography.

WHO'S WHO; Who Is Who of Greek Origin in Institutions of Higher Learning in the United States and Canada. Compiled and edited by Nicholas D. Iliopoulos. New York, Greek Orthodox Archdiocese of North and South America, 1974.

A directory of educators of Greek origin arranged alphabetically by name. Gives addresses, education, publications, specialization, and present position.

Audiovisual Material

MAPS

GREECE.

A booklet of maps of Greece, one showing the major divisions of the country, another indicating main road connections and distances, and a schematic map of rail and air networks. Each division of Greece then has its own separate enlarged map.

MAP OF GREECE. Athens, National Tourist Organization of Greece, 1972.

A road map of Greece showing the entire country on one side and selected enlarged areas on the verso, including Crete, Rhodes, the Ionian Islands, and the areas around Athens and Thessalonika. Symbols show the locations of airports, hotels, camping sites, historical sites, resorts, and other places of interest to tourists. An inset map gives railway networks, air routes, and domestic shipping routes. In color. Approximately 25 by 28 inches.

FILMS

ANCIENT CIVILIZATIONS: CRETE. Super 8mm. Color and silent. 4 minutes. Coronet Instructional Media, 1974.

Illustrates Crete's accomplishments in architecture, trade, and writing and shows Cretan influence on the development of ancient Greece. With captions.

ANCIENT CIVILIZATIONS: GREECE. Super 8mm. Color and silent. 4 minutes. Coronet Instructional Media, 1974.

Describes the political, social, and geographic structure of the city-states of ancient Greece. Assesses the influence of Greek culture on Western civilization. With captions.

THE ANCIENT GAMES. 16mm. Color and sound. 28 minutes. By ABC Sports. Released by ABC Media Concepts, 1972.

Re-creates the historic Pythian games which were second in importance only to the Olympic games. Reenacted at Delphi, site of the original games. Former Olympic decathlon gold medalists Bill Toomey and Rafer Johnson compete in the five events of the pentathlon.

ANCIENT GREECE. 16mm. Color and sound. 10 minutes. Coronet Instructional Media, Chicago, 1976.

Shows the Parthenon, the Academia, the Plain of Marathon, Delphi, and the Athenian countryside while pointing out the achievements of the ancient Greeks in philosophy, athletics, politics, and the arts.

APOLLO STILL LIVES HERE. 16mm. Color and sound. 18 minutes. A.C. and R. Public Relations, Incorporated, 437 Madison Avenue, New York, New York 10022.

ATHENS, CITY OF EVERLASTING APRIL. 16mm. Color and sound. 22 minutes. A.C. and R. Public Relations, Incorporated, 437 Madison Avenue, New York, New York 10022.

It's warm in Greece when it's cold elsewhere, so one can visit Athens in December for a perfect summer holiday. There's a fashion show on New Year's Eve featuring bathing suits! And swimming, sailing, and water skiing, and the world-famous sights, of course - the Acropolis, the Parthenon, the statue of Athena, and the temple of Olympian Zeus.

ATHENS, BIRTHPLACE OF DEMOCRACY. 16mm. Color and sound. 18 minutes. By Paul Hoefler Productions. Mar/Chuck Film Industries, Mount Prospect, Illinois, 1971.

A visit to Athens brings into perspective almost 7,000 years of Greek history and cultural development.

BUTTERFLIES AND BEACHES. 16mm. Color and sound. 17 minutes. A.C. and R. Public Relations, Incorporated, 437 Madison Avenue, New York, New York 10022.

Two attractive young girls visit two Greek islands - Rhodes and Crete - where they find both butterflies and beaches. On Rhodes there's shopping for handmade tiles, windmills, outdoor cafes, historical remains of the Crusades, the Place of the Grand Masters, and the Sanctuary of Athena. On Crete, one sees the Place of Knossos, a Venetian fortress, beautiful churches, Greek dancing, flowers and jewelry.

CRETAN BALLAD. 16 and 35mm. Color and sound. 14 minutes. A.C. and R. Public Relations, Incorporated, 437 Madison Avenue, New York, New York 10022.

This is Crete, belonging to Greece, and surely one of the most famous and celebrated of islands. From Crete comes the legend of the Minotaur, and the remains of the royal palace of Knossos are here to support it. The influence of the Minoan civilization remains the strongest, though others followed. You see present-day Crete, too, with its beaches, stupendous cliffs, modern hotels - civilized and hospitable.

CRETE AND MYCENAE. 16mm and 35mm. Color and sound. 54 minutes. By Hans-Joachim Hossfeld, 1970. Universal Education and Visual Arts, 1973.

Presents photographs showing the archaeological findings at Knossos and elsewhere on Crete, as well as Mycenae on the Greek mainland, in order to compare the cultural history of the Minoan civilization with that of Mycenae.

CYCLADES. 16mm. Color and sound. 24 minutes. A.C. and R. Public Relations, Incorporated, 437 Madison Avenue, New York, New York 10022.

THE FEAST NEVER ENDS. 16 and 35mm. Color and sound. 22 minutes. A.C. and R. Public Relations, Incorporated, 437 Madison Avenue, New York, New York 10022.

Somewhere in Greece at any time of the year you'll find a festival celebrating a special occasion. The film starts in Athens with the Easter festival, the most important one of the year. The churches are beautifully decorated with flowers, there are candle-light processions, and the women wear their colorful traditional costumes. Also shows scenes in Corfu, Crete, Delphi, and Iannina.

FESTIVALS IN GREECE. 16mm. Color and sound. 10 minutes. A.C. and R. Public Relations, Incorporated, 437 Madison Avenue, New York, New York 10022.

Shows scenes of ancient Greek plays, operatic music, and modern dance. Opens with a scene from Euripides' "The Bacchae" at the theater of Epidaurus, and goes from there to the Herod Atticus theater in Athens. You hear an aria from Verdi's "Macbeth," you see an imaginative modern dance troupe, a bit of Puccini's "Turandot," Ashkenazy playing Beethoven, a scene from Euripides' "Electra," and one from Aristophanes' "Lysistrata." There's a great deal of cultural excitement in this brief film.

GLORY WAS . . . GLORY IS! 16mm. Color and sound. 14 minutes. A.C. and R. Public Relations, Incorporated, 437 Madison Avenue, New York, New York 10022.

You're in the Peloponnesus now. In the agora there are the remains of the Temple of Apollo, the Gate of Lions, and the tomb of Agamemnon etched into a mountain. The theater of Epidaurus, built in the fourth century B.C., is used today for performances of the great Greek plays. And there's Olympia, where the Olympics began 2,500 years ago. And the Temple of Zeus and wonderful gnarled old olive trees.

GREECE AND ITS BEAUTIFUL ISLANDS. 16mm and Super 8mm. Color and sound. 9 minutes. Castle Films, 1972.

Surveys the major attractions of Greece, including scenes of the islands and cities which show both contemporary Greece and the ruins of past civilizations.

GREECE, THE LAND AND THE PEOPLE. 16mm. Color and sound. 11 minutes. Coronet Instructional Media, Chicago, 1977.

A Greek man and woman show the people, industries, agriculture, and fishing in their homeland, as well as the arts and sciences of its ancient beginnings.

THE GREEKS. 16mm. Color and sound. 29 minutes. Also issued as video recording. By Polonius Film Services. International Film Bureau, Chicago, 1976.

Surveys Greek history and culture from the early Aegean civilizations to the conquests of Alexander.

THE GREEKS HAVE A NEW WORD. 16mm. Color and sound. 11 minutes. A.C. and R. Public Relations, Incorporated, 437 Madison Avenue,

New York, New York 10022.

This film is about modern and ancient Athens, with a population of 2,000,000 people today. Its most famous tourist attraction is the Acropolis, the hill on which the Parthenon stands. Also shows Constitution Square, beaches, water-skiing in the Aegean Sea, native dances, and a brief trip to Corfu.

THE HILL OF THE GODS. 16mm. Color and sound. 12 minutes. A.C. and R. Public Relations, Incorporated, 437 Madison Avenue, New York, New York 10022.

This is one of the most famous and celebrated hills in the world - the Acropolis in Athens. You have only to see the Parthenon and two other temples in Athens, the Erechtheum and the temple of Olympian Zeus, to understand why ancient Greek architecture remains one of the wonders of the world. You'll also see today's Athens - as modern as a city can be.

INTRODUCING GREECE. 16mm. Black and white. Sound. 16 minutes. Also issued as a video recording. By Europa Telefilm. North Atlantic Treaty Organization, Brussels. Distributed by National Audiovisual Center, Washington, D.C., 1979.

Describes the country and people of Greece, including geographical features, historical development and achievements, economic life, occupations of the people, and social customs. Explains briefly the role of Greece in the North Atlantic Treaty Organization.

ISLANDS OF FLOWERS. 16mm. Color and sound. 17 minutes. A.C. and R. Public Relations, Incorporated, 437 Madison Avenue, New York, New York 10022.

Now you're in the Ionian Islands of Greece - Corfu, Cephalonia, Ithaca, Zante. The Venetian influence is strong on Corfu. There are open-air shops, modern resort hotels, sculptures of Achilles and other mythical figures. And Cephalonia, Ithaca, and Zante have a flavor all their own and are covered with olive groves and flowers.

MODERN ODYSSEY. 16mm. Color and sound. 21 minutes. A.C. and R. Public Relations, Incorporated, 437 Madison Avenue, New York, New York 10022.

THE 'NERAIDAS' OF GREECE. 16 and 35mm. Color and sound. 25 minutes. A.C. and R. Public Relations, Incorporated, 437 Madison Avenue, New York, New York 10022.

A young woman visiting Greece has an errand to perform. She is to deliver a letter to someone in in Neraida, but learns that there are about a dozen villages in Greece by that name. So you see Greece while she tries to find the right one (which she does, of course). You see modern and ancient Athens, the rugged Greek countryside, steep cliffs, olive groves, modern hotels, the ruins at Knossos, Crete, and Salonica.

RENDEVOUS IN GREECE. 16mm. Color and sound. 18 minutes. A.C. and R. Public Relations, Incorporated, 437 Madison Avenue, New York, New York 10022.

RHODES: AN ISLAND, A STORY. 16mm. Color and sound. 18 minutes. A.C. and R. Public Relations, Incorporated, 437 Madison Avenue, New York, New York 10022.

SPIRIT OF CRETE. 16mm. Color and sound. 26 minutes. A.C. and R. Public Relations, Incorporated, 437 Madison Avenue, New York, New York 10022.

SUMMER IN GREECE. 16 and 35mm. Color and sound. 23 minutes. A.C. and R. Public Relations, Incorporated, 437 Madison Avenue, New York, New York 10022.

A pretty blonde picks up a magazine dropped by a bicyclist and sees an advertisement of Greece. She starts dreaming, and in her dream dances her way through Greece. You see the Acropolis and the Parthenon and other world-famous Greek ruins; and you see Mykonos, Crete, and other out-islands. It's a fanciful way to see Greece.

SWINGIN' NORTH. 16mm. Color and sound. 17 minutes. A.C. and R. Public Relations, Incorporated, 437 Madison Avenue, New York, New York 10022.

This is a visit to Northern Greece. In Salonika, the capital of Macedonia, Ionic, Doric and Corinthian columns are everywhere. There's a beautiful statue of Dionysus riding a panther, and an imposing Venetian tower built in the fifteenth century. Ancient Greek history abounds in the north of Greece, but so do all the modern amenities - beautiful hotels, fabulous restaurants, and night life.

THESSALONIKI AND HALKIDIKI. 16mm. Color and sound. 18 minutes. A.C. and R. Public Relations, Incorporated, 437 Madison Avenue, New York, New York 10022.

TREASURES OF THE GREEK SEAS. 16 and 35mm. Color and sound. 20 minutes. A.C. and R. Public Relations, Incorporated, 437 Madison Avenue, New York, New York 10022.

There's scuba diving in the Greek islands. In fact, there are two marble sarcophagi lying beneath the sea off the coast of the Peloponnesus, and there's a whole city sunk under the Aegean Sea. The rest of the film shows you island hopping by helicopter over Mykonos, Corfu, Rhodes, Crete, Cephalonia, and Ithaca, and Byzantine castles, fortresses build by the Crusaders, and centuries-old monasteries.

WINTER SUN. 16mm. Color and sound. 18 minutes. A.C. and R. Public Relations, Incorporated, 437 Madison Avenue, New York, New York 10022.

YACHTING IN GREECE. 16mm. Color and sound. 18 minutes. A.C. and R. Public Relations, Incorporated, 437 Madison Avenue, New York, New York 10022.

For yachting enthusiasts Greece and its out-islands are a veritable paradise. You see gorgeous yachts, sail boats and motor boats. There are modern marinas throughout the islands for repairs and supplies. Sail past the out-islands - Mykonos, Naxos, and others - and into the Mediterranean Sea.

(For information about borrowing the films, write to A.C.& R.Public Relations, Incorporated, 437 Madison Avenue, New York, New York 10022.)

FILMS ABOUT GREEK AMERICANS

DEMETRI ALEXANDROS' DIVE. 16mm. Color and sound. 9 minutes. Encyclopedia Britannica Educational Corporation, Chicago, 1977.

The story of a young Greek boy who wants to dive for the cross in a traditional community church ceremony but is refused permission because he is too young. Depicts ethnic traditions and aspects of daily life in a Greek-American neighborhood. For primary grades.

A VILLAGE IN BALTIMORE. 16mm. Color and sound. 58 minutes. By Doreen Moses. Hellenic American Neighborhood Action Committee, 1730 21st Street, Northwest, Washington, D.C. 20009, 1981.

Set in a Greek ethnic neighborhood, "Greektown", this film depicts in everyday events the various assimilation levels, particularly of Greek women.

GUATEMALANS
See also: SPANISH-SPEAKING PEOPLES

Embassy and Consulates

EMBASSY OF GUATEMALA
and Permanent Mission to the OSA
2220 R Street, Northwest
Washington, D.C. 20008 (202) 332-2865

CONSULATES GENERAL

333 North Michigan Avenue
Chicago, Illinois 60601 (312) 332-1587

Interstate Building, Room 105
3407 Montrose Boulevard
Houston, Texas 77006 (713) 522-6737

403 West Eighth Street,
Suite 407
Los Angeles, California 90014 (213) 629-1901

Ingraham Building, Suite 945
25 Southeast Second Avenue
Miami, Florida 33131 (305) 377-3201

International Trade Mart,
Suite 1601
2 Canal Street
New Orleans, Louisiana 70130 (504) 525-0013

57 Park Avenue
New York, New York 10016 (212) 686-3837

Flood Building, Room 306
870 Market Street
San Francisco, California 94102 (415) 781-0118

Mission to the United Nations

GUATEMALAN MISSION
57 Park Avenue
New York, New York 10016 (212) 679-4760

Tourist and Travel Offices

GUATEMALA TOURIST COMMISSION
57 Park Avenue
New York, New York 10016 (212) 679-8513

Public Affairs Organizations

ASSOCIATION IN SOLIDARITY WITH
GUATEMALA
Post Office Box 13006
Washington, D.C. 20009 (202) 232-4467
Contact: Curt Wands Founded 1979

Coalition of students, professionals, and working people who wish to promote the self-determination of Guatemala, and to oppose as harmful to that aim, United States intervention in Guatemala. Promotes a tourism boycott of Guatemala until repression ceases. Plans to organize Guatemalan Solidarity groups to disseminate information on conditions in Guatemala and effects of United States intervention.

GUATEMALA NEWS AND INFORMATION BUREAU
Post Office Box 4126
Berkeley, California 94704 (415) 835-0810

Provides news and information on political, economic and social developments in Guatemala.
Publication: Guatemala! (bilingual), bimonthly.

Cultural and Educational Organizations

INTERNATIONAL SOCIETY OF GUATEMALA
COLLECTORS
Post Office Box 246
Troy, New York 12181 (518) 271-7629
Librarian: James C. Andrews Founded 1948

Organization of philatelists interested in the stamps and postal history of Guatemala. Operates primarily through correspondence, although some meetings are held in conjunction with stamp exhibits in which the Society participates. Maintains library of society publications. Affiliated with the American Philatelic Society.
Publications: El Quetzal, quarterly; Membership Directory, irregular; has also published a two-volume Guatemala Handbook, listing and describing stamps of Guatemala.

Newspapers and Newsletters

GUATEMALA NEWSLETTER. Monthly. Guatemala, Asociacion de Amigos del Pais. Apartodo Postal 291. In English.

Each issue devoted to a problem or issue pertinent to Guatemala.

EL QUETZAL. 1949-. Quarterly. Editor: Roger K. Frigstad. Publisher: International Society of Guatemala Collectors, Post Office Box 331, Glenview, Illinois 60025.

Serves collectors of Guatemalan postage stamps with news notes, queries, announcements, and major articles on philately, postal history, and the background history and geography of Guatemala. Includes cumulative ten-year indexes.

Airline Offices

AVIATECA
(Empresa Guatemalteca de Aviacion)
Miami International Airport
Post Office Box 592496
Miami, Florida 33159 (800) 327-9832

Schedules flights from Guatemala City to North American cities and to Honduras, as well as providing domestic services. Other offices in the United States: Houston and New Orleans.

Books and Pamphlets

ANTHROLOGICAL BIBLIOGRAPHY OF ABORIGINAL GUATEMALA AND BRITISH HONDURAS. By Jorge Lines. San Jose, Costa Rica, Tropical Science Center, 1967.

ANTIGUA. Washington, Department of Publications, Organization of American States, 1978.

Features the architecture of this ancient colonial city.

GUATEMALA: TEXTURES OF GUATAMALA. Guatemala Tourist Commission.

A general description of the geography, Mayan legacy, colonial history, handicrafts and culture of Guatemala, with a section on interesting places to visit. Illustrated in color.

GUATEMALA: WHERE COLOR WAS BORN. Guatamala, Guatamala Tourist Commission.

A brochure giving general information for the visitor and including special sections on Antigua, Lake Atitlan, Chichicasternango, Tikal and the various fiestas.

HISTORICAL DICTIONARY OF GUATEMALA. By Richard E. Moore. Metuchen, New Jersey, Scarecrow Press, revised edition, 1973.

A sourcebook for historical and contemporary facts about people, places, events, geography and political organizations. Includes a bibliography.

IMAGE OF GUATEMALA. Washington, Organization of American States, 1972.

Discusses Mayan history, the colonial period and the modern society of Guatemala. Ranges over several geographical regions and cities. A booklet in magazine format with numerous photographs, generally in color.

Audiovisual Material

MAP

MAP OF GUATEMALA. Guatemala, Guatemala Tourist Commission, 1979.

A road map of Guatemala showing the entire country and keyed for main areas of interest and for archeological sites. On the verso there are city maps for Guatemala City and for Quezaltenango also showing locations of points of interest. In color. Approximately 16-1/2 by 21-1/2.

FILMS

ANTIGUA, GUATEMALA: AMERICAN MONUMENT. 16mm. Color and sound. 23 minutes. Also available on video cassette. Museum of Modern Art of Latin America, Washington, D.C., 1978.

A documentary film on one of the oldest cities in

America. In English and Spanish.

GUATEMALA: ADELA'S REBOZO. 16mm. Color and sound. 12 minutes. Exploring the World series. By Joshua Tree Productions. Released by Doubleday Multimedia, Santa Ana, California 1969.

Portrays life in the typical Guatemalan village of Santiago Atitlan by following a young girl as she tries to sell the first rebozo that she has woven. Compares clothing, housing, family relationships, and patterns of living of Guatemala with those of the United States.

GUATEMALA, LAND OF COLOR. 16mm. Color and sound. 25 minutes. Also available on video cassette. Museum of Modern Art of Latin America, Washington, D.C., 1978.

Surveys the variety of culture and some of the sights of the colorful country of Guatemala. In English and Spanish.

IMPRESSIONS OF A GUATEMALA MARKET DAY. 16mm. Color and sound. 10 minutes. By Pyramid Films, Santa Monica, California, 1970.

Provides an impression of the culture and daily life of Guatemala, focusing on the activities of the market.

THIS IS GUATEMALA. 16mm. Color and sound. 24 minutes. By J.W. Redding. Cast-of-One Productions, Dallas, Texas, 1975.

A tour of Guatemala showing areas where various stages of the culture and history of Central America, from the time of the Maya, through the Spanish conquest, to the present, are still visible.

HAITIANS
See also: FRENCH-SPEAKING PEOPLES

Embassy and Consulates

EMBASSY OF HAITI
2311 Massachusetts Avenue
Washington, D. C. 20008 (202) 332-4090

CONSULATES GENERAL

919 North Michigan Avenue
Suite 3311
Chicago, Illinois 60611 (312) 337-1603

Ingraham Building
25 Southeast Second Avenue
Suite 709
Miami, Florida 33131 (305) 377-3547

60 East 42nd Street
Room 1365
New York, New York 10017 (212) 697-9767

654 Ave Nunos Rivera
Suite 909
Hato Rey, Puerto Rico 00918

HONORARY CONSULATES

Post Office Box 80340
Atlanta, Georgia 30366 (404) 455-3434

50 Congress Street
Suite 640
Boston, Massachusetts 02109 (617) 742-6454

1016 Standard Building
Cleveland, Ohio 44113 (216) 771-0280

621 Seventeenth Street
Suite 1741
Denver, Colorado 80293 (303) 534-7392

2121 First National Bank Building
Detroit, Michigan 48226 (313) 965-7962

Post Office Box 4200
Evansville, Indiana 47711 (812) 423-8000

1980 Post Oak Street
Suite 1070
Houston, Texas 77401 (713) 961-9037

1972 Derby Drive
Santa Ana, California 92705 (714) 731-8051

Post Office Box 942
Mobile, Alabama 36601 (205) 433-5424

416 Common Street
New Orleans, Louisiana 70130 (504) 586-8309

211 Harland Road
Norwich, Connecticut 06360 (203) 887-5034

1430 Land Title Building
6801 Lincoln Drive
Philadelphia, Pennsylvania
19110 (215) 563-0700

200 Mahantongo Street
Pottsville, Pennsylvania 17901

441 Cloisters Walk
Kirkwood, Missouri 63122
(Saint Louis) (314) 966-5280

100 Brannan Street
San Francisco, California
94107 (415) 957-1189

First School Building
110 Main Avenue
Passaic Park, New Jersey
(Trenton) 07055 (201) 777-2121

Mission to the United Nations

HAITIAN MISSION
801 Second Avenue, Room 300
New York, New York 10017 (212) 986-9686

Information Offices

HAITIAN REFUGEE INFORMATION CENTERS

32 Northeast 54th Street
Miami, Florida 33127 (305) 757-8538

Maintains a legal hotline (800) 327-7519. For Florida: (800) 423-4337

190 Northeast 46th Street
Miami, Florida (305) 573-1314

Tourist and Travel Offices

HAITI GOVERNMENT TOURIST BUREAU

1270 Avenue of the Americas
New York, New York 10020 (212) 757-3517

150 Southeast Second Avenue
Miami, Florida 33131 (305) 371-9420

919 North Michigan Avenue
Chicago, Illinois 60611 (312) 337-1603

980 South Post Oak Road
Houston, Texas 77056 (713) 961-9037

2311 Massachusetts Avenue, Northwest
Washington, D.C. 20008 (202) 328-1888

G.P.O. Post Office Box
San Juan, Puerto Rico 00936 (809) 753-0825

Fraternal Organization

CHARLEMAGNE PERAUTE CENTER
333 Lincoln Place
Brooklyn, New York 11238 (212) 638-7000
Director: Joseph Etienne Founded 1979

A community center for Haitians in the New York area.

Public Affairs Organizations

AD HOC COMMITTEE FOR HAITIAN CONCERNS
c/o Saint Mary's
646 Monroe
Detroit, Michigan 48226
Chairman: Julio Bateau (313) 961-8711

BOSTON COMMITTEE FOR THE SUPPORT OF HAITIAN REFUGEES
c/o CHAMA
105 Windsor Street
Cambridge, Massachusetts 02139
Chairman: Frantz Minuty (617) 492-6622

COALITION FOR HAITIAN ASYLUM
267 Euclid Avenue
Oakland, California 95610
Chairman: Jackie Ousley (415) 763-6162

COALITION FOR HAITIAN CONCERNS
Post Office Box 95
Willow Grove, Pennsylvania 19090
Chairman: Professor Gerard Ferere (215) 657-3193

COMITE INTERREGIONAL POUR REFUGIES HAITIANS, INCORPORATED
333 Lincoln Place
Brooklyn, New York 11238
Chairman: Father Antoine Adrien (212) 789-3661

COMMITTEE FOR THE DEFENCE OF HAITIAN REFUGEES
c/o Haitian Fathers
333 Lincoln Place
Brooklyn, New York 11238
Chairman: Joseph Etienne (212) 638-7000

United States branch of the organization. Also has an office in Hato Rey, Puerto Rico.

EMERGENCY COALITION FOR HAITIAN REFUGEES
275 Seventh Avenue, 11th Floor
New York, New York 10001
Executive Director: Michael Hooper (212) 596-5500
Founded 1982

Religious, Haitian, labor, civil rights and human rights organizations, and individuals concerned about mistreatment of Haitians seeking asylum in the United States. Goals are: to obtain release of over 2,000 Haitians being held in federal immigration facilities and prisons in the United States and Puerto Rico; to ensure that they receive fair treatment and due process of law in hearings before immigration judges; to end United States Coast Guard interdiction of Haitian boats on the high seas; to deepen the public's understanding of the social, economic, and political causes of Haitian flight from Haiti. Alleges that Haitians have not received equal treatment with other peoples seeking political asylum in the United States.

FRIENDS OF HAITI
Post Office Box 348
New City, New York 10956 (914) 352-3872
Coordinator: Jill Ives Founded 1971

Volunteer students and others interested in generating political and material support in the United States

for the Haitian national liberation struggle, particularly the Mouvement Haitien de Liberation, an anti-imperialist, national liberation movement based in Haiti. To disseminate information on the Haitian social structure and the liberation process, with an emphasis on United States economic, political and military involvement. Activities include conducting research and writing for other publications; producing and distributing printed materials, slideshow and film programs; and fundraising. Maintains data center on Haiti, and the Caribbean; also maintains library of 3,000 volumes.
Publications: Haiti Report, quarterly.

FRIENDS OF HAITIAN REFUGEES
Post Office Box 943
Miami Beach, Florida 33139 (305) 672-5132
Coordinator: Marty Goodman Founded 1980

A support group of the Haitian Refugee Center. Includes progressive and anti-racist groups and individuals united to educate Americans on "the unequal and racially discriminatory treatment of Haitian refugees." Goals are to close the Haitian detention camps; gain political asylum, and end United States support of the current regime. Organizes speaking engagements, press conferences and demonstrations. Maintains collection of books, pamphlets and newspaper clippings on refugees. Has conducted immigration conference.
Publications: Haiti Alert, quarterly.

FRIENDS OF THE HAITIANS
1023 Clouet Street
New Orleans, Louisiana 70017
Chairman: George Lesperance (504) 947-2717

HAITIAN-AMERICANS UNITED FOR PROGRESS
221-05 Linden Boulevard
Cambria Heights, New York 11411
Chairman: Reverend Guy Sansaricq (212) 527-3776

HAITIAN CENTER FOR INFORMATION, DOCUMENTATION AND SOCIAL ACTION
2728 13th Street, Northwest
Washington, D.C. 20009
Director: Guitele Nicoleau (202) 232-1711

Concerned with Haitian refugee problems but also with the preservation of Haitian culture.

HAITIAN TASK FORCE OF KENTUCKY COUNCIL OF CHURCHES
c/o Haitian Center
800 Lexington Building
201 West Short Street
Lexington, Kentucky 40507
Chairman: Judy Kooshian (606) 233-4556

HOSPITALITY HOUSE
Box 509
Alderson, West Virginia 24910
Chairmen: Margaret Louden and Richard Dieter (304) 445-2769

PUSH COALITION TO FREE & RESETTLE THE HAITIAN REFUGEES
c/o PUSH
930 East 50th Street
Chicago, Illinois 60615
Contact: Mrs. Jeanine Raymond (312) 752-4823

WOMEN'S TASK FORCE ON HAITIAN POLITICAL PRISONERS
Post Office Box 2293
Washington, D.C. 20013
Coordinator: Roz Dickson (202) 544-7475

Cultural and Educational Organizations

HAITIAN PHILATELIC SOCIETY
c/o Richard Taylor
5200 Brittany Drive, South, No. 901
Saint Petersburg, Florida 33715 (815) 866-0513
Secretary: Richard Taylor Founded 1975

Persons interested in studying the philately of Haiti. Sponsors exhibits; participates in joint research projects. Maintains library. Affiliated with: American Philatelic Society.
Publication: Haiti Philately, quarterly.

REFUGEE RESOURCE CENTER
200 Park Avenue, South
New York, New York 10003 (212) 674-6844

Refugee Resource Center was developed under a federal grant to the Committee on Migration and Refugee Affairs of the American Council of Voluntary Agencies for Foreign Service. Objectives are to: provide information on refugee resettlement to the general public; interpret the role of the private sector in refugee resettlement; assist in developing communication networks between the voluntary agencies and other participants in the resettlement program, including federal, state and local governments, mutual assistance associations, and other service providers; and facilitate coordinations among national resettlement agencies in order to increase their effectiveness in the resettlement program. Convenes roundtables designed to focus on specific areas of concern to resettlement practitioners. Discussions also focus on refugee placement in local communities, to develop better understanding of the respective roles of state coordinators and voluntary agencies and to respond to needs expressed by other sectors involved in the resettlement effort. Produces and distributes periodic mailings including information on resettlement processing, descriptions of resettlement programs, and reports of the activities of other agencies involved in resettlement. Holds regional conferences.

SOUTHEAST CURRICULA DEVELOPMENT CENTER
1410 Northeast Second Avenue
Miami, Florida 33132 (305) 350-3241

Prepares teaching material in Haitian Creole.

Charitable Organizations

DADE COUNTY COMMUNITY ACTION AGENCY
395 Northwest First Street
Miami, Florida 33128 (305) 579-5600

An independent, non-profit corporation which has resettled the great majority of the Haitian refugees. Helps to locate sponsors, provides orientation for refugees and sponsors, assists in obtaining government supported services in education, employment training, social welfare, health and general assistance.

HAITIAN AND CO-ARTS ASSOCIATION
165 Park Row, Suite 8-D
New York, New York 10038
President and Executive Director: (212) 732-9735
Andre Letellier Founded 1956

Professionals, business executives, clerics, artists and others both in the United States and Haiti. Established as a charitable educational assistance program "to voluntarily contribute to the elimination of hunger, eradication of disease and promotion of literacy of deprived children of the peasants in rural areas of Haiti." Establishes rural and mobile clinics accessible to remote, inhabited villages under a program of community-wide vaccination against polio, diptheria, whooping cough, tuberculosis, yaws, malaria and tetanus. Provides information on these diseases to villages; undertakes educational programs to improve diets and hygiene. Promotes cooperative rural agriculture development programs with the small peasant farmers. Seeks to enhance literacy with greater emphasis placed upon industrial and agricultural technology as well as the introduction of advanced vocational trade development. Plans to construct vocational schools in the five geographical departments of the rural areas of Haiti, which will also provide medical care, food and shelter. United States corporations and individuals donate funds, clothing, medical and dental supplies, drugs, agricultural seeds and educational materials for distribution by the Association. Also attempts to develop public interest in Haiti, by sponsoring cultural endeavors in such fields as folklore, dance, music, history, literature, art, theater, photography and wood sculpture; sponsors sports events and trade exhibits. Formerly (1973) Haiti Voluntary Central Committee.

HAITIAN REFUGEE CENTER, INCORPORATED
32 Northeast 54th Street
Miami, Florida 33137
Director: Fr. Gerard Jean-Juste (305) 757-8538

Provides free legal, immigration and social services to Haitian refugees and indigents. Lobbies for legal status for Haitians and supplies emergency aid to the needy. Maintains a legal hotline (800) 327-7519; for Florida (800) 432-4337.

HAITIAN REFUGEE PROJECT
110 Maryland Avenue, Northeast, Room 108
Washington, D.C. 20002
Co-Directors: Sue Sullivan (202) 544-7475
Fritz Longchamp Founded 1978

Aids Haitian refugees in procedures for obtaining asylum in the United States. Gathers information both in Haiti and in the United States and makes it available to church agencies, the federal government, and the general public. Serves as liaison between refugees and concerned bureaus and organizations. Maintains regional office in Miami, Florida. Supersedes Office of Haitian Refugees Concerns of the National Council of Churches (founded 1976).
Publications: Newsletter, monthly; also publishes Fact Sheets and reports.

National Voluntary Agencies under Contract to the Office of Refugee Resettlement, which have been involved in resettlement of Haitian entrants.

CHURCH WORLD SERVICE
Migration and Refugee Program
475 Riverside Drive, Room 666
New York, New York 10027
Contact: Desma Holcum (212) 870-2164

LUTHERAN IMMIGRATION AND REFUGEE SERVICE
Lutheran Council in the U.S.A.
360 Park Avenue South
New York, New York 10017
Contact: Zdenka Seiner (212) 532-6350

PRESIDING BISHOPS FUND FOR WORLD RELIEF
Episcopal Center
815 Second Avenue
New York, New York 10017
Contact: Marnie Dawson (212) 867-8400

U. S. CATHOLIC CONFERENCE
Migration and Refugee Services

1312 Massachusetts Avenue, Northwest
Washington, D.C. 20005
Contact: Gerry Wynn (202) 659-6625

1250 Broadway
New York, New York 10001 (212) 563-4300

WORLD RELIEF REFUGEE SERVICES
National Association of Evangelicals
Post Office Box WRC
Nyack, New York 10960
Contact: Dennis Ripley (914) 353-1444

A description of the services rendered will be found in the listing for each of the agencies in the Indochinese section.

Religious Organizations

HAITIAN FATHERS
333 Lincoln Place
Brooklyn, New York 11238
Contact: Father Antoine Adrien (212) 789-3661

U.S. Government Programs

OFFICE OF REFUGEE RESETTLEMENT
Cuban/Haitian Entrant Program
Department of Health and Human Services
330 C Street, Southwest
Switzer Building
Washington, D.C. 20201
Chief: Deni Blackburn

In 1980 the Cuban/Haitian Task Force was merged with the Office of Refugee Resettlement in the Department of Health and Human Service. Programs of assistance to entrants administered from this office under block grants to states include cash assistance, aid to families with dependent children, supplemental security income, medical assistance and social services. These may include: an outreach program; English-as-a-Second-Language instruction; vocational assistance in career counseling, job orientation, job placement and follow-up, and assessment; vocational training; skills recertification; day care and transportation necessary for participation in an employability or social service plan; social adjustment services, (information and referral, emergency services, health [including mental health] related services, home management services, orientation services); and transportation and interpreter services. The ORR also maintains a data systems and analysis program and hotlines in Miami (800) 327-3463 and Washington (800) 424-9304 to provide information and referral services in the areas of health, employment, legal and housing assistance and other social services. Hotline staff speak Spanish, Creole and English.

OFFICE OF REFUGEE HEALTH AFFAIRS
Room 18A-30, Parklawn Building
5600 Fisher's Lane
Rockville, Maryland 20857
Contact: Robert F. Knouss, M.D. (301) 443-4130

Coordinates all Public Health Service-supported health programs for Cuban and Haitian entrants. These include medical screening and the services of community health centers, maternal and child health programs, and community mental health centers.

OFFICE OF BILINGUAL EDUCATION AND MINORITY LANGUAGES AFFAIRS
Refugee Children Assistance Programs
Department of Education
Reporters Building - Room 505
400 Maryland Avenue, Southwest
Washington, D.C. 20202
Chief: James H. Lockhart (202) 472-3520

Provides supplementary educational assistance to meet the special educational needs of Cuban and Haitian entrant children who are enrolled in public and non-profit elementary and secondary schools. Program is operated through grants.

Newspapers and Newsletters

HAITI ALERT. Quarterly. Publisher: Friends of Haitian Refugees, Post Office Box 943, Miami Beach, Florida 33139.

Prints articles advocating a change of United States policy towards new Haitian arrivals in this country as well as towards the current regime in Haiti.

HAITI REPORT. Quarterly. Publisher: Friends of Haiti, Post Office Box 348, New City, New York 10956.

Carries articles on Haiti and the liberation movement to change the present government.

UNITE; The Haitian-American Paper. Weekly. 1976. Editor: Louis A. Brun. Publisher: Haitian Unity Council, Box 152, Canal Street Station, New York, New York 10013. In French and English.

A tabloid newspaper devoted to Haitian concerns.

Radio Programs

New York - New York

WPOW - 1111 Woodrow Road, Staten Island, New York 10312, (212) 984-4600. Haitian programs, 3 hours weekly.

New York - Stony Brook

WUSB (FM) - State University of New York, Stony Brook, New York 11794, (516) 246-7900. Haitian programs, 1 hour weekly.

Airline Offices

AIR HAITI, S.A.
North American Headquarters:
3345 Northwest 67th Avenue
Miami International Airport
Miami, Florida 33122 (305) 526-6250

Bookdealers and Publishers' Representatives

THE ANTIQUARIUM
(antiquarian Haitiana)
66 Humiston Drive
Bethany, Connecticut 06525 (203) 393-2723

HOUSE OF BOOKS INCORPORATED
(imports books from Haiti)
Post Office Box 231
Kearny, New Jersey 07032

Books and Pamphlets

CAP HAITIEN AND THE MIGHTY CITADELLE. Washington, D.C., Haiti Government Tourist Bureau.

An illustrated brochure about the place where Columbus first landed and where Christophe, the slave who became king, built the magnificant San Souci Palace and the impregnable Citadelle high on a mountain top as a defense against Napoleon.

THE COMPLETE HAITIANA: A BIBLIOGRAPHICAL GUIDE TO SCHOLARLY LITERATURE 1900-1980. 2 volumes. Millwood, New York, Kraus International, 1982.

HAITI. Hints for Visitors. Port-au-Prince, Haiti National Office of Tourism and Public Relations.

Points out places of interest as well as giving short summaries on history and culture and general information on travel and everyday life in Haiti.

HAITI. Le Grand Value. Port-au-Prince, Haiti National Office of Tourism and Public Relations, 1981.

Colored photographs illustrate the various cities of Haiti and the activities offered. Includes a listing of hotels and prices.

IMAGE OF HAITI. By the General Secretariat, Organization of American States. Washington, D.C., 1972.

Describes the land of Haiti; the nation's history and political development; art, architecture, and handicrafts; literature; music and folklore; education; principal cities; land use; economic development; and tourism. A booklet illustrated with a map and many photographs, some in color.

JACMEL. Port-au-Prince, Haiti National Office of Tourism.

An introduction to the town of Jacmel on the southern coast of Haiti newly accessible by highway where pirates, the Spanish, British and French have lived in turn. Illustrated in color.

PORT-AU-PRINCE. Port-au-Prince, Haiti National Office of Tourism.

Shows the colorful life of Haiti's national capital and main port.

HAITIAN-AMERICANS

CARIBBEAN IMMIGRATION TO THE UNITED STATES. Edited by Roy Bryce-Laporte and Delores Mortimer. Washington, D.C., Research Institute on Immigration and Ethnic Studies, 1976.

A collection of addresses, essays and lectures, centering on Cuban immigration patterns and problems.

ETHNICITY AS DEPENDENCE: THE HAITIAN COMMUNITY IN NEW YORK. By Michael S. Laguerre. New York, 1978.

HAITIAN EMIGRATION: REPORT OF THE SUBCOMMITTEE ON IMMIGRATION, CITIZENSHIP AND INTERNATIONAL LAW OF THE COMMITTEE ON THE JUDICIARY. House of Representatives, 94th Congress. Washington, D.C., Government Printing Office, 1976.

Audiovisual Material

FILMS

HAITI. 16 mm. Color and sound. 21 minutes. By Rosebud Films. ACI Media, New York, 1975.

Traces political and cultural history of Haiti, from 1804 to 20th century American occupation. Explores contemporary Haitian society and lifestyles as well as Haitian art, festivals, and voodoo.

PORTRAIT OF HAITI. 16 mm. Color and sound. 14 minutes. By Hack Swain Productions. Mar/Chuck Film Industries, Mount Prospect, Illinois, 1977.

Presents the history, culture, and religion of Haiti as viewed through the eyes of a contemporary painter of primitive art.

HAWAIIANS

Tourist and Travel Offices

HAWAII VISITORS BUREAU

Waikiki Business Plaza, Suite 801
2270 Kalakaua Avenue
Honolulu, Hawaii 96815 (808) 923-1811

441 Lexington Avenue
New York, New York 10017 (212) 986-9203

180 North Michigan Avenue, Suite 1031
Chicago, Illinois 60601 (312) 236-0632

Brooks Brothers Building
209 Post Street, Suite 615
San Francisco, California 94108 (415) 392-8173

3440 Wilshire Boulevard
Los Angeles, California 90005 (213) 385-5301

Meetings and Convention Division
1511 K Street, Northwest
Room 415
Washington, D.C. 20005 (202) 393-6752

Research Centers and Special Institutes

BERNICE P. BISHOP MUSEUM
1355 Kalihi Street
Post Office Box 6037
Honolulu, Hawaii 96818
Director: Dr. Edward C. Creutz (808) 847-3511
Founded 1889

Independent nonprofit research and educational organization. Supported by federal and local government research grants and contracts, income from trust fund and endowment, foundations, gifts and admission fees. Principal fields of research: Anthropology, botany, entomology, malacology, ichthyology, invertebrate zoology, vertebrate zoology, and history (including maritime) of the Pacific, covering studies on prehistory of Polynesia, Hawaiian archaeology, Hawaiian language, art and culture, Antarctic and western regions of the Pacific, zoo-geography and evolution of Pacific insects, faunal and floral studies in Hawaii and elsewhere in the Pacific, marine borers and Pacific island terrestrial mollusks and materials conservation services to other institutions through the Pacific Regional Conservation Center. Also collaborates with University of Hawaii, Hawaii State Department of Education, Hawaiian Academy of Science and Pacific Science Association. Maintains a scientific information service for scientists working on Pacific problems, a science center, including a planetarium-observatory and extensive archaeological and entomological research collections. Research results published in professional journals, monographs and bulletins. Maintains a major research and reference library of 77,500 volumes on anthropology, history and natural history of Pacific areas. Publications: Bishop Museum Bulletin, irregular; Occasional Papers, irregular; Journal of Medical Entomology, 6 times a year; Pacific Insects Journal, quarterly; Pacific Anthropological Records, irregular.

HAWAII RESEARCH CENTER FOR FUTURES STUDY
University of Hawaii
Social Sciences Research Institute
Honolulu, Hawaii 96822

Integral unit of Social Sciences Research Institute at University of Hawaii, located on its Manoa Campus, and housed administratively within the Institute, to facilitate communication among social scientists whose research leads to exploration of alternatives for Hawaii and other developing areas in the Pacific and Asia.

SOCIAL SCIENCE RESEARCH INSTITUTE
University of Hawaii
2635 South King Street
Honolulu, Hawaii 96822
Director: Professor Donald M. Topping (808) 944-8930

Recently reorganized and renamed organized research unit at University of Hawaii located on its Manoa Campus; formerly known as Pacific and Asian Linguistics Institute. Now initiates and conducts interdisciplinary research in social sciences as well as linguistics through four working groups focusing their primary research efforts on Hawaii, the Pacific Islands, communications and alternative futures. Principal fields of research are in the general theory and specific problems of lexicography, structural semantics and grammatical theory and description of languages and linguistics of the Pacific and adjacent areas, including studies of seven Austronesian languages, contrast of pidgin Hawaiian with a standard variety of English, phonological algorithms needed to convert Korean morphophonemic orthography into phonetic representation, Japanese syntax and computerizable models of language change and linguistic comparison,

also preparation of pedagogical materials for courses in linguistic theory and in languages of the Pacific and of a dictionary and comparative linguistic materials for languages of the Pacific. Collaborates with other departments of the University in periodical seminars related specifically to linguistics.
Publication: Oceanic Linguistics (twice a year).

Museums

BERNICE PAUAHI BISHOP MUSEUM
1355 Kalihi Street
Honolulu, Hawaii 96819 (808) 847-1443
Director: Dr. Edward C. Creutz Founded 1889

Established in 1896 to collect, preserve, store and exhibit specimens of Polynesian antiquities, ethnology and natural history. Maintains library of 88,000 volumes, archives and Hawaiian Immigrant Heritage Preservation Center. Sponsors lectures, films, adult education programs, school loan services, traveling exhibitions and training program for professional museum workers.
Publications: Bulletins; Occasional Papers; Pacific Anthropological Records and other publications.

HALE HOIKEIKE
Post Office Box 1018
Wailuku, Hawaii 96793 (808) 244-3326
Director: Mrs. Virginia Wirtz Founded 1957

Displays pre-missionary era Hawaiian artifacts, early missionary and Hawaiian royalty items in historic Hale Hoikeike, the old Bailey Mission Home, built in 1841. Offers guided tours, lectures and inter-museum loans. Has a museum shop.
Publications: La Perouse in Maui (book); Lahaina Historical Guide; Hale Hoikeike; A House and its People.

HULIHEE PALACE
Alii Drive
Kailua-Kona, Hawaii 96740
Mailing Address:
Post Office Box 838
Kailua-Kona, Hawaii 96740 (808) 329-1877
Curator: Lei Collins Founded 1838

This historic building contains collections of Hawaiian artifacts; household furnishings; portraits; furniture; tapa; featherworks and Hawaiian quilts. Offers guided tours; pageants and concerts by the sea, dance demonstrations and crafts.
Publication: Treasures of the Hawaiian Kingdom.

IOLANI PALACE
Post Office Box 2259
Honolulu, Hawaii 96804
Curator: Henry J. Bartels (808) 536-3552

Museum is comprised of the Iolani Palace and eleven-acre Palace grounds. Its collections include artifacts of the period 1882-1893, the period of the Hawaiian monarchy and original artifacts of Iolani Palace. Offers guided tours of Iolani Palace.
Publications: Newsletter, quarterly.

KAMUELA MUSEUM
Kawaihae-Kohala Junction
Route 19 & 250
Waimea, Hawaii 96743
Mailing Address:
Post Office Box 507 (808) 885-4724
Kamuela, Hawaii 96743 Founded 1968

Collections include artifacts from ancient Hawaii through the monarchy period; objects brought to the islands by ethnic groups in the 1880's; historical military items; rare royal items from the Iolani Palace as well as European and Oriental art objects.

KAUAI MUSEUM
4428 Rice Street
Lihue, Hawaii 96766
Mailing Address:
Post Office Box 248
Lihue, Hawaii 96766 (808) 245-6931
Director: Robert A. Gahran Founded 1960

The museum is housed in the 20th century Wilcox building designed by Hart Wood. It has a Hawaiiana collection with particular emphasis on items dealing with the island of Kauai; and does research in connection with the collection. Maintains a 1,000 volume library of books; pamphlets; photographs dealing with the history of the Island of Kauai available on premises. Hawaiiana books; guided tours; films; arts festivals as well as permanent and temporary exhibitions. The Museum shop sells crafts from the South Pacific.

LAHAINA RESTORATION FOUNDATION
Dickenson and Front Streets
Lahaina, Maui, Hawaii 96761
Mailing Address:
Box 338
Lahaina, Maui, Hawaii 96761 (808) 661-3262
General Manager: James C. Luckey Founded 1962

The historic ship "Carthaginian II", a whaling brig from the nineteenth century recreates the atmosphere of whaling as closed circuit TV brings the latest information on Maui's Humpback whales. Collections include period furniture, art and historical artifacts. Research is conducted in local history, ethnic studies and anthropology. Maintains library of early Hawaiiana, a botanical garden and museum shop. Offers guided tours, lectures, film, ethnic and cultural programs for children. The museum is located in three historical buildings.
Publications: Lahaina Jottings, quarterly.

LYMAN HOUSE MEMORIAL MUSEUM
276 Haili Street
Hilo, Hawaii 96720 (808) 935-5021
Director: Orlando H. Lyman Founded 1932

A history museum containing Hawaiian artifacts; lava specimens; shells and coral from the Pacific Islands; ethnic displays of the seven groups of Hawaii; and missionary family relics. The house (built in 1839 for Reverend and Mrs. Lyman, missionaries) contains Chinese teakwood furniture, art objects, and the original koa floor boards. Lectures on Hawaiian history are held and a library on Hawaiian topics is available to researchers.
Publication: Sarah Joiner Lyman of Hawaii - Her Own Story; The Lymans of Hawaii.

POLYNESIAN CULTURAL CENTER
Kamehamcha Highway (808) 293-9291
Laie, Hawaii 96762 Founded 1963

Founded to present, preserve, perpetuate the arts, crafts, culture and lore of Fijian, Hawaiian, Maori, Marquesan, Tahitian, Tongan, Samoan and other Polynesian peoples. The Center seeks to preserve and dramatize ancient cultures in danger of being swept away by the twentieth-century civilization. Polynesian natives demonstrate traditional way of life in villages of native huts at the Center, which is located on a 42-acre site on the North Shore of the island of Oahu, 38 miles from Waikiki. Visitors are offered guided tours, extemporaneous dancing by Tahitian and other Polynesian maidens, crafts demonstrations and an evening show features 175 performers. Maintains collection of Polynesian artifacts. (Operated by the Church of Jesus Christ of Latter-day Saints). Revenue from the Center is used to provide educational and employment opportunities for Polynesian young people.
Publications: Employee Update, weekly.

PU'UHONUA O HONAUNAU NATIONAL HISTORICAL PARK
Post Office Box 128
Honaunau, Hawaii 96726
Superintendent: Jerry Y. Shimoda (808) 328-2326
Founded 1961

The Park contains the restored Hale-O-Keawe building and a museum of early Hawaiian history located in an early place of refuge. A small library on Hawaiian history and natural history and a museum shop are maintained. Offers guided tours, demonstrations, films, lectures, educational programs and workshops.

QUEEN EMMA SUMMER PALACE
2913 Pali Highway
Honolulu, Hawaii 96817
Regent: Mrs. Reynolds G. Burkland (808) 595-3167
Founded 1915

In the former summer palace of Queen Emma and King Kamehameha IV, built in 1847, relics of the Hawaiian monarchy are displayed, including household furnishings and personal effects of Queen Emma and her family. Hawaiian artifacts, featherwork, tapa and quilts are exhibited. Offers guided tours, demonstrations of arts, crafts and dance of Old Hawaii, films, classes in crafts and language.

Special Libraries and Subject Collections

BERNICE P. BISHOP MUSEUM-LIBRARY
1355 Kalihi Street
Box 19000-A
Honolulu, Hawaii 96819
Librarian: Mrs. Cynthia Timberlake (808) 847-3511
Founded 1889

Subjects: Early voyages, natural and general history, archaeology and ethnology of the Pacific area. Hawaiiana special collections: Manuscripts, historic map collection; largest photo collection in Hawaii containing approximately 360,000 pictures dating from 1845; Hawaiian language newspapers. Holdings: Books, pamphlets, periodicals, newspapers, manuscripts, microfilms, photographs. Library open to public limited hours.

CITY OF REFUGE NATIONAL HISTORICAL PARK LIBRARY
United States National Park Service
Box 128
Honaunau, Hawaii 96726 (808) 328-2326
Librarian: Blossom Sapp Founded 1961

Subjects: Hawaiian culture and history; National Park Service. Holdings: Books and manuscripts. Library open to public for reference use only.

EAST-WEST POPULATION INSTITUTE RESOURCE MATERIALS COLLECTION
East-West Center
1777 East-West Road
Honolulu, Hawaii 96848
Research Materials Specialist: Alice D. Harris
(808) 944-7451
Founded 1969

Subjects: Demography, population problems and policy in Hawaii, Asian countries and Pacific area; family planning programs; environment. Holdings: Books; bound periodical volumes; reprints/papers; films; microfilms; tapes; journals and other serials. Services: Interlibrary loans and copying (through University of Hawaii libraries); library open to public with restrictions.
Publication: Acquisitions List, bimonthly.

HAWAII DEPARTMENT OF ACCOUNTING AND GENERAL SERVICES - PUBLIC ARCHIVES
Iolani Palace Grounds
Honolulu, Hawaii 96813
State Archivist: Agnes C. Conrad
(808) 548-2357
Founded 1906

Subjects: Hawaiian history and government. Special Collections: Captain Cook Collection (on Cook and discovery of Hawaiian Islands). Holdings: Books; bound periodical volumes; newspapers; government publications; manuscripts (private collections); official archives; prints and negatives; maps. Services: Copying; division open to public.

HAWAII NEWSPAPER AGENCY LIBRARY
News Building
605 Kapiolani Boulevard
Honolulu, Hawaii 96801
Chief Librarian: Beatrice S. Kaya (808) 525-7669

Special Collections: Hawaiiana. Holdings: Books and pamphlets; dissertations; reports; microfilm.

HAWAII STATE LIBRARY - HAWAII AND PACIFIC SECTION
478 South King Street
Honolulu, Hawaii 96813
Section Head: Hatsue Matsushige
(808) 548-2346
Founded 1913

Subjects: Hawaiiana; Pacifica. Special Collection: Hawaiian Historical Collection. Holdings: Books; journals and other serials; newspapers; state documents; microfilm. Services: Interlibrary loans; copying; library open to the public.
Publications: Hawaii Documents; Basic Hawaiiana; What to Read about Hawaii; Index to Honolulu Star-Bulletin and Advertiser.

HAWAIIAN HISTORICAL SOCIETY MISSION - HISTORICAL LIBRARY
560 Kawaiahao Street
Post Office Box 2596
Honolulu, Hawaii 96813
Librarian: Barbara E. Dunn
(808) 537-6271
Founded 1893

Subjects: Pacific and round the world voyages; history of Hawaiian Islands and Polynesia; local biography. Special Collections: Newspapers printed in the Hawaiian Islands, 1836-1900. Holdings: Books; journals and other serials; pamphlets; manuscripts; clippings; pictures; microfilms of early newspapers. Services: Copying; library open to public, but it is primarily for researchers.
Publication: Hawaiian Journal of History, annual.

HAWAIIAN MISSION CHILDREN'S SOCIETY - MISSION-HISTORICAL LIBRARY
553 South King Street
Honolulu, Hawaii 96813
Librarian: Mary Jane Knight
(808) 531-0481
Founded 1920

Subjects: Hawaiiana; American missions to Hawaii; voyages and travel. Special Collections: Letters and reports of American missionaries to Hawaii; books on the Hawaiian language, early Hawaiian newspapers and magazines. Holdings: Books and pamphlets; periodicals; manuscripts (cataloged); pictures; journals. Services: Library open to qualified researchers.

KATHRYN E. LYLE MEMORIAL LIBRARY
Lyman House Memorial Museum
276 Haili Street
Hilo, Hawaii 96720
Arch./Librarian: Christina R. N. Lothian
(808) 935-5021

Subjects: Hawaii - history including prehistory, volcanology, flora and fauna, mythology and legends, religions, geology, agriculture; local family genealogies; Pacific Islands; missionaries in Hawaii. Special Collections: Lyman Family; Hilo Boarding School; sugar industry. Holdings: Books; bound periodical volumes; manuscripts, paintings, newspaper clippings, maps, photographs; other historical items of early Hawaii, journals and other serials.

Services: Copying; library open to public for reference use only.
Publications: Sarah Joiner Lyman of Hawaii - Her Own Story - 1832-1885.

UNIVERSITY OF HAWAII LIBRARY
Hawaiian Collection
Hamilton Library
2550 The Mall
Honolulu, Hawaii 98622 — (808) 948-8264
Curator: David Kittelson — Founded 1927

Subjects: Hawaiian Islands; Captain Cook. Special Collections: Rare Hawaiiana. Holdings: Books; journals and other serials. Services: Interlibrary loans; copying; collection open to the public.
Publication: Current Hawaiiana, quarterly.

UNIVERSITY OF HAWAII - SPECIAL COLLECTIONS - PACIFIC COLLECTION
Hamilton Library, 2550 The Mall
Honolulu, Hawaii 96822 — (808) 948-8264
Curator: Renee Heyum — Founded 1959

Subjects: Pacific Islands government, law, linguistics, vernacular texts, literature, anthropology, history; Melanesia, Micronesia, Polynesia. Special Collections: Depository for microfilms issued by PAMBU (Pacific Manuscripts Bureau), Canberra; out-of-state theses; depository for South Pacific Commission; rare Pacific materials. Holdings: Books; journals and other serials. Services: Interlibrary loans; copying; collection open to public.
Publication: Acquisitions List.

Magazines

CULTURE LEARNING INSTITUTE REPORT. 1972-. Quarterly. Editor: William Feltz. Publisher: East-West Culture Learning Institute, East West Center, Honolulu, Hawaii 96848.

Covers the research of the center in cross-cultural influences in the areas of education, psychology, learning, language, and organization.

Radio Programs

Hawaii - Hilo

KIPA - Post Office Box 1602, Hilo, Hawaii 96720, (808) 935-6858. Hawaiian music, 40 hours weekly.

Hawaii - Honolulu

KCCN - 2270 Kalakaua Avenue, Suite 904, Honolulu, Hawaii 96815, (808) 923-0402. Format of Hawaiian programs.

KDEO - 94-1088 Farrington Highway, Waipahu, Hawaii 96797, (808) 671-2851. Contemporary Hawaiian music.

KTUH (FM) - 2500 Campus Road, University of Hawaii, Honolulu, Hawaii 96822, (808) 944-7261. Hawaiian programs, 10 hours weekly.

Hawaii - Kailua, Oahu

KLEI - Post Office Box "C", Kailua, Hawaii 96734, (808) 262-6988. Hawaiian music.

Hawaii - Kealakekua-Kona

KKON - Post Office Box 845, Kealakekua, Hawaii 96750, (808) 323-2434. 2 P.M. - 6 P.M. - all Hawaiian music.

Hawaii - Wailuku

KAOI (FM) - 1728 Kaahumanu Avenue, Wailuku, Hawaii 96793, (808) 244-9145. Special Hawaiian programs.

Commercial and Trade Organizations

HAWAIIAN SUGAR PLANTERS' ASSOCIATION
Post Office Box 1057
Aiea, Hawaii 96701
Vice President and Secretary: Robert L. Cushing — (808) 487-5561 — Founded 1895

1511 K Street, Northwest
Washington, D.C. 20005 — (202) 628-6372

Sugar companies raising sugar cane and manufacturing sugar, and individuals connected with these firms. Seeks to improve and protect the sugar industry of Hawaii. Supports an experiment station.
Publication: Hawaiian Planters' Record, annual; also publishes Hawaiian Sugar Manual.

Festivals, Fairs, and Celebrations

Hawaii - All the Islands

ALOHA WEEK
All Islands, Hawaii

The celebration is based on an ancient custom in Hawaii when the chief of Hawaii accepted taxes on the Name of Lono and the islanders then engaged in a week long festival of thanksgiving to the god for the gifts of the land. Celebrated on all the Hawaiian Islands this pageantry includes street dances, luaus, royal ball (Oahu), parade, canoe race, (Aloha Week Molokai-Oahu Canoe Race), floral floats in parade, and a songfest. There are exhibitions of poi-pounding, tapa-making, lei-stringing, and hala-weaving at a grass-thatched village in Ala Moana Park. Aloha Week king and queen (state wide) are selected. Begun around 1948. Held in late October.
Contact: Aloha Week Headquarters, 680 Ala Moana Boulevard, Room 402, Honolulu, Hawaii 96813.

Hawaii - Hilo

INTERNATIONAL FESTIVAL OF THE PACIFIC
Hilo, Hawaii

Presents a superb view of Polynesian culture and lifestyles. The festival opens with an inspiring lantern-lit parade down the main streets of Hilo. Later a lavish international pageant features ethnic dancing and music. Held for a week in mid-July.

MERRY MONARCH FESTIVAL
Hilo, Hawaii

Named for the last ruling king of Hawaii, David Kalakaua. Music, international pageant, parade, queen coronation, dancing, feasting, Grog Shoppe, a Miss Aloha hula competition, traditional and rock music, arts and crafts show, and cultural exhibits. Held in mid-April for four days. Begun around 1964.
Contact: Hawaii Island Chamber of Commerce, 180 Kinooki Street, Hilo, Hawaii 96720.

Hawaii - Honolulu

FESTIVAL OF TREES
Honolulu, Hawaii

Imaginative exhibits of decorated trees, wreaths and yule items. Sale for the benefit of Queen's Hospital. Traditional and Hawaiian Christmas carols are performed by choral groups. Held for six days in early December.
Contact: Hawaii Visitors Bureau, Suite 801, Waikiki Business Plaza, 2270 Kalakaua Avenue, Honolulu, Hawaii 96815.

KAMEHAMEHA DAY
Honolulu, Hawaii

A state holiday on June 11th honors the eighteenth century Hawaiian King Kamehameha the Great, first to rule over all of the islands. The holiday is celebrated throughout the islands with parades, pageantry, luaus, canoe races, and hula dancing. Held annually in early June.
Contact: Kamehameha Day Celebration, Post Office Box 119, Suite 801, Honolulu, Hawaii 96810.

LEI DAY
Wakiki State Park
Honolulu, Hawaii

Festival in honor of the lei. The leis are exhibited statewide, there are competitions for the best. A Lei-Day Queen and court are chosen. There is a hula pageant with singing, dancing, and chanting at the Waikiki Shell. Held on the first of May.
Contact: Hawaii Visitors Bureau, Suite 801, Waikiki Business Plaza, 2270 Kalakaua Avenue, Honolulu, Hawaii 96815.

SUNSHINE FESTIVAL
Diamond Head Crater
Honolulu, Hawaii

Features folk, rock, and Hawaiian music. Food and crafts booths.
Contact: Hawaii Visitors Bureau, Special Events Department, Honolulu, Hawaii 96815.

Hawaii - Kailua

KONA COFFEE FESTIVAL
Kailua, Hawaii

Pageantry and programs celebrating Hawaii's coffee capitol and featuring ethnic attractions such as dances, music, arts and crafts, food. International bazaar, Polynesian entertainment, coffee products, queen contest, flowers, bon dancing, coffee recipe contest, Kona Coffee Blossom Ball, queen's breakfast, and lantern parade. Held in early November. Contact: Hawaii Visitors Bureau, Special Events Department, Honolulu, Hawaii 96815.

Hawaii - Kamuela

WAIMEA HIGHLAND GAMES
Kamuela, Hawaii

Blend of Scottish and Hawaiian sports and pageantry, dancing, and exhibits. Held in October.
Contact: Pacific Area Travel Association, 228 Grant Avenue, San Francisco, California 94108.

Hawaii - Kauai Island

PRINCE KUHIO FESTIVAL
Kauai Island, Hawaii

Celebrated with pageantry, songs, and dances of the era of Prince Junah Kuhio Kalanianaole, who was the first Hawaiian delegate to Congress. Features ethnic programs, youth activities, sporting events, a parade, and an elaborate royal ball. Held annually in late March.
Contact: Hawaii Visitors Bureau, 444 Rice Street, Lihue, Kauai, Hawaii 96766.

Hawaii - Maui

NA MELE O MAUI
Maui, Hawaii

A glimpse of Hawaiian lifestyles: plants and flowers, arts and crafts, dances and music, fashion show, and luau. Held for four or five days in mid-September.
Contact: Na Mele O Maui, Post Office Box 778, Wailukee, Hawaii 96793.

Hawaii - Waikiki

GREAT HAWAIIAN JUBILEE
Kapiolani Park
Waikiki, Hawaii

Festival for cross-cultural sharing. Activities include traditional hula; Samoan entertainment, crafts, kava ceremony, and food; other events and performing arts activities. Held for two days in early April.
Contact: The State Foundation on Culture and the Arts, 250 South King Street, Room 310, Honolulu, Hawaii 96813.

HULA FESTIVAL
Kapiolani Park Bandstand
Waikiki, Hawaii

Student dancers of all ages are taught traditional Hawaiian dances by the Department of Parks and Recreation. Students from professional schools and individuals perform ancient and modern versions of the dance. Held for a week in early April.
Contact: Hawaii Visitors Bureau, Special Events Department, Honolulu, Hawaii 96815.

Airline Offices

ALOHA AIRLINES, INCORPORATED
Post Office Box 9038
Honolulu, Hawaii 96820 (808) 836-4101

Provides services within the Hawaiian Islands between the islands of Oahu, Kauai, Molokai, Maui, and Hawaii. Other offices in the United States: Chicago, Dallas, Hilo, Kahului, Kailua-Kona, Lihui (Hawaii), Los Angeles, Miami, New York, San Francisco, Seattle, and Waikiki.

HAWAIIAN AIRLINES, INCORPORATED
Post Office Box 9008
International Airport
Honolulu, Hawaii 96820 (808) 525-5511

Links all six major Hawaiian Islands, with one stop on Oahu, Maui, Kauai, Molokai, and Lanai, and three stops on the large island of Hawaii. Other offices in the United States: Boston, Chicago, Dallas, El Segundo (California), Denver, Miami, New York, Phoenix, San Francisco, Seattle, and Washington.

Bookdealers and Publishers' Representatives

BOOKFINDERS OF HAWAII
(Hawaiiana mail order)
150 Haili Street
Hilo, Hawaii 96720

F & I BOOKS
(antiquarian books on Hawaii)
Post Office Box 1900
Santa Monica, California 90406 (213) 394-7886

HONOLULU BOOK SHOPS
(current and antiquarian Hawaiian publications)
1450 Ala Moana Boulevard
Honolulu, Hawaii 96814 (808) 941-2274

ROBERT F. LUCAS
(antiquarian Hawaiian)
Post Office Box 63
Main Street
Blandford, Massachusetts 01008 (413) 848-2061

PETROGLYPH PRESS, LIMITED
(Hawaiian material)
211 Kinoole Street
Hilo, Hawaii 96720 (808) 935-3186

Books and Pamphlets

AIN'T NO BIG THING. Coping Strategies in a Hawaiian-American Community. By Alan Howard. Honolulu, University Press of Hawaii, 1974.

BIBLIOGRAPHY OF THE HAWAIIAN ISLANDS. By James Hunnewell. Boston, 1869, Reprint New York, Kraus Reprint Corporation, 1962.

This early bibliography begins with an introductory sketch of the discovery and civilization of the Hawaiian Islands, followed by a listing of books relating to these Islands.

CULTURE, BEHAVIOR, AND EDUCATION: A STUDY OF HAWAIIAN-AMERICANS. By Ronald Gallimore. Beverly Hills, California, Sage Publications, 1974.

Presents the findings from a five year study of the culture of Hawaiian-Americans in a community in Oahu. Research data was obtained from taped group discussions, observations of naturally occurring situations, life histories of children and a survey of the neighborhood.

GOVERNMENT AND POLITICS IN HAWAII: AN INFORMATION SOURCE SURVEY. By Robert Harmon. Monticello, Illinois, Vance Bibliographies, 1978. (Public Administration Series: Bibliography; P-37)

An introduction to source materials on the government and politics of Hawaii. Divided into nine sections with brief introductions: state and local government, constitutional background and development, Hawaii State Government-Legislative Branch, Hawaii State Government - Executive Branch, Hawaii State Government - Judicial Branch, politics in Hawaii, local government in Hawaii, reference materials and general sources.

HAWAII: THE ALOHA STATE. Honolulu, State of Hawaii, Hawaii Visitors Bureau, and Chamber of Commerce of Hawaii, 1976.

Describes the geography and history of the Hawaiian Islands, the economy, armed forces, government, recreation and sports, volcanoes, transportation, communication, cultural assets, education, religion, festivals, and people of Hawaii. A brochure illustrated with a map and photographs.

HAWAII: THE BIG ISLAND. Honolulu, Hawaii Visitors Bureau, 1980.

Tells about tourist attractions on Hawaii, the largest of the Hawaiian Islands. Includes a large color map of the island and color photographs of places of interest.

HAWAII: THE SUGAR-COATED FORTRESS. By Francine du Plessix Gray. New York, Vintage Books, 1972.

HAWAII'S PEOPLE. By Andrew Lind. Honolulu, University of Hawaii Press, 3rd ed., 1967.

KAUAI: THE GARDEN ISLE OF THE ISLANDS OF HAWAII. Honolulu, Hawaii Visitors Bureau, 1974.

A tourist and travel folder showing places of interest on the island of Kauai. Illustrated with a map and photographs in color.

MAUI: THE VALLEY ISLE OF THE ISLANDS OF HAWAII. Honolulu, Hawaii Visitors Bureau, 1981.

Describes tourist attractions on the second largest of the Hawaiian Islands. Illustrated with a map and photographs in color.

MOLOKAI. Honolulu, Hawaii Visitors Bureau, 1978.

Shows sites of interest to tourists on "the friendly isle" of Molokai the closest in spirit to Old Hawaii where modern development is least in evidence. Includes a map and photographs in color.

OAHU: THE GATHERING PLACE. Honolulu, Hawaii Visitors Bureau, 1981.

Presents tourist attractions on Oahu, including Honolulu, the capital city, and Waikiki. Illustrated with a color map and photographs.

THE POLYNESIAN FAMILY SYSTEM IN KA'U, HAWAII. By Mary Kawena Pukui. Wellington, New Zealand, 1958.

SOME MODERN HAWAIIANS. By Ernest Beaglehole. Honolulu, University of Hawaii, 1939 (1937).

STUDIES IN A HAWAIIAN COMMUNITY. Edited by Ronald Gallimore and Alan Howard. Honolulu, 1962.

Audiovisual Material

FILMS

HAWAII, ENCHANTED ISLE. 16 mm. or Super 8 mm. Color and sound. 9 minutes. Castle Films, 1972.

Surveys the major attractions of Hawaii, including the natural wonders and the capital city, Honolulu.

HAWAII: OUR LITTLE CORNER OF THE WORLD. 16 mm. Color and sound. 27 minutes. By Trans-World International, Chicago. Modern Talking Picture Service, 1977.

An elegant and detailed look at our magnificent 50th state. A Polynesian Pied Piper (actually a Hawaiian conch blower) entices us away for a glimpse of all there is to see and do on five of the Hawaiian Islands including Molokai, this seldom visited but most intriguing of the Islands. Great viewing for singles, families or groups looking for a 'dream vacation.' Free discussion materials available with this film.

HAWAII - OUR SUGAR ISLANDS. 16 mm. Color and sound. 22 minutes. By Vista Productions for California and Hawaiian Sugar Company. Released by West Glen Films, 1975.

Presents a history of the sugar industry of Hawaii, giving an account of the volcanic creation of the islands and of the people living there.

HAWAII: POLYNESIA IN THE U.S.A. 16 mm. Color and sound. 17 minutes. By William Claiborne, Incorporated. Released by CCM Films, Mount Vernon, New York, 1972.

Explores the contrasting ways of life in present-day Hawaii, and examines its historical past, focusing on its discovery by Captain Cook, the reign of Kamehameha, and the early missionaries who played an important role in changing the lives of the people. For elementary grades.

HAWAII REVISITED. 16 mm. Color and sound. 58 minutes (a 26 minute version also issued). Also available as videocassette. By Julian Krainin Productions for The Reader's Digest. Santa Monica, California, Pyramid Films, 1978, made 1977.

Explores the history and geography of the Hawaiian Islands, showing how their present diverse culture came into being. Narrated by James Michener.

HAWAII, STATE OF PARADISE. Super 8 mm. Color. Silent. Approximately 4 minutes. By Universal Education and Visual Arts, Universal City, California, 1969.

Shows views of Honolulu, including Waikiki Beach, the Hawaiian Village, a luau, and water sports.

HAWAII - THE FORTUNATE ISLES. 16 mm. Color and sound. Distributed by Hawaii Visitors Bureau. 29 minutes.

Breathtakingly beautiful scenery, rich treasures of cultural heritage, faces of beautiful people at work and at play, the omnipresent sun and omnipresent sea, the miracle powers of nature, the bustle of a vibrant city, the happy rhythms of a people to whom music is a part of life; that's Hawaii.

HAWAIIAN VOLCANOES. 16 mm. Color and sound. 9 minutes. Also available as videorecording. By United States National Park Service, Division of Audiovisual Arts, Washington. Distributed by National Audiovisual Center, 1979.

Shows eruptions of active volcanoes named Kilauea and Mauna Loa on the island of Hawaii. Includes footage showing cascades and lava foundations, the building of spatter cones, Mauna Loa's famous curtain of fire, and a massive lava flow from Mauna Loa plunging into the sea.

HAWAIIANS' ISLANDS. 16 mm. Color and sound. 30 minutes. By Sunset Films for Hawaiian Airlines, San Francisco, Sunset Films, 1979.

Part I presents a documentary of the history of Hawaiian Airlines using archival photographs, cinema verite, and animation. Part 2 shows tourists' activities on the islands of Oahu, Maui, Hawaii, Molokai, Lanai, and Kauai.

THE ISLANDS OF HAWAII - OUR 50TH STATE. 16 mm. Color and sound. 30 minutes. Distributed by Elliott Whiton Productions. Honolulu, Hawaii, 1974.

LEE SUZUKI: HOME IN HAWAII. 16 mm. Color and sound. 19 minutes. (Many Americans). By Learning Corporation of America, New York, 1973.

Helps develop an understanding of the ways in which people in the United States live in the story of a young Hawaiian boy who plans to help his grandfather run a boat for tourists in Honolulu Harbor. For elementary grades.

THE QUEEN'S DESTINY. 16 mm. Color and sound. 27 minutes. Also available as videocassette. By Films, Incorporated for WNET/13, Wilmette, Illinois, 1977.

Recounts the reign of Queen Liluokulani, the last divine monarch of the Hawaiian Islands.

A TASTE OF PARADISE. 16 mm. Color and sound. 28 minutes. Distributed by Pineapple Growers Association, 1978.

THE WONDERFUL WORLD OF ALOHA. 16 mm. Color and sound. 28 minutes. Distributed by Aloha Airlines, 1974.

THIS IS HAWAII. 16 mm. Color and sound. 28 minutes. Distributed by United Airlines.

Singing star Don Ho takes us on a beautiful tour of the Hawaiian Islands. The camera captures the beauty, color and splendor of this little corner of the world with background music of Hawaiian hit songs. Free discussion materials available with this film.

VOLCANO: THE BIRTH OF A MOUNTAIN. 16 mm. Color and sound. 24 minutes. Distributed by Encyclopedia Britannica Educational Corporation, 1977.

THE VOYAGE OF THE HOKULE'A. 16 mm. Color and sound. 86 minutes. Distributed by National Geographic Society, Washington, D.C., 1976.

HONDURANS
See also: SPANISH-SPEAKING PEOPLES

Embassy and Consulates

EMBASSY OF HONDURAS
4301 Connecticut Avenue, Northwest, Suite 100
Washington, D. C. 20008 (202) 966-7700

CONSULATES GENERAL

1040 West Granville #218
Chicago, Illinois 60660 (312) 338-8335

427 West Fifth Street, #714
Los Angeles, California 90013 (213) 622-1804

14 Northeast First Avenue, Suite 1104
Miami, Florida 33132 (305) 358-3477

203 Carondelet Street, Suite 707
New Orleans, Louisiana 70130 (504) 522-3118

18 East 41st Street, Suite 602
New York, New York 10017 (212) 889-3858

870 Market Street, Room 451
San Francisco, California 94102 (415) 342-0076

4301 Connecticut Avenue, Northwest, Suite 100
Washington, D. C. 20008 (202) 966-7700

CONSULATES

229 Peachtree Street, Northeast
Atlanta, Georgia 30303 (404) 659-8675

6600 East Fourth Avenue
Denver, Colorado 80220 (303) 222-3851

1130 Travis
Houston, Texas 77002 (713) 654-0900

6825 Lindberg Boulevard
Philadelphia, Pennsylvania 19142 (215) 365-6693

Mission to the United Nations

HONDURAN MISSION
415 Lexington Avenue, Room 1310
New York, New York 10017 (212) 697-2772

Information Offices

HONDURAS INFORMATION SERVICE
425 El Coronado South Pasadena
Los Angeles, California 90010 (213) 485-0261

501 Fifth Avenue
New York, New York (212) 490-0766

Airline Offices

TAN-SAHSA AIRLINES
North American Headquarters
Post Office Box 52-2222
Miami, Florida 33152 (305) 526-4332

A merger of two Honduran airlines offering international service from Miami to Mexico, Belize and the Honduras as well as from New Orleans to Panama, Guatemala, Nicaragua, the Gulf Islands and Honduras. Other offices in the United States: Chicago, Los Angeles, Houston and New York.

Books and Pamphlets

GUIDE TO COPAN, HONDURAS; Cradle of the Ancient Maya. Tegucigalpa, Honduras, Instituto Hondureño de Turismo.

Describes the temples, pyramids, and sculptures in the archaeological part at the ancient Maya city of Copan in northwest Honduras. Illustrated with a map and color photographs.

HISTORICAL DICTIONARY OF HONDURAS. By Harvey K. Meyer. Metuchen, New Jersey, Scarecrow Press, 1976.

A sourcebook of historical and contemporary facts and statistics about persons, places, events, geography and political organization.

HONDURAS. Embassy of Honduras. Washington, D.C.

A fact sheet describing Honduras' geography, culture, history, economy and national flag.

HONDURAS. THE BAY ISLANDS. Tegucigalpa, D. C., Honduras, Secretaria de Cultura y Turismo.

An illustrated tourist brochure about the islands north of Honduras in the Caribbean once occupied by pirates. Furnishes transportation and hotel information as well as a map.

HONDURAS. FACTS AND INFORMATION. Tegucigalpa, D. C., Honduras, Secretaria de Cultura y Turismo.

Information is provided on the topography, main cities, climate, cultural life, history, currency, economy, flora, sports, cuisine and folk art. The major towns are described.

AN INTRODUCTORY BIBLIOGRAPHY ON HONDURAS. By Tom L. Martinson. Monticello, Illinois, Council of Planning Librarians, 1972.

RESEARCH GUIDE TO HONDURAS. By Fernando Lanza Sandoval. Mexico, Pan American Institute of Geography and History, 1977.

Audiovisual Material

FILMS

BELIZE-BRITISH HONDURAS. 16 mm. Color and sound. 20 minutes. (Also available as video cassette). Museum of Modern Latin American Art, Washington, D.C., 1971.

Shows general patterns of culture.

HONDURAS-A WORLD INTO ITSELF. 16mm. Color and sound. 20 minutes. Museum of Modern Latin American Art, Washington, D.C., 1976. Also available as video cassette. In English and Spanish. Centers on the folk life of Honduras as well as other aspects of interest to tourists.

TRIUNFO. 16mm. Color and sound. 31 minutes. Made by Amram Nowak Associates. United States Peace Corps., Washington, D.C. Distributed by National Audiovisual Center, 1970.

A young couple, who are finishing their assignment as Peace Corps volunteers with a Honduran fish co-op, help orient their replacements to the job, their responsibilities, the people, and the culture of Honduras.

THE WORLD OF A PRIMITIVE PAINTER. 16mm. Color and sound. 20 minutes. Also available as a video cassette. Museum of Modern Art of Latin America, Washington, D.C., 1971.

Shows the works of the renowned Honduran primitive painter, J. A. Velaquez, in the setting in which he paints, San Antonio and Tegucigalpa. Has received international recognition as well as CINE's Golden Eagle in the United States. In English and Spanish.

HUNGARIANS
(Includes MAGYARS)

Embassy and Consulates

HUNGARIAN EMBASSY
3910 Shoemaker Street, Northwest
Washington, D. C. 20008 (202) 362-6730

Commercial Attache Office
2401 Calvert Street, Northwest
Washington, D. C. 20008 (202) 387-3191

Office of the Commercial Counselor
150 East 18th Street, 35th Floor
New York, New York 10021 (212) 752-3060

Hungarian Commercial Counselor's Office
Prudential Building, Suite 2430
Prudential Plaza
Chicago, Illinois 60601 (312) 856-0274

CONSULATE GENERAL
8 East 75th Street
New York, New York 10021 (212) 879-4126

CONSULATE
3910 Shoemaker Street, Northwest
Washington, D. C. 20008 (202) 362-6795

Mission to the United Nations

HUNGARIAN MISSION
10 East 75th Street
New York, New York 10021 (212) 535-8660

Tourist and Travel Offices

IBUSZ
Hungarian Travel Bureau
630 Fifth Avenue
New York, New York 10111 (202) 582-7412

Fraternal Organizations

AMERICAN HUNGARIAN CATHOLIC SOCIETY
11800 Shaker Boulevard, No. 105
Cleveland, Ohio 44120 (216) 491-8550
Founded 1894

Fraternal benefit life insurance society.

AMERICAN HUNGARIAN FEDERATION
c/o John Taba
10195 Lee Highway
Fairfax, Virginia 22030
Vice President and Treasurer: John Taba
Founded 1906

Americans of Hungarian origin. Formed to acquaint newly arrived Hungarians with the ideals of American democracy and to familiarize the second and succeeding generations with the history, art, literature, and culture of Hungary. Also known as: Amerikai Magyar Szovetseg.

FIRST HUNGARIAN LITERARY SOCIETY
323 East 79th Street
New York, New York 10021 (212) 650-9435
President: E. Rotch

Social and benevolent association for men and women of Hungarian extraction. Formerly called the Hungarian Literary Society.

HUNGARIAN AMERICAN SOCIAL CLUB, INCORPORATED
660 Tonawanda
Buffalo, New York 14207 (716) 877-9771

HUNGARIAN CLUB
1125 Southampton Road
Philadelphia, Pennsylvania 19116 (215) 969-9446

HUNGARIAN REFORMED FEDERATION OF AMERICA
11428 Rockville Pike
Rockville, Maryland 20852 (301) 770-1144
President: Rt. Reverend Arpad George
Founded 1896

Fraternal benefit insurance society for Americans of Hungarian descent.
Publications: Fraternity, quarterly.

HUNGARIAN SCOUT ASSOCIATION IN EXILE
247 Lanza Avenue
Garfield, New Jersey 07026 (201) 772-8810
President: Dr. George Nemethy Founded 1947

Offers educational programs on the Hungarian heritage and folk arts. Trains Scout Leaders. Maintains a library of 5,000 volumes.

Public Affairs Organizations

COORDINATING COMMITTEE OF HUNGARIAN ORGANIZATIONS IN NORTH AMERICA
4101 Blackpool Road
Rockville, Maryland 20853 (301) 871-7018
Executive Secretary: Istvan Gereben Founded 1965

Hungarian organizations in the U. S. and Canada. Promotes the ideals of the 1956 Hungarian revolution; coordinates activities of member organizations and serves as liaison between governments and member organizations. Member of the American-East European Ethnic Conference which is concerned with human rights in Eastern Europe. Prepares and distributes informational material on violations of human rights in Eastern Europe.

HUNGARIAN FREEDOM FIGHTERS' FEDERATION, U.S.A.
201 Raymond Avenue
South Orange, New Jersey 07079 (201) 762-3674
General Secretary: Eva Szorenyi Founded 1957

Hungarian-American political refugees of the 1956 Hungarian Revolt; Hungarian emigrants to the United States before 1956; American-born citizens who believe in the principles of the Hungarian Revolt. Seeks to perpetuate the memory of those who died in 1956 in the fight for freedom against communist oppression. Attempts to educate the American public about the plight of Hungary. Cooperates with representatives of other captive nations and with all democratic organizations whose goals are similar to the Federation's. Celebrates annually the anniversary of the Revolt. Protects and aids Hungarian refugees coming to the United States. Helps in presenting the real face of international communism to the American public. Presents an annual Freedom Award to an American or foreigner who contributes to Hungary's fight for freedom. Maintains a chapel and archives in Berkeley Springs, West Virginia. Maintains archives.
Publications: Fight for Freedom, quarterly; Magyar Szabadsagharcos, and Hungarian Freedom Fighter, both published by local chapters.

WORLD FEDERATION OF HUNGARIAN FREEDOM FIGHTERS
3403 15th Street, Northwest
Washington, D. C. 20009 (202) 234-8021
Vice President & Secretary: Ilona Maria Gyorik Founded 1956

Political refugees of the 1956 Hungarian Revolution, immigrants and individuals who share the Federation's beliefs. Works for the implementation of goals and demands as expressed by the Revolution which are: the immediate withdrawal of Soviet troops from Hungary and restoration of Hungarian sovereignty and national independence corroborated by the 1947 Paris Peace Conference; release of all political prisoners; restoration of the right to self-determination by internationally supervised free election with the participation of multiple political parties; restoration of human rights in every aspect of life, public and private, in Hungary; dedication to serving the principles of human freedom, liberty, human decency and democracy against all forms of totalitarianism. Bestows Freedom Award on those contributing most in a given year to the welfare and eventual liberation of Hungary. Maintains Information Bureau of the Hungarian Freedom Fighters (news agency). Publishes newsletters.

WORLD FEDERATION OF HUNGARIAN JEWS
136 East 39th Street
New York, New York 10016
Executive Vice President: Ervin Farkas (212) 683-5377

Represents Hungarian Jews all over the globe in matters of restitution against the German government. Unites and organizes Hungarian Jews for perpetuating the cultural values of Hungarian Jewry. Represents Hungarian Jewry against Hungarian war criminals. Carries on charitable work such as sending food parcels to Hungary and establishing social centers in Israel. Also known as the World Federation of Jews of Hungarian Descent.

Cultural and Educational Organizations

AMERICAN HUNGARIAN EDUCATORS' ASSOCIATION
c/o Eniko Molnar Basa
707 Snider Lane
Silver Spring, Maryland 20904 (202) 426-6323
President: Eniko Molnar Basa Founded 1975

Educators who are of Hungarian origin, who teach Hungarian or are active in related fields or who conduct research on Hungarian topics, including translators and librarians. Purposes are to further Hungarian cultural activities, particularly by encouraging the inclusion of folk arts, language, literature, folklore and cultural history instruction in school curricula; to provide the possibility of organizing groups and identifying methods to work within members' respective professional organizations; to provide for discussion of common problems; to further Hungarian and related studies in American and Canadian universities and other institutions of learning; to promote and participate in cooperative scholarly ventures. Resources include speakers bureau and costume and artifact museum of folklore. Produces position papers and supportive research on ad hoc basis to answer needs and queries; identifies scholars in the field. Conducts research in ethnic history; maintains immigration archives. Compiles statistics. Maintains library of 70 volumes on Hungarian folk art and literature and German classics.
Publications: American Hungarian Educator (newsletter), 3/year; Directory, annual.

AMERICAN HUNGARIAN LIBRARY AND HISTORICAL SOCIETY
215 East 82nd Street
New York, New York 10028 (212) 744-5298
President: Paul E. Veseny Founded 1955

Maintains a collection of Hungariana. Promotes research and study on the contribution of Hungarian culture to that of the United States. Presents scientific and cultural lectures. Maintains a library of about 3,000 volumes. Publishes studies on Hungarian culture.

AMERICAN HUNGARIAN FOLKLORE CENTRUM
Post Office Box 262
Bogota, New Jersey 07603 (201) 343-5240
Acting Director: Kalman Magyar Founded 1977

Persons interested in the support and promotion of Hungarian studies and folk culture within the scholarly and public life of America. Activities include researching and collecting Hungarian folklore, sponsoring folkdance festivals and organizing folklore projects within Hungarian communities. Conducts charitable programs and children's services. Maintains collection of records and video recordings, biographical archives and museum. A division of the American Hungarian Educators' Association.
Publications: Karikazo (newsletter), quarterly; also publishes articles and books.

AMERICAN LISZT SOCIETY
c/o Dr. David Z. Kushner
Department of Music
University of Florida
Gainesville, Florida 32611 (904) 392-6674
Chairman, Board of Directors: Founded 1967
Dr. David Z. Kushner

Scholars, professional musicians, students, and other interested in the life and works of Franz Liszt (1811-1886), Hungarian pianist and composer. Aim is to develop increased interest in Liszt's music, particularly that which is seldom played, through performances, recording, publications and forums for presentation of scholarly papers. Goals include: presentation of awards and grants in the areas of performance, composition and musicology for the purpose of advanced study and travel. Maintains archive of tapes of festival performances, papers, programs and other Lisztiana at the University of Florida at Gainesville.
Publications: Journal, 3/year.

HUNGARIAN CENTRAL COMMITTEE FOR BOOKS AND EDUCATION
16403 Southland Avenue
Cleveland, Ohio 44111 (216) 671-0669
President: Dr. Gabor Papp Founded 1958

Persons of Hungarian origin. Seeks to raise funds for scholarships to needy students on the high school and university levels through commemorative patriotic programs, fund-raising banquets, concerts, and other charitable programs.
Publications: Insights, quarterly.

HUNGARIAN CULTURAL ASSOCIATION
2212 North Lincoln
Chicago, Illinois 60614 (312) 525-1597

HUNGARIAN HOUSE
213 East 82nd
New York, New York 10028 (212) 650-1974

HUNGARIAN NATIONAL SPORTS FEDERATION
213 East 82nd
New York, New York 10028 (212) 744-8594

HUNGARIAN THEATER AND DANCE COMPANY
24441 Hilliard Boulevard
Westlake, Ohio 44145 (216) 835-2374
Director: Istuan Soltay Founded 1971

Studies Hungarian culture and dramatic art. Performs Hungarian dances, dramas and music. Shows films. Maintains a small library.

SOCIETY FOR HUNGARIAN PHILATELY
Post Office Box 1162
Samp Mortar Station
Fairfield, Connecticut 06430
Secretary: Thomas E. Phillips Founded 1969

Collectors of philatelic material relating to Hungary. Offers translation service; holds quarterly mail auctions.
Publications: News of Hungarian Philately, bimonthly; also publishes monographs devoted to research in specialty areas.

WORLD FEDERATION OF HUNGARIAN ARTISTS
416 East 85th Street, 3A
New York, New York 10028 (212) 988-4221
Executive President: Professor Ernest Gyimesy Founded 1963

Coordinates exhibitions of Hungarian artists in America and around the world. Maintains a collection of catalogs and photographs, a small library and an art gallery.

Foundations

AMERICAN FOUNDATION FOR HUNGARIAN LITERATURE AND EDUCATION, LIMITED
213 East 82nd Street
New York, New York 10028 (212) 249-9360

AMERICAN HUNGARIAN FOUNDATION
177 Somerset Street
New Brunswick, New Jersey 08903 (201) 846-5777
Executive Director: August J. Molnar Founded 1954

Contributors interested in furthering the understanding and appreciation of the Hungarian cultural and historical heritage in the United States. Aids persons and organizations of Hungarian origin. Supports and promotes publications, research, educational programs, and academic studies of Hungarian culture in American universities, colleges, and high schools. Maintains a library and museum collection of about 33,000 books and 500 paintings, rare volumes, and manuscripts. Presents annual George Washington awards to persons who have aided Hungary or Hungarian people and to persons of Hungarian descent who have achieved success in the United States. Plans to build a Hungarian Heritage Center, a research center for the Foundation's library, manuscripts, and museum collection. Formerly American Hungarian Studies Foundation.
Publications: Hungarian Studies Newsletter, three times a year; also publishes Hungarian Reference Shelf Series and bulletin.

CALIFORNIA HUNGARIAN AMERICAN CULTURAL FOUNDATION, INCORPORATED
Northright, California 91324 (213) 349-8933
President: George Ashley Founded 1969

Promotes the Hungarian cultural heritage in America. Maintains a reference library of 5,000 volumes.

HUNGARIAN CULTURAL FOUNDATION
Post Office Box 364
Stone Mountain, Georgia 30086 (404) 377-2600
President: Joseph M. Ertavy-Barath Founded 1966

Persons interested in preserving the Hungarian cultural heritage in the United States and elsewhere in the English-speaking world. Publishes "the best achievements of Hungarian literature and art" in the English language. Organizes exhibits and lectures; awards scholarships; promotes Hungarian studies in institutions of higher learning. Publishes books.

KOSSUTH FOUNDATION
c/o Butler University
Indianapolis, Indiana 46208 (317) 283-9552
President: Dr. Janos Horvath Founded 1957

Seeks to assist Hungarian students living in the United States. Supports research and scholarly publications about Hungary. Builds a cultural bridge between the United States and Hungary to bring about a more cordial atmosphere of sharing ideas and techniques. Named in honor of Lajos Kossuth (1802-1894), Hungarian patriot and statesman. Conducts a Scholar and Technical Expert Exchange Program with countries in Asia, Africa, and Latin America. Maintains a Hungarian Research Library of about 3,000 volumes. Absorbed the Hungarian Student Service.
Publication: The Kossuth Foundation Bulletin, monthly.

Religious Organizations

HUNGARIAN CATHOLIC LEAGUE OF AMERICA
30 East 30th Street
New York, New York (212) 684-3623
President: Msgr. John S. Sabo Founded 1943

Catholics in the United States of Hungarian origin. Aids Hungarian refugees. Supports Hungarian schools and cultural institutions in Western Europe.
Publication: Catholic Hungarian Sunday, weekly.

HUNGARIAN CATHOLIC PRIESTS' ASSOCIATION IN AMERICA
215 Somerset Street
New Brunswick, New Jersey 08901 (201) 545-1427
President: Reverend Julian Fuzner Founded 1974

Priests of Hungarian ancestry and priests of other nationalities who work among Hungarian Catholics in the United States and Canada. Advocates freedom for Hungary and the preservation of national heritage and churches built by Hungarians. Promotes spirituality and contact with the church in Hungary.

HUNGARIAN REFORMED CHURCH IN AMERICA
18700 Midway Avenue
Allen Park, Michigan 48101
Bishop: Rt. Reverend Dezso Abraham

Organized in 1904 in connection with the Reformed Church of Hungary. Formed the Free Magyar Reformed Church in America in 1922 as an autonomous, self-supporting American denomination. In 1958, this group changed its name to Hungarian Reformed Church in America.
Publication: Magyar Egyhaz (Magyar Church), monthly.

Research Centers and Special Institutes

ETHNIC HERITAGE STUDIES PROGRAM
Indiana University at South Bend
1825 Northside Boulevard
South Bend, Indiana 46615
Project Director: Richmond Calvin (219) 237-4486
Founded 1974

The Ethnic Heritage Studies Program is funded by the United States Office of Education to identify, adapt, and disseminate culturally pluralistic curriculum materials for the following ethnic groups: Afro-Americans, Hungarian-Americans, Italian-Americans, Mexican-Americans, Polish-Americans.
Publications in preparation: Bibliography; Ethnic Resource Guide; five local ethnic histories (Afro-, Hungarian-, Italian-, Mexican-, and Polish-American); multi-cultural ethnic materials.

SUBCOMMITTEE ON URALIC LANGUAGES
Columbia University
404 Philosophy Hall
New York, New York 10027 (212) 280-3963
Chairman: Professor Robert Austerlitz Founded 1959

Integral unit of Columbia University. Principal fields of research: Uralic (Hungarian, Finnish, Estonian, etc.) languages, linquistics, folklore and other aspects of culture. Also provides graduate instruction in descriptive and comparative Uralic linquistics and germane fields and compiles theoretically and practically oriented grammars, textbooks and study aids for teaching of Finnish and Hungarian languages.

Research results published in books and professional journals. Maintains a library of 25,000 volumes dealing with Hungarian, Finnish, Estonian and other Uralic subjects.

URALIC AND ALTAIC STUDIES DEPARTMENT
Indiana University
Goodbody Hall
Bloomington, Indiana 47401 (812) 337-2233
Chairman: Professor Denis Sinor Founded 1949

Integral unit of Graduate School at Indiana University. Supported by parent institution and U. S. Government.

Principal fields of research: Uralic (Hungarian, Finnish and Estonian) and Altaic and Inner Asian (Turkish, Uzbek, Mongolian, Korean, Manchu and Tibetan) language and area studies, also teaching of those languages.

Publication: JOURNAL OF ASIAN HISTORY. (Research results also published in books and professional journals.)

Museums

SAINT LADISLAUS HUNGARIAN FOLK ART MUSEUM
1412 East 29th Street
Lorain, Ohio 44055 (216) 277-8187
Director: Reverend Alex Demetzky Founded 1968

Collections include a room each of Matyo, Kalotaszegi and Kalocsai folk art as well as a section devoted to religious art. Offers crafts and dance classes.

Special Libraries and Subject Collections

AMERICAN HUNGARIAN LIBRARY AND HISTORICAL SOCIETY
215 East 82nd Street
New York, New York 10028 (212) 744-5298
President: Paul E. Vesenyi Founded 1955

Maintains a collection of Hungarica. Promotes research and study on the contributions of Hungarian culture to that of the United States.
Publications: Hungarian Digest, quarterly; Studies on Hungarian culture, occasional.

AMERICAN HUNGARIAN STUDIES FOUNDATION LIBRARY
177 Somerset Street
New Brunswick, New Jersey 08903 (201) 846-5777
Executive Director: August J. Molnar Founded 1954

Subjects: Hungarian history and culture. Holdings: Books and periodicals, rare books, works of art.
Publication: Hungarian Studies, triennial.

DR. ANDREW T. UDVARDY REFERENCE LIBRARY
66 Plum Street
New Brunswick, New Jersey Founded 1973

Subjects: Hungarian culture. Holdings: Books, periodicals, art and cultural objects, archives.
Services: Reading room, loans to schools, radio programs, dance and film production.

HUNGARIAN CULTURAL FOUNDATION
755 Columbia Drive, Suite 612
Decatur, Georgia 30030 (404) 377-2600
Librarian: Thomas Szendray Founded 1967

Subjects: Hungarian culture. Holdings: Books, periodicals, audiovisual, archives.

HUNGARIAN FREEDOM FIGHTERS FEDERATION, U.S.A., LIBRARY
201 Raymond Avenue
South Orange, New Jersey 07079 (201) 762-3674
Librarian: Mrs. Hortenzia Pogany Founded 1957

Subjects: Hungarian history and the Hungarian Revolution of 1956. Services: Library is open to qualified researchers with written permission for reference only. (Mailing Address: Post Office Box 214, Union City, New Jersey 07087).

HUNGARIAN RESEARCH LIBRARY
Kossuth Foundation
Butler University
Indianapolis, Indiana 46208
President: Dr. Janos Horvath Founded 1957

Subjects: General Information about Hungary, with strong emphasis on Hungarian culture, social sciences, and American-Hungarian relations.
Special Collections: Hungarica-Americana; the Hungarian Revolution in 1956 and 1848; Hungarian scholars, scientists, and artists in the United States. Holdings: Books; journals and other serials; newspapers; pamphlets; newspaper clippings; manuscripts; documents; photographs; maps; tapes. Services. Interlibrary loans; library open to outside users only by appointment.

SZATHMARY ARCHIVES
2218 North Lincoln Avenue
Chicago, Illinois 60614 (312) 525-1592
Director: Louis Szathmary

Subjects: Hungary and Hungarian Americans.
Holdings: Books, periodicals, audio-visual materials, art, archives. Services: offers school and media presentations, has speakers' bureau; reading room and copying.

VARDY COLLECTION
5740 Aylesboro Avenue
Pittsburgh, Pennsylvania 15217 (412) 422-7176
Founded 1955

Subjects: Hungarian history, especially earlier periods; literary history. Not open to the public.

Newspapers and Newsletters

AMERIKAI-KANADAI MAGYAR ELET (American Hungarian Life). 1959-. Weekly. Editor: Lajos Adam-Halmagyi. Publisher: American Hungarian Life, 3636 Paris Avenue, North, Chicago, Illinois 60634. In Hungarian.

AMERIKAI MAGYAR NEPSZAVA (American Hungarian People's Voice). 1899-. Weekly. Editor: Zoltan Gombos. Publisher: Nepszava, Incorporated, 1220 Huron Road, Cleveland, Ohio 44115. In Hungarian.

Publishes international and national news and events of special interest to Hungarian readers.

AMERIKAI MAGYAR SZO (Hungarian Word). 1952-. Weekly. Editor: Zoltan Deak. Publisher: Hungarian Word, Incorporated, 130 East 16th Street, New York, New York 10003. In Hungarian.

Prints general information, national and international news.

CALIFORNIAI MAGYARSAG (California Hungarians). 1922-. Weekly. Editor: Maria Fenyes. Publisher: Zoltan V. Savados, 105 South Western Avenue, Los Angeles, California 90004. In Hungarian.

Offers news on international and domestic events, as well as news of Hungarian community activities.

CHICAGO ES KORNYEKE (Chicago and Vicinity). 1906-. Weekly. Editor and publisher: Istvan Fekete, 2923C Argyle, Chicago, Illinois 60625. In Hungarian.

Covers international, national, and local news.

DETROITI MAGYAR UJSAG (Detroit Hungarian News). 1911-. Weekly. Editor and publisher: Cornelius A. Navori, 1580 Oak Street, Wyandotte, Michigan 48192. In Hungarian.

KATOLIKUS MAGYAROK VASARNAPJA (Catholic Hungarians' Sunday). 1894-. Weekly. Editor: Dr. Nicholas G. Dengl, O.F.M. Publisher: Catholic Publishing Company, 1739 Mahoning Avenue, Youngstown, Ohio 44509. In Hungarian.

Publishes news items about the Catholic Church in Hungary and news about political, cultural, and social activities and events.

MAGYAR HOLNAP (Hungarian Tomorrow). Monthly. Publisher: Hungarian Freedom Fighters (Guardian) Federation Incorporated, Box 441 Gracie Station, New York, New York 10028. In Hungarian.

MAGYARSAG (Hungarian People). 1925-. Weekly. Editor and publisher: Jeno Szebedinszky, 200 Johnston Avenue, Pittsburgh, Pennsylvania 15207. In Hungarian.

NYOLCADIK TORAS (The Eighth Tribe). Monthly. Editor: Sandor E. Chomos. Publisher: Bethlen Press, Post Office Box 637, Ligonier, Pennsylvania 15658. In English and Hungarian.

NYUGATI ÖRSZEM (West Observer). Monthly. Publisher: Arpad Dobolyi, 3294 Maynard Road, Cleveland, Ohio 44122.

SZABADSAG (Liberty). 1891-. Weekly. Editor: Zoltan Gombos. Publisher: Liberty Publishing Company, 1220 Huron Road, Cleveland, Ohio 44115. In Hungarian.

Provides general, international, national, and local news coverage for Hungarian readers, as well as some literary articles.

SZITTYAKURT. Monthly. Editor: Major Tibor, Post Office Box 35245, Puritas Station, Cleveland, Ohio 44135.

Magazines

AMERIKAI MAGYAR SZEMLE (The American Hungarian Review). 1963-. Quarterly. Editor: Leslie Konnyu. Publisher: The American Hungarian Review, 5410 Kerth Road, Saint Louis, Missouri 63128. In English and Hungarian.

Publishes articles on the arts, sciences, humanities, and Hungarian American historical and cultural relations.

A.M. SZ. HIRADO. Quarterly. Publisher: American Hungarian Federation, Post Office Box 1623, Passaic, New Jersey 07055. In Hungarian.

CARPATHIAN OBSERVER. Biennial. Editor: Louis Lote, Post Office Box 3869, Rochester, New York. Publisher: Committee of Transylvania. In English.

EVANGELIUMI HIRNÖK (Gospel Messenger). 1908-. Semimonthly. Editor: Bela Udvarnoki. Publisher: Hungarian Baptist Union of America. 748 Fordham Road, Palm Bay, Florida 32905. In Hungarian.

Includes inspirational and doctrinal articles as well as news of activities and events of the Hungarian Baptist Union of America.

HUNGARIAN DIGEST. 1976-. Quarterly. Published by the American Hungarian Library and Historical Society, 215 East 82nd Street, New York, New York 10028.

LITERARY HERALD (Irodalmi Hirado). 1955-. Monthly. Editor: Samuel Weiss. Publisher: New York First Hungarian Literary Society, 323 East 79th Street, New York, New York 10021. In Hungarian and English.

MAGYAR EGYHAZ (Magyar Church). 1922-. Monthly. Editor: Reverend Tibor Domotor. Publisher: Magyar Egyhaz Publishing Company, 1657 Centerview Drive, Akron, Ohio 44321. In Hungarian and English.

The official organ of the Hungarian Reformed Church in America, this publication informs members about ecclesiastical events. Also includes devotional and doctrinal articles and news from the congregations.

NOK VILAGA (Women's World). 1932-. Monthly. Editor: Rose Weinstock. Publisher: Nok Vilaga, Incorporated, 150 Fifth Avenue, New York, New York 10011. In Hungarian.

A women's magazine.

SZABADULÁS. Biennial. Editor: Tibor Helcz. 4907 Albart Drive, Syracuse, New York 13215. In Hungarian.

SZEKELY NÉP. Biennial. Editor: Louis Lote, Post Office Box 3869, Rochester, New York 14610. In Hungarian.

A SZIV (The Heart). 1915-. Monthly. Editor: Reverend Joseph Bieleck. Publisher: Hungarian Jesuit Fathers, 76 Locust Hill Avenue, Yonkers, New York 10701. In Hungarian.

Offers devotional and doctrinal articles as well as items on subjects relevant to Roman Catholic interests.

TESTVERISEG (Fraternity). 1923-. Quarterly. Editor: Reverend Imre Bertular. Publisher: Hungarian Reformed Federation of America, 11428 Rockville Pike, Fourth Floor, Rockville, Maryland 20034. In English and Hungarian.

Quarterly magazine free to members of the fraternal life insurance organization.

UJ VILAG (New World). Weekly. Editor: Ferenc Orbán. Publisher: Blanche Orbán, 5017 Melrose Avenue, Los Angeles, California 90038. In Hungarian.

WASHINGTON KRONIKA. 1976-. Quarterly. Editor: Gizella Rona, 1727 Massachusetts Avenue, Northwest, Washington, D. C. 20036. In Hungarian.

Carries articles about Hungarian affairs, both in Hungarian and in the American Hungarian ethnic community.

Radio Programs

California - Corona

KWRM - Box 100, Corona, California 91720, (714) 737-1370. Hungarian programs, 2 hours weekly.

California - Inglewood

KTYM - 6803 West Boulevard, Inglewood, California 90302, (213) 678-3731. Hungarian programs, 1 hour weekly.

Connecticut - Fairfield

WVOF (FM) - Box R, Fairfield University, Fairfield, Connecticut 06430, (203) 259-8020. Hungarian programs, 2 hours weekly.

Indiana - South Bend

WSBT - 300 West Jefferson Boulevard, South Bend, Indiana 46601, (219) 233-3141. Hungarian programs, 1 hour weekly.

New Jersey - New Brunswick

WCTC - Box 100, Broadcast Center, New Brunswick, New Jersey 08903, (201) 249-2600. Hungarian programs, 1 hour weekly.

New Jersey - Trenton

WTTM - 333 West State Street, Trenton, New Jersey 08618, (609) 695-8515. Hungarian programs, 1 hour weekly.

Ohio - Akron

WAUP (FM) - 302 East Buchtel Avenue, Akron, Ohio 44325, (216) 375-7105. Hungarian programs, 1 hour weekly.

Ohio - Chardon

WBKC - Box 266, Chardon, Ohio 44024, (216) 946-0136. Hungarian programs, 3 hours weekly.

Ohio - McKeesport

WEDO - 414 Fifth Avenue, Midtown Plaza Mall, McKeesport, Ohio 15132, (412) 462-9922. Hungarian programs, 1 hour weekly.

Ohio - Willoughby

WELW - 36913 Stevens Boulevard, Willoughby, Ohio 44094, (216) 946-1330. Hungarian programs, 1-1/2 hours weekly.

Television Programs

New York - New York-Newark, New Jersey

WWHT Incorporated, 416 Eagle Rock Avenue, West Orange, New Jersey 07052, (201) 731-9024. Hungarian: time not specified.

Festivals, Fairs, and Celebrations

California - Los Angeles

HUNGARIAN PRESS DAY FESTIVAL
Croatian American Center
Los Angeles, California

Special events include Hungarian Dance Festival, gypsy music, and open-fire goulash. Held annually for one day in late September.
Contact: Southern California Visitors Council, 705 West Seventh Street, Los Angeles, California 90017.

Louisiana - Albany

HUNGARIAN HARVEST DANCE
Saint Margaret Catholic Church
Albany, Louisiana

Albany is America's only rural Hungarian settlement. The dance celebrates both their traditional culture and the harvest. The festival begins with costumed dancers performing traditional Hungarian dances. Fruit decorates the ceiling of the hall; after the dance, everyone is expected to join in grabbing the fruit. Those with fruit are chased by the dancers and must pay a small 'fine' if they are caught. Everyone is welcome to join into the dancing later. Both Hungarian and contemporary American music are played. Held annually in November.
Contact: Louisiana Tourist Commission, Post Office Box 44291, Baton Rouge, Louisiana 70804.

New Jersey - Holmdel

HUNGARIAN FESTIVAL
Garden State Arts Center
Holmdel, New Jersey

Morning folk festivities, exhibits, and sports activities held at the Arts Center Plaza feature Hungarian groups and youths from New Jersey and New York. Hungarian folk art on display includes embroidery, ceramics, tapestry, and wood-carving. A Csardas contest is held. A formal afternoon program on stage features the works of Hungarian composers sung by concert singers and choral groups and played by the Kara-Nemeth Radio Orchestra, as well as the skilled Hungarian Folk Dance Ensemble. Held in mid-September.
Contact: Hungarian Festival Committee, American Hungarian Studies Foundation, Post Office Box 1084, New Brunswick, New Jersey 08903.

Ohio - Toledo

HUNGARIAN WINE FESTIVAL
St. Stephen's Church Hall
Toledo, Ohio

The Hungarian Club of Toledo holds the festival annually to coincide with a similar one in Hungary celebrating that country as the second largest producer of wine next to France. Hungarian wine, food, and gypsy music draw capacity crowds. Over 25 different types of Hungarian pastries are available. Held the first or second weekend in September.
Contact: Jim Szegti, 209 Cherry Street, Toledo, Ohio 43608.

Airline Offices

MALEV (Hungarian Airlines)
North American Headquarters:
Rockefeller Center
630 Fifth Avenue, Suite 2602
New York, New York 10020 (212) 757-6480

Serves international routes from Budapest to 37 major cities in Eastern and Western Europe, the Middle East, and North Africa.

Bookdealers and Publishers' Representatives

BRISTOL INTERNATIONAL CORPORATION
245 Main Street
Bristol, Connecticut 06010 (203) 589-3981

FAM BOOK SERVICE
69 Fifth Avenue
New York, New York 10003 (212) 243-3737

HUNGARIAN BOOKS & RECORDS
11802 Buckeye Road
Cleveland, Ohio 44120 (216) 991-3737

IMPORTED PUBLICATIONS INCORPORATED
320 West Ohio Street
Chicago, Illinois 60610 (312) 787-9017

KEREKES BROTHERS, INCORPORATED
177 East 87th Street
New York, New York 10028 (212) 289-2020

UNIVERSAL DISTRIBUTORS COMPANY
54 West 13th Street
New York, New York 10011 (212) 243-4317

Books and Pamphlets

BALATON, HUNGARY. Budapest, National Board of Tourism, 1979.

Tourist brochure illustrated in color of the sights and recreational offerings of the region around Lake Balaton. Includes some general tourist information about Hungary and a small map of the lake.

BIBLIOGRAPHY ON HUNGARY. By Zoltán Sztaray. New York, Kossuth Foundation, 1960.

Lists books in languages other than Hungarian. Includes bibliographies and general works as well as topical groupings such as history, social and cultural life, economics, religion, literature and language, music, folk arts.

BUDAPEST, HUNGARY. Budapest, National Board of Tourism, 1979.

Color illustrations of the old and the new in the capital city of Hungary make up this tourist brochure. Architecture, night life and thermal baths are featured. There is miscellaneous tourist information and a small map of the central city.

DOCTORAL DISSERTATIONS RELATED TO HUNGARY ACCEPTED IN THE UNITED STATES AND CANADA AND BIBLIOGRAPHIES ON HUNGARY. Athens, Ohio, Ohio University Library, 1974.

GUIDE TO HUNGARIAN STUDIES. By Elemer Bakó. Stanford, California, Hoover Institution Press, 1973.

A two-volume guide with over 4,000 bibliographical entries covering reference works, periodicals, monographs, and journal articles on Hungarian history, culture, and economics. Bibliographical entries are arranged under 20 categories. Cross references provide access to works on more than one subject. Includes sources in Hungarian, English, French, German, and Latin.

HUNGARIAN AUTHORS: A BIBLIOGRAPHICAL HANDBOOK. Cambridge, Belknap Press of Harvard University Press, 1970.

Part one gives a bibliography for authors from 1450-1945 and part two deals with post World War II authors. Appendices list literary awards, societies, newspapers and periodicals as well as scholarly and literary periodicals and a directory of libraries.

HUNGARIAN LITERATURE IN ENGLISH TRANSLATION PUBLISHED IN GREAT BRITAIN 1830-1968: A BIBLIOGRAPHY. By Magda Czigány. London, Szepsi Csombor Literary Circle, 1969.

Includes an annotated bibliography of books and articles on Hungarian literature and a bibliography of books translated into English. There is a chronological index as well as an index of names.

HUNGARY. By Thomas Kabdebó. Oxford and Santa Barbara, Clio Press, 1980.

An annotated bibliography arranged according to categories: geography, flora and fauna, archeology, history, population, nationalities, languages and dialects, religion, philosophy and psychology, social conditions, social services, politics, legal system, foreign relations, economics, trade, industry, agriculture, food and wine, employment, statistics, environment, architecture, education, science and technology, literature, arts, sports, libraries, archives and museums, medicine. Also lists professional periodicals, encyclopedias, directories and bibliographies.

HUNGARY. Budapest, National Board of Tourism, 1979.

General tourist information and a small map of the country accompany the many colored photographs of Hungary's architectural treasures, peasant costumes and life, spas, as well as recreational and gastronomical pleasures.

HUNGARY. Editor: Ferenc Gyulai, Budapest, Budapress, 1981.

Official information booklet printed in several languages and brought up to date every half year. Regular chapters include state administration, political and social organizations, international relations, the economy, budget management, tourism, public health and social welfare, cultural life, sports and a calendar of events.

AN INTRODUCTORY BIBLIOGRAPHY TO THE STUDY OF HUNGARIAN AUTHORS. By Albert Tezla. Cambridge, Harvard University Press, 1964.

HUNGARIAN AMERICANS

ACCULTURATION AND OCCUPATION: A STUDY OF THE 1956 HUNGARIAN REFUGEES IN THE UNITED STATES. By S. Alexander Weinstock. The Hague, Nijhoff, 1970.

A socio-psychological study of a selected sample of individual refugees in an attempt to assess factors affecting their rate of acculturation.

AMERICANS FROM HUNGARY. By Emil Lengyel. Philadelphia, J. B. Lippincott Company, 1948.

Tells about the struggle of Hungarians for freedom, immigration to America, the lives of individual immigrants and their offspring, organizations, religion, occupations, communication, cultural and intellectual activities.

BEG, BORROW AND SQUEAL. By Eugene Endrey. New York, Pageant Press, 1963.

Deals with Hungarian immigration for the general reader.

FROM THE DANUBE TO THE HUDSON; UNITED STATES MINISTERIAL AND CONSULAR DISPATCHES ON IMMIGRATION FROM THE HABSBURG MONARCHY 1850-1900. By Zoltán Kramár. Atlanta, Hungarian Cultural Foundation, 1978.

Description of documents showing how Austria and Hungary discouraged emigration. Gives the official point of view about the dimension and nature of the emigration. Particularly valuable in showing the motivation of the immigrants.

GOLDEN VILLAGE. By Joseph Anthony, Indianapolis, Bobbs-Merrill, 1924.

A novel telling about the difficulties of Hungarian Americans in a rural setting.

A HISTORY OF AMERICAN HUNGARIAN LITERATURE: PRESENTATION OF AMERICAN HUNGARIAN AUTHORS OF THE LAST 100 YEARS AND SELECTIONS FROM THEIR WRITINGS. By Leslie Konnyu. St. Louis, Cooperative of American Hungarian Writers, 1962.

Contains biographical sketches as well as an historical survey of the pioneer generation of writers, the writers between the World Wars and the new post war generation. There are sections also of the Kossuth group of immigrants, Civil War writers, the American Hungarian newspapermen and the role of churches and fraternal organizations.

HUNGARIAN LANGUAGE MAINTENANCE IN THE UNITED STATES. By Joshua A. Fishman. Bloomington, Indiana University Publications, 1966.

THE HUNGARIANS IN AMERICA. By Rezsoe and Margaret Young Grancza. Minneapolis, Lerner Publications, 1969.

For younger readers.

HUNGARIANS IN AMERICA; A Biographical Directory of Professionals of Hungarian Origin in the Americas. Series 3, 4 and 5. Edited by Desi K. Bognav. Mount Vernon, New York, Afi Publication, 1972.

A who's who of prominent Hungarian Americans, giving biographical, educational, and professional data.

HUNGARIANS IN AMERICA, 1583-1974. A Chronology and Fact Book. Compiled and Edited by Joseph Széplaki. Dobbs Ferry, New York, Oceana Publications, 1975.

A chronology of Hungarian immigration from before the American Revolution, stressing the wave of refugees resulting from the Hungarian War of Independence in 1848-49, economic immigration from 1870-1917 and political refugees in the twentieth century. Includes a selection of documents relating to Hungarian immigration at various periods. Includes appendices, a bibliography and an index.

HUNGARIANS IN BRIDGEPORT: A SOCIAL SURVEY. By Hellel Bardin. Bridgeport, Connecticut, University of Bridgeport, 1959.

HUNGARIANS IN THE UNITED STATES; An Immigration Study. By Leslie Konnyu. Saint Louis, American Hungarian Review, 1967.

A general history of Hungarian immigration and the contributions of Hungarians to America. Contains maps and photographs.

HUNGARIANS IN THE UNITED STATES AND CANADA: A BIBLIOGRAPHY. Holdings of the Immigration Research Center of the University of Minnesota. Compiled and edited by Joseph Széplaki. Minneapolis, IHRC, University of Minnesota, 1977.

Includes bibliographies and other reference works, the history of Hungarian Americans, languages, literature, religion, associations, music, serials, manuscript collections.

JOHN XANTUS: HUNGARIAN GEOGRAPHER IN AMERICA (1851-1864). By Leslie Konnyu. Koln, Hungary, American Hungarian, 1965.

A study of the Hungarian naturalist who explored and mapped the Arkansas River.

JOSEPH PULITZER AND HIS WORLD. By James Wyman Barrett. New York, Vanguard, 1941.

A biography of one of the best known Hungarian Americans treating his service in the Civil War, his rise in journalism and his contributions to American public life.

THE MAGYARS IN AMERICA. By D. A. Souders. New York, George H. Doran Company, 1922. Reprinted by R & E Research Associates, San Francisco, 1969.

Part I discusses the European background of the Magyars in Hungary. Part II deals with immigration of Magyars to America, the economic and social conditions they encountered, their religion, and special problems. Appendices include an essay on Americanization from the foreigner's point of view and a list of Magyar publications in the United States.

OUT OF THIS FURNACE. By Thomas Bell. Boston, Little, Brown, 1941.

A novelistic account of a Hungarian American family in Pennsylvania.

THE STORY OF AN IMMIGRANT GROUP IN FRANKLIN, NEW JERSEY. By Janos Makar. Franklin, New Jersey, 1969.

A localized description by an insider.

Audiovisual Material

FILMS

FARMBOY OF HUNGARY. 16 mm. Color and sound. 19 minutes. By Gabor Kalman in cooperation with Vue Touristique Film Studios, Budapest. Released by Barr Films, Pasadena, California, 1974.

Reveals the characteristics, attitudes, and values of rural life in Hungary by following a young boy as he accompanies his uncle to the village market. Shows activities on the family farm and describes the boy's school day.

HUNGARIAN REVOLT OF 1956. 8 mm. Black and white and silent. 4 minutes. Highlights in World History. By Anargyros Film Library, Los Angeles, California, 1970.

Uses scenes of demonstrations and street warfare, Hungarian poets reading in the streets, and the toppling of Stalin's statue to portray the unrest in communist Hungary which culminated in outright rebellion in 1956. Shows Russian tanks suppressing the revolt, and refugees reaching freedom at the Austrian border.

HUNGARY AND ITS PEOPLE. 16 mm. Color and sound. 16 minutes. Your World Neighbors series. By United World Films, Los Angeles, California, 1966.

Describes the geography of Hungary and discusses the effect of communism on the daily lives of the people. Explores Budapest and a small village on the Danube whose enterprises are cooperatively planned and owned.

THE RED DANUBE. 16 mm. Color and sound. 25 minutes. By CTV Television Network, Toronto, 1976.

Correspondent Michael Maclear examines the Hungarian freedom fighters who, in 1956, rebelled against Soviet oppression. He finds that these individuals have unwittingly become supporters of the regime that many gave their lives to overthrow.

The Hungarian Embassy maintains a library of informational and entertainment films and will send a list on request.

FILMS ON HUNGARIAN AMERICANS

REFUGEE. 16 mm. Color and sound. 15 minutes. By Elizabeth Ban. Washington, 1976.

Introduces two members of a Hungarian refugee family and offers their opposing points of view about being a refugee and settling in the United States.

SEARCHING FOR WORDIN AVENUE. 16 mm. Color and sound. 52 minutes. By Media Studies Center, Sacred Heart University, 5229 Park Avenue, Bridgeport, Connecticut 06606, 1980.

Shows the joys and frustrations of Hungarian immigrants in America.

ICELANDERS
See also: SCANDINAVIANS

Embassy and Consulates

EMBASSY OF ICELAND
2022 Connecticut Avenue, Northwest
Washington, D.C. 20008 (202) 265-6653

CONSULATE GENERAL
370 Lexington Avenue
New York, New York 10017 (212) 686-4100

HONORARY CONSULATES

1649 Tully Circle, Northeast
Suite 105
Atlanta, Georgia 30329 (404) 321-0777

131 South Federal Highway
Suite 4
Boca Raton, Florida 33432 (305) 395-1701

77 Franklin Street
Boston, Massachusetts 02110 (617) 482-2010

Post Office Box 299
Boulder, Colorado 80302 (303) 442-3734

221 North La Salle Street
Suite 2700
Chicago, Illinois 60603 (312) 782-6872

11429 Goodmight Lane
Dallas, Texas 75229 (214) 620-7212

606 Northland Towers East
Southfield, Michigan 48075 (313) 569-0707
(Detroit)

8820 Market Street
Camp Hill, Pennsylvania 17011 (717) 761-8084
(Harrisburg)

5220 North Ocean Drive
Hollywood, Florida 33019 (305) 920-6911

2701 Westheimer, Apt. 5A
Houston, Texas 77006 (713) 523-3336

6290 Sunset Boulevard, Suite 1125
Los Angeles, California
90028 (213) 981-6464

3642 47th Avenue, South
Minneapolis, Minnesota
55406 (612) 729-1097

1010 Plaza One
Norfolk, Virginia 23510 (804) 622-3366

310 Northwest Davis Street
Portland, Oregon 97209 (503) 226-4783

3150 20th Avenue
San Francisco, California
94132 (415) 564-4000

5610 20th Avenue, Northwest
Seattle, Washington 98107 (206) 783-4100

Post Office Box 753
270 Crossway Road
Tallahassee, Florida 32304 (904) 878-1144

Mission to the United Nations

ICELAND MISSION
370 Lexington Avenue
New York, New York 10017 (212) 686-4100

Tourist and Travel Office

ICELANDIC NATIONAL TOURIST OFFICE
75 Rockefeller Plaza
New York, New York 10019 (212) 582-2802

Fraternal Organizations

HEKLA CLUB OF MINNEAPOLIS - ST. PAUL AREA
4524 Washburn Avenue, South
Newport, Minneapolis 55410
President: Lily Gudnundson (612) 926-3696

ICELAND HOUSE
2742 Adrian Street
San Diego, California 92110
President: John Long (714) 222-2294

Affiliated with the Icelandic National League.

ICELAND VETERANS
2101 Walnut Street
Philadelphia, Pennsylvania 19103 (215) 568-1234
Caretaker: Dave Zinkoff Founded 1950

Men and women who served in the Armed Forces or Red Cross in Iceland, during World War II or later. Also known as the Forgotten Boys of Iceland (FBI's). Publication: White Falcon, Jr., annual.

ICELANDIC-AMERICAN CLUB OF SOUTHERN CALIFORNIA
17122 Baltar Avenue
Van Nuys, California 91405 (213) 881-5842
President: Holmger Brynjolesson Founded 1945

Persons interested in Iceland, its people and traditions as well as those of Icelandic descent.
Publication: Gustur (newsletter).

ICELANDIC ASSOCIATION OF CHICAGO
1985 Brighton Lane
Huffman Estates, Illinois 60195
President: Asa Thorsteinsdottir (312) 843-3268

A social and cultural group of Icelanders, people of Icelandic descent and those interested in Iceland.
Publication: Chicago Icelander Newsletter.

ICELANDIC ASSOCIATION OF THE DELAWARE VALLEY
960 Jamison Street
Hartsville, Pennsylvania

ICELANDIC ASSOCIATION OF WASHINGTON, D.C., INCORPORATED
2297 Longview Drive
Woodbridge, Virginia 22191 (703) 550-7494
President: Erlingur Ellertson Founded 1968

ICELANDIC CLUB OF GREATER SEATTLE
17508 Clover Road
Bothell, Washington 98011
President: Mrs. Didda Wilson (206) 745-0451

ICELANDIC NATIONAL LEAGUE
Baran Chapter
Cavalier, North Dakota 58276
President: Friman Melsted (701) 265-3193

ICELANDIC SOCIETY OF GREATER GRAND FORKS
Post Office Box 1294
Grand Forks, North Dakota 58201
President: Robert S. T. Johnson (701) 772-8195

ICELANDIC SOCIETY OF NEW YORK
70 Lookout Circle
Larchmont, New York 10538
President: Dr. Kristjan Ragnarsson (914) 834-7530

ICELANDIC SOCIETY OF NORTHERN CALIFORNIA
6179 Shadygrove Drive
Cupertino, California 95014
President: Thor Roff (408) 996-8110

Special Libraries and Subject Collections

OLIN RESEARCH LIBRARY
Cornell University
Fiske Icelandic Collection
Ithaca, New York 14853 (607) 256-6462
Curator: Vilhjalmur Bjarnar Founded 1905

Subjects: Islandica, with special emphasis on the Icelandic language and literature and history.
Holdings: Books, journals, and other serials.
Publication: Islandica, irregular - available on an exchange basis.

Newspapers and Newsletters

CHICAGO ICELANDER NEWSLETTER. Editor: Ludvik Fridriksson. Publisher: Icelandic Association of Chicago, 1985 Brighton Lane, Hoffman Estates, Illinois 60195. In English.

GUSTUR. Irregular. Editor: Jacob Magnusson. Publisher: Icelandic American Association of Southern California, 3200 Oakshire Drive, Los Angeles, California 90064.

Newsletter of the organization.

ICELANDIC CLUB OF GREATER SEATTLE NEWSLETTER. Editor: Ethel Vatnsdal, 6201 24th Avenue, Northwest, Seattle, Washington 98107. In English.

NEWS FROM ICELAND. 1976-. Monthly. Editor: Haraldur J. Hamar. Publisher: Iceland Review, Post Office Box 93, Reykjavik, Iceland. In English.

Contains general news and summaries of economic developments - fisheries, trade, tourism and industry - culled from the press, official press releases and other reliable sources.

Magazines

ATLANTICA & ICELAND REVIEW. 1962-. Quarterly. Editor: Haraldur J. Hamar. Publisher: Atlantica & Icelandic Review, Post Office Box 93, Reykjavik, Iceland. In English.

Provides news and general information on events and interesting people in Iceland, trade, culture, politics, science, food, tourism, fishing, and the economy. Attractively illustrated with many color photographs.

ISLANDICA. 1908-. Annually. Ithaca, New York, Cornell University Library.

Furnishes bibliographical information.

Airline Offices

ICELANDAIR, INCORPORATED
North Atlantic Headquarters:
630 Fifth Avenue
New York, New York 10020 (212) 757-8585

Offers transatlantic service from Chicago and New York to Iceland and Luxembourg. Flies routes from Iceland to Copenhagen, Glasgow, London, Oslo, and Stockholm. Other offices in the United States: Beverly Hills, Chicago, Houston, Miami, San Francisco, and Washington.

Ship Lines

HAFSKIP STEAMSHIP LINE

New York Agent:
Hansen and Tidemann, Incorporated
1 World Trade Building
New York, New York
10048 (212) 432-1910

Norfolk Agent:
Capes Shipping Agencies, Incorporated
1128 West Olney Road
Norfolk, Virginia 23507 (804) 625-3658

ICELAND STEAMSHIP COMPANY, LIMITED
c/o A. L. Burbank
2000 Seaport Avenue
Portsmouth, Virginia 23707 (804) 393-1038

Bookdealers and Publishers' Representatives

THE ANTIQUARIUM (Icelandica, new and antiquarian)
66 Humiston Drive
Bethany, Connecticut 06525 (203) 393-2723

Books and Pamphlets

BIBLIOGRAPHY OF OLD NORSE - ICELANDIC STUDIES. Copenhagen, 1963 ff.

CATALOGUE OF THE ICELANDIC COLLECTION BEQUEATHED BY WILLARD FISKE. Compiled by Halldor Hermannsson. Ithaca, New York, Cornell University Library. Norwood, Massachusetts, Plimpton, 1914. New edition, New York, 1966.

ICELAND. Reykjavik, Iceland Tourist Board.

An illustrated brochure showing scenes of natural beauty and telling about the geological highpoints, nature and wildlife as well as a short resume of the country and its inhabitants.

ICELAND: A WORLD OF DIFFERENCE. Reykjavik, Iceland State Tourist Bureau.

Shows the extremes of fiery craters and frosty glaciers and many places of interest to tourists. Discusses the history, culture, and products of Iceland. The booklet includes a map and many color photographs.

ICELAND SAGA. Special issue of The Unesco Courier, February 1974. Distributed by the Embassy of Iceland.

Tells the story of the "Land of Ice and Fire", the glaciers and geysers, the history of the country and the birth of the sagas, the active volcanic areas, the natural hot springs, and the relation to the sea.

ICELAND - SOME FACTS ON ICELAND. Reykjavik, Icelandair.

A general brochure describing the location and area, the sea, geology and topography, hot springs and glaciers, surface, climate, flora and fauna, the people, economy, communications and trade.

ICELANDIC BOOKS OF THE SIXTEENTH CENTURY (1534-1600). By Halldor Hermannsson. Ithaca, New York, Cornell University Library, 1916. Reprint, New York, Kraus, 1966.

ICELANDIC BOOKS OF THE SEVENTEENTH CENTURY, (1601-1700). By Halldor Hermannsson. Ithaca, New York, Cornell University Library, 1922. Reprint New York, Kraus, 1966.

THE NATIONAL COSTUME OF WOMEN IN ICELAND. By Elsa E. Gudjonsson. Reykjavik, 3rd edition, 1978.

An essay on the history of Icelandic traditional clothing, illustrated in manuscripts and drawings, paintings and photographs.

NORTHERN ICELAND. Land of Contrasts. Akureyri, Iceland, Fjorthungssamband Northendinga.

A fold-out map of the northern part of Iceland shows the location of the many beautiful areas pictured. The booklet describes towns and mountains, sports and outdoor life, fauna and flora, the national heritage and traditions, the coast, industry and culture.

REYKJAVIK, THE SMOKELESS CITY. Reykjavik, Reykjavik Tourist Commission.

Since Reykjavik is heated almost exclusively by boiling water from its hot springs there is a near absence of smoke in Iceland's capital city. This brochure shows pictures of Reykjavik's Old Town, important new architecture, people at play and overviews of the city. A stylized map is furnished.

ICELAND AMERICANS

MODERN SAGAS; The Story of the Icelanders in North America. By Thorstina Walters. Fargo, North Dakota, North Dakota Institute for Regional Studies, North Dakota Agricultural College, 1953.

Relates the story of daring, endurance, and resourcefulness displayed by pioneer groups who started coming to America from Iceland in the early 1870's. Analyzes the roles played by church, school, and community life in assimilation of the settlers. Pictures the home life of the immigrant families with its preservation of old Icelandic traditions, religious convictions, emphasis on integrity, and touch of mysticism and poetry.

THE RISE AND PROGRESS OF THE ICELANDIC CHURCHES IN THE UNITED STATES AND CANADA. By George Francis Patterson. Boston, Unitarian Historical Society, 1932.

Audiovisual Material

FILMS

(All are 16 mm films about 25 minutes long in color with English sound track.)

THE COUNTRY BETWEEN SANDS.

DAYS OF DESTRUCTION. 1974.

The drama of a volcanic eruption in the populated Westmann Islands in 1973. A town of ca. 5,000 inhabitants covered with pumice and lava.

DEATH OF A SETTLEMENT

FIRE ON HEIMAEY. 1975.

A film on the volcanic eruption in the Westmann Islands in 1973. Fighting the lava flow - reconstruction of the town.

FLIGHT OVER ICELAND. 15 minutes.

A view of Reykjavik and different parts of Iceland from the air. Shows the geology of Iceland.

HEKLA. 1949.

A film on the volcanic eruption of Mountain Hekla in 1947.

KING OF THE RIVER. 1978.

A film on salmon fishing in Iceland.

ON TOP OF THE WORLD. 1975.

A film on Reykjavik (the capital) today.

PROSPECT OF ICELAND. 1965.

A general introduction to Iceland.

SPRING IN ICELAND.

Tourist attractions, landscapes, sheep and ponies, etc.

SURTSEY. 1964.

A film on the volcanic eruption off the south coast of Iceland, birth of a new island, Surtsey, in 1963.

THREE FACES OF ICELAND. 1975.

A film on the country and the population, made on the occasion of the eleventh centenary of the settlement of Iceland (874-1974).

(For information about borrowing the films listed above, write to the nearest consulate or the Embassy of Iceland.)

ICELAND. 16 mm. Color and sound. 3 minutes. By Victor Sarin, Canada, 1972.

Presents a variety of impressions of Iceland.

INTRODUCING ICELAND. Videorecording. Black and white. Sound. 18 minutes. By North Atlantic Treaty Organization, Brussels. Distributed by National Audiovisual Center, NATO, Washington, D.C., 1979.

Describes the country and the people of Iceland, including geographical features, historical development and achievements, economic life, occupations of the people, and social customs. Explains briefly the role of Iceland in the North Atlantic Treaty Organization.

THEY SHOULDN'T CALL ICELAND, ICELAND. 16 mm. Color and sound. 28 minutes. By Film Authors. Iceland Tourist Board, New York, 1977, made 1976.

A travelog on Iceland. Also issued in French, German, Norwegian and Spanish.

INDIANS (East Indians)
(Includes HINDUS)
See also: ASIANS

Embassy and Consulates

EMBASSY OF INDIA
2107 Massachusetts Avenue, Northwest
Washington, D.C. 20008 (202) 265-5050

CONSULATES GENERAL

2300 North Michigan Avenue
Chicago, Illinois 60601 (312) 726-0659

3 East 64th Street
New York, New York 10021 (212) 661-8020

215 Market Street
San Francisco, California
94105 (415) 982-7036

Mission to the United Nations

PERMANENT MISSION OF INDIA TO THE UNITED NATIONS
750 Third Avenue
21st Floor
New York, New York 10017 (212) 661-8020

Tourist and Travel Offices

GOVERNMENT OF INDIA TOURIST OFFICE

201 North Michigan Avenue
Chicago, Illinois 60601 (312) 236-6899

3550 Wilshire Boulevard
Suite 204
Los Angeles, California
90010 (213) 380-8855

30 Rockefeller Plaza
North Mezzanine
New York, New York 10020 (212) 586-4901

Fraternal Organizations

ASSOCIATION OF INDIANS IN AMERICA
663 Fifth Avenue
New York, New York 10022
President: Surendra K. Saxena, Ph.D. (212) 682-0326
Founded 1967

Immigrants of Asian Indian heritage living in the United States. Seeks to continue Indian cultural activities in the United States and to encourage Asian-Indian full participation as citizens and residents of America. Promotes Indo-United States economic relations; furthers facilities for travel and tourism between India and the United States; fosters Indian studies programs in American academic institutions. Has conducted a survey of the career profile of Asian Indians. Conducts national conferences on timely subjects; sponsors cultural programs; bestows awards.
Publications: Journal, quarterly.

CULTURAL ASSOCIATION OF BENGAL
101 Iden Avenue
Pelham Manor, New York 10803 (914) 738-5727
President: Dr. Dipak Haldar Founded 1971

Fosters the cultural and social heritage of Bengal, promotes Bengali language and literature in the United States, and promotes cultural exchange between the United States and India and Bangladesh. Conducts classes in language, culture and history for Bengali children; maintains a number of libraries.
Publication: Sangbad Bichitra, monthly.

EELAM TAMILS ASSOCIATION OF AMERICA
66 Glen Street
Somerville, Massachusetts 02145 (617) 666-3125
Secretary General: T. Sri Tharan Founded 1979

Primarily persons who speak Tamil, a Dravidian language of Sri Lanka and India. Works to promote the Tamil language; seeks international publicity of Tamil problems with Sri Lanka. Conducts charitable programs in Sri Lanka; sponsors fund raising activities. Maintains library of documents on Tamil subject matter. Compiles statistics.
Publications: Progress Reports, quarterly.

FEDERATION OF INDIAN ASSOCIATIONS
Post Office Box 1327
Cathedral Station
New York, New York 10025 (212) 866-4623
President: Thomas Abraham Founded 1969

Serves as a nucleus to various existing India organizations and individuals in the United States and Canada. Arranges educational and cultural programs and organizes trips. Established an India Service Center. Promotes international goodwill and understanding. Supports a Student Relief Fund. Holds essay and children's art contests. Annually presents Mahatma Gandhi Award to distinguished individuals in the United States and Canada for their outstanding work for India and her people. Absorbed the Federation of India Student Associations of the United States of America and the Indo-American Sports Association.
Publications: India Digest (journal), semiannual; India Federation News, semiannual.

FRIENDS OF INDIA SOCIETY INTERNATIONAL
9A Clover Road
Maple Shade, New Jersey 08052 (609) 779-9584
Secretary: Madha Upadhyaya Founded 1976

Primarily persons of Indian origin living outside of India. Purposes are: to promote social, economic and political progress within India; to study the short and long term problems of Indians living in and outside of India; to function as a people's channel of communication between India and the countries of their residence; to develop internationally a "correct" image of India and India's culture; to work for the cause of human rights, civil liberties and freedom of expression all over the world; to promote peace and prosperity. Sponsors and supports developmental projects in India. Sponsors meetings, lectures, seminars and symposia.
Publications: Satyavani (newspaper), monthly; Conference Proceedings, biennial; also publishes newsletter, booklets and other material evaluating events in India.

INDIA-AMERICA SOCIETY
Post Office Box 57324
Los Angeles, California 90057
President: K. K. Mehra (213) 447-2882

Publication: Bulletin, quarterly.

TAMIL SANGAM, NEW YORK, INCORPORATED
166 Logan Avenue
Staten Island, New York 10301 (212) 273-8885
President: Dr. P. Kumaresan Founded 1970

Promotes the exchange of ideas between peoples of Tamil and other cultural backgrounds, and the preservation of the Tamil language and literature. Maintains a small collection of books and periodicals.
Publications: Newsletter, monthly; Formal Annual Report.

Cultural and Educational Organizations

AMERICAN VEGAN SOCIETY
Post Office Box H
Malaga, New Jersey 08328 (609) 694-2887
President: H. Jay Dinshah Founded 1960

Individuals interested in the compassionate, harmless way of life found in Veganism and Ahimsa. The Society defines Veganism as reverence for all life, especially avoiding cruelty and exploitation of the animal kingdom, including use of a total vegetarian diet and non-animal clothing. Ahimsa is a Sanskrit word for non-killing, non-harming. AVS outlines six guides, each beginning with a letter of Ahimsa: Abstinence from animal products; Harmlessness with reverence for life; Integrity of thought, word, and deed; mastery over oneself; Service to mankind, nature, and creation; Advancement of understanding and truth. Activities include lectures, meetings, and training members in how to live a better life; maintains educational center. Affiliated with the International Vegetarian Union.
Publications: Ahimsa, quarterly; also publishes books.

HIMALAYAN INTERNATIONAL INSTITUTE OF YOGA SCIENCE AND PHILOSOPHY OF THE U.S.A.
RD 1, Box 88
Honesdale, Pennsylvania 18431
President: Rudolph M. Ballantine, M.D. (717) 253-5551
Founded 1971

People of all ages, walks of life and faiths. Purpose is to help people understand themselves in every way; to teach holistic health care based on a synthesis of Eastern and Western knowledge techniques; and to further the personal growth of modern man and his society. Offers courses and seminars whose underlying philosophy is the practice of "Superconscious Meditation," a systematic method for developing every level of one's consciousness, and the belief that everyone has the power to recreate his life and realize his inner potential through study and practice. Imparts techniques which can be applied to daily life including techniques for regulation of the various aspects of body, mind and emotions; conducts research to establish scientific basis for these techniques. Offers stress management programs, training programs for counselors, therapists and physicians, diet and nutrition programs and training in combined therapy. Sponsors weekend seminars on a wide variety of personal growth topics.

Maintains speakers bureau; operates a children's school and a graduate school which offers masters degrees in Eastern Studies and Comparative Psychology. Has established the Eleanor N. Dana Research Laboratory and the Himalayan Institute Teachers Association, which certifies yoga teachers. Maintains library.
Publications: Himalayan News, bimonthly; Dawn Magazine, quarterly; Research Bulletin of the Himalayan International Institute/Eleanor N. Dana Laboratory, quarterly; also publishes books and tapes.

KRISHNAMURTI FOUNDATION OF AMERICA
Post Office Box 216
Ojai, California 93023
Administrative Officer: Erna Lilliefelt — (805) 646-2726
Founded 1968

Individuals interested in teachings of J. Krishnamurti, Indian author, lecturer, and educator, who believes that the "general disorder and confusion that pervades the consciousness of mankind" can be dispelled through meditation, which brings order to the activity of thought. "As such order comes, the noise and chaos of our consciousness die out." To sponsor public talks of Krishnamurti and to disseminate information on his teachings, his repudiation of all connections with organized religions and ideologies, and his concern with "setting men absolutely and unconditionally free." Has established an elementary school in Ojai, California. Conducts seminars and discussion groups and produces and distributes films, video and audio recordings on Krishnamurti's teachings. Maintains library.
Publications: Bulletin, semiannual; also publishes pamphlets and books.

Religious Organizations

AGNI YOGA SOCIETY
319 West 107th Street
New York, New York 10025 — (212) 864-7752
President: Mrs. Sina Fosdick — Founded 1946

Promotes study and research in Eastern philosophy and comparative religion. Promotes study of esoteric literature and Eastern sources. Associated with the Nicholas Roerich Museum. Publishes books and reprints.

HINDUSTAN BIBLE INSTITUTE
800 West Carson, Suite 22
Torrance, California 90502
American Director: Reverend Len Shockey — (213) 533-6097
Founded 1950

Operates Bible School in Madras, India, to train Indian nationals for mission work. Sponsors training schools, evening classes and correspondence courses for missionary work; offers open-air gospel tours and hospital visitations. Maintains rural medical ministry; operates six orphanages; distributes literature and recordings; broadcasts evangelical programs in three languages in India. Holds three Bible conferences per year in India.
Publications: Newsletter, monthly; Voice of India, quarterly; also publishes book, God of the Untouchables.

INTERNATIONAL SOCIETY FOR KRISHNA CONSCIOUSNESS
3764 Watseka Avenue
Los Angeles, California 90034
Executive Officer: David M. Schiller, Jr. — (213) 559-2874
Founded 1966

Individuals interested in Krishna. Non-sectarian, cultural, religious, philosophical and educational movement which represents tradition rooted in ancient India. Dedicated to teaching self-realization and Krishna consciousness worldwide through the practice of Bhakti-yoga and meditation on the various names of Krishna. Maintains multimedia diorama museum. Sponsors cultural festivals throughout the year.
Publications: Back to Godhead (magazine), monthly; Report (media newsletter), monthly; World Review (newspaper), monthly; also publishes Bala Books (children's stories), Bhaktivedanta Scientific Institute Monograph Series, a cassette tape ministry, religious music on tape, documentary/educational films and videotapes, and books on the philosophical and spiritual classics of India.

RAMAKRISHNA - VIVEKANANDA CENTER
17 East 94th Street
New York, New York 10028
Minister: Swami Adiswarananda — (212) 534-9445
Founded 1933

A religious organization, the Center is an accredited branch of the Ramakrishna Order of India. It functions as a self-sustaining unit, with spiritual guidance from the Order. Its minister , or Swami, is a monk of the Order. Teachings are based on the system of Vedanta, which combines both the religion and the philosophy of the Hindus, especially as explained by Sri Ramakrishna (1836-1886) and his disciple Swami Vivekananda (1863-1902) and demonstrated in their lives. Holds spiritual services; conducts Sunday services and weekly classes. Maintains a library of books on Indian and Western thought and culture.

SANATANA DHARMA FOUNDATION
3100 White Sulphur Springs Road
Saint Helena, California 94574 (707) 963-9487
Spiritual Head: Yogeswhar Muni Founded 1975

The "founding and supervising organization for Sanatana Dharma in the Western World." Sanatana Dharma means the Path of Eternal Truth or the way of living as determined by the way things actually are. Was originally organized by Charles Berner, now known as Yogeswhar Muni. Conducts: Dyad School of Enlightenment; Energy Mastery Program; Sanatana Dharma Spiritual Community; Vyasa School of Sanskrit; School of Yogic Music and Dance; G. C. Berner Library of Spiritual Sciences. The schools are attended by sincere students who wish to become teachers and practitioners of the Sanatana Dharma. The various schools conduct retreats, month-long sessions, yoga training and various types of enlightenment sessions. Maintains Spiritual Sciences Library including scriptures of all religions and hundreds of hours of recorded tape. Absorbed the Institute of Ability.
Publications: Vishvamitra, quarterly.

SELF-REALIZATION FELLOWSHIP
3880 San Rafael Avenue
Los Angeles, California 90065 (213) 225-2471
President: Daya Mata Founded 1920

Persons interested in the scientific practice of yoga "to attain direct personal experience of God." Maintains temples and centers throughout the world. Trains SRF teachers in monastic orders. Supplies 3-1/2 year series of lessons to members. Operates day and residential grade schools, high schools, colleges, a free medical dispensary and hospital in India. Students make Braille copies of some books for the blind.
Publications: Self-Realization Fellowship Lessons, weekly; Service Readings, monthly; Center Bulletin, quarterly; Self-Realization Magazine, quarterly; Yogoda Magazine (published in India), quarterly; also publishes an annual journal in German and Spanish; also publishes books and recordings by Paramahansa Yogananda and Daya Mata.

3HO FOUNDATION
1620 Preuss Road
Los Angeles, California 90035
Executive Director: Shakti Parwha Kaur Khalsa (213) 550-9043
Founded 1969

Operates 108 centers in the United States, Canada, Puerto Rico, Europe, Mexico, South America, Australia, and Japan. Members are students and teachers of Kundalini Yoga, which includes all types of Yoga, and who practice the "Healthy, Happy, Holy way of life" as taught by Yogi Bhajan. Provides nursery school education; sponsors special teacher training courses; is developing elementary schools in Phoenix, Arizona, Washington, D.C. and Los Angeles. Operates speakers bureau; provides lectures, and demonstrations of the Kundalini Yoga technique; teaches gourmet vegetarian cooking. Sponsors drug rehabilitation programs at regional centers. Operates the Kundalini Research Institute to investigate all aspects of the drug rehabilitative and other beneficial aspects of Kundalini Yoga. Also offers legal services and operates free food kitchens. Has a women's division, GGMWA, or Grace of God Movement, Women of America "for the uplift of the dignity and respect of womanhood."
Publications: Beads of Truth, quarterly; Journal of Science and Consciousness for Living in the Aquarian Age, quarterly; Peace Lagoon, a translation of the sacred writings of the Sikhs; Guru Nanak, Guru for the Aquarian Age; Teachings of Yogi Bhajan and Experience of Consciousness.

VEDANTA SOCIETY OF GREATER WASHINGTON, INCORPORATED
7430 Tower Street
Falls Church, Virginia 22046
Executive Secretary: Dr. Shanti Tayal (703) 573-4760
Founded 1968

A religious organization based on the teaching of the Vedas. Affiliated with the Ramakrishna Mission in India.
Publication: Monthly Bulletin, monthly.

VEDANTA SOCIETY OF NEW YORK
34 West 71st Street
New York, New York 10023 (212) 877-9197
Leader: Swami Tathagatananda Founded 1894

Persons interested in the religious philosophy evolved from the teaching of the Vedas, a collection of ancient Indo-Aryan scriptures. Teaches that man's real nature is divine, and the purpose of human life is to recognize this truth through prayer, meditation, spiritual inquiry, or unselfish work. Recognizes different religions to be paths to the same goal, and believes in spiritual transformation of lives rather than proselytizing. Started in New York by Swami Vivekananda, founder of the monastic Ramakrisha Order in India. Conducts public classes, services, lectures, and private interviews for instruction. There are twelve centers in the United States, all under the control of the Ramakrishna Mission.

VEDANTA SOCIETY OF NORTHERN CALIFORNIA
2323 Vallejo Street
San Francisco, California 94123 (415) 922-2323

VEDANTA SOCIETY OF SOUTHERN CALIFORNIA
1946 Vedanta Place
Post Office Box 290
Hollywood, California 90068
Minister: Swami Prabhavananda (213) 465-7114
Founded 1934

Religious organization operating under the spiritual guidance of the Ramakrishna Order of India. Maintains a church, convent, and monastery in Hollywood, a church and convent at Santa Barbara, California, and a monastery at Trabuco Canyon near Santa Ana, California. Promotes the study of the philosophy and religion of Vedanta (religion derived from the Vedas, a body of ancient Hindu scriptures) through public lectures, classes, and personal instruction in prayer and meditation. Sponsors a number of pamphlet and book publications and maintains two bookshops. Affiliated with the Vedanta Society of New York.

VIVEKANANDA VEDANTA SOCIETY OF CHICAGO
5423 South Hyde Park Boulevard
Chicago, Illinois 60615 (312) 667-7882
Director: Swami Bhashyananda Founded 1930

Emphasizes spiritual awakening of the self and service to others. Conducts lectures every Sunday morning, a children's Sunday school, and two weekday evening classes. Publishes weekly and monthly bulletins. Established a monastery-retreat in Ganges, Michigan. Maintains a library of books on religion and philosophy, a bookshop and a museum.
Publications: Yoga for Beginners; Vedanta in Chicago; Meditation; Bulletins, weekly and monthly.

Research Centers and Special Institutes

AMERICAN INSTITUTE OF INDIAN STUDIES
1130 East 59th Street
Chicago, Illinois 60637
President: Edward C. Dimock, Jr. (312) 753-4350
Founded 1961

A cooperative nonprofit organization of American colleges and universities with a special interest in Indian studies, with its executive headquarters located at University of Chicago; formerly located at University of Pennsylvania. Supported by United States Government, foundations and membership dues.

Principal field of research: Furtherance of mutual understanding between United States and India, primarily by advancing scholarly interest and achievement among Americans in all branches of Indian civilization, both ancient and modern, through fellowship studies in India. Maintains centers on campus of Deccan College in Poona, India, and in New Delhi, Calcutta and Madras. Promotes research by American scholars in India. Grants faculty research, faculty training and junior fellowships. Conducts language training program in India.
Publications: Newsletter, quarterly; Annual Report, biennial.

ELEANOR N. DANA RESEARCH LABORATORY
RD 1, Box 88
Honesdale, Pennsylvania 18431 (717) 253-5551

Established by the Himalayan International Institute of Yoga Science and Philosophy of the U.S.A. to conduct research to establish a scientific basis for techniques for the regulation of the various aspects of the body, mind, and emotions.

HIMALAYAN INSTITUTE TEACHERS ASSOCIATION
RD 1, Box 88
Honesdale, Pennsylvania 18431 (717) 253-5551

Established by the Himalayan International Institute of Yoga Science and Philosophy of the U.S.A. Offers training programs to certify yoga teachers.

SOCIETY FOR SOUTH INDIA STUDIES
c/o George L. Hart
Department of South and Southeast Asian Studies
4115 Dwinelle
University of California
Berkeley, California 94720 (415) 642-4564
Treasurer: George L. Hart Founded 1968

Scholars involved in the study of South India. Serves as a clearinghouse of information; sponsors scholarly meetings and symposia. Affiliated with Association of Asian Studies.
Publications: Newsletter, quarterly; also publishes Who's Who in South India Studies.

Museums

INTERNATIONAL SOCIETY FOR KRISHNA CONSCIOUSNESS
3764 Watseka Avenue
Los Angeles, California 90034
Executive Officer: David M. Schiller, Jr. (213) 559-2874

Maintains a multimedia diorama museum.

VIVEKANANDA VEDANTA SOCIETY
5423 South Hyde Park Boulevard
Chicago, Illinois 60615 (312) 667-7882
Librarian: Dixie Ray Founded 1930

Maintains a museum that contains artifacts and works of art representative of the culture of India. Services include tours and speakers.

Special Libraries and Subject Collections

ATMANIKETAN ASHRAM - LIBRARY
1291 Weber Street
Pomona, California 91768 (714) 629-8255
Librarian: Santosh Krinsky Founded 1973

Subjects: Sri Aurobindo, Indian spirituality, Vedanta, Sanskrit studies, Vedic-Upanishadic texts, education. Special Collections: Sri Aurobindo Birth Centenary Library; Collected Works of the Mother; Maha-Bharata (English translation); Readings in Sanitri; Cultural Heritage of India. Holdings: Books; bound periodicals; papers and reprints (cataloged); complete back issue sets of annual, monthly and quarterly journals of Sri Aurobindo Ashram, cassette tapes, journals and other serials. Services: Library open to public by appointment. Also Known As: Auromere. A branch library is located at 1291 Weber Street. Publications: Purna Yoga magazine, annual.

CONSULATE GENERAL OF INDIA - INFORMATION SERVICE OF INDIA LIBRARY
3 East 64th Street
New York, New York 10021 (212) 879-7800
Librarian: Mrs. Pushpa Gupta Founded 1958

Subjects: India: all fields of information. Special Collection: Collected works of Mahatma Gandhi and Sri Aurobindo. Holdings: Books; newspapers, clippings of Indian newspapers, documentary films, genealogical materials, journals, and other serials. Services: Library is open to the public.

LIBRARY OF THE INFORMATION SERVICE OF INDIA
Embassy of India
2107 Massachusetts Avenue, Northwest
Washington, D.C. 20008
Librarian: Baburaj Stephen (202) 565-5050

Subjects: India: philosophy and religion, history, geography, literature, political science, food and agriculture, economics, biography. Special Collections: Rabindranath Tagore collection, Mahatma Gandhi collection; Sri Aurobindo collection. Holdings: Books, newspapers, journals and other serials. Services: Interlibrary loans; library is open to the public.

Newspapers and Newsletters

AMERICAN INSTITUTE OF INDIAN STUDIES NEWSLETTER. Quarterly. Publisher: American Institute of Indian Studies, Foster Hall, University of Chicago, Chicago, Illinois 60637. In English.

CENTER BULLETIN. Quarterly. Publisher: Self-Realization Fellowship, 3880 San Rafael Avenue, Los Angeles, California 90065. In English.

News of the activities of the Self-Realization Fellowship.

EELAM TAMILS ASSOCIATION OF AMERICA PROGRESS REPORTS. Quarterly. Publisher: Eelam Tamils Association of America, 66 Glen Street, Somerville, Massachusetts 02145. In English.

Concerned with persons who speak Tamil, a Dravidian language of Sri Lanka and India.

HIMALAYAN NEWS. Bimonthly. Publisher: Himalayan International Institute of Yoga Science and Philosophy of the U.S.A., RD 1, Box 88, Honesdale, Pennsylvania 18431. In English.

News relating to yoga and the activities of the Institute.

HINDUSTAN BIBLE INSTITUTE NEWSLETTER. Monthly. Publisher: Hindustan Bible Institute, 800 West Carson, Suite 22, Torrance, Colorado 90502. In English.

News and activities of the Hindustan Bible Institute.

INDIA ABROAD. 1970-. Weekly. Editor: Vidya Chandra. Publisher: India Abroad Publications, Incorporated, 60 East 42nd Street, New York, New York 10017. In English.

Publishes news from India.

INDIA-AMERICA SOCIETY BULLETIN. Quarterly. Editor: Sushila Janadass. Publisher: India-America Society, c/o Sushila Janadass, Editor, 1811 North Las Palmas Avenue, Hollywood, California 90028. In English.

INDIA FEDERATION NEWS. Semiannual. Publisher: Federation of Indian Associations, Post Office Box 1327, Cathedral Stations, New York, New York 10025. In English.

News relating to activities of Indian organizations throughout the United States and Canada.

INDIA-WEST. 1975-. Weekly. Editor: Ms. Bina Murarka. Publisher: India-West Publications, Incorporated, 4510 Peralta Boulevard, No. 23, Fremont, California 94536. In English.

Publishes news from India and the United States.

INDIAN OPINION. 1975-. Biweekly. Editor: Rani Chopra. Publisher: S. Poddar, Indians for Democracy, South Print Plaza, Lansing, Michigan 48910, (517) 393-4777. In English.

Newsletter of the Indians for Democracy.

INTERNATIONAL SOCIETY FOR KRISHNA CONSCIOUSNESS REPORT. Monthly. Publisher: International Society for Krishna Consciousness, 3764 Watseka Avenue, Los Angeles, California 90034. In English.

A media newsletter on the activities of the Society.

NEWS & CINE INDIA. 1977-. Weekly. Editor: N. M. Hira. Publisher: Hiba Publishing, 320 East 55th Street, New York, New York 10022. In English.

SATYAVANI. Monthly. Publisher: Friends of India Society International, 9A Clover Road, Maple Shade, New Jersey 08052.

Newspaper primarily for Indian emigrants.

SOCIETY FOR SOUTH INDIA STUDIES NEWSLETTER. Quarterly. Publisher: Society for South India Studies, c/o George L. Hart, Department of South and Southeast Asian Studies, 4115 Dwinelle, University of California, Berkeley, California 94720. In English.

Reports news and activities of scholars involved in the study of South India.

TAMIL SANGAM NEWSLETTER. Monthly. Publisher: Tamil Sangam, New York, Incorporated, 166 Logan Avenue, Staten Island, New York 10301. In English.

News items relating to Tamil people, language and literature.

VEDANTA SOCIETY OF GREATER WASHINGTON MONTHLY BULLETIN. Monthly. Publisher: Vedanta Society of Greater Washington, 7430 Tower Street, Falls Church, Virginia 22046. In English.

Contains news items about the society, its programs and members.

VIVEKANANDA VEDANTA SOCIETY OF CHICAGO BULLETINS. Weekly and Monthly. Publisher: Vivekananda Vedanta Society of Chicago, 5423 South Hyde Park Boulevard, Chicago, Illinois 60615. In English.

WORLD REVIEW. Monthly. Publisher: International Society for Krishna Consciousness, 3764 Watseka Avenue, Los Angeles, California 90034. In English.

A newspaper for individuals interested in Krishna.

Magazines

AHIMSA. Quarterly. Publisher: American Vegan Society, Post Office Box H, Malaga, New Jersey 08328. In English.

Contains articles relating to Ahimsa, a Sanskrit word meaning non-killing, non-harming.

ASSOCIATION OF INDIANS IN AMERICA JOURNAL. Quarterly. Publisher: Association of Indians in America, 663 Fifth Avenue, New York, New York 10022. In English.

BACK TO GODHEAD. Monthly. Publisher: International Society for Krishna Consciousness, 3764 Watseka Avenue, Los Angeles, California 90034. In English.

Magazine containing articles on self-realization and Krishna consciousness.

BEADS OF TRUTH. Quarterly. Publisher: 3HO Foundation, 1620 Preuss Road, Los Angeles, California 90035. In English.

Focuses on Kundalini Yoga.

COLLABORATION. 1974-. Quarterly. Editor: Eric Hughes. Publisher: Matagiri, Mount Tremper, New York 12457. In English.

Carries information on projects worldwide of the followers of Sri Aurobindo. Publishes photographs and poetry by followers.

DAWN MAGAZINE. Quarterly. Publisher: Himalayan International Institute of Yoga Science and Philosophy of the U.S.A., RD 1, Box 88, Honesdale, Pennsylvania 18431. In English.

Articles on the practice and philosophy of yoga.

INDIA DIGEST. Semiannual. Publisher: Federation of Indian Association, Post Office Box 1327, Cathedral Station, New York, New York 10025. In English.

Journal containing articles on India.

INDIAN ENGINEERING EXPORTER. Quarterly. Publisher: India Engineering Export Promotion Council, 333 North Michigan Avenue, Suite 2014, Chicago, Illinois 60601. In English.

Contains information on engineering products from India.

JOURNAL OF SCIENCE AND CONSCIOUSNESS FOR LIVING IN THE AQUARIAN AGE. Quarterly. Publisher: 3HO Foundation, 1620 Preuss Road, Los Angeles, California 90035. In English.

Reports results of research and studies of the beneficial aspects of Kundalini Yoga.

KRISHNAMURTI FOUNDATION OF AMERICA BULLETIN. Semiannual. Publisher: Krishnamurti Foundation of America, Post Office Box 216, Ojai, California 93023. In English.

Disseminates information on teachings of J. Krishnamurti.

NAYA DAUR. 1973-. Quarterly. Editor: Sohail Jalibi. Publisher: 1065 Shady Hill Drive, Columbus, Ohio 43221. In Urdu.

RESEARCH BULLETIN OF THE HIMALAYAN INTERNATIONAL INSTITUTE/ELEANOR N. DANA LABORATORY. Quarterly. Publisher: Himalayan International Institute of Yoga Science and Philosophy of the U.S.A., RD 1, Box 88, Honesdale, Pennsylvania 18431. In English.

Reports results of research and studies on Yoga science and philosophy.

SATSANG. 1973-. Semimonthly. Editor: Vasant V. Paranjpe. Publisher: Agnihotra Press, 1708 Whitehead Road, Woodlawn, Virginia 24381. In English.

Prints religious and philosophical articles and warnings about pollution of the atmosphere and earth.

SELF-REALIZATION MAGAZINE. Quarterly. Publisher: Self-Realization Fellowship, 3880 San Rafael Avenue, Los Angeles, California 90065. In English.

Contains articles relating to yoga and self-realization.

VISHVAMITRA. 1975-. Quarterly. Editor: Narada Muni. Publisher: Sanatana Dharma Foundation, 3100 White Sulphur Springs Road, Saint Helena, California 94574.

Carries discussions of yoga, meditation, and Dharma. Contains articles by the Guru and testimonials.

VOICE OF INDIA. Quarterly. Publisher: Hindustan Bible Institute, 426 West Carson, Carson, California 90702. In English.

Articles relating to the Institute's missionary work in India.

Radio Programs

California - Los Gatos

KRVE (FM) - 227 North Santa Cruz Avenue, Los Gatos, California 95030, (408) 354-6622. Hindu programs, 1/2 hour weekly.

California - San Francisco

KEST - 1231 Market Street, San Francisco, California 94103, (415) 626-5585. Special programs in Hindu.

California - Stockton

KSTN (FM) - 2121 Ralph Avenue, Stockton, California 95206. Hindu programs, 4 hours weekly.

California - Yuba City

KXEZ (FM) - Box 309, Yuba City, California 95991, (916) 673-1600. Punjabi programs, 4 hours weekly.

Colorado - Boulder

KGNU (FM) - Box 1076, Boulder, Colorado 80306, (303) 449-4885. East Indian programs, 3 hours weekly.

Connecticut - West Hartford

WWUH (FM) - University of Hartford, West Hartford, Connecticut 06117, (203) 243-4703. Eastern Indian programs, 1 hour weekly.

Illinois - Chicago

WSBC - 4949 West Belmont Avenue, Chicago, Illinois 60641, (312) 777-1700. Indian programs, 1 hour weekly.

Maryland - Bethesda

WHFS (FM) - 4853 Cordell Avenue, Bethesda, Maryland 20014, (301) 656-0600. East Indian programs, 2 hours weekly.

Massachusetts - Cambridge

WMBR (FM) - 3 Ames Street, Cambridge, Massachusetts 02142, (617) 253-4000. Indian programs, 2 hours weekly.

Michigan - Detroit

WDET (FM) - 655 Merrick, Detroit, Michigan 48202, (313) 577-4204. East Indian programs, 1 hour weekly.

New York - New York

WFUV (FM) - Fordham University, Bronx, New York 10458, (212) 933-2233. Nation of India programs, 1-1/2 hours weekly.

New York - Stony Brook

WUSB (FM) - State University of New York, Stony Brook, New York 11794, (516) 246-7900. Indian programs, 1 hour weekly.

New York - Syracuse

WAER (FM) - 215 University Place, Syracuse, New York 13210, (315) 423-4021. Indian/Pakistan programs, 1 hour weekly.

WYRD - 3000 Erie Boulevard East, Syracuse, New York 13224, (315) 446-7442. Indian programs, 1 hour weekly.

New York - Troy

WRPI (FM) - Troy, New York 12181, (518) 270-6248. Indian programs, 3 hours weekly.

Pennsylvania - California

WVCS (FM) - 428 Hickory Street, California State College, California, Pennsylvania 15419, (412) 938-4330. Hindi programs, 1 hour weekly.

Pennsylvania - Canonsburg

WARO - Box 191, Canonsburg, Pennsylvania 15317, (412) 531-8800 or 745-5400. Hindi programs, 1 hour weekly.

Virgin Islands - Charlotte Amalie

WVWI - Box 5170, Saint Thomas, Virgin Islands, 00801, (809) 774-1000. East Indian programs, 1 hour weekly.

Television Programs

New Jersey - Newark

WNJU-TV - 1020 Broad Street, Newark, New Jersey 07102. Hindi, unspecified.

New Jersey - West Orange

WWHT - 416 Eagle Rock Avenue, West Orange, New Jersey 07052. East Indian, unspecified.

Bank Branches in the U.S.

BANK OF INDIA
277 Park Avenue
New York, New York 10172 (212) 753-6100

Commercial and Trade Organizations

INDIA CHAMBER OF COMMERCE OF AMERICA
c/o Prakash Shah
American Express International Bank
American Express Plaza
New York, New York 10004
Executive Director/Secretary: (212) 323-3197
Prakash Shah Founded 1934

Provides forum for development of economic and commercial relations of an Indo-American nature. Has established a trade center that assists businessmen from India and the United States. Affiliated with: Chamber of Commerce of the United States.

INDIA ENGINEERING EXPORT PROMOTION COUNCIL
333 North Michigan Avenue, Suite 2014
Chicago, Illinois 60601
Regional Manager, North America:
P. K. Banerjee (312) 236-2162

Manufacturers of engineering products in India. Aids members in sales and product promotion, marketing research, advertising and importation of engineering products into the Canadian and United States markets. Provides service to United States importers on the selection and choice of products from India. Publications: Indian Engineering Exporter, quarterly; Directory of Indian Engineering Exporters.

Airline Offices

AIR INDIA
North American Headquarters:
400 Park Avenue
New York, New York 10022 (212) 407-1460

Flies from India to the Arab Middle East, western Europe, and to the United States. Flies east-west routes to Japan or Australia and the South Pacific via Southeast Asia. Also serves an Indian Ocean-East Africa route from India. Other offices in the United States: Chicago, Cleveland, Dallas, Detroit, Los Angeles, Philadelphia, San Francisco, and Washington.

Ship Lines

INDIA SHIPPING COMPANY
157 Tonnele Avenue
Jersey City, New Jersey 07306 (201) 656-0808

Bookdealers and Publishers' Representatives

AUROMERE
(imports books from India)
1291 Weber Street
Pomona, California 91768 (714) 629-8255

CULTURAL INTEGRATION FELLOWSHIP BOOKSTORE
(Arabic, Bengali, Chinese, Hindi, Sanskrit)
3494 21st Street
San Francisco, California 94110 (415) 648-1489

THE EAST AND WEST SHOP
(carries antiquarian books on India)
4 Appleblossom Lane
Newtown, Connecticut 06470 (203) 426-0661

GULHMOHR BOOKS
(imports books from India)
Post Office Box 1414
Los Altos, California 94022

IMPORTED PUBLICATIONS, INCORPORATED
320 West Ohio Street
Chicago, Illinois 60610 (312) 787-9017

INDIA BOOK HOUSE LIMITED
10 Norden Lane
Huntington Station, New York 11746 (516) 271-0548

INDUS BOOKS
(specializes in antiquarian books on India)
Post Office Box 812
Davis, California 95616 (916) 756-4495

INTERNATIONAL PUBLICATIONS SERVICE
(imports books from India)
114 East 32nd Street
New York, New York 10016 (212) 685-9351

R. E. LEWIS, INCORPORATED
(lists books from India)
Post Office Box 1108
San Rafael, California 94902 (415) 461-4161

MATAGIRI
(imports books from India)
Mount Tremper, New York 12457 (914) 679-8322

MEHER BABA LEAGUE BOOKSHOP
(imports books from India)
2131 University Avenue
Room 235
Berkeley, California 94704 (415) 845-4339

NAROPA INSTITUTE BOOKSTORE
(specializes in books from India, Japan and Tibet)
2034 14th Street
Boulder, Colorado 80302 (303) 449-6219

THE OLD GEOGRAPHY COMPANY
(carries antiquarian material from and on India)
354 Front Street
Owego, New York 13827 (607) 687-5943

PARAGON BOOK GALLERY LIMITED
14 East 38th Street
New York, New York 10016 (212) 532-4920

TEC-BOOKS LIMITED (Librairie De Documentation Technique SA)
(specializes in technical books in many languages, including Hindi)
41 William
Pittsburgh, Pennsylvania 12901 (518) 561-0005

THULASI BOOK IMPORTS
(imports books in Sanskrit)
Box 7850
Stanford, California 94305 (415) 968-6345

Books and Pamphlets

ANNOTATED BIBLIOGRAPHY ON THE ECONOMIC HISTORY OF INDIA, (1500 A.D. to 1947 A.D.) By Gokhale Institute of Politics and Economics, Pune, India, Gokhale Institute of Politics and Economics, 1977.

An eleven part bibliography, that is bound into four volumes, on the economic history of India plus Pakistan and Bangladesh. Includes records, reports, acts, Parliamentary papers, census reports, serials, books, articles and theses.

ASPECTS OF INDIAN CULTURE; Select Bibliographies. Edited by H. S. Patil and R. N. Sar. New Delhi, Bhatkal Books International, 1966.

This set of volumes contains reprints of various bibliographies on aspects of Indian art and culture that were originally published in Cultural News from India. The entries have been revised and annotated.

BOOKS FOR THE MULTI-RACIAL CLASSROOM: A SELECT LIST OF CHILDREN'S BOOKS, SHOWING THE BACKGROUNDS OF THE INDIAN SUB-CONTINENT AND THE WEST INDIES. Second revised edition. By Judith Elkin. London Library Association Youth Libraries Group, 1976.

A list, for educators, of the children's books judged to be worthwhile on the geographical, cultural and religious backgrounds of the Indian sub-continent and the West Indies.

BOOKS ON INDIA. Compiled by Nancy C. Scott. Gettysburg, Pennsylvania, Gettysburg College Library, 1966.

A partially annotated bibliography. Supplement I was issued in 1972.

A GUIDE TO REFERENCE MATERIALS ON INDIA. Edited by N. N. Gidwani and K. Navalani. Jaipur, Saraswati Publications, 1974.

A two volume set that provides a listing of reference materials in the field of Indian studies. Covers all types of materials except maps, reports and general world-wide compendia.

INDIA. Washington, D.C., Embassy of India.

A collection of circulars discussing India's land and people, political structure, foreign policy, Hindu religion, family planning, and other topics concerning the country.

INDIA; A Critical Bibliography. By J. Michael Mahar, Tucson, University of Arizona Press, 1964.

A select, graded, annotated list of works, mainly in English that provide a guide to what materials are available on traditional and modern India.

INDIA: AJANTA, ELLORA. New Delhi, Government of India Department of Tourism, 1972.

A brochure about the ancient Buddhist and Hindu temples and monasteries at Ajanta and Ellora near Aurangabad, India. Illustrated with a map and color photographs of the sculptures, paintings, and shrines found in the rock-hewn caves at these archaeological sites.

INDIA: DYNAMIC PROGRESS THROUGH DEMOCRACY. Washington, D.C., Embassy of India, 1982.

Discusses the political structure of India, its economic progress in industrial, agricultural, and scientific areas, and its improvements in education and health. Includes information on customs, cultural achievements, and national emblems. Contains many photographs in color.

INDIA: TEMPLES OF KHAJURAHO. New Delhi, Government of India Department of Tourism, 1973.

Describes the spectacular group of twenty-two temples built by the Chandellas of the warrior Rajput clan in medieval times. Tells the history of the Hindu and Jain shrines at Khajuraho. A brochure illustrated with a map and photographs of the temples and ornamental sculptures.

INDIA: TRAVEL INFORMATION. New York, Government of India Tourist Office.

A booklet presenting information about travel regulations, transportation, foods, products, books on India and accommodations in India.

INDIA AND INDIANS: A BIBLIOGRAPHY; Holdings of the Colgate University Library in Two Volumes. Edited by Ravindra N. Sharma. Hamilton, New York, Colgate University Library, 1974.

Provides a listing of the library's collection on India arranged alphabetically with Library of Congress subject headings. Includes standard bibliographic information.

INDIAN POLITICAL MOVEMENT, 1919-1971: A SYSTEMATIC BIBLIOGRAPHY. By Arun Ghash. Calcutta, India Book Exchange, 1976.

A bibliography of documents, books, pamphlets and selected articles and editorials on the political history of India during 1919-1971. Majority of the documents are from political parties and groups.

INDIAN REFERENCE SOURCES: AN ANNOTATED GUIDE TO INDIAN REFERENCE BOOKS. By Hari Dev Sharma. Indian Bibliographic Centre, 1972.

An annotated listing of reference books published in India, both in Indian languages and English. Only books either in print or easily available in libraries were included in the guide.

MAHARASHTRA AND THE MARATHAS: THEIR HISTORY AND CULTURE; A Bibliographic Guide to Western Language Materials. Compiled by Datta Kharbas. Rochester, New York, University of Rochester Library, 1973.

POPULAR HINDUISM AND HINDU MYTHOLOGY: AN ANNOTATED BIBLIOGRAPHY. By Barron Holland. Westport, Connecticut, Greenwood Press, 1979.

This bibliography covers works on Hinduism and Hindu mythology published up to 1978. Includes monographs, journal articles, chapters of monographs, essays and articles from collections and doctoral dissertations in the major European languages.

A SELECTED AND ANNOTATED BIBLIOGRAPHY OF THE GOVERNMENT, POLITICS AND FOREIGN RELATIONS OF INDIA. Berkeley, California, California University, Human Relations Area Files, 1956.

A bibliography of government documents, secondary works, periodical articles and unpublished materials on political thought, government and administration, political process and foreign relations of India.

SOUTH ASIA, A SELECTED BIBLIOGRAPHY ON INDIA, PAKISTAN, CEYLON. By Patrick Wilson. New York, American Institute of Pakistan Relations, 1957.

A list to introduce the general reader to what is available on South Asia. Foreign booksellers dealing in South Asia publications are noted at the end of the bibliography.

THIS IS INDIA. Madras, India Tourism Development Corporation, 1977.

This colorful illustrated booklet describes modern-day India and its tourist attractions.

TRADITION, SOCIAL CHANGE AND MODERNIZATION IN INDIA: A SELECTED RESEARCH BIBLIOGRAPHY, PART I (1900-1961). PART 2 (1962-1972). By Prakash C. Sharma. Monticello, Illinois, Council of Planning Librarians, 1974.

This bibliography lists studies conducted in the area of traditionalism, social change and modernization in India. The studies have been published from 1900-1972. Both parts of the bibliography are divided into two parts: part one contains the listing of books and monographs and part two covers research articles and periodicals.

INDIAN AMERICANS

ASIANS IN AMERICA: FILIPINOS, KOREANS, AND EAST INDIANS. By Howard Brett Melendy. Boston, Twayne Publishers, 1977. (The Immigrant Heritage of America Series).

Examines the three immigrant groups, Filipinos, Koreans and East Indians and what motivated them to come to America and how they coped in American society. Includes a selective bibliography.

CALIFORNIA AND THE ORIENTAL: JAPANESE, CHINESE AND HINDUS REPORT OF STATE BOARD OF CONTROL OF CALIFORNIA TO GOVERNOR WILLIAM D. STEPHENS, JUNE 19, 1920, REV. TO JANUARY 1, 1922. Sacramento, California State Printing Office, 1922. Reprint, San Francisco, R and E Research Associates, 1970.

A reprint of the report by the State Board of Control of California on the subject of Oriental immigration, population and land ownership.

EAST INDIAN IMMIGRATION ON THE PACIFIC COAST. By Jogesh Misrow. Stamford, California, 1915. Reprint San Francisco, R and E Research Associates, 1971.

A broad look at East Indian immigration with emphasis on its effect on British imperialism and American life. Data for this work was obtained through personal experience of the author, study of documents, reports and other literature on immigration.

INDIAN COMMUNITY REFERENCE GUIDE AND DIRECTORY OF INDIAN ASSOCIATIONS IN NORTH AMERICA. Federation of Indian Associations, 1979.

Provides information on practical questions such as taxes, legal matters, employment, and health services for Indians visiting or living in North America. Also lists the names, addresses, telephone numbers, and officers of hundreds of Indian associations in North America.

INDIAN STUDENTS ON AN AMERICAN CAMPUS. By Richard Lambert. Minneapolis, University of Minnesota Press, 1956.

This book contains the results of studies of Indian students to determine the adjustments the students made while in the United States and when they returned home. A sample interview with a student is included.

THE NEW ETHNICS: ASIAN INDIANS IN THE UNITED STATES. Edited by Parmatma Saran and Edwin Eames. New York, Praeger, 1980.

A collection of papers that were presented at a "conference on the new immigration organized by the Research Institute on Immigration and Ethnic Studies of the Smithsonian Institution in 1976." The purpose of the papers was to show the present condition of Asian Indians in the United States.

Audiovisual Material

FILMS

ARTS OF INDIA. Videocassette. Color and sound. 30 minutes. Stamford, Connecticut, Educational Dimensions Group, 1979.

Shows some important art collections of India.

BUDDHISM-FOOTPRINT OF THE BUDDHA-INDIA. Videocassette. Color and sound. 52 minutes. BBC-TV. Producer: Peter Montagnon; Narrator: Ronald Eyre. New York, Time-Life Multimedia, 1978.

Visits Sri Lanka and India to discover the type of Buddhism practiced throughout Southeast Asia. Includes talks with monks, school children, novices, and housewives who describe their own religious experiences and discuss the high moral standards demanded by Buddhism. Includes study guide. Also issued as motion picture.

FAMILIES OF THE WORLD-INDIA. 16 mm. Color and sound. 19 minutes. United Nations Children's Fund. Evanston, Illinois, Journal Films, 1976.

Explores family life in India. Focuses on a family and its 85 members, who live in a small village. Shows how they share eating, living, and sleeping quarters in the same compound. Points out changes that are taking place in their culture and the dreams of the people for a better future. Includes teacher's guide.

THE FAMILY KRISHNAPPA. 16 mm. Color and sound. 18 minutes. Benchmark Films, A-V Media. Briarcliff Manor, New York, Benchmark, 1977.

Depicts one day in the life of a typical rural family and village in Southern India.

FARM VILLAGE OF INDIA: THE STRUGGLE WITH TRADITION. 16 mm. Color and sound. 21 minutes. By Coronet Instructional Films, Chicago, 1971.

Views of a farmer and his wife on the Ganges Plain trying to improve their life are used to give a glimpse of village life in India. Emphasizes the problems that result from government inefficiencies.

FARMERS OF INDIA. 16 mm. Color and sound. 13 minutes. Russell Wulff. Released by Oxford Films, 1975.

Depicts life in a village of prosperous Hindu farmers through the family of a 14-year-old boy whose father owns 20 acres of land. Points out that the family practices many ancient traditions but is receptive to modern ways.

GANDHI'S INDIA. 16 mm. and videocassette. Black and white. Sound. 20 minutes. BBC-TV, New York. Time-Life Multimedia, 1969.

An account of India's efforts to obtain home rule beginning in the 1800's. Discusses Gandhi's successful leadership of India's independence from Britain, the conflict between Muslim Pakistan and Hindu India, and the birth of modern India and Pakistan.

GANGES RIVER RAFTING. 16 mm. Color and sound. 19 minutes. New York, ABC Sports, 1978.

Actor Robert Duvall journeys down the Ganges. Along the way he befriends the villagers who live along the river and learns about the Indian way of life.

GURDEV BROTHERS-AFTER SCHOOL CHORES. 8 mm. Color. Silent. 4 minutes. Made by Arthur C. Twomey. Released by Sound Book Press Society, 1975.

Shows two Indian brothers as they come home from school to groom the family cow and calf and hoe a small vegetable and flower garden. Loop film in cartridge. With teacher's guide on cartridge container.

GURDEV BROTHERS AT ELEMENTARY SCHOOL. 8 mm. Color. Silent. 4 minutes. Made by Arthur C. Twomey. Released by Sound Book Press Society, 1975.

Shows two young brothers and their daily activities in elementary school in New Delhi. Points out that during a six-day school week students take courses in several languages, including English, Hindi, Sanskrit, Punjabi, as well as courses in math, history, spelling, and art. Loop film in cartridge. With teacher's guide on cartridge container.

GURDEV BROTHERS-BREAKFAST AND SCHOOL. 8 mm. Color. Silent. 4 minutes. Made by Arthur C. Twomey. Released by Sound Book Press Society, 1975.

Shows the daily routines of two young brothers who are members of the Sikh religion. Loop film in cartridge. With teacher's guide on cartridge container.

GURDEV BROTHERS-GAMES AND HOMEWORK. 8 mm. Color. Silent. 4 minutes. Made by Arthur C. Twomey. Released by Sound Book Press Society, 1975.

Shows two Indian brothers playing on a homemade rocking toy and joining in a marble game. Also shows them as they write their homework in the ancient Sanskrit script. Loop film in cartridge. With teacher's guide on cartridge container.

GURDEV BROTHERS VISIT HINDU TEMPLE. 8 mm. Color. Silent. 4 minutes. Made by Arthur C. Twomey. Released by Sound Book Press Society, 1975.

Shows two Indian brothers as they visit the Shri Lakshminarain temple and observe preparations for Divali, the festival of lights. Loop film in cartridge. With teacher's guide on cartridge container.

HERDING CASTES OF CENTRAL INDIA-THE MATHURA, THE HATKAR DHANGARS. 16 mm. Color and sound. 25 minutes. Margaret C. Fairlie. Ithaca, New York. Ithaca College School of Communications, 1978.

Compares and contrasts the daily lifestyles, ceremonial rites, and dance forms of the Mathura and Hatkar Dhangar tribes of central India. Relates their communal activities with their symbolic religious and kinesthetic patterns. Includes study guide.

HINDU DEVOTIONS AT DAWN. 16 mm. Color and sound. 10 minutes. Image of India, number 9. By H. Daniel Smith. Released by Film Marketing Division, Syracuse University, Syracuse, New York, 1969.

Shows a middle-aged Hindu performing his daily devotions to the sun. Explains that these prayers and praises must precede any other ritual undertaking of the day. Filmed within the Tengalai Brahmin community of Srivaisnauas.

HINDU PROCESSION TO THE SEA. 16 mm. Color and sound. 8 minutes. Image of India, number 7. By H. Daniel Smith. Released by Film Marketing Division, Syracuse University, Syracuse, New York, 1969.

Explains that processions of temple deities through the streets of India constitute a prominent part of visible Hinduism, and that each procession is a celebration of one moment in the on-going liturgical year of any given temple. Shows in Madras, India, one of these processions, which has as its object the bathing of the temple deity in the sea.

THE HINDU RITUAL SANDHYA. 16 mm. Color and sound. 19 minutes. Doris Srinivasan. Released by Center for Mass Communication, Columbia University Press, 1972.

A study of the Hindu ritual, Sandhya, which is over 2500 years old, and its ancient cultural heritage. Shows how Sandhya is performed by a Maharashtrian Smarta Brahman, follower of the Sakala school of the Rig Veda. Explains that this practice is an example of cultural continuity in a traditional society.

HINDU RITUALS. 16 mm. Color and sound. 7 minutes. Religions of the Eastern World. By Lew Ayres. Released by International Communication Films, Santa Ana, California, 1968.

A study of the various Hindu rituals and of the importance of the Ganges River on Hindu life. Includes views of ritual bathing in the Ganges and of a formal burning of the dead.

HINDU VILLAGE BOY. 16 mm. Color and sound. 11 minutes. By Atlantis Productions, Thousand Oaks, California, 1970.

Uses events in the life of a Hindu village boy in northern India to show the changes taking place in the lives of the farmers of India, and to explain that technical improvements necessitate changes in vocational and human relationships.

HINDUISM. 16 mm. Color and sound. 21 minutes. Lew Ayres. Irvine, California, Doubleday Multimedia, 1976.

Explains the rituals, symbols, and teaching of Hinduism. Includes sequences on its history, religious beliefs, and practices. Includes teacher's guide.

HINDUISM: THE MANY PATHS TO GOD. 16 mm. Color and sound. 26 minutes. ABC News. Narrator: Edward P. Morgan. Released by Xerox Films, 1974.

Explores several facets of the Hindu religion as practiced in India. Shows how people worship many different gods in festivals, celebrations and in private meditation.

HINDUISM - THE SONG OF GOD. 16 mm. Color and sound. 30 minutes. Hartley Productions, 1975. Made by Elda Hartley.

Intoruces the philosophy and religion of Hinduism, emphasizing the concepts of self-realization as expressed in the Bhagavad gita. Deals with purpose in life, the four yogas, the law of Karma, and the four stages of life.

HINDUISM: 330 MILLION GODS. 16 mm. and videocassette. Color and sound. 52 minutes. BBC-TV. Producer: Peter Montagnon; Narrator: Ronald Eyre; Camerman: John Else. New York, Time-Life Multimedia, 1978.

Visits various sites in India and observes the performance of several types of religious ceremonies. Explores the Hindu approach to God and the complexity of the Hindu religious experience. Includes study guide.

HOLY MEN OF INDIA. 16 mm. Color and sound. 10 minutes. Religions of the Eastern World. By Lew Ayres. Released by International Communication Films, Santa Ana, California, 1968.

Shows events in the day of a Hindu holy man as he meditates, goes through various steps of worship, and demonstrates an unusual series of Yoga practices.

IN INDIA THE SUN RISES IN THE EAST. 16 mm. Color and sound. 18 minutes. By Richard Kaplan Productions. Released by McGraw-Hill Book Company, New York, 1969.

Presents scenes of various aspects of life in urban and rural India.

INDIA. Videocassette and 16 mm. Color and sound. 25 minutes. Arlington, Virginia, Screenscope, 1979.

A look at the human geography of India through the many sights and sounds of teeming cities and thousands of villages.

INDIA: ALONG THE TIBETAN BORDER. 16 mm. Color and sound. 16 minutes. By Lem Bailey Productions. Released by AV-ED Films, Hollywood, California, 1968.

Describes the characteristics of the different areas along the Tibetan border of India and tells about the life of the people there.

INDIA, ASIA'S SUBCONTINENT. 16 mm. Color and sound. 17 minutes. Paul Hoefler Productions. Mount Prospect, Illinois, Mar/Chuck Film Industries, 1969.

Shows some of India's 450 million people as they till the fields, lift water for irrigation, and transport freight and agricultural products to market. Also shows how India's leaders, who are faced with problems of flood and drought, overpopulation, and inadequate funds, are attempting to raise the living standards of the people through the building of dams, education, and the introduction of modern machinery.

INDIA, PEOPLE IN TRANSITION. 16 mm. Color and sound. 17 minutes. Paul Hoefler Productions. Mount Prospect, Illinois, Mar/Chuck Film Industries, 1969.

Presents important concepts relating to the history, religions, and social and political structure of India in order to give students a better understanding of the difficult problems facing India as it makes the transition to the modern state.

INDIA-THE BEWILDERED GIANT. 16 mm. Color and sound. 38 minutes. BBC-TV. Writer: Dom Moraes. New York, Time-Life Multimedia, 1971.

A portrait of contemporary political and social conditions in India. Examines the problems of racial and caste tensions, the predominance of local rather than national loyalties, and the general disorganization following the implementation of communism.

INDIA: THE LAND. 16 mm. Color and sound. 9 minutes. Asia: Lands and People. By Alpha Corporation of America, Mundelein, Illinois, 1968.

Describes the physical geography of India, including the size, climates, land forms, and rainfall patterns. Explains the basic patterns of agriculture and natural resources, and discusses the villages and cities of India.

INDIA: THE PEOPLE. 16 mm. Color and sound. 7 minutes. Asia: Lands and People. By Alpha Corporation of America, Mundelein, Illinois, 1968.

Describes the people of India and explains the divisions in their patterns of life, language, and history. Discusses the religions of India and the nationalistic feeling.

INDIA: THE STRUGGLE FOR FOOD. 16 mm. Color and sound. 18 minutes. Oriental World series. By Vision Associates. Released by McGraw-Hill Book Company, New York, 1968.

Examines the problems of increasing food production in rural India. Shows family life and the daily schedule of activities among farmers in India. Pictures the forces of change and improvement which are reaching the villages under government auspices.

INDIA: URBAN CONDITIONS. 16 mm. Color and sound. 19 minutes. Oriental World Series. By Vision Associates. Released by McGraw-Hill Book Company, New York, 1968.

Shows the problems, frustrations, and general living conditions of a typical workman and his family in a large Indian city. Describes the urgent need for industrial growth in India and the factors which are retarding such growth. Discusses the concept that population growth in India is so rapid that it tends to negate government attempts to increase food production, stimulate industrial growth, and improve the living conditions of the people.

INDIA AND THE INFINITE: THE SOUL OF A PEOPLE. 16 mm. Color and sound. 30 minutes. Cos Cob, Connecticut, Hartley Film Foundation, 1979.

Pictures an India of many paradoxes and extremes: the many religions, the love of ritual and what it symbolizes, and great art and architecture.

THE INDIA TRIP. 16 mm. Color and sound. 50 minutes. By the National Film Board of Canada, New York, 1971.

Presents a journey to Pondicherry, India.

AN INDIAN PILGRIMAGE-KASHI. 16 mm. Color and sound. 30 minutes. South Asian Area Center, University of Wisconsin, Madison. Producer: Joseph W. Elder; Directors: Mira Reym Binford, Michael Camerini. Madison, The Center, 1976.

Presents a documentary on a pilgrimage to the sacred city of Kashi on the Ganges River. Follows two Telegu-speaking Brahmins and their wives who come from south India to perform classical ancestor rites. Shows some of the tenets of Hinduism as the pilgrims are instructed in the correct performance of the rites by a Brahmin Telegu-speaking priest. In Telegu, with English subtitles. Includes film guide.

AN INDIAN PILGRIMAGE-RAMDEVRA. 16 mm. Color and sound. 26 minutes. South Asian Area Center, University of Wisconsin, Madison. Producer: Joseph W. Elder; Directors: Mira Reym Binford, Michael Camerini. Madison, The Center, 1974.

Presents a documentary on a folk pilgrimage to Ramdevra, India. Follows a group of Hindus from Bombay to the grave of Ramdev, a medieval hero and saint of Rajasthan. Shows ways in which the Hindu pilgrims are free to worship, their collective offering at Ramdev's grave, and their interactions with other pilgrims, shoppers, preachers, hawkers, and devotional singers who throng the festival. In Rajasthani, with English subtitles. Includes film guide.

JYOTI. 16 mm. Color and sound. 17 minutes. Film Australia. Ossining, New York, Wombat Productions, 1977.

Follows the everyday activities of a 12-year-old Hindu girl who lives in a self-contained industrial complex outside Bombay.

NEW DELHI DENTIST'S FAMILY - MORNING. 8 mm. Color. Silent. 4 minutes. Made by Arthur C. Twomey. Released by Sound Book Press Society, 1975.

Visits the family of a New Delhi dentist in their middle-class neighborhood. Shows that their life is a blend of modern ways and traditional customs. Loop film in cartridge. With teacher's guide on cartridge container.

NEW DELHI-FRUIT AND VEGETABLE MARKET. 8 mm. Color. Silent. 4 minutes. Made by Arthur C. Twomey. Released by Sound Book Press Society, 1975.

Shows a young Indian girl visiting an outdoor market in New Delhi. Loop film in cartridge. With teacher's guide on cartridge container.

ONE DAY WITH SHIVA. 16mm. Color and sound. 8 minutes. Director: P. R. Zielinski. Montreal, Concordia University, 1975.

An impressionistic documentary of south India.

PIYARE. 16 mm. Color and sound. 10 minutes. Robert and Eileen Zalisk, 1975.

A 12-year-old boy who sells flutes to tourists in Benares, India, talks about himself, his family, and his work. Also issued in super 8 mm.

RANA. 16 mm. Color and sound. 19 minutes. Film Australia. Ossining, New York, Wombat Productions, 1977.

Follows the everyday activities of a young Moslem college student in Old Delhi. Points out the restrictions of her religion and includes interviews with her family.

TEXTILES AND ORNAMENTAL ARTS OF INDIA. 16mm. Color and sound. 12 minutes. Charles Eames and Ray Eames, 1955. Released by Encyclopaedia Britannica Educational Corporation, 1973.

Records and preserves the essence of an exhibition of textiles and ornamental arts of India assembled by Alexander Girard and Edgar Kaufman and presented at the Museum of Modern Art in New York. Includes teacher's guide.

VISHNU'S MAYA. 16 mm. Color and sound. 30 minutes. Saraswati Films, Director and Writer: Thomas Ball, New York, Phoenix Films, 1977.

Visually explores the beauty of India and examines classical Hindu culture.

The Embassy of India maintains a collection of more than 150 short documentaries, which include many films on dance, geography, science, industry and history of India. There are biographies of Ghandi, Nehru, Tagore, artist Nandlal Bose and others. A large number of films are about animals. A few use archival footage, including one on the history of the Indian film industry, 1913-1963. Folk tales are told in animation, live action, and dance.

For further information, contact:

Embassy of India
Information Service
2107 Massachusetts Avenue, Northwest
Washington, D.C. 20008 (202) 265-5050

INDOCHINESE
(Includes CAMBODIANS; HMONG; LAOTIANS; VIETNAMESE)
See also: ASIANS

Mission to the United Nations

MISSION OF THE SOCIALIST REPUBLIC OF VIETNAM TO THE UNITED NATIONS
20 Waterside Plaza
New York, New York 10010 (212) 685-8001

MISSION OF THE KINGDOM OF LAOS
820 Second Avenue, Suite 400
New York, New York 10017 (212) 986-0227

Fraternal Organizations

INDOCHINESE COMMUNITY CENTER
1628 Sixteenth Street, Northwest
Washington, D.C. 20009 (202) 462-4330
Director: Vilay Chaleunrath Founded 1977

Established to foster a sense of solidarity, friendship and mutual assistance through sharing experience among the three Indochinese refugee groups and the American community. Provides comprehensive resettlement services, including employment services, information and referral, orientation, counseling, adjustment of INS status, translation and interpretation, and cultural, social and educational activities.

VIETNAMESE

DALAT UNIVERSITY ALUMNI ASSOCIATION, INCORPORATED
2844 Subtle Lane
Fairfax, Virginia 22031
President: Nguyen Van Son (703) 654-9180

Brings together graduates of Dalat University for fraternal and social activities.
Publication: Thu Nhan, (newsletter), quarterly.

ORGANIZATION OF FREE VIETNAMESE
478 West Hamilton Avenue, Suite 161
Campbell, California 95008 (408) 379-2046
President: Ngo Chi Dung Founded 1975

Fraternal organization of overseas Vietnamese dedicated to the struggle for freedom and human rights in Vietnam.

TRUONG XUAN FRIENDSHIP ASSOCIATION
6604 Lee Highway
Falls Church, Virginia 22046 (703) 241-8298
President: Pham Ngoc Luy Founded 1975

Fraternal organization of Vietnamese dedicated to the ideals of freedom as symbolized by the S.S. Truong Xuan, the Exodus of Vietnamese 'boat people'.

VIETNAMESE CATHOLIC STUDENTS AND PROFESSIONAL ASSOCIATION OF NORTH AMERICA
1628 Sixteenth Street, Northwest
Washington, D.C. 20009
President: Reverend Pham Quang Thuy (202) 462-4330
Founded 1950

Fraternal organization of Vietnamese in the United States, not necessarily of the Catholic faith, dedicated to the welfare and progress of the Vietnamese community in North America.

VIETNAM MUTUAL ASSISTANCE PROGRAM
164 North Mill Street
Pontiac, Michigan 48058 (313) 334-5040
Director: Nghuyen Huy Han (313) 338-1127

Established to encourage mutual cooperation and voluntarism in communities in 28 states across the nation. Provides Mutual Assistance Associations with national goods distribution network of food and personal care products. Plans to distribute audiovisual materials and books. Promotes integration into American society as well as cultural preservation. Was host to a national convention of all Vietnamese Mutual Assistance Associations in August 1982 which included a cultural exhibition and fair and a national olympics for Vietnamese young people in the United States.

VIETNAMESE PARENTS ASSOCIATION
1120 North Harrison Street
Arlington, Virginia 22205 (703) 532-1949
President: Pham Khac Tri Founded 1980

Created to coordinate Vietnamese parent involvement in the educational process of their children. Supports bilingual/multicultural education. There are local groups in many cities in the United States.

VIETNAMESE SENIOR CITIZENS ASSOCIATION
c/o Linh Quang Vien
8500 New Hampshire Avenue, Apartment 141
Silver Spring, Maryland 20903 (301) 445-3898
President: Linh Quang Vien Founded 1978

Organization has members not only in the United States but also abroad (France, Canada, Australia, Zaire, etc.). Dedicated to the upholding of Vietnamese traditions.

VIETNAMESE WOMEN'S ASSOCIATION
Post Office Box 9327
Washington, D.C. 20005 (202) 966-0015

Offers assistance to Vietnamese women refugees as well as social activities and cultural preservation.
Publication: Newsletter, bimonthly.

VIETNAMESE YOUTH EDUCATION ASSOCIATION, INCORPORATED
1306 South 28th Street, #12
Arlington, Virginia 22206
Director: Chu Ba Anh (703) 684-7378

Sponsors Vietnamese language summer school and summer camp; educational seminars and cultural contests. Organizes the Mid-Autumn Children's Festival. Provides information and counseling to Vietnamese students.

CAMBODIANS

CAMBODIAN ASSOCIATION OF AMERICA
602 Pacific Avenue
Long Beach, California 90802
Director: Jean Fernandez (213) 432-5849

Founded to coordinate Cambodian community efforts to improve resettlement opportunities and services to newly arriving refugees and to help integrate the Cambodian communities into the main stream of the new way of life.

FEDERATION OF CAMBODIAN ASSOCIATIONS IN NORTH AMERICA
Post Office Box 242
Alexandria, Virginia 22313 (703) 379-7296
President: Chun Chen Founded 1979

Serves as a communication network between Cambodian refugee and human rights groups. Affiliated with Cambodian Religio-Cultural Association of America.
Publications: Newsletter, weekly.

LAOTIANS

FEDERATION OF LAO ASSOCIATIONS OF THE AMERICAS
Post Office Box 173
Oakdale, Iowa 52319
President: Dr. Bounlieng Phommasouvanh (319) 353-5400

LAO ASSOCIATION
Post Office Box 4494
Falls Church, Virginia 22044
Director: Voradeth Ditthavong (703) 671-9468

Provides orientation, counseling, and crisis intervention services. Engages in cultural and social activities for the Lao community.

LAO FAMILY COMMUNITY, INCORPORATED
1140 South Bristol
Santa Ana, California 92704
Director: Mr. Xeu Vang Vangyi (714) 556-9520

5460 Peaceful Terrace
Alexandria, Virginia 22303
Contact: Ms. Somchanh Vinaya (703) 838-4453

Professional Organizations

VIETNAMESE

VIETNAMESE ASSOCIATION FOR SCIENCE AND TECHNOLOGY
Post Office Box 454
Hyattsville, Maryland 20782
President: Dr. Pham Van Pho

Professional organization of Vietnamese scientists, engineers and computer science personnel dedicated to science information and exchange.

VIETNAMESE ENGINEERING SOCIETY
Richmond, Virginia (804) 275-2278
President: Nghiem Xuan Liem Founded 1975

Professional organization of Vietnamese engineers and computer science personnel.
Publication: English-French-Vietnamese Technical Dictionary.

VIETNAMESE LAWYER ASSOCIATION
1073 Wunderlick Drive
San Jose, California 95129
Attention: Mr. Vu Ngoc Tuyen (408) 446-1251

VIETNAMESE LAWYERS ASSOCIATION
2009 North 14th Street, Suite 705
Arlington, Virginia 22201
President: Dr. Pham Van Thuyet (703) 841-0304

Professional organization of Vietnamese lawyers both trained in Vietnam and in the United States.

VIETNAMESE MEDICAL PERSONNEL ASSOCIATION
3705 George Mason Drive
Falls Church, Virginia (703) 671-3220
President: Dr. Tran Dinh De Founded 1978

Professional association of health personnel trained both in Vietnam and in the United States.

Public Affairs Organizations

CENTER FOR IMMIGRATION POLICY AND REFUGEE ASSISTANCE
Georgetown University
Washington, D.C.
Director: Dr. Harold Bradley, S. J. (202) 625-3221
Founded 1980

Objective is to influence the choices which will be made in developing a humane, reasonable, and enforceable immigration policy for the United States, a nation of immigrants in a world of displaced people. Holds public meetings and seminars where migration issues are discussed by experts in the field. Also promotes experiential learning by involving undergraduates and medical and social welfare personnel in actual refugee resettlement programs through internships. Publishes occasional papers.

COUNCIL OF SOUTHEAST ASIAN REFUGEES
1424 16th Street, Northwest
Suite 404 (202) 667-7910
Washington, D.C. 20036 Founded 1982

A consortium of major refugee organizations from Cambodia, Laos and Vietnam currently operating in the United States. Provides a forum in which various Southeast Asian refugee groups can discuss common issues pertaining to successful resettlement in the United States. Purposes are to advocate for better programs and policies of refugee resettlement; provide input into the formulation and implementation of national and international policies affecting refugees from Southeast Asia; to develop support networks among the various ethnic groups at national, state and local levels; to promote more rapid attainment of economic self-sufficiency in refugee communities through assisting in the development of community-based programs and activities; to identify resources for technical assistance and support; to promote mutual understanding and cooperation among Southeast Asian refugees, other ethnic groups and the American community at large, in order to prevent and alleviate community tensions; to serve as a clearinghouse providing accurate information and appropriate advice to public and private organizations with regard to Southeast Asian culture in general and refugee activities in particular; and to foster cultural preservation programs within each Southeast Asian refugee community with a view to enabling them to significantly contribute to the American cultural heritage.

INDOCHINA PROJECT
Center for International Policy
120 Maryland Avenue, Northeast
Washington, D.C. 20002
Project Director: Donald L. Ranard (202) 546-8181
Founded 1975

Examines the impact of current United States foreign policy on human rights and social and economic needs in present-day Vietnam, Laos and Cambodia. Maintains an information resource center for journalists, members of Congress, church agencies and scholars. Also maintains a speakers bureau.
Publications: Indochina Issues, monthly.

INDOCHINA REFUGEE ACTION CENTER
1424 16th Street, Northwest
Suite 404
Washington, D.C. 20036 (202) 667-7810
Director: Le Xuan Khoa Founded 1979

Objectives are: to make known to the American public the situation in Southeast Asia; to provide a forum and process for planning among public and private organizations seeking to help Indochinese refugees; to provide opportunities for new Americans from Indochina to aid in the development of resettlement policies and programs. Conducts research into the needs of and issues affecting Indochinese refugees. Maintains resource file of newsclippings, public and private agency reports, cultural orientation materials (particularly language and vocational training materials), and reports on refugee mental health and social adjustment needs.
Publications: Published Refugee Resettlement Resource Book and Updates.

NATIONAL COALITION FOR REFUGEE RESETTLEMENT
c/o Secretariat
National Conference on Social Welfare
1730 M Street, Northwest, Suite 911 (202) 785-0817
Washington, D.C. 20036 Founded 1977

The Coalition provides a forum for communication, policy development, and exchange of information among its members -- which include voluntary agencies, national public interest groups and other national organizations engaged in resettlement, and state and local governments. It also serves as a channel of communication between Coalition members and the Federal government. The National Conference on Social Welfare provides secretariat support for the Coalition. Information services provided to its membership include legislative updates, materials on a variety of resettlement concerns, and meetings and conferences devoted to resettlement issues.

NATIONAL IMMIGRATION, REFUGEE, AND CITIZENSHIP FORUM
533 Eighth Street, Southeast
Washington, D.C. 20003
President: Rich Swartz (202) 544-0004

Stimulates and coordinates policy-focused working relationships and information networks spanning the range of issues and interest groups involved in immigration, refugees, and related foreign policy. Comprised of more than 60 groups, the Forum adopts no position on policy questions.

REFUGEE POLICY GROUP
1424 Sixteenth Street, Northwest, Suite 402
Washington, D.C. 20036
Executive Director: Dennis Gallagher (202) 387-3015
Founded 1982

Devoted to policy analysis and research on a broad range of refugee issues, including resettlement, protection, asylum, assistance in developing countries and other refugee-related concerns. Is in the process of establishing a Library Resource Center to collect documentation which will facilitate research in the broad range of topics relevant to refugee needs and to serve as an information center for other agencies and organizations.

VIETNAMESE

BOAT PEOPLE S.O.S. COMMITTEE
6970 Linda Vista Road
San Diego, California 92111
Chairperson: Nguyen Huu Xuong (714) 571-0260
Founded 1980

Professors, journalists and others concerned about the Vietnamese boat people. Objectives are to publicize the plight of the boat people, eliminate the pirate attacks against them in the Gulf of Thailand, and locate the women who are kidnapped by the pirates. Appeals to the communications and news media, the people of Thailand, and Vietnamese families, whether settled or in refugee camps, to aid in the search for the abducted women and girls, many of whom are believed to have been sold in the slave markets of Southeast Asia. Publishes Pirates on the Gulf of Siam (booklet) and membership directory.

COMMITTEE FOR THE DEFENSE OF POLITICAL PRISONERS IN VIETNAM
7706 Random Run Lane, No. 102
Falls Church, Virginia 22042 (703) 698-1982
President: Nguyen Huu Hieu Founded 1978

Former prisoners, families and friends of prisoners, student groups, refugees (particularly "Boat People") and other concerned individuals and organizations. United to: denounce the system of re-education camps in Vietnam; call world attention to and work toward the release of political prisoners in Vietnam detained without charges or trial. Seeks public trials, fixed prison terms and better prison conditions. Urges the Socialist Republic of Vietnam to follow the tenets of the United Nations to "respect the basic principles of freedom and human dignity." Has appealed to the American Red Cross and Amnesty International, U.S.A. Affiliate to send fact-finding missions to Vietnam. Conducts research and documents findings; holds interviews with former prisoners and families of prisoners; disseminates information. Holds press conferences and talks throughout the United States, Canada and Europe. Raises funds to send medicine to prisoners. Maintains archives.
Publications: Thoi Tap (magazine), monthly; also publishes documents and appeals.

MOVEMENT FOR HUMAN RIGHTS IN VIETNAM
13482 El Prado
Garden Grove, California 92640 (714) 971-2631
Chairman: Reverend Do Thanh Ha Founded 1977

Vietnamese refugees and Americans concerned about human rights violations in Vietnam by the present Communist regime. To fight for religious freedom, the release of political prisoners and family reunification in Vietnam. Organizes political rallies; holds conferences and workshops to update activities and objectives. Keeps records of materials concerning human rights; writes appeals and petitions to persons of influence.

VIETNAM VETERANS MEMORIAL FUND
1110 Vermont Avenue, Northwest
Suite 308
Washington, D.C. 20005
Executive Vice President: Donald E. Schaet (202) 659-1151
Founded 1979

Purpose is to erect a national memorial to honor the Americans who served, and particularly those who died, in the Vietnam war. The memorial will make no political statement about the war, but will serve as a means for Americans of diverse political opinions to unite in acknowledging those who served in Vietnam. To be erected on land donated by the federal government in Washington, D.C., the memorial will include landscaped surroundings, a sculpture symbolizing the experience of the Americans who served in Vietnam, and an inscription of the names of all 57,692 Americans who died there. Once the memorial has been built and its maintenance provided for in perpetuity by the Department of the Interior, the Fund will cease to exist.

CAMBODIANS

SAVE CAMBODIA, INCORPORATED
4620 Lee Highway, Suite 100
Arlington, Virginia 20042
Director: Chhang Song (703) 276-8837

Active in job referral and placement as well as accompanying refugees to medical, government and other offices as they find their way into American life. Engages in advocacy for Cambodian refugees. Publication: Cambodia Today.

Cultural and Educational Organizations

ACTION FOR SOUTHEAST ASIANS, INCORPORATED
Providence Building, Suite 205
6521 Arlington Boulevard
Falls Church, Virginia 22042
President: Dr. Tran Minh Tung (703) 241-5695

Action for Southeast Asians, Incorporated, (ASEA) is a nonprofit organization offering mutual assistance in the areas of research, training and technical assistance. The "Learning to Help" Program conducts short-term training for Southeast Asian refugees who are employed in human services in the metropolitan Washington area. The training is designed to enhance their skills as practitioners, and expand opportunities for careers in human services.

CENTER FOR APPLIED LINGUISTICS
3520 Prospect Street, Northwest
Washington, D.C. 20007 (202) 298-9292
Director: G. Richard Tucker Founded 1959

Engages in research, development of teaching and scholarly materials, technical assistance programs and active participation in language policy formulation. Has recently focused on the language and cultural needs of refugees, especially Indochinese. Produces print and audiovisual materials for refugees and sponsors in English and the five major languages of Southeast Asia (Vietnamese, Khmer, Lao, Hmong and Chinese). These provide information and guidance at the "survival level, and deal with topics of immediate concern such as housing, employment, health services, legal issues, and food and nutrition. Also works with language training services in refugee camps in Southeast Asia. Has developed tests for survival and vocational-level skills in English for use with Indochinese and other refugees which can be used by non-specialists to determine language instruction needs.

INDOCHINA CURRICULUM GROUP
11 Garden Street (617) 354-6583
Cambridge, Massachusetts 02138 Founded 1973

To provide materials for high school teachers and students who want to go beyond the textbook version of the Vietnam war and explore the underlying issues of that period and the war's continuing effects on Indochina and the United States. Sponsors workshops upon request; maintains library. Publishes books, filmstrips and tapes.

INDOCHINESE CULTURAL AND SERVICE CENTER
3030 Southwest Second Street
Portland, Oregon 97201 (503) 241-9393

Develops orientation and educational material for Indochinese newcomers. Sponsors a family clinic and refugee affairs service office. Serves as a cultural center for Indochinese in the Portland area.

INDOCHINESE ECONOMIC DEVELOPMENT CENTER
3210 Grace Street, Northwest
Washington, D.C. 20007
Director: Bui Diem (202) 337-0135

Provides community-based economic development, technical and management assistance and advocacy.

NATIONAL CLEARINGHOUSE FOR BILINGUAL EDUCATION
1300 Wilson Boulevard
Suite B2-11
Rosslyn, Virginia 22209 (703) 522-0710
Director: Harpreet Sandhu

Serves as the national information center in the field of bilingual education. Is funded jointly by the National Institute of Education and the Office of Bilingual Education and Minority Languages Affairs, United States Department of Education and is operated by InterAmerica Research Associates, Incorporated. The purposes of the Clearinghouse are to provide information services to bilingual educators through its reference and referral activities; to develop and make available information products to educators, researchers, and others interested in bilingual education; to coordinate information among federally and state funded entities in the bilingual field; to maintain a computerized database to ensure effective processing, retrieval, and dissemination of information; and to coordinate information gathering and processing among bilingual education programs. Maintains a toll-free hotline (800) 336-4560, on-line search service to provide current information on bilingual education, computerized database and information network and field representatives to give assistance at Bilingual Education Service Centers. Has produced informational materials listing publication and services to assist Cambodian, Himong, Lao, Vietnamese and other refugees.
Publication: Forum (newsletter), monthly.

REFUGEE RESOURCE CENTER
American Council of Voluntary Agencies
200 Park Avenue South
New York, New York 10003
Director: Georgianna Gleason (212) 674-6844

Provides information on refugee resettlement to the general public; serves as an information resource for the national voluntary agencies; interprets the role of the private sector in refugee resettlement; assists in developing communication linkages between the voluntary agencies and other participants in the resettlement program. The Resource Center is also coordinating a series of roundtables on resettlement issues.

SOCIETY OF INDOCHINA PHILATELISTS
Post Office Box 531
Chicago, Illinois 60690
Executive Secretary: Mark Isaacs Founded 1970

Individuals interested in studying the postal emissions and postal history of French Indo-China, Laos, North and South Vietnam and Cambodia. Maintains translation service, auction department and new issue service. Grants Best in Show award when applicable. Affiliated with: American Philatelic Society; Society of Philatelic Americans.
Publications: Indo-China Philatelist, six times a year; also publishes membership directory.

VIETNAMESE

NATIONAL ASSOCIATION OF VIETNAMESE AMERICAN EDUCATION
1123 Beverly Road
Jenkintown, Pennsylvania 19046 (215) 884-1023
President: Dr. Vuong G. Thuy Founded 1979

To provide equal educational opportunities for Vietnamese-Americans; to acknowledge and publicize contributions of Vietnamese education and culture in American schools, culture and society, and to encourage appreciation of Vietnamese and American cultures, education and language. Works toward legislative needs of Vietnamese-Americans; attempts to increase an understanding of Vietnam and Indochina through facilitation of information exchange among scholars and professionals. Encourages scholarly excellence and active participation of parents and community members in school and community activities. Offers travel, recreation and education opportunities in the United States and overseas. Holds local, state, regional and national meetings. Sponsors scholarship contests; offers referral service with more than 500 specialists in the fields of education and human services.
Publications: Newsletter, quarterly; Directory, triennial; also publishes bulletin.

CAMBODIANS

CAMBODIAN-AMERICAN HERITAGE, INCORPORATED
5412 Joel Lane
Temple Hills, Maryland 20748
Contact: Tes Saroeum (301) 755-4823

Sponsors artistic dance (Royal Ballet and folk), music, cultural preservation and social gatherings.

Foundations

VIETNAM FOUNDATION
6713 Lumsden Street
McLean, Virginia 22101 (703) 893-7458
President: Pho Ba Long Founded 1975

Board of directors is comprised of professionals in educational and cultural services who promote the integration of Vietnamese immigrants and refugees into American society. Aids in the preservation of Vietnamese cultural heritage in the United States; promotes bilingual and bicultural education and activities; develops and distributes bilingual literature. Focuses efforts on children and their parents, since 50% of the Vietnamese population in the United States is under 19 years of age. Sponsors classes in Vietnamese language and culture and English classes for Vietnamese natives. Maintains counseling service for students and parents; compiles statistics.

Charitable Organizations

AMERICAN RED CROSS
National Headquarters
17th and D Streets, Northwest
Washington, D.C. 20006

Since 1975 the American Red Cross has operated a refugee locator service specializing in the location of Indochinese refugees. A Refugee Locator Unit at the national headquarters in Washington, D.C. works in conjunction with a nationwide network of chapters as well as the national Red Cross and Red Crescent societies of other countries and the Central Tracing Agency of the International Committee of the Red Cross in Geneva. Individuals who wish to initiate a location request concerning a relative or close friend should contact the nearest Red Cross Chapter which will forward the necessary information on a special form to the Refugee Locator Unit. Red Cross staff carry out the field search and personal contact necessary to confirm identity and obtain permission of the person located to release his or her address. The Red Cross also assists with family reunification problems and other humanitarian situations when possible. Persons needing such help should contact the nearest Red Cross chapter. When necessary, requests will be forwarded to the national headquarters for service.
Publications: A Vietnamese-English orientation booklet "Your New Country - a Guide to Language and Life in the United States" may be obtained without charge upon request to any Red Cross Chapter.

AMERICAN REFUGEE COMMITTEE
2110 Nicollet
Minneapolis, Minnesota 55404
Executive Director: Stanley B. Breen (612) 872-7060
Founded 1979

Provides medical relief to Indochinese refugees in Thailand. Offers training for sponsors of refugees; sponsors development support services for Indochinese refugees in the United States. Works with large and small corporations which donate materials, time and funds toward recruiting sponsors. Maintains slide collection. Supports local offices in Minneapolis, Chicago, and Omaha. Publishes orientation handbooks and additional resource material for sponsors.

FRIENDS OF CHILDREN OF VIETNAM
600 Gilpin
Denver, Colorado 80218 (303) 321-8251

HOLT INTERNATIONAL CHILDREN'S SERVICES, INCORPORATED
1195 City View
Box 2880
Eugene, Oregon 97402
Executive Director: David H. Kim (503) 687-2202

Provides care for unaccompanied minors through its sister organization, Holt Sahathai Foundation, in two Khmer refugee holding centers in Thailand.

INDOCHINA AMERICAN RESETTLEMENT AND JOB PROGRAM
810 18th Avenue, Room 206
Seattle, Washington 98122 (206) 325-3277

American Volunteer Agencies involved in the resettlement of refugees. (These agencies are assisted by contracts from the United States State Department).

THE AMERICAN COUNCIL OF VOLUNTARY AGENCIES FOR FOREIGN SERVICE, INCORPORATED
Committee on Migration and Refugee Affairs
200 Park Avenue South
New York, New York 10003 (212) 777-8210
Committee Chairman: Wells Klein
Founded 1945

ACVA provides voluntary agencies with a forum for information exchange, planning and joint action in consultation with the United States government, the United Nations and other organizations active in relief, development and refugee assistance. Council is comprised of forty-six member agencies. Representatives of the voluntary agencies listed in this section meet weekly in New York under the auspices of the ACVA to allocate the refugees who will be resettled by the participating agencies. Maintains Refugee Resource Center.

AMERICAN COUNCIL FOR NATIONALITIES SERVICE
20 West 40th Street
New York, New York 10018
Executive Director: Wells Klein (212) 398-9142

A national non-sectarian, coordinating organization for a network of 30 community-supported social service agencies that assist immigrants, refugees, and the foreign-born in adjusting to American society. These agencies, the majority called International Institutes or Nationalities Service Centers, provide service to the foreign-born in such areas as English language training, immigration counseling, social and educational services, and inter-ethnic programs and activities. ACNS resettles refugees through its network of member agencies, as well as through five local resettlement agencies. At present most of the refugees are Indochinese. The national office sponsors site visits, funding, staff development, public and sponsor-recruiting information, specialized consultant services and technical assistance in English language training, accounting, management and fund raising. Sponsors the United States Committee for Refugees which serves as a non-governmental focal point for information and education activities on behalf of the world refugee situation.
Publications: World Refugee Survey (with the United States Committee for Refugees), annual; Refugee Reports, biweekly.

AMERICAN FUND FOR CZECHOSLOVAK REFUGEES, INCORPORATED
Indochinese Program
1790 Broadway, Room 513
New York, New York 10019
Director, Indochinese Program: Tatiana Uremenko (212) 265-1919
Founded 1948

Has participated in resettlement of refugees from Indochina since 1975 through an Indochinese program. Maintains offices in Boston, Salt Lake City and San Francisco. Provides English language training, employment placement, orientation for refugee and sponsors, medical screening and emergency funds.

BUDDHIST COUNCIL FOR REFUGEE RESCUE AND RESETTLEMENT
City of Ten Thousand Buddhas
Talmadge, California 95481
Director: Douglas Powers (707) 462-0939

A consortium of Buddhist groups (American, Chinese, Japanese, Sri Lankan, Tibetan and Indochinese) which works through an existing network. Provides a three-month recuperation and adjustment course to incoming refugees on the Dharma Realm Buddhist University campus where intensive, vocationally-oriented English language training, orientation and acculturation programs and field trips are offered in order to prepare for resettlement in American life.

CHURCH WORLD SERVICE
Immigration and Refugee Program
475 Riverside Drive, Room 666
New York, New York 10027 (212) 870-2164

5250 Santa Monica Boulevard
Suite 311
Los Angeles, California 90029 (213) 666-2708
Director, Immigration and Refugee Programs: Dale deHaan

The relief and development arm of the Division of Overseas Ministries, National Council of Churches of Christ in the U.S.A. Coordinates the relief, development, and refugee resettlement activities of 32 Protestant, Anglican, and Orthodox denominations in the United States. One of the major resettlement agencies developing resettlement opportunities for Indochinese and other refugees. Committed to the global dimensions and concerns of the refugee situation, and hence works closely with its colleague organization, the World Council of Churches, in Geneva, Switzerland. Espouses the congregational model of resettlement in which a local congregation enables individual refugees or refugee families to become self-sufficient, independent community members. Coordinates international refugee case processing, pre-arrival and port-of-entry reception; distribution of refugee cases to denominational resettlement offices; information services and technical assistance (sponsorship training, consultant services in bi-cultural orientation, language training, social services); public information and national advocacy; and financial and operations management.
Publication: Refugees and Human Rights Newsletter, quarterly; also publishes Refugee Updates.

HEBREW IMMIGRANT AID SOCIETY, INCORPORATED
Indochinese Department
200 Park Avenue South
New York, New York 10003
Director, Indochinese Department: Dail Stolow (212) 674-6800

Works through extensive network of local Jewish Federations and their direct service agencies as well as synagogues, families and individuals, non-sectarian groups and local Indochinese mutual assistance associations. National office provides pre-arrival planning, placement and policy coordination. Monitors local resettlement programs and conducts seminars. Local groups provide orientation, employment assistance, language training, socialization programs and emergency financial and crisis intervention assistance. Follow-up services include family and educational counseling, employment advising, day care and self-help programs.

INTERNATIONAL RESCUE COMMITTEE, INCORPORATED
Indochina Project
386 Park Avenue South
New York, New York 10016
Coordinator, Indochina Project: Robert DeVecchi (212) 679-0010
Founded 1933

1732 "Eye" Street, Northwest
Washington, D. C. 20006
National Resettlement Coordinator: Ray Evans (202) 333-6814

Engages in resettlement and public advocacy of refugees on a world-wide basis. Has offices in Western Europe, Latin America, Canada, Southeast Asia and other parts of the world, as well as 16 regional offices in the United States. Operates medical, educational and other relief programs in refugee camps overseas. Offers information service, policy guidelines and program analysis to regional offices. These provide case-workers, bilingual resettlement officers and placement specialists, language training, and orientation materials.

LUTHERAN IMMIGRATION AND REFUGEE SERVICE
Lutheran Council in the USA
360 Park Avenue South
New York, New York 10010 (212) 532-6350
Director: Ingrid Walter
Founded 1939

A department of the Division of Mission and Ministry of the Lutheran Council in the United States. Handles immigration and refugee affairs through a network of regional consultants who are the link to Lutheran congregations which are the refugee sponsors. The national office coordinates the entire resettlement program by processing cases and providing direct pre- and post-arrival information, interpreter services and immigration counseling. Also offers a foster care program for unaccompanied minors, language training and tutor training workshops and follow-up evaluations. Prepares reports on the special needs of refugee women, statistical analysis of post-settlement patterns and other services. Engages in advocacy for immigrant and refugee groups in the United States. Publications: LIRS Bulletin, quarterly; also publishes orientation and language materials.

PRESIDING BISHOPS FUND FOR WORLD RELIEF
Episcopal Center
815 Second Avenue
New York, New York
Director: Marnie Dawson (212) 867-8400

TOLSTOY FOUNDATION, INCORPORATED
Department of Immigration and Refugee Resettlement
250 West 57th Street
New York, New York 10019
Deputy Director: Alla G. Ivask (212) 247-2922

Primarily engaged in Russian or Slavic refugee resettlement, but participates also in Indochinese resettlement. Provides orientation and processing materials for refugees and sponsors. Regional offices offer language training, day care centers and other services.

U. S. CATHOLIC CONFERENCE
Migration and Refugee Services
1312 Massachusetts Avenue, Northwest
Washington, D.C. 20005
Executive Director: John E. McCarthy (202) 659-6625

1250 Broadway
New York, New York 10001
Associate Director: Robert Wright (212) 563-4300

Has been the major voluntary agency engaged in Indochinese resettlement. Has over 150 diocesan resettlement offices each with professional staff and social services back up. National office provides information, program guidance and technical assistance to diocesan resettlement offices which are the link to parish and individual sponsors. Diocesan offices provide assistance in employment placement, vocational and English language programs, day care programs, temporary housing and legal services.

WORLD RELIEF REFUGEE SERVICES
National Association of Evangelicals
Post Office Box WRC
Nyack, New York 10960
Vice President: Don Bjorl (914) 353-1444

Agency represents 62 Prostestant denominations and operates through ten regional offices as well as two special offices in New York and Miami. The regional offices are in direct contact with local congregations which act as sponsors. National office provides resource materials, training and coordinating services. Maintains a speakers bureau. Provides films and other cross-cultural materials. Has published a Sponsors' Manual, a Resource Manual and a manual for refugees explaining American social customs.

VIETNAMESE

VIETNAMESE REFUGEE FUND, INCORPORATED
6318 Mori Street
McLean, Virginia 22101 (703) 734-0028

Provides information, referral and translation. Sponsors biweekly Vietnamese radio program.

Religious Organizations

VIETNAMESE

OVERSEAS VIETNAMESE SANGHA COUNCIL
5401 16th Street, Northwest
Washington, D.C. 20011
Supreme Patriarch: The Most Venerable Thich Tem Chau (202) 829-2423
Founded 1979

Headquartered in Washington, this council gathers under its authority all the Vietnamese Buddhist priesthood outside Vietnam, not only in the United States but also in France, Japan, Germany, Canada and elsewhere.

VIETNAMESE AMERICAN BUDDHIST ASSOCIATION
7060 Wyndale Street, Northwest
Washington, D.C. 20015
President: Le Thi Bai (202) 966-0015

VIETNAMESE BUDDHIST CONGREGATIONAL CHURCH OF AMERICA
5401 16th Street, Northwest
Washington, D.C. 20011
President: Venerable Thich Tam Chan (202) 829-2423
Founded 1976

Headquartered in Washington, this church has branches in Canada, New Jersey, Pennsylvania, Minnesota, Texas.
Publications: Duoc Tue (The Torch of Wisdom), irregular.

VIETNAMESE BUDDHIST FELLOWSHIP OF AMERICA
863-865 South Berendo Street
Los Angeles, California 90005
Founder: Venerable Dr. Thich Thien An (213) 487-1235
Founded 1972

VIETNAMESE UNITED BUDDHIST CHURCHES IN THE UNITED STATES
863 South Berendo Street
Los Angeles, California 90005
Director: Venerable Thich Man Giac (213) 384-9638

CAMBODIANS

CAMBODIA BUDDHIST SOCIETY
6301 Westbrook Street
New Carrollton, Maryland 20784 (301) 577-7596
Secretary: Yok L. Vat-Ito
Founded 1979

Aim is to preserve the culture, tradition and religion of the Cambodian people so that Buddhist morals are not lost. Assists Cambodian refugees in finding food, lodging, employment and in general, overcome the initial shock of living in another country. Maintains Cambodian Buddhist Temple and celebrates the seven traditional Cambodian Buddhist religious holidays. Conducts research on Cambodian Buddhist literature. Is currently compiling library of materials from Thailand, France and the United States on Cambodian Buddhism.
Publications: Vatt Khmer (newsletter), quarterly.

CAMBODIAN RELIGIO-CULTURAL ASSOCIATION OF AMERICA
Post Office Box 242
Alexandria, Virginia 22313 (703) 360-2623
President: Dr. Lopez Sangwar Founded 1975

To preserve the religious and cultural heritage of Cambodia. Seeks to draw attention to human rights violations in Cambodia. Affiliated with: Federation of Cambodian Associations in North America.

LAOTIANS

LAO BUDDHIST SOCIETY
5248 Clifton Street
Alexandria, Virginia 22312
Director: Vilay Soulatha (703) 354-7021

Provides religious ceremonies, counseling, cultural preservation activities, including Lao language classes for children.
Publication: Bhouthavong Monthly.

Research Centers and Special Institutes

CENTER FOR VIETNAMESE STUDIES
Southern Illinois University at Carbondale
Carbondale, Illinois 62901
Director: Nguyen Dinn-Moa

Recently established research activity at Southern Illinois University on its Carbondale campus.

INDOCHINESE REFUGEE STUDIES CENTER
George Mason University
4400 University Drive
Fairfax, Virginia 22030
Contact: Dr. Nguyen Manh Hung (703) 323-2065 or 323-2275

NATIONAL ASIAN CENTER FOR BILINGUAL EDUCATION
11743 Gateway Boulevard
Los Angeles, California 90064 (213) 474-7173

Develops educational material for Indochinese immigrants. Funded by the United States Department of Education, Office of Bilingual Education and Minority Language Affairs. Materials are available through the National Clearinghouse for Bilingual Education.

NATIONAL CENTER FOR MATERIALS AND CURRICULUM DEVELOPMENT
University of Iowa
N. 310 Oakdale Campus
Oakdale, Iowa 52319
Codirectors: Lawrence M. Stolurow/Alan B. Menkin (319) 353-5400

Develops educational materials in Vietnamese, Khmer and Laotian.

NATIONAL MULTILINGUAL/MULTICULTURAL MATERIALS DEVELOPMENT CENTER
California State Polytechnical University
3801 West Temple Avenue
Pomona, California 91768

Funded by the United States Department of Education, Office of Bilingual Education and Minority Language Affairs. Materials are available through the National Clearinghouse for Bilingual Education.

PACIFIC/ASIAN AMERICAN MENTAL HEALTH RESEARCH CENTER
1001 West Van Buren Street
Chicago, Illinois 60607

Affiliated with the University of Illinois, Chicago Circle Campus. Performs research in the field of refugee mental health and emotional health.
Publication: P/AAMHRC Research Review.

U.S. Government Programs

U.S. COORDINATOR FOR REFUGEE AFFAIRS
Department of State
Washington, D.C. 20520
Ambassador-at-Large: Eugene Douglas (202) 632-5230
Established 1979

The U. S. Coordinator is responsible to the President for overall United States refugee policy, coordination of international and domestic admission and resettlement programs; design of refugee budget strategy with policy guidance to federal agencies, presenting the administration's refugee policy to Congress, advising the President, Secretary of State and the Secretary of Health and Human Services, representing the United States to other governments and international organizations concerning refugee issues and reviewing federal regulations, guidelines and procedures. Policy coordination is carried out through the Interagency for Refugee Affairs comprised of representatives of all federal agencies involved in domestic refugee programs: Departments of Health and Human Services, State,

Labor, Justice, Education and Housing and Urban Development as well as the Office of Management and Budget, National Security Council, Domestic Council, Central Intelligence Agency and Departments of Defense and Commerce.

BUREAU OF REFUGEE PROGRAMS
Department of State
Washington, D. C. 20521
Director: James Purcell (202) 632-0604

Within the Department of State, the Bureau of Refugee Programs is primarily responsible for the development, implementation and operation of policies and programs for the United States' participation in the relief and resettlement of refugees throughout the world, and for the initial resettlement of refugees accepted to the United States. Its work is authorized under the Refugee Act of 1980. The initial domestic placement and resettlement of refugees is carried out primarily by 11 voluntary agencies (see Charitable organizations) and two state agencies, all under contract to the Department of State. These contracts for domestic resettlement are managed by the Bureau of Refugee Programs. Relations between the Department of State and the various voluntary agencies are often carried out under the auspices of the American Council of Voluntary Agencies for Foreign Service, Incorporated which provides a forum in which voluntary agencies can coordinate their refugee resettlement activities. Each participating agency receives a grant of several hundred dollars per refugee for the provision of initial receiption and placement services.

OFFICE OF REFUGEE RESETTLEMENT
Department of Health and Human Services
Switzer Building, Room 1229
330 C Street, Southwest
Washington, D.C. 20201 (202) 472-6510
Director: Phillip Hawkes Established 1980

Responsible for providing assistance to refugees after their initial placement in United States communities, primarily by utilizing existing federal programs. Assistance is rendered in social services, such as language instruction, career counseling, employment placement and development, vocational training, day care and transportation, health, mental health, home management and translation. Cash and medical assistance are provided to refugees in need. Help for unaccompanied minors is also provided. Maintains an automated statistical file on arrivals and location by city of individual refugees.

OFFICE OF BILINGUAL EDUCATION AND MINORITY LANGUAGES AFFAIRS
Refugee Children Assistance Programs
Department of Education
Reporters Building - Room 505
400 Maryland Avenue, Southwest
Washington, D.C. 20202
Chief: James H. Lockhart (202) 472-3520

Provides supplementary educational assistance to meet the special educational needs of Indochinese refugee children who are enrolled in public and non-profit elementary and secondary schools. Program is operated through grants.

INDOCHINESE MATERIALS CENTER
United States Department of Education
324 East 11th Street, 9th Floor
Kansas City, Missouri 64106
Director: James B. Tumy (816) 374-2659

Gathers, maintains, and catalogues a collection of educational materials, curriculum guides, cross-cultural orientation materials, bilingual and ESL manuals, and other documents relevant to the teaching of Indochinese refugees. Also collects and maintains supplementary materials and background information on Indochinese cultures and on problems and issues in domestic resettlement. Each year the Center publishes and disseminates a "Bibliography of Materials on the Education and Resettlement of Indochinese Refugees," containing a comprehensive listing of the materials held in the Center's collection. Materials listed in the bibliography may generally be obtained from their original sources. In addition, the Center provides free copies of many of the supplementary materials listed in the bibliography to educators and others who request them. Approximately 200 items are available.

ACTION
806 Connecticut Avenue, Northwest
Washington, D.C. 20525 (202) 254-3545

Sponsors programs in support of refugee resettlement by awarding grants to mutual assistance and voluntary agencies to develop networks of self-help. Is preparing a volunteer refugee assistance package, a manual intended to give technical assistance in managing volunteers.

Special Libraries and Subject Collections

CORNELL UNIVERSITY
John M. Echols Collection on Southeast Asia
Olin Library
Ithaca, New York 14853
Curator: Giok Po Oey (607) 256-4189

Subjects: Southeast Asia. Holdings: Books; serials; newspapers; microfilm; maps; journals and other serials; newspapers. Services: Interlibrary loans; copying; library open to public for reference use only.

HOWARD UNIVERSITY - BERNARD B. FALL COLLECTION
Founders Library, Room 300A
Washington, D.C. 20059 (202) 636-7261
Curator: Steven I. Yoon Founded 1970

Subjects: Southeast Asia; South and North Vietnam. Holdings: Books; periodicals; pamphlets; vertical file items; microfilm; maps. Services: Copying; collection open to public by appointment.

TACOMA COMMUNITY HOUSE MINI LIBRARY
1311 South M Street (206) 383-3951
Tacoma, Washington 98405 Founded 1910

A special collection of books, periodicals and audio-visual materials documents the history of the Vietnamese in America and provides resources for Indochinese educational and social activities.
Publication: Indochinese Newsletter, monthly.

UNIVERSITY OF MINNESOTA
Southeast Asia Resource Center
University of Minnesota
Minneapolis, Minnesota 55455 (612) 373-2851

Contains significant holdings in Southeast Asian materials.

VIETNAMESE IMMIGRATION COLLECTION
State University of New York
Buffalo, New York 14260

Oral history, interviews, orientation materials and refugee camp newspapers form the nucleus of the collection.

Newspapers and Newsletters

INDOCHINA ISSUES. 1980-. Ten times a year. Publisher: Center for International Policy, 120 Maryland Avenue, Northeast, Washington, D.C. 20002. In English.

Discusses current political problems in Southeast Asia with a view to influencing American public opinion and policy.

INDO-CHINA PHILATELIST. Six times a year. Publisher: Society of Indo-China Philatelists, Post Office Box 531, Chicago, Illinois 60690. In English.

INDOCHINESE REFUGEE UPDATE. Publisher: National Council of Churches of Christ in the United States, Immigration and Refugee Program, 475 Riverside Drive, New York, New York 10115. In English.

NEW HORIZON. Publisher: Access, 6970 Linda Vista Road, San Diego, California 92111.

REFUGEE REPORTS. 1979-. Biweekly. Editor: Rosemary Tripp. Publisher: American Council for Nationalities, 815 Fifteenth Street, Northwest, Suite 610, Washington, D.C. 20005.

Contains news, analysis of federal programs and legislation and discussion of refugee related issues. It is major resource on all facets of domestic refugee resettlement. Formerly called Indochinese Refugee Reports.

VIETNAMESE

CHUONG VIET. Weekly. Publisher: Chuong Viet, 1628 Sixteenth Street, Northwest, Washington, D.C. 20009. In Vietnamese.

DAN CHUA. Editor: Do La Lam. Publisher: Reverend Viet Chau, Post Office Box 13455, New Orleans, Louisiana 70185. In Vietnamese.

DAN CHUNG. Weekly. Publisher: 2339 West First Street, Santa Ana, California 92704. In Vietnamese.

DAN TOC. Weekly. Editor: Ha Tuc Dao. Publisher: Post Office Box 36084, San Jose, California 95158. In Vietnamese.

DAT HUA (The Promised Land). Publisher: Vietnamese Apostolate Association of Catholic Charities, 2929 South Carrolton Avenue, New Orleans, Louisiana 70118. In Vietnamese and English.

Newsletter of the organization.

DAT MOI (New Land). 1975-. Semimonthly. Publisher: Nguyen Van Giang, 2103 South Atlantic Street, Seattle, Washington 98144. In Vietnamese.

Covers developments in Vietnam and the United States.

DIEU HAU. c/o Nguyen Dat Thinh, Post Office Box 26565, San Diego, California 92126.

DONG DUONG. c/o Indochinese Refugee Center, 7402 North 56th Street, Suite 907, Tampa, Florida 33617.

Newsletter of the Center.

DONG TIEN. Weekly. Publisher: 4222 South Broad Avenue, New Orelans, Lousiana 70125. In Vietnamese.

DUOC THIENG. Weekly. Publisher: Post Office Box 0248, Garden Grove, California 92642. In Vietnamese.

DUOC TU BI. Weekly. Publisher: Post Office Box 3048, Santa Fe Springs, California 90670. In Vietnamese.

DUOC TUE. (Torch of Wisdom). Irregular. Publisher: Vietnamese Buddhist Congregational Church of America, 5401 16th Street, Northwest, Washington, D.C. 20011. In Vietnamese.

HOA THINH DON VIET BAO (Washington Vietnamese Newspaper). Weekly. Editor: Nguyen Truong Giang. Publisher: 1230 Rear North Hartford, Arlington, Virginia 22201, or Post Office Box 3652, Arlington, Virginia 22203. In Vietnamese.

HON VIET MOI. Weekly. Publisher: Post Office Box 4279, Glendale, California 91202. In Vietnamese.

KHAI PHONG. Weekly. Publisher: Post Office Box 85250, Hollywood, California 90072. In Vietnamese.

KHANG CHIEN. Weekly. Publisher: Post Office Box 2457, Redwood City, California 94064. In Vietnamese.

NAVAE NEWSLETTER. Quarterly. Publisher: National Association of Vietnamese American Education, 3206 Wynford Drive, Fairfax, Virginia 22031. In English.

Prints articles about the activities of the association and its members.

NGAY NAY. Bimonthly. Editor: Nguyen Thanh Truc. Publisher: 3225 Milam Street, Houston, Texas 77006 or Post Office Box 6667. In Vietnamese.

NGAY NAY (Today). 1979-. Monthly. Managing Editor: Le Hong Long. Post Office Box 12805, Wichita, Kansas 67277. In Vietnamese.

Covers international and national news with emphasis on developments in Vietnam.

NGUOI VIET. Weekly. Editor: Do Nguoi Yen. Publisher: 9393-F Bolsa Avenue, Westminster, California 92683. In Vietnamese.

NGUOI VIET TU DO. 9609 Bolsa Avenue, Westminster, California 92683. In Vietnamese.

QUE HUONG. Monthly. Editor: Duy Sinn. Publisher: Mrs. Le Ngoc Thach, 9937 Westminster Avenue, Garden Grove, California 92044. In Vietnamese.

SAI-GON TUAN BOA. Weekly. Editor: Vu Tai Luc, 9609 Bolsa Avenue, Westminster, California 92683. In Vietnamese.

THA HUONG. Publisher: Tha Huong, 4827 North Kenmore Avenue, Chicago, Illinois 60640. In Vietnamese.

THU NHAN. Publisher: Dalat Alumni Association, Post Office Box 3048, 11769 Telegraph Road, Santa Fe Springs, California 90670. In Vietnamese.

TIN ANH. Weekly. Editor: Vi Thuan. Publisher: 1440 South College Boulevard, Suite 3-B, Anaheim, California 92714. In Vietnamese.

TRANG DEN. Monthly. Editor and Publisher: Viet Dinh Phoung, Post Office Box 192, Glendale, California 91209. In Vietnamese.

VAN HOA GIRO DUC (Cultural and Educational News). 1980-. Six times a year. Editors: Huynh Van Lang and Tran Qui Phiet. Publisher: Vietnam Foundation, 16713 Lumsden Street, McLean, Virginia 22101. In Vietnamese and English.

VAN HOC NGHE THUAT Post Office Box 19555, San Diego, California 92119. In Vietnamese.

VIETNAM HAI NGOAI (Vietnam Overseas). 1976-. Semimonthly. Editor: Vu Luc Thuy. Publisher: Dinh Thach Bich, Post Office Box 33627, San Diego, California 92103. In Vietnamese.

Offers news coverage of developments in Vietnam and activities of interest to the Vietnamese abroad.

VIET NAM TU DO. Weekly. Publisher: 1102 West Seventeenth Street, Suite 118-119, Santa Ana, California 92706. In Vietnamese.

CAMBODIAN

CAMBODIA TODAY. Publisher: Save Cambodia, Incorporated, 4620 Lee Highway, Suite 100, Arlington, Virginia 20042.

Articles are concerned with the current situation in Cambodia, refugee movement and relief as well as resettlement activities in the United States.

CAMBODIAN APPEAL. Monthly. Editor: Saunora Prom. Publisher: Free Cambodia, Incorporated, Post Office Box 242, Alexandria, Virginia 22314. In Khmer and English.

VATT KHMER. Quarterly. Publisher: Cambodian Buddhist Society, 6301 Westbrook Street, New Carrollton, Maryland 20784.

VOICE OF FEDERATION. Weekly. Publisher: Federation of Cambodian Association, Post Office Box 242, Alexandria, Virginia 22314. In Khmer.

LAOTIAN

BHOUTHARONG. Monthly. Publisher: Lao Buddhist Society, 5248 Clifton Street, Alexandria, Virginia 22312. In Laotian.

Newsletter of the association.

LAO SOVEREIGNTY. Biweekly. Editor: Kim Himphavanh, 9890 West 26th Avenue, Apartment #6-B, Lakewood, Colorado 82015 or 3911 East Everett, Takoma, Washington.

XAO LAO. Monthly. Editor and Publisher: Vichi Vongsawat, 746 42nd Street, San Diego, California 92102.

Magazines

JOURNAL OF REFUGEE RESETTLEMENT. 1980-. Quarterly. Editor: Rosemary E. Tripp. Publisher: American Public Welfare Association, 1125 Fifteenth Street, Northwest, Washington, D.C. 20005. In English.

Articles deal primarily with aspects of Indochinese resettlement in the United States and may cover such topics as secondary migration, mental health, religion, cultural, language, problems of women.

VIETNAMESE

CHAN TROI MOI (New Horizon). Publisher: Buddhist Congregational Church, 5401 16th Street, Northwest, Washington, D.C. 20011. In Vietnamese and English.

DOI. Monthly. Editor: Nguyen Sa. Publisher: Post Office Box 4658, Irvine, California 92716. In Vietnamese.

DONG PHUONG (The Orient) FOUNDATION. Monthly. Editor and Publisher: Quoc Nam, Post Office Box 68335, Seattle, Washington 98146. In Vietnamese.

Sponsored by the Vietnam Young Members Association of America. Covers news of the Vietnamese abroad. Features articles on Vietnamese culture.

HON VIET (The Soul of Vietnam). 1976-. Semimonthly. Editor and Publisher: Nguyen Hoang Doan, 7321 Dinwiddle Street, Downey, California 90241. In Vietnamese.

Covers developments in Vietnam and the United States.

HUONG VIET (Remember Vietnam). Irregular. Editor: Bui Tran Phu. Publisher: Vietnam Student Association, 2100 Moorpark Avenue, Room 204, San Jose, California 95128.

HY VONG (Vietnamese Alliance Magazine). c/o Lutheran Service, 2701 Alcott, Suite 460, Denver, Colorado 80211.

LIEN LAC. Monthly. Editor: Reverend Nguyen Van Tinh. Publisher: Saint Patrick's College, Post Office Box 151, Mountain View, California 94042. In Vietnamese.

A magazine for Vietnamese Catholics.

NGUOI VIET (The Vietnamese). 1978-. Weekly. Editors: Do Ngoc Yen and Duy Sinh. Publisher: 1005 North Euclid, Santa Ana, California 92703. In Vietnamese with occasional English inserts.

Provides news coverage of local, national and international events of interest to the Vietnamese refugee community.

NHAN CHUNG. Monthly. Editor: Du Tu Le. Publisher: 4413 West First Street, Santa Ana, California 92703. In Vietnamese.

PHAT GIAO VIETNAM (Vietnamese Buddhism). Monthly. Editor: Venerable Thich Man Giac. Publisher: Confederation of Vietnamese Buddhist Churches of the United States, Venerable Thich Thien An, 863 South Berendo Street, Los Angeles, California 90005.

Provides news coverage of religious activities. Features articles promoting the study of Buddhism.

SUC KHOE VA HANH PHUC GIA DINH (Health and Family Happiness). 1979-. Monthly. Editor: Do Qui Sang. Managing Editor: Le Thanh Tri. 201 North Monterey, Suite 1, Alhambra, California 91801.

Provides family counseling and features health articles.

THOI NAY (The Modern Times). 1977-. Monthly. Editor and Publisher: Nguyen Trong Toai. Managing Editor: Tu Phuong. 1411 East Broadway, Glendale, California 91205. In Vietnamese.

Contains general and scientific articles.

THOI TAP. Monthly. Publisher: Committee for the Defense of Political Prisoners in Vietnam, 7706 Random Run Lane, No. 102, Falls Church, Virginia 22042.

THUC TINH MAGAZINE. Editor: Le Minh Truc. Publisher: Vi Nhan, Post Office Box 20537, Los Angeles, California 90006. In Vietnamese.

TRAI TIM DUC ME MAGAZINE. Publisher: Reverend Nguyen Duc Thiep, Post Office Box 836, Carthage, Missouri 64836. In Vietnamese.

VAN NGHE TIEN PHONG (The Frontier). 1976-. Semimonthly. Editor: Ho Anh. Publisher: Nguyen Thanh Hoang, 3718 North Fourth Street, Arlington, Virginia 22203. In Vietnamese.

Covers world news and developments in Vietnam. Features general articles.

Radio Programs

California - Los Angeles

KMAX (FM) - 3844 East Foothill Boulevard, Pasadena, California 91107, (213) 681-2486.

Contact:
Mr. Joe Marcel
1400 West Ninth Street
Los Angeles, California 90015 (213) 385-7211

California - Mission Viejo

KSBR (FM) - 28000 Marguerite Parkway, Mission Viejo, California 92691, (714) 831-5727. Vietnamese programs, 1/2 hour weekly.

California - Orange County

Contact:
Mr. Nguyen Cat Tuong
Vietnamese Community of Orange County, Incorporated
9107 Bolsa Avenue
Westminster City, California 92683 (714) 894-9875

California - San Diego

Contact:
Mr. Doan Chau Mau
Indochinese Service Center
4379 30th Street
San Diego, California 92104 (714) 298-4634

California - San Francisco

Contact:
Mr. Samboyn Sayasane, Lao Lane Xang Association
3550 Twenty Third
San Francisco, California 94110 (415) 826-8867

District of Columbia

WPFW (FM) - 700 H Street, Northwest, Washington, D.C., (202) 783-3100. Indochinese programs, 1 hour every two weeks.

Minnesota - Minneapolis-Saint Paul

KFAI (FM) - 3104 16th Avenue, South Minneapolis, Minnesota 55407, (612) 721-5011. Cambodian programs, 1/2 hour weekly.

Oklahoma - Edmond

KCSC (FM) - Central State University, Edmond, Oklahoma 73034, (405) 341-2980. Vietnamese programs, 1 hour weekly.

Oklahoma City, Oklahoma

Contact:
Mr. Nguyen Trong
1416 Linwood
Oklahoma City, Oklahoma 73006 (406) 232-3655

Pennsylvania - Harrisburg

WMSP (FM) - 24 South Second Street, Harrisburg, Pennsylvania 17101, (717) 238-6763. Vietnamese programs, 2 hours weekly.

Contact:
Mr. Truong Ngoc Phuong
Indochinese Service Center
21 South River Street
Harrisburg, Pennsylvania 17101 (717) 236-9401

Pennsylvania - Philadelphia

Contact:
Mr. Do Long
Indochinese Community Center
3132 Midvale Avenue
Philadelphia, Pennsylvania 19129 (215) 329-0313

Bookdealers and Publishers' Representatives

ASIA BOOKS
(dictionaries, linguistics and literature related to Vietnam, Cambodia and Laos)
Post Office Box 873
Carbondale, Illinois 62901

BABEL INDOCHINESE RESOURCE CENTER
255 East 14th Street
Oakland, California 94606 (415) 451-0511

CENTER FOR VIETNAMESE STUDIES
Southern Illinois University
Pullman Hall
Carbondale, Illinois 62901 (618) 536-3385

CHICAGO BOARD OF EDUCATION
(educational materials in Vietnamese, Khmer and Lao)
Department of Curriculum
Language Arts Bureau
228 North LaSalle
Chicago, Illinois 60601 (312) 641-4050

CHILDREN'S BOOK AND MUSIC CENTER
(Vietnamese children's books)
2500 Santa Monica Boulevard
Santa Monica, California 90404 (213) 829-0215

DAI NAM COMPANY
(reprints Vietnamese novels, English-Vietnamese and Vietnamese-English dictionaries)
1334 North Pacific Avenue
Glendale, California 91202 (213) 244-0135

DELTA SYSTEMS, INCORPORATED
(learning aids for Vietnamese and Cambodians)
215 North Arlington Heights Street
Arlington Heights, Illinois 60004 (800) 323-8270

EASY AIDS, INCORPORATED
(educational materials in Vietnamese)
256 South Robertson Boulevard
Beverly Hills, California 90211 (213) 659-4210

EVERYBODY'S BOOKSTORE
(books in Vietnamese)
17 Brenham Place
San Francisco, California 94108 (415) 781-4989

GRANDASIA PUBLICATIONS
(books in Vietnamese)
907 Cherry Street, Southeast
Grand Rapids, Michigan 49506 (616) 456-4354

IACONI BOOK IMPORTS
(books in Vietnamese)
300 Pennsylvania Avenue
San Francisco, California 94107 (415) 285-7393

INSTITUTE FOR LANGUAGE STUDY
(books in Vietnamese)
71 Plymouth Street
Montclair, New Jersey 07042 (212) 241-1848

PHILIPPINE AND ASIAN BOOK CENTER
(books in Vietnamese and Lao)
611 Geary Street
San Francisco, California 94102 (415) 673-2660

SONG MOI
(books in Vietnamese)
Post Office Box 2744
Fort Smith, Arkansas 72913 (501) 783-2210

SPOKEN LANGUAGE SERVICES, INCORPORATED
(books in Khmer and Lao)
Post Office Box 783
Ithaca, New York 14850 (607) 257-0500

VIET-MY PUBLISHING COMPANY
(books in Vietnamese)
Post Office Box 99312
Tacoma, Washington 98494

VIETNAMESE PUBLISHING COMPANY, INCORPORATED
(books in Vietnamese)
Post Office Box 1251
Secaucus, New Jersey 07094 (201) 863-8248

ZIELEKS PUBLISHING COMPANY
(Vietnamese books)
11215 Sageland Drive
Houston, Texas 77089 (713) 481-3783

Books and Pamphlets

BIBLIOGRAPHY OF LAOS AND ETHNICALLY RELATED AREAS. By John McKinstry. Laos Project Paper No. 22. Los Angeles, 1961. Reissued by the Micro-Photo Division of Bell and Howell.

BIBLIOGRAPHY OF THE PEOPLES AND CULTURES OF MAINLAND SOUTHEAST ASIA. By John F. Embree and Lillian Ota Dotson. New Haven, Yale University, Southeast Asia Studies, 1950.

Arranged by country with subdivisions for ethnic groups. Includes books and periodicals and bibliographies.

CAMBODIA: AN ANNOTATED BIBLIOGRAPHY OF THE HISTORY, GEOGRAPHY, POLITICS AND ECONOMY SINCE 1954. By Mary L. Fisher. Cambridge, Massachusetts Institute of Technology, Center for International Studies, 1967.

AN INTRODUCTION TO INDOCHINESE HISTORY, CULTURE, LANGUAGE AND LIFE. Edited by John K. Whitmore. Ann Arbor, Michigan, Center for South and Southeast Asian Studies, 1979.

A collection of essays on such aspects of Southeast Asian society and culture as prehistory, language, religion, language and literature, the years of war and family structure. Includes a bibliography.

VIETNAM: A COMPREHENSIVE BIBLIOGRAPHY. By John Hsueh-ming Chen. Metuchen, New Jersey, Scarecrow Press, 1973.

VIETNAM: A GUIDE TO REFERENCE SOURCES. By Michael Cotter. Boston, G. K. Hall, 1977.

INDOCHINESE IN AMERICA

FROM VIETNAM TO AMERICA: A CHRONICLE OF VIETNAMESE IMMIGRATION TO THE UNITED STATES. By Gail P. Kelly. Boulder, Colorado, Westview Press, 1977.

Surveys the arrival and settlement process during the greatest influx of Indochinese refugees.

A GUIDE FOR HELPING INDOCHINESE REFUGEES IN THE UNITED STATES. Washington, D.C., Center for International Policy, Indochina Project.

Describes the process of resettling refugees from arrival through resettlement and sponsorship. Lists resettlement agencies and specific ways to help refugees and their sponsors, giving address and telephone numbers.

A GUIDE TO ORIENTATION MATERIALS FOR INDOCHINESE REFUGEES AND THEIR SPONSORS. A Selected, Annotated Bibliography. Washington, D. C., Center for Applied Linguistics, Orientation Resource Center, 1981.

Bibliography is organized topically: community services, consumer education, culture, education, employment, family planning and child care, finances, health, housing, legal, nutrition, sponsorship and resettlement, transportation and United States, with subdivisions for nationality and other appropriate groupings.

THE INDOCHINESE MUTUAL ASSISTANCE ASSOCIATIONS -- CHARACTERISTICS, COMPOSITIONS, CAPACITY BUILDING NEEDS AND FUTURE DIRECTIONS. By Diana Bui, Le Xuan Khoa and Nguyen Van Hien. Washington, D.C., Indochina Refugee Action Center, 1981.

Analyses the purposes and membership orientation of Indochinese mutual assistance associations, based on a survey of sixty representative groups; shows their needs and resources, their organizational characteristics and network linkage. Appendices include a description of methodology, a sample of the survey questionnaire and a short bibliography.

INFORMATION PACKET FOR INDOCHINESE BILINGUAL PROGRAMS AND RESOURCES. Rosslyn, Virginia, National Clearinghouse for Bilingual Education, 1981.

Gives a survey of Indochinese children in the United States based on statistical data, introduces the kinds of educational material available and gives addresses of publishers, lists other information sources, outlines current Title VII programs and describes search services available from the Clearinghouse.

INFORMATION SERVICES ASSESSMENT REPORT -- INDOCHINESE REFUGEE RESETTLEMENT PROGRAM. By Robert Frankel and Joseph E. Langlois. Washington, D.C., Indochina Refugee Action Center, 1981.

Reviews more than thirty national information providers giving address and short description of the primary information services which each provides. Identifies the types of material being received at the local level. In analyzing and evaluating this data, the study makes recommendations to increase the access to the information networks now existing and points out gaps needing to be filled. Appendices include a list of information providers not reviewed in depth, the questions used in the survey, categories of information and types of dissemination as well as lists of specific needs cited by local organizations.

PROCESSES OF TRANSITION: VIETNAMESE IN COLORADO. Edited by Peter W. Van Arsdale and James A. Pisarowicz. Austin, Texas, High Street Press, 1980.

Examines the phases of Vietnamese migration and settlement, first where sponsors are located, then to ethnic enclaves and finally into mainstream American life.

REFUGEE MATERIALS CENTER BIBLIOGRAPHY. Washington, D.C., United States Department of Education, 1981.

Lists textbooks and workbooks for teaching English to non-English speakers followed by materials for Vietnamese, Cambodians, Laotians, Chinese and other groups. Updated periodically.

REFUGEE RESETTLEMENT IN THE UNITED STATES. An Annotated Bibliography. Washington, D.C., Department of Health and Human Services, Office of Refugee Resettlement, 1981.

Reviews not only Southeast Asian refugee literature but also pertinent materials about Soviet and Cuban refugees which have comprised the major refugee groups in the last twenty years. Arranged alphabetically by author. Indexed according to subject and nationality.

THE REFUSED: THE AGONY OF INDOCHINESE REFUGEES. By Barry Wain. New York, Simon and Schuster, 1981.

Describes the terrible plight of the boat people.

REFUGEE RESETTLEMENT RESOURCE BOOK: A GUIDE TO FEDERAL PROGRAMS AND NATIONAL SUPPORT PROJECTS TO ASSIST IN REFUGEE RESETTLEMENT. Washington, D.C., Office of United States Coordinator for Refugee Affairs and Department of Health and Human Resources' Office of Refugee Resettlement, 1980.

Describes the activities of voluntary and state resettlement agencies as well as the mandates of all parts of federal and national government in participating in refugee resettlement and national private organizations supportive of resettlement. Appendices give relevant documents, list congressional committees concerned with refugee affairs and list regional offices of the voluntary agencies. An Update Service is provided by the Indochina Refugee Action Center.

THE RESETTLEMENT OF INDOCHINESE REFUGEES IN THE UNITED STATES: A SELECTED BIBLIOGRAPHY. Edited by Robert Frankel. Washington, D.C., Indochina Refugee Action Center, and Office of Refugee Resettlement and Office of the United States Coordinator for Refugee Affairs, 1980.

Divided into sixteen subject areas: bibliographies, camps in Southeast Asia, domestic resettlement, legal aspects of refugee status, social/cultural adjustment, orientation to American life, orientation of sponsors, social service providers and teachers, language acquisition, physical health care needs, emotional and mental health, vocational/occupational adaptations, housing needs, children and youth, refugees in the United States, and periodicals.

TRANSITION TO NOWHERE: VIETNAMESE REFUGEES IN AMERICA. By William T. Liu. Nashville, Tennessee, Charter House, 1979.

Describes the flood of Vietnamese refugees in 1975 from their departure from Vietnam to their resettlement. Emphasizes mental health perspective, as well as demographic characteristics and the problem of unaccompanied children. Includes a bibliography.

VIETNAMESE AMERICANS: PATTERNS OF RESETTLEMENT AND SOCIOECONOMIC ADAPTATION IN THE UNITED STATES. By Darrell Montero and Marsha I. Weber. Boulder, Colorado, Westview Press, 1979.

WRAPPED IN THE WIND'S SHAWL: REFUGEES OF SOUTHEAST ASIA AND THE WESTERN WORLD. By Scott C. S. Stone and John E. McGowan. San Raphael, California, Presidio Press, 1980.

A photographic essay showing the migration of refugees from their war-torn homelands in Southeast Asia to the bewildering West.

Audiovisual Material

FILMS AND VIDEOCASSETTES

BOY OF SOUTHEAST ASIA. 16 mm. Color and sound. 17 minutes. 1967. Available from University of Michigan Audio-Visual Center, Ann Arbor, Michigan 48109.

An uncomplicated look at lowland rural life.

CAMBODIAN DANCE. Videocassette. Color and sound. 50 minutes. Produced by Southeast Asia Program, Cornell University. In English and Khmer.

Videotape recorded from performances of Cambodian classical ballet and folk dance at Bailey Hall, Cornell University, on November 10, 1979. Each dance is preceded by an introduction in English. The program includes: Apsara, The Magic Scarf, Elephant Hunting, Sovan Macha, Cambodian Music, Krab, Chhayam, and Dance of Greetings and Best Wishes. Good as preservation of culture for Cambodian refugees and introduction to Cambodian dance and music.

CBS REPORTS: THE BOAT PEOPLE. Videotape cassette/color and sound. 50 minutes. Produced and distributed by CBS News, 1979.

CBS television program documenting the situation of the Boat People, their arrival in Malaysia, and the camp at Pilau Bidong.

FOR OUR TIMES: CAMBODIA A NATION IN PERIL. Videotape cassette. Color and sound. 30 minutes. Produced and distributed by CBS News, November, 1979.

CBS television program presenting clips of Cambodian refugees in the camps and interviews with Reverend Theodore Hesburgh, president of Notre Dame University, and United States government officials.

THE HMONG: A NATION IN EXILE. Audiotape cassette. Color. Produced and Distributed by Allen Bjergo/United States Department of Agriculture, 1979. Available from University of Michigan Audio-visual Center, Ann Arbor, Michigan 48109.

Presents background about the Hmong, why they are refugees, and how they are resettling in Montana.

HUNGRY AND SICK: THE CAMBODIANS. Video-cassette. Color and sound. Produced by the International Red Cross. Distributed by the American Red Cross, 1979. English.

Shows the activities of the International Red Cross in the Sakeo refugee camp, including medical care and the shipping in of relief goods and water.

IN THE YEAR OF THE PIG. Black and white. 101 minutes. Available from University of Michigan Audio-Visual Center, Ann Arbor, Michigan 48109. Cornell University, Ithaca.

Using old newsreel footage, shows the development of war in Indochina through the twentieth century.

INSIDE NORTH VIETNAM. 16 mm. Color and sound. 85 minutes. Available from University of Michigan Audio-Visual Center, Ann Arbor, Michigan 48109, 1965.

Anti-war, but good views of rural Vietnamese farming technology.

MEKONG, A RIVER OF ASIA. 16 mm. Color and sound. 25 minutes. Available from University of Michigan Audio-Visual Center, Ann Arbor, Michigan 48109, 1967.

A look at the river and the lifestyles along its banks-Lao, Thai, Khmer, Vietnamese.

THE MIAO YEAR (Parts I and II). 16 mm. Color and sound. 61 minutes. Produced by Contemporary Films of McGraw Hill Films. Distributed by Southeast Asia Program, Cornell University.

Film documenting the annual cycle of the Hmong (Miao) people. In English. Useful as film ethnography, for preserving record of the traditional life-style of the Hmong refugees and providing orientation about Hmong to sponsors and service providers. An attempt "to tell the story of the Miao." Discusses in brief the history and culture of the Hmong. Includes a sketch of their migration, political and military conflicts, and resettlement in the Western world.

NATURAL RESOURCES OF SOUTHEAST ASIA. 16 mm. Color and sound. 15 minutes. Available from University of Michigan Audio-Visual Center, Ann Arbor, Michigan 48109, 1968.

Discussion of the primary resources of the region.

THE NEW AMERICANS. Videotape cassette. Color and sound. 28 minutes. Produced by David Abramowitz. Distributed by KCET/International Institute of Los Angeles.

A series of four half-hour shows produced for educational television showing Indochinese culture and history, representing the cultures of the Vietnamese, the ethnic Chinese living in Vietnam, the Khmer, the Lao, and the Lao-Hmong. The stated objective for the series is "to offer information on the positive aspects of differences in the people from Indochina . . . through original music, parables, cultural demonstrations and dramatic vignettes that focus on conflicts that occur due to misunderstanding and offering positive solutions to their conflicts." Though the series is geared to children aged 7 to 11, it is also appropriate and interesting for adults.

NIOK. 16 mm. Color and sound. 29 minutes. Available from University of Michigan Audio-Visual Center, Ann Arbor, Michigan 48109, 1961.

A tale of a Cambodian boy and his elephant.

OUR SECRET ARMY. Videotape cassette. Color. 20 minutes. Produced and distributed by CBS News., 1979.

A feature news report on the plight of the Hmong. Shows their situation in the refugee camps and presents background on their involvement with the United States which has brought them to their present state. A concise, strong presentation which shows that the United States is largely responsible for the difficult situation in which the Hmong find themselves and that the United States is not really keeping the promise it made to the people. A rather powerful statement of the necessity for the United States to accept the Hmong (and other Indochinese) refugees.

A QUESTION OF RELIEF. Videotape cassette. Color. 30 minutes. Produced by International Red Cross. Distributed by American Red Cross, 1980.

Shows the efforts of the International Red Cross to enter Cambodia in 1979 to provide relief. Relief activities in Cambodia and along the Thai border are described, particularly the provision of medical treatment and food and the difficulties encountered in providing relief.

SAD SONG OF YELLOW SKIN. 16 mm. Color and sound. 60 minutes. Available from University of Michigan Audio-Visual Center, Ann Arbor, Michigan 48109, 1970.

Mainly life in Saigon, with Vietnamese, Americans, and the degradation therein; a strong film.

SOUTHEAST ASIA: VIETNAM, CAMBODIA, LAOS. 16 mm. Color and sound. 22 minutes. By Coronet Instructional Media, 1973.

Gives a geographic overview of Cambodia, Laos and Vietnam, and points out political and cultural factors that prevail there. Explains that although the people of North and South Vietnam, Cambodia, and Laos have much in common, there are differences in human use of the land.

VIETNAM TODAY. 16 mm. Color and sound. Produced by Sierra World Films, 1975. Distributed by Oxford Films, Division of Paramount Communications.

Film documentary about life in Vietnam showing Vietnamese fisher family, rice farming, local village school, local pagoda, an agricultural training program, and Saigon. Filmed before 1975 and the fall of the Saigon government, it provides a record of some aspects of life which many of the refugees are likely to remember.

TROPICAL RAIN FOREST. 16 mm. Color and sound. 28 minutes. 1962, 16 minutes. Available from University of Michigan Audio-Visual Center, Ann Arbor, Michigan 48109, 1961.

Two films showing the plant and animal life of such environments.

MY VAN FILMS. 2325 15th Avenue, San Francisco, California 94116, (415) 664-1663.

Specializes in Vietnamese-speaking films.

INDOCHINESE IN AMERICA

BEN DA, USA. 16 mm. Color and sound. 28 minutes. By David Hogoboom.

A look at the difficulties of assimilation in the United States faced by Vietnamese refugees in the Texas Gulf Coast area.

THE CHALLENGE OF A NEW BEGINNING. Videotape cassette. Color and sound. 21 minutes. Produced by PolyCom Productions. Distributed by the Illinois Adult Indochinese Refugee Consortium.

Videotape describing activities of the Illinois Adult Indochinese Refugee Consortium. Focuses in particular on problems of refugees who do not know English. Tries to sensitize the American viewer to the problem by showing what it would be like for an American to look for a job in another language situation.

EXPERIENCES OF LONG-TIME VIETNAMESE RESIDENTS IN THE UNITED STATES. Videocassette. I Want To Know . . . series. Produced by the Foreign Service Institute. Distributed by the English Language Resource Center of the Center for Applied Linguistics. In Vietnamese.

Panel discussion with moderator and four Vietnamese refugees. Discussion focuses on their experiences as long-time residents in the United States.

INSTANT REFUGEES. 16 mm. Color and sound. 30 minutes. By Catholic Relief Services. Available from Modern Talking Pictures.

Displaced Kampucheans, Laotians and Thais receive emergency aid and resettlement assistance from Catholic Relief Services. This film shows three stages of refugee life: feeding along the Kampuchea-Thailand border, day to day existence in a refugee camp, and the heartbreak-exhilaration of resettlement. A CINE Golden Eagle Award Winner.

THE PHANS OF JERSEY CITY. 16 mm. Color and sound. 49 minutes. Produced by Abbie H. Fink and Stephen L. Forman. Distributed by Films, Incorporated, Skokie, Illinois, 1979.

A documentary film focusing on the Phan family, a Vietnamese refugee family of 19 members who resettled in the United States in 1975. The film looks at each adult member of the family to show how they have adjusted to life in the United States as well as how they live their daily family life.

REFUGEE. Videotape cassette. Color and sound. 28 minutes. Produced and distributed by Joel Foreman. Public Television Productions, 3310 Glenway Drive, Kensington, Maryland 20795, 1980.

Videotape documentary of the Vietnamese community in Northern Virginia shows episodes of refugees on arrival, at work, in school, and in the community. Presents some background of the history of refugees in the United States.

ROOM FOR A STRANGER. 16 mm. Color and sound. 25 minutes. Produced by Harvey Kopel Films, 1979. Distributed by Lutheran Immigration and Refugee Service.

Features a church community's deliberation about sponsorship. Their discussion is interspersed with the comments of other sponsors and refugees. The film culminates in the arrival of a refugee family and their welcome by the community.

THANH. 16 mm. Color and sound. 9 minutes. By WGBH-TV. Indiana University Audio-Visual Center, Bloomington, 1979, made 1976.

Pham Thanh, a 15-year-old refugee from Vietnam, tells his classmates of the tragedy of seeing American soldiers destroy his village and kill his mother, father and grandmother. He relates his daily struggle to deal with the loneliness, fear and depression that have been part of his life since he was airlifted out of Vietnam 7 years ago.

INDONESIANS

Embassy and Consulates

EMBASSY OF THE REPUBLIC OF INDONESIA
2020 Massachusetts Avenue, Northwest
Washington, D.C. 20036 (202) 293-1745

CONSULATES GENERAL

5 East 68th Street
New York, New York 10021 (212) 879-0600

World Trade Center
351 California Street, Suite 700
San Francisco, California
94102 (415) 982-8966

1990 Post Oak Boulevard
Houston, Texas 77056 (713) 626-3291

CONSULATES

3540 Wilshire Boulevard, Suite 315
Los Angeles, California 90010 (213) 383-5126

Honorary Consulates

PRI Tower - 733 Bishop Street
Post Office Box 3379
Honolulu, Hawaii 96842 (808) 524-4300

Mission to the United Nations

INDONESIAN MISSION
666 Third Avenue
New York, New York 10017 (212) 286-8910

Tourist and Travel Office

PUSAT PROMOSI PARIWISATA INDONESIA
(Indonesian Tourist Promotion Board for North America)
32 Geary Street, Suite 305
San Francisco, California 94108 (415) 981-3585

Fraternal Organization

INDONESIAN COMMUNITY ASSOCIATION
c/o Embassy of Indonesia
2020 Massachusetts Avenue, Northwest
Washington, D.C. 20036 (202) 293-1745
Chairman: Mr. Sambas Wirakusuma Founded 1952

Formed to support the activities of the official representation of Indonesia in the United States through family participation in social activities, lectures, sports and religious holidays. There are groups also in other major areas such as New York associated with the respective consulate.
Publication: Warta IKI (newsletter), quarterly.

Public Affairs Organizations

EAST TIMOR PROJECT
Post Office Box 2197
Washington, D.C. 20013 (202) 667-4094
Coordinator: Arnold Kohen Founded 1978

Seeks to draw public attention to the situations of political prisoners in Indonesia, and to conditions in East Timor, particularly famine. Conducts research. Formerly (1981) Emergency Committee for Human Rights in Indonesia and Self-Determination on East Timor.

TAPOL/USA - CAMPAIGN FOR THE RELEASE OF INDONESIAN POLITICAL PRISONERS
Post Office Box 609
Montclair, New Jersey 07042
President: Professor Richard W. Franke (201) 893-4133
Founded 1975

To inform the public about continuing abridgement of fundamental human rights in Indonesia; to encourage United States citizens to become aware and involved in appropriate actions to help obtain release of political prisoners and restoration of fundamental human liberties in Indonesia. Sponsors seminars and lectures.
Publications: Bulletin, bimonthly; also publishes books and pamphlets.

Cultural and Educational Organizations

INDONESIAN AMERICAN SOCIETY
c/o Major Hal Maynard
8725 Piccadilly
Springfield, Virginia 22151
Chairman: Major Harold Maynard (703) 425-5080

Furthers knowledge and interest in Indonesia through lectures and special activities.

INDONESIAN STUDENTS ASSOCIATION
c/o Embassy of Indonesia
2020 Massachusetts Avenue, Northwest
Washington, D.C. 20036 (202) 293-1745

Founded to serve the needs of young Indonesians studying at American colleges and universities. Branches exist in Washington, San Francisco, Los Angeles and elsewhere.

Research Centers and Special Institutes

CORNELL MODERN INDONESIA PROJECT
Cornell University
Ithaca, New York 14853
Co-Director: Professor George McT. Kahin

Research activity of Center for International Studies at Cornell University, participating in scholarly research in United States on Indonesia's social and political development, including preparation of monographs containing series of biographies and autobiographies of Indonesian historical figures and articles on foreign affairs and Indonesian military, dance and culture.

Newspapers and Newsletters

THE INDONESIA LETTER. 1969-. Monthly. Editor: Arthur C. Miller. Publisher: The Asia Letter, Limited, Post Office Box 54149, Los Angeles, California 90054.

Provides commentary and analysis on the subject of Indonesia and news of its economic, political, social developments and trends.

Bank Branches in the U.S.

BANK INDONESIA
One Liberty Plaza
New York, New York 10006 (212) 227-7300

EXPORT IMPORT BANK INDONESIA
100 Wall Street
New York, New York 10005 (212) 344-4088

BANK NEGARA INDONESIA 1946
100 Wall Street
New York, New York 10005 (212) 943-4750

Commercial and Trade Organizations

AMERICAN-ASEAN TRADE COUNCIL
40 East 49th Street
New York, New York 10017 (212) 688-2755
Secretary: George Peabody Founded 1978

Comprised of the membership of the American Indonesian Chamber of Commerce and the Philippine-American Chamber of Commerce and other ASEAN countries.
Publications: Bulletin, bimonthly.

AMERICAN INDONESIAN CHAMBER OF COMMERCE
Two Park Avenue
New York, New York 10016
Executive Secretary: Boyd R. Compton (212) 683-6170
Founded 1949

Publishes Information Bulletins.

CENTRAL INDONESIAN TRADING COMPANY
30 Vesey Street
New York, New York 10007 (212) 233-5310

INDO-METAL
275 Madison, Room 1905
New York, New York 10016 (212) 532-3307

INDONESIAN CONSORTIUM OF CONSTRUCTION INDUSTRIES - USA
222 Bridge Plaza South, #301
Fort Lee, New Jersey 07024 (201) 461-7275

INDONESIAN INVESTMENT PROMOTION OFFICE
420 Lexington Avenue
New York, New York 10017 (212) 210-8860

INDONESIAN TRADE PROMOTION CENTER
c/o Indonesian Consultate General
5 East 68th Street
New York, New York 10021 (212) 879-0600

350 South Figueroa
Los Angeles, California 90071 (213) 617-9398

PERTAMINA
2029 Century Park East, Suite 1100
Los Angeles, California 90067 (213) 277-3721

P. T. PUPUK KUJANG (fertilizer company)
c/o Pullman Kellog
1300 Three Greenway Plaza East
Houston, Texas 77046 (713) 626-4927

P. T. PUSRI (fertilizer company)
c/o The M. W. Kellog Company
1300 Three Greenway Plaza East
Houston, Texas 77046 (713) 960-4964

Airline Offices

GIA
Garuda Indonesian Airways
9814 Airport Boulevard South, Suite 930
Los Angeles, California 90045 (213) 649-0083

Ship Lines

JAKARTA LLOYD
17 Battery Place
New York, New York 10004 (212) 344-0426

TRIKORA LLOYD
2 World Trade Center
99th Floor
New York, New York 10007 (212) 524-1100

Books and Pamphlets

A BIBLIOGRAPHY OF THE GEOGRAPHICAL LITERATURE ON SOUTHEAST ASIA, 1920-1972. By Alvar Carlson. Monticello, Illinois, Council of Planning Librarians, 1974.

A comprehensive bibliography of the geographical literature published in English. The entries (articles, reports, pamphlets, books, unpublished theses and doctoral dissertations) were written by geographers or were published in geographical periodicals.

A BIBLIOGRAPHY ON LAND, PEASANTS, AND POLITICS FOR MALAYSIA, INDONESIA AND THE PHILIPPINES. Compiled by James C. Scott and Howard Leichter. Land Tenure Center, 1972.

This listing of materials emphasizes the studies which deal with social structure and peasant politics. It is divided by countries and then subdivided into fourteen topics.

THE INDONESIAN ECONOMY, 1950-1967, BIBLIOGRAPHIC SUPPLEMENT. By George Hicks. New Haven, Connecticut, Southeast Asia Studies, Yale University, 1967. Distributed by Cellar Book Shop, Detroit, Michigan.

This bibliography covers writings on the postwar Indonesian economy in Indonesian and English, with data also from government sources. Most of the materials are available in the major Djakarata libraries and those United States libraries participating in the Library of Congress project in Indonesia.

Audiovisual Material

FILMS

THE AURA OF INDONESIA. 16 mm. Color and sound. 12 minutes. By Cine-Mintz, Los Angeles, 1977.

A look at some of Indonesia's customs and scenery.

AZHARI ALI - AN ACEHNESE UNIVERSITY STUDENT. 16 mm. Color and sound. 24 minutes. Asian Neighbors Series: Indonesia. By Film Australia, Sydney, 1974. Released in the United States by Australian Information Service, 1975.

Shows the day-to-day life of a young university student in Indonesia who works five nights a week so that he may study agriculture.

BALI: RELIGION IN PARADISE. 16 mm. Color and sound. 26 minutes. By ABC News. Released by Xerox Films, 1974.

Examines the religious beliefs and practices of the people of Bali.

BALI: THE MASK OF RANGDA. 16 mm. Color and sound. 30 minutes. By Harvey Bellin. Hartley Productions, 1975.

Shows the elaborate ceremonies and dramatic performances in Bali which demonstrate the link between man and God.

A BALINESE GONG ORCHESTRA. 16 mm. Color and sound. 11 minutes. Asian Neighbors Series: Indonesia. By Film Australia, Sydney, 1974. Released in the United States by Australian Information Service, 1975.

Presents explanations and demonstrations of the various component instruments of a Balinese gong orchestra.

EMERALDS OF THE TROPICS. 16 mm. Color and sound. 27 minutes. By Film and Television Communications, McDonnell Douglas Corporation, Santa Monica, California for Garuda Indonesian Airways, 1976.

Shows the architecture, cultures, religions, and beautiful attractions of Bali, Sumatra, Java and the cities of Jogjakarta and Jakarta.

THE FILM WITHOUT A TITLE. 16 mm. Color and sound. 29 minutes. Made and released by Film Authors, for Holland America Cruises, 1974.

Shows some of the scenic highlights of the islands of Indonesia. Also issued in Dutch, French, German.

THE HASANS - A BUGINESE TRADING FAMILY. 16 mm. Color and sound. 23 minutes. Asian Neighbors Series: Indonesia. By Film Australia, Sydney, 1974. Released in the United States by Australian Information Service, 1975.

Examines the work and life of a trading family which operates a fleet of ships in the Java Sea.

INDONESIA. 16 mm. Color and sound. 29 minutes. By Peter Drummond. International Film Foundation, Australia, 1973.

Examines many facets of life in Indonesia, including the contrast of city and country life, the nation's cultural development and traditions, the religious traditions of Islam and Hinduism, and the problems faced by Indonesians in the areas of education and economics.

INDONESIA: A TIME TO GROW. 16mm. Color and sound. 19 minutes. Oriental World series. By Vision Associates. Released by McGraw-Hill Book Company, New York, 1970.

Portrays Indonesia as a country emerging into the modern world. Covers Indonesian traditions, village life, farming, urban growth, and a youth's view of the future of Indonesia. Depicts the life of a typical farm family in Indonesia.

INDONESIA: AN ISLAND NATION'S PROGRESS. 16 mm. Color and sound. 15 minutes. By Paolo Koch. Universal Education and Visual Arts, 1972.

A study of life in Indonesia. Describes the various industries, the sources of recreation for children, and progress in agriculture during recent years.

INDONESIA - EAST OF BALI. 16 mm. Color and sound. 28 minutes. By Tulsa Studios, Oklahoma, 1979, made 1976.

Presents a tour through the islands of Indonesia, featuring unusual attractions such as glass eating, body piercing with spears, giant lizards, and headhunters.

INDONESIA - UNITY IN DIVERSITY. 16 mm. Color and sound. 53 minutes. By Film Australia, Australian Broadcasting Commission and University of Queensland Press. Released by Australian Information Service, New York, 1977, made, 1976.

Provides insight into the historical and cultural background of Indonesia, concentrating on the most populated areas. Also discusses the Indonesian concept of power and the Indonesian Army, an essential ingredient in their society.

THE MAGICAL MOUNTAIN. 16 mm. Color and sound. 52 minutes. By Ruff Cut Productions. Media Vision, Toronto, 1975.

Documents the Indonesian way of life.

MARVEL - A JAKARTA BOY. 16 mm. Color and sound. 17 minutes. Asian Neighbors Series: Indonesia. By Film Australia, Sydney, 1974. Released in the United States by Australian Information Service, 1975.

Examines the life of a young migrant boy in Jakarta, Indonesia. Shows how he works hard so that he can fulfill his life's goal of getting an education.

WET EARTH AND WARM PEOPLE. 16 mm. Color and sound. 59 minutes. By the National Film Board of Canada, New York, 1971.

Presents a view of life in Indonesia. Explains how Indonesia, with the fifth largest population in the world, struggles to find political and social direction for the future.

Documentary films may also be obtained from the Embassy of the Republic of Indonesia, 2020 Massachusetts Avenue, Northwest, Washington, D.C. 20036.

IRANIANS (Persians)
See also: ARABS

Embassy and Consulates

IRAN INTEREST SECTION
Embassy of Algeria
Suite 200
2139 Wisconsin Avenue
Washington, D.C. 20007 (202) 965-2050

Mission to the United Nations

IRANIAN MISSION
622 Third Avenue
New York, New York 10017 (212) 687-2020

Fraternal Organizations

IRANIAN INFORMATION CENTER
16661 Ventura Boulevard
Suite 828
Encino, California 91436 (213) 789-0558

Provides telephone information service for California and for the United States in Farsi and in English.

IRANIAN JEWISH ASSOCIATION OF CALIFORNIA
6112 Wilshire Boulevard
Suite 201
Los Angeles, California 90048 (213) 551-6627

IRANIAN JEWISH FEDERATION
6505 Wilshire Boulevard
Suite 1101
Los Angeles, California 90048 (213) 852-1272

Publication: Shoofar, monthly.

SOCIETY OF ARMENIANS OF IRAN IN LOS ANGELES
221 South Brand Boulevard
Glendale, California 91204 (213) 241-1073

Public Affairs Organizations

COMMITTEE IN SOLIDARITY WITH THE PEOPLE OF IRAN
339 Lafayette Street, Room 301
New York, New York 10012
Executive Officer: Ali Mobarez Founded 1981

Objective is to compile and publish statistics and reports on human rights violations in Iran. Sponsors seminars and cultural programs. Maintains library of 700 volumes.
Publications: Newsletter, irregular.

FRONT FOR LIBERATION OF IRAN
Post Office Box 3090
Falls Church, Virginia 22043

Post Office Box 10295
Beverly Hills, California 90213 (213) 208-1720

Headquartered in France. Sponsors the Iran Center for Documentation to collect and preserve literary works and other items relating to the culture of Iran.
Publications: Frontier, weekly; Jebh-e-Nejat-Iran, weekly.

HUMANIST MOVEMENT OF IRANIAN PEOPLE - RAMA
c/o Dr. Adnan Mazarei
550 South Barrington Avenue
Brentwood, Los Angeles, California 90049
Secretary General: Dr. Adnan Mazarei (213) 476-0435
Founded 1964

Established in Iran, RAMA claims to be the first attempt to organize a humanist group as a political party. Goal is to "liberate humanism from its philanthropic, only moral, academic meaning and transform it into a solid tangible socio-economic doctrine." Also referred to as "applied humanism." Believes that people are living in a transitory historical period and that people will soon witness an "unprecedented economic, social, political and intellectual mutation" that will "transform the entire living condition of mankind." Attempts to apply humanist principles to what it sees as "the new human society." Maintains library of 5,000 volumes.
Publications: Middle East Peoples (magazine); Battle

on Two Fronts for a Humanist Democracy (book); and Humanist Democracy (article series).

IRAN FREEDOM FOUNDATION
Post Office Box 34422
Bethesda, Maryland 20817 (301) 654-7622
President: M. R. Tabatabai Founded 1979

Iranians living in the United States; Americans interested in Iran's future. Social and educational organization which promotes a secular democracy in Iran through increased political socialization of the citizenry. The Foundation maintains that 98 percent of the Iranians living abroad are against the present regime of the Ayatollah Ruholla Khomeini. Strongly believes that the next Iranian leadership should be a democracy and that "no religious man should be at the helm of the affairs of the state." Disseminates educational materials and literature.
Publication: Newsletter, monthly; Bonyad Azadi-e-Iran, monthly.

Cultural and Educational Organizations

IRAN AMERICA FRIENDSHIP FOUNDATION
2025 I Street, Northwest
Washington, D.C. 20006
Administrator: Bahman Lotfi (202) 331-8308

Nonprofit nonpolitical organization that seeks to foster mutual understanding between Iranian and American people, through the promotion of humanitarian activities. Encourages Iranians to form productive enterprises; assists other organizations; provides health services; teaches Persian language and literature to Iranian children.

IRANIAN STUDENTS ASSOCIATION OF THE UNITED STATES
Post Office Box 4000F
Berkeley, California 94704

KOUROSH FOUNDATION
Post Office Box 1144
Norwalk, California 90650
Administrator: Farokh Nojumi (213) 864-0788

Nonprofit organization. Encourages the development of Persian culture.
Publication: Touca (Persian Children's Magazine).

SOCIETY OF FRIENDS OF FARSI LITERATURE
8671 Wilshire Boulevard
Suite 501
Beverly Hills, California 90211 (213) 852-4771

Religious Organizations

ISLAMIC SOCIETY IN AMERICA
781 Bolinas Avenue
Fairfax, California 94930 (415) 454-6666

ZOROASTRIAN CENTER OF SOUTHERN CALIFORNIA
1814 South Bayless Street
Anaheim, California 92802 (714) 533-8990

Research Centers and Special Institutes

AMERICAN INSTITUTE OF IRANIAN STUDIES
c/o Professor William L. Hanaway, Jr.
325 University Museum
University of Pennsylvania
Philadelphia, Pennsylvania 19104
President: Professor William L. Hanaway, Jr. (215) 243-7427
Founded 1967

Composed of educational institutions, foundations, corporations and individuals. Seeks to facilitate research on Iran by both North American and Iranian scholars. Operates the Tehran Research Center (at present inactive) in Tehran, Iran which aids visiting scholars in securing research and residence permits from the Iranian government, facilitating appropriate contacts with Iranian officials and scholars and generally enhancing the work of such scholars while in the country. Maintains a small research and reference library.
Publications: Tehran Center Newsletter, quarterly; also publishes a directory of research in progress with notices of publications and dissertations resulting from that research.

SOCIETY FOR IRANIAN STUDIES
Box J-154
Boston College
Chestnut Hill, Massachusetts 02167 (314) 889-5252
Executive Secretary: Dr. Lois Beck Founded 1967

Scholars and students working in the field of Iranian studies including historians, economists, sociologists, anthropologists, psychologists and literary critics. Aim is to promote scholarship in the field. Conducts

seminars and conferences. Formerly: (1969) Society For Iranian Cultural and Social Studies.
Publications: Iranian Studies (journal), quarterly; also publishes newsletter.

Newspapers and Newsletters

ARYA. Post Office Box 75132, Los Angeles, California 90005. In Farsi.

BONYAD AZADI-E-IRAN. 1979-. Monthly. Publisher: Iran Freedom Foundation, Incorporated, Post Office Box 34422, Bethesda, Maryland 20817. In Farsi.

COMMITTEE IN SOLIDARITY WITH THE PEOPLE OF IRAN NEWSLETTER. Irregular. Publisher: Committee in Solidarity with the People of Iran, 339 Lafayette Street, Room 301, New York, New York 10012. In English.

FRONTIER. Weekly. Distributor: Front For Liberation of Iran, Post Office Box 3090, Falls Church, Virginia 22043. In English. English translated version of Jebh-e-Nejat-Iran.

GAMA. Post Office Box 77183, Los Angeles, California 90007.

IRAN FREEDOM FOUNDATION NEWSLETTER. 1979-. Monthly. Publisher: Iran Freedom Foundation Incorporated, Post Office Box 34422, Bethesda, Maryland 20817. In English. English translated version of Bonyad Azadi-e-Iran.

IRAN NEWS. 1980-. Weekly. Editor and Publisher: Iraj Rostami, 7046 Hollywood Boulevard #610, Los Angeles, California 90028. In Farsi.

IRAN TIMES. 1970-. Weekly. Editor and Publisher: Javad Khakbaz, 2727 Wisconsin Avenue, Northwest, Washington, D.C. 20007. In English and Farsi.

IRAN TRIBUNE. 1980-. Weekly. Editor and Publisher: Parviz Qazi-Saied, 2444 Moorpark Avenue, Suite 322, San Jose, California 95128. In Farsi.

IRANSHAHR. 1980-. Weekly. Editor: Hooshang Shakibai. Publisher: Iranshahr Publishing, Incorporated, 2527 Wilson Boulevard, Arlington, Virginia 22201. In Farsi.

JEBH-E-NEJAT-IRAN. Weekly. Distributors: Front for Liberation of Iran, Post Office Box 3090, Falls Church, Virginia 22043, and Post Office Box 10295, Beverly Hills, California 90213. In Farsi.

KABOB NAMEH. 1441 Truman Street, San Fernando, California 91340. In Farsi.

KEYHAN DAR TABEED. Post Office Box 5235, San Mateo, California 94402. In Farsi.

MELLAT-E-BIDAR. 270 North Canon Drive, Suite 103, Beverly Hills, California 90210. In Farsi.

NEHZAT (The Movement). 839 Royal Ann Lane, Concord, California 94518. In Farsi.

PAN IRAN. Post Office Box 4432, Foster City, California 94404. In Farsi.

PARDIS. Post Office Box 2429, Beverly Hills, California 90213. In Farsi.

PAYAM-E-AZADI (Tidings of Freedom). The Iranian Newspaper. Post Office Box 1312, Canoga Park, California 91304. In Farsi.

PAYAM-E-IRAN. 1981-. Weekly. 18520 Burbank Boulevard, #3, Tarzana, California 91356. In Farsi.

ROOZNAMEH-E-HAREKAT (The Movement Newspaper). Publisher: Harekat Newspaper, 519 Seaver Drive, Mill Valley, California 94941. In Farsi.

SHANZDAHOM AZAR. I.S.A. U.S., Post Office Box 4000F, Berkeley, California 94704. In Farsi.

SOCIETY FOR IRANIAN STUDIES NEWSLETTER. Publisher: Society for Iranian Studies, Box J-154, Boston College, Chestnut Hill, Massachusetts 02167. In English.

Magazines

ELM VA JAMEA (Science and Society). Publisher: Persian Journal for Science and Society, Post Office Box 7353, Alexandria, Virginia 22307. In Farsi.

ENGHLAB VA AZADI (Revolution and Freedom). Publisher: E.S.A., Post Office Box 07101, Detroit, Michigan 48207. In Farsi.

HAGH. Publisher: Post Office Box 160081, Sacramento, California 95816. In Farsi.

IRAN POST. Publisher: Post Office Box 3765, Beverly Hills, California 90212. In Farsi.

IRANIAN STUDIES. Quarterly. Publisher: Society for Iranian Studies, Box J-154, Boston College, Chestnut Hill, Massachusetts 02167. In English.

ISLAMIC REVOLUTION. Monthly. Publisher: Research and Publication Incorporated, Post Office Box 2556, Falls Church, Virginia 22042. In English.

MAJALLEH-E-PEYVAND (The Link Magazine). Monthly. Publisher: Post Office Box 1629, Arlington, Virginia 22210. In English and Farsi.

MELLAT-E-BIDAR (The Awakened Nation). Biweekly. Publisher: Melli Publishing House, Incorporated, 270 North Canon Drive, Suite 103, Beverly Hills, California 90210. In Farsi.

MIDDLE EAST PEOPLES. Publisher: Humanist Movement of Iranian People (RAMA), c/o Dr. Adnan Mazarei, 550 South Barrington Avenue, Brentwood, Los Angeles, California 90049. In English.

NASL-I-NO (The New Generation). Monthly. Editor and Publisher: Ebrahim Safai, 15957 Ventura Boulevard, Suite 430, Encino, California 91436. In Farsi.

PARS. Monthly. Editor: Kamran Shakib, 17641 Van Owen Street, Van Nuys, California 91406. In Farsi.

RAHAVARD. Quarterly. Editor: Hassan Shahbaz, 221 South Gale Drive, Apartment #262, Beverly Hills, California 90211. In Farsi.

RAH-E-ZENDEGHI (The Way of Life). Weekly. Editor and Publisher: Hooshang Mirhashem, 1015 Gayley Avenue, #1111, Los Angeles, California 90024. In Farsi.

SHOOFAR. Monthly. Editor: Homa Sarshar. Publisher: Iranian Jewish Federation, 6505 Wilshire Boulevard, Los Angeles, California 90048. In Farsi.

TOUCA (Persian Children's Magazine). Editor: Cyrus Meshkin. Publisher: Kourosh Foundation, Post Office Box 1144, Norwalk, California 90650. In Farsi.

Radio Programs

California - Los Gatos

KRVE (FM) - 227 North Santa Cruz Avenue, Los Gatos, California 95030, (408) 354-6622. Persian programs, 2 hours weekly.

California - San Francisco

KFAX - 1470 Pine Street, San Francisco, California 94109, (415) 673-4148. Iranian programs, 1 hour weekly (Saturdays at 11:00 a.m.)

Maryland - Laurel

WLMD - Briarwood Drive, Laurel, Maryland 20811, (301) 792-9077. Iranian programs, 1 hour weekly.

New York - New York

WKCR (FM) - 208 Ferris Booth Hall, New York, New York 10027, (212) 280-5223. Iranian programs, 1 hour weekly.

Television Programs

California - Los Angeles

KSCI - Channel 18, 1950 Cotner Avenue, West Los Angeles, California 90025, (213) 479-8081. Iranian programs, 4 hours weekly.

Bank Branches in the U.S.

BANK MELLI IRAN
628 Madison Avenue
New York, New York 10022 (212) 759-4700

BANK SADERAT IRAN
375 Park Avenue
New York, New York 10152 (212) 753-6400

BANK SEPAH-IRAN
650 Fifth Avenue
New York, New York 10019 (212) 974-1777

Airline Offices

IRAN AIR
650 Fifth Avenue
New York, New York 10019 (212) 582-8811

Bookdealers and Publishers' Representatives

DOKAN, INCORPORATED
(carries books, magazines, newspapers and music)
7921 Old Georgetown Road
Bethesda, Maryland 20814 (301) 657-2361

IACONI BOOK IMPORTS
(imports books in Modern Farsi)
300 Pennsylvania Avenue
San Francisco, California 94107 (415) 285-7393

MARK A. KALUSTIAN
(specializes in books on ancient Persia)
259 Pleasant Street
Arlington, Massachusetts 02174 (617) 648-3437

KETAB CORPORATION
(publishes and sells publications in Farsi)
16661 Ventura Boulevard, Suite 828
Encino, California 91436 (213) 789-0558

KI-SA
(sells cassette and 8-track tapes of Iranian music)
Post Office Box 748
Columbia, Maryland 21045 (301) 596-6448

LIBERATION BOOKSTORE
(carries political publications in Farsi, Chinese and Spanish)
1828 Broadway
Seattle, Washington 98122 (206) 323-9222

MAY DAY BOOKS & PUBLICATIONS
(carries political publications in Farsi, Arabic, Chinese and Spanish)
3134 East Davison
Detroit, Michigan 48212 (313) 893-0523

NOOR PUBLISHING COMPANY
(publishes and sells books in Farsi. Quarterly catalog available)
Post Office Box 3251
Falls Church, Virginia 22043 (703) 448-0495

Books and Pamphlets

BIBLIOGRAPHY OF IRAN. 5th edition. By Geoffrey Handley-Taylor. Chicago, Saint James Press, 1969.

Basic bibliography of Iran with a memoir of Mohamad Reza Pahlavi Aryamehr, Shananshah of Iran at the beginning.

A BIBLIOGRAPHY OF PRE-ISLAMIC PERSIA. Edited by James D. Pearson. London, Mansell, 1975.

This bibliography is an attempt to include all the printed literature available in western European languages on Pre-Islamic Persia. Materials are arranged in four sections: languages and literature, history, religion and art and archaeology.

THE ECONOMIC AND SOCIAL DEVELOPMENT OF IRAN. By John Vidergar. Monticello, Illinois, Council of Planning Librarians, 1977.

This bibliography deals with the internal economic and social developments in Iran, especially the problems of industrialization, urbanization and agricultural reform.

IRAN; A Selected and Annotated Bibliography. By Hafez F. Farman. New York, Greenwood Press, 1968.

A general list of materials on Iran that are available in the Library of Congress. Emphasis is placed on publications relating to Iran of the nineteenth and twentieth centuries. The works are divided into three parts: general, Pre-Islamic period and Islamic period.

IRAN: PAST AND PRESENT. 9th edition. By Donald N. Wilber. Princeton, New Jersey, Princeton University Press, 1981.

Encyclopedic text covering development of Iran from earliest known time to its modern role as a major oil-producing nation. Discusses political, social, and economic structure of modern Iran, including the role of the development of national resources in international affairs.

THE IRANIAN DIRECTORY: YELLOW PAGES IN CALIFORNIA, 1982. Encino, California, Ketab Corporation, 1982.

Directory of businesses, institutions, professionals, and individuals who wish to advertise their services to the Iranian community in California. Mainly in Farsi, with some English.

THE LAND OF THE GREAT SOPHY. 3rd edition. By Roger Stevens. London, Methuen, 1979.

A summary of Persian topography, history, religion, and art, followed by a detailed account of the country's ancient cities, monuments, and scenery. Includes updated travel notes for the visitor, as of publication date.

Audiovisual Material

FILMS

ANCIENT CIVILIZATIONS: PERSIA. 8 mm. Color. Silent. 4 minutes. Coronet Instructional Media, 1974.

Chronicles the ascension of the Persian Empire and its ultimate destruction by Alexander the Great. With captions. Loop film in cartridge.

INVADERS AND CONVERTS. 16 mm. Color and sound. 30 minutes. By the British Broadcasting Corporation-TV, London. Released in the United States by Time-Life Films, New York, 1969.

Notes that the Persian culture flourished in spite of a thousand years of invasions by Mongols, and shows examples of Islamic art which reached its zenith in the golden dome of the holy city of Mashad.

IRAN. 16 mm. Color and sound. 18 minutes. By Claude Lelouch. Made by Aria Production, Geneva. Released in the United States by Pyramid Films, 1973.

An extended montage of Iran's people, sports, education, business, industry, and entertainment.

IRAN: BRITTLE ALLY. 16 mm. Black and white. Sound. 54 minutes. Columbia Broadcasting System Reports. By CBS News, New York, 1959.

Examines the problems and prospects of Iran, as of the late 1950's. Probes the efforts of the (former) Shah of Iran to institute agrarian reform, eliminate disease and illiteracy, and at the same time coexist with the Soviet Union.

IRAN: LANDMARKS IN THE DESERT. 16 mm. Color and sound. 27 minutes. Chatsworth Film Distribution Limited. Narrator: Anthony Quayle. Lawrence, Kansas, Centron Educational Films, 1977, c.1973.

Emphasizes the turbulent history of Persia through the ages, as seen through the vivid artistry of architects, painters, and craftsmen of the different periods. Includes sequences on the ancient ruins of Persepolis and on the weaving of Persian carpets. Includes leader's guide. Made in England. Longer version (52 minutes) also issued under title: Landmarks in the desert.

NIGHT FLIGHT TO IRAN - LAND OF SPLENDOUR. 16 mm. Color and sound. 26 minutes. Iran Air. Made by Welebit Productions, New York, Iran Air, 1976.

Shows the beauty of Iran as seen by two very different tourists.

THE SUDDEN EMPIRE. 16 mm. Color and sound. 30 minutes. The Glory That Remains, number 1. By the British Broadcasting Corporation-TV, London. Released in the United States by Time-Life Films, New York, 1969.

Traces the history of the rise and fall of the Achaemenid dynasty, using as a background the courtyards of Persepolis.

THE TEMPTATION OF POWER. 16 mm. Color and sound. 43 minutes. By Icarus Films, New York, 1979, made 1976. Gordien Troeller, Claude Deffarge, and Francois Partant.

A documentary which probes the reasons for widespread discontent among Iran's population during the rule of the Shah. Focuses on elements such as poverty, the roles of the military and police, the demolition of ancient buildings and villages, the erosion of the traditional way of life, land reform, and rapid westernization.

VIDEOTAPES

IRAN VIDEO. 12049 Ventura Place, Studio City, California 91604, (213) 996-2368.

Sells videotapes of Iranian movies, plays and dances.

PARS VIDEO. 16042 Ventura Boulevard, #205, Encino, California 91436, (213) 789-8788.

Sells videotapes of Iranian movies, plays, dances, documentaries, and television programs.

IRAQIS
(Includes ASSYRIANS)
See also: ARABS

Embassy and Consulates

IRAQI INTERESTS SECTION
EMBASSY OF INDIA
1801 P Street, Northwest
Washington, D.C. 20036 (202) 483-7500

Press Office (202) 232-6933

Mission to the United Nations

IRAQ MISSION
14 East 79th Street
New York, New York 10021 (212) 737-4433

Information Offices

PRESS INFORMATION OFFICE
14 East 79th Street
New York, New York 10021 (212) 737-4433

Fraternal Organization

IRAQI CLUB
40 West Seven Mile Road
Detroit, Michigan 48203 (313) 366-5126

Public Affairs Organization

AMERICAN COMMITTEE FOR RESCUE AND RE-SETTLEMENT OF IRAQI JEWS
1200 Fifth Avenue
New York, New York 10029 (212) 427-1246
President: Heskel M. Haddad Founded 1969

"To rescue the Jews of Iraq." Disseminates information to arouse public opinion regarding "the persecution of Jews in Iraq" and raises funds to help their rescue and resettlement. A Committee advertisement in the New York Times of January 29, 1970 asked for immediate restoration of fundamental human rights of Jews in Iraq, release of Jews in jails there and permission for the emigration of those Jews who wished to leave Iraq. As a result of pressure by other governments, the Iraqi government released all Jewish detainees held in Iraqi prisons and allowed a limited number of Jewish families to leave Iraq.
Publications: AMCORR-HOPE.

Cultural and Educational Organizations

ASSYRIAN-AMERICAN NATIONAL FEDERATION
5509 North Clark Street
Chicago, Illinois 60640 (312) 784-4489

Publication: Assyrian Star, bimonthly.

BET NAHRAIN
Post Office Box 4116
Modesto, California 95352 (209) 521-0434
Executor: Dr. Sargon Dadesho Founded 1974

Individuals united internationally to perpetuate the rich heritage of the Assyrian people through radio. TV and printed matter and through athletic and cultural programs. Conducts seminars and classes in ancient Assyrian language. Sponsors Assyrian broadcasting radio station and television network.
Publications: Bet Nahrain Journal, monthly; Radio and TV Newspaper, quarterly.

Religious Organizations

HOLY APOSTOLIC AND CATHOLIC CHURCH OF THE EAST (ASSYRIAN), DIOCESE OF THE UNITED STATES AND CANADA
7444 North Kildare
Skokie, Illinois 60076
Patriarch: His Holiness Mar Dinkha IV, Catholicos Patriarch of the East (312) 673-0022

The official name of the Church is the Holy Apostolic and Catholic Church of the East (Assyrian) and is used in this form and in many variations of this combination of words. It is also known as the East Syrian, Assyrian Orthodox, Persian (Babylonian) and "Nestorian" (misnomer) Church, among others. The Church was founded in 33 A.D. in Edessa (Urhai), state of Oshroene in the Persian Region.

Special Libraries and Subject Collections

BABYLONIAN COLLECTION
Yale University
Sterling Memorial Library
120 High Street
New Haven, Connecticut 06520 (203) 432-4725
Curator: William W. Hallo Founded 1912

Subjects: Assyriology; cuneiform; Sumerian, Akkadian, Hittite, Mesopotamian literature, archaeology, and history; Semitics. Special Collections: Cuneiform texts from the collections of E. I. David, E. J. Banks, J. P. Morgan, Edwin T. Newell, General Theological Seminary. Holdings: Books; bound periodical volumes; reprints (cataloged); cuneiform tablets and inscriptions; cylinder seals and stamp seals; other Ancient Near Eastern artifacts; journals and other serials. Services: Library open to public upon application to the curator.
Publications: Yale Oriental Series - Babylonian Texts; Yale Oriental Series Researches; Babylonian Inscriptions in the Collection of James B. Nies, Yale University; Goucher College Cuneiform Inscriptions; Babylonian Records in the Library of J. Pierpoint Morgan; Yale Near Eastern Researches.

Newspapers and Newsletters

ASSYRIAN STAR. 1933-. Bimonthly. Publisher: Assyrian-American National Federation, Incorporated, 5509 North Clark Street, Chicago, Illinois 60640. Text in Assyrian and English.

Contains articles, book reviews, and items relating to Assyrian interests.

BET NAHRAIN JOURNAL. Monthly. Publisher: Bet Nahrain, Post Office Box 4116, Modesto, California 95352. In English.

Contains items relating to Assyrian interests.

RADIO AND TV NEWSPAPER. Quarterly. Publisher: Bet Nahrain, Post Office Box 4116, Modesto, California 95352. In English.

Contains items relating to Assyrian interests.

Magazines

IRAQ TODAY: A POLITICAL AND CULTURAL FORTNIGHTLY. Biweekly. Editor: Mohieddin Ismail. Publisher: Translation and Foreign Languages Publishing House, Caliphs Street, Post Office Box 4074, Baghdad, Iraq. In English.

Contains articles and news reviews of political and cultural affairs in Iraq.

UR. Quarterly. Editor: Saad al-Bazzaz. Publisher: Iraqi Cultural Centre, 177-178 Tottenham Court Road, London W1P 9LP, England. In English.

Features articles dealing with cultural and political affairs in Iraq. Also includes fiction and reviews of books, films, music and art.

Radio Programs

California - Ceres

KBES (FM) - Box 4116, Modesto, California 95352, (209) 537-0933. Features educational programs in Assyria.

Airline Offices

IRAQI AIRLINES
1211 Avenue of the Americas
New York, New York 10036 (212) 921-8990

Books and Pamphlets

BABYLON. Baghdad, Iraq, Directorate General of Antiquities Ministry of Information, 1972.

A booklet published by the Iraq government on the preservation and restoration of the monuments of

Babylon. The text is in Arabic, German, English, Russian, and French. Photographs and drawings, most in color, show the costumes, architecture, sculpture, mosaic work, building plans, and ruins of the ancient city of Babylon on the Euphrates River in Iraq.

EDUCATION IN THE REPUBLIC OF IRAQ. Baghdad, Ministry of Education, Government of Iraq, 1972.

THE GEOGRAPHY OF IRAQ: A SELECTED BIBLIOGRAPHY. By Elizabeth Lytle. Monticello, Illinois, Council of Planning Librarians, 1977.

A listing of works of research completed since 1950 on the geography of Iraq. Topics covered are: climatology, economic, general, historical, human, medical, physical, political, population, settlement, transportation and urban geography.

GUIDE BOOK TO THE MOSUL MUSEUM. 2nd edition. By the Directorate General of Antiquities, Ministry of Culture and Guidance, Republic of Iraq. Baghdad, Government Press, 1966.

Discusses the history and archaeological sites of the cities of Mosul (at the ruins of Nineveh), Nimrud, and Hatra. A paperback book illustrated with numerous photographs showing the sculpture, cuneiform tablets, wall decorations, and other Mosul Museum pieces from the ancient cities of Iraq.

IRAQ. New York, Arab Information Center, 1973.

Presents information about the geography, history, government, people, economy, foreign trade, transportation and communications, health, education, and sites of interest to tourists in Iraq. A booklet illustrated with photographs.

IRAQ: A TOURIST'S GUIDE. Baghdad, Iraq, Tourism and Resorts Administration.

Discusses the historical background of Iraq, the capital city of Baghdad, the southern and northern regions of the country, resorts, and general information about the geography and people, education, resources, arts, industry, flora and fauna, foods, and transportation in Iraq. A paperback book illustrated with a map and many fine photographs, mostly in color.

NIMRUD. Baghdad, Iraq, Directorate General of Information, Ministry of Culture and Information, 1969.

Describes the ancient city of Nimrud, its history, topography, and sites of special interest.

REVOLUTION AND DEVELOPMENT IN IRAQ: CELEBRATING THE TWELFTH ANNIVERSARY OF THE 17-30 JULY REVOLUTION. By Ministry of Planning, Baghdad, Ministry of Culture and Information, July 1980.

Presents information about Iraq's population, economy, agriculture, industries, education, health, and cultural development. Includes statistics and many illustrations in color.

Audiovisual Material

SLIDES

SET OF SLIDES. 16 mm. Color.

A group of 40 slides showing ancient sculptures and other archaeological treasures, mosques, palaces, and people of present-day Iraq.

(For information about borrowing the slides, write to the Iraqi Interests Section of the Embassy of India.)

FILMS

ANCIENT MESOPOTAMIA. 16 mm. Color and sound. 10 minutes. Chicago, Coronet Instructional Media, 1976.

Depicts the cultural legacy of the Sumerians, Semites, Babylonians, and Assyrians of the ancient Middle East against authentic locales, including Babylon, Ur, and Nineveh. Revised version of the 1953 Coronet motion picture of the same title. Includes study guide.

IRAQ: STAIRWAY TO THE GODS. 16 mm. Color and sound. 27 minutes. Narrator: Anthony Quayle. Chatsworth Film Distributors, Limited, Lawrence, Kansas, Centron Educational Films, 1977, c.1973.

Summarizes the achievements of the Sumerians in ancient Mesopotamia and the fearsome rule of the Assyrians in the Fertile Crescent. Made in England. Longer version (52 minutes) also issued under title: Stairway to the Gods.

NANA: UN PORTRAIT. 16 mm. Color and sound. 25 minutes. By Jamil Simon Productions, Cambridge, Massachusetts, 1973.

Presents a portrait of 80-year-old Nana Zilkha, who was born in Baghdad and now lives in an apartment in New York City. She tells of her life with her husband and seven children and of the people and places she has known. With English subtitles.

IRISH
See also: BRITISH

Embassy and Consulates

EMBASSY OF IRELAND
2234 Massachusetts Avenue, Northwest
Washington, D.C. 20008 (202) 462-3939

CONSULATES GENERAL

535 Boyleston Street
Boston, Massachusetts 02159 (617) 267-9330

400 North Michigan Avenue
Chicago, Illinois 60611 (312) 337-1868

580 Fifth Avenue
New York, New York 10036 (212) 245-1010

681 Market Street
San Francisco, California 94105 (415) 392-4214

Mission to the United Nations

IRISH MISSION
1 Dag Hammerskjold Plaza
885 Second Avenue, 19th Floor
New York, New York 10017 (212) 421-6934

Tourist and Travel Offices

IRISH TOURIST BOARD

590 Fifth Avenue
New York, New York 10036 (212) 869-5500

224 North Michigan Avenue
Chicago, Illinois 60601 (312) 726-9356

681 Market Street
San Francisco, California 94105 (415) 781-5688

IRISH TRAVEL INFORMATION AND BOOKING CENTER
160 East 48th Street
New York, New York 10017 (212) 486-0777

Fraternal Organizations

ANCIENT ORDER OF HIBERNIANS IN AMERICA
Box 700, Riverdale Station
Bronx, New York 10471
National Secretary: John W. Duffy (914) 476-4999
Founded 1836

Fraternal benefit insurance society of American Catholics who are Irish by birth or descent.
Publication: National Hibernian Digest, bimonthly.

ASSOCIATED IRISH ORGANISATIONS
Post Office Box 861
Cincinnati, Ohio 45201
President: Richard Ormond (513) 321-8275

Umbrella organization for all Irish groups in the Cincinnati metropolitan area.

FRIENDLY SONS OF SAINT PATRICK IN WASHINGTON, D. C.
12320 Park Lawn Drive
Rockville, Maryland 20852
President: Louis Boland (301) 881-8600

GAELIC LEAGUE
3549 Quesda Street, Northwest
Washington, D.C. 20015
President: Colin Owens (202) 370-3849

THE GAELIC LEAGUE - IRISH AMERICAN CLUBS, INCORPORATED
2068 Michigan Avenue
Detroit, Michigan 48216
President: Chris Murray (313) 963-8895

IRISH AMERICAN CLUB
Post Office Box 5416
Takoma Park, Maryland 20910 (301) 559-8639
President: Tom Keane
Founded 1948

Irish Americans from Maryland, Virginia and Washington, D.C. Sponsors an Irish Feis annually and also the Saint Patrick's Day Parade in Washington. Brings children from Northern Ireland for three weeks each summer so that they can see that it is possible for various religions to live in harmony.
Publication: Amergael (newsletter, monthly.

IRISH AMERICAN CLUB, EAST
227 Lake Shore Avenue
Euclid, Ohio 44117
President: Mickey Coyne — Founded 1979

IRISH INSTITUTE
82-78 Caldwell Avenue
Middle Village, New York 11379 — (212) 335-8205
President: Kathleen Mulvey — Founded 1950

United States citizens of Irish birth or extraction. Formerly called the Irish Feis Institute.

KNIGHTS OF EQUITY AND FRIENDLY SONS OF SAINT PATRICK
16 Southern Parkway
Rochester, New York 14618
Supreme Secretary: Kenneth T. Power — Founded 1895

Americans who are of Irish ancestry and are practicing Roman Catholics. Purposes are: to advance members spiritually, materially and socially, to teach Irish history and culture; and to help the cause of liberty and freedom for the people of Ireland. Assists orphan homes, homes for the aged and young men interested in priesthood. Provides high school and university scholarships; sponsors Celtic courses at universities and for members. Purchased trophies for Catholic school athletic activities. Bestows annual Celtic Culture Award to member or group most outstanding in advancing Celtic culture. Maintains 2,300 volume library. Formerly: Knights of Equity.
Publications: Lecturers, monthly; News Bulletins, monthly.

SOCIETY OF THE FRIENDLY SONS OF SAINT PATRICK IN THE CITY OF NEW YORK
80 Wall Street, Room 1112
New York, New York 10005 — (212) 269-1770
Secretary: Philip J. Curry — Founded 1784

Men of Irish descent in the New York City area. Conducts charitable activities.

UNITED IRISH COUNTIES ASSOCIATION OF NEW YORK
326 West 48th Street
New York, New York 10036
Executive Secretary: Maureen Mulcany — (212) 265-4226 — Founded 1904

Federation of 32 Irish county associations and two related clubs; each group is represented by 11 delegates. Maintains a placement bureau. Bestows Irishman of the Year Award. Holds annual Irish Feis (cultural festival) in June, a concert in August and a ball in January. Membership is concentrated in the New York City area.

WEST SIDE IRISH-AMERICAN CLUB
9613 Madison Avenue
Cleveland, Ohio 44102 — (216) 961-9632
President: Steve Mulloy — Founded 1931

Promotes Irish culture. Supports a Fife and Drum Corp and a Drill Team.

Public Affairs Organizations

AD HOC COMMITTEE TO SUPPORT IRISH POLITICAL PRISONERS
418 Detroit Street
Ann Arbor, Michigan 48104 — (313) 662-6454
Executive Officer: Dennis O'Hearn — Founded 1980

Primarily engaged in a campaign "to publicize prison conditions in Northern Ireland, the occupation of Northern Ireland by British troops, and its economic domination by England."
Publications: Newsletter, monthly.

AMERICAN COMMITTEE FOR ULSTER JUSTICE
c/o Mark Barrett
129 Third Street
New York, New York 10956 — (914) 634-1160
Executive Officer: Mark Barrett — Founded 1971

Primarily Americans of Irish descent. Purposes are "to bring the truth about British occupation and denial of human rights in the six occupied counties of Ireland to the American public, and publicize the issue before the United States Congress." Maintains a speakers bureau, distributes films, conducts lobbying trips to Washington, D.C.
Publications: Newsletter, monthly.

CELTIC LEAGUE
American Branch:
2973 Valentine Avenue
Bronx, New York 10458 — Founded 1961

Interested individuals and members of political-nationalist and cultural organizations in Celtic countries (Wales, Scotland, Brittany, Ireland, Cornwall, Isle of Man) and throughout the world. Fosters cooperation between national movements in the Celtic countries; seeks to make known the struggle and achievements of

the Celtic national movements; organizes help to prisoners.
Publications: CARN, quarterly.

FRIENDS OF IRELAND
6130 Ram's Horn Drive
McLean, Virginia 22101 (703) 790-5138
Chairman: Michael Brennan Founded 1980

Operates as a special interest group promoting the cause of Irish nationalism in Ulster.

IRISH AMERICAN CONFERENCE
9831 Brookridge Court
Gaithersburg, Maryland 20879 (301) 559-8563
Chairman: James H. McLaughlin Founded 1980

Formed to present a clear picture of the plight of the people in Ireland to America; to educate and promote an objective view of Ireland; to promote justice and unity in Ireland.

IRISH NATIONAL CAUCUS
228 Second Street, Southeast
Washington, D.C. 20003
National Director: Fr. Sean McManus (202) 544-0568
Founded 1974

Persons concerned with the protection of human rights in Northern Ireland. Through lobbying and public education efforts, seeks to make human rights in Ireland an American issue, both legally and morally. Ultimate goal is a just and lasting peace in Ireland. Conducts workshops and seminars; maintains speakers bureau.

NATIONAL ASSOCIATION FOR IRISH FREEDOM
799 Broadway, Room 422
New York, New York 10003 (212) 254-1757
Chairman: Joseph Jamison Founded 1971

Fraternal, political, and cultural organizations in the United States made up primarily of Irish born or Irish Americans. Supports the goals of the Northern Ireland Civil Rights Association and the right of the Irish to self-determination in creating a free and independent nation, without economic or physical boundaries. Encourages seminars and forums on the history of the Irish struggle; compiles statistics and information on the current civil rights struggle in Northern Ireland. Affiliated with the Northern Ireland Civil Rights Association. Supersedes the National Association for Irish Justice founded in 1969.
Publication: Factsheet, bimonthly. Also publishes booklet.

Cultural and Educational Organizations

AMERICAN COMMITTEE FOR IRISH STUDIES
Department of English
Virginia Polytechnic Institute and State University
Blacksburg, Virginia 24061
Secretary: Johann A. Norstedt Founded 1959

Scholars interested in Irish arts, folklore, history, language, literature, and social sciences. Sponsors a microfilm project. Maintains archives of information concerning teaching and research in Irish studies. Affiliated with the International Association for the Study of Anglo-Irish Literature.
Publications: Newsletter, four times an academic year; Current Books of Irish Interest (in Newsletter), annual; Membership Directory, annual.

AMERICAN IRISH BICENTENNIAL COMMITTEE
3917 Moss Drive
Annandale, Virginia 22003
Executive Director: Joseph F. O'Connor (703) 354-4721
Founded 1973

American and Irish organizations and individuals concerned with discovering the full contribution of the Irish people to the formation of the United States. Seeks to stimulate continued Irish cultural contributions to the United States, thus enhancing Irish-American relations. Current projects include recreation of historic events, music concerts, erection of monuments, exhibits of historic documents and memorabilia, folklore festivals and academic exchange programs.
Publications: Stars and Harp (newsletter), semiannual.

AMERICAN IRISH HISTORICAL SOCIETY
991 Fifth Avenue
New York, New York 10028 (212) 288-2263
Director: Thomas M. Bayne Founded 1897

Persons interested in Irish cultural and historical affairs. Presents an annual medal to an outstanding American of Irish lineage. Maintains a library of about 25,000 volumes on Irish history and genealogy and the Irish in America.
Publication: The Recorder, annual.

AN CLAIDEHEAMH SOLUIS - THE IRISH ARTS CENTER
553 West 51st Street
New York, New York 10019 (212) 757-3318
Administrator: Nye Heron Founded 1972

American born, young adults active in Irish arts; interested individuals. To establish in America an awareness of the artistic expression of the Irish people. Aims to provide a forum for the education, research, exploration and development of Irish art forms and for communication through art with people of other national backgrounds. An Claidheamh Soluis means "The Sword of Light." In Irish mythology this sword appeared to the Irish people when they were in great danger. Strives to insure that the Irish culture not only survives, but again becomes the everyday expression of the Irish people. Sponsors The Irish Rebel Theatre. Offers free workshops in traditional Irish music, dance, theatre and the language, and free concerts and Irish dances. Maintains small library on Irish and related subjects.
Publications: Litir Nuacht (newsletter), monthly; An Gael, The Magazine of Irish America, quarterly.

THE BERNARD SHAW SOCIETY
Box 3314
Grand Central Station
New York, New York 10017
Secretary: Douglas Laurie Founded 1962

Individuals and libraries. To present, study and explain the dramas and social philosophy of Bernard Shaw (1856-1950) through lectures, readings, performances, discussions and publications. Readings of Bernard Shaw plays in New York public libraries. Formerly New York Regional Group of the Shaw Society (London); (1979) New York Shavians.
Publications: The Independent Shavian, 3 times a year.

CELTIC CULTURAL SOCIETY, INCORPORATED
9 Morrison Road
Burlington, Massachusetts 01803
President: Peter Molony

COMHALTAS CEOLTOIRI EIREANN
North American Branches:

928 Hawkins Avenue
Lake Grove, New York 11755

239 Grove Street
Waltham, Massachusetts 02154
President: Lawrence Reynolds Founded 1951

Irish musicians, singers, dancers and those who wish to promote the Irish tradition in these areas. Seeks to foster greater bonds of friendship among all lovers of Irish music, particularly the music of the Irish harp and uilleann (or elbow) pipes. Conducts research and educational programs. Holds concerts, festivals and music competitions. Bestows awards; maintains museum, library, and hall of fame.
Publications: Treoir, 6 times a year.

EIRE PHILATELIC ASSOCIATION
Post Office Box 2352
Denver, Colorado 80201
Secretary-Treasurer: Joseph E. Foley, Jr. Founded 1950

Adults interested in philatelic items from Ireland. Holds mail auctions of Irish stamps and other philatelic matter. Gives award of merit for outstanding services toward Irish philately. Holds informal area meetings in conjunction with large stamp exhibits in major United States cities.
Publications: The Revealer, quarterly.

IRISH AMERICAN CULTURAL ASSOCIATION
10415 South Western
Chicago, Illinois 60643 (312) 239-6760
President: Thomas R. McCarthy Founded 1974

People interested in all areas of Irish culture, especially as it relates to their ethnic identity. Objective is to promote the study and appreciation of Irish culture. Sponsors lectures; provides funds for Irish writers, painters, musicians and craftsmen. Sponsors research on various Irish topics. Is establishing Irish-American library.

IRISH AMERICAN CULTURAL CENTER OF SAN FRANCISCO
2123 Market Street
San Francisco, California 94114 (415) 621-2200

IRISH AMERICAN HERITAGE CENTER
410 South Michigan Avenue
Chicago, Illinois 60605 (312) 939-0899
President: Michael Shevlin Founded 1977

Sponsors lectures, exhibits and children's programs. Takes an active role in Irish Family Day. Is raising funds to buy a building to house the center.

IRISH CULTURAL SOCIETY
106 Little Falls Street
Falls Church, Virginia 22046
President: Senator John K. Donovan (703) 532-1770
Founded 1966

IRISH GEORGIAN SOCIETY
American Branch:
455 East 51st Street
New York, New York
(212) 759-7155
Founded 1958

Individual firms and libraries; includes 2,000 members in Ireland, 1,500 in the United States and 700 elsewhere. "To awaken an interest in Ireland's Georgian architecture." Arranges expeditions to buildings of interest, which might eventually be open to tourists; sponsors lectures on architecture, 18th century decor and gardens.
Publications: Bulletin, quarterly; Bound Bulletin, annual; Newsletter, annual; also publishes books and pamphlets.

IRISH MUSIC CLUB OF GREATER BOSTON
160 Spruce Street
North Abington, Massachusetts 02351
President: Denis Donovan

IRISH REBEL THEATER
553 West 51st Street
New York, New York
Director: Jim Sheridan
(212) 757-3318

Concentrates on Irish classical repertory and new Irish playwrights. Associated with the Irish Arts Center.

JAMES JOYCE SOCIETY
41 West 47th Street
New York, New York 10036
Secretary: Philip Lyman
(212) 757-0367

Readers and admirers of the Irish literary figure James Joyce (1882-1941) and his work, including academic persons, students, and others. Seeks to make available Joycean interpretations and commentaries by inviting Joyce scholars to give addresses. Stimulates activity within the membership through the presentation of papers, discussions, and periodic publication of material. Promotes the presentation of Joyce's work in all media: theatre, radio, television, motion pictures, readings, and concerts.

SOCIETY OF INTER-CELTIC ARTS AND CULTURE
96 Marguerite Avenue
Waltham, Massachusetts 02154
Co-Director: Kevin D. Gilligan
(617) 899-2204
Founded 1978

International educational society of individuals and organizations working to promote greater awareness of ancient and contemporary Celtic culture and to establish a permanent network for educational and cultural exchange between North America and the Celtic countries (Brittany, Cornwall, Ireland, Isle of Man, Scotland and Wales). Goals are: to assist in the full restoration of Celtic languages and culture in the Celtic countries; to establish a Celtic studies institute, performing arts center, museum and yearly arts festival in North America; to construct an archetypal Celtic village modeled upon European archaeological sites; to compile, publish and distribute educational materials. Sponsors and promotes seminars, lectures, concerts and educational programs. Maintains library of 600 volumes and 300 periodicals on Celtic literature, art, folklore, archaeology and history.
Publications: Keltica: The Inter-Celtic Quarterly; is compiling data for an International Directory of Celtic Organizations and a Bibliography for Celtic Studies.

UNITED IRISH CULTURAL CENTER
2700 45th Avenue
San Francisco, California 94116
(415) 661-2700
Founded 1975

Meeting place for people of Irish descent with special activities pertaining to their heritage. Maintains a library. Conducts classes. Sponsors lectures on Irish and Irish-American history.

Charitable Organizations

CHARITABLE IRISH SOCIETY
40 Court Street, Room 1217
Boston, Massachusetts 02108
President: Mr. Joseph Maher

Research Centers and Special Institutes

INSTITUTE OF CELTIC STUDIES
Post Office Box 44
Oakland, California 94604
Director: Barbara Ruffner
(415) 893-2972

IRISH AMERICAN CULTURAL INSTITUTE
683 Osceola Avenue
Saint Paul, Minnesota 55105
President: Dr. Eoin McKiernan
(612) 647-5678
Founded 1964

An independent, nonprofit research organization maintaining informal relations with the College of Saint Thomas. Works to stimulate creativity in the arts and sciences in Ireland. Encourages research in all

aspects of Irish civilization in Ireland and abroad, including literary and historical studies on Irish history, literature, archaeology, music, and culture. Sponsors international exchanges of academic staff as well as others related to the arts and sciences. Conducts an annual lecture series by visiting Irish artists, scholars, and other speakers. Presents annual awards for new books in Irish and for Irish artists, painters, musicians and dramatists. Has produced a television series of 53 programs on Irish life and civilization.
Publications: Duchas, monthly; Eire-Ireland, quarterly.

Special Libraries and Subject Collections

AMERICAN IRISH HISTORICAL SOCIETY LIBRARY
991 Fifth Avenue
New York, New York 10028 (212) 288-2263
Director: Thomas M. Bayne Founded 1897

Maintains a collection of books on the Irish in the American colonies and the United States. Also has a large collection of family and local histories, Irish and Irish-American newspapers of the nineteenth and twentieth centuries, collections of letters of Irish-American public figures and photographs. Has a reading room. Maintains speakers and performing arts bureau.

BAPST LIBRARY
Boston College Irish Collection
Chestnut Hill, Massachusetts 02167
Curator: Helen A. Landreth (617) 969-0100

Subjects: Ireland - history, social history, art, archeology, government, education; Gaelic literature; Anglo-Irish literature. Holdings: Books; bound periodical volumes; Gaelic transcripts (cataloged); manuscripts (mostly autographed letters); and other serials. Also has art by Irish and Irish-American artists. Services: Interlibrary loans (limited); copying; collection open to public by appointment.

DUANE LIBRARY
Fordham University - Special Collections
Bronx, New York 10458
Chief Reference Librarian:
Mary Riley (212) 933-2233

Subjects: Literature, history, Gaelic language and literature. Services: Copying; library open to public with restrictions.

ELLEN CLARKE BERTRAND LIBRARY
Bucknell University
Lewisburg, Pennsylvania 17837
Head, Personnel Department: (717) 524-3056
Mary Jane Stoneburg Founded 1846

Subjects: Irish authors. Special Collections: Letters and manuscripts of Oliver S. Gogarty. Holdings: Books and bound periodical volumes; manuscripts. Services: Interlibrary loans; copying; library open to public for reference use only.

FEEHAN MEMORIAL LIBRARY
Saint Mary of the Lake Seminary
Mundelein, Illinois 60060 (312) 566-6401
Librarian: Gloria Sieben Founded 1929

Subjects: Ancient Christian literature; medieval theology; theology. Special Collections: History of Ireland, the Irish language, and Irish Literature. Holdings: Books; journals and other serials; newspapers; reels of microfilm; microcards. Services: Interlibrary loans; copying; library is open to the public for reference use.

IRELAND CONSULATE GENERAL LIBRARY
580 Fifth Avenue
New York, New York 10036
Consulate General: Honorable Sean
Oh'Uiginn (212) 245-1010

Subjects: Economic, social, political, and cultural information on Ireland. Services: Library is open to the public.

IRISH-AMERICAN CULTURAL ASSOCIATION - LIBRARY
10415 South Western
Chicago, Illinois 60643 (312) 239-6760
Librarian: Cynthia L. Buescher Founded 1974

Subjects: Literature, history, biography, art, music. Holdings: Books. Services: Copying; not open to public.

IRISH CULTURAL SOCIETY
106 Little Falls Street (703) 532-1770
Falls Church, Virginia 22046 Founded 1966

Books, periodicals, archives, photographs and manuscripts.

IRISH FAMILY HISTORY SOCIETY - LIBRARY
173 Tremont Street
Newton, Massachusetts 02158
Director: Joseph M. Glynn, Jr. (617) 965-0939

Subjects: Ireland - genealogy, history, literature, heraldry. Special Collections: Lewis's Topographical Dictionary of Ireland. Holdings: Books; tapes on Irish genealogy; maps. Services: Copying; library open to public. Special Indexes: Surname index of members; Irish Family History Index (card). Publications: Newsletter, 5 times a year.

MCLAUGHLIN LIBRARY
MacManus Collection
Seton Hall University
South Orange, New Jersey 07079 (201) 762-9000
Director: Msgr. William Noe Field Founded 1958

Subjects: Every phase of Irish literature and history, politics, and particularly the home rule question. Holdings: Books; bound periodical volumes; autographs, diaries, photographs, clippings, and letters. Services: Collection is open to outside users with permission of the librarian.

MILLER LIBRARY
Colby College - Special Collections
Waterville, Maine 04901
Head, Special Collection: (207) 873-1131
J. Fraser Cocks, III Founded 1938

Subjects: Irish literary renaissance. Special Collections: James A. Healy Collection of Irish Literature. Holdings: Books; bound periodical volumes; letters and manuscripts; microfilm; journals and other serials. Services: Copying; open to public.

O'SHAUGHNESSY LIBRARY
College of Saint Thomas Celtic Library
Saint Paul, Minnesota 55105
Curator: John B. Davenport (612) 647-5720

Maintains a collection of books on Irish language, history, and literature; also some publications on the Scotch and Welsh. Services: Copying; collection is available to qualified users.

UNITED IRISH CULTURAL CENTER
2700 45th Avenue
San Francisco, California 94116 (415) 661-2700
Library Director: Pat Dowling Founded 1975

Subjects: Irish history, poetry, literature, drama; Irish heritage in the United States. Holdings: Books; periodicals, newspapers, audiovisual materials, archives. Services: Lecture series, classes, guided tours, films.

Newspapers and Newsletters

CHICAGO IRISH AMERICAN NEWS. 1977-. Monthly. Editor and Publisher: Bob Burns, Post Office Box A 66218, Chicago, Illinois 60666.

DUCAS. Seven times a year. Editor: Michael E. Coughlin. Publisher: Irish American Cultural Institute, 683 Osceola, Saint Paul, Minnesota 55105,

Provides historical, literary, and other cultural information of interest to Irish Americans, including news of the activities of the institute.

EIRE-IRELAND. 1966-. Quarterly. Editor: Eoin McKiernan. Publisher: Irish American Cultural Institute, 683 Osceola Avenue, Saint Paul, Minnesota 55105.

Prints articles on Irish history, contemporary events, culture and science.

IRISH ADVOCATE. 1893-. Weekly. Editor: James O'Connor. Publisher: Elise O'Connor, 15 Park Row, New York, New York 10038. In English.

An Irish-American weekly printing news from Ireland and activities of Irish Americans in the New York area and the rest of America.

IRISH ECHO. 1928-. Weekly. Editor: John J. Thornton. Publisher: John Grimes, 1860 Broadway, New York, New York 10016. In English.

Publishes news and features of interest to Irish Americans.

IRISH HERALD. 1962-. Monthly. Editor: John Whooley. Publisher: Irish Heritage Center, 2123 Market Street, San Francisco, California 94114.

IRISH PEOPLE. 1971-. Weekly. Editor: Martin Galvin. Publisher: The Irish People, Incorporated, 4951 Broadway, New York, New York.

Carries news of various Irish groups and activities especially in the New York area. Also covers national and international news pertaining to Irish interests.

IRISH WORLD. 1870-. Weekly. Editor: M. P. Ford. Publisher: Irish World, 853 Broadway, New York, New York 10003. In English.

Carries news about Irish interests.

LITIR NUACHT. 1972-. Monthly. Editor: Nye Heron. Publisher: The Irish Arts Center (An Claidheamh Soluis), 553 West 51st Street, New York, New York 10019.

Newsletter of the Irish Arts Center.

RECORDER. 1940-. Annual. Publisher: American Irish Historical Society, 991 Fifth Avenue, New York, New York 10028.

THE REVEALER. 1951-. Quarterly. Editor: John J. Blessington. Publisher: Eire Philatelic Association, 1265 South Bates, Birmingham, Michigan 48009.

Promotes the collection and study of adhesive and other stamps of Ireland. Includes a feature, "Random Notes", containing reports of new discoveries of Irish philately. Includes auction news, literature notes, and signed articles.

Magazines

AISLING. 1973-. Quarterly. Editor and Publisher: Paul Shuttleworth, 2526 42nd Avenue, San Francisco, California 94116.

A poetry magazine for Irish and American poets.

AN GAEL. 1974-. Quarterly. Editor: Kathleen Vitate. Publisher: The Irish Arts Center (An Claidheamh Soluis), 553 West 51st Street, New York, New York 10019.

Features articles on Irish culture and folkways as well as history and politics. Formerly called Ais Eiri.

Radio Programs

Connecticut - Ansonia

WADS - Ansonia Mall, Ansonia, Connecticut 06401, (203) 735-4606. Irish programs, 1 hour weekly.

Connecticut - Fairfield

WVOF (FM) - Box R, Fairfield University, Fairfield, Connecticut 06430, (203) 259-8020. Irish programs, 1 hour weekly.

Connecticut - Greenwich

WGCH - 490 Dayton Avenue, Greenwich, Connecticut 06830, (203) 869-1490. Irish programs, 1 hour weekly.

Maryland - Baltimore

WITH - 5 Light Street, Baltimore, Maryland 21202, (301) 528-1230. Irish programs, 2 hours weekly.

Maryland - Bethesda

WHFS (FM) - 4853 Cordell Avenue, Bethesda, Maryland, (301) 656-0600. Irish programs, 2 hours weekly.

Maryland - Laurel

WLMD - Box 42, Laurel, Maryland 20810, (301) 953-2332. Irish programs, 1 hour weekly.

Massachusetts - Leominster

WLMS - Box 1000, Leominster, Massachusetts 01453, (617) 537-4141. Irish programs, 3 hours weekly.

Massachusetts - Pittsfield

WBRK - Box 987, Pittsfield, Massachusetts 01201, (413) 442-1553. Irish programs, 1 hour weekly.

Massachusetts - Worcester

WNEB - 236 Worcester Center, Worcester, Massachusetts 01608, (617) 756-4672. Irish programs, 1 hour weekly.

New Jersey - South Orange

WSOU (FM) - 400 South Orange Avenue, South Orange, New Jersey 07079, (201) 762-8950. Irish programs, 1 hour weekly.

New York - Auburn

WAUB - Box 160, Auburn, New York 13021, (315) 253-3040. Irish programs, 1-1/2 hours weekly.

New York - Babylon

WNYG - Route 109, Babylon, New York 11704, (516) 661-4000. Irish programs, 1 hour weekly.

New York - Binghamton

WKOP - 32 West State Street, Binghamton, New York 13901, (607) 722-3437. Irish programs, 1 hour weekly.

New York - New Rochelle

WVOX - One Broadcast Forum, New Rochelle, New York 10801, (914) 636-1460. Irish programs, 1 hour weekly.

New York - Oswego

WSGO (AM & FM) - 333 East Seneca Street, Oswego, New York 13126, (315) 343-1440. Irish programs, 1 hour weekly.

New York - Spring Valley

WGRC - 25 Church Street, Spring Valley, New York 10977, (914) 623-8500. Irish programs, 1 hour weekly.

Ohio - Chardon

WBKC - Box 266, Chardon, Ohio 44024, (216) 946-0136. Irish programs, 3 hours weekly.

Rhode Island - Pawtucket

WGNG - 100 John Street, Cumberland, Rhode Island 02864. Irish programs, 2 hours weekly.

Bank Branches in the U.S.

ALLIED IRISH BANKS, LIMITED

405 Park Avenue
New York, New York 10022 (212) 223-1230

3 First National Plaza
Chicago, Illinois 60603 (312) 630-0044

BANK OF IRELAND

640 Fifth Avenue
New York, New York (212) 397-1700

135 South La Salle Street
Chicago, Illinois 60603 (312) 236-6695

Commercial and Trade Organizations

INDUSTRIAL DEVELOPMENT AUTHORITY

200 Park Avenue
New York, New York 10017 (212) 972-1000

1 East Wacker Drive
Chicago, Illinois 60601 (312) 644-7474

IRELAND UNITED STATES COUNCIL FOR COMMERCE AND INDUSTRY, INCORPORATED
460 Park Avenue
New York, New York 10022 (212) 751-2660

IRISH EXPORT BOARD
10 East 53rd Street
New York, New York 10036 (212) 371-3600

IRISH WHISKEY INFORMATION BUREAU
201 East 42nd Street
New York, New York (212) 687-1196

Festivals, Fairs, and Celebrations

California - San Francisco

IRISH FESTIVAL WEEK
San Francisco, California

An exposition of the heritage, culture, and traditions of the Irish. Features dancing and music, as well as dramatic events, art shows, Irish food, and the coronation of Miss Ireland. Held in mid-October.
Contact: San Francisco Convention and Visitors Bureau, Fox Plaza, San Francisco, California 94102, or John Whooley, c/o Irish Center, Incorporated, 2123 Market Street, San Francisco, California 94114.

SAINT PATRICK'S FROLIC
San Francisco, California

A spectacular parade includes floats, dignitaries, drill corps, dancers, musicians, and equestrians. In Zellerbach Plaza an annual snake race takes place. A Saint Patrick's Dance features special Irish entertainment. At the Green and Gold Ball "Miss Shamrock" is crowned, and Irish bands, dancers, and pipers entertain. Ireland's top football and hurling teams compete at Balboa Statium in a Gaelic superbowl. The festival is held annually centered around Saint Patrick's Day, March 17.
Contact: San Francisco Convention and Visitors Bureau, Fox Plaza, San Francisco, California 94102. (415) 626- 5500.

Colorado - Central City

PAT CASEY DAY
Central City, Colorado

Honors the Irish of the old mining camp. Public procession headed by bagpipes marches along Casey's route. An Irish stew dinner is held at the Belvidere, with an exhibition of Irish folk dances. Held in early October.
Contact: Jack Hidahl, Public Relations Coordinator, Central City, Colorado 80427.

Delaware - Wilmington

DELAWARE FEIS.
Concord High School Grounds
Wilmington, Delaware

Features Irish folk music and dancing as well as a craft show and Irish food. Held in August.
Contact: Martin Mulhern, 215 Rodman Road, Wilmington, Delaware 19809, (302) 762-1538.

Georgia - Dublin

SAINT PATRICK'S FESTIVAL
Dublin, Georgia

Irish fun and frolic prevail during festival week. A gala parade, barbecues, a boat show, beauty pageant, and golf tournaments, including the Shamrock invitational, are held. Has taken place annually since 1966 around March 17.
Contact: Chamber of Commerce, 400 Bellevue Avenue, Dublin, Georgia 31021.

Illinois - Chicago

SAINT PATRICK'S DAY PARADE
State Street
Chicago, Illinois

A time-honored Chicago tradition for Saint Pat's Day. Median strips on State Street are painted kelly green, and the Chicago River is "dyed" green for the day. Bands, floats, marching units, costumed entertainers, and politicians gather for a grand parade. Held on March 17.

Iowa - Emmetsburg

SAINT PATRICK'S CELEBRATION
Emmetsburg, Iowa

Named for an Irishman, Emmetsburg is sister city to Dublin. Visiting dignitaries from Dublin are guests of honor at the many events scheduled for them. Activities include the Miss Saint Patrick's Pageant, grand parade, contests, and other events carrying out the Saint Patrick's theme. Held annually in mid-March.
Contact: Saint Patrick's Association, Emmetsburg, Iowa 50536.

Kansas - Summerfield

IRISH FESTIVAL
Summerfield, Kansas

An Irish ethnic celebration held at the end of June.

Missouri - Rolla

SAINT PAT'S CELEBRATION
Rolla, Missouri

Held by students at the University of Missouri at Rolla to honor Saint Patrick, patron saint of engineers. "Saint Pat" arrives in town by handcar,

dressed in green like members of his court. A parade begins with the painting of Main Street green. In a solemn ceremony, Saint Pat dubs members of the graduating class knights in the "Order of Saint Patrick". Visiting dignitaries are made honorary knights. Due reverence is paid the Blarney Stone, and other events include beard judging and shillelagh judging. Held annually in mid-March since 1907.
Contact: Public Information Office, University of Missouri at Rolla, Rolla, Missouri 65401, (314) 341-4259.

Nebraska - O'Neill

SAINT PATRICK'S DAY CELEBRATION
O'Neill, Nebraska

At a lively Saint Patrick's day party the townsfolk celebrate their Irish heritage with costumed dancing, a grand parade, and a closing celebration dance. Hearty Irish meals are washed down with a mug or two of green beer. Held March 17.
Contact: O'Neill Area Chamber of Commerce, 430 East Douglas, Box 407, O'Neill, Nebraska 68763.

New Jersey - Freehold

IRISH FEIS AND SCOTTISH GAMES FESTIVAL
Freehold Raceway
Freehold, New Jersey

Celebrated with step dancing, ballad singing, Irish and Scottish band music, and pipe band competitions. Also features Gaelic football and soccer games and Irish and Scottish field sports. Held in mid-July.
Contact: Freehold Raceway, Freehold, New Jersey 07728.

New Jersey - Holmdel

IRISH FESTIVAL
Garden State Arts Center
Holmdel, New Jersey

A salute to the rich Irish heritage begins with a Pipe Band competition on the Mall in the morning. An afternoon program on stage features singing stars, Irish band music, harpists, and Irish step dancing. Held annually since 1971 in late June.
Contact: Irish Festival, New Jersey Highway Authority, Garden State Parkway, Woodbridge, New Jersey 07095. (201) 442-8600.

Pennsylvania - Barnesfield

GRAND IRISH JUBILEE
Lakewood Park
Barnesville, Pennsylvania

Features traditional Irish music, Ceili dancing, Irish crafts and special food.
Contact: Jubilee, 123 South Main Street, Mahoney City, Pennsylvania 17948.

South Carolina - Charleston

IRISH EMPHASIS FESTIVAL
Charleston, South Carolina

Part of the Founders' Festivals, a continuing series of month-long festivals centering on the ethnic groups which were instrumental in the founding and growth of Charleston. Special exhibits in the Gibbes Art Gallery and Charleston Museum, special ethnic foods offered in local restaurants, and two or three major events. Held for one month in spring.
Contact: Mr. James B. Bagwell, Jr., 313 Pitt Street, Mount Pleasant, South Carolina 29464.

Tennessee - Erin

WEARIN' OF THE GREEN
City Hall
Erin, Tennessee

Since Erin and the surrounding area were settled by people of predominantly Irish descent, the Saint Patrick's Day celebration there is a very festive one. Activities range from beauty contests, parades, and a bicycle rodeo to a gala Irish ball. Held annually the weekend closest to March 17.
Contact: City Hall, Post Office Box 270, Erin, Tennessee 37061.

Tennessee - McEwen

SAINT PATRICK'S IRISH PICNIC AND HOMECOMING
Saint Patrick's Picnic Grounds
McEwen, Tennessee

Held annually for nearly 130 years, the Saint Patrick's Irish Picnic features Irish dancing and music as well as square dancing.
Contact: Tommy Hooper, Route 2, Box 258-A, McEwen, Tennessee 37101.

Texas - Shamrock

SAINT PATRICK'S CELEBRATION
Shamrock, Texas

Real shamrocks abound on floats as lovely colleens vie for the title of "Miss Irish Rose." Celebrates the Irish heritage. Held in March.
Contact: Chamber of Commerce, Post Office Box 588, Shamrock, Texas 79079.

Airline Offices

IRISH INTERNATIONAL AIRLINES
(Aer Lingus - Irish)
North American Headquarters:
122 East 42nd Street
New York, New York 10038 (212) 557-1090

Schedules North Atlantic flights linking Irish and British cities with Montreal, Boston, and Chicago. Offers international service between Ireland, Great Britain, and Western Europe, as well as domestic services between Dublin, Cork, Shannon, and Belfast. Other offices in the United States: Boston, Chicago, Cleveland, Dallas, Detroit, Los Angeles, Philadelphia, San Francisco, and Washington.

Bookdealers and Publishers' Representatives

ABACUS BOOK COMPANY
43 Barnes Road
Stoughton, Massachusetts 02072 (617) 344-6695

ALICORN BOOKS 'N THINGS
(Gaelic)
3428 Balboa
San Francisco, California 94121 (415) 221-5522

AULDSTONE BOOKSHOP
(Irelandia)
R.F.D. 1
Box 200
Glasgow, Virginia 24555 (703) 258-2582

THE CILLEYVILLE BOOKSTORE
(antiquarian)
Box 127
Andover, New Hampshire 03216 (603) 735-5667

ALICE CONWAY
(Irish history)
855 North McKinley
Lake Forest, Illinois 60045

CUMBERLAND LITERARY AGENCY
Post Office Box 50331
Belle Meade Station
Nashville, Tennessee 37205 (615) 794-7253

FACSIMILE BOOKSHOP, INCORPORATED
(Gaelic)
16 West 55th Street
New York, New York 10019 (212) 581-2672

J. M. HAYS
130 Monument Avenue
Old Bennington, Vermont 05201 (802) 442-4693

J.& J.O'Donoghue
(antiquarian Irish and British books)
1927 Second Avenue South
Anoka, Minnesota 55303

SCOTCH HOUSE
(Gaelic)
Box 221397
Carmel, California 93922 (415) 391-1264

Books and Pamphlets

FACTS ABOUT IRELAND. Dublin, Ireland, Irish Department of Foreign Affairs, 1981.

Discusses the geography, climate, history, language, government, religion, legal system, educational system, defense, communications, international relations, finance, resources, industry, trade, tourism, transportation, economics, social services, culture, and other topics concerning Ireland. A paperback book illustrated with many photographs, part colored. A foldout map is attached to the back cover.

A GUIDE TO BOOKS ON IRELAND. Part 1: Prose Literature, Poetry, Music, and Plays. Edited by Stephen Brown. New York, Longmans Green and Company, 1912. New York, Lemma Publishing Corporation, 1970.

A listing of books in English dealing with Ireland published up to 1911 on the subjects of prose literature, poetry, music and plays.

A GUIDE TO IRISH BIBLIOGRAPHICAL MATERIAL: A BIBLIOGRAPHY OF IRISH BIBLIOGRAPHIES AND SOURCES OF INFORMATION. By Alan Eager, 2nd Revised and Enlarged Edition, London, Library Association, 1980.

A reference guide for those interested in Irish studies and research work. Arrangement is based on the Dewey Decimal Classification and includes an author and subject index.

HOLDINGS OF THE CURRAN COLLECTION - IRISH CULTURE AND LITERATURE. Compiled by Patricia Hodge. Pittsburgh, Carlow College, Grace Library, 1974.

An annotated bibliography containing about 200 entries.

IRELAND - FACT SHEETS. Dublin, Department of Foreign Affairs.

A series of informational brochures on such subjects as basic statistics, broadcasting, foreign affairs, economy, Irish language, National flag, emblem and anthem. Some sheets are illustrated and include a bibliography. Updated from time to time.

IRISH ECONOMICS, 1700-1783; A Bibliography with Notes. By Henry Wagner. London, J. Davy and Sons, 1907. Reprint New York, A. M. Kelley, 1969.

Bibliography of books, essays, letters, proposals, etc. on Irish economic history. Each entry is annotated.

MANUSCRIPT SOURCES FOR THE HISTORY OF IRISH CIVILISATION. By Risteard de Hae. Boston, G. K. Hall, 1965.

An 11 volume catalog manuscripts on the history of Irish civilization and their locations. Entries have been placed in four sections: persons, subjects, places, dates. Each entry has an annotation.

SELECT BIBLIOGRAPHY FOR THE STUDY OF ANGLO-IRISH LITERATURE AND ITS BACKGROUNDS: AN IRISH STUDIES HANDBOOK. By Maurice Harmon. Port Credit, Ontario, P. D. Meary, 1977.

An annotated listing of reference sources, primary research materials and a bibliography of background reading.

A SELECT LIST OF REPORTS OF INQUIRIES OF THE IRISH DAIL AND SENATE, 1922-1972. By Percy Ford. Dublin, Irish University Press, 1974.

A list that includes policy reports of inquiries, white papers, etc. to be found in the Dail, Senate, Oirreachtas, and other government publications. Arranged by subject and an appendix that lists the reports of the National Industrial Economic Council.

THE SOURCES FOR THE EARLY HISTORY OF IRELAND; An Introduction and Guide. By James F. Kenney. New York, Columbia University Press, 1929.

Listing of sources on the early history of Ireland prior to the Anglo-Norman invasion up to 1170. Includes books, periodicals, documents and manuscripts.

A TOUCH OF IRELAND. 1982. Dublin, Irish Tourist Board, 1982.

An introduction to Ireland for visitors. Includes many colored photographs of scenes in the country, a detailed centerfold map and information about Dublin, the country as a whole, its historical traiditon, writers, monuments, architecture, festivals and special events, recommended tours, places to stay, transportation information, cuisine and shopping.

IRISH AMERICANS

AMERICA AND IRELAND, 1776-1976: THE AMERICAN IDENTITY AND THE IRISH CONNECTION: THE PROCEEDINGS OF THE U. S. BICENTENNIAL CONFERENCE OF CUMANN MERRIAM, ENNIS, AUGUST 1976. Edited by David Doyle and Owen Edwards. Westport, Connecticut, Greenwood Press, 1980.

THE AMERICAN IRISH. Rev. edition. By William V. Shannon. New York, Macmillan Company, 1966.

Offers an interpretation of the history and culture of the Irish in America and their influence in politics, religion, the theater, literature, and such specialized activities as prizefighting and law enforcement.

AMERICAN OPINION AND THE IRISH QUESTION, 1910-1923: A STUDY IN OPINION AND POLICY. By Francis Carroll. Dublin, Gillard Macmillan, New York, Saint Martin's Press, 1978.

Tries to define the views held by both Irish-Americans and native Americans on the Irish question and shows how these views influenced the revolution in Ireland.

THE ATTITUDES OF THE NEW YORK STATE IRISH TOWARD STATE AND NATIONAL AFFAIRS, 1848-1892. By Florence E. Gibson. New York, Columbia University Press, 1951.

Analyzes the influence of the politically strong Irish minority in New York State, including some of the sensational events involving the Irish during the late 1800's. Discusses anti-British sentiment, Democratic party ties, and political activity of the Irish.

A BIBLIOGRAPHY OF THE IRISH IN THE UNITED STATES. By Walter R. Rose. New York, Tristram Shandy Publications, 1969.

A very brief bibliography.

BOSTON'S IMMIGRANTS: A STUDY IN ACCULTURATION. By Oscar Handlin. Revised edition Cambridge, Massachusetts, Harvard University Press, 1959.

Includes groups other than the Irish, but is important in placing the Irish in an urban setting. Describes the settlement of immigrants in Boston; the factors influencing their economic, physical, and intellectual adjustment and also the factors encouraging or discouraging group togetherness and group conflict. Appendix includes 28 tables.

THE BRITISH AND IRISH IN OKLAHOMA. By Patrick J. Blessing. Norman, University of Oklahoma Press, 1980. (Newcomers to a New Land Series).

Analyzes the role of the Irish and British in Oklahoma and how they contributed to the history of that state. Includes bibliographic essay and tables.

CATHOLIC COLONIZATION ON THE WESTERN FRONTIER. By James P. Shannon. New Haven, Yale University Press, 1957. Reprinted New York, Arno Press, 1976.

A study of religious settlements in western Minnesota - the history of their founding, their role in a national colonization association and the reasons for their growth or decline. Important treatment of the Irish.

COMING OF THE GREEN. By Leonard Patrick O'Connor Wibberley. New York, Henry Holt & Company, 1958.

Recounts the facts of Irish immigration in a lively and readable style filled with personal incidents and Irish lore.

DAYS BEYOND RECALL. By Roger B. Dooley. Milwaukee, Bruce, 1949.

A novel showing upward mobility of ethnic Irish in Buffalo, New York.

FORGOTTEN PIONEERS; Irish Leaders in Early California. By Thomas F. Prendergast. San Francisco, Trade Pressroom, 1942. Reprint Freeport, New York, Books for Libraries Press, 1972.

Points out the significant roles of individual Irishman in settling California and contributing to its development before and after gold rush days.

GOING TO AMERICA. By Terry Coleman. New York, Pantheon Books (Random House), 1972.

Tells the story of the millions of emigrants who left Great Britain and Ireland for America in 1846 through 1855. Explains who they were, why they left home and how, and what happened to them in America.

A HISTORY OF IRISH SETTLERS IN NORTH AMERICA, FROM THE EARLIEST PERIOD TO THE CENSUS OF 1850. By Thomas D'Arcy McGee. Boston, Patrick Donahoe, 1852. Reprinted by R and E Associates, San Francisco, 1970.

Deals with early Irish settlers in American colonies; their part in the American Revolution; Catholic missions in the United States; Irish Americans in education, science, and politics; their role in the War of 1812; the spread of Irish influence and Catholicism; American sympathy for Irish troubles; the "Native American" movement; involvement of the Irish in South American revolutions and the Mexican War; and Irish pioneers in the Midwest.

HISTORY OF THE IRISH IN WISCONSIN IN THE NINETEENTH CENTURY. By Sister Justille McDonald. Washington, D.C. Catholic University of America Press, 1954.

A scholarly account of Irish settlements in Wisconsin.

HOUR OF SPRING. By Mary Deasy. Boston, Little, Brown, 1948.

A novel about middle-class Irish life.

HOW THE IRISH BECAME AMERICANS. By Joseph O'Grady. New York, Twayne Publishers, 1973. The Immigrant Heritage of America Series.

This book describes the Anglo-Irish struggle, the forces that drove the Irish to America, how America influenced that struggle and how it, in turn conditioned the Irishman's life in America. Includes a glossary and bibliographic essay.

IMMIGRATION OF THE IRISH QUAKERS INTO PENNSYLVANIA, 1687-1750. By Albert Cook Myers. Swarthmore, Pennsylvainia, Author, 1902. Reprint Baltimore, Genealogical Publishing, 1969.

Part one treats Quakerism in England and Ireland. Part two deals with the religious and economic causes for emigration, the inducements through Penn and favorable reports, the ways and means of emigration. Part three describes places of settlements, social life of Irish Friends and gives sketches of some prominent Irish Friends. An appendix, bibliography and index are included.

INTERNATIONAL CONFLICT IN AN AMERICAN CITY: BOSTON'S IRISH, ITALIANS, AND JEWS, 1935-1944. By John Stack, Westport, Connecticut, Greenwood Press, 1979.

A study of the Irish and two other ethnic groups of Boston and their reactions to various issues of the time - facism, Nazism, anti-semitism, isolationism and the coming of World War II. Includes a selected bibliography.

IRELAND AND IRISH EMIGRATION TO THE NEW WORLD FROM 1815 TO THE FAMINE. By William F. Adams. New Haven, Yale University Press, 1932. Reprint New York, Russell and Russell, 1967.

Especially useful in giving historical background for the exodus of Irish from their mother country.

IRELAND AND THE AMERICAN EMIGRATION, 1850-1900. By Arnold Schreier. Minneapolis, University of Minnesota Press, 1958. Reprint New York, Russell and Russell, 1970.

The large numbers of people leaving Ireland for the United States had a great effect on both countries. This study looks both at cause and effects.

IRISH-AMERICAN NATIONALISM, 1870-1890. By Thomas N. Brown. Philadelphia, J. B. Lippincott Company, 1966.

Discusses the turbulent, tragic history of Ireland, the flood of Irish immigrants to America, conditions after the Civil War, experiences of Irish nationalists in the United States, repercussions of Irish political events, American aid to Ireland, achievement of political power by Irish Americans, corruption, violence, and achievements of Irish-American nationalists during the late 1800's.

IRISH AMERICANS: IDENTITY AND ASSIMILATION. By Marjorie Fallows. Englewood Cliffs, New Jersey, Prentice-Hall, 1979. (Ethnic Groups in American Life Series).

This book focuses on the lives of the Irish Americans and how they have been affected by social forces. This insight provides an opportunity to analyze the stages involved in the assimilation process.

THE IRISH AMERICANS: THE RISE TO MONEY AND POWER. By Andrew Greeley. New York, Harper and Row, 1981.

A survey discussion of the Irish Catholics - their Celtic heritage, their experiences in the United States upon arriving and the present condition of Irish Catholics in America.

THE IRISH: AMERICA'S POLITICAL CLASS. Selected by James B. Walsh. New York, Arno Press, 1976.

A reprint of twenty-two articles published between 1898 and 1975 on the Irish in American politics.

THE IRISH AND IRISH POLITICIANS; A Study of Cultural and Social Alienation. By Edward M. Levine. Notre Dame, Indiana, University of Notre Dame Press, 1966.

Discusses the values, identity, and social structure of the Irish and Irish politicians in America. Describes the background of English oppression and the potato famine in Ireland, early experiences in the United States, attainment of political power, the significance of Irish Catholicism and the Democratic Party.

THE IRISH DIASPORA IN AMERICA. By Lawrence McCaffrey. Bloomington, Indiana University Press, 1976.

A history of the Irish from their life in Ireland to their immigration to America and their struggle for identity in the new land. A recommended reading section lists books on the subjects of Irish heritage and the American Irish.

THE IRISH EMIGRATION, MARRIAGE AND FERTILITY. By Robert E. Kennedy, Jr. Berkeley, University of California Press, 1973.

Gives a general picture of the Irish immigrant experience, accompanied by tables and a good bibliography.

IRISH EMIGRATION TO THE UNITED STATES. By Stephen Byrne. Catholic Publication Society, 1873. Reprint New York, Arno Press, 1969.

Reprint of a publication written for Irish people intending to emigrate from Ireland. The author divides the book into two parts - the first contains information on the prospects, duties, dangers and mistakes of emigrants and the second part contains the population, area and general information of each state and territory in the United States.

THE IRISH HELPED BUILD AMERICA. By Virginia B. McDonnell. New York, Julian Messner, 1968.

For younger readers.

IRISH IMMIGRANT PARTICIPATION IN THE CONSTRUCTION OF THE ERIE CANAL. By George J. Suejda. Washington, D.C., United States Office of Archaeology and Historical Preservation, 1969.

Contains an account of the author's interviews with Irish immigrants in the land of their adoption during his travels through various states of the union in 1854 and 1855. The interviews tell from what parts of the Emerald Isle the Irishmen came, their present location, and their experiences in America.

IRISH IMMIGRATION IN THE UNITED STATES: IMMIGRANT INTERVIEWS. By Jeremiah O'Donovan. New York, Arno Press, 1969. c. 1864.

An account of the author's interviews with fellow Irish-Americans, discussing Ireland and their new home in America.

THE IRISH IN AMERICA. By Carl Frederick Wittke. Baton Rouge, Louisiana State University Press, 1956.

Presents a history of the Irish in America from colonial days onward, concentrating on the great migrations of the 1830's and 1840's. Tells about their contributions to American life and attempts to dispel stereotyped conceptions of Irish Americans by offering an objective analysis of their experiences and accomplishments in the New World.

THE IRISH IN AMERICA. By James E. Johnson. Minneapolis, Lerner, 1966.

An account of the Irish immigrant experiences and contribution for school children.

THE IRISH IN AMERICA. By John Francis Maguire. London, Longmans, Green, and Company, 1868. American Immigration Collection series. Reprinted by Arno Press and the New York Times, New York, 1969.

Presents the author's personal observations of how the Irish were getting along in America in 1867. Contrasts their economic and agricultural progress in the old and new countries, their religious faith, education, urban and rural living conditions, drinking habits, politics, and family life. Also discusses their role in the Civil War and anti-British feeling among the Irish in America.

THE IRISH IN AMERICA, 1550-1972; A Chronology & Fact Book. Compiled and edited by William D. Griffin. Ethnic Chronology Series number 10, Dobbs Ferry, New York, Oceana Publications, 1973.

The chronology section dates major historical facts in the history of Irish exploration, immigration, and settlement in America and the deeds of individual Irishmen. The document section contains excerpts from letters, newspapers, government documents, speeches, reports, and magazine articles concerning the experiences of Irish Americans. The book also includes statistical tables and a bibliography.

THE IRISH IN NEW ORLEANS, 1800-1860. By Earl F. Niehaus. Baton Rouge, Louisiana State University Press, 1965.

A survey of the social activities of the New Orleans Irish from 1803 to the occupation of the city by Federal forces in 1862.

THE IRISH IN PHILADELPHIA: TEN GENERATIONS OF URBAN EXPERIENCE. By Dennis Clark. Philadelphia, Temple University Press, 1973.

Traces the process by which Irish countrymen became American urbanites. The greater area of Philadelphia as compared with other urban centers receiving large numbers of Irish immigrants, such as Boston and New York, facilitated a more rapid absorption. The author describes the role of the Roman Catholic Church and its manifold resources in augmenting group development.

THE IRISH IN THE UNITED STATES. By John B. Duff. Belmont, California, Wadsworth, 1971.

IRISH PIONEERS IN MARYLAND, 1914-15. By M. J. O'Brien. American - Irish Historical Society Journal, Volume 14, 1914-15.

Author discusses the first Irish settlements in Maryland - their locations, the pioneers involved in the founding of each settlement and its further growth.

IT'S THE IRISH. By Robert Bernard Considine. Garden City, New York, Doubleday & Company, 1961.

Encomium of the Irish in America in their diversity and in spite of adversity.

JEW AND IRISH; Historic Group Relations and Immigration. By Rudolf Glanz. New York, 1966.

LET GO OF YESTERDAY. By Howard Breslin. New York, Whittlesey, 1950.

A novelistic rendering of the Irish ethnic community and the influence of the Roman Catholic Church.

MAGGIE: A GIRL OF THE STREETS. By Stephen Crane. New York, Appleton, 1896.

A novel depicting the devastating effects of slum life among the Irish.

MOONDYNE. By John Boyle O'Reilly. Boston, Pilot Publishing Company, 1879.

A novel describing the very bad living conditions in which Irish immigrants lived in the nineteenth century.

NEIGHBORS IN CONFLICT: THE IRISH, GERMANS, JEWS, AND ITALIANS OF NEW YORK CITY, 1929-1941. By Ronald H. Bayor. Baltimore, John Hopkins University Press, 1978.

This book seeks to analyze the origin, development, manifestation, and culmination of group conflict within a multi-ethnic urban setting in New York City. The Irish were one of four ethnic groups studied during the 1930's.

A PORTRAIT OF THE IRISH IN AMERICA. By William D. Griffin. New York, Charles Schribner's Sons, 1981.

A pictorial account of the Irish people's history from their homeland to America. Each photograph or illustration has a detailed caption accompanying it.

REAL LACE: AMERICA'S IRISH RICH. By Stephen Birmingham. New York, Harper and Row, 1973.

Story of a select group of Irish - the rich, Irish Catholics: how they rose from rags to riches and then fell back to rags.

THE SAN FRANCISCO IRISH, 1848-1880. By R. A. Burchell. Berkeley, University of California Press, 1980.

In the period of greatest social change the Irish found opportunity for rapid acceptance in San Francisco. Material success, lack of a rigid social system and a sense of importance assisted the Irish in feeling at home.

SHANTY IRISH. By Jim Tulle. New York, Boni, 1928.

A novel showing Irish-American life in the Midwest.

SOME ASPECTS OF EMIGRATION FROM IRELAND TO THE NORTH AMERICAN COLONIES BETWEEN 1660 AND 1775. By Audrey Lockhart. New York, Arno Press, 1976.

A dissertation concerned with very early emigration to the North American colonies. Gives background information about Ireland, describes the kind of people emigrating, including criminals and indentured servants, tells about the voyage itself and reception and absorption of the immigrants.

A SURVEY OF THE LITERATURE CONCERNING THE IRISH-AMERICAN EXPERIENCE FOR THE URBAN PLANNER. By John Foley. Monticello, Illinois, Council of Planning Librarians, 1974.

A listing of materials to aid in reviewing the social and cultural history of the Irish-American.

THAT MOST DISTRESSFUL NATION; The Taming of the American Irish. By Andrew M. Greeley. Chicago, Quadrangle Books, 1972.

Tells the ethnic history of the American Irish and how success has tamed them and caused a loss of their sense of distinction as a group. Discusses the historical background of the Irish, church and family characteristics, the arrival of Irish immigrants in America, and their experiences here.

TO THE GOLDEN DOOR; The Story of the Irish in Ireland and America. By George Potter. Boston, Little, Brown and Company, 1960.

A study of the great wave of Irish immigration to the United States during the years of the potato failures in Ireland from 1825 to 1854. Part One: Where They Came From; Part Two: How They Got Across the Ocean; Part Three: What Befell Them in America.

WHAT BRINGS SO MANY IRISH TO AMERICA? By Hibernicus, Pseud. New York, 1845. Reprint San Francisco, R and E Research Associates, 1972.

The author explains the causes of Irish emigration and the good and bad of residing in America. Written during the height of the Irish flood of emigration.

Audiovisual Material

FILMS

BIMSE AG RINCE (WE DANCE). 16 mm. Color and sound. 26 minutes. Embassy of Ireland, 1975.

This film contains many fine sequences of traditional Irish dancing as well as sequences showing excerpts from Siamsa Tire's performance. "Siamsa Tire" is a folk and drama group based near Listowel, County Kerry. The commentary is in English.

A CHANGE OF SEASON: IRELAND AND THE IRISH WAY. 16 mm. Color and sound. 24 minutes. By Stony Brook, New York, Puffin Films Corporation, 1979.

Presents a look at the Irish people, the Irish countryside and traditional Irish music.

CONNEMARA AND ITS PONIES. 16 mm. Color and sound. 27 minutes. Produced by David Shaw Smith.

A visual essay of Connemara from spring to autumn with pony breeding as its theme. Fine shots include the birth of a foal, rabbits at play and fox cubs. Traditional bargaining at the Maam Cross Fair is also depicted. The background music is largely traditional; the commentary is very much in harmony with the mood of the film.

CRADLE OF GENIUS. 16 mm. Black and white. Sound. 40 minutes.

The setting for this 1962 Academy Award nominee is the burnt-out shell of the old Abbey Theatre. Against this backgrop characters and incidents of the Abbey's history, such as the riots on the opening night of "Juno and the Paycock", are recalled. An excellent commentary written and spoken by Frank O'Connor is interspersed with the personal reminiscences of actors such as Siobhan MacKenna, Eithne Dunne, Cyril Cusack, Gabrial Fallen, Maureen Delany, Sheelagh Richards, and the playwright Padhraic Colum. The highlight of the film is a conversation between the Playwright Sean O'Casey and Barry Fitzgerald.

DA VINCI'S DREAM. 16 mm. Color and sound. 11 minutes. Directed by Declan Langan, Embassy of Ireland, 1978.

A group of people who share Leonardo da Vinci's dream of free flight leave the city behind and once out in the hills, take to the air in hang gliders. The film was made to give the viewer the feeling of being aloft, cameras are mounted on the gliders and give a breathtaking view of mountains and the sea as they glide in the airstreams above the Wicklow Mountains and Achill Island. Has won several awards.

DRESDEN IN DRUMCOLLIHER. 16 mm. Color and sound. 25 minutes. Embassy of Ireland, 1978.

This film is about a firm in County Limerick which manufactures Dresden type figurines in porcelain. It traces the manufacturing process from Irish sculptural models to the finished products and it gives a picture of the immensely skilled work involved.

ERRIGAL. 16 mm. Color and sound. 12-1/2 minutes. Directed by Patrick Carey, 1968.

Depicts the various moods evoked by Mount Errigal in County Donegal. The film is a visual essay set against music composed by Brian Boddell.

GOLDEN GALLONS. 16 mm. Color and sound. 22 minutes. Directed by Kieran Hickey, Embassy of Ireland, 1967.

This film produced for An Bord Bainne (Irish Dairy Produce Board) deals with the development and marketing of quality Irish dairy produce throughout the world and especially in Britain.

A HUNDRED THOUSAND WINGS. 16 mm. Color and sound. 40 minutes. Embassy of Ireland, 1975.

Some 360 species of wild birds have been recorded in Ireland of which 135 breed in the country. Three-quarters of the world population of the Greenland Whitefronted Gooses winter in Ireland and a large proportion of the world's stormy petrels breed on the southern and western coasts of Ireland. These and many other species are shown in this film in their colorful and often dramatic surroundings in locations such as Donegal, the Skelligs, Puffin Island, North Bull Island and the internationally important Wildlife reserve in County Wexford.

INVITATION TO ART. 16 mm. Black and white. Sound. 25 minutes.

Beginning with a brief description of the country, which stresses its island nature and its restlessness, the film then goes on to document the history of Irish art beginning with the Golden Monastic Age. Such works of genius as the Tara Broach, the Ardagh Chalice, illuminated manuscripts, the ruins of Cashel and Clonmacnoise are depicted. From Norman castles the film takes us to eighteenth century Georgian Dublin. Works of the eighteenth and nineteenth century painters - James Barry, Frederick Burke, Natanial Hone, and Paul Henry - are discussed. Much time is devoted to the work of Jack Yeats (brother of the poet). The school of twentieth century Irish stained glass is also studied.

INVITATION TO IRELAND. 16 mm or super 8 mm. Color and sound. 9 minutes. By Castle Films, 1970.

Shows the major attractions of Ireland, including scenes of the countryside and of how the people live and play.

IRELAND. 16 mm. Color and sound. 15 minutes. Directed by Colm O' Laoghaire, 1968.

A geography film for schools dealing with the economic structure of the country, based on the life of a young schoolboy living in rural Ireland. The film takes in a wide cross section of Irish life, ranging from Dermot's father's farm to his aunt's home in the Gaeltacht (Irish-speaking area) to a visit to Dublin.

IRELAND. 16 mm. Color and sound. 20 minutes. By Boulton-Hawker Films, Hadleigh, England, 1966. Released in the United States by International Film Bureau.

Shows the physical characteristics of Ireland and examines their influence on the people and the economy. Also studies the division of Ireland by religion which results in a north-south border.

IRELAND, A STATE OF MIND. 16 mm. Color and sound. 22 minutes. By Sheridan-Elson Communications, Incorporated for Irish Tourist Board. Released by GLL-TV Enterprises, 1978.

A travelog of many outstanding sites in Ireland.

IRELAND - THE HERITAGE OF THE PAST. 16 mm. Color and sound. 10 minutes. Embassy of Ireland, 1974.

The history of Irish architecture is traced from the cairns and passage graves of the Stone Age through the oratories, monasteries and castles of the Middle Ages to the great houses and streetscapes of the 18th century.

IRELAND - ISLE OF SPORT. 16 mm. Color and sound. 33 minutes. Directed by Kenneth Fairburn, 1963.

This is a Caltex film on the great variety of sports in Ireland including hurling, Gaelic football, rugby, the hunt, horse-show jumping, horse and dog racing, athletics, etc.

IRELAND - NO MORE YESTERDAYS. 16 mm. Color and sound. 25 minutes.

Industrial expansion and economic development in Ireland are the theme of this film.

IRISH BOY - THE STORY OF SEAN. 16 mm. Color and sound. 15 minutes. By B.A.C. Enterprises, Dublin, 1971. Produced in collaboration with the Department of Foreign Affairs, Republic of Ireland. Released in the United States by Encyclopaedia Britannica Educational Corporation, 1972.

Illustrates rural life in Ireland as exemplified by the life of a family living on a small dairy farm. Compares rural life with urban life in Ireland. For elementary grades.

ISLAND. 16 mm. Color and sound. 30 minutes. Embassy of Ireland, 1978.

This is a beautifully photographed survey of the daily lives of the people of Tory Island, County Donegal. The various occupations of the islanders are observed from a range of perspectives, and the mix is very pleasing indeed. Many sequences are delightfully composed of bright, natural colors, and arranged with love and humor. Boatbuilding, turfcutting, housekeeping, dancing, are all recorded and woven into a narrative showing the simplicity and variety of life of an island that might appear bleak to the casual eye.

LEADING THE WAY. 16 mm. Color and sound. 38 minutes. Directed by Joe Mendoza, 1963.

This Esso documentary about mechanization on Irish farms won the Golden Ear of Corn Award at the Agriculture Film Festival in Berlin in 1964. Through interviews with five farmers it shows how mechanization can be applied to both the small farms in County Kerry to the relatively large farms of the East.

THE LIGHT OF OTHER DAYS. 16 mm. Color and sound. 49 minutes. Embassy of Ireland.

The film is a panorama of Irish social life from the death of Parnell in 1891 to the beginning of the era of change heralded by the arrival of the motor car. One of the most comprehensive collections of late 19th and early 20th century photography to have been preserved in its entirety forms the basis of the film. In "The Light of Other Days" these pictures seem to come alive. We are shown work and recreation, transport and tourism, fashion and furnishings, the unchanging pattern of country life and the rapid development of the cities. The film reminds us that this was a time of marked social divisions between classes - although the growth of popular seaside resorts and cheap travel meant that holidays were no longer the privilege of the few, only the rich could afford such distractions as golfing and motoring. The melodies of Thomas Moore and music from street pianos of the period are skillfully combined with the photographs to record the way of life.

THE LITTLE PEOPLE. 16 mm. Color and sound. 20 minutes. Embassy of Ireland, 1971.

All over Ireland, in remote and out of the way places, small factories and workshops have been springing up, bringing back life to small towns and villages which might otherwise have faded away. They concentrate on high quality produce for export, and are helped along by the Government sponsored Kilkenny Design Workshops set up to encourage the highest standards of design in Ireland. The film gives a historical sketch of the background against which these firms grew up and shows the rural revolution which they have brought about. They may be individually small, but as the ironic title of the film suggests, these firms collectively make a contribution to Ireland's expanding economy which is far from small.

THE NATIONAL GALLERY. 16 mm. Color and sound. 25 minutes. Directed by Norris Davidson. Embassy of Ireland.

The National Gallery of Ireland houses a remarkable collection of paintings which is sampled in this colorful film. As well as reflecting the glories of the collection, the film traces briefly the history of the Gallery and glances at its many activities, including restoration and art education.

RHAPSODY OF A RIVER. 16 mm. Color and sound. 12 minutes. Produced by Louis Marcus, 1966.

This film, shot in the valley of the River Lee, depicts one day in the life of the countryside and city of Cork.

REFLECTIONS OF IRELAND. 16 mm. Color and sound. 20 minutes. By Patrick Carey for Irish Tourist Board, 1977. Released in the United States by Cecropia Films, Atlanta, 1979.

This film graphically depicts the beauty of the Western Province of Connaught. Musical accompaniment is by the Chieftains. There is no spoken commentary.

SHANNON - PORTRAIT OF A RIVER. 16 mm. Color and sound. 27 minutes. Directed by George Fleixhamn, 1973.

Traces the course of the Shannon, the longest river in Ireland, and manages to depict a wide range of Irish scenery ranging from the tranquil beauty of Lough Ree to the rugged cliffs of Moher (800 feet). En route to the sea the river passes the towns of Athlone and Carrick-on-Shannon and the ancient monastic settlement of Clonmacnoise.

THESE STONES REMAIN. 16 mm. Color and sound. 27 minutes.

A very beautiful film dealing with the evolution of Irish stone carving from the earliest times to the twelfth century.

THE TREASURES OF IRELAND. 16 mm. Color and sound. 57 minutes. By Pamela Ilott. Embassy of Ireland, 1972.

This film receptures the period when Ireland was a major center of European art, education and civilization. It traces motifs in Irish art from the Boyne Valley stones through bronze-age ornaments to the arrival of the Celts and then through Christian art as far as the Cross of Cong. Numerous outdoor shots in ancient monasteries, on the Rock of Cashel and on the island of Skellig Michael enhance the visual attraction of the film and place the works of art in the context in which they emerged.

YEATS COUNTRY. 16 mm. Color and sound. 17 minutes. Directed by Patrick Carey, 1965.

This is an exceptionally beautiful film made to commemorate the centenary of William Butler Yeats' birth. His poetry is read against the background which inspired it.

FILMS ON IRISH AMERICANS

GOODBYE HOME. 16 mm. Color and sound. 30 minutes. By Douglas Kirkland, 1972. National Film Board of Canada.

Examines the history of Irish emigration.

THE IRISH. 16 mm. Color and sound. 30 minutes. By Saul Rubin and Elaine Attias for National Communications Foundation, 1975. Released by Macmillan Films, Mt. Vernon, New York, 1977.

Tells the story of the arrival of Irish settlers in America, showing their origins, their problems in a new land, their entry into city politics, and their contributions to American culture.

ITALIANS

Embassy and Consulates

EMBASSY OF ITALY
1601 Fuller Street, Northwest
Washington, D.C. 20009 (202) 328-5500

CONSULATES GENERAL

101 Tremont Street
Boston, Massachusetts 02108 (617) 542-0483

625 North Michigan Avenue
Chicago, Illinois 60611 (312) 943-0703

10960 Wilshire Boulevard, Suite 800
Los Angeles, California 90024 (213) 479-5253

708 Cotton Exchange Building
231 Carondelet Street
New Orleans, Louisiana 70130 (504) 524-2272

690 Park Avenue
New York, New York 10021 (212) 737-9100

2128 Locust Street
Philadelphia, Pennsylvania 19103 (215) 732-7436

2590 Webster Street
San Francisco, California 94115 (415) 931-4924

CONSULATES

Cleveland Plaza, Suite 354
Euclid Avenue at 12th Street
Cleveland, Ohio 44115 (216) 861-1585

1200 Sixth Avenue, Suite 800
Detroit, Michigan 48226 (313) 963-8560

209 World Trade Building
1520 Texas Street
Houston, Texas 77002 (713) 222-7860

200 Southeast First Street
Miami, Florida 33131 (305) 371-5393

VICE CONSULATE

17 Academy Street
Newark, New Jersey 07102 (201) 643-1448

Mission to the United Nations

ITALIAN MISSION
809 United Nations Plaza, 3rd Floor
New York, New York 10017 (202) 687-6001

Tourist and Travel Offices

ENIT-ITALIAN GOVERNMENT TOURIST OFFICE

630 Fifth Avenue
New York, New York 10020 (212) 245-4822

500 North Michigan Avenue
Chicago, Illinois 60601 (312) 644-0990

360 Post Street
San Francisco, California 94108 (415) 392-6206

ITALIAN STATE RAILWAYS
666 Fifth Avenue
New York, New York 10020 (212) 397-2667

Fraternal Organizations

AMERICAN ITALIAN CONGRESS
111 Columbia Heights
Brooklyn, New York 11201 (212) 852-2929
General Director: John N. La Corte
Founded 1949

Federation of Italian-American organizations. Attempts to promote more active participation in civic, cultural, and philanthropical projects and coordinate activities. Presents awards to college students. Maintains an Italian Hall of Fame and Brooklyn Hall of Fame. Sponsors essay contests. Maintains a library of about 700 volumes of historical material, including a special Italian history-biography section.
Publications: Italian-American Review, annual; also publishes Brooklyn Review Magazine and other materials.

AMITA
Post Office Box 140
Whitestone, New York 11357 (212) 767-7667
President: Lucile DeGeorge Founded 1956

AMITA stands for American-Italian Women of Achievement. Founded to bestow awards to successful women in the arts, business, and professions, and in the United States Armed Forces. Grants annual achievement awards to American women of Italian lineage, and quinquennial awards to American women of other ethnic backgrounds. Distributes annual scholarship grants to students regardless of race, color, creed, or national origin.
Publication: AMITA Gold Book, annual.

ITALIAN AMERICAN WAR VETERANS OF THE UNITED STATES
115 South Meridian Road
Youngstown, Ohio 44509 (216) 782-5142
Executive Officer: Dominic Butch Founded 1931

Persons of Italian-American extraction who served in the United States Armed Forces during World War I, World War II, the Korean Conflict, or the Vietnam Conflict. State and local organizations sponsor community, veterans, social and cultural programs. Participates in veteran rehabilitation and community service programs. Opposes Communism and Fascism. Promotes recognition of contributions Italians have made to American history and contemporary living. Sponsors National Essay Contest.
Publications: The Torch, quarterly; National Directory, annual.

ITALO AMERICAN NATIONAL UNION
1400 Winston Plaza
Melrose Park, Illinois 60160
Executive Director: Paschal J. Pavani (312) 343-9885
Founded 1895

Fraternal benefit life insurance society for Americans of Italian origin or legal relationship. Bestows annual awards: Man of the Year; Renaissance and Leonardo da Vinci. Offers many scholarships and provides aid to senior citizen homes.
Publications: Newsletter, monthly; Bulletin, quarterly.

SONS OF ITALY SUPREME LODGE
1520 Locust Street
Philadelphia, Pennsylvania 19102
Executive Director: Peter M. Borromeo (215) 732-7575

Awards scholarships and sponsors charity programs. Maintains Garibaldi-Meucci Museum in Staten Island, New York.

UNICO NATIONAL
72 Burroughs Place
Bloomfield, New Jersey 07003 (201) 748-9144
President: Renato R. Biribin Founded 1922

Active members and associate national members are business and professional people of Italian lineage or married to an Italian-American. Sponsors educational, cultural and civic programs; maintains the Mental Health Research Foundation; makes contributions towards research in Cooley's Anemia, a blood disease affecting children; conducts seminars; bestows scholarships; presents high school athletic awards; sponsors literary contest. Maintains library and athletic Hall of Fame. Absorbed (1947) National Civic League.
Publications: Unico National Magazine, monthly.

UNITED ITALIAN AMERICAN LEAGUE
210 East 61st Street
New York, New York 10021
National President: Paul P. Rao, Jr. (212) 964-8866

Federation of Italo-American civic and political organizations. Seeks to foster better understanding between the American people and Americans of Italian descent.

Professional Organizations

AMERICAN ASSOCIATION OF TEACHERS OF ITALIAN
SUNY at Stony Brook
Stony Brook, New York 11794 (514) 246-8676
President: Joseph A. Tursi Founded 1924

Professional society of college and secondary school teachers and others interested in Italian language and culture.
Publication: Italica, quarterly (spring issue includes directory of members). Also publishes a handbook.

ASSOCIATION OF STUDENT AND PROFESSIONAL ITALIAN-AMERICANS
Post Office Box 3672, Grand Central Station
New York, New York 10017
President: Pasquale D'Onofrio Founded 1957

College graduates or persons with equivalent education; students. To assist Italian-American professionals and Italian exchange students to further their careers and studies; to encourage communication among them and create an atmosphere of mutual understanding; to foster responsible leadership within the Italian-American Community; to promote interest in Italian culture through educational and social activities. Programs include guest speakers, dinner discussions, dances, theatre and opera parties, museum visits and picnics.

GRADUATES OF ITALIAN MEDICAL SCHOOLS
c/o Mario E. Milite
360 East 194th Street
Bronx, New York 10458 (212) 364-3164
Secretary: Mario E. Milite, M.D. Founded 1966

Physicians of any national origin who graduated from schools in Italy. Purposes are scientific and social. Maintains placement service and charitable program. Publications: Newsletter, five times a year; Membership Directory, biennial.

ITALIAN ACTORS UNION
1674 Broadway
New York, New York 10019
Executive Secretary: S. A. Carollo (212) 245-1347
Founded 1938

Publication: Bulletin, quarterly.

ITALIAN AMERICAN LIBRARIANS CAUCUS
Six Peter Cooper Road, Apt. 11G
New York, New York 10010 (212) 228-8438
President: C. M. Diodati, Jr. Founded 1974

Political and national Italian and non-Italian American organizations, primarily business, government, public and academic information scientists. To provide guidelines and studies on Italian and Italian American materials and populations particularly relevant to libraries and information centers.
Publications: Bulletin, semiannual; Writings on Italian Americans, updated biennially.

NATIONAL COUNCIL OF COLUMBIA ASSOCIATIONS IN CIVIL SERVICE
299 Broadway, Room 1500
New York, New York 10007
Executive Secretary: Alphonse F. D'Andrea (212) 962-5780
Founded 1938

Italo-American civil service employees in the New York area. Conducts social, charitable, educational, self-improvement, public service and anti-defamation programs. Is concerned with accurate portrayal of Italo-Americans in text books and the mass media. Awards scholarships; sponsors promotion classes. Formerly Grand Council of Columbia Associations in Civil Service.

SOCIETY FOR ITALIAN-AMERICAN SCIENTISTS AND PHYSICIANS
Box 492
Gaithersburg, Maryland 20760
President: Donald M. Valerino, Ph.D. (301) 926-2487

Limited to Italian-American scientists and physicians who have made outstanding contributions to their fields. To promote highest standards of research, education and medicine; to encourage careers in science and medicine and offer guidance in career goals; to focus public attention on members and their accomplishments; to strengthen ties of friendship among Italian-American scientists and physicians. Plans to present awards and form hall of fame.
Publications: Newsletter, annual.

Public Affairs Organizations

AMERICAN COMMITTEE ON ITALIAN MIGRATION
373 Fifth Avenue
New York, New York 10016
Executive National Secretary: Reverend Joseph A. Cogo (212) 679-4650
Founded 1952

Seeks liberalization of immigration laws and their implementation by assisting Italian immigrants in filing immigration petitions and aiding in the smooth assimilation of Italian immigrants into the United States society.
Publications: Newsletter, bimonthly; Nuova Via, bimonthly.

AMERICANS OF ITALIAN DESCENT
104 East 40th Street, Suite 306
New York, New York 10016 (212) 697-8850
President: Joseph Calio Founded 1966

To combat defamation and discrimination; provide technical assistance to individuals and organizations in obtaining a wide range of social services; to foster cultural activities; provide educational counseling, books and other materials. Publishes Italian Heroes of American History and Writings on Italian-Americans. Formerly: American Italian Anti-Defamation Leagues.

APOSTOTATE FOR THE ITALIAN-SPEAKING
75 Greene Avenue (212) 638-5500
Brooklyn, New York 11238 Founded 1974

Sponsored by the Diocese of Brooklyn to aid in legal problems connected to immigration.

ITALIAN AMERICAN FORUM
2626 Pennsylvania Avenue, Northwest
Washington, D.C. 20037
President: Dr. Elio E. Grandi Founded 1978

Political interest group which seeks to improve opportunities for Italian Americans. Compiles a data bank of Italian American registered voters in states with large Italian populations. Lobbies at all levels of government. Currently inactive.

NATIONAL ITALIAN AMERICAN FOUNDATION
1019 19th Street, Northwest
Suite 730
Washington, D.C. 20036
Executive Director: Alfred Rotondaro (202) 293-1713
Founded 1975

United States citizens of Italian ancestry. Activities include: research and education concerning Italian art, culture, sciences and social history; seminars, regional meetings, lecture series, studies; plays and musical events. Acts as liaison with Congress and other agencies. Compiles statistics; maintains speakers bureau and biographical archives. Presents awards. Local groups are known as Friends of the National Italian American Foundation. Formerly (1978) Italian American Foundation.
Publications: Washington Newsletter, monthly.

Cultural and Educational Organizations

AMERICA-ITALY SOCIETY
667 Madison Avenue
New York, New York 10021
Executive Director: Mrs. Hedy Giusti Lanham (212) 838-1560
Founded 1949

Fosters friendship between Italy and the United States based upon mutual understanding of their respective contributions to science, art, music, literature, law, and government. Conducts cultural exchanges between Italy and the United States through lectures, distribution of publications, concerts, and art shows. Assists staffs of American institutions and foundations in establishing professional contacts in Italy. Maintains a current roster of Americans concerned with Italian affairs. Also sponsors Italian language and cooking schools.
Publications: Newsletter, quarterly; also publishes Attenzione, magazine.

AMERICAN INSTITUTE FOR VERDI STUDIES
Department of Music
New York University
Faculty of Arts and Science
24 Waverly Place, Room 268
New York, New York 10003 (212) 598-3431
Director: Dr. Martin Chusid Founded 1976

Persons interested in the work of Giuseppe Verdi (1813-1901), Italian composer. Resources include archives of letters, literature relating to the work of Verdi. Presents concerts; sponsors occasional courses at New York University. Maintains library of 3,000 volumes of books, articles, librettos, records, music and 15,000 letters and other documents.
Publications: Newsletter, semiannual; also publishes scholarly papers and Congress Report.

AMERICAN ITALIAN HISTORICAL ASSOCIATION
209 Flagg Place
Staten Island, New York 10304 (212) 667-6628
President: Francis X. Femminella Founded 1966

Academicians (historians, sociologists, anthropologists, educators) and lay persons interested in collecting, preserving, publishing, and popularizing material about the settlement and history of the Italians in the United States and Canada. Awards prizes and fellowships to scholars of Italian-American history. Presents the Leonard Covello Award annually for a scholarly article on an Italian-American topic. Sponsors seminars and conferences. Maintains archives containing manuscripts, organizational records, and published materials relating to Italian-American history.
Publications: Newsletter, quarterly; Proceedings, annual; also publishes bibliography and other materials on the Italian-American experience.

ARTURO TOSCANINI SOCIETY
Post Office Box 7312
Burbank, California 91505
Founder-President: Clyde J. Key Founded 1968

Admirers of Arturo Toscanini attempt to preserve and perpetuate the memory of Toscanini. Makes available to members recordings of Toscanini's works not otherwise available. Maintains a library of published books and records plus transcriptions and tapes of Toscanini's concerts and rehearsals.
Publications: Bulletin, quarterly; The Maestro, annual.

COMITATO NAZIONALE PER LE ONORANZE A GIOVANNI DA VERRAZZANO
John Jay Homestead
Post Office Box A. H.
Jay Street
Katonah, New York 10536
Vice President: Lino S. Lipinsky De Orlov (914) 232-3667
Founded 1956

Membership is by election only to the Italian national committee for the commemoration of Giovanni da Verrazzano, who discovered New York Bay in 1524. Conducts research into the history of medieval navigation and exploration. Maintains a library at Chianti, Florence, Italy. Italian officer and address: Count Bino Sanminiatelli, President, Palazzo Firenze, Piazza Firenze 27, Rome, Italy. Maintains biographical archives and presents awards. The Committee participated in the dedication of the Verrazzano-Narrows Bridge in New York City in 1964. Engaged in donating and erecting monuments to Verrazzano in Dieppe, France, and Providence, Rhode Island. United States and Italian postage stamps have been issued in honor of Verrazzano. Also known as the Italian National Committee for the Commemoration of Giovanni da Verrazzano.

COMMITTEE FOR THE MONUMENT OF GARIBALDI

Formed on July 4, 1882, the date when the Italian patriot died, to erect a memorial statue in Washington Square in New York City. The statue was moved about fifteen feet in October, 1970 and workmen discovered a container holding a June 4, 1882 copy of Il Progresso Italo-Americana, comments from Victor Hugo and George Sands and the notation that the mementoes had been placed there by the Committee.

CONFERENCE GROUP ON ITALIAN POLITICS
Department of Political Science
University of Nebraska
Lincoln, Nebraska 68588
Executive Secretary: Raphael Zariski (402) 472-2346
Founded 1975

Professors, students, journalists, diplomatic officials and civil servants. Promotes professional study, criticism and research in Italian political processes and issues.
Publications: Newsletter, semiannual; Membership List, annual.

DANTE ALIGHIERI SOCIETY OF SOUTHERN CALIFORNIA
2501 Crest Drive
Manhattan Beach, California 90266 (213) 547-3877
President: Rosario Armato Founded 1957

Friends of Italian culture. Named in honor of Dante Alighieri (1265-1321), Italian poet. Aim is to keep alive Italian history, art, and culture by sponsoring the production of Italian drama, music, and dance; lectures and exhibitions of paintings, sculpture, and architecture; poetry readings; debates and seminars on the Italian Renaissance and its place in world history. International headquarters is in Rome, Italy; independent branches are located all over the world.

DANTE SOCIETY OF AMERICA
Boylston Hall
Harvard University
Cambridge, Massachusetts 02138
Secretary-Treasurer: Anthony J. De Vito
Founded 1881

Teachers, scholars, and others interested in the study of Dante (Italian poet, 1265-1321, author of the Divine Comedy) and in furthering scholarship in the field. Dante Prizes are awarded annually at undergraduate and graduate levels. Maintains a library of about 200 volumes of basic texts concerning Dante.
Publication: Dante Studies (journal), annual.

ISTITUTO ITALIANO DI CULTURA (ITALIAN CULTURAL INSTITUTE)
686 Park Avenue
New York, New York 10021
Director: Marco Miele (212) 879-4242

The cultural agency of the Italian Ministry of Foreign Affairs. Serves as a center of documentation and information on Italy. Promotes cultural relations between Italy and the United States. Maintains a library of about 29,000 books and 150 periodicals, with an extensive audiovisual department.
Publication: Newsletter (with a bibliographical supplement), bimonthly.

THE ITALIA PHILATELIC SOCIETY
c/o Collectors Club
22 East 35th Street
New York, New York 10016
President: Domenico Facci Founded 1976

Collectors of stamps from Italy, the Italian states, Italian colonies, San Marino and Vatican City. Sponsors seminars on forgeries; maintains small library of catalogs and research volumes. Bestows awards. Plans to publish newsletter and monographs.

ITALIAN AMERICAN STAMP CLUB
Post Office Box 210
Milwaukee, Wisconsin 53201 (414) 263-1636
President: Mary Ann Sarsfield Founded 1980

Collectors of Italian philately. Provides for the display and exhibition of philatelic materials and exchanges philatelic information with emphasis on Italian philately.
Publications: Newsletter, monthly.

ITALIAN CULTURE COUNCIL
c/o Patricia A. McDorman
1781 Walker Avenue, Apt. D
Irvington, New Jersey 07111
Executive Director: Patricia A. McDorman (201) 374-6418
Founded 1963

Professors, teachers, publishers; universities, societies; other individuals and groups concerned with the Italian language and culture. Disseminates information on Italian language and culture. Supplies materials and specific information to groups interested in fostering the study of Italian in United States schools. Serves as an information center for administrators, boards of education, teachers, students, and the general public. Provides speakers in New Jersey or the New York City area for informal talks on Italian history and culture.
Publications: ICC Source Book of Information (collection of monthly bulletins from 1965-1972), with Annual Supplements; has also published booklets, flyers, folders to aid in preparing ethnic festivals, and a survey, Colleges and Universities Offering Italian in the United States.

ITALIAN HISTORICAL SOCIETY OF AMERICA
111 Columbia Heights
Brooklyn, New York 11201 (212) 852-2929
Director: John LaCorte Founded 1949

Founded to perpetuate the Italian heritage in America and to gather historical data on Americans of Italian descent. Sponsored the First Italian Heritage Cultural Festival in New York City in June, 1972, in order to promote greater appreciation of the basic human values, and to encourage youths to become more meaningfully involved in the enhancement of man's dignity. Maintains music scholarship fund and library.
Publications: Italian-American Review, quarterly; Italian American Newsletter, irregular; also publishes Italian American Almanach.

LEONARDO DA VINCI SOCIETY
35 East Central Avenue
Maywood, New Jersey 07607 (201) 845-5449
President: Anthony Gaglioti Founded 1961

Men and women in the Bergen County, New Jersey, area. Named in honor of Leonardo da Vinci (1452-1519), Florentine painter, sculptor, architect, engineer, and scientist. Seeks to diffuse the Italian language, literature, culture, and traditions. Sponsors cultural, educational, travel, and social activities. Prepares exhibits. Conducts Italian classes. Presents medallions to students for achievement in high school Italian, a scholarship to an outstanding college student majoring in Italian, and prizes for art.
Publication: Scriptores, semiannual.

PIRANDELLO SOCIETY
c/o Dr. Anne Paolucci
St. John's University
Jamaica, New York 11439 (212) 767-8380
President: Dr. Anne Paolucci Founded 1958

To encourage the study of Italian author Luigi Pirandello's (1867-1936) works, particularly his plays. Bestows awards and maintains speakers bureau.
Publications: Pirandello Newsletter, three times a year.

SOCIETY FOR ITALIAN HISTORICAL STUDIES
Boston College
Chestnut Hill, Massachusetts 02167
Executive Secretary-Treasurer: Alan J. Reinerman (617) 969-0100

College and university professors and graduate students. Attempts to encourage the study and teaching of Italian history. Aims to promote research and publication of studies dealing with the history of Italy and with relations between the United States and Italy. Seeks grants-in-aid for students and scholars. Awards prizes to Americans making original contributions in the field. Presents the Helen and Howard R. Marraro Prize annually. Sponsors conferences and lectures, and facilitates exchange of technical and professional information on Italian historical subjects.
Publications: Newsletter, annual; also publishes annual membership list.

VENICE COMMITTEE
International Fund For Monuments
3624 Legation Avenue, Northwest
Washington, D.C. 20015
Executive Secretary: James A. Gray (202) 726-5225
Founded 1969

Individuals devoted to the rescue of Venice, Italy, and its art treasures. Seeks to restore and preserve paintings, sculpture, and architectural treasures in Venice.
Publications: Anthology Guide to Venice and booklets.

Charitable Organizations

BOYS' TOWNS OF ITALY
24 West 57th Street
New York, New York 10019
Executive Director: Janet T. Garry
(212) 581-7380
Founded 1945

An American agency to raise funds for child care institutions throughout Italy, including boys' towns, girls' towns, children's homes, day nurseries, and rehabilitation centers. The organization was founded by Rt. Rev. Msgr. J. P. Carroll-Abbing who started the first shelter for homeless boys in a bombed-out villa in Rome. Formerly called American Relief for Italy.
Publication: News, monthly.

ITALIAN CHARITIES OF AMERICA
83-20 Queens Boulevard
Elmhurst, New York 11373
Executive Director: John J. Alliegro
(212) 478-3100
Founded 1936

Young adult group of Italian charities in America made up of persons of Italian birth or descent. Renders service to the community and nation in the form of scholarships to deserving students, camping for underprivileged youngsters, leadership training, youth guidance, and emergency welfare assistance. Sponsors Senior Center for senior citizens. Offers classes in dancing, Italian and Spanish. Maintains library of 3,000 volumes in the areas of fiction, non-fiction, reference, legal and documentary.

ITALIAN WELFARE LEAGUE
250 West 57th Street, Suite 1131
New York, New York 10019
Executive Secretary: Rosalie M. Gianbalva-Avakian
(212) 247-7956
Founded 1920

Founded to assist Italian immigrants in America. Offers grants to hospitals and scholarships to graduate students of Italian background for study at Columbia University School of Social Work.

Religious Organizations

ASSOCIATION OF EVANGELICALS FOR ITALIAN MISSIONS
314 Richfield Road
Upper Darby, Pennsylvania 19082
Editor: Dr. Anthony F. Vasquez
(215) 334-1282
Founded 1968

Persons of Italian Baptist origin and members of Italian Evangelical churches; churches affiliated with the American Baptist Convention. Fosters evangelization in Italian Baptist churches. Maintains a benevolence fund to help churches, groups, and Evangelical organizations in Italy. Gathers information for ministerial placement. Awards an annual citation to an outstanding Evangelical layman or minister. Affiliated with the Evangelical Baptist Christian Union of Italy. Formed by merger of the American Federation of Italian Evangelicals and Italian Baptist Association of America.
Publication: New Aurora, monthly.

ITALIAN CATHOLIC FEDERATION CENTRAL COUNCIL
1801 Van Ness Avenue, Suite 330
San Francisco, California 94109
Administrative Director: Mariano J. Barsotti
(415) 673-8240
Founded 1924

Catholics of Italian birth or descent. Conducts religious, patriotic, social, cultural, and charitable activities. Awards 50 scholarships annually.
Publication: Il Bolletino, monthly.

Research Centers and Special Institutes

AMERICAN ACADEMY IN ROME
41 East 65th Street
New York, New York 10021
Executive Secretary: Ruth D. Green
(212) 535-4250
Founded 1894

To promote the study and practice of the fine arts and the investigation of the archaeology, literature and history of the classical and later periods by granting fellowships in architecture, design/photography, landscape architecture, musical composition, painting, sculpture, art history, literature, Italian and classical studies and post-classical humanistic studies to United States citizens for use at the Academy in Rome, Italy. Maintains library of 85,000 volumes on Classical Literature, Archaeology and Fine Arts. Absorbed (1913) American School of Classical Studies in Rome.

Publications: Memoirs (research), annual; Papers and Monographs (research), annual.

CENTER FOR ITALIAN STUDIES
University of Connecticut
Storrs, Connecticut 06268 (203) 486-3156
Director: Dr. Norman Kogan Founded 1966

Carries out studies on modern Italy in all its aspects: political, historical, social, cultural, literary, and artistic. Also provides advanced instruction and research training of graduate students at the University interested in various aspects of modern Italy. Research results are published in professional journals.

INSTITUTE FOR MEDITERRANEAN ART AND ARCHAEOLOGY
18 East Fourth Street, No. 909
Cincinnati, Ohio 45202 (606) 341-1860
Dean: Dr. Alfonz Lengyel Founded 1972

Purposes are: to excavate in Toscana; to develop an archaeological institute at the University of Siena (Italy); to organize exchange of scholars. Has developed a degree program on classical art and archaeology; organizes summer course and excavation in Italy. Maintains library. Formerly 1975 Toscan-American Archaeological Association; 1978 Tuscan-American Institute for Mediterranean Archaeology.
Publications: Bulletin, annual.

THEMATIC INDEX OF SIXTEENTH CENTURY ITALIAN MUSIC
State University of New York at Binghamton
Vestal Parkway East
Binghamton, New York 13901 (607) 798-2591
Director: Dr. Harry B. Lincoln Founded 1965

Principal field of research is in sixteenth century Italian music, also other repertoires as demand and capacity permit, including development of thematic indexes of printed and manuscript sources using data processing and computer techniques to work out an index system of music input language from which intervallic order and other information can be extracted and by which many anonymous works can be identified and borrowings can be cited, also research and development of special typography for high-speed computer printer to permit publication of music on preprinted staff paper.

Museums

THE GARIBALDI AND MEUCCI MEMORIAL MUSEUM
420 Tomkins Avenue
Rosebank
Staten Island, New York 10305
Director: Lino S. Lipinsky de Orlov (212) 442-1608

Contains paintings, prints and photographs of the Risorgimento Wars in Italy, as well as guns, sabers, military uniforms, and decorations. The collection in the home of Antonio Meucci, an inventor of the telephone, includes early working models of his 1841 telephone.

Special Libraries and Subject Collections

CALIFORNIA STATE UNIVERSITY AT SAN FRANCISCO LIBRARY
Frank V. de Bellis Collection
1630 Holloway Avenue
San Francisco, California 94132 (415) 469-1649
Curator: Serena de Bellis Founded 1963

Subjects: Italian and Roman civilizations, including history, literature, fine arts, and science. Holdings: Books; bound periodicals; sheet music, manuscripts, and reports; pamphlets; recorded tapes, phonorecords; Italic, Etruscan, and Roman artifacts. Services: Library is open to qualified scholars. Publications: The Frank V. de Bellis Collection (revised edition, 1967); catalog of artifacts: Exhibition of the Frank V. de Bellis Etruscan, Greco-Roman Collection.

CENTER FOR MIGRATION STUDIES - LIBRARY
209 Flagg Place
Staten Island, New York 10304
Librarian/Archv.: Nancy F. Avrin (212) 351-8800

Subjects: Human migration and ethnic group relations, especially strong in Italian-American affairs. Holdings: Monographs, periodicals, newspapers, archival collections, photographs. Services: Collection is available for public use; photocopying permitted.

ISTITUTO ITALIANO DI CULTURA LIBRARY
686 Park Avenue
New York, New York 10021 (212) 879-4242
Head: Professor Marco Miele Founded 1959

Subjects: Italian philosophy; social sciences concerning Italy; Italian language; science and technology; Italian arts; Italian literature; Italian history, geography, and biography. Holdings: Books; journals and other serials; clippings; photographs; films; slides, magnetic tapes; cassettes; filmstrips; phonorecords. Services: Interlibrary loans; copying; library open to visitors; card required for borrowing privileges.
Publications: Monthly Newsletter, mailed upon request to libraries, cultural institutions, and scholars.

LIBRARY OF THE ITALIAN RISORGIMENTO
Garibaldi and Meucci Memorial Museum
John Jay Homestead, Box AH
Katonah, New York 10536
Director: Lino S. Lipinsky de Orlov (914) 232-3667
Founded 1956

Contains a collection of books on the history of the Italian Unification Wars and mementoes of Garibaldi. The library is open to the public.

PATERNO LIBRARY (CASA ITALIANA)
Columbia University
1161 Amsterdam Avenue
New York, New York 10027
Library Assistant: Robert Connolly (212) 280-2307
Founded 1927

Maintains a collection of books on Italian literature and culture. Provides interlibrary loans and copying services.

Newspapers and Newsletters

ACIM DISPATCH. 1953-. Bimonthly. Editor: Reverend Joseph Cago. Publisher: American Committee on Italian Migration, 373 Fifth Avenue, New York, New York 10016.

Newsletter of the American Committee on Italian Migration. Publishes news of the organization and on issues pertaining to immigration.

AGENDA, THE ITALIAN AMERICAN NEWS. 1975-. Weekly. Editor: Joseph Preite. Publisher: Italian-American News Incorporated, 26 Court Street, Brooklyn, New York 11242.

AMERICA-ITALY NEWSLETTER. Quarterly. Editor: Hedy Giusti Lanham. Publisher: America-Italy Society, Incorporated, 667 Madison Avenue, New York, New York 10021. In English.

Publishes news about events and activities sponsored by the Society.

THE AMERICAN CITIZEN. 1923-. Quarterly. Editor and Publisher: Victor Failla, Post Office Box 944, 8262 Hascall Street, Omaha, Nebraska 68124. In Italian and English.

Covers international, national, and local news of special interest to the Italian-American community.

AMERICAN ITALIAN HISTORICAL ASSOCIATION--NEWSLETTER. 1966-. Quarterly. Editor: George Pozzetta. Publisher: American Italian Historical Association, 209 Flagg Place, Staten Island, New York 10304.

Designed "to promote the study of the Italian American experience in North America." Carries communications from readers concerning significant or nostalgic events arising from their immigration. Provides news from chapters. Includes reports of research in progress and schedules of activities.

BOYS' TOWN OF ITALY NEWS. Monthly. Editor: Janet T. Garry. Publisher: Boys' Town of Italy, 24 West 57th Street, New York, New York 10019. In English.

Newsletter of the organization.

BOLLETTINO DELLA FEDERAZIONE CATTOLICA ITALIANA (Bulletin of the Italian Catholic Federation). 1924-. Monthly. Editor: Mario J. Cugia. Publisher: Italian Catholic Federation, 1801 Van Ness Avenue, Suite 330, San Francisco, California 94109. In English and Italian.

Carries news items on activities of the various branches of the Italian Catholic Federation, as well as articles on travel and religious matters, and book reviews.

BULLETIN OF THE ITALIAN AMERICAN CHAMBER OF COMMERCE. 1907-. Bimonthly. Editor: Leonora LiPuma Turner. Publisher: Italian American Chamber of Commerce, 126 West Grand Avenue, Chicago, Illinois 60610.

COLORADO. 1923-. Weekly. Editor and Publisher: Francis Mancini, 3630 Ontario Place, Denver, Colorado 80211. In English.

Covers general, national, and local news.

CONNECTICUT ITALIAN BULLETIN. 1949-. Irregular. Editor: Ven Sequenzia. Publisher: Connecticut Italian Publishing Company, Incorporated, Post Office Box 1264, Hartford, Connecticut 06105. In Italian and English.

IL CORRIERE DEL BERKSHIRE (The Berkshire Courier). 1930-. Weekly. Editor: Enzo Marinaro. Publisher: Courier Printing and Publishing Company, 24-26 First Street, Pittsfield, Massachusetts 01202. In Italian.

THE ECHO. 1896-. Weekly. Editor and Publisher: Jean Russi, 243 Atwells Avenue, Providence, Rhode Island 02903. In English and Italian.

Covers local and group news of interest to Italian Americans.

FLORIDA ITALIAN BULLETIN. 1968-. Irregular. Editor: Ven Sequenzia. Publisher: European Cultural Bureau, Post Office Box 181, Hollywood, Florida 33022. In Italian and English.

LA GACETA. 1922-. Weekly. Editor and Publisher: Roland Manteiga, 2015 15th Street, Tampa, Florida 33605. In Spanish, Italian, and English.

GIUSTIZIA (Justice). 1918-. Monthly. Editor: Lino Manocchia. Publisher: International Ladies' Garment Workers Union, 1710 Broadway, New York, New York 10019. In Italian.

A union publication for Italian-speaking employees of the garment industry.

ISTITUTO ITALIANO DE CULTURA -- NEWSLETTER. 1968-. Irregular. Editor: Dr. Marco Niele. Publisher: Italian Cultural Institute, 686 Park Avenue, New York, New York 10023.

Covers cultural events in Italy including art, books, music, theater, films, architecture; reports exhibits and performances of Italian interest in the United States; gives announcements of courses, contests, congresses, and prizes in Italy.

ITALIAN HERITAGE NEWSLETTER. 1968-. Monthly. Editor and Publisher: Joseph A. Tigani, Box 114, Rowayton, Connecticut 06853.

ITALIAN TRIBUNE. 1931-. Weekly. Editor: Joan Alagna. Publisher: Ace Alagna Publications, 427 Bloomfield, Newark, New Jersey 07107. In English.

ITALO-AMERICAN TIMES. 1964-. Bimonthly. Editor: Rudy Damonte. Publisher: Italo-American Times Publishing Company, Post Office Box 1492, Baychester Station, Bronx, New York, New York 10469. In English.

Provides news coverage of international, national and local events, reports on developments in Italy, and other news of special interest to Italian Americans.

L'ITALO AMERICANO DI LOS ANGELES (Los Angeles Italian American). 1908-. Weekly. Editor: Mario Trecco. Publisher: Scalabrini League, Incorporated, 6399 Wilshire Boulevard, Los Angeles, California 90012. In Italian.

MIDDLETOWN BULLETIN. 1948-. Weekly. Editor: Max B. Corvo. Publisher: Middletown Bulletin, Incorporated, 790 Ridge Road, Middletown, Connecticut 06457. In English and Italian.

Covers general, national, and local news.

LA PAROLA DEL POPOLO (The Word of the People). 1908-. Bimonthly. Editor: Egidio Clemente. Publisher: La Parola del Popolo Publishing Company, 6740 West Diversey, Chicago, Illinois 60635. In Italian and English.

Provides news and commentaries on economic, social, and political affairs of Italy and the United States. A pro-labor Democratic Socialist publication.

IL PENSIERO (The Thought). 1904-. Semimonthly. Editor and Publisher: Antonio Lombardo, 10001 Stonell Drive, Saint Louis, Missouri 63123. In Italian and English.

Offers news coverage of events in Italy and activities of interest to Italian communities in the United States.

IL POPOLO ITALIANO (The Italian People). 1935-. Monthly. Editor and Publisher: Arnold R. Orsatti, 6510 Ventnor Avenue, Ventnor City, New Jersey 08406. Trenton Editor: Maurice Perilla.

In addition to general news, prints information about Italian community activities in South New Jersey. Has combined with La Nuova Capitale of Trenton and also carries that name in its title.

POST-GAZETTE. 1896-. Weekly. Editor and Publisher: Phyllis F. Donnaruma, 5 Prince Street, Boston, Massachusetts 02113. In English.

Publishes general, international, national, and local news.

IL PROGRESSO ITALO-AMERICANO (Italian-American Progress). 1880-. Daily. Editor: Fortune Pope. Publisher: Il Progresso Italo-Americano Publishing Company, Incorporated, 260 Audubon Avenue, New York, New York 10033. In Italian.

Provides international, national, and local news coverage, with emphasis on events in Italy.

SOCIETY FOR ITALIAN HISTORICAL STUDIES--NEWSLETTER. 1955-. Annual. Editor: Professor Alan J. Reinerman. Publisher: Society for Italian Historical Studies, c/o Alan J. Reinerman, Boston College, History Department, Chestnut Hill, Massachusetts 02167.

Serves the teachers and students of Italian history who make up this academic society affiliated with the American Historical Association. Carries reports of the annual meeting of the society and notices of conferences, awards and grants, appointments and promotions, doctoral dissertations and projected activities. Includes announcements of publications on Italian history.

SONS OF ITALY NEWS. 1930-. Weekly. Editor: Ralph Ferruzzi. Publisher: Grand Lodge of Massachusetts, Order of Sons of Italy in America, 126 Cambridge Street, Boston, Massachusetts 02114. In English.

Covers news concerning member lodges in Massachusetts and their activities.

SONS OF ITALY TIMES. 1936-. Weekly. Editor: Joseph L. Monte. Publisher: Grand Lodge of the Order of the Sons of Italy in America, 1520 Locust Street, Philadelphia, Pennsylvania 19102. In English and Italian.

A fraternal newspaper covering news about lodges throughout Pennsylvania. Includes editorials on topics such as pollution, politics, legal matters, and education.

LA TRIBUNA ITALIANA (The Italian Tribune). 1933-. Monthly. Editor and Publisher: Gino Cacchione, 7171 North 42nd Street, Milwaukee, Wisconsin 53209. In Italian.

LA TRIBUNA ITALIANA D'AMERICA (Italian Tribune of America). 1909-. Weekly. Italian Editor: Ferruccio Serdoz. English Editor and Publisher: Edward Baker, 3455 Twelve Mile Road, Warren, Michigan 48093. In Italian and English.

Covers international, national and local news as well as items of special interest to the Italian American community.

LA VOCE ITALIANA (The Italian Voice). 1934-. Weekly. Editor and Publisher: Emilio Augusto, 77-79 Mill Street, Paterson, New Jersey 07501. In Italian.

Publishes general, national, and local news.

LA VOCE ITALIANA. Monthly. Editor and Publisher: Emanuel Blumbery, Reading, Pennsylvania. In Italian.

LA VOCE DEL POPOLO (Voice of the People). 1910-. Weekly. Editor: Victor Viberti. Publisher: Pious Society of Saint Paul, 7050 Pinehurst, Dearborn, Michigan 48126. In Italian and English.

Magazines

ATTENZIONE. 1979-. Monthly. Editor: Joan Schlesinger. Publisher: Leda Giovannetti Sanford, 10 East 49th Street, New York, New York 10017. In Italian.

A magazine especially for Italian American interests, publishing news and cultural articles.

LA FOLLIA DI NEW YORK (Folly). 1893-. Monthly. Editor: Michael Sisca. Publisher: Italian National Magazine Company, 125 East 95th Street, New York, New York 10028. In Italian.

Publishes articles on Italian culture, and literature, etc.

FORUM ITALICUM (Italian Forum). 1967-. Three times a year. Editor: M. Ricciardelli. Publisher: Forum Italicum, 2022 Park Boulevard, Tonawanda, New York 14150. In English and Italian.

Contains articles about the culture, language, and literature of Italy, as well as essays, poetry, news, and book reviews.

I-AM. 1976-. Monthly. Editor: Ron de Paolo. Publisher: I-Am Publishing Corporation, 3 East 54th Street, New York, New York 10022. (Subscriptions to: Box 6350, Marion, Ohio 43302).

Positive accent is given to being American and being Italian by featuring articles about Italy, and about the Italian American experience. Carries book reviews.

IDENTITY. 1977-. Monthly. Editor: Raffaele Donato. Publisher: Identity, 420 Madison Avenue, New York, New York 10017.

A magazine for the American aware of or searching for his Italian heritage.

ITALIAN AMERICAN REVIEW. 1952-. Quarterly. Editor: Dr. John J. LaCorte. Publisher: American Italian Historical Society, 111 Columbia Heights, Brooklyn, New York 11201.

Deals with the contributions of Italians in America and keeps readers informed of coming events in the Italian American community.

ITALIAN AMERICANA. 1974-. Biennial. Editors: Bruno Arcudi and Richard Gambino. Publisher: State University College at Buffalo, 1300 Elmwood Avenue, Buffalo, New York 14222.

ITALIAN QUARTERLY. 1957-. Quarterly. Editor: Carlo L. Golina. Publisher: University of California at Riverside, College of Letters and Sciences, University of California, Riverside, California 92502. In English.

Publishes articles on Italy and Italian culture, including literature, art, music, economics, education, and politics.

ITALICA. 1924-. Quarterly. Editor: Olga Ragusa. Publisher: American Association of Teachers of Italian, Department of Italian, Rutgers College, New Brunswick, New Jersey. In Italian and English.

Features articles promoting the study of Italian language and literature.

IL LEONE (The Lion). 1929-. Monthly. Editor: Phil Corauls. Publisher: Grand Lodge of California, Order of Sons of Italy in America, 5051 Mission Street, San Francisco, California 94112. In Italian.

A magazine providing general articles and fraternal news.

IL MESSAGGERO (The Messenger). 1921-. Monthly. Editor: Dr. J. B. Bisceglia. Publisher: National Religious Press, 544 Wabash, Kansas City, Missouri 64124. In Italian and English.

Publishes religious and educational material and articles of interest to Italian Americans in Kansas City.

IL MONDO LIBERO (The Free World). 1956-. Monthly. Editor: Dr. G. Oberdam Rizzo. Publisher: Free World International Academy, Incorporated, 2844 Syracuse Street, Dearborn, Michigan 48124. In Italian and English.

Features cultural articles on literature, science, and the arts, as well as poetry and news of current events.

THE NEW AURORA (The New Dawn). 1903-. Bimonthly. Editor: Anthony F. Vasquez. Publisher: Excelsior Press, 314 Richfield Road, Upper Darby, Pennsylvania 19082. In English and Italian.

Contains articles on religious topics of an international and informational nature for Italian Americans. Sponsored by the Association of Evangelicals for Italian Missions.

OSIA NEWS. 1946-. Monthly. Editor: Albert A. Maino. Publisher: Supreme Lodge of Order of Sons of Italy in America, 41 Austin Street, Worcester, Massachusetts 01609. In English.

UNICO MAGAZINE. 1948-. Monthly. Editor: Hugo Senerchia. Publisher: Unico National, 72 Burroughs Place, Bloomfield, New Jersey 07003.

UNIONE (Union). 1890-. Biweekly. Editor: Victor Frediani. Publisher: Frediani Publishing Company, 1719 Liberty Avenue, Pittsburgh, Pennsylvania 15222. In Italian.

A fraternal magazine sponsored by the Order of Italian Sons and Daughters of America.

Radio Programs

California - Inglewood

KTYM - 6803 West Boulevard, Inglewood, California 90302, (213) 678-3731. Italian programs, 3 hours weekly.

California - Los Gatos

KRVE (FM) - 227 North Santa Cruz Avenue, Los Gatos, California 95030, (408) 354-6622. Italian programs, 2 hours weekly.

California - Mount Shasta

KWSD (AM & FM) - Box 448, Mount Shasta, California 96067, (916) 926-2124. Italian programs, 1 hour weekly.

California - San Francisco

KEST - 1231 Market Street, San Francisco, California 94103, (415) 626-5585. Italian programs

KUSF (FM) - 2130 Fulton Street, San Francisco, California 94117, (415) 666-6206. Italian programs, 6 hours weekly.

California - Santa Barbara

KKIO - 1919 State Street, Santa Barbara, California 93101, (805) 963-5896. Italian programs, 1 hour weekly.

Colorado - Boulder

KGNU (FM) - Box 1076, Boulder, Colorado 80306, (303) 449-4885. Italian programs, 2 hours weekly.

Connecticut - Bristol

WBIS - 1021 Farmington Avenue, Bristol, Connecticut 06010, (203) 583-9265. Italian programs, 1 hour weekly.

Connecticut - Greenwich

WGCH - 1490 Dayton Avenue, Greenwich, Connecticut 06830, (203) 869-1490. Italian programs, 1 hour weekly.

Connecticut - Hartford

WCCC (FM) - 11 Asylum Street, Hartford, Connecticut 06103, (203) 549-3456. Italian programs, 1 hour weekly.

WRTC (FM) - Trinity College, Hartford, Connecticut 06106, (203) 527-0447. Italian programs, 3 hours weekly.

Connecticut - Middletown

WCNX - Box 359, River Road, Middletown, Connecticut 06457, (203) 347-2565. Italian programs, 1 hour weekly.

Connecticut - Monroe

WMNR (FM) - 1014 Monroe Turnpike, Monroe, Connecticut 06468, (203) 268-9667. Italian programs, 3 hours weekly.

Connecticut - Naugatuck

WNVR - Mallane Lane, Naugatuck, Connecticut 06770, (203) 729-2291. Italian programs, 1 hour weekly.

Connecticut - New Britain

WRYM - 1056 Willard Avenue, Newington, Connecticut 06111, (203) 666-5646. Italian programs, 25 hours weekly.

Connecticut - New London

WNLC - Box 1031, New London, Connecticut 06320, (203) 442-5328. Italian programs, 1 hour weekly.

Connecticut - Norwalk

WNLK - Box 1350, Norwalk, Connecticut 06852, (203) 838-5566. Italian programs, 1 hour weekly.

Connecticut - Southington

WNTY - 440 Old Turnpike Road, Southington, Connecticut 06489, (203) 628-0311. Italian programs, 5 hours weekly.

Connecticut - Stamford

WSTC - 117 Prospect Street, Stamford, Connecticut 06901, (203) 327-1400. Italian programs, 1 hour weekly.

Connecticut - Westport

WMMM - Box 511, Westport, Connecticut 06880, (203) 227-5133. Italian programs, 5 hours weekly.

Florida - Fort Lauderdale

WAVS - 2727 East Oakland Plaza, Fort Lauderdale, Florida 33306, (305) 561-1190. Italian programs, 3 hours weekly.

Florida - Largo

WSST - Box 800, Largo, Florida 33540, (813) 581- 9424. Italian programs, 1/2 hour weekly.

Florida - Tampa

WMNF (FM) - 305 South Boulevard, Tampa, Florida 33606, (813) 258-6791. Italian programs, 1 hour weekly.

Illinois - Chicago

WEDC - 5475 North Milwaukee Avenue, Chicago, Illinois 60630, (312) 631-0700. Italian programs, 4 hours weekly.

WSBC - 4949 West Belmont Avenue, Chicago, Illinois 60641, (312) 777-1700. Italian programs, 7 hours weekly.

WUIC (FM) - Box 4348, Chicago, Illinois 60680, (312) 996-2720. Italian programs, 1-1/2 hours weekly.

WLUW (FM) - 820 North Michigan Avenue, Chicago, Illinois 60611, (312) 670-2788. Italian programs, 3 hours weekly.

Illinois - Cicero

WCEV - 5356 West Belmont Avenue, Cicero, Illinois 60641, (312) 282-6700. Italian programs, 13-1/2 hours weekly.

Illinois - La Grange

WTAQ - 9355 West Joliet Road, La Grange, Illinois 60525, (312) 352-1300. Italian programs, 14 hours weekly.

Illinois - Oak Park

WOPA (AM & FM) - 408 South Oak Avenue, Oak Park, Illinois 60302, (312) 848-5760. Italian programs, 10 hours weekly.

Maryland - Baltimore

WITH - 5 Light Street, Baltimore, Maryland 21202, (301) 528-1230. Italian programs, 1 hour weekly.

Maryland - Bethesda

WHFS (FM) - 4853 Cordell Avenue, Bethesda, Maryland 20014, (301) 656-0600. Italian programs, 1 hour weekly.

Massachusetts - Brookline

WUNR (AM & FM) - 275 Tremont Street, Boston, Massachusetts 02116, (617) 357-8677. Italian programs, 15 hours weekly.

Massachusetts - Framingham

WKOX - 100 Mount Wayte Avenue, Framingham, Massachusetts 01701, (617) 879-2222. Italian programs, 1/2 hour weekly.

Massachusetts - Lynn

WLYN (FM) - Box 631, Lynn, Massachusetts 01903, (617) 595-6200. Italian programs, 18 hours weekly.

Massachusetts - Newton

WNTN - 143 Rumford Avenue, Newton, Massachusetts 02166, (617) 969-1550. Italian programs, 2 hours weekly.

Massachusetts - Pittsfield

WBEC - 211 Jason Street, Pittsfield, Massachusetts 01201, (413) 499-3333. Italian programs, 1 hour weekly.

Massachusetts - Worcester

WCUW (FM) - 910 Main Street, Worcester, Massachusetts 01610, (617) 753-1012. Italian programs, 1 hour weekly.

WNEB - 236 Worcester Center, Worcester, Massachusetts 01608, (617) 756-4672. Italian programs, 1 hour weekly.

Michigan - Garden City

WCAR - 32500 Park Lane, Garden City, Michigan 48135, (313) 525-1111. Italian programs, 5 hours weekly.

Missouri - Columbia

KOPN (FM) - 915 East Broadway, Columbia, Missouri 65201, (314) 874-1139. Italian programs, 1 hour weekly.

Missouri - Jackson

KJAS - Box 312, Jackson, Missouri 63755, (314) 243-8179. Italian programs, 1 hour weekly.

Missouri - Saint Louis

WEW - 1701 South Eighth Street, Saint Louis, Missouri 63104, (314) 436-7777. Italian programs, 1-1/2 hours weekly.

Nebraska - Omaha

KIOS (FM) - 3219 Cuming Street, Omaha, Nebraska 68131, (402) 556-2770. Italian programs, 1 hour weekly.

New Jersey - Elizabeth

WJDM - 9 Caldwell Place, Elizabeth, New Jersey 07201, (201) 965-1530. Italian programs, 2 hours weekly.

New Jersey - Hammonton

WRDI - 1168 5 White Horse Pike, Hammonton, New Jersey 08037, (609) 561-1900. Italian programs, 2-1/2 hours weekly.

New Jersey - Hazlet

WVRM (FM) - Airport Plaza, Highway 36, Hazlet, New Jersey 07730, (201) 739-1777. Italian programs, 1 hour weekly.

New Jersey - Long Branch

WWUU (FM) - 156 Broadway, Long Branch, New Jersey 07740, (201) 222-1071. Italian programs, 5 hours weekly.

New Jersey - New Brunswick

WRSU (FM) - 126 College Avenue, New Brunswick, New Jersey 08903, (201) 937-7800. Italian programs, 1 hour weekly.

New Jersey - South Orange

WSOU (FM) - 400 South Orange Avenue, South Orange, New Jersey 07079, (201) 762-8950. Italian programs, 1 hour weekly.

New Jersey - Trenton

WTTM - 333 West State Street, Trenton, New Jersey 08618, (609) 695-8515. Italian programs, 2 hours weekly.

New York - Amsterdam

WKOL - Box 3, Amsterdam, New York 12010, (518) 843-1570. Italian programs, 2 hours weekly.

WMVQ (FM) - 279 West Main Street, Amsterdam, New York 12010, (518) 842-0101. Italian programs, 2 hours weekly.

New York - Attica

WBTF (FM) - 35 Main Street, Attica, New York 14011, (716) 591-1490. Italian programs, 4 hours weekly.

New York - Auburn

WAUB - Box 160, Auburn, New York 13021, (315) 253-3040. Italian programs, 1-1/2 hours weekly.

New York - Babylon

WNYG - Rt. 109, Babylon, New York 11704, (516) 661-4000. Italian programs, 8 hours weekly.

New York - Baldwinsville

WBXL (FM) - East Oneida Street Complex, Baldwinsville, New York 13027, (315) 635-3949. Italian programs, 2 hours weekly.

WSEN (AM & FM) - Box 1050, Baldwinsville, New York 13027, (315) 635-3971. Italian programs, 2 hours weekly.

New York - Beacon

WBNR - 475 South Avenue, Beacon, New York 12508, (914) 831-1260. Italian programs, 1 hour weekly.

New York - Binghamton

WKOP - 32 West State Street, Binghamton, New York 13901, (607) 722-3437. Italian programs, 1 hour weekly.

New York - Cortland

WKRT (AM & FM) - Box 746, Cortland, New York 13045, (607) 756-2828. Italian programs, 1 hour weekly.

WNOZ (FM) - Box 746, Cortland, New York 13045, (607) 756-2828. Italian programs, 1 hour weekly.

New York - Ellenville

WELV (AM & FM) - 22 North Main Street, 309 Ellenville, New York 12428, (914) 626-0123. Italian programs, 1 hour weekly.

New York - Geneva

WECQ (FM) - Box 213, 609 West Washington Street, Geneva, New York 14456, (315) 789-1101. Italian programs, 1 hour weekly.

New York - Gloversville

WENT - North Harrison Street, Ext, Gloversville, New York 12078, (518) 725-7175. Italian programs, 2 hours weekly.

New York - Hampton Bays

WWHB (FM) - Box 751, Hampton Bays, New York 11946, (516) 728-9229. Italian programs, 1/2 hour weekly.

New York - Islip

WLIX - 138 West Main Street, Bayshore, New York 11706, (516) 666-2200. Italian programs, 4 hours weekly.

New York - Jamestown

WJTN - Box 1139, Jamestown, New York 14701, (716) 487-1151. Italian programs, 1 hour weekly.

New York - Kingston

WKNY - 212 Fair Street, Kingston, New York 12401, (914) 331-1490. Italian programs, 1 hour weekly.

New York - Lancaster

WXRL - 5360 William Street, Lancaster, New York 14086, (716) 684-4142. Italian programs, 1 hour weekly.

New York - Little Falls

WLFH - 341 South Second Street, Little Falls, New York 13365, (315) 823-1230. Italian programs, 1 hour weekly.

New York - New Rochelle

WVOX - One Broadcast Forum, New Rochelle, New York 10801, (914) 636-1460. Italian programs, 4 hours weekly.

New York - New York

WBNX - Box 1380, Carlstadt, New Jersey 07072, (212) 594-1380. Italian programs, 3-1/2 hours weekly.

WFUV (FM) - Fordham University, Bronx, New York 10458, (212) 933-2233. Italian programs, 1 hour weekly.

WPOW - 1111 Woodrow Road, Staten Island, New York 10312, (212) 984-4600. Italian programs, 5 hours weekly.

New York - Niagara Falls

WHLD - Box 398, Niagara Falls, New York 14302, (716) 265-3421. Italian programs, 6 hours weekly.

New York - North Syracuse

WSOQ - Box 20, North Syracuse, New York 13212, (315) 699-8200. Italian programs, 2 hours weekly.

New York - Oswego

WSGO (AM & FM) - 333 East Seneca Street, Oswego, New York 13126, (315) 343-1440. Italian programs, 2 hours weekly.

New York - Patchogue

WALK - Box 230, Patchogue, New York 11772, (516) 475-5200. Italian programs, 3 hours weekly.

New York - Poughkeepsie

WSPK (FM) - Box 1703, Poughkeepsie, New York 12601, (914) 462-5800. Italian programs, 1 hour weekly.

New York - Rochester

WMJQ (FM) - 850 Midtown Tower, Rochester, New York 14604, (716) 232-7550. Italian programs, 2 hours weekly.

WDKX (FM) - 1337 East Main Street, Rochester, New York 14609, (716) 288-5470. Italian programs, 1 hour weekly.

WPXN - 201 Humboldt Street, Broadcast Center, Rochester, New York 14610, (716) 288-0120. Italian programs, 2 hours weekly.

WVOR (FM) - 1225 Midtown Tower, Rochester, New York 40340, (716) 454-3942. Italian programs, 2 hours weekly.

New York - Schenectady

WWWD - 422 Liberty Street, Schenectady, New York 12305, (518) 393-3622. Italian programs, 1 hour weekly.

New York - Spring Valley

WGRC - 25 Church Street, Spring Valley, New York 10977, (914) 623-8500. Italian programs, 1 hour weekly.

New York - Stony Brook

WUSB (FM) - State University of New York, Stony Brook, New York 11794, (516) 246-7900. Italian programs, 1/2 hour weekly.

New York - Utica

WBVM - Box 1550, Utica, New York 13503, (315) 797-0803. Italian programs, 4 hours weekly.

New York - Watkins Glen

WGMF - 421 North Franklin Street, Watkins Glen, New York 14891, (607) 535-2779. Italian programs, 2 hours weekly.

Ohio - Akron

WAUP (FM) - 302 East Buchtel Avenue, Akron, Ohio 44325, (216) 375-7105. Italian programs, 2 hours weekly.

Ohio - Ashtabula

WFUN - Box 738, Ashtabula, Ohio 44004, (216) 993-2126. Italian programs, 2 hours weekly.

Ohio - Bellaire

WBHR (FM) - Board of Education of Bellaire City School District, 35th and Guernesey Street, Bellaire, Ohio 43906, (614) 676-9247. Italian programs, 1 hour weekly.

Ohio - Cleveland

WBOE (FM) - 10600 Quincy Avenue, Cleveland, Ohio 44106, (216) 421-7373. Italian programs, 1 hour weekly.

WZAK (FM) - 1303 Prospect Avenue, Cleveland, Ohio 44115, (216) 621-9300. Italian programs, 7 hours weekly.

Ohio - Niles

WNIO - Box 625, Niles, Ohio 44446, (216) 545-4024. Italian programs, 2 hours weekly.

Ohio - Steubenville

WLIT - Box 1798, Steubenville, Ohio 43952, (614) 264-7771. Italian programs, 2 hours weekly.

Ohio - Struthers

WKTL (FM) - 111 Euclid Avenue, Struthers High School, Struthers, Ohio 44471, (216) 755-1435. Italian programs, 1 hour weekly.

Ohio - Uhrichsville

WBTC - 2305 North Water Street, Ext., Uhrichsville, Ohio 44683, (614) 922-2700. Italian programs, 1 hour weekly.

Ohio - Warren

WTCL - 1295 Lane West Road, Southwest, Warren, Ohio 44481, (216) 373-1570. Italian programs, 2 hours weekly.

Ohio - Willoughby

WELW - 36913 Stevens Boulevard, Willoughby, Ohio 44094, (216) 946-1330. Italian programs, 1/2 hour weekly.

Ohio - Youngstown

WBBW (AM & FM) - 418 Knox, Youngstown, Ohio 44502, (216) 744-4421. Italian programs, 1 hour weekly.

Pennsylvania - Altoona

WVAM - 2727 West Albert Drive, Altoona, Pennsylvania 16602, (814) 944-9456. Italian programs, 1 hour weekly.

Pennsylvania - Ambridge

WMBA - 304 Duss Avenue, Ambridge, Pennsylvania 15003, (412) 266-1110. Italian programs, 1 hour weekly.

Pennsylvania - Chester

WDNR (FM) - 1000 Widener University, Chester, Pennsylvania 19013, (215) 499-4437. Italian programs, 1 hour weekly.

WQIQ - 12 Kent Road, Ashton, Pennsylvania 19014, (215) 874-4321. Italian programs, 1 hour weekly.

Pennsylvania - Ebensburg

WEND - 102 South Center Street, Ebensburg, Pennsylvania 15931, (814) 472-8801. Italian programs, 1 hour weekly.

Pennsylvania - Erie

WERG (FM) - Box 236, Gannon University, Erie, Pennsylvania 16541, (814) 871-7325. Italian programs, 3 hours weekly.

WQLN (FM) - Box 10, Erie, Pennsylvania 16512, (814) 868-4654. Italian programs, 2 hours weekly.

Pennsylvania - Jeanette

WBCW - 111 South Fourth Street, Jeanette, Pennsylvania 15644, (412) 527-5656. Italian programs, 1 hour weekly.

Pennsylvania - Jenkintown

WIBF (FM) - The Benson East, Jenkintown, Pennsylvania 19046, (215) 886-2000. Italian programs, 15 hours weekly.

Pennsylvania - Loretto

WAMQ - Box 103, Loretto, Pennsylvania 15940, (814) 472-8700. Italian programs, 1 hour weekly.

Pennsylvania - McKeesport

WEDO - 414 Fifth Avenue, Midtown Plaza Mall, McKeesport, Pennsylvania 15132, (412) 462-9922. Italian programs, 1 hour weekly.

Pennsylvania - New Kensington

WKPA - 810 Fifth Avenue, New Kensington, Pennsylvania 15068, (412) 337-3588. Italian programs, 1-1/2 hours weekly.

Pennsylvania - Philadelphia

WRCP - 2043 Locust Street, Philadelphia, Pennsylvania 19103, (215) 564-2300. Italian programs, 1 hour weekly.

WTEL - 4140 Old York Road, Philadelphia, Pennsylvania 19140, (215) 455-9200. Italian programs, 7 hours weekly.

Pennsylvania - Pittsburgh

WDUQ (FM) - Pittsburgh, Pennsylvania 15219, (412) 434-6030. Italian programs, 1 hour weekly.

WPIT - 200 Gateway Towers, Pittsburgh, Pennsylvania 15222, (412) 281-1900. Italian programs, 1 hour weekly.

WYEP (FM) - 4 Cable Place, Pittsburgh, Pennsylvania 15213, (412) 687-0200. Italian programs, 1 hour weekly.

Pennsylvania - Pittston

WARD - Box 1540, Pittston, Pennsylvania 18640, (717) 655-5521. Italian programs, 1 hour weekly.

Pennsylvania - Red Lion

WGCB - Box 88, Red Lion, Pennsylvania 17356, (717) 244-5360. Italian programs, 1 hour weekly.

Rhode Island - Pawtucket

WGNG - 100 John Street, Cumberland, Rhode Island 02864, (401) 725-9000. Italian programs, 2 hours weekly.

Rhode Island - Providence

WRIB - Providence, Rhode Island, (401) 434-0406. Italian programs, 5 hours weekly.

Texas - Dallas

KNON (FM) - 4415 San Jacinto, Dallas, Texas 75204, (214) 823-7490. Italian programs, 1 hour weekly.

Vermont - Rutland

WHWB - Box 518, West Proctor Road, Rutland, Vermont 05701, (802) 773-3315. Italian programs, 1 hour weekly.

Washington - Blaine

KARI - Box X, Blaine, Washington 98230, (206) 332-5500. Italian programs, 2 hours weekly.

West Virginia - Fairmont

WTCS - Box 1549, Fairmont, West Virginia 26554, (304) 366-3700. Italian programs, 3 hours weekly.

West Virginia - Weirton

WEIR - 3578 Penn Avenue, Weirton, West Virginia 26062, (304) 723-1430. Italian programs, 1 hour weekly.

Wisconsin - Kenosha

WLIP - Box 659, Kenosha, Wisconsin 53141, (414) 657-6162. Italian programs, 2 hours weekly.

Wisconsin - Milwaukee

WEMP - 11800 West Grange Avenue, Hales Corners, Milwaukee, Wisconsin 53130, (414) 529-1250. Italian programs, 1 hour weekly.

Television Programs

California - Sacramento

KMUV-TV - Box B, 500 Media Place, Sacramento, California 95813, (916) 929-0300. Italian: unspecified.

California - San Francisco

KEMO-TV - 2500 Marin Street, San Francisco, California 94124, (415) 285-6420. Italian: unspecified.

KTSF-TV - 185 Berry Street, San Francisco, California 94107, (415) 495-4995. Italian: unspecified.

Florida - Fort Lauderdale

WKID - 2090 Southwest 30th Avenue, Pembroke Park, Florida 33009, (305) 454-5100. Italian: no time specified.

Illinois - Chicago

WCIU-TV - Board of Trade Building, Chicago, Illinois 60604, (312) 663-0260. Italian: unspecified.

Massachusetts - Boston

WQTV - 390 Commonwealth Avenue, Boston, Massachusetts 02215, (617) 267-1530. Italian: unspecified.

Michigan - Windsor, Ontario - Detroit

CBET - 825 Riverside Drive West, Windsor, Ontario N9A 5K9, (519) 254-2831. Italian: 1 hour a week.

New York - New York-Newark, New Jersey

WNJU-TV - Symphony Hall, 1020 Broad Street, Newark, New Jersey 07102, (201) 643-9100. Italian: unspecified.

New York - New York

WNYE-TV - 112 Tillary Street, Brooklyn, New York 11201, (212) 596-4425. Italian: unspecified.

Bank Branches in the U.S.

BANCA COMMERCIALE ITALIANA S.p.A.

Chicago Branch:
115 South La Salle Street
Chicago, Illinois 60603 (312) 346-1112

Los Angeles Branch:
555 South Flower Street
Los Angeles, California 90071 (213) 624-0440

New York Branch:
280 Park Avenue
New York, New York 10017 (212) 661-8500

BANCA NAZIONALE DEL LAVORO

Los Angeles Branch:
707 Wilshire Boulevard
Suite 4950
Los Angeles, California

New York Branch:
25 West 51st Street
New York, New York 10019 (212) 581-0710

BANCA NAZIONALE DELL' AGRICOLTURA

New York Branch:
100 Wall Street
New York, New York 10005 (212) 269-8740

BANCA POPOLARE DI MILANO
153 East 53rd Street
New York, New York 10022 (212) 758-5040

BANCA POPOLARE DI NOVARA
430 Park Avenue
New York, New York 10022 (212) 755-1300

BANCO DI NAPOLI

New York Branch:
277 Park Avenue
New York, New York 10017 (212) 644-8400

BANCO DI ROMA

Chicago Branch:
230 West Monroe
Chicago, Illinois 60606 (312) 368-8855

Los Angeles Branch:
400 Montgomery Street
San Francisco, California 94104 (415) 398-6500

New York Branch:
100 Wall Street
New York, New York 10005 (212) 952-9300

BANCO DI SICILIA
250 Park Avenue
New York, New York 10177 (212) 599-6200

CREDITO ITALIANO, S.A.

Los Angeles Agency:
707 Wilshire Boulevard
Los Angeles, California 90017

New York Branch:
375 Park Avenue
New York, New York 10152 (212) 546-9600

Commercial and Trade Organizations

AMERICAN CHAMBER OF COMMERCE IN ITALY - MILAN
Main Office
Via Agnello 12
I-20121 Milan, Italy
General Secretary: Herman H. Burdick
Founded 1915

Promotes development of trade between the United States and Italy. Disseminates information; examines questions pertaining to commercial and industrial relations; sponsors seminars and workshops. Maintains research library.
Publications: Italian American Business, monthly; Newsletter, monthly; Membership Directory, annual.

ITALIAN CHAMBER OF COMMERCE
327 South La Salle
Chicago, Illinois 60604
Executive Director: Leonora LiPluma Turner
(312) 427-3014
Founded 1907

Promotes trade between Italy and the United States and aids Italian organizations.
Publication: Bulletin, bimonthly.

ITALIAN TRADE COMMISSION
499 Park Avenue
New York, New York 10048
Trade Commissioner: Lucio Caputo (212) 980-1500

Promotes imports of Italian products. Programs include Italian Wine Promotion Center, Italian Tile Center and Italian Leathergoods Promotion Center.

ITALO-AMERICAN TRADE CENTER
21 West 86th Street
New York, New York 10024 (212) 595-3330

ITALY-AMERICA CHAMBER OF COMMERCE
350 Fifth Avenue
New York, New York 10001
Executive Secretary: Arthur A. De Santis
(212) 279-5520
Founded 1887

Publications: Trade With Italy, bimonthly; Directory, biennial.

Festivals, Fairs, and Celebrations

California - San Francisco

COLUMBUS DAY CELEBRATION
Telegraph Hill, Ghirardelli Square
Aquatic Park, Washington Square
San Francisco, California

After a solemn high mass, a procession of the Madonna del Lume proceeds to Fisherman's Wharf for fleet blessing ceremonies. A bazaar, the crowning of "Queen Isabella," followed by a "You are There" interview with the Queen and her Court; a civil ceremony at Columbus' statue, aquatic pageant, and Columbus Day Banquet and Coronation Ball add to the festivities. Other activities include softball, bocce ball, and soccer matches, a children's art contest, carnival with

fun rides, and a grand Columbus Day parade with jugglers, jesters, actors, acrobats, swordsmen, "surprise guests", puppeteers, a calliope, bands, baton twirlers, drill corps, equestrian and antique autos. Held annually in mid-October.
Contact: San Francisco Convention and Visitors Bureau, 1390 Market Street, San Francisco, California 94102. (415) 626-5500.

Delaware - Wilmington

ITALIAN FESTIVAL
Saint Anthony's High School
Wilmington, Delaware

Celebrates the Italian heritage of the community with traditional foods, music and sports events. Held in June.
Contact: Father Roberto Balducelli, Saint Anthony's High School, Ninth and Scott Streets, Wilmington, Delaware 19805.

Illinois - Chicago

OUR LADY OF MOUNT CARMEL FEAST
Lake Street and North Avenue
Melrose Park, Illinois

A religious celebration which has been held annually since 1894. A field mass is followed by a three mile procession and then there is a festival featuring Italian food and games, handicrafts, and folklore.
Contact: Our Lady of Mount Carmel Rectory, 1101 North 23rd Avenue, Melrose Park, Illinois 60160.

Indiana - Clinton

LITTLE ITALY FESTIVAL
Clinton, Indiana

Folk dancing, strolling musicians, Italian singers and Italian foods await visitors to Indiana's Little Italy Town. The festival set up along the Wabash River also includes traditional grape stomping, a puppet show and gondola rides as well as costume and "Moustache" contests, spaghetti and pizza eating contests, a tour of the coal mines, a celebrity auction, wine tasting and the state bocce ball championships. Held in late August or early September.
Contact: Publicity Chairman, Little Italy Festival, 849 North Street, Clinton, Indiana 47842.

Indiana - Merrillville

ITALIAN FESTIVAL
Michelangelo Picnic Grounds
Merrillville, Indiana

Gourmet Italian food as well as pizza and more familiar Italian specialities are at the center of this community festival. There are also Italian folk dancing groups, carnival ridges, games and other entertainment. Held in June.
Contact: Merrillville Chamber of Commerce, Merrillville, Indiana 46410.

Louisiana - Independence

LITTLE ITALY FESTIVAL
Catholic School Grounds
Independence, Louisiana

Italian music, food and refreshments, parade, dancing exhibitions, and street dancing are featured in this community celebration. Held in late April.
Contact: John M. Masaracchia, Post Office Box 826, Independence, Louisiana 70443.

Massachusetts - Boston

FEAST OF SAINT JOSEPH
North End
Boston, Massachusetts

A colorful religious festival featuring food and wine stands, Italian music and entertainment. Held in late July.
Contact: Little Italy City Hall, 20 Parmenter Street, Boston, Massachusetts 02113. (617) 742-9547.

FEAST OF THE FISHERMAN
Madonna del Saccorso
North End
Boston, Massachusetts

A street festival of religious significance. Booths offer Italian specialties such as fresh seafood, pastries, wine and main dishes. Chances are sold for a trip to Italy. The music is provided by an Italian band and singers. Held in mid-August.
Contact: Little Italy City Hall, 20 Parmenter Street, Boston, Massachusetts 02113. (617) 742-9547.

Massachusetts - Sagamore

ITALIAN FIESTA
Keith Memorial Field
Sagamore, Massachusetts

Games and contests are included in the events celebrating the town's Italian heritage. Held annually for 2 days in early September.
Contact: Massachusetts Department of Commerce and Development, Division of Tourism, Box 1775, Boston, Massachusetts 02105.

Michigan - Charlevoix

CHARLEVOIX VENETIAN FESTIVAL
Charlevoix, Michigan

As in Venice there is a yacht parade which takes place on Round Lake. There is also a street parade and a carnival. Special attractions include a Venetian foot race, a queen contest, water hose fight, greased pole climb, various sports events, exhibitions by gymnastics groups, singers and dancers. All types of Italian food are sold. The festival began in 1931 and is held annually at the end of July.
Contact: Charlevoix Chamber of Commerce, Charlevoix, Michigan 49720.

Missouri - Kansas City

ITALIAN FESTIVAL
Crown Center Square
Kansas City, Missouri

This old world festival features food, music, dance, and entertainment in the Italian atmosphere. Held for three days in mid-August.
Contact: Convention and Visitors Bureau of Greater Kansas City, 1221 Baltimore, Kansas City, Missouri 64105.

Missouri - Saint Louis

HILL DAY
Saint Ambrose Church
Saint Louis, Missouri

An ethnic celebration honoring Saint Louisians of Italian ancestry in the city's "Hill" region. Features street dancing, arts, crafts, Italian food, and a grape stomping contest. Held in mid-August.
Contact: Convention and Visitors Bureau of Greater Saint Louis, 500 Broadway Building, Saint Louis, Missouri 63102. (314) 421-1023.

New Jersey - Holmdel

ITALIAN FESTIVAL
Garden State Arts Center
Holmdel, New Jersey

A colorful morning program includes Piazza Stati d'Giardino, a typical Italian street scene complete with cafe expresso, Italian pastries, tortoni and spumoni, music, and the gay Tarantella. Italian-American arts and crafts are exhibited and sold. An afternoon stage program features stars of the stage, screen, television, and Metropolitan Opera. A fashion show by Italian American designers, choral music, and a talent show of teenagers are also presented. Held annually since 1971 in late June.
Contact: Italian Festival, New Jersey Highway Authority, Garden State Parkway, Woodbridge, New Jersey 07095. (201) 442- 8600.

New York - Lewistown

ARTPARK ITALIAN FESTIVAL
Artpark
Lewistown, New York

Bocce and pignata are featured along with Italian food and an evening entertainment.
Contact: Artpark Italian Festival, Lewistown Chamber of Commerce, Lewistown, New York 14092.

New York - New York

COLUMBUS DAY PARADE
Fifth Avenue
New York, New York

The parade honors the Italian who discovered America by emphasizing the many aspects of Italian contributions to the country. Held in October.
Contact: New York Convention Center and Visitors Bureau, 90 East 42nd Street, New York, New York 10017. (212) 687-1300.

FESTIVAL OF SAINT ANTHONY
Sullivan Street
Little Italy
New York, New York

A street festival lasting ten days during June. The visitor can eat his way through meat, fish and seafood specialities, pastries and confections, buy handicrafts and religious objects, dance and sing or listen to music.
Contact: New York Convention Center and Visitors Bureau, 90 East 42nd Street, New York, New York 10017. (212) 687-1300.

FEAST OF SAN GENARRO
Mulberry Street
Little Italy
New York, New York

The streets are decorated with lights and lined with booths selling souvenirs and southern Italian (especially Neopolitan) food. Italian singers aboard floats serenade the spectators. Both Italian and American music is played during the festival. The statue of San Genarro is carried in procession. Started in 1925. Held annually for ten days in September. Contact: New York Convention and Visitors Bureau, Incorporated, 90 East 42nd Street, New York, New York 10017.

Oklahoma - McAlester

ITALIAN FESTIVAL
McAlester, Oklahoma

The rich cultural heritage brought by Italian coal miners in the 1880's is carefully preserved by their descendants. The festival features authentic Italian folk music, dances, and colorful native costumes. Delicious ethnic culinary specialties are served. Held in late September.
Contact: Chamber of Commerce, Post Office Box 759, McAlester, Oklahoma 74501. (918) 423-2550.

West Virginia - Clarksburg

ITALIAN HERITAGE FESTIVAL
Clarksburg, West Virginia

Held at the end of the summer. Features Italian food and music, traditional handcrafts and games.
Contact: Clarksburg Chamber of Commerce, Clarksburg, West Virginia 26301.

Airline Offices

ALITALIA
North American Headquarters:
666 Fifth Avenue
New York, New York 10019 (212) 262-4422

Serves worldwide routes extending from Italy across the North Atlantic to eight North American cities; across the South Atlantic to seven South American countries; to Japan and Australia via Russia and the major capitals of South Asia; to Middle East countries; to East and South Africa; and to virtually every European country. Other offices in the United States: Atlanta, Boston, Buffalo, Camillus (New York), Chicago, Cincinnati, Cleveland, Crawfordsville (Indiana), Dallas, Denver, Detroit, East Meadow (New York), Hartford, Houston, Los Angeles, Metaire (Louisiana), Miami, Milwaukee, Minneapolis, Newark, Philadelphia, Pittsburgh, Saint Louis, San Diego, San Francisco, Seattle, Tampa, Tulsa, and Washington.

ITAVIA (Aerolinee Itavia, S.p.A.)
United States Headquarters:
437 Madison Avenue
New York, New York 10022 (212) 466-1557

Provides domestic services within Italy and international scheduled and charter services to Europe and the Mediterranean.

Ship Lines

COSTA LINE, INCORPORATED

1 Biscayne Tower
Miami, Florida 33131 (305) 358-7395

733 Third Avenue
New York, New York 10017 (212) 682-3505

Cargo Services:
26 Broadway
New York, New York 10004 (212) 480-8282

530 West Sixth Street, Suite 1208
Los Angeles, California 90014 (213) 627-4015

Departs from Miami, Florida, for short cruises to Nassau and Freeport. Sails from Port Everglades, Florida, for Caribbean and South America ports.

ITALIAN LINE
1 Whitehall Street
New York, New York 10004 (212) 344-5657

Cruise ships depart from Port Everglades, Florida, and from New York City for the Mediterranean or Caribbean Seas.

Bookdealers and Publishers' Representatives

ADLER'S FOREIGN BOOKS, INCORPORATED
162 Fifth Avenue
New York, New York 10010 (212) 691-5151

THE AMERICAN CLASSICAL COLLEGE PRESS
Post Office Box 4526
Albuquerque, New Mexico

ANGELESCU BOOK SERVICE
1800 Fairfield
Detroit, Michigan 48221 (313) 861-5342

CAVALLI-ITALIAN BOOKSTORE
1441 Stockton Street
San Francisco, California 94133 (415) 421-4219

ALLAN ELSNER'S BOOKSHOP
900 First Avenue
New York, New York 10022 (212) 688-4577

EUROPEAN PUBLISHERS REPRESENTATIVES
11-03 46th Avenue
Long Island City, New York
11101 (212) 937-4606

LA GALERIA DE LOS ARTESANOS, ON THE PLAZA
Box 1657
Las Vegas, New Mexico 87701 (505) 425-8331

IACONI BOOK IMPORTS
300 Pennsylvania Avenue
San Francisco, California 94107 (415) 285-7393

INSTITUTE OF MODERN LANGUAGES BOOKSTORE
2125 S Street, Northwest
Washington, D.C. 20009 (202) 565-2580

R. E. LEWIS, INCORPORATED
Post Office Box 1108
San Rafael, California 94902 (415) 461-4161

LIBRERIA DEL MAESTRO
522 Columbus Avenue
San Francisco, California 94133 (415) 392-5800

MIDDLEBURY COLLEGE STORE
5 Hillcrest Road
Middlebury, Vermont 05753 (802) 388-7722

REGENCY BOOK SERVICE
Post Office Box 84
Boston, Massachusetts 02101

RIZZOLI INTERNATIONAL BOOKSTORE
712 Fifth Avenue
New York, New York 10019 (212) 397-3740

SCHOENHOF'S FOREIGN BOOKS, INCORPORATED
1280 Massachusetts Avenue
Cambridge, Massachusetts 02138 (617) 547-8855

F.A.O. SCHWARZ
745 Fifth Avenue
New York, New York 10022 (212) 644-9400

SHERMAN'S
332 Park Avenue
Baltimore, Maryland 21201 (301) 837-3363

SKY BOOKS INTERNATIONAL, INCORPORATED
48 East 50th Street
New York, New York 10022 (212) 688-5086

SPEEDIMPEX USA, INCORPORATED
23-16 40th Avenue
Long Island City, New York
11101 (212) 786-4706

TEC-BOOKS LIMITED (Librairie De Documentation Technique SA)
41 William
Pittsburgh, Pennsylvania 12901 (518) 561-0005

U. S. GAMES SYSTEMS, INCORPORATED
38 East 32nd Street
New York, New York 10016 (212) 685-4300

UNIVERSAL BOOKSTORE
5458 North Fifth Street
Philadelphia, Pennsylvania 19120 (215) LI9-2897

S. F. VANNI PUBLISHERS & BOOKSELLERS
30 West 12th Street
New York, New York 10011 (212) 675-6336

YALE COOPERATIVE CORPORATION
77 Broadway
New Haven, Connecticut 06520 (203) 772-0670

Books and Pamphlets

ARCHAEOLOGY. New York, Italian Cultural Institute.

A booklet about archaeological treasures of Italy.

BIOGRAPHIES. New York, Italian Cultural Institute.

Contains biographical sketches of eminent Italians.

BOOKS TRANSLATED FROM THE ITALIAN AND BOOKS OF ITALIAN INTEREST PUBLISHED IN THE UNITED STATES OF AMERICA. New York, Italian Cultural Institute.

A series of bibliographies issued by the Italian Cultural Institute, the cultural agency of the Italian Ministry of Foreign Affairs. (Also known as the Istituto Italiano di Cultura.) The bibliographies cover books published from 1959 to 1965; in 1966 and 1967; in 1968 and 1969; in 1970 and 1971; in 1972 and 1973.

ECONOMICS. New York, Italian Cultural Institute.

Discusses Italy's economic situation.

FOR STUDENTS AND TRAVELERS. New York, Italian Cultural Institute.

Describes places of interest to travelers and others interested in learning about Italy.

GENERAL INFORMATION FOR TRAVELERS TO ITALY. New York, Italian Government Travel Office, 1981.

An abundance of information from official regulations to the location of flea markets, accommodations in various cities, camping, university courses for foreigners, sports and cultural events, travel within the country by air, rail, steamer, car and bus.

GOVERNMENT AND POLITICS. New York, Italian Cultural Institute.

Discusses the political situation in Italy and the form of government.

HISTORY. New York, Italian Cultural Institute.

Tells about the history of Italy under fascist domination, after World War II, and during the modern era.

HOW TO FIND OUT ABOUT ITALY. By Franklin S. Stych. Oxford, New York, Pergamon Press, 1970.

Indicates the sources of information on the life and the culture of Italy, not only printed materials but also libraries, archives, societies and institutions. Arrangement is based on the Dewey Decimal Classification.

ITALIAN IMMIGRANTS ABROAD: A BIBLIOGRAPHY ON THE ITALIAN EXPERIENCE OUTSIDE ITALY IN EUROPE, THE AMERICAS, AUSTRALIA, AND AFRICA. By Vittorio Briani. Detroit, B. Ethridge Books, 1979.

Listing of sources on the study of Italian emigration to various parts of the world. Some entries are annotated. First half of the book contains English books and the rest of the book is in Italian.

ITALY. New York, Italian Cultural Institute.

A booklet about the land and people of Italy and their way of life.

ITALY. By Piero Buscaroli. Rome, ENIF, Italian State Tourist Department, 1978.

A booklet with many colored illustrations showing the scenic beauties of the country in all four seasons, describing art and archeological treasures, festivals and folklore and giving information on shopping, camping, holiday villages, spas, gastronomy and transportation. Includes a map.

STUDIES ON ITALY, 1943-1975; Select Bibliography of American and British Materials in Political Science, Economics, Sociology, and Anthropology. By Peter Lange. Torino, Fondazione Giovanni Angelli, 1977.

Listing of books, articles, data and research studies carried out on subjects concerning Italy. Divided into three sections: political, sociology and cultural anthropology, and economics.

ITALIAN AMERICANS

THE AMERICAN ITALIANS: THEIR HISTORY AND CULTURE. By Andrew F. Rolle. Belmont, California, Wadsworth Publishing Company, 1972.

A readable account with bibliographies.

AMERICANS BY CHOICE. By Angelo M. Pellegrini. New York, Macmillan Company, 1956.

Presents sketches of six Italian Americans: a peasant mother, a winegrower, a bootlegger, a mother of winegrowers, a roving parasite, and a ditchdigger. Tells about their backgrounds, life styles, and adventures.

THE ASSIMILATION OF ETHNIC GROUPS: THE ITALIAN CASE. By James A. Crispino. Staten Island, New York, Center for Migration Studies, 1980.

A study of Italian Americans in Bridgeport, Connecticut, and its suburbs, in which the author investigated the seven types of assimilation. Deals primarily with third generation Italians.

ASSIMILATION OF THE ITALIAN IMMIGRANT. New York, Arno Press, 1975. (The Italian American Experience).

Contains reprint of two publications: Guide for the Immigrant Italian in the United States of America and The Italians: A Study of the Countrymen of Columbus, Dante and Michelangelo.

BLOOD OF MY BLOOD; The Dilemma of the Italian-Americans. By Richard Gambino. Garden City, New York, Doubleday and Company, 1974.

A personal view combined with written records interprets the story of Italian immigrants in America. Discusses family ties, reasons for leaving Italy, living and working conditions in the United States, customs, attitudes, religion, education, and assimilation.

BOYS IN LITTLE ITALY: A COMPARISON OF THEIR INDIVIDUAL VALUE ORIENTATIONS, FAMILY PATTERNS, AND PEER GROUP ASSOCIATIONS. By Albert S. Alissi. San Francisco, R and E Research Associates, 1978.

A study that demonstrates the existence of subsystems within an Italian-American neighborhood and a comparison of delinquent boys with other groups of neighborhood boys.

THE BUSINESS OF CRIME: ITALIANS AND SYNDICATE CRIME IN THE UNITED STATES. By Humbert S. Nelli. New York, Oxford University Press, 1976.

A history of Italians in American crime during the period from the murder of the Police Chief in New Orleans in 1890 to 1941.

THE CHILDREN OF COLUMBUS; An Informal History of the Italians in the New World. By Erik Amfitheatrof. Boston, Little, Brown and Company, 1973.

Part One, The Crucible, discusses the part played by Italian explorers in America, upheavals in Italy, political exiles, and Italian participation in the American Civil War. Part Two, The Great Migration, deals with Italian immigration from 1870 to the 1970's, describing reasons for immigration, living conditions in the United States, labor troubles, crime, achievements, and the present status of Italian Americans.

DAGO RED. By John Fante. New York, Viking Press, 1940.

A collection of short stories about young people growing up in the mixed Italian-American tradition in a small town near Denver.

A DOCUMENTARY HISTORY OF THE ITALIAN AMERICANS. Edited by Wayne Moquin with Charles Van Doren. New York, Praeger Publishers, 1974.

Conveys the diversity of Italian American life through selected readings from newspapers, magazines, letters, parish and organization papers. Arranged under the following topics: The Italian Presence in the New World, 1492-1850; Immigration and Patterns of Settlement, 1850-1929; Making a Living, 1890-1930; The Quasi-Public Utility: Organized Crime and the Italian American, 1890-1973; The Controversy over

Italian Immigration: Violence and Polemic, 1890-1924; Emergency of the Italian American.

ETHNIC ALIENATION: THE ITALIAN-AMERICANS. By Patrick J. Gallo. Rutherford, New Jersey, Fairleigh Dickinson University Press, 1974.

A sociological study based on interviews with Italian Americans in Patterson, New Jersey, and Brooklyn, New York, compared with a control group of Episcopalians in New Jersey. Analyzes community and family life of three generations of Italian Americans, touching on urbanization, assimilation, religion, class, structure, political activities, the economic situation, and the political and social alienation felt by Americans of Italian descent.

ETHNIC AND POLITICAL ATTITUDES: A DEPTH STUDY OF ITALIAN AMERICANS. By Michael Parenti. New York, Arno Press, 1975.

A group of 18 Italian-American males were interviewed to explore the ways in which ethnic attitudes and experiences influence and interact with political opinions and values.

FAMILY AND COMMUNITY: ITALIAN IMMIGRANTS IN BUFFALO, 1880-1930. By Virginia Yans-McLaughlin. Ithaca, Cornell University Press, 1977.

Story of Italian immigrant families and how they affected cities to which they migrated. Also considers what happens to the family's internal and external relationships.

FOUR CENTURIES OF ITALIAN AMERICAN HISTORY. 5th edition. Revised edition. By Giovanni E. Schiavo. New York, Vigo Press, 1958.

A standard work on the Italian Americans.

THE GOLDEN DOOR: ITALIAN AND JEWISH IMMIGRANT MOBILITY IN NEW YORK CITY, 1880-1915. By Thomas Kessner. New York, Oxford University Press, 1977.

This book analyzes how well the Jews and Italians survived and established upward mobility in New York during their first 35 years there.

HALF BITTER, HALF SWEET; An Excursion into Italian-American History. By Alexander DeConde. New York, Charles Schribner's Sons, 1971.

A standard work which recounts and analyzes the relationships between Italy and the United States over more than two centuries and discusses the conditions in Italy leading to migration and the experiences of Italian immigrants in America in finding work and housing, taking part in politics and war and being assimilated. Includes a descriptive bibliography.

THE IMMIGRANT UPRAISED; Italian Adventurers and Colonists in an Expanding America. By Andrew F. Rolle. Norman, Oklahoma, University of Oklahoma Press, 1968.

Offers a new interpretation of the Italian immigrant experience by showing how Italians who migrated to the American West suffered little discrimination, were readily assimilated, and were upraised to wealth and power.

IMMIGRANTS AND UNIONS, A CASE STUDY, ITALIANS AND AMERICAN LABOR, 1870-1920. By Edwin Fenton. New York, Arno Press, 1975.

A study of the southern Italian, rural immigrant and his presence in the labor movement and the effect that he had on it. Also discusses the various occupations that Italians held. Includes appendix, critical essay on authorities and a bibliography.

IMMIGRANT'S RETURN. By Angelo M. Pellegrini. New York, MacMillan, 1953.

An autobiographical narrative of the author's return to Italy.

THE IMMIGRANTS SPEAK: ITALIAN AMERICANS TELL THEIR STORY. By Salvatore LaGumina. New York, Center for Migration Studies, 1979.

Personal histories of various Italian Americans who have a wide range of occupations from the miner to the lawyer.

INTERNATIONAL CONFLICT IN AN AMERICAN CITY: BOSTON'S IRISH, ITALIANS, AND JEWS, 1935-1944. By John F. Stack, Jr., Westport, Connecticut, Greenwood Press, 1979.

A study of the Irish, Italians, and Jews of Boston as they reacted to various events or issues of the 30's and 40's.

ITALIAN-AMERICAN AUTHORS AND THEIR CONTRIBUTION TO AMERICAN LITERATURE. By Olga Peragallo. New York, S.F. Vanni, 1949.

An annotated bibliography listing Italian-American authors who wrote in English and contributed to American literature. Arranged alphabetically, each entry contains the following information: biography, bibliography, comments and sources.

ITALIAN AMERICAN BUSINESS - ANNUAL DIRECTORY ISSUE. Edited by Gabriella Gabet. Milan, American Chamber of Commerce in Italy, 1982.

Italian and American businesses interested in developing trade and investment within and between the two countries. Entries include name of Italian company, address, phone, cable address, telex, names and titles of key personnel, a coded product/service list, names of American companies represented, name of American parent company. A second section lists American firms represented in Italy, giving company name and location, products, Italian firm and address, coded to indicate relationship (subsidiary, affiliate). Frequency: Annual, October.

THE ITALIAN-AMERICAN CHILD, HIS SOCIOLINGUISTIC ACCULTURATION. By Lawrence Biondi. Washington, Georgetown University Press, 1975.

The author's study examines the process of language development in monolingual and bilingual Italian-American children in Boston's North End.

THE ITALIAN AMERICAN COMMUNITY, 1875-1960: A SELECTED BIBLIOGRAPHY. By Susan Limper. Monticello, Illinois, Council of Planning Librarians, 1977.

A short listing of dissertations, periodical articles, books and bibliographies on Italian Americans.

THE ITALIAN-AMERICAN EXPERIENCE. Edited by Francesco Cordasco. 39 vols. New York, Arno Press/New York Times, 1975.

A source collection of the literature and archives of the Italian American past. Included are materials of Italian emigration; recollections and reminiscences; polemics in behalf of and opposed to the migration; tracts, texts, and settlement house literature which sought to solve the "Italian problem"; Italian American novels; observations and reform recommendations of Italian immigrants; and unpublished doctoral dissertations. Included are original anthologies: ASSIMILATION OF THE ITALIAN IMMIGRANT; ITALIANS IN THE CITY: HEALTH AND RELATED NEEDS; ITALIANS IN THE UNITED STATES: A REPOSITORY OF RARE TRACTS AND MISCELLANEA; and PROTESTANT EVANGELISM AMONG ITALIANS IN AMERICA.

THE ITALIAN-AMERICAN EXPERIENCE; An annotated and Classified Bibliographical Guide, with Selected Publications of the Casa Italiana Educational Bureau. By Francesco Cordasco. New York, B. Franklin, 1974.

A selective, annotated bibliographical guide of 338 major entries. Includes the texts of early studies (1931-34) of the Casa Italiana Educational Bureau: Leonard Covello, THE CASA ITALIANA EDUCATIONAL BUREAU--ITS PURPOSE AND PROGRAM; Leonard Covello, THE ITALIANS IN AMERICA; William B. Shedd, ITALIAN POPULATION IN NEW YORK; and John J. D'Alesandre, OCCUPATIONAL TRENDS OF ITALIANS IN NEW YORK CITY.

THE ITALIAN AMERICAN FAMILY; The Southern Italian Family's Process of Adjustment to an Urban America. By Lydio Tomasi. Staten Island, New York, Center for Migration Studies, 1972.

Discusses how socio-economic changes can help or hinder a family system. Begins with a basic look at the Southern Italian family and continues with a discussion of the various generations and their attitudes.

ITALIAN-AMERICAN HISTORY. By Giovanni Schiavo. New York, Vigo Press, 1947.

Two volume set that consists of a series of fifteen chapters dealing with the history of the Italians in America from Columbus to the 1940's. Some topics covered are religious activities, artists, fraternal and social organizations and the sociology of the Italians in America.

THE ITALIAN AMERICAN NOVEL: A DOCUMENT OF THE INTERACTION OF TWO CULTURES. By Rose Basile Green. Rutherford, New Jersey, Fairleigh-Dickenson University Press, 1974.

Examines early autobiographies, fiction dealing realistically with urban concentration of Italians and fiction in which general human themes are presented in literary form.

THE ITALIAN-AMERICANS. By Luciano J. Iorizzo and Salvatore Mondello. New York, Twayne Publishers, 1971.

Surveys the experiences of Italian immigrants on the farms, in big cities, and in small towns of the United States, using Italians of Oswego, New York, as examples of newcomers in small towns. Integrates Italian immigration with major patterns in American history from colonial to modern times.

ITALIAN AMERICANS. By Joseph Lopreato. New York, Random House, 1970.

Discusses the social, political, and economic realities of existence for Italians who immigrated to America from about 1880 on. Deals with reasons for migrating, patterns of settlement, problems of adjustment, family relations, religious participation, difficulties of cultural contact with other groups, and achievements in terms of occupation, education, and income.

ITALIAN AMERICANS: A GUIDE TO INFORMATION SOURCES. By Francesco Cordasco. Detroit, Gale Research Company, 1978. (Ethnic Studies Information Guide Series, Volume 2).

Exhaustive annotated bibliography and directory of information about Italian Americans arranged in sections: general reference works, the social sciences, history and regional studies, applied sciences, and the humanities. Includes a retrospective and current list of Italian American periodicals, a list of major fraternal, professional and religious organizations and an appendix of audiovisual materials. Indexed according to author, title and subject.

ITALIAN AMERICANS: A STUDY GUIDE AND SOURCE BOOK. By Alberto Meloni. San Francisco, R and E Research Associates, 1978. C. 1977

ITALIAN-AMERICANS AND RELIGION: AN ANNOTATED BIBLIOGRAPHY. By Silvano M. Tomasi. New York, Center for Migration Studies, 1978.

An annotated bibliography of the religious aspects of the history of Italians.

THE ITALIAN AMERICANS: TROUBLED ROOTS. By Andrew F. Rolle. New York, Free Press, 1980.

This book analyzes the dynamics of the Italian Americans using their historical experience in America as illustration.

THE ITALIAN CONTRIBUTION TO AMERICAN DEMOCRACY. By John H. Mariano. Boston, Christopher Publishing House, 1921. Reprint New York, Arno, 1975.

A sociological study of Italian life in New York City; examining socio-economic conditions, psychological traits, social organization, and how the Italian's contribute to American democracy.

THE ITALIAN EMIGRATION OF OUR TIME. By Robert F. Foerster. Cambridge, Massachusetts, Harvard University Press, 1919. Reprint New York, Arno Press, 1975.

Particularly strong in describing conditions in Italy which led to emigration to America and other countries.

THE ITALIAN EXPERIENCE IN THE UNITED STATES. Edited by Silvano M. Tomasi and Madeline H. Engel. Staten Island, New York, Center for Migration Studies, 1970.

Presents ten articles on various aspects of Italian immigration to the United States. Discusses basic characteristics and trends, the impact of Italians and Americans on each other, the process of assimilation, and the return migration to Italy.

ITALIAN FASCIST ACTIVITIES IN THE UNITED STATES. By Gaelano Salvemini. Edited with an introduction by Philip V. Cannistraro. New York, Center for Migration Studies, 1977.

A previously unpublished study of the major organizations, methods, and persons in the Italian Fascist Movement in the United States from 1922 to 1936. The author was a leading figure in the Italian anti-fascist resistance.

THE ITALIAN IN AMERICA. By Eliot Lord, John J. D. Trenor, and Samuel J. Barrows. New York, B. F. Buck and Company, 1905. Reprinted by Books for Libraries Press, Freeport, New York, 1970.

Discusses the flow of emigration of Italians to America from 1880 on; their cultural heritage; settlement in American cities; economic situation; work experiences in mining, farming, and other occupations; congested living conditions; education and assimilation; and political development.

THE ITALIAN IN AMERICA; A Social Study and History. By Lawrence Frank Pisani. New York, Exposition Press, 1957.

Shows the part played by Italians in American history from exploration and early settlement to the 1950's. Tells about their occupations, personality traits, community life, religion, amusements, literature, arts and science, and their impact on America.

THE ITALIAN IN AMERICA; The Progressive View, 1891-1914. Edited by Lydio F. Tomasi. New York, Center for Migration Studies, 1972.

A collection of articles about Italian Americans originally published from 1891 to 1914 in the progressive magazine, Charity, sponsored by the Charity Organization Society of New York. The first section, The Immigrant: His Problem and Ours, discusses social and economic conditions in urban and rural areas and the reactions of Americans to mass immigration. The second section, The Italian in America: 1891-1914, deals with problems of health, labor, criminality, charity, housing, and philanthropists' views concerning the problems.

ITALIAN NAME PLACES IN THE UNITED STATES WITH HISTORICAL AND DESCRIPTIVE ANNOTATIONS AND INFORMATION. By Ernest L. Biagi. Philadelphia, Adams, 1970.

ITALIAN OR AMERICAN? The Second Generation in Conflict. By Irvin L. Child. New Haven, Connecticut, Yale University Press, 1943.

Examines the psychological reactions to acculturation of a group of second-generation male Italians in an American city (New Haven).

AN ITALIAN PASSAGE: IMMIGRANTS TO THREE AMERICAN CITIES, 1840-1930. By John Walker Briggs. New Haven, Yale University Press, 1978.

The author examines immigrant experience in three medium-sized cities; Rochester and Utica, New York and Kansas City, Missouri. Numerous tables throughout the book.

ITALIAN WOMEN IN INDUSTRY. By Louise C. Odencrante. New York, Russell Sage Foundation, 1919. Reprint New York, Arno, 1977.

An inside look at Italian women and their work; their incomes, home life and the standards they have established. A group of women from lower Manhattan were used for the study.

THE ITALIANS; How They Live and Work. By Andrew Bryant. New York, Frederick A. Praeger, 1969.

THE ITALIANS IN AMERICA. By Philip M. Rose. New York, George H. Doran Company, 1922. Reprint New York, Arno Press/New York Times, 1975.

Written under the auspices of the Interchurch World Movement, and "undertaken to show, in brief outline, the social, economic, and religious background . . . and to present the experience--social, economic and religious--of the Italians in America, with special reference to the contact with religious institutions in the United States."

THE ITALIANS IN AMERICA. By Ronald P. Grossman. Minneapolis, Lerner Publications Company, 1966.

For young readers.

ITALIANS IN AMERICA: ANNOTATED GUIDE TO NEW YORK TIMES ARTICLES, 1890-1940. By Ivan H. Light. Monticello, Illinois, Council of Planning Librarians, 1975.

Divided into two parts; Part 1 lists articles giving title, and date. Part 2 lists articles giving title, date and annotation.

THE ITALIANS IN AMERICA, 1492-1972; A Chronology and Fact Book. Compiled and edited by Reverend Anthony F. LoGatto. Ethnic Chronology Series No. 4. Dobbs Ferry, New York, Oceana Publications, 1973.

Gives dates and important events concerning Italian explorers and immigrants in the chronology section. Presents excerpts from journals, reports, letters, speeches, and official records in the documents section. Lists eminent Italian Americans under various categories in the appendices. Also includes a bibliography.

THE ITALIANS IN CHICAGO. By Carroll D. Wright. Washington, Government Printing Office, 1897. Reprint New York, Arno Press, 1970.

A government report dealing with the social and economic condition of the Italians in Chicago. Largely made up of tables with a fifty page analysis of the data.

ITALIANS IN CHICAGO: 1880-1930: A STUDY IN ETHNIC MOBILITY. By Humbert S. Nelli. New York, Oxford University Press, 1970.

"The new urban surroundings profoundly affected other traditions and viewpoints, although immigrants themselves believed that in America they were re-creating homeland village life. In the process they created a myth that they have nurtured to the present." A challenging study, the conclusions of which are controversial.

THE ITALIANS IN CHICAGO; A Study in Americanization. By Giovanni E. Schiavo. Preface by Jane Addams. Chicago, Italian American Publishing Company, 1928. Reprint New York, Arno Press/ New York Times, 1975.

Explores the problems of Italians in slum districts of the city and also in "American" neighborhoods. Discusses the Americanization of business and professional people of Italian descent.

THE ITALIANS IN MILWAUKEE, WISCONSIN: GENERAL SURVEY. By George La Piana. Milwaukee, Associated Charities, 1915. Reprint San Francisco, R and E Research Associates, 1970.

A basic discussion of the Italians in Milwaukee and their way of life (housing, food expenses, education, etc.). Also discusses the public and private charities for the Italians in Milwaukee.

THE ITALIANS IN MISSOURI. By Giovanni Schiavo. Chicago, Italian American Publishing Company, 1929. Reprint New York, Arno Press/New York Times, 1975.

A study of Italian life in the border state of Missouri. The author includes statistics on Italians in St. Louis and Kansas City; on occupations; social organizations; educational, religious, and recreational activities; and on politics. Also included are a wide range of photographs and a "Business Directory of the Italians in Kansas City."

THE ITALIANS IN OKLAHOMA. By Kenny L. Brown. Norman, University of Oklahoma Press, 1980.

One book in a series titled "Newcomers to a New Land" which looks at the role of major ethnic groups who have contributed to the history of Oklahoma.

ITALIANS IN THE CITY: HEALTH AND RELATED SOCIAL NEEDS. Edited by Francesco Cordasco. New York, Arno Press/New York Times, 1975.

Reprints four seminal papers: Antonio Mangano, THE ITALIAN COLONIES OF NEW YORK CITY (1903); Antonio Stella, THE EFFECTS OF URBAN CONGESTION ON ITALIAN WOMEN AND CHILDREN (1908); John C. Gebhart, THE GROWTH AND DEVELOPMENT OF ITALIAN CHILDREN IN NEW YORK CITY (1924); and SOME HEALTH PROBLEMS OF ITALIANS IN NEW YORK CITY: A PRELIMINARY SURVEY (1934).

ITALIANS IN THE UNITED STATES; A Bibliography of Reports, Texts, Critical Studies and Related Materials. By Francesco Cordasco and Salvatore LaGumina. New York, Oriole Editions, 1972.

Lists books, journal articles, dissertations, and pamphlets in sections dealing with topics such as Italian emigration to America, Italian-American history, regional studies, etc. Includes over 1,400 items, some of which are annotated.

ITALIANS IN THE UNITED STATES: A REPOSITORY OF RARE TRACTS AND MISCELLANEA. Edited by Francesco Cordasco. New York, Arno Press/New York Times, 1975.

A dimensionally diverse profile of Italian experience in the United States, originally assembled by an archivist at the New York Public Library and preserved in a slipcase. The tracts, brochures, monographs, and miscellanea include the Italy America Society CONSTITUTION (1920), annual report (1920), list of members (1920) and BULLETIN (1924).

THE ITALIANS OF NEW YORK: A SURVEY. Federal Writers' Project, New York, Random House, 1938. Reprint New York, Arno Press, 1969.

Story of the Italians in New York from the arrival years ago to the present time. Discusses their customs and way of life in America plus their contributions to society.

THE ITALIANS OF OMAHA, WRITERS' PROGRAM IN THE STATE OF NEBRASKA. Omaha, Independent Printing Company, 1941. Reprint New York, Arno Press, 1975.

A story of the Italians who immigrated to Omaha beginning in the 1860's when they were employed in the building of the Union Pacific Railroad. Shows their economic development and integration into community life.

THE ITALIANS OF PHILADELPHIA. By Ernest L. Biagi. New York, Carlton Press, 1967.

THE ITALIANS OF SAN FRANCISCO, 1850-1930. By Deanna P. Gumina. New York, Center for Migration Studies, 1978.

THE ITALIANS OF SAN FRANCISCO; Their Adjustment and Acculturation. By Paul Radin. San Francisco, R and E Associates, 1970.

This study tries to show two things; the nature of the process by which the Italians were assimilated to American standards of living and what factors are involved in the changes that take place when an immigrant group comes into contact with another group.

THE ITALIANS; Social Backgrounds of an American Group. By Francesco Cordasco and Eugene Bucchioni. Clifton, New Jersey, Augustus M. Kelley Publishers, 1974.

A collection of journal articles and book excerpts dealing with the exodus from Italy to the United States from about 1880 on; Italian communities in America; responses to American life; employment, health, and social conditions; and the education of Italian children.

ITALICA-DIRECTORY ISSUE. Edited by Olga Ragusa. American Association of Teachers of Italian, Department of Italian, Columbia University, New York, New York 1983.

Issued annually.

THE ITALO-AMERICAN STUDENT IN THE AMERICAN PUBLIC SCHOOL: A DESCRIPTION AND ANALYSIS OF DIFFERENTIAL BEHAVIOR. By Richard O. Ulin. New York, Arno Press/New York Times, 1975.

Studies the academic and school-related performance of a selected group of Italian-American second and third generation boys in a Massachusetts high school.

JEW AND ITALIAN; Historic Group Relations and the New Immigration (1881-1924). By Rudolf Glanz. New York, Ktav Publishing Company, 1971.

The author compares two ethnic groups, Jews and Italians, in terms of their family structure and education, the help extended to immigrants by those already citizens, and occupational patterns.

LA GUARDIA, A FIGHTER AGAINST HIS TIMES, 1882-1933. By Arthur Mann. Chicago, University of Chicago Press, 1969.

The biography of a leading Italian American who became mayor of New York City.

LOVE AND PASTA. By Joe Vergara. New York, Harper and Row, 1969.

Tells the story of Rosario, who left southern Italy for the United States at fourteen, the American family he raised, and his three sons' attempts to Americanize him.

MARIA. By Michael De Capite. New York, John Day, 1943.

An autobiographical novel spanning three generations of Italian life in Cleveland.

NEIGHBORHOOD IN CONFLICT: THE IRISH, GERMANS, JEWS AND ITALIANS OF NEW YORK CITY, 1929-1941. By Ronald H. Bayor. Baltimore, Johns Hopkins University Press, 1978.

The book tries to analyze the roots and development, the various manifestations and the culmination of group conflict within a multi-ethnic urban setting.

THE NEIGHBORHOOD; The Story of Baltimore's Little Italy. By Gilbert Sandler. Baltimore, Bodine, 1974.

A portrait of the community, its roots, history, institutions and prospects for the future. The greatest part of the text is devoted to portraying the atmosphere and history of Little Italy. Includes numerous photographs and sketches.

NO BRIGHTER BANNER. By Michael de Capite. New York, John Day, 1944.

The Italian American hero spends his childhood and young adult years in the slums, then after education and the possibilities of American society have liberated him, turns to a critical evaluation of American culture.

PASCAL D'ANGELO, SON OF ITALY. By Pascal D'Angelo. New York, Macmillan, 1924.

Autobiographical account of the perplexity experienced in confronting urban American life.

PEASANTS AND STRANGERS: ITALIANS, RUMANIANS AND SLOVAKS IN AN AMERICAN CITY, 1890-1950. By Josef J. Barton. Cambridge, Massachusetts, Harvard University Press, 1975.

A comparative study of the three immigrant groups in Cleveland in process of formation and assimilation.

PEASANTS NO MORE; Social Class and Social Change in an Underdeveloped Society. By Joseph Lopreato. San Francisco, Chandler Publishing Company, 1967.

Analyzes social change in southern Italy as a consequence of emigration.

A PICTORIAL HISTORY OF THE ITALIAN PEOPLE. By Massimo Salvadore. New York, Crown Publishers, 1972.

PIETY AND POWER: THE ROLE OF ITALIAN PARISHES IN THE NEW YORK METROPOLITAN AREA, 1880-1930. By Silvano M. Tomasi. New York, Center for Migration Studies, 1975.

An examination of the process of assimilation of Italian immigrants in the New York metropolitan area from the viewpoint of the institutional aspect of religious experience. Based on data from the dioceses of New York, Newark, Brooklyn and Boston.

ROSA; The Life of an Italian Immigrant. By Marie Hall Ets. Minneapolis, University of Minnesota Press, 1970.

Provides an authentic expression of the motives, reactions, and destiny of a young Italian woman who immigrated to the United States in 1884, by assembling the accounts Rosa gave about her early life. Shows how a young wife and mother coped with the tasks of maintaining a household and rearing a family in a foreign land.

SAN FRANCISCO SCAVENGERS: DIRTY WORK AND THE PRIDE OF OWNERSHIP. By Stewart E. Perry. Berkeley, University of California Press, 1978.

Examines the daily work activities of the men of the Sunset Scavenger company of San Francisco, which is a business owned by Italian-Americans.

SOCIAL AND RELIGIOUS LIFE OF ITALIANS IN AMERICA. By Enrico C. Sartorio. Boston, Christopher Publishing House, 1918. Reprint Clifton, New Jersey, August M. Kelley, 1974.

Written by an Italian during the period of the great immigrations. Deals with the twin dynamics of conflict and acculturation in the Italian communities and with the vote of the churches from the viewpoint of a Protestant minister.

THE SOCIAL BACKGROUND OF THE ITALO-AMERICAN SCHOOL CHILD; A Study of the Southern Italian Family Mores and their Effect on the School Situation in Italy and America. By Leonard Covello. Totowa, New Jersey, Rowman and Littlefield, 1972.

A major study of ethnicity, of the context of poverty, of a minority's children, and the challenges to the American school. Part 1: Social Background in Italy; part 2: The Family as the Social World of the Southern Italian Contadino Society; part 3: Italian Family Mores and Their Educational Implications; part 4: Summary and Conclusions.

SONS OF ITALY; A Social and Religious Study of the Italians in America. By Antonio Mangano. New York, Russell and Russell (Atheneum Publishers), 1917. Reissued 1972.

Contributes a contemporary overview of the social and cultural life of Italians in urban America. Tells of the life styles, strengths, contributions, and virtues of the Italian poor in a hostile society.

SOUL OF AN IMMIGRANT. By Constantine Panunzio. New York, Macmillan, 1921.

An autobiography which reveals how bad conditions were in Italy and the dreams of success in America which led to emigration. Portrays in realistic detail the hardships and intolerance faced by the immigrant in America and the way industry exploited them.

THE STORY OF THE ITALIANS IN AMERICA. By Michael A. Musmanno. Garden City, New York, Doubleday and Company, 1965.

Outlines the achievements of Italians in America from Columbus and Verrazano to Joe DiMaggio. Discusses the hardships encountered and the contributions made by men and women of Italian descent in many fields of endeavor - art, music, education, religion, law, medicine, sports, science, business, military and government.

STREET CORNER SOCIETY; The Social Structure of an Italian Slum. 3rd edition. By William Foote Whyte. Chicago, University of Chicago Press, 1961.

Analyzes an Italian slum district in Boston's North End. Deals with the structure and leadership of informal groups called "corner boys" and their relationships with racket, police, and political organizations.

THEY CAME FROM ITALY; The Story of Famous Italian Americans. By Barbara Marinacci. New York, Dodd Mead and Company, 1967.

For young readers.

THREE CIRCLES OF LIGHT. By Pietro di Donato. New York, Messner, 1960.

Portrays immigrant Italian life set in the Italian section of West Hoboken, New Jersey.

THE TWO ROSETOS. By Carla Bianco. Bloomington, Indiana, University Press, 1974.

A study of acculturation and social change in an Italian-American enclave in Pennsylvania and its parent village in southern Italy. Oral tradition in both communities is studied: folk songs, adaptations of older ballads, personal historical accounts, proverbs, sayings, and folktales. The study is broadened by comparisons with Italian-American enclaves elsewhere in North America.

UNITED STATES-ITALY TRADE DIRECTORY. Italy-America Chamber of Commerce, New York.

Lists importers of Italian commodities, Italian manufacturers represented in the United States, and United States companies with business interests in Italy. Arranged by activity. Updated biennially.

THE URBAN VILLAGERS; Group and Class in the Life of Italian-Americans. By Herbert J. Gans. New York, Free Press, 1962.

Reports on a study of an inner city Boston neighborhood called the West End and the native-born Americans of Italian parentage who lived there among other ethnic groups. Explains the behavior patterns and values of the Italian-American working class subculture.

VENDETTA: A TRUE STORY OF THE WORST LYNCHING IN AMERICA, THE MASS MURDER OF ITALIAN-AMERICANS IN NEW ORLEANS IN 1891 . . . By Richard Gambino. Garden City, New York, Doubleday, 1977.

The story of the slaughter of eleven Italian men by citizens who were avenging the death of a local police chief.

WAIT UNTIL SPRING, BANDINI. By John Fante. New York, Stackpole, 1938.

Stories about an Italian laborer and his family living in Colorado.

WOP! A Documentary History of Anti-Italian Discrimination in the United States. Edited by Salvatore J. LaGumina. Ethnic Prejudice in America series. San Francisco, Straight Arrow Books, 1973.

Explores the factors leading to anti-Italian discrimination and the effects as manifested in the United States before and after 1880. Contains excerpts and cartoons from books, newspapers, reports, and journal articles.

WRITINGS ON ITALIAN-AMERICANS. Edited by Carmine Diodati, Jean Coleman, and Joseph Valletutti. New York, New York Public Library, 1975.

An annotated bibliography including selected materials on Italian Americans available in public libraries. Arranged by topics: collections; history; influences affecting the immigrant; personalities; periodicals; new theatre and cinema; Italian-American artists, business people, laborers, politicians, writers, and scholars.

Audiovisual Material

MAP

MAP OF ITALY. Embassy of Italy.

Shows major and secondary roads connecting important cities and towns. Indicates air and steamer transportation. Approximately 15 x 11.

FILMS

ANCIENT ROME. 16 mm. Color. Sound. 11 minutes. By Coronet Instructional Media, Chicago, Illinois, 1977.

Shows the remains of the Appian Way, the Colosseum, Domitian's Palace, the Forum, and Sacra Via in Rome in order to recall a culture that contributed many ideas to Western civilization.

DUCE. 16 mm. Black and white. Sound. 14 minutes. Screen News Digest, volume 14, number 7. By Hearst Metrotone News, New York, 1972.

Deals with the rise and fall of Benito Mussolini and his fascist empire. Focuses on the march on Rome, the founding of the Fascist Party in Italy, the invasion of Ethiopia by Italy, and the entrance of Italy into World War II.

FANTASTIC FACTS OF ITALY. 16 mm. Color. Silent (with a lecture cued to the film). 95 minutes. By Douglas Productions, Detroit, Michigan, 1965.

Describes the features of Rome related to important epochs of history and describes interesting aspects of modern Italy found in its other large cities.

THE FOUNTAINS OF ROME (VALLE GIULIA AND THE TRITON). By Ottorino Resphighi. 16 mm. Color and sound. 7 minutes. Music in Motion. By Musilog Corporation, Santa Barbara, California. Released by Bailey Films, Santa Monica, California, 1968.

Uses photographs of fountains and buildings of Rome to illustrate portions of the Fountains of Rome, by Respighi.

THE FOUR DAYS OF NAPLES. 35 mm. Black and white. Sound. 114 minutes. By Titanus, Rome, in cooperation with Metro. Released in the United States by Metro-Goldwyn-Mayer, New York, 1962.

A dramatization which documents events that followed the Nazi surrender to the Allies in September, 1943. Points out the Nazi reprisals on the people of Naples and the rise of resistance fighters to counter them.

HEARTBREAK COUNTRY: ITALY'S SOUTH. 16 mm. Black and white. Sound. 30 minutes. The Twentieth Century series. By Columbia Broadcasting System News, New York, 1965.

Describes the life of poverty, malnutrition, and ignorance which characterizes the southern Italian towns of Lavello and Tricarico. Discusses the unsuccessful government land reform initiated in 1963 and the renewed attempts of the government to develop industry in southern Italy.

THE HERO AS ARTIST. Cassette. Color. Sound. 52 minutes. By British Broadcasting Corporation. Time-Life Multimedia, New York, 1971.

Surveys the development of Western civilization in Italy beginning in 1500 as seen in the demise of city states such as Florence and the rise of Rome as a world power. Examines the work of Michelangelo, Raphael, and Bramante.

INTRODUCING ITALY. Cassette. Black and white. Sound. 21 minutes. North Atlantic Treaty Organization; made by Europa Telefilm. NATO, Brussels. Distributed by National Audiovisual Center, Washington, D.C. 1979.

Describes the country and people of Italy, including geographical features, historical development and achievements, economic life, occupations of the people, and social customs. Explains briefly the role of Italy in the North Atlantic Treaty Organization.

AN ITALIAN FAMILY: LIFE ON A FARM. 16 mm. Color. Sound. 21 minutes. By Encyclopaedia Britannica Educational Corporation, 1975.

Presents geographic and cultural aspects of Italy with an account of one family living on a small farm, who, unlike many Italians seeking modernization, avoid mechanization in preference for a simple way of life.

THE ITALIAN RENAISSANCE: ITS MIND AND ITS SOUL. 16 mm. Color and sound. 14 minutes. World History Series. By Centron Educational Films, Lawrence, Kansas, 1971.

Examines the era of the Italian Renaissance. Questions whether this period was a universal and democratic rebirth of knowledge for all men or merely an intellectual revolution of the elite. Includes paintings by Da Vinci, Michelangelo, Raphael, Titian, and others.

ITALY: BAMBINI ITALIANI. 16 mm. Color. Sound. 18 minutes. Ontario Educational Communications Authority, Toronto, 1969. Released in the United States by NBC Educational Enterprises, 1972.

Deals with daily life of young people in Italy. Illustrates life in school and at play by showing young boys in three villages near Rome: Macaressi, Fregina, and Terracina. For elementary grades.

ITALY INVADES ETHIOPIA, 1935. Super 8 mm. Black and white. Silent (with film notes). 4 minutes. By Anargyros Film Library, Los Angeles, California, 1973.

Describes aggressive acts of the Fascist government in Italy prior to World War II, focusing on the invasion of Ethiopia in 1935.

ITALY - TANNA, A GIRL OF SICILY. 16 mm. Color and sound. 16 minutes. By Frith Films, Hollywood, California, 1960.

Describes the life of a Sicilian girl and her family, showing the family home above the bay and Tanna's companionship with friends at home and on a shopping trip through Taormina. Describes the economic life of the community. Includes scenes of the crater of Mount Etna and Taormina's ancient Greek amphitheater.

ITALY, THE LAND AND THE PEOPLE. 16 mm. Color and sound. 16 minutes. Coronet Instructional Media, Chicago, Illinois, 1977.

Visualizes the cities and farmlands of Italy, showing through the eyes of the people the physical and economic characteristics of Italy's major geographic regions, as well as some of the people's traditions and culture.

ITALY - THE POST-WAR RENAISSANCE. 16 mm. Color and sound. 17 minutes. Today's People in Our Changing World series. By Carl Dudley, Dudley Pictures Corporation. Released by United World Films, Hollywood, California 1963.

A pictorial study of Italy featuring views of many famous cities and historic treasures in art and culture. Explores the city of Rome, showing its Forum, Appian Way, Colosseum, and Saint Peter's Basilica.

ITALY: THE ROAD TO TORINO. 16 mm. Color and sound. 20 minutes. By Wharton International Films. Released by Universal Education and Visual Arts, Universal City, California, 1970.

A study of life on the Italian sea coast. Shows that change is found everywhere by following a boy who leaves his home to escape poverty and a hard life just before a superhighway is built, improving conditions in the hamlet he left.

ITALY TODAY. 16 mm. Color and sound. 18 minutes. By Wharton International Films. Released by CCM Films, Mount Vernon, New York.

Considers the social, economic, and historical reasons behind Italy's recovery from World War II. Explains the way in which the problem presented by the barren southlands, the mezzogiorno, was treated.

JOHNINE'S WINTER JOURNAL. 16 mm. Color and sound. 29 minutes. Made and released by McDonnell Douglas Corporation, Santa Monica, California, 1973.

A traveling reporter conducts a winter tour through Italy in order to encourage foreign visitors to visit Italy during the winter months.

THE MANWATCHER. Videorecording. Color and sound. 52 minutes. BBC-TV. Time-Life Video, New York, 1980.

Analyzes the rich vocabulary of hand movements with which Italians augment their speech. Reveals the meanings of signals that human beings unwittingly, but effectively, convey to the world.

NAPLES TO CASSINO. Videorecording. Black and white. Sound. 26 minutes. United States Department of the Army. Distributed by National Audiovisual Center, Washington, D.C., 1980.

Shows scenes of fighting during the drive of Allied forces from Naples to Cassino, Italy, during World War II.

THE PATH TO ROME. 16 mm. Color and sound. 54 minutes. By Fred Meyer Films, Scottsville, New York, 1972.

Retraces the path taken in 1902 by Hilaire Belloc on a pilgrimage from Toul to Rome. Compares the path as it is today to the path of the 1902 journey.

FILMS ON ITALIAN AMERICANS

THE FEAST OF SAN GENNARO. 16 mm. Color and sound. 16 minutes. Scott Morris Films, New York, 1978.

A documentary offering impressions of a traditional Italian street festival in New York City's Little Italy.

ITALIAN AMERICAN. 16 mm. Color and sound. 26 minutes. National Communications Foundation. Macmillan Films, Mount Vernon, New York, 1977.

Profiles the experiences of Italian-American immigrants through the eyes and lives of one couple, Catherine and Charlie Scorsese. Includes informal footage of the family at the dinner table, reminiscences about the Scorsese family in Sicily and New York, and treasured family snapshots.

ITALIAN AMERICANS. Super 8 mm. Color. Silent. 4 minutes. Ethnic Groups series. By Ealing Corporation, Cambridge, Massachusetts, 1970.

Includes scenes of four generations of Italian Americans at a traditional Sunday dinner in New York's Little Italy.

SILVER HARVEST. 16 mm. Color and sound. 25 minutes. By Steve Rosen for the Monterey Savings and Loan Association, Monterey, California, 1979.

A documentary on the Italian fishing families that came to Monterey, California to fish schooling sardines in the 1930's. Shows special equipment that was designed and emphasizes the unique heritage which developed.

WHAT CAN I TELL YOU: A PORTRAIT OF THREE GENERATIONS OF WOMEN. 16 mm. Color and sound. 55 minutes. Centre Productions, Boulder, Colorado, 1979, made 1978.

Focuses on three generations of women from an Italian-American family, who offer anecdotes and personal perspectives on their self-images and family relationships and on such topics as marriage, children, working, and independence. Depicts each woman as a unique individual who has evidenced the need to express life fully.